THE LAW OF FREEDOM OF INFORMATION

THE LAW OF FREEDOM OF INFORMATION

by

JOHN MACDONALD QC
CLIVE H JONES

With

ROSS CRAIL
COLIN BRAHAM

and contributions from

Stephen Schaw Miller
Ian Peacock
Jane Evans-Gordon
Adrian Pay
David Warner
Mark Hubbard
Colette Wilkins
Edwin Simpson
James Bailey
Sandra Corbett

The authors are barristers from New Square Chambers, London

OXFORD
UNIVERSITY PRESS

OXFORD
UNIVERSITY PRESS

Great Clarendon Street, Oxford OX2 6DP

Oxford University Press is a department of the University of Oxford.
It furthers the University's objective of excellence in research, scholarship,
and education by publishing worldwide in

Oxford New York

Auckland Bangkok Buenos Aires Cape Town Chennai
Dar es Salaam Delhi Hong Kong Istanbul Karachi Kolkata
Kuala Lumpur Madrid Melbourne Mexico City Mumbai Nairobi
São Paulo Shanghai Taipei Tokyo Toronto

Oxford is a registered trade mark of Oxford University Press
in the UK and in certain other countries

Published in the United States
by Oxford University Press Inc., New York

British Library Cataloguing in Publication Data
Data available

Library of Congress Cataloging in Publication Data
Data available

ISBN 0–19–924994–6

1 3 5 7 9 10 8 6 4 2

Typeset by Hope Services (Abingdon) Ltd
Printed in Great Britain
on acid-free paper by
Biddles Ltd., Guildford and King's Lynn

FOREWORD

I am delighted to have been asked by John Macdonald QC to contribute a
Foreword to *The Law of Freedom of Information*. Freedom of information seems
set to become one of the most fertile subjects in English civil law. The procreators
of this fertility are the Freedom of Information Act 2000 and the Human Rights
Act 1998. The boundaries of the civil rights growing out of this fertile statutory
soil will be explored, and are already being explored, by judges, professional and
academic lawyers, politicians, journalists and others. In doing so, the assistance of
the comprehensive exposition of freedom of information law to be found in this
book will be invaluable. The book has been written as a practioners' book but the
commendably simple, clear language of the text will make its exposition of the law
as accessible to non-lawyers as to lawyers. John Macdonald and his team from
New Square Chambers, Lincoln's Inn, are to be congratulated.

Richard Scott
16 January 2003

PREFACE

This book has been written for those who are responsible for providing information and those who seek information and their respective advisers.

Freedom of Information is a new subject. It has arrived late in the United Kingdom and though we now have the Freedom of Information Act 2000 it does not come fully into force until January 2005 when people will be able to exercise the statutory *right to know.*

Much information, however, is already available under Local Government legislation, under environmental regulations and under the Open Government Code which was introduced in 1994 and is supervised by the Ombudsman. Much can also be obtained from the institutions of the European Union. The current position is summed up in chapter 4.

We provide an overview of the Act in chapter 3 and a detailed commentary on the Act in chapters 5–8, but we have gone on to set the *right to know* in its broader legal context. Thus we discuss the relationship of the Freedom of Information Act to the Human Rights Act and the Data Protection Act, the law of confidentiality, secrecy, whistle-blowing and money laundering. We hope the reader will find it helpful to have these related subjects gathered together in one volume.

In the absence of any United Kingdom precedents we have considered what happens overseas, where we believe the experience of other countries is likely to assist those who have to make difficult decisions about what should be disclosed, and those who are seeking information which is not readily forthcoming. Overseas cases will be of greatest help where the overseas legislation is similar to the United Kingdom Act. Chapter 9 therefore compares our Act with Freedom of Information regimes in the United States, Canada, Australia, New Zealand and Ireland. The layout of the chapter follows that of the overview in chapter 3. In chapter 25 we describe their statutory provisions, country by country, adding in the legislation in Sweden, France and the Netherlands.

The Freedom of Information Act does not stand alone. It is part of a new constitutional settlement which includes the Human Rights Act and devolution to Scotland, Wales and from time to time to Northern Ireland. Parts of the Freedom of Information Act extend throughout the United Kingdom, but Scotland now has its own Act. We have dealt at length with the position in Scotland because the way freedom of information develops in one part of the United Kingdom is likely to have an impact on other parts. We also have a chapter on the special position of Wales and Northern Ireland.

The business community has made great use of the United States Freedom of Information Act. Richard Thomas, the new Information Commissioner, has written: 'As sophisticated companies know, a treasure trove of reports, surveys, statistics, analyses, opinions and recommendations has been amassed by various organs of government over the past decades . . . Provided their own genuine secrets remain secret, businesses have a strong interest in ensuring maximum access to information held by government and public authorities.' We address the specific threats and opportunities for business in Part F.

Though Freedom of Information is a new subject we are not the first to write about it, and we have learned much and quoted extensively from those who have gone before, in particular from Professor Patrick Birkinshaw, from Richard Clayton and Hugh Tomlinson, from Maurice Frankel and the Campaign for Freedom of Information and from Professor Robert Hazell and the Constitutional Unit at University College, London. We have found their work illuminating and helpful. We are sure our readers will too.

We should also like to thank Lee Hughes and all at the Lord Chancellor's Department, the Public Record Office and the Information Commissioner's Office for their unfailing help and courtesy and the speed with which they have dealt with our enquiries.

Finally we should like thank the clerks and staff at New Square Chambers, Lucy Plaskett, Lyn Cole, who came from Isle-en-Dodon and enabled us to return the proofs in good order, and everyone at Oxford University Press. We are very fortunate in our publishers, who have been enthusiastic and supportive throughout and are expert in producing books to the highest standards.

The law is as stated at December 2002.

John Macdonald
Lincoln's Inn
January 2003

CONTENTS—SUMMARY

E RELATIONSHIP WITH OTHER STATUTES

F FREEDOM OF INFORMATION AND
THE COMMERCIAL WORLD

G PRIVACY, CONFIDENTIALITY AND HUMAN RIGHTS

H DEVOLUTION

I THE EUROPEAN UNION AND OTHER PARTS OF THE WORLD

J THE FUTURE

APPENDICES

I: Practical Guides

II: Materials

CONTENTS

A AN INTRODUCTION TO THE FREEDOM OF
INFORMATION ACT 2000

1. The Historical Background

C THE STATUTORY SCHEME

5. Access to Information Held By Public Authorities

7. Enforcement

8. Historical Records

D A COMPARATIVE VIEW

9. A Comparison with Freedom of Information Elsewhere

E RELATIONSHIP WITH OTHER STATUTES

10. Data Protection

F FREEDOM OF INFORMATION AND THE COMMERCIAL WORLD

17. Implications for Business

G PRIVACY, CONFIDENTIALITY AND HUMAN RIGHTS

20. Privacy and Confidentiality

21. The Human Rights Act 1998

J THE FUTURE

26. The Future

APPENDICES

I: Practical Guides

II: Materials

TABLES OF CASES

TABLES OF LEGISLATION

TABLE OF TREATIES AND CONVENTIONS

Part A

AN INTRODUCTION TO THE FREEDOM OF INFORMATION ACT 2000

1

THE HISTORICAL BACKGROUND

A. Introduction

The White Paper

Unnecessary secrecy in government leads to arrogance in governance and defective decision making

So starts the White Paper[1] presented to Parliament in December 1997 entitled **1.01** 'Your Right to Know—The Government's Proposals for a Freedom of Information Act'. The White Paper proposed radical changes in the approach of public authorities to questions of disclosing or withholding information. In the Prime Minister's words 'The traditional culture of secrecy will only be broken down by giving people in the United Kingdom the legal right to know'.[2]

---

[1] Cm 3818, para 1.1.
[2] ibid, preface.

3

Summary of Bill

1.02 The Bill when it was published did not live up to the White Paper and the disappointment which was forcefully expressed by many who had campaigned for a Freedom of Information Act tended to obscure the real merits of the government's proposals. Lord Falconer, the Minister of State at the Cabinet Office, summarized the main thrust of the Bill in a few sentences when he moved the second reading in the House of Lords on 20 April 2000.[3] He said:

> All information held by any public authority will fall into the scope of the Bill, and will be available on request, unless an exemption applies. And even if an exemption applies, in almost all cases the authority must disclose the information where the wider public interest outweighs the need to maintain the exemption.
>
> The Bill creates an information commissioner who will have the task of enforcing its provisions. So people will not have to take expensive court action to enforce their rights. The commissioner will do that and access to the commissioner will be free of charge. . .
>
> . . . the Bill creates a delicate balance of rights, balancing the right to know against the right to privacy and the right to confidentiality.

That statement reflects the official view of what the Bill intended and the statute achieved, and on a fair assessment, there is a reasonable basis for that view.

B. The Historical Perspective

Late start

1.03 There is no doubt the United Kingdom lagged behind other countries in the process of ending secrecy within central government. The United States, for example, has had a Freedom of Information Act since 1966[4] and Australia led the way for Commonwealth countries in 1982 followed by Canada and New Zealand also in 1982. In the United Kingdom neither statute nor common law developed an overall concept of freedom of information prior to the 2000 Act, though there has been considerable piecemeal legislation dealing with subjects as diverse as land registration, medical records and access to local government information. Indeed one of the themes of the White Paper was the need to draw the strings of such legislation together.

1.04 Writing in 1972, HWR Wade drew attention to 'the difficulties which British law puts in the way of the ordinary citizen trying to obtain or use information in government hands'. Wade strikingly comments:

---

[3] *Hansard*, HL (series 5) vol 612, cols 823–830 (20 April 2000).
[4] Significantly amended by the Electronic Freedom of Information Act Amendments 1996—5 USC 552 (Supp II 1996).

This ought to be a topic of administrative law, but it will not become one until Britain, like the United States, gives the public some sort of legal right against the government, and subscribes to the healthy American philosophy of 'the public's right to know'.[5]

Shift in attitudes

The context in which Wade wrote those comments was a period of some ten years **1.05** during which there was a significant shift in British attitudes to the provision of legal and administrative remedies for the citizen,[6] extending in some fields to the establishment of legal rights (which, as noted in the last paragraph, did not include freedom of information, though the Franks Report on section 2 of the Official Secrets Act 1911 was published in 1972). The change was reflected in British acceptance of the right of individual petition under the European Convention of Human Rights (1966), the setting up of the Parliamentary Commissioner for Administration (1967), the enactment of anti-discrimination laws (1968, 1975 and 1976), and the liberalization of the law relating to Crown privilege.[7]

High tide of secrecy

Before those changes twentieth century Britain was characterized by the absence **1.06** of such rights and remedies. Indeed those years saw the high tide of governmental secrecy, through the operation (until 1989) of section 2 of the Official Secrets Act 1911, and of Crown privilege. The 1911 Act invoked the criminal law to prevent disclosure effectively of all government information.

The main offence created by section 2 was the offence committed by a person **1.07** who, having in his possession any information which he had obtained owing to his position as a person holding office under Her Majesty or a contract on behalf of Her Majesty, communicated that information to any person other than a person to whom he was authorized to communicate it. 'In ordinary language,' it was explained in the Franks Report, 'it is an offence under section 2(1)(a) for a Crown servant or Government contractor to make an unauthorised disclosure of information which he has learnt in the course of his job.'[8] This measure was

---

[5] B Schwartz and HWR Wade, *Legal Control of Government* (1972) 81. Wade's subsequent approach was consistent with this comment: in HWR Wade and C Forsyth, *Administrative Law* (7th edn, 1994), the topic does not appear; in the 8th edn (2000) the new Freedom of Information Act is discussed at 64–66.

[6] A Lester and D Pannick, *Human Rights Law and Practice*, (1999) 3 at para 1.09.

[7] *Conway v Rimmer* [1968] AC 910. After that decision the proper term is no longer 'Crown privilege' but 'public interest immunity'; see P Craig, *Administrative Law* (4th edn, 1999) 822–825.

[8] Departmental Report on section 2 of the Official Secrets Act 1911, (Cmnd 5104 1972), App IB n 2. See also ch 12 below.

inimical to open government because it embraced all official information, irrespective of whether there was or was not a good reason to protect its secrecy.

1.08 Section 2 of the 1911 Act was described by the Franks Report[9] as having a

> catch-all quality. It catches all official documents and information. It makes no distinctions of kind, and no distinctions of degree. All information which a Crown servant learns in the course of his duty is 'official' for the purposes of section 2, whatever its nature, whatever its importance, whatever its original source. A blanket is thrown over everything; nothing escapes.

1.09 Section 2 continued until 1989 to cause problems for the courts. In *R v Peter Anthony Galvin*[10] it was argued that documents in the public domain should be excluded from the scope of section 2. The Court of Appeal found itself unable to accept this argument. The wording of the section prevented the court from reaching such a conclusion. The fact that the Ministry had widely circulated the document in question, a manual relating to the Rolls Royce Olympus aero-engine, did not itself mean that the document was no longer protected by section 2. The Court of Appeal was, however, able to achieve a sensible result and allow the appeal because the jury had not been asked to decide whether such widespread dissemination of the manual had or might have occurred on the basis of an implied authorization for anyone who came into possession of the manual to make such use of it as that person thought fit.

1.10 The House of Lords went much further in *A-G v Guardian Newspapers (No 2)*,[11] the *Spycatcher* case. The Crown relied on the signing of a declaration that the Official Secrets Act 1911 continued to apply to Peter Wright, a former member of the Security Service, as part of its application for an injunction to restrain publication of Mr Wright's book. The House of Lords held that in seeking to restrain the disclosure of government secrets the Crown must demonstrate that disclosure was likely to damage or had damaged the public interest before relief could be granted: that since the worldwide publication of *Spycatcher* had destroyed any secrecy as to its contents, and copies of it were readily available to anyone who wished to obtain them, the continuation of injunctions was not necessary. Significantly the House also emphasized that members and former members of the security service owed a lifelong duty of confidence to the Crown and the vast majority of them would not disclose confidential information to the newspapers.

1.11 The 1911 Act has now been replaced by the Official Secrets Act 1989. In *R v Shayler*[12] the House of Lords held that restrictions placed on past and present members of the security service were not absolute, but were confined to disclosure

---

[9] Departmental Report on section 2 of the Official Secrets Act 1911 (n 8 above), para 17.
[10] (1988) 86 Cr App Rep 85.
[11] [1990] AC 109.
[12] [2002] 2 WLR 754.

without lawful authority. Refusal of such authority could be challenged in the courts and so the restrictions were not a contravention of Mr Shayler's right of freedom of expression. Mr Shayler is taking the case to the European Court of Human Rights. The courts have thus striven for and now (with the 1989 Act in place) to some extent achieved a proper balance on questions of official secrecy.

Crown privilege

Under the law of Crown privilege, the government could refuse to produce docu-   **1.12**
ments in court. Before the Second World War it appeared to be accepted that the Crown's power to refuse disclosure was not absolute, but in 1942 the law 'took a sharp wrong turning when the House of Lords laid down . . . that a ministerial claim of privilege was unquestionable in law . . . In particular, the House ruled that the minister might say that the evidence belonged to a class of documents which the public interest required to be withheld from production'.[13] After a number of government concessions (privilege would no longer be claimed for certain categories of report), and some stirrings of judicial rebellion, the House of Lords in 1968[14]

> shattered the basis of the unrestricted 'class' privilege, and . . . successfully ordered the production of documents against the objections of the Crown. . . . [I]n every case the court had the power and the duty to weigh the public interest of justice to litigants against the public interest as asserted by the government. In many cases this could be done only by inspecting the documents, which could properly be shown to the court, but not to the parties, before the court decided whether to order production.[15]

Curbing the Crown

The absence of legal rights and remedies (noted in paragraphs 1.05 and 1.06   **1.13**
above) might seem surprising in the light of the great changes that had taken place over the preceding four centuries, including in particular the curbing of the monarch's powers.

The most drastic manifestations of such curbing were, of course, those which took   **1.14**
place in the seventeenth century, with the execution of one king and the casting out of another. While it is true that first the Civil War and Interregnum, then the Bill of Rights of 1688–89 and the Act of Settlement of 1700, changed the constitutional and political landscape, they did not greatly enhance the liberties of the subject, who in any event remained a subject, not a citizen.

---

[13] Schwartz and Wade (n 5 above) 192, referring to *Duncan v Cammell Laird & Co* [1942] AC 624.
[14] *Conway v Rimmer* [1968] AC 910.
[15] HWR Wade and C Forsyth, *Administrative Law*, (8th edn, 2000) 829.

1.15 Successive governments, dissimilar in other respects, shared a considerable disinclination to encourage the free flow of information. For example, in 1637 a decree of Star Chamber provided that no book could be printed unless licensed, and made it an offence to print, import or sell any seditious or offensive books or pamphlets. Star Chamber was abolished in 1641, but two years later Parliament passed an equally repressive order which Milton described as the 'immediate image' of the decree of 1637, and which called forth his *Areopagitica*.[16]

1.16 The constitutional settlement after the departure of James II at first appears, especially because it included a Bill of Rights, to be a substantial constitutional reordering, which imposed significant limits on royal power. However, as Maitland pointed out (in 1887–88):[17]

> William III as King of England had very great powers . . . All the old prerogatives existed save in so far as they had been expressly abolished by statute, and they were wide, and it was intended that William should exercise them. It was no honorary president of a republic that the nation wanted, but a real working, governing king— a king with a policy—and such a king the nation got.

1.17 Almost a century later, Kenyon made a similar assessment:[18]

> The failure to curb the King's sweeping powers of appointment to office, in Church and State, in local and central government, in the judiciary and the armed forces, was decisive for the maintenance of royal power and influence down the eighteenth century.

Parliament

1.18 When consideration is given to the long term effects of the constitutional reordering, having allowed for the waning of royal power in the nineteenth century, the question remains as to who were the ultimate beneficiaries:

> The 'glorious bloodless' revolution was won by Parliament; and although the Bill of Rights . . . and the Act of Settlement . . . recognised some important personal rights and liberties, the terms of the constitutional settlement were mainly concerned with the rights and liberties of Parliament. The alliance of Parliament and the common lawyers ensured that the supremacy of the law would mean the supremacy of Parliament; or, more realistically, the supremacy of the central government in Parliament . . . .[19]

1.19 That constitutional result prevailed until the second half of the twentieth century.[20] Its nature was not changed nor its form severely modified by either the gradual extension of the franchise, in the century after 1830, to virtually the entire

---

[16] Birkinshaw: *Freedom of Information* (3rd edn, 2000) 106.
[17] FW Maitland, *Constitutional History of England* (1965 edn) 388.
[18] JP Kenyon, *Stuart England* (1978) 264.
[19] Lester and Pannick (n 6 above) para 1.03.
[20] See para 1.05 above.

adult population, or by the prodigious growth of bureaucracy, which began earlier and continued for longer.[21]

Citizens' rights

It can be seen, therefore, that until the changes referred to in para 1.05 above, there was no context of citizens' rights into which a right to information could fit: there were instead 'liberties of the subject', which were 'residual and negative in their nature—the individual's freedom to do what he or she likes, unless forbidden by the common law or by statute'.[22] Hence Dicey's characterization of 'the right to personal liberty, as understood in England' as 'in substance a person's right not to be subjected to imprisonment, arrest, or other physical coercion in any manner that does not admit of legal justification'. Similarly he identified 'the right to freedom of discussion' as follows: 'Any man may . . . say or write whatever he likes, subject to the risk of, it may be, severe punishment if he publishes any statement (either by word of mouth, in writing, or in print) which he is not legally entitled to make'.[23]   **1.20**

As indicated in para 1.05 above, from about 1966 citizens began to acquire legal rights and remedies, some piecemeal but others wide ranging, as with the individual right to petition Strasbourg in 1966 and the enactment of the Human Rights Act 1998.   **1.21**

C. The Development of Administrative Law

Landmark cases

In the 1960s citizens looked to the courts rather than Parliament to exercise some restraint over the executive, and the courts in a series of far-reaching decisions reasserted the principles of judicial review. Constitutional reform moved up the political agenda, and the demand for the enactment of a freedom of information Act was an important part of that campaign.   **1.22**

The resurgence of judicial review started to change the attitude towards the release of information. First, in *Ridge v Baldwin*[24] the principles of natural justice were given their proper application, providing a broad foundation for a kind of code of   **1.23**

---

[21] See the discussion in Birkinshaw (n 16 above) 108–112.
[22] Lester and Pannick (n 6 above) para 1.02.
[23] AV Dicey, *Law of the Constitution* (10th edn) 207–8, 240. As to the limitations of residual rights and liberties, see R Clayton, H Tomlinson and C George, *Law of Human Rights* (2000) paras 1–21 to 1–23.
[24] [1964] AC 40.

administrative due process.[25] Secondly in *Conway v Rimmer*,[26] as noted above, the House of Lords rejected the view that the Crown could claim privilege for a whole class of documents and refuse to produce them in litigation regardless of their contents. The House inspected the documents and ordered their disclosure. Thirdly in *Anisminic v Foreign Compensation Commission*[27] the notion of unfettered administrative discretion was firmly rejected.

1.24 In that case the Foreign Compensation Commission had rejected a claim for compensation for a property already sold to a foreign buyer on the erroneous ground that the statutory Order in Council required that the successor in title should have been of British nationality at a certain date. The majority of the House of Lords held that this error destroyed the Commission's jurisdiction and rendered its decision a nullity, since on a true view of the law it had no jurisdiction to take the successor in title's nationality into account. By asking itself the wrong question, and by imposing a requirement which it had no authority to impose, it had overstepped its powers. Thenceforward, as Lord Browne-Wilkinson explained in *R v Hull University Visitor, ex p Page*,[28] it was to be taken that Parliament had only conferred the decision-making power on the footing that it was to be exercised on the correct legal basis: a misdirection in law in making the decision therefore rendered the decision ultra vires. The fundamental principle is that the courts will intervene to ensure that the powers of public decision-making bodies are exercised lawfully.

Procedural reform

1.25 The development of judicial review gathered pace in the mid 1970s with the procedural reforms which followed an inquiry which the Law Commission undertook, at the request of the Lord Chancellor,[29] into the form and procedure of judicial remedies. The Law Commission in its report[30] advocated that existing non-statutory remedies in administrative law should be sought in a unified application for judicial review. This reform was introduced by the Rules of the Supreme Court (Amendment No 3) Order which took effect in January 1978.

1.26 The vast majority of applications under the new procedures relied on the rules laid down in *Associated Provincial Picture Houses v Wednesbury Corporation*[31] and asked not only whether the authority had acted reasonably but in Lord Greene's words:[32]

---

[25] See Wade and Forsyth (n 15 above) 17.
[26] [1968] AC 910.
[27] [1969] 2 AC 147.
[28] [1993] AC 682.
[29] Lord Gardiner.
[30] Cmnd 6407, 1976.
[31] [1948] 1 KB 223.
[32] ibid at 233–4.

whether they had taken into account matters which they ought not to take into account or conversely, have refused to take into account or neglected to take into account matters which they ought to take into account.

The application of this test has resulted in decision-makers having not only to **1.27** explain their decisions but also to produce information and documentation relevant to the decision-making process. For example in the case of *R v Secretary of State for the Home Department, ex p Doody*[33] Lord Mustill observed that:

> I find in the more recent cases on judicial review a perceptible trend towards an insistence on greater openness, or if one prefers the contemporary jargon 'transparency', in the making of administrative decisions.

Reasons

In that case Lord Mustill explained that it is to be presumed that administrative **1.28** powers are to be exercised fairly and that fairness will often require that a person who may be adversely affected by the decision should have the opportunity to make representations. Representations cannot be properly made unless the person concerned is informed of the matters which are relevant to the decision. Fairness requires the decision maker to inform that person of the gist of the case he has to meet.[34] The House of Lords applied those principles and decided that life prisoners were entitled to know the factors that the Home Secretary would take into account when deciding the appropriate period to be served, so that they might make proper representations. Their Lordships were clear, however, that English law did not recognize a general obligation to give reasons for administrative decisions.[35]

In the absence of a general obligation the courts have given contrasting signals. In **1.29** *R v Kensington & Chelsea RBC, ex p Grillo*[36] the Court of Appeal considered it wrong to impose a duty to give reasons in a housing case where the Housing Act 1985, sections 65 and 69 did not require a local authority to give reasons for a decision that accommodation offered to a homeless person was suitable.[37]

In *R v Secretary of State for the Home Department, ex p Fayed*,[38] however, the Court **1.30** of Appeal held that the duty of fairness meant that the Secretary of State should inform Mr Fayed, an applicant for naturalization of the nature of any matters weighing against him and give him the opportunity to address such matters even

---

[33] [1994] 1 AC 531, HL at 561.
[34] See *Kanda v Government of Malaya* [1962] AC 322, 327.
[35] [1994] 1 AC 531, 561.
[36] (1996) 28 HLR 94.
[37] It is notable that the superseding statute, the Housing Act 1996, alters that position and provides for a review and appeal mechanism; see ss 184(3), 202 and 204.
[38] [1998] 1 WLR 763.

though the British Nationality Act 1991, section 44(2) provided that reasons for decisions did not have to be given.

1.31 Sedley J summarized the position in *R v Higher Education Council, ex p Institute of Dental Surgery*[39] in a passage which remains good law:

> In summary then: (1) there is no general duty to give reasons for a decision, but there are classes of case where there is such a duty. (2) One such class is where the subject matter is an interest so highly regarded by the law (for example, personal liberty), that fairness requires that reasons, at least for particular decisions, be given as of right. (3) (a) Another such class is where the decision appears aberrant. Here fairness may require reasons so that the recipient may know whether the aberration is in the legal sense real (and so challengeable) or apparent; (b) it follows that this class does not include decisions which are themselves challengeable by reference only to the reasons for them. A pure exercise of academic judgement is such a decision. And (c) procedurally, the grant of leave in such cases will depend upon prima facie evidence that something has gone wrong. The respondent may then seek to demonstrate that it is not so and that the decision is an unalloyed exercise of an intrinsically unchallengeable judgment.

1.32 Thus the judicial development of administrative law has, in those cases where reasons for decisions are now required, imposed openness on government.

D. The Campaign and Piecemeal Legislative Progress

The first Bills

1.33 In 1977 the Labour government introduced the 'Croham Directive', named after the then head of the civil service, which instructed heads of departments to provide factual and analytical material used as the background to major policy studies. Very little was in fact disclosed under the directive.

1.34 Freedom of information Bills drawn up by the Outer Policy Unit were introduced into the House of Commons in 1978 by Clement Freud MP and in 1981 by Frank Hooley MP. In 1984 David Steel introduced another Bill drafted by the Campaign for Freedom of Information. None of these Bills made significant progress.

1.35 In 1984 the government did start to move. The Data Protection Act was passed,[40] which gave individuals the right to see information held about themselves on computer. This was followed by the Local Government (Access to Information) Act 1985,[41] which started life as a private member's Bill introduced by Robin

---

[39] [1994] 1 WLR 242, 263.
[40] See ch 10 below.
[41] See ch 15 below.

Squire MP and came into force on 1 April 1986. It gave the public substantial rights of access to council meetings, reports, and papers.

Tisdall and Ponting: cases for concern

In 1984 Sarah Tisdall, a clerk in the Foreign and Commonwealth Office, was **1.36** prosecuted under section 2 of the Official Secrets Act for leaking information about the government's plans to handle the public relations aspects of the arrival of cruise missiles in Britain. She was convicted and sentenced to six months in prison. The next year Clive Ponting, a senior Ministry of Defence official, was also prosecuted under section 2 for leaking information which concerned the sinking of the *Belgrano* in the Falklands Islands conflict. Mr Ponting's defence, that he was acting in the public interest, was rejected by the trial judge as having no basis in law. The jury, however acquitted Mr Ponting.

The Campaign for Freedom of Information

The Campaign for Freedom of Information made real advances in 1987 and 1988 **1.37** when three Bills which it had drafted received the Royal Assent. First, the Access to Personal Files Act 1987 gives people the right to see manually held social work and housing records about themselves. Secondly, the Access to Medical Reports Act 1988 gives people the right to see any report produced by their own doctor for an employer or insurance company. Thirdly, the Environment and Safety Information Act 1988 gives people the right to see enforcement notices issued when organizations breach laws dealing with environmental protection and safety.

In 1988 the Campaign for Freedom of Information also drafted the private mem- **1.38** ber's Bill which was introduced by Richard Shepherd MP to reform section 2 of the Official Secrets Act. This Bill, which was prompted by concern aroused by the Tisdall and Ponting prosecutions, provided that offences should only be commit- ted where serious injury to the national interest was proved, and it created a pub- lic interest defence, allowing a defendant to argue that a disclosure benefited the public. This went too far for the Conservative government which ensured, by imposing a three-line whip, that it was defeated. They introduced their own Bill to amend section 2 the next year.

The Official Secrets Act 1989 repealed section 2 and replaced it with a narrower **1.39** measure which protects information about security, defence, international rela- tions and law enforcement.[42] The 1989 Act contains some absolute offences for which a person can be convicted without evidence that a disclosure has caused harm. There is no public interest defence.

---

[42] See ch 12 below.

1.40   The Access to Health Records Act 1990, which was introduced as a private member's Bill by Doug Henderson MP, allowed people to see information put on their medical records after November 1991.[43] This was another Bill which was promoted by the Campaign for Freedom of Information. The Campaign was beginning to have some effect, albeit in a piecemeal fashion. In the 1992 general election the Labour Party and the Liberal Democrats both promised a Freedom of Information Act and the Conservatives promised to reduce official secrecy.

1.41   After the election Mark Fisher MP introduced The Right to Know Bill with all party support. The Bill was given an unopposed second reading and completed its committee stage before being talked out.

1.42   The Environmental Information Regulations came into force in 1993. The Regulations, which were passed pursuant to a European Directive, provide a right of access to information about the environment held by public bodies.[44] The Campaign for Freedom of Information expressed the view that the Regulations are deeply flawed.[45] The main shortcomings which the Campaign noted result from (a) the excessively broad exemptions, (b) the inadequate definition of the bodies to whom the Regulations apply, and (c) the lack of any effective enforcement mechanism.

E. The 1994 Code of Practice

The Code

1.43   In July 1993 the government published a White Paper entitled *White Paper on Open Government*. This was followed by the *Code of Practice on Access to Government Information* which came into force on 4 April 1994.[46]

1.44   The Code, which was revised in 1997, applies to those government departments and other bodies which are within the jurisdiction of the Ombudsman.[47] It provides a formal access right, clear exemptions, a public interest 'override' and independent enforcement by the Ombudsman. Whitehall departments have since the Code was introduced had their own open government staff, internal guidance and monitoring arrangements as well as the reports from the Ombudsman.[48] Even

---

[43]   See ch 11 below.

[44]   The Regulations are considered in detail in ch 16 below.

[45]   'Freedom of Access to Information on the Environment': The Campaign For Freedom of Information's evidence to the House of Lords European Communities Committee, Sub-Committee C, 22 February 1996, published on the Campaign's website: http://www.cfoi.org.uk, 25 March 2002.

[46]   The provisions of the Code are discussed in detail in ch 4 below.

[47]   As listed in Sch 2 to the Parliamentary Commissioner Act 1967.

[48]   The use which has been made of the Code is discussed in ch 4 below.

with this exposure the Code is not well known within Whitehall. Hence the emphasis the Lord Chancellor's Department has placed on the steep learning curve which Whitehall faces with the Freedom of Information Act 2000 due to come fully into force by January 2005.

F. The Campaign Continued

Open government

In June 1995 a Code of Practice on openness in the National Health Service came **1.45** into force.[49]

In 1996 the Select Committee on The Parliamentary Commissioner for **1.46** Administration published a report entitled *Open Government* and recommended that a Freedom of Information Act should be introduced. This was the first time that a select committee had done so.

In October 1996 the Labour Party and the Liberal Democrats set up a joint **1.47** Consultative Committee under the chairmanship of Robin Cook MP and Robert Maclennan MP to consider whether there might be sufficient common ground to enable the parties to reach agreement on a legislative programme for constitutional reform. The Joint Committee reported in the spring of 1997. It recorded that both parties were committed to a Freedom of Information Act, and concluded that the proposed legislation would 'shift the balance decisively in favour of a presumption that government information should be made publicly available unless there is justifiable reason not to do so'.

G. The Advance of Information Technology

The technological revolution

By the 1990s technological advance had reached the point where it was far more **1.48** feasible to store information in an organized manner and to retrieve any part of it speedily. Public authorities increasingly stored information in the memory banks of their computers. The easiest form of access to this information would be on-line, but where that was not feasible the authority could have the information available on CD-ROM or disc. These new practical possibilities led in the United States to the Freedom of Information Act Amendments 1996,[50] and in the UK (as in all advanced countries) they enabled a freedom of information system to be set

---

[49] See ch 11 below.
[50] See ch 25 below.

up or operated much more expeditiously than had been possible in the days of manual records.

H. The 1997 White Paper

A change in the official culture

1.49 The 1997 White Paper[51] identified a need to move forward into a new relationship between government and governed where openness became 'part of the official culture rather than an irksome imposition'.[52] It proposed 'legislation designed to replace [the Code of Practice's] piecemeal and inadequate system with clear and consistent requirements which would apply across government'.[53]

1.50 The legislation foreshadowed in the White Paper was bolder in some respects than the statute as finally enacted. The most immediately apparent difference was that the White Paper proposed seven exemptions, whereas the statute specifies twenty-three. Secondly, where a damage test was required in order that information could be exempted, the White Paper test was that disclosure of the relevant information would cause 'substantial harm'.[54] In the statute it is a sufficient ground for withholding information that disclosure would 'prejudice' or be likely to prejudice particular interests. Clearly it is easier for public authorities to meet the 'prejudice' test. Thirdly, there is the matter of ministerial certificates issued in order to prevent disclosure of the relevant information. The White Paper said[55] that the government had considered the possibility of ministerial certificates but had decided against it, 'believing that a government veto would undermine the authority of the Information Commissioner and erode public confidence in the Act'. By virtue of section 53 of the Act,[56] however, 'the accountable person' in relation to the relevant authority can give the Information Commissioner a certificate stating that he has, on reasonable grounds, formed the opinion that the information ought not to be released. The accountable person is a member of the Cabinet or a Law Officer (or a specific senior minister in one of the devolved governments). The decision to issue such a certificate is subject to judicial review. Fourthly, the White Paper, unlike the statute, did not include provision for an Information Tribunal. The White Paper envisaged that any challenge to the Commissioner's decision would be made to the High Court by way of judicial review;[57] the statute introduces an intermediate level of appeal in the form of the Tribunal.

---

[51] Cm 3818; see para 1.01 above.
[52] ibid, Preface by the Prime Minister and para 7.1.
[53] ibid, para 1.6.
[54] ibid, para 3.7.
[55] ibid, para 5.18.
[56] See paras 7.103–7.108 below.
[57] Cm 3818, para 5.16.

Even though the statute is appreciably more cautious in its approach than the **1.51** White Paper it nevertheless heralds a change in the 'official culture'.[58] Instead of routinely keeping matters secret, 'government and other public bodies will need to justify a failure to disclose relevant information upon request. The relationship between citizen and state is being significantly altered'.[59]

---

[58] See para 1.49 above.
[59] HWR Wade and C Forsyth, *Administrative Law*, (8th edn, 2000) 64.

2

THE DEBATE IN PARLIAMENT

A. Introduction

The scope of this chapter

The Freedom of Information Bill was reported on in July 1999 by the House of **2.01**
Commons Public Administration Committee and a House of Lords Select
Committee whose chairman was Lord Archer of Sandwell (Labour). The Bill
underwent significant amendments in its passage through Parliament. This chapter considers the following main issues which were debated: the public interest
test; the need for an executive override or veto on disclosure; non-disclosure and
the need for prejudice; disclosure where investigations are taking place; the environment; safeguarding the formulation of government policy and the conduct of
public affairs. It identifies in respect of each issue the salient points which were
made by Ministers, and gives some account of differing views where these help to
clarify the position of the government.

The principles stated in *Pepper v Hart*

This approach is designed to assist members of the public service, and to guide **2.02**
practitioners to the statements which may be admissible to construe the Act under
the principles laid down in *Pepper v Hart*.[1] In that case Lord Browne-Wilkinson
stated the modern rule in these terms:

---

[1] [1993] AC 593 at 634.

> In my judgment, subject to the questions of the privileges of Parliament reference to Parliamentary material should be permitted as an aid to the construction of legislation which is ambiguous or obscure or the literal meaning of which leads to absurdity. Even in such cases references in court to Parliamentary material should only be permitted where such material clearly discloses the mischief aimed at or the legislative intention lying behind the ambiguous or obscure words. In the case of statements made in Parliament, as at present advised I cannot foresee that any statement other than the statement of the Minister or other promoter of the Bill is likely to meet these criteria.

B. The Main Issues

The public interest test

2.03 The general framework of the Act is to be found within the Bill as originally presented; namely to create a statutory duty to disclose information, subject to the exemptions set out in Part II of the Bill. One of the main arguments in Parliament was about how, and in what way, the public interest should determine whether or not information is disclosed. When the Bill was first introduced public authorities were given a discretion to consider whether, in the public interest, information, which fell within one of the exemptions, should be disclosed. To this main argument was allied the question of what should be the role of the information commissioner. Significant changes were made to the government's proposals during the course of the Bill.

2.04 Those arguments in turn gave rise to a number of further questions.

(a) Should a public interest test apply across the board?
(b) Should the commissioner be restricted to recommending disclosure or should the commissioner have the power to insist on disclosure?
(c) Should the public interest be weighted and if so which way?
(d) Who should have the final say?[2]
(e) Should there be time limits on determining public interest questions?
(f) How far should the factual part of policy advice be subject to the public interest test?[3]

2.05 The Home Secretary, Jack Straw, addressed the first two of those issues on 4 April 2000 in the debate at the report stage in the Commons, when he outlined the way in which the government had changed their original proposals for a public interest test. He said:[4]

---

[2] This is considered in paras 2.12–2.20 below.
[3] This is considered in paras 2.26–2.32 below.
[4] *Hansard,* HC (series 6) vol 347, col 918 (4 April 2000).

I shall describe how the basic scheme of the Bill works. . . Under clause 1 there is a statutory duty to disclose information. Under part II, there are a series of exemptions and exceptions. Some are class exemptions—for example, in respect of policy advice to Ministers—some are total exclusions, which most notably include the security and intelligence agencies, and there are others. Most are determined by a prejudice test.

The first and most important thing to say about that part of the scheme of the Bill is that where there is a dispute about whether information that is sought comes within the exemptions or exclusions under part II, the matter goes to the commissioner and—subject only to appeal to the tribunal and in very limited circumstances, to a court—the commissioner's decision is final. Ministers have no discretion whatever—no veto, no override, nothing. If the commissioner orders a disclosure and says that the information is not exempt or excepted, it has to be disclosed. It is only when the commissioner or the tribunal have themselves said that information that is being sought is not required to be disclosed under clause 1 and part II that the question of the so-called discretionary proposal under clause 13 kicks in. Amendment No 1 relates to clause 13[5]. . .

Originally under clause 13, we proposed that the commissioner would have power to make a recommendation for disclosure, but not be able to order it. The disclosure test, which is first on the public authority, is one of balancing the public interest in disclosure against the public interest in the information not being disclosed. As a result of many representations. . . I recognised the concern in the House about the fact that in the scheme of a statutory right to know it looked slightly odd that there should be provision only for the commissioner to make a recommendation. It was up to the public authority whether to accept it. Two objections were made to that: the first was that only a recommendation could be made and the second, which flowed from that fact, was the level at which a decision would in practice be taken by the public authority as to whether to accept the recommendation might be quite low.

As a result of the representations, we have in many ways fundamentally changed the structure of clause 13 . . . we have made it a duty, not a discretion, on the public authority to consider whether the public interest in disclosure outweighs the public interest in the matter not being disclosed. Where the public authority decides that the balance of public interest is in favour of disclosure, it is under a duty to disclose. If it comes to a contrary view, the matter can go to the commissioner and he can order disclosure. That is the scheme of the Bill.

At the committee stage in the House of Lords Lord Goodhart (Liberal Democrat) **2.06**
sought to clarify the role of the information commissioner and asked whether in respect of the public interest test it would be purely one of judicial review,[6] that is of deciding whether the public authority had erred in law when reaching its decision or otherwise made a perverse decision? Replying, Lord Falconer said:

the position has always been that the commissioner could substitute her own view for that of the authority.[7]

---

[5] Clause 13 became s 2.
[6] *Hansard,* HL (series 5) vol 617, col 906 (17 October 2000).
[7] *Hansard,* HL (series 5) vol 617, col 907 (17 October 2000).

2.07   The third of the issues identified at paragraph 2.04 above was addressed when the government at the committee stage in the Lords introduced a new wording of the balancing test in applying considerations of public interest:

> . . . in all the circumstances of the case, the public interest in disclosing the information outweighs the public interest in maintaining the exemption. . .

Lord Falconer denied at committee stage that this raised burden of proof issues.[8] However, at Lords report stage a Liberal Democrat amendment was accepted which was designed to give greater precedence to public interest considerations. In introducing the amendment, the human rights lawyer Lord Lester of Herne Hill (Liberal Democrat) said:

> These amendments require the public authority, the information commissioner and ultimately the courts to ask and answer a key question: in all the circumstances of the case, does the public interest in maintaining the exclusion of the duty to confirm or deny outweigh the public interest in disclosing whether the public authority holds the information? In other words, the starting point is the public right of access and the public interest in disclosure, and it is for the public authority to justify non-disclosure on the basis that public disclosure is outweighed in the circumstances of the case by the public interest in non-disclosure.
>
> The burden of proof, as we lawyers would say, is placed upon the public authority to show that there is some pressing need for non-disclosure and that the restriction on the public right of access is necessary in the sense of being a proportionate way of meeting that need.

2.08   Lord Falconer replied that the government was interested in seeking to achieve a change of culture in relation to freedom of information and that the amendments:

> will result in an important and significant shift towards greater openness. They will put beyond doubt the Government's resolve that information must be disclosed except where there is an overriding public interest in keeping specific information confidential. Perhaps I may repeat that: information must be disclosed except where there is an overriding public interest in keeping specific information confidential.[9]

2.09   The Lords returned to this in the third reading debate. Lord Lester's explanation and the Minister's reply which accepts the central point Lord Lester is making are illuminating. Lord Lester said:[10]

> I should like to try to explain, for the last time I am sure, why I believe that the Bill as it stands now provides a proper constitutional and legal framework for balancing the competing public interests. My starting point is Article 10 of the European Convention on Human Rights, which guarantees the right to free speech, subject to necessary exemptions.
>
> Article 10 does not segment information and ideas into little categories. What it does is to treat all information and ideas as being the subject matter of the right of

---

[8]   *Hansard,* HL (series 5) vol 617, col 914 (17 October 2000).
[9]   *Hansard,* HL (series 5) vol 619, col 143 (14 November 2000).
[10]   *Hansard,* HL (series 5) vol 619, cols 825–827 (22 November 2000).

freedom of communication and receipt of information and ideas. It then subjects that right to necessary exceptions. Those exceptions are scrutinised carefully as exceptions to a fundamental right, using the well-known principles of proportionality.

The other relevant convention right in Article 8 is to personal privacy, which is one of the exceptions that has to be balanced against free speech.[11] Again, it does not seek to segment the subject; it balances these two fundamental rights using proportionality. So if we had no freedom of information Bill but simply the European Convention of Human Rights as our framework, the information commissioner/the Data Protection Commissioner, being the same person, would be balancing free speech on the one hand covering information and ideas against personal privacy on the other.

But the great weakness of Article 10 as a touchstone is that it has not been interpreted by the European Court of Human Rights yet as giving a general right of access to official information. So although it applies to the balance between free speech and a fair trial, free speech and copyright, or free speech and official secrecy, it does not guarantee a positive right of the public to government information.

One of the most important things that we have achieved in this House in relation to the Bill is that we have repaired the weakness in Article 10, effectively by writing in to Article 10 a right of public access to information and ideas—not subject to particular categories, but subject only to necessary exceptions. There are two kinds of exceptions: those that are absolute, where there is no balancing, and those that are qualified; for example, those that we are considering at present under Clause 35, which are not absolute but are subject to a public interest test.

It will not, ultimately, be for the Minister, for myself, for the noble and learned lord, Lord Archer of Sandwell, or indeed for the Campaign for Freedom of Information to decide what Clause 2 means: it will be a matter for the courts. I find it inconceivable that the information commissioner and the courts will apply a different standard to the freedom of information legislation from that applied to the Data Protection Act, which is the other side of the coin. . .

I find it inconceivable that the proportionality principle will not apply. There is no way in which that test is other than a harm test—a substantial harm or prejudice test. What are the information commissioner and the courts doing when they weigh the right of access to government information against necessary exceptions? They are weighing whether there is a sufficiently substantial prejudice or harm to another facet of the public interest to justify, on an objective basis, curtailing the right of public access to information. . .

Lord Falconer said:[12]   **2.10**

The structure of the Bill now involves exemptions but also, under clause 2, provisions whereby the public authority should disclose the information unless there is a public interest in maintaining the exemption. . .

. . . I hope that I have made clear on previous occasions—if I have not done so, I make it clear on this occasion—that in the case of a piece of information to which an exemption applies but which falls under the provisions of Clause 2, it is necessary for the public authority to consider in each case whether or not the Clause 2 discretion

---

[11] For a full discussion of these convention rights see ch 21 below.
[12] *Hansard*, HL (series 5) vol 619, col 831 (22 November 2000).

requires disclosure of the document or the information. It has to be considered on a case-by-case basis.

2.11 Amendments to impose a definite time limit by which public authorities would make a decision on the public interest test (the fifth issue identified in paragraph 2.04) were unsuccessful, but a Liberal Democrat amendment agreed by the government requires a public authority to give an estimate of the time it will take to reach a decision under clause 2.[13] Lord Bassam of Brighton (Labour) said,[14] for the government, that a failure to comply with the estimate would render the authority liable to a practice recommendation from the commissioner.[15]

The need for an executive override or veto on disclosure

2.12 This issue is about who has the last word. The government's view was that, even where the information commissioner had decided that there was a public interest in an exempt document being disclosed, there might be circumstances where the government should be allowed to overrule the commissioner and keep the information secret. This was a matter which was keenly debated in both Houses.

2.13 The following are the principal questions which were raised.

(a) To what situations would the veto apply?

(b) Does it apply to the preliminary question whether a request falls within an exemption?

(c) To which public authorities would it apply?

(d) What safeguards are there?

(e) Should the power be exercised only by members of the Cabinet?

(f) Should it be a collective decision?

(g) Should reasons be given?

(h) Is the veto subject to judicial review?

(i) Should the veto be subject to a serious harm test?

(j) Should there be enhanced Parliamentary scrutiny?

2.14 The Home Secretary, Jack Straw, dealt with many of these questions in his contribution to the debate at the report stage in the Commons. He said:[16]

> We have moved away from discretionary disclosure: we have placed a duty on the Minister to release information if he or she judges that public interest is in favour of disclosure, not against it; and we have given the commissioner the power to order disclosure.
>
> The issue remains what happens if, notwithstanding the commissioner's order, the public authority continues to believe, for sound reasons, that the information

---

[13] Freedom of Information Act 2000, s 17(2).

[14] *Hansard,* HL (series 5) vol 619, col 190 (14 November 2000).

[15] Under s 48 of the 2000 Act.

[16] *Hansard,* HC (series 6) vol 347, col 921 (4 April 2000).

should not be disclosed. Most regimes that we have surveyed have some sort of executive override of one sort or another, and we propose to have one . . . we propose that the decision in respect of any public authority, other than a local government authority should be made by a Minister of the Crown. . .

However, I have received representations to the effect that decisions in respect of the Executive override both by central government and separately, in respect of local government, would not be made at a high enough level. Where central government is concerned, I accept the burden of the argument that has been put to me. Therefore I propose—it will have to be done in the other place, but it will be done—that those parts of the amendments that speak of Ministers of the Crown will be replaced by a definition of a Cabinet Minister . . . In future such decisions will be made by a Cabinet Minister or the Attorney-General, rather than by any Minister of the Crown.

The second issue relates to collective responsibility. Ministers make two sorts of decisions. The vast range of decisions are made collectively and Ministers are collectively responsible for them in any event. However, some decisions are, by legal expectation and practice, made not collectively but in a quasi-judicial role. . .

It is neither possible nor necessary to write into the Bill that the decisions made by a Cabinet Minister must be made only after consultation and agreement with all of his or her Cabinet colleagues—not least because some of the decisions are quasi-judicial. In practice it would be an extremely unwise Cabinet Minister who chose to issue an exemption certificate amounting to a veto of a decision made by the commissioner to order disclosure without consulting his or her Cabinet colleagues. That might lead to that Cabinet minister's speedy demise and the receipt of his or her P45 by return of post.

To reinforce these arrangements, I propose that there should be written into the ministerial code—which is a published document available in the Library of the House and, I believe on the internet—guidance on how decisions relating to Executive exemption certificates should be made and the way in which other colleagues should be consulted, other than on quasi-judicial decisions.

The Home Secretary was asked by Robert Maclennan MP (Liberal Democrat) **2.15** why if he was prepared to set out rules for consultation in an informal way he was not prepared to follow the New Zealand pattern and legislate for consultation? Mr Straw replied:

The briefing that I have had about the position in New Zealand is that an individual decision was taken on seven occasions. Since decisions have been taken collectively, that figure is down to one. I do not believe that there will be many occasions when a Cabinet Minister—with or without the backing of his colleagues—will have to explain to the House or publicly, as necessary, why he has decided to require information to be held back which the commissioner said should be made available. The changes that I am suggesting will make a significant difference in practice to the behaviour of Ministers.

Subsequent government amendments introduced in the House of Lords limited **2.16** the veto to information relating to government departments, the National Assembly for Wales and any public authority designated by order. The order is subject to the affirmative resolution procedure and is likely to cover bodies such as police authorities, security and law enforcement bodies. Local authorities are not expected to be included within the definition.[17]

2.17 In the second reading in the House of Lords Lord Falconer said[18] it was important to note the limitations on the executive override provision. First, it is not a general override of the commissioner's decisions; it applies only to decisions taken under clause 13.[19] Secondly, the Minister must explain publicly why he has chosen to disagree with the commissioner. Thirdly, the decision is subject to judicial review and the commissioner will have locus to seek such a review. Thus, this is not an easy provision for Ministers to use. Moreover, he said, the government were committed to tabling an amendment at Committee to restrict the use of the override to Cabinet Ministers or the Attorney-General and to explore ways to reflect on the face of the Bill that the decision to use the executive override would be taken collectively.

2.18 Lord Falconer was asked by Baroness Hilton (Labour)[20] whether he believed that a politician is the appropriate person to judge objectively public interest questions in relation to information within his own department? Lord Falconer replied:

> My Lords, an objective conclusion is reached by the information commissioner who has to rule on whether the Minister is right in that respect. If the Minister overrides what is said by the information commissioner, he or she must explain why. The Minister must have the support of Cabinet colleagues and his or her decision is subject to judicial review. It is for this House to decide whether or not Cabinet ministers would regularly overrule the information commissioner and persuade all their Cabinet colleagues to take a political risk in relation to that matter.

2.19 At the report stage of the Bill Lord Falconer summed up the Government's position in this way:[21]

> . . . the Government believe that there will be certain cases dealing with the most sensitive issues where a senior member of the Government, able to seek advice from his Cabinet colleagues, should decide on the final question of public interest in relation to disclosure.
>
> We believe that Cabinet Ministers are accountable in a way in which the commissioner cannot be. It is right that responsibility and accountability should rest at that level for this very important aspect of the freedom of information regime. As noble Lords have pointed out in the course of this short debate, a provision in Clause 52[22] requires the person exercising the override to specify the reasons for doing so. That is the purpose of the override, and that is the basic way it works.

---

[17] See Research paper 00/89 published by Parliament and Constitution Centre, House of Commons Library, 16.
[18] *Hansard*, HL (series 5) vol 612, col 828 (20 April 2000).
[19] Now s 2 of the 2000 Act.
[20] *Hansard*, HL (series 5) vol 612, col 890–891 (20 April 2000).
[21] *Hansard*, HL (series 5) vol 619, col 258 (14 November 2000).
[22] Now s 53(6) of the 2000 Act.

In the third reading debate in the Lords Lord Falconer accepted[23] an amendment **2.20** providing for the accountable person to lay a copy of the exemption certificate before each House of Parliament or the appropriate devolved assembly. He said the government had always made it absolutely clear that the relevant Minister should be accountable to Parliament.

Non-disclosure and the need for prejudice

The Bill as first presented and the Act create some exemptions to the duty to give **2.21** access to information which depend upon 'harm tests' for their operation. The term 'harm tests' refers to the need to demonstrate some form of prejudice as a justification for withholding information under an exemption. Examples can be found in the Act at sections 26 (defence), 27 (international relations) and 31 (law enforcement). Attempts were made in Committee in the Lords to extend 'harm tests' to security matters. These attempts were not successful.

In the second reading debate Lord Falconer dealt with the importance which the **2.22** government attached to harm tests where they do apply. In opening the debate he said:[24]

> Finally, on the subject of exemptions, I want to emphasise the strength of the prejudice test. Prejudice is a term used in other legislation relating to the disclosure of information. It is a term well understood by the courts and the public. It is not a weak test. The commissioner will have the power to overrule an authority if she feels that any prejudice caused by a disclosure would be trivial or insignificant. She will ensure that an authority must point to prejudice which is 'real, actual or of substance'.

The Minister did not think that adding the words 'substantial or significant' was a sensible way forward. What he was saying was that the commissioner would spell *real, actual or of substance* out of the word *prejudice*.

Lord Falconer returned to the 'harm test' in his reply. He said:[25] **2.23**

> A number of noble Lords said that the reference should be to 'substantial harm'. That was the kind of test they were looking for. The word that was chosen where we are dealing with a harm test is 'prejudice'. To all lawyers present—there are depressingly few—'prejudice' will mean some real harm to government. . . It is something real, and it is harm. Should it be 'substantial harm', or should it be 'prejudice'? That sounds like the kind of discussion that a lawyer would like to enter into, but it does not cut to the heart of the debate. It sounds much more theological, if I may use that word in this context, rather than cutting to the fundament of the Bill.

---

[23] *Hansard*, HL (series 5) vol 619, col 845 (22 November 2000).
[24] *Hansard*, HL (series 5) vol 612, col 827 (20 April 2000).
[25] *Hansard*, HL (series 5) vol 612, col 889 (20 April 2000).

Disclosure where investigations are taking place

2.24 The question of the 'harm test' was also raised in the Lords in connection with the investigations exemption[26] concerning investigations and proceedings conducted by public authorities. Lord Goodhart, for the Liberal Democrats, argued that a harm test was unnecessary, since the clause was subject to the newly strengthened public interest test in clause 2.[27] Lord Falconer did not agree and explained that it was appropriate to apply a harm test first in order to decide whether the information qualified as exempt information. If so, the public interest test provided by section 2 could then be applied. He set out the government interpretation of the clause:[28]

> Clause 29(1), first, provides an exemption in respect of material held by an authority which is in the course of investigating existing criminal proceedings.
>
> The purpose of the exemption, with which most people would agree, is that witnesses and people under investigation should not feel inhibited in relation to the material they provide. They should not feel that in addition to the risk of having to give evidence in court there may be an additional risk in relation to trial by press or whatever.
>
> However, Clause 29(1) is subject to Clause 2, the public interest test. If an authority comes within any of the subsections of Clause 29 [and wishes] not to disclose under Clause 2, as I have said and as a result of the amendments advanced by the Liberal Democrats, there must be a good reason for not disclosing. The Noble Lord, Lord Brennan, rightly identified the health-and-safety-at-work-type situation where, for example, the body was not necessarily considering prosecution but might prosecute if it found something wrong. It would therefore be covered by Clause 29 and would receive information about standards of care and safety in every case.
>
> Jenny Bacon,[29] balancing the public interest and disclosure in Clause 2 against any harm that may be done, is perfectly entitled under the provisions of the Bill as it is presently to say that the public interest is plainly in favour of disclosure. But, as a result of the amendments tabled by the Liberal Democrats, it goes further than that. There must be a good reason for Jenny Bacon not to disclose the information. That good reason must be, for example, prejudicing an existing prosecution; deterring witnesses; or making it harder for them to obtain information subsequently in relation to investigations of important matters.

The environment

2.25 Lord Falconer in the second reading debate[30] explained that clause 73[31] gave the Secretary of State the power to make regulations to enable the United Kingdom to ratify the Aarhus Convention on access to environmental information. These

---

[26] Freedom of Information Bill, cl 29 and s 30 of the 2000 Act.

[27] Freedom of Information Act 2000, s 2.

[28] *Hansard,* HL (series 5) vol 619, col 219 (14 November 2000).

[29] The former director-general of the Health and Safety Executive.

[30] *Hansard,* HL (series 5) vol 612, col 829 (20 April 2000).

[31] Freedom of Information Act 2000, s 74.

regulations would replace the existing Environmental Access Regulations made under the European Communities Act 1972. The new regulations would provide wider access than under the current system. The government had taken the decision not to integrate the provisions of the Convention into the Bill itself. However, he said, the Bill's provisions would continue to have effect on access to environmental information. For example, if information were not available under the new regulations the provisions of Clause 13 of the Bill would require disclosure if it were in the public interest.

Formulation of government policy advice and the conduct of public affairs

There was debate about the scope of these exemptions for the formulation of government policy and prejudice to the effective conduct of public affairs which are now in sections 35 and 36 of the Act. In particular there was debate about whether factual information should come within the exemptions. There was also discussion about the meaning of the phrase in what is now section 36 where information was considered exempt 'in the reasonable opinion of a qualified person', and whether the reasonableness of decisions in this area could only be challenged by way of judicial review. The question was also asked whether in relation to scientific data a public interest test or a harm test is more appropriate and more generally whether there is a public interest in maintaining the principle of an exemption for policy matters, and whether this means that harmless scientific information will not be disclosed? **2.26**

The government introduced amendments to clause 33 of the Bill, which became section 35 of the Act: first, to remove the phrase 'in the reasonable opinion of a qualified person' in relation to the release of statistical information and secondly, to provide that statistical information would not be regarded as relating to government policy or ministerial communications once a decision had been taken on the overall policy. **2.27**

Jack Straw in his contribution in the debate at the report stage of the Bill in the House of Commons made clear that the public interest test in clause 2 of the Bill[32] would ensure that there was a significant route for the release of factual and background information, including that which had informed policy discussions.[33] **2.28**

The point was taken up by Lord Falconer in the second reading debate in the House of Lords. He explained that clause 33[34] provided a class exemption for the formulation and development of government policy, and that the public interest disclosure provisions in clause 13[35] would apply to this exemption and ensure that **2.29**

---

[32] Now s 2 of the 2000 Act.
[33] *Hansard*, HC (series 6) vol 347, col 1021 (5 April 2000).
[34] Clause 33 was the basis for s 35.
[35] The public interest test is in s 2 of the 2000 Act.

information would be disclosed where it was in the public interest to do so. He went on to say:[36]

> There has also been discussion as to whether factual and background information used in the decision-making process should be available as of right. No one disagrees that good government can only be achieved if there can be a full and frank exchange of views between Ministers, and between Ministers and their advisers. No one disagrees either that, wherever possible, factual information which is used to provide an informed background to decision-taking should be made available. But the dividing line between facts and opinions, or advice, is simply not that clear. Of course there will be many instances where facts, such as statistics, or research papers, will be freely available—and indeed may already be in published documents. But there will be occasions where 'facts' are part of the discussion or argumentation about options under consideration and where it will not be possible to disentangle facts from opinion or advice. On these occasions the disclosure of such information would, of itself, affect the decision-taking process. Thus there will be a need to withhold such information on a few occasions. To deal with that point, the Government have left the disclosure of factual information relating to policy decisions to Clause 13, albeit with a strong steer towards disclosure set out in that clause.

2.30 In replying to the debate Lord Falconer dealt with the main themes which had run through the debate.[37] Dealing with 'blanket exemptions' Lord Falconer said:

> There have been complaints that there are blanket exemptions; for example, that under Clause 33,[38] in respect of which there has been substantial debate, all information relating to the formulation or development of government policy is exempt; and it is asked why do we not simply provide that kind of exemption on a harm basis as well, rather than on a class basis.
>
> I take Clause 33 as an example to indicate how the Bill works. The provision demonstrates that what applies to the class exemption in that Clause applies also to every other substantive class exemption. It must be determined whether the information relates to the formulation or development of government policy; if so, it is exempt as a class. However, under Clause 13 the Minister is obliged to consider whether the public interest in maintaining the exemption is outweighed by the public interest in disclosing information which would otherwise be exempt. The exemption having been established, the Minister is nevertheless obliged to consider whether the public interest in disclosure outweighs the existence of the exemption.
>
> In relation to Clause 33, much reference has been made to the fact that when a Minister makes a policy decision there will be a good deal of factual background material, the disclosure of which will cause absolutely no harm but will assist the citizen in seeing how government operate. Indeed there will be. Under Clause 13(5)[39] it is specially provided that in making any decision under subsection (3) or (4) in a case where the information is exempt, the Minister must have regard to the public interest in communicating to the applicant the factual information which has been

---

[36] *Hansard,* HL (series 5) vol 612, col 827 (20 April 2000).
[37] *Hansard,* HL (series 5) vol 612, cols 887–893 (20 April 2000).
[38] Freedom of Information Act 2000, s 35.
[39] ibid, s 35(4).

used, or is intended to be used, to provide an informed background to decision-taking.

Therefore, in relation to the Clause 33 exemption, the Minister must consider whether the public interest in disclosure outweighs the exemption. He is specifically directed by the terms of Clause 13 to the public interest in disclosing the factual background that is relevant to the decision-taking.

The 'reasonable opinion of a qualified person' test was retained for section 36 of the Act, the 'prejudice to effective conduct of public affairs' exemption. Lord Falconer also dealt with this.[40] He said that once one accepted that there should be some protection to enable open and frank conversations to take place between officials and Ministers in central government, it seemed right that the same protection should be given to public authorities which were not part of central government. That was one important part of Clause 35. The other important part of Clause 35 concerned the fact that around 50,000 bodies would be covered by the Bill; they would be under an obligation to give people the right to know. However situations may arise which could not be foreseen where some sort of exemption should be given to prevent disclosure which would be prejudicial to the effective conduct of public affairs. The test proposed referred to the reasonable opinion of a qualified person because if one were dealing with a situation that was not targeted, it was right that an individual of high standing and great responsibility in the organization should make the decision as to whether or not Clause 35 should be invoked.

2.31

The Minister went on to say:[41]

2.32

> All of Clause 35 is subject, as the noble Lord, Lord Goodhart, rightly said, to Clause 2; namely the balancing of public interest. The noble Lord, Lord Goodhart, rightly said in relation to the phrase 'in the reasonable opinion of a qualified person' that the information commissioner cannot interfere unless there is some procedural irregularity in the exercise of the discretion or the judgment is so perverse that no reasonably qualified person could have come to it. However, when it comes to Clause 2, the information commissioner is entitled to substitute her view for that of the public authority as regards where the balance lies between the exemption on the one hand and the public interest and disclosure on the other. In the light of the amendments put in by the Liberal Democrats earlier tonight, the balance will start in favour of disclosure unless there is a good reason against disclosure. It seems to me that that is a reasonable structure. A reference to, 'the reasonable opinion of a qualified person' provides sensible protection. It is sensible that there should be a clause such as Clause 35 to cover bodies other than central government and to deal with 50,000 public authorities which may have particular concerns in relation to it.

---

[40] Freedom of Information Bill, cl 35 and s 36 of the 2000 Act.
[41] *Hansard*, HL (series 5) vol 619, col 240 (14 November 2000).

3

AN OVERVIEW

A. Introduction

Scope of the chapter

The Freedom of Information Act 2000 is unlikely to be used as a model for new **3.01** recruits to the Office of Parliamentary Counsel. It is an unnecessarily complicated piece of legislation. Part B of this chapter faces up to this fact, and tries to give a simple overview of the Act; it suggests the questions public authorities are going to have to ask when someone seeks information; and identifies the provisions concerning practice, procedure and implementation. Part C of the chapter looks at the principles which the courts are likely to apply when construing the Act. Finally there are examples of the day-to-day challenges which public authorities will face and a broad range of illustrations of the kind of ways in which individuals and businesses are likely to try to use the Act.

B. The Framework and Scheme of the Act

(1) Parts I and II and Schedule 1

A statutory right to information

The most important reform which the Act makes comes in section 1(1). It estab- **3.02** lishes a statutory right of access to information held by public authorities. Its importance was recognized by the Home Secretary, Jack Straw, who said it:

lays down for the first time in our constitutional history that the public have a right to know about the work of government and all other public authorities.[1]

There are two limbs to the statutory right. Any person making a request is entitled:

(a) to be informed in writing by the public authority whether it holds information of the description specified in the request, and

(b) if that is the case, to have that information communicated to him.

The duty under (a) is described[2] as *the duty to confirm or deny*.

3.03 'Public authorities' are listed in the first Schedule. It is a long list, divided into seven parts: (i) general, (ii) local government, (iii) the National Health Service, (iv) maintained schools and other educational institutions, (v) police, (vi) other public bodies and offices, and (vii) other public bodies and offices—Northern Ireland. The authorities range from *any government department* to *the Zoos Forum*. The Lord Chancellor has power to add to the list,[3] but in relation to Scotland the power is strictly limited.[4]

3.04 The person making the inquiry is not entitled to have any information he wants. There are exemptions set out in Part II: a general exemption in section 21, which excludes information accessible to the applicant by other means, and specific exemptions in sections 22 to 44. The scheme, however, is a general right with exemptions, not a limited right. This may affect the question of where the burden of proof lies.

3.05 The framework is that the rights granted in section 1(1) are expressed to have effect subject to section 2, which in turn sets out the effect of the exemptions. These provisions are complex.[5] There are two questions: first, is there a duty to disclose whether the authority has the information, and second, should the information be handed over? In each case it is necessary to consider the individual section in Part II which specifies the exemption in conjunction with section 2. The provisions must be examined in some detail because they raise a series of questions which public authorities will have to answer when they are asked for information under the Act.

---

[1] The historical background is discussed in ch 1 above.
[2] See the Freedom of Information Act 2000, s 1(6). The Act is in Appendix C.
[3] ibid, s 4.
[4] ibid, s 80.
[5] The complexity may have arisen because of the way the Bill was amended at a late stage in the House of Lords. See House of Commons Research Paper 00/89.

Three types of exemption

There are three types of exemption found in Part II.[6] First there are provisions **3.06** which confer absolute exemption. These exempt all information within a wide class. The only question is whether the information falls within the class; there is no public interest test. If the information falls within the class there is no duty to disclose the information nor to say whether the authority holds it. The absolute exemptions are specified in section 2(3). They are set out in section 21 (information accessible to the applicant by other means); section 23 (information supplied by, or relating to, bodies dealing with security matters); section 32 (court records); section 34 (Parliamentary privilege); section 36 (information held by the House of Commons or the House of Lords); section 40 (personal data); section 41 (information provided in confidence) and section 44 (statutory prohibitions on disclosure). The force of this last exemption is somewhat modified by section 75 which gives the Lord Chancellor power by order to repeal or amend any existing statute or statutory instrument which is capable of preventing the disclosure of information under section 1 of the Act. There are over 300 legislative provisions which contain restrictions on disclosure. The Lord Chancellor's Department is undertaking a review of them. It remains to be seen after the review what use will be made of this power.

The second type of exemption is like the first except that it is not absolute. Again **3.07** it relates to all information in a wide class, regardless of whether the particular disclosure is harmful. It is, however, not enough for the public authority to decide that information properly falls into the class: it has to go on to consider whether the public interest test in section 2 means that the information should be disclosed. This class comprises exemptions for information intended for future publication (section 22), national security (section 24) investigations and proceedings (section 30), communications with the Royal Family (section 37), environmental information (section 39),[7] the formulation of government policy and ministerial communications (section 35), and legal professional privilege (section 42).

The third type of exemption applies where disclosure can be shown to prejudice **3.08** interests which are singled out in the Act, namely defence (section 26), international relations (section 27), relations within the United Kingdom (section 28), the economy (section 29), law enforcement (section 31),[8] audit functions (section 33), the conduct of public affairs (section 36), health and safety (section 38) and

---

[6] These three types are identified in the Campaign for Freedom of Information's briefing on the House of Lords third reading of the Bill.

[7] This is not a true exception, see para 3.21 below.

[8] The law enforcement exception is wide: it includes the detection of crime, the prosecution of offenders, the administration of justice, the collection of taxes, immigration controls and security in prisons.

commercial interests (section 43(2)). If prejudice *cannot* be shown, the information must be disclosed. If prejudice *is* established, the information will still have to be disclosed under the public interest test set out in section 2, if the balance of public interest favours disclosure.

Section 2—the public interest test

3.09 Section 2 has an elaborate structure, but in essence it does two things. First, it identifies the exemptions in Part II which are absolute. The rights in section 1 do not apply to this exempt information. Secondly, it provides a public interest test for all other exceptions.

3.10 The right to be informed whether a public authority holds information does not apply if:

> in all the circumstances of the case, the public interest in maintaining the exclusion of the duty to confirm or deny outweighs the public interest in disclosing whether the public authority holds the information.

The right to the communication of information held by the authority does not apply if:

> in all the circumstances of the case, the public interest in maintaining the exemption outweighs the public interest in disclosing the information.

Lord Falconer, speaking on behalf of the government at the report stage of the Bill in the House of Lords, said that the amendments then made to section 2:

> put beyond doubt the Government's resolve that information must be disclosed except where there is an overriding public interest in keeping specific information confidential.[9]

3.11 There was a lively public debate following the report stage in the House of Lords as to whether on the wording of section 2 it would be possible for government departments to argue in the case of *class exemptions* that the public interest would be harmed by any disclosure from within the relevant class of documents, regardless of the consequences of the disclosure of the actual information.[10] We consider this argument in detail elsewhere,[11] but it seems to be contradicted by the passage cited from Lord Falconer with its emphasis on *specific information*. Further, if the argument was right it would be difficult to see why only some class exemptions are made 'absolute'.

---

[9] *Hansard,* HL (series 5) vol 619, col 143 (14 November 2000).

[10] See the Campaign for Freedom of Information's briefing dated 21 November 2000 and a letter in the *Guardian* dated 16 November 2000 from Lords Goodhart and Lester.

[11] The discussion in Parliament is considered at paras 2.07–2.10 above.

Formulation of government policy and the conduct of public affairs

Two of the most far-reaching exemptions concern the formulation of government **3.12** policy (section 35) and the conduct of public affairs (section 36). Section 35 is restricted to information held by a government department[12] or by the National Assembly for Wales. It does not extend to local authorities. Section 36 applies to information held by all public authorities.

Information is exempt if it is held by a government department and relates to the **3.13** formulation or development of government policy, ministerial communications, the provision of advice by the Law Officers or any request for the provision of such advice or the operation of a ministerial private office.[13]

Section 35(2) provides that once a decision on government policy has been taken, **3.14** any statistical information used to provide an informed background to the taking of the decision is not to be regarded as relating to the formulation of policy or to ministerial communications.

Section 35 does not confer an absolute exemption, so the public interest test has **3.15** to be applied. The test is reinforced by section 35(4) which provides that in applying the test regard shall be had to the particular public interest in disclosure of factual information which has been used, or is intended to be used, to provide informed background to decision-taking. If these words are to have any meaning they must weigh the scales of the public interest test in favour of disclosure of such factual information.

Section 36 applies to information the disclosure of which in the reasonable opin- **3.16** ion of a qualified person would, or would be likely:

(a) to prejudice the maintenance of the convention of the collective responsibility of Ministers, or the work of the Executive Committee of the Northern Ireland Assembly, or the work of the executive committee of the National Assembly for Wales;
(b) to inhibit the free and frank provision of advice, or the free and frank exchange of views for the purposes of deliberation, or would otherwise prejudice, or would be likely to otherwise prejudice, the effective conduct of public affairs.

This is very wide. It is not confined to government departments, it applies to all **3.17** public authorities. The decision under this section is to be taken not by the public authority itself but by a *qualified person*. This is to ensure that the decision is taken at a high level. The qualified person must act *reasonably*.

---

[12] 'Government department' is defined by s 84.
[13] 'Government policy', 'the Law Officers', 'ministerial communications' and 'ministerial private office' are defined in s 35(5).

3.18 The exemption is absolute in so far as it relates to the House of Commons and the House of Lords. The qualified person for the House of Commons is the Speaker. The qualified person for the House of Lords is the Clerk of the Parliaments. Section 36(7) provides that a certificate signed by the Speaker or the Clerk that information falls within the section is conclusive. This must mean that certificates signed by other qualified persons are not conclusive.

3.19 Section 36(5)(a) identifies a *qualified person* in respect of a government department in the charge of a Minister of the Crown as any Minister of the Crown. Section 36(5)(b) to (n) identifies a range of other *qualified people* in respect of different authorities, including the Mayor of London and the Comptroller and Auditor General. The *qualified person* in respect of information held by public authorities not specifically identified means (section 36(5)(o)):

    (i)   a Minister of the Crown,

    (ii)   the public authority, if authorised for the purposes of this section by a Minister of the Crown, or

    (iii) any officer or employee of the public authority who is authorised for the purpose of this section by a Minister of the Crown.

3.20 We consider below what are the consequences of the qualified person having to reach a *reasonable opinion*.

Environmental information

3.21 The Aarhus Convention on access to information, public participation in decision-making and access to justice in environmental matters was signed on 25 June 1998. Under Article 4 of the Convention each party is to ensure that public authorities, in response to a request for environmental information, make such information available to the public, within the framework of national legislation. Section 74 of the Act provides that the Secretary of State may make regulations for the purpose of implementing the information provisions of the Convention. The provisions of the Convention are similar to, but not the same as, the provisions of the Act.[14] Section 39 of the Act provides that information is exempt information if an authority is required to make it available in accordance with the regulations: this means that when the regulations are made the disclosure of environmental information will be made under the Convention and not under the Act. Environmental information, therefore, is not exempt.

Certificates for security information

3.22 In wartime, even in a war against terrorism, it is easy to believe that careless talk costs lives. It is not surprising that the Act gives added protection to the confiden-

---

[14] See paras 16.48–16.69 below.

tiality of information about security. The exemptions about security matters which are in sections 23 and 24 are strengthened by providing that a certificate signed by a Minister is conclusive evidence that the information falls within the exemptions. There are however two safeguards. First, the certificate has to be signed by a member of the Cabinet or by the appropriate Law Officer. Secondly, the certificates can be challenged under section 60.

Section 60 provides that the Information Commissioner or the applicant for the information concerned may appeal to the Information Tribunal[15] about the certificate. The Tribunal has a free hand to quash a certificate given under section 23(2) if it concludes that the information to which it applies was not supplied by or related to the security bodies listed in section 23(3). The Tribunal may quash a certificate under section 24(3) if it concludes, applying judicial review principles, that the Minister did not have reasonable grounds for issuing the certificate. **3.23**

Where a certificate contains a general description of the information to which it applies the Tribunal is given power under section 60(4) and (5) to determine to what information it does apply. **3.24**

Other certificates

The Speaker, in the case of the House of Commons, and the Clerk of the Parliaments, in the case of the House of Lords, can issue certificates which are conclusive where questions of Parliamentary privilege arise[16] or where information is held by either House in its conduct of public affairs.[17] **3.25**

Other qualifications on the statutory right

Exemptions apart, there are three other ways in which the statutory right may be curtailed. First, the person seeking information may have to pay for it. Section 9 provides that a public authority may charge fees in accordance with regulations made by the Lord Chancellor, though the section envisages that no fees may be charged in prescribed cases.[18] Secondly, cost may also excuse a public authority from complying with a request for information,[19] if the authority estimates that the cost of complying would exceed the appropriate limit, being such sum as may be prescribed,[20] it seems, by regulations to be made by the Lord Chancellor.[21] **3.26**

---

[15] The role of the Commissioner and the Tribunal are considered at paras 3.36–3.55 below.
[16] Section 34(3).
[17] Section 36(5), (7).
[18] Section 9(4)(a).
[19] Section 12(1).
[20] Section 12(3).
[21] Section 12(5).

3.27 Thirdly, a public authority does not have to comply with a request, if the request is vexatious, or if a person repeats a request without allowing a reasonable time to elapse.[22] The Act does not define 'vexatious'.

The questions the public authority must ask

3.28 At this point it is convenient to consider what are the questions which a public authority must ask when it receives a request for information. The decision-making process on the release of information has a number of stages. When it first considers the matter[23] the questions which the public authority must ask are:

(a) Does it have the information which is sought?

(b) Have any certificates been issued which help to answer the questions which the authority faces?

(c) Is the information exempt under any of the grounds set out in Part II of the Act? If it is *not* the authority is under a duty to say that it has the information and to release it.

(d) Does the information fall within any of the absolute exemptions specified in section 2(3)?

If the answer is yes it should not be disclosed, at any rate at this stage.[24]

If the answer is no:

(e) Should the authority
  (i) disclose that it holds the information?
  (ii) hand it over?

(f) In either case does the information fall within an exemption which is triggered by *prejudice*?

If the answer is yes:

(g) Has there been prejudice? If the answer is no the information must be disclosed.

If the answer is yes, or if the information falls within one of the class exemptions the public interest test must be applied.

(h) Is the balance of public interest in favour of disclosure
  (i) of the existence of the information?
  (ii) of the information?

If the answer is yes there is a duty to disclose.

(i) Is this a case where the other qualifications on the statutory right should be applied:
  (i) is a payment to be made?
  (ii) does the cost of supplying the information exceed the appropriate limit?
  (iii) is the request vexatious?

---

[22] Section 14.
[23] For the position on appeal see paras 3.51–3.55 below.
[24] The authority's decision may be overruled by the Commissioner or the Tribunal.

Proper procedures

Public authorities are required by the Act to have proper procedures in place, both **3.29** to publish information and to deal with the questions which will arise under the Act.[25] Proper procedures will involve referring all requests for information to a designated officer or team who have access to legal advice. The answer to the majority of questions will be straightforward, but the procedure will have to provide for the most difficult questions to be considered at the highest level of the authority.

Timetables

What is more, the authority is under a strict timetable. Section 10(1) provides that **3.30** the authority must comply with section 1(1) promptly and in any event not later than the twentieth working day following the date of receipt of the request. Where the applicant has to pay for the information, the time during which payment is awaited does not count as part of the 20 days. The Lord Chancellor has power to extend the 20-day period to up to 60 days by regulation, but as the government originally proposed a 40-day response time in the Bill and reduced this to 20 days the Lord Chancellor is not likely to rush to make regulations extending the time.

Refusal of request for information

A public authority which refuses to give information must within the 20-day **3.31** period give the applicant a notice specifying the exemption on which it relies and stating why the exemption applies. The authority must give the applicant such a notice even in the case where the Act provides that no duty under section 1(1)(a) or (b) arises.

(2) Section 18, Schedule 2 and Part III

Regulation

The regulation of freedom of information is in the hands of the Information **3.32** Commissioner and the Information Tribunal, with the Secretary of State[26] and the Lord Chancellor having particular functions. There is an appeal on a point of law to the High Court.

---

[25] See ss 19 and 20 and 45 and 46.

[26] ie one of Her Majesty's Principal Secretaries of State: see the Interpretation Act 1978, s 5, Sch 1. The Bill was introduced by the Home Secretary but responsibility for freedom of information now comes under the Lord Chancellor's Department. All the functions of the Secretary of State (save for the regulation-making power under s 74) were transferred to the Lord Chancellor by the Transfer of Functions (Miscellaneous) Order 2001, SI 2001/3500, arts 3 and 8, Sch 1 para 12, Sch 2 para 8, which came into force on 26 November 2001.

3.33 The Information Commissioner and the Information Tribunal are the pre-existing Data Protection Commissioner and Data Protection Tribunal with their roles expanded to cover both Acts.[27] The form of the legislation is dictated to some extent by the fact that Parliament legislated for data protection before freedom of information. The records of the Commissioner and the Tribunal are public records for purposes of the Public Records Act 1958.[28] The Tribunal is under the direct supervision of the Council on Tribunals.[29]

Codes of practice

3.34 Section 45 provides that the Lord Chancellor shall, after consultation with the Commissioner, issue a code of practice which shall be laid before each House of Parliament and must include provisions relating to:

(a) the provision of advice and assistance to applicants;

(b) the transfer of requests by one authority to another by which the information is or may be held;

(c) consultation with persons to whom the information requested relates or persons whose interests are likely to be affected by the disclosure of information;

(d) the inclusion in public authority contracts of terms relating to the disclosure of information; and

(e) procedures for dealing with complaints.

3.35 Section 46 provides that the Lord Chancellor shall issue a code of practice to relevant authorities in connection with the keeping, management, and destruction of their records. The Codes of Practice which the Lord Chancellor has issued are included in Appendix D and Appendix E below.

General functions of the Commissioner

3.36 The general functions of the Commissioner are to:[30]

(a) promote good practice, the observance of the requirements of the Act and the provisions of the codes;

(b) disseminate information to the public about the operation of the Act, good practice and other matters within the scope of his functions and to give advice as to any of those matters;

(c) assess, with the consent of any public authority, whether it is following good practice;

---

[27] Section 18.

[28] See the Public Records Act 1958; Sch 1, Pt II of the Table in para 3, as amended by the Freedom of Information Act 2000, Sch 2, Pt 1, para 3(1).

[29] See the Tribunals and Inquiries Act 1992, Sch 1, Pt 1, para 14.

[30] Freedom of Information Act 2000, s 47.

(d) consult the Keeper of Public Records about the promotion of the observance of the section 46 code in relation to public records.

Good practice is defined in section 47(6) to mean such practice in the discharge of   **3.37**
a public authority's functions under the Act as appears to the Commissioner to be desirable and includes (but is not limited to) compliance with the requirements of the Act and the provisions of the codes of practice.

Recommendations as to good practice

The Commissioner may give a practice recommendation in writing to a public   **3.38**
authority under section 48, where it appears its practice does not conform with the code, specifying the provisions of the code with which it does not conform and specifying the steps it should take to promote such conformity.

The Commissioner is required to report annually to each House of Parliament.[31]   **3.39**

(3) Parts IV and V and Schedules 3 and 4

Enforcement

The Commissioner has the key role in enforcing the Act and is given real power,   **3.40**
subject only to the ministerial veto on decision notices and enforcement notices provided for by section 53.

Decision notices

First, it is the Commissioner who decides under section 50 of the Act whether a   **3.41**
request for information made to a public authority has been dealt with in accordance with the requirements of Part 1 of the Act. Any person who has applied for information may apply to the Commissioner for such a decision. The Commissioner is bound to make a decision unless the complainant has not exhausted the complaints procedure of the authority, or there has been undue delay in making the application, or the application is frivolous or vexatious.

When the Commissioner has made a decision he is required to serve a *decision*   **3.42**
notice on the complainant and the public authority. If the Commissioner decides that a public authority has failed to communicate information, or to provide confirmation or denial that it holds information, where it is required so to do, the decision notice must specify the steps which must be taken by the authority in order to comply with the Act and the period within which the steps must be taken. The decision notice must contain particulars of the right to appeal conferred by section 57. The time specified for taking any steps must not expire before the time for appealing.

---

[31] Section 49.

Information notices

3.43   Secondly, section 51 provides that the Commissioner may serve an *information notice* on a public authority (a) if he has received an application under section 50 or (b) if he reasonably requires any information for the purpose of determining whether an authority has complied with the requirements of Part 1 of the Act, or is conforming with the codes of practice. The notice will require the authority, within such time as is specified, to furnish the Commissioner with the information he requests. If the Commissioner serves a notice under (b) he must give his reasons for regarding the information as relevant. Again the information notice must contain particulars of the right to appeal and the time specified for giving the notice must not expire during the appeal period. The section does not allow the Commissioner to obtain information which is covered by some legal professional privilege.[32]

3.44   In section 51 *information* includes unrecorded information. This and section 75(2) are the only sections where *information* is given this particular definition. Elsewhere it means '*information recorded in any form*'.[33]

Enforcement notices

3.45   Thirdly, section 52 provides that the Commissioner may serve an *enforcement notice* on a public authority if it has failed to comply with any requirement of Part 1, requiring the authority to take specific steps within a specific time to remedy matters. The notice must specify the requirements with which the authority has failed to comply. The notice must also state the Commissioner's reasons for reaching such a conclusion. Again the notice must contain particulars of the right to appeal, and the authority must be able to appeal before it is required to comply with the notice.

The ministerial veto

3.46   When the Information Commissioner issues a decision or enforcement notice requiring the disclosure of information from a government department this may be subject to a ministerial override, or veto, where specified conditions are met.[34] The conditions are that in respect of a government department a member of the Cabinet, or the Attorney-General, certifies that he has on reasonable grounds formed the opinion that in respect of the request concerned there was no failure to comply with the Act. There are comparable provisions allowing certificates to be given where notices are served on the National Assembly for Wales or on any public authority designated by an order made by the Lord Chancellor. In other words, in each of these cases the decision of the Commissioner can be overruled.

---

[32]   Section 51(5).
[33]   Section 84.
[34]   Section 53.

The certificate has to be given not later than the twentieth working day following **3.47** the effective date. The effective date means the day on which the notice was given to the public authority or where an appeal is brought, the date on which that appeal is determined or withdrawn.

There are safeguards. First, the person giving the certificate has to lay a copy of the **3.48** certificate before each House of Parliament.[35] Secondly, where a certificate is given in respect of a decision notice the accountable person, for example a member of the Cabinet, has to inform the complainant under section 50 of the reasons for his opinion. Thirdly, there is nothing in the Act which prevents the Commissioner or the complainant seeking on judicial review to have the certificate quashed, on for example the ground that the reasons which the accountable person has given are capricious.

Powers of entry and inspection

The Commissioner is given wide powers of entry and inspection which are set out **3.49** in Schedule 3. It is an offence to obstruct a person in the execution of a warrant issued under Schedule 3.[36]

Contempt of court

Section 54 gives the High Court power to enforce the Commissioner's decisions **3.50** by dealing with an authority which fails to comply with a notice as if it had committed a contempt of court.[37] This means the court can impose a prison sentence of up to two years. This can be an effective sanction, but the position of public servants is protected because the court is required to consider any evidence or statement offered in defence and the Act does not confer any civil right of action on the citizen who has failed to obtain information to which he or she is entitled.

Appeals

Section 57 entitles a complainant or a public authority to appeal to the Tribunal **3.51** against a decision notice and also enables a public authority to appeal to the Tribunal against any information notice or enforcement notice served upon it.

Section 58 sets out two grounds on which the Tribunal can allow an appeal: (a) if **3.52** a notice is not in accordance with the law and (b) if it considers that the Commissioner ought to have exercised his discretion differently. The Tribunal may review any finding of fact on which the notice in question is based.

---

[35] Section 53(3).
[36] Schedule 3, para 12.
[37] The Commissioner may certify in writing to the court that a public authority has failed to comply with a notice. The court may then inquire into the matter, and will no doubt usually do so on the application of the Commissioner or the applicant.

3.53 Section 59 provides that any party may appeal from the decision of the Tribunal on a point of law to the High Court.

3.54 Section 60 deals with appeals against certificates issued in relation to national security matters.[38]

3.55 Section 61 introduces Schedule 4 which amends the Data Protection Act 1998, Schedule 6, relating to appeal proceedings; consequently appeals under Part V of the 2000 Act are dealt with in accordance with the procedures in the amended Schedule 6 to the 1998 Act.

(4) Part VI and Schedule 5

Historical records and records in the Public Record Office

3.56 The Public Records Act 1958, s 3(1) imposes a duty on every person responsible for public records to make arrangements for the selection and safekeeping of those records which ought to be permanently preserved. The 2000 Act makes no changes to the existing system of selecting records for transfer to the Public Record Office.

3.57 What do change are the rules under which 'historical records'[39] can be inspected. Access to records will depend not on their being 30 years old or more, as now, but on whether they 'fall to be disclosed in accordance with the Freedom of Information Act 2000'.[40]

3.58 People will have greater access to historical records than to current documents. Some of the exemptions in Part II of the Act do not apply to historical records. Section 63 provides that information in a historical record cannot be exempt by virtue of section 28 (relations within the United Kingdom), 30(1) (investigations and criminal proceedings conducted by public authorities), 32 (court records), 33 (audit functions), 35 (formulation of government policy), 36 (prejudice to effective conduct of public affairs), 37(1)(a) (communications with the Royal Family), 42 (legal professional privilege) or 43 (commercial interests). Section 63 also specifies how long information can remain exempt under the honours[41] and law enforcement[42] exemptions (60 years and 100 years respectively).

3.59 Information contained in a historical record in the Public Record Office cannot be exempt on the grounds that it is accessible to the applicant by other means or

---

[38] For a fuller discussion see para 3.23 above and para 3.83 below.

[39] Section 62 defines the terms *'historical record'* for the purposes of Part VI of the Act. A record becomes a *historical record* at the end of the period of thirty years beginning with the year following that in which it was created. *Year* means a calendar year.

[40] Public Records Act 1958, s 5, as amended by Sch 5 to the 2000 Act.

[41] Freedom of Information Act 2000, s (1)(b).

[42] Section 31.

is intended for future publication.[43] Information which was supplied by, or relates to, bodies dealing with security matters which is contained in a historical record in the Public Record Office is not subject to an absolute exemption.[44]

Section 65 provides that where a historical record is also a public record as defined **3.60** by the Public Records Act 1958, a public authority must consult the Lord Chancellor before refusing a request for information contained in it unless it falls within an absolute exemption. Section 66 makes provision for consultation as to the exempt status of certain public records.

(5) *Part VII and Schedule 6*

Freedom of information and data protection

The Information Commissioner oversees both the Freedom of Information Act **3.61** 2000 and the Data Protection Act 1998. Both laws relate to aspects of information policy. The scheme of the 2000 Act is that this joint responsibility will allow the Information Commissioner to provide an integrated and coherent approach to information handling and will provide a single point of contact for public authorities and the public. The two laws come together at the point where personal information is considered for disclosure.

The Freedom of Information Act 2000 extends access rights to personal informa- **3.62** tion which already existed under the Data Protection Act 1998. Section 69 introduces a new section 9A in the 1998 Act which makes provision for access to unstructured personal data held by public authorities.

The way the two Acts work is that a request by an individual for information **3.63** about himself will be exempt under the Freedom of Information Act and will continue to be handled as a 'subject access request' under the Data Protection Act. In certain circumstances such a request may involve the release of associated third party information.

Where an applicant specifically requests information about a third party, the **3.64** request falls within the remit of the Freedom of Information Act. However, the authority must apply the *data protection principles*[45] when considering the disclosure of information relating to living individuals. An authority must not release third party information if to do so would mean breaching one of the principles.

---

[43] Section 64(1).
[44] Section 64(2).
[45] The data protection principles are considered in detail at paras 10.16–10.34 below.

(6) Part VIII and Schedules 7 and 8

Disclosure of information between Commissioner and ombudsmen

3.65 Section 76 allows the Commissioner to disclose to one of a range of named ombudsmen any information which appears to the Commissioner to relate to a matter which could be the subject of an investigation by that ombudsman. Schedule 7 provides for the Parliamentary Commissioner to disclose to the Commissioner any information which appears to the Parliamentary Commissioner to relate to matters in respect of which the Commissioner might exercise his enforcement powers or which relates to the commission of an offence under the Act or the Data Protection Act 1998. There are similar provisions in Schedule 7 for disclosure by the other ombudsmen.

The offence of altering records with intent to prevent disclosure

3.66 Section 77 makes it an offence to alter, deface, block, erase, destroy or conceal records held by a public authority with the intention of preventing disclosure to an applicant who has made a request for the information and is entitled to receive it. The offence applies to the public authority and any person who is an officer or employee or is subject to the direction of the authority. A government department is not liable to prosecution under the Act but section 77 and paragraph 12 of Schedule 3 apply to a person in the public service of the Crown as they apply to any other person.[46]

The voluntary disclosure of information

3.67 Nothing in the Act is to be taken to limit the powers of a public authority to disclose information held by it.[47]

Defamation

3.68 Section 79 provides that for the purposes of the law of defamation, the disclosure of information under the Act is covered by qualified privilege, in cases where the information was supplied to the public authority by a third person.

Interpretation and repeals

3.69 Section 84 is the interpretation section. Repeals are set out in Schedule 8.

---

[46] Section 81(3)
[47] Section 78.

Commencement

Section 87(1) sets out the provisions of the Act which came into force on 30   **3.70**
November 2000, the day the Act was passed. Section 87(2) sets out the provisions
of the Act which came into force on 1 February 2001. Section 87(3) provides the
rest of the Act shall come into force at the end of the period of five years beginning
with the day on which the Act was passed or on such day before the end of that
period as the Lord Chancellor may appoint.

The Lord Chancellor announced to the House of Lords on 13 November 2001   **3.71**
that the Act will be implemented in full by January 2005; eleven months before
the deadline set out in section 87(3) of the Act. The timetable is set out in the Lord
Chancellor's first annual report to Parliament on the implementation of the Act
made in November 2001.

The publication scheme provisions of the Act, which require every public author-   **3.72**
ity to adopt and maintain a scheme for the publication of information by the
authority,[48] will be implemented first, on a rolling programme, according to the
timetable shown below.

November 2002:	Central government (except the Crown Prosecution Service and the Serious Fraud Office), Parliament, National Assembly for Wales, and non-departmental public bodies currently subject to the Code of Practice on Access to Government Information.
February 2003:	Local government (except police authorities).
June 2003:	Police, police authorities, Crown Prosecution Service, Serious Fraud Office, armed forces.
October 2003:	Health Service.
February 2004:	Schools, universities, remaining non-departmental public bodies.
June 2004:	Remaining public authorities.

The individual right of access to information will be brought into force for all   **3.73**
public authorities in January 2005.

Public authorities in Northern Ireland will either be required to apply publication   **3.74**
schemes at the same time as their counterparts in England and Wales, or alternative arrangements will be made. This is a matter for further discussion between the
Lord Chancellor's Department and the Northern Ireland Assembly.

---

[48] See para 3.98 below.

C. Principles of Construction to be Applied

The scope of this part of this chapter

3.75 This part of this chapter takes an overview of the constitutional principles, both those recognized by the common law and those deriving from the practice of the European Court of Human Rights, which the courts will apply in construing the Freedom of Information Act 2000. These principles are discussed throughout the book. It also considers how the rights created by the Act fit into the constitutional framework of the United Kingdom now that the Human Rights Act 1998 is part of the constitutional arrangements.

Accountability

3.76 The principle of accountability means that information is held by government, not for its own benefit, but for the benefit of the public. Ministers in the United Kingdom are accountable for their actions both to Parliament and to the law. The principle is summed up by Lord Scott of Foscote in his essay on confidentiality.[49]

> At the heart of the principle of accountability lies the obligation of Ministers to give information about the activities of their departments and about the actions and omissions of their civil servants . . . unless there is an acceptable public interest reason for withholding information, the constitutional principle of accountability requires that if information about government or its activities is sought the information should be disclosed.[50]

3.77 The reason for this is that it is desirable in a democracy that information should be readily available to the public, so that people can understand the basis for the decisions which are taken by the executive, and judge the competence, fairness and honesty of those who govern them. The principle reinforces one of the main purposes of the Act.

3.78 It is one of the characteristics of the Westminster constitution that Ministers are Members of Parliament. The development of party politics and the whip system has meant that a government with a majority in the Commons can usually get its own way. Notwithstanding this, one of the main functions of Parliament is to control the executive and to do this Parliament needs the best possible access to information. Despite the conflicts imposed by the whip system, Members of Parliament have consistently recognized that Parliament should be on the side of openness. This can be seen in the development of select committees which followed the influential report by the Select Committee on Procedure in 1978.

---

[49] Published in *Freedom of Expression and Freedom of Information*, Essays in honour of Sir David Williams (OUP, 2000).

[50] See further ch 20, part E below.

The principle recognizes that it is important in a democracy that the executive **3.79** makes information available to Parliament. It is also important that it makes information available to the courts, when they are exercising their judicial review function. When a court is considering the questions raised in *Associated Provincial Picture Houses Limited v Wednesbury Corporation*,[51] whether the authority has acted reasonably, and whether it has taken the relevant factors into account, it is important to know what information the authority had to hand.

Surprisingly, however, the courts have been slow to order discovery of documents, **3.80** interrogatories or cross-examination in judicial review proceedings.[52] The litigant was probably better off before the introduction of Order 53 in 1977, when judicial review was often obtained by means of an action for a declaration in the Chancery Division, where discovery and cross-examination were available as of right. The right to know under the Act should help the courts and individuals who seek to challenge decisions of the executive to see the full background to the decision which is challenged.

Exhaustion of available remedies

It is convenient to consider this topic here, though the exhaustion of available **3.81** remedies is not a principle but rather a procedural hurdle. The Act is designed so that individuals can enforce their rights without having to embark on expensive legal actions. An applicant who is dissatisfied with the answer of a public authority has to go through the authority's complaints procedure before he can ask the Information Commissioner for a decision.[53] The applicant must exhaust the available remedies before turning to the courts. The vast majority of cases will be determined through internal complaints procedures or by the Commissioner. For the rest there is a general right of appeal from the Commissioner to the Information Tribunal, with an appeal to the High Court on a point of law. Test cases are however likely to be very much the exception.

The primacy of the rule of law

The desire to give people a right to know, which can be enforced without elabo- **3.82** rate legal machinery, is an important part of the statutory scheme, but it is not the whole picture. It has to be balanced against the principle that the exercise of any power should be subject to the rule of law (and so subject in the final analysis to the supervision of the courts).[54] This is clearly so in respect of the powers which arise under the Act. Whilst the decisions which are made by public authorities will

---

[51] [1948] 1 QB 223.
[52] See HWR Wade and C Forsyth, *Administrative Law*, (8th edn, 2000) 643.
[53] Section 50(2) of the 2000 Act.
[54] See *Anisminic v Foreign Compensation Commission* [1969] 2 AC 147, S de Smith, H Woolf and J Jowell, *Judicial Review of Administrative Action* (5th edn, 1995) 253, and para 1.19 above.

be judged in the first instance by the Commissioner in an informal way, the implementation of the public right to know is ultimately subject to the rule of law.

3.83 Section 60 expressly provides that where a certificate has been issued by a Minister in respect of national security matters the Commissioner or the applicant may appeal to the Tribunal, and the Tribunal may quash a certificate, under section 23(2) on any ground, and under section 24(3), applying judicial review principles.

3.84 There is no comparable express provision with respect to certificates issued under section 36(7) by the Speaker of the House of Commons or the Clerk of the Parliaments as to information held by the Commons and the Lords, but it is likely that the courts will apply the principle of primacy of the rule of law if there is evidence that the certificate has been improperly obtained.

3.85 The use of the word 'reasonable' in section 36(2) which provides that information is exempt if, in the reasonable opinion of a qualified person, disclosure would be likely to prejudice the conduct of public affairs, signals that this test is subject to judicial review.

3.86 The government made clear in the Bill's passage through Parliament that the executive override, or ministerial veto, in section 53 is subject to judicial review.[55]

The principle of proportionality

3.87 In human rights law the task which is inherent in the whole of the European Convention on Human Rights is to seek to strike a fair balance between the demands of the general interest of the community and the requirements of the protection of the individual's fundamental rights.[56] An authority's response to a request from an individual should be proportionate and no more than proportionate. It is not proportionate to use a sledgehammer to crack a nut.

3.88 The principle of proportionality in the principle by which the courts balance conflicting human rights, or determine how far a permitted exception is to be allowed to curtail a human right.

3.89 The principle is of importance in drawing the line between Article 10 of the European Convention on Human Rights which guarantees the right to free speech, subject to necessary exceptions, and the right to personal privacy in Article 8.

3.90 The Freedom of Information Act supplements the individual's rights under Article 10, by effectively writing into Article 10 a right of public access to informa-

---

[55] See para 2.17 above and *Hansard*, HL (series 5) vol 612, col 828 (20 April 2000).
[56] *Sporrong and Lonroth v Sweden* (1982) 5 EHRR 35 at 52.

tion and ideas, subject only to necessary exceptions. Some of these are absolute, but most are subject to the public interest test under section 2 of the Act. The principle of proportionality is the tool the courts are likely to use to balance the public interest.

The European Court of Human Rights has held that a restriction on a freedom **3.91** guaranteed by the Convention must be proportionate to the legitimate aim pursued.[57] There must be a reasonable relationship of proportionality between the means employed and the legitimate objectives pursued by the contested limitation.[58] Lester and Pannick say that:

> A measure will satisfy the proportionality test only if three criteria are satisfied:
> (1) the legislative objective must be sufficiently important to justify limiting a fundamental human right;
> (2) the measures designed to meet the legislative objective must be rationally connected to that objective—they must be no more than is necessary to accomplish the legitimate objective—they must not be arbitrary, unfair or based on irrational considerations;
> (3) the means used to impair the right or freedom must be no more than is necessary to accomplish the legitimate objective—the more severe the deleterious effects of a measure, the more important the objective must be if the measure is to be justified in a democratic society.[59]

The Information Commissioner and the courts, in determining where the public **3.92** interest lies under section 2 of the Act, will be weighing whether there is sufficient prejudice to the public interest to justify, on an objective basis, curtailing the right of public access to information. They will be applying the same test as the courts apply in balancing Articles 10 and 8 of the European Convention on Human Rights. The principle of proportionality and striking the balance between Articles 8 and 10 is considered further in chapter 21, where the extent to which proportionality should inform judicial review is also discussed in the light of Lord Cooke of Thorndon's observation in *R v Home Secretary (Daly)*:[60]

> It may well be, however, that the law can never be satisfied in any administrative field merely by a finding that the decision under review is not capricious or absurd.

The margin of appreciation

The principle of proportionality must be distinguished from the doctrine of **3.93** *margin of appreciation*. The doctrine of margin of appreciation means that an

---

[57] *Handyside v United Kingdom* (1976) 1 EHRR 737 at 754, para 49.
[58] *Fayed v United Kingdom* (1976) 1 EHRR 737 at 754, para 49.
[59] A Lester and D Pannick, *Human Rights Law and Practice* (1999) 69 at para 3.10.
[60] [2001] UK HL 26, [2001] 2 AC 532 at para 32.

international court is reluctant to substitute its judgment for that of the domestic authorities. The European Court of Human Rights has recognized that:

> By reason of their direct and continuous contact with the vital forces of their countries, the national authorities are in principle better placed than an international court to evaluate local needs and conditions.[61]

Domestic authorities are therefore given a discretionary area of judgment, but that is subject to the ultimate supervision of the European Court of Human Rights.

3.94 The doctrine of the margin of appreciation does not apply when a national court is considering the Human Rights Act.[62]

D. Day-to-day Challenges for Local Authorities

The scope of parts D and E of this chapter

3.95 Throughout 2002 the Lord Chancellor's Department has held seminars at regional centres to discuss the implementation of the Act and in particular publication schemes which have to be in place for central government departments in November 2002 and for local authorities in February 2003. Public authorities have been represented at these seminars, or 'roadshows' at a senior level. The seminars underlined the wide range of problems which will arise under the Act. In this part of this chapter consideration is given to the day-to-day challenges which public authorities will face. In part E examples are given of the sort of information which concerned citizens are likely to seek, so that the reader can see the broad scope of the Act.[63]

The basic approach

3.96 Public authorities receive thousands of requests for information every week. The Freedom of Information Act will apply to all of them, not just to enquiries which are clearly labelled as being made under the Act. This means that most members of staff will need to know the broad structure of the Act, the duties which it imposes on authorities, and the time scale within which authorities have to respond to requests. The approach which members of staff should take will be to give members of the public information they seek unless there is a good reason not to do so. All members of staff should know to whom in the authority they should

---

[61] *Buckley v United Kingdom* (1996) 23 EHRR 101 at 129, para 75.

[62] Lester and Pannick (n 59 above) 74 at para 3.21.

[63] Many of the examples are based on case studies published by the Campaign For Freedom of Information. The authors have been greatly helped by the Campaign's work.

turn if they are in doubt as to whether information should be given. Clear lines of communication are very important.

Publication schemes

The key to coping with the Act is for an authority to have its records in order, to **3.97** know what information it holds and how to track it down, and to publish the information which the public is likely to want on a regular basis. If requested information is published all that the authority will have to do is to say so.

Publication schemes are designed to ensure that authorities do publish relevant **3.98** information. The better the publication scheme the easier life will be for the authority. The better the scheme the more money the authority will save. Complying with requests for information which has not been published will inevitably be time consuming and expensive, and only a small part of the expense will be recovered from the applicant. The contents of publication schemes are considered in detail in chapter 4 below.

E. What Concerned Citizens Will Want to Know

It is possible to get some idea of the way in which people will use the Act by con- **3.99** sidering the attempts of the Campaign for Freedom of Information and others to extract information from the government and by looking at the experience in other countries. Here is a broad range of such examples.

Examples given in Parliament

Lord Falconer on the second reading of the Bill in the House of Lords[64] gave exam- **3.100** ples of the practical way in which the Bill would benefit individuals:

> This Bill gives parents the right to know how schools apply their admission criteria, how health authorities determine the health care priorities for their areas and how administrative decisions over a very wide range of issues, such as planning, immigration and the award of grants are taken. Everyone will benefit from this Bill. It will deliver a more responsive, better informed and accountable public service.

To this one can add examples taken from cases where information was in short **3.101** supply: why hospitals and schools are to be closed, what housing stock does a local authority or a housing association own, when was it built, and by what method.[65]

---

[64] *Hansard,* HL (series 5) vol 612, col 830 (20 April 2000).
[65] This would be relevant to someone who has purchased a council house which was system built and has proved defective.

Sellafield

3.102 The safety of nuclear installations is a matter of widespread public concern. The Campaign for Freedom of Information has long been concerned at the lack of information about nuclear installations. In April 1994 the Campaign wrote an article which first appeared in the *Observer* supplement on censorship under the title 'Addicted to Secrecy, Lies and Distortion'. One of the examples used in the article was Sellafield:

> In 1957 fire broke out at the Windscale nuclear reactor in Cumbria causing what at the time was the world's worst nuclear accident. Milk sales from more than 200 square miles around the plant were banned and it is now estimated that, on the most pessimistic assumptions, as many as 1000 fatal cancers and a similar number of non fatal cases may eventually result.
>
> An immediate official inquiry was held—but its report was to remain secret for three decades. Publicly, prime minister Harold Macmillan said disclosure would damage national security. Privately the Ministry of Defence acknowledged that there was 'no security objection' to publication. But Macmillan wanted the facts concealed from the Americans, fearing that if they learnt of Britain's nuclear incompetence they would block future collaboration. The truth about the fire was only revealed in 1988, when the report was finally made public under the 30-year rule.
>
> Windscale, today known as Sellafield, is now home to the THORP nuclear reprocessing plant. What are the chances of a new accident? The answer is another secret. The Health and Safety Executive refuses to release the risk assessment. The public supposedly has a right to environmental information under new regulations. But the HSE claims that it deals only with safety and not the environment, and shrugs off the duty to disclose.

3.103 This is an area where the Act will make a real difference. After Chernobyl the foolishness of trying to conceal accidents at nuclear installations is clear. In fairness there have always been those within government and the nuclear industry who have argued for greater openness. In the future (national security apart), the public will have a right to know unless there is a public interest in concealment. The case for concealment will be a difficult case to argue.

BSE and foot and mouth disease

3.104 The Inquiry Report into BSE chaired by Lord Phillips[66] found that:

> Gathering of data about the extent of the spread of BSE was impeded in the first half of 1987 by an embargo within the SVS [State Veterinary Service] on making information about the new disease public. This should not have occurred.[67]
>
> The evidence demonstrates a clear policy of restricting the disclosure of information about BSE.[68]

---

[66] Report, evidence and supporting papers of the Inquiry into the emergence and identification of Bovine Spongiform Encephalopathy (BSE) and variant Creutzfeldt-Jakob Disease (vCJD) and the action taken in response to it up to 20 March 1996, HC 887-1 ('the BSE Report').

[67] The BSE Report, Vol 1, Executive Summary, xix.

[68] ibid, Vol 3, ch 2 para 2.175.

The BSE Report makes clear that information was being disclosed at best on a **3.105** need to know basis. The inquiries currently taking place into the outbreak of foot and mouth disease disclose a similar picture. Farmers and consumers are likely to use the Act to get more information about the administration of agriculture.

The BSE Report makes it clear where the public interest lay in the BSE case. The **3.106** Report says:

> We can see why there were concerns that reports of a possible TSE [Transmissible Spongiform Encephalopathy] in cattle might harm the industry and, in particular, the export market. But this did not justify suppression of information needed if disease surveillance was to operate effectively.[69]

The Report was also highly critical of the Government's campaign of reassurance **3.107** about BSE. This failed to acknowledge (a) the uncertainty of the government's scientific advisers and (b) the fact that the reassurance was entirely based on the assumption that BSE controls were being rigorously applied. Yet the reassurance continued to be given even as it became clear that controls were not properly observed.

For example, in October 1995, the Chief Medical Officer, Sir Kenneth Calman, **3.108** was quoted in a Department of Health press release as saying that 'beef and other meats are safe to eat'. The Inquiry concluded that at the time Sir Kenneth knew there had been reports of the failure to comply with BSE regulations in slaughter-houses, and that this unqualified statement was unjustified.[70]

The Campaign for Freedom of Information has expressed concern that govern- **3.109** ment may seek to block the disclosure of information in similar circumstances by relying on the class exemptions in sections 35 (policy advice), 36 (the conduct of public affairs), or 30 (investigations and proceedings conducted by public author-ities). All of these exemptions are subject to the public interest test. The Campaign argues that *after* a disaster has struck, the public interest in disclosure is obvious. But before anything goes wrong, the public interest may be difficult to establish, particularly if conventional wisdom asserts there is no problem, the information is complex or its significance is unclear. There is some truth in this, but it probably undervalues the change in public attitudes which has been brought about by the BSE and foot and mouth disease disasters. It will be for the Information Commissioner to determine where the public interest lies and for the courts to ensure, if necessary, that the purpose of the Act is implemented. One thing is clear: the government will have to disclose much more information about the administration of agriculture than it has done in the past. As Tony Blair (when he was Leader of the Opposition) said in 1996:

---

[69] ibid, Vol 6, ch 6 paras 6.347–6.350.
[70] ibid, Vol 6, ch 6 paras 6.347–6.350.

> When a health scare like BSE occurs, the public want to know the facts, people want to know what the scientific advice is in full, and they need to be sure that the public interest has always come first. They want to know if there was a relaxation of regulations which resulted in public safety being compromised . . . the whole sorry saga of how this matter has been handled has resulted in loss of public trust in government . . . the only way to begin to restore people's trust is therefore to be completely open about what the risks are.[71]

The contrast with the United States

3.110 In 1991 the Campaign for Freedom of Information gave examples of information which was then available in the United States under their Freedom of Information Act, but was not available here. Here are three of them. First, British cruise liners crossing the Atlantic were checked by health inspectors in both countries. The British reports were secret; the US reports were widely publicized. Secondly, it is possible to learn more about environmental problems at a US Air Force base in England than about pollution from an ordinary British factory. The Campaign obtained records of oil spills at USAF bases at Lakenheath and Mildenhall in Suffolk. In October 1990 alone there were 19 spillages at Lakenheath, though most did not cause external pollution. Such information is not available for British owned premises. Thirdly, American officials inspect British pharmaceutical companies who export to the US to ensure that the products are sterile and manufactured to the highest standards. Their inspection reports are available under the US Freedom of Information Act. A Department of Health official who had released the equivalent British report would have committed a criminal offence and could have been jailed for two years. If a company's licence was suspended because its products were substandard even purchasers of drugs such as health authorities would not be informed. In the most serious cases, unsafe products would be recalled. All this is set to change.

Business

3.111 Businesses have a strong need to know about government activity. In the United States and Canada it is the business community which has made the most use of the legislation. It is likely that business here will make full use of the Act. Richard Thomas, the Director of Public Policy at Clifford Chance, the international law firm and the new Information Commissioner, has written:[72]

> . . . as sophisticated companies know, a treasure trove of reports, surveys, statistics, analyses, opinions and recommendations has been amassed by the various organs of government over the past decades. Information relating to such matters as market intelligence, customer needs, personnel issues, public procurement, registers, and existing government policy can all be useful. Government contractors have a partic-

---

[71] Speech at the Campaign for Freedom of Information annual awards, 25 March 1996.
[72] In *Freedom of Expression and Freedom of Information* (n 49 above) 397.

ular interest in understanding government's needs. Published information—including that obtained through Parliamentary Questions—is only the tip of the iceberg . . . but many businesses are ignorant about just how much information is held by government which could help commercially.

Richard Thomas makes the point that a great deal of government information is **3.112** already obtainable under the open government code,[73] though there remains a great deal of information which is not freely available. He lists examples where Clifford Chance or its clients have encountered problems in accessing information which include:

(a) internal guidance used by regulatory authorities;
(b) rules dealing with corporate hospitality;
(c) decisions of tribunals associated with financial regulators;
(d) details of licences issued by a regulatory authority;
(e) reasons for decisions on mergers and other competition issues;
(f) factual responses to governmental criticism of private pension providers;
(g) details of prospective public sector contracts;
(h) current and historical guidance on the announcement of contract awards during election periods;
(i) formal ministerial correspondence relating to the powers of a state-owned company;
(j) framework documents relating to the future of Next Steps Agencies;
(k) details of corporate criminal convictions.

These are the sorts of areas where businesses are likely to seek and gain information when the Act comes fully into force in January 2005.

---

[73] See further in ch 4 below.

Part B

THE PRESENT

4

FREEDOM OF INFORMATION UNTIL JANUARY 2005

A. Introduction

The way we live now

The Lord Chancellor announced to the House of Lords on 13 November 2001 **4.01** that the right of access to information under the Freedom of Information Act 2000 will be brought into force for all public authorities in January 2005. That does not mean that those who want information, or those who want to give information have to fold their arms and wait patiently for the witching hour on

31 December 2004. There are many other statutory provisions which give people the right to information and the *Code of Practice on Access to Government Information* ('the Code'),[1] which was introduced by the then Conservative Minister of Science and Public Service, William Waldegrave, on 4 April 1994 (and revised in January 1997) remains in force until 2005. The Code itself is one of Whitehall's better kept secrets.[2] The Parliamentary Commissioner ('the Ombudsman') in his annual report for 2001–2[3] says it is clear that awareness of the Code, beyond Whitehall and those with a particular interest in information issues, remains largely non-existent. No doubt the Ombudsman is right about that but the Code points the way to open government and, given some publicity, is likely to prove an increasingly effective way of obtaining information.

The scope of this chapter

4.02 This chapter deals with the provisions of the Code, the way in which it has been enforced by the Ombudsman and the effect which the adoption of publication schemes by public authorities is having on the flow of information. It also summarizes the other statutory provisions which may assist a person seeking information before the right of access under the Act comes into force, and explains whereabouts in this book these provisions are discussed in more detail.

B. The Code

The aims of the Code

4.03 Paragraph 1 of the Code states that the approach to release of information should in all cases be based on the assumption that information should be released except where disclosure would not be in the public interest, as specified in Part II of the Code. This statement of purpose is important and when it is viewed in the context that Parliament has enacted that people will have a right to information from 2005, it suggests that good practice will require public authorities to disclose now information which they will have to disclose under the Act, unless there are compelling reasons not to do so.

4.04 The aims of the Code are set out in paragraph 2. They are:

- to improve policy-making and the democratic process by extending access to the facts and analyses which provide the basis for the consideration of proposed policy;

---

[1] The Code is in Appendix C.

[2] The Campaign for Freedom of Information comments that the government gave little publicity to the Code's launch. The fact the Campaign says that the Code was brought into force on a bank holiday during the parliamentary recess guaranteed an inauspicious launch: *Testing the Open Government Code of Practice* http://www.cfoi.org.uk/copbriefing.html (25 March 2002).

[3] HC 897 para 5.10.

- to protect the interests of individuals and companies by ensuring that reasons are given for administrative decisions, except where there is statutory authority or established convention to the contrary; and
- to support and extend the principles of public service established under the Citizen's Charter.

These aims are balanced by the need:

- to maintain high standards of care in ensuring the privacy of personal and commercially confidential information; and
- to preserve confidentiality where disclosure would not be in the public interest or would breach personal privacy or the confidences of a third party, in accordance with statutory requirements and Part II of the code.

Commitments

Paragraph 3 of the Code contains five commitments: **4.05**

(a) to supply facts and analysis with major policy decisions;
(b) to open up internal guidelines about departments' dealings with the public;
(c) to supply reasons for administrative decisions;
(d) to provide information under the Citizen's Charter about public services, what they cost, targets, performance, and redress; and
(e) to respond to requests for information.

Documents and response times

There is no commitment that pre-existing documents, as distinct from informa-   **4.06**
tion, will be made available in response to a request. The Code does not require departments to acquire information they do not possess, to provide information which is already published, or to provide information which is provided as part of an existing charged service other than through that service.[4] This rule, which was criticized by the Campaign for Freedom of Information,[5] is to some extent offset by the Ombudsman's opinion about summarizing information. In his annual report for the year 2000–1 he said that although the Code gives entitlement only to information, the Ombudsman's view is that if release is appropriate, the information contained in a document (such as a report) can most sensibly be made available in that format. In some cases this approach will not work, either because the information is widely scattered or because it has been accepted that some of the information in the particular document should be withheld. In that case the provision of a summary of the relevant information is often the most appropriate way forward. The Ombudsman has welcomed an increasing willingness to use such an approach, which was used in varying ways in a number of cases

---

[4] The Code, para 4.
[5] *Testing the Open Government Code of Practice,* (n 2 above).

during the year 2000–1.[6] Under the Freedom of Information Act 2000 a person will be entitled to information recorded in any form.[7]

4.07 Paragraph 5 of the Code provides that information will be provided as soon as practicable. The target response time to simple requests for information is 20 working days from the date of receipt. 20 working days is also the response time laid down in the Act.[8] Some departments have set themselves tighter deadlines under the Code. The Public Record Office's target is 10 working days; the Cabinet Office, the Employment Service, the Government Office for the South West and the Department for Trade and Industry have a target of 15 working days, and the Department for Culture, Media and Sport has a target of 18 working days. It is encouraging that the Lord Chancellor's Department reports that in 2000, the bodies covered by the Code met either the 20-day deadline set out in the Code or their own, more stringent, deadlines in 96.2 per cent of cases.[9]

The scope of the Code

4.08 Paragraph 6 of the Code provides that it applies to those government departments and other bodies which come within the jurisdiction of the Ombudsman (as listed in Schedule 2 to the Parliamentary Commissioner Act 1967). The Code applies to agencies within departments and to functions carried out on behalf of a department or public body by contractors. The security and intelligence services are not within the scope of the Code, nor is information obtained from or relating to them.

4.09 The scope of the Code has changed considerably over the last three years. 1999 saw the Ombudsman's jurisdiction extended by over 150 bodies, but it also saw both the Scottish Executive and the Welsh Assembly introduce their own Codes. The *Code of Practice on Access to Scottish Executive Information* is similar to the UK Code and covers the Scottish Executive and Scottish public authorities within the jurisdiction of the Scottish Parliamentary Commissioner for Information. The Code of the National Assembly for Wales, the *Code of Practice on Public Access to Information*, was prepared and adopted in accordance with the Assembly's Standing Order (Number 17) and against a background of the provisions of the draft UK Freedom of Information Bill. In March 2000, ahead of the passage of the Freedom of Information Act 2000, the First Minister for Wales announced his

---

[6] See the *Parliamentary Commissioner's Annual Report 2000–1* HC 5 para 5.8. and cases A2/01, A29/00 (in HC 126) and A6/00.

[7] Section 84.

[8] Section 10(1).

[9] *Code of Practice on Access to Government Information Monitoring Report for 2000* by the Lord Chancellor's Department, para 15 and note 3, http://www.lcd.gov.uk/foi/codprac/00/01 intr.htm (30 August 2002).

proposals for greater openness in the National Assembly and these included a review of the existing Code. A revised Code was approved, in draft, by the First Minister and his Cabinet and was then formally adopted by the Assembly on 8 May 2001. Most public bodies in Northern Ireland, including departments, follow the provisions of the UK Code, working on the presumption that information should be made widely available whenever possible.[10]

Charges

Paragraph 7 of the Code provides that public bodies will make their own arrange- **4.10** ments for charging. A great deal of information will be provided free of charge. The *Guidance on Interpretation of the Code* published by the Cabinet Office[11] makes clear that:

> Departments should not charge for the provision of information which it is necessary for the public to have as part of fair and accountable performance of their functions. Information explaining:
>
> (a) benefits, grants, rights and entitlements;
> (b) the standards and availability of services;
> (c) the reasons for administrative decisions made in an applicant's case;
> (d) the ways in which the citizen may exercise rights to appeal or complain about a decision;
> (e) regulatory requirements affecting affairs of a business or commercial interests; and
> (f) the main points of existing departmental policies or initiatives,
>
> should usually be available free of charge.
>   There may be a charge if a request for information does not come within one of these categories and causes additional work.

Charges may consist of a flat rate to cover straightforward requests, with an extra **4.11** payment for any additional work. Applicants will be asked before the work starts whether they are willing to pay the charge. The government's aim is stated to be that where charges are made they should strike a balance between the interests of the applicant and those of the taxpayer. There is, however, considerable discrepancy between charging policies of various departments. These are listed in Appendix 4 to the *Monitoring Report for 2000*, published by the Lord Chancellor's Department.[12] The most generous appear to be the Lord Chancellor's Department, the Public Record Office and parts of the Northern Ireland Office which allow five hours free work, and then charge only for additional time; and the Cabinet Office, the Department of National Heritage and the Scottish Office, which waive the first £100 of all fees.

---

[10] ibid, paras 3-6.
[11] 2nd edn, Part 1 paras 72, 73.
[12] See n 9 above.

4.12 The Campaign for Freedom of Information has suggested that all departments should bring their charges into line with these departments and that fees should be waived where there is a public interest in the disclosure of the information.[13] Applicants should ask for details of charges from the public authority when they make their requests. The Campaign's advice urges people not to be put off by the charges. They say:

- Certain types of request under the code must be granted free of charge.
- You must be told of the charges in advance and asked if you will agree to them.
- Departments often decide not to ask a fee—even though their charging policy may allow them to do so.
- You may be able to reduce or avoid charges by making your request more specific, or narrower, so that it involves less work.
- You can—and should—challenge unreasonable charges by complaining via an MP to the Ombudsman. Some departments' charging schemes appear inherently unreasonable. Do not accept charges just because they are in line with published charging arrangements.[14]

Limitations of the Code

4.13 The Code is non-statutory and cannot override provisions contained in statutory rights of access to information or records, nor can it override statutory prohibitions on disclosure.[15] The Code is not intended to override statutory provisions on access to public records, whether over or under 30 years old.[16] The Code only applies to government-held information. It does not apply to or affect information held by courts or contained in court documents.[17]

Investigations of complaints

4.14 Paragraph 11 of the Code is in the following terms:

Complaints that information which should have been provided under the Code has not been provided, or that unreasonable charges have been demanded, should be made first to the department or body concerned. If the applicant remains dissatisfied, complaints may be made through a Member of Parliament to the Ombudsman. Complaints will be investigated at the Ombudsman's discretion in accordance with the procedures in the 1967 Act.

4.15 If an applicant thinks his request has not been answered properly, or the response has taken too long, or he has been charged too much he must first ask the body who provided the information to review its decision. In 2000 there were 5,969

---

[13] *Testing the Open Government Code of Practice* (n 2 above).
[14] The Campaign for Freedom of Information's paper, *Testing the Open Government Code of Practice*, http://www.cfoi.org.uk/copbriefing.html (30 August 2002).
[15] The Code, para 11.
[16] ibid, para 9.
[17] ibid, para 10.

requests for information under the Code and in 50 cases there were internal reviews. The internal review procedure varies from department to department. When the Code was first introduced there was much criticism of the elaborate procedures some departments, for example the Northern Ireland Office, adopted. However, the *Guidance on Interpretation of the Code*[18] now makes it clear that internal reviews:

> should in all cases be a single stage process. The aim should be to ensure that the applicant has been fairly treated under the provisions of the Code, that any exemptions have been properly applied and that charges are reasonably and consistently applied. It is good practice for such review to be conducted by someone not involved in the original decision.

Between January 2001 and April 2002 Michael Buckley, the Ombudsman, **4.16** reported on 23 cases.[19] On 25 January 2001 he said:

> While some government departments have clear and efficient procedures for dealing with requests for information under the Code, others fail to realise that they should deal with all requests in the way laid down in the Code. Given that the Code has been in operation for nearly seven years there can be no excuse for this. Often, with a creative and imaginative approach departments can release useful information by anonymising and summarising information without breaching any confidentiality they might owe to the supplier of that information. This approach would be very much in keeping with the spirit of the Code.

The Lord Chancellor's Department in its monitoring report for 2000 expresses **4.17** the hope that this criticism will not be relevant for its next report, and notes that as part of the awareness training currently being conducted concerning the Freedom of Information Act, government departments and other bodies covered by the Code are being reminded of the importance of ensuring that they meet the Code's requirements—if bodies are not meeting the Code's requirements now, they will have great difficulty meeting the more rigorous obligations placed upon them when the Act is fully implemented. This is a theme which the Lord Chancellor's Department is also pressing home in the road shows on the Freedom of Information Act which it has been holding for public authorities during 2002. In this new climate there is clearly the opportunity for public authorities to make as much information as possible available and there is no need to wait until January 2005 to answer proper enquiries.

The public interest

Part II of the Code is concerned with exemptions. The general approach is set out **4.18** in the preamble which is in these terms:

---

[18] 2nd edn, Part 1 para 72, 73.
[19] See para 4.36 below.

The following categories of information are exempt from the commitments to provide information under the Code. In those categories which refer to harm or prejudice, the presumption remains that information should be disclosed unless the harm likely to arise from disclosure would outweigh the public interest in making the information available.

References to harm or prejudice include both actual harm or prejudice and risk or reasonable expectation of harm or prejudice. In such cases it should be considered whether any harm or prejudice arising from disclosure is outweighed by the public interest in making the information available.

The exemptions will not be interpreted in a way which causes injustice to individuals.

4.19 The test is expressed in straightforward language. In the Act[20] the test is the other way round:

in all the circumstances of the case, the public interest in maintaining the exemption outweighs the public interest in disclosing the information.

The significance of this change was discussed in the debates in the House of Lords.[21] Lord Falconer said the wording put beyond doubt the government's resolve that information must be disclosed except where there was an overriding public interest in keeping the specific information confidential.[22] When departments come to decide whether they should disclose information under the Code, they are likely to apply Lord Falconer's test both before and after 1 January 2005.

Exemptions

4.20 The Code lists 15 exemptions. They are set out in the following paragraphs together with a reference to the comparable provisions in the Act.

4.21 **1. Defence, security and international relations**

Information whose disclosure would harm national security or defence. Information whose disclosure would harm the conduct of international relations or affairs. Information received in confidence from foreign governments, foreign courts or international organisations.

The comparable provisions are sections 26, 23, 24 and 27 of the Act.

4.22 **2. Internal discussion and advice**

Information whose disclosure would harm the frankness and candour of internal discussion, including:

• proceedings of Cabinet and Cabinet committees;
• internal opinion, advice, recommendation, consultation and deliberation;

---

[20] Section 2(2)(b).
[21] See paras 2.07–2.10 above.
[22] *Hansard,* HL (series 5) vol 619, col 143 (14 November 2000).

- projections and assumptions relating to internal policy analysis; analysis of alternative policy options and information relating to rejected policy options;
- confidential communications between departments, public bodies and regulatory bodies.

The comparable sections of the Act are 35 and 36.

3. Communications with the Royal Household   4.23

Information relating to confidential communications between Ministers and Her Majesty the Queen or other members of the Royal Household, or relating to confidential proceedings of the Privy Council.

The comparable sections of the Act are 37 and 41.

4. Law enforcement and legal proceedings   4.24

Information whose disclosure could prejudice the administration of justice (including fair trial), legal proceedings or the proceedings of any tribunal, public inquiry or other formal investigations (whether actual or likely) or whose disclosure is, or has been, or is likely to be addressed in the context of such proceedings.

Information whose disclosure could prejudice the enforcement or proper administration of the law, including the prevention, investigation or detention of crime, or the apprehension or prosecution of offenders.

Information relating to legal proceedings or the proceedings of any tribunal, public inquiry or other formal investigation which has been completed or terminated, or relating to investigations which have or might have resulted in proceedings.

Information covered by legal professional privilege.

Information whose disclosure would harm public safety or public order, or would prejudice the security of any building or penal institution.

Information whose disclosure would harm public safety or public order, or would prejudice the security of any person or identify the source of information or assistance given in confidence for law enforcement or security purposes.

Information whose disclosure would increase the likelihood of damage to the environment, or rare or endangered species and their habitats.

The comparable sections of the Act are 31, 30, 32 and 42.

5. Immigration and nationality   4.25

Information relating to immigration, nationality, consular and entry clearance cases. However, information will be provided, though not through access to personal records, where there is no risk that disclosure would prejudice the effective administration of immigration controls or other statutory provisions.

The comparable section of the Act is 31.

6. Effective management of the economy and collection of tax   4.26

Information whose disclosure would prejudice the assessment or collection of tax, duties or National Insurance contributions, or assist tax avoidance or evasion.

Sections 29 and 31 are the comparable sections.

4.27 **7. Effective management and operations of the public service**

Information whose disclosure could lead to improper gain or advantage or would prejudice:

- the competitive position of a department or other public body or authority;
- negotiations or the effective conduct of personnel management, or commercial or contractual activities;
- the awarding of discretionary grants.

Information whose disclosure would harm the proper and efficient conduct of the operations of a department or other public body or authority, including NHS organisations, or any regulatory body.

Sections 31, 36 and 43 are the comparable sections

4.28 **8. Public employment, public appointments and honours**

Personnel records (relating to public appointments as well as employees of public authorities) including those relating to recruitment, promotion and security vetting.
   Information, opinions and assessments given in confidence in relation to public employment and public appointments made by Ministers of the Crown, by the Crown on the advice of Ministers or by statutory office holders.
   Information, opinions and assessments given in relation to recommendations for honours.

Sections 36, 37, 40 and 41 are the comparable sections.

4.29 **9. Voluminous or vexatious requests**

Requests for information which are vexatious or manifestly unreasonable or are formulated in too general a manner, or which (because of the amount of information to be processed or the need to retrieve information from files not in current use) would require unreasonable diversion of resources.

Sections 12 and 14 are the comparable sections.

4.30 **10. Publication and prematurity in relation to publication**

Information which is or will soon be published, or whose disclosure, where the material relates to a planned or potential announcement or publication, could cause harm (for example, of a physical or financial nature).

The comparable sections are 21 and 22.

4.31 **11. Research, statistics and analysis**

Information relating to incomplete analysis, research or statistics, where disclosure could be misleading or deprive the holder of priority of publication or commercial value.
   Information held only for preparing statistics or carrying out research, or for surveillance for health and safety purposes (including food safety), and which relates to individuals, companies or products which will not be identified in reports of that research or surveillance, or in published statistics.

Sections 35, 36, 38 and 43 are the comparable sections.

12. Privacy of an individual   **4.32**

Unwarranted disclosure to a third party of personal information about any person (including a deceased person) or any other disclosure which would constitute or could facilitate an unwarranted invasion of privacy.

Section 40 is the comparable section.

13. Third party's commercial confidences   **4.33**

Information including commercial confidences, trade secrets or intellectual property whose unwarranted disclosure would harm the competitive position of a third party.

Section 43 is the comparable section.

14. Information given in confidence   **4.34**

Information held in consequence of having been supplied in confidence by a person who:

- gave the information under a statutory guarantee that its confidentiality would be protected; or
- was not under any legal obligation, whether actual or implied, to supply it, and has not consented to its disclosure.

Information whose disclosure without the consent of the supplier would prejudice the future supply of such information.

Medical information provided in confidence if disclosure to the subject would harm their physical or mental health, or should be made by a medical practitioner.

Sections 41 and 40 are the comparable sections.

15. Statutory and other restrictions   **4.35**

Information whose disclosure is prohibited by or under any enactment, regulation, European Community law or international agreement.

Information whose release would constitute a breach of Parliamentary Privilege.

The comparable sections are 44 and 34.

C. The Ombudsman's Investigations

The Ombudsman's general approach

In the period from January 2001 to April 2002 the Ombudsman has investigated   **4.36**
23 cases. No doubt the number would be higher if applicants had direct access to the Ombudsman, but these recent cases not only give a clear indication of the way the Code is working, but also provide guidance as to the way the Information Commissioner is likely to act, on taking over the Ombudsman's role in January 2005 when the Act comes fully into force.

4.37 A study of the cases is likely to reassure both those who fear that the Act will make little difference, and those who anticipate that the Act will make the business of government much more difficult. The Ombudsman has shown good judgment and those on both sides of the argument should be encouraged.

4.38 The Ombudsman in his annual report for 1997–8 listed complaints which he had upheld and complaints which he had rejected.

4.39 Information released as a result of his investigations included:

    (a) a list of animal carcass incinerator operators who held contracts with the Ministry for Agriculture, Fisheries and Food for the disposal of BSE infected cattle;[23]

    (b) the human rights content of training provided in the United Kingdom for Indonesian military personnel;[24]

    (c) the A36 Salisbury Bypass reassessment report;[25]

    (d) details of fees paid to lawyers in the second inquest into the *Marchioness* disaster;[26]

    (e) a report about the refurbishment and upgrading of a senior RAF officer's official residence;[27]

    (f) an expert adviser's report into the financial viability of the project for a proposed museum;[28] and

    (g) the reasons why the Sports Council for Wales decided not to award a grant to an athlete.[29]

4.40 In the following cases the Ombudsman accepted that the Code exemptions cited by departments were valid, or that the department did not have the information requested:

    (a) information about the export of military, security and para-military goods, arms and ammunition (there was no evidence that the department held the information);[30]

    (b) information about defects found during inspections of the reactor pressure vessel at Sizewell B nuclear power station (the information was protected by statute);[31]

---

[23] A33/96 in HC 132.
[24] Parliamentary Commissioner, Access to Official Information: investigations completed, 4th report, session 1999–2000, case no A42/96.
[25] ibid, case no A30/96.
[26] ibid, case no A5/97.
[27] ibid, case no A32/96.
[28] ibid, case no C431/96.
[29] ibid, case no A6/97.
[30] ibid, case no A21/96.
[31] ibid, case no A37/96.

(c) a copy of an accident report held by the Health and Safety Executive (the information was either protected by statute if provided under a statutory power or by absence of the consent of the provider if given voluntarily);[32] and

(d) an assessment of the economic validity of the Thermal Oxide Reprocessing Plant at Sellafield (the information was withheld on the grounds of commercial and other kinds of confidentiality).[33]

The Ombudsman's investigations have not all been plain sailing. The Ombudsman in his most recent annual report[34] writes of a frustrating year in policing the Code. This is partly because for the first time since the Code came into force in 1994, a department refused, in a case about declarations of interest, to accept a recommendation by the Ombudsman that information should be released, and partly because of delay by some departments involved in Code investigations. **4.41**

The Ombudsman points out that a refusal to act in accordance with a recommendation undermines not only the Code but also the Ombudsman's independent role investigating complaints. He adds that it has become apparent that in some cases departments are resisting the release of information not because they have a strong case under the Code for doing so but because to release the information could cause them embarrassment or political inconvenience. **4.42**

No doubt the Ombudsman has had a frustrating year, but the totality of his work shows that steady progress is being made in moving towards open government and that that is a trend which will continue. The Ombudsman's success in the Hinduja brothers case, which is discussed next, is at least as important as the isolated case about declarations of interest in which the government (perhaps in a moment of aberration) has refused to accept his recommendation.[35] **4.43**

Legal proceedings—the *Hinduja* case

The thoroughness with which the Ombudsman has conducted his enquiries is well illustrated by one of the higher profile cases he has considered: the refusal by the Home Office to release information to a journalist relating to one of the Hinduja brothers.[36] **4.44**

---

[32] ibid, case no A34/96.

[33] ibid, case no A29/95.

[34] Annual Report 2001–2, HC 897 para 5.3.

[35] It seems that the Prime Minister was involved in both decisions (*The Times*, 12 July 2002 reports that the Secretary to the Cabinet informed the Public Administration Committee that the decision not to co-operate with the Ombudsman in the declarations of interest case was taken at the highest level; as to the decision in the Hinduja case see para 4.52 below). If this is so the Prime Minister's second decision is to be preferred. Even Homer can nod once.

[36] Parliamentary Commissioner, Access to Official Information: investigations completed, February–April 2002, HC 844, 15 case no A33/01.

4.45 The journalist on 26 January 2001 asked the Home Office if they could provide him with the information contained in a telephone conversation regarding the naturalization application of Srichand Hinduja between the Rt Hon Peter Mandelson MP, at the time Minister without Portfolio in the Cabinet Office, and the Minister for Immigration and Nationality at the Home Office, Mike O'Brien. The journalist also requested the dates of all letters written by Keith Vaz MP to the Home Office regarding the Hinduja brothers since May 1997 and for the information contained in them.

4.46 Jack Straw, the then Home Secretary, replied on 23 February 2001. He said that the Prime Minister had asked the former Treasury Solicitor, Sir Anthony Hammond QC, to review the full circumstances surrounding approaches to the Home Office in connection with the possibility of an application by Srichand Hinduja in 1988. Sir Anthony aimed to complete his inquiry as quickly as possible. In the light of this the Home Secretary said that he was satisfied that exemption 4(a) of the Code applied. Exemption 4(a) concerns information whose disclosure could prejudice the administration of justice (including fair trial), legal proceedings or the proceedings of any tribunal, public enquiry or other formal investigation. The journalist asked the Ombudsman to investigate the matter.

4.47 Interesting points about the case include the tenacity with which the Ombudsman established what information was available and inspected it, and his decision that the Home Secretary was wrong in his view that exemption 4(a) applied.

4.48 On 17 July 2001 a member of the Ombudsman's staff investigated the case papers held by the Immigration and Nationality Directorate and found that several key documents detailed in Sir Anthony's report were not present on the immigration files, nor did they appear on the contents lists attached to the files.

4.49 The Ombudsman experienced great difficulty in gaining access to the papers from Mr Mandelson's and Mr O'Brien's private offices. In September he wrote to the Secretary of the Cabinet and asked if he could ensure matters were taken forward. On 7 November 2001, in the continued absence of a reply from either the Cabinet Office or the Home Office, the Ombudsman wrote to the Permanent Secretary at the Home Office telling him that the Ombudsman would have to discontinue his investigation owing to a serious lack of co-operation from both Departments. He also said that he had formed the provisional view that the Home Office were not justified in citing exemption 4(a).

4.50 On 21 November the Permanent Secretary of the Home Office replied. He said that no papers had been retained in Mr O'Brien's private office and that copies of any relevant papers were held with the immigration papers for GP Hinduja and SP Hinduja which the Ombudsman had already examined. The Permanent

Secretary also said that he had asked the Cabinet Office about any papers that they held; in reply they said that:

> This ground was gone over extensively by the Hammond Inquiry, and Sir Anthony had full access to the papers which were held by the Government from that period. His report made clear that he found no evidence in Cabinet Office papers of the alleged conversation taking place, let alone a record of what was said.

The Ombudsman was not put off by this reply. He writes in paragraph 4.13 of his **4.51** report:

> Throughout this part of my investigation I had received no direct communication from the Cabinet Office. However my interpretation of their comments, quoted by the Permanent Secretary in his letter to me . . . was that they appeared to be withholding papers, which they readily acknowledged existed, from my investigation. I was deeply concerned at this development. Such a refusal strikes at the very heart of my Office's function. . . I found myself in the position of being quite unable to confirm whether or not there was any information regarding the telephone conversation that could, and should, have been disclosed to Mr M [the journalist]. It was on the basis of these facts, and acting within the requirements of the Parliamentary Commissioner Act 1967, that I submitted a draft report of my investigation to the Home Office.

This produced an immediate response. The Permanent Secretary at the Home **4.52** Office apologized for the fact that the Ombudsman's staff had been shown incomplete files. He said that owing to an administrative error papers which the Ombudsman had referred to as not being present on the files were in fact held on 'associated folders'. The Permanent Secretary said that all the relevant papers had now been collated and were available for inspection. The Secretary of the Cabinet said that he was writing, with the agreement of the Prime Minister, to say that Cabinet Office was now content for the Ombudsman's staff to inspect the papers made available to Sir Anthony Hammond for his Inquiry.

The Ombudsman stated from his examination of the papers that the entirety of **4.53** the evidence still remained inconclusive; but he concluded, as did Sir Anthony Hammond, that it is likely on balance that Mr Mandelson did speak directly to Mr O'Brien. However, the Ombudsman said it was clear from the papers examined by his staff that there was no direct evidence of such a conversation. He therefore concluded that there was no information which could be disclosed under the Code because there was no evidence that such information existed.

The Ombudsman went on to conclude that the Home Office could not rely on **4.54** exemption 4(a). The Ombudsman said:[37]

> My understanding, which the Home Office have confirmed, is that the review conducted by Sir Anthony had no statutory basis. While I accept that the review

---

[37] Parliamentary Commissioner, *Access to Official Information: investigations completed*, HC 844, para 4.21.

operated on a different level to any ordinary internal departmental inquiry that might have been set up to consider these issues, it is clear to me that Exemption 4(a) is intended to cover legal proceedings and other formal proceedings which have an identifiable link to the regulated or related matters. It is also, in my view, a point of considerable importance that the bodies referred to in Exemption 4(a) conduct their proceedings (save in exceptional circumstances) in public; Sir Anthony Hammond's inquiry was conducted in private. I have given careful consideration to the Home Office's arguments, but I remain unpersuaded by them.

4.55 This success of the Ombudsman in eventually extracting proper replies from the departments bodes well for future investigations by the Information Commissioner. Indeed he will be in a stronger position than the Ombudsman after January 2005, because he will be able to issue an information notice and the courts can treat any failure to comply with such a notice as a contempt of Court.[38]

The public interest test—the *Ilisu Dam* cases

4.56 In the year 2000–1 the Ombudsman completed two investigations into requests for information relating to the Ilisu Dam project in Turkey, in both of which he had to consider the public interest. The background to the cases was that from 1999 a large dam was planned on the River Tigris 65 kms upstream from the borders of Iraq and Syria. The power plant was to be built by a consortium led by Sulzer Hydro of Switzerland with Balfour Beatty leading the civil engineering works element of the project. On 21 December 1999 the Secretary of State for Trade and Industry announced that he was minded to grant export credit facilities to Balfour Beatty conditional on the Turkish authorities agreeing to address the concerns the British government had about the environmental and social impact of the project.

4.57 The first investigation[39] concerned a request by Friends of the Earth for information from the Export Credits Guarantee Department ('the ECGD') about Balfour Beatty's application for export credit support. The Ombudsman concluded that although exemption 13 (third party commercial confidences) applied to the information sought, the harm test within that exemption operated in this case in favour of disclosure. He was unable, however, to recommend disclosure because of legal advice that the information was protected by the law of confidence. This finding is therefore an example of a case where the non-statutory Code cannot override the law.

4.58 In the second case the request for information was made by Bowen Wells MP (Conservative), the then chairman of the House of Commons Select Committee on International Development. He asked to see all the correspondence between

---

[38] Section 54 of the Act.
[39] Parliamentary Commissioner, Access to Official Information: investigations completed, HC 126, case no A31/00.

the Foreign and Commonwealth Office ('the FCO') and the Department of Trade and Industry ('the DTI') concerning the Ilisu Dam up to 1 February 2000. Mr Wells sought to establish whether or not the FCO, in their representations to the DTI about the issue, raised the question of human rights not only in respect of those directly affected by the construction of the dam in terms of their need for resettlement, but also in the wider context of the effect of the Ilisu Dam project itself on the general issues of human rights and conflict in that particular region of Turkey. Ministers and officials had given the Select Committee on International Development conflicting accounts of the exchanges between departments.

The FCO in arguing the case for withholding the information requested by Mr **4.59** Wells quoted exemptions 2 and 1(b) but relied chiefly on exemption 2.

Exemption 1(b) deals with information whose disclosure would harm the con- **4.60** duct of international relations or affairs. The FCO argued that there was information in the papers covering certain matters involving Her Majesty's Government and Turkey which if disclosed would cause harm. The Ombudsman was satisfied that, to the extent that there was such information in the papers he had examined (and in his view there was comparatively little), that was so.

Turning to exemption 2, the material which the Ombudsman had examined con- **4.61** sisted of fact (much already in the public domain); but it also contained a great deal of advice, opinion and comment in respect of a subject with wide implications. It was also a live issue: the government had yet to decide whether or not to lend its support to the project. On that basis therefore the Ombudsman concluded that there was clearly a powerful argument for saying that, in respect of a complex and highly sensitive issue on which government policy was not yet finalized, the government should continue to be allowed to think in private. The Ombudsman said he was sympathetic to that argument, and to the point that releasing the correspondence between the departments might well affect the candour with which those debating similar issues in the future feel that they can record their views.

The Ombudsman, however said that there seemed to be substantial counter- **4.62** arguments to that view in the particular case. In considering the disclosure or otherwise of information under exemption 2, he had to evaluate the harm that might be caused by its release. That harm, if any, had to be balanced against the public interest that there might be in having the information disclosed. The Ombudsman found no doubt in his mind that there was a valid public interest in obtaining a clear answer to the question which Mr Wells had posed; and on balance he concluded that the public interest in the case outweighed any harm which might be caused by disclosure of the information.

The Ombudsman therefore concluded that while the documents involving corre- **4.63** spondence at ministerial and official level should not themselves be released, the essential elements of information sought by Mr Wells should be released to him. The Ombudsman therefore annexed to his report a summary of the exchanges between the FCO and the DTI in respect of human rights issues arising from the Ilisu Dam project. The Permanent Secretary of the FCO agreed to the release of the summary which showed that on 16 March 1999 the FCO provided the ECGD with brief lines to take in response to correspondence about the project, covering the policy towards the Kurds and human rights abuses in south-east Turkey.

Policy advice and the Ministerial Code of Conduct

4.64 The case in which the Home Office refused to accept the recommendation of the Ombudsman concerned the Ministerial Code of Conduct.[40] The attitude of the government is not easy to understand, even though the Code is obviously a sensitive subject. In retrospect it seems a very clear case.

4.65 Anthony Robathan MP, the Conservative member for Blaby, asked the Home Secretary by Parliamentary question on how many occasions since May 1997 Ministers in his department had made a declaration of interest to their colleagues under the Code and how many times Ministers had sought the advice of the Permanent Secretary about potential conflicts of interest.

4.66 In refusing to disclose the information the Home Office cited exemption 2 (internal discussion and advice) and exemption 12 (privacy). The Home Office argued under exemption 2 that the Ministerial Code was particularly sensitive and that any disclosure in this area could harm the frankness and candour of future discussions. The Ombudsman agreed that matters considered under the Ministerial Code were potentially sensitive particularly when they related to a conflict between a Minister's public duties and his or her private interests. However, the Ombudsman said Mr Robathan did not request the details of any declarations made or of advice sought, but simply the number of occasions on which they were made. The question in the case was therefore whether or not the release of that information alone would affect the confidentiality of future discussions. The Ombudsman did not believe that it would. The Ombudsman also held that no privacy issue arose in the case. He was plainly right.

Policy advice

4.67 In other circumstances the Ombudsman has stressed the importance of the policy advice exemption. In case no A2/02[41] Mr and Mrs B complained through their

---

[40] Parliamentary Commissioner, *Access to Official Information: investigations completed*, HC 353, case no A28/01.

[41] Parliamentary Commissioner, *Access to Official Information: investigations completed July 2001–January 2002*, HC 585.

accountant to the Adjudicator's office about the manner in which the Inland Revenue had handled their tax affairs. The Adjudicator investigated their complaint but did not recommend an increase in the level of consolatory payment already made by the Inland Revenue. Mr and Mrs B then requested sight of all the correspondence in whatever form that had passed between the Adjudicator's office and the Inland Revenue relating to their complaint.

The Ombudsman in his assessment said: **4.68**

> I have carefully examined all the correspondence which passed between the Adjudicator's Office and the Inland Revenue regarding Mr and Mrs B's complaint. Having done so I am in no doubt that the Adjudicator's Office engaged in an exchange of views and considerable discussion with the Inland Revenue relating to Mr and Mrs B's tax affairs. It seems to me that for this exchange to be worthwhile, it needed to be both frank and unambiguous or there would be little value in engaging in the process. This, it seems to me, is particularly the case given that Mr and Mrs B's problems with the Inland Revenue had already been the subject of considerable debate and discussion between the accountant and the Inland Revenue without a satisfactory conclusion being reached for either party. Therefore the need for clear and straightforward opinion and comment between the Adjudicator's Office and the Inland Revenue would seem obvious.

The Ombudsman went on to consider the harm test which applies to exemption **4.69** 2 and said that a balance needed to be struck between preserving the integrity of the deliberative process and ensuring that complainants received enough information to be satisfied that their complaint had been properly investigated. He said that it was clear that the Adjudicator's reasoning and the conclusions reached by the Adjudicator were explained in great detail. The Ombudsman did not therefore uphold the complaint.

The Ombudsman expressed similar views about exemption 2 in case no A32/01,[42] **4.70** a case where Mr D asked HM Customs and Excise for a copy of an internal investigation report relating to the way his VAT case had been handled. The Ombudsman said that the purpose of exemption 2 was to allow departments the opportunity to consider matters, particularly those which were likely to prove contentious, on the understanding that their thinking would not be exposed in such a way as to fetter their deliberations by inhibiting the frank expression of opinion. He said the authors of reports such as these must be allowed to provide an objective assessment of a case without having to worry that their views would be disclosed to a wider audience. The Ombudsman however held that a significant amount of the report was factual information and he could see no reason why those factual elements should not be released to Mr D without undermining the effectiveness of Customs' internal process of consideration. Customs

---

[42] ibid.

accepted this recommendation and agreed to release an edited version of their report to Mr D.

4.71 In these cases the Ombudsman has given practical guidance to departments about how they should apply the policy making exemption and has been keen to encourage departments to release as much information as possible.

Crime prevention and national security

4.72 One of the lessons which the Ombudsman has sought to draw from the cases he has investigated is that some information in sensitive areas such as crime prevention and national security can be released safely if departments take a realistic view of potential harm in relation to public interest disclosure.[43]

4.73 Two investigations in 2000 illustrate the Ombudsman's point. The first (no A3/00[44]) concerned a man who asked the Home Office for a complete copy of *The Internet Detective*, a guide to internet crime for crime investigators. He was offered a censored copy of the book with the operationally sensitive parts removed. When he protested that the media had been given a less heavily censored version, the Home Office apologized and made the same version available to him. The Ombudsman accepted that the department were entitled to withhold some parts of a particular chapter, but recommended that the rest of the chapter should be released and it was.

4.74 The second case (no A.2/00[45]) involved the Ministry of Defence ('MoD'). The Ombudsman took the view that the MoD's refusal to supply a man with copies of annual performance reports for MoD itself and for the Royal Air Force was partially justified. Some of the information had already been published, but some related to the UK's nuclear capacity and to security and intelligence matters. It was accepted by the Ombudsman that harm could be caused to national security if such material was released, but he concluded that other less sensitive material which had not been previously published could be safely released. It was released.

Exemption 9—voluminous or vexatious requests

4.75 The Ombudsman in his report for 2001–2 said that exemption 9 is one of the most difficult exemptions to apply. It is, he said, clearly a matter of judgment as to whether requests from a particular claimant can be said to be voluminous or vexatious. Such judgments are made more difficult by the fact that complainants, perhaps understandably, almost never perceive them as either.

---

[43] See a press release issued by the Parliamentary Commissioner dated 25 May 2000, available at http://www.ombudsman.org.uk/pca/press (30 August 2002).

[44] Parliamentary Commissioner, Access to Official Information: investigations completed, 4th report, session 1999-2000.

[45] ibid.

In case A.14/00[46] the Charity Commission refused a request for a large quantity **4.76** of information about the affairs of an animal welfare charity on the grounds that the request was too general and also that some of the information would consti- tute an invasion of privacy. The Ombudsman upheld the Charity Commission's decision.

The Ombudsman also upheld the decision of the Medicines Control Agency **4.77** ('MCA') in case no A24/01.[47] Mrs R asked the MCA to provide her with what she described as 'the unexpurgated papers and associated papers' concerning changes that had occurred to clomipramine, tranxene and other identified drugs between 1985 and 1996. The MCA refused Mrs R's request, citing exemption 9. The refusal was upheld on an internal review. The Permanent Secretary said that the MCA had refused to provide Mrs R with the information she sought because it would take too much time to check the contents of each document in 12 volumes, establish whether the information contained in it could be disclosed, then photo- copy and reconstitute the 12 files. The Ombudsman said that having himself examined these files he endorsed this assessment. Indeed it was clear to him that the task of simply copying the documents (without even taking into account the nature of the information contained in them and whether or not disclosure of any of it might be appropriate) would in itself require a considerable diversion of resources. Further he did not see how the MCA would be able to make a decision on whether or not to release the information contained in the relevant papers without consulting the two pharmaceutical companies concerned and where nec- essary taking legal advice. The Ombudsman accepted that that task would also involve a considerable diversion of resources and therefore exemption 9 had been correctly applied.

The MCA, with the consent of one of the pharmaceutical companies, gave Mrs R **4.78** a PLUS report, being a computerized summary of information in respect of tranx- ene. Mrs R did not regard this information as satisfactory. The other pharmaceu- tical company was not prepared to agree to the release of information in that format and said that any disclosure of it would be a breach of section 118 of the Medicines Act 1968. This section makes the disclosure of any information with respect to any manufacturing process an offence unless it is done in the perfor- mance of a duty. The Ombudsman's staff asked the MCA to explain how they interpreted section 118 of the 1968 Act. The MCA said that in their view, while that section clearly imposed a restriction on the disclosure of information obtained or supplied under the Act, that restriction did not apply where the dis- closure was made in the performance of a duty. The MCA, as a body coming

---

[46] Parliamentary Commissioner, Access to Official Information: investigations completed Nov 1999–March 2000, HC 494.
[47] Parliamentary Commissioner, Access to Official Information: investigations completed January–June 2001, HC 160.

within the jurisdiction of the Ombudsman, took the view that the commitment to releasing information laid down by the Code was in fact just such a duty. The Ombudsman, however, did not resolve this issue. His finding was that the MCA were justified in withholding the information sought by Mrs R under exemption 9 of the Code.

The Legal Aid Commission cases

4.79 Two cases against the Legal Aid Commission have also turned on exemption 9. In case no A.14/01[48] Mr P sought information which fell into two categories: the representations which had been made against the continuance of his certificate by his opponent and the Commission's entire case file. Section 38 of the Legal Aid Act 1988 states that the Commission shall not disclose information provided to them without the consent of the persons who provided the information. The Commission relied on this section and the Ombudsman's role in this part of the case was therefore limited to satisfying himself that this claim was properly made. Mr P's case file was voluminous and the Commission relied on exemption 9. The Ombudsman decided that in the light of Mr P's very general request for information he considered it would be unreasonable to expect the Commission to divert resources to identifying and collating the information sought.

4.80 In case no A.9/02[49] the Ombudsman took the view that the request of a complainant against the Legal Services Commission, whose correspondence took up 25 files and who between January and June 2001 had sent the Commission over 400 e-mails, many of which were lengthy and sought information about a range of different subjects, was an exemption 9 case.

4.81 The Ombudsman summed up his attitude to exemption 9 in his annual report for 2001–2 in this way:

> although each case will need to be dealt with on its individual merits, the Ombudsman recognises that sometimes departments will have done all that can reasonably be expected of them in responding to requests for information, and that there is an equal responsibility upon those who make requests to ensure that they do not make excessive demands upon departments.

It is always sensible for people making requests under the Code to narrow their questions and focus on the information they really want.

Confidence, privacy and premature publication

4.82 In January 2000 the Department of Health ('DoH') published *Protecting Children, Supporting Parents: A Consultation Document on the Physical Punishment*

---

[48] Parliamentary Commissioner, Access to Official Information: investigations completed January–June 2001, HC 160, at p 18.
[49] Parliamentary Commissioner, Access to Official Information: investigations completed February–April 2002, HC 844.

of Children. This document invited people and organizations to submit their views on certain questions raised in it. The document stated:

> We may wish to cite, or quote from, some of the responses we receive. Please make clear whether or not you would be willing to have your view published, on a named basis, in any subsequent document that may be produced. We will assume that you are happy to be quoted unless you tell us to the contrary.

In case no A.13/02[50] Mr F wrote to the DoH and asked to see all the responses to the consultation document where the respondents had not requested that their replies be treated in confidence. He also asked to be told how many respondents had asked for their replies to be treated in confidence, and for the number of those responses to be divided between individuals and organizations. The DoH declined to release this information relying on exemptions 10 (premature publication) and 14 (information given in confidence).

4.83 The Ombudsman held that the part of the request which sought the number of responses received where confidentiality was requested was a request for purely factual information and to provide it would not breach any duty of confidentiality. The Ombudsman dealt with the second strand of Mr F's request in this way:

> DoH have argued that respondents who did not request confidentiality were giving their permission for DoH to quote from their replies only in the context of a future DoH publication, not for their responses to be made available on any broader basis. While I can see merit in this argument, is it sufficient of itself to justify withholding the information? I think not. In my view, by choosing not to request confidentiality, respondents were indicating a willingness for any part of their reply to be included in any analysis DoH might prepare for publication, on a named basis, and for any person including Mr F, to read part or all of such a response in such a publication. Given this fact, is it reasonable for DoH to assume that those respondents would be unwilling for Mr F or anyone else for that matter to be given a sight of their responses? I cannot see that it is. By choosing not to request confidentiality respondents have indicated their willingness in principle to allow anyone to read any part of their replies. From the respondents' perspective I cannot see any essential difference between being content for Mr F to have sight of all or part of their response via a DoH publication and being content for him to have sight of it as originally submitted. On balance I do not therefore find that Exemption 14 applies in this case.

The Ombudsman, however, said that before disclosing the information the Department should ensure that the addresses of the respondents were obscured. The Ombudsman thought there was a difference between respondents being content for their replies to be published on a named basis and for their addresses also to be disclosed, especially when the replies concerned such an emotive and contentious issue.

---

[50] Parliamentary Commissioner, Access to Official Information: investigations completed July 2001–January 2002, HC 585 at p 22.

4.84 The Ombudsman said that exemption 10 was designed to prevent requesters obtaining information prior to its official publication and possibly obtaining an unfair benefit or advantage over others by doing so. The Ombudsman concluded that that was not going to happen in this case because the department only ever intended to publish part of the material. In the event the department agreed to publish on its website all the replies received where confidentiality had not been requested and to give details of the numbers of responses they had received where confidentiality was requested.

4.85 The exemptions which figure most frequently in cases submitted to the Ombudsman are 12, 13, and 14. The common feature of these three exemptions is that they relate to information which has been provided to the body holding it under some expectation of confidentiality or in the belief that personal privacy will not be breached. The Ombudsman in his 2000–1 report recognizes that, in such cases, it is important to take account of the basis on which information has been provided. He does, however, expect to see that an attempt has been made to establish whether or not those submitting the information or those to whom it relates still wish confidentiality or privacy to be maintained; this is particularly important if the information was provided some time previously.

4.86 In case no A.25/00[51] the Medical Devices Agency ('MDA') refused to provide the names of specialists referred to in the minutes of a meeting of an advisory group of which the complainant was a member, on the grounds that they would not reveal the identities of external experts without their permission. They had not however sought such permission: when they did so, all three experts agreed to the release of their names. The Permanent Secretary said that the MDA had been concerned that releasing the details the complainant had requested might ultimately expose the individuals concerned to unwarranted intrusion in the form of extended correspondence. He also considered that such a disclosure might deter other individuals from assisting the MDA in the future. The Ombudsman recognized the strength of these arguments. However, he considered that ultimately it is for the individuals concerned to decide whether or not they wish their details to be disclosed.

The euro

4.87 Unsurprisingly a number of applications for information which have been referred to the Ombudsman have concerned the euro. A typical case is no A.6/02[52]

---

[51] Parliamentary Commissioner, *Access to Official Information: investigations completed January–June 2001*, HC 160 at p 28.

[52] Parliamentary Commissioner, *Access to Official Information: investigations completed July 2001–January 2002*, HC 585 at p 41. See also the Parliamentary Commissioner, *Access to Official Information: investigations completed February–April 2002*, HC 844 at 11 and 24, cases no A.5/02 and no A.11/02.

where Mr H wrote to the Treasury and asked, under the Code, for a list of any studies that they had commissioned or undertaken on the impact of the euro on competition or trade in the United Kingdom or the eurozone since May 1997. The Treasury refused to supply the information and relied on exemptions 2 (policy advice) and 10 (premature publication). The Ombudsman acknowledged the sensitivity of the issue, but did not see how exemption 2 could apply to the specific information that Mr H had requested. The Ombudsman said that all Mr H had asked for was a list of titles; he had not asked for those studies or for any information contained in them. The disclosure of a list would not reveal any advice, recommendation, opinion or indeed any projections or assumptions relating to internal policy or analysis. The Ombudsman did not consider that the disclosure of the specific information Mr H sought could have any adverse effect of any kind on the frankness and candour of future deliberations on this matter.

4.88 The Ombudsman had more sympathy with the Treasury's arguments on exemption 10. The Ombudsman recognized the strength of the argument that the public interest would be best served by publication of a full assessment of the five economic tests rather than by a disclosure of a partial analysis of any one or more components of that assessment. The Treasury's argument was that the disclosure of even the number and the titles of internal studies they have undertaken would be misleading and damaging because of the speculative and destabilizing inferences that could be drawn by the markets and the media from the disclosure of partial information.

4.89 The Ombudsman recognized in principle that the disclosure of some study titles might cause the type of harm suggested by the Permanent Secretary, but having looked again at the titles being sought he found it difficult to see how the disclosure of these particular titles could in themselves cause harm. The Ombudsman said this:

> I am aware, however, that Exemption 10 recognises that market sensitivity is one of the factors that may make the disclosure of information inappropriate before a planned announcement and I am therefore prepared to accept that the disclosure of a partial list of work undertaken by the Treasury could be misleading and therefore potentially destabilising.
>
> I have also taken into account the Treasury's publication of a paper to the Select Committee which was issued to coincide with the Chancellor's speech to the CBI annual conference on 4 November 2001. The paper, which is headed 'Preliminary and technical work to prepare for the assessment of the Five Tests for UK Membership of the Single Currency', sets out the contents and scope of the work that is currently being undertaken by the Treasury. Having considered this paper against the list of studies sought by Mr H I am satisfied that it provides a reasonably comprehensive overview of the areas of work being undertaken by the Treasury in preparation for the five economic tests assessment. I welcome the Treasury's publication of this information and would encourage the publication of similar updates on a regular basis. To my mind disclosure of such information not only helps public

understanding of such an important and sensitive issue but also improves the transparency and accountability of the Government, one of the aims of the Code.

D. Publication Schemes

Introduction

4.90 The Public Record Office has put out a striking leaflet which asks these questions: *Request for Information? Do we have anything on this subject? If we do, where is it?* The point the Public Record Office is making is that any freedom of information legislation is only as good as the quality of the records to which it provides access. A well-ordered authority will manage its records, so that it knows what information it holds, where it is, how much of it is in the public domain, and the reasons, if any, why the remainder is not to be made public.

4.91 Section 19 of the Act places a duty on public authorities to adopt and maintain publication schemes which must be approved by the Information Commissioner. Such schemes must set out:

(a) the classes of information the authority publishes;
(b) the manner in which the information is published; and
(c) details of any charges.

Timing

4.92 The Lord Chancellor announced to the House of Lords on 13 November 2001 that publication schemes will be introduced on a rolling programme, according to the timetable which is set out at paragraph 3.72 above. This means that from November 2002 the amount of information in the public arena will increase significantly.

Thoughts and pilot schemes

4.93 The Information Commissioner published her initial thoughts on publication schemes on 31 May 2001[53] and has set up a series of pilot schemes with the Public Record Office, the Department for International Development, the Health and Safety Executive, the Medicines Control Agency and the Ministry of Defence. Between them the Commissioner's thoughts and the pilot schemes, which are examined in this part of this chapter, give some indication of the changes which are taking place.

---

[53] *Freedom of Information Act 2000, Preparing for Implementation, Publication Schemes*, The Information Commissioner, vol 2, 31 May 2001.

The scope of a publication scheme

The provisions of section 19 raise a number of questions. First, what is the scope **4.94** of a publication scheme? The Act provides no guidance as to this, but the Commissioner suggests that whilst an authority might wish to adopt a minimalist scheme, for example stating that it publishes an annual report every July, the link between schemes and section 21 suggests it is in the interests of the authority to include as much information as possible. (Section 21 states that information is exempt from the Act if it is accessible to the applicant by other means.) The requirement to consider the public interest in openness when producing a scheme, also appears to support a more detailed approach. Section 19(3) of the Act states:

> In adopting or reviewing a publication scheme, a public authority shall have regard to the public interest—
>
> (a) in allowing public access to information held by the authority, and
> (b) in the publication of reasons for decisions made by the authority.

In essence a publication scheme is a catalogue of all the information which an authority holds which it is prepared to make public. The scheme may itself contain key information; it will in any event explain to the individual how he can obtain access to this information which is in the public domain.

Classes of information—the Ministry of Defence's pilot publication scheme

The second question which arises is how to define classes of information. The **4.95** Information Commissioner has given some very general guidance to the effect that it can be done by subject or by reference to the structure of the authority, but it is perhaps helpful to see how departments have in fact defined classes of information. The Ministry of Defence pilot scheme, for example, says:

> Our intention is to publish as much information as possible on subjects in which there is known to be public interest. However, exemptions under the Freedom of Information Act may prevent some information from being released. The Ministry of Defence publishes or intends to publish information under the classes listed below:
>
> **Defence Policy**
> Information about the UK's defence policy and strategy, our capabilities, relationship with allies, other countries, Parliament and other Government departments, and legislation that we sponsor or in which we have a primary interest.
>
> **The Armed Forces and their Activities**
> Information about the RN, Army, RAF and their reserve forces, including their organisation, capability and equipment, the conduct of operations and training, and the strategic and political framework within [which] these are undertaken.

Personnel

Information about policy and practice concerning serving and former personnel—military and civilian—including numbers, terms and conditions of service, recruitment, pay, rewards, training, welfare and health.

Buying and Supporting Equipment and Services

Information about the equipment and services we buy including logistic support arrangements and policy and plans for the replacement or acquisition of equipment and services.

Sales and Export Support

Information about the sale of MOD land, equipment, services, and information, and the support to British industry.

Finance and Resource Accounting

Information about financial and accounting policy and management systems, budgets and investment plans.

Planning and Performance Management

Information about management and planning, targets, incentives, performances and initiatives for promoting efficiency and good practice.

Research, Science and Technology

Information about research conducted on behalf of MOD including equipment, medical and academic research work.

Supporting Services and Infrastructure

Information about other supporting activities and infrastructure including the defence estate, security, contingency planning, the MOD Police, communications, information use and management, safety, health, environment and fire.

In addition, individual departments [within the MoD] may elect to include extra classes particular to their area of activity.

Exploring the Ministry of Defence's pilot scheme

4.96 The Information Commissioner has said that if a publication scheme is to be structured according to broad headings or classes, in the way that the MoD has chosen, these must be supported by a mechanism for identifying and locating the specific material covered, whether in the form of a catalogue/database or other link to the material. The Ministry of Defence pilot scheme is published on the Ministry's website.[54] It has a facility to browse or search for information within the pilot publication scheme. The scheme has been structured so that applicants will be able to see what is available either by selecting one of the categories of activity in which the department is involved (these categories match the classes of information), or by choosing an area of the organization. Applicants are also able

---

[54] http://www.foi.mod.uk (30 August 2002).

to specify a type of information (such as speeches) and to search by entering key words.

To pursue the MoD example, an applicant seeking to explore the MoD pilot pub-   **4.97**
lication scheme who seeks information under one of the suggested headings, for example, '*Gulf veteran*' will be offered amongst other things, access to 20 research papers, 10 reports, three policy papers, correspondence and budget information. To explore the quality of information available the authors took as a random sample the report (which is in fact a memorandum) listed under the title '*Organophosphate pesticide use Feb 97*'. A copy of this and the other reports can be downloaded from the MoD website.

A memorandum on organophosphates

The memorandum concerns an investigation into why proper and timely advice   **4.98**
was not provided to MoD Ministers between July 1994 and September 1996 on the subject of organophosphate (OP) pesticide used by British troops during Op GRANBY (the UK name for the coalition campaign which led to the liberation of Kuwait in 1991). The memorandum sets out the findings of the investigation and includes supporting material concerning the key events in the evolution of the MoD's handling of this issue.

The findings of the investigation were: **4.99**

A. The answers to six Parliamentary Questions (PQs) in 1994 concerning pesticide usage during Op GRANBY were incorrect because Ministers were given flawed advice by Service and Civil Service staff, who had obtained and used inaccurate information when preparing the draft answers.

B. The submission of flawed advice concerning pesticides to Ministers in July 1994 and again in November 1994, together with repeated submissions of the same inaccurate information at later dates, constituted a fundamental failure of the working practices adopted by Service and Civil Service staff within the area of MoD concerned.

C. As a result of internal confusion about the subject, MoD gave incomplete information to HCDC [The House of Commons Defence Committee] in a memorandum dated 9 December 1994 concerning the non-OP pesticides which had been used during Op GRANBY.

D. In the course of 1995, MoD Service and Civil Service staff received a number of indications that during the Gulf War British troops might have obtained locally and also used some OP pesticides, but this information was neither assessed nor followed up properly.

E. No later than early June 1996, some MoD Service and Civil Service staff knew that OP pesticides had been used more extensively during Op GRANBY than had previously been reported and that this new information would embarrass the Department. However, appropriate action was not taken.

F. Although new information concerning OP pesticide usage during Op GRANBY had emerged much earlier, MoD Service and Civil Service staff failed to provide Ministers with appropriate written advice on the subject until 25 September

1996. Thereafter Parliament was informed at the earliest opportunity that incorrect statements had been made.

4.100 The supporting material under the heading '*Possible Sources of Information— Internal*' suggests further avenues for an applicant to explore. This part of the material is in these terms:

Departmental Records

52. If undertaken, a search of the appropriate Departmental records during this period might have revealed information about pesticide use during Op GRANBY. Broadly there are three possible areas to consider.

53. Each area of MoD keeps its own working files. Those areas of MoD with responsibility for particular aspects of pesticide matters could have been contacted and asked to consult their records from the period of Op GRANBY. This should have produced contemporary documents with relevant information. (Some documents of this type were used to underpin the OPPIT Report.[55])

54. The existence of Post Operational Reports (PORs) from Op GRANBY should always have been known to the department, not least on the basis that it is standard practice to write such reports, and therefore they were always potentially available to be consulted about particular issues. Details of the Environmental Health (EH) PORs from Op GRANBY were given in the OPPIT Report (see paragraph 3.G.9-16). Had these PORs been consulted, it would have been clear that there had been local purchase of pesticide.

55. Finally, there were, and still are, within MoD the Service Historical Branches (SHBs), whose role is to record operations such as Op GRANBY. Hence they have considerable expertise both as regards the events themselves and related records. Pesticide issues do not feature in higher level reporting from the theatre, but there was always the possibility of information being in relevant in-theatre files and the appropriate SHB could have been contacted for advice. It must be noted that research in these numerous and un-indexed records can be very time consuming.

Missing Documents

56. As part of this investigation, it was established that one folder of documents, which may have been of relevance to the investigation, had been lost. This folder was formerly in the possession of a division in MoD HQ.

4.101 It is appreciated that many readers are unlikely to be in need of detailed information about Gulf War syndrome, but the example taken does show that the Ministry of Defence is disclosing real information in its pilot publication scheme and that information describes further records which the Department keeps which could be made the subject matter of further inquiries under the Code or from 1 January 2005 under the Act.

4.102 The Information Commissioner stressed that an authority which includes a class of information in its scheme implies a willingness to make public all information

---

[55] Some may find the Whitehall use of initials excessive. It has not been possible to determine for what OPPIT stands.

in that class. Listing minutes of a particular meeting would imply that such minutes will be publicly available in their entirety. The Commissioner states:

> It is the Commissioner's view that an authority would not be able to rely on another exemption to withhold information, which it has said in its publication scheme that it will publish.

Presumably the Commissioner means that authorities should be careful not to include a class of information in their scheme if it is likely that the authority may wish to rely on an exemption in relation to some information which falls within the class, at any rate without making its intention clear in its entry.[56]

The form in which information is to be published

Some authorities will doubtless continue to publish information in traditional, printed form. Increasingly, however, it is likely that the preferred medium of publication will be electronic. In considering whether to approve a publication scheme and in monitoring its effectiveness, the Commissioner will seek to be satisfied: that websites are reasonably easy to navigate; that the authority has taken full advantage of the technology, for instance by regularly updating information; and that provision has been made to make information available to those who do not have access to the internet or who have special needs. **4.103**

Conclusion

From November 2002 when the first publication schemes come into effect it will be clear from searching publication schemes that a significant step has been taken towards a more open society. **4.104**

E. Existing Statutory Provisions for the Disclosure of Information

First, to sum up: this chapter has shown that there is much that those seeking information from government today can do: they can search publication schemes; they can ask for the information using the Code; they can remind civil servants that with the Act coming fully into force in 2005 it would be good practice to make information available if it will be available under the Act; if Whitehall does not provide the information they can ask the Ombudsman for help; or they can use the range of statutes which have been passed in recent years to provide access to particular sorts of information. This part of this chapter lists the principal statutes and says where in this book the statutes are discussed in greater detail. **4.105**

---

[56] The Ministry of Defence makes a general reservation about exemptions at the start of their pilot publication scheme: see para 4.95 above.

Data protection

4.106   Under the Data Protection Act 1998 individuals are now entitled to have access to any data held on them in any structured manner. This will include medical and education records (unless the Secretary of State exempts such information by Order). Significantly this will also include employment records. Chapter 10 sets out the origin and background to the Data Protection Act 1998, and briefly runs through its main provisions including the important definitions; the rights of individuals to access data relating to themselves and if necessary, to have it corrected or erased; control of data users including registration and enforcement; and the role and powers of the Information Commissioner and the Information Tribunal. Finally the chapter sets out the relationship between the 1998 Act and the Freedom of Information Act 2000.

Medical records

4.107   In 1988 the Access to Medical Reports Act 1988 gave individuals the right to see, and if thought fit to veto, reports sought by employers or insurers from the individual's doctor. Two years later the Access to Health Records Act 1990 provided a right of access to health records produced manually. The Data Protection Act 1998 extended these rights. The individual's rights to see medical records and the provisions of the Code on Openness in the National Health Service are discussed in chapter 11.

Local government

4.108   Individuals already have substantial rights of access to minutes of council meetings, reports and papers. These rights were first introduced by the Local Government (Access to Information) Act 1985. The possibilities are discussed in chapter 15.

The environment

4.109   The Environment and Safety Information Act 1988 gave people the right to see enforcement notices issued when organizations broke laws dealing with environmental protection and safety. This was a modest start, but the need to protect the environment extends across national frontiers, and the matter was taken up by the European Union which set European standards on the freedom of access to information on the environment in EC Directive 90/313/EEC. The United Kingdom implemented the directive by enacting the Environmental Information Regulations 1992.[57] These regulations are still in force. The matter was taken further by the Aarhus Convention on *Access to Information, Public Participation in*

---

[57] SI 1992/3240.

Decision-Making and Access to Justice in Environmental Matters which was signed on 25 June 1998.[58] The Secretary of State has power under section 74 of the Act to make regulations to implement the provisions of the Convention. Draft regulations have been published. These matters are discussed in chapter 16.

Individuals concerned about the environment may also want to use the provisions **4.110** of the Coal Industry Acts which give the right to information about areas which have been mined.

The Land Registration Acts

The Land Registration Acts provide for the registration of the title to land in **4.111** England and Wales. There is a discussion of what information can be obtained under these statutes in chapter 16.

The Registration and Census Acts

A considerable amount of information about births, deaths and marriages can be **4.112** obtained under the various Registration Acts, and the Census Act 1920 gives extensive statistical information about life in the United Kingdom: see chapter 16.

The European Union

On 6 December 1993 the Council and the Commission of the European Union **4.113** approved a Code of Conduct concerning public access to Council and Commission Documents,[59] designed to establish the principles governing access to documents held by them. The Code contains the following principle: 'The public will have the widest possible access to documents held by the Commission and the Council'. This was followed by Regulation (EC) 1049/2001 of the European Parliament and the Council of 30 May 2001[60] regarding public access to European Parliament, Council and Commission documents. The regulation is applicable from 3 December 2001. The European dimension is discussed in chapter 24.

Conclusion

The years since 1997 have seen significant reforms in the constitutional arrange- **4.114** ments in the United Kingdom and the Freedom of Information Act 2000 has been an important part of these changes. This chapter has examined the many ways in which the citizen can obtain information from public authorities before

---

[58] Cm 4736.
[59] [1993] OJ L340/41.
[60] [2001] OJ L145/0043-0048.

the Act comes fully into force in 2005. Those who have sought information will know that one of the most important factors in determining whether they are successful is the attitude of those who are in a position to give information. Here there is evidence of change, there is an acceptance throughout the government machine that the citizen does need to know if democracy is working well.

Part C

THE STATUTORY SCHEME

5

ACCESS TO INFORMATION HELD BY PUBLIC AUTHORITIES

A. Introduction

The long title

5.01 The long title of a statute normally contains a general statement indicating its scope and purpose. The statement should provide a plain guide to the statute's general objective. As such it is important because the interpretation of a statute depends upon knowing what the legislative object was.[1] The long title to the Freedom of Information Act 2000 states that it is:

> An Act to make provision for the disclosure of information held by public authorities or by persons providing services for them . . .

5.02 This statement identifies the general purpose in the broadest of terms. Whilst it is clear that the Act provides for disclosure, it does not give any indication as to the extent of such provision. It does not include a positive assertion that the purpose is to achieve a right of access whenever possible. This broad statement reflects a statute which creates a general right of access subject to a number of exceptions.

The absence of a preamble or objects clause

5.03 The use of a long title only is to be contrasted with the approach of other countries which have included in their freedom of information statutes a detailed preamble or objects clause for the purpose of ensuring that their provisions are construed in a manner which achieves the specified objects: for example Australia, Canada and New Zealand.[2]

5.04 The Australian Freedom of Information Act 1982 contained an objects clause[3] which identified the object as being 'to extend as far as possible the right of the Australian community to access to information in the possession of the Government of the Commonwealth'. It expressly required its provisions to be interpreted accordingly and that this should be achieved by the provisions of the statute being interpreted in ways which would:

(a) make information about the operations of public authorities and departments available;
(b) ensure that rules and practices which affected the dealings of the public with departments and public authorities were readily available;
(c) create a general right of access to information in documentary form in the possession of Ministers, departments and public authorities with exceptions

---

[1] See the speech of Lord Simon of Glaisdale in *Black-Clawson Limited v Papierwerke AG* [1975] AC 591, 647.

[2] See paras 25.01, 25.43 and 25.203 below.

[3] Freedom of Information Act 1982, s 3.

and exemptions being only those necessary for the protection of essential public interests and people's private and business affairs.

Such a practice is not normally followed by Parliament. Indeed it is often sug- **5.05** gested, and rightly, that such an approach is unnecessary when the courts in any event will usually adopt a purposive construction. However, there was cause to argue for a different approach within the context of the Act. The White Paper, *Your Right To Know* emphasized that the statute needed to achieve a change in culture and the question arises whether this is a statute in which it would have been appropriate to identify the objects for that purpose alone. The aim of a more specific objects clause would have been to ensure that the statute is construed in accordance with the specified purposes not just by the courts but also by those public officials who will have to apply the legislation.

The experiences of Australia are to be noted in this context. Some 13 years after **5.06** the passing of the Commonwealth Freedom of Information Act it was observed in a report of the Commonwealth Ombudsman that 'many government agencies still do not operate within the legal framework and certainly not the "spirit" of the Act'.[4] This observation was made notwithstanding the existence of an objects clause.

Whilst it is not right to assume that the same will apply to the operation of the **5.07** Freedom of Information Act, it is a precedent which should be viewed with caution. It is important that the Act is construed from the premise that its purpose is to provide access to information. It is arguable that a more detailed objects clause could have been extremely useful and beneficial for the operation of the Act and would assist in changing the traditional culture of secrecy. Those making requests for information and facing intransigence would have been able to point to an authoritative statement of support for the adoption of an open approach except where the statute expressly provided otherwise.

There are, of course, two sides to this debate. One of the problems of an objects **5.08** clause is that it might prove to be deficient; as has been said to be the case in Australia.[5] More importantly perhaps, Parliament has adopted its traditional approach within the scheme of a statute that makes provision for Codes of Practice and for an Information Commissioner to ensure that the purpose of the Act is implemented. Time will tell whether an objects clause is also needed but it is clear that Parliament has recognized the need to control its implementation.

---

[4] Commonwealth Ombudsman, *Annual Report 1994–95*, (AGPS, Canberra, 1995), 33.
[5] See paras 25.06 and 25.07 below.

B. A General Right of Access to Information

The right

5.09 Section 1(1) of the Act provides that:

Any person making a request for information to a public authority is entitled—

(a) to be informed in writing by the public authority whether it holds information of the description specified in the request [which section 1(6) of the Act designates as 'the duty to confirm or deny'], and

(b) if that is the case, to have that information communicated to him.

5.10 The Act creates a 'general right of access to information held by public authorities' subject to various exclusions and limitations. The right is conferred by section 1 upon 'any person' without restriction as to identity, nationality or place of residence. Applications for access to information can be made, therefore, by limited companies, by public authorities themselves and by persons resident abroad. Whilst the Freedom of Information Bill originally included a right for public authorities to enquire into the motives for an application, there is no such right or requirement within the Act. It is also to be noted that nothing in the Act is to be taken to limit the powers of a public authority to disclose information held by it.[6]

5.11 The phrase 'general right of access to information held by public authorities' appears in the side note to section 1 of the Freedom of Information Act and is, perhaps, slightly misleading. The right created by section 1 will only arise if a request for information in writing satisfying the statutory requirements[7] is made.

5.12 Furthermore, the right is not an unqualified right of access. As section 1(2) of the Act provides, it is subject to the provisions of sections 2, 9, 12, and 14. The operation of these sections is considered in detail below but the effect is that compliance with a request may be avoided in the following circumstances:

(a) if one or more of the exemptions in Part II of the Act applies (section 2);

(b) if fees payable by an applicant for the provision of information are not paid (section 9);

(c) if the estimated cost of complying with the request exceeds a certain limit (section 12);

(d) if it is a vexatious or repeated request (section 14).

5.13 As appears from paragraph 5.09 above section 1(1) of the Act contains two limbs. Even if an authority is justified in refusing to communicate the information requested, it may still have to admit to holding it.

---

[6] Freedom of Information Act 2000, s 78.

[7] ibid, s 8(1).

Exemptions

The general right of access to information held by public authorities is made **5.14** expressly subject to the exemption of various categories of information under Part II of the Act. Exemptions will be dealt with in detail in the following chapter but at this stage it is necessary to refer to section 2 of the Act.

Section 2 provides for the 'effect of the exemptions in Part II'. It divides the **5.15** exemption provisions into two classes. The first consists of those provisions which confer what is called 'absolute exemption'. These are listed in section 2(3) and concern the following categories of information:

(a) information accessible to an applicant by other means (section 21);
(b) information supplied by, or relating to, bodies dealing with security matters (section 23);
(c) information in court records, etc (section 32);
(d) information protected by Parliamentary privilege (section 34);
(e) information held by the House of Commons or the House of Lords disclosure of which would prejudice effective conduct of public affairs (section 36);
(f) personal information (section 40);
(g) information provided in confidence (section 41);
(h) information disclosure of which is prohibited by law (section 44).

The significance of absolute exemption is that section 1(1)(a) of the Act does not **5.16** apply[8] whenever one of the above-mentioned sections states that the duty to confirm or deny does not arise. In those circumstances the authority is under no duty to confirm or deny whether it holds the information. There is no public interest or other test to be met.

Similarly section 2(2)(a) of the Act provides in respect of absolute exemptions that **5.17** there is no duty to communicate the information requested in accordance with section 1(1)(b) of the Act. Again, there is no public interest or other test, just a blanket exclusion.

This is to be contrasted with the exemption provisions of Part II of the Act which **5.18** are not absolute. These conditional exemptions (a term not used in the Act) include, for example, information intended for future publication (section 22), information concerning defence (section 26) and information concerning international relations (section 27). In conditional exemption cases where it is provided that the duty to confirm or deny does not arise, a further test is set. Section 2(1)(b) of the Act provides that the duty to confirm or deny does not apply to this information if:

---

[8] ibid, s 2(1)(a).

in all the circumstances of the case, the public interest in maintaining the exclusion of the duty to confirm or deny outweighs the public interest in disclosing whether the public authority holds the information.

5.19 In the case of conditional exemptions, the section 1(1)(b) duty to communicate the information requested is only excluded if:

in all the circumstances of the case, the public interest in maintaining the exemption outweighs the public interest in disclosing the information.[9]

The application of the public interest test is considered in detail in the next chapter.

5.20 In the light of these restrictions and exemptions it can be observed that the Act does not go as far as to create a general right of access to information. Critics of the statute may suggest that this explains why the long title is so generally worded. However, there must always be limitations on a statutory right of access both in principle and in practice. Certain areas of government have to retain some secrecy; defence and foreign policy are two areas for which it is obvious that there cannot be an open house but there are many others including information provided in confidence. It is necessary to have exemptions.

5.21 Equally there are administrative burdens which must be recognized and eased so far as possible. Each request will take time to answer and there are those who will abuse the right to request information just as there are those who will wish to restrict it. Requests which require employees to trawl through e-mails and other records for references to particular topics may be unreasonably troublesome. There need to be mechanisms to deal with fees, costs and vexatious or repeated requests. The fact that there is not a general right of access is therefore not a valid criticism in itself. The question is whether the statute achieves an acceptable balance between the competing public interests in access and non-disclosure.

C. Public Authorities

Information held by public authorities

5.22 The Act confers a right of access to information held by public authorities[10] and nothing in the Act is to be taken to limit the powers of a public authority to disclose information held by it.[11]

---

[9] Freedom of Information Act 2000, s 2(2)(b).
[10] ibid, s 1.
[11] ibid, s 78.

Public authorities are defined in section 3 of the Act as meaning: **5.23**

(a) all bodies, persons or holders of office listed within Schedule 1 to the Act; or
(b) any person designated as a public authority by order of the Lord Chancellor for the purposes of the Act pursuant to section 5 of the Act; or
(c) a publicly owned company as defined by section 6 of the Act.

Section 3(2) of the Act provides that information is held by a public authority for **5.24** the purposes of the Act if:

(a) it is held by the authority otherwise than on behalf of another person, or
(b) it is held by another person on behalf of the authority.

The Act is therefore concerned with information that a public authority has or **5.25** keeps rather than with ownership of the information. As a result it will have a very wide application, subject to the specific statutory exemptions provided for within Part II of the Act.

An authority cannot escape the ambit of the Act by simply transferring its **5.26** information to third parties. Information which is archived or held by a contracting party will still be subject to the general right of access because it is held on behalf of the public authority. This provision closes what might otherwise have been a loophole enabling a public authority to avoid a duty to disclose by ensuring that information is held by another person. Public authorities which store information or otherwise transfer it to third parties who hold it on their behalf should ensure that in practice they can recover that information in sufficient time to comply with their statutory obligations.

Information received from third parties, including the public, will be 'held by a **5.27** public authority' and therefore will be covered by the Act unless held on behalf of the provider. Circumstances in which information is held on behalf of another person will occur if the public authority is acting as a bailee, voluntary or involuntary, and is obliged to return the information upon demand. In other words when the public authority holds the information as a custodian, as opposed to holding the information in the normal performance of its obligations and duties.

Those supplying information to public authorities should be aware of the provi- **5.28** sions of section 3(2) of the Act and therefore of the potential application of the Act to the information provided. However, as will be seen later in this and the next chapter, the Act makes certain provision for the protection of third parties. For example, section 41 of the Act confers absolute exemption for information the disclosure of which would constitute an actionable breach of confidence. The fact that the exemption is absolute will provide comfort to persons who provide information on a confidential basis and third parties will be well advised to make clear that this is the basis upon which the information is supplied should they wish and be able to benefit from the exemption.

Schedule 1

5.29 Those bodies qualifying as public authorities by virtue of their inclusion within Schedule 1 to the Act fall into the following seven categories:[12]

Part I   A general category incorporating: all government departments; the House of Commons; the House of Lords; the Northern Ireland Assembly; the National Assembly for Wales; the armed forces of the Crown except for the special forces and any unit or part of a unit for the time being required by the Secretary of State to assist the Government Communications Headquarters in the exercise of its functions.

Part II   Local government—which includes county councils, all other local authorities in England and Wales, the Greater London Authority and an extensive list of bodies responsible for various aspects of local government.

Part III   The National Health Service—this Part not only includes bodies such as health authorities, special health authorities, primary care trusts, community health councils, the Dental Practice Board and the Public Health Laboratory Service Board established under sections 8, 11, 16A, 20, 37 of and Schedule 3 to the National Health Service Act 1977 together with National Health Service trusts established under section 5 of the National Health Service and Community Care Act 1990 but also includes:

(a) persons providing general medical services, general dental services, general ophthalmic services or pharmaceutical services under Part II of the National Health Service Act 1977 in so far as information relates to the provision of those services; and

(b) any person providing personal medical services or personal dental services under arrangements made under section 28C of the National Health Service Act 1977 in so far as information relates to the provision of those services.

Part IV   Maintained schools and other educational institutions—covering governing bodies of maintained schools, institutions within the further education sector, universities receiving public support under section 65 of the Further and Higher Education Act 1992 and other higher education providers.

Part V   The police—including police authorities established under section 3 of the Police Act 1996, the Metropolitan Police Authority, a chief officer of

---

[12] See Freedom of Information Act 2000, Sch 1 and ch 23 below for a more detailed consideration of the operation of the Act in Wales and Northern Ireland.

police of a police force in England and Wales, the British Transport Police and the Ministry of Defence Police.

Part VI   Other public bodies and offices including, for example: the Adjudicator for the Inland Revenue and Customs and Excise; the Arts Council of Wales; the British Museum; the Civil Procedure Rule Committee; the Design Council; the Health and Safety Executive; the Law Commission; the Overseas Service Pensions Scheme Advisory Board and the Post Office.

Part VII   Other public bodies and offices of Northern Ireland.

Automatically ceasing to be a public authority

Section 4(4) of the Act provides that any body listed in Parts VI or VII of the   **5.30** Schedule shall cease to be a public authority for the purposes of the statute by virtue of its entry in Schedule 1 if either of the conditions set out in section 4(2) and (3) ceases to be satisfied.

The first condition which is contained within section 4(2) is that: **5.31**

the body [defined in section 84 of the Act as including an unincorporated association] or office—

(a) is established by virtue of Her Majesty's prerogative or by an enactment or by subordinate legislation, or
(b) is established in any other way by a Minister of the Crown in his capacity as Minister, by a government department or by the National Assembly for Wales.

The second condition which is contained within section 4(3) is: **5.32**

(a) in the case of a body, that the body is wholly or partly constituted by appointment made by the Crown, by a Minister of the Crown, by a government department or by the National Assembly for Wales, or
(b) in the case of an office, that appointments to the office are made by the Crown, by a Minister of the Crown, by a government department or by the National Assembly for Wales.

The conditions are therefore concerned with establishment and appointment. In   **5.33** both cases the body or office must be established and appointed by (in summary) the Crown, legislation or the government.

Specified information

In some cases the listing in Schedule 1 is in respect of specified information only.   **5.34** For example: the Common Council of the City of London is included in Part II in respect of information held in its capacity as a local authority, police authority or port health authority; the Bank of England is included in Part VI in respect of information held for purposes other than those of its functions with respect to monetary policy, financial operations intended to support financial institutions for the purposes of maintaining stability and the provision of private banking and related services; and the BBC and the Channel Four Television Corporation are included within Part VI only in respect of information held for purposes other than those of journalism, art or literature.

5.35 Section 7(1) of the Act expressly provides that where the listing of a public authority is limited to specified information, Parts I to V of the Act do not apply to any other information held by that authority. That information is therefore excluded from the scope of the right of access to information created by section 1 of the Act and the consequential provisions of sections 2 to 61 of the Act.

Amendment of Schedule 1

5.36 Section 4 of the Act confers two discretionary powers upon the Lord Chancellor which enable him to amend Schedule 1 to the Act. The first of those powers is concerned with adding to the list, whilst the second is concerned with removal from the list. The powers of addition and removal are supplemented by the provisions of section 7 of the Act in order to permit amendments limited to specified information.

5.37 Section 4(1) provides that the Lord Chancellor may amend Schedule 1 by order to add a reference to any body or office-holder not already listed provided that both of the conditions specified by section 4(2) and (3) of the Act apply. Those conditions are referred to at paragraphs 5.31 and 5.32 above.

5.38 The amendment may be made either by specific reference to the person, body or office to be added or by reference to a specified description of person, body or office.[13] One order has already been made adding a number of bodies to Parts VI and VII of Schedule I including the Criminal Injuries Compensation Authority, the Electoral Commission and the Strategic Rail Authority.[14]

5.39 There must be consultation with the National Assembly for Wales if an addition to Parts II, III, IV, or VI of Schedule 1 refers to a body or to an office-holder whose functions are exercisable only or mainly in or as regards Wales. Similarly there must be consultation with the First Minister and deputy First Minister in Northern Ireland if the order relates to a Northern Ireland body or a Northern Ireland office-holder.

5.40 Section 7(2) of the Act enables the Lord Chancellor to exercise the powers of amendment conferred by section 4(1) of the Act by listing the public authority being added in relation to information of a specified description only.

---

[13] Freedom of Information Act 2000, s 4(6).
[14] The Freedom of Information (Additional Public Authorities) Order 2002, SI 2002/2623.

More generally section 7(3) permits the Lord Chancellor by order to limit the **5.41** types of information which can be obtained from public authorities already listed in Schedule I and to remove or amend any limitation to information of a specified description contained in a current entry.

Concern was expressed in the course of Parliamentary debate about the use to **5.42** which the power to introduce new limitations might be put. Lord Bassam of Brighton, Parliamentary Under-Secretary of State for the Home Office, described it as a 'just-in-case' provision to be inserted just in case a listed body should acquire new functions involving the holding of information in respect of which 'it would be inappropriate and damaging to apply freedom of information principles'.[15] He gave as an example the hypothetical scenario of the Bank of England adding insurance to the banking and related services which it provides to its private customers which are already expressly excluded from the scope of the Act.

In certain cases there must be consultation with the following bodies before the **5.43** powers of amendment conferred by section 7(3) of the Act can be exercised:

(a) the National Assembly for Wales, if the order relates to the National Assembly for Wales or a Welsh public authority;
(b) the Presiding Officer of the Northern Ireland Assembly, if the order relates to the Assembly;
(c) the First Minister and Deputy First Minister in Northern Ireland, if the order relates to a Northern Ireland department or a Northern Ireland public authority.[16]

Section 4(5) of the Act confers upon the Lord Chancellor a discretionary power to **5.44** amend Schedule 1 by removing the entry of any body or office from Part VI or VII if that body or office has ceased to exist.

Section 4(5) of the Act also enables the Lord Chancellor to amend Schedule 1 by **5.45** removing the entry of any body or office from Part VI or VII of Schedule 1 if either of the conditions specified in section 4(2) and (3) of the Act no longer applies to it. This overlaps with the automatic cessation provision of section 4(4) of the Act but is clearly distinct in that the public authority ceases to be a public authority by virtue of that subsection whether it is removed from the list or not. The list can be amended at the same time or afterwards by the Lord Chancellor in order to maintain its accuracy.

No order may be made by the Lord Chancellor pursuant to the amending powers **5.46** to include within Schedule 1 to the Act: the Scottish Parliament; any part of the Scottish Administration; the Scottish Parliamentary Corporate Body or any

---

[15] *Hansard*, HL (series 5) vol 619, col 182 (14 November 2000).
[16] Freedom of Information Act 2000, s 7(4).

Scottish public authority with mixed functions or no reserved functions within the meaning of the Scotland Act 1998.[17]

Designation orders

5.47 Section 5 of the Act confers power on the Lord Chancellor by order to designate as a public authority for the purposes of the statute a person who is neither currently listed in Schedule 1 nor capable of being added to it pursuant to section 4(1). Where the section 4(1) power is available, by virtue of the criteria in section 4(2) and (3)[18] being satisfied, that is the means which must be employed to extend the range of the Act. In other cases, the section 5 power can be exercised, but only if the person in question appears to the Lord Chancellor to exercise functions of a public nature, or is providing a service the provision of which is the function of a public authority under a contract with that public authority. The making of an order under section 5 must have been preceded by consultation with every person to whom the order relates or with persons appearing to represent them.

5.48 An order made in respect of a person who appears to the Lord Chancellor to exercise functions of a public nature must specify the functions in respect of which the designation is to have effect. Designation does not affect any other functions and information concerning non-specified functions is therefore excluded from the general right of access to information created by section 1 of the Act and the consequential provisions of sections 2 to 61 of the Act.[19] Examples of potential candidates include the Press Complaints Commission and private companies which run prisons.

5.49 Similar provision is made for persons providing a service that is the function of a public authority under a contract with that public authority. The service must be specified in the order and nothing in Parts I to V of the Act applies to information that does not relate to the provision of that service.[20]

5.50 Inclusion by designation will prevent potential arguments concerning information held by the providers of contracted out services. In some cases the contractor will hold information which has to be delivered up by reason of other statutory provisions, for example housing files where advice and assessment services under the Housing Act 1996 have been contracted out. In other cases the information held by third party contractors will be held on behalf of a public authority with the result that section 3(2) of the Act will apply and the public authority will be treated as holding the information itself. However there will also be cases where the information held by the contractor would fall outside the scope of the

---

[17] Freedom of Information Act 2000, s 80.
[18] See paras 5.31 and 5.32 above.
[19] Freedom of Information Act 2000, s 7(5).
[20] ibid, s 7(6).

Act without designation. This might apply, for example, in many cases where a contractor has successfully tendered to carry out local authority services.

A designation order can be made in respect of either a specified person or office or **5.51** a specified description of persons and offices. It cannot be made in respect of: the Scottish Parliament; any part of the Scottish Administration; the Scottish Parliamentary Corporate Body or any Scottish public authority with mixed functions or no reserved functions as defined within the Scotland Act 1998.[21]

Publicly-owned company

A 'publicly-owned company' is automatically included within the ambit of the **5.52** Act without having to be listed in Schedule 1. This is because section 3(1)(b) of the Act includes publicly-owned companies within the definition of public authority.

The phrase 'publicly-owned company' is defined by section 6 of the Act as mean- **5.53** ing a company, including any body corporate, which is:

(a) wholly owned by the Crown, having no members other than Ministers of the Crown, government departments or companies wholly owned by the Crown (or persons acting on their behalf); or

(b) wholly owned by a public authority listed in Schedule 1 to the Act, other than a government department or any authority listed only in relation to particular information, so that its membership is exclusively made up of that public authority or companies wholly owned by that public authority (or persons acting on their behalf).

Section 7(8) of the Act gives the Lord Chancellor power to make an order in **5.54** respect of a publicly-owned company which identifies information which is excluded from the provisions of Parts I to V of the Act. The 'excluded information' is exempt from the right of access created by section 1 of the Act.[22]

Government departments

'Government department' is defined in section 84 of the Act as including a **5.55** Northern Ireland department, the Northern Ireland court service and 'any other body or authority exercising statutory functions on behalf of the Crown'. This includes, for example, government agencies such as the Passport Agency. Expressly excluded from the definition are the Security Service, the Secret Intelligence Service, the Government Communications Headquarters, the National Assembly for Wales, and various Scottish bodies enumerated in section 80(2) of the Act.

---

[21] ibid, s 80.
[22] ibid, s 7(7).

5.56   Section 81(1) of the Act provides that for the purposes of the Act each government department is to be treated as a person separate from any other government department.

5.57   This provision could have had the result that each government department could rely upon section 41 of the Act in order to claim that information provided to it by another department was exempt information. That is because section 41 provides that information is exempt if obtained by a public authority from any other person including another public authority and its disclosure would constitute an actionable breach of confidence. This result is avoided by section 81(2) of the Act which provides that:

(a) section 81(1) does not enable a government department which is not a Northern Ireland department to claim for the purposes of section 41(1)(b) of the Act that the disclosure of any information by it would constitute a breach of confidence actionable by any other government department which is not a Northern Ireland department; and

(b) section 81(1) does not enable a Northern Ireland department to claim for those purposes that the disclosure of information by it would constitute a breach of confidence actionable by any other Northern Ireland department.

5.58   Although government departments are to be treated as persons, section 81(3) of the Act provides that they are not liable to prosecution under the Act. However, persons in the service of the Crown can be prosecuted for the offences of altering records with intent to prevent disclosure[23] and of obstructing the execution of a warrant for entry and inspection,[24] as can a person acting on behalf of either House of Parliament or on behalf of the Northern Ireland Assembly.

D. The Information

The request

5.59   Section 84 of the Act defines 'information' as follows:

'information' (subject to sections 51(8) and 75(2)) means information recorded in any form

5.60   This is a very wide definition that will include documentation, computer data, recordings, plans and photographs. However, 'information' does not include unrecorded information save in the particular contexts of two sections, neither of

---

[23]   Freedom of Information Act 2000, s 77.
[24]   ibid, Sch 3, para 12.

which is directly concerned with the right of access. Section 51 permits the Information Commissioner to require a public authority to furnish him with unrecorded information in the exercise of his investigative powers for the purposes of enforcing compliance with the Act.[25] Section 75 empowers the Lord Chancellor to amend or repeal other enactments which prohibit the disclosure of information.

Requests cannot be made which will require officers or employees of a public **5.61** authority to provide information within their own or some other person's knowledge unless it has been recorded. Furthermore the right is to obtain access to the information itself and not to the document or record which contains it. That means that the request for access should describe the information required as opposed to a document or other form of record. This has the advantage that a public authority must provide access (subject to the Act's exemptions) to all records containing the information requested. It cannot restrict access to a particular document referred to in the request. It also means that an applicant will be entitled to disclosure of all the non-exempt information contained in a relevant record even if the record also contains exempt information which the authority can withhold.

Date of information to be provided

Section 1(4) of the Act provides that the information which can be the subject of **5.62** a request and which is to be communicated is the information in question which 'is held at the time the request is received'. Account 'may be taken' of any amendment or deletion to that information if made between the time when the request is received and the time the information is to be communicated. Such account may only be taken, however, if the amendment or deletion would have been made regardless of the request.

It is to be observed, therefore, that the right to receive information does not **5.63** include information received or produced after the date of the request. This is a surprising provision and one which is rather unsatisfactory. Later information may be very pertinent to the request and it is to be hoped that public authorities will take the view that it is sensible to provide it in order to avoid further requests and complaints. Such an approach would be consistent with the duty to provide advice and assistance prescribed by section 16 of the Act considered at paragraphs 5.72 to 5.74 below.

There are no statutory restraints upon how far back the information may go **5.64** and the subject matter of a request for access may be current or past. However,

---

[25] See ch 7 below, especially at paras 7.31–7.38.

the information available may have been reduced in the ordinary course of an authority's management of its records. As the White Paper, *Your Right to Know* at paragraph 6.12 recognized:

> A Freedom of Information Act can only be as good as the quality of the records which are subject to its provisions. Statutory rights of access are of little use if reliable records are not created in the first place, if they cannot be found when needed, or if the arrangements for their eventual archiving or destruction are inadequate.

The Act implicitly acknowledges this fact by including within section 46 a requirement that the Lord Chancellor provides guidance upon the keeping, management and destruction of public authority records.

Form of the request

5.65 The request for information must be in writing and state the name of the applicant and an address for correspondence.[26] There is no requirement for the request to be addressed to any specific person. The request must describe the information requested.[27] Although there is no obligation to state that the request is made under the Act and it is for the public authority to recognize that the Act applies, it would be prudent to do so. Public authorities for their part will need to be alert to the possibility that any communication in writing or sent by electronic means may contain a request for information within the meaning of the Act, which will have to be responded to in accordance with the provisions of the Act.

5.66 Section 8(2) of the Act provides that the text of the request can be transmitted by electronic means but will only be treated as satisfying the requirement of writing if it is received in legible form and is capable of being used for subsequent reference. Whether an e-mail address is sufficient for the purpose of satisfying the section 8(1) requirement that an address must be stated is a moot point. The problem with an e-mail address is that the public authority may not be able to provide the information to the applicant by that means; for example where it is held in hard copy only. This may lead to disputes. Whilst it is unlikely that *Hansard* can be adverted to on this point of construction, it is to be observed that the original promoters did not consider an e-mail address sufficient. The pragmatic approach for a public authority to take will be to advise the applicant of any practical problems it faces in communicating information. However, it is suggested that on a strict construction of the section 'address' must mean a place for communication and not part of the ethereal world of the Internet.

5.67 It is to be noted that the duty to advise and assist created by section 16 of the Act applies whether or not the request is made in the form required by section 8 of the

---

[26] Freedom of Information Act 2000, s 8(1).
[27] ibid, ss 1(1) and 8(1).

Act. Therefore requests which are made, for example, orally should result in the public authority advising the applicants of the need to make their application in writing.

Communication

The authority may communicate the information by any means which are reasonable in the circumstances[28] unless a preference has been stated. Section 11(1) of the Act provides that the request may indicate a preferred method for communication selected by the applicant out of the following options: **5.68**

(a) a copy of the information in a permanent form or some other form acceptable to the applicant;
(b) a reasonable opportunity to inspect a record containing the information; and
(c) a digest or summary of the information in a permanent form or another form acceptable to the applicant.

The public authority is obliged to comply with that preference 'so far as reasonably practicable' having regard to all the circumstances including the cost. The public authority must notify the applicant of its reasons if it decides that it is not reasonably practicable to comply with the expressed preference.[29] In those circumstances the information should be communicated by any means which are reasonable in the circumstances.[30] **5.69**

Section 11(1) of the Act could lead to difficulty for public authorities, although it is intended to provide a sensible solution to the question of how best to provide information. On the face of it the three options ought to be acceptable to applicants. However there could be disputes over whether the opportunity to inspect which an authority offers is reasonable or whether the digest or summary prepared by the authority is sufficient. The test is an objective one in both cases. The phrase 'acceptable to the applicant' refers to the form in which the digest or summary is to be provided, not to its content. There will no doubt be occasions when it will be contended that a digest or summary hides the details that a copy of the information or inspection would provide. **5.70**

At the end of the day any such disputes will fall to be resolved by the Information Commissioner and perhaps the Information Tribunal under Part IV of the Act. It is unlikely that there will be a need to take the matter further by way of judicial review. The Information Commissioner can be expected to reach a satisfactory, unchallengeable reasoned decision having seen the information itself as well as the digest or summary. **5.71**

---

[28] ibid, s 11(4).
[29] ibid, s 11(2) and (3).
[30] ibid, s 11(4).

E. Advice and Assistance

The section 16 duty

5.72 Exercise or effective exercise of the right of access depends in part upon an ability to describe the desired information. There is nothing necessarily wrong in that. After all, public authorities can only provide access to information once they understand what information is required. However, it is a potential weakness of the Act in light of the view taken in the White Paper that there was a culture of secrecy that had to be overcome. Those who wish to maintain that culture could try taking a narrow approach to construction when considering requests. What needs to be avoided is the adoption by public authorities of a defensive attitude to requests which leads to a restrictive interpretation of their scope. Requests must not be thwarted by a public authority arbitrarily reducing the ambit of the information sought.

5.73 The Act seeks to avoid such an approach. The sections governing the right of access to information should be read together with section 16 of the Act which provides that:

(1) It shall be the duty of a public authority to provide advice and assistance, so far as it would be reasonable to expect the authority to do so, to persons who propose to make, or have made, requests for information to it.

(2) Any public authority which, in relation to the provision of advice or assistance in any case, conforms with the code of practice under section 45 is to be taken to comply with the duty imposed by subsection (1) in relation to that case.

5.74 Section 16 of the Act therefore makes it a statutory duty for public authorities to provide advice and assistance to those who are proposing to make or have made requests for information so far as it would be reasonable to expect the authority to do so.

The section 45 Code

5.75 The extent of that duty is one of the matters covered by the Code of Practice issued by the Lord Chancellor under section 45 of the Act providing guidance to public authorities on the discharge of their functions under Part I of the Act. It was clearly necessary for the code to address this issue of concern and ensure that the duty is performed in a way which will prevent unhelpful, restrictive interpretation of requests. An officer or employee of a public authority should not be able to adopt such an approach if, for example, the Code were expressly to require him to explain what additional or alternative information might be available and made the subject of a request.

5.76 The section 45 Code of Practice was laid before Parliament on 20 November 2002. It is reproduced in Appendix D to this book. In connection with section 16 of the

Act it requires all public authorities to publish their procedures for dealing with requests. It states that a public authority should ensure that appropriate assistance is given to a person unable to frame his request in writing in order to enable the request to be made. Suggested methods of help include identifying another person or agency who could assist (such as the Citizens Advice Bureau) or (in exceptional circumstances) offering to take a note over the telephone which would constitute a written request once it had been sent to, verified and returned by the applicant. That provision is aimed at helping people who are unable, for example through disability or illiteracy, to express their desire for information in written form. What of applicants who can reduce their requests to writing, but do so in unclear terms? Paragraph 9 of the Code says that when an application does not describe the information sought in a way which would enable the recipient authority to identify or locate it, or the request is ambiguous, the authority should as far as practicable provide assistance to enable the applicant to describe the information sought more clearly.

The Code makes clear that the object of providing such assistance is to clarify the **5.77**
nature of the information required and not the aims of or motives for the request. The examples of such assistance it gives are:

(a) providing outlines of the different kinds of information which may be relevant;
(b) providing access to detailed catalogues and indexes which may assist; and
(c) providing a general response setting out options for further information which could be provided on request.

However the Code also states that if, notwithstanding the assistance provided, a **5.78**
satisfactory description is still not forthcoming, the authority is not expected to seek further clarification. The authority should explain why it cannot take the request further, whilst disclosing such information as has been identified and found in the course of the application (subject to any claims for exemption). This guidance appears to have in mind the problem that a public authority's resources cannot be committed to endless attempts at clarification, although there may be a danger that this guidance is construed too literally.

Public authorities may consider that there is an opportunity to reduce their work- **5.79**
load and place the burden upon others by advising those making requests to obtain assistance from, for example, the Citizens Advice Bureau. Such advice must be given responsibly. First, it is reasonable to presume that a public authority will only take such steps where there is a problem. Secondly, in those circumstances it may well be best for all concerned to ensure that third party assistance is available. Thirdly, there is no reason to believe that bodies such as the Citizens Advice Bureau will not be able to provide valuable assistance. Finally, the authority will need to explain why it cannot take the request further and this will enable the applicant to seek further help from the third party.

F. Fees and Costs

The discretion

5.80 Section 9 of the Act gives public authorities a discretion to charge a fee for complying with section 1(1). Section 9(3) and (5) provide that public authorities must act in accordance with regulations made by the Lord Chancellor when determining whether to charge a fee, unless a fee is prescribed by another enactment. Those regulations may provide in particular for circumstances in which no fee is to be charged, a maximum charge and methods of calculation.[31]

5.81 A public authority which exercises its discretion under section 9 of the Act and decides to charge a fee in accordance with the regulations must give notice in writing to the applicant, a 'fees notice', stating that a fee of an amount specified in the notice is to be charged for compliance with the public authority's duty under section 1(1) of the Act.[32] There is no guidance concerning the exercise of the discretion in the Act but a public authority must act as a reasonable authority (that is in the *Wednesbury* sense) in reaching its decision.

Time for compliance

5.82 The applicant has three months beginning with the day on which the fees notice is given to pay the fee. If that period expires without payment having been made the public authority no longer owes a duty under section 1(1) of the Act.[33]

5.83 If a fees notice is served and the fee is paid in time, the calculation of the period for compliance with section 1(1) of the Act excludes the working days from the day on which the fees notice is given to the day on which the fee is received.[34]

5.84 A public authority is exempted from the obligation to communicate information[35] in a case in which it estimates that the costs of complying with the request for information would exceed the 'appropriate limit'.[36] However, the public authority will not be exempt from complying with the duty to confirm or deny unless the estimated cost of compliance with that duty on its own would exceed the appropriate limit.[37]

---

[31] Freedom of Information Act 2000, s 9(4).
[32] ibid, s 9(1).
[33] ibid, s 9(2).
[34] ibid, s 10(2).
[35] ie ibid, the s 1(1)(b) duty.
[36] ibid, s 12.
[37] ibid, s 12(2).

The appropriate limit is such amount as may be prescribed by regulations made **5.85** by the Lord Chancellor.[38] The regulations may prescribe different amounts in respect of different cases and provide for the method of estimation. They may also deal with cases of one person making two or more requests to the same authority, and with cases of requests being made to the same authority by different persons who appear to the authority to be acting in concert or in pursuance of a campaign. In such circumstances the regulations may provide that the estimated cost of compliance with any one of such requests should be calculated as the estimated total cost of complying with all of them.[39]

When the cost of compliance with a request exceeds the appropriate limit, so that **5.86** section 1(1) of the Act does not apply, and the communication of the information is not otherwise required by law, section 13 of the Act provides that the public authority may nevertheless provide the information at a fee to be determined in accordance with regulations made by the Lord Chancellor.[40] The regulations may set a maximum fee and may lay down the method of calculation.[41]

The draft fees regulations

Draft fees regulations[42] have been prepared and circulated. They do not prescribe **5.87** any circumstances in which authorities are prohibited from charging any fees. Their principal provisions are as follows.

(a) The costs to be taken into account by a public authority when determining any fee to be charged under section 9(1) or section 13(1) are (i) *the prescribed costs* and (ii) *the disbursements* that the authority would incur (or reasonably estimates it would incur) in complying with the relevant request.

(b) 'Prescribed costs' are the costs reasonably incurred by a public authority in:

- determining whether it holds information of the description specified in the request
- locating and retrieving any such information
- giving effect to any preference expressed by the applicant as to the method of communicating it to him.

The cost of staff time associated with those activities is included, but the cost of staff time taken up in determining whether the authority is obliged to comply with the request is specifically excluded.

---

[38] ibid, s 12(3)–(5).
[39] ibid, s 12(4).
[40] ibid, s 13(3) expressly excludes the operation of this provision if a fee is chargeable for supplying the information under any other enactment.
[41] ibid, s 13(2).
[42] Entitled the Freedom of Information (Fees and Appropriate Limit) Regulations. A copy is to be found in Appendix J to this book.

(c) 'Disbursements' means any costs directly and reasonably incurred by a public authority in:

- informing the applicant whether it holds information of the description specified in the request
- communicating any such information to him.

(d) The maximum fee chargeable to an applicant under section 9(1) is the sum of:

   (i)   10% of the prescribed costs; and
   (ii) the disbursements relating to his request.

(e) The appropriate limit for the purposes of section 12[43] is £550. In estimating the cost of compliance with a request for the purposes of deciding whether it would exceed the appropriate limit, disbursements are to be left out of account.

(f) The maximum fee chargeable to an applicant under section 13(1) is the sum of:

   (i)   10% of the prescribed costs up to £550;
   (ii) 100% of the prescribed costs in so far as they exceed £550; and
   (iii) the disbursements relating to his request.

(g) The circumstances in which the estimated cost of complying with one request is to be taken as the estimated total cost of complying with that and one or more other requests[44] are that:

- the requests are for information which is on the same subject matter or otherwise related
- the last of the requests is received by the authority before the twentieth working day following the date of receipt of the first of them
- it appears to the authority that the requests have been made in an attempt to ensure that the prescribed costs of complying separately with each of the requests would not exceed the appropriate limit.

The section 45 Code

5.88 The section 45 Code of Practice indicates that in circumstances where cost is the only obstacle to disclosure of requested information, the public authority should try to find some compromise solution. For example, it says that where an applicant who has been given a fees notice is not prepared to pay the notified fee, the authority should consider whether there is any information that might be of interest to him which is available free of charge. Where the cost of compliance with a request would exceed the appropriate limit and the authority is not willing

---

[43] See para 5.84 above.
[44] Pursuant to the regulation-making power in the Freedom of Information Act 2000, s 12(4).

to provide the information on a discretionary basis because of the cost of doing so, it should consider providing the applicant with an indication of what information it could give within the cost ceiling. And where an authority is excused compliance with a request because the regulations made under section 12(4) of the Act apply and the aggregated costs of compliance with that and the related requests would exceed the appropriate limit, the authority should consider whether the information could be disclosed in another, more cost-effective manner; such as publishing it on its website and notifying the applicants of the website reference.

G. Time for Compliance and Transfers

Time for compliance

The time for compliance with a request in accordance with the requirements of **5.89** section 1(1) of the Act depends upon whether the public authority in exercise of its discretion gives the applicant a fees notice under section 9 (that is, a notice in writing stating that a quantified fee is to be charged for compliance).

The basic position when no fees notice is given is that the public authority must **5.90** both inform the person making the request whether it holds information of the description specified in the request, and if it does, communicate that information promptly.[45]

Section 10 of the Act provides a maximum time period for such compliance of not **5.91** later than the twentieth working day following receipt.[46] That period can be altered by the Lord Chancellor by regulations subject to a maximum limit of the sixtieth working day following the date of receipt of the request.[47] Such regulations may prescribe different days in relation to different cases and confer a discretion on the Commissioner.[48] The reference to a discretion is, however, rather puzzling bearing in mind that it applies to regulations under section 10(4) of the Act which makes no reference to the Commissioner. It is to be inferred that the discretion would be a discretion to extend time limits for compliance in specified classes of case, but the subsection is ambiguous.

It is important to note that the overriding requirement is that of promptitude. **5.92** Authorities are not entitled to take the full allowance of twenty working days to comply with requests whether they need that length of time or not. What would

---

[45] ibid, s 10.
[46] 'Working day' is defined in ibid, s 10(6) as any day other than a Saturday, Sunday, Christmas Day, Good Friday or a day which is a bank holiday under the Banking and Financial Dealings Act 1971 in any part of the UK.
[47] ibid, s 10(1) and (4).
[48] ibid, s 10(5).

constitute prompt compliance in any particular case will depend on all the circumstances. However, the basic position is subject to three possible variations. The first occurs when the public authority reasonably requires further information in order to identify and locate the information requested and gives notice of that fact to the applicant. In those circumstances section 1(3) of the Act provides that the obligation to comply with the duty to confirm or deny will not arise and the time will not start to run unless and until that further information is provided. Section 10(6) of the Act provides that the date of provision of that information (rather than the date of receipt of the request) will count as the date of receipt for the purposes of section 10.

5.93　The second possibility is that the information requested is subject to an exemption. If the provision in question is one of those conferring absolute exemption, it makes no difference. If on the other hand it has to be decided whether the public interest in maintaining the exclusion of the duty to confirm or deny outweighs the public interest in disclosing whether the public authority holds the information (section 2(1)(b)) and/or whether the public interest in maintaining the exemption outweighs the public interest in disclosing the information (section 2(2)(b)), then the time for complying with the duty to confirm or deny, or the duty to communicate information, or both (as the case may be), is extended for 'such time as is reasonable in the circumstances' to enable that decision to be made: section 10(3). However, the time for serving a notice under section 17(1) stating that an exemption provision is being relied on is not extended.

5.94　Section 17(2) of the Act requires an estimate to be given of the expected date of a decision concerning the balance of public interest and the Lord Chancellor's Code of Practice made pursuant to section 45 of the Act advises that this should be a realistic and reasonable estimate and should be complied with unless there is good reason not to. Failure to do so should result in an explanation and an apology. The Code also provides that public authorities should aim to make all decisions within 20 working days wherever possible.

5.95　The third possibility is that the public authority is exempt from complying with the request for information because it estimates that the cost of compliance will exceed the 'appropriate limit'.[49]

5.96　If a fees notice is served, the period for compliance with section 1(1) of the Act is extended by the number of working days in the period beginning with the day on which the fees notice is given and ending with the day on which the fee is received. Therefore the giving of the fees notice stops the running of the clock until it restarts on the day after payment of the fees.[50]

---

[49] Freedom of Information Act 2000, s 12.
[50] ibid, s 10(2).

The provisions governing time for compliance therefore provide a rather cumber- **5.97**
some and complicated system which could result in delays. In particular there is
scope for delay when considering whether a conditional exemption applies. The
extent to which this may cause difficulties cannot be predicted and may largely
depend upon the number of requests being received by a public authority. It is to
be remembered in this context that the Act has to allow for the administrative burden which compliance may impose on public authorities with limited resources at
their disposal.

Transferring requests

It may sometimes be the case that an applicant makes a mistake about the identity **5.98**
of the public authority which holds the information he wants, and addresses his
request to the wrong authority. The Act does not make express provision for the
transfer of requests from one public authority to another. In such a case the
scheme of the Act is to:

(a) require the authority receiving the request to fulfil its duty to confirm or deny
    under section 1 of the Act by saying that it does not hold the information
    sought;
(b) rely upon that public authority to provide advice and assistance pursuant to
    its obligations under section 16 of the Act; and
(c) provide that the Code of Practice to be issued by the Lord Chancellor in
    accordance with section 45 of the Act shall include guidance upon transfer-
    ring requests.[51]

The section 45 Code says that in most such cases the authority receiving the orig- **5.99**
inal request will consider that the most helpful way of assisting the applicant
would be to contact him, explain that there is another public authority which it
believes to hold the information he seeks, provide him with contact details for that
authority, and suggest that he make a fresh request to that authority. However, the
Code also provides that the authority may consider it more appropriate to transfer the original request directly to that other authority. That should only be done
where the other authority has been consulted and has confirmed that it holds the
information sought. Consideration should be given to whether the transfer is
appropriate and whether the applicant is likely to have grounds for objection
before a transfer is made. If the authority reasonably concludes that objection is
unlikely, it may transfer the request without reverting to the applicant, provided
the applicant is informed and it complies with its obligation to advise whether it
holds any of the requested information. Otherwise the consent of the applicant to
the transfer should be sought.

---

[51] ibid, s 45(2)(b) and see Part VI of the Code.

5.100 The Code also provides that a request may only be transferred in so far as it relates to information not held by the transferring authority and the authority must still comply with the request as to the information which it holds. A transferred request is to be treated by the receiving authority in the same way as an original request by the applicant. Time for compliance will run from the date the request is received. The authority making the transfer has no further responsibility for handling the request. All transfers should be dealt with promptly.

H. Vexatious and Repeated Requests

Vexatious requests

5.101 Section 14 of the Act exempts a public authority from complying with a vexatious request. It is also specified within section 14(2) that a public authority does not have to comply with a request which is identical or substantially similar to a previous request by the same person unless a reasonable period has elapsed between compliance with the previous request and the making of the current request.

5.102 The Oxford English Dictionary defines the word 'vexatious' in relation to legal actions as meaning 'instituted without sufficient grounds for the purpose of causing trouble or annoyance to the defendant'. It has been said in the context of striking out proceedings that a claim is vexatious if it is such that no reasonable person could properly treat it as being made in good faith.[52]

5.103 Generally speaking, however, the motives of an applicant for information under the Act are irrelevant and it is questionable whether enquiry into the purpose of a request or the good faith of the applicant is permissible. There is a distinction to be drawn between the concept of a vexatious application and that of a vexatious applicant.

5.104 In the course of the Freedom of Information Bill's passage through Parliament, the government rejected a proposed amendment which would have introduced the concept of vexatious applicants. In the words of Lord Bach:[53]

> The notion of a 'vexatious request' in subsection (1) of Clause 12 is intended to capture such things as supplementary requests from the same individual for further and further clarification of an original request beyond the point where any further information could reasonably be provided. In this case, the request can be said to be vexatious because no further information can be supplied.
>
> The notion of a vexatious applicant—which the amendment seeks to add—on the other hand requires the authority to come to a conclusion as to the motives of the applicant: in the words of the amendment, whether the applicant has 'reasonable

---

[52] *Norman v Matthews* (1916) 85 LJKB 857.
[53] Then a government whip in the House of Lords.

grounds' for making the request. But what would constitute reasonable grounds—that the applicant had an interest, or needed to know the information?

This Bill will give to people for the first time a statutory right to information. The idea that people have to establish an interest or need to know the information before they have the right to request the information undermines the reasoning behind a general right of access. The Bill is intended to end the 'need to know' culture. The amendment would introduce it again by the back door. The Government's proposals will create a right of access which we hope will be 'applicant blind'. The Bill does not empower authorities to scrutinise an applicant's reasons for making a request. We believe that the amendment would fatally undermine this important principle.[54]

In Standing Committee, Mike O'Brien (then Parliamentary Under-Secretary of State for the Home Department) said:[55]   **5.105**

The word vexatious refers to applications that abuse the right in some way—for example, a request that returns to a theme that has habitually been brought up but which has been dealt with previously is arguably vexatious.

It is therefore the nature and effect of the request, rather than the intentions of the   **5.106**
applicant, which should determine whether the request is an abuse of the right of access and therefore a vexatious one. An example might be wasting an authority's time by requesting information which it obviously would not have.

Repeated requests

There are likely to be fewer difficulties of interpretation so far as section 14(2) is   **5.107**
concerned, although there will be scope for factual disputes about what constitutes a 'substantially similar request' and how long is a 'reasonable interval' between requests.

It is suggested that in the context of a statute the purpose of which is to provide   **5.108**
disclosure of information, the words 'substantially similar' should not be given too broad an interpretation.

The length of a 'reasonable interval' will depend on all the circumstances. As was   **5.109**
acknowledged by Lord Bach[56] and Mike O'Brien[57] in the course of debate, where information is of a sort which could be expected to change rapidly, it could be a matter of days or even hours.

---

[54] *Hansard*, HL (series 5) vol 617, cols 1014-1015 (17 October 2000).
[55] Proceedings of Standing Committee B on the Freedom of Information Bill, col 118 (18 January 2000).
[56] *Hansard*, HL (series 5) vol 617, col 1014 (17 October 2000).
[57] Proceedings of Standing Committee B on the Freedom of Information Bill, col 124 (18 January 2000).

I. Refusal of the Request

Section 17

5.110 Section 17 of the Act requires written notice to be given to the applicant when a public authority refuses to disclose requested information. There are four different types of notice:

(a) The first type of notice is to be given when any Part II provision is relied upon to claim either that the duty to confirm or deny is excluded or that the information is exempt.

(b) The second type of notice is appropriate when an authority is relying on one of the Part II provisions which does not confer absolute exemption, but has not yet decided where the balance of public interest lies.

(c) The third type of notice is a statement of reasons for claiming that the public interest in maintaining the exclusion of the duty to confirm or deny, or in maintaining an exemption, outweighs the public interest in disclosing whether the authority holds particular information, or in disclosing information as the case may be.

(d) The fourth type of notice is issued when a public authority claims that the section 12 or section 14 exemption applies (that is, that the cost of compliance would exceed the appropriate limit, or that the request is vexatious or repeated).

5.111 The first type of notice must state that the authority is relying on a claim that a provision of Part II relating to the duty to confirm or deny is relevant to the request, or that the information sought is exempt information, specify the exemption relied upon, and state why the exemption applies if that would not otherwise be apparent.[58] A statement as to why the exemption applies need not be made if, or to the extent that, it would involve disclosure of information which would itself be exempt information.[59]

5.112 The second type of notice must include all the information that has to be included in the first type of notice and indicate that no decision as to the balance of public interest has yet been made. It must also contain an estimate of the date by which a decision is expected.[60] In the case of a public record[61] which has been transferred under the Public Records Act 1958 to the Public Record Office or another appointed place of deposit, the decision as to where the balance of public interest lies will be that of the 'responsible authority' (usually the authority which

---

[58] Freedom of Information Act 2000, s 17(1).
[59] ibid, s 17(4).
[60] ibid, s 17(2).
[61] As defined in the Public Records Act 1958, Sch 1: see para 5.170 below.

transferred the record) rather than the records authority which has custody of it: section 66(3) and (4) of the Act.[62] The responsibility for notifying the applicant, however, remains with the records authority.

Section 17(3) of the Act comes into play once a decision has been made as to the **5.113** balance of public interest which is adverse to the applicant. The reasons for that decision may be included in the first form of notice. Alternatively, when the authority has initially given a notice of the second type, it may state the reasons in a separate and subsequent notice (the third type) given within such time as is reasonable in the circumstances.

A statement as to why the balance is in favour of maintaining the exclusion need **5.114** not be made if, or to the extent that, it would involve disclosure of information which would itself be exempt information.[63]

The fourth type of notice (that is, one stating that section 12 or section 14 of the **5.115** Act is relied upon) must be given within the time for complying with section 1(1) of the Act.[64]

There is an exception to the requirement to give the fourth type of notice[65] in cases **5.116** in which section 14 of the Act is relied upon (that is, in respect of vexatious or repeated requests) if the fourth type of notice has been given in relation to a previous request. In that case no further notice need be given if it would be unreasonable in all the circumstances to expect a further such notice to be served. However, bearing in mind that applicants who make requests of a vexatious or repeated nature are likely to complain over the absence of a notice and to dispute the question of reasonableness, it is suggested that as a matter of practice it may be best not to invoke this provision but to serve a notice of the fourth type in every case.

All four types of notice must contain particulars of any procedure provided by the **5.117** public authority for dealing with complaints about the handling of requests for information or state that the authority does not provide such a procedure. They must also contain particulars of the right conferred by section 50 of the Act, that is the right to apply for a decision by the Information Commissioner as to whether a request for information has been dealt with in accordance with the requirements of Part I of the Act.[66] The absence of such particulars will invalidate the notice, although the breach may be waived should it have no practical effect and the matter reach the courts. The likely effect, however, will be that applicants will complain that they were unaware of their right to have access to the complaints

---

[62] Discussed in paras 8.30–8.35 below.
[63] ibid, s 17(4).
[64] ibid, s 17(5).
[65] ibid, s 17(6).
[66] ibid, s 17(7). See ch 7 below (especially part D) for discussion of the forms of redress available to dissatisfied applicants.

procedure and/or the Commissioner and will be out of time to exercise their right should the notice be treated as valid. In those circumstances it is likely that the absence of such particulars will result in the notice being held invalid so that the rights of complaint and appeal will not have been lost.

J. Publication Schemes

Section 19

5.118 An obvious problem for those wishing to exercise the right of access is to know where to start and which type of information to ask for. The Act does not intend people to have to start from scratch and to be without assistance. A convenient starting point for any member of the public wanting access to particular information held by a public authority will be its publication scheme. If the information is referred to there, then it will not be necessary to follow the formal request procedure appropriate for exercising the section 1 right. Indeed the section 1 duty to communicate will not apply to that information because it will be accessible by other means, attracting the section 21 exemption.[67]

5.119 Every public authority must have a *publication scheme* drawn up in compliance with section 19 of the Act and approved by the Information Commissioner. The scheme is to be published in such manner as the public authority thinks fit.[68] The scheme must specify:[69]

(a) classes of information which the public authority publishes or intends to publish;

(b) the manner in which information of each class is, or is intended to be, published; and

(c) whether the material is, or is intended to be, available to the public free of charge or on payment.

5.120 Each public authority is required to publish information in accordance with its scheme and to review the scheme from time to time.[70] A public authority shall have regard when adopting or reviewing a scheme to the public interest in allowing public access to information it holds and in the publication of reasons for decisions it makes.[71] Section 78 provides that nothing in the Act is to be taken to limit the powers of a public authority to disclose information held by it. The exercise of the right conferred by section 1 is not intended to constitute the exclusive means

---

[67] See ch 6, paras 6.13–6.18 below for details.
[68] Freedom of Information Act 2000, s 19(4).
[69] ibid, s 19(2).
[70] ibid, s 19(1)(b) and (c).
[71] ibid, s 19(3).

of access to information in the possession of a public authority. On the contrary, the Act not only permits but strongly encourages the voluntary release of information through the device of publication schemes. The Act neither prescribes any particular information which must be published, nor restricts what may be published, pursuant to a scheme. The only limitations on an authority's freedom to include as much or as little as it chooses are prohibitions on disclosure in other enactments and the necessity to obtain the Information Commissioner's approval for its scheme.

Model publication schemes

It was clearly necessary for the Act to include a provision ensuring that the publi- **5.121** cation schemes drawn up by the authorities themselves are monitored. The Act gives the Information Commissioner the role of approving schemes, including model publication schemes. The Commissioner when approving a scheme proposed by a public authority may restrict his approval to expire at the end of a specified period.[72] The Commissioner also has a discretionary power to give notice to a public authority at any time revoking his approval of its scheme. Revocation will take effect at the end of the period of six months beginning with the day on which such notice is given.[73] Reasons must be given to the public authority for a refusal to approve a proposed publication scheme or for a revocation of approval.[74]

Model publication schemes apply to public authorities falling within particular **5.122** classes. They may be prepared by the Commissioner or by other persons, apparently without limitation. If the Commissioner approves a model scheme it may be approved upon terms that the approval expires at the end of a specified period. An approved model scheme may be adopted by a public authority falling within the specified class without requiring individual approval from the Commissioner provided it is adopted without modification. Any modifications require the Commissioner's approval.[75]

The Commissioner has similar powers of revocation of approval in respect of a **5.123** model scheme as apply to publication schemes generally. He may publish a notice of revocation at any time and in such manner as he thinks fit. Revocation will take effect at the end of the period of six months beginning with the day on which such notice is published.[76]

---

[72] ibid, s 19(5).
[73] ibid, s 19(6).
[74] ibid, s 19(7).
[75] ibid, s 20(1)–(3).
[76] ibid, s 20(4).

5.124 Reasons must be given by the Commissioner for:[77]

(a) a refusal to approve a proposed model scheme (when the reasons must be given to the person who applied for approval);

(b) a refusal to approve any modifications to an approved model scheme (when the reasons must be given to the applicant authority);

(c) revocation of an approved model scheme (when the reasons must appear within the notice of revocation itself).

5.125 There is no statutory right of appeal from decisions of the Commissioner in relation to publication schemes. Decisions can only be challenged by an application for judicial review. Chapter 4 above contains some further discussion of publication schemes including the timetable for their introduction (commencing in November 2002).[78]

K. The Lord Chancellor's Code of Practice

Section 45

5.126 A further means of ensuring that access to information is given in accordance with the terms of the Act is provided by section 45(1) of the Act. This subsection requires the Lord Chancellor[79] to issue a Code of Practice which provides guidance to public authorities on the practice which in his opinion it would be desirable for them to follow in the discharge of their functions under Part I of the Act.

5.127 There must be consultation with the Information Commissioner before the Code is issued and the Code must be laid before each House of Parliament.[80] Section 45(1) confers a discretionary power to revise the Code from time to time but there must be prior consultation with the Information Commissioner. The revised Code must also be laid before each House of Parliament.[81]

5.128 Section 16(2) of the Act provides that a public authority is to be taken to have complied with its duty to provide advice and assistance in a particular case if it conforms to the Code of Practice.

---

[77] Freedom of Information Act 2000, s 20(5)–(7).

[78] In paras 4.90–4.104 above.

[79] As originally enacted, s 45 placed this responsibility on the Secretary of State. However, it was transferred to the Lord Chancellor with all the other functions of the Secretary of State under the Act (save for the regulation-making power under s 74) and s 45 was amended accordingly by the Transfer of Functions (Miscellaneous) Order 2001, SI 2001/3500, arts 3 and 8, Sch 1, para 12, Sch 2, para 8, which came into force on 26 November 2001.

[80] Freedom of Information Act 2000, s 45(4) and (5).

[81] ibid, s 45(4) and (5).

Guidance in the Code

The Code may make different provisions for different public authorities[82] but **5.129** must contain guidance on:[83]

(a) the provision of advice and assistance to those who propose to make or have made requests for information;

(b) the transfer of requests by one public authority to another public authority which holds or may hold the information requested;

(c) consultation with persons to whom requested information relates or persons whose interests are likely to be affected by disclosure;

(d) the inclusion of terms relating to disclosure of information in contracts entered into by public authorities;

(e) the provision by public authorities of procedures for dealing with complaints about their handling of requests for information.

The Code will provide an opportunity to try to avoid the continuation of a **5.130** culture of secrecy and to ensure that employees of public authorities act in the spirit of the statute. Although a Code of Guidance is not enforceable as such and public authorities will not be bound to follow it, it will have to be taken account of by a public authority when performing its functions. Failure to do so can constitute an error of law.[84] The adoption of an alternative approach will at least require an explanation and may establish a prima facie error of law which would be susceptible to challenge by way of judicial review.

Section 47(1) of the Act provides that the Information Commissioner will be **5.131** under a duty to promote good practice generally and the observance of the Code in particular. The Commissioner will have power to give practice recommendations to public authorities which are not conforming with the Code, although those recommendations are not directly enforceable.

The Code

The Code approved by Parliament on 20 November 2002 is arranged under **5.132** twelve sub-headings.[85]

I. Introduction

The Code acknowledges that it does not have statutory force but emphasizes that the Information Commissioner can issue a 'good practice' recommendation under section 48 of the Act if it appears to him that an authority's practice does not

---

[82] ibid, s 45(3).
[83] As provided in ibid, s 45(2).
[84] See by reference to the Code of Guidance under homelessness legislation, s 182 of the Housing Act 1996, the decision of the Court of Appeal in *De Falco, Silvestri v Crawley BC* [1980] QB 460.
[85] The Code is reproduced in full in Appendix D to this book.

comply with the Code, and reminds authorities of the effect of section 16(2) of the Act (namely, that compliance with the Code in relation to the provision of advice or assistance in a particular case will be taken as compliance with the authority's duty to provide advice and assistance in that case). However, it recognizes that there will be instances in which a public authority may, having taken account of the Code, decide for good reason that its provisions should not be applied. The obligation of public authorities is to comply with the provisions of the Act and any regulations made under it, and the Code is only a guide to how the obligation is in general to be performed.

II.   The provision of advice and assistance to persons making requests for information

5.133   Some aspects of this part of the Code have already been mentioned in connection with section 16 of the Act (at paragraphs 5.75 to 5.79 above). It begins (in paragraph 5) by reminding public authorities that the advice and assistance which it is their duty under that section to provide includes, but is not necessarily limited to, the steps set out in the Code. In other words, the Code is not exhaustive; it does not (and indeed could not) cover all the situations which might arise in which an applicant (or prospective applicant) for information needs advice or assistance which it would be reasonable to expect the authority to give.

5.134   The Code advises in paragraph 6 that an authority's procedures for dealing with requests should be both published and referred to in its publication scheme. Contact addresses (including an e-mail address where possible), and telephone numbers, should be provided. Paragraph 7 reminds public authority employees that not everyone will be aware of the Act or the regulations made under it, and that they will need to draw them to the attention of applicants who appear to be unaware of them.

5.135   Paragraph 8 considers the situation of a person who is unable to put a request in writing as required by section 8 of the Act. There could be many and diverse reasons for this, of which physical and mental disabilities, illiteracy, and linguistic difficulties are the most obvious, and the Code stresses the need for flexibility in tailoring the advice and assistance offered to suit the particular circumstances of individual applicants. It suggests that appropriate assistance could include directing the applicant to another person or agency, such as a Citizens Advice Bureau, or offering to take a note of the application. If the latter course is adopted, the Code advises that the note should be sent to the applicant for confirmation and that it will constitute a request in writing once verified and returned, with the result that the timetable for compliance will start when the written confirmation is received.

5.136   If the authority cannot identify the information being applied for because the request provides insufficient detail or is ambiguous, paragraph 9 of the Code advises that the authority should try to clarify the request. It should not, so the Code expressly advises, seek to determine the aims or motivation of the applicant. 'Care should be taken not to give the applicant the impression that he or she is obliged to disclose the nature of his or her interest or that he or she will be treated differently if he or she does.' Appropriate assistance in this context might involve outlining the kinds of information available, providing detailed catalogues and indexes, or giving a general response setting out options for further requests.

Paragraph 12 of the Code states that once such assistance has been provided the authority 'is not expected to seek further clarification' if the applicant still fails to describe the information requested in a way which would enable the authority to identify and locate it. Nevertheless, any information which has been successfully identified should be provided, together with an explanation of why the request cannot be taken further and details of the complaints procedure and the right to apply for a decision by the Commissioner under section 50 of the Act.   **5.137**

Paragraphs 13 and 14 of the Code draw attention to cases in which the giving of access is hindered by considerations of cost. Where a request is refused pursuant to section 12 of the Act because the 'appropriate limit' would be exceeded and the authority is not prepared to comply on a discretionary basis, the authority is advised to consider indicating what information could be provided within the cost ceiling. Where a fees notice has been given and the applicant indicates that the fee will not be paid, public authorities are advised to consider whether there is any information that may be of interest that is available free of charge.   **5.138**

The Code at paragraph 15 advises that an authority is not expected to provide assistance when a request is vexatious within the meaning of section 14 of the Act.   **5.139**

III. Handling requests for information which appear to be part of an organized campaign

Paragraph 16 addresses the situation arising where a number of related requests have a cumulative compliance cost[86] in excess of the 'appropriate limit' prescribed pursuant to section 12 of the Act. The authority is advised to consider whether the information could be disclosed in another, more cost effective manner: for example by publication on its website.   **5.140**

IV. Timeliness in dealing with requests for information

Paragraph 17 of the Code draws attention to section 10(1) of the Act (which requires section 1(1) of the Act to be complied with promptly and in any event not later than the twentieth working day after the date of receipt of the request) and points out that authorities should not delay responding until the end of the 20 working days if the information could reasonably be provided earlier.   **5.141**

---

[86] See paras 5.85 and 5.87 above on the circumstances in which costs can be aggregated.

5.142   The Act does not prescribe a particular time limit within which a public authority must determine where the balance of public interest lies on an application for information subject to a non-absolute exemption, but defines it by reference to what is reasonable in the circumstances.[87] However, the giving of a time estimate is required by section 17(2) of the Act. The Code at paragraph 18 advises public authorities to give realistic and reasonable estimates and to comply with those estimates unless there is good reason not to, while aiming to make all decisions within 20 working days wherever possible. Applicants should be kept informed if estimates have to be revised. Public authorities are advised to apologize to applicants when the estimate is exceeded and to keep a record of such instances in order that any problem can be identified and remedied.

V. Charging fees

5.143   The Code at paragraphs 19–20 has little to say on this topic. It points out that the power to charge fees in accordance with regulations made under sections 9, 12, and 13 of the Act is discretionary; the regulations will not apply to material made available under a publication scheme (section 19 of the Act), or to information which is reasonably accessible to the applicant by other means as defined by section 21 of the Act, or where fees are prescribed by other enactments (section 9(5) of the Act). In cases of charges falling outside the Act public authorities should check that the correct fees are charged.

VI. Transferring requests for information

5.144   The guidance provided on this subject is set out in detail in paragraphs 5.99 and 5.100 above. There will, of course, be cases where the authority receiving the original request does not know where the information is to be found, and is unable either to advise the applicant where to reapply or to effect a direct transfer. In those circumstances, paragraph 30 of the Code tells authorities to consider what advice, if any, they can provide to the applicants to enable them to pursue their requests.

VII. Consultation with third parties

5.145   The Code at paragraph 31 draws attention to the principle that information must be disclosed unless one of the Act's specific exemptions applies, regardless of how disclosure would affect the rights or interests of third parties. The guidance offered in paragraph 32 is to seek consent (in so far as practicable) from third parties whose rights would be infringed by disclosure where an exemption provision does apply, such as section 41 (actionable breach of confidence) or section 40 (personal information). Consultation is also recommended where third party views may assist in determining whether an exemption applies or where the balance of public interest lies, unless the cost would be disproportionate (paragraphs 34 to

---

[87] Freedom of Information Act 2000, s 10(3).

36). Where numerous third parties are involved, paragraph 38 suggests consulting a representative organization or sample. However, paragraph 40 emphasizes that the decision as to whether information should be disclosed is always that of the authority itself; a third party's refusal of consent is not determinative. Nor is it an excuse for not complying with the requirements of the Act that a third party has failed to respond to consultation (paragraph 39), although time taken in consultation would obviously be a relevant factor in assessing what length of time is reasonable for deciding public interest issues for the purposes of section 10(3) of the Act.

Paragraph 37 lists three situations in which consultation will be unnecessary: **5.146**

(a)   where the authority has another legitimate ground under the Act for refusing access and intends to rely on it;
(b)   where the third party's views could make no difference to the outcome, for example because there is some other statute requiring or prohibiting disclosure;
(c)   where no exemption applies and the authority has no choice but to disclose.

VIII.   *Freedom of information and public sector contracts*

The Code (at paragraph 41) advises public authorities that they cannot contract   **5.147** out of the Act and should reject terms which purport to restrict the disclosure of information that would be disclosable under the Act. The terms of a contract cannot override the statutory obligations created by the Act.

Paragraph 42 refers to the possibility that non-public authority contractors may   **5.148** require confidentiality clauses. The guidance given is that these should be rejected wherever possible. However, when non-disclosure provisions have to be agreed, in exceptional cases, a proposed option is for the contract to contain a schedule which identifies clearly the information subject to them. Public authorities should only agree to such provisions if the information is truly confidential (paragraph 43) and there are good reasons to do so (paragraph 44).

According to paragraph 45 public authorities will need to consider whether con-   **5.149** tracts should include non-disclosure clauses in respect of information which they provide to the contractors that would be exempt from disclosure under the Act. Such clauses should be drafted narrowly and terms of secrecy should not otherwise be imposed on contractors.

IX.   *Accepting information in confidence from third parties*

Paragraph 47 of the Code seeks to prevent authorities from accepting information   **5.150** in confidence unless it is necessary to obtain such information in the exercise of the authority's functions, the information would not otherwise be given, and it is truly confidential. Acceptance of terms of confidentiality should, it says, be capable of being justified to the Commissioner.

X. Consultation with devolved administrations

5.151 Paragraph 48 of the Code says that consultation should take place before information provided by or directly concerning a devolved administration is disclosed, unless it would be futile (for example, because there is no applicable exemption) or disproportionate.

XI. Refusal of request

5.152 Section 17(1) of the Act requires a public authority refusing a request in reliance on an exemption to serve a notice stating why the exemption applies, if that would not otherwise be apparent. Paragraph 50 of the Code warns public authorities against merely paraphrasing the wording of the exemption in purported fulfilment of this obligation (unless the provision of further information would amount to a disclosure of exempt information). Similarly, in giving reasons for a decision that the public interest in maintaining exemption outweighs the public interest in disclosure,[88] the factors weighed in the balancing exercise, both for and against, should be specified (unless this would amount to a disclosure of exempt information).

5.153 Paragraph 51 of the Code advises that records of refusals should be kept and collated for monitoring purposes.

XII. Complaints procedure

5.154 Paragraph 52 of the Code advises that all public authorities should have a complaints procedure in place before their duties in respect of publication schemes come into effect,[89] for the use of anyone who perceives there to be non-compliance with those schemes, and also, in due course, persons dissatisfied with the way in which their access requests have been handled.

5.155 Paragraph 54 of the Code reminds public authorities of their statutory obligation under section 17(7) of the Act to notify applicants of their rights of complaint when refusing a request for information. Paragraph 55 advises that any reply expressing dissatisfaction should be treated as a complaint and dealt with under the complaints procedure, even if the applicant does not expressly ask for a review. All complaints should be acknowledged, with a target date being given for determination.

5.156 Paragraph 56 says the complaints procedure must be fair and impartial. It should enable decisions to be reversed or amended where appropriate. It should be capable of producing a prompt decision and should not be unnecessarily bureaucratic. A complaint concerning a request for information should (where practicable) be handled by a person who was not party to the original decision. If

---

[88] Under Freedom of Information Act 2000, s 17(3).
[89] See para 5.194 below for the timetable.

the original decision was taken by someone in such a senior position that it cannot realistically be reviewed (for example a Minister), the internal review procedure may be waived, enabling the complainant to approach the Commissioner directly (paragraph 57).

Paragraph 59 provides that public authorities may set their own target dates for **5.157** dealing with complaints but they should be reasonable, defensible and subject to regular review. Target times and rates of success in meeting them should be published.

Paragraph 58 of the Code stresses that the complainant should always be **5.158** informed of the outcome and if the complaint results in information being disclosed, paragraph 61 provides that disclosure should take place as soon as practicable. If it transpires that the authority's procedures were not properly followed, an apology should be given and steps should be taken to prevent such errors recurring. If the complaint is dismissed, paragraph 63 provides that the applicant should be informed of the right to apply to the Commissioner and given details of how to do so.

Paragraph 60 requires that records of complaints be kept and monitoring proce- **5.159** dures be put in place.

L. The Code of Practice on Record Management

Record-keeping obligations: other jurisdictions

In other jurisdictions, freedom of information statutes are complemented by pri- **5.160** mary legislation imposing statutory duties in respect of information management. For example, Queensland law obliges public authorities to make and keep full and accurate records of their activities and ensure the safe custody and preservation of records in their possession. Disposal of any public records without the authority of the state archivist or other legal authority, justification or excuse is prohibited, and punishable by fine.[90] In Victoria, those in charge of public offices are required to ensure that full and accurate records of the business of their respective offices are made and kept.[91] The Australian Law Reform Commission has recommended[92] the inclusion, in a proposed new Archives and Records Act, of a requirement for Commonwealth agencies and departments to create, maintain and make accessible full and accurate records.

---

[90] Queensland Public Records Act 2002, ss 7, 8, 13.
[91] Victoria Public Records Act 1973, s 13.
[92] *Australia's Federal Record—a review of the Archives Act 1983* (ALRC, 85) para 4.27.

5.161 The US Federal Records Act provides that:

> The head of each Federal Agency shall make and preserve records containing adequate and proper documentation of the organisation, functions, policies, decisions, procedures, and essential transactions of the agency and designed to furnish the information necessary to protect the legal and financial rights of the government and of persons directly affected by the agency's activities.

In his Annual Report to Parliament for the year 2000-01, the Canadian Information Commissioner advocated the introduction of legislation on the American model imposing statutory duties to make and preserve records as part of a strategy for resuscitating what he described as 'the terminally ill information management structure' of that country's government.

The Lord Chancellor's Code of Practice on record management

5.162 Here, there was some pre-existing legislation on the subject of public record-keeping, in the form of the Public Records Act 1958 and the Public Records Act (Northern Ireland) 1923, which (rather than being repealed and replaced) will be amended with a view to its integration into the new freedom of information regime.[93] The Act itself stops short of directly imposing obligations on public authorities either to record information in a form which can be kept or to retain records for a minimum period of time. What it does instead is make indirect provision for setting standards and improving systems through the mechanism of a code of practice, to be issued and periodically revised by the Lord Chancellor, 'providing guidance to relevant authorities as to the practice which it would, in his opinion, be desirable for them to follow in connection with the keeping, management and destruction of their records'.[94] In exercising those functions, the Lord Chancellor is specifically required[95] to have regard to the public interest in allowing public access to information held by relevant authorities. He must consult the Information Commissioner and the appropriate Northern Ireland Minister before issuing or revising any such code,[96] and is to lay it before each House of Parliament.[97]

5.163 Promotion of the observance of any such code by public authorities is one of the Information Commissioner's functions.[98] If it appears that the practice of a public authority does not conform with provisions of the Code, the Commissioner may issue a written practice recommendation under section 48 of the Act specifying the relevant provisions and the steps which ought in the

---

[93] See ch 8 below.
[94] Freedom of Information Act 2000, s 46(1).
[95] By ibid, s 46(3).
[96] ibid, s 46(5).
[97] ibid, s 46(6).
[98] ibid, s 47(1)(b).

Commissioner's opinion to be taken to promote conformity. Deficiencies in practice might come to attention through an authority agreeing to an assessment under section 47(3) of the Act, or the service of a formal information notice under section 51 of the Act asking questions about its practices for the purpose of determining whether they conform with the Code, or incidentally in the course of considering a complaint under section 50 of the Act;[99] or they might be directly reported to the Commissioner by a member of the public or even an insider. It is to be observed, however, that no sanction is prescribed for failing to implement a practice recommendation. The Commissioner is required to consult the Keeper of Public Records and the Deputy Keeper of the Records of Northern Ireland in respect of promoting the observance of the code, and before giving a practice recommendation, in relation to any records which are 'public records' within the meaning of the Public Records Acts.[100]

The Lord Chancellor issued a Code of Practice under section 46 of the Act in **5.164** November 2002. It is reproduced in Appendix E to this book. As might be expected, it is considerably more detailed than any statutory provisions could reasonably be expected to be (albeit not as detailed as the various records management standards published by the British Standards Institute and Public Record Office which are commended in the text of the Code and listed in Annexe A).[101] It is divided into two parts.

Part One sets out practices for relevant authorities to follow in relation to the **5.165** keeping, management and destruction of their records, in accordance with section 46(1). Arguably, it goes beyond that (and beyond the Lord Chancellor's statutory remit) by including a paragraph concerned with record *creation*, calling for each operational or business unit of an authority to have in place an adequate system for documenting its activities. Whether that is so depends on whether the word 'keeping' in the context of section 46 is to be interpreted broadly, as embracing record creation as well as record maintenance, or narrowly, as meaning only the latter. From a linguistic viewpoint, either is a possible reading; but the term would fall to be construed against the background of its usage by those professionally involved in the field of record management, such as the Public Record

---

[99] See ch 7 below for details of those procedures.

[100] Freedom of Information Act 2000, ss 47(5) and 48(3)–(4). For the meaning of 'public records', see para 5.170 below.

[101] The Public Record Office has produced model action plans for central government departments and local authorities to assist them in achieving compliance with the Code. Full texts are to be found on its website at http://www.pro.gov.uk/recordsmanagement/access/default.htm (25 October 2002). Model action plans have also been prepared for the higher education sector (funded by the Joint Information Systems Committee) and the police (by the Association of Chief Police Officers) drawing on the Public Record Office models, and can be accessed via links from the Public Record Office website. A model action plan for the health sector is to follow.

Office, who understand it in the wider sense. Other aspects of best practice emphasized in Part One of the Code are:

- recognition of records management as a distinct corporate function, with its own defined objectives and the organization and resources to achieve them
- an integrated approach to records management, freedom of information, data protection and other information management issues
- an overall policy statement on records management
- lead responsibility for records management to be given to a designated senior staff member
- appropriate staff training and development programmes
- a record audit
- easily understood rules for referencing and indexing
- a system controlling the movement and location of records to promote easy retrieval
- clean, tidy and secure storage accommodation
- clearly established policies for records appraisal and disposal.

5.166   The Code provides at paragraph 9 that records should be closed as soon as they are no longer used except for reference, but that, as a general rule, they should be closed after five years in any event, with a new file being opened if the matter remains active. Closure should be noted in the appropriate index or database and upon the file itself. There should be an appraisal system in place for the purposes of deciding whether closed files should be disposed of or preserved and ensuring consistency in such decisions. The system should identify the documents designated for destruction, the authority for their destruction, and the dates when they are to be destroyed. A record of destruction should be kept. Scheduled destruction should be delayed in the case of a record known to be the subject of a request for information under the Act until either the request has been met or the Act's complaint and appeal procedures have been exhausted.

5.167   The process of record selection may be a difficult one involving a balancing exercise between retaining information which might be required and ensuring that record storage is manageable. The Code at paragraph 9.6 advises that there should be a selection policy which identifies the functions from which records are likely to be selected for permanent preservation and the lengths of time for which other records should be retained. This should be linked to schedules indicating dates for review and disposal for all records including electronic ones.

5.168   The Code recommends that records selected for permanent preservation and no longer in regular use by an authority should be transferred as soon as possible to an archival institution with adequate storage and public access facilities.

Transfer of records

As contemplated by section 46(2) of the Act, the Code also includes guidance as **5.169** to the practices to be adopted in relation to the transfer of records under section 3(4) of the Public Records Act 1958,[102] and section 3 of the Public Records Act (Northern Ireland) 1923, and the review of records before they are transferred under those provisions. This guidance is to be found in Part Two and is considered in more detail below.[103]

Relevant authorities and public records

The Code of Practice issued under section 46 of the Act will apply to 'relevant **5.170** authorities', which means[104] not just public authorities within the meaning of the Act,[105] but any other office or body whose 'administrative and departmental records' are 'public records' for the purposes of the Public Records Act 1958 or its Northern Irish equivalent. 'Public records' are defined in the First Schedule to the Public Records Act 1958.[106] Principal categories are:

(a) administrative and departmental records belonging to Her Majesty in right of Her Majesty's Government in the United Kingdom, in particular:
   (i)   records of, or held in, any government department; and
   (ii) records of any office, commission, or other body or establishment under the Government;[107]
(b) administrative and departmental records of the bodies and establishments individually listed in the Table at the end of paragraph 3;[108] and
(c) records of courts and tribunals.

Local authorities are included within the scope of the Act but not that of the Public **5.171** Records Act 1958, although that does not mean they have no statutory record-keeping responsibilities. Principal councils have to make 'proper arrangements'

---

[102] See ch 8 below.
[103] ibid.
[104] Freedom of Information Act 2000, s 46(7).
[105] As defined in ibid, s 3 and Sch 1.
[106] 'Records' include not only written records, but records conveying information by any other means whatsoever: Public Records Act 1958, s 10(1).
[107] Subject to certain exceptions, notably Welsh public records and records of any government department or body wholly or mainly concerned with Scottish affairs. However, the provisions of the Public Records Act 1958 are to apply to Welsh public records as if they did fall within the statutory definition until an order transferring responsibility for them to the National Assembly for Wales is made by the Lord Chancellor under the Government of Wales Act 1998, s 117: s 116 of that Act.
[108] This list is less extensive than that in Sch 1 to the Freedom of Information Act 2000. However, ibid, Sch 5, para 4 amends the Public Records Act 1958, Sch 1 to allow the Table in para 3 to be augmented by the addition (by Order in Council) of any other body or establishment which is, or could be, specified in the Parliamentary Commissioner Act 1967, Sch 2.

with respect to any documents belonging to them or in their custody.[109] In March 2000, the then Department of the Environment, Transport and the Regions issued guidance to local authorities on the performance of that duty.[110] Welsh principal councils must make, maintain and keep under review schemes setting out their arrangements for the proper care, preservation and management of records in their ownership or custody which have been retained for reference and research purposes or because of their likely historical interest.[111]

Practical suggestions

5.172 The following practical suggestions, although not found within the Code, may be of some assistance to authorities:

(a) each unit or department should identify the records which need to be made and maintained in the ordinary course of its work;

(b) each employee should be aware of the types of record required to be made and the methods of keeping the records required of him or her;

(c) records should be made as contemporaneously as possible, and should always be legible, and files should normally be compiled chronologically;

(d) records should identify their author and the reason for their creation;

(e) the maker of a record should identify those parts of the record which contain information received from third parties and note the circumstances in which such information was given;

(f) the maker of a record should mark those parts of the record which may be subject to privilege or confidentiality or in respect of which access may be restricted for any other reason, indicating any relevant statutory exemptions;

(g) the record-keeping should be reviewed regularly in order to ensure good practice is being maintained.

M. Alteration of Records

Criminal offence

5.173 Section 77 of the Act creates a criminal offence of altering records with intent to prevent disclosure. The offence is committed by the public authority or any person employed by or an officer of or subject to the direction of a public authority if:

(a) a request for information has been made;

---

[109] Local Government Act 1972, s 224(1).
[110] See http://www.local-regions.dtlr.gov.uk/section224/index.htm (25 October 2002).
[111] Local Government (Wales) Act 1994, s 60.

(b) the applicant would have been entitled (subject to payment of any fee) to communication of any information in accordance with section 1 of the Act or section 7 of the Data Protection Act 1998;

(c) that person alters, defaces, blocks, erases, destroys or conceals any record held by the public authority; and

(d) has the intention in so doing of preventing the disclosure by that authority of all, or any part, of the information which the applicant would have been entitled to have communicated to him.

The proceedings can be instituted in England and Wales only by the Information **5.174** Commissioner or by or with the consent of the Director of Public Prosecutions. In Northern Ireland they can be instituted only by the Commissioner or by or with the consent of the Director of Public Prosecutions for Northern Ireland.[112] A person guilty of an offence is liable on summary conviction to a fine not exceeding level 5 on the standard scale (currently £5,000).[113]

Application

The section only applies when a request for information has been made and there- **5.175** fore will not catch a pre-emptive act of alteration, destruction or concealment motivated by fear or expectation of a future request, or even one committed in the knowledge that a particular request is about to be made and with the specific intent of frustrating it. Similarly upon a strict construction of the section it does not cover the case of information brought into existence after the date of the request and before a new request applicable to that information is made.

The reasons for this may be practical rather than theoretical. There will be **5.176** difficulties in any event in detecting offences under the section, certainly without the help of inside informants; and proof to the criminal standard of the requisite intention could be almost impossible outside the context of a specific request. Routine destruction of records is universal and unavoidable in the ordinary course of record management. But once a request had been made, the destruction of a relevant record without a good alternative explanation would give rise to an inference that prevention of disclosure was the purpose.

Destruction

The Lord Chancellor's Code of Practice on record management prescribes that **5.177** the destruction of a record should be delayed if it is known to be the subject of a request for information until disclosure has taken place or the complaint and appeal provisions of the Act have been exhausted. Deliberate non-compliance with such official guidance could lend strength to an inference of malpractice.

---

[112] Freedom of Information Act 2000, s 77(4).
[113] ibid, s 77(3).

However, the government resisted pressure for the introduction of a statutory obligation to protect records identified as the subject of a request from destruction or alteration.

5.178 In successfully seeking the withdrawal of a proposed amendment to that effect when the Freedom of Information Bill was being debated in the House of Lords,[114] Lord Falconer of Thoroton said that freedom of information should not hamper normal records management procedures, such as getting rid of ephemeral or irrelevant documents in accordance with disposal policy, or updating rapidly changing information (especially electronic data).

5.179 The saving in section 1(4) of the Act (for amendments and deletions made between receipt of a request and the time for communication of the information sought which would have been made regardless of the receipt of the request) would appear to legitimize routine acts of alteration, if not destruction, done in full knowledge of a relevant request. The saving was justified by Lord Falconer on the basis that authorities could not carry out their work properly if files (especially electronic ones) were 'frozen' pending satisfaction of requests. It would seem to follow that a prosecution under section 77 of the Act for amendment or deletion would fail if the defendant could show that the same amendment or deletion would have been made at the same time in the ordinary course of departmental practice, request or no request.

Condition for the offence

5.180 Section 77 of the Act also makes it a condition that the applicant would have been entitled (subject to payment of any fee) to communication of information under section 1 of the Act or under section 7 of the Data Protection Act 1998. The offence will therefore not have been committed if exemption from having to communicate the information could have been claimed, or if section 12 or section 14 of the Act applied. The burden of proving that that was not the case and the applicant would have been entitled to receive the information will rest on the prosecution in accordance with general principle.

Offence

5.181 Section 77 applies to a person who:

(a) alters, defaces, blocks, erases, destroys or conceals any record held by the public authority, and
(b) does so with the intention of preventing the disclosure by that authority of all, or any part, of the information to the communication of which the applicant would have been entitled.

---

[114] At Committee stage: see *Hansard*, HL (series 5) vol 617, col 922 (17 October 2000).

The offence is therefore not defined in terms of the act of alteration, destruction   **5.182**
or concealment having been successful in its object of preventing the disclosure
sought. Nor is it even necessary that the record tampered with should have been
the record containing the relevant information. A bungled attempt to prevent disclosure is sufficient to attract the penalty; it is the intention to defeat a legitimate
exercise of the right to access which is the essence of the offence.

Provisions in Schedule 3 to the Act for the issue to the Information Commissioner   **5.183**
of warrants to enter premises and inspect and seize documents and other materials and equipment[115] apply where he is able to satisfy a circuit judge by information on oath that there are reasonable grounds for suspecting that an offence
under section 77 has been or is being committed.

The persons to whom section 77(1) of the Act applies are defined in section 77(2),   **5.184**
which reads 'subsection (1) applies to the public authority and to any person who
is employed by, is an officer of, or is subject to the direction of, the public authority'.[116] Government departments, while 'public authorities' within the meaning of
the Act,[117] are however given specific immunity from prosecution under the Act
by section 81(3).

N. The Aarhus Convention[118]

On 25 June 1998 the government signed the Convention on Access to   **5.185**
Information, Public Participation in Decision Making and Access to Justice in
Environmental Matters at the town of Aarhus in Northern Denmark. Section 74
of the Act confers power on the Secretary of State to make regulations to
implement the provisions of Article 4 of the Aarhus Convention,[119] which will
replace the rights of access to environmental information conferred by the
Environmental Information Regulations 1992.

In particular the regulations may:[120]   **5.186**

(a) enable charges to be made for making such information available;

---

[115] See ch 7 below for a detailed account of these provisions.
[116] Including persons in the public service of the Crown: Freedom of Information Act 2000,
s 81(3).
[117] ibid, Sch 1, Pt I, para 1.
[118] There is a detailed discussion of the Convention in ch 16, paras 16.48–16.69 below.
[119] Including Arts 3–9 so far as they relate to Art 4.
[120] Except that pursuant to section 80 of the Act they shall not apply to or affect information held
by the Scottish Parliament, any part of the Scottish Administration, the Scottish Parliamentary
Corporate Body or any Scottish public authority with mixed functions or no reserved functions as
defined within the Scotland Act 1998.

(b) provide that any obligation imposed by the regulations in relation to the disclosure of information is to have effect notwithstanding any enactment or rule of law;

(c) make provision for a code of practice to be issued by the Secretary of State;

(d) provide for sections 47 and 48 of the Act to apply to such a code with such modifications as may be specified;

(e) provide in relation to compliance with any requirement of the regulations for any of the provisions of Parts IV and V of the Act to apply, with such modifications as may be specified;

(f) contain transitional or consequential provisions (including provision modifying any enactment) as the Secretary of State considers appropriate.

O. Defamation

5.187 There can be no claim of defamation against a public authority as a result of the non-malicious disclosure of information to an applicant for information pursuant to section 1 of the Act if the information was supplied to the public authority by a third person.[121] However this statutory privilege does not apply either to information created by the public authority (that is, not supplied to it by a third person) or to publication with malice of information supplied to it by a third person.

P. Secondary Legislation

5.188 Section 82 of the Act provides that any power of the Lord Chancellor or Secretary of State to make an order or regulations under the Act shall be exercisable by statutory instrument. A statutory instrument containing an order under sections 5, 7(3) or (8), 53(1)(a)(iii), or 75, or regulations under sections 10(4) or 74(3) shall not be made unless a draft of the instrument has been laid before and approved by resolution of each House of Parliament.[122]

5.189 A statutory instrument which contains an order under section 4(1) or a regulation under any other provision than those identified within section 82(2)(b) shall be subject to annulment in pursuance of a resolution of either House of Parliament unless it also contains orders or regulations which make it subject to the requirement that a draft of the instrument be laid before and approved by resolution of each House of Parliament.

---

[121] Freedom of Information Act 2000, s 79.
[122] ibid, s 82(2).

An order made under section 4(5) of the Act shall be laid before Parliament after **5.190**
being made. If a draft of an order under sections 5 or 7(8) would be treated for the
purposes of the Standing Orders of either House as a hybrid instrument apart
from section 82(5) of the Act, it shall proceed in that House as if it were not such
an instrument.

Q. Funding

Avoiding conflict with the Treasury, section 85 of the Act provides that the fol- **5.191**
lowing shall be paid out of money provided by Parliament:

(a) any increase in the expenses of the Lord Chancellor in respect of the
Commissioner, the Tribunal or any of its members attributable to the Act;
(b) any administrative expenses attributable to the Act of the Secretary of State or
the Lord Chancellor;
(c) any other expenses incurred by a Minister of the Crown or government
department or by either House in consequence of the Act; and
(d) any increase attributable to the Act in the sums which are payable under any
other Act out of money so provided.

R. Commencement

The commencement provisions are to be found in section 87(1) of the Act and are **5.192**
as follows:

(a) from 30 November 2000:

    (i)   sections 3 to 8 and Schedule 1;
    (ii)   section 19 so far as relating to the approval of publication schemes;
    (iii) section 20 so far as relating to the approval and preparation by the
Commissioner of model publication schemes;
    (iv) sections 47(2) to (6), 49, 74, 75, 78 to 85 and 87;
    (v)   paragraph 4 of Schedule 5 and section 67 so far as relating to that para-
graph;
    (vi) paragraph 8 of Schedule 6 and section 73 so far as relating to that para-
graph;
    (vii) Part I of Schedule 8 and section 86 so far as relating to that paragraph;
    (viii) all provisions conferring power to make any order, regulations or codes
of practice.

(b) From 1 February 2001:

    (i)   sections 18(1), 76 and Schedule 7;

(ii)   paragraphs 1(1), 3(1), 4, 6, 7, 8(2), 9(2), 10(a), 13(1), 13(2), 14(a), 15(1) and 15(2) of Schedule 2 and section 18(4) so far as relating to those provisions;

(iii)   Part II of Schedule 8 and section 86 so far as relating to that Part.

(c)   The rest of the Act at the end of five years beginning with 30 November 2000 (that is, 29 November 2005) or on such day before the end of that period as the Lord Chancellor may appoint.

5.193   On 13 November 2001 the Lord Chancellor announced to the House of Lords that the Act will be in force in full by January 2005. The timetable is set out in the Lord Chancellor's first annual report to Parliament on the implementation of the Act made in November 2001.

5.194   The following timetable has been made for public authorities to adopt and maintain a publication scheme pursuant to section 19 of the Act:

(a)   November 2002—central government (except the Crown Prosecution Service and the Serious Fraud Office), Parliament, National Assembly for Wales, non-departmental bodies currently subject to the Code of Practice on Access to Government Information;

(b)   February 2003—local government (except police authorities);

(c)   June 2003—police, police authorities, the Crown Prosecution Service, the Serious Fraud Office and armed forces;

(d)   October 2003—Health Service;

(e)   February 2004—schools, universities, remaining non-departmental bodies;

(f)   June 2004—remaining public authorities.

5.195   The timetable for Northern Ireland is a matter for discussion between the Lord Chancellor's Department and the Northern Ireland Assembly.

6

EXEMPT INFORMATION

A. Introduction

Scope of the chapter

It should come as no surprise that legislation providing for the disclosure of **6.01** information as a 'right' contains extensive exempting provisions. The Freedom of Information Act 2000 ('the Act') does not disappoint. Part II, consisting of sections 21 to 44, sets out the circumstances in which information is 'exempt information'. Some of the exemptions are absolute ones, protecting a class of information entirely; others rely on the application of a prejudice test or upon other harmful consequences of disclosure.[1]

6.02 As has already been seen,[2] the right to disclosure contained in section 1 of the Act operates in two stages. First, the entitlement that a public authority 'confirm or deny' whether it holds the information specified in an application, under section 1(1)(a); and, secondly, the distinct entitlement 'to have that information communicated', under section 1(1)(b). This chapter deals with information in respect of which one or both of these duties does not arise, as provided for by section 2.

6.03 It should also be noted that, in addition to the exemptions contained in Part II of the Act, there are other provisions of the Act which may result in a public authority not being obliged to comply with a request for information: section 12, which excuses a public authority from compliance where the cost of doing so exceeds a prescribed limit, and section 14, which excuses a public authority from complying with vexatious or repeated requests. These sections are dealt with in chapter 5 above.[3]

B. The General Operation of Section 2

The effect of exemptions

6.04 The effect of the exemptions in Part II is provided for by section 2(1) and (2):

> 2. (1) Where any provision of Part II states that the duty to confirm or deny does not arise in relation to any information, the effect of the provision is that where either—
> (a) the provision confers absolute exemption, or
> (b) in all the circumstances of the case, the public interest in maintaining the exclusion of the duty to confirm or deny outweighs the public interest in disclosing whether the public authority holds the information,
> section 1(1)(a) does not apply.
> (2) In respect of any information which is exempt information by virtue of any provision of Part II, section 1(1)(b) does not apply if or to the extent that—
> (a) the information is exempt information by virtue of a provision conferring absolute exemption, or
> (b) in all the circumstances of the case, the public interest in maintaining the exemption outweighs the public interest in disclosing the information.

6.05 The effect of these subsections is to draw a distinction between two categories of exempt information. First, there is information subject to an 'absolute exemp-

---

[1] For comparison with the approach to exemptions in other legal systems, see paras 9.26 to 9.28 below (New Zealand), para 9.29 below (the United States), paras 9.30 to 9.32 below (Australia), paras 9.33 to 9.36 below (Canada) and para 9.37 below (Ireland).

[2] See para 3.02 above.

[3] See paras 5.84–5.86 (s 12) and paras 5.101–5.109 (s 14) above.

tion'.[4] Secondly, there is information in respect of which, in all the circumstances of the case, the public interest in maintaining the exclusion of the duty to confirm or deny,[5] or in maintaining the exemption,[6] outweighs the public interest in disclosing whether the public authority holds the information,[7] or the public interest in disclosing the information itself.[8] Information subject to absolute exemption is considered in part C of this chapter, and information in respect of which an authority must embark upon the balancing exercise in part D. It can be observed at once that, in cases where a balancing exercise is called for, the question must be approached on the basis of 'all the circumstances of the case'; and that the two-stage operation of the general right to disclosure creates the possibility of a situation where the duty under section 1(1)(a) (to confirm or deny) might arise, but the duty under section 1(1)(b) (actually to communicate the information) might not.

Third party rights

A person may request information from a public authority, the disclosure of **6.06** which would affect a third party.[9] The Act imposes no statutory obligation on the public authority in such circumstances to consult that third party before disclosing the information. However, by virtue of section 45(2)(c), the code of practice issued by the Lord Chancellor[10] must include provision relating to 'consultation with persons to whom the information requested relates or persons whose interests are likely to be affected by the disclosure of information'.[11]

If a third party, who is consulted by the public authority following the code of **6.07** practice, objects to the disclosure of the information but the public authority proposes to disclose the information under the Act in any event, then the third party has no mechanism under the Act to challenge or prevent disclosure. In those circumstances the third party will have to make a claim for judicial review of the public authority's decision to disclose the information and an injunction to restrain disclosure or rely on any private law rights by virtue of which it may be able to restrain disclosure.

---

[4] Freedom of Information Act 2000, s 2(1)(a) and 2(2)(a).
[5] ibid, s 2(1)(b).
[6] ibid, s 2(2)(b).
[7] ibid, s 2(1)(b).
[8] ibid, s 2(2)(b).
[9] For comparison with the treatment of third party rights in other legal systems, see paras 9.90 to 9.92 below.
[10] The references to the Secretary of State in the original section 45 have been replaced with references to the Lord Chancellor by virtue of the Transfer of Functions (Miscellaneous) Order 2001 (SI 2001/3500).
[11] See ch 5 above for discussion of what the Code provides in this respect.

6.08 If the public authority discloses the information without first consulting the third party (either in breach of the code of practice or because the code of practice does not require the third party to be consulted in the circumstances of the case), then the person concerned will have no redress under the Act. The third party's remedies would again be a claim for judicial review (together with an injunction to restrain further disclosure if appropriate) or to rely on any private law rights arising as a result of the disclosure.

6.09 Third party rights are further discussed below in connection with those individual exemptions (such as sections 41 (information provided in confidence) and 43 (commercial interests)) where issues of third party rights are most likely to arise.[12]

C. Absolute Exemption

The effect of absolute exemption

6.10 Where a provision of the Act confers absolute exemption, an applicant is not entitled (a) to a confirmation or denial that an authority has the information sought to the extent that the provision states that the duty to confirm or deny does not arise; or (b) to the communication of the information to the extent that the information is exempt by virtue of the provision. In those circumstances no question of whether the public interest in maintaining the exclusion of the duty to confirm or deny, or in maintaining the exemption, outweighs the public interest in disclosing whether the public authority holds the information, or the public interest in disclosing the information itself, will arise. However, the public authority must, within the time for complying with section 1(1), give the applicant a notice specifying the exemption on which it relies and stating why the exemption applies.[13]

The categories of absolute exempt information

6.11 By virtue of section 2(3) the following sections create absolute exemptions:

(a) section 21 (information accessible to applicant by other means);
(b) section 23 (information supplied by, or relating to, bodies dealing with security matters);
(c) section 32 (court records, etc);
(d) section 34 (Parliamentary privilege);

---

[12] See paras 6.78 to 6.81, 6.172 and 6.236 to 6.237 below.
[13] Freedom of Information Act 2000, s 17(1). The authority in giving this notice is not obliged to make a statement which would involve the disclosure of information which would itself be exempt information.

(e) section 36 (prejudice to effective conduct of public affairs) (so far as relating to information held by the House of Commons or the House of Lords);

(f) section 40 (personal information) (save to a limited extent);

(g) section 41 (information provided in confidence); and

(h) section 44 (prohibitions on disclosure).

The operation of each of the sections in this list will now be considered in turn. It **6.12** should be noted first that, as a result of the opening words of section 2(3), the remaining provisions of Part II of the Act (considered in part D below) are *not* to be regarded as conferring absolute exemption.

Section 21: information accessible to applicant by other means

Section 21(1) creates an absolute exemption in relation to information which is **6.13** accessible to the public by other means. The exact scope of the exemption is that information which is reasonably accessible to the applicant otherwise than under section 1 is exempt information.[14] For the purposes of the section (a) information may be reasonably accessible to the applicant even though it is accessible only on payment; and (b) information is to be taken to be reasonably accessible to the applicant if it is information which the public authority or any other person is obliged by or under any enactment to communicate (otherwise than by making the information available for inspection) to members of the public on request, whether free of charge or on payment.[15]

Further, for the purposes of the section, information, which is held by a public **6.14** authority and which is not information which the public authority or any other person is obliged by or under any enactment to communicate (otherwise than by making the information available for inspection) to members of the public on request (whether free of charge or on payment), is not to be regarded as reasonably accessible to the applicant merely because the information is available from the public authority itself on request, unless the information is made available in accordance with the authority's publication scheme and any payment required is specified in, or determined in accordance with, the scheme.[16]

The effect of section 21 (in conjunction with section 2(3)) is to confer absolute **6.15** exemption on information that is reasonably accessible to the applicant by other means: public authorities are not to become the natural first-choice source for *any* information whatsoever. It is also expressly provided that the fact that payment may be required to obtain the information by another means does not prevent the absolute exemption from being conferred;[17] but it seems that, if the cost of so

---

[14] ibid, s 21(1).
[15] ibid, s 21(2).
[16] ibid, s 21(3).
[17] ibid, s 21(2)(a).

obtaining the information is excessive, that could render the information not *reasonably* accessible by the alternative means. It should not be forgotten that the public authority can itself charge a fee in connection with the provision of information under section 1.[18]

6.16 Information which is available by virtue of other legislation (other than information which is required to be available for inspection) is deemed to be reasonably accessible to the applicant and therefore absolutely exempt.[19] Other information held by a public authority (that is, information *not* made available by virtue of other legislation), but which is in fact available on request from the authority, will only be absolutely exempt from the entitlements of section 1 if it is made available in accordance with the authority's publication scheme, and if any payment required is specified in, or determined in accordance with, that scheme.[20] Where material is made generally available, in accordance with a publication scheme, in this way, the consequence of its absolute exemption will be that the authority will not be obliged to provide information contained in the material pursuant to individual requests.

6.17 It should be noted that the section creates no exemption in relation to the duty to confirm or deny. Accordingly, where a request is made for information which is reasonably accessible to the applicant by other means, the public authority will still be under a duty to confirm or deny whether it holds the requested information. One would expect that, in stating why the exemption in section 21 applies to a request for information,[21] the public authority would point the applicant towards where the information is reasonably available to them by other means.

6.18 The Canadian Access to Information Act provides more simply that the Act does not apply to published materials, materials available for purchase, or material in the public archives, libraries or museums.[22]

Section 23: information supplied by, or relating to, bodies dealing with security matters

6.19 Section 23 creates an absolute exemption in relation to information supplied by, or relating to, certain bodies dealing with security matters. The exact scope of the exemption is that information held by a public authority is exempt if it was directly or indirectly supplied to the public authority by, or relates to, any of certain specified bodies.[23] The duty to confirm or deny does not arise if, or to the

---

[18] Freedom of Information Act 2000, s 9. Considered in ch 5 above.

[19] For further discussion of such other legislation, see ch 16 below.

[20] Publication schemes are provided for by the Freedom of Information Act 2000, ss 19 and 20, and considered in chs 4 and 5 above.

[21] The public authority would be obliged to do this by virtue of ibid, s 17(1)(c).

[22] For a comparison with other countries, see para 9.39 below.

[23] Freedom of Information Act 2000, s 23(1).

extent that, compliance with the duty would involve the disclosure of any information (whether or not already recorded) which was directly or indirectly supplied to the public authority by, or relates to, any of the specified bodies.[24]

The bodies which are specified are: **6.20**

(a) the Security Service;
(b) the Secret Intelligence Service;
(c) the Government Communications Headquarters;
(d) the special forces;
(e) the Tribunal established under section 65 of the Regulation of Investigatory Powers Act 2000;
(f) the Tribunal established under section 7 of the Interception of Communications Act 1985;
(g) the Tribunal established under section 5 of the Security Service Act 1989;
(h) the Tribunal established under section 9 of the Intelligence Services Act 1994;
(i) the Security Vetting Appeals Panel;
(j) the Security Commission;
(k) the National Criminal Intelligence Service; and
(l) the Service Authority for the National Criminal Intelligence Service.[25]

'The Government Communications Headquarters' is defined to include any unit **6.21** or part of a unit of the armed forces of the Crown which is for the time being required by the Secretary of State to assist the Government Communications Headquarters in carrying out its functions.[26] The special forces are those units of the armed forces of the Crown the maintenance of whose capabilities is the responsibility of the Director of Special Forces or which are for the time being subject to the operational command of that Director.[27]

A certificate signed by a Minister of the Crown certifying that the information to **6.22** which it applies was directly or indirectly supplied by, or relates to, any of the specified bodies is, subject to a right of appeal under section 60, conclusive evidence of that fact.[28] In New Zealand the Prime Minister has a similar power to issue a certificate that making information available would be likely to prejudice the security or defence of New Zealand. To the knowledge of the New Zealand Law Commission the power has only been exercised once.[29] For comparison of national security and defence exemptions in other jurisdictions, see paragraphs 9.41 to 9.45 below.

---

[24] ibid, s 23(5).
[25] ibid, s 23(3).
[26] ibid, s 23(4).
[27] ibid, s 84.
[28] ibid, s 23(2) and s 60.
[29] *Review of the Official Information Act 1982* (New Zealand Law Commission Report 40, 1997) para 280.

6.23 A document purporting to be such a certificate shall be received in evidence and deemed to be such a certificate unless the contrary is proved.[30] A document which purports to be certified by or on behalf of a Minister of the Crown as a true copy of such a certificate issued by that Minister shall in any legal proceedings be evidence (or, in Scotland, sufficient evidence) of that certificate.[31] Such a certificate can only be signed by a Minister who is a member of the Cabinet or by the Attorney-General, the Advocate General for Scotland or the Attorney-General for Northern Ireland.[32] These provisions save a public authority, in legal proceedings, from the inconvenience of having to obtain evidence that a certificate was signed by its purported signatory.

6.24 In accordance with its import, this section calls for little explanation. Its effect is to confer absolute exemption upon all information directly or indirectly supplied by, or relating to, certain bodies[33] dealing with security matters.[34] A certificate signed by a Minister of the Crown is conclusive proof that the information is of the type in question,[35] although an appeal is possible to the Information Tribunal within the provisions of section 60 of the Act.[36] It should be noted that the bodies specified in the section are not themselves public authorities within the scope of the Act.

6.25 During the Committee stage of the Bill in the House of Lords, there was some discussion of whether a certificate under section 23 (or section 24) could ever be exempt itself under the Act. Lord Falconer of Thoroton, the Minister of State at the Cabinet Office, said that he could not conceive that that would be the case and continued:

> The purpose of the evidential certificate proving the exemption is that it is intended to be produced in public to the information commissioner or to the appropriate authority. I cannot conceive that it could be exempt because it is intended to be made, in effect, public.[37]

6.26 Whilst this answer accords with common sense, it is not clear that it is correct under the Act. If a Minister certifies that particular information held by a public authority relates to, say, the security service, then information contained in or relating to the certificate also relates to the security service and, as such, is on the face of it exempt under section 23. The consequence of this in practice is likely to be that, where a Ministerial certificate is relied on as an answer to a request for

---

[30] Freedom of Information Act 2000, s 25(1).
[31] ibid, s 25(2).
[32] ibid, s 25(3).
[33] Specified in ibid, s 23(3) and 23(4).
[34] ibid, s 23(1).
[35] ibid, s 23(2).
[36] See ch 7 below.
[37] *Hansard*, HL (series 5) vol 617, col 1259 (19 October 2000).

information, it will undoubtedly be made 'public' in the sense of being communicated to the information commissioner or appropriate authority. However, if a request for information asks for, say, details of all certificates issued under section 23(2), the requested information would appear to be exempt under section 23.

As a certificate under 23(2) is subject to a right of appeal under section 60, it is **6.27** thought that it will not be sufficient for the Minister making the certificate merely to certify that the relevant exemption is required for the purpose of safeguarding national security and that the Minister should give reasons as to why that is the case—in the absence of reasons it will be impossible for the Tribunal to determine whether or not to quash the certificate under section 60.[38]

Section 32: court records, etc

Section 32 creates absolute exemptions in relation to information contained in **6.28** court records and other similar documents.[39] Section 32(1) provides that information held by a public authority is exempt if it is held only by virtue of being contained in:

(a) any document filed with, or otherwise placed in the custody of, a court for the purposes of proceedings in a particular cause or matter;

(b) any document served upon, or by, a public authority for the purposes of proceedings in a particular cause or matter; or

(c) any document created by (i) a court, or (ii) a member of the administrative staff of a court, for the purposes of proceedings in a particular cause or matter.[40]

Section 32(2) provides that information held by a public authority is exempt if it **6.29** is held only by virtue of being contained in:

(a) any document placed in the custody of a person conducting an inquiry or arbitration, for the purposes of the inquiry or arbitration; or

(b) any document created by a person conducting an inquiry or arbitration, for the purposes of the inquiry or arbitration.[41]

---

[38] The court applied similar reasoning in holding in *Alexander Machinery (Dudley) Ltd v Crabtree* [1974] ICR 120, NIRC that industrial tribunals (now employment tribunals) (from a decision of which there is an appeal on a point of law) should give reasons for their decisions sufficient to enable the parties to know that the tribunals have not erred in law. The court stated at 122 that 'in the absence of reasons it is impossible to determine whether or not there has been an error of law. Failure to give reasons therefore amounts to a denial of justice and is itself an error of law.'

[39] For comparison with the treatment of such material in other legal systems, see paras 9.49 to 9.51 below.

[40] Freedom of Information Act 2000, s 32(1).

[41] ibid, s 32(2).

6.30 The duty to confirm or deny does not arise in relation to information which is (or if it were held by the public authority would be) exempt information by virtue of section 32.[42]

6.31 In the section:

(a) 'court' includes any tribunal or body exercising the judicial power of the State;

(b) 'proceedings in a particular cause or matter' includes any inquest or post-mortem examination;

(c) 'inquiry' means any inquiry or hearing held under any provision contained in, or made under, an enactment; and

(d) except in relation to Scotland, 'arbitration' means any arbitration to which Part I of the Arbitration Act 1996 applies.[43]

6.32 It should be noted that courts are not themselves public authorities under the Act. The government departments responsible for the organization of courts and tribunals are public authorities but they may be unlikely to hold documents in relation to particular causes or matters. However, bodies such as the police, the Legal Services Commission and the Legal Services Ombudsman are also public authorities under the Act and are more likely to hold documents in relation to particular causes or matters.

6.33 The term 'court' is defined to *include* any tribunal or body exercising the judicial power of the state. Whereas domestic courts are, of course, exercising the judicial power of the state, bodies such as the European Court of Justice and the European Court of Human Rights will not be. The fact that the definition of 'court' is inclusive means that it is at least arguable that those bodies qualify as courts for the purposes of section 32.

6.34 Statements of case, witness statements, experts' reports and skeleton arguments will clearly all be within the scope of section 32(1). Where a public authority is involved in litigation it is thought that the section will also be wide enough to encompass documents which are provided to the public authority by the other parties to the litigation under their disclosure obligations.

6.35 It should be noted that the section applies to information which is held by a public authority *only* by virtue of it being contained in the various documents. Where a public authority is involved in litigation, its own statements of case or witness statements may well contain information which is held in another form by the public authority, not just by virtue of it being contained in documents falling within the scope of section 32. For example, if a public authority is involved in litigation concerning a written agreement, it is likely to hold information con-

---

[42] Freedom of Information Act 2000, s 32(3).
[43] ibid, s 32(4).

cerning that agreement in any event (because it will have a copy of the agreement). In those circumstances a request for information concerning the agreement would not be exempt simply because the information requested was contained in the authority's statement of case.

As a result of this the information which is more likely to fall within the section is **6.36** (a) information which is known to the public authority only as a result of it being contained in the documents served on it by another party in litigation; or (b) information which, whilst it was held by the public authority, was only recorded in connection with the litigation.[44] An example of the second of these categories would occur where an employee of the authority recalls an incident but does not record that recollection until asked to produce a witness statement in connection with litigation.[45]

The other effect of this section is that it is left to the court to control access to doc- **6.37** uments filed with the court. There are a number of relevant provisions of the Civil Procedure Rules ('CPR'). By virtue of CPR 5.4(1) a party to proceedings may be supplied from the records of the court with a copy of any document relating to those proceedings (including documents filed before the claim was commenced) provided that they pay any prescribed fee and file a written request for the document. By virtue of CPR 5.4(2) any other person who pays the prescribed fee may, during office hours, search for, inspect and take a copy of (a) a claim form which has been served; (b) any judgment or order given or made in public; and (c) any other document if the court gives permission.[46]

Where a court hearing is held in public, members of the public may obtain a tran- **6.38** script of any judgment given or a copy of any order made (subject to payment of the appropriate fee).[47] Where a judgment is given or an order is made in private, if any member of the public who is not a party to the proceedings seeks a transcript of the judgment or a copy of the order, they may seek the leave of the judge who gave the judgment or made the order.[48]

---

[44] It might be argued that such information, although only recorded in connection with the litigation, was still held by the public authority before being so recorded and so falls outside the scope of the exemption created by ibid, s 32(1). However, it is thought that the better view is that information is not held for the purposes of the section until it is in recorded form.

[45] Drafts of such a witness statement will not fall within the scope of ibid, s 32 but will be conditionally exempt by virtue of s 42 (legal professional privilege).

[46] It should be noted that these provisions do not currently apply to proceedings in the county court pending the installation of facilities for a computer search to be made: PD(5) Court Documents, 4.5. Where a member of the public applies for a copy of counsel's written opening or skeleton argument which has been accepted by the judge in lieu of an oral hearing, they are prima facie entitled to it: *GIO Personal Investment Services Ltd v Liverpool and London Steamship Protection and Indemnity Association Ltd* [1999] 1 WLR 984, CA.

[47] PD(39) Miscellaneous Provisions Relating to Hearings, 1.11.

[48] ibid, 1.12.

6.39   Further, a witness statement which stands as evidence-in-chief in a trial is open to inspection during the course of the trial unless the court directs otherwise.[49] Any person may ask for a direction that a witness statement is not open to inspection.[50] However, the court will not make such a direction unless it is satisfied that a witness statement should not be open to inspection because of

(a)   the interests of justice;
(b)   the public interest;
(c)   the nature of any expert medical evidence in the statement;
(d)   the nature of any confidential information (including information relating to personal financial matters) in the statement; or
(e)   the need to protect the interests of any child or patient.[51]

The court may exclude from inspection words or passages in the statement.[52]

6.40   The documents covered by the section are only documents relating to a particular cause or matter. Accordingly, if, for example, a police force holds information as to the conviction rates in its area, such information will not fall within the scope of the section.

Section 34: Parliamentary privilege

6.41   Section 34 creates an absolute exemption designed to protect Parliamentary privilege.[53] The scope of the exemption is that information is exempt if exemption from disclosure is required for the purpose of avoiding an infringement of the privileges of either House of Parliament.[54] The duty to confirm or deny does not apply if, or to the extent that, exemption from the duty is required for the purpose of avoiding an infringement of the privileges of either House of Parliament.[55]

6.42   Parliamentary privilege is the term used to describe the rights and immunities enjoyed by the House of Lords and the House of Commons and their members which exceed those enjoyed by other bodies and individuals. Parliamentary privilege is claimed by the Houses of Parliament as being necessary for them to carry out their functions effectively without external interference. It arises largely at

---

[49] CPR 32.13(1). The right to inspect witness statements does not extend to documents referred to in such statements: *GIO Personal Investment Services Ltd v Liverpool and London Steamship Protection and Indemnity Association Ltd* [1999] 1 WLR 984, CA.
[50] CPR 32.13(2).
[51] CPR 32.13(3).
[52] CPR 32.13(4).
[53] For comparison with the treatment of such matters in other legal systems, see paras 9.53 and 9.54 below.
[54] Freedom of information Act 2000, s 34(1).
[55] ibid, s 34(2).

common law but also partly by statute.[56] In 1705 both Houses of Parliament agreed that they had no power to create any new privileges.[57]

The most significant privileges are: 6.43

(a) the right of freedom of speech and proceedings in Parliament;
(b) the right of exclusive cognizance of Parliament's own proceedings;
(c) the right to control publication of its proceedings;
(d) the right of freedom from arrest; and
(e) the right to punish for breach of privilege and contempt.[58]

The right of freedom of speech and proceedings in Parliament. By virtue of   6.44
Article 9 of the Bill of Rights 1689 freedom of speech and debates or proceedings
in Parliament are not to be impeached or questioned in any court or place out of
Parliament. This has the effect that members of either House of Parliament will
incur no liability for anything said in the course of debates or proceedings in
Parliament. This extends to both civil liability (such as for defamation) and criminal liability (such as for breach of the Official Secrets Acts). The privilege will also
extend to those who participate in the proceedings of Parliament. 'Proceedings in
Parliament' include proceedings in either House of Parliament and in committees
and will extend to asking questions and giving written notice of questions. The
privilege will prevent a party to legal proceedings from questioning in those proceedings words spoken or actions done in Parliament by suggesting, whether by
direct evidence, cross-examination, inference or submission, that they were
untrue or misleading or were instigated for improper motives, although *Hansard*
can be relied on to prove as a matter of history what has taken place in
Parliament.[59] Receiving evidence of the proceedings of Parliament for the purposes of construing a statute does not involve impeaching or questioning those
proceedings.[60] The privilege does not prevent either House from taking action
against members who exercise their freedom of speech in ways that offend the
House.

The right of exclusive cognizance of Parliament's own proceedings.[61] This right   6.45
means that it is for the Houses of Parliament to control their own proceedings and
the court will not entertain arguments as to the adequacy or otherwise of the proceedings followed by Parliament. Accordingly, the court refused to intervene
where it was alleged that the House of Commons had acted in breach of a statute

---

[56] See, for example, Article 9 of the Bill of Rights 1689.
[57] 17 Lords Journals 677; 14 Commons Journals 555, 560.
[58] For information on other privileges reference should be made to *Erskine May's Parliamentary Practice*.
[59] *Prebble v Television New Zealand Ltd* [1995] 1 AC 321, PC.
[60] *Pepper v Hart* [1993] AC 593, HL.
[61] This right can be seen as an aspect of the right to freedom of speech rather than a separate privilege in its own right.

governing its own internal procedure by refusing to allow a member to take the oath and had excluded him from the House in order to enforce that refusal.[62] Similarly, the court would not investigate allegations that a private Act of Parliament had been procured by fraud.[63] The privilege even extends to the licensing of the catering arrangements in Parliament.[64] The privilege also means that no member of either House of Parliament can be compelled to give evidence in court regarding proceedings in the House without the leave of the House. Similarly, no clerk, officer or shorthand writer of the House of Commons may give evidence in respect of proceedings without leave. A party in court proceedings who wishes to produce evidence given to the House of Commons or any of its committees or who wishes to refer to any other document in the custody of officers of the House must petition the House of Commons for permission to do so. However, the House of Commons resolved in 1980 to give leave for reference to be made in court proceedings to the Official Report, published reports and public evidence taken by committees without the party wishing to make such a reference needing to petition the House for leave.[65]

6.46 **The right to control publication of its proceedings.**[66] Each House of Parliament has the right to control publication of its proceedings. In 1971 the House of Commons resolved that it would not entertain any complaint of contempt of the House or breach of privilege in respect of the publication of the debates and proceedings of the House or of its committees except when any such debates or proceedings had been conducted with closed doors or in private, or when such publication had been expressly prohibited by the House.[67]

6.47 **The right of freedom from arrest.** Members of both Houses of Parliament are free from civil arrest. Since the abolition of imprisonment for debt this privilege has been of less significance. Where it continues to be of significance is in the fact that the privilege means that members cannot be compelled by service of a witness summons to give evidence in court proceedings. The privilege will also extend to those who give evidence to Parliament or its committees and to officers and others engaged in business before Parliament.

6.48 **The right to punish for breach of privilege and contempt.** Each House of Parliament has the right to punish breaches of privilege or other contempts.

---

[62] *Bradlaugh v Gossett* (1884) 12 QBD 271.

[63] *British Railways Board v Pickin* [1974] AC 765, HL.

[64] *R v Graham Campbell, ex p Herbert* [1935] 1 KB 594, where the court held that it had no jurisdiction to intervene even if liquor had been sold without a licence in the precincts of the House of Commons.

[65] 236 Commons Journal 823.

[66] This right can be seen as an aspect of the right to freedom of speech rather than a separate privilege in its own right.

[67] 226 Commons Journals 548–549.

Members of either House may by punished by expulsion, suspension, imprisonment or reprimand. Others may be punished by imprisonment or reprimand.[68]

When a claim is made that there has been a breach of Parliamentary privilege, the **6.49**
court has distinguished between two questions. The first is as to the scope of
Parliamentary privilege, in other words what the privilege is of which breach is
alleged. The second question is whether there has been a breach of that privilege.
The court now takes the view that it is for it to determine the scope of
Parliamentary privilege but has always taken the view that it is for Parliament to
determine whether there has been a breach of a privilege recognized by the court.[69]
The result of this is that, whereas the court would refuse to uphold a claim based
on the breach of a hitherto unrecognized privilege, it will not interfere with a
claim that there has been a breach of a well-established privilege.

It seems likely that the most frequent circumstances in which information will **6.50**
be exempt under section 34 will be where the exemption will be required for the
purpose of avoiding an infringement of the right of Parliament to control the
publication of its own proceedings. For example, a public authority may hold a
draft copy of a select committee report which has not yet been published or
information concerning select committee proceedings held in private. In those
circumstances the information concerned may well be exempt.

It is difficult to envisage in what circumstances information might be exempt due **6.51**
to the exemption being required to avoid infringing some of the other
Parliamentary privileges discussed above; it is hard to see how disclosure of
information might infringe the rights of freedom of speech, exclusive cognizance
of Parliament's own proceedings or freedom from arrest.

A certificate signed by the appropriate authority certifying that exemption from **6.52**
disclosure, or from the duty to confirm or deny is, or at any time, was required for
the purpose of avoiding an infringement of the privileges of either House of
Parliament shall be conclusive evidence of that fact.[70] In this context the appropriate authority is, in relation to the House of Commons, the Speaker of that
House and, in relation to the House of Lords, the Clerk of the Parliaments.[71]

The Act contains no right of appeal against a certificate under section 34(3) certi- **6.53**
fying that exemption from disclosure is required for the purpose of avoiding an
infringement of the privileges of either House of Parliament. The fact that a
certificate is conclusive evidence of the requirement of exemption means that it is
likely to be very difficult to challenge such a certificate.

---

[68] The last time either House committed anyone to prison for contempt was in 1880.
[69] *Pepper v Hart* [1993] AC 593, 645, HL, where it was said that 'it is for the courts to decide
whether a privilege exists and for Parliament to decide whether such privilege has been infringed'.
[70] Freedom of Information Act 2000, s 34(3).
[71] ibid, s 34(4).

6.54 On the face of it a certificate, which referred to a request for particular information and merely certified that exemption from disclosure under the Act was required for the purpose of avoiding an infringement of the privileges of either House of Parliament without specifying the privilege concerned or giving reasons as to why the exemption was required, would appear to comply with the Act and would be unlikely to be open to challenge.[72] However, it will undoubtedly be good practice for a certificate under section 34(3) to specify the privilege which would be infringed by the disclosure of the requested information and to give reasons as to why that is the case. If this practice is followed, in the light of the principles referred to above,[73] it is thought that it would be open to the Information Commissioner to refuse to accept a certificate as conclusive if the certificate purported to rely on a privilege which had not hitherto been recognized. On the other hand, the Information Commissioner would be likely to accept a certificate relying on a well-established privilege as conclusive even if the reasons given were manifestly unreasonable or inadequate.

Section 36: prejudice to effective conduct of public affairs

6.55 Section 36 creates an exemption designed to protect the effective conduct of public affairs.[74] It is a conditional exemption save in respect of information held by the House of Commons or the House of Lords, in which cases it is absolute. Section 36 is discussed in full in the section on conditional exemptions at paragraphs 6.196 to 6.208 below.

6.56 The reason why the exemption created by section 36 is an absolute exemption only in respect of information held by the House of Commons or the House of Lords is presumably in recognition of Parliamentary privilege.[75]

Section 40: personal information

6.57 Section 40 provides exemptions in respect of personal information, or, more accurately, 'personal data'.[76] So far as public authorities[77] are concerned, the meaning

---

[72] Although administrative law, in some circumstances, recognizes a duty on the part of a decision-maker to give reasons, it is thought that the court would be unlikely to imply such a duty in respect of certificates under section 34(3) given the court's acceptance that it is for Parliament to decide whether or not its privileges have been infringed.

[73] At para 6.49 above.

[74] For comparison with the treatment of such matters in other legal systems, see paras 9.55 to 9.61 below.

[75] See the comment of Mike O'Brien, Parliamentary Under-Secretary of State for the Home Office at *Hansard*, HL (series 6), vol 340, col 787 (7 December 1999): 'We must protect parliamentary privilege, so we have had to add some exemptions for them. Because we have broadened the Bill, we have had to add some narrow exemptions.'

[76] Defined by the Freedom of Information Act 2000, s 40(7) to have the same meaning as in the Data Protection Act 1998, s 1(1). For that meaning, see further at paras 10.08 to 10.12 below.

[77] Within the meaning of the Freedom of Information Act 2000, s 3.

of 'data' is extended by section 68 of the Act,[78] to include not only information stored automatically (that is, by computer) and manually processed data stored in a 'structured' form (for example a handwritten card index system, ordered by surname) but also to include manually processed data in an 'unstructured' form. Data is 'personal' if it enables a living individual to be identified from it, or from it and other information in the hands of the controller of the information.[79]

The purpose of the exemptions provided for by section 40 is not to prevent the release of such information, but rather to recognize that a regime governing the processing, including the release, of such information already exists under the Data Protection Act 1998.[80] That regime is considered in detail in chapter 10 below. The (unnecessarily complex) structure of section 40 is, however, outlined here, referring the reader as appropriate to the detailed treatment in chapter 10.[81]   **6.58**

Section 40 operates by distinguishing between applications for information made by the person to whom personal information relates (the 'data subject'), and applications by a third party (someone other than the 'data subject').   **6.59**

Section 40(1)

Where the applicant is the 'data subject', section 40(1) creates an absolute exemption. The effect of this is to remove such applications entirely from the regime of the Act, leaving them subject instead to the existing regime of the Data Protection Act 1998. The effects of that regime, considered in detail below in chapter 10, are essentially threefold. First, to give 'data subjects' rights of access to, and certain other rights of control over,[82] personal information which concerns them.[83] Secondly, to regulate the use that is made of information contained in personal data (through the application of 'data protection principles').[84] And, thirdly, to provide that there should be impartial supervision of those who hold the data (now undertaken by the Information Commissioner and the Information Tribunal, whose jurisdiction extends across the fields of both freedom of information and data protection).[85]   **6.60**

---

[78] See para 3.62 above.

[79] See para 10.08 below. For the precise meaning of 'data controller' see para 10.14 below.

[80] Implementing the Council Directive (EC) 95/46 on data protection. The Data Protection Act 1998 replaced, with effect from 1 March 2000, the Data Protection Act 1984, which had previously implemented the Council of Europe Data Protection Convention of 1981 (Treaty No 108).

[81] For comparison with the treatment of personal information in other legal systems, see paras 9.64 to 9.67 below.

[82] For example, the right to prevent processing for the purposes of direct marketing.

[83] See paras 10.35 to 10.66 below. The right of access is, of course, subject to a number of exemptions, including on grounds of national security, in relation to crime and taxation, and certain other matters: see paras 10.68 to 10.83 below.

[84] See paras 10.16 to 10.34 below.

[85] See paras 10.84 to 10.99 below.

Section 40(2)

6.61 Where the applicant is not the data subject, but a third party, matters are a little more complicated. Such applications are to be dealt with under the Act, but because the release of personal information to a third party raises issues of data protection, very broad exemptions apply to such requests,[86] and these exemptions are defined by reference to the 1998 Act. Wherever an application for 'personal data' is made by someone other than the 'data subject', the information to which it relates will be exempt from disclosure under the Act where either of two conditions are satisfied.[87]

6.62 These two conditions are considered in detail elsewhere,[88] but, with some simplification, their general effect can be described as follows. Where disclosure by the public authority of the data sought would contravene any of the 'data protection principles' it is absolutely exempt.[89] Where the data falls within the original form of section 1(1) of the 1998 Act (that is, it is information stored in a computer or it is manually processed data stored in a 'structured', rather than 'unstructured', form)[90] then disclosure is also prevented if it would contravene the right to prevent processing likely to cause damage or distress.[91] The exemption is not, however, in such a case, absolute, but is subject to the public interest test. The same is true if the information in question is exempt from the data subject's own right of access under the 1998 Act:[92] it is again exempt, but the exemption is subject to the public interest test. Further, the duty to confirm or deny is excluded where an application is made by someone other than the data subject if compliance would contravene any of the data protection principles, or section 10 of the 1998 Act, or where the data is exempt from disclosure to the data subject under the 1998 Act.[93]

Section 41: information provided in confidence

6.63 Section 41 creates an absolute exemption for certain information provided in confidence.[94] By section 41(1) information is exempt if (a) it was obtained by the public authority from any other person (including another public authority); and (b) the disclosure of the information to the public (otherwise than under the Act)

---

[86] Further to the Freedom of Information Act 2000, s 40(2).

[87] The two conditions are set out in ibid, s 40(3) and 40(4) respectively.

[88] See paras 10.103 and 10.104 below.

[89] In this context the exemptions provided by the Data Protection Act 1998, s 33A(1) (inserted by the Freedom of Information Act 2000, s 70) do not apply.

[90] ie information falling within the Data Protection Act 1998, s 1(1)(a)–(d), but not information (unstructured manual data) falling within ibid, s 1(1)(e), itself added to the definition by the Freedom of Information Act 2000, s 68.

[91] Pursuant to the Data Protection Act 1998, s 10.

[92] Pursuant to ibid, s 7(1)(c).

[93] Freedom of Information Act 2000, s 40(5).

[94] For comparison with the treatment of such information in other legal systems, see paras 9.68 to 9.76 below.

by the public authority holding it would constitute a breach of confidence action-able by that or any other person. The duty to confirm or deny does not arise if, or to the extent that, the confirmation or denial that would have to be given to com-ply with the duty would (apart from the Act) constitute an actionable breach of confidence.[95]

It should be noted that the exemption only applies to information obtained by the public authority from another person—it cannot be used by a public authority to justify withholding disclosure of the authority's own confidential information. **6.64**

Further, information provided by one government department to another will in general not be exempt information within the scope of section 41. This is because, although section 81(1) provides that for the purposes of the Act each government department is to be treated as a person separate from any other government department, section 81(2) provides that that provision does not enable (a) a gov-ernment department which is not a Northern Ireland department to claim for the purposes of section 41(1)(b) that the disclosure of any information by it would constitute a breach of confidence actionable by any other government department (not being a Northern Ireland department); or (b) a Northern Ireland department to claim for those purposes that the disclosure of information by it would consti-tute a breach of confidence actionable by any other Northern Ireland department. It should be noted that this still leaves open the possibility that information pro-vided by a Northern Ireland department to a government department which is not a Northern Ireland department, and vice versa, might still be exempt informa-tion within the scope of section 41. **6.65**

The exemption only applies if disclosing the information would constitute an actionable breach of confidence. It is clear that this is to be judged at the time the public authority considers a request for information. **6.66**

It was suggested during the Committee stage of the Bill in the House of Lords that a breach of confidence would only be actionable if the person bringing the claim for breach of confidence against the public authority would be successful in their claim.[96] Accordingly, if a claim would fail because, although the information was provided to the public authority in confidence, it is now in the public domain, the information would not fall within the scope of the exemption in section 41. **6.67**

A claim for breach of confidence is a claim whereby a party can, in some circum-stances, restrain the disclosure of information by another party.[97] There are three requirements to be met for such a claim to be established: **6.68**

---

[95] Freedom of Information Act 2000, s 41(2).
[96] Lord Falconer of Thoroton, Minister of State at the Cabinet Office, *Hansard*, HL (series 5) vol 617, col 92 (17 October 2000).
[97] For further discussion on the law of confidence, see ch 20 below.

(a) that the information, disclosure of which is sought to be restrained, has the necessary quality of confidence about it;

(b) that the information was imparted to the other party in circumstances importing an obligation of confidence; and

(c) that disclosure of the information would be to the detriment of the party seeking to restrain disclosure.[98]

6.69 In relation to personal information concerning individuals it has been suggested that a test for the first requirement is that disclosure would be highly offensive to a reasonable person of ordinary sensibilities.[99] Another test is whether there is a private interest worthy of protection.[100] Information relating to a person's health, personal relationships or finances is likely to meet the requirement.[101] However, trivial information will not meet the requirement of having the necessary quality of confidence about it.[102] Information which is already public knowledge or in the public domain will also not meet the requirement.[103]

6.70 As has been said, the second requirement that must be met is that the information was imparted to the party whom it is sought to restrain in circumstances importing an obligation of confidence. The most straightforward way in which such an obligation can arise is as a result of a contract. There are also certain relationships in which obligations of confidence will arise (either as implied terms of a contract or independently of any contract). Examples are the relationships between spouses[104] and between employers and their employees,[105] doctors and their patients,[106] banks and their customers,[107] journalists and their sources,[108] lawyers and their clients, priests and their supplicants and teachers and their pupils. Sexual relationships outside marriage will also give rise to obligations of confidence, although the more stable the relationship the greater will be the

---

[98] This formulation of the three requirements is taken from *Campbell v MGN Ltd* [2002] EWCA Civ 1373, CA. Slightly different formulations can be found in other cases.

[99] *Australian Broadcasting Corporation v Lenah Games Meats Property Ltd* (2001) 185 ALR 1, High Court of Australia.

[100] *A v B plc* [2002] 3 WLR 542, CA.

[101] *Australian Broadcasting Corporation v Lenah Games Meats Property Ltd* (2001) 185 ALR 1, High Court of Australia.

[102] *Attorney-General v Guardian Newspapers Ltd (No 2)* [1990] 1 AC 109, HL.

[103] ibid.

[104] *Argyll v Argyll* [1967] 1 Ch 302, Ch D.

[105] *Faccenda Chicken Ltd v Fowler* [1987] Ch 117, CA.

[106] *Hunter v Mann* [1974] QB 767, CA; *W v Egdell* [1990] Ch 359, CA.

[107] *Tournier v National Provincial and Union Bank of England* [1924] 1 KB 461, CA.

[108] As recognized by the Contempt of Court Act 1981, s 10 which provides that: 'No court may require a person to disclose, nor is any person guilty of contempt of court for refusing to disclose, the source of information contained in a publication for which he is responsible, unless it be established to the satisfaction of the court that disclosure is necessary in the interests of justice or national security or for the prevention of disorder or crime.' For a detailed discussion of this section, reference should be made to specialist textbooks.

significance to be attached to it.[109] Even in the absence of such a relationship, if one person imparts information of a confidential nature to another person, that other person may well come under an obligation of confidence in respect of it.

It should also be noted that the information need not have been imparted to the   **6.71**
party whom it is sought to restrain by the party bringing the action for breach of confidence. A third party who receives confidential information from a person who is under a duty of confidence in respect of it, knowing that it has been disclosed to them in breach of that duty, will also come under a duty of confidence in respect of the information.[110] It has also been suggested that someone who finds what is clearly a personal diary or a confidential document is likely to come under a duty of confidence in respect of it.[111]

There has been some debate as to the extent to which the third requirement, that   **6.72**
the disclosure of the information would be to the detriment of the party seeking to restrain disclosure, needs to be met. So far as private bodies or individuals are concerned the fact that information given in confidence is to be disclosed to persons whom the confider would prefer not to know of it is likely to be sufficient detriment in itself.[112] Where the Crown (and presumably other public authorities) are seeking to restrain disclosure, it is likely that a more specific detriment will need to be shown.[113]

Even if the three requirements discussed above are met, an action for breach of   **6.73**
confidence will fail if disclosure is in the public interest. This is often referred to as the 'public interest defence' to an action for breach of confidence.[114]

In considering whether a public interest defence to a claim for breach of   **6.74**
confidence arises, the public interest in protecting the confidence has to be balanced against the public interest in disclosure. The public interests in the detection or prevention of wrongdoing, in preventing a miscarriage of justice or in the maintenance of public safety have all been recognized as public interests which can outweigh the public interest in protecting the confidence.[115] It should be

---

[109]   *A v B plc* [2002] 3 WLR 542, CA.

[110]   *Attorney-General v Guardian Newspapers Ltd (No 2)* [1990] 1 AC 109, HL; *Douglas v Hello! Ltd* [2001] QB 967, CA.

[111]   *Attorney-General v Guardian Newspapers Ltd (No 2)* [1990] 1 AC 109, HL.

[112]   ibid, where Lord Keith gave the example of an anonymous donor to a worthy cause who wished to preserve their anonymity.

[113]   ibid.

[114]   Some commentators have suggested that it is more accurate to think of a fourth requirement—an action for breach of confidence will only succeed if restraining disclosure is in the public interest—as no duty of confidence will arise if it is not in the public interest to prevent disclosure.

[115]   See the summary given by Millett J in *Price Waterhouse v BCCI Holdings (Luxembourg) SA* [1992] BCLC 583, 601.

noted that, in some cases, the public interest may justify only limited disclosure.[116]

6.75 In a number of recent cases the court has had to balance the public interest in protecting a confidence and the right to respect for a person's private and family life, home and correspondence under Article 8 of the European Convention on Human Rights against the right to freedom of expression under Article 10 of the European Convention.[117] In such cases the fact that restraining disclosure of the information would interfere with the freedom of expression of others (and in particular the freedom of the press) is a matter to be weighed in the balance irrespective of whether the disclosure itself is desirable in the public interest.[118] The court has recognized that public figures are entitled to have their privacy respected in the appropriate circumstances but that because of their public positions they must expect and accept that their actions will be more closely scrutinized by the media.[119] If a public figure has courted publicity, they will have less ground to object to intrusion into their private lives.[120] Thus, a model who had publicly stated that she did not take drugs could not restrain disclosure of the information that she was in fact a drug addict (although she would have been able to do so but for her public statement).[121]

6.76 Accordingly, if any claim for breach of confidence brought against the public authority would be defeated by the public interest defence, the information will not be exempt under section 41.

6.77 Section 41 creates an absolute exemption: there is no scope for the public authority to decide that the public interest in disclosure outweighs the public interest in maintaining the confidence. However, the fact that in some circumstances a prima facie breach of confidence will not be actionable because the public authority will be able to rely on a public interest defence means that in some circumstances confidential information should be disclosed under the Act.

6.78 If a public authority were proposing to disclose under the Act information obtained in confidence from another person, there is no statutory obligation on the public authority to consult with that other person before disclosing the information. However, by virtue of section 45(2)(c), the code of practice issued by

---

[116] See, for example, *W v Egdell* [1990] Ch 359, CA where a psychiatrist was justified in submitting a psychiatric report to the relevant authorities but would not have been justified in making wider disclosure.

[117] See, for example, *Douglas v Hello! Ltd* [2001] QB 967, CA; *A v B plc* [2002] 3 WLR 542, CA; *Theakston v MGN Ltd* [2002] EMLR 398, QBD; *Campbell v MGN Ltd* [2002] EWCA Civ 1373, CA.

[118] *A v B plc* [2002] 3 WLR 542, CA.

[119] ibid.

[120] ibid.

[121] *Campbell v MGN Ltd* [2002] EWCA Civ 1373, CA.

the Lord Chancellor must include provision relating to 'consultations with persons to whom the information requested relates or persons whose interests are likely to be affected by the disclosure of information'. It is thus likely that a person who has provided information in confidence to a public authority will be consulted by the public authority before it discloses the information.

If, when consulted, the person informs the public authority that they are happy **6.79** for the information to be disclosed, then the public authority will no longer be able to rely on any exemption under section 41 of the Act: the disclosure of the information will not be an actionable breach of confidence because the person concerned has consented to what might otherwise have been a breach of confidence.

If, on the other hand, the person informs the public authority that they object to **6.80** the disclosure of the information but the public authority proposes to disclose the information under the Act in any event, then the person has no mechanism under the Act to prevent disclosure. However, if the public authority has wrongly concluded that information within the scope of section 41 is not exempt, then its disclosure would be an actionable breach of confidence and the person concerned should be able to obtain an injunction to prevent disclosure.

If the public authority discloses the information without first consulting the **6.81** person who provided it in confidence (either in breach of the Lord Chancellor's code of practice or because that code of practice does not require the person to be consulted in the circumstances of the case), then the person concerned will have no redress under the Act. However, again if the public authority has wrongly concluded that information within the scope of section 41 is not exempt, then its disclosure will have been an actionable breach of confidence. If the information has already been disclosed, then the person's remedy may be limited to damages (although an injunction against further disclosure might be available).

Section 44: prohibitions on disclosure

Section 44 creates an absolute exemption so as to ensure that where information **6.82** is subject to some prohibition on disclosure it will be exempt.[122] Section 44(1) provides that information is exempt if its disclosure (otherwise than under the Act) by the public authority holding it (a) is prohibited by or under any enactment; (b) is incompatible with any Community obligation; or (c) would constitute or be punishable as a contempt of court. By virtue of section 44(2), the duty to confirm or deny does not arise if the confirmation or denial that would have to be given to comply with the duty would (apart from the Act) fall within any of the paragraphs of section 44(1).

---

[122] For comparison with the treatment of such matters in other legal systems, see para 9.77 below.

6.83 The effect of this section is to ensure that public authorities do not find themselves in the invidious situation where the Act requires them to disclose certain information but as a result of another enactment, Community obligation, rule of court or court order they are obliged not to do so. As a result of section 44 the other obligation on the public authority (prohibiting disclosure) will take precedence.

6.84 It should be noted that if an enactment, Community obligation, rule of court or court order only gives a public authority a discretion as to whether or not to disclose certain information, the information will not be exempt under section 44.

Existing statutory prohibitions on disclosure

6.85 There are more existing bars to disclosure than one might imagine: 400 or so, Lord Falconer of Thoroton (then Minister of State, Cabinet Office) told the House of Lords when the clause of the Freedom of Information Bill which became section 44 was being debated at Committee stage.[123] Some 250 (not all of which are still in force) were listed in Annexe B to the 1993 White Paper, *Open Government*.[124] An up-to-date list was produced for the purposes of the Lord Chancellor's report to Parliament on 27 November 2002 on the review of legislation restricting the disclosure of information, as to which see further below.[125] According to that report, some 381 items of primary and secondary legislation containing provisions prohibiting the disclosure of information had been identified.

6.86 Probably the best known are those contained in the Official Secrets Acts discussed in chapter 12 below.[126] Targeted at specific categories of information, sometimes highly specific, most (in order to be properly understood) have to be read in the context of the particular statute or statutory instrument in which they appear. They take many different forms and cover a strikingly diverse range of subject matter, but some common themes emerge.

6.87 At one end of the spectrum are provisions which were clearly intended to serve a national purpose. For example, the prohibitions in the Representation of the People Act 1983, section 66, on communicating any information obtained as to the identity of the candidates for whom particular voters have cast their votes at elections, were designed to maintain the secrecy of the ballot, a basic democratic principle enshrined in Article 3 of the First Protocol to the European Convention for the Protection of Human Rights and Fundamental Freedoms (1950). The

---

[123] *Hansard*, HL (series 5) vol 617, col 905 (17 October 2000).

[124] Cm 2290.

[125] See paras 6.92 to 6.98 and 6.106 below. On the Lord Chancellor's report, see further http://www.lcd.gov.uk/foi/foidoirpt2.htm (still to be posted at this address on 2 December 2002). An earlier report to Parliament on 1 May 2002 on the progress of the review is at http://www.lcd.gov.uk/foi/foidoirpt.htm (2 December 2002).

[126] The question of whether the Official Secrets Acts are enactments which might prohibit the disclosure of information for the purposes of s 44 is not entirely clear cut, although the better view is that they are. This question is discussed further in part C of ch 12 below.

rationale for its having been made unlawful for members of the Armed Forces to make unauthorized disclosures of information relating to any matter upon which information would or might be useful to an enemy[127] is also obvious. At the other end of the spectrum are provisions purely for the protection of individuals, exemplified by the prohibitions on disclosure of information about particular persons having undergone certain types of medical procedures or treatments which might incur social stigma (such as termination of pregnancy[128] and fertility treatment[129]), and on disclosure of spent convictions.[130]

The majority lie somewhere between, the result of a balancing exercise or arguably a **6.88** trade-off between public benefit and private interests. Generally speaking, what they do is limit the uses to which information garnered by the government and other bodies from individuals and businesses (typically under compulsion of law) can be put. Uses other than for the particular purposes of the statute conferring the power to collect the information are forbidden. The arguments for imposing such restrictions, and (as is frequently the case) criminal sanctions for their breach, were forcefully put as follows in the Franks Report[131] of 1972 (at paragraphs 196 and 197):

> A considerable number of the statutes which require the giving of information, or which confer powers of entry or inspection, contain provisions expressly prohibiting unauthorised disclosures of the information obtained in these ways. The principle behind these provisions is that when the State requires the citizen to provide or reveal information which may be of a personal and confidential nature, or which should be kept confidential for commercial reasons, then the State should give the citizen a guarantee that this information will be properly protected. . . . In our view there are proper reasons for maintaining the protection of criminal sanctions. Here is a point where the requirements of government and the interests of the citizen wholly coincide. The Government is requiring more and more information from citizens and bodies. This information is given willingly and frankly only on the assurance, implicit or explicit, that it will be kept confidential. The Government cannot function effectively without this information. The people have the right to expect their confidences to be safeguarded by the Government. Any breakdown of this trust between Government and people could have considerable adverse repercussions on the government of the country.

Personal and confidential information supplied under compulsion of law includes **6.89** the information in census returns, tax returns, and social security records. Thus there are offences of unauthorized disclosure of personal census information,[132] information relating to particular persons held in the exercise of tax functions,[133]

---

[127] Army Act 1955, s 60; Air Force Act 1955, s 60; Naval Discipline Act 1957, s 34.
[128] Abortion Act 1967, s 2.
[129] Human Fertilization and Embryology Act 1990, s 33.
[130] Rehabilitation of Offenders Act 1974, s 9.
[131] *The Report of the Departmental Committee on Section 2 of the Official Secrets Act 1911* (Cmnd 5104).
[132] Census Act 1920, s 8.
[133] Finance Act 1989, s 182.

and information acquired in the course of employment in social security admin-istration or adjudication.[134]

6.90   As for keeping information obtained in the exercise of statutory powers confiden-tial for commercial reasons, there are numerous examples of prohibitions such as restrictions on the publication of information obtained for regulatory[135] or statis-tical[136] purposes. Statutes conferring powers of entry and inspection for the pur-poses of enforcing environmental, public health, and consumer protection legislation typically contain provisions prohibiting disclosure of information relating to trade secrets or manufacturing processes obtained by officials in the course of exercising those powers (otherwise than in performance of their duty), on pain of a criminal penalty.[137]

6.91   One other category of statutory prohibitions on disclosure of information relates to information obtained in the course of investigations, presumably to encourage frankness within the context of the investigation. Examples are prohibitions on disclosure of information given in connection with investigations by the Equal Opportunities Commission,[138] the Commission for Racial Equality,[139] and the Parliamentary Commissioner for Administration.[140]

The review of existing bars to disclosure

6.92   Parliament could, in the interests of transparency, have included in a schedule to the Act a comprehensive list of all the legislative provisions which are prohibitive or restrictive of the disclosure of information by public authorities. Such was the course chosen by the Canadian Parliament, which delimited the scope of the mandatory exemption from disclosure for records containing information the disclosure of which was restricted by and pursuant to other statutory provisions[141] by specifying what those other provisions were.[142]

6.93   It is true that the adoption of such a system would have entailed amending the Act every time one of the listed provisions was repealed or a new provision of that kind was enacted. That might have been inconvenient (although no more so than amending Schedule 1 from time to time by adding and removing the names of public authorities[143]), but would have had the advantage of showing on the face of

---

[134] Social Security Administration Act 1992, s 123.

[135] eg, under the Secretary of State's power to require a company to produce its documents: Companies Act 1985, ss 447, 449.

[136] eg, Agricultural Statistics Act 1979, s 3 and Statistics of Trade Act 1947, s 9.

[137] eg, Environmental Protection Act 1990, Sch 3, para 3(2); Food Safety Act 1990, s 32(7); Trade Descriptions Act 1968, s 28(5).

[138] Sex Discrimination Act 1975, s 61.

[139] Race Relations Act 1976, s 2.

[140] Parliamentary Commissioner Act 1967, s 11.

[141] Access to Information Act 1982, s 24(1).

[142] ibid, Sch II.

[143] Under the Freedom of Information Act 2000, s 4.

the Act itself how many enactments fall within section 44(1)(a) at any given time and what they are. Instead, Parliament opted for a general form of wording which would cover any enactment prohibitive of disclosure for the time being in force, following the precedent set by the United States[144] and New Zealand.[145]

One reason for going down this route may have been the government's avowed **6.94** intention to review all the existing statutory bars to the release of information. During the passage of the Freedom of Information Bill through Parliament, David Lock (then Parliamentary Secretary, Lord Chancellor's Department) stated in Standing Committee[146] that the government was committed to providing a wide-ranging freedom of information regime and considering the repeal of any such bars in other legislation as could no longer be justified, but to do so would require a long hard examination of every such provision and much cross-departmental liaison. The clear implication was that it would be a slow process, and not one which could be accomplished within the timescale planned for the Bill's becoming law.

In the House of Lords, at Committee stage, Lord Falconer confirmed that the gov- **6.95** ernment recognized that some statutory bars to the release of information had outlived their usefulness and a review was currently ongoing.[147] It may have been thought that there would be little purpose in including in the Act express reference to provisions of which some would not long survive its coming into force. Other reasons may have been the sheer number of provisions in question, and the risk of overlooking some.

In Canada, a review by Parliamentary Committee of every provision set out in the **6.96** Access to Information Act, Schedule II, culminating in a report to Parliament on whether and to what extent they were necessary, was mandated by express statutory provision.[148] The review was duly carried out by the House of Commons Standing Committee on Justice and Solicitor-General, who concluded that section 24 and Schedule II were unnecessary as the interests safeguarded by the provisions there set out could all be adequately protected by other existing exemptions in that Act. They recommended[149] the repeal of section 24 and Schedule II (subject, however, to the insertion of a new provision specifically exempting income tax records and information supplied by individuals, corporations and labour unions for statistical purposes as a guarantee to the public of the absolute confidentiality of those particular matters), and the amendment of the

---

[144] United States Code, Title 5, § 552(b)(3).
[145] Official Information Act 1982, s 18(c) and s 52(3)(b).
[146] *Hansard*, Standing Committee B, Freedom of Information Bill, col 385 (1 February 2000).
[147] *Hansard*, HL (series 5) vol 617, col 905 (17 October 2000).
[148] Access to Information Act 1982, s 24(2).
[149] *Open and Shut: Enhancing the Right to Know and the Right to Privacy* (Ottawa, March 1987) 116.

statutes referred to in Schedule II to bring them into line with the Access to Information Act.

6.97 That recommendation has not been implemented. Rather, as noted by the Canadian Information Commissioner in his Annual Report to Parliament for 2000-01,[150] the number of statutory provisions listed in Schedule II as restricting disclosure had grown from 40 in 1983 to 66 as at 31 December 2000, in a process he dubbed 'secrecy creep' and denounced as derogating 'by the back door' from the public's right to access.

6.98 It would, of course, have been impossible as a matter of constitutional principle for Parliament in enacting the Act to bind future Parliaments by precluding the passage of subsequent enactments prohibiting or restricting the disclosure of information, consistently with the provisions of the Act or otherwise. The most that could have been done would have been for the Act itself to repeal pre-existing statutory bars to disclosure, or amend them consistently with its provisions, as was originally envisaged in the White Paper, *Your Right to Know* (Cm 3818) paragraph 3.20. Any future legislation containing a prohibition on the disclosure of information will of course have been passed by Parliament in full knowledge that it would preclude the right of access under the Act, and (it is to be assumed) after having due regard to that conflict.

The power to repeal or amend existing statutory bars to disclosure

6.99 What the Act does instead is to confer power on the Lord Chancellor[151] to make such repeals or amendments, by statutory instrument. This meant that the passage into law of the Freedom of Information Bill could proceed while the review was still in progress, but no further primary legislation would be required to implement its outcome. The power is conferred by section 75 which was one of the provisions selected for bringing into force on the day the Act was passed.[152] The condition for its exercise is that it appears to the Lord Chancellor that an enactment prohibiting the disclosure of information held by a public authority is by virtue of section 44(1)(a) capable of preventing the disclosure of information under section 1. 'Information' in the context of this section includes unrecorded information.[153]

6.100 Section 44(1)(a) expressly provides that information is exempt if its disclosure (otherwise than under the Act) by the public authority is prohibited by or under any enactment. On the face of it any enactment prohibiting the disclosure of

---

[150] At p 59.

[151] The references to the Secretary of State in the original s 75 have been replaced with references to the Lord Chancellor by virtue of the Transfer of Functions (Miscellaneous) Order 2001 (SI 2001/3500).

[152] By the Freedom of Information Act 2000, s 87(1)(g).

[153] ibid, s 75(2).

information held by a public authority would by virtue of section 44(1)(a) appear to prevent the disclosure of information under section 1. The question therefore arises as to why the words 'is capable of preventing' were used in section 75 rather than simply 'prevents'.

A possible explanation is that an enactment may prohibit the disclosure of information falling within the scope of one of the other exemptions under the Act. It might be argued that such an enactment does not prevent the disclosure of information under section 1 *by virtue of section 44(1)(a)*, as the information would (or might) not be disclosed under the Act in any event by virtue of one of the other exemptions. It is thought that the use of the words 'is capable of preventing' in section 75 should ensure that such an enactment falls within the scope of section 77.[154] **6.101**

Where the condition for the exercise of the powers is satisfied, the Lord Chancellor may repeal by order the relevant enactment or amend it, but only for the purpose of removing or relaxing the prohibition on disclosure. Section 75(3) confers ancillary powers to make such modifications of enactments as are in the Lord Chancellor's opinion consequential upon, or incidental to, that amendment or repeal, and to include such transitional provisions and savings as appear to him appropriate. An order made under section 75 may also make different provision for different cases.[155] **6.102**

The power is exercisable only in relation to enactments contained in Acts passed before or in the same Parliamentary session as the Act, or in Northern Ireland legislation or subordinate legislation passed or made before the passing of the Act on 30 November 2000.[156] Accordingly, the Lord Chancellor does not have power to amend or repeal Acts passed after the session in which the Act was passed or Northern Ireland legislation or subordinate legislation passed after the Act was passed: one presumes that it was thought that, if such legislation contains a prohibition on the disclosure of information, any such prohibition would have been passed by Parliament in the full knowledge that it would interfere with the rights under the Act. **6.103**

There is a potential ambiguity in section 75(2)(b)—the section could be read so that the reference to subordinate legislation includes only Northern Ireland subordinate legislation. However, the reference to subordinate legislation is overwhelmingly likely to be interpreted so as to cover all subordinate legislation, and **6.104**

---

[154] It might be argued that an enactment which prohibited the disclosure of information which, in all circumstances, would not be disclosed under the Act by virtue of one of the other exemptions, would fall outside the scope of ibid, s 75 as there were no circumstances in which the enactment was capable of preventing the disclosure of information by virtue of ibid, s44(1)(a). However, it is thought that the court would strive to avoid such a construction of s 75.

[155] ibid, s 75(3).

[156] ibid, s 75(2).

that is clearly the understanding of the Lord Chancellor's Department which has already earmarked a number of provisions in statutory instruments for repeal under the section.

6.105 The discretion is subject to Parliamentary control in that no order can be made under section 75 unless a draft of the instrument has been laid before, and approved by a resolution of, each House of Parliament.[157] The discretion is also limited by the fact that, as was pointed out by David Lock in Standing Committee,[158] many of the existing bars on disclosure are necessary to implement European Community legislation, and will for that reason be inviolate.

6.106 In his report to Parliament on the progress of the review of statutory bars to disclosure,[159] the Lord Chancellor said that some 97 items of legislation had so far been identified as candidates for repeal or amendment. Examples are section 11 of the Atomic Energy Act 1946 (which makes communication without Ministerial consent of information about plant used for the production of atomic energy a criminal offence) and section 44 of the British Nationality Act 1981 (which provides that the Home Secretary does not have to give reasons for discretionary decisions under the Act, such as refusing an application for British citizenship).[160] The review is ongoing with 201 items continuing to be under review. The primary criteria for retaining provisions prohibiting disclosure have been identified by the government as:

(a) the item fulfils an international obligation;[161]
(b) the information being protected may be held by a person or body not covered by the Freedom of Information Act 2000;[162]
(c) the information being protected has been collected under compulsion;[163] or
(d) the information is protected as part of a specific and limited access regime.[164]

Disclosure incompatible with a Community obligation

6.107 As has already been commented above[165] a number of the existing bars on disclosure contained in enactments give effect to the obligations of the United Kingdom

---

[157] Freedom of Information Act 2000, s 82(2)(a).
[158] *Hansard*, Standing Committee B, Freedom of Information Bill, col 473 (10 February 2000).
[159] See para 6.85 above.
[160] For an illustration see *R v Secretary of State for the Home Department, ex p Al-Fayed (No 1)* [1998] 1 WLR 763, CA.
[161] The report identifies 57 items for retention as requisite for the fulfilment of international obligations.
[162] The report identifies 12 items for retention as protecting information which may be held by bodies and individuals not covered by the Freedom of Information Act 2000.
[163] The report identifies seven items for retention as protecting information which has been gathered under compulsion.
[164] The report identifies three items for retention as protecting information as part of a limited and specific access regime.
[165] See para 6.105 above.

under European Community law. Where the disclosure of information is prohibited by such an enactment the information will be exempt by virtue of section 44(1)(a).

There are, however, provisions of Community law which have direct effect—that **6.108** is they give rise to rights of, or obligations on, individuals which can be enforced in the United Kingdom courts whether or not there is United Kingdom legislation giving effect to the relevant provisions of Community law. A provision of Community law will have direct effect if it creates an unconditional and sufficiently precise obligation.[166] If the disclosure of information by a public authority is incompatible with such a provision, then the information concerned will be exempt by virtue of section 44(1)(b).

Disclosure of information as a contempt of court

A public authority may be subject to a court order requiring it not to disclose par- **6.109** ticular information. In those circumstances, the disclosure of that information will be a contempt of court and the information will be exempt by virtue of section 44(1)(c). It should also be noted that, if the court has granted an order against a party restraining it from disclosing information pending the trial of a claim, it may be a contempt of court for a third party, with knowledge of the court order, to disclose the information as the disclosure of the information may undermine the court order and thereby interfere with the administration of justice.[167]

If a public authority holds a document which has been disclosed to it by a party to **6.110** litigation in which the public authority has been involved, the public authority may use the document only for the purpose of that litigation except where (a) the document has been read to or by the court, or referred to, at a hearing which has been held in public; (b) the court gives permission; or (c) the party who disclosed the document and the person to whom the document belongs agree.[168] Accordingly, if a request is made for information which is held by the public authority solely because it is contained in such a document it would be a contempt of court for the public authority to disclose the information. In those circumstances, the information will be exempt by virtue of section 44(1)(c).

---

[166] Reference should be made to specialist textbooks for a detailed discussion of the circumstances in which Community law has direct effect.

[167] *Attorney-General v Times Newspapers Ltd* [1992] 1 AC 191, HL.

[168] Civil Procedure Rules Part 31.22.

D. Conditional Exemption

The effect of conditional exemption

6.111 As has been said, where a provision of Part II does not confer an absolute exemption, the information subject to the provision will be exempt where, in all the circumstances of the case, the public interest in maintaining the exclusion of the duty to confirm or deny,[169] or in maintaining the exemption,[170] outweighs the public interest in disclosing whether the public authority holds the information,[171] or the public interest in disclosing the information itself.[172] An exemption which is not absolute will be referred to as a conditional exemption.

6.112 It should be emphasized that this balancing exercise must be carried out 'in all the circumstances of the case'.[173] This means that a public authority must consider each request for information individually and will not be able to adopt rigid guidelines which will lead to particular categories of requests being rejected without any scope for allowing for the particular circumstances of the case.

6.113 The Act does not contain any general guidance on the factors to be taken into account in carrying out the balancing exercise. This is unsurprising given the wide variety of different circumstances that are likely to arise.[174]

The categories of conditionally exempt information

6.114 The following sections create conditional exemptions:

(a) section 22 (information intended for future publication);

(b) section 24 (national security);

(c) section 26 (defence);

(d) section 27 (international relations);

(e) section 28 (relations within the United Kingdom);

(f) section 29 (the economy);

(g) section 30 (investigations and proceedings conducted by public authorities);

(h) section 31 (law enforcement);

(i) section 33 (audit functions);

(j) section 35 (formulation of government policy);

---

[169] Freedom of Information Act 2000, s 2(1)(b).

[170] ibid, s 2(2)(b).

[171] ibid, s 2(1)(b).

[172] ibid, s 2(2)(b).

[173] Lord Falconer of Thoroton, Minister of State at the Cabinet Office, *Hansard*, HL (series 5) vol 619, col 831 (22 November 2000).

[174] For a discussion of how similar public interest tests have been applied in other legal systems, see paras 17.41 to 17.46 below.

(k) section 36 (prejudice to effective conduct of public affairs) (save so far as relating to information held by the House of Commons or the House of Lords);

(l) section 37 (communications with Her Majesty, etc and honours);

(m) section 38 (health and safety);

(n) section 39 (environmental information);

(o) section 40 (personal information) (to a limited extent);

(p) section 42 (legal professional privilege);

(q) section 43 (commercial interests).

The operation of each of these sections will be considered in turn below. Before **6.115** doing so it is worth making some general observations regarding conditional exemptions.

First, it should be noted that a number of the exemptions apply only to informa- **6.116** tion where its disclosure under the Act would, or would be likely to, prejudice particular interests. These will be referred to as prejudice-based exemptions. In contrast the other conditional exemptions apply to all information in a particular class regardless of whether any prejudice is caused to any interest. These exemptions will be referred to as class-based exemptions.

Prejudice-based exemptions

Prejudice-based exemptions can be found in section 24 (national security); sec- **6.117** tion 26 (defence); section 27(1) (international relations); section 28 (relations within the United Kingdom); section 29 (the economy); section 31 (law enforcement); section 33 (audit functions); section 36 (prejudice to effective conduct of public affairs); section 38 (health and safety); and section 43(2) (commercial interests).

In each of these sections, with three exceptions, the test for whether or not **6.118** information is exempt is whether its disclosure under the Act would, or would be likely to, prejudice the particular interest or interests referred to in the section. The three exceptions are:

(a) section 24, where the test is whether the exemption is required for the purpose of safeguarding national security;

(b) section 36(2)(b), where the test is whether the disclosure of the information under the Act would, or would be likely to, inhibit:
   (i) the free and frank provision of advice; or
   (ii) the free and frank exchange of views for the purposes of deliberation; and

(c) section 38, where the test is whether the disclosure of the information under the Act would, or would be likely to:
   (i) endanger the physical or mental health of any individual; or
   (ii) endanger the safety of any individual.

6.119 It should be noted that, for the information to fall within the scope of the various sections, any prejudice is sufficient: there is no requirement for the prejudice to be significant, serious or substantial. The Act has been much criticized because of the lack of any such requirement.

6.120 During the Parliamentary consideration of the Bill the government emphasized its view that prejudice means prejudice that is actual, real or of substance and that the Information Commissioner would have power to overrule the public authority in cases where any prejudice caused by the disclosure would be trivial or insignificant.[175]

6.121 Lord Falconer went on to say:

> We do not think that reliance on undefined terms such as 'substantial' or 'significant' is a sensible way forward. We do not know how they will be interpreted by the commissioner or the courts. We can never deliver absolute certainty, but we can avoid making uncertainty worse by adding ill-defined terminology into the Bill.[176]

6.122 For conditional prejudice-based exemptions, the force of the criticism that there is no requirement for any prejudice caused by disclosure to be substantial or significant is to an extent blunted because, in many cases, where disclosure would cause insubstantial or insignificant prejudice only, the public interest test will come down in favour of disclosure. However, there will be other cases where, notwithstanding that the prejudice caused by disclosure would be insubstantial or insignificant, the public interest test will come down in favour of maintaining the exemption and such cases would have been decided differently with a more rigorous test for prejudice.

6.123 It should also be noted that the prejudice has to be at least likely: the mere possibility of prejudice will not suffice.

6.124 It has already been noted that the public interest test has to be applied on a case by case basis. It is less clear whether the test of whether prejudice would be caused by disclosure under the Act also has to be applied on a case by case basis. In particular, whereas disclosure to one applicant for the information might be likely to cause prejudice, disclosure to another may not.

6.125 To give an example, a request for information concerning the effectiveness of army rifles may engage the exemption created by section 26: disclosure of the information might prejudice the effectiveness of the armed forces. If the applicant for information is someone with known sympathies with, say, a group in Afghanistan opposed to the presence of British armed forces operating there, it

---

[175] Mike O'Brien, Parliamentary Under-Secretary of State for the Home Office, *Hansard*, HC (series 6) vol 347, col 1067 (5 April 2000); Lord Falconer of Thoroton, Minister of State at the Cabinet Office, *Hansard*, HL (series 5) vol 612, col 827 (20 April 2000).

[176] *Hansard*, HL (series 5) vol 612, col 827 (20 April 2000).

might well be said that disclosure of the requested information would be likely to prejudice the effectiveness of the armed forces. However, if the applicant for information is a retired army colonel whose hobby is a keen interest in army rifles and who is unlikely to disseminate the information, it is much less clear that the disclosure of the requested information would be likely to cause any prejudice.

It is thought that the correct approach to the prejudice test would be to consider **6.126** whether widespread public disclosure of the relevant information would cause, or would be likely to cause, the relevant prejudice[177]—a public authority disclosing information to the retired army colonel might be concerned about setting a precedent when faced with a later request for the same information from a sympathizer with the Afghan group referred to above.

In relation to prejudice-based exemptions the duty to confirm or deny is generally **6.127** excluded if complying with the duty would prejudice the interest concerned. This means that the confirmation or denial that the information is held must itself have the relevant effect before the duty to confirm or deny is excluded. The effect of this is that, if a wide request for information is made, the duty to confirm or deny is less likely to be excluded than if a narrow request for information is made.

To go back to the example referred to above concerning a request for information **6.128** concerning the effectiveness of army rifles, whereas the information itself might (subject to the public interest test) be exempt under section 26, merely confirming or denying whether any such information is held cannot really be said to be likely to prejudice the effectiveness of the armed forces so that the duty to confirm or deny is unlikely to be excluded under the section. On the other hand, if the request is for information concerning significant specified problems with army rifles, confirming or denying whether any such information is held would (subject to the public interest test) be more likely to prejudice the effectiveness of the armed forces and so be excluded under the section.

Class-based exemptions

Class-based exemptions can be found in section 22 (information intended for **6.129** future publication); section 27(2) (international relations); section 30 (investigations and proceedings conducted by public authorities); section 35 (formulation of government policy); section 37 (communications with Her Majesty, etc and honours); section 39 (environmental information); section 40 (personal information); section 42 (legal professional privilege); and section 43(1) (commercial interests).

---

[177] The government appears to take this view. Lord Falconer suggested during the Committee stage of the Bill in the House of Lords that the public interest test should be looked at objectively without reference to the motive of the person applying for the information: *Hansard*, HL (series 5) vol 617, col 921 (17 October 2000).

6.130   Class-based exemptions are based on the assumption that any disclosure of information falling within the scope of the exemption will be harmful. To the extent that this assumption is not well founded in a particular case and no harm would, in fact, be caused by the disclosure of the information, it would be expected that the public interest test would result in the information being disclosed.

Section 22: information intended for future publication

6.131   Section 22 creates a conditional exemption for certain information held by a public authority which is intended for future publication.[178] Information requested from a public authority will be exempt information by virtue of this section if three conditions are met:

(a)   the information is held by the public authority with a view to its publication, by the authority or any other person, at some future date (whether determined or not);

(b)   the information was already held with a view to such publication at the time when the request for information was made; and

(c)   it is reasonable in all the circumstances that the information should be withheld from disclosure until the date referred to in paragraph (a).[179]

The duty to confirm or deny does not arise if, or to the extent that, complying with the duty would involve the disclosure of any such information (whether or not already recorded).[180]

6.132   In contrast to a number of the exemptions under the Act the effect of this section is not to prevent the disclosure of information for all time on the grounds that the disclosure of such information is or may be against the public interest.

6.133   What this section does, however, do is to allow public authorities to manage the publication of information. For example, where a public authority has commissioned a report a date may have been set for the publication of the report. This section will prevent applicants for information under the Act gaining advance notice of the content of the report prior to publication provided that it is reasonable in all the circumstances that the information should be withheld from disclosure until the publication of the report.

6.134   If a request is made for information some time before publication of the report, the report may still be in the process of being finalized. It might be said that a draft report is not being held with a view to publication as it is not the draft report

---

[178]   For comparison with the treatment of such information in other legal systems, see para 9.40 below.

[179]   Freedom of Information Act 2000, s 22(1).

[180]   ibid, s 22(2).

which will be published. However, it is thought that the information contained in the draft report will be held by the public authority with a view to publication so that that information will be (subject to the public interest test) exempt under section 22.

It should be noted that the section applies whether or not the date of publication **6.135** has been determined and whether or not publication is to be by the public authority to whom the request is made or by some other person. The information must, however, already have been held with a view to publication at the time the request was made: this provision is to prevent public authorities from avoiding responding to a request for, say, the disclosure of embarrassing information by deciding upon receipt of the request that the information will be published at some future (and perhaps more politically expedient) date.

Section 22 creates a class-based exemption: see paragraphs 6.129 and 6.130 **6.136** above.

Section 24: national security

As stated above section 23 creates an absolute exemption in relation to informa- **6.137** tion held by a public authority supplied by or relating to certain specified bodies dealing with security matters.[181] Section 24 creates a conditional exemption in relation to certain other information, where the exemption is required for the purpose of safeguarding national security.[182]

Information will be exempt information under section 24(1) if (a) it does not fall **6.138** within the scope of section 23(1) (information supplied by or relating to bodies dealing with security matters); and (b) an exemption from the right to have the information disclosed is required for the purpose of safeguarding national security. The duty to confirm or deny does not arise if, or to the extent that, exemption from the duty is required for the purpose of safeguarding national security.[183]

Like section 23, section 24 provides that a certificate signed by a Minister of the **6.139** Crown certifying that exemption from the duty to disclose, or from both the duty to confirm or deny and the duty to disclose, is, or at any time was, required for the purpose of safeguarding national security shall be conclusive evidence of that fact.[184] Such a certificate is subject to an appeal to the Information Tribunal.[185] Such a certificate may identify the information to which it applies by means of a

---

[181] See paras 6.19 to 6.27 above.
[182] For comparison with the treatment of such information in other legal systems, see paras 9.41 to 9.45 below.
[183] Freedom of Information Act 2000, s 24(2).
[184] ibid, s 24(3).
[185] ibid, ss 24(3) and 60.

general description and may be expressed to have prospective effect.[186] This means that a certificate could have extraordinarily wide ranging effect. For example, a certificate could provide that an exemption in relation to any information supplied by, or relating to, the armed forces or the immigration service either existing at the time of the certificate or coming into existence in the future was required for the purpose of safeguarding national security.

6.140 This is a conditional exemption but it is envisaged that only in fairly extraordinary circumstances would a public authority decide that the public interest in maintaining the exemption did not outweigh the public interest in disclosing the information—the public authority would have to come to the view that the public interest in disclosure was such as to justify endangering national security.

6.141 It is also theoretically possible that, notwithstanding a Ministerial certificate, a public authority could decide that the public interest in disclosure outweighed the public interest in maintaining the exemption. It is difficult to envisage circumstances in which a public authority might so decide. However, if it did, the Act seems to provide no mechanism for the Minister to prevent disclosure of the information.

6.142 The provisions referred to in paragraph 6.23 above apply to certificates under section 24(3) in the same way as they apply to certificates under section 23(2).

6.143 Section 24 creates a prejudice-based exemption: see paragraphs 6.117 to 6.128 above. However, it should be noted that the test is quite a strict one, the exemption must be required for the purpose of safeguarding national security and not merely desirable for that purpose.

Section 26: defence

6.144 Section 26 creates a conditional exemption for certain information held by a public authority relating to defence.[187] The exact scope of the exemption is that information is exempt if its disclosure under the Act would, or would be likely to, prejudice (a) the defence of the British Islands or of any colony, or (b) the capability, effectiveness or security of any relevant forces.[188] The duty to confirm or deny does not arise if, or to the extent that, compliance with the duty would, or would be likely to prejudice any of those matters.[189] 'Relevant forces' are defined as (a) the armed forces of the Crown, and (b) any forces co-operating with those forces, or any part of those forces.[190]

---

[186] Freedom of Information Act 2000, s 24(4).
[187] For comparison with the treatment of such information in other legal systems, see paras 9.41 to 9.45 above.
[188] Freedom of Information Act 2000, s 26(1).
[189] ibid, s 26(3).
[190] ibid, s 26(2).

This wide definition of 'relevant forces' would extend to the forces of other states **6.145** co-operating with British armed forces, in, for example, United Nations peace-keeping missions or joint NATO training exercises, or to, say, the armed forces of the United States when co-operating with British armed forces during the Gulf War.

Section 26 creates a prejudice-based exemption: see paragraphs 6.117 to 6.128 **6.146** above.

Section 27: international relations

Section 27 creates conditional exemptions for certain information held by a pub- **6.147** lic authority relating to international relations.[191] The section creates two differ-ent categories of exempt information. First, information is exempt under the section if its disclosure under the Act would, or would be likely to, prejudice:

(a) relations between the United Kingdom and any other state;
(b) relations between the United Kingdom and any international organization or international court;
(c) the interests of the United Kingdom abroad; or
(d) the promotion or protection by the United Kingdom of its interests abroad.[192]

Secondly, information is exempt if it is confidential information obtained from a state other than the United Kingdom or from an international organization or international court.[193]

The various terms used in the section are widely defined. The section provides **6.148** that 'state' includes the government of any state and any organ of its government, and that references to a state other than the United Kingdom include references to any territory outside the United Kingdom.[194] 'International organization' means any international organization whose members include any two or more states, or any organ of such an organization.[195] 'International court' means any international court which is not an international organization and which is estab-lished (a) by a resolution of an international organization of which the United Kingdom is a member, or (b) by an international agreement to which the United Kingdom is a party.[196]

---

[191] For comparison with the treatment of such information in other legal systems, see para 9.46 below.
[192] Freedom of Information Act 2000, s 27(1).
[193] ibid, s 27(2).
[194] ibid, s 27(5).
[195] ibid.
[196] ibid. The War Crimes Tribunal in the Hague and the new International Criminal Court would fall within the definition of 'international court'.

6.149 For the purposes of the section any information obtained from a state, organization or court is confidential at any time while the terms on which it was obtained require it to be held in confidence or while the circumstances in which it was obtained make it reasonable for the state, organization or court to expect that it will be so held.[197]

6.150 It should be noted that, in deciding whether information obtained from a state, organization or court is confidential, the focus is on the terms on or circumstances in which the information was obtained and whether those terms or circumstances required or led to a reasonable expectation that the information would be held in confidence. However, information is only confidential while that requirement or reasonable expectation continues. Thus, if information supplied in confidence by another state to the United Kingdom had entered the public domain in that other state, it might well be argued that the terms on which the information was supplied no longer required that it be held in confidence.

6.151 The most obvious example of such confidential information is perhaps intelligence information shared with the United Kingdom security service by the intelligence service of another state. However, the exemption created by section 27(2) is potentially of wide ranging effect.

6.152 The duty to confirm or deny does not arise if, or to the extent that, complying with the duty:

(a) would, or would be likely to, prejudice any of the matters mentioned in section 27(1); or

(b) would involve the disclosure of any information (whether or not already recorded) which is confidential information obtained from a state other than the United Kingdom or from an international organization or international court.[198]

6.153 Section 27(1) creates a prejudice-based exemption: see paragraphs 6.117 to 6.128 above. Section 27(2) creates a class-based exemption: see paragraphs 6.129 and 6.130 above.

Section 28: relations within the United Kingdom

6.154 Section 28 creates a conditional exemption relating to certain information held by a public authority relating to relations within the United Kingdom.[199] The scope of the section is that information is exempt if its disclosure under the Act would, or would be likely to, prejudice relations between any administration in the

---

[197] Freedom of Information Act 2000, s 27(3).

[198] ibid, s 27(4).

[199] For comparison with the treatment of comparable information in other legal systems, see para 9.47 below.

United Kingdom and any other such administration.[200] The duty to confirm or deny does not arise if, or to the extent that, compliance with the duty would, or would be likely to prejudice such matters.[201] 'Administration in the United Kingdom' means (a) the government of the United Kingdom, (b) the Scottish Administration, (c) the Executive Committee of the Northern Ireland Assembly, or (d) the National Assembly for Wales.[202] It should be noted that local authorities (and the Greater London Assembly) are excluded from this definition. Presumably, if English regional assemblies come into being, they too will be excluded from the scope of the section.

6.155 During the Committee stage of the Bill in the House of Lords the government gave two examples of information which might be exempt under this section. The first was where a government department kept a thumbnail sketch of the strengths and weaknesses of the individual members of an executive. The second was where a government department held comments on a devolved administration's policy proposals or Acts.[203]

6.156 Section 28 creates a prejudice-based exemption: see paragraphs 6.117 to 6.128 above.

Section 29: the economy

6.157 Section 29 creates a conditional exemption in relation to certain information concerning the economy.[204] The exact scope of the exemption is that information is exempt if its disclosure under the Act would, or would be likely to, prejudice (a) the economic interests of the United Kingdom or of any part of the United Kingdom, or (b) the financial interests of any administration in the United Kingdom.[205] In this section 'administration in the United Kingdom' has the same meaning as in section 28 concerning relations within the United Kingdom.[206]

6.158 The duty to confirm or deny does not arise if, or to the extent that, compliance with the duty would, or would be likely to, prejudice any of the matters referred to in the previous paragraph.[207]

6.159 This section would clearly cover, for example, information concerning the contents of a forthcoming Budget or an imminent interest rate change. If such

---

[200] Freedom of Information Act 2000, s 28(1).

[201] ibid, s 28(3).

[202] ibid, s 28(2).

[203] Lord Falconer of Thoroton, Minister of State at the Cabinet Office, *Hansard*, HL (series 5) vol 617, col 1280 (19 October 2000).

[204] For comparison with the treatment of such information in other legal systems, see para 9.48 below.

[205] Freedom of Information Act 2000, s 29(1).

[206] ibid, s 29(1)(b). See para 6.154 above.

[207] ibid, s 29(2).

matters were widely known before being announced, it would enable people to make arrangements to minimize the effect of forthcoming tax or interest rate changes to the likely prejudice of the UK's economy.

6.160 During the Committee stage of the Bill in the House of Lords the government gave an example of information which might be exempt as prejudicing the economic interests of part only of the United Kingdom. That is where a public authority, such as the Department of Trade and Industry, held documents setting out the advantages and disadvantages of investing in different regions. Disclosure of such information to an overseas investor contemplating setting up a factory in a particular region might deter the overseas investor from investing.[208]

6.161 Section 29 creates a prejudice-based exemption: see paragraphs 6.117 to 6.128 above.

Section 30: investigations and proceedings conducted by public authorities

6.162 Section 30 creates two related conditional exemptions concerning certain investigations and proceedings conducted by public authorities.[209]

6.163 The scope of the first exemption is that information held by a public authority is exempt if it has at any time been held by the authority for the purposes of:

(a) an investigation which the public authority has a duty to conduct with a view to it being ascertained:
  (i) whether a person should be charged with an offence; or
  (ii) whether a person charged with an offence is guilty of it;
(b) any investigation which is conducted by the authority and in the circumstances may lead to a decision by the authority to institute criminal proceedings which the authority has power to conduct; or
(c) any criminal proceedings which the authority has power to conduct.[210]

6.164 Information falls within the scope of the second exemption if two conditions are met. The first condition is that information held by a public authority is exempt if it was obtained or recorded by the authority for the purposes of its functions relating to:

(a) investigations of the type referred to in the previous paragraph;
(b) criminal proceedings which the authority has power to conduct;
(c) investigations (other than investigations of the type referred to in the previous paragraph) which are conducted by the authority for any of certain specified

---

[208] Lord Falconer of Thoroton, Minister of State at the Cabinet Office, *Hansard*, HL (series 5) vol 617, col 1287 (19 October 2000).
[209] For comparison with the treatment of such information in other legal systems, see paras 9.49 to 9.51 below.
[210] Freedom of Information Act 2000, s 30(1).

purposes and either by virtue of Her Majesty's prerogative or by virtue of powers conferred by or under any enactment; or

(d) civil proceedings which are brought by or on behalf of the authority and arise out of such investigations.[211]

The specified purposes are those listed in paragraph 6.178 below.[212] The second condition that must be met for the information to be exempt is that the information relates to the obtaining of information from confidential sources.[213]

In relation to the institution or conduct of criminal proceedings or the power to conduct them, references to the public authority in the section include references: **6.165**

(a) to any officer of the authority;

(b) in the case of a government department other than a Northern Ireland department, to the Minister of the Crown in charge of the department; and

(c) in the case of a Northern Ireland department, to the Northern Ireland Minister in charge of the department.[214]

'Criminal proceedings' are widely defined to include: **6.166**

(a) proceedings before a court-martial constituted under the Army Act 1955, the Air Force Act 1955 or the Naval Discipline Act 1957 or a disciplinary court constituted under section 52G of the Naval Discipline Act 1957;

(b) proceedings on dealing summarily with a charge under the Army Act 1955 or the Air Force Act 1955 or on summary trial under the Naval Discipline Act 1957;

(c) proceedings before a court established by section 83ZA of the Army Act 1955, section 83ZA of the Air Force Act 1955 or section 52FF of the Naval Discipline Act 1957 (summary appeal courts);

(d) proceedings before a Courts-Martial Appeal Court; and

(e) proceedings before a standing civilian court.[215]

'Offence' is also defined to include any offence under the Army Act 1955, the Air Force Act 1955 or the Naval Discipline Act 1957.[216]

The words of the section are amended in relation to its application to Scotland to take account of the different arrangements for the prosecution of offences in Scotland.[217] **6.167**

---

[211] ibid, s 30(2)(a).
[212] ibid.
[213] ibid, s 30(2)(b).
[214] ibid, s 30(4).
[215] ibid, s 30(5).
[216] ibid.
[217] ibid, s 30(6).

6.168 The first exemption relates only to information held in relation to particular investigations or proceedings. Accordingly, it would cover, for example, information obtained by the police during the course of the investigation of a particular crime—the thinking behind such an exemption being that disclosure of the information might well prejudice the investigation. If someone is subsequently charged with the crime, the exemption would cover the information which led to them being so charged and the evidence which suggests that they are responsible for the crime. This will prevent the accused using the Act to sidestep the rules of disclosure which govern criminal proceedings.

6.169 However, the first exemption would not, for example, cover statistics held by a police force as to the conviction rates in their particular area—such information does not relate to particular investigations or proceedings.

6.170 It should be noted, however, that the exemption is not subject to any time limit: on the face of it it continues even after any criminal proceedings are concluded. The fact that they have been concluded will be something to be taken into account in applying the public interest test.

6.171 The second exemption is not restricted to particular investigations or proceedings but is only engaged when the information relates to the obtaining of information from confidential sources. The thinking behind this exemption is undoubtedly that people would be deterred from providing information to the police if information which might enable them to be identified would be disclosed under the Act. It would also be wide enough to cover statistics held by a police force as to the number of informers with whom they were in contact.

6.172 It should be noted that, if a public authority concludes that the public interest requires the disclosure of information notwithstanding that it relates to the obtaining of information from confidential sources, it is under no statutory obligation to consult any confidential sources who may be affected by the disclosure. However, the code of practice issued by the Lord Chancellor under section 45 must contain guidance as to consultation with persons whose interests are likely to be affected by the disclosure of the information.

6.173 It should also be noted that the investigations referred to in section 30(2)(a)(iii), as well as being conducted for certain specified purposes, have to be conducted either by virtue of Her Majesty's prerogative or by virtue of powers conferred by or under an enactment. This will mean that, if, for example, a local authority sets up an inquiry which may reveal illegality but is not an inquiry which it has express power to conduct under legislation, information obtained or recorded by the authority for the purposes of that inquiry and relating to the obtaining of information from confidential sources will not be exempt.[218]

---

[218] For a discussion of issues arising from such inquiries, see part D of ch 15 below.

The duty to confirm or deny does not arise in relation to information which is (or **6.174** if it were held by the public authority would be) exempt by virtue of the section.[219]

This is a class-based exemption: see paragraphs 6.129 and 6.130 above. It can be **6.175** seen that it covers a very wide class of information without any requirement of prejudice or the likelihood of prejudice being caused by the disclosure.

Section 31: law enforcement

In addition to the wide class-based exemption created by section 30, section 31 **6.176** creates a prejudice-based conditional exemption with regard to certain information relating to law enforcement.[220]

The scope of the exemption is that information which is not exempt information **6.177** by virtue of section 30 is exempt information if its disclosure under the Act would, or would be likely to, prejudice:

(a) the prevention or detection of crime;
(b) the apprehension or prosecution of offenders;
(c) the administration of justice;
(d) the assessment or collection of any tax or duty or of any imposition of a similar nature;
(e) the operation of the immigration controls;
(f) the maintenance of security and good order in prisons or in other institutions where persons are lawfully detained;
(g) the exercise by any public authority of its functions for any of certain specified purposes;
(h) any civil proceedings which are brought by or on behalf of a public authority and arise out of an investigation conducted for any of the certain specified purposes by or on behalf of the authority by virtue of Her Majesty's prerogative or by virtue of powers conferred by or under an enactment; or
(i) any inquiry held under the Fatal Accidents and Sudden Deaths Inquiries (Scotland) Act 1976 to the extent that the inquiry arises out of an investigation of the type referred to in item (h) above.[221]

The specified purposes are as follows: **6.178**

(a) the purpose of ascertaining whether any person has failed to comply with the law;
(b) the purpose of ascertaining whether any person is responsible for any conduct which is improper;

---

[219] Freedom of Information Act 2000, s 30(3).
[220] For comparison with the treatment of such information in other legal systems, see paras 9.49 to 9.51 below.
[221] Freedom of Information Act 2000, s 31(1).

(c) the purpose of ascertaining whether circumstances which would justify regulatory action in pursuance of any enactment exist or may arise;

(d) the purpose of ascertaining a person's fitness or competence in relation to the management of bodies corporate or in relation to any profession or other activity which he is, or seeks to become, authorized to carry on;

(e) the purpose of ascertaining the cause of an accident;

(f) the purpose of protecting charities against misconduct or mismanagement (whether by trustees or other persons) in their administration;

(g) the purpose of protecting the property of charities from loss or misapplication;

(h) the purpose of recovering the property of charities;

(i) the purpose of securing the health, safety and welfare of persons at work; and

(j) the purpose of protecting persons other than persons at work against risk to health or safety arising out of or in connection with the actions of persons at work.[222]

6.179 The duty to confirm or deny does not arise if, or to the extent that, compliance with the duty would, or would be likely to, prejudice any of the matters referred to in paragraph 6.177 above.[223]

6.180 This section has a wider range than section 30 but the exemption only arises if disclosure will, or is likely to, prejudice the various matters specified in the section. Unlike the exemption created by section 30(1) the exemption is not limited to particular cases. Thus, for example, information as to deficiencies in the collection of taxes or the operation of immigration controls would (subject to the public interest test) fall within the scope of the exemption.

6.181 In so far as a request for information under either section 30 or section 31 relates to a particular investigation, the information requested is quite likely to be personal information under section 40 and exempt by virtue of that section.

6.182 As has been said section 31 creates a prejudice-based exemption: see paragraphs 6.117 to 6.128 above.

Section 33: audit functions

6.183 Section 33 creates a conditional exemption designed to safeguard the effectiveness of the audit functions of certain public authorities.[224] The only public authorities which can rely on the exemption are those which have functions in relation to (a) the audit of the accounts of other public authorities; or (b) the examination of the

---

[222] Freedom of Information Act 2000, s 31(2).

[223] ibid, s 31(3).

[224] For comparison with the treatment of such information in other legal systems, see para 9.52 below.

economy, efficiency and effectiveness with which other public authorities use their resources in discharging their functions.[225]

The scope of the exemption is that information held by such a public authority is exempt information if its disclosure would, or would be likely to, prejudice the exercise of any of the authority's functions in relation to any of the matters referred to in the previous paragraph.[226] **6.184**

The duty to confirm or deny does not arise in relation to such a public authority if, or to the extent that, compliance with the duty would, or would be likely to, prejudice the exercise of any of the authority's functions in relation to any of those matters.[227] **6.185**

The most obvious bodies to fall within the scope of the section are the Audit Commission for Local Authorities and the National Health Service in England and Wales, the Auditor-General for Wales, the National Audit Office and the Northern Ireland Audit Office. However, the large number of inspectorates which exist in relation to public services (such as the social services inspectorate or the magistrates' courts service inspectorate) will also fall within the scope of the section. It should be noted that bodies within the scope of the section will often publish reports on the effectiveness of other public authorities so that a certain amount of the information held by them will be made public in due course. **6.186**

Section 33 creates a prejudice-based exemption: see paragraphs 6.117 to 6.128 above. **6.187**

Section 35: formulation of government policy, etc

Section 35 creates a class-based conditional exemption designed to protect the effective formulation of government policy.[228] The scope of the exemption is that information held by a government department[229] or by the National Assembly for Wales is exempt information if it relates to: **6.188**

(a) the formulation or development of government policy;
(b) Ministerial communications;
(c) the provision of advice by any of the Law Officers or any request for the provision of such advice; or
(d) the operation of any Ministerial private office.[230]

---

[225] Freedom of Information Act 2000, s 33(1).
[226] ibid, s 33(2).
[227] ibid, s 33(3).
[228] For comparison with the treatment of such information in other legal systems, see paras 9.55 to 9.61 below.
[229] For the definition of 'government department', see Freedom of Information Act 2000, s 84.
[230] ibid, s 35(1).

6.189 The duty to confirm or deny does not arise in relation to information which is (or if it were held by the public authority would be) exempt information under the section.[231]

6.190 The wide scope of the section is narrowed by section 35(2) which provides that once a decision as to government policy has been taken, any statistical information used to provide an informed background to the taking of the decision is not to be regarded (a) as relating to the formulation or development of government policy; or (b) as relating to Ministerial communications.

6.191 Further, section 35(4) provides that, in relation to information which is exempt because it relates to the formulation or development of government policy, in determining whether the exclusion of the duty to confirm or deny outweighs the public interest in disclosing whether the public authority holds the information, or in determining whether the public interest in maintaining the exemption outweighs the public interest in disclosing the information, regard shall be had to the particular public interest in the disclosure of factual information which has been used, or is intended to be used, to provide an informed background to decision-taking.

6.192 In section 35 'government policy' includes the policy of the Executive Committee of the Northern Ireland Assembly and the policy of the National Assembly for Wales.[232] The term 'the Law Officers' is defined as the Attorney-General, the Solicitor-General, the Advocate General for Scotland, the Lord Advocate, the Solicitor-General for Scotland and the Attorney-General for Northern Ireland.[233]

6.193 'Ministerial communications' are defined as any communications (a) between Ministers of the Crown; (b) between Northern Ireland Ministers, including Northern Ireland junior Ministers; or (c) between Assembly Secretaries including the Assembly First Secretary.[234] It is also provided that 'Ministerial communications' include, in particular, proceedings of the Cabinet or of any committee of the Cabinet, proceedings of the Executive Committee of the Northern Ireland Assembly, and proceedings of the executive committee of the National Assembly for Wales.[235] A 'Northern Ireland junior Minister' is a member of the Northern Ireland Assembly appointed as a junior Minister under section 19 of the Northern Ireland Act 1998.[236]

6.194 The term 'Ministerial private office' is defined as any part of a government department which provides personal administrative support to a Minister of the Crown,

---

[231] Freedom of Information Act 2000, s 35(3).
[232] ibid, s 35(5).
[233] ibid.
[234] ibid.
[235] ibid.
[236] ibid.

to a Northern Ireland Minister or a Northern Ireland junior Minister or any part of the administration of the National Assembly for Wales providing personal administrative support to the Assembly First Secretary or an Assembly Secretary.[237]

As has been said section 35 creates a class-based exemption: see paragraphs 6.129 and 6.130 above. **6.195**

Section 36: prejudice to effective conduct of public affairs

Section 36 creates a further exemption designed to protect the effective conduct **6.196** of public affairs.[238] The section applies to (a) information which is held by a government department or by the National Assembly for Wales and which is not exempt by virtue of section 35; and (b) information which is held by any other public authority.[239]

The scope of the section is that such information is exempt information if, in the **6.197** reasonable opinion of a qualified person, disclosure of the information under the Act:

(a) would, or would be likely to, prejudice:
   (i) the maintenance of the convention of the collective responsibility of Ministers of the Crown; or
   (ii) the work of the executive committee of the Northern Ireland Assembly; or
   (iii) the work of the executive committee of the National Assembly for Wales;
(b) would, or would be likely to, inhibit:
   (i) the free and frank provision of advice; or
   (ii) the free and frank exchange of views for the purposes of deliberation; or
(c) would otherwise prejudice, or would be likely otherwise to prejudice, the effective conduct of public affairs.[240]

The duty to confirm or deny does not arise in relation to information to which the **6.198** section applies (or would apply if held by the public authority) if, or to the extent that, in the reasonable opinion of a qualified person, compliance with the duty would, or would be likely to, have any of the effects mentioned in the previous paragraph.[241]

It will be noted that the exemption of information under this section is dependent **6.199** on the reasonable opinion of a qualified person. There is one exception to this,

---

[237] ibid.
[238] For comparison with the treatment of such information in other legal systems, see paras 9.55 to 9.61 below.
[239] Freedom of Information Act 2000, s 36(1).
[240] ibid, s 36(2).
[241] ibid, s 36(3).

which is that in relation to statistical information the section is to be applied as if the words 'in the reasonable opinion of a qualified person' were omitted.[242]

6.200   The term 'qualified person':

(a)   in relation to information held by a government department in the charge of a Minister of the Crown, means any Minister of the Crown;

(b)   in relation to information held by a Northern Ireland department, means the Northern Ireland Minister in charge of the department;

(c)   in relation to information held by any other government department, means the commissioners or other person in charge of that department;

(d)   in relation to information held by the House of Commons, means the Speaker of that House;

(e)   in relation to information held by the House of Lords, means the Clerk of the Parliaments;

(f)   in relation to information held by the Northern Ireland Assembly, means the Presiding Officer;

(g)   in relation to information held by the National Assembly for Wales, means the Assembly First Secretary;

(h)   in relation to information held by any Welsh public authority other than the Auditor-General for Wales, means:

(i)   the public authority; or

(ii)   any officer or employee of the authority authorized by the Assembly First Secretary;

(i)   in relation to information held by the National Audit Office, means the Comptroller and Auditor-General;

(j)   in relation to information held by the Northern Ireland Audit Office, means the Comptroller and Auditor-General for Northern Ireland;

(k)   in relation to information held by the Auditor-General for Wales, means the Auditor-General for Wales;

(l)   in relation to information held by any Northern Ireland public authority other than the Northern Ireland Audit Office, means:

(i)   the public authority; or

(ii)   any officer or employee of the authority authorized by the First Minister and deputy First Minister in Northern Ireland acting jointly;

(m)   in relation to information held by the Greater London Authority, means the Mayor of London;

(n)   in relation to information held by a functional body within the meaning of the Greater London Authority Act 1999, means the chairman of that functional body; and

---

[242]   Freedom of Information Act 2000, s 36(4).

(o) in relation to information held by any public authority not falling within any of items (a) to (n) above, means:

    (i) a Minister of the Crown;

    (ii) the public authority, if authorized for the purposes of the section by a Minister of the Crown; or

    (iii) any officer or employee of the public authority who is authorized for the purposes of the section by a Minister of the Crown.[243]

6.201 Any authorization for the purposes of section 36 (a) may relate to a specified person or to persons falling within a specified class; (b) may be general or limited to particular classes of case; and (c) may be granted subject to conditions.[244]

6.202 A certificate signed by the Speaker of the House of Commons or the Clerk of the Parliaments certifying that in his or her reasonable opinion (a) disclosure of information held by either House of Parliament; or (b) compliance with the duty to confirm or deny by either House would, or would be likely to, have any of the effects mentioned in paragraph 6.197 above shall be conclusive evidence of that fact.[245]

6.203 This section creates an absolute exemption so far as information held by the House of Commons or the House of Lords is concerned. Otherwise it creates a conditional exemption.

6.204 Section 36 has a potentially wider scope than section 35: whereas section 35 is limited in its scope to 'central government' section 36 applies to all public authorities. However, section 36, unlike section 35, is a prejudice-based exemption.

6.205 Further, before information (other than statistical information) is exempt under the section, a qualified person has to have stated that in their reasonable opinion prejudice would, or would be likely to, be caused. This has the effect that exemption under the section will not be claimed without a decision by someone of sufficient seniority that it should be claimed. The purpose of this provision is presumably to prevent the exemption being claimed too readily.

6.206 However, whereas, if there was no requirement for the reasonable opinion of a qualified person before the exemption was claimed, the Information Commissioner could reach his or her own view as to whether prejudice would, or would be likely to, be caused, the government suggested during the Committee stage in the House of Lords[246] (it is thought correctly) that the Information Commissioner would only be able to intervene at that stage on a judicial review basis—that no reasonable qualified person could come to the conclusion that

---

[243] ibid, s 36(5).
[244] ibid, s 36(6).
[245] ibid, s 36(7).
[246] Lord Falconer of Thoroton, Minister of State at the Cabinet Office, *Hansard*, HL (series 5) vol 618, col 306 (24 October 2000).

prejudice would, or would be likely to, be caused. (It would, of course, be open to the Information Commissioner to reach his or her own view on the application of the public interest test.)

6.207 The exclusion of the requirement for the reasonable opinion of a qualified person in relation to statistical information is presumably to ensure that the Information Commissioner has a wider power of intervention in forming his or her own view as to whether disclosure of the statistical information would, or would be likely to, cause prejudice. However, perversely, the lack of such a requirement means that it is easier for a public authority to claim that statistical information is exempt under section 36 than other information.

6.208 As has been said section 36 creates a prejudice-based exemption: see paragraphs 6.117 to 6.128 above.

Section 37: communications with Her Majesty, etc and honours

6.209 Section 37 creates a conditional exemption in relation to information relating to royal communications and honours. The exact scope of the exemption is that information is exempt if it relates to (a) communications with Her Majesty, with other members of the Royal Family or with the Royal Household; or (b) the conferring by the Crown of any honour or dignity.[247]

6.210 The duty to confirm or deny does not arise in relation to information which is (or if it were held by the public authority would be) exempt information by virtue of section 37(1).[248]

6.211 This is a class-based exemption: see paragraphs 6.129 and 6.130 above.

Section 38: health and safety

6.212 Section 38 creates a conditional exemption in relation to information the disclosure of which might endanger health and safety.[249] The scope of the exemption is that information is exempt if its disclosure under the Act would, or would be likely to, (a) endanger the physical or mental health of any individual; or (b) endanger the safety of any individual.[250] The duty to confirm or deny does not arise if, or to the extent that, compliance with the duty would, or would be likely to, have either of those effects.[251]

---

[247] Freedom of Information Act 2000, s 37(1).

[248] ibid, s 37(2).

[249] For comparison with the treatment of such information in other legal systems, see para 9.62 below.

[250] Freedom of Information Act 2000, s 38(1).

[251] ibid, s 38(2).

An example of information falling within the scope of the section would be **6.213** information held by a public authority as to where a convicted paedophile recently released from prison was living. The disclosure of such information might endanger the safety of the person. Of course, this information would also be likely to be exempt as personal information under section 40.

However, the section might also be used to justify refusing the disclosure of **6.214** information concerning any dangers caused by 'triple-jab' MMR (measles, mumps, rubella) vaccination—the public authority might take the view that disclosing the information would endanger the health of individuals if it led to parents refusing to have their children vaccinated.

A further example might be information as to the layout of a property which **6.215** might be vulnerable to terrorist or criminal attack—disclosing the detailed plans of a nuclear power station or a bank's safes might endanger the safety of those working at the power station or the bank if it enabled terrorists to plan an attack on the power station or criminals to plan a robbery of the bank.

It is not clear what is the difference between health and safety—it is difficult to **6.216** envisage something which might endanger the safety of an individual which did not also endanger the physical or mental health of the individual.

Section 38 creates a prejudice-based exemption: see paragraphs 6.117 to 6.128 **6.217** above.

Section 39: environmental information

Section 39 creates a conditional exemption in relation to certain environmental **6.218** information.[254] The scope of the section is that information is exempt if the public authority holding it (a) is obliged by regulations under section 74 to make the information available to the public in accordance with the regulations; or (b) would be so obliged but for any exemption contained in the regulations.[252] The duty to confirm or deny does not arise in relation to information which is (or if it were held by the public authority would be) exempt information by virtue of section 39(1).[253] Section 39(3) provides that the provision in section 39(1)(a), that information is exempt if the public authority is obliged by regulations under section 74 to make the information available to the public in accordance with the regulations, does not limit the generality of section 21(1) (which creates an exemption in relation to information reasonably accessible to the applicant by other means).

---

[252] ibid, s 39(1).
[253] ibid, s 39(2).
[254] For comparison with the treatment of environmental information in other legal systems, see para 9.63 below.

6.219   The power given to the Secretary of State by section 74 to make by regulations provision relating to environmental information is discussed in chapter 16 below. It will be noted that like a number of the sections in Part II of the Act[255] section 39 does not create a true exemption, in the sense that the purpose of the section is not to prevent the disclosure of the information within its scope altogether, but to ensure that disclosure of the information within its scope is dealt with under another regime for the disclosure of information rather than the Act.

6.220   It should also be noted that, unlike a number of the other sections which do not create true exemptions,[256] section 39 creates a conditional exemption. The effect of this is that there may be circumstances in which information would be disclosed pursuant to a request under the Act even if the public authority concerned is obliged by regulations under section 74 in any event to make the information available to the public. Further, there may be circumstances where information will be disclosed under the Act even if it is exempt from disclosure under the regulations.

6.221   Section 39 creates a class-based exemption: see paragraphs 6.129 and 6.130 above.

Section 40: personal information

6.222   The exemption created by section 40 is largely an absolute exemption and has been dealt with at paragraphs 6.57 to 6.62 above. However, there are some circumstances in which it creates a conditional exemption only. These have been considered at paragraph 6.62 above.

Section 42: legal professional privilege

6.223   Section 42 creates a conditional exemption in relation to information subject to legal professional privilege. The scope of the exemption is that information in respect of which a claim to legal professional privilege (or, in Scotland, to confidentiality of communications) could be maintained in legal proceedings is exempt.[257] The duty to confirm or deny does not arise if, or to the extent that, complying with the duty would involve the disclosure of any such information (whether or not already recorded).[258]

6.224   The scope of legal professional privilege is discussed later in this book.[259] As will be seen, legal professional privilege falls into two categories: advice privilege and

---

[255]   Freedom of Information Act 2000, ss 21 and 22 and, to an extent, s 40.
[256]   ibid, s 21 and, to an extent, s 40.
[257]   ibid, s 42(1).
[258]   ibid, s 42(2).
[259]   See paras 18.45 to 18.51 below.

litigation privilege. It is thought that information which is 'without prejudice'[260] will not fall within the scope of section 42—this ground for withholding disclosure of documents in litigation is usually treated as being separate from legal professional privilege.

It should be noted that information only falls within the scope of the section if a **6.225** claim to legal professional privilege could be maintained in legal proceedings. This means that, if the information falls within the scope of the limited circumstances where legal professional privilege does not arise (for example, a document which came into existence in pursuance of fraud or crime or where the privilege has been waived), the information will not be exempt.

Section 42 creates a conditional exemption only. It will be seen[261] that, subject to **6.226** very limited exceptions, legal professional privilege can be maintained in proceedings regardless of the circumstances. In particular, there is no scope for the court in proceedings to decide that the privilege should be overridden because of a wider public interest in disclosure. In contrast, there may be circumstances in which a public authority decides, applying the public interest test, that the public interest in disclosure outweighs the public interest in upholding the privilege. It is thought that the circumstances in which this will happen will be rare—there is a considerable public interest in a party being able to communicate with its lawyers and prepare for litigation in the knowledge that those communications or preparations will not be disclosed.

To give an example, a tenant of a local authority may be suing the local authority **6.227** for damages in respect of disrepair to the tenant's property. The local authority may have taken external legal advice as to the level of damages the tenant is likely to recover, which advice will be subject to legal professional privilege. If, during settlement negotiations, the tenant were to request information as to that external legal advice, it is thought that the public interest test would favour maintaining the exemption—disclosure would give the tenant an unfair advantage in its proceedings against the local authority which would be contrary to the public interest. However, once the proceedings have been concluded, that public interest will not arise and disclosure under the Act may be more likely, although the public authority would still have to consider the possible inhibiting effect disclosure might have—communications between public authorities and their legal advisers may become less candid if it was contemplated that those communications might subsequently be disclosed.

Section 42 creates a class-based exemption: see paragraphs 6.129 and 6.130 **6.228** above.

---

[260] See paras 18.52 and 18.53 below.
[261] See paras 18.48 to 18.50 below.

Section 43: commercial interests

6.229 Section 43 creates two different conditional exemptions designed to protect commercial interests. The first exemption is a class-based one: information is exempt if it constitutes a trade secret.[262] The second exemption is a prejudice-based one: information is exempt if its disclosure under the Act would, or would be likely to, prejudice the commercial interests of any person (including the public authority holding it).[263] The duty to confirm or deny does not arise if, or to the extent that, complying with that duty would, or would be likely to, prejudice the commercial interests of any person.[264]

6.230 The term 'trade secret' is not defined in the Act. However, it is a term familiar from the common law to describe certain information confidential to business, although no clear definition of the term has emerged from the authorities.

6.231 In *Faccenda Chicken Ltd v Fowler*[265] the court distinguished between trade secrets of an employer, which employees are under an implied obligation not to disclose or use either during or after their employment; and other confidential information of the employer, which employees are under an implied obligation not to disclose or use during their employment but are free to disclose or use after their employment. The court[266] described as falling within the trade secret category 'secret processes of manufacture such as chemical formulae . . . or designs or special methods of construction . . . and other information which is of a sufficiently high degree of confidentiality as to amount to a trade secret'.

6.232 In *Lansing Linde Ltd v Kerr*[267] Staughton LJ defined trade secrets as information used in a trade or business of which the owner limits the dissemination or at least does not encourage or permit widespread publication and which if disclosed to a competitor would be liable to cause real (or significant) harm to the owner of the secret.

6.233 The House of Lords Select Committee which considered the draft Freedom of Information Bill suggested that a 'trade secret' is 'information of commercial value which is protected by the law of confidence'.[268] The problem with such a definition is that whether a particular piece of information will be protected by the law of confidence may depend on the circumstances of the proposed disclo-

---

[262] Freedom of Information Act 2000, s 43(1).
[263] ibid, s 43(2).
[264] ibid, s 43(3).
[265] [1987] 1 Ch 117, CA.
[266] ibid at 136.
[267] [1991] 1 WLR 251, 260, CA.
[268] Report from the Select Committee appointed to consider the Draft Freedom of Information Bill, 27 July 1998, para 45.

sure: for example, the court will more readily restrain disclosure by a current employee than a former employee.[269]

Whether information constitutes a trade secret will depend on all the circum- **6.234** stances of the case. Manufacturing processes and formulae are likely to be trade secrets. Information about customers, prices and costs may well constitute trade secrets.

It should be noted that the duty to confirm or deny is not excluded in relation to **6.235** information purely on the basis that the information constitutes a trade secret. However, in a situation where the duty to confirm or deny would involve the public authority disclosing a trade secret, it might be presumed that the duty to confirm or deny would be excluded on the basis that complying with the duty would, or would be likely to, prejudice the commercial interests of the person whose trade secret it is.

Where a public authority is proposing to disclose under the Act information **6.236** which constitutes a trade secret or which would, or would be likely to, prejudice the commercial interests of another person, there is no statutory obligation on the public authority to consult the person whose trade secret it is or whose commercial interests will, or are likely to, be prejudiced. However, the code of practice issued by the Lord Chancellor under section 45 must include provision relating to such consultation.[270]

If, having been consulted, the person objects to the proposed disclosure but the **6.237** public authority still intends to make it, there is no mechanism under the Act enabling the person to protect their interests. If the information is confidential information, the person may, however, be able to obtain an injunction to prevent disclosure. Alternatively, the person may be able to claim judicial review of the public authority's decision to disclose the information and an injunction to restrain that disclosure.

It is likely that most trade secrets and much information, the disclosure of which **6.238** would cause prejudice to commercial interests, will also be confidential information. As such, it is likely to be subject to the absolute exemption created by section 41.[271]

As has been said the exemption created by section 43(1) is a class-based one (see **6.239** paragraphs 6.129 and 6.130 above) and the exemption created by section 43(2) is a prejudice-based one (see paragraphs 6.117 to 6.128 above).

---

[269] *Faccenda Chicken Ltd v Fowler* [1987] 1 Ch 117, CA.
[270] Freedom of Information Act 2000, s 45(2)(c).
[271] See paras 6.63 to 6.81 above.

7

ENFORCEMENT

A. Introduction

The enforcement regime of the Act[1] can be seen as operating on two levels, the **7.01** general and the specific.

At the general level, the Act and the Codes of Practice are designed to bring about **7.02** a change of culture in public authorities to ensure that public authorities keep better records and make them readily available to members of the public. The Lord Chancellor has issued a Code of Practice setting out guidance to public authorities relating to the provision of access to information and a Code of Practice setting out guidance to public authorities relating to record management. The greatest responsibility for bringing about this change in culture will be borne by the Information Commissioner who is under a duty to promote good practice under the Act, which includes compliance with the provisions of the Codes of Practice. The Information Commissioner has extensive powers to achieve this aim including the use of information notices to determine whether a public authority

---

[1] Parts IV (Enforcement) and V (Appeals) of the Act.

is complying with the Act (and good practice) and a power to apply for search warrants. The Information Commissioner will report to Parliament on an annual basis on the extent to which public authorities have adopted this change of culture.

7.03 At the specific level, the Act aims to ensure that any individual application under the Act is decided properly and impartially; and further that public authorities are forced to give effect to such decisions. Any applicant requesting information can apply to the Information Commissioner for a decision as to whether a public authority has properly discharged its functions in providing access to information and can, thereafter, appeal to the Information Tribunal. Once a decision has been made by the Information Commissioner, a public authority which does not give effect to the decision can be held in contempt of court.

7.04 The enforcement regime reflects a balance between the competing interests of the various parties who are likely to be involved in an application under the Act. First, applicants under the Act want a quick and efficient resolution to their applications; similarly, they want effective penalties to ensure that recalcitrant authorities comply with their obligations under the Act. On the other hand, public authorities, which will bear the brunt of the administrative burden of the Act, will want as much time to deal with applications as possible; further, public authorities may be expected to show some reluctance in making available information to which the public had, hitherto, no right of access. In addition, there are the interests of third parties, whose interests may be affected by disclosure of information under an application, but who are not parties to an application under the Act.

7.05 There are three significant areas of the enforcement regime where the Act has deviated significantly from the path set out in the White Paper. First, the Act provides for a ministerial veto whereas the White Paper was of the view that a ministerial veto would undermine the role of the Information Commissioner and would erode public confidence. Secondly, where the White Paper eschewed any appeal procedure beyond the Information Commissioner (other than judicial review), the Act provides an appeal by way of rehearing to an Information Tribunal and a further appeal to the High Court on a point of law. The White Paper saw in appeals an opportunity for recalcitrant authorities to delay the provision of information; the Act may provide such opportunities. Thirdly, whereas the White Paper emphasized the need to protect the interests of third parties who may be affected by disclosure, the Act is all but silent as to how that protection is to be achieved.

7.06 Whilst it is difficult to predict how successful the enforcement regime will be, some features can be noted by comparing these Parts of the Act both with the proposals in the White Paper and with the procedures and experiences of jurisdictions overseas. Another useful area of comparison is the Data Protection Act

1998, the enforcement regime of which has marked similarities to that of the Act. Whilst an explanation of the workings of these Parts of the 2000 Act is the primary aim of this chapter, this chapter does also attempt to highlight some of those notable features.

B. Codes of Practice

Codes of Practice: general

The Act provides for two Codes of Practice to be issued (and updated): one in re- **7.07** lation to dealing with requests for information under the Act and the other in relation to records management. The use of statutory Codes of Practice or Codes of Guidance is a familiar feature in modern public law legislation.[2] The provisions of the Codes of Practice under the Act do not have statutory force. The Codes of Practice are expressed to be by way of 'guidance' as to the practice 'which it would be desirable' for public authorities to follow.

The Information Commissioner is under a duty to promote the following of good **7.08** practice by public authorities which includes compliance with the provisions of the Code of Practice.[3] To that end, the Information Commissioner may serve information notices in order to ascertain whether a public authority is complying with a Code of Practice. However, the Information Commissioner's powers in relation to enforcing compliance with Codes of Practice are limited. If it appears to him that the practice of a public authority does not conform with that proposed by the Code, he may issue a practice recommendation.[4] However, the Information Commissioner cannot enforce compliance with the Code of Practice by means of an enforcement notice.[5] In contrast to an enforcement notice, a practice recommendation does not, it seems, have any binding legal effect on the public authority. A public authority which does not comply with the Codes of Practice can, however, expect to have decisions which it makes relating to requests for information regularly quashed by the Information Commissioner, Information Tribunal or the courts.[6]

---

[2] For example, under the Data Protection Act 1998; the Housing Act 1996; the Town and Country Planning Act 1990.

[3] Section 47(1) and (6) of the Act. See similarly, under s 51, Data Protection Act 1998, the Information Commissioner is under a duty to encourage the development of Codes of Practice for guidance as to good practice under that Act; 'good practice' is defined under the Data Protection Act 1998 as 'such practice in the processing of personal data as appears to the Commissioner to be desirable having regard to the interests of the data subjects and others and includes (but is not limited to) compliance with the requirements of the Act'.

[4] See paras 7.27–7.29 below.

[5] See paras 7.39–7.44 below.

[6] See *De Falco v Silvestri* [1980] QB 460.

The Code of Practice on dealing with requests for information

7.09   The Lord Chancellor has issued a Code of Practice providing guidance to public authorities as to the practice which it would, in his opinion, be desirable for them to follow in connection with the discharge of the authorities' functions relating to the provision of access to information held by them.[7]

7.10   The Act specifies a non-exhaustive list of five areas as to which the Code of Practice must make provision. These are:

(a)   the provision of advice and assistance by public authorities to persons who propose to make, or have made, requests for information;

(b)   the transfer of requests for information between public authorities;

(c)   consultation with parties to whom the information requested relates or parties whose interests are likely to be affected by the disclosure of information;

(d)   the inclusion in public authority contracts of terms relating to the disclosure of information; and

(e)   the provision by public authorities of procedures for dealing with complaints about the handling by them of requests for information.[8]

7.11   Parliament has approved the Code of Practice on the Discharge of Public Authorities' Functions under Part I of the Act which was presented by the Lord Chancellor on 20 November 2002.[9] The Code of Practice provides guidance for each of the five specified areas.[10] It is preceded by a foreword which is not part of the Code itself. It also provides guidance in relation to the timeliness of dealing with requests for information; guidance on fees and guidance on receiving information in confidence from third parties.

7.12   The Code of Practice may be revised from time to time[11] and may make different provision for different public authorities.[12] The Lord Chancellor must consult the Information Commissioner before revising the Code of Practice.[13] Any revision to the Code of Practice must be laid before both Houses of Parliament.[14]

---

[7]   Section 45(1) of the Act.

[8]   ibid, s 45(2)(a) to (e).

[9]   The Code of Practice is available from the Lord Chancellor's website at http://www.lcd. gov.uk/foi/codesprac.htm. The Code of Practice is reproduced at Appendix D.

[10]   See paras 5.133–5.139 above (advice and assistance); paras 5.99–5.100 above (transfers); paras 7.58–7.66 (complaints procedure); 5.147–5.149 above (contract terms); paras 7.120–7.136 (consultation with third parties).

[11]   Section 45(1) of the Act.

[12]   ibid, s 45(3). For example, it might be desirable for a smaller public authority to have a less extensive complaints procedure.

[13]   ibid, s 45(4).

[14]   ibid, s 45(5).

The Code of Practice on record-keeping

The Lord Chancellor has issued a Code of Practice providing guidance to relevant **7.13** authorities as to the practice which it would, in his opinion, be desirable for them to follow in connection with the keeping, management and destruction of their records.[15] A relevant authority is a public authority or a body which is not a public authority but whose administrative and departmental records are public records.[16] There is a Code of Practice which has been made available. Chapter 8 deals with this aspect of the Act and this Code of Practice in detail.[17]

The Code of Practice may be revised from time to time[18] and may make different **7.14** provision for different relevant authorities.[19] The Lord Chancellor is obliged to consult the Information Commissioner (and, in relation to Northern Ireland, the appropriate Northern Ireland Minister), before revising any Code of Practice.[20] Any revision to the Code of Practice must be laid before both Houses of Parliament.

C. Information Commissioner

Introduction

The Information Commissioner is the independent office holder who was for- **7.15** merly known as the Data Protection Commissioner.[21] The first Information Commissioner is the former Data Protection Commissioner, Elizabeth France. Richard Thomas of Clifford Chance has been named to succeed Elizabeth France with effect from 2 December 2002.

The White Paper expressed the view that the appointment of an independent of- **7.16** fice holder was preferable to an officer accountable to Parliament (like the Parliamentary Ombudsman under the Code of Practice on Access to Government Information) because of the wide application of the Act, which extends to bodies which are not directly accountable to Parliament. Further, it guarantees independence in the exercise of the Information Commissioner's functions.[22] The establishment of the post of Information Commissioner reflects the practice adopted

---

[15] ibid, s 46(1).

[16] ibid, s 46(7). Public records, in this context, means records which are public records for the purposes of the Public Records Act 1958 or the Public Records Act (Northern Ireland) 1923.

[17] The Code of Practice is available from the Lord Chancellor's website at http://www.lcd. gov.uk/foi/codesprac.htm. The Code of Practice is reproduced at Appendix E.

[18] Section 46(1) of the Act.

[19] ibid, s 46(4).

[20] ibid, s 46(5).

[21] ibid, s 18; s 6(1), Data Protection Act 1998 as amended by Sch 2 to the 2000 Act.

[22] White Paper, *Your Right to Know* etc (Cm 3818, 1997) para 5.7.

in a number of other jurisdictions.[23] Adopting this system, rather than having the legislation administered solely by the courts, makes the procedure for challenging decisions of public authorities cheaper and more readily available. Further, the Information Commissioner can and does have a more extended rôle than merely enforcing the legislation: he is also responsible for promoting, monitoring and reporting on freedom of information.

7.17 The Act amended the Data Protection Act 1998 such that the Data Protection Commissioner became the Information Commissioner.[24] The Information Commissioner, therefore, has the dual rôle of enforcing and promoting both freedom of information and data protection. This was not envisaged in the White Paper.[25] It is readily seen that the two regimes have aims which have the potential to conflict.[26] In the Information Commissioner's annual report for the year ending 31 March 2001, it was stated:

> On 30th January 2001 I took responsibility for freedom of information. . . At this stage there is little to report . . . The significant change is that the UK does now have two sets of statutory rights and obligations which I said last year I considered to be important if we are to ensure that public bodies give due weight to both the public's right to know and the individual's right to respect for private life. There will be difficult decisions to take at the interface. Those will present challenges for my Office once individual rights under the Freedom of Information Act are in place.[27]

7.18 As was indicated above, the Information Commissioner has the greatest responsibility for the effective implementation of freedom of information. The Information Commissioner expects the staff to double in number over five years and has £5million to spend on information technology over two years.[28]

7.19 The Information Commissioner's rôle falls to be analysed in two parts:

(a) in the context of a specific request for information, the Information Commissioner is the first arbiter of whether or not a public authority has complied with the Act in refusing to disclose information and his decision has similar effect to a court order; and

---

[23] For example, in New Zealand, the Ombudsman under the Official Information Act 1982. By contrast, in the United States of America under the Freedom of Information Act, responsibility for enforcing freedom of information is that of the courts alone. See further ch 9.

[24] Section 18 and Sch 2 to the 2000 Act, in particular paras 13–21. The office of Information Commissioner is regulated by the Data Protection Act 1998, Sch 5.

[25] Cm 3818 (n 22 above) paras 4.12–4.13.

[26] The most important interface between the freedom of information regime and the data protection regime is Section 40 of the Act.

[27] Annual Report of the Information Commissioner for the Year Ending 31 March 2001, Commissioner's Foreword.

[28] Annual Report of the Information Commissioner for the Year Ending 31 March 2001, 17.

(b) generally, he is to promote compliance with and raise awareness of the rights and obligations under the Act.[29]

The first aspect of the rôle will be considered in detail later in this chapter in part D. It is convenient to analyse the second aspect of the rôle by considering, first, the obligations and then the powers conferred upon the Information Commissioner to fulfil those obligations.

Statutory obligations of the Information Commissioner

The Information Commissioner has a statutory duty to promote the following of **7.20** good practice by public authorities and, in particular, to perform his functions under the Act so as to promote the observance by public authorities of the re-quirements of the Act and the provisions of the Codes of Practice.[30] The Information Commissioner has targeted an initial level of awareness for public authorities of their obligations under the Act of 14.0 per cent by March 2002[31] and 25.0 per cent by March 2003.[32]

Good practice includes, but is not limited to, compliance with the Codes of **7.21** Practice issued by the Lord Chancellor. The Information Commissioner is enti-tled to be consulted by the Lord Chancellor in relation to the drafting of the Codes of Practice.[33]

The Information Commissioner is obliged to arrange for the dissemination of **7.22** information to the public about the operation of the Act, good practice and any other matters within the scope of his functions.[34] The Information Commissioner has targeted a level of awareness for individuals of their rights under the Act of 11.0 per cent by March 2002[35] and 15.0 per cent by March 2003.[36]

The Information Commissioner is also responsible for the approval of public au- **7.23** thorities' publication schemes and may approve model publication schemes.[37]

---

[29] In the White Paper, Cm 3818 (n 22 above) para 1.7, 'there will be an independent Information Commissioner, who will police the Act, and handle appeals.'

[30] Section 47(1) of the Act. Compare the duty of the Information Commissioner under s 51, Data Protection Act 1998 namely (a) promoting good practice and observance of the Data Protection Act 1998 by data controllers; (b) encouraging the development of Codes of Practice for guidance as to good practice; (c) disseminating information about the Act.

[31] Annual Report of the Information Commissioner for the Year Ending 31 March 2001, 49.

[32] Annual Report of the Information Commissioner for the Year Ending 31 March 2002, 31.

[33] Sections 45(5) and 46(5)(b) of the Act.

[34] ibid, s 47(2). The Information Commissioner's website is currently at www.dataprotection. gov.uk

[35] Annual Report (n 31 above) 49.

[36] ibid, 31.

[37] Sections 19 and 20 of the Act. Publication schemes are discussed in detail in ch 5 above at paras 5.90–5.104.

7.24 The Information Commissioner is obliged to lay annually before each House of Parliament a general report on the exercise of his functions under the Act[38] and may lay before Parliament such other reports as he thinks fit.[39] There is a similar provision under the Data Protection Act 1998.[40] The Information Commissioner has published a combined report for the years ending March 2001 and March 2002 under both the Data Protection Act 1998 and the Freedom of Information Act 2000.

7.25 The Information Commissioner is a public authority to whom the provisions of the Act apply.[41]

Statutory powers of the Information Commissioner

Practice assessments

7.26 The Information Commissioner may, with the consent of any public authority, assess whether the authority is following good practice.[42] It can be seen that such an assessment could be initiated either by the Information Commissioner to assess compliance with good practice, or by a public authority in order to obtain an audit of their information procedures to ensure that they are compliant with the Act. The Act makes provision for the Information Commissioner to charge for an assessment of whether a public authority is complying with good practice.[43] It is, perhaps, surprising that the Information Commissioner requires the consent of a public authority before undertaking an assessment of the public authority's good practice. A public authority's withholding of consent would, doubtless, be a matter which the Information Commissioner would report to Parliament in the annual general report.[44] By contrast, under the Data Protection Act 1998,[45] any member of the public can request that the Information Commissioner carry out an assessment of whether a data controller was complying with the provisions of that Act. On receiving such a request, the Information Commissioner is obliged to carry out such an assessment.

Practice recommendations

7.27 If it appears to the Information Commissioner that the practice of a public authority does not conform with the Codes of Practice he may issue a practice recommendation specifying the steps which ought in his opinion to be taken for

---

[38] Section 49(1) of the Act.
[39] ibid, s 49(2).
[40] Data Protection Act 1998, s 52(1), (2).
[41] Schedule 1, Part VI of the 2000 Act.
[42] Section 47(3) of the Act.
[43] ibid, s 47(4).
[44] Under ibid, s 49 (see para 7.24 above).
[45] Data Protection Act 1998, s 42.

promoting such conformity.[46] A practice recommendation must be in writing and refer to the particular provisions of the relevant Code of Practice.[47] The Information Commissioner is required to consult the Keeper of the Public Records (or the Deputy Keeper of the Records of Northern Ireland) before giving a practice recommendation relating to conformity with the Lord Chancellor's Code of Practice on record-keeping.[48] The Act is silent as to the consequences of a public authority failing to comply with a practice recommendation. In contrast to non-compliance with a decision notice, information notice or an enforcement notice,[49] it is not a contempt of court for a public authority not to comply with a practice recommendation. It would seem, in principle, open to the Information Commissioner to issue judicial review proceedings for an order of mandamus to compel a public authority to comply with a practice recommendation. One would expect the issuing of practice recommendations and any failures by public authorities to comply with practice recommendations to be matters to which the Information Commissioner will refer in the annual report. The foreword to the Code of Practice states in relation to practice recommendations:

> A practice recommendation is simply a recommendation and cannot be enforced by the Information Commissioner. However, a failure to comply with a practice recommendation may lead to a failure to comply with the Act. Further, a failure to take account of a practice recommendation may lead to an adverse comment in a report to Parliament by the Commissioner.[50]

7.28 This view is confirmed by the following statement from Lord Bassam of Brighton (Labour) on behalf of the government at the Committee Stage in the House of Lords:

> I fully accept that compliance with the published codes of practice would not be enforceable in the courts in the same way that a statutory duty might be. As the provision is drafted, the information commissioner has the power to look at compliance and issue practice recommendations. I believe it would be an exceptional authority which wilfully ignored such a recommendation, particularly given the commissioner's powers to name and shame in any report that she might make to Parliament. An additional point is that the code of practice could be referred to in any test case which was the subject of judicial review. The power of naming and shaming should not be underestimated in regard to public sector bodies keen to keep the confidence of the public they serve.[51]

7.29 It should be emphasized that it is through practice recommendations rather than enforcement notices that the Information Commissioner will promote

---

[46] Section 48(1) of the 2000 Act.
[47] ibid, s 48(2).
[48] ibid, s 48(3) and 48(4).
[49] Under ibid, ss 50, 51 and 52 respectively (see paras 7.67–7.77; 7.31–7.38; 7.39–7.44 below).
[50] Paragraph 6 of the Foreword to the Code of Practice under ibid, s 45.
[51] *Hansard*, HL (series 5) vol 617, col 944 (17 October 2000).

compliance with the Codes of Practice. An enforcement notice can only be served by the Information Commissioner in relation to a failure to comply with any of the requirements of Part I of the Act.[52]

Decision notices

7.30   A person who is dissatisfied with a public authority's response to a request for information may apply to the Information Commissioner for a decision notice.[53] Decision notices can only be issued in the context of an individual request for information and are, therefore, discussed in part D below, under the heading 'Enforcement'.

Information notices

7.31   If the Information Commissioner has received an application for a decision[54] or requires any information for the purpose of determining whether a public authority has complied with or is complying with any of the requirements of Part I of the Act or either of the Codes of Practice,[55] he may serve an information notice on the public authority.[56] An information notice will thus either be served in the context of a particular request for information by a particular applicant or will be served on the Information Commissioner's own initiative. An information notice may require the public authority to provide the Information Commissioner with information relating to the application or to compliance with Part I of the Act or the Codes of Practice.[57] The information notice will specify the period within which the public authority is required to supply the information and may specify the form in which the Information Commissioner requires the information to be provided.[58]

7.32   Where the information notice is served in the context of an application for a decision, the information notice must contain a statement that the Information Commissioner has received such an application.[59] No further details of the application need be given. The Information Commissioner does not need to state why he wants the information.

7.33   If the information notice is served for the purpose of determining whether a public authority has complied with or is complying with any of the requirements of Part I or either of the Codes of Practice, the information notice must state that the Information Commissioner regards the information as relevant to such a determination and must give reasons why the Information Commissioner regards the

---

[52]   Section 52(1) of the Act.
[53]   Section 50 and paras 7.67–7.77 below.
[54]   Under s 50.
[55]   Under ss 45 or 46.
[56]   ibid, s 51(1). Compare Data Protection Act 1998, s 43.
[57]   Section 51(1) of the 2000 Act.
[58]   ibid.
[59]   ibid, s 51(2)(a).

information as relevant to that determination.[60] It has been seen above that the Information Commissioner may carry out a practice assessment to assess whether a public authority is following good practice but only with the consent of the public authority.[61] However, the power to serve information notices to determine whether or not a public authority is complying with the Act or the Code of Guidance seems, on the face of it, unlimited. The Information Commissioner has confirmed the view that there is no limit on the Information Commissioner's power to serve information notices.

In the context of an information notice, 'information' includes unrecorded **7.34** information[62] including, for example, the state of knowledge of officers of the public authority.

There is a right of appeal to the Information Tribunal against an information **7.35** notice.[63] The information notice must give particulars of the right of appeal.[64]

Any time period specified in an information notice for compliance with a re- **7.36** quirement to provide information must not expire before the end of the period within which an appeal can be brought against the notice. If an appeal is brought, the public authority does not need to furnish the information until the outcome of the appeal.[65]

An information notice cannot require the disclosure of information in respect of **7.37** any communication between a professional legal adviser and his client (a) in connection with the giving of legal advice to the client with respect to his obligations, liabilities or rights under the Act; or (b) made in connection with or in contemplation of proceedings under or arising out of the Act.[66]

If a public authority in receipt of an information notice fails to comply with **7.38** it within the specified time period, the public authority can be made subject to proceedings for contempt of court.[67]

Enforcement notices

The Information Commissioner can serve on a public authority an enforcement **7.39** notice requiring the authority to take such steps as may be specified, if he is 'satisfied' that a public authority has failed to comply with any of the requirements of

---

[60] ibid, s 51(2)(b).

[61] ibid, s 47(3). 'Good practice' includes but is not limited to compliance with the Act and the Codes of Guidance.

[62] ibid, s 51(8). For the purposes of the rest of the Act, 'information' is defined by s 84 as 'information recorded in any form'.

[63] ibid, s 57.

[64] ibid, s 51(3).

[65] ibid, s 51(4).

[66] ibid, s 51(5).

[67] ibid, s 54. Contrast the specific offence created by the Data Protection Act 1998, s 47.

Part I of the Act.[68] It seems that whether or not the Information Commissioner does serve an enforcement notice in such circumstances is entirely at his discretion, subject to his statutory duty to promote compliance with the Act and the Codes of Practice. In the most recent Annual Report, the Information Commissioner has referred to the establishment of an Enforcement Board to decide whether or not enforcement action should proceed, on the basis of reasonable and consistent criteria.[69]

7.40 It should be noted that it is a precondition to the service of an enforcement notice that the Information Commissioner is satisfied that a breach of the Act has occurred; the Information Commissioner cannot serve an enforcement notice in relation to an anticipated breach of the Act. Further, the requirement that the Information Commissioner must be 'satisfied' that a breach of the Act has occurred, entails some threshold level of knowledge. It appears that this means that the Information Commissioner need not satisfy himself of the actual existence of the breach before issuing an enforcement notice, but must be able to show that it did appear to him that a breach had occurred.[70]

7.41 Significantly, the service of an enforcement notice is limited to enforcing the requirements of Part I; the Information Commissioner cannot serve an enforcement notice in relation to failure to comply with either of the Codes of Practice.[71]

7.42 The enforcement notice must contain a statement of the requirement or requirements of Part I with which the Information Commissioner is satisfied that the public authority has failed to comply and his reasons for reaching that conclusion.[72]

7.43 There is a right of appeal to the Information Tribunal against an enforcement notice.[73] The enforcement notice must inform the public authority of the right of appeal.[74] Any time period specified in the enforcement notice for complying with the enforcement notice must not expire before the end of the period within which an appeal can be brought against the enforcement notice.[75]

7.44 If a public authority in receipt of an enforcement notice fails to take the steps specified in it within the specified time, the public authority may be subject to proceedings for contempt of court.[76]

---

[68] Section 52 of the 2000 Act. Compare the Data Protection Act 1998, s 40.

[69] Annual Report of the Information Commissioner for the Year Ending March 2002, 13.

[70] See *R v Rochester City Council, ex p Hobday* [1989] 2 PLR 38, a decision relating to planning enforcement notices.

[71] Contrast an information notice under s 51 of the Act and a practice recommendation under s 48 of the Act.

[72] ibid, s 52(2)(a).

[73] ibid, s 57.

[74] ibid, s 52(2)(b).

[75] ibid, s 52(3).

[76] ibid, s 54. Contrast the specific offence created by the Data Protection Act 1998, s 47.

Search warrants

The Information Commissioner can apply to a circuit judge for a warrant en- **7.45**
abling him to enter premises and inspect documents.[77] The White Paper said the
following:

> There have been a number of cases overseas where public officials have deliberately
> altered, destroyed or withheld records from review. Although such cases are rare,
> and while there is no evidence of similar abuses having occurred under the Code [of
> Practice on Access to Governmental Information], we will therefore allow the
> Information Commissioner to apply for a warrant to enter and search premises and
> examine and remove records. . .[78]

The circuit judge must be satisfied by evidence on oath that there are reasonable **7.46**
grounds for suspecting:

(a) that a public authority has failed or is failing to comply with:
  (i) any of the requirements of Part I of the Act; or
  (ii) so much of a decision notice as requires steps to be taken; or
  (iii) an information notice or an enforcement notice; or
(b) that an offence of altering, defacing, blocking, erasing, destruction or concealment of records[79] is being committed.[80]

The circuit judge must also be satisfied that there are reasonable grounds for sus- **7.47**
pecting that evidence of such a failure to comply or of the commission of the
offence is to be found on any premises specified in the information.[81]

A warrant must not be issued unless the circuit judge is satisfied that the **7.48**
Information Commissioner:

(a) has given seven days' notice in writing to the occupier of the premises demanding access; and
(b) that either:
  (i) access was demanded at a reasonable hour and was unreasonably refused;
    or
  (ii) entry was granted, but the occupier unreasonably refused to allow the
    Information Commissioner to inspect or seize documents or inspect or
    operate equipment; and
(c) that the Information Commissioner has notified the occupier of the application for a warrant and the occupier has had the opportunity of being heard by

---

[77] Section 55 and Sch 3 to the 2000 Act. Compare the similar powers under the Data Protection
Act 1998, s 50, Sch 9. In the year ending March 2001, the search powers under the Data Protection
Act were exercised nine times.
[78] White Paper, *Your Right to Know* (n 22 above) para 5.14.
[79] Section 77 of the Act; see paras 7.118–7.119 below.
[80] ibid, Sch 3, para 1(1).
[81] ibid.

the circuit judge on the question of whether or not a warrant should be issued.[82]

7.49 However, if the circuit judge is satisfied that the case is one of urgency or that compliance with the above provisions would defeat the object of the entry, then those provisions do not apply.[83] In an appropriate case, therefore, the Information Commissioner can apply for a warrant without any notice.

7.50 The warrant authorizes the Information Commissioner to:

(a) enter and search the premises;

(b) to inspect and seize documents or other material found there which may be evidence of a failure to comply or the commission of an offence; and

(c) to inspect, examine, operate and test any equipment found there in which information held by the public authority may be recorded.[84]

7.51 It is an offence to obstruct the Information Commissioner in the execution of a warrant or to fail to give such assistance as is reasonably required without reasonable excuse.[85]

D. Enforcement

A comparison with other jurisdictions

7.52 Different jurisdictions have chosen different methods of enforcing an individual's 'right to know'. The various enforcement regimes are usually a combination of one or more of the following:

(a) an internal review by the public authority which has received the request for information. This may or may not be a mandatory precondition for pursuing other methods of reviewing a refusal;

(b) a review by an independent Commissioner or Ombudsman charged with the function of enforcing freedom of information legislation (ie a figure similar to the Information Commissioner). This decision may or may not be binding on the public authority;

(c) a right of 'appeal' to the judiciary. The nature of the 'appeal' may be a complete rehearing; a process akin to a judicial review; or a pure appeal on a point of law. The 'appeal' may be to a 'normal' court, a specialist tribunal, or an administrative court.

---

[82] Schedule 3, para 2(1) of the Act.
[83] ibid, Sch 3, para 2(2).
[84] ibid, Sch 3, para 1(2).
[85] ibid, Sch 3, para 12.

By way of brief summary,[86] the following jurisdictions have the following features: **7.53**

(a) France:
    (i) a complaint to the Commission (which is an obligatory precondition to bringing judicial proceedings) whose decision, however, is not binding on the public authority;
    (ii) an appeal to an administrative court akin to judicial review in that the function of the administrative court is to determine whether the public authority's decision was illegal and, if so, the public authority's decision will be quashed and it will be required to make a fresh decision.

(b) Canada:
    (i) a review by the Commissioner whose decision is not binding on the public authority;
    (ii) a judicial review.

(c) Ireland:
    (i) an internal review which is mandatory where it is available;
    (ii) a review by the Commissioner whose decision is binding on the parties;
    (iii) an appeal to the High Court on a point of law.

(d) Australia:
    (i) an internal review; and
    (ii) any of: an appeal to the Administrative Appeals Tribunal; a judicial review; or a review by the Ombudsman.

(e) Sweden: an appeal by way of a rehearing to a court (except in cases where the refusal is by Parliament or the government, in which case the appeal is to the government itself).

(f) New Zealand:
    (i) right of complaint to the Ombudsman; and thereafter
    (ii) judicial review.

(g) USA:
    (i) an internal review; and
    (ii) an appeal by way of rehearing to the courts who will substitute their own decision. Additionally, the court, if it is of the view that the withholding of information has been arbitrary or capricious, will initiate proceedings to determine whether or not disciplinary action is warranted against the employee or officer responsible.

As will be seen in more detail below, the UK has: **7.54**

(a) a mandatory internal review;
(b) a review by the Information Commissioner whose decision has legally binding effect on the public authority;

---

[86] For a fuller discussion of other jurisdictions, see chs 9 and 25 below.

(c) an appeal, by way of rehearing, to the Information Tribunal;

(d) an appeal on a point of law to the courts.

7.55 The effect of different combinations of these procedures is difficult to predict. It also depends, to a considerable extent, on other features of the legislation and judicial procedure in the jurisdiction in question and, moreover, on the degree to which public authorities embrace or reject the whole concept of freedom of information.

7.56 However, the following broad propositions appear to have held true:

(a) an excess of procedural stages leads to expense and delay in making information available;

(b) a right of recourse to the court only is likely to deter applicants from challenging refusals because of expense.

7.57 Two features of the regime under the Act call for immediate comment:

(a) the extensive appeal procedure, which may cause both delay and expense; but also

(b) the provision that a decision of the Information Commissioner has legally binding effect (which is a feature to be welcomed).

In relation to the first feature the White Paper stated:

> Overseas experience shows that where appeals are allowed to the Courts, a public authority which is reluctant to disclose information will often seek leave to appeal simply to delay the implementation of a decision.[87]

Complaints procedure

7.58 The first step for a person who is dissatisfied with a decision of a public authority is to exhaust any complaints procedure provided by the public authority in question. The advantages of an internal review procedure are stated in the White Paper *Your Right to Know*:

> Internal review will be the first step in the FOI appeals process. It will provide a quick, low cost and simple mechanism for resolving many complaints. It should also ease the burden on the Information Commissioner. . . Generally, an internal review will be a precondition for making a complaint to the Information Commissioner. . .[88]

7.59 A further advantage is that it enables a public authority to monitor its own decision-making.[89] There are, however, disadvantages. First, the necessity for an internal review may be questioned: it increases the time taken for a disclosure de-

---

[87] White Paper, *Your Right to Know* (n 22 above) para 5.17.

[88] ibid, para 5.8.

[89] See para 60, Code of Practice.

cision to be finally decided and adds to the administrative burden on public authorities. Secondly, it is likely to engender a culture of junior officers erring towards non-disclosure of information, with the reassurance that an erroneous decision against disclosure can be reversed by a more senior officer (whereas, of course, an erroneous decision to disclose cannot usually be reversed).

If a person has not exhausted the complaints procedure, the Information **7.60** Commissioner is entitled to refuse to entertain an application for a decision. Section 50(2) provides 'the Information Commissioner *shall* make a decision *unless* it appears . . . (a) that the complainant has not exhausted any complaints procedure which is provided by the public authority in conformity with the code of practice under section 45'. It is understood that the effect of this provision is that the Information Commissioner may, at his discretion, consider an application for a decision notwithstanding the fact that an internal complaints procedure has not been exhausted.[90]

The Lord Chancellor's Code of Practice relating to access to information provides **7.61** guidance to public authorities as to the provision of a complaints procedure.[91]

The Code of Practice provides that all public authorities should have in place a **7.62** complaints procedure for dealing with complaints from people who consider that their request has not been properly handled, or who are otherwise dissatisfied with the outcome of the consideration of their request, and the issue cannot be resolved in discussion with the official dealing with the request. The complaints procedure should be in place by the date on which its duties in respect of the publication scheme provisions of the Act come into effect.[92]

The complaints procedure must be communicated to an applicant when com- **7.63** municating any decision on a request for information.[93] It should provide a fair and impartial means of dealing with, handling problems and reviewing decisions and it should be possible to amend or reverse decisions previously taken.[94] Where practicable, the complaints procedure should be handled by a person who was not party to the original decision.[95] The complainant should be informed of the outcome of the complaints procedure but there is no requirement in the Code of Practice that the public authority give reasons for its decision after an internal review.[96]

---

[90] See also ibid, para 51.
[91] Section 45(2)(e) of the Act.
[92] Paragraph 52 of the Code of Practice. See ch 4 above for the timetable in accordance with which the Act will come into force. The provisions relating to publication schemes will be in force before the provisions relating to requests for information.
[93] Section 17(7) of the Act. Paragraph 54 of the Code of Practice.
[94] Paragraph 56 of the Code of Practice.
[95] ibid, para 57.
[96] ibid, para 58.

7.64 Public authorities should publish target times for dealing with complaints and information as to how successful they are in meeting those targets, and the Code of Practice further states that target times should be *'reasonable, defensible and subject to regular review'*.[97] However, the Code of Practice does not specify time limits within which a public authority must come to a decision. The Code of Practice provides:

> In all cases . . . the complainant should be informed of the authority's target for determining the complaint. Where it is apparent that determination of the complaint will take longer than the target time. . . the authority should inform the applicant and explain the reason for the delay.[98]

The lack of a fixed time limit is, perhaps, surprising given the strict 20-day time limit for compliance with a request.[99] It gives rise to the possibility of a public authority delaying the further process of a request by failing to carry out their complaints procedure speedily.[100] It may be that, where an applicant has requested an internal review, but the internal review decision has been unreasonably delayed, the applicant may nevertheless proceed to ask the Information Commissioner for a decision notice.[101] Otherwise, in order to compel a public authority to carry out the internal complaints procedure, it appears that an applicant would have to proceed by way of judicial review.[102]

7.65 Records should be kept of complaints and their outcomes and public authorities should monitor these records and, if appropriate, change their policies if decisions are being regularly reversed. Where the outcome of a complaint is that the public authority's procedures have not been followed by an individual, the authority should apologize to the applicant. Where the outcome of a complaint is that the original decision is upheld, the applicant should be informed of his right to apply to the Commissioner for a decision and be given details of how to make an application.[103]

7.66 Given that the internal review will be by the public authority which has refused the request for information, it might, with some justification, be said that an internal review will never be fair and impartial. The internal review procedure will not, however, contravene Article 6 of the European Convention on Human

---

[97] Paragraph 59 of the Code of Practice.

[98] ibid, para 58.

[99] Section 10 of the Act.

[100] The White Paper, *Your Right to Know* (n 22 above) stated 'We see independent review and appeal as essential to our Freedom of Information Act. We favour a mechanism which is readily available, freely accessible, and quick to use, capable of resolving complaints in weeks not months.'

[101] Since the complaints procedure will not be in conformity with the Code of Practice; see s 50(2)(a).

[102] Section 50(2)(a) entitles the Information Commissioner to refuse an application for a decision notice until the complainant has exhausted the complaints procedure.

[103] Paragraphs 60 to 63 of the Code of Practice.

Rights because there is a right of application to the Information Commissioner for a decision as to whether the request has been dealt with in accordance with the Act and the subsequent right of appeal to the Information Tribunal (who can review findings of fact).[104]

Application for decision by the Information Commissioner

A person who has made a request for information may apply to the Information **7.67** Commissioner for a decision whether, in any specified respect, the request has been dealt with in accordance with the requirements of Part I of the Act.[105] It should be noted that it appears that the application can only be made by the person who has made the request; an application cannot be made, for example, by a third party who feels that information was disclosed which should not have been.

An application to the Information Commissioner for a decision can be made in **7.68** respect of any alleged failure to comply with the requirements of Part I. The most common complaint will be that the public authority has wrongly refused a request for information, relying on section 1(1) of the Act. However, an application to the Information Commissioner could be grounded on, for example, an excessive fee,[106] a failure to make a decision within the specified time limits,[107] an unjustifiable failure to provide the information in the applicant's preferred form,[108] a failure to provide advice and assistance[109] or a failure to specify the exemption on which a refusal is based or why that exemption applies.[110]

The Information Commissioner is required to make a decision on an application **7.69** unless it appears to him:

    (a) that the complainant has not exhausted any complaints procedure which is provided by the local authority in conformity with the [Lord Chancellor's] code of practice under section 45;
    (b) that there has been undue delay in making the application;
    (c) that the application is frivolous or vexatious; or
    (d) that the application has been withdrawn or abandoned.[111]

'Undue delay' is not defined under the Act but it seems likely that the 20-day time limit for processing an application and the time limit for appealing to the Information Tribunal would be relevant to construing 'undue delay'. The phrase 'frivolous or vexatious' is familiar in relation to the former power to strike out cases

---

[104] See *R v Secretary of State for Environment, Transport and the Regions, ex p Alconbury Developments Ltd* [2001] UKHL 23.
[105] Section 50(1) of the Act.
[106] ibid, s 9.
[107] ibid, s 10.
[108] ibid, s 11.
[109] ibid, s 16.
[110] ibid, s 17.
[111] ibid, s 50(2).

under Order 18, rule 19(1)(b) of the Rules of the Supreme Court.[112] There is a similar provision in the New Zealand freedom of information legislation.[113] Section 14 of the (UK) 2000 Act provides that a public authority is not obliged to answer a 'vexatious' request for information.

7.70   The Information Commissioner must either notify the complainant that he has not made a decision for any of the above reasons or must serve a 'decision notice' on the complainant and the public authority.[114] Notably, the Information Commissioner is under no statutory obligation to provide reasons with the decision notice.[115]

7.71   For the purposes of making a decision, the Information Commissioner may require the public authority to make any information available that he wants by serving an information notice.[116]

7.72   If the Information Commissioner decides that a public authority has either (a) failed to communicate information, or to provide confirmation or denial, in a case where it is required to do so by section 1(1), or (b) has failed to comply with any of the requirements of section 11 (the means by which communication of information is to be made) and section 17 (refusal of request), the decision notice must specify the steps which must be taken by the authority for complying with that requirement and the period within which they must be taken.[117]

7.73   It is clear that the Information Commissioner's review is by way of rehearing. The Information Commissioner will not only decide whether or not a particular request falls within an exemption but will also come to his own view as to where the public interest lies. For example, if a public authority refuses to disclose information on the basis that disclosure would be prejudicial to health and safety,[118] the Information Commissioner can substitute his own view as to whether or not the disclosure would be prejudicial to health and safety and can also substitute his own view as to whether or not the public interest in disclosure outweighs that prejudice.

7.74   There are no adverse consequences for a public authority if its decision is reversed by the Information Commissioner other than the reversal itself. There are no costs

---

[112] The phrase is not retained in CPR 3.4 but it is likely that there remains an inherent jurisdiction to strike out claims which are frivolous or vexatious; most frivolous or vexatious claims will be an abuse of the court's process and liable to be struck out under CPR 3.4(2)(b).

[113] Section 18(h), Official Information Act 1982 is in similar terms. The Ombudsmen have issued guidance as to the interpretation of that provision by reference to English and New Zealand case law on striking out (Practice Guideline Number 9).

[114] Section 50(3) of the 2000 Act.

[115] Contrast s 51(2)(b) of the Act (information notices); and s 52(1)(a) (enforcement notices).

[116] See paras 7.31–7.38 above.

[117] Section 50(4) of the Act.

[118] The exemption in ibid, s 38.

consequences since the application for a review by the Information Commissioner is a free procedure. This may well be contrasted with the position under, for example, the United States Freedom of Information Act where the court has the power to order disciplinary action against an officer or employee of a public authority who has acted capriciously or arbitrarily in refusing information.[119]

Both the complainant and the public authority have a right of appeal to the Information Tribunal.[120] The decision notice must contain particulars of the right of appeal.[121] **7.75**

Any time period specified in a decision notice for compliance with a requirement must not expire before the end of the period within which an appeal can be brought against the notice. If an appeal is brought, the public authority does not have to carry out any of the steps which would be affected by the appeal until the outcome of the appeal.[122] **7.76**

If a public authority is served with a decision notice which requires steps to be taken and the public authority fails to take those steps within the specified timescale, the public authority may be subjected to proceedings for contempt of Court.[123] **7.77**

E. Appeals

Introduction

So far as the White Paper was concerned, the rôle of the courts in a request for information was limited to judicial review of the Information Commissioner: **7.78**

> We do not propose that there should be a right of appeal to the Courts. However, a disclosure order of the Information Commissioner (or a decision not to grant an order) would be subject to judicial review (the question of whether the Commissioner has properly exercised his or her powers in reaching a reasonable decision. This is in contrast to a right of appeal to the courts on the substantive question of whether the decision was the right one or not.). We have decided to take this approach because we believe it to be in the best interests of the FOI applicant. Overseas experience shows that where appeals are allowed to the Courts, a public authority which is reluctant to disclose information will often seek leave to appeal simply to delay the implementation of a decision. The cost of making an appeal to the courts would also favour the public authority over the individual applicant.[124]

---

[119] Freedom of Information Act 1966, 5 USC sec 522.
[120] The right of appeal is conferred by s 57 of the 2000 Act.
[121] ibid, s 50(5).
[122] ibid, s 56(6).
[123] ibid, s 54.
[124] White Paper, *Your Right to Know* (n 22 above) para 5.16.

7.79 In contrast to the proposals in the White Paper, the Act provides for both an appeal by way of rehearing from the Information Commissioner's decision to the Information Tribunal and a further appeal on a point of law to the High Court.

Appeals against notices

7.80 Both the complainant and the public authority in question have a right of appeal to the Information Tribunal against a decision notice.[125] A public authority also has a right of appeal to the Information Tribunal against an information notice or an enforcement notice.[126]

7.81 The Information Tribunal will allow the appeal if it finds that the notice against which the appeal is brought is not in accordance with the law or, to the extent that the notice involved an exercise of discretion by the Information Commissioner, he ought to have exercised his discretion differently.[127] The Information Tribunal may review any finding of fact on which the notice in question was based.[128] In effect, therefore, the Information Tribunal is the final arbiter, subject to the 'executive override',[129] of all questions of fact and discretion including, for example, where the public interest lies (since subsequent appeals are limited to points of law). This is to be welcomed since the Information Tribunal is pre-eminently well-qualified to decide on such questions since it both comprises specialists in this area and represents the interests of those who request information and public authorities equally.[130]

7.82 It should be noted that the Information Tribunal has power to substitute such other notice as could have been served by the Information Commissioner. A similar power under the Data Protection Act 1998 has been used on a number of occasions to vary an enforcement notice under that Act, where the scope of the enforcement notice went beyond that which was required to prevent breaches of data protection principles.[131]

7.83 The Information Tribunal is the body formerly known as the Data Protection Tribunal.[132] The Data Protection Act 1998 is amended accordingly.[133]

---

[125] Section 57(1) of the Act.
[126] ibid, s 57(2).
[127] ibid, s 58(1). Similarly, s 49(1), Data Protection Act 1998.
[128] Section 58(2) of the 2000 Act. Similarly, s 49(2), Data Protection Act 1998.
[129] Section 53 of the 2000 Act. See paras 7.103–7.108 below.
[130] See para 7.84 below.
[131] See, for example, *CCN Systems Limited v CCN Credit Systems Limited* Case DA/90 25/49/9. (The judgment can be found in the *Encyclopaedia of Data Protection*.)
[132] Section 18 of the 2000 Act; s 6(3), Data Protection Act 1998 as amended by Sch 2 to the 2000 Act.
[133] Schedules 2 and 4 of the 2000 Act.

The Information Tribunal consists of a chairman and an equal number of mem-   **7.84**
bers appointed to represent the interests of those who make requests for information and persons to represent the interests of public authorities.[134] An appeal is
decided by a majority of the members hearing the appeal.[135]

The Lord Chancellor may make rules for governing the procedure of the   **7.85**
Information Tribunal.[136] The Lord Chancellor has made rules of procedure for
appeals in data protection matters.[137]

The Lord Chancellor published in March 2002 a *Consultation Paper on Proposals for*   **7.86**
New Procedural Rules for Appeals and Hearings before the Information Tribunal. The
Consultation Paper contained suggested draft procedural rules applicable to both
appeals under the Freedom of Information Act 2000 and the Data Protection Act
1998.[138] It contained a notable provision (in paragraphs 26 and 27) that the default
position for freedom of information appeals is that they are to be before Parliament
heard on paper only. However, on 1 November 2002, the Lord Chancellor laid
before parliament the Information Tribunal (Enforcement Appeals) (Amendment)
Rules 2002[139] which simply had the effect of extending the ambit of the existing
Data Protection Tribunal (Enforcement Appeals) Rules 2000 to both freedom of
information and data protection appeals. It may be inferred that this is a temporary
measure, brought about by the necessity to have the procedural rules in place by the
time that publication schemes are required for some public authorities, and that
more extensively amended rules will follow in the near future.

---

[134] Data Protection Act 1998, Sch 6, para 4(1A), 2, as amended by the 2000 Act, Sch 4, para 3.
The Data Protection Act 1998, s 6(6) is amended by the 2000 Act, Sch 2, para 12, to cater for the
appointment of members to represent the interests of applicants and members to represent the
interests of public authorities.

[135] Data Protection Act 1998, Sch 6, para 5.

[136] Data Protection Act 1998, Sch 6, para 7, as amended by the 2000 Act, Sch 4, para 4. Under
the Data Protection Act 1998, it was provided that the rules may, in particular, make provision as
to (a) the period in which an appeal can be brought and the burden of proof on an appeal; (b) the
summoning of witnesses; (c) securing production of documents and material; (d) the operation and
testing of any equipment or material; (e) the hearing of an appeal wholly or partly in private; (f) the
hearing of an appeal in the absence of the appellant or determining an appeal without a hearing; (g)
enabling an appeal against an information notice to be determined by the chairman or deputy chairman; (h) enabling preliminary issues to be dealt with by the chairman or deputy chairman; (i) costs;
(j) the publication of reports of decisions; (k) such ancillary powers as thought necessary. The
amendments in the 2000 Act add provision for: (aa) joinder of third parties; (bb) directing that an
appeal under the Act be heard together with an appeal under the Data Protection Act 1998.

[137] The Data Protection Tribunal (Enforcement Appeals) Rules 2000, SI 2000/189.

[138] See the Lord Chancellor's *Consultation Paper on Proposals for New Procedural Rules for Appeals
and Hearings before the Information Tribunal* (March 2002): 'We propose to produce a single set of
rules that will cover both appeals under the Data Protection Act 1998 and appeals under the
Freedom of Information Act 2000. We consider that appeals made under either legislation are not
sufficiently distinguishable to necessitate two different sets of rules and that it will be less confusing
and more logical for there to be only one set of rules in operation. We welcome views on this proposal.' (para 3).

[139] SI 2002/2722 which came into force on 30 November 2002.

7.87 Under the Data Protection Tribunal (Enforcement Appeals) Rules 2000, the power to award costs is limited to cases where the appeal or the decision was manifestly unreasonable or where a party has acted frivolously, vexatiously, improperly or unreasonably or has failed to comply with directions or has caused avoidable delay.[140]

7.88 There is no statutory time limit for bringing an appeal to the Information Tribunal. The procedural rules in the subordinate legislation provide for the time limit. Under the Data Protection Tribunal (Enforcement Appeals) Rules 2000, the time limit is 28 days from the date of service of the notice, although the Information Tribunal has a discretion to allow an appeal after the expiry of the time limit.

7.89 If a public authority brings an appeal, it is not obliged to carry out any steps required by a decision notice, information notice or enforcement notice until the determination of the appeal.[141]

Appeal to the High Court

7.90 Any party[142] to an appeal to the Information Tribunal may appeal to the High Court on a point of law.

7.91 The procedure is governed by the Civil Procedure Rules Part 52. Permission to appeal is not required. An appeal notice must be filed at the High Court within 28 days after the date of the decision of the Information Tribunal.[143] The appellant is also required to serve a copy of the appeal notice on the Information Tribunal.[144]

7.92 The appeal to the High Court is on a point of law. The High Court will not interfere with a finding of fact of the Information Tribunal or the exercise of discretion by the Information Tribunal save in the most exceptional circumstances.[145]

7.93 In contrast to an appeal to the Information Tribunal, an appeal to the High Court does not automatically suspend the effect of the notice in question. Prima facie, a public authority is obliged to comply with the notice in question under threat of contempt proceedings, even if it has lodged an appeal in the High Court.

---

[140] Data Protection Tribunal (Enforcement Appeals) Rules 2000 (n 137 above) reg 25.

[141] Freedom of Information Act 2000, ss 50(6) (decision notices); 51(4) (information notices); 52(3) (enforcement notices).

[142] This might include not only the public authority and the person requesting the information, but also a third party provided that they were a party to the proceedings in the Information Tribunal (see para 7.132 below).

[143] Practice Direction to CPR Part 52: PD (52) 17.3. If a statement of reasons follows the decision, the time limit is calculated from the date on which the statement is received by the appellant.

[144] PD (52) 17.5.

[145] CPR 52.11. *Tanfern Limited v Cameron MacDonald (Practice Note)* [2000] 1 WLR 1311.

An appeal from the High Court lies to the Court of Appeal but only with the per- **7.94**
mission of the Court of Appeal, which will not be forthcoming unless the appeal
raises an important point of principle or practice or there is some other compelling reason for the Court of Appeal to hear it.[146]

National security appeals

The Act makes specific and separate provision for an appeal against a national se- **7.95**
curity certificate[147] to the Information Tribunal which is available either to the
Information Commissioner or to any applicant whose request for information is
affected by the issue of the certificate.

The Act provides for two types of national security certificate. A national secu- **7.96**
rity certificate is a certificate signed by a Minister of the Crown which either (1)
certifies that information to which it applies has been supplied by one of a number of specified bodies which deal with security matters (for example, GCHQ,
the Secret Intelligence Service or the special forces), or (2) that information to
which it applies must be exempted for the purpose of safeguarding national
security.[148]

In relation to the former type of national security certificate, the Information **7.97**
Tribunal may quash the certificate if it finds that the relevant information was not
exempt information, because it was not, supplied by one of the specified bodies
dealing with national security.[149]

In relation to the latter type of national security certificate, the Information **7.98**
Tribunal may quash the certificate if the Minister of the Crown did not have reasonable grounds for issuing the certificate, applying the principles of judicial review.[150]

In addition to the rights of appeal identified above, in relation to the latter type of **7.99**
national security certificate, if the certificate identifies the relevant information by
way of a general description, any party to proceedings under the Act may appeal
to the Information Tribunal, which may determine that the certificate does not
apply to the information in question.

The Lord Chancellor is required to appoint, from amongst the chairman and **7.100**
deputy chairmen, persons who are capable of hearing national security appeals

---

[146] *Colley v Council for Licensed Conveyancers* (CA, 17 July 2001); *Tanfern Limited v Cameron MacDonald* [2000] 1 WLR 1311. Access to Justice Act 1999, s 55(1). *Clark (Inspector of Taxes) v Perks* [2000] 4 All ER 1. CPR 52.13.
[147] Section 60 of the Act.
[148] ibid, ss 23 and 24.
[149] ibid, s 60(2).
[150] ibid, s 60(3).

(under both the Act and the Data Protection Act). A national security appeal will be heard by three of these designated persons.[151]

7.101 On 1 October 2001, the National Security Information Tribunal heard its first appeal (under section 28(4) of the Data Protection Act 1998), in the case of *Baker v Secretary of State for the Home Department*,[152] where the Tribunal quashed a national security certificate because it was too wide in its terms.

7.102 No appeal lies beyond the Information Tribunal on a national security matter.

F. The Ministerial Veto

7.103 In the ordinary course of a request under the Act and subject to rights of appeal to the Information Tribunal and the courts, the Information Commissioner is the final arbiter as to whether or not information is to be disclosed (subject to an appeal on a point of law). Section 53 of the Act creates a controversial exception, which has been referred to in the Information Commissioner's media release as the 'executive override'. A decision notice or enforcement notice ceases to have effect if, no later than 20 days after the effective date, an 'accountable person' in relation to the public authority certifies in writing that he has, on reasonable grounds, formed the opinion that there was no failure to disclose.[153] An 'accountable person' is either a Minister of the Crown who is a member of the Cabinet or the Attorney-General.[154]

7.104 The 'executive override' is limited to requests to governmental departments and the Welsh National Assembly but may be extended to other public authorities by order of the Lord Chancellor.[155]

7.105 The accountable person must lay a copy of the certificate before Parliament.[156] The accountable person, on or as soon as reasonably practicable after giving such a certificate, must inform the complainant of the reasons for his opinion[157] save in so far as giving reasons would involve the disclosure of exempt information.[158]

---

[151] Data Protection Act 1998, Sch 6, paras 2, 3, as amended by the 2000 Act, Sch 4.

[152] [2001] UKHRR 1275.

[153] Section 53(2) of the Act.

[154] ibid, s 53(8). In Northern Ireland, the accountable person is the First Minister and deputy First Minister acting jointly. In Wales, the accountable person is the Assembly First Secretary.

[155] ibid, s 53(1). Section 53(5) provides that where such an order relates to a Welsh public authority, the Northern Ireland Assembly or a Northern Ireland public authority, the Secretary of State is obliged to consult with the Welsh National Assembly, the Presiding Officer of the Northern Ireland Assembly or the First Minister and deputy First Minister in Northern Ireland, respectively.

[156] ibid, s 53(3), or the Welsh National Assembly or the Northern Ireland Assembly, as appropriate.

[157] ibid, s 53(6).

[158] ibid, s 53(7).

The requirement to lay a copy of the certificate before Parliament is clearly aimed **7.106** at ensuring that the executive veto is rarely used,[159] since unjustifiable use of the veto will result in criticism by the opposition and the public. To that extent, there is a degree of accountability in the exercise of the executive override.

The inclusion of the 'executive override' is in direct conflict with the recommen- **7.107** dation in the White Paper. The White Paper stated:

> In a number of countries with FOI legislation, Ministers are given the discretion to override the disclosure powers of the appeals body. For example, they can certify that particular documents lie outside the appeals process or they can veto a finding of the relevant Ombudsman. We have considered this possibility, but have decided against it, believing that a government veto would undermine the authority of the Information Commissioner and erode public confidence in the Act. We believe that our proposals strike the right balance between the sometime competing public interests in disclosing and withholding information.[160]

This reflects the experience of other jurisdictions. Many jurisdictions with free- **7.108** dom of information legislation operate effectively without any sort of executive override (for example, USA, Canada, and South Africa). The freedom of information legislation in both New Zealand and Australia did provide for an executive override. In the embryonic stages of the Australian Bill, the following was said:

> There is no justification for such a system tailored to the convenience of ministers and senior officers in a Freedom of Information Bill that purports to be enacted for the benefit of, and to confer rights of access upon, members of the public. This can only confirm the opinion of some critics that the bill is dedicated to preserving the doctrine of executive autocracy.[161]

The New Zealand legislation originally provided for a power of veto exercisable by any Cabinet Minister individually but in the wake of heavy criticism, the power of veto was greatly restricted by amendments introduced in 1987 (such that, amongst other restrictions, the veto was only exercisable by, in effect, the Cabinet collectively). If it was expected that political accountability would dissuade governments from exercising the executive override, the contrary seems to be the case; in both jurisdictions, the executive override seems to have been exercised needlessly on a number of occasions and any resulting criticism was easily weathered. That conclusion is reflected in the UK's own recent experience, where the Home Office's refusal to comply with a recommendation of the Parliamentary

---

[159] In Australia, the Ministerial veto under the Freedom of Information Act 1982 was used 55 times during the first four years of operation.

[160] White Paper, *Your Right to Know* etc, (Cm 3818, 1997) para 5.18.

[161] Senate Standing Committee on Constitutional and Legal Affairs, *Freedom of Information* (Australian Government Publishing Service, Canberra) paras 15.19–15.20.

Ombudsman under the Open Government Code has attracted little criticism, despite it being the first example of such a refusal.[162]

G. Contempt Proceedings

7.109 If a public authority fails to comply with (a) so much of a decision notice as requires steps to be taken; (b) an information notice; or (c) an enforcement notice, the Information Commissioner may certify in writing to the High Court that the public authority has failed to comply with the notice.[163] The High Court may inquire into the matter and, after hearing any witness who may be produced against or on behalf of the public authority, and after hearing any statement that may be offered in defence, deal with the authority as if it had committed a contempt of court.[164]

7.110 In relation to an information notice, a public authority which, in purported compliance with an information notice, either makes a statement which it knows to be false in a material respect, or recklessly makes a statement which is false in a material respect, is to be taken to have failed to comply with the notice.[165]

7.111 Given that failure to comply with a notice can be punished as a contempt of court, it is important that the notice in question is clear in its requirements. In the context of planning enforcement notices, it has been said that the relevant question is 'does the notice tell (the person on whom it is served) fairly what he has done wrong and what he must do to remedy it?'[166] Similarly, in the case of breach of a court order and, in particular, breach of an injunction, a court will be reluctant to accede to a committal application where the order in question is not sufficiently precisely phrased.

7.112 In contrast to enforcement under the Freedom of Information Act, section 47 of the Data Protection Act 1998 created a specific criminal offence of failure to comply with an enforcement notice, information notice or special information notice under that Act. An offence under section 47 can either be brought summarily in the magistrates' court or on indictment in the Crown Court. On conviction, the offender is liable only to a fine. That section of that Act also created a statutory defence, whereby a person would escape liability by establishing that he exercised all due diligence to comply with the notice in question.

---

[162] For a more detailed analysis of the arguments against the executive override, see the Campaign for Freedom of Information in Scotland's *Further Written Evidence to the Justice 1 Committee* (28 December 2001), to which the author is indebted for the contents of this paragraph.

[163] Section 54(1) of the Act. In Scotland, the Court of Session exercises the functions of the High Court.

[164] ibid, s 54(3).

[165] ibid, s 54(2).

[166] *Miller Mead v Minister of Housing and Local Government* [1963] 2 QB 196.

The Data Protection Act 1998 also made specific provisions as to the criminal li- **7.113** ability of officers of bodies corporate providing that where an offence has been committed by a body corporate and is proved to have been committed with the 'consent or connivance' of or to be 'attributable to any neglect' on the part of any director, manager, secretary or similar officer of the body corporate (or any person purporting to act as such), he, as well as the body corporate is guilty of the offence and liable to be proceeded against and punished accordingly.[167]

The 2000 Act, instead of creating a specific offence, relies on the established law **7.114** of contempt. The clear intention seems to be that notices issued by the Information Commissioner are to have the effect of an order of the court. It seems clear that the contempt is a 'civil contempt' (as a breach of a court order would be) rather than a 'criminal contempt'.[168] The standard of proof is, nevertheless, the criminal standard.[169] For a civil contempt, the better view is that nothing more needs to be proved than that the contemnor did the act which was the breach of the order (or notice); a specific intention either to breach the terms of the order (or notice) does not need to be proved.[170]

The wording of section 54 suggests that the court has a discretion as to whether **7.115** or not to examine an instance of non-compliance with a notice which has been certified by the Information Commissioner. The phrase 'may inquire into the matter' further suggests that the court will hear argument from both the Information Commissioner and the public authority. It is to be inferred that the court will hear evidence from both the Information Commissioner and the public authority as to whether the notice in question has been complied with. If the inquiry is in relation to non-compliance with a decision notice, it is possible that evidence from the person requesting the information would be sought. However, it is clear that the person requesting the information cannot initiate the inquiry under section 54 but must rely upon the assistance of the Information Commissioner.

A contempt of court is punishable by the committal to custody of the contemnor **7.116** for a fixed period of up to two years[171] or by a fine of an unlimited amount. A Minister of the Crown may be liable for civil contempt even though the Crown

---

[167] Data Protection Act 1998, s 61. Exactly the same wording appears in the Health and Safety at Work Act 1974, s 37(1).

[168] This is confirmed by contrasting the wording 'as if it had committed a contempt of court' with the wording 'as if it were a criminal contempt of court' in the Bail Act 1976, s 6(5) and the Juries Act 1974, s 20(2). In *R v Reader* (1987) 84 Cr App R, CA, it was held that an offence under the Bail Act 1976, s 6(5) was not itself a contempt of court.

[169] *Dean v Dean* [1987] 1 FLR 517, CA.

[170] A. Arlidge, D. Eady and ATH Smith, *Arlidge, Eady and Smith on Contempt* (2nd edn, 2000) 754 et seq.

[171] Contempt of Court Act 1981, s 14.

itself may not.[172] Employees and officers of a public authority which is found to have failed to comply with a notice are not liable for contempt unless it can be said that they have knowingly assisted a breach of the notice.[173]

H. Miscellaneous

No right of action against a public authority

7.117 Section 56 of the Act provides that 'this Act does not confer any right of action in civil proceedings in respect of any failure to comply with any duty imposed by or under the Act'.[174] It is understood that this simply precludes a party from bringing an action for damages against a public authority or the Information Commissioner for negligence or breach of statutory duty, for example.

Alteration of records

7.118 Section 77 creates a criminal offence of altering, defacing, blocking, erasing, destroying or concealing a record. The constituent elements of the offence are:

(a) a request for information must have been made to a public authority;

(b) the applicant requesting the information would have been entitled to the communication of information under section 1 of the Act (or section 7 of the Data Protection Act 1998);

(c) a relevant person alters, defaces, blocks, erases, destroys or conceals any record held by the public authority;

(d) such alteration etc is done with the intention of preventing the disclosure by the authority of all, or any part, of the information to the communication of which the applicant would have been entitled.[175]

It seems that it would be a defence to such a charge that, for example, either the person would not have been entitled to the information (because, for example, an exemption applied) or that the alteration happened without the requisite *mens rea.*

7.119 A relevant person is the public authority and any person who is employed by, is an officer of, or is subject to the direction of, the public authority.[176] A person guilty of the offence is liable to a fine not exceeding £5,000.[177] Proceedings can only be

---

[172] *Re M* [1994] 1 AC 337.

[173] *Marengo v Daily Sketch and Sunday Graphic Limited* [1948] 1 All ER 406. However, it is arguable that RSC Ord 45, r 5(1) applies such that an order for committal can be sought against any officer, if a public authority fails to comply with a notice.

[174] The same wording appears in the Consumer Protection Act 1987, s 41(2).

[175] Section 77(1) of the Act.

[176] ibid, s 77(2).

[177] ibid, s 77(3).

initiated either with the consent of the Director of Public Prosecutions or by the Information Commissioner.[178]

I. Third Parties

As was noted in the introduction to this chapter, although the usual request for **7.120** information under the Act will involve two parties, the applicant and the public authority, in many cases the decision as to disclosure or non-disclosure will substantially affect the interests of third parties. This will occur most frequently in two contexts: (i) personal information which is private to an individual; or (ii) commercial information which is confidential. Both of these situations are, in principle, covered by absolute exemptions[179] under the Act.

On this subject the White Paper stated: **7.121**

> Public authorities hold a great deal of information concerning individuals, companies and other organisations (referred to collectively as 'third parties') which will be potentially releasable under the Act. We would welcome views on whether a mechanism should be established to allow third parties to appeal against decisions to release information which they believe would cause 'substantial harm' to their interests and, if so, what structure the mechanism should have. The need for such appeals is most likely to arise in areas of personal privacy, commercial confidentiality, or when the information requested was supplied in confidence by the third party.[180]

In the context of personal privacy, the White Paper had stated: **7.122**

> The right of the individual to personal privacy is a fundamental human right . . . At the same time, the right to personal privacy cannot be absolute—there may be cases where disclosure of personal information may be in the public interest. Such cases could well raise difficulties between the potentially conflicting interests of the individual, the applicant and the public authority holding the information. This is an issue which an FOI Act may need to acknowledge through a mechanism to allow third party appeals against impending disclosure.[181]

In the context of commercial confidential information, the White Paper had **7.123** stated:

> . . . the Act will cover information and records of any date before it comes into force. This will make it particularly important to ensure adequate protection for people or organisations whose communications with public authorities were covered by explicit undertakings of confidentiality, or at least a reasonable expectation that the law of confidentiality applied to them.

---

[178] ibid, s 77(4).
[179] ibid, ss 40 and 41.
[180] White Paper, *Your Right to Know* (n 160 above) para 5.19.
[181] ibid, para 3.11(3).

7.124 A flowchart entitled *Processing an FOI Access Appeal* annexed to the White Paper indicated that:

> A third party may be allowed to challenge decisions to disclose information which it believes would cause 'substantial damage' to its interests;

and that

> . . . a third party may apply for Judicial Review of the Information Commissioner's decision.

7.125 In the context of any given request for information, there are four stages at which third parties might be expected to want their interests to be represented:

(a) the decision process of the public authority (including the internal review);
(b) the application to the Information Commissioner;
(c) the appeal to the Information Tribunal;
(d) the appeal to the High Court (and subsequent appeals).

Wrongful disclosure at any of these stages may cause a third party irreparable harm.

7.126 Section 3(2)(a) of the Act excludes information from the ambit of the Act if it is held by a public authority 'on behalf of' another person. Further, there are exemptions which are intended to protect the interests of third parties: most clearly, section 40 (personal information); section 41 (information provided in confidence) and section 43 (commercial interests). A public authority (and, similarly, the Information Commissioner or the Information Tribunal) should, therefore, consider the interests of third parties.

7.127 It is striking, however, that the Act is all but silent as to how third parties, themselves, should go about protecting their interests, especially given the prominence that these interests were given in the White Paper. There are, however, some pointers concealed in the detail. It is clear that much of the burden of safeguarding third parties' interests will be borne by the Code of Practice rather than the Act itself. This is, in itself, regrettable since, as observed above, the Code of Practice does not have statutory force. The Act makes it mandatory for the Code of Practice to provide guidance to public authorities as to, first, consultation with third parties to whom the information requested relates or persons whose interests are likely to be affected by the disclosure of information[182] and, secondly, the inclusion in contracts of terms relating to the disclosure of information.[183]

7.128 The Code of Practice states:

> In some cases the disclosure of information pursuant to a request may affect the legal rights of a third party, for example where information is subject to the common law

---

[182] Section 45(2)(c) of the Act.
[183] ibid, s 45(2)(d).

duty of confidence or where it constitutes 'personal data' within the meaning of the Data Protection Act 1998. Public authorities must always remember that unless an exemption provided for in the Act applies in relation to any particular information, they will be obliged to disclose that information in response to a request.[184]

These two sentences make it explicit that, if no exemption applies, the public authority is obliged to disclose the information *even if,* by disclosing the information, it would be infringing third parties' legal rights.

The Code of Practice goes on to outline a number of principles. First, where information could be disclosed but for the fact that it affects third party rights, the third party should be approached to see whether they consent to disclosure, unless it is clear to the public authority that such consent would not be forthcoming.[185] Secondly, where the views of a third party may assist the authority to determine whether information is exempt from disclosure under the Act or where the public interest lies, consultation should take place[186] unless (i) the public authority does not intend to make disclosure (relying on another legitimate ground); (ii) the views of the third party would have no effect on the decision of the authority; (iii) the cost of consultation is disproportionate.[187] It is implicit in the Code of Practice that where the information may affect the legal rights of third parties, the public authority should consult the third party unless it intends to refuse disclosure.

7.129

The Code of Practice also provides that, as a matter of practice, public authorities should refuse to include confidentiality clauses in contracts and should refuse to accept information 'in confidence' from third parties.[188]

7.130

The Act is completely silent as to the extent to which the Information Commissioner should consult third parties. Third parties may not initiate the application to the Information Commissioner.[189] The Information Commissioner is not even obliged to inform interested third parties of his decision.

7.131

The Act amends the Data Protection Act 1998 such that it is made explicit that regulations governing the procedure of the Information Tribunal will make provision for the joinder of any other person to an appeal to the Information Tribunal.[190] This provision seems designed to ensure that third parties are entitled

7.132

---

[184] Code of Practice, para 31.

[185] ibid, para 32.

[186] ibid, para 35.

[187] ibid, paras 36 and 37.

[188] ibid, para 47.

[189] Section 50(1) of the Act. Although 'any person' would seem apt to include a third party, the subsequent use of the word 'complainant' makes it clear that 'any person' means the person who made the request.

[190] Data Protection Act 1998, Sch 6, para 7(2)(aa), as inserted by the 2000 Act, Sch 4, para 4(3).

to have their interests represented at the appeal. Third parties, however, may not lodge the appeal itself.[191]

7.133   Provided that a third party is a party to the Information Tribunal proceedings, it may appeal the decision of the Information Tribunal to the High Court.[192]

7.134   Other than the above, it is clear that a third party must look outside the Act in order to safeguard its interests. The Act does not preclude a third party from seeking remedies arising from the law of confidentiality or from, for example, Article 8 of the European Convention on Human Rights.

7.135   It is a consequence of the nature of the subject matter of the Act, namely information, that damages after a wrongful disclosure will rarely be an adequate remedy. The most effective means for a third party to safeguard its interests will, in the usual course of events, be applying for an injunction. The balance of convenience will usually favour the third party, because of the simple fact that disclosure cannot be reversed. Alternatively, or additionally, a third party could seek a judicial review of a public authority's decision or that of the Information Commissioner.

7.136   One can easily imagine a number of situations where the lack of any real integration of mechanisms to protect third party rights will lead to some difficulties or uncertainties. For example, through a public authority's oversight, a commercial entity's confidential information may be disclosed without it even being notified of an application under the Act, leaving only a possible action for damages. A public authority may refuse to disclose information on the basis that it is confidential but the Information Commissioner may decide otherwise (or even that there is a countervailing public interest in disclosure); assuming that the Information Commissioner is wrong, the public authority is faced with the choice of disclosing the information and risking being sued for damages by the third party or risk being found in contempt of court; the third party, cannot, it seems, compel the public authority to appeal the decision nor can it appeal the decision itself. These are troubling problems which will need to be addressed.

---

[191]   Section 57(1) of the 2000 Act: '. . . the complainant or the public authority may appeal to the Tribunal against the notice'.
[192]   ibid, s 59.

8

HISTORICAL RECORDS

A. The Public Records Act 1958: Transfer to the Public Record Office

Section 3(1) of the Public Records Act 1958 imposes a duty on every person **8.01** responsible for 'public records' to make arrangements for the selection and safe-keeping of 'those records which ought to be permanently preserved'. By section 3(2), that duty is to be performed under the guidance of the Keeper of Public Records, an official appointed by the Lord Chancellor[1] to take charge (under his direction) of the Public Record Office.[2] Public records selected for permanent preservation are required by section 3(4) to be transferred not later than 30 years[3] after their creation[4] to the Public Record Office or such other place of deposit appointed by the Lord Chancellor as he may direct.[5]

---

[1] Overall responsibility for the execution of the Public Records Act 1958 and supervising the care and preservation of public records is placed on the Lord Chancellor by s 1(1).

[2] ibid, s 2(1).

[3] Subject to exceptions: see paras 8.07–8.10 below.

[4] Where records created at different dates are, for administrative purposes, kept together in a single file or other assembly, all the records in that file or other assembly are treated for the purposes of the Public Records Act 1958 as having been created at the date of creation of the latest of them: s 10(2).

[5] Power to appoint other places of deposit for classes of public records is conferred on the Lord Chancellor by ibid, s 4. The power has been delegated to the Keeper of Public Records in the Public Record Office's Executive Agency Framework Agreement (amended 1997). Records in appointed places of deposit are held on behalf of the Lord Chancellor.

8.02 'Public records' are defined in Schedule 1 to the Public Records Act 1958.[6] Principal categories are:

(a) administrative and departmental records belonging to Her Majesty in right of Her Majesty's Government in the United Kingdom, in particular
   (i) records of, or held in, any government department; and
   (ii) records of any office, commission, or other body or establishment under the government;[7]
(b) administrative and departmental records of the bodies and establishments individually listed in the Table at the end of paragraph 3;[8] and
(c) records of courts and tribunals.

8.03 The Freedom of Information Act 2000 (referred to in this chapter as 'the 2000 Act') makes no changes to section 3 of the Public Records Act 1958,[9] and the existing system of selecting certain records for transfer to the Public Record Office will continue, at least for the time being.[10]

8.04 Only pre-1660 documents automatically qualify for permanent preservation, under section 3(3) of the Public Records Act 1958. Those records which have been rejected are to be destroyed or otherwise disposed of in accordance with section 3(6). The section lays down no other criteria for selecting and rejecting records as worthy of preservation, leaving it to the judgment of the persons responsible. Nor does the Code of Practice on record management issued by the Lord Chancellor pursuant to section 46 of the 2000 Act,[11] which stipulates merely

---

[6] 'Records' include not only written records, but records conveying information by any other means whatsoever: s 10(1).

[7] Subject to certain exceptions, notably Welsh public records and records of any government department or body wholly or mainly concerned with Scottish affairs. However, the provisions of the Public Records Act 1958 are to apply to Welsh public records as if they did fall within the statutory definition until an order transferring responsibility for them to the National Assembly for Wales is made by the Lord Chancellor under the Government of Wales Act 1998, s 117: s 116 of the 1998 Act.

[8] This list is less extensive than that in Sch 1 to the 2000 Act. However, Sch 5, para 4, to the 2000 Act amends the Public Records Act 1958, Sch 1 to allow the Table in para 3 to be augmented by the addition (by Order in Council) of any other body or establishment which is, or could be, specified in the Parliamentary Commissioner Act 1967, Sch 2.

[9] Or to the Public Records Act (Northern Ireland) 1923, s 3. The 2000 Act does however extend to Northern Ireland and contains provisions relating to the Public Record Office of Northern Ireland and to public records within the scope of that statute which parallel the provisions for England (and Wales) discussed in this chapter, as too does the Code of Practice on record management issued by the Lord Chancellor pursuant to s 46 of the 2000 Act (as to which see ch 5 above and paras 8.04, 8.10, 8.18, 8.36, 8.40–8.46, 8.50 below).

[10] Consideration is being given to the possibility of new national archives legislation which might revise the law governing the preservation of public records and extend it to local authority records. A consultation paper may be issued in due course.

[11] A copy of the *Lord Chancellor's Code of Practice on the Management of Records under section 46 of the Freedom of Information Act 2000* is included in Appendix E below.

that each relevant authority[12] should maintain a selection policy stating in broad terms the functions from which records are likely to be selected for permanent preservation and the periods for which other records should be retained. The only express restriction on destruction is that it should be delayed in the case of a record known to be the subject of a request under the 2000 Act until either disclosure has taken place or the complaint and appeal provisions have been exhausted.

Current departmental practice is for selection to take place in two stages. Each government department has its own Departmental Record Officer who is responsible for the management of its records and carries out the selection process under the guidance of the Public Record Office through the central Records Management Department. 'First Review' usually takes place five years after a departmental file is closed, when records considered to be valueless are destroyed. Those which it is thought might be needed in future for administrative or research purposes are kept for another 10 to 20 years before being assessed for permanent preservation on 'Second Review'.[13] **8.05**

Only a minority of records make it as far as Second Review. In the 1993 White Paper *Open Government*,[14] the following statistics were given for the 35 largest government departments:[15] some 23,000 feet of records subjected to Second Review each year, compared with some 155,000 feet receiving First Review. Those figures were exclusive of another category, records scheduled for automatic destruction after a fixed period of time as being 'ephemeral' and not even meriting a First Review—for which no measurements were given. The quantity annually transferred to the Public Record Office was stated as about 5,000 to 6,000 feet of records. **8.06**

Retention of public records in exceptional cases

Although the basic rule is that transfer is to take place within 30 years of creation, there is a proviso to section 3(4) of the Public Records Act 1958, which allows records to be retained for longer if in the opinion of the person responsible for them they are required for administrative purposes or there is some other special reason for retaining them, and the Lord Chancellor gives his approval. It should be noted that not all records retained by authorities for administrative purposes beyond 30 years are destined for ultimate transfer to the Public Record Office; **8.07**

---

[12] 'Relevant authorities' are public authorities within the meaning of the 2000 Act and all other offices and bodies whose administrative and departmental records are public records for the purposes of the Public Records Act 1958: s 46(7) of the 2000 Act.

[13] See the Public Record Office website, under 'The Public Records System': http://www.pro.gov.uk/about/access/system.htm 30 August 2002.

[14] Cm 2290.

[15] ibid, para 9.7.

some (such as staff files) are not considered worthy of permanent preservation and will eventually be destroyed when no longer needed.

8.08 Individual applications for approval of retention beyond 30 years are referred to the Advisory Council on Public Records for its advice. Constituted under section 1(2) of the Public Records Act 1958, that body exists to advise the Lord Chancellor on public records matters. In addition to the Master of the Rolls, who is ex officio designated as chairman, it consists of unpaid appointees of the Lord Chancellor who are chosen to represent a variety of interests, such as representatives of the main political parties, former civil servants, academics, archivists, librarians, journalists, historians and other researchers. They usually meet four times a year.

8.09 There are some categories of record for the retention of which a blanket authorization has been given on the basis that they are especially sensitive: security, intelligence, and defence-related material. However, according to chapter 9 of the White Paper *Open Government*, all records retained for other than administrative reasons are to be reviewed regularly with a view to their being released if the sensitivity has passed. The test to be applied is whether release would cause actual damage in one of three ways:

(a) it would harm defence, international relations, national security (including the maintenance of law and order) or the economic interests of the United Kingdom and its dependent territories;

(b) it would involve a disclosure of information supplied in confidence which would or might constitute a breach of good faith;

(c) it would involve disclosing personal information about individuals the disclosure of which would cause them or their descendants either substantial distress or endangerment from a third party.

8.10 The Code of Practice on record management says that it is on the basis of that guidance (or subsequent revisions of government policy on retention) that the Advisory Council will consider future applications for retention of documents within departments after 30 years. The criteria for retention will, therefore, remain non-statutory, instead of being put onto a statutory footing as was envisaged in the White Paper *Your Right to Know*.[16]

8.11 Retained records will not be immune from the individual access provisions of the 2000 Act. However, most records satisfying the above criteria would be likely to fall within one of the exemptions.

---

[16] Cm 3818, para 6.7.

B. Access to Records in the Public Record Office

Statutory rights to access—the end to the 30-year rule

The respect in which the Public Records Act 1958 is significantly affected by the **8.12** 2000 Act is, naturally, the provision it makes for public access to records in the Public Record Office (and other appointed places of deposit). Section 5 of the 1958 Act will be radically amended[17] when the 2000 Act is brought fully into force.

In its current form, section 5 places a duty on the Keeper of Public Records to **8.13** arrange reasonable facilities for the public to inspect and obtain copies of public records in the Public Record Office (with equivalent arrangements being made for other appointed places of deposit), but not before the expiry of 30 calendar years[18] following the year of their creation[19] (except in the case of documents to which the public had already had access before the transfer). This is the so-called '30-year rule' which results every New Year's Day in the block release of documents to the public and consequent press coverage of the most sensational and interesting among them.

There are exceptions to the 30-year rule laid down in the current section 5 of the **8.14** Public Records Act 1958. The Lord Chancellor may prescribe a different period, either longer[20] or shorter, for any particular class of records. In the case of extensions of time, it is invariably the practice for the Advisory Council to be consulted. The criteria governing the so-called 'extended closure' of records, as reviewed in 1992, are set out in the White Paper *Open Government.*[21] The basic guiding principle is that the period will only be extended if release would cause actual damage in one of the ways identified at paragraph 8.09 above. There will be other records which were not made available to the public after the expiry of 30 years because of specific prohibitions in statute or instrument;[22] or because the Lord Chancellor was notified by the person responsible for their permanent preservation under section 3 of the Public Records Act 1958 that they contained information obtained from members of the public in circumstances such that their opening would or might be a breach of good faith and approval for their opening has not been given by that person and the Lord Chancellor.[23]

---

[17] By the Freedom of Information Act 2000, Sch 5, para 2.
[18] Originally 50 years, until reduced by the Public Records Act 1967 as from 1 January 1968.
[19] See n 4 above for the meaning of 'creation'.
[20] For example census returns are closed for 100 years.
[21] Cm 2290, ch 9 and Annexe C.
[22] Public Records Act 1958, s 5(3) and Sch 2 (and see ch 6 above on statutory prohibitions of disclosure).
[23] ibid, s 5(2).

8.15 Some records are transferred and released before the expiry of 30 years, in a process known as 'accelerated opening'. Moreover, members of the public may request, and may be granted, access to documents still held in departments, whether more or less than 30 years old.

8.16 Once Schedule 5 to the 2000 Act comes into force, the '30-year rule' will cease to exist. Section 5 of the Public Records Act 1958 will be amended to read as follows:

> (3) It shall be the duty of the Keeper of Public Records to arrange that reasonable facilities are available to the public for inspecting and obtaining copies of those public records in the Public Record Office which fall to be disclosed in accordance with the Freedom of Information Act 2000.
>
> (5) The Lord Chancellor shall as respects all public records in places of deposit appointed by him under this Act outside the Public Record Office require arrangements to be made for their inspection by the public comparable to those made for public records in the Public Record Office.

8.17 Under the terms of the new section 5, access to records in the Public Record Office (and other appointed places of deposit), whether transferred before or after the 2000 Act comes fully into force, will depend not on their being 30 years old or more, but on whether they 'fall to be disclosed in accordance with the Freedom of Information Act 2000'.

'Historical records'—the removal of exemptions

8.18 It does not follow that the thirtieth anniversary of the creation of a record will lose all significance; Part VI of the 2000 Act invests it with a new and different importance. Section 62(1) provides that a record becomes a 'historical record' at the end of the period of 30 years beginning with the year following that in which it was created.[24] Where records created at different dates are kept in one file or other assembly for administrative purposes, the date of creation of them all will be the date when the latest was created.[25] To counter the potential for abuse by leaving files open and adding extra documents to them over many years, so as to postpone the commencement of the 30-year period, the Code of Practice on record management prescribes that files should be closed after five years even if action is continuing and another file has to be opened.

8.19 A number of exemptions which would otherwise apply to requests for information under the 2000 Act are removed by section 63 of that Act in respect of 'historical records'. That is the case whether or not they are 'public records' subject to the regime of the Public Records Act 1958 and irrespective of whether they are in the custody of the Public Record Office. These are:

---

[24] 'Year' means 'calendar year': Freedom of Information Act 2000, s 62(3).
[25] ibid, s 62(2): cf Public Records Act 1958, s 10(2) (n 4 above).

- section 28: disclosure prejudicial to relations between administrations within the United Kingdom
- section 30(1): investigations and proceedings conducted by public authorities
- section 32: court records
- section 33: audit functions of public authorities
- section 35: information relating to formulation of government policy etc
- section 36: prejudice to effective conduct of public affairs
- section 37(1)(a): communications with Her Majesty or other members of the Royal Family or Household
- section 42: legal professional privilege
- section 43: commercial interests.

Other exemptions to be removed, but at a later stage, are: **8.20**

- section 37(1)(b), information concerning the conferring of honours: after the end of the period of 60 years beginning with the year following that in which the record was created
- section 31, information under the heading of law enforcement: after the end of the period of 100 years beginning with the year following that in which the record was created.

Whilst these provisions are intended to reflect the fact that the sensitivity of **8.21** records decreases with the passage of time,[26] a sizeable number of exemptions will remain which are not removed after any period:

- section 23: information supplied by intelligence services
- section 24: safeguarding national security
- section 26: prejudice to defence
- section 27: prejudice to international relations
- section 29: prejudice to economic/financial interests
- section 34: upholding Parliamentary privilege
- section 38: endangering health/safety
- section 40: personal data
- section 41: information supplied in confidence
- section 44: information disclosure of which is prohibited by an enactment or incompatible with a European Community obligation, or would be a contempt of court.

Of those, five are absolute exemptions[27] (sections 23, 34, 40, 41 and 44), save that section 23 is made non-absolute in the case of historical records in the Public

---

[26] *Your Right to Know* (Cm 3818) para 6.4.
[27] Section 2(3) of the 2000 Act.

Record Office.[28] Section 40 is, however, self-limiting, in that the lifespan of 'personal data' is concurrent with the lifetime of the data subject.[29]

8.22 The aspiration expressed in paragraph 6.9 of the White Paper *Your Right to Know*, that an upper time limit of 100 years be imposed on the withholding of material to ensure that no information would be left indefinitely undisclosed, has therefore not been achieved. Under the guidelines for extended closure of records set out in the 1993 White Paper *Open Government* at Annexe C, 100 years was the maximum recommended closure period, and that recommended in relation to records containing information disclosure of which would harm defence, international relations, or national security, and to most documents containing information supplied in confidence, was 40 years.

A new role for the Public Record Office

8.23 Under the current section 5 of the Public Records Act 1958, the Public Record Office is concerned with providing the general public with physical access to records for the purposes of inspection and copying, as opposed to responding to requests for information. In contrast, the scheme of the Freedom of Information Act is for a public authority to identify in response to an individual request whether the specific information requested is held, and to communicate that specific information to that individual, subject to exemptions. Whilst the method of performance may involve inspection of the record containing the information itself, it need not and even such inspection is limited to the information requested.[30] It is not a case of having open access to the relevant documents. The question arises whether and if so to what extent the new freedom of information regime will change the role of the Public Record Office from one of providing general access to documents for public inspection to one of providing individual access to information requested.

8.24 Section 5 in its new form will continue to be expressed in terms of making facilities available to the public for inspecting and obtaining copies of public records, which, on its own, would suggest that the role of the Public Record Office will not change. However, the duty will be specifically limited to public records 'which fall to be disclosed in accordance with the Freedom of Information Act 2000'. Under the 2000 Act nothing falls to be disclosed until after a request for information has been made under section 1 and the duty to confirm or deny created by that section has been complied with. Those words might suggest that the *obligation* of the Public Record Office will be to furnish information which it holds in transferred public records in response to individual requests and in accordance with the pro-

---

[28] By s 64(2) of the 2000 Act.
[29] See the definition in the Data Protection Act 1998, s 1(1).
[30] Freedom of Information Act 2000, s 11.

cedures laid down in the 2000 Act, although not *prohibiting* it from making any records available otherwise than in response to a request made under that Act.

The view that there will be a change of role is supported by the fact that the Public **8.25** Record Office is a government department and as such a public authority for all purposes of the 2000 Act. It will, therefore, be liable to comply with individual requests for information made in accordance with the 2000 Act. Further, as will be seen in the next section, the 2000 Act prescribes an elaborate procedure for handling requests for information contained in records in its custody.

However, if the Public Record Office's only duties were to be those arising under **8.26** the 2000 Act itself, the new section 5(3) would be redundant, which suggests that it was intended to add something. And it does go beyond what the 2000 Act requires, in two respects. That Act does not contemplate, let alone require, communication of information to anyone other than the person asking for it, let alone the public at large. Nor does it make it mandatory for a public authority to allow inspection or copying of any records.

There are two other considerations which point towards the new section 5 being **8.27** intended to impose a duty over and above those imposed by the 2000 Act. One is the express exclusion, in relation to historical records in the Public Record Office, of the section 21 and section 22 exemptions.[31] This presupposes that but for the exclusion, the information in such records would or might be 'reasonably accessible to the applicant otherwise than under section 1' or 'held with a view to its publication'. That would not be the case if the Public Record Office only had to make information available to individuals as and when they asked for it under the 2000 Act. Secondly, it seems an improbable intention to impute to the legislature that access to documents which prior to that Act's coming into force were readily available in the Public Record Office (or but for its coming into force would have become so) should be made more difficult or complicated. Yet that would be the effect of making the use of the 2000 Act's procedures compulsory, including the provisions for requests to be in writing (section 8) and the giving of a written confirmation or denial as to whether the information is held (section 1), with the time lapse between request and compliance contemplated in section 10.

Those considerations suggest that the legislative intention behind the new section **8.28** 5 is that in addition to complying with specific requests for information made in strict accordance with the 2000 Act, the Public Record Office should carry on providing all the same services and facilities (including online services and facilities)[32]

---

[31] ibid, s 64(1).
[32] The Public Records Act 1958, s 2(4) confers a general power to do all such things as appear to the Keeper of Public Records necessary or expedient to maintain the utility of the Public Record Office. Specific examples are given, which include the compilation and making available of indexes and guides to the records in its custody.

that it does under the current section 5, but in relation to a differently defined class of documents. The emphasis laid on public inspection in the new section 5(5),[33] respecting other appointed places of deposit, tends to confirm this. The words 'which fall to be disclosed in accordance with the 2000 Act' could be interpreted as referring to those records which would fall to be disclosed on a hypothetical application for access to the information in them made under the 2000 Act, or in other words, those records in respect of which either no exemptions apply or the public interest nonetheless favours disclosure, such that the 2000 Act would not allow the information in them to be withheld. There is no problem in principle with this interpretation; the difficulty arises in practice. When, how, and by whom, would those records which 'fall to be disclosed in accordance with the 2000 Act' be identified? Could it be done otherwise than in the context of a specific request?

8.29 The obvious place to look for assistance in answering those questions, and resolving the issue of interpretation of the new section 5, is in the provisions of the 2000 Act which deal specifically with records in the Public Record Office.

Requests for information in transferred public records

8.30 Section 66 of the 2000 Act applies to information which is (or if it existed, would be) contained in 'transferred public records', and requires the 'appropriate records authority' to consult the 'responsible authority' before deciding whether any such information falls within any provision of Part II of the 2000 Act relating to the duty to confirm or deny, or is exempt information. This requirement does not, however, apply to any information which the responsible authority has 'designated as open information for the purposes of the section'.

8.31 The term 'open information' is undefined and there are no express provisions as to how such a designation is to be made, or on what criteria it is to be based.

8.32 The other terms are defined, in section 15 of the 2000 Act, as having the following meanings:[34]

(a) 'transferred public record' means a public record which has been transferred to the Public Record Office or to another place of deposit appointed by the Lord Chancellor under the Public Records Act 1958[35]

(b) 'appropriate records authority' means the Public Record Office, or the Lord Chancellor in relation to other appointed places of deposit, depending on the location of the transferred public record in question;[36]

(c) 'responsible authority' means:

---

[33] See para 8.16 above.
[34] Omitting those parts of the definitions which relate to Northern Ireland.
[35] Freedom of Information Act 2000, s 15(4).
[36] ibid, s 15(5).

(i) in the case of a record transferred from a government department in the charge of a Minister of the Crown to the Public Record Office or other appointed place of deposit, the Minister who appears to the Lord Chancellor to be primarily concerned;

(ii) in the case of a record transferred from any other person to the Public Record Office or other appointed place of deposit, the person who appears to the Lord Chancellor to be primarily concerned.[37]

Not all 'responsible authorities' will be public authorities within the meaning of the 2000 Act. Section 66(6) provides, however, that such authorities are to be treated as 'public authorities' for the purposes of Parts III to V of that Act in so far as relates to the duty imposed by section 15(3)[38] and the imposition of any requirements to furnish information relating to compliance with Part I in connection with information to which section 66 of the 2000 Act applies.

Section 66 of the 2000 Act also identifies two situations in which it is specified that the responsible authority shall itself make decisions in respect of information contained in a transferred public record which has not been 'designated as open information': **8.33**

(a) first, where such information falls within a Part II provision relating to the duty to confirm or deny which is not identified in section 2(3) of the Act as conferring absolute exemption, it is for the responsible authority to determine the question arising under section 2(1)(b) of the Act as to whether the public interest in maintaining the exclusion of the duty outweighs the public interest in disclosing whether the information is held;[39]

(b) secondly, where such information is exempt information but not subject to an absolute exemption, the exercise under section 2(2)(b) of the Act of balancing the public interest in maintaining the exemption against the public interest in disclosing the information is to be carried out by the responsible authority.[40]

In either situation, section 15(1) of the 2000 Act requires the appropriate records authority to send a copy of any relevant request to the responsible authority within the period for complying with section 1(1).[41] Section 15(3) obliges the responsible authority to inform the appropriate records authority of its decision under section 66(3) or (4) within such time as is reasonable in all the circumstances. If the decision is adverse to the applicant, and he complains successfully **8.34**

---

[37] ibid.
[38] See para 8.34 below.
[39] Section 66(3) of the 2000 Act.
[40] ibid, s 66(4).
[41] Presumably as a matter of good practice it should be sent at the outset, to facilitate the consultation process and the decision as to which, if any, exemptions apply.

to the Information Commissioner, both authorities have a right of appeal to the Tribunal.[42]

8.35 One of the circumstances relevant to the time it is reasonable to take for the purposes of section 15(3) is the need to consult the Lord Chancellor if the responsible authority is minded to withhold the information.[43] The Lord Chancellor therefore retains some say in what public records are to be disclosed, but only in a consultative capacity. In contrast, under the old regime, extension or abridgement of the 30-year period was a matter for his discretion;[44] and furthermore, there were no set statutory criteria for how that discretion was to be exercised. Under the new regime, the conditions for claiming exemption from disclosure and the periods for which exemption can be claimed[45] are laid down in the 2000 Act itself and can only be altered by primary legislation.

8.36 It is unclear if the Lord Chancellor will continue to consult his Advisory Council about every request referred to him, as was formerly his practice in relation to applications for extensions of the 30-year period. It seems reasonable to expect that he will, especially given the role envisaged for the Advisory Council in the Code of Practice on record management, namely the scrutinizing of schedules prepared by public authorities when they review information to be released in order to identify the information which it is proposed should be withheld.[46] The 2000 Act adds a new sub-section, (2A), to the Public Records Act 1958, section 1, specifically extending the Advisory Council's remit to questions of the application of the 2000 Act to information in public records over 30 years old.[47]

8.37 Section 65 of the 2000 Act gives the Lord Chancellor another residual role to play in deciding whether or not to release information subject to one of the non-absolute exemptions: the right to be consulted before a public authority refuses a request for any such information which is contained in a historical record which is also a public record within the meaning of the Public Records Act 1958 (but not a transferred one to which section 66 of the 2000 Act applies instead). This situation could only arise where retention of a public record beyond 30 years had previously been approved by the Lord Chancellor in the exercise of his power under the Public Records Act 1958, section 3(4).[48]

---

[42] Section 57(3) of the 2000 Act.
[43] ibid, s 66(5).
[44] Under the Public Records Act 1958, s 5(1): see para 8.14 above.
[45] See paras 8.18–8. 21 above.
[46] See para 8.41 below.
[47] Freedom of Information Act 2000, Sch 5, para 1.
[48] See para 8.07 above.

'Open information'

The above provisions establish a procedure which on the face of it is inconsistent **8.38** with there being general access[49] to any transferred public records containing information which has not been 'designated' by the responsible authority as 'open information'. It is, however, not inconsistent with records containing information which has been so designated being made available to the general public for inspection and copying under the new section 5 of the Public Records Act 1958 without the necessity of a formal request under the 2000 Act.

As previously stated, the 2000 Act, unhelpfully, neither defines the term 'open **8.39** information', nor offers any enlightenment as to when or how information is to be so designated. That is somewhat surprising. What would seem to be envisaged is notification being given by the responsible authority to the appropriate records authority at, or perhaps after, the date of transfer that no exemptions from disclosure apply and no consideration need be given to claiming any. Such a procedure has the potential to save time and expense which would otherwise be wasted if consultation had to take place every time a request was received. In relation to future transfers, it would clearly be sensible for responsible authorities to make such designations where possible before handing over their records.

While there is no statutory requirement for that to be done as a matter of routine **8.40** (or at all), the Code of Practice on record management seems to recognize this necessity. Part Two stipulates that authorities subject to the Public Records Act should ensure they operate effective arrangements to determine which records ought to be selected for permanent preservation and which of those ought to be released to the public; the purpose of the review for release is to consider which information must be available to the public on transfer because no exemptions under the 2000 Act apply, and (where exemptions do apply) whether the information should nonetheless be released in the public interest.

The Code provides that if a review results in the identification of specified **8.41** information which the authority considers ought not to be released under the terms of the 2000 Act, it is to prepare a schedule, identifying the information precisely, citing the relevant exemption(s), explaining why the information may not be released and identifying either a date at which release would be appropriate or a date at which the case for release should be reconsidered. That schedule is to be submitted to the Public Record Office for review and advice, and considered by the Advisory Council in the circumstances described in paragraph 8.44 below. Information not included in the schedule is presumably intended to count as having been 'designated as open information' within the meaning of section 66(1) of

---

[49] As opposed to access given to a particular individual in response to a request made under the 2000 Act: see para 8.24 above.

the 2000 Act. However, that expression does not appear in the Code, which employs slightly different terminology. It says that records transferred before they are 30 years old are to be 'designated for immediate release' unless an exemption applies. There will be no formal review of such designations.

8.42 The language of the Code, in particular the references to 'release to the public', suggests that records in respect of which it has been decided that no exemptions apply are to be made available to the public for inspection and copying without more, like the blocks of records released each New Year's Day under the 30-year rule.

8.43 Similarly, according to the Code, a record in respect of which a future date for release has been specified in the relevant schedule (as being the date on which an exemption from access under the 2000 Act will cease to apply pursuant to section 63) is to become 'automatically available' to members of the public on that day. This would suggest that such records are to be treated as from that date as if the information contained in them had been 'designated as open information' for the purposes of section 66 of the 2000 Act (and the new section 5 of the Public Records Act 1958). Strictly speaking, however, at the date of transfer that information would have been designated as not open, and a further designation as open, or a consultative exercise under section 66, would seem to be needed after the expiry of the relevant period.

8.44 According to the Code, authorities when carrying out their reviews of records for release to the public should consider, and indicate in their schedules of information proposed to be withheld, first, which information must be made available on the relevant records becoming 'historical' and the dates when that will occur, and secondly, which information they consider merits protection beyond 30 years, for how much longer, and why. The case for withholding records for more than 30 years is to be considered by the Advisory Council, which, it is said, may respond in a variety of ways:

(a) by accepting that the information may be withheld for longer than 30 years and earmarking the records for release or re-review at the date identified by the authority;

(b) by accepting the principle of withholding the information for more than 30 years but asking the authority to reconsider the date for release or re-review;

(c) by questioning the basis on which it is deemed that the information may be withheld beyond 30 years and asking the authority to reconsider altogether;

(d) by advising the Lord Chancellor that it is not satisfied with the response received from the authority;

(e) by taking such other action as it deems appropriate within its role as defined in the Public Records Act 1958.

None of the first three responses would have any legally binding force, and it is **8.45** difficult to imagine quite what the consequences of the latter two might be; the Advisory Council has no teeth and the Code will have no statutory force. It must, however, be questionable whether in any event a date for release or re-review could effectively be fixed far into the future, save in the case of an absolute exemption. The balance of public interest might change during the intervening period. Moreover, should an individual request the information under the 2000 Act before the date arrived, the matter would have to be considered afresh in the circumstances then pertaining. If the decision were in favour of disclosure, questions would then arise as to whether the information should be regarded as 'designated as open' for the purposes of section 66, and made generally available to the public in advance of the date originally specified.

The Code of Practice has nothing to say about designating 'as open information', **8.46** or 'for release', the content of records which have already been transferred. There are of course two classes of such records: those which have been made available for public inspection and those which as yet have not. What the Code does say is that requests for information in transferred public records will be dealt with on a case by case basis in accordance with the provisions of the 2000 Act, which brings one back to section 66.

Section 66(2) requires consultation with the responsible authority before decid- **8.47** ing whether any exemptions apply. In the case of a record which has not yet been made available to the public, such consultation has an obvious purpose: to find out whether in the opinion of the responsible authority any exemptions apply. These records can be dealt with, and decisions can be taken as to whether the information they contain falls to be disclosed under the 2000 Act, on a case by case basis. Section 66 does not say that if the outcome of a consultation exercise is a decision that no exemptions apply, the information becomes 'open information' such that the procedure under that section will never again have to be gone through; but that would seem to be implicit. The contrary would fly in the face of common sense.

What of records which have been released to the public in the past? It is conceiv- **8.48** able that if the question of their disclosure were to arise for consideration afresh after the coming into force of the 2000 Act, in accordance with the new criteria it lays down, the withholding of some might be justifiable.[50] But they are already in the public domain. It cannot be the intention of the legislature that the Public Record Office should be able to refuse a request for information in such records, or withdraw them from public inspection. In the case of that class of records, a sensible purposive construction of section 66 and the new section 5 of the Public

---

[50] See paras 8.20–8.21 above.

Records Act 1958 would be that the duty to make arrangements for inspection and copying exists without the need to apply the procedures and requirements of the 2000 Act.

8.49 It is therefore suggested that it will be the duty of the Keeper of Public Records under the new section 5(3) of the Public Records Act 1958 (and that of the Lord Chancellor under section 5(5), as amended), to make available to the general public for inspection and copying without the necessity of consultation or a formal request under the 2000 Act, the following classes of transferred public record:

(a) records the information in which has been 'designated as open information' by the responsible authority on or after transfer;

(b) records which have already been made available to the public before the 2000 Act comes fully into force, under the current section 5 of the 1958 Act, and are therefore in the public domain as at that date;

(c) other records the information in which has been specifically requested under the 2000 Act, and been the subject of a previous decision that no exemptions from disclosure under that Act apply to it.

8.50 In respect of all other transferred public records, the procedures and requirements of the Freedom of Information Act 2000 will need to be complied with before individual or general public access is given. This will involve the application of the consultation provisions of section 66 of that Act. It is to be noted that the foreword to the Code of Practice on record management envisages that it will be complemented by memoranda of understanding setting out how the consultation requirements of section 66 will be put into effect. It may be that such memoranda, which will presumably be between responsible authorities and appropriate records authorities, will address and clarify situations (including those identified above) which are not expressly covered by the 2000 Act or the Code.

Part D

A COMPARATIVE VIEW

9

A COMPARISON WITH FREEDOM OF INFORMATION ELSEWHERE

A. Introduction

Scope of the chapter

9.01 The Freedom of Information Act 2000 (in this chapter described as the 2000 Act) provides the people of this country[1] for the first time with a general right of access to information held by public authorities. This right has existed in Sweden since the eighteenth century, in the United States since 1966, in France and the Netherlands since 1978, in Australia since 1982, in Canada and New Zealand since 1983,[2] and in Ireland since 1998.[3] The government acknowledged in the White Paper[4] that the United Kingdom can learn much from the experience of these mature democracies. For those concerned with the practical implementation of the 2000 Act it is important to stress the many similarities in the different legislative provisions. All the statutes are concerned with the disclosure of information as a matter of right, with exemptions prohibiting the release of certain kinds of information and with machinery for appeal against refusal to supply information.

9.02 In this chapter the broad themes which are common to all these freedom of information regimes are examined.[5] Consideration is given to how the different acts in different countries have worked in practice, and particular attention is paid to those provisions which are similar to the UK provisions. Problems which have arisen are identified, and the way in which different courts have dealt with them is discussed. Freedom of information laws now exist in over 40 countries across the world.[6] In chapter 25 below there is a summary of the main provisions of the legislation in Australia, Canada, France, Ireland, the Netherlands, New Zealand, Sweden and the United States, country by country. These are the countries which are referred to in the White Paper and which influenced the shape of the UK legislation. This chapter in contrast concentrates on the practice in the United States, Ireland, Australia, Canada and New Zealand, countries which share a common tradition.

---

[1] The Act extends to the whole United Kingdom, though Scotland is to have its own Freedom of Information law which will cover much of the ground there; see ch 22 below.

[2] The Canadian Access to Information Act 1982 and New Zealand Official Information Act 1982 did not come into force until 1983.

[3] The Irish Freedom of Information Act 1997 came into force in 1998.

[4] *Your Right To Know* (Cm 3818, 1997) para 1.3.

[5] The chapter follows much the same pattern as the overview in ch 3 above.

[6] These include Australia, Belgium, Belize, Bosnia and Hertzegovina, Bulgaria, Canada, Czech Republic, Denmark, Estonia, Finland, France, Greece, Hungary, Iceland, Ireland, Israel, Japan, Latvia, Lithuania, Netherlands, New Zealand, Norway, Poland, Portugal, Slovakia, South Africa, South Korea, Spain, Sweden, Thailand, Trinidad and Tobago, Ukraine, United Kingdom, USA.

B. Access to Official Information as of Right

Disclosure as a matter of right

Access to information as of right, *the right to know*, is one of the principles which **9.03** is common to all countries which have freedom of information legislation. These countries no longer rely on the judgment of civil servants to release or withhold information: the right to know places the onus on the government to justify with-holding information from the public. The 2000 Act gives *any person* making a request for *information* to a public authority the right to be informed whether the authority holds the information, and if it does to have the information commu-nicated to him.

Purpose clauses

The first point to note is that the Freedom of Information Acts in Canada,[7] **9.04** Australia[8] and New Zealand have purpose clauses; those in the UK, Ireland and the United States do not. Sections 4 and 5 of the New Zealand Official Information Act for example provide:

4. Purposes

The purposes of this Act are, consistently with the principle of the Executive Government's responsibility to Parliament:

(a) To increase progressively the availability of official information to the people of New Zealand in order—
   (i) To enable their more effective participation in the making and administra-tion of laws and policies; and
   (ii) To promote the accountability of Ministers of the Crown and officials, —
and thereby to enhance respect for the law and to promote the good government of New Zealand:

(b) To provide for proper access by each person to official information relating to that person:

(c) To protect official information to the extent consistent with the public interest and the preservation of personal privacy.

5. Principle of availability

The question whether any official information is to be made available, where that question arises under this Act, shall be determined, except where this Act otherwise expressly requires, in accordance with the purposes of this Act and the principle that the information shall be made available unless there is good reason for withholding it.

Campaigners for Freedom of Information were disappointed that the 2000 Act **9.05** did not contain a purpose clause which said that information should be made

---

[7] Access to Information Act 1982, s 2.
[8] Freedom of Information Act 1982, s 3.

available unless there is good reason for withholding it. Instead we have the long title:

> An Act to make provision for the disclosure of information held by public authorities or by persons providing services for them.

Somehow this does not have the same ring about it. Traditionally, however, UK legislation does not rely on purpose clauses, and it would be easy to exaggerate the difference which the absence of a purpose clause will make. UK judges will be ready to draw on constitutional principles as a guide to defining the purpose of the legislation. As Lord Scott has written:

> Ministers are accountable for what they do as Ministers and for what is done in the departments of which they are in charge. At the heart of the principle of accountability lies the obligation of Ministers to give information about the activities of their departments and about the actions and omissions of civil servants.[9]

And Lord Cooke of Thorndon said in *R (Daly) v Home Secretary:*[10]

> The truth is, I think, that some rights are inherent and fundamental to democratic civil society. Conventions, constitutions, bills of rights and the like respond by recognising rather than creating them.

Nevertheless when making comparisons between the United Kingdom legislation and that of Canada, Australia and New Zealand it is necessary to remember that UK judges do not have the assistance of a purpose or objects clause.

Who enjoys the right and what use has been made of it?

9.06 The 2000 Act gives the right to information to 'any person'. This follows the example of Australia, Ireland and the United States where the wording is also 'any (or every) person' and is not limited to any particular class of persons, such as citizens and permanent residents, as was originally the case in Canada,[11] or 'the properly and directly concerned persons' specified by the Administrative Procedure Act 1946, which was the predecessor in the United States to the 1966 Freedom of Information Act.

9.07 The Hon John Reid, the Information Commissioner in Canada, in his report for the year to 31 March 2001, said that the most surprising feature of the Access to Information Act was the modest use made of it; initial predictions of 50,000 re-

---

[9] Richard Scott's essay on 'Confidentiality' in J Beatson and Y Cripps (eds), *Freedom of Expression and Freedom of Information: Essays in Honour of Sir David Williams* (OUP, 2000) 267.

[10] [2001] 2 WLR 1622 at 1636.

[11] The right was extended in 1989 to all individuals and corporations present in the country, which makes it similar in scope to the right conferred by the New Zealand Official Information Act 1982, s 12. The Task Force set up by the Canadian government to review the operation of that country's Act recommends a further extension to make it a universal right: *Access to Information: Making it Work for Canadians* (June 2002) (hereafter *the Canadian Task Force report*), at 19.

quests a year (based on experience in the United States) were proved excessive and it took ten years to reach the 50,000 mark.[12] However, there has been what is described in the *Canadian Task Force report*[13] as a 'significant jump' in the past two years, with the number of requests exceeding 20,000 for the first time in 2000–01. In Ireland there has been a quicker take up rate with 11,539 requests in 1999, 13,705 in 2000, and 15,428 in 2001.

There is some interesting material in *The Access to Information Act 10 years on*, a report published by the Canadian Information Commissioner's Office in 1994, about patterns of use of the Act. Up to then, the largest user group had been business (43% in 1992–3), many people trying to get hold of information that would help them win government contracts. (Another category of business use is by persons or companies who obtain government information in order to sell it on at a profit. The Information Commissioner sees nothing wrong in that; he says they pay taxes and anyway the government could exploit its information itself if it chose.[14]) The next largest group was individuals (39% in 1992–3), followed by media (7–10%) with special interest groups, academics (about 2%), and lawyers making up the rest. Use by Parliamentarians had been minimal. There were striking examples of multiple uses of the Act, notably by one Ken Rubin (who claimed to have made some 3,000 requests, 400 complaints to the Commissioner and 30 Federal Court challenges in the first ten years, largely to do with health, safety and environmental matters, for example air crashes, food poisoning, possible siting of cruise missiles in Canada) and a Montreal tax lawyer called Claude Désy (who is said to have made over 4,500 requests of Revenue Canada, with 2,679 complaints to the Commissioner, obtained 234,234 pages of information, and occupied 10 Revenue Canada staff in servicing his requests; he sold the information in a newsletter claiming that he was trying to open up tax rulings that should have been made public, an activity regarded by some as 'a blatant abuse of the spirit of the Act'). The statistics for the year 2000–1[15] show that business users still predominate, with 40.9% of requests emanating from them. 31.5% came from the general public (which includes Parliamentarians, estimated to have made about 10%), 16% from organizations, 10.8% from the media and 0.8% from academics. The Task Force agreed with the Commissioner that there is nothing wrong in commercial usage of the Act, but recommended the introduction of a differential fee structure, with higher charges for requests the purpose of which is to further private commercial interests, as in the United States and New Zealand.[16]

9.08

---

[12] The *Information Commissioner's report 2000–1*, 17.
[13] *The Canadian Task Force report*, 9.
[14] *The Information Commissioner's report 2000–1*, 17–18.
[15] *The Canadian Task Force report*, 9.
[16] ibid, 79.

9.09   The business community is by far the largest user group in the United States, principally seeking information on business competitors, with individuals and the
media lagging far behind. Antonin Scalia[17] commented in 1982 that the legislation had been 'promoted as a boon to the press, the public interest group, the
little guy; they have been used most frequently by corporate lawyers'.[18] A satellite
industry has grown up of 'data brokers' or 'surrogate requesters' who acquire
information under the statute for selling on to interested parties.

9.10   In Ireland, early experience has been rather different. Individuals, many of them
seeking personal information, have formed by far the largest proportion of requesters: on average about 64%. The proportion of requests which are for purely
personal information has remained fairly constant at around the 45% mark.
Business users accounted for only 8% in 2001. Media usage of the Act has risen
from 14% in 1999 to 20% in 2001, a trend which the Irish Information
Commissioner in his annual report for 2000 described as 'encouraging'. He there
gave the example of one national daily newspaper which in March 2001 had published 15 separate articles on topics such as arts funding, the environment, treatment of asylum seekers, food safety and taxation policy based on information
obtained under the Act. He also praised journalists for using the Act in a more se-
rious-minded way to produce well-researched stories on issues of importance,
rather than the sensational but trivial stories which had initially tempted them.
However, in his 2001 report he sounded a more cautionary note, reminding the
media of their 'responsibility to present an accurate and complete picture of the
released information' and warning them to avoid 'confusing their own self-inter-
est with the public interest', observing that a perception on the part of some public servants that their work is misrepresented by selective, unfair or sensationalist
reporting is hardly conducive to their having a positive attitude towards freedom
of information.

9.11   The predominance of requests for personal information has been significantly
more striking in Australia, where (although there have until recently been no
available statistics showing a breakdown of requests by type) the ratio has been
generally accepted as about 9:1.[19] The Australian Law Reform Commission and
Administrative Review Council in their joint review of the Australian Act[20] found
that over 90% of requests were being made to four agencies that received mainly
requests for applicants' own personal information: the Australian Taxation Office

---

[17]   Then a professor of law, from 1986 a Justice of the Supreme Court of the United States.
[18]   *The Freedom of Information Act has no clothes*: Regulation: AEI Journal on Government and
Society (March/April, 1982) 16, reprinted in RG Vaughn (ed) *Freedom of Information* (2000).
[19]   The Commonwealth Ombudsman's report *Needs to Know: Own motion investigation into the
administration of the Freedom of Information Act 1982 in Commonwealth agencies* (Report under the
Ombudsman Act 1976, s 35A, June 1999) (hereafter *the Needs to Know report*) para 3.23.
[20]   Australian Law Reform Commission Report 77, *Open Government: A Review of the Federal
Freedom of Information Act 1982* (1995) (hereafter *the Australian Law Reform Commission report*).

('ATO'), and the Departments of, respectively, Veterans' Affairs, Immigration and Ethnic (now Multicultural) Affairs, and Social Security (now known as Centrelink).[21] The previous estimates were borne out by the Attorney-General's annual report on the operation of the Act for 2000–1, the first to distinguish between requests for personal information and requests for other types of information. The former accounted for 89.67% of all requests during the year ending 30 June 2001, with requests to the three departments named above adding up to 86.66% of the total number of requests for the year (given as 35,439).[22] Requests to the ATO had fallen dramatically following a change of practice in 1996–7 which led to it making many documents available outside the framework of the Act.[23] The Commonwealth Ombudsman noted[24] in 1999 that the success rate of requests for personal information was much higher than for other types of requests, thought it reasonable to assume that many of the former might have been suitable for informal disclosure outside the Act, and expressed the view that:

> the unnecessary handling of requests for personal information under the Act inflates reported FOI activity and would seem to serve no useful purpose, particularly in agencies which handle predominantly personal information.

The reasons for the relatively small number of requests for other types of informa- **9.12** tion were unclear, according to *the Australian Law Reform Commission report.* [25] Possible deterrents to use of the Act were said to include lack of public awareness of its existence; the potential costs of pursuing a request; frustration with delays; the way in which requests could develop into legalistic, adversarial contests; and a lack of confidence in the system. The report identified as a major weakness the absence of an independent person or organization with overall responsibility for overseeing the administration of the Act and monitoring agencies' performance of their obligations under it.[26] It concluded that the existence of such a person would raise the profile of the legislation and boost public confidence in it by improving performance standards and proposed the creation of a new statutory office of Freedom of Information Commissioner with those functions.

In New Zealand, no official statistics are compiled in relation to the numbers of **9.13** requests made or the patterns of use of the legislation. There is no requirement for records of requests to be kept and private research indicates that many departments and bodies subject to the Official Information Act do not bother to keep

---

[21] ibid, para 2.10.
[22] *Attorney-General's annual report 2000–1*, 2–4. The total number of requests over the lifetime of the Australian Act (1 December 1982 to 30 June 2001) was given as 600,658. These figures did not include applications which failed to satisfy the statutory requirements for the making of a valid request.
[23] *The Needs to Know report*, para 3.7.
[24] ibid, paras 3.22–3.25, 3.37–3.44.
[25] *The Australian Law Reform Commission report*, paras 2.10–2.12.
[26] ibid, ch 6.

any.[27] A 1997 study[28] suggested that use by the general public is low by comparison with political parties and the media, but no generalizations could safely be drawn from the limited range of survey data on which it was based.

Information or records

9.14 The 2000 Act gives a right to *information*, as opposed to those of the United States, Canada, and Ireland where the right is to see *records*, and the Australian statute which is concerned with *documents*. *Information*, however, is defined in section 84 as 'information recorded in any form', whereas the Irish definition of 'record' includes 'any form or thing in which information is held or stored',[29] and the Australian definition of 'document' includes as a catch-all category 'any other record of information',[30] so perhaps there is not much difference. It has been held[31] that an access request made under the Australian Act is not defective because it is expressed simply as a request for information; in context, such a request is to be read as a request for the document(s) containing that information. In Canada *'record'* is defined to include:[32]

> any correspondence, memorandum, book, plan, map, drawing, diagram, pictorial or graphic work, photograph, film, microfilm, sound recording, videotape, machine readable record, and any other documentary material, regardless of physical form or characteristics, and any copy thereof.

Further, any record requested under the Canadian Act that does not exist but can be produced from a machine readable record under the control of a government institution using computer hardware and software and technical expertise normally used by the institution is deemed to be a record under its control.

9.15 The 2000 Act is more liberal in one respect. Under section 51 the Information Commissioner may serve an information notice which requires the furnishing of 'unrecorded information'. This is a wide power and is closer to the position in New Zealand. Official information is defined in section 2 of the New Zealand Act by reference to various categories of information. In *Commissioner of Police v Ombudsman*,[33] at first instance, Jeffries J said:

> Perhaps the most outstanding feature of the definition is that the word 'information' is used which dramatically broadens the scope of the whole Act. The stuff of what is held by Departments, Ministers or organizations is not confined to the written word

---

[27] D Clemens, *Requests made under the Official Information Act 1982: a survey at the agency level* (February 2001).

[28] EH Poot, *The impact of the Official Information Act 1982 on the policy development process* (1997).

[29] Freedom of Information Act 1997, s 2(1).

[30] Freedom of Information Act 1982, s 4.

[31] *Young v Wicks* (1986) 79 ALR 448.

[32] Access to Information Act 1982, s 3.

[33] [1985] 1 NZLR 578, 586.

but embraces any knowledge, however gained or held, by the named bodies in their official capacities. The omission, undoubtedly deliberate, to define the word 'information' serves to emphasise the intention of the legislature to place few limits on relevant knowledge.

The Official Information Act 1982 is enforced in New Zealand primarily by the   **9.16**
Ombudsmen. Sir Brian Elwood, the Chief Ombudsman, writing in 1999[34] said:

> The wide definition of what constitutes official information has ensured that the principle of open government has become a central feature of New Zealand's public administration and has had a profound effect upon the quality of the information and documents generated by public officials.

The practice of the Ombudsmen has been, in the absence of formal notes or   **9.17**
records, to ask one or more persons involved in the decision-making process to provide a written account of what was said or the reasons expressed orally for reaching that decision.[35] It will be possible for the Information Commissioner in the UK to ask for the like information in an appropriate case, though it has to be stressed that this is a matter for the discretion of the Commissioner; applicants have no right to demand this.

Who is bound by the Act?

Public authorities who are bound by the 2000 Act are defined in section 3 and   **9.18**
listed in Schedule 1; the Lord Chancellor has power to add to the list.[36] The pattern is similar in Canada,[37] New Zealand[38] and Ireland.[39] In Ireland, for example, the public bodies listed in the Schedule can broadly be described as (i) government departments, (ii) other national bodies, (iii) local authorities and (iv) health boards. The Minister of Finance has power to add to the list. The Irish Act has been extended to a considerable number of other bodies since coming into operation—for example, public voluntary hospitals from Autumn 1999 and universities and regional assemblies from Autumn 2001.

In Canada the Information Commissioner has been critical of the way the gov-   **9.19**
ernment has kept the list of public authorities up to date. The Commissioner pointed out in his 2000–1 report[40] that there are no prescribed principles dictating what institutions should be added to Schedule I and there is no duty, only a power under section 77(2) of the Canadian Act, to add to the list at all. That, he

---

[34] *The New Zealand Model—The Official Information Act 1982*, conference paper presented at the Conference 'FOI and the Right to Know', held in Melbourne on 19–20 August 1999.
[35] I Eagles, M Taggart and G Liddell, *Freedom of Information in New Zealand* (1992), 21.
[36] 2000 Act, s 4.
[37] Access to Information Act 1982, s 3 and Sch I.
[38] Official Information Act 1982, s 2 and Sch 1.
[39] Freedom of Information Act 1997, s 2 and Sch 1.
[40] At pp 54–57.

said, has resulted in an obsolete Schedule I, listing institutions that no longer exist and not listing ones that ought to be there. The 2000 Act is subject to the same limitations, though the UK may not throw up the same problems. He favours legislative criteria for inclusion and a statutory obligation to add any institution for the time being satisfying them, with a right to complain to the Information Commissioner about the presence or absence of institutions and with the Federal Court having a power of review and a power to order additions and removals. In his 2001–2 report[41] he has returned to the theme, complaining that the right of access continues to be eroded through the creation of new institutions to carry out public functions (such as the Waste Management Organization to manage nuclear fuel waste) which are not subject to the access legislation. The Commissioner, the Hon John Reid, is a former Minister, and as such his criticisms carry added force. *The Canadian Task Force report*[42] accepts that there should be legislative criteria for inclusion in Schedule I to aid a more consistent and principled approach to its composition, but urges a need for flexibility to take account of the diversity of non-governmental organizations through which public services are nowadays delivered. It suggests partial subjection to the Act in some cases, for example excluding private commercial activities but covering activities of a public nature performed in partnership with or on behalf of the government.

9.20 Elsewhere, newly established bodies satisfying a generally worded definition in the freedom of information legislation automatically become subject to its provisions (unless expressly excluded). In the United States the Act is a federal statute which applies to agencies within the executive branch of the federal government. 'Agencies' is defined[43] as including 'any executive department, military department, Government corporation, Government controlled corporation or other establishment in the executive branch of Government (including the Executive Office of the President), or any independent regulatory agency'. The Australian Act too features the concept of 'agency', there defined as including departments of the Australian Public Service corresponding to Commonwealth Departments of State and 'prescribed authorities' (which are bodies and holders of offices established for public purposes by enactment or Order in Council, or prescribed by regulations for the purposes of the Act). Official documents of Commonwealth Government Ministers are also caught.

How requests for information are made

9.21 Section 8 of the 2000 Act requires a request for information to be in writing, although 'writing' includes a text which is transmitted in electronic form. There are

---

[41] At pp 11–12.
[42] At pp 22–24.
[43] United States Code, Title 5, s 551(1) and s 552(f)(I).

similar provisions in Australia,[44] Canada[45] and Ireland.[46] Section 12 of the New Zealand Official Information Act makes no reference to writing. In the United States the Electronic Freedom of Information Act effected a substantial change of emphasis. The classic means of obtaining information for the previous 30 years had entailed (a) making a request, and (b) waiting for an answer. The 1996 Amendments now required the agencies to anticipate requests and make broad categories of records immediately available to the public, both at agency record depositories and, using telecommunications technology, via the requester's home computer.[47]

When may authorities decline to say whether they hold information, and when must they justify refusing its release?

The 2000 Act is structured so that public authorities have to answer two questions: (i) does the authority have the information? and (ii) should it disclose it? In refusing a request the authority has to say why any exemption applies.[48] This is not dissimilar to the Irish legislation, which requires a notice refusing a request for access to state the reasons for refusal, the statutory provisions on which the refusal is based, the findings on any material issues relevant to the decision, and particulars of any matter relating to the public interest taken into consideration for the purposes of the decision.[49] Those details need not be given in a limited number of situations, where the statute specifically prohibits disclosure of whether the record exists: if, for example, the head of the public body concerned is satisfied that such disclosure would prejudice law enforcement or the defence of the state.[50] The way in which Irish public bodies carry out their obligation to give reasons for refusing access has been the subject of criticism by that country's Information Commissioner. Indeed, in the report of his investigation into the first three years of the Irish Act's operation,[51] he identified as 'the biggest deficiency in handling requests' a 'widespread failure, when refusing information, to give reasons which meet the requirements of the Act', and suggested that such failures might be occurring in about 50% of cases. Particular problems he highlighted were a tendency in relying on an exemption to give no indication why it was applicable, or simply to paraphrase its wording, and failure to provide the requester with a schedule listing the records in issue with details of the exemption claimed for each.

9.22

---

[44] Freedom of Information Act 1982, s 15.
[45] Access to Information Act 1982, s 6.
[46] Freedom of Information Act 1997, s 7.
[47] ME Tankersley, 'How the Electronic Freedom of Information Act Amendments of 1996 update public access for the information age' (1998) 50 Admin Law Rev 421–458 at 423, reprinted in Vaughn (n 18 above) 59.
[48] 2000 Act, s 17.
[49] Freedom of Information Act 1997, s 8(2).
[50] ibid, ss 23(2), 24(3).
[51] Conducted pursuant to the Freedom of Information Act 1997, s 36(2).

9.23　In Australia, Ministers and agencies refusing access requests must serve notices giving particulars of their reasons and findings on any material questions of fact (referring to the material on which these were based).[52] *The Australian Law Reform Commission report* recommended the addition of a specific requirement to list factors taken into account in applying any relevant public interest test. In a handful of cases a different type of notice may be given, stating that the existence of the requested document is neither confirmed nor denied but assuming its existence it would be exempt and giving such particulars of the reasons for so doing as is possible without disclosing any exempt matter.[53] That can be done where information as to the existence or non-existence of the document would or could reasonably be expected to damage the security, defence or international relations of the Commonwealth, its relations with states, law enforcement, or the protection of public safety. In practice, problems akin to those reported in Ireland appear to have been encountered in this jurisdiction. Submissions for the purposes of the Australian Law Reform Commission review[54] indicated that statements of reasons were 'often of a poor standard', sometimes merely referring to an exemption without explaining how it applied to the relevant document and not always even specifying which exemption was claimed for which document. However, the only solution the report could propose was that the new Commissioner should monitor the quality of statements provided and 'name and shame' poorly performing agencies in his annual report. The Ombudsman in *the Needs to Know report*[55] was also critical of agencies in this regard, observing that his office's examination of departmental files 'indicated widespread misunderstanding of the decision-making requirements of section 26'.

9.24　The Canadian Act is less complicated and less stringent. In Canada the head of a government institution may either (a) say that the record does not exist or (b) say that it does but specify a particular provision of the Act on which the refusal is based or (c) decline to say if it exists or not but specify the provision on which a refusal could 'reasonably be expected to be based' if it does.[56] There is no separate duty to confirm or deny in Canada and there is no requirement to state reasons for refusing to say if the requested record exists or refusing to give access to it. The legislation is simpler too, and more flexible, in New Zealand, where under section 10 of the Official Information Act 1982 the recipient of a request may give written notice to the applicant that he neither confirms nor denies the existence or non-existence of the information sought, if satisfied that an interest protected under section 6 or section 9(2)(b) would be likely to be prejudiced by disclosing whether

---

[52]　Freedom of Information Act 1982, s 26.
[53]　ibid, ss 25, 33, 33A, 37(1).
[54]　Referred to at para 7.19 of the report (n 20 above).
[55]　See n 19 above, paras 3.29–3.32.
[56]　Access to Information Act 1982, s 10.

it exists. Subject to section 10, an applicant whose request is refused is to be given the reason and (if he asks for them) the grounds in support of that reason, unless to give them would itself prejudice a protected interest: section 19. All jurisdictions, however, agree that there are circumstances in which it may be damaging to the public interest to disclose whether information exists.

C. Exemptions: The General Approach

The United Kingdom

The exemptions in the 2000 Act are detailed and numerous. They are numerous   **9.25**
in part because the draughtsman has dealt separately with matters which in other jurisdictions are brought together under a general proposition. This makes the 2000 Act appear one of the more restrictive when the reality is that all countries tend to exclude much the same matters from disclosure. We have seen[57] that the UK exemptions are of three types, (i) absolute (ii) class exemptions and (iii) exemptions where some particular interest may be prejudiced. Disclosure of types (ii) and (iii) is subject to a public interest test.

New Zealand

There the objective is that information shall be made available unless there is good   **9.26**
reason for withholding it.[58] Sections 6 and 7 set out good reasons which are conclusive. They apply where making the information available would be likely to prejudice interests of the state (such as defence), or endanger a person's safety. Section 9 sets out other good reasons for withholding information unless in the circumstances of the particular case the withholding of the information is outweighed by other considerations which render it desirable, in the public interest, to make the information available. Section 9 reasons apply when withholding the information is necessary to achieve a specified purpose, such as protecting privacy or Cabinet confidentiality or (in three cases) to avoid a certain kind of prejudice. All the substantive exemptions are framed by reference to the consequences of disclosure, rather than categories of information, and their application has accordingly to be judged on a case by case basis depending on the particular circumstances. They reflect a conscious decision to retain flexibility by the Danks Committee which prepared the legislation:

> Judgments cannot, in our view, be properly and satisfactorily made all at one time by legislation. We were faced early in our work, with the choice of trying to design a once and for all static mechanism, with a complex set of exceptions, or a more flexible

---

[57] See ch 3, paras 3.06–3.08 above.
[58] Official Information Act 1982, s 5.

mechanism, operating by reference to principles and competing criteria that reflect a continuing shift away from a presumption of secrecy. We opted for a flexible process.[59]

The grounds for refusal of requests are brought together in section 18 and also include administrative grounds, for example that the information requested is or will soon be publicly available, or that the information requested cannot be made available without substantial collation or research. These are dealt with as separate substantive exemptions in the 2000 Act.

9.27 Sir Brian Elwood, the New Zealand Chief Ombudsman, has said that only a limited range of information is withheld pursuant to the conclusive reasons relating to such matters as prejudice to the government's international relationships or the maintenance of law. Sir Brian went on to say:[60]

> Most information is withheld at least initially because of the necessity of avoiding one of the prejudices identified in section 9. The more difficult, sometimes agonizing task, is to determine whether the public interest in the release of particular information outweighs the prejudice which has been identified, should the information be released. It is rare indeed for the holder of information once having established a prejudice under section 9 to then proceed to acknowledge that the reason for withholding it is outweighed by the public interest. The task of determining the public interest and the weight to be accorded to it, inevitably falls to the review body, in New Zealand the Ombudsmen.

Sir Brian Elwood says that the High Court in New Zealand has given some guidance. He refers to *TV3 Network Services v BSA*,[61] a privacy case, where Eichelbaum CJ says:

> it is necessary to draw attention to the distinction between matters properly within the public interest, in the sense of being of legitimate concern to the public, and those which are merely interesting to the public on a human level—between what is interesting to the public and what it is in the public interest to be made known.

In the UK the task of determining the public interest will in the first place rest with the Information Commissioner.

9.28 In *Commissioner of Police v Ombudsman*,[62] the New Zealand Court of Appeal considered the meaning of the word 'likely' in the formula 'would be likely to prejudice (or damage)' stated interests found in section 6 of the Official Information Act (which is directly comparable to the common wording of some of the exemption provisions in the 2000 Act). It was interpreted as meaning not that the prejudice or damage is more likely than not to eventuate, but that there is 'a serious or real and substantial risk, a risk that might well eventuate' (per Cooke P at 391), or

---

[59] *Towards Open Government*, The Committee on Official Information's report (1980).
[60] *The New Zealand Model—The Official Information Act 1982*, a paper presented at the conference on 'FOI and the Right to Know' held in Melbourne on 19–20 August 1999.
[61] [1995] 2 NZLR 720 at 733.
[62] [1988] 1 NZLR 385.

'a distinct or significant possibility' (per McMullin J at 404), 'a real risk . . . something that might well happen' (per Casey J at 411). Cooke P added 'whether such a risk exists must be largely a matter of judgment . . . if the decision-maker is in two minds in the end, he should come down on the side of availability of information', but that statement was made against the background of the specific wording of the principle at the end of section 5 of that Act, which has no parallel in the UK Act.[63]

The United States

In the United States the federal agencies are authorized by statute to withhold   **9.29** information within nine broad categories:

(a) classified national defence and foreign policy information;
(b) internal agency rules and practices;
(c) information the disclosure of which is prohibited by another federal statute;
(d) trade secrets and privileged or confidential commercial or financial information;
(e) inter-agency or intra-agency communications that are protected by legal privilege;
(f) information (personnel, medical and similar files) involving matters of personal privacy;
(g) certain records or information compiled for law enforcement purposes if disclosure would result in specified kinds of harm;
(h) information relating to the regulation or supervision of financial institutions;
(i) certain geological and geophysical information and data.

It is to be noted that even if the information sought is within one of the statutory exemptions, the relevant agency may, as a matter of administrative discretion, disclose it.

Australia

Here, too, there is no binding obligation to withhold any exempt documents, but   **9.30** the exemption provisions in Part IV of the Freedom of Information Act 1982 (sections 33–47A) differ from their American counterparts in that (like the UK exceptions) they are much more specifically drawn. Internal working papers will be exempt if disclosure would reveal the deliberative processes of an agency or Minister or of the government and would be contrary to the public interest.[64] There is another exemption for documents disclosure of which would be contrary to the public interest by reason of its potential economic effects.[65] Exemptions for

---

[63] See para 9.04 above.
[64] Freedom of Information Act 1982, s 36.
[65] ibid, s 44.

the protection of Commonwealth–state relations, financial and property interests of the Commonwealth and agency operations are subject to a public interest balancing test.[66] The remaining sections make no express reference to the public interest. Some require a reasonable expectation of injury or prejudice to a stated interest (such as security, defence, or law enforcement). Others (for example those relating to Parliamentary privilege, Cabinet and Executive Council documents, legal professional privilege, contempt of court, breach of confidence and statutory prohibitions on disclosure) do not.

9.31 Conclusive exemption certificates can be issued by Ministers under sections 33 (damage to security, defence and international relations), 33A (damage to Commonwealth–state relations), and 36 (internal working documents), and by the Secretary to the Department of the Prime Minister and Cabinet and Secretary to the Executive Council under sections 34 and 35 (Cabinet and Executive Council documents respectively). There is no provision in the Act for a decision to issue such a certificate to be reviewed or overturned; power is given to the Administrative Appeals Tribunal to determine whether there are reasonable grounds[67] for claiming the exemption, but even if it concludes there to be none the appropriate Minister is under no obligation to revoke the certificate. If he decides against doing so he has to explain his reasons to the applicant and to Parliament, but only in so far as that does not involve referring to any exempt matter.[68] However, it was recently held by the Federal Court in *Shergold v Tanner* that a decision to sign such a certificate is amenable to judicial review under the Administrative Decisions (Judicial Review) Act 1977, so long as the challenge is to the manner in which the decision was arrived at, as opposed to the matters which the certificate asserts. The decision was upheld on appeal to the High Court of Australia.[69]

9.32 The certification provisions have been well used, especially in the early years of the Act's operation (more than 50 times in 1982–6).[70] Despite their controversial nature, *the Australian Law Reform Commission report* considered retention to be justified under sections 33 and 34 but not section 33A. Total repeal of section 35 was proposed. Opinion was divided as to section 36, the Commission (but not the

---

[66] Freedom of Information Act 2000, ss 33A, 39, 40.

[67] For discussion of what is meant by 'reasonable grounds', see *Dept of Industrial Relations v Burchill* (1992) 105 ALR 327 (was the view expressed by the certificate 'reasonably open'?); *Australian Doctors Fund Ltd v Commonwealth* (1994) 126 ALR 273; and *Shergold v Tanner* (2001) 179 ALR 150, 184 *per* Finkelstein J, Federal Court ('the Tribunal need only determine whether a reasonable person in the position of the Minister could have arrived at the decision; that is, was there some basis in fact which justified the making of the decision?') .

[68] Freedom of Information Act 1982, ss 58, 58A.

[69] (2002) 188 ALR 302.

[70] See the Attorney-General's annual reports and the 1987 report on the Act of the Senate Standing Committee on Legal and Constitutional Affairs.

Council) being in favour of abolition in that case, and as to whether the lifespan of certificates should continue to be unlimited (the Commission favoured a maximum duration of two years). A change in the review provisions was regarded as unnecessary, the obligation to justify to Parliament a refusal to revoke a certificate for which the Tribunal had found there to be no reasonable grounds being described as 'a considerable and sufficient discipline' for Ministers. However, the report castigated the 'not uncommon' practice of issuing certificates only *after* substantive appeals against refusals of access had been lodged with the Tribunal as an abuse of the certification provisions, although stopping short of advocating its prohibition and placing faith instead in the deterrent effect of its being exposed in the proposed new Commissioner's annual reports.[71] With regard to exemptions generally, *the Australian Law Reform Commission report* concluded that the protection afforded by Part IV of the Act was in some instances unnecessary or too wide[72] but did not propose any major amendments. Some of its more significant recommendations are mentioned below under specific heads of exemption. Although they were reflected in the Freedom of Information Amendment (Open Government) Bill 2000[73] ('the Australian Amendment Bill'), the Senate Legal and Constitutional Legislation Committee, which conducted an inquiry into that Bill, did not support their enactment, on the basis that alternative exemption systems not based on individual categories should be explored as part of a longer-term revision of the Act before any changes are made in this regard.[74]

Canada

In Canada there are many exemptions. Most are in form discretionary, opening **9.33** with the words 'The head of a government institution may refuse to disclose any record requested under this Act which . . .', but some are mandatory, replacing the word 'may' with 'shall'. In the discretionary cases there is no express equivalent of the requirement in section 2 of the 2000 Act to balance public interests. There has been much criticism in Canada of these provisions.

In March 1987 the Standing Committee on Justice of the Canadian House of **9.34** Commons and the Solicitor-General produced a unanimous report[75] on the Freedom of Information Act and the Privacy Act. The report advocated the abolition of all mandatory exemptions (except for Cabinet confidences) and making the test for all discretionary exemptions a reasonable expectation of significant injury to the stated interest. This recommendation was not implemented. The

---

[71] *Australian Law Reform Commission report* (n 20 above) paras 8.17–8.20.
[72] ibid, para 8.6.
[73] See ch 25 below, at para 25.05.
[74] *Inquiry into the Freedom of Information Amendment (Open Government) Bill 2000* (April 2001) (hereafter *the Senate Inquiry report*), paras 3.36, 3.64, 3.137.
[75] *Open and Shut—Enhancing the Right to Know and the Right to Privacy* hereafter *the Open and Shut report*.

Information Commissioner in his 2000–1 report favoured the introduction of an injury test for all exemptions except section 19 (personal information) and a 'public interest override'.

9.35 The 'public interest override' is a feature of most Canadian provincial access statutes. It means an obligation to disclose information without having to be asked for it. The expression is also used to mean a proviso to an exemption which disapplies it when in the public interest to do so. The Ontario Freedom of Information and Protection of Privacy Act exemplifies both senses: it has (i) a general override requiring the head of an institution to disclose as soon as practical to the public or persons affected any record where he has reasonable and probable grounds to believe it is in the public interest to do so and the record reveals a grave environmental, health or safety hazard to the public, and (ii) specific overrides disapplying certain exemptions (advice, relations with other governments, third party information, economic interests, dangers to health/safety, personal information) where there is a compelling public interest in disclosure clearly outweighing the purpose of the exemption. The British Columbia and Alberta Acts[76] have a general override for circumstances where there is a risk of significant harm to the environment, health or safety or any other reason for which disclosure is clearly in the public interest.

9.36 The Canadian Information Commissioner would make it compulsory to disclose any information in which the public interest in disclosure outweighs any of the interests protected by the exemptions.[77] He points out that the sister statute, the Privacy Act, authorizes governmental release of personal information without consent when the public interest in disclosure clearly outweighs any invasion of privacy that would result.[78] The Task Force saw no necessity to change the existing pattern.[79] It believes that there is implicit in every discretionary exemption a need to consider what possibility of harm there would be in disclosure, and a balancing of the public interest in disclosure against the public interest in protecting the information. Any problems in applying the exemptions can be cured by training decision-makers how to do so properly; it is a matter of education and attitudes, not defects in the drafting of the legislation.

Ireland

9.37 The Irish provisions as to exempt records are detailed and complex, and not unlike those in the United Kingdom. Some provide for an absolute exemption.[80] Other records are only exempt if, in the opinion of the head of the public body

---

[76] Sections 25, 31 respectively.
[77] Page 72 of his 2000–1 report.
[78] Privacy Act 1982, s 8(2)(m)(i).
[79] *The Canadian Task Force report* (n 11 above) pp 42–44.
[80] Freedom of Information Act 1997, ss 22, 26(1)(b), 32.

concerned, prejudice or an adverse effect or a significant adverse effect could reasonably be expected to result from disclosure, such as prejudice to the prevention,
detection, or investigation of offences, an adverse effect on the security or defence
of the state, or a serious adverse effect on the government's ability to manage the
economy.[81] A number of provisions require the head of the public body concerned
not to disclose whether or not a record exists where the head is satisfied that the
disclosure of the existence or non-existence of the record would be contrary to the
public interest or itself have a prejudicial or adverse effect. A number of other
provisions disapply exemptions in a case where, in the opinion of the head of the
department concerned, the public interest would, on balance, be better served by
granting, than by refusing to grant, the request.

D. Particular Exemptions

In this part of this chapter the intention is to set out the American and **9.38**
Commonwealth provisions which come closest to the provisions of the 2000 Act.

Information accessible to applicant by other means

The first absolute exemption in the 2000 Act is for information which is accessible **9.39**
to the applicant in some other way.[82] The Canadian Act provides more simply[83]
that the Act does not apply to published materials, materials available for purchase, or to material in the public archives, libraries or museums. So too the Irish
Act does not apply to records that are available for inspection, or copies of which
are available, to members of the public, whether upon payment or free of charge,[84]
and there is a closely comparable provision in Australia.[85]

Information intended for future publication

Section 22 of the 2000 Act provides that information intended for future publi- **9.40**
cation is exempt. Canada and Ireland have similar provisions but both have a time
limit within which the publication has to take place: 90 days in Canada[86] and 12
weeks in Ireland.[87] Section 18(d) of the New Zealand Act provides that a request
may be refused if the information is or will soon be publicly available. The

---

[81] ibid, ss 23(1)(a), 24(1), 31(1)(a).
[82] Freedom of Information Act 2000, ss 2(3) and 21.
[83] Access to Information Act 1982, s 68.
[84] Freedom of Information Act 1997, s 46(2).
[85] Freedom of Information Act 1982, s 12(1).
[86] Access to Information Act 1982, s 26.
[87] Freedom of Information Act 1997, s 10(1)(d).

Australian Act permits deferment of access to a document which there is a legal requirement to publish until the time limit for its publication has passed.[88]

National security and defence

9.41 Section 23 of the 2000 Act provides that information supplied by or relating to bodies dealing with security matters is exempt. It is an absolute exemption. Section 24 provides that other information is exempt if the exemption is required for safeguarding national security. A Minister can certify that either exemption applies and the certificate is conclusive evidence, subject to an appeal to the Information Tribunal under section 60. Under section 26 information is exempt if its disclosure would be likely to prejudice defence.

9.42 The United States Act[89] does not apply to security and defence matters that (a) are specifically authorized under criteria established by an executive order to be kept secret in the interest of national defence or foreign policy and (b) are in fact properly classified pursuant to such executive order. This gives the courts the final say. Exceptions relating to national security and defence in Canada are in sections 15 and 16(2) of the Access to Information Act 1982. As in the case of all other exemptions under that Act a decision to withhold access under these sections is subject to investigation by the Information Commissioner and review by the courts. However, following the terrorist attacks on New York and Washington on 11 September 2001, the Canadian Parliament passed the Anti-terrorism Act 2001, which added a new section to the Access to Information Act (section 69.1) altogether excluding from its operation information disclosure of which has been prohibited by the issue of a certificate under section 38.13 of the Canada Evidence Act. Such a certificate may be issued by the Attorney-General for the purpose of protecting national defence or security, or information obtained in confidence from or about a foreign entity. Its issue has the effect of discontinuing any existing proceedings before the Commissioner or the courts in which access to the relevant records is being sought. A party to the proceeding may apply to the Federal Court of Appeal for an order varying or cancelling the certificate, but the Court's jurisdiction is limited to determining whether the information subject to the certificate relates to national defence or security, or information obtained in confidence from or in relation to a foreign entity. If and to the extent that the Court determines that the information does so relate, it is obliged to confirm the certificate. The Information Commissioner among others opposed the introduction of this

---

[88] Freedom of Information Act 1982, s 21.

[89] United States Code, Title 5, s 552(b)(1). Note the related provisions ('exclusions') under s 552(c), especially (c)(3): 'Whenever a request is made which involves access to records maintained by the Federal Bureau of Investigation pertaining to foreign intelligence or counterintelligence, or international terrorism, and the existence of the records is classified information as provided in subsection (b)(1), the Bureau may, as long as the existence of the records remains classified information, treat the records as not subject to the requirements of this section.'

measure. In his 2001–2 report[90] he argues that it was unnecessary because sensitive intelligence information was already amply protected by the exemptions in sections 13 and 15 of the Canadian Act, and sets out his concerns about the breadth of the Attorney-General's powers. The judicial review provisions he describes as 'window dressing' in as much as they do not authorize an independent assessment of the sensitivity of the information or the purpose of the certificate.

New Zealand has a single provision which deals with security and defence: section 6(a) provides that good reason for withholding information exists if making the information available would be likely to prejudice the security or defence of New Zealand. If the Prime Minister certifies that to be the case, the Ombudsman cannot recommend disclosure, but only that the holder of the relevant information reconsider.[91] To the knowledge of the New Zealand Law Commission, the power had only once been exercised.[92]   **9.43**

In Australia a document is exempt if its disclosure would, or could reasonably be expected to, cause damage to (amongst other things) the security or defence of the Commonwealth.[93] A minister is given power, where he is satisfied that a document is exempt for one of these reasons, to sign a certificate which establishes conclusively that the document is exempt.[94]   **9.44**

In Ireland a request for information which could reasonably be expected to affect adversely the security or defence of the state may be refused[95] and a Minister of the government, if he is satisfied that the record is of sufficient sensitivity or seriousness, may certify conclusively that the record is an exempt record.[96] There are safeguards on this certification. The Taoiseach and other designated Ministers have power to review certificates, Ministers have to report annually the number of certificates issued by them, and certificates only remain in force for a maximum of two years (but can be renewed). There is also a right of appeal against a certificate to the High Court on a point of law.[97] Only two such certificates were issued in 2000 and one in 2001 and it appears that none had been issued prior to that.   **9.45**

International relations

Under section 27 of the 2000 Act information is exempt if its disclosure would be likely to prejudice relations between the United Kingdom and any other state, or   **9.46**

---

[90] At pp 11, 15–20.
[91] Official Information Act 1982, s 31.
[92] *Review of the Official Information Act 1982*, New Zealand Law Commission Report 40 (1997) (hereafter *the New Zealand Law Commission report*) para 280.
[93] Freedom of Information Act 1982, s 33.
[94] See para 9.31 above.
[95] Freedom of Information Act 1997, s 24.
[96] ibid, s 25.
[97] ibid, s 42(2).

international organization, or if it is confidential information obtained from another state or organization. Most countries have such exemptions. Sections 13 and 15(1) of the Canadian Act are very close to the wording of the 2000 Act. In New Zealand section 6(a) and (b) of the Official Information Act 1982 provides that a conclusive reason for withholding information exists if making the information available would be likely to prejudice international relations[98] or the entrusting of information to the government of New Zealand on a basis of confidence by the government of any other country, or any international organization. The United States Act, as has been seen, does not apply to matters that are specifically authorized under criteria established by an executive order to be kept secret in the interests of foreign policy which are in fact properly classified pursuant to such an executive order.[99] A reasonable expectation of damage to international relations is another reason for exempting a document under section 33 of the Australian Act, with its conclusive certification provisions. That section also applies if disclosure would divulge any information communicated in confidence by a foreign government or international organization.

Relations within the United Kingdom

9.47 The exemption for international relations is matched by an exemption for information disclosure of which would prejudice relations between any administration in the United Kingdom and any other such administration.[100] There is a similar provision in Canada relating to information the disclosure of which could reasonably be expected to be injurious to the conduct by the government of Canada of federal-provincial affairs.[101] If damage to relations between the Commonwealth of Australia and one of the states would, or could reasonably be expected to, ensue from disclosing a document, access can be withheld unless disclosure would, on balance, be in the public interest.[102] In Ireland there is an exemption for records which could reasonably be expected to prejudice the functions and negotiations of public bodies: this exemption is subject to a public interest test.[103]

---

[98] A s 31 certificate may be issued as to this: see para 9.43 above.
[99] United States Code, Title 5, s 552(b)(1).
[100] Freedom of Information Act 2000, s 28.
[101] Access to Information Act 1982, s 14.
[102] Freedom of Information Act 1982, s 33A.
[103] Freedom of Information Act 1997, s 21.

The economy

Information is exempt if its release is likely to prejudice the economic interests of **9.48**
the United Kingdom.[104] Australia,[105] Canada,[106] New Zealand,[107] and Ireland[108] all
have exemptions that are designed to protect the economic interest of their countries. The 2000 Act is the most succinct, it is also the Act which gives greatest protection to the government. The others require something more than *prejudice* to
found the exemption. In Australia the disclosure has to have a *substantial adverse
effect* on the government's ability to manage the economy; in Canada it has to be
reasonably expected to be materially injurious to the ability to manage the economy;
in New Zealand it must be likely to *damage seriously* the economy; in Ireland it is
to have a *serious adverse effect* on financial interests of the state or the ability of the
government to manage the national economy. According to *the Australian Law
Reform Commission report*,[109] the Australian exemption is rarely used and super-
fluous; in every previous case to have reached the appeal stage in which it had been
relied upon, the relevant documents had been found on appeal to be exempt
under another provision. Its repeal was accordingly advocated.

Legal matters

A number of exemptions relate to legal matters. Section 30 of the 2000 Act covers **9.49**
investigations and proceedings conducted by public authorities. Section 31 is
concerned with law enforcement where disclosure is likely to prejudice the prevention and detection of crime, the apprehension or prosecution of offenders, the
administration of justice, the assessment or collection of tax, the operation of immigration controls, and the maintenance of security and good order in prisons.
Section 32 deals with court records (an absolute exemption), and section 42 deals
with legal professional privilege. Section 44(1)(c) of the 2000 Act provides that
disclosure of information is exempt if it would constitute or be punishable as a
contempt of court. This is also an absolute exemption.

In the United States the right to information does not apply to records or informa- **9.50**
tion compiled for law enforcement purposes, but only to the extent that the production of such records and information:

(a) could reasonably be expected to interfere with enforcement proceedings;
(b) would deprive a person of a right to a fair trial or an impartial adjudication;

---

104 Freedom of Information Act 2000, s 29.
105 Freedom of Information Act 1982, s 44.
106 Access to Information Act 1982, s 18.
107 Official Information Act 1982, s 6(e).
108 Freedom of Information Act 1997, s 31.
109 See n 20 above at para 9.28.

(c) could reasonably be expected to constitute an unwarranted invasion of personal privacy;

(d) could reasonably be expected to disclose the identity of a confidential source;

(e) would disclose techniques and procedures for law enforcement investigations or prosecutions; or

(f) could reasonably be expected to endanger the life or physical safety of any individual.[110]

9.51 In New Zealand good reason for withholding information exists where disclosure is likely to prejudice the maintenance of the law, including the prevention, investigation, and detection of offences, and the right to a fair trial.[111] Information is exempt where the withholding of it is necessary to maintain legal professional privilege unless the balance of public interest favours disclosure[112] and a request for information may be refused where making it available would constitute contempt of court.[113] The New Zealand exemptions are not as specific as those in the 2000 Act but they cover much the same ground. The same can be said of Australia and Canada. Exempt documents in Australia include documents affecting enforcement of the law, documents subject to legal professional privilege and documents the disclosure of which would be a contempt of court.[114] In Canada section 16 of the Access to Information Act 1982 provides exemptions for records relating to law enforcement and investigations and section 23 exempts documents subject to solicitor and client privilege. In Ireland there are comparable provisions in sections 22 and 23 of the Freedom of Information Act 1997.

Audit

9.52 Information which would prejudice the audit functions of a public authority is exempt under section 33 of the 2000 Act. There are close parallels in Canada where section 22 of the Access to Information Act provides that the head of a government institution may refuse to disclose any record requested that contains information relating to testing or auditing procedures if the disclosure would prejudice the use or results of particular tests or audits; Ireland where access can be refused if, in the opinion of the head of the public body concerned, it could reasonably be expected to prejudice the effectiveness of tests or audits conducted by the body and would not serve the public interest better than non-disclosure;[115] and Australia where a document is exempt if its disclosure would or could reason-

---

[110] United States Code, Title 5, s 552(b)(7).

[111] Official Information Act 1982, s 6(c). The Attorney-General may issue a certificate under s 31 precluding an Ombudsman's recommendation of disclosure in such cases.

[112] ibid, s 9(2)(h).

[113] ibid, s 18(c).

[114] Freedom of Information Act 1982, ss 37, 42 and 46.

[115] Freedom of Information Act 1997, s 21(1)(a).

ably be expected to prejudice particular audits, or audit procedures generally, and would not be on balance in the public interest.[116]

Parliamentary privilege

Information in the United Kingdom is exempt if the exemption is required for the **9.53** purpose of avoiding an infringement of the privileges of either House of Parliament.[117] There is a similar provision in Australia: section 46 of the Freedom of Information Act 1982 provides that a document is exempt if public disclosure would infringe the privileges of the Parliament of the Commonwealth or of a state. In New Zealand a request for information may be refused if making it available would constitute contempt of the House of Representatives.[118] In Ireland the head of a public body is required to refuse a request if the record sought consists of (i) the private papers of a representative of the European Parliament or (ii) opinions, advice, recommendations, or the results of consultations, considered by either House of the Oireachtas[119] or a committee appointed by either such House, and certain other classes of parliamentary papers are altogether excluded from the scope of the legislation.[120] Freedom of Information legislation in Canada does not apply to Parliament[121] and in the United States it does not apply to Congress.

Section 34(3) of the 2000 Act gives the Speaker in the Commons and the Clerk of **9.54** the Parliaments in the Lords power to issue a certificate that exemption is required to avoid an infringement of Parliamentary privilege. Such a certificate is conclusive. There is no comparable provision in Australia, New Zealand or Ireland.

Constitutional conventions

Two of the most important exemptions in the 2000 Act relate to the formulation **9.55** of government policy (section 35) and prejudice to the effective conduct of public affairs (section 36). The exemptions reflect long-standing constitutional practice that advice to government should not be disclosed.

Under section 35 information held by a government department or by the **9.56** National Assembly for Wales is exempt information if it relates to (a) the formulation or development of government policy; (b) ministerial communications; (c) the provision of advice by any of the law officers; or (d) the operation of any private office. Statistical information is not to be included in (a) or (b) once a decision on government policy has been taken. The Act specifically provides that in

---

[116] Freedom of Information Act 1982, s 40.
[117] Freedom of Information Act 2000, s 34.
[118] Official Information Act 1982, s 18(c).
[119] The Irish Parliament.
[120] Freedom of Information Act 1997, ss 22(1)(c), 46(1)(e).
[121] *The Canadian Task Force report* (n 11 above) recommends that it should, subject to the safeguarding of privilege.

making any determination about such information regard shall be had to the particular public interest in the disclosure of factual information which has been used, or is intended to be used, to provide an informed background to decision-taking.

9.57 Section 36 applies to all public authorities. Information is exempt if in the reasonable opinion of a qualified person it would (i) prejudice the collective responsibility of ministers; (ii) be likely to inhibit the free and frank provision of advice or the free and frank exchange of views for the purpose of deliberation; or (iii) otherwise be likely to prejudice the effective conduct of public affairs. In the case of statistical information the words *in the reasonable opinion of a qualified person* are omitted from the test.

9.58 New Zealand also has generous exemptions to protect constitutional conventions. If the withholding of information is necessary to protect the confidentiality of communications with the Queen or her representative, or collective or individual ministerial responsibility, or the political neutrality of officials or the confidentiality of advice tendered by Ministers or officials, or to maintain the effective conduct of public affairs through the free and frank expression of opinions or the protection of Ministers from improper pressure or harassment, the information is exempt.[122] These exemptions are close to the United Kingdom provisions and both the New Zealand and the United Kingdom exemptions are subject to a public interest test.[123] Exemptions in Australia apply to Cabinet documents, Executive Council documents and internal working documents disclosure of which would reveal deliberative processes of an agency or Minister or of the government,[124] and in Ireland to records relating to meetings of the government and the deliberations of public bodies.[125] The exemption in section 19 of the Irish Act does not extend to factual information relating to a decision of the government that has been published, or records relating to a decision taken by the government more than five years prior to request. The section 20 exemption is subject to a number of exceptions, including one for factual information, and to what the Irish Information Commissioner has described[126] as 'a fairly strong test', namely that the granting of the request must, in the opinion of the head of the public body concerned, be positively contrary to the public interest. Nonetheless, in his report on the first three years of the Act's operation the Commissioner expressed concern that the test was not being properly applied and was being confused with the pub-

---

[122] Official Information Act 1982, s 9(2)(f) and (g).
[123] Save in the United Kingdom in respect of information held by the House of Commons or the House of Lords.
[124] Freedom of Information Act 1982, ss 34–36.
[125] Freedom of Information Act 1997, ss 19–20.
[126] See the Minutes of Evidence taken before the House of Lords Select Committee on the draft Freedom of Information Bill: HL Paper (1998–99) no 97 at p 72.

lic interest balancing test to be found in other sections. He also criticized decision-makers for unjustifiably withholding materials relating to deliberative processes until after conclusion of the processes in question.

The Australian Law Reform Commission report considered the absolute exemption **9.59** for Cabinet documents to be justified in the interests of upholding the convention of collective Ministerial responsibility and the confidentiality of Cabinet deliberations (subject to the introduction of a 20-year time limit from the date of creation of such documents), but that all Executive Council documents deserving of secrecy would be covered by some other exemption.[127] As for section 36, it was thought that its title ('internal working documents') gave a misleading impression of the width of the exemption and should be replaced by 'documents revealing deliberative processes', but its substance met with approval despite having been the subject of heavy criticism by applicants and commentators for being a 'catch-all' provision.[128] Suggestions that the exemption should be narrowed to apply only to material relating to policy formulation, as opposed to all 'thinking processes', were rejected on the basis that the distinction would be a difficult one to draw in practice.[129]

In Canada section 69 of the Access to Information Act provides that the Act does **9.60** not apply to confidences of the Queen's Privy Council for Canada, which is defined to include the Cabinet and Cabinet committees. Section 69(1) provides that such confidences include:

(a) memoranda the purpose of which is to present proposals or recommendations to the Cabinet;
(b) discussion papers the purpose of which is to present background explanations;
(c) the agenda and records recording deliberations or decisions;
(d) records used for or reflecting communications or discussions between ministers on matters relating to the making of government decisions or the formulation of government policy;
(e) records the purpose of which is to brief ministers in relation to matters that are before or are proposed to be brought before Cabinet;
(f) draft legislation.

The section does not apply to confidences which are more than 20 years old, or to confidences within item (b) if the discussion papers relate to decisions which have been made public or, where the decisions have not been made public, if four years have passed since the decision was made.[130]

---

[127] *Report* (n 20 above) paras 9.7–9.14.
[128] ibid, para 9.15.
[129] The view that what 'deliberative processes' means is policy forming processes has been advanced but rejected: see, for example, *Re Waterford and Dept of the Treasury (No 2)* (1984) 5 ALD 588, *Kavvadias v Commonwealth Ombudsman (No 2)* (1984) 2 FCR 64, 74–8 and *Re Subramanian and Refugee Review Tribunal* (1997) 44 ALD 435, AAT.
[130] Access to Information Act, s 69(3)(b).

9.61   This section is said to have been Prime Minister Pierre Trudeau's price for proceeding with the Bill in 1982.[131] The clause has been controversial from the first, both because its terms were considered too wide and because its application was thought not to be subject to independent review.[132] In *Information Commissioner of Canada v Minister of Environment Canada and Ethyl Canada Inc*[133] Blanchard J held that Cabinet discussion papers should have been released. The papers related to the banning of the use of MMT (an octane enhancer used in motor vehicle fuels). On advice from the Privy Council Office, access was refused on the grounds that the documents were not *discussion papers* (which were liable to disclosure once the decision had been taken), but portions of 'memoranda' which were protected under section 69(1)(a) of the Act. It emerged during the trial that in 1984, shortly after the Act was passed, *discussion papers* as a separate class of documents had been abolished, and the material which would formerly have been put in them began to be incorporated as an analysis section in *memoranda* presenting proposals to the Cabinet. The judge upheld the view of the Commissioner that the Cabinet could not circumvent the intention of Parliament in this way and prevent the release of documents which the law required to be made available to the public. What mattered was the content of the documents not what label the Privy Council Office chose to put upon them. This case illustrates that the courts are likely to have little sympathy with Ministers and civil servants who try to frustrate the Act.

Health and safety

9.62   Information is exempt under section 38 of the 2000 Act if its disclosure would be likely to endanger the physical or mental health of any individual, or endanger the safety of any individual. This is matched in Canada where the disclosure of information which could reasonably be expected to threaten the safety of individuals is exempt.[134] That disclosure would or could reasonably be expected to endanger the life or physical safety of any person is a sufficient ground for exemption in Australia.[135] In New Zealand too, among the good reasons for not disclosing information are if the disclosure would be likely to endanger the safety of any person,[136] or if withholding the information is necessary to avoid prejudice to mea-

---

[131]   *The Access to Information Act: A Critical Review* prepared by Sysnovators Ltd of Ottawa for the Information Commissioner of Canada (1994) 34.

[132]   See *the Open and Shut Report* (n 75 above) and the Information Commissioner's report for the year to March 2001. The Task Force accepted that documents in this class should be brought within the scope of the Act and made the subject of an exemption rather than an exclusion, with a reduction in the protection period to 15 years, and a narrowing of the definition (*the Canadian Task Force report* (n 11 above) 45–47).

[133]   [2001] 3 FC 514 (appeal pending).

[134]   Access to Information Act 1982, s 17.

[135]   Freedom of Information Act 1982, s 37(1)(c).

[136]   Official Information Act 1982, s 6(d).

sures protecting the health or safety of members of the public, and the public interest does not favour disclosure.[137] The United States has a somewhat narrower exemption. The US Act does not apply to records or information compiled for law enforcement purposes disclosure of which could reasonably be expected to endanger the life or physical safety of any individual.[138]

Environmental information

The duty to disclose environmental information already exists in the United **9.63** Kingdom and arises under the provisions of the Aarhus Convention of 25 June 1998, rather than under the 2000 Act. Section 39, which excludes as exempt information matters which a public authority is bound to disclose under the regulations made in relation to the Convention, is not a true exemption. No other country has similar provisions. This is an oddity of the way the UK legislation is drafted. Indeed, one of the main features of freedom of information legislation around the world is to encourage the disclosure of information which governments hold about the environment.

Personal information

Personal information is protected from disclosure.[139] In Canada there is a general **9.64** provision requiring the head of a government institution to refuse to disclose any record that contains personal information as defined in section 3 of the Privacy Act, unless disclosed in accordance with section 8 of that Act (which permits disclosure in certain circumstances, one of which is that the public interest in disclosure clearly outweighs any invasion of privacy it would involve). In New Zealand section 9(2)(a) of the Official Information Act 1982 protects the privacy of natural persons, including that of deceased natural persons, subject to a public interest test. In Ireland personal information is generally exempt,[140] but can be released if the public interest in disclosure outweighs the public interest in the subject's right to privacy being upheld.

In the United States the Act does not apply to information involving matters of **9.65** personal privacy or to records and information compiled for law enforcement purposes disclosure of which could reasonably be expected to constitute an unwarranted invasion of personal privacy.[141] There are authorities for the propositions that disclosure will be ordered if it would contribute to a public interest purpose, and that once having found an invasion of privacy the court should weigh the seriousness of the invasion against whatever gain would accrue to the

---

[137] ibid, s 9(c).
[138] United States Code, Title 5, s 552(b)(7).
[139] Section 40 of the 2000 Act.
[140] Freedom of Information Act 1997, s 28.
[141] United States Code, Title 5, s 552(b)(6) and (7).

public from disclosure to decide if it is 'unwarranted'.[142] However, the Supreme Court decision in *US Dept of Justice v Reporters Committee for Freedom of the Press*[143] seems to place limits on the public interest in the disclosure of personal information. That case concerned a request for access to FBI-held 'rap sheets' (criminal history records) for certain persons alleged to have had corrupt dealings with a member of Congress. It was held that the purpose of the freedom of information legislation was to shed light on agencies' performance of their statutory duties and information (such as rap sheets) which was not directly revelatory of government activities fell outside the ambit of the public interest the legislation was intended to serve.

9.66   In Australia documents are exempt if to disclose them would involve the unreasonable disclosure of personal information about any person, living or dead (other than the applicant for access).[144] There is authority that the word 'unreasonable' imports a public interest test similar to those which are made express in the Canadian, New Zealand and Irish Acts. See, for example, *Colakovski v Australian Telecommunications Cpn*[145] where Lockhart J said that the concept of 'unreasonableness' in this context 'must have as its core public interest considerations', including the public interest in maintaining personal privacy. The Australian Administrative Appeals Tribunal has adopted the test of balancing competing public interests (in the preservation of privacy and the public gain from disclosure respectively) in deciding what would be an 'unreasonable' disclosure of personal information.[146] *The Australian Law Reform Commission report*[147] advocated redrafting this section of the Australian Act to clarify its meaning, and tie it in with the later Privacy Act, by providing that a document is exempt if it contains personal information disclosure of which would constitute a breach of Information Privacy Principle 11 (which forbids disclosure of personal information to third parties save in limited circumstances) and would not, on balance, be in the public interest. *The Senate Inquiry report* supported an amendment along those lines in the case of this particular exemption.[148]

9.67   Section 40 of the 2000 Act is in line with these provisions but more restrictive of disclosure. Any information to which a request for information relates is exempt if it constitutes personal data of which the applicant is the data subject, or if the disclosure contravenes the data protection principles, or if it is likely to cause damage or distress. While the data protection principles allow the release of

---

[142]   *Dept of Air Force v Rose* 425 US 352 (1976), *Ferry v CIA* 458 F Supp 664 (1978), *Committee on Masonic Homes of RW Grand Lodge v NLRB* 556 F2d 214 (1977).

[143]   489 US 749 (1989).

[144]   Freedom of Information Act 1982, s 41.

[145]   (1991) 100 ALR 111.

[146]   See eg *Re Scholes and Australian Federal Police* (1996) 44 ALD 299, AAT.

[147]   See n 20 above, para 10.7.

[148]   See n 74 above at paras 3.52, 3.65.

information in certain narrowly defined circumstances which may serve a public interest purpose, they do not allow it by reference to general considerations of public interest.[149]

Confidence

A number of exemptions relate to information supplied in confidence. Section 41 **9.68** of the 2000 Act provides that if the disclosure of information would constitute a breach of confidence actionable by the person who supplied the information it is absolutely exempt. Section 42 deals with legal professional privilege which has already been considered.[150] Section 43 provides that information is exempt if it constitutes a trade secret, or if its disclosure under the Act would be likely to prejudice the commercial interests of any person (including the public authority holding it).

The United States

The United States Act does not apply to: 'trade secrets and commercial or finan- **9.69** cial information obtained from a person and privileged or confidential'.[151] The majority of cases on this exemption have turned on whether the information sought fell within the 'commercial or financial information' category.[152]

Australia

In Australia a document is an exempt document if its disclosure would disclose **9.70** trade secrets, or any other information having a commercial value that would be, or could reasonably be expected to be, destroyed or diminished if the information was disclosed, or other information the disclosure of which would or could reasonably be expected to affect adversely a person's business or professional affairs or the business, commercial or financial affairs of an organization or undertaking.[153] There is a separate exemption for documents the disclosure of which under the Act would constitute an actionable breach of confidence.[154]

Canada

In Canada there are detailed provisions relating to confidential information. **9.71** Section 13 of the Access to Information Act 1982 deals with information obtained in confidence from other governments, from other states and from the provinces. Section 18, which deals with the economic interests of Canada, provides that the head of a government institution may refuse to disclose any record

---

[149] See ch 10 below.
[150] See paras 9.49–9.51 above.
[151] United States Code, Title 5, s 552(b)(4).
[152] AC Aman and WT Mayton: *Administrative Law* (2nd edn, 2001) 669–671.
[153] Freedom of Information Act 1982, s 43.
[154] ibid, s 45.

that contains trade secrets or financial, commercial or technical information that belongs to the government of Canada or a government institution and has substantial value or which could reasonably be expected to prejudice the competitive position of a government institution. Section 20 contains a mandatory exception for records containing third party trade secrets; other confidential information supplied by a third party of a financial, commercial, scientific or technical nature; information the disclosure of which could reasonably be expected to prejudice a third party's competitive position, or interfere with a third party's contractual 'or other' negotiations, or 'result in material financial loss or gain to a third party'; *unless* (i) the record contains the results of product or environmental testing carried out by a government institution or (ii) its disclosure would be in the public interest as relating to public health or safety or environmental protection and the interest in disclosure 'clearly outweighs in importance' the prejudice to the third party: proviso (ii) does not apply to trade secrets.

9.72 The Canadian courts have consistently said that the test for what is 'confidential information' is objective and that government institutional undertakings to keep information confidential are not determinative of their disclosure obligations under the Access to Information Act 1982 and cannot override its specific provisions. In *Information Commissioner of Canada v President of Atlantic Canada Opportunities Agency*[155] the information requested was details of jobs created by firms with funding assistance from the Opportunities Agency. The Agency refused to disclose the information on the basis that the information was supplied in confidence by the firms which had received grant/loan aid. A survey had been carried out for the Agency by Price Waterhouse, which had promised the firms that their responses would be kept confidential. The Court of Appeal said that that undertaking had not been authorized by the Agency but in any event could not have been determinative of the Agency's disclosure obligations under the Act.[156]

9.73 In his 2000–1 report the Hon John Reid, the Information Commissioner, described the section 20 exemption as 'one of the most used, abused and litigated'. He said the Act is too cautious in extending protection to private business; especially in the days of government downsizing and privatization when more and more matters affecting the public interest are dealt with in the private sector:

> Government officials and private firms should not be able to agree among themselves to keep information secret. Yet section 20(1)(b) comes perilously close to giving authority for just such a cozy arrangement.[157]

---

[155] (1999) 250 NR 314, Federal Court of Appeal.

[156] The Court of Appeal cited: *Ottawa Football Club v Canada (Minister of Fitness and Amateur Sports)* [1989] 2 FC 480, *Information Commissioner for Canada v Immigration and Refugee Board (Canada)* (1997) 140 FTR 140, and *Canada Broadcasting Cpn v National Capital Commission* (1998) 147 FTR 264.

[157] Pages 74–6 of the report.

New Zealand

In New Zealand provisions about confidence are subject to a public interest test. **9.74** The Official Information Act 1982 provides[158] that good reason exists for withholding information where it is necessary to:

- protect information where the making available of the information would disclose a trade secret or be likely unreasonably to prejudice the commercial position of the person who supplied or who is the subject of the information;
- protect information which is subject to an obligation of confidence or which any person has been or could be compelled to provide under the authority of any enactment where the making available of the information (i) would be likely to prejudice the supply of similar information or information from the same source and if it is in the public interest that such information should continue to be supplied, or (ii) would be likely otherwise to damage the public interest;
- enable a Minister or any department or organization holding the information to carry out, without prejudice or disadvantage, commercial activities;
- enable a Minister or any department or organization holding the information to carry on without prejudice or disadvantage negotiations (including commercial and industrial negotiations);
- prevent the disclosure or use of official information for improper gain or improper advantage.

Accordingly, the existence of an obligation of confidence is not of itself sufficient to ensure protection in this jurisdiction.

Ireland

Subject to exceptions, information obtained in confidence (section 26) and com- **9.75** mercially sensitive information (section 27) are exempt under the Irish Freedom of Information Act 1997. There are, however, two classes of information obtained in confidence. One consists of information disclosure of which would constitute a breach of a legal duty of confidence, refusal of access to which is mandatory. The other consists of information given in confidence and on the understanding that it would be treated as confidential, which is to be disclosed unless the head of the public body concerned considers that its disclosure would be likely to prejudice the future giving of similar information and would not serve the public interest better than non-disclosure. A practical problem identified by the Irish Information Commissioner in his report on the first three years of the Act's operation was the difficulty of determining when information is given in confidence or is subject to a legal duty of confidence.

---

[158] At s 9(2)(b), (ba), (i), (j), (k).

Given the volume of business transacted by public bodies, it is not surprising that express assurances of confidentiality are relatively rare. This means that decision makers often have to decide whether an assurance of confidence was implied. This is not an easy task particularly since the decision maker may not be able to establish with certainty the precise circumstances in which the information was given to the public body and the use to which the provider of the information intended it to be put. Even where express assurances of confidentiality are given problems can arise. Some such assurances may be inappropriate, or their scope may be misleading, as where, for example, information is given to a public body and it is intended that active use will be made of it to the detriment of another person. In such cases, if active use is made of the information then fair procedures may require disclosure of the substance of the information to the person affected regardless of any prior assurances given to the provider of the information.

He recommended that to avoid uncertainty, public bodies should develop and publish clear guidelines on the collection and use of information from third parties and a clear policy on when confidentiality would be assured.

9.76 The complexity of the law in this area, and the difficulties agencies face in applying it, were also acknowledged in *the Australian Law Reform Commission report.*[159] However, a proposal to make the relevant section of the Australian Act self-contained by including a statement of the elements of a breach of confidence was rejected, on the basis that the exemption should be left to develop in line with the general law. Instead, it recommended that the proposed new Freedom of Information Commissioner should provide decision-makers with detailed assistance as to the circumstances in which a duty of confidence arises to help them distinguish between information which is legally protected and information which, while it may be described as 'confidential', is not. *The Canadian Task Force report*[160] observes that many third party complaints arise because informants are unaware that the information they provide to government will be accessible under the legislation, and recommends that they should be forewarned in advance of providing it.

Prohibitions on disclosure

9.77 Under section 44 of the 2000 Act information is exempt if its disclosure by the public authority holding it:

(a) is prohibited by or under any enactment, [or]
(b) is incompatible with any [European] Community obligation.

The section also deals with contempt of court which has already been considered. The comparable provision in the United States is drawn more tightly. The Act does not apply to matters specifically exempted from disclosure by statute pro-

---

[159] See n 20 above at paras 10.32–10.33.
[160] See n 11 above at p 61.

vided that such statute (a) requires that the matters be withheld from the public in such manner as leaves no discretion on the issue, or (b) establishes particular criteria for withholding or refers to particular types of matters to be withheld.[161] The United States Act does not, of course, refer to Community obligations. The comparable provision in New Zealand is section 18(c) of the Official Information Act 1982, and that in Ireland is section 32 of the Freedom of Information Act 1997. The Australian and Canadian Acts both have schedules listing enactments prohibitive of disclosure which prevent the access provisions from applying.

E. Answering Requests

Timetables

Section 10(1) of the 2000 Act provides that a public authority must comply with **9.78** a request promptly and within 20 working days, and section 17 provides that if the public authority refuses a request it must give the applicant a notice which specifies any exemption on which the authority relies and specifies why the exemption applies. New Zealand has the same time limit, with power to extend it where the request is for a large quantity of official information.[162] In Canada the head of the institution receiving the request has 30 days to give notice whether access will be given and if so to give it; or 15 days to transfer the request to another institution with a greater interest in the record, for example because it produced it. There is no similar provision in the 2000 Act for passing on a request to another authority. In Canada time can be extended for a reasonable period if fees are charged and required to be paid before access is given, or if the institution needs more time to search or consult, or if it serves notice of the request on an affected third party.[163]

The Information Commissioner in Canada complained in his 2000–1 report[164] of **9.79** 'an ignominious 18 year record of disrespect for the requirement that responses to access requests be timely' and said 'strong medicine' was needed to deal with delays, which were the subject of 50 per cent of the complaints to him. This has apparently been a problem from the beginning. He noted that the exemption in section 26 (for information that is going to be published) is open to abuse and is used as a device to buy time; institutions say something is going to be published and then when the time allowed for publication is about to expire, change their minds and claim some other exemption. The Commissioner proposed reducing the 90 days allowed in Canada for publication to 60 days and providing that if the

---

[161] United States Code, Title 5, s 552(b)(3).
[162] Official Information Act 1982, ss 15 and 15A.
[163] Access to Information Act 1982, ss 7–9.
[164] See pp 18, 59 and 77–78.

information is not published within that time it must be released forthwith. According to his 2001–2 report,[165] there has been a significant drop in the proportion of complaints concerned with delay (down to about 29 per cent in the year under report), which he attributes to an increased allocation of resources to access to information units and the measures taken by him to combat delay, including tabling in Parliament 'report cards' grading the performance of departments in this respect. However, he expresses anxiety that this improvement may have been achieved at the expense of careful critical assessment of whether exemptions apply. He also highlights[166] what he calls a 'troubling new development' whereby some departments have begun to take undue advantage of the provisions for extending time in reliance on the decision of the Federal Court in *Attorney-General of Canada and Janice Cochrane v Information Commissioner of Canada.*[167] That case arose out of a three-year extension by Citizenship and Immigration Canada ('CIC') which the Commissioner had found not to be reasonable. Nonetheless, the judge held that the Commissioner and the Court were powerless to do anything about it, their jurisdiction to intervene[168] depending on there having been a refusal of access, which there had not been. A deemed refusal would occur if access was not given 'within the time limits set out in the Act'[169] but that meant within the time as extended by CIC, however unreasonably.

9.80 In the United States, agencies are required to respond to a request within 20 business days and (if the response is favourable) to provide the document within a reasonable time thereafter, with provision for a 10-day extension in certain circumstances.[170] There is provision for expedited processing in cases where the requester demonstrates a 'compelling need', that is where delay could reasonably be expected to pose a threat to an individual's life or safety, or the request is made by a person primarily engaged in disseminating information to the public and the information sought is urgently needed to inform the public about some actual or alleged federal government activity.[171]

9.81 The time limit in Australia for notifying an applicant of a decision on his access request is 30 days[172] and in Ireland it is as soon as may be, but not later than four weeks after receipt of a request.[173] There are provisions in both cases for time to be extended to allow mandatory consultation with third parties to take place.[174]

---

[165] See pp 13–14, 33.
[166] ibid, pp 12, 27–29, 80–82.
[167] 2002 FCT 136, Kelen J (appeal pending).
[168] Under Access to Information Act 1982, ss 30(1) and 41.
[169] ibid, s 10(3).
[170] United States Code, Title 5, s 552(a)(6)(A), (B).
[171] ibid, s 552(a)(6)(E).
[172] Freedom of Information Act 1982, s 15.
[173] Freedom of Information Act 1997, s 8.
[174] See para 9.91 below.

Delay in processing applications has also been one of the most common problems experienced under the Australian regime.[175] Nevertheless, in light of the advances in information technology since the 30-day limit was introduced, *the Australian Law Reform Commission report* optimistically recommended a reduction to 14 days. The Ombudsman took the view that unless and until there were considerable improvements in record management, such a deadline would be unrealistic.[176] Some of the participants in the Senate Committee inquiry into the Australian Amendment Bill agreed and submitted that to impose time limits which could not be complied with could bring the legislation into disrepute. The Committee considered that the balance should be struck at 21 days (with a three-year delay before bringing the reduction into force).[177] The New Zealand Law Reform Commission (which found 'tardiness in responding to requests' to be a major problem) considered that shortening the time limits in that country's Act (to 15 working days) would prompt agencies to take more seriously their primary obligation to respond 'as soon as reasonably practicable' instead of treating the 20-day outside limit as the benchmark.[178]

Fees

Section 9 of the 2000 Act provides that fees charged by public authorities must be **9.82** determined in accordance with regulations made by the Lord Chancellor, which may provide that no fee is payable in prescribed cases.[179] The authority has to serve a fees notice informing the applicant how much the fee will be.

In Canada a person who makes a request for access to a record may be required to **9.83** pay at the time the request is made such application fee, not exceeding Canadian $25, as may be prescribed by the regulations; and before any copies are made such fee as reflects the cost of reproduction. In addition the head of a government institution may require payment for every hour in excess of five hours that is reasonably required to search for a record, or prepare any part of it for disclosure, and may require that payment is made before access is given.[180] One of the improprieties of which the Hon John Reid, the Canadian Information Commissioner, complained in his 2000–1 report[181] was giving inflated fee estimates to deter access requests, especially from 'troublesome requesters'. However, fees can be waived and according to *the Canadian Task Force report*,[182] in about two-thirds of

---

[175] *The Australian Law Reform Commission report* (n 20 above) para 7.12.
[176] *The Needs to Know report* (n 19 above) paras 3.77–3.84.
[177] *The Senate Inquiry report* (n 74 above) paras 3.116–3.127.
[178] *The New Zealand Law Commission report* (n 92 above) para 169.
[179] The rule of thumb by which the fees are charged is that the fee should not exceed 10% of the cost of answering the request.
[180] Access to Information Act 1982, s 11.
[181] At pp 20–22.
[182] See n 11 above at 10, 83.

cases they are either formally waived or just not collected. The lack of any set criteria for waiver, or consistency in the practice, was the subject of adverse comment. Fees recovered amount to approximately 1.8 per cent of the costs of administering the system.

9.84 In Australia application fees and other charges prescribed under regulations have to be paid before a person is given access, but such fees may be reduced or waived for any reason, including but not limited to financial hardship to the applicant and the public interest in access being given. A decision not to grant an applicant's request for reduction or waiver can be reviewed by the Administrative Appeals Tribunal.[183] According to *the Australian Law Reform Commission report*,[184] the charging provisions had proved one of the most controversial aspects of the legislation, heavily criticized by applicants and agencies alike. Agencies complained that the system was so complicated, time-consuming and expensive to administer that it was not worth bothering to levy the charges. It was estimated in 1994–5 that a mere 3.7 per cent of the overall cost of compliance with the statute was recouped from applicants. According to the Attorney-General's report for 2000–1,[185] the total amount collected in that year represented only 1.54 per cent of the aggregate costs of administering the Act. It is general practice not to charge for personal information.[186] Applicants, on the other hand, complained that the costs were too much and that some agencies gave exaggerated estimates to deter them. Particular bones of contention were that charges were payable for decision-making time (which was seen as open to abuse) and in respect of documents which were ultimately withheld as exempt. *The Senate Inquiry report* records[187] evidence that the fee regime has been one of the main reasons for the low level of use of the Australian Act by the media, one particular example cited being of a request to the Department of Defence for which the initial fee estimate was $110,000. The Ombudsman noted an increasing discrepancy between the charges notified to applicants and the amounts subsequently collected, and thought the data lent weight to the concern that some agencies might be setting unreasonably high charges to process requests.[188] In the year to 30 June 2001, agencies notified a total of $1,099,380 in charges, of which only $126,052 (11.47 per cent) was collected.[189] The solutions proposed in *the Australian Law Reform Commission report* included abolishing the charge for decision-making time in all cases, restricting charges to documents actually obtained, making access to applicants' own personal information absolutely free, and introducing a fixed scale of costs.

---

[183] See Freedom of Information Act 1982, ss 18, 29, 30A, 58.
[184] See n 20 above at ch 14.
[185] At para 1.34.
[186] ibid, para 1.31; *the Needs to Know report* (n 19 above) para 4.4.
[187] See n 74 above at paras 3.132–3.133.
[188] *The Needs to Know report* (n 19 above) at paras 4.12–4.14.
[189] The Attorney-General's 2000–1 report, para 1.33.

In New Zealand the department, Minister or organization decides what charge is **9.85** to be made if the request for information is granted. The charge has to be reasonable and regard may be had to the cost of the labour and materials in making the information available and to any costs incurred pursuant to a request of the applicant to make the information available urgently.[190] There are no regulations governing what charges may be made, but the government periodically issues guidelines, and control is exercised through the Ombudsman's power of review.

In Ireland fees are based on the estimated cost of the search for and retrieval of the **9.86** record concerned, plus the estimated cost of any copying.[191] Search fees are calculated at a prescribed hourly rate. The head of a department has power to waive or reduce fees if the disclosure is one which would assist the understanding of an issue of national importance, or the administrative costs of collection would outweigh the amounts chargeable. In his report on the first three years of the Act's operation,[192] the Information Commissioner noted that fees were in practice charged in only a very small percentage of cases, largely due to the administrative inconvenience involved in collection.

In the United States, agencies are required to publish regulations specifying 'rea- **9.87** sonable standard charges' which may be imposed in respect of three categories of requests:

(a) where records are requested for commercial use, charges may be made for document search, duplication and review;
(b) where records are sought by educational or non-commercial scientific institutions, the charges are limited to document duplication; and
(c) where records are requested other than under (a) or (b) above, the charges are limited to search and duplication.

Agencies may waive or reduce fees 'if disclosure of the information is in the public interest because it is likely to contribute significantly to public understanding of the operations or activities of the government and is not primarily in the commercial interest of the requester'.[193]

Exemption where cost of compliance exceeds appropriate limit

A public authority in the United Kingdom can refuse a request if the cost of com- **9.88** plying is disproportionate.[194] There is a comparable provision in New Zealand where a request may be refused if the information cannot be made available

---

[190] Official Information Act 1982, s 15.
[191] Freedom of Information Act 1997, s 47.
[192] Under the Freedom of Information Act 1997, s 36(2).
[193] United States Code, Title 5, s 552(a)(4)(A).
[194] Freedom of Information Act 2000, s 12.

without substantial collation or research.[195] In Ireland a request may be refused if compliance would cause a substantial and unreasonable interference with, or disruption of, other work of the public body concerned,[196] which is very similar to the position in Australia.[197]

Vexatious requests

9.89 Section 14(1) of the 2000 Act provides that a public authority does not have to comply with a request for information if the request is vexatious. There is no definition of vexatious. There is a similar provision in New Zealand. Section 18(h) of the Official Information Act 1982 provides that a request may be refused if it is frivolous or vexatious or the information requested is trivial. There is no judicial authority on this particular provision, but in a practice guide issued by the Ombudsmen for the benefit of holders of official information, they explain that they have followed the interpretation given to the words in the context of striking out legal proceedings:

> In essence, for a request to be refused on these grounds a requester must be believed to be patently abusing the rights granted by the legislation for access to information rather than exercising those rights in a bona fide manner.

However, the guide goes on to emphasize that it is the nature of the particular request and the circumstances in which it is made that determine whether it is frivolous or vexatious, not the identity of the maker; the section does not create an equivalent of the vexatious litigant. In Ireland a request may be refused if the request is, in the opinion of the head of the relevant public body, frivolous or vexatious.[198] The Canadian Act currently has no such provision, but the Task Force favours introducing one.[199] In contrast, *the Australian Law Reform Commission report* rejected a proposal to amend the Australian Act to permit refusal of access on this basis, despite a high level of support for it among agencies, on account of 'vexatious' being 'a vague concept. . .likely to result in unpredictable implementation' and 'the potential for agencies to invoke such a provision to avoid requests merely because they regard them as nuisances'. The furthest it was prepared to go was to propose a limited amendment allowing an agency to refuse to process repeat requests for material to which access has already been legitimately refused.[200]

---

[195] Official Information Act 1982, s 18(f).
[196] Freedom of Information Act 1997, s 10(1)(c).
[197] Freedom of Information Act 1982, s 24.
[198] Freedom of Information Act 1997, s (10)(1)(e).
[199] *The Canadian Task Force report* (n 11 above) 73.
[200] See n 20 above at para 7.18. The Australian Amendment Bill included such a clause.

Rights of third parties

The 2000 Act makes no provision for the protection of third parties who might be **9.90** adversely affected by disclosure of information; that matter is left to be dealt with by non-statutory means, that is in the Lord Chancellor's Code of Practice under section 45. This is similar to the position in New Zealand, where the Danks Committee[201] was concerned about the complexity and rigidity of a statutory scheme and thought that the adoption of good practice should ensure that account was taken of relevant third party interests. The New Zealand Law Commission noted[202] that as anticipated by the Danks Committee, providers of information are in practice consulted before its release, and the courts have entertained an application for judicial review by an affected third party of an Ombudsman's recommendation for disclosure.[203]

In contrast, the Australian,[204] Irish[205] and Canadian[206] statutes impose obligations **9.91** on public bodies to notify third parties of requests that may affect them, and to take account of any representations they may make, and confer rights on such parties to appeal against decisions to disclose. Experience has shown that those obligations can be onerous to discharge, especially when large numbers of potentially affected third parties are involved. In giving evidence to the House of Lords Select Committee on the Freedom of Information Bill, the Irish Information Commissioner recalled a request to the Revenue Commissioners for information about the tax affairs of charities which necessitated consulting some 6,000 charities.[207] In his report for 2000–1[208] the Canadian Information Commissioner lamented the 'unwieldy procedural apparatus which contributes to delay and administrative burden', and the impracticality of complying with the direct notice and consultation requirements in cases of multiple third parties (126,000, in one particular instance).

> Faced with those situations, departments are tempted to take the path of least resistance. They simply refuse to disclose the information and pass the dissatisfied requester over to the Commissioner, along with all the notice and consultation headaches.

He favoured forms of public notice or advertisement where practicable, as do the Canadian Task Force.

---

[201] Supplementary report (1981) para 71.
[202] *The New Zealand Law Commission report* (n 92 above) paras 210–211.
[203] *Wyatt Co (NZ) Ltd v Queenstown—Lakes DC* [1991] 2 NZLR 180.
[204] Freedom of Information Act 1982, ss 26A, 27, 27A, 58F, 59, 59A.
[205] Freedom of Information Act 1997, ss 29, 34, 42.
[206] Access to Information Act 1982, ss 27–29, 35, 44.
[207] HL Paper (1998–99) no 97 at p 74.
[208] At pp 75–6.

9.92 Where a third party in the United States wishes to prevent an agency from handing over information concerning him to a requester, he can apply for judicial review of the agency's decision. This form of litigation is known as a reverse Freedom of Information Act suit.[209]

F. Advice, Schemes and Codes

Advice and assistance

9.93 In the United Kingdom there is a duty on public authorities to provide advice and assistance to those seeking information, though the duty does not go beyond complying with the Code issued by the Lord Chancellor under section 45 of the 2000 Act.[210] This is close to section 13 of the New Zealand Official Information Act 1982 which places a duty on every department, Minister and organization to give reasonable assistance to a person who wishes to make a request. Compare also section 6(2) of the Irish Freedom of Information Act 1997 and section 15(3) of the Australian Freedom of Information Act 1982. Section 6(2) of the Irish Freedom of Information Act 1997 obliges public bodies to give reasonable assistance to all persons seeking records under the Act in relation to making their requests, and to help disabled requesters generally to exercise their rights under the Act. Section 15(3) of the Australian Freedom of Information Act 1982 provides that agencies are under a duty to take reasonable steps to assist persons who wish to make a request, or have made a request which does not comply with the statutory requirements, to make a request which does so comply.

Publication schemes

9.94 Section 19 of the 2000 Act places a duty on every public authority to adopt a scheme for the publication of information, approved by the Information Commissioner, and to publish information in accordance with the scheme. This provision comes into force for Whitehall departments in November 2002 and for others at four monthly stages thereafter. The scheme must specify the classes of information the authority publishes or intends to publish, the manner in which information in each class is published and whether or not a fee is charged. The authority in adopting a scheme has to have regard to the public interest in allowing public access to information held by the authority, and the publication of reasons for decisions made by the authority.

---

[209] See *Chrysler Corp v Brown*, 441 US 281 (1979); *Campaign for Family Farms v Glickman*, 200 F 3d 1180 (8th Cir 2000).

[210] Freedom of Information Act 2000, ss 16, 45. See Appendix D below for this Code.

Publication schemes in the United Kingdom are backed up by the Code of **9.95** Practice which the Lord Chancellor, after consultation with the Information Commissioner, has issued[211] and laid before both Houses of Parliament. The Code must include provisions relating to:

(a) the provision of advice and assistance to applicants;
(b) the transfer of requests;
(c) consultation with persons to whom the information relates, or whose interests are likely to be affected by the disclosure of information; and
(d) procedures for dealing with complaints.

An obligation to publish information is a feature of all freedom of information **9.96** regimes. The underlying objectives are to assist members of the public to take advantage of the rights conferred on them by the law and to enable them to conduct their dealings with public bodies on an informed basis.

The United States

The United States Code provides that each agency shall publish in the Federal **9.97** Register for the guidance of the public:

(a) descriptions of its central and field organization and the established places at which the public may obtain information;
(b) statements of the general course and method by which its functions are channelled and determined;
(c) rules of procedure, descriptions of forms available and instructions as to the scope and contents of all papers, reports or examinations;
(d) substantive rules and statements of general policy formulated and adopted by the agency;
(e) each amendment, revision or repeal of the foregoing.

Except to the extent that a person has actual and timely notice thereof, a person may not be adversely affected by a matter required to be published in the Federal Register and not so published. [212]

Canada

In Canada the designated Minister is required to publish once a year a description **9.98** of the organization and responsibilities of each government institution; a description of all classes of records under its control; a description of all manuals used in administering or carrying out any of the programmes or activities of the institution; and the title and address of the appropriate officer to whom requests for access should be sent. The publication (known as *Info Source*) is kept up to date by

---

[211] Freedom of Information Act 2000, s 45. See Appendix D below for this Code.
[212] United States Code, Title 5, s 552(a)(1).

regular bulletins and has to be made available throughout Canada.[213] It does not appear to have had its intended impact. One of the conclusions drawn by the Canadian Task Force from its researches and consultations was that:

> After 20 years the Act is still not well understood by the public, requesters, third parties who supply information, or even the public service. There is a pressing need for more education about access to information.[214]

9.99 Another theme of *the Canadian Task Force report*[215] is that the formal request process under the Access to Information Act cannot meet all the needs of Canadians for government information, nor is it an efficient way of delivering information; it is too time-consuming and not cost-effective. There is 'a need to move from a reactive approach to a program delivery concept of access to information', using electronic means of communication. Similar views had already been expressed by the Hon John Reid in his 2000–1 report, namely that more efforts should be made to release information voluntarily and routinely into the public domain, without waiting for a request; that a public register of released information should be set up, to avoid unnecessary duplication of requests; and that the government should be obliged to create 'pathways to information' by disseminating information about sources of information. He also had much to say about information management (defined by him as policies, standards, and practices for the creation, maintenance, selection for preservation, and disposal of records). He thought that Canada needed further legislation on this and pointed out that legislation in other jurisdictions was more explicit in requiring appropriate records to be made and kept.[216] He thought that Canada should introduce statutory duties to make and preserve records on the American model and a statutory framework governing record keeping and reporting requirements and procedures. The Task Force found that 'Everyone is in agreement that there is a crisis in information management in the federal government, as well as in every jurisdiction we have studied'.[217] Among the causes they identified were reductions in resources and the growth of alternative informal methods of communication such as e-mail and voicemail.

Australia

9.100 Section 8 of the Australian Freedom of Information Act requires the Minister responsible for an agency to cause to be published statements setting out particu-

---

[213] Access to Information Act 1982, s 5.

[214] *The Canadian Task Force report* (n 11 above) 3.

[215] ibid, 5, 133–139.

[216] He referred among others to the US Federal Records Act and to the recommendation of the Australian Law Reform Commission for a 'requirement to create, maintain and make accessible full and accurate records' in a proposed new Archives and Records Act; and he also praised the Australian Standard AS 4390—Records Management (1996)—which is being adopted by the International Organization for Standardization for other jurisdictions.

[217] *The Canadian Task Force report* (n 11 above) 141.

lars of its organization, functions and decision-making powers; any arrangements for public participation in the formulation of policy or the administration by the agency of any enactment or scheme; the categories of publicly available documents that are maintained in its possession; the facilities for enabling the public to obtain physical access to its documents; and its procedures for handling requests for access to documents. Copies of documents used by agencies in making decisions or recommendations under or for the purposes of enactments and schemes administered by them which affect members of the public are to be made available for inspection and purchase under section 9. *The Australian Law Reform Commission report* recorded[218] that compliance with these sections was 'patchy' and the information disclosed under them was not easily accessible and rarely used. It recommended that compliance be monitored by the proposed new Commissioner and the availability of the information be better publicized. The Ombudsman has been even more forthright in his criticism, remarking[219] that the majority of statements reviewed by his staff were inadequate and in most cases the details of the categories of documents in the possession of the agency were 'so broad as to be meaningless'.

New Zealand

In New Zealand it is the State Services Commission which has the duty of pub- **9.101** lishing in respect of each Department and each organization:

(a) a description of its structure, functions and responsibilities including those of its statutory officers or advisory committees;
(b) a general description of the categories of documents held by it;
(c) a description of all manuals, and similar types of documents which contain policies, principles, rules or guidelines in accordance with which decisions or recommendations are made in respect of any person or body of persons in his or its personal capacity; and
(d) particulars of the officer or officers to whom requests for official information should be sent.[220]

Ireland

There are similar provisions for the publication of information about public **9.102** bodies in sections 15 and 16 of the Irish Freedom of Information Act 1997.

---

[218] See n 20 above at paras 7.7–7.8.
[219] In *the Needs to Know report* (n 19 above) paras 3.100–3.101.
[220] Official Information Act 1982, s 20.

G. Enforcement and Appeals

United Kingdom

9.103 In the United Kingdom the Information Commissioner has the key role in enforcing the Act. He decides whether a request for information has been dealt with in accordance with the Act and he issues a decision notice saying what steps, if any, a public authority must take to comply with the Act. He may back up his decision by serving an enforcement notice. He also has wide powers of entry and inspection. Failure to comply with an enforcement notice is dealt with as a contempt of court.

9.104 The Commissioner's decision is subject to a ministerial veto, but it is plain this will only be used in exceptional circumstances. The veto has to be exercised by a member of the Cabinet or the Attorney-General, and it has to be laid before both Houses of Parliament. The Minister is required to state reasons for his decision, which can be the subject of judicial review.

9.105 There is an appeal from the decision of the Commissioner to the Information Tribunal, with a further appeal on a point of law to the High Court. The Tribunal can set aside the decision of the Commissioner and has limited power to set aside certificates which are issued in relation to national security measures.

9.106 The enforcement procedures in the United Kingdom are likely to prove effective.

9.107 In addition to the functions of adjudication and enforcement in particular cases, the Information Commissioner has other tasks to perform: promoting good practice on the part of public authorities, publicizing the Act, providing advice about it, and assisting the Lord Chancellor with regard to the codes of practice.[221] It is interesting to note that in other countries where there is no person or body with equivalent powers, a need for one has been felt. The Canadian Task Force advocates expanding the role of that country's Commissioner to encompass mediation between requesters and institutions, educating the public about the Act, training public servants in its administration, conducting institutional practice assessments, and providing advice on legislation and guidelines.[222] The New Zealand Law Commission also identified 'a need for the administration of the Act to be enhanced' by the adoption of a more co-ordinated and systematic approach to overseeing compliance generally, reviewing the operation of the legislation and educating government and the public in its use, although it considered the appropriate body to assume overall responsibility for these functions to be the

---

[221] See the Freedom of Information Act 2000, Parts III and IV, in particular ss 45–48.
[222] *The Canadian Task Force report* (n 11 above) 92–100.

Ministry of Justice.[223] The Australian Law Reform Commission's proposals for the establishment of a Freedom of Information Commissioner[224] have already been mentioned.[225] They envisaged that he would have no formal investigative powers or power to review decisions, but would audit agencies' freedom of information practices, issue guidelines and provide training to agencies concerning the interpretation and administration of the Australian Act, provide information, advice and assistance to applicants, agencies and third parties in respect of requests, publicize the Act in the community, and provide legislative policy advice about it.

United States

A person is able to appeal against an agency's decision. The initial step is an administrative appeal, which is an internal process. Any further challenge has to be pursued in the federal courts. The court conducts a complete rehearing of the case, and the agency carries the burden of justifying its refusal to supply the information sought. **9.108**

The court may order the agency to supply the information sought or require it to provide a *Vaughn* index,[226] that is, an itemized index in which the agency sets out its detailed justification of its claims, correlating each document (or part thereof) sought to be withheld with a specific exemption under the Act. It seems likely that the United Kingdom authorities will follow this procedure. In the United States it has provided an incentive to greater disclosure. **9.109**

Canada

The procedure in Canada is somewhat closer to that in the United Kingdom. In Canada it is a function of the Information Commissioner to receive and investigate complaints from applicants, but although he has wide powers of investigation and no record to which the Act applies can be withheld from his inspection, he can only make recommendations and, unlike the UK Commissioner, he cannot enforce his decisions. If his recommendations are ignored, the matter has to go to the court and is at large. The court can order disclosure. There is no Canadian equivalent of the UK Information Tribunal. **9.110**

---

[223] *The New Zealand Law Commission report* (n 92 above) paras 37–50.

[224] *The Senate Inquiry report* came to the conclusion that the functions should instead be conferred on the Commonwealth Ombudsman and carried out by a specialized unit within his office (n 74 above, paras 3.113–3.115). This was somewhat ironic, considering that the Ombudsman had previously in the Act's history been given a monitoring role (by Part VA, introduced by amendments in 1983 and repealed in 1991) but it had been taken away again because his office lacked the funding and personnel to perform it.

[225] At para 9.12 above.

[226] So called after the order in *Vaughn v Rosen* 484 F 2d 820 (1973).

9.111 The Canadian Task Force found 'overwhelming support' among the people who made submissions to it and participated in its public consultations for the Commissioner's being invested with full order-making powers, on the basis that binding decisions would be obtained more quickly and at less expense than under the present system.[227] Another advantage in the opinion of the Task Force was that it would result in a more consistent body of jurisprudence and make future outcomes more predictable. Its report encourages the government to consider moving towards this change.

Australia

9.112 Part VI of the Freedom of Information Act 1982 deals with the review of decisions. Section 54 provides for an internal review of a decision of an agency taken other than by the responsible Minister or principal officer. In other cases, or if dissatisfied with the outcome of the internal review, the applicant may apply to the Administrative Appeals Tribunal under section 55 to have the decision reviewed on its merits. The Tribunal has power to substitute its own decision for that of the agency or Minister, except where there is in force a conclusive certificate of exemption under sections 33 to 36, in which case all it can do is determine whether there are reasonable grounds for claiming the exemption. If a Minister does not accept a finding of the Tribunal which is adverse to his certification, it is not binding upon him, but he must notify the applicant of the reasons for his decision and place a copy of these before both Houses of Parliament. The Tribunal has no discretion to order disclosure of exempt documents. There is an appeal on a point of law from the Tribunal to the Federal Court. Another possibility is to complain to the Commonwealth Ombudsman under section 57, although he does not have power to investigate decisions taken by Ministers and can only make non-binding recommendations to agencies if he finds maladministration. Nor is the jurisdiction of the Federal Court under the Administrative Decisions (Judicial Review) Act 1977 ousted by the Act: see *Shergold v Tanner*[228] for discussion of the interrelationship between the various remedies.

New Zealand

9.113 New Zealand relies on the Ombudsmen rather than the courts to review decisions about the disclosure of documents. The New Zealand approach was summarized by the Danks Committee in this way:

> The system we favour involves the weighing of broad considerations and the balancing of competing interests against one another, and against individual interests. If the general power to determine finally whether there should be access to official

---

[227] *The Canadian Task Force report* (n 11 above) 113–114.
[228] (2001) 179 ALR 150, FCA, (2002) 188 ALR 302, HC of A.

information were given to the courts, they would have to rule on matters with strong political and policy implications. This is not a normal or traditional function of the Courts in New Zealand, and the judges themselves have shown a reluctance to embrace it.[229]

The scheme of the Act is to allow the Ombudsman to investigate the dispute using **9.114** traditional inquisitorial processes. These lead to a recommendation rather than a formal determination. The recommendation gives rise to a statutory duty on the authority to comply. This duty can be overridden but only by a decision of the Cabinet, expressed in an Order in Council.[230] Every such Order in Council has to set out the reasons and grounds for overriding the Ombudsmen's recommendation. There is a further safeguard in that the applicant for the information can seek judicial review of the Order in Council from the High Court (with an appeal to the Court of Appeal), on the basis that it is ultra vires or wrong in law.[231] As the statute was originally enacted, the power was vested in individual Ministers, and could be exercised for reasons which were not relied on before the Ombudsman (which is no longer the case). Prior to the introduction of the current system in 1987, 14 recommendations (out of a total of 92) were overridden;[232] the tally since then is none.

Over the years a climate of compliance with Ombudsman's recommendations has **9.115** developed in New Zealand. Sir Brian Elwood says that during his term of office as Chief Ombudsman, he has known of only three situations where a recommendation has not been complied with. In order to avoid the need for the Ombudsman to be seen to be enforcing his own recommendations it has been accepted that the Attorney-General (or Solicitor-General), in the public interest, will institute proceedings in the High Court to enforce compliance with the statutory duty. Experience has shown that once that occurs, the organization against whom the Ombudsman's recommendation is directed, complies. There have been no recent examples of failure to comply with an Ombudsman's recommendation.[233]

Ireland

Section 33 of the Irish Freedom of Information Act established the office of **9.116** Information Commissioner. The first Commissioner was also the Ombudsman. The Commissioner can review, and reverse, decisions to refuse a request for access to a record and other decisions adverse to requesters.[234] Any right to review by the public body itself must have been exercised before application is made to the

---

[229] Supplementary report (1981).
[230] Official Information Act 1982, s 32.
[231] ibid, ss 32B and 32C.
[232] *New Zealand Law Commission report* (n 92 above) para 353.
[233] *The New Zealand Model—The Official Information Act 1982*, a paper presented at the conference 'FOI and the Right to Know' held in Melbourne on 19–20 August 1999.
[234] Freedom of Information Act 1997, s 34.

Commissioner. Most refusals of requests for access under the Act can be referred to a more senior official of the public body concerned, under section 14. In 2001 about 9 per cent of decisions proceeded to internal review (compared with 14 per cent in 1998, 11 per cent in 1999 and 7 per cent in 2000), according to the Information Commissioner's reports. However, in his report on the first three years of the Act's operation the Commissioner expressed reservations about the effectiveness of such reviews, saying that some of those which he had examined for the purposes of the review bore all the hallmarks of rubber-stamping while a larger proportion (almost 40 per cent) did not meet the requirements of the Act in terms of quality of response. The Commissioner was asked to review the decisions on some 5 per cent of requests at first, falling to 3 per cent by 2001. There is no Information Tribunal, on the United Kingdom model, in Ireland. An appeal lies to the High Court on a point of law from the decision made by the Commissioner on a review.[235] There are wider provisions for appeals from decisions made by the Commissioner in his capacity as the head of the Office of the Information Commissioner (a public body within the scope of the Act) in relation to records held by that Office. Subject to appeal, the Commissioner's decisions are binding.

---

[235] Freedom of Information Act 2000, s 42.

PART E

RELATIONSHIP WITH OTHER STATUTES

10

DATA PROTECTION

A. Introduction

Although the Freedom of Information Act 2000 and the Data Protection Act **10.01**
1998 ('the 1998 Act') would appear to be at odds with one another in that the former notionally ensures that information held by public authorities or bodies is
made freely available while the latter ensures that it is not, in fact both statutes
protect the confidentiality of personal information, thereby upholding the individual's right to privacy under both the Council Directive (EC) 95/46 on the protection of individuals with regard to the processing of personal data and on the
free movement of such data and the European Convention for the Protection of
Human Rights as now enshrined in the Human Rights Act 1998. Generally
speaking, the 1998 Act also provides for freedom of information but this freedom
is restricted to the private individual about whom personal data are kept. Unlike
the Freedom of Information Act 2000 and the Human Rights Act 1998, the 1998

Act applies only to natural persons; companies and other non-living persons are not protected by the 1998 Act at all. Of course, the right to privacy is not absolute and must be balanced against other human rights, notably the right to freedom of expression. In addition, and more prosaically, the right to privacy must be balanced against the commercial and social interests in utilization of personal information.

10.02 This chapter will set out the origin of and background to the 1998 Act, and, briefly, run through its main provisions including the important definitions; the rights of individuals to access data relating to themselves and, if necessary, to have them corrected or erased; control of data users, including registration and enforcement; and the roles and powers of the Information Commissioner and the Information Tribunal. Finally, the relationship between the 1998 Act and the Freedom of Information Act 2000 will be considered.

B. The Data Protection Acts—Origins and Purpose

10.03 Prior to 1984 there was no right to privacy as such in English law.[1] From about 1961 this absence became of great concern and was recognized as a serious flaw in our system of justice, which required rapid remedy, and steps were taken to this end. In addition to two White Papers[2] on the topic there were produced a Law Commission working paper and draft Bill, two Parliamentary reports and no fewer than seven Parliamentary Bills. Further, in May 1981 the United Kingdom signed the Council of Europe's Convention for the protection of individuals with regard to automatic processing of personal data. All this activity produced (albeit perhaps not rapidly) the Data Protection Act 1984, a groundbreaking statute in the law of privacy and confidence although somewhat limited in scope. This was followed, reasonably quickly, by the Access to Personal Files Act 1987,[3] the Access to Medical Reports Act 1988[4] and, somewhat later, by the Access to Health Records Act 1990[5] and now the Data Protection Act 1998. The intention is to balance the individual's right to privacy against the social and commercial needs to utilize personal information and against the right to freedom of expression.

---

[1] See ch 20 below.

[2] *Report of the Younger Committee on Privacy* in 1972 (Cmnd 5012); *Report of the Lindop Committee* in 1978 (Cmnd 7341).

[3] This Act was repealed by the 1998 Act although any application made under it prior to its repeal is to be dealt with under the regulations made under it (1998 Act, Sch 14, para 19). Further, to the extent that records previously governed by the Access to Personal Files Act 1987 are temporarily exempted from the 1998 Act by virtue of Sch 8 of that Act, the 1987 Act will apply.

[4] See ch 11 below.

[5] ibid.

As stated, the Data Protection Act 1984 ('the 1984 Act') was replaced by the Data **10.04** Protection Act 1998 ('the 1998 Act') which became law by Royal Assent on 16 July 1998. This was the United Kingdom's implementation of the Council Directive (EC) 95/46 on the protection of individuals with regard to the processing of personal data and on the free movement of such data. The Act came fully into effect on 1 March 2000.[6] It considerably expanded the statutory protection of individual privacy and individuals' rights to access, and, to a degree, to control personal information held about them. One of the biggest changes is that whereas the 1984 Act was restricted to electronically processed data, the 1998 Act extends the legislation to cover many paper and other non-computerized (for example microfiche) records too. In addition, individuals are given wider rights and remedies for breaches both of those rights and of the data protection principles.

This will have a major impact in that individuals are now entitled to have access **10.05** to any data about them held in any structured manner. This will include medical and education records (unless the Secretary of State exempts such information by order).[7] Significantly, this will also include employment records such as job application forms (and any comments written on them), reports, recommendations, reviews, bonus recommendations, e-mails and virtually any other document containing personal data about an employee. The Information Commissioner (as the Data Protection Commissioner is now known) has produced a draft Code of Practice for employers to assist them in complying with the Act.[8]

Transitional provisions are contained in section 72 of and Schedule 13 to the 1998 **10.06** Act. These prevent some of the 1998 Act's provisions having full effect until 24 October 2007 by modifying sections 12, 32, 34, 53 and paragraph 8 of Part II of Schedule 1 to the 1998 Act.[9] Of course, the 1984 Act still applies in such cases.

C. The Data Protection Act 1998

The 1998 Act cannot be described as user friendly, and has been described as a **10.07** cumbersome and inelegant piece of legislation.[10] Essentially, it controls the processing of data by prescribing eight principles which must be complied with by

---

[6] But there are transitional provisions running until 23 October 2007. See paras 10.18 et seq below.

[7] 1998 Act, s 38.

[8] This is available from the Office of the Information Commissioner.

[9] See para 10.18 et seq below.

[10] *Campbell v Mirror Group Newspapers* [2002] EWCA Civ 1373 at para 72, TLR 16 October 2002. At para 97 it was stated that because the 1998 Act was based on a European Directive and was not the product of a Parliamentary draftsman the court must adopt a purposive approach to construction.

data controllers.[11] Processing is defined very broadly and extends to merely holding or accessing personal data.[12] The 1998 Act confers rights on data subjects and provides for a system of regulation and enforcement. It is divided into six parts and has sixteen Schedules. The parts and their contents are, broadly, as follows:

Part I   The application of the 1998 Act and definitions of data, personal data, sensitive personal data, data controllers and the data protection principles.

Part II   Rights of data subjects and others.

Part III   Regulation of data controllers, duties of data controllers, some functions and powers of the Information Commissioner.

Part IV   Exemptions.

Part V   Enforcement by the Information Commissioner.

Part VI   Miscellaneous and general matters including other functions of the Information Commissioner, provisions relating to offences, further definitions, application to the Crown, power of the Secretary of State to make regulations.

Data covered by the 1998 Act

10.08 The 1998 Act covers only 'personal information'. Personal information means any information at all relating to a particular living individual which may permit that individual to be identified from the relevant information or from that and other information which is in or is likely to come into the possession of the data controller (section 1(1)). It expressly includes expressions of opinion and intention. It has been said, albeit obiter, that a photograph taken on a private occasion and held in digital form would be personal information for the purposes of the 1998 Act.[13] The High Court of Ireland has held that the correct test to apply to determine whether data 'relates to' a subject is whether there is a sufficiently substantial link between the requester's personal information (as defined in the statute) and the record in question. The test is satisfied if the data subject is named in the record:

> If the record contains an express reference to the requester, be it however insubstantial or trivial, then clearly it 'relates to personal information' about the requester . . . Where the record does not name or has no express reference to the requester a substantial link will be established if the record relates to something in which the requester has a substantial personal interest, as distinct from something in which he has an interest as a member of the general community or of a large scale class of the same.[14]

---

[11] See paras 10.16 et seq below.
[12] 1998 Act, s 1.
[13] *Douglas & Ors v Hello! Ltd* [2001] QB 967 at para 56.
[14] *EH v The Information Commissioner* [2001] IEHC 182.

The data covered by the 1998 Act extend to any personal information being **10.09** processed by automatically operating equipment in response to an instruction so to process (section 1(1)(a)); any information recorded for the purpose of being so processed (section 1(1)(b)); any information recorded in a filing system in such a manner that information relating to an individual is readily accessible (section 1(1)(c)); any other information which is held on an accessible health, education or public record (section 1(1)(d) and section 68); and, finally, any recorded information held by a public authority and not falling within paragraphs (a) to (d). Processing includes obtaining, recording or just holding personal information as well as manipulating it (section 1).[15]

Section 1(1)(a) of the 1998 Act most obviously covers all computer records or **10.10** files; however, it would also cover sorting machines used to process data on punched cards (should these still be in use anywhere) and machines such as automatic telephone logging systems. Section 1(1)(b) extends the scope of the Act to cover information that has been prepared for processing even though it may not yet have been processed. This would cover any information stored on a disk or other recording medium for use in a computer or other automatic processing machine and almost certainly extends to paper, digital, audio, photographic and other records which have been compiled to be scanned into or otherwise entered on a computer. Section 1(1)(c) refers to all paper filing records such as those maintained by most businesses which contain correspondence and copies of other documents relating to their customers. It is not necessary for such files to be arranged by reference to names; the sub-section extends to any arrangement which permits access to information about an individual. For example, bank files arranged by reference to the type of account would be caught, as would retailers' files arranged by reference to products bought. 'Recorded' information, although not defined, will include manuscripts, photographs and audio and videotapes.

Section 1(1)(d) is a catch-all provision relating to accessible records which are **10.11** those records most commonly kept about people, that is, health, education and public records, which are not covered by sub-sections (a), (b) and (c), namely unstructured files or records. While education records are only available if they are held by a school maintained by a local education authority or a special school within the meaning of section 6(2) of the Education Act 1996 (Schedule 11 to the 1998 Act), records held by virtually anyone whose practice may be described as 'medical' fall within the sub-section (section 68(2) and section 69). Thus records held by private schools are not covered but those held by a private general practitioner or osteopath are. The reference to 'an accessible public record' gives effect

---

[15] In *Campbell v Mirror Group Newspapers* [2002] EWCA Civ 1373 at para 107, TLR 16 October 2002, Lord Phillips MR held that publication within the media falls within the definition of processing.

to *Gaskin v UK*,[16] in which the European Court of Human Rights held that the failure of a local authority to permit an individual to have access to social security records was a breach of Article 8 of the Convention. However, the term 'accessible public record'[17] is limited in scope, as it applies only to records held by a Housing Act local authority for the purpose of the authority's tenancies, or information held by a local social services authority for the purpose of its social services functions.[18]

10.12　Completely unstructured records relating to matters such as planning applications or permissions were not originally subject to the 1998 Act. However, the scope of the 1998 Act is extended quite considerably by the insertion of section 1(1)(e)[19] to include all recorded information held by a public authority.[20] Section 1(1)(e) will apply to all public authorities which are subject to the Freedom of Information Act 2000. Section 1(1)(e) is subject to the restrictions provided for by section 7 of the Freedom of Information Act 2000.[21]

10.13　Some information is deemed to be particularly sensitive and is singled out for special protection. This includes information on racial or ethnic origin, political opinions, religious or similar beliefs, membership of a trade union, physical or mental health or condition, sexual life, criminal offences or alleged offences together with any criminal proceedings and their outcomes.[22] A photograph could amount to sensitive personal data by disclosing the race or ethnic origins of a data subject, but not where the subject 'is proud to be a leading black fashion model and it is part of her lifestyle and profession to be photographed as a black woman'.[23] However, it was held in the same case that information as to the nature of and details of therapy received at Narcotics Anonymous together with captioned photographs clearly fell within the definition of sensitive personal data as being information on physical or mental health or condition.[24]

Application of the 1998 Act

10.14　The 1998 Act applies to every data controller[25] (as distinguished from a data processor) established in the United Kingdom in respect of data processed in the

---

16　Series A No 160, (1989) 12 EHHR 36.

17　1998 Act, s 68(1)(c).

18　ibid, Sch 12.

19　By the Freedom of Information Act 2000, s 68(2), but note the exemptions applying to this data by virtue of the 1998 Act, s 33A, inserted by the Freedom of Information Act 2000, s 70: see para 10.77 below. In any event, s 1(1)(e) will not come into force until 30 November 2005 unless an earlier order is made.

20　Defined in the Freedom of Information Act 2000, s 3(1).

21　See ch 5 above.

22　1998 Act, s 2.

23　*Campbell v Mirror Group Newspapers* (2002) HRLR 28 at paras 85–86.

24　ibid, at para 87.

25　The Commissioner has issued guidance on the meaning of data controller (12 January 2000).

context of that establishment,[26] and to every data controller established outside the United Kingdom and outside any other state in the European Economic Area[27] who processes data on equipment in the United Kingdom (unless the data are simply passing through en route from one person to another both of whom are established outside the United Kingdom): section 5(1)(b). Any data controllers falling within section 5(1)(b) are obliged to nominate a representative within the United Kingdom[28] to enable enforcement both of individual rights and of the 1998 Act. A data controller is defined in section 1 as the person who determines the purposes for which and the manner in which the data are, or are to be, processed. If a person making the determination does so jointly or in common with other persons then each is a separate data controller.[29] This definition includes any self-employed person using a computer, whether personally or through a third party, on which is kept any personal information about individual clients. It includes reports and opinions. A data controller does not have to be a living person as there is no intention contrary to the definition of a person contained in the Interpretation Act 1978 section 5, Schedule 1. The 1998 Act applies to the Crown.[30] The only exception to this definition is found in section 1(4) and refers to persons upon whom there is a statutory obligation to process particular data.

Section 5(3) sets out who is to be treated as being established within the United Kingdom. In addition to living persons ordinarily resident in, and bodies incorporated under the law of any part of, the United Kingdom, partnerships and other unincorporated associations formed under the law of any part of the United Kingdom are included, as is any person who maintains an office, branch or agency through which an activity or a regular practice is conducted within the United Kingdom. **10.15**

Data protection principles

Section 4 of the 1998 Act imposes a duty on data controllers to comply with the data protection principles ('the Principles') in relation to all personal data. The appropriateness of all dealings with personal information is judged by reference to the Principles; they are fundamental to data control. Enforcement of the 1998 Act by the Information Commissioner is inevitably based on a breach of one or more of the Principles. The Data Protection Registrar (as the Commissioner then was) produced an 'Introduction to the Data Protection Act 1998' which contains guidance on likely interpretation of the Principles. **10.16**

---

[26] 1998 Act, s 5(1)(a).
[27] ie a contracting party to the Agreement on the European Economic Area signed at Oporto on 2 May 1992 as adjusted by the Protocol signed at Brussels on 17 March 1993.
[28] 1998 Act, s 5(2).
[29] ibid, s 1(1).
[30] ibid, s 63, but note immunity from prosecution under s 63(5).

10.17 The Principles are set out in Part I of Schedule 1 to the 1998 Act. There are eight of these, dealing with the acquisition, retention, processing and transfer of data and with their quality, accuracy and confidentiality. In addition, the sixth Principle deals with the data subject's rights under the Act. Part II of Schedule 1 provides for the interpretation of the Principles.

10.18 It was recognized that it would not be possible for data controllers to comply with the Principles overnight, particularly in respect of non-automated or manual data. Accordingly, the 1998 Act provided for limited exemptions in respect of some automated data and most manual data between 24 October 1998 and 23 October 2001, the first transitional period. As this period has now passed no further reference will be made to it. Between 24 October 2001 and 23 October 2007 inclusive, the second transitional period,[31] exempt manual data are not subject to the first data protection principle[32] except in so far as it requires compliance with paragraph 2 of Part II of Schedule 1 (provision of information to the data subject on the use to which data will be put, including disclosure to third parties, and the identity of the data controller and any representative). Exempt manual data are not subject to the second, third, fourth and fifth data principles at all. Finally, such data are not subject to the general rights of data subjects to have inaccurate personal data rectified, blocked, erased and/or destroyed under section 14(1) to (3). Such data are exempt only until 23 October 2007, the end of the second transitional period.

10.19 What are exempt manual data? They are manual data that either were held immediately prior to 24 October 1998 or form part of an accessible health, education or public record.[33] Manual data are defined simply as non-automated data. It should be noted that otherwise relevant manual data held or processed solely for the purposes of historical research are exempted under paragraphs 15 to 18 of Schedule 8 and not under paragraph 14.

10.20 This exemption provides additional time to those holding old manual records to enable them to comply with the data protection principles. It also provides such additional time to public authorities such as local government, schools, hospitals and GPs.

10.21 Some data are generally exempt from the provisions of the data protection principles. The first, second, third, fourth and fifth principles are 'non-disclosure provisions'.[34] Non-disclosure provisions do not apply to data required for national security,[35] data processed for the purposes of journalism, literature or

---

[31] 1998 Act, Sch 8, para 1(2).
[32] Personal data shall be processed fairly and lawfully.
[33] 1998 Act, s 1(1)(d), s 68 and Sch 8, para 14.
[34] ibid, s 27(3), (4).
[35] ibid, s 28.

art[36] and data processed by an individual solely for domestic, family or household purposes (so personal diaries, filofaxes and Christmas card lists are safe).[37]

The First Principle: Personal data shall be processed fairly and lawfully and, in particular, shall not be processed unless—(a) at least one of the conditions in Schedule 2 is met, and (b) in the case of sensitive personal data, at least one of the conditions in Schedule 3 is also met.

The conditions precedent to the processing of personal data are contained in **10.22** Schedule 2 to the 1998 Act. At least one of the conditions must be met. They are as follows:

- the data subject consents (paragraph 1);
- the processing is necessary for the performance of a contract with the data subject or the taking of steps at the request of the data subject with a view to entering into a contract (paragraph 2);
- the processing is necessary for compliance with any non-contractual legal obligation (paragraph 3);
- the processing is necessary to protect the vital interests of the data subject (paragraph 4);
- the processing is necessary for the administration of justice, the exercise of statutory functions, the exercise of functions of the Crown, a Minister of the Crown or a government department, or the exercise of other public functions exercised in the public interest (paragraph 5);
- the processing is necessary in the legitimate interests of the data controller or a third party to whom the data are disclosed unless such processing would unwarrantedly prejudice the rights, freedoms or legitimate interests of the data subject (paragraph 6).[38]

The Secretary of State may by order specify other circumstances in which the last condition is to be taken to be satisfied. No order has been made to date. The Court of Appeal has considered the effect of paragraph 6 in the context of defamatory statements posted anonymously on an Internet site.[39] It held that a data controller could legitimately refuse to reveal the identity of an alleged defamer (or,

---

[36] ibid, s 32.

[37] ibid, s 36.

[38] While publication of a person's drug addiction may be in the legitimate interests of a newspaper, details of therapy or medical treatment are not: *Campbell v Mirror Group Newspapers* (2002) HRLR 28 at para 112.

[39] *Totalise plc v The Motley Fool Ltd* [2002] 1 WLR 1233. The case involved a *Norwich Pharmacal* application against the data controller seeking an order for the disclosure of the identity of an anonymous defamer. The hearing before the Court of Appeal was limited to the issue of costs.

presumably, any other data subject) without a court order where there may be a balancing exercise to be carried out between the legitimate interests of the third party applicant, the data controller and/or the data subject. The Court of Appeal went on to give guidance as to what a data controller should do when faced with such a demand or application. He should notify the data subject of the application and should offer to pass on in writing any reasons put forward by the data subject for not having his or her identity disclosed. Indeed the Court of Appeal suggested that a court might require this to be done before making an order for disclosure of identity in order to protect rights not only under the 1998 Act but also under the Human Rights Act 1998.

10.23 Schedule 3 contains the conditions relevant to the processing of sensitive personal data. It will be recalled that these data consist of information on a data subject's race or ethnic origin, political opinions, religious or similar beliefs, trade union membership, physical or mental health, sex life, criminal record or alleged criminal offences, or any criminal proceedings taken against him together with the outcome and sentence.[40] There are ten conditions at least one of which must be met before processing of sensitive personal data may be considered fair for the purposes of the first data protection principle. These are as follows:

- explicit consent of data subject
- processing is necessary for exercising or performing any right or obligation conferred or imposed by law in connection with employment
- processing is necessary to protect the vital interests of a person and consent cannot be given, cannot reasonably be obtained or has been unreasonably refused; the last applies only when the vital interests are those of another person
- processing is by a political, philosophical, religious or trade union body or association, which is non-profit making
- data are in the public domain as a result of the data subject's deliberate actions
- processing is necessary for legal proceedings, legal advice and/or establishing, exercising or defending legal rights
- processing is necessary for the administration of justice, or the exercise of functions of the Crown, a Minister of the Crown or a government department
- processing is necessary for medical purposes
- processing is of racial or ethnic origin data for monitoring purposes
- as prescribed by the Secretary of State.[41]

10.24 Many of these conditions are qualified in some way, so reference must be made to the detailed provisions of the Schedule. Some qualifications follow closely the wording of similar statutory exemptions, such as that in section 35(2) dealing with legal proceedings; therefore cases and commentary applicable to one should

---

[40] 1998 Act, s 2.
[41] See the Data Protection (Processing of Sensitive Personal Data) Order 2000, SI 2000/417.

be relevant to the other. Paragraphs 1 to 4 inclusive of Part II of Schedule 1 set out some of the matters relevant to the fair processing of data. The interpretation includes guidance on when the acquisition of the data may be fair or unfair, including as to the means by which the data are obtained, and the information to be given to the data subject at the time the data are first processed. The Secretary of State may by order prescribe other conditions and has done so.[42]

Data must be obtained fairly. This means that the use to which data are to be put **10.25** must be disclosed to the data subject.[43] For example, where members of the public buy goods from mail order companies, whether by filling in an order form or over the telephone, they must be informed if their names will be included on a mailing list and passed to third parties. This information must be provided prior to the data subject disclosing his or her name and address.[44] Where data are obtained from a third party, fair processing of data requires that the data controller (presumably the receiving data controller) notify the data subject of his identity, the purpose for which the data are to be processed, and any other information necessary to ensure that the data are processed fairly in the particular circumstances.[45] This must be done at the time of first processing of the data or as soon as practicable thereafter.[46] It should be remembered that 'processing' includes obtaining and holding of data. The surreptitious taking of photographs of a person attending a Narcotics Anonymous meeting is not fair obtaining of data.[47] Paragraph 2(1)(b) of Part II of Schedule 1 to the 1998 Act does not apply if the provision of the specified information would involve a disproportionate effort,[48] or where the recording or disclosure of the information is necessary for compliance with a non-contractual legal obligation of the data controller.[49] The Commissioner has indicated some of the factors that will be taken into account in determining whether or not compliance would involve a 'disproportionate effort': these are cost (including postage and man-hours), time necessary for compliance and ease or difficulty of compliance. These factors will always be balanced against both the benefit to the data controller and the effect on the data subject.[50] This exception may apply to a data controller who purchases or otherwise obtains a large mailing list, thereby blunting the effect of this protection so it becomes relatively

---

[42] See the Data Protection (Conditions under Paragraph 3 of Part II of Schedule 1) Order 2000, SI 2000/185.

[43] 1998 Act, Sch 1, Part II, para 2(1)(a) and (3)(c).

[44] *Innovations (Mail Order) Ltd v Data Protection Registrar* (decision of the Data Protection Tribunal, 1994).

[45] 1998 Act, Sch 1, Part II, para 2(1)(b), (3).

[46] ibid, para 2(1)(b) and (2).

[47] *Campbell v Mirror Group Newspapers* (2002) HRLR 28 at paras 103–105.

[48] 1998 Act, Sch 1, Part II, para 3(2)(a).

[49] ibid, para 3(2)(b).

[50] *The Data Protection Act 1998: An Introduction* (paper by Data Protection Commissioner) para 1.12.2.

notional.[51] Data must also be processed lawfully. Morland J has held that data are obtained unlawfully if published in breach of confidence.[52]

10.26 In addition to the general exemptions (see paragraph 10.21 above) there are other more limited exemptions from the First Principle in respect of data processed for the purposes of discharging statutory functions relating to the prevention and detection of crime or the collection of tax or duty;[53] data on a subject's mental or physical health or processed for social work purposes;[54] data processed for the purpose of regulating financial services or other professions;[55] personal data required by statute to be made available to the public.[56] Further, section 37 and Schedule 7 provide for various miscellaneous exemptions relating to, for example, the armed forces and the judiciary. The full extent and application of these exemptions cannot be adequately addressed in a work of this nature as they are somewhat complex: reference should be made to Part IV of the Act. An example of disclosure, which nevertheless constituted 'fair processing' and so did not breach the First Principle, was the disclosure by the police to a local education authority of two allegations of improper behaviour towards children, which did not lead to criminal proceedings. The disclosure was made in relation to a vetting inquiry in respect of an applicant for headship of an infants' school. It was held that such disclosure was necessary for the taking of steps at the request of the applicant with a view to entering a contract and it was necessary for the exercise of a public function in the public interest. Further, being sensitive personal data, the disclosure was held to be necessary for the exercise of the statutory duties of both the police and a constable and for the prevention of crime.[57]

10.27 The Information Commissioner has provided guidance on the fair processing of data. For example, the then Data Protection Registrar produced the leaflet 'Data Protection Guidance for Direct Marketers'.[58]

The Second Principle: Personal data shall be obtained only for one or more specified and lawful purposes, and shall not be further processed in any manner incompatible with that purpose or those purposes.

---

[51] However, see the Data Protection (Conditions under Paragraph 3 of Part II of Schedule 1) Order 2000, SI 2000/185, which imposes further conditions before this exemption may be relied upon.

[52] *Campbell v Mirror Group Newspapers* (2002) HRLR 28 at para 106; but perhaps he meant processed unlawfully.

[53] ibid, s 29.

[54] ibid, s 30.

[55] ibid, s 31.

[56] ibid, s 34.

[57] *R(A) v Chief Constable of C and D* [2001] 1 WLR 461, referred to also in ch 15 below at paras 15.74 et seq.

[58] This is available from the Information Commissioner's Office.

The purpose(s) for which data are processed must be both specified and lawful. **10.28**
Guidance as to the interpretation of this principle is provided in paragraphs 5 and
6 of Part II of Schedule 1 to the 1998 Act. Purposes are specified if they are contained in a notice given by the data controller to the data subject pursuant to paragraph 2 of Part II of Schedule 1 or if they are notified to the Information
Commissioner under Part III of the 1998 Act. Part III of the 1998 Act requires
data controllers to be registered[59] and the requirements for registration include
specification of the purpose or purposes for which data will be processed.[60]

**The Third Principle: Personal data shall be adequate, relevant and not excessive
in relation to the purpose or purposes for which they are processed.**

No guidance is given in Part II of Schedule 1 as to the interpretation of this prin- **10.29**
ciple. Clearly it is considered self-explanatory. In order for personal data to be adequate they should be complete in that they should contain all the data necessary
for the purpose for which they are processed. For example, if data indicate that a
county court judgment has been entered against a person, they must also show
any discharge of that judgment, particularly if the purpose for which the data are
held is credit control. Records of job applications should contain all relevant experience and qualifications. What is relevant will depend on the purposes for
which the data are processed. For example, information on health may be relevant
to job applications, as are academic qualifications and references; however, it is
unlikely that details of membership of political parties or social organizations
would be. Data must not be excessive. Data are excessive if they are held just in
case they may come in useful in some unspecified way at some unspecified time in
the future. This must be distinguished from holding data on a contingent basis,
for example details of the blood groups of employees engaged in dangerous work
in case of accident.[61] Clearly, any irrelevant data would also be excessive. Much
historic data may be considered excessive. In addition to the general exemptions
set out at paragraph 10.21 above, other data exempt from the third data protection principle are data processed for the detection or prevention of crime or assessing or collecting tax or duty;[62] data required by any enactment to be made
available to the public;[63] disclosures required by law or in connection with legal

---

[59] 1998 Act, s 17.
[60] ibid, ss 18 and 16(1)(d).
[61] *Registrar's Guidelines*, Third Series 1994: Guideline 4.
[62] 1998 Act, s 29(3).
[63] ibid, s 34.

proceedings.[64] Finally, the Secretary of State may make further exemptions by order.[65]

The Fourth Principle: Personal data shall be accurate and, where necessary, kept up to date.

10.30 The concept of accuracy should require no explanation; however, the circumstances in which data need not be up to date call for consideration. Data need only be kept up to date where 'necessary'. Paragraph 7 of Part II of Schedule 1 provides assistance in interpretation. This states that a data controller is not in breach of the fourth principle provided that his records accurately record the data as supplied to him, whether by the data subject or a third party, and provided that he has taken reasonable steps to ensure the accuracy of the data 'having regard to the purpose or purposes for which they were obtained' and, where a data subject has notified him that in the data subject's view the data are inaccurate, the data indicate that fact. For exemption purposes the fourth principle is a non-disclosure provision.[66] The same exemptions apply to this principle as apply to the third principle (see paragraphs 10.21 and 10.29 above).

The Fifth Principle: Personal data processed for any purpose or purposes shall not be kept for longer than is necessary for that purpose or those purposes.

10.31 This principle clearly requires no interpretation as there is no reference to it in Part II of Schedule 1. The length of time that may be considered necessary for a particular purpose will be a question of fact in each case. The fifth data protection principle is another non-disclosure provision; therefore the relevant exemptions may be found at paragraphs 10.21 and 10.29 above. In addition, processing personal data only for research purposes will not constitute a breach of this principle even if they are kept indefinitely.[67] Clearly data must be regularly reviewed to ensure continuing compliance.

The Sixth Principle: Personal data shall be processed in accordance with the rights of data subjects under this Act.

---

[64] 1998 Act, s 35.
[65] ibid, s 38(2).
[66] ibid, s 27(3), (4)(b).
[67] ibid, s 33(3).

This principle is somewhat limited in scope in that by virtue of paragraph 8 of Part **10.32** II of Schedule 1, a person can only be in breach of this principle if he is in breach of one or more of sections 7, 10, 11 and 12 of the 1998 Act, which set out the rights of data subjects.[68] The only data which are exempted from this principle are data required for national security,[69] data processed for the purposes of journalism, literature or art[70] and data processed by an individual solely for domestic, family or household purposes.

The Seventh Principle: Appropriate technical and organizational measures shall be taken against unauthorized or unlawful processing of personal data and against accidental loss or destruction of, or damage to, personal data.

Proportionality would appear to be the key to this principle. The interpretation **10.33** guidance given at paragraph 9 of Part II of Schedule 1 indicates that the level of security required depends on the state of technological development and the cost of providing it balanced against the harm that might be caused by a breach of the 1998 Act and the nature of the data to be protected. A data controller can be held responsible for the acts of his employees and of independent contractors who process data on his behalf.[71] In the case of the former, he must take reasonable steps to ensure their reliability if they have access to personal data. In the case of the latter, he must use a data processor which provides guarantees of its own compliance with the seventh principle and take reasonable steps to ensure actual compliance by the processor. A contract between the parties is required which must be in, or evidenced in, writing, which requires the data processor to act only on instructions from the data controller, and which expressly requires the data processor to comply with similar obligations to those imposed by the seventh principle.[72] The only two exemptions from this principle are for data processed for the purpose of national security and data processed by an individual for domestic purposes. Note that the Commissioner may only enforce this principle against a data controller and not against a data processor who is not himself a data controller.

The Eighth Principle: Personal data shall not be transferred to a country or territory outside the European Economic Area unless that country or territory

---

[68] See paras 10.35 et seq below.
[69] 1998 Act, s 28.
[70] ibid, s 32.
[71] ibid, Sch 1, Part II, paras 10 and 11.
[72] ibid, para 12.

ensures an adequate level of protection for the rights and freedoms of data subjects in relation to the processing of personal data.

10.34 Clearly the key question raised by this principle is the meaning of 'adequate'. Paragraph 13 of Part II of Schedule 1 sets out the factors relevant to the determination of adequacy. These are the nature of the personal data, the country or territory of origin and final destination of the information contained in the data, the purposes and period for which the data will be processed, the law, international obligations and relevant codes of conduct or other rules in the country or territory in question, and the security measures taken in respect of the data in that country or territory. Paragraph 15 of Part II of Schedule 1 provides that where a Community finding has been made on the adequacy of levels of protection in a country outside the European Economic Area, the question must be determined in accordance with that finding. A 'Community finding' means a decision of the European Commission under the procedure provided for in Article 31(2) of the Data Protection Directive.[73] In addition to processing for the purposes of national security, journalism, literature and art and domestic use there are nine cases where the eighth principle has no application at all.[74] These are that the transfer is:

- with the consent of the data subject
- necessary for the performance of a contract between the data controller and the data subject or for taking steps at the latter's request with a view to entering into such a contract
- necessary for the conclusion or performance of a contract between the data controller and a third person which is entered into at the request or in the interests of the data subject
- necessary in the public interest (this is something which may be regulated by the Secretary of State by order)
- necessary for the purposes of legal proceedings, advice etc
- necessary to protect the vital interests of the data subject
- part of personal data on a public register (and the transferred data will be subject to the same protection as in this country)
- made on terms of a kind approved by the Information Commissioner
- authorized by the Information Commissioner.

Clearly, there is a lot of scope for a nanny state approach to the interpretation of these criteria, particularly when determining what is in the interests of a data subject.

---

[73] 1998 Act, para 15(2). Decisions have been made in respect of the USA, Switzerland, Hungary and Canada.

[74] 1998 Act, Sch 1, Part II, para 14 and Sch 4.

Rights of data subjects

Data subjects have the following rights in respect of their own personal informa-   **10.35**
tion:

- right of access[75]
- right to prevent processing likely to cause damage or distress [76]
- right to prevent processing for the purposes of direct marketing[77]
- right to prevent automated decision-taking in relation to the data subject[78]
- right to have exempt manual data which are inaccurate or incomplete rectified, blocked, erased or destroyed or to require the data controller to cease holding exempt manual data in a way incompatible with the data controller's legitimate purposes[79]
- right to have inaccurate data rectified, blocked, erased or destroyed [80]
- right to compensation.[81]

These rights are enforceable in the first instance by giving the data controller a re-   **10.36**
quest or notice in writing.[82] 'In writing' includes any mode of notice in which the
words are visible because there is no contrary intention in the 1998 Act.[83] Further,
section 64 permits the transmission of notices and requests under Part II by electronic means,[84] provided that the notice or request is received in legible form and
is capable of being used for subsequent reference.[85] Accordingly, Part II notices
and requests may be sent by fax or e-mail. It would appear that text messages to a
data controller's mobile telephone would also be sufficient provided the message
could be stored for an indefinite period.

If the service of a notice or request does not resolve a problem, an individual may   **10.37**
apply to court for an appropriate order.[86] It should be noted that the relevant sections all state that the court 'may' make an order and not that it 'shall' do so. It follows that the court always has discretion as to what order, if any, it should make.
In addition, any individual suffering damage as a result of any contravention of

---

[75] ibid, s 7.
[76] ibid, s 10.
[77] ibid, s 11.
[78] ibid, s 12.
[79] ibid, s 12A.
[80] ibid, s 14.
[81] ibid, s 13.
[82] ibid, ss 7(1)–(2), 10(1), 11(1), 12(1)–(2), 12A(1).
[83] Interpretation Act 1978, s 5, Sch 1.
[84] 1998 Act, s 64(1)(a).
[85] ibid, s 64(2)(b)–(c).
[86] ibid, ss 7(9), 10(4), 11(2), 12(8), 12A(3) and 14(1). The introduction of the right to apply to
a court in the face of a refusal to supply personal information rectified the United Kingdom's breach
of Art 8 of the Convention of Human Rights in this respect (*MG v United Kingdom* [2002] 3 FCR
289, ECHR).

the 1998 Act is entitled to compensation from the defaulting data controller.[87] An individual may also recover damages for any distress suffered.[88]

10.38 If data are being processed for any of the special purposes[89] and an application to court has been made or is anticipated a data subject might apply to the Information Commissioner for assistance.[90] 'Assistance' in this context means bearing the costs of any legal advice obtained by or on behalf of a data subject and/or the costs of litigation.[91] Unsurprisingly, the Commissioner may only grant such assistance if the matter is one of substantial public importance.[92]

10.39 The High Court and the county court have concurrent jurisdiction under Part II of the 1998 Act.[93] In Scotland, the Court of Session and the sheriff have concurrent jurisdiction.

Right of access

10.40 Section 7 gives all individuals the right to be informed by any data controller to whom an application is made whether or not personal data on the applicant are being processed (remembering that processing includes obtaining, recording and holding) by that data controller.[94] If the data controller is processing such data, then the applicant is entitled to be given a description of the data, the purposes for which they are held, and the recipients or classes of recipients to whom they might be disclosed.[95] The applicant is also entitled to receive, in an intelligible form, the information constituting such personal data, and to be told the source of those data so far as is known to the data controller and the logic involved in any automated decision-making in relation to the applicant[96] (unless that logic amounts to a trade secret).[97] 'Trade secret' is not statutorily defined; therefore recourse must be had to the common law.[98] For example, many shops offer instant credit on the basis of completion of an application form and a quick check, usually of a computer database. Any person who is refused credit in such or similar circumstances is entitled to find out why (as, indeed, are those who are granted such credit). This latter right exists where any decision significantly affecting the data subject is taken by reference to or in reliance on automated data processing.[99]

---

[87] 1998 Act, s 13.
[88] See para 10.67 below.
[89] Journalistic, artistic and literary purposes: 1998 Act, s 3.
[90] ibid, s 53.
[91] ibid, s 53(6) and Sch 10.
[92] ibid, s 53(2).
[93] ibid, s 15(1).
[94] ibid, s 7(1)(a).
[95] ibid, s 7(1)(b).
[96] ibid, s 7(1)(c), (d).
[97] ibid, s 8(5).
[98] See *Lansing Linde Ltd v Kerr* [1991] 1 All ER 418.
[99] See also rights in relation to automated decision-taking, paragraphs 10.54–10.59 below.

Any application under section 7 must be in writing and, sometimes, must be paid **10.41**
for.[100] Any fee charged by the data controller is subject to a prescribed maximum.[101] At present, it appears that an applicant must specifically ask for each separate item of information set out at section 7(1). If this is not done the data
controller may limit the information supplied to that specifically requested.
However, the Secretary of State may by regulation provide that any request is
deemed to extend to all such items of information either in prescribed cases or
generally.[102] No such regulation had been made at the time of writing. Where a request for information is made to a credit reference agency, the request is deemed
to be limited to a request for personal data relevant to the applicant's financial
standing unless the request shows a contrary intention.[103] Section 159 of the
Consumer Credit Act 1974, as amended by section 62 of the 1998 Act, must
be referred to, as regulations governing the form in which information must be
supplied may have been made.

A data controller must comply with a request for information promptly (subject **10.42**
to paragraph 10.43 below) and in any event within 40 days of receipt of either the
request or the information required under section 7(3) (if any) and fee, whichever
is the later.[104] Any supply of information constituting personal data[105] must be in
a permanent form unless the applicant agrees otherwise or it is not possible or
would involve a disproportionate effort to supply it in such a form.[106] Such a supply must contain an explanation of any terms used that are not otherwise intelligible. The information supplied may be by reference to either the relevant data at
the date the request is received or the relevant data at the time the information is
supplied. However, in the latter case, any intervening amendments or deletions
must be ones that would have been made regardless of the receipt of the request.[107]

A data controller does not have to comply with a request for information in all cir- **10.43**
cumstances. He is entitled to require information to satisfy himself as to the identity of the applicant and to enable him to locate the relevant information.[108] Such
a requirement must be reasonable. In addition the data controller may refuse the
request if the required information and/or fee are not provided by the applicant.
The data controller may also refuse to comply with a request for information if the

---

[100] 1998 Act, s 7(2).
[101] ibid, s 7(2)(b), (10) and the Data Protection (Subject Access) (Fees and Miscellaneous
Provisions) Regulations 2000, SI 2000/191 as amended by the Data Protection (Subject Access)
(Fees and Miscellaneous Provisions) (Amendment) Regulations 2001, SI 2001/3223.
[102] 1998 Act, s 8(1).
[103] ibid, s 9.
[104] ibid, s 7(8).
[105] ibid, s 7(1)(c).
[106] ibid, s 8(2).
[107] ibid, s 8(6).
[108] ibid, s 7(3).

disclosure of that information would involve the disclosure of information about another individual who can be identified from the information to be disclosed, unless either the third party consents to disclosure or, in all the circumstances, it is reasonable for him to comply with the request without such consent.[109] When determining whether or not to supply information in the absence of the consent of a third party, the data controller (and the court) must have regard to the matters set out in section 7(6): these are (a) any duty of confidentiality owed to the third party, (b) any steps taken to obtain the consent of the third party, (c) whether the third party is capable of giving consent and (d) any express refusal of consent by the third party. This ground for non-compliance is not a blanket exemption. A data controller must provide as much information as he can without disclosing the identity of the third party.[110] He must edit the information so as not to identify the third party provided this can be done without disproportionate effort. Finally, a data controller does not have to comply with a request if he has previously complied with an identical or similar request from that applicant unless a reasonable interval has elapsed between the two requests.[111] In determining whether an interval is reasonable, regard is to be had to the nature of the data, the purpose for which the data are processed, and the frequency with which the data are altered.[112]

10.44   Failure to comply with a request for information under section 7 is a breach of the sixth data protection principle. If a data controller fails to comply with a request for information under section 7 the applicant may apply to court for an order requiring compliance[113] and may obtain compensation if the failure to comply causes damage or distress to the applicant.[114] In determining such an application the court may require the relevant data to be disclosed to it together with the logic mentioned in section 7(1)(d). However, the court shall not require this information to be disclosed to the applicant or his legal representatives unless and until the application is determined in his favour.[115]

10.45   Of course, there are many exemptions from the right to access data under section 7, which is a 'subject information provision' for the purpose of exemptions.[116] The relevant exemptions are those relating to national security,[117] preventing or detecting crime, or assessing or collecting tax or duty,[118] mental and physical health

---

[109]   1998 Act, s 7(4).
[110]   ibid, s 7(5).
[111]   ibid, s 8(3).
[112]   ibid, s 8(4).
[113]   ibid, s 7(9).
[114]   ibid, s 13.
[115]   ibid, s 15(2).
[116]   ibid, s 27(2)(b).
[117]   ibid, s 28.
[118]   ibid, s 29.

and social work,[119] regulation of financial services and other professions,[120] journalism, literature and art,[121] research,[122] information statutorily required to be made available to the public,[123] and personal domestic use.[124] In addition there are various miscellaneous exemptions in section 37 and Schedule 7. The Secretary of State may make further exemptions by order[125] but none have been made at the date of writing. If a data controller cannot bring himself within one of the above exemptions he must comply with the request even if another statute or rule of law prohibits or restricts the disclosure or authorizes the withholding of the information.[126]

Right to prevent processing likely to cause damage and distress

An individual has the right to prevent any or all processing of data which is likely **10.46** to cause substantial damage and/or distress to himself or another where such damage or distress is unwarranted,[127] provided that none of the conditions in Schedule 2, paragraphs 1 to 4 are met, as to which see paragraph 10.49 below. The data subject must give a written notice to the data controller ('the data subject notice'), which must allow a reasonable period for compliance. What a reasonable period may be will depend on all the circumstances of the case. No doubt there will be cases where such a period would be very short, for example where immediate action is threatened on the basis of incorrect data such as an alleged debt that is not in fact owed by the data subject. The notice may require the data controller to cease processing or not to begin processing the relevant data. It may be limited to processing in a specified manner or for a specified purpose. The notice must specify the reasons for considering that the processing will cause distress and/or damage. While only a data subject may serve a notice under this section, it is not necessary that he be the person suffering or likely to suffer damage or distress.

Within 21 days of receiving a data subject notice the data controller must reply to **10.47** the relevant individual in writing, stating either that he has complied or intends to comply with the data subject notice[128] or that he does not intend to comply either in whole or in part.[129] In the latter case he may only refuse to comply in whole or in part on the basis that the data subject notice is unjustified and he must give his reasons for regarding it to be unjustified.

---

[119] ibid, s 30.
[120] ibid, s 31.
[121] ibid, s 32.
[122] ibid, s 33.
[123] ibid, s 34.
[124] ibid, s 36.
[125] ibid, s 38(1).
[126] ibid, s 27(5).
[127] ibid, s 10(1), (2).
[128] ibid, s 10(3)(a).
[129] ibid, s 10(3)(b).

10.48 The court may compel a data controller to comply with a data subject notice if it appears both that the notice is justified and that the data controller has failed to comply with it.[130] This is not an all or nothing power in the court; if the notice is partly justified the court may order compliance to the extent that it is justified. In the absence of an indication by the data controller that he does not intend to comply with a data subject notice, it is unlikely that a court would make an order pursuant to this section unless the data controller concerned fails to respond within the permitted 21 days of receipt of the notice. However, if it is clear that the data controller does not intend to comply with the data subject notice there does not appear to be any reason why an application cannot be made to the court within the 21 day period. In any event, this sub-section does not exclude the court's jurisdiction to grant an injunction against a data controller in appropriate circumstances.

10.49 This section does not apply in certain cases. The section does not apply if any of the conditions in paragraphs 1 to 4 inclusive of Schedule 2 are met. Those are:

- that the data subject has given consent (paragraph 1);
- that the processing is necessary either for the performance of a contract to which the data subject is a party (paragraph 2(a)) or for the taking of precontractual steps at the request of the data subject (paragraph 2(b));
- that the processing is necessary for compliance with any legal obligation to which the data controller is subject, other than one imposed by contract (paragraph 3);
- that the processing is necessary to protect the vital interests of the data subject (paragraph 4).

10.50 As section 10 is a 'non-disclosure provision',[131] this right is not exercisable if the data controller can rely on the general exemptions relating to national security (section 28), detection of crime or taxation (section 29(3)), journalism, literature and art (section 32), a statutory obligation to make the data available to the public (section 34), an obligation to disclose under an enactment, rule of law, court order or for the purposes of legal advice and proceedings (section 35), or pure domestic use (section 36). Further, the Secretary of State may provide for exemptions in other cases, but no order had been made at the time of writing.

Right to prevent processing for the purposes of direct marketing

10.51 Section 11 confers a right on any individual to prevent the use of personal data for the purposes of direct marketing, that is 'the communication of any advertising or marketing material which is directed to particular individuals'.[132] This right is

---

[130] 1998 Act, s 10(4).
[131] ibid, s 27(4)(c).
[132] ibid, s 11(3).

exercised by the service of a written notice on the data controller requiring him to cease or not to begin processing the relevant data for those purposes. The data controller must be given a reasonable time to comply with the notice. Although what is reasonable will depend on all the circumstances, it is difficult to see why it should take longer than one or two weeks for a data controller to comply. As stated above, a notice in writing includes any visible form of communication[133] and may be served electronically.[134]

As processing includes holding data,[135] a data controller using personal data solely **10.52** for the purposes of direct marketing must procure the removal of the relevant data from his files and not simply ensure that no direct mailing takes place whilst retaining the personal data. This right may be exercised even if the individual has previously consented to the use of his personal data for these purposes. A court order requiring compliance with any notice served may be obtained, if appropriate.[136] For the purposes of an application to court, a failure to comply with a notice under this section is itself a breach of the sixth data protection principle.[137] Reference should also be made to orders made under the Telecommunications Act 1984 in respect of direct marketing by fax and telephone.[138]

The only qualifications on this right are the exemptions relating to national secu- **10.53** rity[139] and domestic use.[140] However, circumstances in which such exemptions may be applicable are likely to arise rarely.

Rights in relation to automated decision-taking

An automated decision is one based solely on the processing by automatic means **10.54** of personal data in respect of an individual for the purpose of evaluating matters relating to him such as his performance at work, creditworthiness, reliability or conduct.[141] This list of examples is not exhaustive. Subject to any applicable exemptions, section 12 gives individuals the right to ensure that no automated decisions which significantly affect them are taken by or on behalf of a data controller. This right is protected in two ways. First, if an individual becomes aware that an automated decision is likely to be taken he may give the data controller a

---

[133] Interpretation Act 1978, s 5, Sch 1.
[134] 1998 Act, s 64.
[135] ibid, s 1(1).
[136] ibid, s 11(2).
[137] ibid, s 4(2), Sch 1, Part II at para 8.
[138] Telecommunications (Data Protection and Privacy) Regulations 1999, SI 1999/209, as amended by the Telecommunications (Data Protection and Privacy) (Amendment) Regulations 2000, SI 2000/15.
[139] 1998 Act, s 28.
[140] ibid, s 36.
[141] ibid, s 12(1).

written notice requiring the latter to ensure that an automated decision is not taken in relation to that individual.[142]

10.55 Secondly, as people do not always know that such a decision is likely to be taken or, indeed, has been taken, section 12(2) requires a data controller to notify the individual involved, as soon as reasonably practicable, that an automated decision significantly affecting him has been taken.[143] This obligation does not apply if the data subject has served a notice under section 12(1), as the data controller may not take an automated decision in these circumstances. Oddly perhaps, there is no requirement that this notification be in writing or in any particular form. It is suggested that it would be prudent to give such a notice in writing, if only for evidential purposes. The individual may, by written notice, require the data controller either to reconsider the decision or to take a new decision on a non-automated basis.[144] On receipt of such a notice the data controller has 21 days to give the data subject a further written notice specifying the steps he intends to take to comply with the notice. No time within which these steps must be taken is prescribed. However, given that the object of the section is to prevent the data subject from being prejudiced by an automated decision, it is likely that the steps must be taken sufficiently promptly to permit the objectionable decision to be retaken effectively.

10.56 Non-compliance with either a section 12(1) or section 12(2)(b) notice may be remedied by an application to court,[145] and compensation for any damage or distress suffered as a result of a breach of this provision may be awarded (section 13).

10.57 Decisions which meet the conditions set out in sections 12(6) and 12(7) are exempt from the effects of sections 12(1) and (2). Those conditions are that the decision is taken in the course of steps taken for the purpose of considering whether to enter into a contract with the data subject,[146] or with a view to entering into such a contract,[147] or in the course of performing such a contract,[148] or the decision is authorized or required by or under statute.[149] In addition, the effect of the decision must be to grant a request of the data subject,[150] or steps must have been taken to safeguard the legitimate interests of the data subject by, for example, allowing him to make representations.[151]

---

[142] 1998 Act, s 12(1).
[143] ibid, s 12(2)(a).
[144] ibid, s 12(2)(b).
[145] ibid, s 12(8).
[146] ibid, s 12(6)(a)(i).
[147] ibid, s 12(6)(a)(ii).
[148] ibid, s 12(6)(a)(iii).
[149] ibid, s 12(6)(b).
[150] ibid, s 12(7)(a).
[151] ibid, s 12(7)(b).

The effect of this section, therefore, is not to prevent completely the taking of au- **10.58**
tomated decisions but to provide redress if such a decision is unfavourable. This
allows, for example, the grant of credit by computer without service of notices but
does not permit its refusal unless the applicant has been protected under section
12(7)(b). In many cases the practical consumer benefits of this will be difficult to
see. An obvious example is the instant credit offered by many retailers. In such
cases credit is granted or refused on the basis of certain information loaded into a
computer. While one may see the attraction of permitting credit to be granted in
this way, the refusal of credit in a public environment may be distressing and
embarrassing. This distress or embarrassment will not be alleviated by the subsequent service of a section 12(2)(b) notice.

Section 12(5)(b) permits the Secretary of State to prescribe other circumstances in **10.59**
which automated decisions may be exempt but none had been prescribed at the
time of writing. Some of the general exemptions also apply, namely, those relating
to national security,[152] journalism, literature and art[153] and domestic use.[154]

Rights in relation to exempt manual data

Exempt manual data[155] are not subject to the general right to rectification, block- **10.60**
ing, erasure or destruction of inaccurate or incomplete personal data bestowed by
section 14.[156] As inaccurate data could cause great damage and distress section
12A provides more limited rights in respect of such data during the period of exemption.[157] An individual may, by notice in writing ('a section 12A notice'), require a data controller to rectify, block, erase or destroy exempt manual data which
are inaccurate or incomplete.[158] In addition, an individual may, by a section 12A
notice, require a data controller to cease holding exempt manual data in a way
which is inconsistent with the latter's legitimate interests.[159] The second right offers some protection for individual privacy in cases where excessive personal data
are held which are no longer, or may never have been, necessary for the lawful purposes of the data controller. This is necessary because exempt manual data are not
subject to the second data protection principle.

Any notice served pursuant to this section must state the data subject's reasons for **10.61**
believing that the data are inaccurate or incomplete, alternatively, for believing
that they are held in a manner incompatible with the data controller's legitimate

---

[152] ibid, s 28.
[153] ibid, s 32.
[154] ibid, s 36.
[155] For the meaning of this phrase see paras 10.18–10.20 above.
[156] 1998 Act, Sch 8, para 14(2)(c).
[157] 24 October 2001 to 23 October 2007 inclusive.
[158] 1998 Act, s 12A(1)(a).
[159] ibid, s 12A(1)(b).

purposes.[160] Whether or not data are inaccurate will be a matter of fact. Whether or not they are incomplete, however, is a mixed question of fact and law because section 12A(5) provides that data are only incomplete if they would contravene the third or fourth data protection principles had those principles applied. There is no time limit within which the data controller must either respond to the section 12A notice or comply with it. However, on any application to court to force compliance with the section 12A notice, the court must be satisfied that the data controller has failed to comply; therefore the data controller must be given a reasonable time in which to comply. If the court is satisfied that the section 12A notice is justified, or partly justified, and there has been a failure to comply, it may make an order requiring the appropriate degree of compliance.[161] A failure to comply with a section 12A notice is itself a breach of the sixth data protection principle, one of the few that applies to exempt manual data.

10.62 The usual exemptions apply to this section, namely: national security,[162] journalism, literature and art,[163] personal data required by statute to be made available to the public,[164] and domestic use.[165]

Rectification, blocking, erasure and destruction of inaccurate data

10.63 Where a data controller is holding or otherwise processing inaccurate personal data, the data subject may apply to court for an order requiring the data controller to rectify, block, erase or destroy the offending data.[166] This includes the original data and any other personal data that include an expression of opinion based on the inaccurate data. Unusually, there is no requirement to serve a written notice or request prior to making an application under this section. Nonetheless, a data subject should take all reasonable steps to obtain a non-judicial remedy prior to making an application pursuant to this section if only for the purposes of compliance with the spirit of the Civil Procedure Rules.

10.64 The right to rectification, etc exists even if the inaccurate data have been obtained from the data subject himself or from a third party. However, in these cases the court's discretion is wider. Provided that the data controller has taken reasonable steps to ensure the accuracy of the data and the data contain an indication of any view of the data subject as notified to the data controller to the effect that the data are inaccurate,[167] the court may, as an alternative to rectification etc, order that the

---

[160] 1998 Act, s 12A(2).
[161] ibid, s 12A(3).
[162] ibid, s 28.
[163] ibid, s 32.
[164] ibid, s 34.
[165] ibid, s 36.
[166] ibid, s 14(1). For brevity, these four remedies are hereafter referred to as 'rectification, etc'.
[167] ibid, Sch 1, Part II, para 7.

data be supplemented by a statement of the true facts.[168] The court must approve the statement of the true facts. Further, even if the requirements of paragraph 7 of Part II of Schedule 1 have not been complied with, at all or in part, the court may simply make an order requiring such compliance with or without a supplementary statement of the true facts.[169] In determining the question of what steps are reasonable for the purposes of ensuring the accuracy of any data obtained regard must be had to the purpose(s) for which the data were obtained and further processed.[170] Where inaccurate data have been rectified etc voluntarily, or the court so orders, it may also order the data controller to notify third parties to whom the inaccurate data have been disclosed of the rectification, etc but it should only do so where such notification is reasonably practicable.[171]

10.65 Whether or not data are inaccurate, a court may order their rectification, etc if it is satisfied that the data subject has suffered damage as a result of a data controller's contravention of any of the requirements of the 1998 Act such as to entitle the data subject to compensation under section 13 and that there is a substantial risk that there will be further contraventions and further damage for the purposes of section 13.[172] Again, in these circumstances the court may also order that third parties should be notified of the rectification, etc of the data, where reasonably practicable to do so.[173]

10.66 As section 14(1) to (3) is a non-disclosure provision,[174] this right is not exercisable if the data controller can rely on the general exemptions relating to national security,[175] detection of crime and taxation,[176] journalism, literature and art,[177] a statutory obligation to make the data available to the public,[178] an obligation to disclose under an enactment, rule of law, court order or for the purposes of legal advice and proceedings,[179] or pure domestic use.[180] In addition, the Secretary of State may make further exemptions[181] but none had been made at the time of writing.

---

[168] ibid, s 14(2)(a).
[169] ibid, s 14(2)(b).
[170] ibid, Sch 1, Part II, para 7(a).
[171] ibid, s 14(3).
[172] ibid, s 14(4).
[173] ibid, s 14(5).
[174] ibid, s 27(3), (4)(c).
[175] ibid, s 28.
[176] ibid, s 29(3).
[177] ibid, s 32.
[178] ibid, s 34.
[179] ibid, s 35.
[180] ibid, s 36.
[181] ibid, s 38(2).

Compensation

10.67 Section 13 significantly expands individuals' rights to compensation in that financial recovery can now be made in respect of any damage caused by any contravention of the 1998 Act.[182] Damage in this context does not include distress because the section makes separate provision for compensation for distress.[183] Compensation may be payable for distress caused by a breach of the provisions of the 1998 Act. However, compensation for distress is only recoverable if either it is accompanied by damage or the contravention relates to processing for special purposes, that is journalistic, artistic or literary purposes.[184] It is thought that damage must mean financial loss or damage to one's reputation for these purposes. Recently, the Court of Appeal stated that a newspaper article, which 'trashed' an individual in a highly offensive and hurtful manner, could found an award of aggravated damages for distress.[185]

Exemptions

10.68 As law making operates on a broadly utilitarian basis both in this country and in the EC there are thought to be occasions when the greater good takes precedence over individual rights. Sometimes the greater good's precedence is deemed to be absolute, as in cases of national security; in other cases a balancing exercise has been undertaken or is required to be undertaken by the relevant authority, for example in cases of processing of data for the purposes of journalism, literature or art. Indeed, even in the case of national security any exemption must be proportionate to the need.

10.69 Section 27(1) of the 1998 Act identifies two types of 'provisions' for the purposes of exemptions: subject information provisions and non-disclosure provisions.[186] There are two subject information provisions in the 1998 Act: the first data protection principle to the extent that it requires compliance with paragraph 2 of Part II of Schedule 1,[187] and section 7.[188] The non-disclosure provisions are again, the first data protection principle (but this time except to the extent that it requires

---

[182] 1998 Act, s 13(1).

[183] ibid, s 13(2).

[184] ibid, ss 13(2)(b) and 3.

[185] *Campbell v Mirror Group Newspapers* [2002] EWCA Civ 1373 at para 139, TLR 16 October 2002. However, as the Court of Appeal reversed the first instance decision on liability this is obiter. See also text and nn 218, 220 below.

[186] 1998 Act, s 27(2), (3) and (4).

[187] Together these provide that data are only processed fairly if the data subject is provided with information relating to the data controller and the purposes for which the data are processed within a relevant period.

[188] Right of access to personal data.

compliance with the conditions in Schedules 2 and 3),[189] the second, third, fourth and fifth data protection principles, and sections 10 and 14(1) to (3) of the 1998 Act.[190]

National security

Unsurprisingly, safeguarding national security overrides all the data protection principles, all individual rights and all statutory obligations.[191] A certificate signed by a Minister of the Crown conclusively determines any question as to whether national security is at issue.[192] The certificate may restrict the exemption only to certain parts of the 1998 Act or to certain personal data. Alternatively, it may be couched in very broad and general terms.[193] However, anyone who is personally affected by the issue of such a certificate has the right to appeal to the Information Tribunal against the certificate.[194] In such an application the Tribunal's role is restricted to reviewing the decision of the Minister; the only action it may take is to quash the certificate and it may only do that if it finds that the Minister did not have reasonable grounds for granting the certificate.[195] An indication of the courts' approach may be gleaned from a recent decision of the House of Lords in relation to a national security exemption in an immigration appeal.[196] In that case it was stated that national security need not involve a direct threat to the United Kingdom; it could involve a threat to another state. The question of national security involves a large element of policy, so the decision is that primarily of the Secretary of State and not the court. The Secretary of State may have regard to precautionary and preventative principles. The material before him does not have to meet the civil standard of proof on the question; it must simply be material on which he could reasonably and proportionately conclude that there is a real possibility of activities harmful to national security. Presumably, a certificate could be quashed on the basis that it was disproportionately wide. In addition, where there are proceedings under the 1998 Act on foot in which a data controller is seeking to rely on a certificate of this type couched in general terms, any party to the proceedings may appeal to the Tribunal for a determination that the certificate does not apply to the personal data which are the subject of the proceedings.[197] Short of

10.70

---

[189] The 1998 Act Sch 2 imposes conditions for the processing of personal data while Sch 3 imposes further conditions for the processing of sensitive personal data.

[190] ibid, s 10 confers the right to prevent processing likely to cause damage or distress while s 14(1)–(3) confers the right to rectification, blocking, erasure and destruction of inaccurate data.

[191] ibid, s 28(1), (11).

[192] ibid, s 28(2). Only a Cabinet Minister, the Attorney-General or the Lord Advocate may issue a certificate: s 28(10).

[193] ibid, s 28(2), (3). This was intended to permit Ministers to be proportionate in their use of such certificates (HC Official Report; SC D (Data Protection Bill) 19 May 1998).

[194] 1998 Act, s 28(4).

[195] ibid, s 28(5).

[196] *Secretary of State for the Home Department v Rehman* [2001] 3 WLR 877.

[197] 1998 Act, s 28(6), (7).

a statement by the relevant Minister that the relevant certificate does not cover the subject data, it would appear that the issue must be one of construction of the certificate. The section also contains provisions as to evidence and the constitution and procedure of the Tribunal.[198]

Crime and taxation

10.71 This exemption (set out in section 29) covers the processing of personal data for the purposes of the prevention or detection of crime, the apprehension or prosecution of offenders, or the assessment or collection of any tax, duty or similar imposition. It is not restricted to the police and revenue authorities but extends to any user registered for the purpose, for example a private detective. It is suggested that National Insurance would fall within the phrase 'similar imposition'. Proportionality is a relevant consideration for this exemption as it is only available to the extent that compliance with the full obligations of the 1998 Act would prejudice any of the purposes to which the section refers. Such processing is exempt from the first data protection principle, which requires data to be processed fairly and lawfully, except to the extent to which it requires compliance with the conditions in Schedules 2 and 3.[199] However, as one of the conditions contained in both Schedules is that the processing is necessary 'for the exercise of any functions conferred on any person by or under any enactment or . . . for the exercise of any functions of the Crown, a Minister of the Crown or a government department. . .'[200] it is unlikely that this qualification will cause the relevant data controller any significant difficulty. Such processing is also exempt from the right to access personal data conferred by section 7.[201] In both cases the exemption applies only to the extent that the relevant provisions would be likely to prejudice any of the stated purposes. Prejudice must be likely and not just possible.[202]

Health, education and social work

10.72 Section 30 empowers the Secretary of State to make orders exempting certain personal data from the subject information provisions or modifying those provisions. The relevant personal data are:

(a) information on the physical or mental health of the data subject;[203]

(b) personal data relating to persons who are or have been pupils at a school and the data controller in respect of which is a teacher at the school or the proprietor of it;[204]

---

[198] 1998 Act, s 28(8), (9) and (12).
[199] ibid, s 29(1).
[200] ibid, Sch 2 para 5(b), (c); Sch 3, para 7(b), (c).
[201] ibid, s 29(1).
[202] *Equifax Europe Ltd v Data Protection Registrar* [Case DA/90 25/49/7].
[203] 1998 Act, s 30(1). See also ch 11 below.
[204] ibid, s 30(2).

(c) information processed by government departments, local authorities, voluntary organizations[205] or other bodies designated under the order and appearing to him to be processed in the course of, or for the purposes of, carrying out social work in relation to the data subject or other individuals.[206]

There is no qualification to the power to make an order as far as the first two categories are concerned. However, in the last case the Secretary of State may only make an order to the extent that the full application of the provisions would be likely to prejudice the carrying out of social work. To date orders have been made in relation to personal data consisting of information as to the physical or mental health or condition of the data subject,[207] information constituting educational records,[208] and information constituting a social work record.[209] The orders also relate to information processed by a court consisting of information supplied in a report or other evidence given to a court by various public bodies and/or officers under various statutes. **10.73**

Regulatory activity

This exemption applies only to the subject information provisions,[210] so that for data processed for regulatory purposes there is no right of access under section 7, nor is the data controller required to ensure that the data subject is provided with, or has readily made available to him, the information set out in paragraph 2 of Part II of Schedule 1 pursuant to the first data protection principle. Again, the exemption is available only to the extent necessary to avoid prejudice to the discharge of the regulatory functions. This section is very widely drafted and covers virtually every conceivable regulatory body, whether or not created by or under a statute, including government departments and those performing a function 'which is of a public nature and is exercised in the public interest'.[211] It also covers the Director General of Fair Trading and all Parliamentary and local government Commissioners and Ombudsmen.[212] Generally speaking, the 'relevant functions' extend to anything involving the protection of the public, whether from financial wrongdoing or otherwise, and range from the protection of charities to the protection of workers and businesses.[213] Undoubtedly, bodies controlling the professions such as the Bar Council, the General Medical Council, and the Institute **10.74**

---

[205] No doubt this would cover organizations like the NSPCC.
[206] 1998 Act, s 30(3).
[207] Data Protection (Subject Access Modification) (Health) Order 2000, SI 2000/413.
[208] Data Protection (Subject Access Modification) (Education) Order 2000, SI 2000/414.
[209] Data Protection (Subject Access Modification) (Social Work) Order 2000, SI 2000/415.
[210] 1998 Act, s 27.
[211] ibid, s 31(3).
[212] ibid, s 31(4).
[213] ibid, s 31(2), (4) and (5).

of Chartered Accountants may avail themselves of this exception when exercising their regulatory functions.

Journalism, literature and art

10.75 This is a significant new exemption introduced by the 1998 Act. It did not exist under the 1984 Act, and is designed to balance rights of privacy against the right to freedom of expression. Personal data processed only with a view to publication of journalistic, literary or artistic material (special purposes[214]) is not subject to any of the data protection principles except the seventh (protection of the data from unauthorized or unlawful processing and against loss, damage and destruction), nor do data subjects have any rights in respect of such data.[215] However, to avail himself of the exemption the data controller must hold a reasonable belief that:

(a) the publication would be in the public interest, with particular regard to the public interest in freedom of expression;[216] and

(b) in all the circumstances, compliance with the relevant provision of the 1998 Act is incompatible with the special purposes.[217]

Public interest does not mean anything that may be of interest to the public, a balancing exercise is necessary. As Lord Phillips MR, delivering the judgment of the court, recently held:

> . . . the fact that an individual has achieved prominence on the public stage does not mean that his private life can be laid bare by the media. We do not see why it should necessarily be in the public interest that an individual who has been adopted as a role model, without seeking this distinction, should be demonstrated to have feet of clay.[218]

Factors relevant to the issue of reasonableness of belief in relation to the public interest include the data controller's compliance with any relevant code of conduct and compliance with any code which the Secretary of State, by order, designates for the purposes of this provision.[219] Section 32 is ambiguous in that it is not clear whether it applies only to pre-publication processing or whether it covers publication itself and subsequent processing. The general view of writers on the topic was that the exemption applied only to pre-publication processing; however the

---

[214] ibid, s 3.

[215] ibid, s 32(1), (2), save for the right to compensation for a breach of the seventh data protection principle.

[216] ibid, s 32(1)(b).

[217] ibid, s 32(1)(c).

[218] *Campbell v Mirror Group Newspapers* [2002] EWCA Civ 1373 at para 41, TLR 16 October 2002.

[219] ibid, s 32(3). These are the Code on Fairness and Privacy (Broadcasting Standards Commission, June 1998); ITC Programme Code (Independent Television Commission, Autumn 1998); Press Complaints Commission Code of Practice (December 1997); The Producers' Guidelines (BBC, November 1996); The Programme Code (Radio Authority, March 1998).

Court of Appeal recently held that the exemption extends to publication and post publication as well.[220] A court must stay proceedings for the enforcement of rights[221] under the 1998 Act in any case where a data controller claims, or it appears to the court, that the data are being processed only for the special purposes and with a view to publication of any material which had not been previously published by the data controller at a time 24 hours before the stay is being considered. The stay remains until either the Information Commissioner makes a determination under section 45 of the 1998 Act or the data subject's claim is withdrawn. Slightly oddly, section 45 only provides for the Commissioner to determine that the processing is *not* only for the special purposes. There is no provision requiring or empowering the making of a determination that the processing is only for the special purposes. However, no doubt the Information Commissioner would notify the parties in writing if he were not going to make a section 45 determination. See paragraphs 10.84 to 10.99 below for the Information Commissioner's powers.

Research, history and statistics

Data processed only for research purposes, including historical and statistical pur- **10.76**
poses, are exempted from many of the 1998 Act's provisions. In order to be classified as being used for research purposes, it is necessary that the data are not processed to support decisions or measures relating to particular individuals[222] and are not processed in such a way that substantial damage or distress is caused to any data subject.[223] Research data are effectively exempt from the second and fifth data protection principles, in that research purposes are deemed not incompatible with any other purpose for which the data were originally obtained, and such data may be kept indefinitely.[224] Data subjects have no rights of access to research data provided the research results or resulting statistics are not made available in a form which identifies any one or more of the data subjects.[225] Finally, data may be disclosed to other researchers, the data subject or a person acting on his behalf, or at the request or with the consent of the data subject or a person acting on his behalf without losing their status as research data.[226] Where the person making the disclosure has reasonable grounds for believing it to be made in one of these ways, the character of research data will not be lost even if, for example, the data subject did not in fact give his consent to the disclosure.[227]

---

[220] *Campbell v Mirror Group Newspapers* [2002] EWCA Civ 1373 at para 128, TLR 16 October 2002.

[221] For example, to prevent the disclosure of personal data under s 10.

[222] 1998 Act, s 33(1)(a).

[223] ibid, s 33(1)(b).

[224] ibid, s 33(2), (3).

[225] ibid, s 33(4).

[226] ibid, s 33(5).

[227] ibid, s 33(5)(d).

Manual data held by public authorities

10.77 Section 33A of the 1998 Act is inserted by section 70 of the Freedom of Information Act 2000. It exempts unstructured manual personal data (not being an accessible record[228]) held by public authorities from most of the provisions of the 1998 Act but not, by and large, from the fourth data protection principle (data must be accurate and up to date) or from the sixth principle with regard to access to data and rights to rectification of inaccurate data. In addition data subjects retain rights to access, rectification etc of inaccurate data, and compensation in respect of breaches of the fourth and sixth data protection principles. Until these provisions come into force data subjects have no rights in relation to these data as they were not covered by the 1984 Act.

Information available to the public by or under any enactment

10.78 This section[229] disapplies most of the provisions of the 1998 Act in a case where a data controller is required to make personal information available to the public by or under any enactment other than the Freedom of Information Act 2000. For example, the 1998 Act does not permit a refusal to provide a copy of a company's register of members pursuant to section 356(6) of the Companies Act 1985.[230] The important words are 'available to the public'. Where an enactment requires information to be available to a limited class of persons this exemption does not apply. As has been remarked by the Data Protection Registrar, it is difficult to see why a data user should not be obliged to maintain accurate data just because he is required to publish it.

Disclosures required by law or made in connection with legal proceedings etc

10.79 Rather obviously, a data controller cannot rely on the non-disclosure provisions of the 1998 Act for the purposes of refusing disclosure of personal data when such disclosure is required by or under any enactment, rule of law or court order.[231] Disclosure under the Civil Procedure Rules cannot be avoided or restricted by reliance on the 1998 Act. Further, any documentation obtained by a party and/or his lawyers by a means which constitutes or involves a breach of the Principles will not be covered by legal professional privilege even if obtained for the purposes of litigation.[232] This exemption preserves the court's power to make an order requir-

---

[228] 1998 Act, s 68.
[229] ibid, s 34.
[230] *Pelling v Families Need Fathers Ltd* [2001] EWCA Civ 1280, NLC 2010814 (1.08.01).
[231] 1998 Act, s 35(1).
[232] *Dubai Aluminium Co Ltd v Sayed Reyadi Abdulla Nasser Al Alwani* The Times, 6 January 1999.

ing a third party to disclose the identity of a tortfeasor and is not restricted to legal proceedings involving the data controller.[233]

Further, the non-disclosure provisions do not apply to the disclosure of any data **10.80** when that disclosure is necessary for the purposes of or in connection with any legal proceedings or for the purposes of obtaining legal advice or is otherwise necessary for the purposes of establishing, exercising or defending legal rights.[234] This exemption permits the disclosure of any personal data to one's legal advisers and tax or other advisers for the stated purposes. It probably also applies to McKenzie friends. It also permits such disclosure to other parties in any legal action or to any person against whom a legal right is being exercised, established or defended. This will allow disclosure of personal data in any forum for the resolution of disputes including tribunals, arbitrations and mediations. However, the existence of a legal dispute does not permit the disclosure of personal data at large. It should also be noted that the exemption is restricted to the non-disclosure provisions.[235]

Domestic purposes

The 1998 Act provides a blanket exemption for personal data processed for **10.81** strictly personal purposes, that is for the purposes of an individual's personal, family or household affairs including recreational purposes. Users of address lists for purposes such as Christmas cards or parties do not have to comply with any of the provisions of the 1998 Act. Personal diaries are also safe so that one may continue to be as rude and unfair about one's acquaintances as one wishes without fear of discovery, at least under the provisions of the 1998 Act. In the Commissioner's view the term 'recreational purposes' does not exempt any records kept by individuals for the purposes of amateur sporting clubs, churches and the like as the data controller in such cases is the club or association.[236]

Miscellaneous exemptions

Schedule 7 contains miscellaneous exemptions relating to topics such as educa- **10.82** tional or employment references, the armed forces, and Crown honours. Some of these are very important: reference should be made to the Schedule for the full list. Regulations relating to some of these matters have been introduced by statutory instrument.[237]

---

[233] *Totalise plc v The Motley Fool Ltd* [2002] 1 WLR 1233.
[234] 1998 Act, s 35(2).
[235] See ibid, s 27.
[236] Guideline No 6.
[237] Data Protection (Corporate Finance Exemptions) Order 2000, SI 2000/184.

Powers to make further exemptions by order

10.83   As stated above, the Secretary of State has power to make further exemptions by order.[238] Such an exemption may only be made if the Secretary of State considers it necessary for safeguarding the interests of the data subject or rights and freedoms of any other individual, and must be limited to the extent necessary to achieve the purpose. Sub-section (1) applies to exemptions from subject information provisions while sub-section (2) applies to non-disclosure provisions. In order for the former power to arise, the disclosure of the relevant information must be prohibited or restricted by or under an enactment. An order has been made under this section exempting various data relating to such matters as fertilization treatment, adoption and parental records, statements and records of special educational needs.[239]

The Information Commissioner and Information Tribunal

10.84   The Information Commissioner oversees and enforces both the 1998 Act and the Freedom of Information Act. His dual role is intended to ensure a consistent approach to the implementation of both statutes. The Commissioner reports directly to Parliament, and has an international role as well as a national one. This section is confined, however, to a description of his functions and powers within the United Kingdom.[240]

10.85   Any data controller processing or intending to process personal data by means of automatic equipment must register with the Commissioner before he may lawfully process the data.[241] Generally speaking, data controllers processing data only by manual means do not have to register[242] unless the processing is particularly likely to cause substantial damage or distress to, or otherwise to prejudice significantly the rights and freedoms of, data subjects.[243] Keepers of public registers do not have to register either.[244] The Secretary of State may make further exemptions from the duty to register by order.[245] The registrable particulars are contained in section 16 and include such information as name, address, purpose of processing, and description of data processed. There is a continuing duty to notify the

---

[238] 1998 Act, s 38.
[239] Data Protection (Miscellaneous Subject Access Exemptions) Order 2000, SI 2000/419.
[240] Although it is worth noting that the Commissioner has recently authorized the transfer of personal data by data controllers in the EU to data controllers in third countries under a decision of the European Commission in Directive (EC) 95/46. This was the first exercise of the power conferred upon the Commissioner by Sch 4, para 9 of the 1998 Act.
[241] ibid, s 18(1).
[242] ibid, s 17(2).
[243] ibid, s 22(1).
[244] ibid, s 17(4).
[245] ibid, s 17(3).

Commissioner of any changes to the registrable particulars.[246] Failure to register and failure to notify changes to registrable particulars constitute criminal offences,[247] although it is a defence to show the exercise of due diligence in complying with the relevant duty.[248]

The Commissioner's functions cover a wide range of activities. He is responsible, **10.86** for example, for the maintenance of the Data Protection Register.[249] He is required to keep the notification regulations under review, and if necessary to propose their amendment to the Secretary of State.[250] One of his principal tasks is to educate the public about the importance of data protection, and to take any other steps likely to promote respect for the principles on which the 1998 Act is based. A television and leaflet campaign consumed a large part of the Commissioner's budget in 2000, and among the most recent initiatives are a study on website compliance and the publication of a guide to data protection auditing. In particular, once he has consulted the relevant trade associations he may produce and distribute codes of practice, which must be laid before both Houses of Parliament.[251] The Commissioner has recently produced a CCTV code of practice, as well as a code on the use of employee data.

For present purposes, however, the Commissioner's most important function is to **10.87** enforce the provisions of the 1998 Act. The Commissioner has developed a number of non-statutory procedures to assist in this task, but if the Commissioner is not able to persuade a data controller informally to alter his practices the Commissioner has a considerable battery of statutory powers to compel him to do so. Just as important, the Commissioner has an almost unfettered discretion as to how those powers should be exercised in any given case.

If all else fails, it is primarily for the Commissioner to decide whether to prosecute **10.88** any offence under the 1998 Act.[252] There has been a steady stream of prosecutions over the last few years, primarily of unregistered data users, although in the less serious cases the current policy is to administer a formal caution. Where the principal offender is a company, the Commissioner may also prosecute one or more of its directors or managers if he believes that he can prove that the offence was committed with their consent or connivance or is attributable to their neglect.[253] This is potentially a significant provision, although as yet it does not appear to have

---

[246] ibid, s 20.
[247] ibid, s 21.
[248] ibid, s 21(3).
[249] ibid, s 19.
[250] ibid, s 25.
[251] ibid, ss 51, 52.
[252] ibid, s 60. The Director of Public Prosecutions may also mount prosecutions, but in practice he is likely to defer to the Commissioner.
[253] ibid, s 61.

been invoked in practice. Prosecutions are almost invariably conducted in the magistrates' courts, which have regularly imposed fines of £1000 or more.

10.89 Many of the Commissioner's investigations concern the unlawful procurement of information by private investigators and tracing agents. In order to obtain evidence of an offence, subject to certain safeguards the Commissioner may apply to the Crown Court for a warrant to enter any premises in which he has reasonable grounds to suspect either that an offence has been or is being committed or that any of the data protection principles has been or is being contravened.[254] Upon entry into the premises, the Commissioner's officers are entitled to inspect and test any equipment, and to inspect and seize any documents found there. These are extensive powers; the seizure of documents can have a particularly disruptive effect on the operation of a business.

10.90 The Commissioner is likely to invoke these powers, however, only as a last resort. His primary tools are not search and seizure or criminal prosecution, but the issue of one or other of three forms of statutory notice. These are information notices, special information notices and (most importantly) enforcement notices. Each type of notice is subject to controls peculiar to it, but all must inform the recipient of the notice of the basis on which it has been issued and of his right of appeal against it to the Information Tribunal. In each case also, the notice is stayed or suspended until any appeal has been determined. The members of the Tribunal are appointed by the Lord Chancellor and must be legally qualified. An appeal may be heard by the chairman of the Tribunal and two other members, of whom one must have been appointed to represent the interests of data subjects, and the other, the interests of data controllers.[255] The Tribunal may overturn the Commissioner on the facts or the law or both, and may substitute its own view on the merits for his. There is a right of appeal from the Tribunal to the High Court only on a matter of law.[256]

Information notices

10.91 Anyone who believes that he is 'directly affected' by any processing of personal data is entitled to ask the Commissioner under section 42 to assess whether it is 'likely or unlikely' that the processing is being carried out in accordance with the 1998 Act. In practice, most requests for assessment are made by individuals who are concerned about the manner in which their personal data have been processed. There has recently been a sharp increase in the number of requests, of which there

---

[254] 1998 Act, s 50 and Sch 9. Unless it is satisfied that the case is urgent or that notice would defeat the object of the search, the court can only issue the warrant if the suspect has already declined to provide access to his premises or has unreasonably declined to co-operate with a search: ibid. Nine no-notice search warrants were issued in 2001.

[255] ibid, Sch 6, para 4.

[256] ibid, s 49(6).

were almost 9000 in the year to 31 March 2001. About 40 per cent of all complaints relate to consumer credit or allege breaches of the Telecommunications Regulations.

In many cases the Commissioner will deal with the matter informally, but receipt **10.92** of a request entitles him to serve an 'information notice' or a 'special information notice' on the relevant data controller. The Commissioner may also serve an information notice even if he has not received a request, provided that he 'reasonably requires' information to determine whether the data controller has complied or is complying with data protection principles.[257] The notice must inform the recipient into which of these categories it falls, and if it falls into the second must explain why the Commissioner considers that the information sought by the notice is relevant to the determination whether a data protection principle has been or is being complied with.[258] Without that information, the data controller cannot sensibly decide whether to appeal against the notice.

The notice can require the data controller to furnish the Commissioner within the **10.93** period specified in the notice with whatever information is specified in the notice. The Commissioner cannot require the recipient to disclose information which is subject to legal professional privilege or would reveal evidence of his commission of any offence other than one created by the 1998 Act itself. Subject to those qualifications, however, the Commissioner can require the disclosure of any information he chooses, although disproportionate requests may well attract (successful) appeals.

Unless the Commissioner has received a section 42 request, 'special' information **10.94** notices can be served only in the much narrower circumstances which obtain where personal data have been processed for journalistic, artistic or literary purposes.[259] In these cases the individual's right of privacy obviously has to be balanced against the public interest in freedom of expression. In an attempt to strike that balance, the 1998 Act in certain circumstances exempts data processed for any of these 'special' purposes from all but the seventh of the data protection principles.

The exemption operates in an unusual way. If a data controller is prosecuted for **10.95** an offence under the 1998 Act and 'claims' that the relevant data are being processed only for a special purpose with a view to the publication of material which the data controller has not published before, the court must stay the proceedings however spurious it considers the claim to be. The stay remains in place unless and until the Commissioner has determined that the claim is without substance.

---

[257] ibid, s 43(1).
[258] ibid, s 43(2).
[259] ibid, s 3.

10.96 If the Commissioner has not yet made that determination but has reasonable grounds to suspect that the relevant data are either not being processed for a special purpose or are not being processed for first publication, he is entitled to serve a 'special information notice' requiring the data controller to provide the information specified in the notice.[260] The data controller must provide the information within a specified period, subject to the same qualifications as apply to an 'ordinary' information notice.

Enforcement notices

10.97 If as a result of information obtained in response to an information notice or from any other source the Commissioner is 'satisfied' that a data controller has contravened or is contravening any of the data protection principles, he may serve an enforcement notice on the data controller requiring him to comply with the relevant principle. For that purpose the notice may require the data controller either to take or to refrain from taking particular steps, or to refrain from processing personal data at all or in a particular manner or for a particular purpose.[261] Where inaccurate data are held in contravention of the fourth data protection principle the notice may require the data controller not only to rectify the data, but also to rectify or destroy any other data held by him expressing an opinion which appears to the Commissioner to be based on the inaccurate data.

10.98 Since an enforcement notice might otherwise remain in force indefinitely, the 1998 Act entitles the Commissioner at any time to cancel or vary the notice if and to the extent that he 'considers' that the notice need no longer be complied with to ensure the observance of the relevant data protection principle.[262] If the Commissioner does not do so of his own initiative, the data controller can himself apply to the Commissioner to cancel or vary the notice to reflect a change of circumstances since the notice was first served upon him. He may appeal to the Information Tribunal in the usual way if the Commissioner declines to do so.[263]

10.99 The Commissioner will not normally serve an enforcement notice unless a non-statutory 'preliminary' notice has failed to achieve the desired result. A preliminary notice may result, for example, in the offer of a suitable undertaking by the data controller which avoids the need for more formal action. Used effectively, in both its statutory and non-statutory form the enforcement notice offers the Commissioner a versatile and potent tool. It can be adapted to meet almost any situation, modified as the situation itself changes, and monitored over a period of time to ensure real improvements in the relevant data processing practices. In

---

[260] 1998 Act, s 44.
[261] ibid, s 40.
[262] ibid, s 41.
[263] ibid, s 48(2), 49(3).

2000, for example, the Commissioner issued notices against two (related) companies which were believed to have distributed direct marketing material in breach of the Telecommunications Regulations. Both companies appealed against the notices, but without prejudice discussions prior to the hearing of their (consolidated) appeals resulted in an agreement under which both companies submitted to the first of the notices served on each of them, and accepted the terms of a new notice to be served on them in lieu of the second. The Tribunal approved the compromise, and the Commissioner has since continued to monitor the companies' compliance with the notices.

D. The 1998 Act and the Freedom of Information Act 2000

As stated at the outset, despite apparent contradictions, the Data Protection Act 1998 and the Freedom of Information Act 2000 are compatible and complementary although there are some differences. The three main differences are set out below: **10.100**

Freedom of Information Act 2000	Data Protection Act 1998
Applies only to information held by public authorities	Applies to personal data processed by all data controllers whether public authorities or not
Any person may apply for information on any other person	Only living individuals may apply and only for information about themselves
Generally speaking, only non-personal information may be obtained if it relates to a living individual	Only covers personal data relating to living individuals

The main provision governing the relationship between the two Acts is section 40 of the Freedom of Information Act 2000 entitled 'Personal Information'. This section appears in Part II of the 2000 Act and is one of the exemption sections. The heading would be more accurately stated as 'personal data' because that is how personal information is referred to within the section. Personal data in section 40 has the same meaning as in section 1(1) of the 1998 Act,[264] so there is no scope for conflict in that respect.   **10.101**

One cannot apply under the Freedom of Information Act for personal data of which one is the data subject as this information is wholly exempt from the Act;[265]   **10.102**

---

[264] ibid, s 40(7).
[265] ibid, s 40(1).

351

therefore the 1998 Act is the sole source of rights of access to one's own personal data. This sub-section confers a complete exemption from the duty imposed on public authorities by section 1(1)(a) of the Act. Further, in such a case the public authority is not even under a duty to confirm or deny whether it holds such information.[266]

10.103 Section 40(2) to (4) contains the exemptions relating to personal data on another living individual. Frankly, mud is as a mountain spring compared with these provisions. In order to be exempted from the Act the personal data must satisfy one of two conditions.[267] In fact the sub-sections are easier to understand if they are treated as creating three conditions (splitting the first condition) as follows:

Condition 1A:[268]   The data fall within section 1(1)(a) to (d) of the 1998 Act, *and* disclosure would contravene any of the data protection principles or section 10[269] of the 1998 Act.

Condition 1B:[270]   The data fall within section 1(1)(e)[271] of the 1998 Act and disclosure would contravene any of the data protection principles. For these purposes one assumes that all the data protection principles apply as the section directs us to disregard the exemptions applicable to such data under section 33A of the 1998 Act.

Condition 2:[272]   The data subject would himself not be entitled to have access to the data under section 7(1)(c) of the 1998 Act.

10.104 Conditions 1A and 1B have the effect of imposing the same restrictions on access to all types of personal data, as defined in section 1(1) of the 1998 Act, despite the fact that data falling within section 1(1)(a) to (d) are treated differently under the 1998 Act from data falling within section 1(1)(e) (being largely exempted from its provisions).[273] The combined effect of Conditions 1 and 2 means that under the Act personal data about third parties may be obtained by members of the public from public authorities provided that the public authority would be permitted under the 1998 Act to disclose such data to both the data subject himself and to the third party. To determine whether or not it may disclose personal data under the Act a public authority must look to the non-disclosure provisions of the 1998 Act,[274] which are, for these purposes, the first to fifth data protection principles

---

[266] 1998 Act, s 40(5)(a).
[267] ibid, s 40(2)(b).
[268] ibid, s 40(3)(a).
[269] The right to prevent processing likely to cause damage or distress.
[270] ibid, s 40(3)(b).
[271] Inserted by ibid, s 68, ie unstructured manual data held by a public authority that is not an accessible record within the meaning of s 68.
[272] ibid, s 40(4).
[273] See paras 10.12 and 10.77 above re the combined effect of s 1(1)(e) and s 33A.
[274] As defined by the 1998 Act, s 27(3)(4).

and section 10, and to the exemptions from section 7,[275] namely, data processed for the purposes of national security, the prevention and detection of crime or the assessing or collecting of tax or duty etc, mental or physical health and/or social work, financial regulation or that of other professions, special purposes, research. Other exemptions appear in section 37 and Schedule 7 and the Secretary of State may make further exemptions by order under section 38(1). The transitional exemptions from the provisions of the 1998 Act contained in Part III of Schedule 8 to that Act are to be disregarded for these purposes.

Further, the duty to confirm or deny whether third party personal data are held **10.105** does not arise if the giving of the confirmation or denial would itself amount to a breach of the data protection principles or section 10 of the 1998 Act, or would constitute information which is exempt from the data subject's right to be informed under section 7(1)(a).

In conclusion, there is no tension between these two Acts: the 2000 Act does **10.106** not undermine the protection provided by the 1998 Act. Information which is protected by the 1998 Act may not be obtained under the 2000 Act. The fact that the Commissioner is responsible for enforcement of both Acts should ensure a coherent and integrated approach to the protection and disclosure of personal data.

---

[275] Which is defined in ibid, s 27(2)(b) as a subject information provision.

11

MEDICAL RECORDS

A. Introduction

Since the Data Protection Act of 1984 individuals have been entitled to have **11.01** access to certain computerized or automated records including records relating to their health. In 1988 the Access to Medical Reports Act gave individuals the right to see, and if they thought fit veto, reports sought by employers or insurers from their doctors. Two years later the Access to Health Records Act of 1990 provided a right of access to health records produced manually, though it did not have retrospective effect and applied only to records made after 1 November 1991.[1]

In 1992, in line with the then government's aim of introducing a more con- **11.02** sumerist ethos into public services, the Department of Health produced a document entitled *The Patients' Charter and You: A Charter for England.* This document, revised in 1995, set out the rights of those receiving or entitled to receive treatment within the NHS. Included in the rights identified in *The Patients' Charter* was a reference to the right of access to health records. In that regard the Charter provided as follows:

> You have the **right** to . . . have access to your health records and to know that everyone working for the NHS is under a legal duty to keep your records confidential.

---

[1] Save to the limited extent that records produced before the implementation date should be made available in order to render intelligible records made after 1 November 1991.

Though the Charter referred in bold type to a *right* of subject access to health records without any limit of time as to when they were created, in 1992 when the Charter was produced there was no legally enforceable right to see health records produced manually before November 1991. The Charter has been superseded by a document entitled *Your Guide to the NHS*[2] which sets out what are referred to as 'core principles', one of which is that:

> The NHS will respect the confidentiality of individual patients and provide open access to information about services, treatment and performance.

11.03 In 1995 the NHS Executive produced a *Code of Practice on Openness in the NHS*. In common with the *Code of Practice on Access to Government Information* introduced in 1994 (and which the NHS Code complements), the *Code of Practice on Openness in the NHS* ('the Code') is non-statutory. Its stated basic principle is to encourage the practice of responding positively to requests for information except in circumstances identified in the Code, and this has been taken to extend the right of patients to see manual records created prior to November 1991 subject to the exceptions and exemptions set out in the Code. Though the Code, like the Charter and its successor, has no statutory effect, it does provide for complaint to be made, ultimately, to the Health Service Ombudsman.

11.04 The Data Protection Act of 1998 marked a considerable advance in the statutory right of individuals to see their health records. Subject to specified exceptions individuals acquired the right to see their health records whether manual or automated and whenever created. The Data Protection Act 1998 was passed to implement Council Directive (EC) 95/46. It received Royal Assent on 16 July 1998 and its provisions came into force on 1 March 2000.

11.05 The Data Protection Act 1998 repealed the Access to Health Records Act 1990 save to the extent that that Act concerns applications by personal representatives or others who may have a claim as a result of a patient's death for access to the records of the deceased patient.

11.06 Whilst this chapter deals primarily with an individual's right to see his or her own medical records, the consideration of medical records in the context of freedom of information would be incomplete without reference to the rights of third parties to access such records. In part F below consideration is given to the protection afforded to medical records by the obligation of confidence arising from the doctor-patient relationship and the right to respect for privacy guaranteed in Article 8 of the Convention for the Protection of Human Rights and Fundamental Freedoms.[3]

---

[2] http://www.nhs.uk/nhsguide (29 August 2002).
[3] Human Rights Act 1998, Sch 1.

B. Code of Practice on Openness in the NHS

Scope of the Code

In a written answer in May 1994 the Health Secretary, Dr Brian Mawhinney,[4] **11.07** advised the House of Commons that the remit of the task force established to consider the question of open government in the NHS was to 'establish a fair balance between effective management of health service business on the one hand and access for the public to information and involvement in decision-taking on the other, to provide a Code of Practice on Openness in the NHS.' The Code applies to Regional Health Authorities, Family Health Service Authorities, District Health Authorities, Special Health Authorities, NHS Trusts, the Mental Health Act Commission and Community Health Councils. It also covers family doctors, dentists, optometrists and community pharmacists.

Much of the information to be made available under the Code is general informa- **11.08** tion about NHS services, performance and policies, but the Code also sets out the need for those subject to it to provide information as to how people can have access to their own personal health records. Paragraph 5 of the Code, headed 'Information which must be provided', requires the relevant health authorities to provide information 'about how people can have access to their own personal health records'. On its own this would do no more than require health authorities to advise patients of their right to information under the relevant statutory provisions. Indeed, paragraph 8 of the Code, which deals specifically with personal health records, merely observes that 'people normally have a right to see their own records' and continues:

> Depending on who made the records, patients can obtain access through the relevant Trust, Health Authority, family doctor or dentist. Access must be given within the timetable in the Access to Health Records Act 1990 (or, for records held on computer), the Data Protection Act 1984. Under these Acts, patients may be charged for access to their records.

This suggests that where access to personal health records is concerned the Code **11.09** sets out only to ensure that patients are aware of their statutory rights to information: paragraph 5 refers only to the need to inform people as to *how* they can have access to their own health records and paragraph 8 to the fact that people *normally* have a right to see their own health records. Further, the timetable for providing information and the charges for information are stated to be as provided under the relevant statutes and not under the Code. In the case of manual records created before November 1991 there is no timetable for charging or providing information outside the Code. Despite this, it appears that the Code has enjoyed a broad

---

[4] *Hansard*, HC (series 5), vol 244, col 209 (25 May 1994).

interpretation when it comes to accessing personal health records. In giving evidence to the Parliamentary Select Committee on Public Administration[5] Maurice Frankel, director of the Campaign for Freedom of Information, was asked whether the freedom of information legislation would enable patients to get hold of their own health records. In answer Mr Frankel pointed out that patients already had access to manual records made after 1 November 1991 and to computerized records whenever made. He went on:

> The gap in relation to medical records is to the pre November 1991 material, some of which is already accessible, although nobody knows about this, under the Code of Practice on Openness in the NHS. The Health Service Ombudsman has made clear that he accepts requests for information from pre 1991 health records can be dealt with under the Code of Practice.

The basic principle of the Code, namely that the NHS should respond positively to requests for information except in certain circumstances *identified in the Code*,[6] suggests that there are grounds for regarding the Code as extending a patient's right of access to his medical records and extending the right of access to pre-November 1991 manual health records.

Procedure for requests

11.10   Requests for information under the Code may be made in writing or in person. The Code requires a prompt response to a request: it should be acknowledged within four working days and where possible, the information should be provided within 20 days. It is *information* which has to be supplied, not copies of documents themselves, though the Code points out that in some cases it may be simpler to provide a copy where documents contain nothing but the information requested. If information is not to be provided under the Code, the Code requires an explanation to be given within 20 days of the receipt of the request. In addition, it is one of the general principles of the Code that where it is not possible to provide information reasons should be given for not providing the information.

Exemptions

11.11   Information need not be provided if it falls within one of the nine exemptions set out in paragraph 9 of the Code. These are as follows:

(1) Personal information. People have a right of access to their own health records but not normally to information about other people.
(2) Requests for information which are manifestly unreasonable, or far too general, or would require unreasonable resources to answer.

---

[5] Minutes of Evidence, Tuesday 20 January 1998; answer to question 1.
[6] *Code of Practice on Openness in the NHS*, para 1.

(3) Information about internal discussion and advice, where disclosure would harm frank internal debate, except where this would be outweighed by the public interest.

(4) Management information, where disclosure would harm the proper and effective operation of the NHS organization.

(5) Information about legal matters and proceedings, where disclosure would prejudice the administration of justice and the law.

(6) Information which could prejudice negotiations or the effective conduct of personnel management or commercial or contractual activities. This does not cover information about internal NHS contracts.

(7) Information given in confidence. The NHS has a common law duty to respect confidences except when it is clearly outweighed by the public interest.

(8) Information which will soon be published or where disclosure would be premature in relation to a planned announcement or publication.

(9) Information relating to incomplete analysis, research or statistics where disclosure could be misleading or prevent the holder from publishing it first.

Complaints procedure

The Code provides that in the first instance complaints about the provision of **11.12** information should be made to the local individual responsible for the operation of the Code.[7] That individual should be a senior officer directly accountable to the Chief Executive of the organization, and each NHS organization must publish the name of the individual who has responsibility for the operation of the Code.[8] If the complainant remains dissatisfied he may complain to the Chief Executive of the organization or the Chief Executive of the Family Health Services Authority in the cases of family doctors, dentists, pharmacists and optometrists. Complaints must be acknowledged within four working days and replied to within 20 working days.

Where a complainant remains dissatisfied after complaining to the relevant Chief **11.13** Executive, he may appeal to the Health Service Ombudsman. This is the final level of appeal under the Code. There is no charge to lodge a complaint with the Ombudsman but there is also no obligation on the Ombudsman to investigate the complaint. The Ombudsman cannot award damages but he can cause a decision to be changed. There appear to be relatively few complaints taken to the Ombudsman under the *Code of Practice on Openness in the NHS*. For example, in the year 1999 to 2000 of the 262 grievances taken to the Ombudsman just seven concerned alleged breach of the Code.[9]

---

[7] ibid, para 10.
[8] ibid, para 6.
[9] Health Service Commissioner Annual Report 1999–2000 http://www.ombudsman.org.uk/hsc/document/hc542.htm (24 August 2002).

C. Access to Health Records and the Data Protection Act 1998

Health records to which the Data Protection Act 1998 applies

Computerized records

11.14 The Data Protection Act 1998 applies to information which is processed automatically or recorded to be so processed. 'Processing' is widely defined and includes merely holding the information.[10]

Manual records

11.15 The significant difference between the Data Protection Act 1998 and its 1984 predecessor is its application to manual records. Manual health records will be within the Data Protection Act 1998 where:

- the information forms part of an 'accessible record' as defined by section 68 of that Act;[11] or
- the information is recorded as part of a 'relevant filing system' or with the intention that it should form part of a relevant filing system;[12] or
- (with effect from 30 November 2005)[13] the information is recorded information held by a public authority and does not fall within any of paragraphs (a) to (d) of section 1(1) of the Data Protection Act 1998.[14]

Manual record—accessible record

11.16 Most health records will fall within the Data Protection Act 1998 as a result of the definition of 'accessible record' in section 68; this provides that 'accessible record' includes 'health record', and 'health record' is a record which:

(a) consists of information relating to the physical or mental health or condition of an individual, and

(b) has been made by or on behalf of a health professional in connection with the care of that individual.[15]

11.17 Most professionals concerned with mental or physical health care fall within the definition of 'health professional' which appears at section 69 of the Data Protection Act 1998, namely:

---

[10] Data Protection Act 1998, s 1(1).
[11] ibid, s 1(1)(d).
[12] ibid, s 1(1)(c).
[13] Unless an earlier enabling order is made; Freedom of Information Act 2000, s 87(3).
[14] Freedom of Information Act 2000, s 68(2).
[15] Data Protection Act 1998, s 68(2).

(a) a registered medical practitioner (and this includes any person who is provisionally registered under section 15 or 21 of the Medical Act 1983 and is engaged in such employment as is mentioned in sub-section (3) of that section);

(b) a registered dentist as defined by section 53(1) of the Dentists Act 1984;

(c) a registered optician as defined by section 36(1) of the Opticians Act 1989;

(d) a registered pharmaceutical chemist as defined by section 24(1) of the Pharmacy Act 1954 or a registered person as defined by Article 2(2) of the Pharmacy (Northern Ireland) Order 1976;

(e) a registered nurse, midwife or health visitor;

(f) a registered osteopath as defined by section 41 of the Osteopaths Act 1993;

(g) a registered chiropractor as defined by section 43 of the Chiropractors Act 1994;

(h) any person who is registered as a member of a profession to which the Professions Supplementary to Medicine Act 1960 for the time being extends;

(i) a clinical psychologist, child psychotherapist or speech therapist;

(j) a music therapist employed by a health service body;

(k) a scientist employed by such a body as head of a department.

The above list does not include psychotherapists dealing with adults or certain classes of alternative health practitioner. The records of such practitioners would fall within the Data Protection Act 1998, however, if they were made on behalf of one of the other professionals identified above.

The record must have been made '*in connection with*' care, not 'for the purpose' of care, which might have invited a narrow interpretation. This suggests that almost every record made by a relevant health professional will fall within the ambit of the access provisions of the Data Protection Act 1998. **11.18**

Since X-ray or MRI images contain information relating to the physical or mental condition of the individual, these too will fall within the access provisions of the Data Protection Act 1998. The Act does not appear to allow charges to be made for photocopies in addition to the standard access fee[16] and in view of the fee limits discussed below,[17] the cost of meeting requests for copies of x-rays and MRI scans may be considerable. In *Hubble v Peterborough Hospital NHS Trust*[18] it was argued for the Trust, without success, that an x-ray was not a health record within section 68(2) of the Act or data within section 1. It seems to have been argued that disclosure of copy x-rays would not be communication of information 'in an intelligible form'[19] because expert help would be required to interpret them. It was **11.19**

---

[16] cf the Access to Health Records Act 1990, under which the cost of copying could be recovered from the applicant.

[17] See paras 11.36–11.39 below.

[18] Leicester County Court, 21 March 2001, Mr Recorder Butler.

[19] Data Protection Act 1998, s 8(2)(a) requires an explanation to be provided where information would not be intelligible without one.

accepted that expert help was required to interpret x-rays but the suggestion that this put the record outside the Act was rejected; the requirement that explanation be given where information would otherwise be unintelligible was intended to enhance the right to disclosure and not limit it.

11.20 Accessible health records have been accessible under the Data Protection Act 1998 since its implementation on 1 March 2000. The transitional provisions do not apply to health records which are 'accessible records' within the meaning of the Act.[20]

Manual record—relevant filing system

11.21 There will be few health records which do not fall within the Data Protection Act 1998 as a result of the definition of 'accessible record' discussed above.[21] However, for those records which do not fall into this category the manual record may form part of a 'relevant filing system' and fall within the Act's ambit for that reason.

11.22 Data will fall within the 'relevant filing system' definition if the set of information is *structured* either by reference to individuals or by reference to criteria relating to individuals in such a way that specific information relating to a particular individual is readily accessible. Thus information which is recorded only chronologically and not readily accessible by reference to name or other criteria which would identify the sender or recipient would not be 'structured'.

11.23 Guidance from the Information Commissioner recognizes that it is not wholly clear how this definition translates in practical terms to all conceivable situations.[22] The fact that there must be a set of information suggests a grouping together of things by reference to a distinct identifier, that is a common theme or element. It is not necessary for the information to be filed to be part of a set. The information must be specific information about an individual and it must be readily accessible. The government's view of what records were intended to be covered by this provision was made clear by Lord Williams of Mostyn[23] on 16 March 1998:[24]

> We do not wish the definition to apply to miscellaneous collections of paper about individuals, even if the collections are assembled in a file with the individual's name or other unique identifier on the front, if specific data about the individual cannot be readily extracted from that collection. . .we want to catch only those records from which specific information about individuals can be readily extracted.

---

[20] Data Protection Act 1998, Sch 8, Part II, para 3(2) and 3(1)(a).
[21] Starting at para 11.16.
[22] Data Protection Act 1998 Legal Guidance—Information Commissioner http://www.dataprotection.gov.uk para 2.1.2 (24 August 2002).
[23] Under-Secretary of State, Home Office.
[24] *Hansard*, HL (series 5) vol 587, cols 467–468 (16 March 1998).

The Information Commissioner suggests that in deciding whether or not **11.24** information is readily accessible, a data controller should assume that a set of manual information referenced to individuals or criteria relating to individuals and which is specific to an individual is caught by the Data Protection Act 1998 if it is, as a matter of fact, generally accessible at any time to one or more people within the data controller's organization in connection with the day-to-day operation of that organization.

Where manual health records are accessible only on the ground that they are held **11.25** in a 'relevant filing system,' the transitional provisions of the Data Protection Act 1998 are relevant.

Unstructured files—the Freedom of Information Act

Where a *structured* manual record is made by a health professional who does not **11.26** fall within the section 69 definition[25] it will be caught by section 1(1)(c) of the Data Protection Act 1998. Where the record is *unstructured,* the extension of section 1 of the Act by the Freedom of Information Act section 68(2) may be relevant. Section 68(2) adds to the categories of data falling within the Data Protection Act 1998:

> recorded information held by a public authority.

The definition of public authority appears at section 3 of the Freedom of Information Act.[26]

Applications for access under the Data Protection Act 1998

The main section dealing with subject access is section 7, which provides as fol- **11.27** lows:

> (1) Subject to the following provisions of this section and to sections 8 and 9, an individual is entitled—
>> (a) to be informed by any data controller whether personal data of which that individual is the data subject are being processed by or on behalf of that data controller;
>> (b) if that is the case, to be given by the data controller a description of—
>>> (i) the personal data of which that individual is the data subject,
>>> (ii) the purposes for which they are being or are to be processed, and
>>> (iii) the recipients or classes of recipients to whom they are or may be disclosed;
>> (c) to have communicated to him in an intelligible form—
>>> (i) the information constituting any personal data of which that individual is the data subject, and
>>> (ii) any information available to the data controller as to the source of those data.

---

[25] See para 11.17 above.
[26] See ch 5 above.

Who may apply?

11.28   It seems clear from section 7(1) that an individual is entitled to information concerning the data of which *that individual* is the data subject. There appears to be no entitlement to information concerning the data relating to any other data subject.

Children, parents and incompetent adults

11.29   The position of those with parental responsibility or who care for incompetent adults with regard to access to the records of those in their care is unclear under the Data Protection Act 1998. Children can apply to see their own records provided they have the capacity to make the application, namely 'sufficient understanding and intelligence to understand fully what is proposed'.[27] There seems to be no reason why they should not also consent to their records being made available to their parents. Uncertainty arises, however, when the patient lacks the legal capacity to give such consent.

11.30   Department of Health guidance[28] advises that as a general rule a person with parental responsibility will have the right to apply for access to a child's health record, but where a child is capable of making decisions about his medical treatment the consent of the child must be sought before a person with parental responsibility can be given access. Where, in the view of the appropriate health professional, the child patient is not capable of understanding the nature of the application, the holder of the record is entitled to deny access if it is not felt to be in the patient's best interests. The source of the right of a parent to access a young child's records is not specified. It does not appear to be a right conferred by the Data Protection Act 1998.

11.31   Subject to certain safeguards one can well see that it is desirable for those who are likely to be consulted about medical treatment for others to have the same access to relevant health records as would a legally competent patient in respect of his own records. It appears that one must look beyond the Data Protection Act 1998 in considering whether those with parental responsibility or carers of others incapable of making their own applications for access under the Act are entitled to access to the medical records of those in their care. Whether there is a common law right of access to health records, and if so the extent of such right, has yet to be fully explored. The Court of Appeal in *R v Mid Glamorgan Family Health Services Authority, ex p Martin,*[29] did not (like Popplewell J at first instance) reject the possibility that a patient might have a common law right of access to medical records,

---

[27]   *Gillick v West Norfolk and Wisbech AHA* [1985] 3 All ER 402, 437.
[28]   *Patient Confidentiality and Caldicott Guardians. Frequently Asked Questions:* see http://www.doh.gov.uk/ipu/confiden/faq.htm
[29]   [1995] 1 WLR 110.

but had no need to reach a firm view. Mr Martin was challenging the decision of two authorities to grant access only to a medical adviser who was to decide whether providing access to the records was in Mr Martin's 'best interests'. This was sufficient, said the Court of Appeal. The European Commission declared Mr Martin's application manifestly ill-founded.[30]

Prior to the repeal of the relevant sections by the Data Protection Act 1998, the   **11.32** Access to Health Records Act 1990 provided that a person having parental responsibility for a child (England and Wales) or pupil (Scotland) could apply for access to the child or pupil's health records. The Data Protection Act 1984 gave the Secretary of State power to make regulations in this regard: he did not do so.[31] There appears to be no provision for parental or carer subject access in the Data Protection Act 1998. It is curious, then, that the Data Protection (Subject Access Modification) (Health) Order 2000 refers to a person with parental responsibility or appointed by the court to manage the affairs of a data subject incapable of managing his own affairs enabled 'by any enactment or rule of law to make a request on behalf of a data subject'.[32] To what this refers is far from clear.

Information to be provided

Under section 7 of the Data Protection Act 1998, subject to the data controller   **11.33** being satisfied as to the applicant's identity and receiving the appropriate fee[33] and, of course, the exemptions which are discussed below, the applicant is entitled:

- to be informed whether personal data of which he is the subject are being processed (which includes being held or stored);[34]
- to a description of the data held, the purposes for which they are processed and to whom the data may be disclosed;[35]
- to a copy of the information constituting the data in intelligible form, if this is possible without disproportionate effort;[36]
- to information as to the source of the data.[37]

Access is to be granted to all records irrespective of when they were created. The Data Protection Act 1998 does not grant a right to inspect the records themselves though it is the policy of the Department of Health to permit access to the records.

---

[30] *Trevor H Martin v United Kingdom* (Appn no 27433/95) [1996] EHRLR 442 and see the discussion of the CA decision by Dermot Feenan (1996) MLR 101.
[31] Data Protection Act 1984, s 21(9).
[32] SI 2000/413, article 5(3), (4).
[33] See paras 11.36–11.39 below.
[34] Data Protection Act 1998, s 7(1)(a).
[35] ibid, s 7(1)(b).
[36] ibid, s 7(1)(c)(i), s 8(2).
[37] ibid, s 7(1)(c)(ii).

How to apply

11.34 The request for access must be made in writing, which includes transmission by electronic means: an e-mailed request is acceptable.[38] Application is made to the data controller, the person holding the information. The application should provide the data controller with such information as he may reasonably require to satisfy himself as to the identity of the person making the request and to locate the information sought.[39] There is no need for the applicant to state why the information is sought.

Time limit for response

11.35 Access requests must be dealt with promptly and in any event before the end of 40 days;[40] an alternative access period may be introduced by statutory instrument, but to date none such has been made. The Campaign for Freedom of Information considers this period too long, pointing out[41] that it compares unfavourably to response times under comparable provisions. Health service providers have complained that the period is too short, particularly when the need for data controllers to consult health professionals before granting access is taken into account.

Fees

11.36 Data controllers are not obliged to charge for providing access to data, but may do so subject to prescribed limits.

11.37 Where a permanent copy of information stored in computerized form[42] is sought, the maximum fee which may be levied is £10.[43]

11.38 In the case of access to health records which are not held on computer, the subject access fee for a copy of information in permanent form is £50.[44] This fee was due to fall to £10 from 24 October 2001 with the result that there would be no difference between the subject access fee in the cases of computerized and other health records. Compliance advice from the Office of the Information Commissioner in March 2001 noted that concern had been expressed to the Information Commissioner as to the cost to NHS bodies of responding to requests for

---

[38] ibid, s 7(2)(a) and s 64(2).

[39] ibid, s 7(3).

[40] ibid, s 7(8) and (10).

[41] Campaign for Freedom of Information Response to Home Office Consultation on Council Directive (EC) 95/46 on data protection.

[42] ie where information is 'being processed by means of equipment operating automatically in response to instructions given for that purpose [or] is recorded with the intention that it should be processed by means of such equipment'; Data Protection Act 1998, s 1(1)(a) and (b).

[43] The Data Protection (Subject Access) (Fees and Miscellaneous Provisions) Regulations 2000, SI 2000/191, as amended by the Data Protection (Subject Access) (Fees and Miscellaneous Provisions) (Amendment) Regulations 2001, SI 2001/3223.

[44] ibid.

information under section 7 of the Data Protection Act 1998. The Information Commissioner's view was that the subject access fee should be set no higher than that necessary to deter vexatious requests and that a fee of up to £10 satisfied the requirement of the Council Directive upon which the Data Protection Act 1998 was based that access should be available to subjects 'without excessive expense'.[45] However, on 27 September 2001 the Lord Chancellor's Department announced the government's decision that the charges levied by the NHS for providing individuals with access to their health records would continue 'at current levels for the time being', with the result that the maximum fee remains £10 for records held on computer and £50 for paper records and other media.[46] The press release refers to the need to strike a balance between ensuring that cost is not a barrier to access to health records and allowing the NHS to recoup costs 'so that essential resources are not diverted from providing direct patient care'. Though the press release refers to charges 'by the NHS' the fee regulations make no distinction between the NHS and other bodies or persons holding health records.

Where a request for subject access is restricted to data which form part of a health **11.39** record and that record was at least partially created within the 40 days preceding the request, and no permanent copy of the information is to be provided, no fee for subject access may be charged. There is no express provision for any fee to be charged for copying or despatching copies of records.[47]

Exemptions and partial exemptions

Access likely to cause serious harm to the data subject or any other person

Where a data subject seeks access to personal data consisting of information as to **11.40** his physical or mental health, the Data Protection (Subject Access Modification) (Health) Order 2000[48] provides partial exemption from the right of subject access to the extent that the same would be likely to cause serious harm to his or any other person's physical or mental health or condition.[49] Only the harmful data can be withheld, not the whole record.

In deciding whether serious harm might be caused to the data subject or any other **11.41** person, data controllers who are not health professionals must first consult the person who appears to be the appropriate health professional on the question of whether or not the exemption applies.[50] The appropriate health professional is the person who is currently or was most recently responsible for the clinical care of the data subject in connection with the matters to which the information the subject

---

[45] Council Directive (EC) 95/46.
[46] Press Release 331/01.
[47] cf Access to Health Records Act 1990.
[48] SI 2000/413.
[49] ibid, art 5(1).
[50] ibid, art 5(2).

of the request relates; where there is more than one, the most suitable should be consulted. Where the data controller has a recent written opinion from the appropriate health professional in connection with the relevant subject access it may not be necessary for the data controller to consult further on the access request being received.[51]

Information identifying or relating to a third party

11.42   Information in response to a subject access request may include information relating to or identifying a third party. Clearly a balance has to be struck between the rights of the third party and the rights of the applicant. The Data Protection Act 1998 allows the data controller to withhold the information which would make identification of a third party possible.[52] Although section 7(4) alone suggests that there is no obligation to comply with a request where third party information would be disclosed, section 7(5) makes it plain that section 7(4) is not to be construed as excusing a data controller from communicating so much of the information sought as can be communicated without disclosing the identity of the third party, whether by the omission of names, identifying particulars or otherwise. This is, then, only a partial exemption from the disclosure obligations.

11.43   If the third party has consented to the disclosure of the information to the person making the request, *or* it is reasonable in all the circumstances to comply with the request without the consent of the other individual, there is not even a partial exemption from the disclosure obligations.[53] In deciding whether it is reasonable to comply with the request in the absence of consent, regard is to be had to any duty of confidentiality owed to the third party, any steps taken by the data controller to obtain the third party's consent, whether the third party is capable of giving consent, and any express refusal of consent.[54]

11.44   Compliance advice from the Office of the Information Commissioner[55] advises that the data controller may at the very least need to take steps to seek consent to demonstrate that it was reasonable to make disclosure without consent. This may not always be appropriate, for example where the seeking of such consent would involve a disclosure of personal data about the applicant to the third party. The guidance recommends that the following questions be asked by data controllers when dealing with subject access requests:

- Does the information being accessed contain information about a third party?
- If so, would its disclosure reveal the identity of the third party?

---

[51] SI 2000/413, (n 48 above) art 7.
[52] Data Protection Act 1998, s 7(4)–(6).
[53] ibid, s 7(4).
[54] ibid, s 7(6).
[55] *Data Protection Act 1998: Subject Access Rights and Third Party Information*: see http://www.dataprotection.gov.uk/dpr/dpdoc.nsf (1 December 2002).

- In deciding this has other information which the data subject has/may get been taken into account?
- To what extent can the information be edited so it can be given promptly without revealing the third party's identity?[56]
- Has the third party previously given the information to the person making the request?
- If, or to the extent that, the information will identify the third party, has the third party consented to the disclosure?
- If not, should consent be sought?
- Is it reasonable to disclose the third party information without consent?
- Is the third party information confidential or sensitive or harmful?
- Is the third party information of particular importance to the data subject?

In deciding whether a third party can be identified from the information being disclosed the data controller is to have regard to any other information which the applicant has or is likely to acquire.[57]

The partial exemption does not apply where the third party is a health professional **11.45** who has been involved in the data subject's care.[58]

Information in certain court reports

There is a total exemption from section 7 of the Data Protection Act 1998 in the **11.46** case of personal data processed by a court and consisting of information supplied in a report or other evidence given to the court by a local authority, Health and Social Services Trust, probation officer or other person in the course of any proceedings to which the Family Proceedings Courts (Children Act 1989) Rules 1991, the Magistrates' Courts (Children and Young Persons) Rules 1992, the Magistrates' Courts (Criminal Justice (Children)) Rules (Northern Ireland) 1999, the Act of Sederunt (Child Care and Maintenance Rules) 1997, or the Children's Hearings (Scotland) Rules 1996 apply where, in accordance with a provision of any of those Rules, the information may be withheld by the court in whole or in part from the data subject.[59]

Research

Where information is being processed for research, historical or statistical pur- **11.47** poses it need not be disclosed under the Data Protection Act 1998 subject access provisions provided certain conditions are met, namely:

---

[56] Though the 1998 Act requires the third party to be identified where the third party consents or where it would be reasonable to do so without consent: s 7(4).
[57] Data Protection Act 1998, s 8(7).
[58] The Data Protection (Subject Access Modification) (Health) Order 2000, SI 2000/413.
[59] ibid, art 4.

- that the results of the research do not identify any data subject;[60]
- that the processing is not done in a way which would be likely to cause substantial damage or distress to any data subject;[61]
- that the processing is not taking place to support measures or decisions with respect to particular individuals.[62]

Infertility treatment

11.48 Information falling within sections 31 and 33 of the Human Fertilization and Embryology Act 1990 (information about the provision of treatment services, the keeping or use of gametes or embryos and whether identifiable individuals were born in consequence of treatment services) is exempt.[63]

Regulatory bodies

11.49 Personal data processed for the purposes of discharging certain regulatory functions are also exempted from the subject access provisions in any case to the extent to which the application of those provisions to the data would be likely to prejudice the proper discharge of those functions.[64] One of the regulatory functions included in the Data Protection Act 1998, section 31 is any relevant function designed to protect members of the public against malpractice or other seriously improper conduct by, or the unfitness or incompetence of, persons authorized to carry on any profession or other activity.[65] This would include, for example, the disciplinary activities of the General Medical Council. Personal data processed for the purpose of the discharge of any function conferred on the Health Service Commissioner for England, Wales or Scotland is also exempt.

Multiple requests

11.50 If a data controller has previously complied with a section 7 subject access request by an individual, the data controller is not obliged to comply with a subsequent identical or similar request under that section by that individual unless a reasonable interval has elapsed between compliance with the previous request and the making of the current request. In determining whether requests are made at reasonable intervals regard shall be had to the nature of the data, the purpose for which the data are processed, and the frequency with which the data are altered.[66]

---

[60] Data Protection Act 1998, s 33(4).

[61] ibid, s 33(1)(b).

[62] ibid, s 33(1)(a).

[63] ibid, s 38(1) and the Data Protection (Miscellaneous Subject Access Exemptions) Order 2000, SI 2000/419.

[64] Data Protection Act 1998, s 31(1).

[65] ibid, s 31(2)(a)(iii).

[66] ibid, s 8(3) and 8(4).

No notification required where information withheld

There is no requirement for an applicant to be told that information has been **11.51**
withheld under any of the subject access exemptions in the Data Protection Act
1998. Where information is given there is no need to tell the applicant that it is incomplete. Where information is withheld altogether it is sufficient for the data
controller to give an ambiguous reply along the lines of 'We hold no information
which we are required to disclose'. This is also the position under the Access to
Health Records Act 1990. The Access to Medical Reports Act 1988[67] requires an
individual to be told when information is being withheld, as does the *Code of
Practice on Openness in the NHS.*

There can be little doubt that the absence of a requirement to notify an applicant **11.52**
that information has been withheld will limit the opportunities to challenge decisions by data controllers to withhold information. Where information might be
sought in the alternative under the *Code of Practice on Openness in the NHS*[68] this
might be mentioned in the request for access with a view to ensuring that reasons
and an explanation are given where information is not provided.

Non-compliance—remedies

In the event of non-compliance the applicant may ask the Information **11.53**
Commissioner to conduct an assessment of the relevant decision under section
42(2) of the Data Protection Act 1998. The Commissioner can issue enforcement
notices requiring access to be provided.

Dissatisfied applicants are also entitled to apply to the court. Application is made **11.54**
under section 7(9) of the Data Protection Act 1998 and the court can order the
data controller to comply with the request.

An individual who suffers damage by reason of any contravention of the Data **11.55**
Protection Act 1998 by a data controller is entitled to compensation for that damage. Compensation for distress is only available where damage has also been
caused. Compensation for distress alone is not available.[69] The data controller will
have a defence if he can prove that he took such care as in all the circumstances was
reasonably required to comply with the relevant requirement.[70]

The court has power to order a data controller to rectify, block, erase or destroy **11.56**
data which are inaccurate.[71]

---

[67] Section 7(3)(a) and (4)(a).
[68] See paras 11.07–11.11 above.
[69] Data Protection Act 1998, s 13.
[70] ibid, s 13(3).
[71] ibid, s 14.

D. Access to Medical Reports Act 1988

11.57 The Access to Medical Reports Act 1988 gives an individual certain rights in respect of medical reports sought by employers or insurance companies. Where such a report is sought from or prepared by a medical practitioner who is or has been responsible for the clinical care of that individual it is covered by the Act. 'Care' includes examination, investigation or diagnosis for the purposes of, or in connection with, any form of medical treatment.

11.58 The long title of the statute provides that it is 'An Act to establish a right of access by individuals to reports relating to themselves provided by medical practitioners for employment or insurance purposes,' but it should be noted that the Act does *not* apply to reports by independent doctors who have not previously cared for or treated the individual concerned. Thus a report by an independent doctor acting on behalf of the employer or insurance company does not fall within the Access to Medical Reports Act unless that doctor had previously had a doctor-patient relationship with the individual concerned. This is a significant limitation on the scope of the Act.

11.59 The Access to Medical Reports Act prevents employers or insurers contacting an individual's doctor for a report without the written consent of the individual.[72] The individual must also be told of his rights under the Act. One of those rights is the right to be shown the report before it is sent. There is no charge for access to the report but a 'reasonable fee' may be charged if the individual seeks a copy.[73]

11.60 Where an individual has elected to see a report before it is supplied to the employer or insurance company, the medical practitioner may not supply it unless the individual has advised the practitioner that he consents.[74] The individual may ask for amendments to be made. If the practitioner is not prepared to make the amendments the individual is entitled to have his views attached to the report.[75]

11.61 If an individual has not sought access to a report before it is supplied to the employer or insurer, he may seek access to it for a period of six months from the date of supply of the report.[76]

11.62 Access to the report may be refused if, in the opinion of the practitioner, it would be likely to cause serious harm to the physical or mental health of the individual or others,[77] or where it would be likely to reveal information about a third party or

---

[72] Access to Medical Reports Act 1988, s 3.
[73] ibid, s 6(3).
[74] ibid, s 5(1).
[75] ibid, s 5(2).
[76] ibid, s 6.
[77] ibid, s 7(1).

information as to the identity of a third party who has supplied information (unless the third party has consented or is a health professional involved in the care of the individual).[78]

An individual is entitled to be told that his request for access has been denied **11.63** under one of the exemptions[79] (contrast the position under the Data Protection Act 1998 and the Access to Health Records Act 1990). Where access is denied, the individual may apply to the county court for an order that the doctor must provide him with access under the Act.[80]

E. Access to Health Records Act 1990

Most of the provisions of the Access to Health Records Act 1990 have been re- **11.64** pealed by the Data Protection Act 1998.[81] The statute now applies only to applications for access to records by the personal representatives of a patient who has died or by a person who may have a claim arising out of the patient's death.[82] Personal representatives have no right of access to medical records under the Data Protection Act 1998. The definition of 'personal data' in that Act is 'data which relate to a living individual'.

The Access to Health Records Act 1990 applies only to records created after 1 **11.65** November 1991.[83] Unlike the Data Protection Act 1998, it does not have retrospective effect. However, access may be given to earlier records where the holder of the record is of the opinion that access to the same is necessary to make intelligible any part of the record to which access is required under the Act.[84]

The application for access must be made in writing and identify the patient. Since **11.66** the application will now always be made by someone other than the patient, the application must include information sufficient to establish that he or she is entitled to make the application.[85] There is no need to state why access is sought.[86]

Where there is a right of access to a record or part of a record under the Access to **11.67** Health Records Act, the applicant is permitted to inspect the record or relevant part and if required should be supplied with a copy of the record or the relevant

---

[78] ibid, s 7(2).
[79] ibid, s 7(3).
[80] ibid, s 8.
[81] Data Protection Act 1998, Sch 16, Part 1.
[82] Access to Health Records Act 1990, s 3(1)(f).
[83] ibid, s 5(1)(b).
[84] ibid, s 5(2).
[85] ibid, s 3(6).
[86] But note that access shall not be given to any part of the record which would disclose information which is not relevant to any claim which may arise out of the patient's death: ibid, s 5(4).

part.[87] If no part of the accessible record was made more than 40 days before the application, then access must be given within 21 days. In any other case the time limit is 40 days.[88] Any information expressed in terms which are not intelligible without explanation should be explained at the time of providing access or supplying a copy.[89]

11.68 As to fees, in the case of records made in the period of 40 days immediately preceding the date of the application, there is no fee for access. In the case of records made earlier than this the fee is £10.[90] Where copies are supplied the fee should not exceed the cost of making the copy and (where applicable) the cost of posting it to the applicant. In the case of copies of x-rays or scans the fees could be substantial.[91]

11.69 There are some limitations on access under the Access to Health Records Act. Access shall not be given to any part of a health record which, in the opinion of the holder of the record, would disclose information:

(a) which is not relevant to any claim which may arise out of the patient's death;[92]

(b) likely to cause serious harm to the physical or mental health of any individual;[93]

(c) relating to or provided by an individual, other than the patient, who could be identified from that information (unless that person has consented or was a health professional concerned).

As in the case of the Data Protection Act 1998, where access is excluded under the Act all the record holder need do is inform the applicant that he does not hold any information which he is required by law to disclose.

11.70 Dissatisfied applicants are entitled to apply to the court for an order that the holder of the record comply with the Act.[94]

---

[87] Access to Health Records Act 1990, s 3(2).
[88] ibid, s 3(5).
[89] ibid, s 3(3).
[90] ibid, s 3(4)(a) and Data Protection Act 1984, s 21.
[91] But see S Burn, 'Civil Litigation: charges for records and reports' 94/15 LS Gaz (16 April 1997) 30, from which it seems that charges under the Access to Health Records Act are likely to be below the fees otherwise charged to solicitors seeking access to health records on behalf of their clients.
[92] Access to Health Records Act 1990, s 5(4).
[93] ibid, s 5(1)(a)(i).
[94] ibid, s 8.

F. Confidentiality

The principles

Medical records inevitably contain personal information which a patient would **11.71** regard as confidential. The law recognizes an important public interest in maintaining professional duties of confidence. Where, as in the doctor-patient relationship, one party gives information to another in confidence there is a common law duty not to disclose that information to a third party voluntarily without the permission of the party giving the information.[95] Where the law requires disclosure of information, for example as in the case of *Hunter v Mann* where the Road Traffic Act 1972, section 168(2) required a person to give information which might lead to the identification of a driver guilty of an offence, it was no answer to the duty to give information that the party in receipt of the same was a doctor who had received the information in confidence.

In *W v Egdell*[96] W was a detainee in a secure hospital following his conviction for **11.72** manslaughter on the grounds of diminished responsibility. Dr Egdell was the author of a medical report, prepared on the instructions of W's solicitors. Dr Egdell's report did not support W's application for conditional discharge and it drew attention to matters unfavourable to W which had not been noted in other medical reports. W's solicitors refused to send a copy of Dr Egdell's report to those responsible for W's care but withdrew the application for conditional discharge. Without the consent of W or his solicitors Dr Egdell sent a copy of the report to the hospital where W was detained urging disclosure to the Home Office. W's solicitors brought an action for injunctive relief and damages for breach of confidence. The Court of Appeal stressed that it was not the private interests of the doctor and patient which fell to be considered, but the public interests for and against disclosure. It was held that the balance lay in favour of restricted disclosure of vital information to the director of the hospital and to the Secretary of State who had the duty of safeguarding public safety.

The recognition of the right to privacy enshrined in Article 8 of the Convention **11.73** for the Protection of Human Rights and Fundamental Freedoms[97] further supports the individual's right to maintain the confidentiality of his medical records yet this too requires the court to perform a balancing act. Article 8(2) provides that:

> There shall be no interference by a public authority with the exercise of [the right to respect for private and family life . . . home and correspondence] except such as is in

---

[95] *Hunter v Mann* [1974] 1 QB 767.
[96] [1990] 1 All ER 835.
[97] Human Rights Act 1998, Sch 1.

accordance with the law and is necessary in a democratic society in the interests of national security, public safety or the economic well being of the country, for the prevention of disorder or crime, for the protection of health or morals, or for the protection of the rights and freedoms of others.

Before the balancing exercise can take place the interference with privacy must be:

• in accordance with the law. It would not be possible to pray in aid one of the interests identified in Article 8(2) unless disclosure is also in accordance with the law. Thus, if disclosure would breach the common law duty of confidence or any provision of the Data Protection Act 1998, for example, disclosure would not be permissible.
• necessary in a democratic society for one of the stated reasons. This introduces the notion of proportionality.

Some relevant case law

11.74 The European Court of Human Rights considered the question of disclosure of medical records in *Z v Finland*[98] and *MS v Sweden*.[99] In *Z v Finland* in particular the Court's approach to the balancing exercise, its analysis of both the public interest considerations and the manner in which Z's interests might be safeguarded whilst still permitting disclosure, shows how the proportionality concept works in practice. Z's medical records were seized by the police and two doctors were compelled to give evidence of Z's medical history at the trial of Z's husband. Though the proceedings were held in camera the published judgment contained Z's name and medical condition. Z claimed that each of these matters breached her rights under Article 8, together with the fact that the Court had ordered that the documents seized need remain confidential for only ten years. Z's complaints in relation to the seizure of documents and giving of evidence at trial were unsuccessful but she succeeded in connection with both the publication of her name and condition in the judgment and the time limit. The judgment emphasized the need to balance competing interests and included the following observations:[100]

> . . . the Court will take into account that the protection of personal data, not least medical data, is of fundamental importance to a person's enjoyment of his or her right to respect for private and family life as guaranteed by Article 8 of the Convention. Respecting the confidentiality of health data is a vital principle in the legal systems of all the Contracting Parties to the Convention. It is crucial not only to respect the sense of privacy of a patient but also to preserve his or her confidence in the medical profession and in the health services in general. Without such protection, those in need of medical assistance may be deterred from revealing such information of a personal and intimate nature as may be necessary in order to receive

---

[98] (1997) 25 EHRR 371.
[99] (1997) 3 BHRC 248.
[100] (1997) 25 EHRR 371 at 405.

appropriate treatment and, even, from seeking such assistance, thereby endangering their own health and, in the case of transmissible diseases, that of the community. . .

The interests in protecting the confidentiality of such information will therefore weigh heavily in the balance in determining whether the interference was proportionate to the legitimate aim pursued.

In refusing to uphold Z's complaint concerning the giving of medical evidence to the Finnish court and the seizure of medical records, the European Court of Human Rights was much influenced by the fact that the Finnish court had put safeguards in place against the abuse of the information, namely by holding the proceedings in camera and ordering in advance that the evidence be kept confidential. There was, however, no justification for publishing the applicant's name and medical condition in the judgment or for limiting the ban on disclosure of records to ten years.

In *MS v Sweden*[101] MS alleged violation of Article 8 when, in the absence of her **11.75** consent, her medical records were disclosed to the social insurance office in connection with a claim for disability pension. Acknowledging the importance of confidentiality to medical records containing personal and sensitive data the Court nevertheless was satisfied that there had been no violation of Article 8 since the information was of importance to the application of the Insurance Act under which the claim to a pension was made and the receiver of the information was under a duty to maintain confidentiality, an effective and adequate safeguard against abuse.

In *A Health Authority v X*[102] the health authority in question sought disclosure of **11.76** medical records to investigate certain serious complaints against two general practitioners. Two of the practitioners' patients refused to authorize the disclosure of their records to the health authority. The health authority applied for disclosure. Munby J was satisfied that the gravity of the matters to be investigated and the purpose for which disclosure was sought meant that there was a compelling public interest justifying disclosure but included in the order for disclosure a number of conditions intended to safeguard the confidentiality of the material in the records by limiting the use to which the records could be put save with the prior leave of the Court. The health authority objected to the conditions and appealed. The Court of Appeal had no hesitation in rejecting the appeal and upholding the conditions imposed by Munby J. The Court of Appeal emphasized that the conflict between the private/public interest in the confidentiality of medical records should be decided by a judge and not the health authority.[103]

---

[101] (1997) 3 BHRC 248.
[102] [2001] 2 FCR 634.
[103] [2002] 2 All ER 780, 788.

The Health and Social Care Act 2001

11.77 The Health and Social Care Act 2001 includes two sections (tucked away in Part 5 under 'Miscellaneous and Supplementary') of particular relevance to the confidentiality of medical records and their use within the health service. Section 60 provides that regulations may be made by the Secretary of State to make

> such provision for and in connection with requiring or regulating the processing of prescribed patient information for medical purposes as he considers necessary or expedient—
> (a) in the interests of improving patient care, or
> (b) in the public interest.

11.78 The NHS Executive Information Policy Unit has produced a document setting out background information to section 60 of the Health and Social Care Act 2001.[104] This states that there are situations where informed consent cannot be obtained for disclosure yet the public good outweighs issues of privacy. Research projects may involve tens of thousands of patients where contact requesting consent to the use of identifiable patient data would be impracticable or where excluding data where consent had been withheld would so bias the data that it would lose all value. The guidance states that the Act and regulations are intended 'largely as a transitional measure whilst consent or anonymisation procedures are developed'. Each use of the power under the Act is to be reviewed annually.[105]

11.79 The draft regulations prepared under section 60 of the Health and Social Care Act 2001[106] provoked a storm of protest. In particular, the *Independent on Sunday* ran its coverage of the proposed regulations under the headline 'Ministers to snoop on patients' private medical records'.[107] There can be no doubt that the regulations, which came into force on 1 June 2002, override the common law duty of confidentiality in certain circumstances. Regulation 4 is clear on that point:

> Anything done by a person that is necessary for the purpose of processing confidential patient information in accordance with these Regulations shall be taken to be lawfully done despite any obligation of confidence owed by that person in respect of it.

11.80 The regulations authorize the use of confidential patient information in the absence of consent in, broadly, two situations: research (regulation 2) and communicable disease and other risks to public health (regulation 3). There are important safeguards in the regulations. Processing pursuant to the section 60 regulations must be authorized by the Secretary of State and, in the case of research, also by a research ethics committee. Regulation 7 provides further safeguards: processing

---

[104] http://www.doh.gov.uk/ipu/confiden/act/s60bg.htm (28th August 2002).
[105] Health and Social Care Act 2001, s 60(4).
[106] The Health Service (Control of Patient Information) Regulations 2002, SI 2002/1438.
[107] 5th May 2002.

must be in the interest of patients or the wider public, it must be impracticable to obtain consent or to satisfy the purpose using anonymized data, any non-essential particulars identifying an individual that are not essential must be removed and access to the information by persons other than those authorized under the regulations or for any other persons must be prevented. There will be a public register identifying the activities carried out with section 60 support. Further, the only persons entitled to process confidential patient information under the regulations are health professionals or persons who in the circumstances owe a duty of confidentiality which is equivalent to that which would arise if that person were a health professional.[108] Persons in possession of confidential information as a result of the section 60 regulations are obliged to make available information on the steps taken to comply with the regulations on request by any person or body.[109] It was with some justification, then, that the Department of Health described the press coverage of the regulations as 'both ill informed and alarmist'.[110] It should be noted that neither section 60 of the Health and Social Care Act 2001 nor the regulations under it deprive patients of their rights under the Data Protection Act 1998 or, more particularly, the Human Rights Act 1998 and the protection afforded by Article 8 of the Convention for the Protection of Human Rights and Fundamental Freedoms discussed at paragraphs 11.73 to 11.76 above.

---

[108] The Health Service (Control of Patient Information) Regulations 2002, SI 2000/1438, reg 7(2).
[109] ibid, reg 7(1)(e).
[110] Department of Health Guidance Letter (May 2002) http://www.n-i.nhs.uk/dataprotect/ related articles 28 August 2002.

12

SECRECY

A. Introduction

Secrets are irresistible to governments and children. For children, much of the excitement inherent in a secret lies in telling it to other people. On the whole, persons in government, often for good reason, take a contrary view: state secrets should not, without due authority, be disseminated outside a closed circle until they have become sufficiently stale. This chapter concerns the protection of state secrets in the United Kingdom, principally under the Official Secrets Act 1989, and the relationship of that Act with the Freedom of Information Act.[1] **12.01**

In his book, *Not in the Public Interest* published in 1965, David Williams wrote that the Official Secrets Acts 1911 to 1939 'were passed ostensibly to combat espionage. They have been used to guard official information of all kinds. And so widely were they drafted that many forms of conduct are capable of being brought within their terms. The security of the State need not be in the remotest degree endangered.'[2] At the time he was writing other constitutional conventions and legal rules also **12.02**

---

[1] For wider discussions of the law relating to official secrets, see amongst others G Robertson, *Freedom, the Individual and the Law* (7th edn, 1993) ch 4; AC Bradley and KD Ewing, *Constitutional and Administrative Law* (13th edn, 2002) ch 25; P Jackson and P Leopold, *O Hood Phillips & Jackson: Constitutional and Administrative Law* (8th edn, 2001) ch 26; G Robertson and A Nicol, *Media Law* (4th edn, 2002) ch 11; D Feldman, *Civil Liberties and Human Rights in England and Wales* (2nd edn, 2002) ch 15.

[2] D Williams, *Not in the Public Interest* (London, 1965) 94.

prevented access to information held by the administration. The responsibility to answer for the activity of a department's civil servants was the Minister's under the convention of ministerial responsibility to Parliament,[3] whereby the anonymity of civil servants was preserved and direct scrutiny of their activity precluded. The inaccessibility of information in the government's possession was reinforced by Crown privilege, as the right of the Crown to withhold evidence in the public interest was then known. This doctrine, as well as being capable of depriving individual litigants of a remedy where this could not be justified in the national interest, hindered the development of administrative law by severely restricting the evidence and therefore the material for analysis in those cases where issues relating to administrative action came before the courts.[4] Some, but not all, of the reluctance felt by officials to disclose information may have been caused by the lingering effects of attitudes adopted during the Second World War and hardened by the Cold War.

12.03 In the generation which has passed since *Not in the Public Interest* was published, much has changed. The writers of a leading textbook refer to 'the sea-change in attitudes towards administrative law'.[5] Crown privilege, rebranded as public interest immunity, has been much cut back: *Duncan v Cammell Laird & Co Ltd*[6] was overruled in 1968[7] and, in the aftermath of the furore caused by the Matrix Churchill prosecutions, the government announced that it would only seek to withhold evidence where the content of the particular evidence in question led Ministers to believe that its disclosure would cause real harm to the public interest.[8] Parliamentary scrutiny of administrative activity has been enhanced by the establishment of the modern system of select committees and, since 1967,[9] has been assisted by the Parliamentary Commissioner for Administration, the Ombudsman, to whom information must be produced regardless of any obligation to maintain secrecy.[10] Although the convention of Ministerial responsibility remains, civil servants do on occasion give direct accounts of their actions, for example to select committees. Law's empire now extends to the Security and Intelligence Services and their activities. In 1965 the Security Service was 'a body unrecognised by law';[11] since 1989 its existence and purpose have been put on a statutory basis.[12] Since 1994 the Intelligence Services, publicly unmentionable in

---

[3] D Williams, *Not in the Public Interest* (London, 1965) ch 3.
[4] ibid, ch 10.
[5] H Woolf and J Jowell, *Judicial Review of Administrative Action* (5th edn, 1995) para 1–011.
[6] [1942] AC 624.
[7] *Conway v Rimmer* [1968] AC 910.
[8] *Hansard*, HC (series 5) vol 287, cols 949–958; *Hansard*, HL (series 5) vol 576, cols 1507–1517 (18 December 1996).
[9] Parliamentary Commissioner Act 1967.
[10] ibid, s 8(3).
[11] Williams (n 2 above) 135.
[12] Security Service Act 1989.

1965, have also been the subject of statute.[13] And, with the intention of ensuring compatibility with the requirements of the European Convention on Human Rights, comprehensive legislation governs the interception of communications,[14] the practice of which was, in 1965, 'also unrecognised by law'. Thus, many matters, previously unjusticiable, or even wholly hidden, have been rendered susceptible to forms of scrutiny and legal process.

Nor has the law relating to official secrets gone unreformed. Before 1989 any dis-   **12.04**
cussion about freedom of information in the United Kingdom or access to docu-
ments held by its government started by addressing, and customarily deploring,[15] section 2 of the Official Secrets Act 1911. This notoriously wide provision, under which, on one estimation, over 2,000 differently worded charges could be brought,[16] effectively prohibited the unauthorized disclosure of any information in the possession of central government and of some other organs of the state and exposed anyone who disclosed or received such information to prosecution. The range of information to which section 2 related, or was capable of relating, could not be justified by reference to the security of the realm, the protection of subjects or any other similar object. It formed an obstacle to freedom of information, and its demolition was the necessary first step if access to information held by the government was to be granted. Section 2 of the 1911 Act was repealed by the Official Secrets Act 1989 and replaced by measures crafted to protect categories of information the secrecy of which can, with reason, be considered necessary in the interests of the state and its citizens.

The constitutional context into which the Freedom of Information Act 2000 fits   **12.05**
is, therefore, far different from that obtaining and described by David Williams in 1965 or faced by the Franks Committee in 1971. In particular, by 2000 the pre-liminary action of repealing section 2 of the Official Secrets Act 1911 had already been taken by the Official Secrets Act 1989. No further reform of the Official Secrets Acts was felt necessary before legislating for freedom of information and in the White Paper, *Your Right to Know,* the government simply expressed its concern 'to preserve the effectiveness of the Official Secrets Act'.[17] In the result the Freedom of Information Act 2000 was enacted without containing any amend-ment or repeal of any measure contained in the Official Secrets Acts.

For the purpose of the present book, this raises two principal questions. First,   **12.06**
what information is protected by the Official Secrets Act 1989? And secondly,

---

[13] Intelligence Services Act 1994.
[14] Regulation of Investigatory Powers Act 2000.
[15] For a catalogue of reasons to do so, see D Hooper, *Official Secrets: the Use and Abuse of the Act* (1987).
[16] *Report of the Departmental Committee on Section 2 of the Official Secrets Act 1911* (Cmnd 5104, 1972), referred to in this chapter as '*the Franks Report*' after its chairman, para 16.
[17] Cm 3818, para 3.19.

how does the protection of that information under that Act correlate with the duty imposed by the Freedom of Information Act on public authorities to disclose information which they hold?

B. The Official Secrets Act 1989

Overview

12.07 The primary purpose of the Official Secrets Act 1989 is to ensure that protected information remains within the circle of secrecy occupied by those who form part of the apparatus of government. The 1989 Act is therefore the principal focus of attention for present purposes in that its main concern is to prevent the unauthorized release of information by officials and other insiders as opposed to those measures, such as section 1 of the 1911 Act, whose main aim may be said to be preventing outsiders from gaining illegitimate access to certain forms of official information.

12.08 The 1989 Act was preceded by a White Paper entitled, *Reform of Section 2 of the Official Secrets Act 1911*.[18] In that White Paper the government expressed its objectives as follows:

> The central concern of any reform of section 2 is to determine in what circumstances the unauthorised disclosure of official information should be criminal . . . What justifies the application of the criminal law, where disclosure is not caught by section 1 of the 1911 Act, is the degree of harm to the public interest which may result. The objective of the Government's proposals is to narrow the scope of the present law so that the limited range of circumstances in which the unauthorised disclosure of official information needs to be criminal are clearly defined.[19]

12.09 But that aim had been set in 1972 by the Departmental Committee on Section 2 of the Official Secrets Act 1911 headed by Lord Franks which identified the need to restrict the application of the criminal law for the protection of official information as follows:

> We believe that most of those who have given evidence to us, and most reasonable people, would accept as a proper basis for the employment of criminal sanctions the unauthorised disclosure of official information which would be likely to cause serious injury to the security of the nation or the safety of the people. If criminal sanctions are justified at all, they are justified for this purpose. If they are to be reserved for what is important, they should not go any wider. We have therefore adopted this as our touchstone.[20]

---

[18] Cm 408. In this chapter this is referred to as '*the 1988 White Paper*'. In *R v Shayler* [2002] UKHL 11, para 11, Lord Bingham of Cornhill said that 'this White Paper was the immediate precursor of the Official Secrets Act 1989 and its recommendations bear directly on the interpretation of the Act.' See also ibid, para 20.

[19] 1988 White Paper, para 14.

[20] *Franks Report*, para 119.

Although the reform made by the 1989 Act may form part of what might be seen **12.10** as a trend, sketched above, towards rationalizing state powers in Britain, the fact that the reform happened when it did is generally ascribed to official recognition that the wide embrace of section 2 of the 1911 Act was not merely inimical to easy theoretical justification but was proving rebarbative to juries and therefore unpredictable in its practical application and effect. The acquittal of Clive Ponting, a civil servant in the Ministry of Defence, when tried on charges brought under section 2, is often referred to as showing that section 2 had lost whatever moral underpinning is required to render a law publicly acceptable. The charges against Clive Ponting related to the leaking of information concerning the movements of the *Belgrano* during the Falklands conflict. In his defence Clive Ponting sought to justify his actions as being to the public good. Although his acquittal may have prompted reform of section 2, not only does disclosure of information relating to defence remain prohibited under the 1989 Act but also no defence of acting in the public interest is afforded by that Act to a person charged with an offence under it. In material respects, therefore, the law has not been changed. Indeed, since the 1989 Act clearly excludes any public interest defence, whereas under the 1911 such a defence was thought arguable, the reform reduces the range of possible defences.

However, whatever may have been the catalyst for the reforms made by the 1989 **12.11** Act, the general objectives which the government set in the 1988 White Paper are difficult to criticize. Any state which upholds its responsibilities to its citizens requires some secrecy laws in order to maintain its capacity to protect those citizens. Secrecy laws which fulfil the objectives set by the 1988 White Paper would be likely to be laws to which the citizens of a democratic state could subscribe without accepting too gross an incursion into their liberties by their governors.

Sections 1 to 4, the primary group of measures contained in the 1989 Act, aim at **12.12** maintaining the circle of secrecy within which the government, its officials and other persons appointed by the government or its officials operate. Persons within the circle of secrecy are the primary holders of protected information. They are current and former Crown servants, government contractors, members of the security and intelligence services and any person who has been notified that he is subject to the provisions of section 1(1) of the 1989 Act. Save when lawfully authorized to do so and subject to certain conditions and defences, such persons commit an offence if they disclose protected information to persons outside the circle of secrecy.

In most but not all cases, an element of the offence is that the disclosure must be **12.13** damaging to the interest which the prohibition is designed to protect.[21] In those

---

[21] Official Secrets Act 1989, ss 1(3), 2(1) and 3(1).

cases[22] where the prosecution does not have to prove that the disclosure was damaging to the relevant protected interest, there are reasonable grounds for accepting that harm will, or is likely to, follow from disclosure. In this way, the Act seeks to fulfil the justification for invoking the criminal law by applying only in situations where the safety of the realm is at stake.

12.14 Recognizing that information is fluid and prone to escape, the 1989 Act also seeks to prevent any person outside the circle of secrecy who comes into possession of protected information from making further disclosure of it. Hence it is also an offence for persons, other than Crown servants, government contractors and those to whom section 1(1) applies, to make damaging disclosures of protected information which has been disclosed to them without lawful authority or which has been entrusted to them on terms of confidence.[23]

12.15 Finally, for the better protection of official secrets, the Act creates offences covering the wrongful retention of documents by Crown servants, the wrongful failure by government contractors to return documents and the failure by Crown servants and government contractors to take care to prevent unauthorized disclosures of documents.[24]

12.16 Although the measures contained in the 1989 Act are more specific than those contained in section 2 of the 1911 Act, criticism continues to be levelled at the 1989 Act for still leaving the decision whether disclosure is in the public interest to the government.[25] And, for better or worse, no defence of acting in the public interest is afforded by the 1989 Act.

The categories of information protected by the 1989 Act

12.17 There are four categories of information which are protected by the Official Secrets Act 1989:

(a) information relating to security and intelligence;
(b) information relating to defence;
(c) information relating to international relations and confidential information obtained from foreign states and international organizations; and
(d) information relating to crimes and special investigation powers.

Security and intelligence

12.18 Security or intelligence in this context comprises the work of, or work in support of, the security and intelligence services or any part of them. Information relating

---

[22] Official Secrets Act 1989, ss 1(1) and 4(1).
[23] ibid, s 5(1)–(3).
[24] ibid, s 8.
[25] See Feldman (n 1 above) 889–895. For authority on the question of who defines the public interest in relation to section 1 of the 1911 Act, see *Chandler v DPP* [1964] AC 763.

to security or intelligence includes information held or transmitted by those services or by persons in support of, or of any part of, them.[26]

The 1989 Act does not explain what the security and intelligence services are. But the following services are recognized by statute: the Security Service,[27] the Secret Intelligence Service and General Communications Headquarters.[28] **12.19**

Defence

The matters falling within the category of information relating to defence are the size, shape, organization, logistics, order of battle, deployment, operations, state of readiness and training of the armed forces of the Crown; the weapons, stores or other equipment of those forces and the invention, development, production and operation of such equipment and research relating to it; defence policy and strategy and military planning and intelligence; plans and measures for the maintenance of essential supplies and services that are or would be needed in time of war.[29] **12.20**

International relations

International relations are defined as comprising the relations between states, between international organizations or between one or more states and one or more such organizations and include any matter relating to a state other than the United Kingdom or to an international organization which is capable of affecting the relations of the United Kingdom with another state or with an international organization.[30] 'International organization' means an organization of which only states are members and includes a reference to any organ of such an organization.[31] **12.21**

In addition to information relating to international relations, protection is also afforded to any confidential information which has been obtained from a state other than the United Kingdom or an international organization.[32] **12.22**

Crime and special investigations

Save that it all relates to promotion of law and order, the content of the fourth category of information is more varied. It includes information the unauthorized disclosure of which: **12.23**

(a) results in the commission of an offence;

---

[26] Official Secrets Act 1989, s 1(9).
[27] Security Service Act 1989, s 1(1).
[28] Intelligence Services Act 1994, ss 1(1) and 3(1).
[29] Official Secrets Act 1989, s 2(4).
[30] ibid, s 3(5).
[31] ibid, s 13(1) and see s 13(2) and (3) for further refinement.
[32] ibid, s 3(1)(b).

(b)   facilitates an escape from legal custody or the doing of any other act prejudicial to the safekeeping of persons in legal custody; or

(c)   impedes the prevention or detection of offences or the apprehension or prosecution of suspected offenders.[33]

It is not only information which actually causes one of the effects mentioned which is protected, but also any information which is such that its unauthorized disclosure would be likely to have any of those effects. It will be apparent that the information referred to here is defined by its actual or likely effect and that such effect is inherently adverse to the interests of law and order. As is discussed in paragraph 12.38 et seq below, in respect of other categories of information unauthorized disclosure of which is prohibited, an element of the offence is that the disclosure is damaging to the interest which keeping the information secret is intended to protect. But in the case of the information mentioned in this paragraph, that element of damage is necessarily present because the relevant information is defined by its actual or likely adverse effect and that effect intrinsically involves prosecution must also specifically prove that the damage is of good order.

12.24   Also protected is information obtained by, or relating to the obtaining of information by, the interception of communications under warrant or by action authorized under legislation relating to the security and intelligence services.[34]

The offences under sections 1(3), 2, 3, and 4

12.25   Apart from the special provisions of section 1(1) relating to members and former members of the security and intelligence services and persons who have been notified that they are subject to section 1(1), the primary offence of making an unauthorized disclosure of information within one of the protected categories is committed, subject to any available defence, where a currently serving or former Crown servant or government contractor discloses the information without lawful authority and the information is or has been in his possession by virtue of his position as such. Apart from section 1(1) and offences under section 4, the prosecution must also specifically prove that the disclosure is damaging to a relevant interest.

Crown servants and government contractors

12.26   The first element in the primary offence to address is the definition of 'Crown servant' and 'government contractor'. These definitions are also important in the context of determining when and to whom protected information may lawfully be disclosed by virtue of section 7.

---

[33]   Official Secrets Act 1989, s 4(2)(a).
[34]   ibid, s 4(3).

Crown servants

Persons who count as Crown servants for the purpose of the Official Secrets Act **12.27**
1989 are listed in section 12.

The list includes members of the UK and devolved administrations. Thus, **12.28**
'Crown servant' includes a Minister of the Crown.[35] No definition is given of
'Minister of the Crown' in the Official Secrets Act 1989 but as defined by section
8(1) of the Ministers of the Crown Act 1975 it means the holder of an office in
Her Majesty's Government in the United Kingdom and includes the Treasury, the
Board of Trade and the Defence Council. A member of the Scottish Executive or
a junior Scottish Minister is a Crown servant.[36] As regards the Welsh administration, the Assembly First Secretary and each of the Assembly Secretaries, who in
practice but without clear authority, tend to refer to themselves as First Minister
and Ministers respectively, are Crown servants for the purposes of the 1989 Act.[37]

Any person employed in the civil service of the Crown is a Crown servant. For this **12.29**
purpose the civil service includes Her Majesty's Diplomatic Service, Her Majesty's
Overseas Civil Service, the civil service of Northern Ireland and the Northern
Ireland Court Service.[38] A distinction was drawn in the Security Service Act 1989
as originally passed[39] between members of the Security Service and officials of the
department of the Secretary of State, meaning by the latter phrase the officials in
any department of state on account of the doctrine of the indivisibility of the office of Secretary of State, and a similar distinction was observed in the Intelligence
Services Act 1994.[40] But that distinction was made for different purposes and
members of those services are still employed in the civil service of the Crown and
therefore Crown servants within section 12(1)(c).

Service as the holder of any office in the Scottish Administration which is not a **12.30**
Ministerial office, or as a member of the staff of the Scottish Administration constitutes service in the Home Civil Service and therefore falls within the ambit of
the definition.[41] Similarly service as a member of the Welsh Assembly's staff is service in Her Majesty's Home Civil Service and is equally covered.[42]

---

[35] ibid, s 12(1)(a).
[36] Scotland Act 1998, s 125 and Sch 8, para 26(2).
[37] Government of Wales Act 1998, s 53(4).
[38] Official Secrets Act 1989, s 12(1)(c).
[39] Security Service Act 1989, s 4(4) repealed by the Regulation of Investigatory Powers Act 2000,
s 82 and Sch 5.
[40] Intelligence Services Act 1994, s 8(4) repealed by the Regulation of Investigatory Powers Act
2000, s 82 and Sch 5.
[41] Scotland Act 1998, s 51(2).
[42] Government of Wales Act 1998, s 34(2).

12.31 Any member of the naval, military or air forces of the Crown including any person employed by an association established for the purposes of Part XI of the Reserve Forces Act 1996 is a Crown servant.[43]

12.32 Even though police officers are not appointed or paid by the Crown, it was held in *Lewis v Cattle*[44] that a police officer held office under Her Majesty for the purpose of the Official Secrets Acts then in force. Whatever view might be taken of that decision, the position is now rendered clear by the statutory definition of 'Crown servant' which includes any constable and any other person employed or appointed in or for the purposes of any police force, including the Police Service of Northern Ireland and the Police Service of Northern Ireland Reserve.[45] 'Constable' in this context means the office of constable, which has a long history in common law,[46] as opposed to the rank of constable in the police.

12.33 Power is conferred on the Secretary of State to extend the definition by order.[47] Any person who is a member or employee of a prescribed body or a body of a prescribed class and is either himself prescribed for the purposes of section 12(1)(f) of the 1989 Act or belongs to a prescribed class of members or employees of any such body counts as a Crown servant. And so does any person who is the holder of a prescribed office or who is the employee of such a holder and is either prescribed for the purposes of section 12(1)(g) of the Act or belongs to a prescribed class of such employees.

12.34 The principal order made by the Secretary of State is the Official Secrets Act 1989 (Prescription) Order 1990.[48] The schedules to this order set out the prescribed bodies and offices. Prescribed offices for the purpose of section 12(1)(g) include the Comptroller and Auditor-General, members of the National Audit Office, and the Parliamentary Commissioner for Administration.

12.35 Other bodies and offices have been prescribed from time to time.[49] The Scottish Parliamentary Commissioner for Administration[50] and the Auditor-General for Scotland[51] are prescribed offices for the purpose of section 12(1)(g).

---

[43] Official Secrets Act 1989, s 12(1)(d).

[44] [1938] 2 KB 454.

[45] Official Secrets Act 1989, s 12(1)(e) as amended by the Police (Northern Ireland) Act 2000, s 78 and Sch 6, para 9.

[46] See 36(1) *Halsbury's Laws of England* (4th edn, Re-issue) paras 201–205.

[47] Official Secrets Act 1989, s 12(1)(f) and (g) and s 13(1).

[48] SI 1990/200 as amended by SI 1993/847.

[49] eg, by the Official Secrets Act 1989 (Prescription) (Amendment) Order 1993, SI 1993/847.

[50] Scotland Act 1998 (Transitory and Transitional Provisions) (Complaints of Maladministration) Order 1999, SI 1999/1351, art 17(8).

[51] Scotland Act 1998 (Consequential Modifications) (No 1) Order 1999, SI 1999/1049, art 3 and Sch 1, para 18.

Government contractors

A government contractor is any person who is not a Crown servant but who pro- **12.36**
vides, or is employed in the provision of, goods or services for certain purposes or
under certain agreements or arrangements. The purposes in question are those of
any Minister, of any of the services, forces or bodies mentioned above or of the
holder of any office prescribed by the Secretary of State pursuant to the power
mentioned above. The relevant agreements or arrangements are those certified by
the Secretary of State as being ones to which the government of a state other than
the United Kingdom is a party or which are subordinate to, or made for the purposes of implementing, any such agreement or arrangement.[52]

Northern Ireland Ministers

By an amendment made by the Northern Ireland Act 1998,[53] section 12(5) was **12.37**
added to the Official Secrets Act 1989 providing that that Act should apply to the
First Minister and deputy First Minister in Northern Ireland and to Northern
Ireland Ministers and junior Ministers as it applies to persons falling within the
definition of Crown servant. Thus such office-holders are not Crown servants but
are subject to the Official Secrets Act 1989 as if they were.

Requirement that the unauthorized disclosure be damaging

In the cases of unauthorized disclosure by former or current Crown servants or **12.38**
government contractors of information relating to security or intelligence, defence and international relations under sections 1(3), 2(1) and 3(1) respectively,
the offence is only committed if the unauthorized disclosure in question is damaging to the relevant protected interest. What is meant by a damaging disclosure
is defined differently with respect to each of these provisions. In each case damage
is defined not only in terms of damage or effects actually caused but also of damage or effects which are likely to be caused.

Thus in respect of the offence concerning unauthorized disclosure of information **12.39**
relating to security or intelligence, a disclosure is damaging if:

(a) it causes damage to the work of, or any part of, the security and intelligence
    services; or
(b) it is of information which is such that its unauthorized disclosure would be
    likely to cause such damage or which falls within a class or description of
    information, documents or articles disclosure of which would be likely to
    have that effect.[54]

---

[52] Official Secrets Act 1989, s 12(2).
[53] Northern Ireland Act 1998, s 99, Sch 13, para 9. During a suspension of the Northern Ireland
Assembly, no person continues to hold office as a Northern Ireland Minister or Junior Minister;
Northern Ireland Act 2000, s 1(4).
[54] Official Secrets Act 1989, s 1(4).

12.40 Where the information relates to defence, a disclosure is damaging if:

(a) it damages the capability of, or of any part of, the armed forces of the Crown to carry out their tasks, or leads to loss of life or injury to members of those forces or serious injury to the equipment or installations of those forces;

(b) it otherwise endangers the interests of the United Kingdom abroad, seriously obstructs the promotion or protection by the United Kingdom of those interests, or endangers the safety of British citizens abroad; or

(c) it is of information which is such that its unauthorized disclosure would be likely to have any of those effects.[55]

12.41 Where the information relates to international relations or is confidential information obtained from a foreign state or an international organization, a disclosure is damaging if:

(a) it endangers the interests of the United Kingdom abroad, seriously obstructs the promotion or protection by the United Kingdom of those interests or endangers the safety of British citizens abroad; or

(b) it is of information which is such that its unauthorized disclosure would be likely to have any of those effects.[56]

12.42 In the 1988 White Paper, the government proposed that there should be no test of harm in relation to confidential information obtained from a foreign state or international organization. For when such confidential information was disclosed without lawful authorization:

> the harm arising . . . is not simply the disruption of relations between the Government and other government or the organisation concerned. There is a wider damage to the standing of the United Kingdom in relation to all governments and international organisations.[57]

But, in the 1989 Act, it is an element of the offence of making an unauthorized disclosure of such confidential information that the disclosure be damaging. However the task of the prosecution is eased because the fact by itself that the information is confidential, or the nature or contents of the information disclosed, may be sufficient to establish that its disclosure is likely to have one or more of the relevant harmful effects.[58]

12.43 As mentioned in paragraph 12.23 above, the requirement that an unauthorized disclosure be damaging is inherent in that category of information disclosure of which results in the commission of an offence or has other effects adverse to the maintenance of law and order and therefore there is no need for any further re-

---

[55] Official Secrets Act 1989, s 2(2).
[56] ibid, s 3(2).
[57] Cm 408, para 51.
[58] Official Secrets Act 1989, s 3(3).

quirement that the disclosure be damaging in relation to information mentioned in section 4(2).

Finally and exceptionally there is information, identified in section 4(3), which is **12.44** obtained from the interception of communications or by reason of action authorized by warrants issued under the Regulation of Investigatory Powers Act 2000.[59] No requirement of damage applies in this case. In the 1988 White Paper the government explained its view that interception of communications was:

> an exceptional but vital instrument which is used, for the protection of society, when all other means are not available. The effectiveness of interception would be much reduced if details of the practice were readily available.[60]

And it is important not only that the means whereby interception is practised is protected from disclosure but that the information thereby gathered is also kept secret. Although perhaps the more obvious reason for keeping the information secret is that it would then be more useful to the authorities in their battles with crime and terrorism, the given reason was different and addressed the interest of those whose communications were intercepted:

> Interception inevitably involves interference, without their knowledge, with the privacy of those whose communications are intercepted. Such interference is acceptable in the public interest only if those responsible for interception maintain the privacy of the information obtained.[61]

Disclosure of information relating to the interception of communications is now **12.45** also prohibited by section 19 of the Regulation of Investigatory Powers Act 2000.

Section 1(1)

The offences so far mentioned are those which may be committed by persons who **12.46** are or have been Crown servants or government contractors. Special provision is also made for any person who is or has been a member of the security and intelligence services or who is or has been a person notified that he is subject to the provisions of section 1(1) of the 1989 Act. Such a person is guilty of an offence if without lawful authority he discloses any information, document or other article relating to security or intelligence which is or has been in his possession by virtue of his work as a member of those services or in the course of his work while the notification is or was in force.[62]

The reference here to disclosing information includes a reference to making any **12.47** statement which purports to be a disclosure of such information or is intended to

---

[59] Or under the Security Services Act 1989 or the Intelligence Services Act 1994.
[60] Cm 408, para 30.
[61] ibid, para 30.
[62] Official Secrets Act 1989, s 1(1).

be taken by those to whom it is addressed as being such a disclosure.[63] In the 1988 White Paper, it was explained that:

> as a general policy, Governments do not comment on assertions about security and intelligence: true statements will generally go unconfirmed and false statements will normally go undenied. As a result, and because of the particular credibility attaching to statements about security or intelligence by members of the services concerned, the circulation of misinformation by a member of the services may, in a different way, be as harmful as his disclosure of genuine information.[64]

12.48 Section 1(1) of the 1989 Act gives formal recognition and legal effect to the practice of making people sign the Official Secrets Acts. Before the 1989 Act was passed individuals to whom sensitive information was to be given were required to sign the Official Secrets Acts. This practice had no particular legal effect, although the fact that a person had signed an acknowledgement that he was bound by the Acts might assist in showing his knowledge that he should not disclose information. The purpose appears to have been to achieve the useful, but psychological, effect of impressing on the signatory the importance of maintaining confidentiality. Under the 1989 Act notifying a person that he is subject to section 1(1) of that Act has the specific legal significance that it renders that person liable to prosecution under that sub-section if he discloses any information relating to security or intelligence which has come into his possession in the course of his work while the notification is in force.

12.49 A notice that a person is subject to section 1(1) may be served if, in the opinion of a Minister of the Crown, the work undertaken by the person in question is or includes work which is connected with the security and intelligence services and its nature is such that the interests of national security require that he should be subject to the provisions of section 1(1).[65] The notification must be effected by a notice in writing served on the person to be notified by the Minister who decided that the notice was justified. It remains in force for five years, unless revoked, but may be renewed for further periods of five years by the service of a further notice.[66]

12.50 Revocation is effected by notice in writing served by the Minister. The Minister is obliged to serve a notice of revocation as soon as, in his opinion, the work undertaken by the person in question ceases to be such as to require him to be subject to section 1(1).[67] Thus, it would appear that, where a Minister has served a notice subjecting a person to section 1(1), the Minister must keep under review whether the nature of that person's work continues to justify his being subject to section 1(1). After revocation the person in question remains liable to prosecution under

---

[63] Official Secrets Act 1989, s 1(2).
[64] Cm 408, para 43.
[65] Official Secrets Act 1989, s 1(6).
[66] ibid, s 1(7).
[67] ibid, s 1(9).

section 1(1) in respect of relevant information which came into his possession in the course of his work while the notification was in force, but he is not so liable in respect of any information which comes into his possession thereafter.[68]

Lawful disclosure

In the 1988 White Paper, the government stated that: **12.51**

> Crown servants will in the normal course of their duties properly disclose informa-
> tion in the categories which the Government proposes should be covered in new leg-
> islation. The same is true of government contractors. It is obviously not intended
> that such disclosures should be caught by the new legislation, and references to dis-
> closures in the following paragraphs should accordingly be read as excluding disclo-
> sures of that kind.[69]

Effect was given to this in the 1989 Act by providing that the absence of lawful au-   **12.52**
thority is an element in the offences created by that Act. In the case of Crown servants and persons in respect of whom a notification for the purpose of section 1(1)
is in force but who are neither Crown servants nor government contractors, a disclosure is made with lawful authority if, but only if, it is made in accordance with
the relevant person's official duty.[70]

The Act does not assist in determining what the scope of the relevant official duty   **12.53**
is. Obviously disclosures between Crown servants in the ordinary course of their
carrying out the tasks with which they are charged will fall within that duty. In the
case of a Minister of the Crown, his official duty may involve making or authorizing the wider publication of protected information. His disclosure in appropriate
circumstances would fall within his official duty. What the bounds of the official
duty are will effectively have to be determined by the government of the day.
Disclosure in his memoirs would clearly be outside any Crown servant's official
duty.[71]

As regards government contractors, a disclosure is made with lawful authority if,   **12.54**
and only if, it is made in accordance with an official authorization or it is made for
the purposes of the functions by virtue of which the relevant person is a government contractor and without contravening an official restriction.[72] In this context
'official authorization' and 'official restriction' mean an authorization or restriction duly given or imposed by a Crown servant or government contractor or by or
on behalf of a prescribed body or a body of a prescribed class.

---

[68] ibid, s 1(1).
[69] Cm 408, para 36.
[70] Official Secrets Act 1989, s 7(1).
[71] See further R Brazier, *Ministers of the Crown* (1997) 310.
[72] Official Secrets Act 1989, s 7(2).

12.55 And as regards other persons, a disclosure is made with lawful authority if and only if it is made either to a Crown servant for the purposes of his functions as such or in accordance with an official authorization.[73]

12.56 The defendant in *R v Shayler*,[74] being a former member of the security service, fell into the category of other persons. Thus he might only lawfully disclose the information in point in the circumstances defined in section 7(3) and therefore required official authorization before making a general publication of the information in his possession which he had gained while serving in the security service. Lord Bingham of Cornhill said that:

> Consideration of a request for authorisation should never be a routine or mechanical process; it should be undertaken bearing in mind the importance attached to the right of free expression and the need for any restriction to be necessary, responsive to a pressing social need and proportionate.[75]

12.57 David Shayler had not sought such authorization, but the House of Lords recognized that had he done so and been refused authorization, he would have had standing to seek judicial review of the decision to refuse authorization. In reviewing the decision to refuse authorization the court would conduct the more rigorous and intrusive review, described by Lord Steyn in *R(Daly) v Secretary of State for the Home Department*[76] which is appropriate where a Convention right, recognized by the Human Rights Act 1998, is at stake.

12.58 Section 7(3) does not apply to serving Crown servants and therefore the possibility that they might seek and obtain official authorization under section 7(3)(b) to disclose protected information does not apply to them. This is not surprising since, if a serving Crown servant formed the view that some protected information should be disclosed, the only course properly available would be for him to raise the matter internally, either to his superiors in the ordinary line of management or, in an appropriate case, to one of those office-holders mentioned by Lord Bingham in connection with section 7(3)(a). Disclosure in those ways would be in accordance with the Crown servant's official duty, albeit it would not necessarily be in the course of his ordinary duties.

Statutory defences

12.59 For each of the offences which may be committed by a Crown servant or government contractor who makes an unauthorized and, where required, damaging disclosure of protected information, a defence is afforded if he can prove either:

---

[73] Official Secrets Act 1989, s 7(3).
[74] [2002] UKHL 11, [2002] 2 WLR 754.
[75] ibid, para 30.
[76] ibid, paras 26–28. (*R (on the application of Daly) v Secretary of State for the Home Department* [2001] UKHL 26, [2001] 2 AC 532.)

(a) that he did not know, and had no reasonable cause to believe, that the information related to the relevant category of protected information; or

(b) (except in the fourth category of information relating to crime or special investigation powers) that he did not know, and had no reasonable cause to believe, that the disclosure would be damaging.

The latter defence does not apply in the case of charges under section 1(1) because there is no requirement that the disclosure be damaging in that instance. Nor does it apply in the case of the fourth category of information because in that case too there is no independent requirement that the disclosure be damaging.

A defence is also afforded where the person charged can show that he believed that **12.60** he had lawful authority to make the disclosure and had no reasonable cause to believe otherwise.[77] Lawful authority to disclose information is mentioned further below.

Each of the defences contains a subjective and an objective element. Proof of cred- **12.61** ible naivety on the defendant's part will not, therefore, suffice. All of the statutory defences made available in respect of the offences which may be committed under sections 1 to 4 of the 1989 Act put the burden of proof on the accused. In the 1988 White Paper this was justified on the basis that:

> In general it is reasonable to assume that a Crown servant knows the value of the information that comes to him in the course of his duties, and that, if he discloses information likely to cause harm he knows what he is doing.[78]

The same principle applies to government contractors. But the 1988 White Paper stated that the opposite presumption applies in the case of persons who are not Crown servants or government contractors. By virtue of section 5(3)(b), where some person other than a Crown servant or government contractor is charged under section 5[79] with making an unauthorized disclosure of protected information, it is for the prosecution to prove that the accused knew, or had reasonable cause to believe, that an unauthorized disclosure would be damaging. Since the prosecution need only prove that the accused had reasonable cause to believe that the disclosure would be damaging, it may be open to argument whether the statute gives full weight to the principle recognized in the 1988 White Paper. The prosecution must also prove that the accused knew or had reasonable cause to believe that the information was protected from disclosure by sections 1 to 4 of the 1989 Act.[80]

---

[77] Official Secrets Act 1989, s 7(4).
[78] 1988 White Paper, para 56.
[79] See at para 12.75 below.
[80] Official Secrets Act 1989, s 5(2).

12.62 The 1988 White Paper rejected the suggestion that there should be a defence that a disclosure had been made in the public interest.[81] In *R v Shayler*[82] the defendant sought to rely on just such a defence. The House of Lords ruled that no defence based on public interest was afforded by the Official Secrets Act 1989. The further argument that that absence rendered the Official Secrets Act 1989 incompatible with the European Convention on Human Rights also failed. This is discussed below.

Consent of the Attorney-General to prosecutions

12.63 Subject to one exception, no prosecution for an offence under the Official Secrets Act 1989 may be instituted in England and Wales without the consent of the Attorney-General.[83] The exception concerns offences in respect of information mentioned in section 4(2), that is, information disclosure of which results in the commission of an offence, facilitates an escape from legal custody, prejudices the safekeeping of persons in custody or impedes the prevention or detection of offences or the apprehension or prosecution of offenders. Prosecutions in England and Wales for an offence in respect of such information require the consent of the Director of Public Prosecutions.[84]

Interference with the right to free expression

12.64 The Official Secrets Act 1989 constitutes an interference with the right to freedom of expression which is protected by Article 10 of the European Convention on Human Rights. But Article 10 does not confer an absolute right. Article 10(2) states that the exercise of the freedom of expression:

> may be subject to such formalities, conditions, restrictions or penalties as are prescribed by law and are necessary in a democratic society, in the interests of national security, territorial integrity or public safety, for the prevention of disorder or crime, for the protection of health or morals, for the protection of the reputation or rights of others, for the protection of information received in confidence, or for maintaining the authority and impartiality of the judiciary.

In the *Shayler* case[85] the House of Lords recognized that the provisions of sections 1(1) and 4(1) under which David Shayler, a former member of the security service, was charged represented an interference with his right to freedom of expression. The issue addressed by the House was whether those sections were incompatible with the Convention. This issue arose because the construction of the sections was clear and did not permit of any reading which would enable

---

[81] 1988 White Paper, paras 58–61.
[82] [2002] UKHL 11, [2002] 2 WLR 754.
[83] Official Secrets Act 1989, s 9(1).
[84] ibid, s 9(2).
[85] [2002] UKHL 11, [2002] 2 WLR 754.

David Shayler to present by way of defence his case that he had disclosed protected information in the public interest.[86]

Whether the provisions of the Official Secrets Act 1989 are compatible with the **12.65** Convention right to freedom of expression depends on whether those measures can be justified by reference to the requirements of Article 10(2). They have therefore to be prescribed by law, directed to one or more of the objectives specified in Article 10(2) and shown by the state to be necessary in a democratic society. The concept of proportionality is relevant to the third of these points. Lord Bingham stated:

> 'Necessary' has been strongly interpreted: it is not synonymous with 'indispensable', neither has it the flexibility of such expressions as 'admissible', 'ordinary', 'useful', 'reasonable' or 'desirable'. One must consider whether the interference complained of corresponded to a pressing social need, whether it was proportionate to the legitimate aim pursued and whether the reasons given by the national authority to justify it are relevant and sufficient under article 10(2).[87]

Their Lordships' speeches address whether the interferences are prescribed by law and directed to a legitimate aim but the main focus is directed upon the question whether the ban on disclosure imposed by the Act on members and former members of the security and intelligence services is necessary in a democratic society. The critical point is whether the nature of the ban is such that it extends beyond what can be justified under the Convention.

The House held that the prohibition on disclosure is justified because it is not an **12.66** absolute ban but is a ban on disclosure without lawful authority. Hence the provisions contained in section 7(3), under which persons other than currently serving Crown servants or government contractors may be authorized to disclose protected information, were central. The underlying issue was whether these methods of making a lawful disclosure were such that there were sufficient means in a democratic society for former members of the security and intelligence services, or other former Crown servants, to draw attention to abuses or other deficiencies which they had discovered in the course of their service.

By virtue of section 7(3) there are two ways in which a person holding protected **12.67** information may lawfully disclose it: he may disclose it to a Crown servant for the purposes of that Crown servant's functions as such or he may seek official authorization to disclose the information and, if such authorization is obtained, disclose the information in accordance with that authorization. Crown servants to whom

---

[86] The House of Lords eschewed discussion of whether there was a defence of necessity to the charges on the basis that the facts presented by David Shayler did not raise that issue. The views on the availability of that defence expressed in the Court of Appeal ([2001] EWCA Crim 1977, [2001] 1 WLR 2206), which on the facts were obiter dicta in any event, would seem open to further debate.

[87] [2002] UKHL 11, para 23 (references removed), [2002] 2 WLR 754, 770–771.

a former member of the security service might appropriately make disclosure include the staff counsellor appointed to hear concerns raised by any member of the security and intelligence services whose anxieties cannot be allayed by means of the ordinary processes of the relations between management and staff; where the lawfulness of some activity is in question, the Attorney-General, the Director of Public Prosecutions or the Metropolitan Police Commissioner; and, where the concern relates to maladministration or misbehaviour short of unlawfulness, to the Prime Minister or various Secretaries of State, the secretariat of the Parliamentary Intelligence and Security Committee or the staff of the Comptroller and Auditor-General, the National Audit Office and the Parliamentary Commissioner for Administration.[88]

12.68   The second available course is to seek official authorization to disclose the information. It is in this connection that the availability of recourse to the court arises. The initial stage is an internal decision by the Crown servant to whom the application for authorization has been made.

> Whoever is called upon to consider the grant of authorisation must consider with care the particular information or document which the former member seeks to disclose and weigh the merits of that request bearing in mind (and if necessary taking advice on) the object or objects which the statutory ban on disclosure seeks to achieve and the harm (if any) which would be done by the disclosure in question.[89]

Some factors, identifying agents or compromising informers, would justify refusal; others might not. The right to freedom of expression should be borne in mind. And a decision to refuse authorization is subject to judicial review and, as discussed further below, since a Convention right under Article 10 is at stake, such review would be approached on the basis of intensive scrutiny that is applicable where such rights are at stake.

12.69   In his speech, Lord Hope of Craighead suggested that the court should, on such a review, address the following questions. (1) What, with respect to the information sought to be disclosed, was the justification for the interference with the right to freedom of expression? (2) If the justification was that this was in the interests of national security, was there a pressing social need for that information not to be disclosed? And (3) if there was such a need, was the interference with the Convention right which was involved in withholding authorization for the disclosure of that information no more than was necessary?[90] Only Lord Scott of Foscote expressed agreement with Lord Hope's reasons and so this approach does not have the approval of the House. Further, since on the facts the appeal was not an appeal on a judicial review of a refusal to grant authorization, anything said

---

[88] *R v Shayler* [2002] UKHL 11, (n 87 above), para 27.
[89] ibid, para 30.
[90] ibid, para 79.

about how such a review should be conducted is obiter dicta. But perhaps, on such a review, this approach may be followed.

The prohibition on disclosure without authorization creates a procedural difficulty **12.70** for an applicant seeking review of the decision to refuse authorization. Can he disclose the relevant information to his own lawyers so as to enable them to pursue the review? Various means of meeting this difficulty might be available. Authorization under section 7(3)(b) to make disclosure to the lawyers concerned is the starting point. Documents may be redacted or anonymized. Undertakings may be sought from the lawyers that they would not disclose the information. Counsel could even be appointed to represent the applicant's interests in the applicant's absence and with access to material not made available to the applicant himself.[91]

The conclusion of the House of Lords was that the availability of the means dis- **12.71** cussed of making lawful disclosures to Crown servants and of seeking authorization to make wider disclosures renders the interference with the freedom of expression of a former member of the security service which the Official Secrets Act 1989 represents compatible with the Convention. Opinions may differ as to the probability that taking any or all of the steps suggested would have the result that official wrongdoing would be properly addressed. Unlikely as some would think it to be, the possibility that official wrongdoing would go unchecked despite all these steps being taken was recognized by Lord Bingham. But underlying the decision is the acceptance that the matters at stake are such that, even in a democratic society, that possibility has to be accepted.[91a]

The defendant in *R v Shayler* was a former member of the security service who had **12.72** retained information which had come into his possession while he was serving as a member of that service. But an application for authorization under section 7(3)(b) to make disclosure might also be made by other outsiders, such as journalists, into whose possession protected information has come. For unauthorized disclosure by them may also be an offence under section 5. Given that the interests in issue will be of a similar nature, it would seem likely that the same approach would be followed on any review of a decision to refuse authorization.

Offences committed by persons who receive protected information

The 1989 Act created a number of offences which might be committed by persons **12.73** who received protected information and then made unauthorized further disclosures of it. These offences obviously form an important aspect of the law from the point of view of journalists and others who wish to root out information about the doings of government. But they are not central to the questions currently

---

[91] ibid, para 34.
[91a] It is understood that David Shayler will pursue his case further by way of application to the European Court of Human Rights in Strasbourg.

addressed in that they concern restrictions on the use of information by persons outside the circle of secrecy. In the context of freedom of information the primary concern is with gaining access to that information in the first place. Nonetheless the relevant offences are set out in the following paragraphs.

Information protected by sections 1 to 4 of the Official Secrets Act 1989

12.74 As it was put in *the Franks report*, 'a secret is a secret'.

> Whoever lets out . . . a secret [which requires protection], the same damage is done to the nation. Every citizen who knowingly handles a secret of this kind ought to protect it. If a civil servant has failed to protect a secret, there is no justification for the view that a citizen who thereby comes into possession of that secret, and who knows that it is a secret, should be free to compound the failure of the civil servant, and to harm the nation, by passing on the secret as he pleases.[92]

12.75 Subject to various conditions which are mentioned in the following paragraphs, section 5(2) renders it an offence for any person into whose possession any information, document or article protected against disclosure by any of sections 1 to 4 comes to disclose it without lawful authority knowing, or having reasonable cause to believe, that it is protected against disclosure by those provisions and that it has come into his possession as a result of one of a number of specified routes of communication. Those routes are that the information has been disclosed to him or another by a Crown servant or government contractor without lawful authority, that it has been entrusted to him by a Crown servant or government contractor on terms requiring it to be held in confidence or in circumstances in which the Crown servant or government contractor could reasonably expect that it would be held in confidence, or that it has been disclosed to him or another without lawful authority by someone to whom it was so entrusted.

12.76 No offence can be committed under section 5(2) where the disclosure by the person into whose possession the information has come would be an offence under any of sections 1 to 4. Thus an offence under section 5 may only be committed by a person who is not within the categories of persons who are subject to the prohibitions against unauthorized disclosures contained in sections 1 to 4.

12.77 A person does not commit an offence under section 5(2) by disclosing information protected against disclosure by sections 1, 2 or 3 unless the disclosure which he makes is damaging and he makes it knowing, or having reasonable cause to believe, that it would be damaging. What counts as a damaging disclosure is to be determined according to the same test as would apply to an unauthorized disclosure by a Crown servant under the section which pertains to the information disclosed. Thus, in contrast to the position where an unauthorized disclosure is made by a Crown servant or government contractor, it is for the prosecution to prove

---

[92] *The Franks Report*, para 230.

that the person making the disclosure knew or had reasonable grounds to believe that the disclosure would be damaging.[93] But if the information is information to which section 4 applies the condition mentioned in this paragraph does not apply.

Where the relevant information was disclosed to a person by a government con-   **12.78**
tractor without lawful authority or by some other person to whom the information had been entrusted expressly or implicitly in confidence by a Crown servant or government contractor, no offence is committed by the person receiving the information unless the disclosure was by a British citizen or took place in the United Kingdom, any of the Channel Islands, the Isle of Man or a colony.

Information obtained in contravention of section 1 of the Official Secrets Act 1911

A person is guilty of an offence if without lawful authority he discloses any   **12.79**
information, document or other article which he knows, or has reasonable cause to believe, to have come into his possession as a result of a contravention of section 1 of the Official Secrets Act 1911. In outline, section 1 of the 1911 Act renders it an offence for a person, for any purpose prejudicial to the safety or interests of the State, to approach or enter any prohibited place, to make a sketch or other document which might be useful to an enemy, or to obtain, collect, record, publish or communicate to anyone any secret official code or pass word or other document which might be useful to an enemy. Enemies include potential enemies as well as those against whom a state of war exists.[94] Although the heading of section 1 is 'Penalties for spying', by virtue of the definition of prohibited place the section is capable of embracing cases of sabotage as well as espionage.[95]

Information entrusted in confidence to other states or international organizations

Section 6 provides for the protection of information which relates to security or   **12.80**
intelligence, defence or international relations and which has been communicated in confidence by or on behalf of the United Kingdom to another state or to an international organization. If such information comes into a person's possession as a result of its having been disclosed, whether to him or someone else, without the authority of that state or organization or, in the case of an organization, a member of it, then the person into whose possession the information has come is guilty of an offence if he makes a damaging disclosure of the information knowing, or having reasonable cause to believe, that the information relates to one of the protected categories of information and was communicated in confidence as mentioned above, that it has come into his possession as a result of an unauthorized disclosure, and that its disclosure would be damaging. The offence may only be committed where the disclosure would not constitute an offence under any of sections 1 to 5 of the Act.

---

[93] See the 1988 White Paper, para 57.
[94] *R v Parrott* (1913) 8 Cr App Rep 186.
[95] *Chandler v DPP* [1964] AC 763.

12.81   In relation to section 6, official authorizations rendering a disclosure lawful may, in addition to the methods mentioned above, be given by or on behalf of the state or organization concerned or, in the case of an organization, a member of it.[96]

C. Official Secrets and the Freedom of Information Act

12.82   The principal point of impact between the Official Secrets Acts and the Freedom of Information Act concerns the exemption of information the disclosure of which is capable of forming an element of one of what have been described above as the primary offences under the Official Secrets Act 1989. That is to say information within the four categories of information with which sections 1 to 4 of that Act are concerned: security and intelligence, defence, international relations and certain matters relating to crime and special investigation powers. The first step here is to identify which exemptions are relevant. The starting point is the exemption created by section 44(1)(a): the exemption of information if its disclosure (otherwise than under the Freedom of Information Act) by the public authority holding it is prohibited by or under any enactment. The question, therefore, is whether the provisions of the Official Secrets Act 1989 constitute prohibitions within the meaning of that exemption. But that is not the only exemption which is relevant. For there are a series of exemptions, each specific to particular relevant topics, which either encompass or coincide with the categories of information unauthorized disclosure of which is prohibited by the Official Secrets Acts. Those exemptions are:

(a)   section 23(1), exempting information which was supplied by any of the security services;

(b)   section 24(1), exempting information which is required to be exempt from disclosure for the purpose of safeguarding national security;

(c)   section 26(1), exempting information the disclosure of which would, or would be likely to, prejudice the defence of the British Islands or of any colony or the capability, effectiveness or security of the armed forces of the Crown or any forces co-operating with those forces;

(d)   section 27(1), exempting information the disclosure of which would, or would be likely to, prejudice international relations;

(e)   section 27(2), exempting information obtained in confidence from other states or certain international bodies;

(f)   section 30(1) and (2), exempting information relating to certain investigations and proceedings; and

(g)   section 31(1), exempting information relating to law enforcement.

---

[96] Official Secrets Act 1989, s 7(6).

The material difference between all of these other topic-specific exemptions and **12.83** the exemption contained in section 44 is that the exemption conferred by section 44 is an absolute exemption. Of the others, only the exemption under section 23 relating to information supplied by any of the specified security services is an absolute exemption. Therefore if an applicant requested information which fell within the range of those other exemptions, the public authority holding the information would have to address the question whether the public interest in maintaining the exemption outweighs, in all the circumstances of the case, the public interest in disclosing the information before claiming the exemption. But that question would not arise if the relevant exemption were the absolute exemption under section 44.

A second possible difference concerns the question whether a public authority **12.84** holding information of a category which is protected by the Official Secrets Act 1989 is obliged to refuse to disclose it when requested to do so. In general it would appear that a public authority is not obliged to claim that information is exempt where an exemption is available under the Freedom of Information Act. But if a public authority is prohibited by statute from disclosing information, then it would seem that that prohibition represents the principal obligation which the public authority should observe when asked, whether under the Freedom of Information Act or otherwise, to reveal the relevant information.

Hence there is some practical importance to the question whether the Official **12.85** Secrets Act 1989 contains prohibitions which are relevant for the purpose of section 44(1)(a).

The material part of section 44 provides that: **12.86**

> information is exempt information if its disclosure (otherwise than under the Freedom of Information Act) by the public authority holding it is prohibited by or under any enactment.

Those words might be construed as requiring that the other legislation referred to should contain a prohibition on disclosing information which is binding, according to the terms of that other legislation, on the public authority which holds the information. That might, at first blush, seem to be the literal reading of section 44. Two questions arise. The first is whether the Official Secrets Act 1989 contains prohibitions on disclosure, and the second is whether it contains prohibitions which are binding on public authorities. The second is the more difficult question.

Sections 1 to 4 of the Official Secrets Act 1989 concern disclosures of relevant **12.87** information made without lawful authority. No offence is committed where the disclosure is made with lawful authority. But it is a feature of statutory prohibitions on disclosure that the prohibition is subject to exceptions which, when their conditions are satisfied, render the disclosure lawful.

12.88 Further, each of the measures contained in those sections of the 1989 Act does not, at least as a matter of form, prohibit disclosure of relevant information but renders it criminal to make disclosure without lawful authority in defined circumstances. The absence of an express prohibition on making disclosure of information within the identified categories could be taken as a ground for denying that there is any prohibition on the disclosure of the relevant information. Other statutes, for example section 449(1) of the Companies Act 1985, do make such provision. But this is only a difference of drafting. The Official Secrets Act 1989 plainly contains a prohibition at some level on disclosure of relevant information.

12.89 There can, therefore, be little doubt that the Official Secrets Act 1989 contains prohibitions on the disclosure of information. But, as will be recalled, the structure of sections 1 to 4 of the 1989 Act is to create an offence which is committed when a person within one of a series of defined categories makes, without lawful authority, a disclosure of protected information which has come into his possession by virtue of his position. The difficulty to which this gives rise is that the bodies which count as public authorities for the purpose of the Freedom of Information Act are not, save in some limited cases, persons within those categories of persons who are subject to sections 1 to 4 of the 1989 Act. For example, individual civil servants who are Crown servants within the meaning of the 1989 Act and therefore subject to the prohibitions comprised in sections 1 to 4 of that Act are not themselves public authorities for the purpose of the Freedom of Information Act; but, of course, the government department whose staff such civil servants form is a public authority subject to the Freedom of Information Act. For the most part, there is a clear difference between the persons who are subject to the restrictions of the Official Secrets Act 1989 and those who are public authorities within the Freedom of Information Act. But there is some, though limited, overlap. For instance, a chief officer of police of a police force in England or Wales is both a public authority within the Freedom of Information Act and a Crown servant for the purpose of the Official Secrets Act 1989. And so is the Parliamentary Commissioner for Administration.

12.90 The official view appears to be that the Official Secrets Act 1989 does contain prohibitions on disclosure of information held by public authorities. Section 75 of the Freedom of Information Act enables the Lord Chancellor to repeal or amend any enactment which prohibits the disclosure of information by a public authority. In May 2002 the Lord Chancellor's Department published an *Interim Report on Statutory Provisions concerning Disclosure of Information*.[97] Amongst the primary legislation listed as prohibiting the disclosure of official information is the

---

[97] For further discussion of this, see ch 6 above.

Official Secrets Act 1989.[98] But that interim report, made after the Act had been passed, would not be admissible for the purpose of construing section 44.

If section 44 is read as requiring that the prohibition contained in the other legis- **12.91** lation be binding on the public authority to which a request for information is made before that public authority may rely on the exemption, then the prohibitions contained in sections 1 to 4 of the Official Secrets Act 1989 will only be relevant in those limited cases in which the public authority is a Crown servant (or falls within one of the other categories of person who are subject to those sections). This is a feasible reading of the Freedom of Information Act because it would entail that, save in those limited cases, the question whether information protected by the Official Secrets Act 1989 should be disclosed under the Freedom of Information Act would depend on whether the information fell within one of the other exemptions contained in the Freedom of Information Act, such as those relating to national security, defence, international relations and so forth. If the Official Secrets Act 1989 does contain prohibitions which render the information to which those prohibitions relate exempt under section 44, then the other relevant topic-specific exemptions would seem to have very little practical application because in a very large number of, if not most, instances in which they might apply they will be trumped by the section 44 exemption. That consideration militates against construing section 44 in such a way as to treat the prohibition contained in the Official Secrets Act 1989 as applying to public authorities.

But it would seem curious if the prohibitions contained in the Official Secrets Act **12.92** 1989 did not operate so as to preclude disclosure by a public authority under the Freedom of Information Act. For the information disclosure of which is prohibited by the Official Secrets Act 1989 comprises, or ought to comprise, the highest of all state secrets, and the need to protect such information must be at least as high as it is for any other official information disclosure of which is prohibited. And, as mentioned in paragraph 12.03 above, in the White Paper preceding the Freedom of Information Act, the government expressed its intention to preserve the effectiveness of the Official Secrets Act.[99]

At root these difficulties arise from the different purposes which the Official **12.93** Secrets Act 1989 and the Freedom of Information Act 2000 serve. The first defines serious offences the commission of which renders the offender liable to imprisonment; the second establishes an administrative scheme to render publicly available appropriate information held by public authorities. It is clear that the Official Secrets Act 1989 contains prohibitions on the disclosure of certain categories of information. But, for the purpose of the Freedom of Information Act the scope of the relevant prohibition has to be deduced from the offences

---

[98] In the section concerning the Home Office.
[99] *Your Right to Know* (Cm 3818), para 3.19.

contained in the criminal statute. In making that deduction some of the precision, necessary in the definition of an offence, has to be left behind. Hence, although only certain persons are competent to commit the relevant offences, it is possible to deduce from the provisions creating those offences a prohibition which should be taken, for the purpose of section 44(1)(a), as operating upon public authorities. It would appear to follow that a public authority holding information disclosure of which is prohibited by the Official Secrets Act 1989 must observe that prohibition and so is obliged to claim that it is exempt and to refuse to disclose it.

12.94 But, perhaps, this need not be the end of the matter. For, as discussed above, the decision in *R v Shayler*[100] that the prohibition imposed by the Official Secrets Act 1989 was compatible with the Convention depended on the fact that authorization to disclose protected information could be granted in appropriate instances. Hence the prohibition was not absolute but could, where appropriate, be lifted. This renders it questionable whether a public authority, faced with a request under the Freedom of Information Act for information, should claim the exemption under section 44 just because it is protected under the 1989 Act and without due consideration of whether the information in point requires that protection from disclosure. For, as Lord Bingham made clear, where a person holding protected information[101] which he wishes to disclose seeks official authorization to disclose it, the decision whether to allow or refuse disclosure should not result from a routine or mechanical process of consideration: in each case the impact on freedom of expression and the justification for the restriction must be addressed. Where the request arises externally from a person seeking such information, it may be that a similar process of consideration should be applied to the question whether the exemption should be claimed so as to withhold the information from him.

---

[100] [2002] UKHL 11, [2002] 2 WLR 754.

[101] Such a person may either be an insider seeking authorization so as to avoid offending under ss 1 to 4 or an outsider who has received information through one of the channels mentioned in s 5(1).

13

WHISTLE-BLOWING

A. Introduction

Whistle-blower: Slang for an informer. It derives from the phrase 'to blow the whistle on', meaning to stop a corrupt practice in the same way as a referee blows his whistle to stop play after a foul in football. A whistle-blower is usually someone in a business or a government office, who exposes a malpractice or a cover-up to the press. Often such a person is asked to leave his job.

Brewer's Dictionary of Twentieth Century Phrase and Fable (1996 edition)

The particular definition quoted above neatly (if somewhat euphemistically) en- **13.01** capsulated the dilemma in which people stumbling upon wrongdoing within their own organizations have in the past found themselves. Should they speak out, perhaps at great personal cost, or keep quiet at the risk of others? During the 1980s and 1990s, there were a series of disasters which it appeared might have been averted if only insiders had communicated their concerns. To take just one example, the Cullen Inquiry into the Piper Alpha oil platform explosion[1] heard evidence from trade union witnesses that a 'fear factor' had permeated the workforce

---

[1] The Public Inquiry into the Piper Alpha Disaster (Cm 1310).

in the UK sector of the North Sea fields. Workers had not wanted to put their continued employment in jeopardy by raising a safety issue that might be seen as embarrassing to management, and those on short-term contracts had been vulnerable to being 'not required back'. They had therefore suffered unsafe working practices in silence.

13.02 That was the background against which the Public Interest Disclosure Act 1998[2] was enacted. Introduced as a Private Member's Bill by Richard Shepherd MP, it received support from all quarters: the government, opposition parties, the Confederation of British Industry, the Institute of Directors, the Trades Union Congress, consumer groups, the legal, medical, and accountancy professions. When introducing the Bill into the House of Lords, Lord Borrie gave the following explanation of its genesis and object.[3]

> The official reports in recent years into the Zeebrugge ferry disaster, the rail crash at Clapham Junction, the explosion on Piper Alpha and the scandals at BCCI, Maxwell, Barlow Clowes and Barings have all revealed that staff were well aware of the risk of serious physical or financial harm but that they were either too scared to raise their concern or that they did so in the wrong way or with the wrong person. This culture, which encourages decent ordinary citizens to turn a blind eye when they suspect serious malpractice in their workplace, has not only cost lives and ruined livelihoods, but it has also damaged public confidence in some of the very organisations on which we all depend.
>
> The purpose of this Bill is to give a clear signal to people in places of work up and down the country that if they suspect wrongdoing, the law will stand by them provided they raise the matter in a responsible and reasonable way.

13.03 Nowhere in the Public Interest Disclosure Act 1998 itself is the colloquialism 'whistle-blowing' (or any cognate expression) to be found. 'Blowing the whistle' had made a previous appearance in a different statutory context, namely the Pensions Act 1995, sections 48 and 147, but only in sidenotes and inverted commas. The draftsman of the Public Interest Disclosure Act preferred a more formal and dignified approach, perhaps so as not to detract from the seriousness of the subject matter. It was, however, inevitable that it would become popularly known as the 'whistle-blowing legislation'.

B. Mandatory Whistle-blowing

Pension schemes

13.04 Section 48 of the Pensions Act 1995 had been enacted as part of a parcel of measures designed to restore confidence in the security of occupational pension

---

[2] 1998 c 23.
[3] *Hansard*, HL (series 5) vol 589, col 889 (11 May 1998).

schemes, which had been undermined by the Maxwell affair.[4] It imposes a positive duty on actuaries and auditors of occupational pension schemes to 'blow the whistle' by giving a written report to the Occupational Pensions Regulatory Authority if they have reasonable cause to believe that there is or has been a breach of any legal duty relevant to the administration of such a scheme on the part of trustees, managers, employers, professional advisers or other prescribed persons, which breach is likely to be of material significance in the exercise of the Authority's functions.[5]

By way of sanction for failure to comply, the Authority may make a (revocable) **13.05** order disqualifying the defaulter from acting as actuary or auditor of any occupational pension scheme,[6] or impose a financial penalty.[7] Section 48(4) says that any other professional adviser, trustee, manager or person involved in the administration of an occupational pension scheme 'may' give a report to the Authority if he has reasonable cause to believe that there is or has been such a breach. The section affords protection against potential actions for breaches of other duties (such as the duty of confidentiality) in relation to the content of reports given under its aegis.[8] A duty to report material breaches of statutory requirements to the Inland Revenue is imposed on auditors and actuaries of appropriate personal pension schemes by the Pensions Schemes Act 1993, section 33A.[9]

Duties of auditors of financial institutions

Those provisions were not novel or unique. Whistle-blowing obligations had **13.06** been imposed on auditors (albeit not by that name) in a number of statutory instruments made during early 1994. They were the fruit of a recommendation in the Bingham Report on the collapse of BCCI,[10] which related only to auditors of institutions authorized under the Banking Act 1987 to carry on a deposit-taking business (that being the remit of the inquiry), but was extended by analogy to other regulated areas of the financial sector.

The Accountants (Banking Act 1987) Regulations 1994[11] required auditors of **13.07** authorized institutions (and reporting accountants) to report to the Bank of England[12] when they had reasonable cause to believe that any of the minimum

---

[4] So Lord Mackay of Ardbrecknish (Minister of State, Department of Social Security) told the House of Lords at Second Reading: *Hansard*, HL (series 5) vol 560, col 975 (24 January 1995).

[5] Pensions Act 1995, s 48(1).

[6] ibid, s 48(8)–(13).

[7] ibid, s 48(7) and s 10.

[8] ibid, s 48(3) and (5).

[9] Inserted by the Pensions Act 1995, s 147.

[10] *Inquiry into the Supervision of the Bank of Credit and Commerce International* (HC (1992–93) no 198), para 3.45.

[11] SI 1994/524, made under the Banking Act 1987, s 47.

[12] Subsequently to the Financial Services Authority: SI 1998/1129.

criteria for authorization in the Banking Act 1987, Schedule 3 were not or might not be fulfilled. Auditors of persons authorized to carry on investment business were put under an obligation to communicate to the relevant regulator matters which they had reasonable cause to believe were (or were likely to be) of material significance for determining whether such persons were fit and proper persons to carry on investment business, or whether disciplinary action should be taken or powers of intervention exercised to protect investors from significant risk of loss.[13] Auditors of building societies and friendly societies were respectively required to furnish to the Building Societies Commission, or Friendly Societies Commission, information of which they became aware in that capacity which was such as to give them reasonable cause to believe that any of the criteria of prudent management in the Building Societies Act 1986, section 45(3), or the Friendly Societies Act 1992, section 50(3), were not or might not be satisfied.[14] Finally, a duty was imposed on auditors of insurance companies to which Part II of the Insurance Companies Act 1982 applied, to communicate to the Secretary of State such matters of which they became aware in that capacity as they had reasonable cause to believe would or might be of material significance to him in determining whether to exercise any of his powers of intervention under that Act.[15]

13.08   Detailed amendments were made to each of those instruments by the Financial Institutions (Prudential Supervision) Regulations 1996.[16] In each case, the range of matters required to be reported was expanded to include, broadly speaking, (a) matters giving reasonable cause to believe that (i) a necessary authorization could be withdrawn from the institution, or (ii) there was, or might be (or have been), a contravention of any provision of the applicable Act (or any rules or regulations made under it), which was likely to be of material significance to the regulator, or (iii) the continuous functioning of the institution might be affected; and (b) matters preventing an auditor from stating in his report that the annual accounts had been prepared in accordance with relevant requirements, or gave a true and fair view. Information in the relevant categories which had been acquired by auditors while acting in another capacity (that of auditors to other, closely linked, bodies) was brought into the net of the reporting requirements.

---

[13] The Auditors (Financial Services Act 1986) Rules 1994, SI 1994/526, made under the Financial Services Act 1986, s 109.

[14] The Building Societies (Auditors) Order 1994, SI 1994/525, made under the Building Societies Act 1986, s 82, and Friendly Societies (Auditors) Order 1994, SI 1994/132, made under the Friendly Societies Act 1992, s 79.

[15] The Auditors (Insurance Companies Act 1982) Regulations 1994, SI 1994/449, made under the Insurance Companies Act 1982, s 21A.

[16] SI 1996/1669, reg 22, Sch 4, implementing Council Directive (EC) 95/26.

Effect of the Financial Services and Markets Act 2000

The legislative framework has been changed again by the Financial Services and **13.09**
Markets Act 2000,[17] with its unitary regulation system. Banks, investment businesses, building societies, friendly societies and insurance companies have all been
brought under the single regulatory umbrella of the Financial Services Authority
with effect from 1 December 2001.[18] Part XXII (sections 340 to 346) relates to auditors and actuaries of persons authorized for the purposes of that Act to carry on
regulated activities.[19] Sections 342(5) and 343(5)[20] empower the Treasury to make
regulations prescribing circumstances in which such an auditor or actuary must
communicate to the Financial Services Authority matters of which he has become
aware in that capacity or while acting as auditor or actuary for a person with close
links[21] to the authorized person.

The Financial Services and Markets Act 2000 (Communications by Auditors) **13.10**
Regulations 2001[22] were made in exercise of those powers on 17 July 2001, to
come into force simultaneously with section 19 of the Act (the general prohibition on carrying on regulated activities without being either authorized or exempt
for the purposes of the Act). That occurred on 1 December 2001.[23] However,
Article 18 of the Financial Services and Markets Act 2000 (Miscellaneous
Provisions) Order 2001[24] makes transitional savings in respect of the predecessor
legislation. It provides that notwithstanding their repeal, the relevant statutory
sections[25] and the regulations made under them continue to have effect (subject to
modifications) in relation to any matter of which an auditor becomes aware in his
capacity as auditor that relates to things done (or not done) before 1 December
2001. All reports are to be directed to the Financial Services Authority whether
made under the old or the new provisions.

---

[17] 2000 c 8.

[18] The Financial Services and Markets Act 2000 (Commencement No 7) Order 2001, SI
2001/3538.

[19] Defined in the Financial Services and Markets Act 2000, s 22, Sch 2 and Financial Services and
Markets Act 2000 (Regulated Activities) Order 2001, SI 2001/544.

[20] Brought into force on 25 February 2001 by Financial Services and Markets Act 2000
(Commencement No 1) Order 2001, SI 2001/516.

[21] See the Financial Services and Markets Act 2000, s 343(8), for the meaning of that expression.

[22] SI 2001/2587.

[23] By virtue of SI 2001/3538.

[24] SI 2001/3650.

[25] That is the Banking Act 1987, s 47, the Financial Services Act 1986, s 109, and the Insurance
Companies Act 1982, s 21A (repealed with the entirety of those Acts by art 3 of the Financial
Services and Markets Act 2000 (Consequential Amendments and Repeals) Order 2001 (SI
2001/3649) as from 1 December 2001) and the Building Societies Act 1986, s 82 and the Friendly
Societies Act 1992, s 79 (repealed as from 1 December 2001 by the Financial Services and Markets
Act 2000 (Mutual Societies) Order 2001, SI 2001/2617, art 13, Schs 3 and 4).

13.11   As their title suggests, the Financial Services and Markets Act 2000 (Communications by Auditors) Regulations 2001 apply only to auditors. They prescribe five sets of circumstances in which the auditor of an authorized person must communicate to the Financial Services Authority information or opinion on matters of which he has become aware in either of the specified capacities.

(a)   He reasonably believes that as regards that authorized person (i) there is or has been (or may be or have been) a contravention of (1) a requirement imposed by or under the Financial Services and Markets Act itself, relating to authorization or the carrying on of a regulated activity, or (2) a requirement imposed by or under another statute contravention of which constitutes an offence which the Authority has power to prosecute under the Act,[26] and (ii) that contravention may be of material significance to the Authority in deciding whether to exercise any of its functions under the Act in respect of that authorized person.

(b)   He reasonably believes that such information or opinion may be of material significance to the Authority in determining whether that person satisfies the threshold conditions for permission to carry on a regulated activity.[27]

(c)   He reasonably believes that person is not, may not be, or may cease to be, a going concern.

(d)   He is precluded from stating in his report that the annual accounts (or other statutorily required financial reports) of that person have been properly prepared in accordance with the applicable legislative provisions, or give a true and fair view of matters.

(e)   He is required to state in his report in relation to that person any of the facts referred to in the Companies Act 1985, section 237(2), (3) or (4A).

13.12   Sections 342(3) and 343(3) provide that an auditor or actuary will not contravene any duty to which he is subject merely by giving the Financial Services Authority information or opinion on matters of which he has become aware in his capacity as auditor or actuary of an authorized person (or a person with close links to an authorized person), so long as he is acting in good faith and reasonably believes that the information or opinion is relevant to any of the Authority's functions. These provisions[28] apply whether the information or opinion is proffered voluntarily, or

---

[26] Financial Services and Markets Act 2000, s 402 confers power on the Financial Services Authority to institute proceedings under the Criminal Justice Act 1993, Pt V (insider dealing) and such money laundering regulations as may be prescribed by the Treasury. The Financial Services and Markets Act 2000 (Regulations Relating to Money Laundering) Regulations 2001, SI 2001/1819 prescribe the Money Laundering Regulations 1993 (SI 1993/1933) for this purpose.

[27] See the Financial Services and Markets Act 2000, s 41, Sch 6 for the threshold conditions.

[28] Modelled on the Banking Act 1987, s 47(1), the Financial Services Act 1986, s 109(1), (5), and the Insurance Companies Act 1982, s 21A(1): cf the Building Societies Act 1986, s 82(8) and the Friendly Societies Act 1992, s 79(8).

in response to a request from the Authority, or in compliance with the duty imposed by regulations made under the sections.

Consequences of breach of whistle-blowing duties

Auditors and actuaries who fail to comply with duties imposed on them under the **13.13**
Financial Services and Markets Act (including duties to whistle-blow imposed by regulations under sections 342 and 343) will be liable to disqualification by the Financial Services Authority from acting for any authorized person: section 345.

There is no provision to the effect that a breach of such duties will be actionable at **13.14**
the suit of a private person who suffers loss as a result. The contrast with sections 71 and 150 (which do explicitly provide for authorized persons who contravene certain provisions of the Act or rules made by the Authority to incur such liabilities in damages) suggests that the omission is deliberate and no such action is intended to lie.[29]

As to whether a common law duty of care might be superimposed on the statutory **13.15**
duty, it has been said[30] that:

> ... the liability of professional advisers, including auditors, for failure to provide accurate information or correct advice can, truly, be said to be in a state of transition or development. As the House of Lords has pointed out, repeatedly, this is an area in which the law is developing pragmatically and incrementally. It is pre-eminently an area in which the legal result is sensitive to the facts...

However, the decision of the House of Lords in *Caparo Industries plc v Dickman*,[31] and perhaps even more in point, that of the Privy Council in *Deloitte Haskins & Sells v National Mutual Life Nominees Ltd*[32] do not afford much support for imposing tortious liabilities on auditors who do not blow the whistle.

C. The Public Interest Disclosure Act 1998

Scheme of the Public Interest Disclosure Act

The Public Interest Disclosure Act 1998 does not impose whistle-blowing oblig- **13.16**
ations or compel anyone to disclose information of any kind. It does not confer on anyone a right to ask for or obtain information. Its contribution to freedom of information is indirect. What it is intended to do is promote and encourage

---

[29] See *X (Minors) v Bedfordshire County Council* [1995] 2 AC 633, HL for general discussion of circumstances in which breach of statutory duty is actionable.

[30] In *Coulthard v Neville Russell* [1998] 1 BCLC 143, 155 CA, *per* Chadwick LJ.

[31] [1990] 2 AC 605 (and see Buxton LJ's discussion of that decision in *Andrew v Kounnis Freeman* [1999] 2 BCLC 641, 654–5, CA).

[32] [1993] AC 774.

disclosures of certain kinds of information which are perceived to be in the public interest, by conferring on persons making such disclosures a measure of protection against potential adverse consequences of their speaking out.

13.17 The only persons to qualify for protection are 'workers', within the special statutory meaning given to the word.[33] Whilst as insiders they are best placed to detect and blow the whistle on malpractice, they have the most to lose by doing so. The aim of the legislation is to remove, so far as possible, the disincentives. The protection afforded is against victimization by their employers. In *ALM Medical Services Ltd v Bladon*, the first case on the legislation to reach the Court of Appeal, Mummery LJ put it as follows:[34]

> The self evident aim of the provisions is to protect employees from unfair treatment (i.e. victimisation and dismissal) for reasonably raising in a responsible way genuine concerns about wrongdoing in the workplace. The provisions strike an intricate balance between (a) promoting the public interest in the detection, exposure and elimination of misconduct, malpractice and potential dangers by those likely to have early knowledge of them, and (b) protecting the respective interests of employers and employees.

13.18 The legislation does not confer immunity from actions by third parties, such as co-workers or customers or clients of the employer, in connection with disclosures within its scope. Nor does it provide a whistle-blower with a special statutory defence to claims for, say, breach of confidence or defamation arising out of a protected disclosure. So far as concerns persons other than his employer, he would have to rely on general common law defences including the 'public interest' defences.

13.19 The Public Interest Disclosure Act operates within the framework of pre-existing employment legislation by inserting a new Part (Part IVA)[35] and adding other provisions[36] into the Employment Rights Act 1996, adopting procedures and remedies established by that Act and its predecessor statutes. Proceedings are commenced in an employment tribunal and appeals (on questions of law only)[37] lie in the first instance to the Employment Appeal Tribunal.

Timing of disclosures

13.20 The Public Interest Disclosure Act was passed on 2 July 1998, but the majority of its provisions were not brought into force until 2 July 1999.[38] That does not mean that only disclosures made on or after 2 July 1999 can qualify for protection. In

---

[33] See para 13.21 below. The meaning of the term 'employer' is correspondingly extended.
[34] [2002] IRLR 807.
[35] Public Interest Disclosure Act 1998, s 1; Employment Rights Act 1996, ss 43A–43L.
[36] Public Interest Disclosure Act 1998, ss 2–15.
[37] Employment Tribunals Act 1996, s 21.
[38] Public Interest Disclosure Act 1998 (Commencement) Order 1999, SI 1999/1547.

Edgar v Met Office,[39] the Employment Appeal Tribunal was asked to decide an appeal on a preliminary point as to whether the London Central Employment Tribunal had jurisdiction to entertain Mr Edgar's complaint that he had been victimized by reason of his making a protected disclosure on 11 March 1999. Consistently with a previous decision of the Scottish Employment Appeal Tribunal, *Stolt Offshore Ltd v Miklaszewicz*,[40] it was held that the complaint could proceed. The crucial date is that of the act by the employer which is alleged to have constituted victimization (11 February 2000, in that case). It is not the date of the disclosure. Thus in the *Stolt Offshore Ltd* case the relevant date was that at which Mr Miklaszewicz was informed his employment was being terminated on the ground of redundancy, not the date of his disclosure about the company's affairs to the Inland Revenue which he alleged to be the real reason for his dismissal; the year 2000, not 1993. An appeal by the company failed in the Court of Session, which confirmed that as it was the dismissal which triggered his right to invoke the statutory remedies it was as at that time that the criteria for a protected disclosure fell to be applied to his earlier action. A submission that revelations to the Inland Revenue in 1993 could not count as disclosure to a 'prescribed person' within the meaning of section 43F[41] because they were not prescribed for the purposes of that section until 1999 was rejected.

Who counts as a 'worker'?

The general definition of 'worker' for the purposes of the Employment Rights Act 1996 is to be found in section 230(3). It includes not just employees,[42] but any individual who contracts personally to do work or perform services for another, unless he is carrying on a profession or business undertaking and that other is a client or customer. In the particular context of Part IVA and its associated provisions, the concept is broadened[43] to include individuals who fall into any of the following four categories:

13.21

(a) individuals who are introduced or supplied to do work by a third party such as an agency, and whose terms of engagement are substantially determined not by them but by the persons for whom they work or the third parties;[44]

(b) independent contractors who undertake for the execution of work in a place not under the control or management of the other party to the contract, for

---

[39] [2002] ICR 149.

[40] [2001] IRLR 656, Scottish EAT, [2002] IRLR 344, Ct of Session.

[41] See paras 13.43–13.44 below.

[42] Defined as persons working under contracts of employment, that is contracts of service or apprenticeship: Employment Rights Act 1996, s 230(1), (2).

[43] ibid, ss 43K, 47B(3), 230(6).

[44] Where it is the third party which substantially determines the terms, that party will be 'the employer' for the purposes of the legislation: ibid, s 43K(2)(a).

the purposes of that other's business, and would satisfy the general definition with the omission of the word 'personally';

(c) doctors, dentists, ophthalmologists, and pharmacists working in the National Health Service;[45]

(d) individuals provided with work experience pursuant to a training course or programme, or training for employment (otherwise than on a course run by an educational establishment).[46]

Excepted categories of worker

13.22 The legislation applies across the private and public sectors, including to persons in the employment of the Crown,[47] but there are, inevitably, exceptions. It does not apply to members of the armed forces,[48] or to the Parliamentary staffs.[49] Employments for the purposes of the Security Service, the Secret Intelligence Service, and the Government Communications Headquarters are outside its scope, as originally was any other Crown employment certified by a Minister as requiring to be excluded for the purpose of safeguarding national security.[50] The certification procedure has since been abolished,[51] such that there is no bar to Crown employees outside the three specified agencies presenting complaints to employment tribunals under the whistle-blowing legislation. However, the Employment Tribunals Act 1996, section 10 (as amended)[52] will continue to provide that if on a complaint of unfair dismissal under section 111 of the Employment Rights Act 1996, it is shown that the action complained of was taken for the purpose of safeguarding national security, the tribunal shall dismiss the complaint (albeit now without the provision that a Ministerial certificate shall be conclusive evidence of that).[53]

13.23 Another exception was made for the police.[54] In the course of Parliamentary debates on the Public Interest Disclosure Bill the government spokesman, Ian

---

[45] The health authority is 'the employer': ibid, s 43K(2)(b).

[46] In such a case the person providing the work experience or training is 'the employer': ibid, s 43K(2)(c).

[47] ibid, s 191 (as amended by the Public Interest Disclosure Act 1998, s 10).

[48] ibid, s 192.

[49] ibid, ss 194, 195.

[50] ibid, s 193 (as amended by the Public Interest Disclosure Act 1998, s 11).

[51] By the Employment Relations Act 1999, s 41 and Sch 8, brought into force on 16 July 2001: Employment Relations Act 1999 (Commencement No 8) Order 2001, SI 2001/1187, as amended by Employment Relations Act 1999 (Commencement No 8) (Amendment) Order 2001, SI 2001/1461.

[52] By the Employment Relations Act 1999, s 41 and Sch 8, brought into force on 16 July 2001 (see n 51 above).

[53] See Employment Tribunals Act 1996, ss 10–10B for the special rules governing tribunal proceedings in cases involving national security and confidential information.

[54] Employment Rights Act 1996, s 200 (as amended by the Public Interest Disclosure Act 1998, s 13).

McCartney (Minister of State, Department of Trade and Industry) explained their exclusion by saying that they were office-holders subject to a separate regulatory regime, but twice referred to a government commitment that the existing regulatory regime would be examined and amended as necessary to ensure a level of protection equivalent to that in the Bill.[55] 'There will be no disparity in the treatment of police officers, or in their capacity to whistleblow in the circumstances set out in the Bill.' No changes to police regulations followed, but the promise has been kept. When section 37 of the Police Reform Act 2002 comes into force, it will insert a new section into the Employment Rights Act 1996, section 43KA, the effect of which will be to confer the full benefit of the statutory code of protection on the police.

The rationale for the total exclusion of the intelligence agencies was stated by the Minister as follows:[56]   **13.24**

> Anyone who works in them could have access to sensitive information, even when that is not part of their main duties. The ethos of these agencies is secrecy, and blowing the whistle to an outsider is contrary to that ethos . . . It is not the case that workers in the agencies will have no means of expressing legitimate concerns. They will be able to raise them under well-established internal procedures. If an intelligence agency employee believes that his or her concerns are not being adequately dealt with, they can raise the matter with the staff counsellor, who has a broad remit across the three security agencies . . . and can act quickly and effectively to resolve any concerns that may be raised. In addition, there are internal disciplinary, security and audit procedures that can be used to investigate possible illegalities and problems. Furthermore, all Crown servants are subject to the Crown Office guidance document 'Giving Evidence or Information about Suspected Crimes'. Taken together, these procedures provide the type of safeguard that will encourage people in the security services to raise matters of concern in a responsible manner consistent with the aims of the Bill.

Part IVA of the Employment Rights Act 1996

The scheme of Part IVA is as follows: **13.25**

(a) to limit the ambit of 'protected disclosure' to 'workers' as defined by the extended definition;

(b) to define a 'protected disclosure' by reference to a 'qualifying disclosure';

(c) to define a 'qualifying disclosure' by reference to its subject matter;

(d) to limit 'protected disclosures' to 'qualifying disclosures' made to specified persons or in specified circumstances (unless concerned with 'exceptionally serious failures').

---

[55] *Hansard,* HC (series 5) vol 310, cols 1143–44 (24 April 1998): see also Standing Committee D, Public Interest Disclosure Bill, cols 17–18 (11 March 1998).

[56] *Hansard,* HC (series 5) vol 310, cols 1141–42 (24 April 1998).

Qualifying disclosures

13.26   Section 43A of the Employment Rights Act 1996 defines a 'protected disclosure' as a 'qualifying disclosure' made by a worker in accordance with sections 43C to 43H of the statute. Section 43B(1) defines a 'qualifying disclosure' as any disclosure[57] of information which, in the reasonable belief of the worker making the disclosure, tends to show one or more of the following (which the statute calls 'relevant failures'[58]):

(a) that a criminal offence has been committed, is being committed or is likely to be committed;

(b) that a person has failed, is failing or is likely to fail to comply with any legal obligation to which he is subject;[59]

(c) that a miscarriage of justice has occurred, is occurring or is likely to occur;

(d) that the health or safety of any individual has been, is being or is likely to be endangered;

(e) that the environment has been, is being or is likely to be damaged;

(f) that information tending to show any of the above has been, is being or is likely to be deliberately concealed.

13.27   There is no territorial limitation on the scope of section 43B(1); on the contrary, section 43B(2) expressly declares it to be immaterial where in the world a relevant failure has occurred, is occurring or would occur, and what law applies or would apply to it. An actual or potential breach of a legal obligation imposed by a foreign jurisdiction would fall within category (b). (However, breaches of non-statutory guidance or codes of practice issued by or on behalf of the United Kingdom government[60] would not per se constitute breaches of legal obligations.)

13.28   It is also immaterial (although the statute does not spell this out in terms) whose acts or omissions constitute a relevant failure. They may be, but do not have to be, acts or omissions of the employer of the worker making the disclosure, or fellow workers of his. That is implicit in the absence of any requirement for the 'relevant

---

[57] The word 'disclose' may connote ignorance of the information on the part of the recipient prior to its being communicated to him. So that a worker who would otherwise qualify for protection is not deprived of it by the information he imparts already being known to the person he chooses to tell, the Employment Rights Act 1996, s 43L(3) provides that in any case where the person receiving information is already aware of it, 'disclosure of information' is to be read as meaning 'bringing the information to his attention'.

[58] Employment Rights Act 1996, s 43B(5).

[59] In *Parkins v Sodexho Ltd* [2002] IRLR 109, the Employment Appeal Tribunal held that this category includes a breach by the employer of a term of the worker's contract of employment.

[60] Such as the codes of practice issued under the Freedom of Information Act 2000, ss 45, 46, as to which see ch 5 above.

failure' to be in any way associated with his employment (and in the wording of section 43C(1)(b)[61]).

There does not have to be a 'relevant failure'. It is sufficient that the worker has a **13.29** reasonable belief that the information tends to show such a failure. The requirement that his belief be reasonable introduces an element of objectivity. If no reasonable person could think that particular information tended to show a relevant failure, then its disclosure could not be protected however well-intentioned.

There are two situations in which a disclosure of information cannot be a qualify- **13.30** ing disclosure even if the section 43B(1) conditions are satisfied. One occurs where information has been disclosed in the course of obtaining legal advice. A further disclosure by the recipient of the information (that is the legal adviser) will not be a qualifying disclosure if legal professional privilege could be claimed in respect of the information in legal proceedings.[62] The other occurs where the person making the disclosure commits a criminal offence in so doing.[63] The most obvious example would be a breach of the Official Secrets Act 1989,[64] but there are currently many other statutory prohibitions on disclosure of information, the majority of which carry a criminal penalty for infringement.[65]

Disclosures constituting criminal offences

For the latter exception to apply, there does not need to have been an actual **13.31** conviction. Although that is the clearest-cut method of establishing guilt for the purposes of section 43B(3), an employer can rely on the sub-section by way of defence in a claim for victimization even if the applicant escapes prosecution for the relevant disclosure. There was anxious debate in the House of Lords[66] about this clause of the Public Interest Disclosure Bill and the deterrent effect it might have on would-be whistle-blowers. An amendment was proposed to limit the operation of section 43B(3) to cases in which the worker had acted in the knowledge that disclosure constituted a criminal offence, or recklessly as to whether that was so. Lord Borrie, who promoted the Bill in the House of Lords, did not support the amendment,[67] saying that it was inappropriate to seek to make a disclosure involving what was currently a criminal offence appear to be in the public interest. He preferred to rely on the promised review of existing statutory bars to disclosure, and the statement of intention in the White Paper *Your Right to Know*[68]

---

[61] See para 13.41 below.
[62] Employment Rights Act 1996, s 43B(4).
[63] ibid, s 43B(3).
[64] See ch 12 above.
[65] See ch 6 above.
[66] At Committee stage: *Hansard*, HL (series 5) vol 590, cols 612–619 (5 June 1998).
[67] ibid, cols 616–618.
[68] Cm 3818, at para 3.20.

that the forthcoming Freedom of Information Act would, where appropriate, repeal or amend them.[69]

13.32 Lord Borrie also agreed with the opinion expressed earlier in the debate by Lord
Nolan[70] that if the question of whether a criminal offence had been committed
arose in a civil tribunal, the criminal standard of proof should still be applied.
They cited a judgment given by Lord Lane when he was Lord Chief Justice in a
case[71] where it was held that the Solicitors Disciplinary Tribunal should have
applied the criminal standard of proof in disciplinary proceedings concerning an
allegation of criminal conduct.

> Having in mind the situations that may arise under this Bill, the consequences for
> the reputation and employability of an employee who is dismissed because he is
> thought to have committed an offence of some kind will be no less grave than those
> for a professional such as a solicitor who is struck off as a result of allegations of a se-
> rious crime affecting his professional integrity.

Whether the courts will draw that analogy between disciplinary proceedings and
employment tribunal proceedings remains to be seen. A similar result could perhaps be arrived at by a different route. In *R v Home Secretary, ex p Khawaja*,[72] the
House of Lords heard conjoined appeals by persons who had been detained as illegal entrants on the basis that they had obtained leave to enter by committing an
offence of deception. It was held that on their applications for judicial review, it
was for the immigration officers to prove that leave to enter had been obtained by
deception, but to the civil standard.[73]

> ... the choice between the two standards is not one of any great moment. It is largely
> a matter of words ... The flexibility of the civil standard of proof suffices to ensure
> that the court will require the high degree of probability which is appropriate to
> what is at stake ... A preponderance of probability suffices; but the degree of prob-
> ability must be such that the court is satisfied.[74]

Persons to whom protected disclosures are to be made

13.33 The Public Interest Disclosure Act was not designed as a charter for whistle-
blowing to all and sundry. Inherent in the provisions of sections 43C to 43H is a
notion of proportionality; the extent of the disclosure should be commensurate
with the seriousness of the relevant failure in question, and no wider than reason-

---

[69] See ch 6 above.
[70] *Hansard*, HL (series 5) vol 590, col 614 (5 June 1998).
[71] *Re A Solicitor* [1993] QB 69, DC.
[72] [1984] 1 AC 74.
[73] Consistently with the position apparently established in *Hornal v Neuberger Products Ltd*
[1957] 1 QB 247, CA, namely that when a question of whether a criminal offence has been committed arises in civil proceedings, the civil standard of proof is the applicable one.
[74] [1984] 1 AC 74, 112–114, *per* Lord Scarman; and see *R v Hants CC, ex p Ellerton* [1985] 1
WLR 749.

ably necessary for it to be dealt with effectively. The specified categories of recipient are: the employer or other responsible person (section 43C); a legal adviser (section 43D); a Minister of the Crown (section 43E); and a prescribed person (section 43F). However, Part IVA also provides for 'disclosure in other cases' (section 43G) and for 'disclosure of exceptionally serious failure' (section 43H). Neither of those sections prescribes any particular class of recipients.

In practice, the exercise of assessing to whom disclosure may safely be made will **13.34** involve fine judgments and recourse sometimes to legal advice. As Lord Borrie himself acknowledged, 'This Bill will become a statute which will not be easy for the ordinary worker in the workplace to interpret without some help'.[75] One available source of assistance for people concerned about malpractice in the workplace and uncertain what to do about it is the confidential helpline[76] operated by Public Concern at Work, the charity which played a large part in preparing the Public Interest Disclosure Bill and now disseminates information about the legislation and promotes the adoption of whistle-blowing policies.

Good faith

The minimum requirement for protection applicable in all situations bar one is **13.35** that the worker be acting 'in good faith'. The exception is for disclosure to a legal adviser in the course of obtaining legal advice.[77] This may be—but does not necessarily have to be—on the question whether the information could safely be communicated to anyone else.

There is no guidance to be found in the statute as to the meaning of 'good faith' **13.36** but it is a concept well known to the courts. A claim is made 'in good faith' when it is made 'honestly and with no ulterior motive'.[78]

Another criterion for the applicability of each of sections 43F, 43G and 43H[79] is **13.37** that the worker making the disclosure in question reasonably believes that the information disclosed, and any allegation contained in it, are substantially true. The inclusion of that express requirement in those sections, in contrast to its omission from sections 43C to 43E, tends to suggest that a belief in the truth of the information disclosed (and any allegation contained in it) is not necessary for

---

[75] *Hansard*, HL (series 5) vol 589, col 904 (11 May 1998).
[76] Helpline 020 7404 6609: website http://www.pcaw.co.uk
[77] Employment Rights Act 1996, s 43D.
[78] *Central Estates (Belgravia) Ltd v Woolgar* [1971] 3 WLR 571, 575, CA, *per* Lord Denning MR, albeit in the different statutory context of leasehold reform. In similar vein Sir Richard Scott V-C said in relation to the equitable duties of receivers that he did not think the concept of good faith should be diluted by treating it as capable of being breached by conduct that is not dishonest or otherwise tainted by bad faith. 'In my judgment the breach of a duty of good faith should in this area as in all others require some dishonesty or improper motive, some element of bad faith, to be established.': *Medforth v Blake* [2000] Ch 86, 103, CA.
[79] Employment Rights Act 1996, ss 43F(1)(b)(ii), 43G(1)(b), 43H(1)(b).

a disclosure to qualify for protection under those earlier sections. However, a worker who put about information which he did not at least think on credible grounds might be true, such as to call for investigation, would surely have difficulty satisfying the 'good faith' criterion for the purposes of section 43C or section 43E, while one who acted in the knowledge or belief that the information he was communicating was false must fail.

13.38   During debate on the Bill, Lord Borrie said:[80]

> This Bill is meant to encourage any worker in any workplace who discovers a malpractice of some kind . . . to disclose those matters in the public interest. It is not concerned with a worker who wishes to disclose some malpractice for his own ends, possibly to try to gain a private advantage. As the title of the Bill[81] clearly indicates, it is concerned with the public interest.

An analogy can be drawn with the defence of qualified privilege in defamation cases. That defence protects the maker of a statement the making of which was in the public interest, but the protection is forfeited if the maker's dominant motive was desire to injure the person defamed (malice), or to obtain some private advantage.[82]

13.39   The concept of malice was mentioned in passing by the Employment Appeal Tribunal at the preliminary hearing of the employer's appeal in *ALM Medical Services Ltd v Bladon*,[83] when some 'general remarks' were uttered which, it was said, might give some assistance to tribunals.

> Obviously enough, the purpose of this part [Part IVA] is to give protection to those employees who, in broad terms, in good faith and for good reason, make disclosures about their employer's business. However, the legislature obviously intended that these provisions should not give licence to malicious and unjustified complaints by employees against their employers and an effort is therefore made in these provisions to ensure that the protection given to employees is limited by defined requirements of good faith and reasonableness.

Mr Bladon had succeeded at first instance in a claim for unfair dismissal for having made a protected disclosure while employed as a charge nurse in a nursing home. He had expressed concerns, first to his employer and then to Social Services, about patient welfare and care at the home. The Employment Appeal Tribunal refused to allow the employer's appeal to proceed to a full hearing on the ground that it had no reasonable prospect of success. The Court of Appeal allowed the employer's appeal against that decision and remitted the case to the Tribunal

---

[80] *Hansard*, HL (series 5) vol 590, col 616 (5 June 1998).

[81] The long title reads 'An Act to protect individuals who make certain disclosures of information in the public interest; to allow such individuals to bring action in respect of victimisation; and for connected purposes'.

[82] *Reynolds v Times Newspapers Ltd* [2001] 2 AC 127, 194–5, HL; *Horrocks v Lowe* [1975] AC 135, 149–50, HL.

[83] See para 13.17 above.

for rehearing, but on a ground which had not been fully developed in the Employment Appeal Tribunal, namely that the Tribunal had erred in excluding certain relevant evidence which the employer had wished to call. The judgments in the Court of Appeal contained no criticism of the Employment Appeal Tribunal's approach to the other points which were taken before it.[84]

An example of a situation in which a worker might be said to have acted for an   **13.40** ulterior motive (or 'his own ends') would be if he made a disclosure of some past breach of legal obligation not because he genuinely feared that it might be repeated with harmful consequences, but in order to embarrass his employer or get a colleague into trouble. The question arises whether it is only if that was his sole or 'dominant' motive that he could be found to have misused the statutory protection and lost the benefit of it, or merely having mixed motives could disqualify him. A suggestion to the latter effect in the Kennedy report on the paediatric unit at Bristol Royal Infirmary,[85] made in relation to the whistle-blowing activities of Dr Steven Bolsin, has been rejected by the government.[86] By analogy with the authorities on qualified privilege, it is suggested that the former approach is the one which the courts are in due course likely to endorse.[87]

Internal disclosures—sections 43C and 43E

Provided that the minimum 'good faith' requirement is met, a worker may with   **13.41** impunity transmit information falling within Employment Rights Act 1996, section 43B(1) to the following persons:

(a) in all cases, to his employer;[88]
(b) where his employer has authorized him to use a procedure for making such disclosures to some other person, to that person in accordance with that procedure;[89]

---

[84] See also paras 13.46, 13.50, and 13.51 below.

[85] *Learning from Bristol* (Cm 5207) at Annex A, para 194.

[86] In a letter dated 5 October 2001 from John Hutton (Minister of State, Department of Health) to Public Concern at Work confirming agreement with that organization's interpretation of 'good faith' (namely that an ulterior or improper motive can only prevent protection if it is found to be the dominant or primary motive for the disclosure). In the Parliamentary debate on the government's response to the Kennedy report, the Minister reiterated (in reply to a question from Ross Cranston MP) that the government's legal advice supported that interpretation and confirmed that Dr Bolsin would have been protected under the Public Interest Disclosure Act had it been in force at the relevant time: *Hansard*, HC (series 5) vol 378, cols 497–8, 508 (17 January 2002).

[87] cf *Shillito v Van Leer* [1997] IRLR 495, in which the Employment Appeal Tribunal upheld a rejection of Mr Shillito's claim to have been disciplined for performing his functions as a health and safety representative contrary to the Employment Protection (Consolidation) Act 1978 s 22A (now the Employment Rights Act 1996, s 44). Among the real reasons for the employer's action as found by the tribunal was that he had acted 'in bad faith'. 'This was not a case of mixed motives but of an intention solely to embarrass the company and not to perform his health and safety function.'

[88] Employment Rights Act 1996, s 43C(1)(a).

[89] ibid, s 43C(2).

(c) where he reasonably believes that the relevant failure relates solely or mainly to the conduct of a person other than his employer, or any other matter for which a person other than his employer has legal responsibility, to that other person;[90]

(d) where his employer is an individual appointed by a Minister under an enactment, or a body any of whose members are so appointed, to *a* (perhaps surprisingly, not *that*) Minister.[91]

13.42 The relatively relaxed criteria for that range of disclosures reflect two of the main strands of thinking behind the Public Interest Disclosure Act.[92] One was to encourage workers to raise concerns internally in the first instance, giving those responsible a fair chance to put matters right without outside intervention or unwelcome publicity. The other was to encourage employers to facilitate internal raising of concerns and take notice of concerns so raised, in the knowledge that failure to do so would justify their being more widely aired.[93] The Public Interest Disclosure Act imposed no duty on employers to establish whistle-blowing procedures for their staff, or to take any action in response to disclosures made under section 43C (or section 43E), but has given them a strong incentive to do both.

Disclosure to prescribed persons—section 43F

13.43 If a worker prefers for any reason whatsoever not to raise his concern internally, he may be able to take advantage of section 43F of the Employment Rights Act 1996. For that section to apply, good faith by itself is not enough. He must reasonably believe that the relevant failure which is concerning him falls within the description of matters in respect of which one of the persons prescribed by the Secretary of State for Trade and Industry for the purpose of receiving disclosures under the section is prescribed. If so, he may report it to that prescribed person, but only if he also reasonably believes that the information disclosed, and any allegation contained in it, are substantially true. It would seem that not too strict an interpretation will be placed on the expression 'substantially true'. By analogy with the approach of the Employment Appeal Tribunal in *ALM Medical Services Ltd v Bladon* to the expression 'substantially the same information' in the context of section 43G,[94] a broad, common-sense approach is likely to be adopted. In *Holden v*

---

[90] Employment Rights Act 1996, s 43C(1)(b).
[91] ibid, s 43E.
[92] See the second report of the Nolan Committee on Standards in Public Life as quoted by Lord Borrie when introducing the Bill to the House of Lords: *Hansard*, HL (series 5) vol 589, col 889 (11 May 1998).
[93] Under s 43G: see paras 13.49–13.51 below.
[94] See para 13.50 below.

Connex South Eastern Ltd,[95] Mr Holden successfully claimed that he had been victimized and unfairly dismissed from his employment as a train driver for making protected disclosures (some in the form of reports to HM Railway Inspectorate) about health and safety issues, including incidents of signals passed at danger. The respondent contended that his disclosures were unprotected because not all of the allegations contained in his reports had been correct. The Tribunal expressed itself satisfied that he had reasonably believed his allegations to be substantially true, having 'relied on information within his own knowledge and that received after making appropriate enquiry which he received from credible sources'. Having noted that Mr Holden was at a disadvantage compared to the respondent, which held detailed information about the incidents, the Tribunal continued 'Where such a situation exists, it would be wrong to construe the legislation in such a narrow way as made it necessary for every allegation in any disclosure to have to be proved to 100%; that would defeat the object of the legislation . . .'.

To date, only one order has been made under section 43F. The Public Interest **13.44** Disclosure (Prescribed Persons) Order 1999[96] lists a variety of persons, bodies and authorities with an interest in receiving information about 'relevant failures' of one kind or another, and power to act on it. Their fields cover a broad range of matters, as the following examples illustrate: the Director of the Serious Fraud Office, the Criminal Cases Review Commission, the Health and Safety Executive, the Environment Agency, the Commissioners of Inland Revenue and Customs and Excise, the Financial Services Authority, the Comptroller and Auditor General of the National Audit Office, the Charity Commissioners, and the Rail Regulator. An omission to note is that of the police. The coverage is not comprehensive: one addition which experience has already shown might usefully be made to the list is that of social services. Two of the earliest cases under the legislation to reach the tribunals, *ALM Medical Services Ltd v Bladon*[97] and *Everett v Miyano Care Services Ltd,*[98] involved disclosures to social services of concerns about maltreatment of residents at a nursing home and a care home respectively. In each case the tribunal had to apply the more exacting criteria set by section 43G, with the differing results discussed below.[99]

---

[95] London South Employment Tribunal, Case No 2301550/00 (15 April 2002). The decision is being appealed as to both liability and quantum.
[96] SI 1999/1549.
[97] See paras 13.17 and 13.39 above.
[98] Brighton Employment Tribunal, Case No 3101180/00 (6 April 2000).
[99] At 13.50, 13.51 and 13.53 below.

External disclosures—sections 43G and 43H

Common factors

13.45 Where a worker has no prescribed person to turn to, an external disclosure must be brought within either section 43G ('disclosure in other cases') or section 43H ('disclosure of exceptionally serious failure') to qualify for protection. In addition to the 'good faith' requirement, there are three other criteria common to those sections:

(a) the worker must reasonably believe that the information disclosed, and any allegation contained in it, are substantially true (cf section 43F);

(b) he must not make the disclosure for purposes of personal gain (but in determining whether that is the case, any reward payable by or under any enactment is to be disregarded);[100]

(c) in all the circumstances of the case, it is reasonable for him to make the disclosure.

Section 43H : 'exceptionally serious failures'

13.46 Section 43G prescribes a number of factors to which particular regard must be had in assessing the reasonableness of the worker's conduct in making the disclosure.[101] Section 43H is less prescriptive, specifying one only: the identity of the person to whom it was made.[102] That is perhaps unsurprising, given the remaining criterion for the applicability of that section: that the relevant failure be 'of an exceptionally serious nature'. What kinds of relevant failure count as 'exceptionally serious' is, of course, a matter of judgment as to which opinions may legitimately vary, and only time will tell what the tribunals think, although there are some—such as those posing a real risk to life—which it is difficult to imagine not being so characterized. In *ALM Medical Services Ltd v Bladon*, the Employment Appeal Tribunal said that it was far from clear that, had it been necessary for the tribunal to consider section 43H, they would not have concluded it applied.

> Patients were at risk here and, in particular . . . there was a complaint that patients' record cards were not being kept up to date and . . . medication records were not being kept . . . It is difficult to imagine anything more obviously important for a worker in a nursing home establishment to have concern about than the care of patients or residents . . .

13.47 The express reference to the identity of the recipient of the information serves as a reminder that section 43H is not intended to give workers carte blanche even in exceptionally serious cases. If, say, a telephone call to the police or the social services is all that is necessary to set investigations in train, a worker giving the story

---

[100] Employment Rights Act 1996, s 43L(2).
[101] ibid, s 43G(3): see paras 13.51–13.52 below.
[102] ibid, s 43H(2).

to the local newspaper is liable to forfeit the statutory protection. There may be circumstances in which going straight to the press can be justified, but they are likely to be few and far between. It is well established in comparable common law contexts that it does not follow from a communication of information being in the public interest that communicating it to the public is necessarily appropriate. For example, both Lord Griffiths and Lord Goff of Chieveley warned against potential abuse of the public interest defence to an action for breach of confidence in their judgments in the *Spycatcher* case.[103] Lord Griffiths said:

> Even if the balance comes down in favour of publication, it does not follow that publication should be to the world through the media. In certain circumstances the public interest may be better served by a limited form of publication perhaps to the police or some other authority who can follow up a suspicion that wrongdoing may lurk beneath the cloak of confidence. Those authorities will be under a duty not to abuse the confidential information and to use it only for the purpose of their inquiry.

Section 43G: conditions for applicability

13.48 The scope of section 43G is not restricted to relevant failures of any specified degree of seriousness, although seriousness is one of the factors to which a tribunal is required to have regard in determining whether a disclosure was reasonable for the purposes of that section.[104] However, the section cannot be relied on unless, in addition to the four criteria set out above in paragraph 13.45, one of the three conditions specified in section 43G(2) is satisfied.[105]

13.49 Those conditions are as follows:

(a) the worker reasonably believed at the time that he would be subjected to a detriment by his employer if he made disclosure to him or to a prescribed person; or

(b) there was no prescribed person and the worker reasonably believed it to be likely that evidence relating to the relevant failure would be concealed or destroyed if he made disclosure to the employer; or

(c) the worker had previously made disclosure of substantially the same information to the employer[106] or a prescribed person in accordance with section 43F.

---

[103] *A-G v Guardian Newspapers Ltd (No 2)* [1990] 1 AC 109, 268–9, 282–3, HL.
[104] Employment Rights Act 1996, s 43G(3)(b): see further para 13.52 below.
[105] ibid, s 43G(1).
[106] In this connection, it should be noted that a worker who makes a qualifying disclosure to a person other than his employer in accordance with a procedure authorized by his employer is to be treated as having made the disclosure to his employer: s 43C(2).

Previous disclosure to employer

13.50   The expression 'substantially the same information' is undefined,[107] but its meaning was considered by the Employment Appeal Tribunal in *ALM Medical Services
Ltd v Bladon*. The Tribunal had found the third condition to be satisfied by Mr
Bladon's having sent a fax to his employer setting out his concerns. One of the
grounds of appeal was that there were differences between the complaints made in
the fax and his subsequent telephone call to social services, such that the Tribunal
had erred in law in considering that the information disclosed on those occasions
was 'substantially the same'. This was rejected as unarguable. It was sufficient that
the causes of concern put forward on each occasion were that patients were being
put at risk by failures of care. It mattered not if the examples given were not identical. In the words of Judge Collins:

> . . . the phrase is not to be construed technically having regard to the purpose of the
> legislation as I have stated it broadly. The legislature is endeavouring to strike a bal-
> ance protecting the rights of employees while ensuring that employers are not the
> object of malicious and unjustified complaints. It would, in our judgment, be
> wholly inappropriate for tribunals to embark upon an exercise of a nice and detailed
> analysis of the disclosure to the employer, compared with the disclosure to the out-
> side body, for the purpose of deciding whether the test in section 43G(2)(c) has been
> made out. The correct approach, in our judgment, is for tribunals to adopt a com-
> monsense broad approach when deciding whether or not the disclosure is 'substan-
> tially the same'.

13.51   Section 43G(3)(e) provides that it is mandatory when assessing reasonableness
under section 43G(1) in a previous disclosure case to take account of any action
which was taken or might reasonably have been expected as a result of the previous disclosure. It appears implicit that the employer or prescribed person should
normally be given a reasonable time to respond. However, the length of time it is
reasonable to allow is a question of fact, and in cases of urgency it may not be very
long at all. Another ground of appeal rejected as unarguable by the Employment
Appeal Tribunal in *ALM Medical Services Ltd v Bladon* was that the Tribunal had
been perverse to conclude that the disclosure to social services had been reasonable in view of the short lapse of time between the date of the fax, 22 August 1999,
and 31 August 1999, the date of the telephone call to the local authority. A second
matter of which account is required to be taken in the case of a previous disclosure
to an employer is whether the worker complied with any authorized procedure.[108]
If there is a whistle-blowing procedure and the worker chooses not to follow it, he
does so at his own risk. Conversely, an employer who does not establish such a

---

[107]   Except inasmuch as s 43G(4) provides that the addition of information about the action
taken (or not taken) by the employer or prescribed person in response to the earlier disclosure is not
to prevent the later disclosure from being of substantially the same information.
[108]   Employment Rights Act 1996, s 43G(3)(f).

procedure takes the chance that internal disclosures will be made to people without the requisite authority to deal with them, or dealt with inefficiently, with the result that a worker's then going outside the organization may not be unreasonable. By this indirect means the statute promotes the institution, and use, of such procedures, without making them obligatory.

Reasonableness of disclosure

Section 43G(3) identifies other factors to which regard must be had when determining whether disclosure was reasonable in all the circumstances. These apply in any case where reliance is placed on the section. One is whether the relevant failure was continuing, or likely to recur.[109] It is obviously easier to justify disclosure where there is ongoing danger or malpractice, although there may also be a public interest in the exposure of past iniquities. Another is whether the making of the disclosure constituted a breach of a duty of confidentiality owed by the employer to some third party.[110] This provision was introduced by way of government amendment during the passage of the Public Interest Disclosure Bill. Examples given in support were the situations of a patient whose medical records were released by a doctor's receptionist, or a bank employee who revealed details of a customer's account. Regard must also be had to the identity of the person to whom disclosure is made[111] and to the seriousness of the relevant failure.[112]   **13.52**

The need for a worker minded to make a disclosure to an outsider to stop and think carefully before doing so was illustrated by the case of *Everett v Miyano Care Services Ltd*.[113] Miss Everett was refused interim relief[114] on the basis that while the Tribunal Chairman was satisfied that the subject matter of her disclosure (danger to health or safety) qualified for protection, and the disclosure was the principal reason for her dismissal, he had serious doubts on the evidence whether she could bring herself within section 43G. She had admitted not having even thought of talking to her employer about her concerns, and said that if she had thought of that, and had regard to the complaints procedure in its handbook, she would have had no reason not to tell the director because he had always been approachable.   **13.53**

---

[109] ibid, s 43G(3)(c).
[110] ibid, s 43G(3)(d).
[111] ibid, s 43G(3)(a).
[112] ibid, s 43G(3)(b).
[113] See para 13.44 above.
[114] See para 13.69 below.

Rights and remedies

The right not to be unfairly dismissed

13.54 If the only, or principal, reason for an employee[115] being dismissed (or selected for redundancy when other employees in a similar position were not) is that he had made a protected disclosure, that dismissal is automatically unfair. The reasonableness of the employer's action does not arise for consideration. That is the effect of the Employment Rights Act 1996, sections 103A and 105(6A), which were respectively inserted by the Public Interest Disclosure Act 1998, sections 5 and 6. This is so from the outset of any particular employment, on account of exceptions to the general rule that a minimum qualifying period of service is required to bring an unfair dismissal claim.[116] Nor is any upper age limit applied to claims under these heads.[117]

13.55 The concept of dismissal is, of course, not confined to termination of an employment contract by the employer. It also applies to termination by the employee in circumstances where the employer's conduct has been such as to entitle him to terminate the contract without notice, that is to say constructive dismissal,[118] and to non-renewal of a fixed term contract.[119]

Proving the reason for dismissal

13.56 In all three situations it has to be established that the reason for the dismissal was the making of a protected disclosure, as to which the statute assists the employee by providing[120] that, in determining whether a dismissal is fair or unfair, it is for the employer to show the reason (or, if more than one, the principal reason) for the dismissal. That this applies even where the employee is alleging that the reason for his dismissal was one of those which renders a dismissal automatically unfair (such as the making of a protected disclosure)[121] was affirmed by the Court of Appeal in *Maund v Penwith District Council*.[122]

13.57 In that case the employee had been ostensibly dismissed for redundancy but alleged the real reason to have been his trade union activities, which would have

---

[115] For the meaning of 'employee', see para 13.21 above. The Employment Rights Act 1996, s 191(4) makes clear that Crown servants are to be treated as employees for the purposes of the unfair dismissal provisions in Part X of the Act.

[116] See the Employment Rights Act 1996, s 108(3)(ff) (inserted by the Public Interest Disclosure Act 1998, s 7(1)) and (h).

[117] Employment Rights Act 1996, s 109(2)(ff) (inserted by the Public Interest Disclosure Act 1998, s 7(2)) and (h).

[118] Employment Rights Act 1996, s 95(1)(c).

[119] ibid, s 95(1)(b).

[120] ibid, s 98(1).

[121] Under ibid, s 103A, see para 13.54 above.

[122] [1984] ICR 143.

rendered the dismissal automatically unfair.[123] The industrial tribunal had held that this was for the employee to establish, but the Employment Appeal Tribunal and Court of Appeal disagreed. In the words of Griffiths LJ:

> If an employer produces evidence to the tribunal that appears to show that the reason for the dismissal is redundancy, as they undoubtedly did in this case, then the burden passes to the employee to show that there is a real issue as to whether that was the true reason. The employee cannot do this by merely asserting in argument that it was not the true reason: an evidential burden rests upon him to produce some evidence that casts doubts upon the employer's reason. The graver the allegation, the heavier will be the burden. Allegations of fraud or malice should not be lightly cast about without evidence to support them.
>
> But his burden is a lighter burden than the legal burden placed upon the employer; it is not for the employee to prove the reason for his dismissal, but merely to produce evidence sufficient to raise the issue or, to put it another way, that raises some doubt about the reason for the dismissal. Once this evidential burden is discharged, the onus remains upon the employer to prove the reason for the dismissal.

That authority was applied by the London (North) Employment Tribunal in **13.58** *Fernandes v Netcom Consultants (UK) Ltd.*[124] Mr Fernandes had been employed by the respondent, a wholly-owned subsidiary of a United States corporation belonging to a large international telecommunications group, initially as an accountant and subsequently as chief financial officer for the respondent and its UK sister companies. One of his duties was to scrutinize expenses met by other employees out of company funds to check that they had been legitimately incurred on company business. The respondent's managing director failed to provide receipts for his expenditure and 'fobbed off' Mr Fernandes with promises to do so. In January 1997 Mr Fernandes had faxed a letter expressing concern about this state of affairs to his contact at the US parent corporation, who had responded by destroying the fax and warning Mr Fernandes to 'look after your butt'. In November 1999, by which time the unaccounted for expenditure exceeded £300,000 and the company was getting into serious financial difficulties, Mr Fernandes tried again, this time sending a letter and supporting documentation by courier to the boards of the US corporation and its parent, a Luxembourg company. His own dismissal followed.

According to the respondent company, both at the time and at the tribunal hearing, that was because of gross misconduct consisting allegedly of authorizing the misappropriation of monies by the managing director and not making payments of corporation tax and pension fund contributions on time. It was submitted on behalf of Mr Fernandes that looking at the respondent's conduct as a whole, in particular the pressure to resign placed on him before any question of a

---

[123] Under what was then the Employment Protection (Consolidation) Act 1978, s 58: see now the Trade Union and Labour Relations (Consolidation) Act 1992, s 152.
[124] Case No 2200060/00 (18 May 2000).

disciplinary hearing had been raised, and the relatively lenient treatment of the managing director, it was to be inferred that his whistle-blowing was the real reason. The Tribunal referred to the *Maund* case and observed:

> . . . it is extremely unlikely that any employer will come to the Tribunal and admit that it dismissed for an impermissible reason. Therefore, where the employee has performed a protected act and a dismissal follows, it is only common sense for the Tribunal to look to the employer for an explanation and to scrutinise that explanation closely. If the explanation is unsatisfactory, then the Tribunal may infer that the reason for dismissal was the protected act.

On the evidence it had heard, the Tribunal found that inference to be 'irresistible'.

13.60   There is, however, an exception to the general rule that the burden of proving the reason for dismissal rests on the employer. That applies when dismissal occurs within the minimum qualifying period of service necessary for ordinary unfair dismissal claims.[125] In that situation, the employee must establish that the tribunal has jurisdiction to hear his claim, which can only be done by his demonstrating that the reason for the dismissal was one of those attracting exemption from the requirement for a minimum qualifying period.[126] That did not affect Mr Fernandes, whose employment had lasted four years, but did apply to the applicant in *Azmi v Orbis Charitable Trust*,[127] as the Tribunal expressly recognized. Ms Azmi's employment was still in its three-month probationary stage when she first voiced concerns about the administration of the respondent's funds and its compliance with charity law to the executive director, and although her probation period was extended while investigation took place, she was then told that her position would not be confirmed due to 'poor performance'. Her claim was nonetheless successful, the Tribunal accepting that the executive director 'did not appreciate having such matters brought to his attention and used the excuse of performance to remove [her]'.

Constructive dismissal

13.61   The burden of proving dismissal itself rests, however, on the employee, and when constructive dismissal is alleged, he has the task of demonstrating that he was entitled to terminate the contract without notice. That entitlement can only derive from the employer's committing a breach of a term of the employment contract which the employee is entitled to treat as a repudiation by the employer of its contractual obligations.[128]

---

[125]   Under the Employment Rights Act 1996, s 108. That period is currently a year.
[126]   *Smith v Hayle Town Council* [1978] ICR 996.
[127]   Case No 2200624/99 (4 May 2000).
[128]   *Malik v Bank of Credit and Commerce International SA* [1998] AC 20, 34, HL, *per* Lord Nicholls of Birkenhead, confirming the principle established in *Western Excavating (ECC) Ltd v Sharp* [1978] QB 761, CA.

An employee who has blown the whistle on management or colleagues may find **13.62** that his working environment becomes intolerable, for example through his being 'sent to Coventry'. The term of the employment contract which his employer is at risk of breaching is the implied term that the employer will not, without reasonable and proper cause, conduct itself in a manner calculated or likely to destroy or seriously damage the relationship of trust and confidence between the parties.[129]

It has been said[130] that any conduct likely to destroy or seriously damage the rela- **13.63** tionship of trust and confidence between employer and employee must go to the root of the contract (so as to amount to a repudiation). It is not necessary to show that the employer intended to repudiate the contract; the tribunal's function is to look at the employer's conduct as a whole and determine whether its effect, judged reasonably and sensibly, was such that the employee could not be expected to have put up with it.[131] It is the cumulative impact of the employer's conduct which has to be assessed; a series of acts or incidents may together amount to a repudiatory breach of the term although taken individually they would not.[132] That approach will catch an employer who attempts, without committing any major breach of contract, to 'squeeze out' an employee by making his life so uncomfortable that he resigns.[133]

Examples of early claims for unfair dismissal under section 103A of the **13.64** Employment Rights Act 1996 succeeding on the basis of that line of authority are *Boughton v National Tyres & Autocentre Ltd*,[134] *Mr A v X Ltd*[135] and *Holden v Connex South Eastern Ltd*.[136] Mr Boughton had reported to the respondent's regional manager his belief that a criminal offence might be committed by the manager of the depot at which he worked, handing over a tape on which he had recorded conversations with the depot manager. A few days later the tape was handed back to him by the depot manager. The Tribunal found that Mr Boughton was subsequently ostracized by the depot manager and deputy manager to such an extent that he handed in his notice. The respondent was held to have breached the implied term of mutual trust and confidence by failing to

---

[129] The formulation adopted in *Malik v BCCI* (n 128 above) derived from a series of earlier cases including *Courtaulds Northern Textiles Ltd v Andrew* [1979] IRLR 84, EAT; *Woods v WM Car Services (Peterborough) Ltd* [1981] ICR 666, EAT, affirmed [1982] ICR 693, CA; *Lewis v Motorworld Garages Ltd* [1986] ICR 157, CA; *Imperial Group Pension Trust Ltd v Imperial Tobacco Ltd* [1991] 1 WLR 589.

[130] By Arnold J in *Courtaulds Northern Textiles Ltd v Andrew* (n 129 above) at 86 and Browne-Wilkinson J in *Woods v WM Car Services (Peterborough) Ltd* (n 129 above) at 672: see also *Morrow v Safeway Stores plc* [2002] IRLR 9, EAT.

[131] *Woods v WM Car Services (Peterborough) Ltd* (n 129 above) at 670–1.

[132] ibid; see also *Lewis v Motorworld Garages Ltd* (n 129 above) at 167, 169.

[133] *Woods v WM Car Services (Peterborough) Ltd* (n 129 above) at 671.

[134] Bury St Edmunds Employment Tribunal, Case No 1500080/00 (15 September 2000).

[135] Liverpool Employment Tribunal, Case No 2102023/00 (9 March 2001).

[136] See para 13.43 above.

conduct an adequate investigation into Mr Boughton's disclosure and handling the matter with 'extreme insensitivity'. The regional manager had 'swept Mr Boughton's complaint under the carpet', not honoured confidentiality so far as the tape was concerned, given no consideration to possible alternative employment or other measures to address the difficulties Mr Boughton was likely to face in continuing to work at that particular depot, and (in what the Tribunal described as 'the final insult to injury') told him that if he had any problems in the future to raise them with the depot manager. The respondent was also found to have breached an implied term of the employment contract to provide reasonable support for Mr Boughton in the circumstances.[137]

13.65 The protected disclosure made by Mr A to the chief executive of his employer had been of serious allegations of sexual harassment of junior members of staff by a senior manager. The Tribunal found that instead of being complimented on his proper behaviour, he had suffered humiliating treatment in the course of the ensuing investigation and unwarranted disciplinary action for having allegedly breached confidentiality by telling other employees (which he had not); that the purpose had been to intimidate him into keeping quiet about the matter; and that the respondent's conduct had been 'totally inappropriate'. He had both suffered detriment within the meaning of section 47B of the Employment Rights Act 1996[138] and been constructively dismissed by the respondent's breach of the implied trust and confidence term. Mr Holden was found to have been the object of a 'sustained campaign' to force him to resign because of his health and safety activities and protected disclosures. The respondent had looked at his conduct 'in minute detail' and issued disciplinary charges against him where in the normal course the conduct complained of would not have merited disciplinary action.

Remedies for unfair dismissal: compensation

13.66 Another respect in which ex-employees making claims for unfair dismissal[139] in reliance on these provisions are favoured over most other classes of applicant is that there is no statutory ceiling on the amount of compensation employment tribunals can award them on finding their complaints well-founded.[140] This approach to compensation did not feature in the Public Interest Disclosure Act

---

[137] cf *Wigan Borough Council v Davies* [1979] ICR 411, in which the Employment Appeal Tribunal upheld a tribunal decision that Miss Davies had been constructively dismissed by the employer's breach of contract in failing to provide her with reasonable support to ensure she could carry out her duties without disruption and harassment from other employees. She had made herself unpopular by not taking their side in a dispute with management and they had reacted by refusing to talk to or cooperate with her.

[138] See para 13.70 below.

[139] Under the Employment Rights Act 1996, ss 94, 111.

[140] Thus Mr Fernandes was awarded a total of £293,441 (calculated on the basis that he was unlikely at the age of 59 to obtain comparable alternative employment). Mr A was awarded £139,677 on his claim against X Ltd.

itself, because the government had not then been persuaded to endorse it. However, a provision was included[141] which gave the Secretary of State power to make regulations adjusting the basis of compensation in cases of unfair dismissal for making protected disclosures. Regulations removing the limit with effect from 2 July 1999 were made in June 1999,[142] to be superseded as from 25 October 1999 by the Employment Relations Act 1999, section 37(1). The effect of those enactments was to insert into the Employment Rights Act 1996 new section 124(1A), providing that the limit[143] imposed by section 124(1) on the amount of a compensatory award under section 123[144] or compensation under section 117[145] shall not apply where a person is deemed unfairly dismissed by virtue of section 103A or section 105(6A).

13.67 For full details of the provisions and principles in accordance with which compensation is calculated, readers should consult specialist employment law texts. The following is an outline of the main points.

(a) It consists of two elements, a basic award and a compensatory award.[146]

(b) The basic award is calculated on the same basis as a statutory redundancy payment: that is, half a week's pay for every year of employment below the age of 22, a week's pay for every year of employment between the ages of 22 and 41, and one and a half weeks' pay for every year of employment above the age of 40 up to a maximum of 20 years' employment (counting backwards from the effective date of termination).[147] The basic award may be reduced to such extent as the tribunal considers just and equitable if it finds that the complainant unreasonably refused an offer of reinstatement or that any conduct of the complainant before the dismissal was such as to warrant a reduction.[148]

(c) The compensatory award is of such amount as the tribunal considers just and equitable in all the circumstances, having regard to the loss sustained by the complainant in consequence of the dismissal in so far as that loss is attributable to action taken by the employer.[149]

(d) Such loss includes any expenses reasonably incurred by the complainant in consequence of the dismissal, and the loss of any benefit which he might

---

[141] Employment Rights Act 1996, s 127B, inserted by the Public Interest Disclosure Act 1998, s 8(4); repealed by the Employment Relations Act 1999, ss 37(2), 44, Sch 9(11) as from 25 October 1999.

[142] The Public Interest Disclosure (Compensation) Regulations 1999, SI 1999/1548.

[143] Currently £52,600: Employment Rights (Increase of Limits) Order 2002, SI 2002/10.

[144] See para 13.67 below.

[145] Awarded in the event of an order for reinstatement or re-engagement being made but not fully complied with: see para 13.68 below.

[146] Employment Rights Act 1996, s 118(1).

[147] ibid, s 119.

[148] ibid, s 122.

[149] ibid, s 123(1).

reasonably be expected to have had but for the dismissal.[150] The tribunal will calculate actual losses up to the date of the hearing and estimate future losses in the event of the complainant's having obtained no, or less remunerative, alternative employment. Fringe benefits such as pension rights, medical insurance, or a company car will all be taken into account.

(e) The complainant must have acted so as to mitigate his loss.[151]

(f) If the tribunal finds that the complainant's own conduct to any extent caused or contributed to his dismissal, it shall reduce the compensatory award by such proportion as it considers just and equitable having regard to that finding.[152] However, no reduction can be made on this account unless the conduct in question was 'culpable or blameworthy'.[153]

> That concept does not necessarily involve any conduct of the complainant amounting to a breach of contract or a tort . . . it also includes conduct which, while not amounting to a breach of contract or a tort, is nevertheless perverse or foolish, or, if I may use the colloquialism, bloody-minded. It may also include action which, though not meriting any of those more pejorative epithets, is nevertheless unreasonable in all the circumstances. I should not, however, go as far as to say that all unreasonable conduct is necessarily culpable or blameworthy; it must depend on the degree of unreasonableness involved.[154]

It would seem to follow that no reduction could be made on account of conduct dismissal for which is automatically unfair (such as making a protected disclosure), because no such conduct can be characterized as culpable or blameworthy in the light of its special statutory status.

(g) In *Johnson v Unisys Ltd*,[155] Lord Hoffmann said that to construe 'loss' as meaning financial loss only[156] is too narrow a construction; he could see no reason why, in an appropriate case, compensation could not be awarded for distress, humiliation or damage to reputation in the community or family life, as well as for loss flowing from psychiatric injury consequent on an unfair dismissal. Comprised within the award made in *Holden v Connex South Eastern Ltd*[157] was a sum of £13,000 for injury to feelings and also a sum of £5,000 by way of aggravated damages (which appears to be unprecedented for an unfair dismissal claim).

---

[150] Employment Rights Act 1996, s 123(2).
[151] ibid, s 123(4).
[152] ibid, s 123(6).
[153] *Nelson v BBC (No 2)* [1980] ICR 110, CA, approving *Morrish v Henlys (Folkestone) Ltd* [1973] ICR 482, NIRC.
[154] *Nelson v BBC (No 2)* (n 153 above) 121, *per* Brandon LJ.
[155] [2001] 2 WLR 1076, HL.
[156] As was done in *Norton Tool Co Ltd v Tewson* [1973] 1 WLR 45, NIRC.
[157] See para 13.43 and n 95 above.

Reinstatement and re-engagement

Compensation is not the only available remedy; orders for reinstatement and re-   **13.68**
engagement may be made under Employment Rights Act 1996, sections 113 to
115, but only where the complainant expresses a wish for the tribunal to make
such an order.[158] The tribunal in exercising its discretion under section 113 will
have to take into account the practicability of the employer's complying with any
such order and any contribution made by the employee to his dismissal.[159] Factors
relevant to practicability include hostility on the part of fellow workers[160] and the
likelihood that an employee's loss of trust and confidence in his employer would
result in an unsatisfactory working relationship. An order for reinstatement or re-
engagement cannot in any event be enforced if the employer will not comply.[161]
The complainant's only remedy in those circumstances is to apply[162] for compensation for unfair dismissal (calculated on the usual basis), together with an additional award (of between 26 and 52 weeks' pay) which may, however, be
disallowed if the employer can satisfy the tribunal that compliance was not after
all practicable.[163] If the order is complied with, but not fully (if, for example, the
employer re-engages the complainant, but on less favourable terms than were
specified by the tribunal), the complainant may be compensated for loss caused by
the non-compliance.[164]

Interim relief

An employee who would like his job back can apply for interim relief under sec-   **13.69**
tions 128 and 129 of the Employment Rights Act 1996[165] so long as he acts
quickly enough: no later than seven days from the effective date of termination.
The tribunal's powers under section 129 to order reinstatement, re-engagement
or continuation of a contract of employment pending determination or settlement of a complaint only arise if it appears to the tribunal 'likely' that on determining the complaint the tribunal will find that the only or principal reason for
dismissal was the making of a protected disclosure. That test has been interpreted
by the Employment Appeal Tribunal as requiring the tribunal to ask itself
whether the applicant has established that he has 'a pretty good chance' of success,
which involves achieving a higher degree of certainty in the tribunal's mind than

---

[158] Employment Rights Act 1996, s 112(3).
[159] ibid, s 116(1), (3).
[160] cf *Meridian Ltd v Gomersall* [1977] ICR 597, EAT, where the tribunal had regard to the probability that the factory atmosphere had been 'poisoned against' the applicant and her fellow workers 'had been (wrongly) led to think unkindly of her'.
[161] *O'Laoire v Jackel International Ltd* [1990] ICR 197, CA.
[162] Under the Employment Rights Act 1996, s 117(3).
[163] ibid, s 117(4).
[164] ibid, s 117(1), (2).
[165] As amended by the Public Interest Disclosure Act 1998, s 9.

showing just 'a reasonable prospect' of success.[166] However, the tribunal does not have to go so far as to form a judgment about what the reason for dismissal was.[167] Interim relief was granted in *Fernandes v Netcom Consultants Ltd* but refused in *ALM Medical Services Ltd v Bladon* and *Everett v Miyano Care Services Ltd.*

Right not to be subjected to detriment

13.70 Not every worker whose contract is terminated for making a protected disclosure is eligible for relief under the Employment Rights Act 1996, sections 94 and following, which apply only to employees. Nor is every employee on whom retribution is visited for making a protected disclosure; the measures may stop short not only of actual dismissal, but even of entitling him to treat himself as having been constructively dismissed, or he may not wish to take that step. What every worker[168] does have is a 'right not to be subjected to any detriment by any act, or any deliberate failure to act, by his employer done on the ground that the worker has made a protected disclosure': Employment Rights Act 1996, section 47B(1).[169] If that right is infringed, he may present a complaint to an employment tribunal, under the Employment Rights Act 1996 section 48(1A).[170] By these provisions whistle-blowers were fitted into the framework of protection against the infliction of detriment already offered by Part V of that Act to various other classes of workers, for example those performing statutory functions potentially adverse to their employers' interests (such as being health and safety representatives) or those refusing to work on Sundays. Part V and Part X are, however, mutually exclusive and section 47B does not apply to a worker who is an employee and suffers detriment amounting to dismissal: section 47B(2).

13.71 Section 47B (like section 103A) only mentions workers who *have made* protected disclosures. They say nothing about workers who may have been dismissed or subjected to other detriments for having threatened, or intended, or attempted, to make such disclosures. This is to be contrasted with those provisions which confer protection from victimization on other grounds in the Employment Rights Act 1996, Part V and elsewhere which cover workers or employees *proposing* to do protected acts in addition to those who actually *do* them.[171]

---

[166] *Taplin v C Shippam Ltd* [1978] ICR 1068, concerning a claim for interim relief under a statutory predecessor of ss 128–129 (Employment Protection Act 1975, s 78) by an applicant alleging unfair dismissal on the ground of trade union activities.

[167] In *Parkins v Sodexho Ltd* [2002] IRLR 109 the Employment Appeal Tribunal allowed an appeal against the refusal of interim relief on the ground that the tribunal had erred in doing just that and deciding in the employer's favour.

[168] As defined in the Employment Rights Act 1996, ss 230(3) and 43K: see para 13.21 above.

[169] Inserted by the Public Interest Disclosure Act 1998, s 2.

[170] Inserted by the Public Interest Disclosure Act 1998, s 3.

[171] See, by way of example, the Employment Rights Act 1996, ss 45, 101 (proposal to refuse to do shop work on Sundays); ss 46, 102 (proposal by employee trustee of occupational pension scheme to perform functions of trustee); the Trade Union and Labour Relations (Consolidation) Act 1992, s 152 (proposal to join a trade union or take part in trade union activities).

Any worker who claims to have been subjected to a detriment in contravention of **13.72** section 47B may present a complaint to an employment tribunal.[172] No qualifying period of service or age limit is imposed. The complaint ought to be presented within three months of the act (or failure to act) to which it relates, although the tribunal has power to extend the period if satisfied that to do so was not reasonably practicable.[173] There are detailed rules for calculating the commencement date of the limitation period. Where the act or failure complained of was one of a series of similar acts or failures, time begins to run from the last of them. If an act extends over a period, the last day of that period is 'the date of the act', and 'the date of [a] failure to act' is the date on which the employer decided not to do the act in question.[174] In the absence of contrary evidence, such a decision is deemed to have been taken when another act inconsistent with that act is done, alternatively, on the expiry of the period within which the employer might reasonably have been expected to do that act if it was going to be done.

Burden of proof

Three things have to be established for such a complaint to succeed: that the **13.73** worker suffered a detriment; that the detriment was caused by an act (or deliberate failure to act) on the part of his employer; and that the act (or omission to act) was 'done on the ground that' the worker had made a protected disclosure. On ordinary principles, the burden of proof would be on the worker to establish all three. However, in respect of the third the statute shifts the burden to the employer, providing that on such a complaint 'it is for the employer to show the ground on which any act, or deliberate failure to act, was done'.[175] It seems reasonable to assume that by analogy with section 98(1) of the Employment Rights Act 1996, tribunals should adopt a similar approach to that advocated by the Court of Appeal in *Maund v Penwith District Council*[176] in respect of reasons for dismissal.

Meaning of 'detriment'

'Detriment' is undefined. In the context of section 6 of the Sex Discrimination **13.74** Act 1975 (which makes it unlawful to discriminate by subjecting a person to detriment on the ground of sex), it has been said that 'subjecting to detriment' does not mean anything more than 'putting under a disadvantage'[177] and that it is a question of fact rather than law whether particular treatment has that effect. Brightman LJ said in the same case that a detriment exists if a reasonable worker

---

[172] Employment Rights Act 1996, s 48(1A).
[173] ibid, s 48(3).
[174] ibid, s 48(4).
[175] ibid, s 48(2).
[176] See para 13.57 above.
[177] *Ministry of Defence v Jeremiah* [1980] QB 87, 99, CA, *per* Brandon LJ.

would or might take the view that the treatment in question was in all the circumstances to his detriment. In a later Court of Appeal case concerning alleged racial discrimination,[178] Bingham LJ said the phrase 'subjecting to any other detriment' in section 4(2) of the Race Relations Act 1976 was 'to be given its broad, ordinary meaning', and that it was 'plain that almost any discriminatory conduct by employer against employee in relation to the latter's employment will be rendered unlawful by section 4(2)'. However, detriment must be more than de minimis: cf *Peake v Automotive Products Ltd*,[179] in which the Court of Appeal rejected a claim that a rule allowing women employees to leave factory premises five minutes earlier than their male colleagues was a detriment to the latter.

13.75 For a non-employee worker, termination of his contract would be the strongest form of detriment to which he could be subjected; but any worsening of the terms on which, or conditions in which, a worker is employed or otherwise engaged, or unjustified disciplinary action, could count. So could passing him over for promotion, or withholding an increase in pay or other benefits which he might reasonably have expected to receive,[180] or avoidably exposing him to harassment by co-workers or third parties.[181]

Remedies for subjection to detriment

13.76 If a tribunal finds a complaint under section 48(1A) well-founded, it must make a declaration to that effect,[182] and may award the complainant compensation.[183] The primary measure of compensation is what the tribunal considers to be just and equitable in all the circumstances, having regard to the infringement of section 47B and any loss attributable to it.[184] There are supplementary provisions modelled on section 123 of the Employment Rights Act 1996.[185] The loss is to include expenses reasonably incurred by the complainant in consequence of the act or omission and any benefits he might reasonably be expected to have received but for the act or omission; the duty to mitigate applies; and there is to be a reduction

---

[178] *Barclays Bank plc v Kapur* [1989] IRLR 387.

[179] [1978] QB 233.

[180] Compare *Clymo v Wandsworth London Borough Council* [1989] ICR 250, EAT (where it was said not to be a detriment to refuse advantages not offered to others in the same grade of employment, such as the perk of a company car or the right to work overtime) and *Iske v P & O European Ferries (Dover) Ltd* [1997] IRLR 401, EAT (not being offered an advantage to which the complainant had no statutory or contractual right could be a detriment if others were offered it).

[181] cf *Burton v De Vere Hotels Ltd* [1997] ICR 1, EAT, the case in which it was held that the complainants had been subjected to the detriment of harassment on racial grounds contrary to the Race Relations Act 1976, s 4(2) by their employer's allowing them to be made the object of offensive remarks by Bernard Manning.

[182] Employment Rights Act 1996, s 49(1)(a).

[183] ibid, s 49(1)(b).

[184] ibid, s 49(2).

[185] See para 13.67 above.

for contributory fault.[186] The statute says[187] that where the detriment consists of the termination of a contract other than a contract of employment, compensation must not exceed that which would be payable had the worker been an employee dismissed for making a protected disclosure. Following the removal of the limit on compensation for such employees,[188] it would seem to follow that other workers whose contracts are terminated can also recover up to their full losses.

In addition to financial losses, it has been held by the Employment Appeal **13.77** Tribunal in the context of analogous provisions in the Trade Union and Labour Relations (Consolidation) Act 1992, section 146[189] that compensation can be awarded for injury to feelings (which would seem to be confirmed by *Johnson v Unisys Ltd*[190]). Such an award was made in *Mr A v X Ltd*[191] (in respect of the unwarranted disciplinary action taken by the respondent before Mr A handed in his notice, which the Tribunal found to be a detriment within section 47B of the Employment Rights Act 1996) in the amount of £5,000, together with £3,000 for the 'moderate' psychiatric injury caused by the respondent's treatment of him. It awarded an additional £5,000 by way of aggravated damages 'because of the respondent's high handed and unsympathetic behaviour'.

Protected disclosures and breaches of confidentiality

Section 43J of the Employment Rights Act 1996 makes void any provision in any **13.78** agreement between a worker and his employer in so far as it purports to preclude the making of a protected disclosure by the worker. Specific reference is made to compromise agreements whereby the worker agrees to refrain from instituting or continuing proceedings under the Employment Rights Act or at common law for breach of contract. A worker who has already been dismissed or subjected to detriment for making a protected disclosure cannot be bought off and restrained from repeating it (or making further disclosures) so long as he satisfies the criteria for the application of one of sections 43D to 43H.

It of course does not follow that, but for section 43J, protected disclosures would **13.79** necessarily constitute breaches of the implied (if not express) duty of confidentiality owed to an employer by its employee or someone in a similar position. The public interest defence to breach of confidence actions extends to such persons.[192]

---

[186] Employment Rights Act 1996, s 49(3)–(5).
[187] ibid, s 49(6).
[188] ibid, s 124(1A); and see para 13.66 above.
[189] *Cleveland Ambulance NHS Trust v Blane* [1997] ICR 851.
[190] See para 13.67 above.
[191] See paras 13.64–13.65 above.
[192] See for example *Initial Services Ltd v Putterill* [1968] 1 QB 396, CA; *Lion Laboratories Ltd v Evans* [1985] 1 QB 526, CA; *Re A Company* [1989] 1 Ch 477.

13.80 Nor does it follow that a disclosure which is not protected within the meaning of the Public Interest Disclosure Act 1998 will inevitably be an actionable breach of confidence. For example, the subject matter might not have been 'exceptionally serious' (section 43H), and while the worker might have believed that if he spoke to his employer first he would be subjected to a detriment, or relevant evidence would be destroyed, he might not be able to show 'reasonable grounds' for that belief (section 43G(2)(a) or (b)). It could, however, still be held to have been in the public interest for him to have reported his concerns to, say, the police or to an appropriate regulatory or supervisory authority which happened not to be on the list of prescribed persons.

13.81 An employee who is actually or constructively dismissed for whistle-blowing could claim for wrongful dismissal at common law, or unfair dismissal under the Employment Rights Act 1996, section 98, even if it was not automatically unfair by virtue of section 103A. It would still be open to him to argue that the disclosure was in the public interest and so he had committed no breach of his obligations such as to justify termination of his contract, or constitute misconduct or amount to 'some other substantial reason' for dismissal,[193] or alternatively that the employer acted unreasonably in treating it as a sufficient reason for dismissal.[194] It remains to be seen whether tribunals would be unsympathetic to such a claim, thinking either that the complainant could and should have taken care to bring himself within the statutory code of protection, or that by prescribing certain criteria for protection Parliament has shown where the line is to be drawn and an employee who cannot satisfy them has overstepped that line and must take the consequences.

13.82 The position of an employee who cannot rely on the Public Interest Disclosure Act 1998 is, of course, inferior in other ways: the minimum qualifying period of service and compensation limits apply,[195] and he is unlikely to obtain redress for detriments falling short of dismissal, certainly ones which do not constitute breaches of contract (such as a failure to promote or provide a perk). Workers who are not employees are in a worse position still; the only remedy they could seek would be damages for the unexpired terms of their contracts in the event of repudiation.

Concluding remarks

13.83 The legislation introduced by the Public Interest Disclosure Act 1998 is still in its infancy. Tribunal decisions to date (including those discussed above) illustrate its workings in practice and use is certainly being made of it. The number of com-

---

[193] Employment Rights Act 1996, s 98(1)(b), (2)(b).
[194] ibid, s 98(4).
[195] See paras 13.54, 13.66 above.

plaints presented under sections 103A and 47B of the Employment Rights Act 1996 now exceeds one thousand, although only a minority have reached a full hearing. More difficult to gauge is how well the legislation is serving the preventative function envisaged for it, and how far it has succeeded in encouraging a 'culture of openness'. The majority of disclosures which the Public Interest Disclosure Act was designed to promote will be made internally or directed to Ministers or appropriate regulatory bodies and never become public knowledge. It is of the nature of the Act that the full measure of its success is destined to remain secret.

14

MONEY LAUNDERING

A. Introduction

The previous chapter addressed two aspects of 'whistle-blowing': the protection **14.01** afforded by the Public Interest Disclosure Act 1998 to employees (and other 'workers') who reveal matters of public concern (voluntary whistle-blowing), and the positive obligations imposed on auditors and actuaries of occupational and personal pension schemes and providers of financial services to disclose to the relevant regulator concerns which they may have about the administration of such schemes and businesses (mandatory whistle-blowing).

In this chapter consideration is given to further aspects of 'whistle-blowing', both **14.02** mandatory and voluntary, in the context of revealing suspicions of money laundering to the appropriate authorities. In a work of this nature it is not possible to give more than a brief overview of the main statutory provisions and their operation. For a more considered view of this area of the law attention is drawn to the specialist works on the subject.[1]

---

[1] eg AR Mitchell, K Taylor and SM Talbot, *Confiscation and the Proceeds of Crime* (3rd edn, 2002).

B. The International Dimension to Money Laundering Legislation

14.03 In the age of the global economy the laundering of the proceeds of drug trafficking, terrorism and organized crime is seen as a problem of international significance which must be tackled at an international level.

14.04 The international dimension to the prevention and detection of money laundering is to be found in:

(a) the UN Convention against the Illicit Traffic in Narcotic Drugs and Psychotropic Substances 1988 (the Vienna Convention 1988);

(b) the Council of Europe Convention on laundering, tracing, seizure and confiscation of the proceeds of crime 1990; and

(c) Council Directive (EEC) 91/308 on the prevention of the use of the financial system for the purpose of money laundering;

each of which laid the foundations of modern domestic legislation in this area. The interrelationship of these international measures is perhaps best demonstrated in the statement by the representatives of the governments of the member states who met to adopt Council Directive (EEC) 91/308 which is appended to the text of the Directive. It reads:

> The representatives of the Governments of the Member States, meeting within the Council,
>
> Recalling that the Member States signed the United Nations Convention against illicit traffic in narcotic drugs and psychotropic substances, adopted on 19 December 1988 in Vienna;
>
> Recalling also that most Member States have already signed the Council of Europe Convention on laundering, tracing, seizure and confiscation of proceeds of crime on 8 November 1990 in Strasbourg;
>
> Conscious of the fact that the description of money laundering contained in Article 1 of Council Directive 91/308/EEC derives its wording from the relevant provisions of the aforementioned Conventions;
>
> Hereby undertake to take all necessary steps by 31 December 1992 at the latest to enact criminal legislation enabling them to comply with their obligations under the aforementioned instruments.

The Vienna Convention

14.05 The signatories to the Vienna Convention 1988 each agreed, in Article 3(1), to adopt measures to establish as criminal offences:

> (b) (i) The conversion or transfer of property, knowing that such property is derived from any offence or offences established in accordance with subparagraph (a) of this paragraph [relating to the cultivation, manufacture and possession of illicit drugs] or from an act of participation in such offence or

offences, for the purpose of concealing or disguising the illicit origin of the property or of assisting any person who is involved in the commission of such an offence or offences to evade the legal consequences of his actions;

(ii) The concealment or disguise of the true nature, source, location, disposition, movement, rights with respect to, or ownership of property, knowing that such property is derived from an offence or offences established in accordance with subparagraph (a) of this paragraph or from an act of participation in such an offence or offences;

(c) Subject to its constitutional principles and the basic concepts of its legal system:

(i) The acquisition, possession or use of property, knowing, at the time of receipt, that such property was derived from an offence or offences established in accordance with subparagraph (a) of this paragraph or from an act of participation in such offence or offences.

14.06 Article 5 of the Convention required the signatory states to enact measures to enable illicit drugs and the proceeds of their sale to be confiscated. To that end Article 5(2) required each signatory state to:

adopt such measures as may be necessary to enable its competent authorities to identify, trace, and freeze or seize proceeds, property, instrumentalities or any other things referred to in paragraph 1 of this article [the substances, materials and equipment used to commit offences defined in accordance with Article 3(1) and the proceeds of those offences] for the purpose of eventual confiscation.

14.07 Article 5(3) required each signatory state to:

. . . empower its courts or other competent authorities to order that bank, financial or commercial records be made available or seized. A Party shall not decline to act under the provisions of this paragraph on the ground of bank secrecy.

14.08 The principal features of the Vienna Convention were adopted into domestic law by the Criminal Justice (International Co-operation) Act 1990. Section 14 of that Act[2] provided:

(1) A person is guilty of an offence if he—

(a) conceals or disguises any property which is, or in whole or in part directly or indirectly represents, his proceeds of drug trafficking; or

(b) converts or transfers that property or removes it from the jurisdiction, for the purpose of avoiding prosecution for a drug trafficking offence or the making or enforcement in his case of a confiscation order.

(2) A person is guilty of an offence if, knowing or having reasonable grounds to suspect that any property is, or in whole or in part directly or indirectly represents, another person's proceeds of drug trafficking, he—

(a) conceals or disguises that property; or

(b) converts or transfers that property or removes it from the jurisdiction, for the purpose of assisting any person to avoid prosecution for a drug trafficking offence or the making or enforcement of a confiscation order.

---

[2] Criminal Justice (International Co-operation) Act 1990, s 14 was repealed by the Drug Trafficking Act 1994 (and again, by the Proceeds of Crime Act 2002).

    (3) A person is guilty of an offence if, knowing or having reasonable grounds to suspect that any property is, or in whole or in part directly or indirectly represents, another person's proceeds of drug trafficking, he acquires that property for no, or for inadequate, consideration.

    (4) In subsections (1)(a) and (2)(a) above the references to concealing or disguising any property include references to concealing or disguising its nature, source, location, disposition, movement or ownership or any rights with respect to it.

14.09   Such measures were not new to English law. The laundering of the proceeds of drug trafficking had already been outlawed by the Drug Trafficking Act 1986.[3] Section 11 of the Prevention of Terrorism (Temporary Provisions) Act 1989[4] had made similar provision for the laundering of 'terrorist funds'.

14.10   Each of those Acts had also made provision for the voluntary disclosure of information relating to money laundering. However, the legislation was merely permissive. There was no duty on those involved in transactions involving the illegal proceeds of drugs or terrorism to disclose to the authorities their suspicions about the source of the funds involved, although if such disclosure was made the Acts afforded the 'whistle-blower' a statutory defence to any claim for breach of contract. That was to change.

Council Directive (EEC) 91/308

14.11   Almost simultaneously with the coming into force of the Criminal Justice (International Co-operation) Act 1990[5] the member states of the European Union adopted Council Directive (EEC) 91/308 to control money laundering on a Europe-wide level.[6]

14.12   The recitals to the Directive reveal something of the rationale behind the measures adopted by the Council of Ministers. In particular it was noted that:

> Whereas preventing the financial system from being used for money laundering is a task which cannot be carried out by the authorities responsible for combating this phenomenon without the co-operation of credit and financial institutions and their supervisory authorities; whereas banking secrecy must be lifted in such cases; whereas a mandatory system of reporting suspicious transactions which ensures that information is transmitted to the above mentioned authorities without alerting the customers concerned, is the most effective way to accomplish such co-operation; whereas a special protection clause is necessary to exempt credit and financial institutions, their employees and their directors from responsibility for breaching restrictions on disclosure of information . . .

14.13   The desire of governments to override rules on bank secrecy in the interests of identifying and preventing money laundering was not a new one. The need for

---

[3] This Act was repealed by the Criminal Justice (International Co-operation) Act 1990.
[4] This Act was repealed by the Terrorism Act 2000, s 2.
[5] The Act came into force on 28 June 1991.
[6] On 10 June 1991.

such measures was expressly recognized by the signatory states in Article 5(3) of the Vienna Convention.[7] However, the recitals to the Directive signalled an intention to go further. The provisions of the Vienna Convention had required only that the signatories enact measures to allow the courts to order the production or seizure of bank, financial or commercial records to enable laundered funds to be traced and seized. Under the provisions of Council Directive (EEC) 91/308 financial institutions were now to be obliged, on their own initiative, to disclose to the relevant authorities any suspicion which they might have about the source of funds with which they were dealing.

Article 6 of the Directive requires that: **14.14**

> Member States shall ensure that credit and financial institutions and their directors and employees co-operate fully with the authorities responsible for combating money laundering:
> —by informing those authorities, on their own initiative, of any fact which might be an indication of money laundering,
> —by furnishing those authorities, at their request, with all necessary information, in accordance with the procedures established by the applicable legislation.
> The information referred to in the first paragraph shall be forwarded to the authorities responsible for combating money laundering of the Member State in whose territory the institution forwarding the information is situated. The person or persons designated by the credit and financial institutions in accordance with the procedures provided for in Article 11(1) shall normally forward the information. Information supplied to the authorities in accordance with the first paragraph may be used only in connection with the combating of money laundering. However, Member States may provide that such information may also be used for other purposes.

The obligation of disclosure created by Article 6 required that some protection be **14.15** afforded to financial institutions to protect them against its consequences. Article 9 of the Directive puts in place that protection. It provides:

> The disclosure in good faith to the authorities responsible for combating money laundering by an employee or director of a credit or financial institution of the information referred to in Articles 6 and 7 shall not constitute a breach of any restriction on disclosure of information imposed by contract or by any legislative, regulatory or administrative provision, and shall not involve the credit or financial institution, its directors or employees in liability of any kind.

C. Domestic Legislation

The provisions of the Vienna Convention, the 1990 Council of Europe **14.16** Convention and Council Directive (EEC) 91/308 have been incorporated into

---

[7] See para 14.07 above.

domestic law by means of a number of different measures enacted over a period of years. Prior to the commencement of Part 7 of the Proceeds of Crime Act 2002 the main statutory provisions in England and Wales relating to money laundering were fourfold:

(a) Part VI of the Criminal Justice Act 1988 (as amended by the Criminal Justice Act 1993), which was concerned with the laundering of the proceeds of crime generally;

(b) Part III of the Drug Trafficking Act 1994, which created various offences in connection with the proceeds of drug trafficking;

(c) Part III of the Terrorism Act 2000, which created specific offences in relation to terrorist funding; and

(d) the Money Laundering Regulations 1993,[8] which impose obligations on financial institutions to establish systems and training, and to implement procedures, for identifying potential money laundering transactions.

14.17 The three Acts followed essentially the same pattern in their definition of money laundering offences. However, there was one important exception. The power of voluntary disclosure (with its attendant protection for the whistle-blower) previously found in both the Drug Trafficking Act 1986 and the Prevention of Terrorism (Temporary Provisions) Act 1989 was retained in each of the three statutes. In contrast, a positive obligation to disclose suspicions of money laundering, established in Article 6 of Council Directive (EEC) 91/308, was imposed only in relation to the laundering of the proceeds of drug trafficking and terrorist property (by the 1994 and 2000 Acts respectively).

14.18 The reasoning behind this distinction is not clear and, it is suggested, may have led those subject to the duty of disclosure into difficulty. An organization may well have suspicions that funds with which it is dealing are 'dirty' but it is unlikely to know—or be in a position to know—the source of those funds. That, after all, is the purpose of money laundering. Without knowledge or suspicion of the source of the funds in question an organization would not know whether it was under a positive obligation of disclosure or merely entitled to make such disclosure voluntarily. However, in the context of the legislation, it may be that the omission of a positive obligation of disclosure from the Criminal Justice Act 1988 was of no great consequence since an individual who suspected that money laundering was taking place is likely to have wanted to reveal those suspicions for fear that the source of the funds concerned was drug trafficking or terrorism.

14.19 This area of potential difficulty has now been removed by the introduction of the Proceeds of Crime Act 2002 which has done away with the distinction between the laundering of drug money and that of the proceeds of other criminal conduct.

---

[8] SI 1993/1933.

Under the 2002 Act a positive obligation to disclose suspicions of money laundering is imposed on those organizations falling within the definition of the 'regulated sector'.[9] In all other cases the protection for those making voluntary disclosure of their suspicions is retained.

Offences relating to the proceeds of crime

Sections 93A to 93D of the Criminal Justice Act 1988 established four offences related to the laundering of the 'proceeds of criminal conduct'. The term 'criminal conduct' was defined in section 93A(7) to mean conduct constituting an offence to which Part VI of the Act applied or which would have constituted such an offence if it had been committed in England and Wales. **14.20**

Section 93A of the Act created the primary offence of money laundering. Section 93A(1) made it an offence to enter into or be concerned in any arrangement whereby: **14.21**

    (a) the retention or control by or on behalf of another ('A') of A's proceeds of criminal conduct is facilitated (whether by concealment, removal from the jurisdiction, transfer to nominees or otherwise); or

    (b) A's proceeds of criminal conduct—
        (i) are used to secure that funds are placed at A's disposal; or
        (ii) are used for A's benefit to acquire property by way of investment, knowing or suspecting that A is a person who is or has been engaged in criminal conduct or has benefited from criminal conduct . . .

Section 93B made it an offence to acquire, use or have possession of property which was known to be, or directly or indirectly to represent (in whole or part), another person's proceeds of criminal conduct. It was also an offence, by virtue of section 93C, to conceal, disguise, convert or transfer any property which represented the proceeds of criminal conduct for the purpose of avoiding prosecution for an offence under Part VI of the Act. **14.22**

The last of the four relevant sections, section 93D, made it an offence to 'tip off' another about an investigation into suspected money laundering. **14.23**

Offences in connection with the proceeds of drug trafficking

Part III of the Drug Trafficking Act 1994 created a series of similar offences specifically in relation to laundering the proceeds of drug trafficking. **14.24**

Section 49 of that Act mirrored the provisions of section 93C of the 1988 Act and created the offence of concealing, disguising, converting or transferring any property which represented (whether in whole or in part and whether directly or indirectly) the proceeds of drug trafficking for the purpose of avoiding prosecution for **14.25**

---

[9] See Sch 9 to the 2002 Act.

a drug trafficking offence or avoiding the making or enforcement of a confiscation order.

14.26 Section 50 of the Act established the offence of assisting another person to retain the benefit of the proceeds of drug trafficking. The main ingredients of the offence were defined in identical terms to those of the similar offence created by section 93A of the 1988 Act.

14.27 In a similar vein the offence (found in section 93B of the 1988 Act) of acquiring, using or having possession of property which was known to be, or directly or indirectly to represent (in whole or part), another person's proceeds of criminal conduct was reproduced, in relation to drug trafficking, in section 51 of the 1994 Act.

14.28 Section 52 of the Act created the offence of failing to disclose to the police knowledge or a suspicion of the laundering of the proceeds of drug trafficking.

14.29 Similarly section 53 of the Act made it an offence to 'tip off' another about an investigation into suspected drug money laundering.

The Proceeds of Crime Act 2002

14.30 The Proceeds of Crime Act 2002 received the Royal Assent on 24 July 2002. That Act introduces wide-ranging provisions relating to the confiscation of the proceeds of crime, including the establishment of the Assets Recovery Agency under the direction of the Home Secretary. Part 7 of the Act[10] operates to streamline the offences of money laundering found in the previous legislation. Its primary effect is to remove the distinction between the laundering of drug money and the laundering of the proceeds of other crime.

14.31 Part 7 of the 2002 Act creates three primary offences relating to money laundering, which apply whatever the source of the 'criminal property' in question. Those offences are:

(a) concealing, disguising, converting or transferring criminal property or removing it from the jurisdiction: section 327;

(b) entering into or being concerned in arrangements to facilitate the acquisition, retention, use or control of criminal property: section 328; and

(c) acquiring, using or having possession of criminal property: section 329.

'Criminal property' is defined by section 340(3) of the Act as property constituting a person's benefit from criminal conduct or which represents such a benefit (in whole or in part, whether directly or indirectly) and which the alleged offender knows or suspects constitutes or represents such a benefit. In line with the previ-

---

[10] Which is scheduled to come into force shortly.

ous legislation conduct is criminal if it amounts to an offence in the United Kingdom or would do so if the offence had been committed here. The provisions of this part of the Act now extend the offences of money laundering to include the laundering of the proceeds of crime by the criminal himself as well as by others.

Section 327 of the 2002 Act replaces section 49 of the Drug Trafficking Act 1994 **14.32** and section 93C of the Criminal Justice Act 1988. The section provides that:

(1) A person commits an offence if he:
 (a) conceals criminal property;
 (b) disguises criminal property;
 (c) converts criminal property;
 (d) transfers criminal property;
 (e) removes criminal property from England and Wales or from Scotland or from Northern Ireland.

By virtue of section 327(3):

concealing or disguising criminal property includes concealing or disguising its nature, source, location, disposition, movement or ownership or any rights with respect to it.

Section 327(2) provides certain exceptions from the commission of the offences **14.33** established by section 327(1). These are:

(a) that the person concerned made an 'authorized disclosure' under section 338 of the Act and obtained the appropriate consent;[11]
(b) that the person concerned intended to make such an authorized disclosure but has a reasonable excuse for not having done so; and
(c) that the act in question was done in carrying out a function relating to the enforcement of any provision of the Act or of any other enactment relating to criminal conduct or the benefit of such conduct.

The offences created by section 93A of the Criminal Justice Act 1988 and section **14.34** 50 of the Drug Trafficking Act 1994 are simplified and replaced by section 328 of the 2002 Act. Section 328 makes it an offence to enter into or to be concerned in any arrangement which the person concerned knows or suspects will facilitate the acquisition, retention, use or control of criminal property by or on behalf of another person. The commission of this offence is subject to the same exceptions as are provided for by section 327.[12]

Section 329 of the 2002 Act reintroduces and streamlines the offences of acquir- **14.35** ing, using or possessing criminal property found in section 93B of the Criminal Justice Act 1988 and section 51 of the Drug Trafficking Act 1994. Section 329 provides:

---

[11] See paras 14.46 to 14.48 below.
[12] See para 14.33 above.

(1) A person commits an offence if he:
   (a) acquires criminal property;
   (b) uses criminal property;
   (c) has possession of criminal property.

As with sections 327 and 328 of the 2002 Act, exceptions to the commission of the offence are provided by sub-section 2. These are in identical terms save that section 329(2) also makes it a defence to the charge of acquiring, using or having possession of criminal property that the property was acquired for adequate consideration.

14.36 Rather than seek to define what amounts to 'adequate consideration' section 329(3) defines what is 'inadequate consideration', namely consideration which is significantly less than the value of the property or the value of its use or possession. The provision of goods or services which it is known or suspected may help another to carry out criminal conduct is not consideration.

14.37 As with the earlier legislation an offence of 'tipping off' is created by section 333 of the 2002 Act. That section makes it an offence (in circumstances where the alleged offender knows or suspects that a protected or authorized disclosure has been made under sections 337 and 338[13]) to make any disclosure which is likely to prejudice any investigation which might follow the making of the section 337 or 338 disclosure.

14.38 It is a defence to a charge of tipping off under section 333 that:

(a) the person concerned did not know that the disclosure was likely to prejudice any investigation; or

(b) the disclosure in question was done in carrying out a function relating to the enforcement of any provision of the Act or of any other enactment relating to criminal conduct or the benefit of such conduct; or

(c) the person making the disclosure is a professional legal adviser and the disclosure is made to his client (or a representative of that client) in connection with giving the client legal advice or the disclosure is made to any person in connection with legal proceedings or contemplated legal proceedings. However, this defence will not avail the lawyer who makes the disclosure with the intention of furthering some criminal purpose.

Offences in relation to terrorist property

14.39 The laundering of 'terrorist property'[14] remains subject to its own legislative control, in the form of section 18 of the Terrorism Act 2000. That section makes it an

---

[13] See paras 14.44 to 14.48 below.

[14] 'Terrorist property' is defined by section 14 of the 2000 Act as meaning: '(a) money or other property which is likely to be used for the purposes of terrorism (including any resources of a proscribed organization), (b) proceeds of the commission of acts of terrorism, and (c) proceeds of acts carried out for the purposes of terrorism'.

offence to enter into or be concerned in any arrangement which facilitates the retention or control by or on behalf of another person of terrorist property by concealing that property, removing it from the jurisdiction, transferring it to nominees or in any other way. By virtue of section 18(2) the onus is on the defendant to show that he did not know, and had no reasonable cause to suspect, that the arrangement in which he was involved related to terrorist property.

A mandatory obligation to disclose to a police officer a belief or suspicion that **14.40** another person has committed an offence under sections 15 to 18 is imposed by section 19 of the 2000 Act. The section applies to those who acquire relevant information about terrorist activities in the course of their trade, profession, business or employment.[15] However, professional legal advisers are exempt from the duty if the information is acquired by them in 'privileged circumstances'.[16]

A person who forms a belief or suspicion that money or property is terrorist prop- **14.41** erty within the meaning of the Act but who is not under a duty to disclose that information by virtue of section 19(1)(b) may nonetheless rely on the power found in section 20 to permit him to disclose his belief or suspicion. The power created by this section overrides any statutory or common law restrictions on the disclosure of information.

It is an offence, by virtue of section 36 of the Act, to disclose to another anything **14.42** which is likely to prejudice a 'terrorist investigation'[17]—including an investigation resulting from the disclosure of information by virtue of sections 19 and 20. Similarly it is an offence to interfere with any material which is likely to be relevant to the investigation.

D. Blowing the Whistle on Money Laundering

Voluntary whistle-blowing

It was a theme common to the money laundering provisions of both the Criminal **14.43** Justice Act 1988 and the Drug Trafficking Act 1994, as well as the Terrorism Act 2000, that provision was made for the voluntary (as opposed to compulsory) disclosure of suspicions of money laundering. In each case the statutory power of disclosure overrode any statutory or common law restriction upon the disclosure of information. Similar provisions are retained in the Proceeds of Crime Act 2002.

---

[15] Terrorism Act 2000, s 19(1)(b).

[16] ibid, ss 19(5) and 19(6).

[17] 'Terrorist investigation' is defined by s 32 of the 2000 Act to mean an investigation of '(a) the commission, preparation or instigation of acts of terrorism, (b) an act which appears to have been done for the purposes of terrorism, (c) the resources of a proscribed organization, (d) the possibility of making an order under section 3(3) [proscribing terrorist organizations], or (e) the commission, preparation or instigation of an offence under this Act.'

14.44   Section 337 of the Proceeds of Crime Act 2002 (which applies to both voluntary and mandatory disclosure) can be seen to be aimed at encouraging those outside the 'regulated sector'[18] who find that they (or those for whom they work) are dealing with funds or investments which originate from criminal activities to reveal that fact. Under the terms of that section:

    (1)   A disclosure which satisfies the following three conditions is not to be taken to breach any restriction on the disclosure of information (however imposed).

    (2)   The first condition is that the information or other matter disclosed came to the person making the disclosure (the discloser) in the course of his trade, profession, business or employment;

    (3)   The second condition is that the information or other matter:

        (a)   causes the discloser to know or suspect, or

        (b)   gives him reasonable grounds for knowing or suspecting, that another person is engaged in money laundering.

    (4)   The third condition is that the disclosure is made to a constable, a customs officer or a nominated officer as soon as is practicable after the information or other matter comes to the discloser.

    (5)   A disclosure to a nominated officer is a disclosure which:

        (a)   is made to a person nominated by the discloser's employer to receive disclosures under this section, and

        (b)   is made in the course of the discloser's employment and in accordance with the procedure established by the employer for the purpose.

14.45   Thus:

    (a)   a person who in the course of his trade, business, profession or employment;

    (b)   becomes privy to information which causes him to know or suspect or to have reasonable grounds to know or suspect that another person is engaging in money-laundering;

is entitled to make his knowledge or suspicion known to a police officer, a customs officer or a 'nominated officer' appointed by his employer to receive such information in accordance with the employer's procedures. If he does so that disclosure will not amount to a breach of any duty owed by him, whether statutory, contractual or in tort.

14.46   Similarly section 338 of the Act makes provision for the making of 'authorized disclosures'. In the context of this part of the 2002 Act the expression 'authorized disclosure' may be thought to be something of a misnomer since the making of a disclosure under section 338 is not, itself, an authorized act. Section 338 provides that a disclosure is authorized if:

    (a)   it is a disclosure to a constable, a customs officer or a nominated officer by the alleged offender that property is criminal property,

---

[18] 'Regulated sector' is defined in para 14.52 below. It should be noted that nominated officers in businesses outside the regulated sector may be subject to an obligation to make disclosure in the appropriate circumstances. See s 332 of the 2002 Act at paras 14.57 and 14.58 below.

(b) it is made in the form and manner (if any) prescribed for the purposes of this subsection by order under section 339, and

(c) the first or second condition set out below is satisfied.

The conditions referred to are:

(i) that the disclosure is made before the offender does the prohibited act;[19] or

(ii) that the disclosure is made after the doing of the prohibited act in circumstances where there was good reason for failing to make the disclosure before doing that act and where the subsequent disclosure was made on the discloser's own initiative and as soon as practicable after he did the act concerned.

Despite the description 'authorized disclosure' given to a disclosure made under section 338 of the Act, a discloser obtains a defence to a charge of money laundering brought under sections 327, 328 or 329 of the 2002 Act only where, as the result of that disclosure, he obtains the (actual or deemed) consent of the police officer, customs officer or nominated officer to whom the disclosure was made to do the prohibited act concerned.[20] Sections 335 and 336 of the 2002 Act govern the giving of consent to do an act otherwise prohibited by sections 327 to 329.[21]   **14.47**

Section 338(4) provides that an authorized disclosure is not to be treated as a breach of any restriction on the disclosure of information, however that restriction is imposed.   **14.48**

In the context of terrorism, section 20 of the Terrorism Act 2000 operates to provide protection to those who voluntarily reveal wrongdoing. The section is entitled 'Disclosure of information: permission' and provides: **14.49**

> 20.—(1) A person may disclose to a constable—
>> (a) a suspicion or belief that any money or other property is terrorist property or is derived from terrorist property;

---

[19] 'Prohibited act' in this context is defined by s 338(6) to mean any of the acts mentioned in ss 327(1), 328(1) or 329(1) (the primary money laundering offences created by the 2002 Act).

[20] In each case sub-section (2) of the relevant section affords a defence where the alleged offender 'makes an authorized disclosure under section 338 and (if the disclosure is made before he does the act mentioned in subsection (1)) he has the appropriate consent'.

[21] Section 335 provides that a person is to be treated as having the appropriate consent where he has made an authorized disclosure to a police or customs officer and either: (i) he obtains consent from that officer to do the act; or (ii) he does not receive notice within 7 working days after the disclosure is made that consent to do the act in question is refused; or (iii) he receives notice within 7 working days that consent is refused but the moratorium period of 31 days from the date of the disclosure has expired. By virtue of section 336 a nominated officer may give his consent to the doing of a prohibited act provided that he has made disclosure to the Director General of the NCIS and: (iv) he has obtained consent for the act to be done; or (v) he has not received notice within 7 working days after the disclosure is made that consent to do the act in question is refused; or (vi) he receives notice within 7 working days that consent is refused but the moratorium period of 31 days from the date of the disclosure has expired. It is an offence, punishable by up to 5 years' imprisonment, for a nominated officer to give consent to act in circumstances where these conditions are not satisfied.

(b) any matter on which the suspicion or belief is based.

(2) A person may make a disclosure to a constable in the circumstances mentioned in section 19(1) and (2).[22]

(3) Subsections (1) and (2) shall have effect notwithstanding any restriction on the disclosure of information imposed by statute or otherwise.

(4) Where—

(a) a person is in employment, and

(b) his employer has established a procedure for the making of disclosures of the kinds mentioned in subsection (1) and section 19(2), subsections (1) and (2) shall have effect in relation to that person as if any reference to disclosure to a constable included a reference to disclosure in accordance with the procedure.

Mandatory whistle-blowing

14.50 It was in the context of the enforced disclosure of wrongdoing that the Drug Trafficking Act 1994, the Criminal Justice Act 1988 and the Terrorism Act 2000 parted company from one another. Unlike either the Drug Trafficking Act 1994 or the Terrorism Act 2000, Part VI of the Criminal Justice Act 1988 did not impose any obligation to reveal suspicions of money laundering where the source of funds in question was neither drugs nor terrorism. Such disclosure was made on a purely voluntary basis.

14.51 That inconsistency in approach has been removed by the enactment of the Proceeds of Crime Act 2002. The duties of disclosure imposed by the 2002 Act apply whatever the source of the funds. There are three categories of obligation:

(a) that imposed upon those working in the regulated sector;

(b) that imposed upon 'nominated officers' working in the regulated sector; and

(c) that imposed upon 'nominated officers' who do not work in the regulated sector.

Failure to disclose: regulated sector

14.52 The 'regulated sector' is defined in Schedule 9 to the Act. The definition encompasses banks, building societies and other credit and financial institutions. It also extends to the operation of bureaux de change and businesses engaged in the transmission of money by any means or the cashing of cheques made payable to their customers. As the Home Office Explanatory Note[23] on the intended operation of the Act highlights, the definition of businesses and organizations within the regulated sector broadly reflects those organizations found in article 4 of the Money Laundering Regulations 1993.

---

[22] See para 14.59 below.

[23] Explanatory Notes to the Proceeds Of Crime Act 2002 (HMSO, ISBN 010 562 902 2).

The obligation of disclosure imposed by section 330 of the 2002 Act creates an of- **14.53**
fence (punishable by imprisonment for up to five years following conviction on
indictment) in circumstances where:

(a) the person in question knows or suspects or has reasonable grounds for know-
    ing or suspecting[24] that another person is engaged in money laundering; and

(b) the information or other matters on which that knowledge or suspicion is
    based or which give rise to reasonable grounds for knowing or suspecting that
    money laundering is taking place came to him in the course of a business in
    the regulated sector; and

(c) he does not disclose his knowledge or suspicion to the nominated officer or to
    a person authorized by the Director-General of the National Criminal
    Intelligence Service ('NCIS') in the prescribed manner as soon as is practic-
    able after that information became known to him.

A defence is afforded by section 330(6) and (7). **14.54**

(a) It is not an offence to fail to make the required disclosure if the person con-
    cerned had a reasonable excuse for not disclosing the information concerned.

(b) Similarly, it is a defence for a professional legal adviser to show that the
    information in question came to his or her knowledge in circumstances
    which give rise to privilege.

(c) By virtue of sub-section (7) no offence is committed where the person con-
    cerned did not know or suspect that money laundering was taking place and
    his employer has not provided him with training of the type specified by the
    Secretary of State.

For the purposes of section 330(5) disclosure to a nominated officer is disclosure **14.55**
to a person nominated by his employer to receive that information made in the
course of the discloser's employment in accordance with the relevant procedures
of his employer.

Failure to disclose: nominated officers in the regulated sector

It is an offence, by virtue of section 331 of the 2002 Act, for a nominated officer **14.56**
who knows or suspects or has reasonable grounds for knowing or suspecting that
money laundering is taking place as the result of information given to him following a disclosure made under section 330, to fail to make the necessary disclosure to the person nominated by the Director-General of the NCIS as soon as
practicable after the information became known to him. The only defence open

---

[24] It should be noted that the provisions of s 330(2)(b) extend criminal culpability to include
negligence on the part of the person concerned where, objectively, there were reasonable grounds
for suspecting money laundering.

to a nominated officer in these circumstances is to show that he had a reasonable excuse for not making the disclosure.

Failure to disclose: other nominated officers

14.57   As has previously been identified,[25] outside the regulated sector the Act makes provision for disclosure of suspicions of money laundering to be made voluntarily. Where such voluntary disclosure is made the Act affords protection to the 'whistle-blower'. Under the terms of section 337(4) such disclosure may be made to a police officer, customs officer or to an officer nominated for that purpose by the discloser's employer. Similarly section 338 of the Act makes provision for the making of 'authorized disclosures'.

14.58   Under the provisions of section 332 of the 2002 Act a person nominated to receive disclosures made under either section 337 or section 338:

(a) who knows or suspects that another is engaged in money laundering;

(b) as the result of information given to him following a 'protected' or 'authorized' disclosure; and

(c) who does not, as soon as practicable, disclose that information to the person authorized by the Director-General of the NCIS to receive it;

commits an offence punishable by up to five years' imprisonment.

The duty of disclosure under the Terrorism Act 2000

14.59   Section 19 of the Terrorism Act 2000 imposes a similar obligation to disclose information. That section is entitled 'Disclosure of Information: Duty' and provides (so far as is relevant):

(1) This section applies where a person—
    (a) believes or suspects that another person has committed an offence under any of sections 15 to 18, and
    (b) bases his belief or suspicion on information which comes to his attention in the course of a trade, profession, business or employment.

(2) The person commits an offence if he does not disclose to a constable as soon as is reasonably practicable—
    (a) his belief or suspicion, and
    (b) the information on which it is based.

(3) It is a defence for a person charged with an offence under subsection (2) to prove that he had a reasonable excuse for not making the disclosure.

---

[25] See paras 14.44 and 14.45 above.

E. Protecting the Whistle-blower

The mandatory duty of disclosure imposed by both the Drug Trafficking Act **14.60** 1994 and the Terrorism Act 2000 extended further than the duty created by Article 6 of Council Directive (EEC) 91/308. That latter duty is limited in its operation to 'credit and financial institutions'[26] and their directors and employees' whereas the corresponding duty imposed by the Drug Trafficking Act 1994 and the Terrorism Act 2000 was not subject to the same limitation. In each case the obligation applied to those who derived their belief or suspicion that the laundering of drug or terrorist money was taking place from information acquired by them in the course of any trade, profession, business or employment.

Arguably the context in which the duty of disclosure was imposed by the drug **14.61** trafficking and terrorism legislation may suggest that the difference in approach between the 1991 Directive and the UK Acts was more apparent than real since, in practice, the requirements of the UK legislation were likely to impact primarily on organizations operating within the financial sector.

Nevertheless it is to be noted that the introduction of the Proceeds of Crime Act **14.62** 2002 has brought the United Kingdom legislation (save as regards terrorism) more into line with the terms of the 1991 Directive. As has been noted the duty of disclosure imposed by the 2002 Act extends only to those working in the regulated sector (save in the case of nominated officers in businesses outside the regulated sector) in contrast to the provisions of the earlier legislation which imposed the obligation upon all those who acquired the relevant information in the course of any trade, business, profession or employment.

As the provisions of the Home Office guidance[27] on the operation of the Proceeds **14.63** of Crime Act 2002 make clear, the terms of section 337(1) afford protection to those who 'blow the whistle' on money laundering voluntarily as well as pursuant to the duties imposed by the Act, provided that the conditions imposed by that section are observed. Those conditions are:

---

[26] Article 1 of the Directive defines 'credit institution' as 'a credit institution, as defined as in the first indent of Article 1 of Directive 77/780/EEC, as last amended by Directive 89/646/EEC, and includes branches within the meaning of the third indent of that Article and located in the Community, of credit institutions having their head offices outside the Community.' 'Financial institution' is defined as 'an undertaking other than a credit institution whose principal activity is to carry out one or more of the operations included in numbers 2 to 12 and number 14 of the list annexed to Directive 89/646/EEC, or an insurance company duly authorized in accordance with Directive 79/267/EEC, as last amended by Directive 90/619/EEC, in so far as it carries out activities covered by that Directive; this definition includes branches located in the Community of financial institutions whose head offices are outside the Community'.

[27] Explanatory Notes (n 23 above) para 491.

(2) The first condition is that the information or other matter disclosed came to the person making the disclosure (the discloser) in the course of his trade, profession, business or employment.

(3) The second condition is that the information or other matter:
   (a) causes the discloser to know or suspect, or
   (b) gives him reasonable grounds for knowing or suspecting that another person is engaged in money laundering.

(4) The third condition is that the disclosure is made to a constable, a customs officer or a nominated officer as soon as is practicable after the information or other matter comes to the discloser.

Disclosure which satisfies the three conditions of the section is not to be taken to be a breach of any restriction on the disclosure of information, however imposed. This wide-ranging protection covers any duty imposed by statute, contract or in tort imposing a prohibition on the making of such disclosure. The protection afforded to those who make an authorized disclosure pursuant to section 338 of the Act is in identical terms.[28]

14.64 Similarly section 20(3) of the Terrorism Act 2000 provides that the power to make voluntary disclosure of suspected money laundering:

> shall have effect notwithstanding any restriction on the disclosure of information imposed by statute or otherwise.

In each case the statutory exclusion of liability is as wide as it is possible to imagine.

14.65 Section 19 of the Terrorism Act 2000 is the exception to the general rule in that, unlike sections 337 and 338 of the Proceeds of Crime Act 2002, it makes no express provision for an exemption from liability following a disclosure made pursuant to the statutory duty. However, in the context of a statutory obligation to disclose suspicions of wrongdoing, it is suggested that this omission does not deprive the unwitting launderer of terrorist funds of protection. Like its counterpart in the 2002 Act, section 19 of the Terrorism Act 2000 creates a positive statutory duty to disclose suspected criminal activity. It has long been recognized that an express statutory duty of this type will override any contractual or other duty to keep confidential such information. In a decision concerning the duty of confidence owed by a solicitor to his client the Court of Appeal concluded that:

> What we are concerned with here is the contractual duty of confidence, generally implied though sometimes expressed, between a solicitor and client. Such a duty exists not only between solicitor and client, but, for example, between banker and customer, doctor and patient and accountant and client. Such a duty of confidence is subject to, and overridden by, the duty of any party to that contract to comply with the law of the land. If it is the duty of such a party to a contract, whether at common law or under statute, to disclose in defined circumstances confidential information,

---

[28] See para 14.48 above.

then he must do so, and any express contract to the contrary would be illegal and void. For example, in the case of banker and customer, the duty of confidence is subject to the overriding duty of the banker at common law to disclose and answer questions as to his customer's affairs when he is asked to give evidence on them in the witness box in a court of law. I think that similar provisions as to disclosure apply to doctors under the National Health Act.[29]

Thus, in omitting an express exclusion of liability, it may perhaps be considered that, section 19 of the Terrorism Act 2000 most closely follows the existing law. Furthermore the express statutory defence to liability following disclosure found in section 337 of the Proceeds of Crime Act 2002 may be seen as unnecessary to protect those who find themselves bound to make disclosure about money laundering since such protection arises from the existence of the statutory duty to disclose.

Protecting banks who blow the whistle on money launderers

It may readily be recognized that it is banks and other financial institutions on whom the legislation governing money laundering is most likely to impact. Similarly it may be considered that it is banks which have the most to gain from the protection afforded by the statutes to those who do blow the whistle. **14.66**

After a period of uncertainty during the nineteenth century it was confirmed by the Court of Appeal in 1924 in the decision in *Tournier v National Provincial and Union Bank of England*[30] that there exists an implied duty of confidentiality in the relationship of banker and customer. At page 483 of the judgment Atkin LJ said: **14.67**

> Is there any term as to secrecy to be implied from the relationship of banker and customer? I have myself no doubt that there is.

He went on to attempt to define the extent of the duty of confidentiality which he considered existed. He expressed it in this way:

> The first question is: To what information does the obligation of secrecy extend? It clearly goes beyond the state of the account, that is whether there is a debit or a credit balance, and the amount of that balance. It must extend at least to all the transactions that go through the account, and to the securities, if any, given in respect of the account; and in respect of such matters it must, I think, extend beyond the period when the account is closed, or ceases to be an active account . . . I further think that the obligation extends to information obtained from other sources than the customer's actual account, if the occasion upon which the information was obtained arose out of the banking relations of the bank and its customers . . .

In reaching the decision on the existence of the duty of confidentiality the Court of Appeal recognized that it must be seen as a qualified, and not an absolute, duty. In the course of his judgment Bankes LJ put it in these terms: **14.68**

---

[29] *Parry-Jones v The Law Society* [1969] 1 Ch 1, 9, *per* Diplock LJ.
[30] [1924] 1 KB 461.

> At the present day I think it may be asserted with confidence that the duty is a legal one arising out of contract, and that the duty is not absolute but qualified. It is not possible to frame any exhaustive definition of the duty. The most that can be done is to classify the qualification, and to indicate its limits.[31]

14.69   The qualifications to the duty of confidentiality were classified by Bankes LJ under four heads:

> (a) where disclosure is under compulsion by law; (b) where there is a duty to the public to disclose; (c) where the interests of the bank require disclosure; (d) where the disclosure is made by the express or implied consent of the customer.[32]

14.70   These qualifications establish important limits on the extent of the duty of confidentiality owed by banks to their customers. In particular it is to be noted that, in defining the duty, the Court of Appeal was swift to recognize an exception where the law expressly imposed a duty to make disclosure. Thus in the case of a disclosure made pursuant to the statutory duty created by sections 330 to 332 of the Proceeds of Crime Act 2002 or section 19 of the Terrorism Act 2000 a bank will be entitled to rely on that obligation to override the duty of confidence owed to its customer, even without the express protection provided by the former of the two Acts. These statutory exceptions to the duty of confidentiality are not novel. In his report into the banking industry,[33] Professor RB Jack identified 19 occasions when banks are under a statutory duty to disclose the activities of their customers.

14.71   However, the position may be seen to be different where suspicions of money laundering are disclosed to the authorities not under the compulsion of statute but voluntarily. Notwithstanding the qualifications identified by the Court of Appeal in the *Tournier* case, the duty of confidence remains an important feature of the relationship between a bank and its customer. Thus a bank wishing to make voluntary disclosure of the state of its customer's account because it suspects that he is involved in money laundering finds itself in a difficult position. Without the assistance of statute such disclosure could only properly be made if it could be shown that the bank owed the public a duty to make the disclosure or if it could be said that the bank's interests required it to be made. Fortunately for the banking industry Parliament has removed this difficulty by providing those who decide to reveal their suspicions of money laundering voluntarily with a statutory exemption from liability.

---

[31] *Tournier v National Provincial and Union Bank of England* [1924] 1 KB 461, 471–472.
[32] ibid, 473.
[33] Review Committee, *Banking Services: Law and Practice* (Cmnd 622, 1979).

F. Conclusion

The laundering of the proceeds of crime, drug trafficking and terrorism is a grow- **14.72**
ing international problem which requires an international solution. For the countries of Europe the attempt to solve the problem of money laundering has taken
three forms; the Vienna Convention 1988, the Council of Europe Convention on
laundering, tracing, seizure and confiscation of the proceeds of crime 1990, and
Council Directive (EEC) 91/308.

In the United Kingdom those provisions initially found their way into domestic **14.73**
law in three distinct pieces of legislation dealing respectively with the proceeds of
crime generally, drug money, and terrorist property. That division has now narrowed to two separate enactments. The common theme of each of the Acts is the
creation of a statutory *power* as well as a statutory *duty* to disclose to the authorities suspicions or beliefs that money laundering is taking place. In each case where
such disclosure is made the statutes afford a statutory defence to liability arising
from the making of the disclosure. For those who would otherwise be bound by
duties of confidence owed to their clients this statutory defence is of importance.

15

LOCAL GOVERNMENT

A. Introduction

This chapter is concerned with access to meetings and documents of local au-   **15.01**
thorities (part B), and with the duties and discretions of local authorities to disclose information (part C). The particular problems relating to the publication of
local authority reports, which are the subject of a Law Commission Consultation
Paper,[1] are considered at the end of the chapter (part D).

It should be noted at the outset that, apart from the Freedom of Information Act   **15.02**
2000 itself,[2] the applicable statutory provisions in this field are to be found in the
Local Government (Access to Information) Act 1985, the Local Government Act
2000 and the Data Protection Act 1998.[3] The interrelationship of these statutes is

---

[1] Law Commission, *Publication of Local Authority Reports* (Law Com No 163, 2002).
[2] See, for example, the obligations of local authorities to produce publication schemes: ch 4
above.
[3] See ch 10 above.

neither simple nor settled,[4] and the government is undertaking a comprehensive review of access to information held by local authorities with the aim of providing a clear and comprehensive code: in September 2002 the Office of the Deputy Prime Minister produced a policy paper, *Access to Information in Local Government*. This invited comments from councils and user-groups.[5]

B. Access to Meetings and Documents of Local Authorities

Part VA of the Local Government Act 1972

15.03 The Local Government (Access to Information) Act 1985 inserted a new Part VA, comprising sections 100A to 100K, into the Local Government Act 1972. Part VA applies to 'principal councils', which are defined[6] so as to include the councils of non-metropolitan counties, district or London boroughs, Welsh counties and county boroughs, as well as joint authorities, joint boards and joint committees, and in addition special cases such as the Common Council of the City of London and the Broads Authority.[7] Part VA extends (with modifications) to committees and sub-committees of those bodies.[8] The provisions also apply (again with modifications) to community health councils.[9]

15.04 The substantive effect of section 100A is that normally meetings of principal councils, their committees and sub-committees must be open to the public. There are two significant exceptions, which relate to 'confidential' and 'exempt' information.

15.05 Whenever it is likely that confidential information would be disclosed to members of the public in breach of an obligation of confidence, the council must exclude the public from the meeting. In this context 'confidential information' means (a) information furnished to the council by a government department on terms which forbid the disclosure of the information to the public, and (b) information the disclosure of which to the public is prohibited by or under any enactment or by a court order.[10]

15.06 Whenever it is likely that 'exempt information' would be disclosed to members of the public the council 'may' exclude the public from the meeting.[11] 'Exempt

---

[4] The current legal position 'is somewhat in a state of flux': Law Com No 163 (n 1 above) 124, para B8.

[5] ibid, 129, paras B8 and B25, and see the Deputy Prime Minister's written answer to the Parliamentary Question from Andy Love (Labour), *Hansard*, HC (series 5) vol 389, col 999 (23 July 2002).

[6] See the Local Government Act 1972, s 270(1) (as amended).

[7] ibid, and s 100J.

[8] ibid, s 100E.

[9] Community Health Councils (Access to Information) Act 1988, s 1.

[10] Local Government Act 1972, s 100A(2) and (3).

[11] ibid, s 100A(4).

information' is defined in section 100I of the 1972 Act, and in Schedule 12A to that Act. The section provides that the descriptions of exempt information are those 'for the time being specified in Part 1 of Schedule 12A of the Act', subject to qualifications contained in Part II;[12] the Secretary of State may by order vary the descriptions.[13] The descriptions presently specified include a number of particular forms of personal and commercial information, as well as information relating to legal proceedings and action in connection with the prevention, investigation or prosecution of a crime.

Public notice of meetings

Principal councils must give public notice of the time and place of a meeting by posting it at the council offices at least three clear days before the meeting or, if the meeting is convened at shorter notice, then at the time it is convened. While the meeting is open to the public (that is, so long as the meeting is not dealing with items of business concerning confidential or exempt information) (i) the council does not have power to exclude members of the public (without prejudice to the power of exclusion to suppress or prevent disorderly conduct at the meeting), and (ii) duly accredited newspaper[14] representatives must, as far as practicable, be afforded reasonable facilities for taking a report and for telephoning the report at their own expense.[15] **15.07**

Copies of agendas and reports

Copies of the agenda and of any report for a council meeting must be open to inspection by members of the public at least three clear days before the meeting or when the meeting is convened, if convened at shorter notice. The whole of a report or any part of it can, however, be withheld if it relates to items during which, in the opinion of the proper officer, the meeting is not likely to be open to the public. Items which are added to the agenda at a late stage must be open for inspection from the time that they are so added.[16] **15.08**

An item of business may not be considered at a meeting unless the rules as to availability for public inspection have been complied with or, by reason of special circumstances (which must be specified in the minutes) the chairman of the meeting is of the opinion that the item should be considered as a matter of urgency.[17] **15.09**

Where the whole or any part of a report for a meeting is not open for public inspection every copy of the report or part must be marked 'Not for publication', **15.10**

---

[12] ibid, s 100I(1).
[13] ibid, s 100I(2) and (3).
[14] Which for the purpose of Part VA includes radio and television news organizations: s 100K.
[15] ibid, s 100A(6) and (8).
[16] ibid, s 100B(1), (2) and (3).
[17] ibid, s 100B(4).

and there must be stated on it a description, in terms of the Schedule 12A categories,[18] of the exempt information by virtue of which the council is likely to exclude the public during the relevant item.[19]

15.11 At a meeting open to members of the public there must be provided a reasonable number of copies of the agenda and relevant reports for their use. If the press make such a request they must be supplied with a copy of the agenda and the relevant reports, such further statements or particulars as are necessary to indicate the nature of items included in the agenda and, if the proper officer thinks fit, copies of any other documents supplied to members of the council in connection with the item.[20]

Certain documents to remain open for public inspection

15.12 After a meeting, certain specified documents must be open to public inspection for a period of six years, beginning with the date of the meeting. The documents are:

(a) the minutes, or a copy of the minutes, of the meeting, excluding so much of the minutes of proceedings during which the meeting was not open to the public as discloses exempt information;

(b) a written summary made by the proper officer so as to provide a fair and coherent record of proceedings without disclosing exempt information, where the exclusion of part of the minutes has the result that the published part does not provide such a record;

(c) a copy of the agenda; and

(d) a copy of so much of any report for the meeting as relates to any item during which the meeting was open to the public.[21]

15.13 Where copies of the whole or part of a report are required to be open to public inspection, those copies must each include a copy of a list of the background papers for the report or the part of the report, and at least one copy of each of the documents included in that list must also be open to public inspection.[22] Copies of the documents must remain open for inspection for a period of four years from the date of the meeting.[23]

15.14 Nothing in section 100D requires any document which discloses exempt information to be included in the lists, and nothing requires or authorizes the inclusion in the list of any document which, if open to inspection, would disclose

---

[18] See para 15.06 above.
[19] Local Government Act 1972, s 100B(5).
[20] ibid, s 100B(6) and (7).
[21] ibid, s 100C.
[22] ibid, s 100D(1).
[23] ibid, s 100D(2).

confidential information within the meaning of section 100A(2).[24] 'Background papers' are those documents which disclose any facts or matters on which, in the opinion of the proper officer, a report or an important part of the report is based, and which have, in his opinion, been relied on to a material extent in preparing the report; they do not include any published works.[25]

Councillors' additional rights of access to documents

By a further amendment to the Local Government Act 1972, the Local **15.15** Government (Access to Information Act) 1985 gave to all members of principal councils additional rights of access to documents.[26] Such members are entitled to inspect any document which is in the possession or under the control of a principal council and contains material relating to any business to be transacted at a meeting of the council or its committees and sub-committees. That entitlement, however, does not apply where it appears to the proper officer that a document discloses exempt information within certain specified categories (which the Secretary of State may amend by order).[27]

At common law councillors are entitled to see confidential documents only when **15.16** they establish a 'need to know'. In *R v Birmingham City Council, ex p O*,[28] the applicants were foster parents of a child, and applied to the council to adopt the child. A councillor who was not herself a member of the social services committee became concerned that the applicants might not be suitable to adopt the child; she sought to see the relevant files of the social services department. The deputy director of social services indicated that the files would be shown to the councillor, and this proposed course was approved by the council itself. The applicants sought judicial review by way of an order prohibiting the disclosure of the files to the councillor. The Divisional Court refused the application, but the Court of Appeal, by a majority, allowed the appeal on the ground of the public interest in maintaining the confidentiality of the files. The House of Lords allowed the local authority's appeal, deciding that the councillor was entitled to see the files. However, the House of Lords held that a councillor had no automatic right of access to documents of a committee of which she was not a member: she had to establish (as she had succeeded in establishing in the instant case) a 'need to know': Lord Brightman referred to the 'general principle . . . that a councillor is entitled by virtue of his office to have access to all written material in the possession of the local authority of which he is a member, provided he has good reason for such

---

[24] ibid, s 100D(4).
[25] ibid, s 100D(5).
[26] ie, additional to the rights of members at common law.
[27] Local Government Act 1972, s 100F and s 100I.
[28] [1983] 1 AC 578.

access'.[29] The 'need to know' test continues to be relevant for this reason. Section 100F improves the position of a councillor who is not a member of the relevant committee or sub-committee: there is no requirement, in general, to show a 'need to know'. However, it appears that a councillor, whether or not a member of the relevant committee, can be denied access to exempt information *unless* he can establish a 'need to know'. In other words, the 'need to know' trumps the 'exempt information' provisions.[30]

Duties and powers of councils to publish information

15.17 The relevant provisions (apart from the Freedom of Information Act)[31] are to be found in the Local Government Act 1972 and the Local Government, Planning and Land Act 1980.

15.18 Under section 100G of the 1972 Act (as inserted by the Local Government (Access to Information) Act 1985) every principal council must maintain, first, a register stating (a) the name and address of every member of the council for the time being and the ward or division which he or she represents; (b) the name and address of every member of each committee or sub-committee of the council for the time being. Secondly, the council must maintain a list (a) specifying the powers which are for the time being exercisable by officers, and (b) stating the title of the officer by whom each of the powers is exercisable. Thirdly, the council must keep at its offices a written summary of the rights to attend meetings of the council (and its committees and sub-committees) and to inspect and copy and to be furnished with documents by virtue of specified statutory provisions. Fourthly, all these documents must be open to inspection by the public at the council's offices.

15.19 Part II of the Local Government, Planning and Land Act 1980 (sections 2 to 4) places a duty on local authorities[32] to publish information concerning the discharge of their functions. The provisions envisage that the detailed means of carrying out the duty will be specified in codes of recommended practice issued by the Secretary of State.[33] The codes that have so far been issued include those relating to the publication of (a) annual reports and financial statements by local authorities, and (b) information about the handling of planning applications.[34]

15.20 Finally, local authorities are given, by virtue of section 142 of the Local Government Act 1972 (as amended by the Local Government Act 1986) powers

---

[29] [1983] 1 AC 578 (n28 above), 593. See also *R v Hackney LBC, ex p Gamper* [1985] 1 WLR 1229, where the court held that a councillor's right to attend meetings, like his right of access to documents, depended on whether he had a 'need to know'.

[30] See the discussion in *Encyclopaedia of Local Government Law*, para 2–206.14.

[31] See eg the obligation of local authorities to produce publication schemes: ch 4 above.

[32] Local Government, Planning and Land Act 1980, s 2(1).

[33] ibid, s 2(2) to (10).

[34] See *Encyclopaedia of Local Government Law* (n 30 above) paras 3-55 to 3-60.

(not duties) to provide information relating to the functions of the authorities and to the services provided within each local authority area whether by the authority itself or by any of the official or voluntary bodies mentioned in the section.

Local Government Act 2000

Part II of the Local Government Act 2000 introduced new executive structures for **15.21** local authorities. The authorities could choose to operate in the traditional way with decisions made by the council and its committees, or they could choose one of the new models. These were: (i) a mayor and cabinet executive, (ii) a leader and cabinet executive, and (iii) a mayor and council manager executive.[35]

Key decisions

Where a local authority chooses to discharge its executive functions under one of **15.22** the new models, new regulations apply in respect of access to information and decisions made by members of the executive.[36] The general principle of the Regulations is for the public to have access to meetings, documents and decisions where an executive, a committee or an individual is to take a 'key decision'. 'Key decision' is defined in regulation 8(1) of the Regulations as an executive decision which is likely:

(a) to result in the local authority incurring expenditure which is, or . . . making . . . savings which are, significant having regard to the local authority's budget for the service or function to which the decision relates; or

(b) to be significant in terms of its effects on communities living or working in an area comprising two or more wards or electoral divisions in the area of the local authority.

Paragraph 2 of regulation 8 provides that in accordance with section 38 of the **15.23** Local Government Act 2000, 'in determining the meaning of "significant" for the purposes of paragraph 1 regard shall be had to any guidance for the time being issued by the Secretary of State'.[37]

The Secretary of State has since issued the *Local Government Act 2000 Guidance to* **15.24** *English Local Authorities* ('*Guidance*'). Chapter 7 is headed 'Accountable decision-making', and begins with this general statement:

The principal aims of executive arrangements are to make decision making more efficient, transparent and accountable so that local authorities can be more open and responsive to the needs and aspirations of the communities they serve. Central to

---

[35] Local Government Act 2000, s 10, s 11.

[36] Local Authorities (Executive Arrangements) (Access to Information) (England) Regulations 2000, SI 2000/3272 ('the Regulations'). Local Authorities (Executive Arrangements) (Decisions, Documents and Meetings) (Wales) Regulations 2001, SI 2001/2290 (W178).

[37] Section 38(1) of the Act provides that a local authority 'must have regard to any guidance for the time being issued by the Secretary of State for the purposes of this Part'.

executive arrangements there will need to be effective access for the public to decision making and decision makers.[38]

Paragraph 7.3 provides, in part:

All decisions of a local authority (whether they are the responsibility of the executive or not) will need to be made in accordance with the following principles: . . . a presumption in favour of openness.

15.25 The questions whether a decision is a 'key decision' and whether council expenditure or saving is 'significant'[39] are discussed in *Guidance*, paragraphs 7.15 to 7.22. For example (paragraph 7.20), 'a council should regard as key a decision to close a school or carry out roadworks (such as introducing or altering traffic calming measures) in a neighbourhood, notwithstanding the threshold of financial significance and that there may be an impact in only one ward'.

Recording executive decisions and inspection of documents following decisions

15.26 These subjects are dealt with in Part II of the Regulations.

15.27 Regulation 3 contains the provision as to recording executive decisions made at meetings. As soon as reasonably practicable after a meeting, whether public or private, at which an executive decision has been made, the proper officer, or, if the proper officer was not present at the meeting, the person presiding, must ensure that a written statement is produced in respect of every executive decision made at the meeting.[40] The statement must include: (a) a record of the decision; (b) a record of the reasons for the decision; (c) details of any alternative options considered and rejected at the meeting; (d) a record of any conflict of interest declared by any member of the decision-making body and (in respect of any declared conflict of interest); (e) a note of any dispensation granted by the local authority's standards committee.[41]

15.28 Regulation 4 deals with recording executive decisions made by individuals, who must comply with essentially the same requirements as those set out in paragraph 15.27 above.[42]

15.29 As soon as is reasonably practicable after an officer has made a key decision,[43] he must produce a written statement which meets essentially the same requirements.[44]

---

[38] *Guidance*, para 7.1.
[39] See para 15.22 above.
[40] The Regulations, reg 3(1).
[41] ibid, reg 3(2).
[42] ibid, reg 4(1) and (2).
[43] See para 15.22 above.
[44] The Regulations, reg 4(4).

Regulations 5 and 6 concern inspection of documents. After an executive decision **15.30** has been made at a public or private meeting, or after an individual member has made an executive decision or an officer has made a key decision,[45] the proper officer must ensure that (a) any records prepared in accordance with regulations 3 or 4, and (b) any report (not including a draft report) considered at the meeting or by the relevant member or officer, is available for inspection by members of the public, as soon as reasonably practicable, at the offices of the relevant local authority.[46] Copies of the documents must be supplied to any newspaper which requests them.[47]

When a copy of the whole or part of a report for a public or private meeting is **15.31** made available for inspection by members of the public in accordance with regulations 5 or 11,[48] at the same time a copy of a list compiled by the proper officer of the background papers and at least one copy of each document in the list must also be available for public inspection.

Part III of the Regulations specifies additional requirements in respect of key de- **15.32** cisions and public meetings. Subject to regulation 21,[49] a meeting or part of a meeting must be held in public where the council leader, mayor or council manager, or any other person likely to preside at the meeting, reasonably believes that:

(a) the decision to be made at that meeting or part of the meeting will be a key decision; or

(b) a matter which is likely to be discussed at that meeting or part of a meeting relates to a decision included in the current forward plan,[50] where that decision is likely to be made at a meeting of the decision-making body concerned within 28 days of the meeting, and an officer, other than a political adviser or assistant or council manager, will be present at that meeting or part of the meeting where the matter is discussed; or

(c) a matter relating to a key decision to be made by the decision-making body concerned is to be discussed with an officer (other than a political adviser or assistant) present, or a decision is made at that meeting or part of the meeting in relation to which a notice under Regulation 15[51] has been given.[52]

For the purposes of sub-paragraph (b) and (c) of regulation 7(1), 'meeting' does **15.33** not include a briefing meeting, that is, a meeting the principal purpose of which

---

[45] See para 15.22 above.
[46] The Regulations, reg 5(1).
[47] ibid, reg 5(2). 'Newspaper' includes radio and television news organizations: reg 2.
[48] As to ibid, reg 11 see para 15.36 below.
[49] For ibid, reg 21 see para 15.49 below.
[50] See para 15.39 below.
[51] See para 15.42 below.
[52] See the Regulations, reg 7(1).

is for an officer to brief a decision-maker or members on matters concerned with the making of an executive decision.[53]

15.34 Regulation 8 defines a 'key decision'.[54]

15.35 Regulation 9 applies to key decisions which are intended to be made by an executive member or an officer. Where such a decision-maker receives a report which he intends to take into consideration when he makes a key decision, he must not make that decision until the report has been available for public inspection for at least three clear days.[55] Subject to regulation 21,[56] the member or officer making the decision must ensure that the proper officer makes the report, together with a list and copies of background papers, available for public inspection as soon as is reasonably practicable after that officer or member receives it.[57] Where a report has been submitted to an executive member or officer with a view to it being considered by him when he makes a key decision, the person who submitted the report must, as soon as is reasonably practicable, supply a copy of it to the chairman of every relevant overview and scrutiny committee,[58] or to every committee member if there is no chairman.[59]

15.36 Regulations 10 and 11 contain provisions as to agendas and connected reports for public meetings. An item of business can only be considered at a public meeting where a copy of the agenda, or the relevant part of it, has been available for public inspection as required by regulation 11[60] for at least three clear days before the meeting, or, where the meeting is convened at shorter notice in accordance with regulations 15 or 16,[61] a copy of the agenda including the item has been available for inspection by the public from the time that the meeting was convened.[62]

15.37 The agenda and every report for a public meeting must be made available for public inspection when they are made available to the decision-maker. That must be done at least three clear days before the meeting (or, where the meeting is convened at shorter notice, at the time the meeting is convened). Copies of such agendas and reports must be supplied to newspapers on request.[63]

---

[53] The Regulations, reg 7(2). As to 'principal purpose', see reg 7(3): the Secretary of State may issue guidance as to the meaning of this phrase.

[54] See para 15.22 above.

[55] The Regulations, reg 9(1).

[56] See para 15.49 below.

[57] The Regulations, reg 9, paras (2) and (4).

[58] 'Overview and scrutiny committee': under any of the new forms of executive, authorities are required to establish committees, consisting of councillors, with power to review and scrutinize actions and decisions of the executive: Local Government Act 2000, s 21.

[59] The Regulations, reg 9(3).

[60] See para 15.37 below.

[61] See paras 15.42 and 15.43 below.

[62] The Regulations, reg 10.

[63] ibid, reg 11(1), (5) and (7). 'Newspaper': see n 47 above.

If the proper officer thinks fit, the whole or part of any such report can be excluded **15.38** from public inspection. Where a report or part of it is so excluded, the provisions of Part VA of the Local Government Act 1972 apply.[64]

Forward plans

Key decisions[65] are subject to specific publicity requirements. The executive **15.39** leader, section 11(2) mayor[66] or council manager must instruct the proper officer to publish a document which states:

(a) that key decisions are to be made on behalf of the local authority;

(b) that a plan (to be known as the 'forward plan') containing particulars of the matters in respect of which those decisions are to be made, will be prepared monthly by the local authority;

(c) that a forward plan will contain details of the key decisions likely to be made by the authority for the four-month period following publication of the forward plan;

(d) that each current forward plan may be inspected at all reasonable hours and free of charge at the local authority's offices;

(e) that each forward plan contains a list of the documents submitted to the decision-makers for consideration in relation to the matters in respect of which decisions are to be made;

(f) the address from which copies of, or extracts from, documents listed in the forward plan are available;

(g) that other relevant documents may be submitted to the decision-makers;

(h) the procedure for requesting details of any such documents as they become available;

(i) the dates in each month in the following 12 months on which each forward plan will be published and available to the public at the local authority's offices.

The documents must be published in at least one local newspaper annually between 21 and 14 days before the first forward plan of that year comes into effect.[67]

A forward plan must be prepared by the executive leader or the section 11(2) **15.40** mayor or council manager containing details of all matters likely to be the subject of key decisions for a period of four months, and the first such plan will have effect from the first working day of any month. It must be updated on a monthly basis, and a new forward plan produced at least 14 days before it comes into effect. Any matters outstanding from the previous plan are to be included in the

---

[64] See paras 15.03 to 15.15 above.
[65] Defined in the Regulations, reg 8; see para 15.22 above.
[66] ie an elected mayor as specified in the Local Government Act 2000, s 11(2).
[67] The Regulations, reg 12.

new plan. The most recent plan is to be taken to have superseded any earlier plan.[68]

15.41 Each forward plan must contain those of the particulars specified in regulation 14(2) as are available when the plan is prepared or which the person preparing the plan can be reasonably expected to obtain. The specified particulars are:

(a) the matter in respect of which the decision is made;

(b) the identity of the decision-maker;

(c) the date on which, or the period within which, the decision is to be made;

(d) the identity of the principal groups to be consulted;

(e) the means by which any such consultation is proposed to be undertaken;

(f) how and when representations may be made to the executive or the decision-maker; and

(g) a list of the documents submitted to the decision-maker for consideration.[69]

15.42 Regulation 15 provides for a general exception which, when it applies to any matter, removes the need to comply with regulation 14. The exception is directed at these circumstances: where inclusion of a matter in the forward plan is impracticable and the matter would be a key decision, that decision can only be made where the proper officer has informed the chairman of the relevant overview and scrutiny committee or, where there is no chairman, each member, by notice in writing, of the matter about which the decision is to be made. The proper officer must make a copy of the notice available for public inspection, and three days must have elapsed following the day on which the proper officer made the notice available.[70]

15.43 Where the date by which an executive decision that would be a key decision makes compliance with regulation 15 impracticable, the decision is only to be made where the decision-maker has obtained agreement from the chairman of the relevant overview and scrutiny committee that the decision is urgent and cannot be deferred. If that chairman is unable to act, or if there is no such person, agreement may be obtained from the chairman or (if there is no chairman) the vice-chairman of the relevant authority.[71]

Additional rights of members concerning documents

15.44 Part IV of the Regulations provides for additional rights of members of local authorities and members of overview and scrutiny committees. First, access to documents is dealt with. Any document which is in the possession or under the control of the executive of a local authority and contains material relating to any

---

[68] The Regulations, reg 13.

[69] ibid, reg 14.

[70] ibid, reg 15.

[71] ibid, reg 16.

business to be transacted at a public meeting must be available for inspection by any member of the authority. Any such document which contains material relating to (i) any business transacted at a private meeting, or (ii) any decision made by an individual member in accordance with executive arrangements, or (iii) any key decision made by an officer in accordance with executive arrangements must be available for inspection by any member when the meeting concludes or immediately after the decision has been made. The foregoing rights do not apply where it appears to the proper officer that compliance would involve the disclosure of exempt information or of advice provided by a political adviser or assistant.[72]

A member of an overview and scrutiny committee is entitled to a copy of any document which is in the possession or under the control of the executive and contains material relating to (i) any business transacted at a private meeting or a public meeting of a decision-making body of the authority, or (ii) any decision made by an individual member of the executive in accordance with executive arrangements, or (iii) any key decision that has been made by an officer in accordance with executive arrangements. Again, those rights do not apply to any document or part of a document which contains exempt or confidential information, unless that information is relevant to (i) any action or decision the officer is reviewing or scrutinizing or which is relevant to any review contained in any programme of work of such a committee or sub-committee, or (ii) any document or part of a document containing advice provided by a political adviser or assistant.[73]   **15.45**

Reports to the local authority

Regulations 19 and 20 concern reports to the local authority. First, where an executive decision has been made and was not treated as a key decision, but the relevant overview and scrutiny committee consider that it should have been so treated, the committee may require the relevant executive to submit a report to the local authority within a reasonable period. The report must include details of the decision and the reasons for it.[74]   **15.46**

Secondly, the executive leader, the elected mayor or the council manager must submit quarterly reports to the local authority containing details of each executive decision taken during the preceding three months where the making of the decision was agreed as urgent in accordance with Regulation 16.[75]   **15.47**

Part V of the Regulations, under the heading 'General Provisions Relating to Information' deals with three disparate matters: (a) information which need not be disclosed because it is confidential or exempt or consists of political advice,   **15.48**

---

[72] ibid, reg 17.
[73] ibid, reg 18
[74] ibid, reg 19.
[75] ibid, reg 20.

(b) the availability of documents for inspection, and (c) the creation of new criminal offences.

Exemptions

15.49 First, the various exemptions. Nothing in the Regulations is to prevent the exclusion of the public from a meeting of a decision-making body that is exercising an executive function where:

(a) it is likely, in view of the nature of the proceedings or the business to be transacted, that if members of the public were present confidential information would be disclosed to them in breach of the obligation of confidence;

(b) a resolution has been passed, by the decision-making body concerned, excluding the public during the transaction of an item of business where it is likely, in view of the nature of the item, that if members of the public were present exempt information or the advice of a political adviser or assistant would be disclosed to them;

(c) a lawful power is used to exclude a member or members of the public in order to maintain orderly conduct or to prevent misbehaviour at a meeting.

A resolution concerning exempt information must identify the proceedings or part of the proceedings to which it applies and state by reference to the descriptions in Schedule 12A to the 1972 Act[76] the particular exemption invoked. An exclusion of the public by reference to any of the three categories (confidential, exempt, political) can apply only to the part or parts of the meeting during which it is likely that one or more of those categories of information would be disclosed.[77]

15.50 Where a member of an executive or an officer makes an executive decision in accordance with executive arrangements, nothing in the Regulations requires the disclosure of documents to the public where they contain confidential information or in the opinion of the member or officer making the decision would be likely to give rise to disclosure of exempt information or the advice of a political adviser or assistant.[78]

15.51 Nothing in the Regulations requires a decision-making body or decision-maker to permit the taking of any photographs of any proceedings, or the use of any means to enable persons not present to see or hear any proceedings (whether at the time or later) or the making of any oral report on any proceedings as they take place.[79]

---

[76] See para 15.06 above.
[77] The Regulations, reg 21.
[78] ibid.
[79] ibid.

Availability of documents for inspection

The second matter dealt with in Part V of the Regulations is the availability of **15.52**
documents for inspection at the offices of the local authority. Any document required by regulations 5, 6 or 11[80] to be available for public inspection must be so
available at all reasonable hours at the local authority's offices and, in the case of
regulation 6 documents, upon payment by the person seeking to inspect them of
any reasonable fee required by the authority. Where a document is to be available
for inspection by a person, he may make a copy of the whole or part of the document or may require a copy of the whole or part of the document to be supplied
to him upon payment of any reasonable fee required by the authority. This provision does not require or authorize the infringement of any copyright, except that,
where the authority is the owner of the copyright, nothing done pursuant to the
provision will constitute an infringement of the copyright. Where any document
required by the Regulations to be open to public inspection is supplied to, or
available for inspection by, members of the public, or supplied to a newspaper
under regulation 11(7), the publication thereby of any defamatory matter is privileged unless the publication is proved to be made with malice. Any written record
of an executive decision or any report required by regulation 5 to be available for
public inspection must be retained by the local authority and made available
for public inspection for at least six years from the date of the relevant decision.
Background papers subject to regulation 6 are similarly required to be retained,
though in this case for four years.[81] The rights conferred on any person by the
Regulations to inspect, copy or be supplied with documents are additional to any
such rights that that person may have.[82]

New criminal offences

The third and last matter dealt with in Part V concerns the creation of new crim- **15.53**
inal offences. A person who has custody of a document required by regulations 5,
6 or 11 to be available for public inspection commits an offence if without reasonable excuse he intentionally obstructs any person exercising a right conferred
under the Regulations to inspect or copy a document or refuses to supply a document in accordance with regulation 22(2). The penalty on summary conviction is
a fine not exceeding level 1 on the standard scale.[83]

---

[80] See paras 15.30, 15.36 and 15.37 above.
[81] Compare paras 15.12 and 15.13 above.
[82] The Regulations, reg 22.
[83] ibid, reg 23.

C. Duties and Discretions of Local Authorities to Disclose Information

15.54   Local authorities (like police authorities) need to take account of a complex inter-action of statutory and other duties and discretions affecting disclosure of information, particularly in the fields of child protection and the prevention of crime.[84] The recent case law indicates that some of the issues which frequently arise (and may be difficult to resolve) are those concerning the Children Act 1989, the Data Protection Acts 1984 and 1998 and the Human Rights Act 1998.

The *North Wales* case

15.55   It is noteworthy, however, that the leading case concerning disclosure by a public authority of information potentially damaging to individuals in order to protect the public, and in particular children, reflects the application of broad principles rather than statute. In *R v Chief Constable of the North Wales Police, ex p AB*[85] ('the *North Wales* case') the applicants for judicial review were a married couple released from prison after serving long sentences for sexual offences against a number of children. They obtained a caravan and moved to a site in the area of the respon-dent police authority ('the NWP'). The NWP had formulated a policy, set out in a document, for addressing the risk of reoffending by convicted paedophiles. The headnote to the *North Wales* case stated that the policy provided that information acquired by the police about such offenders could be released on a 'need to know' basis to protect a potential victim, after specific consideration of the particular case and with the agreement of senior officers and advisers. After receiving a po-lice report from the area where the applicants had served their sentences which in-dicated that they presented a considerable risk to children and vulnerable people, NWP officers met with members of the local authority social services department and the probation service. After discussion the view was reached that the appli-cants' continued presence on the caravan site during the forthcoming Easter hol-idays, when large numbers of children would be there, would add to the risk, and that the applicants should be invited to move from the site before the holidays; if they did not do so consideration would be given to informing the site owner of the applicants' background. The applicants were accordingly invited to move and warned of the possible disclosure if they remained. They decided to stay. Pursuant to the policy, an officer of the NWP, after discussion with senior officers, showed the site owner material from the local press relating to the applicants' convictions.

---

[84]   See the helpful article by David Feldman, 'Information and Privacy' in J Beatson and Y Cripps (eds), *Freedom of Expression and Freedom of Information* (2000) especially at 316–324.

[85]   [1999] QB 396.

That disclosure was challenged unsuccessfully in the Divisional Court and the Court of Appeal.

The Home Secretary and the National Association for the Care and Resettlement **15.56**
of Offenders ('NACRO') were joined as parties to the proceedings. In the Divisional Court the Secretary of State submitted, with the support of the NWP and NACRO, that a policy adopted by the police to guide its conduct when problems of this sort arose should observe three important principles:

(1) There is a general presumption that information should not be disclosed, such a presumption being based on a recognition of (a) the potentially serious effect on the ability of the convicted people to live a normal life; (b) the risk of violence to such people; and (c) the risk that disclosure might drive them underground.
(2) There is a strong public interest in ensuring that the police are able to disclose information about offenders where that is necessary for the prevention or detection of crime, or for the protection of young or other vulnerable people.
(3) Each case should be considered carefully on its particular facts, assessing the risk posed by the individual offender; the vulnerability of those who may be at risk; and the impact of disclosure on the offender. In making such assessment, the police should normally consult other relevant agencies (such as social services and probation services).[86]

In his judgment in the Divisional Court Lord Bingham of Cornhill CJ said: **15.57**

I accept the first of these principles as an important and necessary principle underlying such a policy. When, in the course of performing its public duties, a public body (such as a police force) comes into possession of information relating to a member of the public, being information not generally available and potentially damaging to that member of the public if disclosed, the body ought not to disclose such information save for the purpose of and to the extent necessary for performance of its public duty or enabling some other public body to perform its public duty. . . . This principle does not in my view rest on the existence of a duty of confidence owed by the public body to the member of the public, although it might well be that such a duty of confidence might in certain circumstances arise. The principle, as I think, rests on a fundamental rule of good public administration, which the law must recognise and if necessary enforce.

As to the second principle, Lord Bingham said:[87] **15.58**

. . . if the police, having obtained information about an individual which it would be damaging to that individual to disclose, and which should not be disclosed without some public justification, consider in the exercise of a careful and bona fide judgment that it is desirable or necessary in the public interest to make disclosure, whether for the purpose of preventing crime or alerting members of the public to an apprehended danger, it is proper for them to make such limited disclosure as is judged necessary to achieve that purpose.

---

[86] ibid, at 409 (judgment of the Lord Chief Justice).
[87] ibid, at 410.

15.59 Lord Bingham also endorsed the third principle as being necessary and important. He added:[88]

> It would plainly be objectionable if a police force were to adopt a blanket policy of disseminating information about previous offenders regardless of the facts of the individual case or the nature of the previous offending or the risk of further offending. While it is permissible for a public body to formulate rules governing its general approach to the exercise of a discretion (see *British Oxygen Company Ltd v Board of Trade* [1971] AC 610), it is essential that such rules should be sufficiently flexible to take account of particular or unusual circumstances, and in a situation such as the present, where the potential damage to the individual and the potential harm to members of the community are so great and so obvious, it could never be acceptable if decisions were made without very close regard being paid to the particular facts of the case. The consultation of other agencies, assuming that time permits, is a valuable safeguard against partial or ill-considered conclusions.
>
> It seems to me that these principles are consistent with the statutory policy expressed in section 28(1) of the Data Protection Act 1984 and with the policy recognised by the court in *Reg v Brown (Gregory)* [1994] QB 547 and *Hellewell v Chief Constable of Derbyshire* [1995] 1 WLR 804.
>
> Judged against these tests, the policy adopted by the NWP is not in my judgment open to legal challenge. The policy recognised the general principle that police information about former paedophile offenders should not be disclosed unless the public interest required it. It acknowledged that disclosure could only be justified for the protection of a member of the public who might otherwise become the victim of crime and who might be in need of protection. It was implicit in the policy that each case would be considered on its merits, and explicit that clearance at the highest level should be obtained before disclosure was made. I detect no legal flaw in the policy.

15.60 Buxton J gave a judgment agreeing with the judgment of the Lord Chief Justice.

15.61 The Court of Appeal affirmed the decision below. Lord Woolf MR, giving the judgment of the Court, emphasized[89] that each case must be judged on its own facts. 'However, in doing this, it must be remembered that the decision to which the police have to come as to whether or not to disclose the identity of paedophiles to members of the public, is a highly sensitive one. Disclosure should only be made when there is a *pressing need* for that disclosure' (emphasis added). Developing this point Lord Woolf added:[90]

> The fact that the convictions of the applicants had been in the public domain did not mean that the police as a public authority were free to publish information about their previous offending absent any public interest in this being done. As Lord Bingham CJ stated, before this happens it must at least be a situation where in all the circumstances it is desirable to make disclosure. Both under the [European] Convention and as a matter of English administrative law, the police are entitled to

---

[88] [1999] QB 396 (n 85 above) at 410–411.
[89] ibid, at 428.
[90] ibid, at 429.

use information when they reasonably conclude this is what is required (after taking into account the interests of the applicants), in order to protect the public and in particular children.

Lord Woolf concluded:[91]

> We agree with the Divisional Court that the policy of the NWP was not unlawful nor was the action of the police in giving effect to that policy.

It will be seen that the phrase 'pressing need' is one that the courts have frequently returned to. **15.62**

Subsequent court decisions

In *Re L (Sexual Abuse: Disclosure)*[92] the Court of Appeal heard the appeals of two men against the decision of judges in separate cases to give leave to disclose findings made against them in care proceedings. The proposed disclosure was in one case to a local authority: the appellant had been found by the judge to pose 'a considerable threat to the children of single female adults with whom he might cohabit but not to children generally'.[93] In the other case the proposed disclosure was to the area football league, since the appellant coached junior football teams at a local club used by two children whom the judge considered were at risk of serious harm unless some protective measures were kept in place.[94] **15.63**

In the Court of Appeal, Butler-Sloss LJ (who gave the only substantive judgment) discussed the relevant provisions of the Children Act 1989. Section 17 required the local authority to safeguard and promote the welfare of children within its area who were in need. Section 47 set out the local authority's duty to investigate circumstances where children in its area were at risk to enable the authority to decide whether it should take any action to safeguard or promote the child's welfare.[95] **15.64**

Butler-Sloss LJ recognized that there would be occasions when one local authority would have the duty to pass on information about abuse and abusers to other local authorities. However, neither section 17 nor section 47 placed upon a local authority the general duty to inform other areas of the movement of those found guilty in care or other family proceedings of sexual abuse. In the cases before the Court of Appeal there were no pending investigations either by the police or any other agency in respect of which the information sought to be disclosed might be of assistance. Accordingly the balance was clearly against disclosure.[96] **15.65**

---

[91] ibid, at 430.
[92] [1999] 1 WLR 299.
[93] ibid, at 301.
[94] ibid.
[95] ibid, at 303–304.
[96] ibid.

15.66 Butler-Sloss LJ referred in addition to the *North Wales* case,[97] and in particular to Lord Woolf's statement that disclosure should only be made when there was a pressing need for it.[98] Butler-Sloss LJ continued:

> Although the facts in [the *North Wales* case] are entirely different from those in the present appeals, the caution urged by Lord Woolf MR that 'disclosure should only be made when there is a pressing need' is of general application and supports my conclusion as to non-disclosure.[99]

15.67 In *Woolgar v Chief Constable of Sussex Police*,[100] the claimant was the matron of a nursing home who was arrested after a patient died in her care. The police interviewed her under caution and, at the end of their investigation, they informed her and the local health authority regulation and inspection unit that there was insufficient evidence to charge her with any criminal offence. The unit was concerned about other allegations against the claimant and referred the matter to the regulatory body for nursing, the United Kingdom Central Council for Nursing (the UKCC). The UKCC contacted the police for relevant information. The police practice was to ask for authority from persons such as the claimant who had provided statements, and if authority was given to disclose the statements. The claimant refused her consent. The UKCC maintained its request, the police decided to disclose the material despite the claimant's refusal of consent, and the claimant sought an injunction restraining disclosure.

15.68 On the claimant's appeal from the judge's refusal to grant her an injunction the Court of Appeal weighed in the balance the two conflicting interests: the public interest in ensuring the free flow of information to the police for the purposes of criminal proceedings which required that information given in confidence would not be used for some collateral purpose, and the countervailing public interest in protecting public health and safety which entitled the police to disclose to a professional or regulatory body operating in that field confidential information which the police reasonably believed was relevant to an inquiry being conducted by that body. The Court of Appeal dismissed the claimant's appeal, refusing to invalidate the police decision to disclose the information, Kennedy LJ adding that 'the primary decision as to disclosure should be made by the police who have the custody of the relevant material, and not by the court.'[101]

---

[97] [1999] QB 396; see para 15.55 above.
[98] [1999] 1 WLR 299 at 305.
[99] ibid, at 306.
[100] [2000] 1 WLR 25.
[101] ibid, at 37.

In reaching this conclusion, the Court considered (among other authorities) *Re* **15.69**
L[102] and the *North Wales* case,[103] referring in particular to the passages from the
judgments of Lord Bingham and Lord Woolf cited above.[104]

In *R v Local Authority and Police Authority in the Midlands, ex p LM,*[105] the appli- **15.70**
cant owned a bus company which had a contract to run a school bus service for a
local education authority. He was asked to complete a form which entitled the
local authority to run a police check on him. The check revealed, as a result of
information disclosed by the police and the social services authority, that there
had been two incidents which had come to the attention of the police, seven and
ten years earlier. Both concerned allegations that LM had sexually abused children. In neither were proceedings brought against him. Nevertheless LM's contract was terminated. LM's company then entered into a school bus contract with
another local council. In addition, LM wished to take up a voluntary post with the
youth service. He requested assurances from the police and social services authorities that, when the council checked, the allegations would not be disclosed again.
The authorities having refused such assurances, LM sought judicial review of their
decisions.

In granting the applications and quashing the decisions, Dyson J noted the statu- **15.71**
tory duties and powers of local authorities relating to the protection of children,
in particularly sections 17, 27 and 47 of the Children Act 1989. Furthermore local
authorities were obliged by section 7 of the Local Authorities Social Services Act
1970 to act under general guidance issued by the Secretary of State. Such guidance
included '*Working Together under the Children Act 1989: a guide to arrangements
for inter-agency co-operation for the protection of children from abuse.*' It was not disputed before Dyson J that the social services department concerned had the power
to disclose information about allegations of sexual abuse of children if it genuinely
and reasonably believed that such disclosure was necessary to protect children
from the risk of sexual abuse.[106]

Dyson J held that, in exercising the power to disclose, the relevant authority must **15.72**
apply the principles set out in the *North Wales* case.[107] A blanket approach was im-
permissible; each case must be considered on its own facts. As Lord Woolf had said
in *North Wales,*[108] disclosure should only be made if there was a 'pressing need'.[109]

---

[102] See para 15.63 above.
[103] See para 15.55 above.
[104] See paras 15.57 to 15.61 above.
[105] [2000] 1 FLR 612.
[106] ibid, at 619.
[107] [1999] QB 396.
[108] ibid, at 428.
[109] *ex p LM* [2000] 1 FLR at 622.

15.73   As to the instant case, Dyson J held that the two authorities had not followed the correct approach when deciding to disclose the allegations to the council. They had not considered the particular facts of the case but had adopted a blanket approach. They had not adopted the pressing need test. Had they applied that test, a decision to disclose would still have been unlawful, since there was no real and cogent evidence of a pressing need to disclose.[110]

15.74   In *R (A) v Chief Constable of C*[111] the High Court considered a disclosure question which had some features in common with those of *ex p LM*.[112] The applicant applied for a job with a local authority which involved working with children. A conditional offer of employment was made. The relevant police authority was then asked by the council to carry out a child access vetting inquiry. In doing so it obtained information from another police authority about previous police investigations into the applicant's alleged inappropriate behaviour with children; the investigators found insufficient evidence to warrant criminal proceedings. That information was passed on to the council, which subsequently withdrew its conditional offer of employment. The applicant sought judicial review of the decisions to disclose made by the two police authorities: the first respondent authority, which held the 'non-conviction information',[113] had disclosed it to the second respondent authority, which had in turn disclosed it to the council that was the applicant's prospective employer. The main grounds of the applicant's challenge were that the decisions to disclose were unlawful because they were contrary to the relevant Home Office guidance (Circular 9/93, *Protection of Children: Disclosure of Criminal Background of Those with Access to Children*) or to the Data Protection Acts 1984 and 1998.

15.75   In refusing the application Turner J held that the passing of sensitive personal information between one police authority and another did not amount to a 'decision' which attracted an obligation that should be judged according to the principles of procedural fairness. Turner J contrasted the case before him with the *North Wales* case.[114] In that case, he said:

> information passed from agencies (police and probation) . . . into the public domain. In such a case it is easy to identify the stage at which procedural fairness should operate. It is . . . less easy to identify the existence of such a stage when information is merely passed from one police force, when both were doing no more than act as a local division of an agency which has national responsibility, to another which shows identical characteristics. . . . So long as, in the instant case, no public authority had taken a decision which had, or could have had, the effect of prejudicing any of the applicant's rights, the scope for imposing an obligation on those authorities

---

[110]   *ex p LM* [2000] 1 FLR, at 624, 625, and 626.
[111]   [2001] 1 WLR 461.
[112]   See n 106 above.
[113]   [2000] 1 WLR 461 at 463.
[114]   [1999] QB 396.

that they should act with procedural fairness was limited, if it existed at all. The public authority to private individual divide, which is readily identifiable as the stage at which procedural fairness should be found to operate, is not present.[115]

Addressing the position of the second respondent police authority, when it passed **15.76** the information to the council, Turner J said:

> There cannot be the slightest doubt that the local education authority had a lawful interest and a 'pressing need' to receive the information which was in the possession of the . . . police since it was or could be important as affecting the decision which it was required to make. In one sense, the local education authority was the body best qualified to decide what, if anything, it would make of the information with which it was being provided. If it was uncertain about the strength of the complaints and needed to know more in order that it could make an informed decision, it was always at liberty to ask for assistance from the communicating police force for its opinion about that matter. It would thereafter be for it to decide whether, or to what extent, the non-conviction material should inform its decision. Before it did, it would, of course, have to provide the applicant with at least the gist of that information and offer him the opportunity to make representations about it. But I am not concerned with the mechanics of a situation which is not before me and which, on the evidence, never happened. There is evidence before the court that the decision of the education authority was not related in any way to the non-conviction material available to it.[116]

So far as the respondent police authorities were concerned no procedural impro- **15.77** priety arose from their decisions (namely, that of the first authority to disclose to the second, and that of the second to disclose to the council).[117]

As to the applicant's challenge based on the Home Office guidance,[118] Turner J **15.78** held that the circular, though it encouraged confidentiality by prescribing a means of limiting the opportunity for sensitive personal data to reach the public domain, imposed no fetters on the obligations of police authorities to pass information between each other.[119]

Furthermore the Data Protection Acts 1984 and 1998 did not avail the applicant. **15.79** The relevant information did not fall within the ambit of the Data Protection Act 1984 because it was manually, not automatically, processed, and although it was 'sensitive personal data' under section 2 of the Data Protection Act 1998 it was exempted from the first data protection principle under Part 1 of Schedule 1 to the Act because it was data being processed for the prevention and detection of crime or other exempted purposes under Schedules 2 and 3 or because its processing was 'necessary for the exercise of any functions conferred on a constable by any rule of

---

[115] [2001] 1 WLR at 476, 477, and 478.
[116] ibid, at 478.
[117] ibid.
[118] See para 15.74 above.
[119] [2001] 1 WLR at 478, 479.

law' in accordance with paragraph 10 of article 2 of the Data Processing (Processing of Sensitive Personal Data) Order 2000, and in those circumstances neither Act was contravened.[120]

15.80 One of the authorities relied upon by the applicant was *ex p LM*,[121] where Dyson J had quashed the decisions of the relevant authorities. *Ex p LM* was a case which concerned disclosure by two authorities, a police authority and a social services department, to a third authority, a county council. Unlike the *North Wales*[122] case and *R (A) v Chief Constable*,[123] *ex p LM* did not involve disclosure to private individuals, or to the general public. Indeed, Dyson J addressed this point directly.[124] He said that in the *North Wales* case, Lord Woolf 'referred to the requirement of a pressing need for disclosure to "members of the public". But that was because on the facts of that case the persons to whom disclosure was made were members of the public. The same principle, however, applies regardless of the identity of the person or persons to whom disclosure is to be made'. Turner J, however, gave particular weight to the 'public authority to private individual divide, which is readily identifiable as the stage at which procedural fairness should be found to operate. . . .'.[125] It appears that he considered Dyson J not to have given effect to this distinction, and for that reason was unable to follow Dyson J's dicta.[126] Turner J added:

> In fairness, it is not apparent that, any more than in the present case, [Dyson J] was assisted by detailed submission on the question whether or when a duty should be held to arise, rather than the circumstances and manner in which it could be exercised. The consequences of that judgment, if it were literally applied, seems to me, respectfully, to fall foul of the caution against 'over-judicialising' the administrative process.[127]

15.81 It remains to be seen which judicial approach prevails in the longer term, though for the present it is to be noted that Turner J found a 'pressing need' to disclose in the factual circumstances he was considering, while Dyson J was confident that there was no such need in the quite different circumstances of *ex p LM*.

D. Publication of Local Authority Reports

15.82 Following an inquiry under the chairmanship of Sir Ronald Waterhouse into the abuse of children in care in North Wales, a report ('the Waterhouse Report') was

---

[120] [2001] 1 WLR at 475.
[121] [2000] 1 FLR 612; see paras 15.69 to 15.72 above.
[122] [1999] QB 396.
[123] [2001] 1 WLR 461.
[124] [2001] 1 FLR at 622.
[125] [2001] 1 WLR at 477.
[126] ibid, at 471 and 477. Dyson J's dicta are to be found at [2000] 1FLR 612, 622.
[127] [2001] 1 WLR at 477.

published in February 2000.[128] The Waterhouse Report expressed concern that in some circumstances local authorities might be unduly inhibited from acting in the wider public interest. They might be constrained, by the threat of legal action or loss of insurance cover, from publicizing failures in service delivery and from acting on inquiry recommendations and identifying necessary reforms in the light of the results of inquiries conducted by them or on their behalf.

The Waterhouse Report recommended that the Law Commission should exam- **15.83**
ine the legal issues surrounding the publication of local authority reports and consider whether there was a need to reform the law. The matter was in consequence referred to the Law Commission in February 2001.

The Commission completed a consultation paper at the end of March 2002.[129] As **15.84**
the paper points out:

> If the effect of the law is to impede publication of the report of the inquiry, then there are several adverse results. Whatever has gone wrong will be more likely to occur again if steps are not taken to prevent it. The authority which set up the inquiry could learn from the report—but if the report is not published, other authorities and bodies which could also benefit from the report will not be prompted to improve their own practices. The facts in relation to the individual complaint ought to be put into the public domain, but if the report is not published they may not be.[130]

The Commission's provisional conclusions on the problems are listed in three cat- **15.85**
egories:

(a) admissions of liability in breach of the local authority's insurance contract,
(b) waiver of rights, entitling the insurer to avoid the contract, and
(c) the risk of precipitating an action for defamation and 'the degree of uncertainty about the unavailability of the common law defence of qualified privilege [which] is likely to promote an overly cautious approach to publication'.[131]

The Commission's provisional conclusions on the solutions are (a) an Agreement **15.86**
to be drawn up by the insurers and local authorities, (b) a Code of Practice for the conduct of local authority ad hoc inquiries, and (c) possible legislative reform of the law of defamation.[132] As to (a) the Commission notes that some progress has already been made. As to (b), a Code of Practice is being developed. As to defamation, the Commission has put to consultees for their consideration a proposed

---

[128] *Lost in care: Report of the Tribunal of Inquiry into the abuse of children in care in the former county council areas of Gwynedd and Clwyd since 1974* (HC (2001–02) no 201).
[129] Law Commission, *Publication of Local Authority Reports* (Law Com No 163).
[130] ibid, para 2.
[131] ibid, paras 7 to 9.
[132] ibid, para 10.

legislative reform extending statutory qualified privilege to any local authority inquiry report where the inquiry and the report observe acceptable standards of fairness. The Commission also raises the possibility of an additional, and wider, legislative reform which would enable local authorities to set up formal inquiries, with powers to summons witnesses, require the production of documents and take evidence on oath.[133]

---

[133] Law Com No 163 (n 129 above) paras 11 to 15.

16

THE ENVIRONMENT
AND OTHER STATUTES

A. The Environment

Introduction

Protection of the environment is a matter of international concern. Pollution does **16.01** not respect state boundaries. It is therefore no surprise that the European Union[1] has taken the lead in ensuring greater access to information about the environment held by public authorities. Council Directive 90/313 (EEC) of 7 June 1990 on the freedom of access to information on the environment recites that access to information held by public authorities will improve environmental protection. It also states that it is necessary to guarantee to any natural or legal person throughout the Community free access to available information held by public authorities concerning the state of the environment, including activities or measures adversely affecting the environment, and those designed to protect it. The Directive

---

[1] The European Economic Community (EEC) came into being under the Treaty of Rome in 1957. In 1965 the Merger Treaty amalgamated the institutions of the EEC and the European Coal and Steel Community and the European Atomic Energy Community. From 1965 the three communities shared a single constitutional structure. In 1992 the Treaty of Union was signed at Maastricht. The three communities remained distinct, but collectively were called the European Union (EU). At the same time the EEC became the European Community (EC).

required member states to bring into force the laws, regulations and administrative provisions which were necessary to comply with the Directive by 31 December 1992.

16.02 In the United Kingdom there was much to be done. The Environmental Protection Act 1990 had granted public access to various pollution registers, but this modest provision did not match up to the Directive. The government therefore brought in the Environmental Information Regulations 1992 and the consequence of this was that people in the United Kingdom acquired rights to information about the environment before they acquired any general right to know. A further result of this is that rights to information about the environment are dealt with outside the Freedom of Information Act 2000 ('the Act').

16.03 This part of this chapter considers:

- the Environmental Protection Act 1990
- the 1990 Directive
- the Environmental Information Regulations 1992
- the Environmental Information (Amendment) Regulations 1998
- the Aarhus Convention 1998
- the 2002 draft Directive on public environmental information which is intended to replace the 1990 Directive and is expected to come into force in the winter of 2002–3
- the draft Environmental Information Regulations 2002, which are proposed to implement the Aarhus Convention and the new Directive, and are expected to come into effect in the winter of 2002–3.

The Environmental Protection Act 1990

16.04 The Environmental Protection Act 1990 required 'enforcing authorities' responsible for controlling pollution (local authorities or the Environment Agency) to maintain registers. The registers contain details of applications to release pollution, the authorization itself, results of monitoring pollution and the enforcement action taken. Section 20(7) of the 1990 Act provides that it shall be the duty of each enforcing authority (a) to secure that the registers maintained by them under this section are available at all reasonable times, for inspection by the public free of charge, and (b) to afford to members of the public facilities for obtaining copies of entries, on payment of reasonable charges. Section 21 provides for the exclusion from the registers of information affecting national security and section 22 provides for the exclusion of certain confidential information.[2] Registers relating to

---

[2] The Environmental Protection Act 1990, ss 1 to 28 have been repealed by the Pollution Prevention and Control Act 1999, s 6, but the repeal does not come into force until the Secretary of State by order so appoints. The substantive provisions relating to registers will be maintained under regulations to be made under the 1999 Act, s 2, Sch 1.

water pollution are maintained by the Environment Agency under the Water Act 1989.

The 1990 Directive

Article 1 of the Council Directive on the freedom of access to information on the   **16.05** environment states that the object of the Directive is to ensure freedom of access to, and dissemination of information on the environment held by public authorities and to set out the basic terms and conditions on which such information should be made available.

Article 2 defines 'information' and 'public authorities'. 'Information relating to   **16.06** the environment' means:

> any available information in written, visual, aural or data-base form on the state of water, air, soil, fauna, flora, land and natural sites, and on activities (including those which give rise to nuisances such as noise) or measures adversely affecting or likely to affect these, and on activities or measures designed to protect these, including administrative measures and environmental management programmes.

'Public authorities' means:

> any public administration at national, regional or local level with responsibilities, and possessing information, relating to the environment with the exception of bodies acting in a judicial or legislative capacity.

The substantive provisions of the Directive are contained in Article 3. It provides   **16.07** that member states shall ensure that public authorities are required to make available information relating to the environment to any natural or legal person at his request and without having to prove an interest. Member states are left to define the practical arrangements under which such information is effectively made available and they may provide for a request to be refused where it affects:

- the confidentiality of the proceedings of public authorities, international relations and national defence
- public security
- matters which are, or have been sub judice, or under enquiry (including disciplinary enquiries), or which are the subject of preliminary investigation proceedings
- commercial and industrial confidentiality, including intellectual property
- the confidentiality of personal data and/or files
- material supplied by a third party without that party being under a legal obligation to do so
- material the disclosure of which would make it more likely that the environment to which such material related would be damaged.

The Article, however, provides that information held by public authorities shall   **16.08** be supplied in part where it is possible to separate out the information on items concerning the interests referred to in the Article. Article 3.3 provides that a request for information may be refused where it would involve the supply of unfinished documents or data or internal communications, or where the request is manifestly unreasonable or formulated in too general a manner. Public authorities are required to respond as soon as possible and at the latest within two months. Importantly the reasons for a refusal must be given.

16.09   Article 4 provides for dissatisfied applicants to seek judicial review. Article 5 allows member states to charge for supplying information but such charges may not exceed the reasonable cost.

16.10   Member states have to ensure that bodies with public responsibilities for the environment, which are under the control of public authorities, make available the information which they hold on the same basis.[3]

16.11   Article 7 provides that member states shall take the necessary steps to provide general information to the public on the state of the environment by such means as the periodic publication of descriptive reports.

The Environmental Information Regulations 1992

16.12   The United Kingdom government implemented the Directive through the Environmental Information Regulations 1992.[4]

The construction of the Regulations

16.13   Regulation 2 deals with the construction of the Regulations. First, they apply to any information which 'relates to the environment' and is held by a relevant person in an accessible form. The Regulations do not apply to information held for legislative or judicial functions. Information 'relates to the environment'[5] if, and only if, it relates to any of the following, that is to say:

(a)   the state of any water or air, the state of any flora or fauna, the state of any soil or the state of any natural site or other land;

(b)   any activities or measures (including activities giving rise to noise or any other nuisance) which adversely affect anything mentioned in sub-paragraph (a) above or are likely adversely to affect anything so mentioned;

(c)   any activities or administrative or other measures (including any environmental management programmes) which are designed to protect anything so mentioned.

---

[3]   Council Directive 90/313 (EEC), Article 6.
[4]   SI 1992/3240.
[5]   This definition is based on the Directive but it is not the same as the definition in the Directive.

The guidance on the implementation of the Environmental Information Regulations[6] paragraph 17 explains this definition. The 'state' in sub-paragraph (a) should be taken to include physical, chemical and biological conditions at any time (that is, past, present or future.) 'Water' should be taken to include underground and surface water (both natural and in man-made structures); surface water to include inland waters (that is, rivers, canals, lakes), estuaries and seas. 'Air' extends to the limits of the atmosphere and should be taken to include the air within buildings and other natural and man-made structures above or below the ground. 'Fauna and flora' should be taken to include species both living and dead. 'Land' should be taken to include all land surfaces, buildings, land covered by water, and underground strata. 'Soil' should be taken to include the in situ upper layer of the mantle rock in which plants grow. A 'natural site' should be taken to include areas identified by reason of their flora, fauna, geological or physiographical features (for example Sites of Special Scientific Interest) or general environmental quality (for example Areas of Outstanding Natural Beauty). Paragraph 18 makes it clear there is no geographical restriction: the information may relate to anywhere in the world.   **16.14**

Regulation 2 also defines 'relevant persons' as: **16.15**

(a) all such Ministers of the Crown, Government departments, local authorities and other persons carrying out functions of public administration at a national, regional or local level as, for the purposes of or in connection with their functions, have responsibilities in relation to the environment; and

(b) any body with public responsibilities for the environment which does not fall within sub-paragraph (a) above but is under the control of a person falling within that sub-paragraph.

'Information' includes anything contained in any records; 'records' includes registers, reports and returns, as well as computer records and other records kept otherwise than in a document; and 'statutory provision' means any provisions made by or under any enactment.   **16.16**

These definitions are more elaborate than those in the Directive.   **16.17**

Paragraph 12 of the Guidance explains that because circumstances vary and change the government is unable to give a definitive list of organizations subject to the requirements of the Regulations. So organizations will need to take a view themselves. The Guidance adds that in cases of dispute it will be for the courts to decide. In *R v British Coal, ex p Ibstock Building Products Limited*[7] it was accepted that the Regulations did apply to the British Coal Corporation, which was a privatized body. In *R v Secretary of State for the Environment, Transport and the Regions and Midland Express Limited, ex p Alliance Against the Birmingham Northern Relief*   **16.18**

---

[6] See: http://www.defra.gov.uk/environment/pubaccess/guidance (19 September 2002).

[7] [1995] JPL 836.

Road,[8] a case about the disclosure of documents to protesters against the relief road, Sullivan J agreed with Harrison J in the *British Coal Corporation* case that a broad interpretation should be given to the scope of environmental information under the regulations.[9]

The obligation to make environmental information available

16.19 A relevant person who holds any information to which the Regulations apply is under a duty to the person who requested the information to make it available.[10] The duty is subject to a number of administrative provisions set out in regulation 3 and to the exceptions set out in regulation 4.

16.20 The administrative provisions require that the request be dealt with as soon as possible and within two months. If the request is refused the relevant person has to give reasons in writing.[11] A request may be refused where it is manifestly unreasonable or is formulated in too general a manner.[12] A charge which is reasonably attributable to the supply of the information may be made, and the supply of the information may be made conditional on the payment of the charge.[13] The relevant person only has to make the information available in such a form and at such time and places as may be reasonable.[14]

The exceptions

16.21 The exceptions to the right to information are contained in regulation 4 which has been amended by the Environmental Information (Amendment) Regulations 1998 so as to align fully the exceptions in regulation 4(2) with the derogations in Article 3(2) of the 1990 Directive.

16.22 Regulation 4(1) provides:

> Nothing in these Regulations shall—
> (a) require the disclosure of any information which is capable of being treated as confidential; or
> (b) authorize or require the disclosure of any information which must be so treated.

16.23 Regulation 4(2) (as amended) lists those circumstances where the release of information may be refused, it is discretionary. It provides:

> For the purpose of these Regulations, information is to be capable of being treated as confidential, if and only if, it is information the disclosure of which—
> (a) would affect international relations, national defence or public security;

---

[8] [1999] JPL 231.
[9] Both the cases are considered further at paras 16.39 and 16.42 below.
[10] SI 1992/3240, reg 3(1), (6).
[11] ibid, reg 3(2).
[12] ibid, reg 3(3).
[13] ibid, reg 3(4).
[14] ibid, reg 3(5).

(b) would affect matters which are, or have been, an issue in any legal proceedings or in any enquiry (including any disciplinary inquiry), or are the subject matter of any investigation undertaken with a view to any such proceedings or enquiry;

(c) would affect the confidentiality of the deliberations of any relevant person;

(d) would involve the supply of a document or other record which is still in the course of completion, or of any internal communication of any relevant person;

(e) would affect the confidentiality of matters to which any commercial or industrial confidentiality attaches, including intellectual property.

Unfinished documents

Paragraph 53 of the Guidance points out that bodies may carry out their own studies including inspection, testing, evaluation, monitoring and research; data may be collected in the process. It is reasonable that access to documents and data should await the completion of the study or report so that analysis and interpretation can proceed unhindered. Of course this does not stop a body granting premature access if it so wishes. If a study is aborted any interim reports and any completed data should be released as soon as possible.   **16.24**

Paragraph 54 of the Guidance says that the test as to what constitutes a completed data set is problematic. If a study depends on a scientifically selected sample of cases, then the data set is not complete until a satisfactory level of responses has been achieved. The satisfactory level of response will normally have been specified as part of the study requirement or is the level at which data collection is closed down on the grounds of cost or practicality. If a study depends on making a series of tests until an hypothesis is accepted or rejected, so that the number of items tested cannot be specified in advance, then the data set is completed once sufficient items have been tested to confirm or reject the hypothesis. In the case of a longitudinal survey, each individual stage of the survey should normally be regarded as if it were a separate survey and data released at the end of each stage. Data which are part of regular routine monitoring should not be regarded as part of an unfinished set but should normally be released as soon as practicable after they are collected, or according to a planned and published timetable. For example, the Guidance suggests, if readings are taken on an hourly or daily basis, it might be reasonable to release them at least once a month.   **16.25**

In *Maile v Wigan Metropolitan Borough Council*[15] Eady J held that a data base which comprised raw data concerning potentially contaminated sites did not have to be disclosed because he accepted evidence that the data was not completed and appeared to have inaccuracies and therefore came within the confidentiality provisions of regulation 4(2). The judge said 'it would be highly unsatisfactory to reveal to the public material which had variously been described as inchoate, embryonic and hypothetical'.   **16.26**

---

[15] [2001] Env LR 11.

Must be treated as confidential

16.27 Regulation 4(3) lists those circumstances where requested information must be treated as confidential. The first category (a) is information which falls within regulation 4(2) and disclosure of which would contravene any other statutory provision or rule of law or would involve the breach of an agreement. This is a catch-all provision. An example would be the Radioactive Substances Act 1960 which makes it a criminal offence to disclose commercial information to third parties. The other categories are:

(b) personal information contained in records held in relation to an individual who had not given his consent to its disclosure;

(c) information which has been supplied by a person who—

    (i) was not under, and could not have been put under, any legal obligation to supply it;

    (ii) did not disclose it in circumstances such that the relevant person is entitled apart from the Regulations to disclose it;

    (iii) has not consented to its disclosure;

(d) information the disclosure of which would, in the circumstances, increase the likelihood of damage to the environment affecting anything to which the information relates.

16.28 The Guidance[16] suggests for example that information about the location of nesting sites, rare habitats or endangered species should be withheld to avoid the risk of damage.

Regulation 5

16.29 Regulation 5 provides that where any environmental information not covered by the Regulations is required by any statutory provision to be made available to any person, arrangements for doing so must be sufficient to satisfy the requirements imposed by the Directive; that is, that the response must be made promptly, that reasons must be given and that charges must be reasonable.

The guidelines on publicity

16.30 The Guidance states that the public needs to know the range and extent of environmental information held by bodies. To this end the Guidance says each body should consider reviewing and stating from time to time the principal areas in which it holds environmental information; special mention could be made of any statutory public registers maintained, giving the subject matter covered and the location of each register. It would also help if bodies publicized the name and address of a contact point or information co-ordinator for enquiries and assistance.

---

[16] At para 70.

The Regulations do not require the comprehensive publication of environmental **16.31** information. The Guidance makes clear that it will be open to each body to publish, at its discretion, any information which it holds and to make an appropriate charge for such reports. The Guidance states that in accordance with Article 7 of the 1990 Directive the Department of the Environment already publishes an annual *Digest of Environmental Protection and Water Statistics*, an annual *Statistical Bulletin* and *The UK Environment*. The last of these is broader in coverage than the *Digest*, less technically oriented, and aimed at a wider audience. A number of other government departments publish reports on particular environmental subjects: for example, the Department of Transport publishes its *Transport Statistics Great Britain*. Enquiries could be referred, where appropriate, to these published documents.

As a footnote to the Environmental Protection Act 1990 the Guidance notes:[17]   **16.32**

> The Government has legislated to establish public registers of environmental information about activities regulated by particular environmental control authorities. The registers are generally accessible during normal working hours and inspection is free of charge. Information held on these registers is presented in a variety of formats: from a collection of papers to structured computer files. To maintain and improve their user friendliness, bodies should keep registers up to date and strive towards greater standardisation and consistency of contents.

Paragraph 72 of the Guidance in a section on enforcement states an action to en- **16.33** force the duty provided for in regulation 3(6) may be taken in the national courts which in turn, and in appropriate circumstances, may need to refer questions of Community law to the European Court of Justice.

Criticisms of the Regulations

The Guidance demonstrates an openness of approach which is refreshing. The **16.34** Regulations themselves have, however, had a mixed reception amongst campaigners for greater openness. Friends of the Earth[18] produced a guide in 1994 for local campaigning groups on using the access regime to obtain environmental information, which can be taken as a positive response. The Campaign for Freedom of Information in its evidence to the House of Lords European Communities Committee, Sub-Committee[19] is critical.

The Campaign's evidence states: **16.35**

> Our overriding view of the regulations is that they are deeply flawed. Their main shortcomings result from (a) the excessively broad exemptions (b) the inadequate definition of the bodies to whom the Regulations apply, and (c) the lack of any effective enforcement mechanism. Although the Code of Practice itself has serious

---

[17] At para 26.
[18] The Friends of the Earth website is at http://www.foe.org.uk
[19] http://www.cfoi.org.uk/envregslordsev (25 March 2002).

shortcomings, we now advise individuals seeking environmental information from central government to apply for it under both the Regulations and the Code of Practice. This enables them to challenge any refusal by complaint to the Parliamentary Ombudsman under the Code: no realistic appeal mechanism exists under the Regulations.

16.36 The evidence points out that the exemptions' most obvious defect is that they contain no harm test, and compares the weak drafting of regulation (4)(1)(e) which exempts 'information relating to matters to which any commercial or industrial confidentiality attaches or affecting any intellectual property' with the much narrower definition for commercial confidentiality in section 22(1) of the Environmental Protection Act 1990 which exempts information if its disclosure in a register 'would prejudice to an unreasonable degree the commercial interests of . . . [the] individual or person [to whom it relates]'. The Campaign wonders what justification there can be for the broader, ill-defined definition in the Regulations.

16.37 Another issue that arose in correspondence between the Campaign and Ministers was the view of the Health and Safety Executive that it was subject to the Regulations only where it had explicit, statutory environmental responsibility and not in relation to other functions (such as those relating to the nuclear industry). This was at odds with the view expressed in the Department of the Environment's Guidance on the Regulations,[20] that a person subject to the Regulations was subject to them in respect of *any* environmental information held by it. Since the Department of the Environment was the lead department the Campaign had assumed that it spoke on behalf of the whole government. The Campaign was astonished to be told by the Employment Secretary that lawyers at both the Health and Safety Executive and the Department of Employment did not accept the Department of the Environment's view. The informant added:

> I note that the Department of the Environment guidance suggests a different interpretation of the law but, in the absence of that, I believe that HSE is right in following legal advice.

The Campaign found it a bizarre reflection on collective responsibility that Ministers were unable or unwilling to resolve their differences and in effect were content to leave the matter unresolved unless a third party brought the matter before a court.

16.38 The Campaign for Freedom of Information comments:

> The cost of bringing such an action deterred us from doing so, although we believe it would have been well-founded legally. The cost would also generally prevent any ordinary citizen and most environmental organisations from enforcing their rights.

---

[20] At para 15.

Cost is a very serious concern and the Campaign's view is borne out by the scarcity of reported decisions on the Regulations. It is therefore important to note that in regulation 9 of the draft Environmental Information Regulations 2002 (which are considered in detail below) the enforcement provisions of the Act are applied to the new regulations.

Cases on the Regulations

R v British Coal Corporation, ex p Ibstock Building Products Ltd[21] involved an application for judicial review of the continuing refusal of the respondent, the British Coal Corporation, to disclose information in its possession relating to the alleged dumping of naval munitions in 1947 down mineshafts beneath the applicant's land known as Ibstock Brick Works. The real information that was required by the applicant was the identity of the person who had informed British Coal that the dumping had occurred so that a view could be taken as to the reliability of the information. On 21 June 1993 leave was granted by Macpherson J to enable the applicant to apply for an order of mandamus requiring British Coal to supply that information to the applicant. On 7 July 1993 British Coal disclosed the identity of the informant to the applicant. The applicant had thereby obtained the information which he needed. The sole issue before the court was therefore who should pay the costs.

16.39

It was accepted by both parties that the presence of munitions in the mineshafts was information relating to the state of the land within regulation 2(2). The point at issue was whether the name of the informant was information relating to the state of the land. As the editors of the Journal of Planning Law point out[22] the most important part of Harrison J's judgment is his approach to this issue of the scope of environmental information. Environmental information basically covers information *relating* to the state of the land, water or air and flora or fauna. By holding that this extends beyond bare information and includes information by which to judge the quality of the information Harrison J has given a broad interpretation of the kind of information that can be required.

16.40

The judge rejected a submission that the information was confidential information because it related to the dumping of naval ordnance secretly by night down the mineshaft and this was information relating to matters affecting national defence or public security within the meaning of regulation 4(2)(a). The judge held there was no evidence that the dumping of munitions in 1944 affected national defence or security in 1994, in fact such evidence as there was was to the contrary effect. The judge also held that the name of the informant was not exempted from disclosure as personal information under regulation 4(3)(b).

16.41

---

[21] [1995] JPL 836.
[22] [1995] JPL 841.

16.42   *R v Secretary of State for the Environment, Transport and the Regions and Midland Expressway Limited, ex p Alliance Against the Birmingham Northern Relief Road*[23] was a case which arose out of the inquiry into the Birmingham northern relief road. The proposal was that the road would be designed, built, financed and operated by Midland Expressway Limited ('Midland') pursuant to a concession agreement with the Secretary of State made under the New Roads and Streets Works Act 1991. Midland as the concessionaire would recover its costs by charging tolls to the users of the road in accordance with a toll order made under the 1991 Act.

16.43   The proposal to build the road was very controversial and the public inquiry lasted over 200 days. The Secretary of State in his decision letter dated 23 July 1997 stated that he proposed to make the necessary orders. The Alliance was concerned that in taking his decision the Secretary of State might have been influenced by the prospect of having to pay compensation to Midland under the terms of the agreement if he had decided not to proceed with the road. There was some discussion about the agreement at the Inquiry but the Inspector had not been allowed to see or reveal full details of the agreement on the grounds of commercial confidentiality. The Inspector stated in his conclusions that he considered the situation unsatisfactory since it was unlikely to have inspired confidence in all those who had attended the inquiry that all relevant factors were properly revealed and discussed.

16.44   In August 1997 the Alliance wrote to the Department and requested a copy of the concession agreement under the Environmental Information Regulations. The Department refused to hand over the agreement and claimed it was commercially confidential within the exception in regulation 4(2)(e). The Alliance applied for judicial review of that decision.

16.45   Sullivan J inspected the agreement and came to the conclusion that only parts of it fell within the confidentiality exception in regulation 4(2)(e). He held that the Alliance was entitled to see the other parts of the agreement. He therefore quashed the Secretary of State's decision but he did not make an order for the agreement to be handed over, he said it was for the Secretary of State to decide how he should respond to the request.

16.46   The most significant thing about the case is the judge's finding that on the principal issues the court was not limited to a review on *Wednesbury* grounds. He held that the language of the Regulations was clear: whether information relates to the environment, is capable of being treated as confidential, and if so whether it falls within any of the categories in regulation 4(3) are all factual questions to be determined in an objective manner. There is a clear distinction between resolving

---

[23]   [1999] JPL 231.

the primary issues of fact, whether the information sought does relate to the environment, and whether it is capable of being treated as confidential, and deciding whether if the information does fall within regulation 4(1)(a) it should be disclosed. The latter is a discretionary decision reviewable only on *Wednesbury* grounds.

Sullivan J found that while it is unusual for the court to have to resolve disputed **16.47** factual issues in applications for judicial review,[24] questions of precedent fact can arise, and that this was a precedent fact case. The editors of the Journal of Planning Law conclude that Sullivan J's judgment on the whole gives a reading to the 1990 Directive and the Regulations which is favourable to open government and transparency.

The Aarhus Convention

On 25 June 1998 the United Nations Economic Commission for Europe **16.48** ('UNECE') Convention on Access to Information, Public Participation in Decision-making and Access to Justice in Environmental Matters was adopted at a European Environmental Ministers meeting at Aarhus, Denmark. 37 UNECE members, including all 15 EU member states and the European Commission, signed the Convention. The Convention covers three 'pillars': access to information, public participation, and access to justice in environmental matters. It entered into force on 30 October 2001.

Section 74 of the Freedom of Information Act 2000 enables the information and **16.49** access to justice provisions of the Aarhus Convention to be met in England, Wales and Northern Ireland so as to enable the United Kingdom to be in a position to ratify the Convention. The European Commission, as a signatory to the Convention on behalf of the European Community, also needs to ensure that EU legislation is consistent with the Aarhus Convention. To do this the Commission in July 2000 proposed a new Directive on Public Access to Environmental Information to replace the 1990 Directive.

The main provisions of the Aarhus Convention

The preamble

The main information and associated access to justice provisions of the Aarhus **16.50** Convention are within a short compass. The preamble is an impressive statement of the need for access to environmental information. A few quotations give the flavour of the piece and show that the parties were not afraid to face up to politically sensitive issues:

---

[24] See the discussion in S De Smith, H Woolf and J Jowell, *Judicial Review of Administrative Action* (5th edn, 1998) 252.

Recognising that, in the field of the environment, improved access to information and public participation in decision-making enhance the quality and the implementation of decisions, contribute to public awareness of environmental issues, give the public the opportunity to express its concerns and enable public authorities to take due account of such concerns . . .

Acknowledging that public authorities hold environmental information in the public interest . . .

Noting the importance of adequate product information being provided to consumers to enable them to make informed environmental choices,

Recognizing the concern of the public about the deliberate release of genetically modified organisms into the environment and the need for increased transparency and greater public participation in decision-making in this field . . .

Have agreed as follows.

The Objective

16.51 Article 1 states the Objective:

In order to contribute to the protection of the right of every person of present and future generations to live in an environment adequate to his or her health and well-being, each Party shall guarantee the rights of access to information, public participation in decision-making, and access to justice in environmental matters in accordance with the provisions of this Convention.

Definitions

16.52 Article 2 defines 'Party', 'public authority', 'environmental information', 'the public', and 'the public concerned'. 'Public authority' is given a wide meaning to include government at all levels and other persons having direct or delegated public administrative functions in relation to the environment.

16.53 'Environmental information' means any information in written, visual, aural, electronic or any other material form on:

(a) The state of elements of the environment, such as air and atmosphere, water, soil, land, landscape, and natural sites, biological diversity and its components, including genetically modified organisms, and the interaction among these elements;

(b) Factors, such as substances, energy, noise, and radiation, and activities or measures, including administrative measures, environmental agreements, policies, legislation, plans and programmes, affecting or likely to affect the elements of the environment within the scope of subparagraph (a) above, and cost-benefit and other economic analyses and assumptions used in environmental decision-making;

(c) The state of human health and safety, conditions of human life, cultural sites and built structures, inasmuch as they are or may be affected by the state of the elements of the environment or, through these elements, by the factors, activities or measures referred to in subparagraph (b) above.

Article 4: Access to environmental information

Article 3 contains general provisions about the implementation of the   **16.54**
Convention. The eight paragraphs of Article 4 contain the operative provisions
about access to environmental information. This is the base from which United
Kingdom law stems.

Article 4(1) provides: **16.55**

> Each Party shall ensure that, subject to the following paragraphs of this article, pub-
> lic authorities, in response to a request for environmental information, make such
> information available to the public, within the framework of national legislation,
> including where requested and subject to paragraph (b) below, copies of actual doc-
> umentation containing or comprising such information:
>> (a) Without an interest having to be stated;
>> (b) In the form requested unless:
>>> (i) It is reasonable for the public authority to make it available in another
>>> form, in which case reasons shall be given for making it available in that
>>> form; or
>>> (ii) The information is already publicly available in another form.

Article 4(2) provides that the information shall be made available as soon as pos-   **16.56**
sible and at the latest within one month of the request, unless the volume and
complexity of the information justify an extension of the period to two months.
The applicant shall be informed of any extension and the reasons for it.

Article 4(3) provides that the request may be refused if the public authority does   **16.57**
not hold the information; or the request is manifestly unreasonable; or the request
concerns material in the course of completion; or the request concerns internal
communications of public authorities where such an exception is provided for in
the national law or customary practice, taking into account the public interest
served by disclosure.

Article 4(4) provides that: **16.58**

> A request for environmental information may be refused if the disclosure would ad-
> versely affect:
>> (a) The confidentiality of the proceedings of public authorities, where such con-
>> fidentiality is provided for under national law;
>> (b) International relations, national defence or public security;
>> (c) The course of justice, the ability of a person to receive a fair trial or the ability
>> of a public authority to conduct an enquiry of a criminal or disciplinary
>> nature;
>> (d) The confidentiality of commercial and industrial information, where such
>> confidentiality is protected by law in order to protect a legitimate economic
>> interest. Within this framework, information on emissions which is relevant
>> for the protection of the environment shall be disclosed;
>> (e) Intellectual property rights;
>> (f) The confidentiality of personal data and/or files relating to a natural person

where that person has not consented to the disclosure of the information to the public, where such confidentiality is provided for in national law;

(g) The interests of a third party which has supplied the information requested without that party being under or capable of being put under a legal obligation to do so, and where that party does not consent to the release of the material; or

(h) The environment to which the information relates, such as breeding sites of rare species.

The aforementioned grounds for refusal shall be interpreted in a restrictive way, taking into account the public interest served by disclosure and taking into account whether the information requested relates to emissions into the environment.

16.59 Article 4(5) provides that where an authority does not hold the information itself it shall inform the applicant of the authority to which it believes it is possible to apply for the information.

16.60 Article 4(6) provides that each Party shall ensure that if information exempted from disclosure can be separated out without prejudice to the confidentiality of the information exempted, public authorities make available the remainder of the information which has been requested.

16.61 Article 4(7) provides that a refusal of a request shall be in writing if the request was in writing or the applicant so requests, and shall state the reasons for the refusal and give information on access to the review procedure provided in accordance with Article 9.

16.62 Article 4(8) provides that each Party may allow its public authorities to make a reasonable charge for supplying information but must make available a schedule of charges.

Collection and dissemination of environmental information

16.63 Article 5 places a duty on the Parties to the Convention to provide for the collection and dissemination of environmental information. In particular Article 5(1)(c) provides that in the event of any immediate threat to human health or the environment, whether caused by human activities or due to natural causes, all information which could enable the public to take measures to prevent or mitigate harm arising from the threat and is held by a public authority is to be disseminated immediately and without delay to members of the public who may be affected.

16.64 Article 5(2) requires the Parties to ensure that the way in which environmental information is made available to the public is transparent and that it is effectively accessible inter alia by establishing and maintaining practical arrangements such as (i) publicly accessible lists, registers or files; (ii) requiring officials to support the public in seeking access to information under the Convention; (iii) the identification of points of contact and providing access to the environmental information contained in lists, registers or files free of charge.

Article 5(3) requires environmental information to become progressively **16.65** available in electronic databases which are easily accessible to the public through public telecommunications networks.

Access to justice

Access to justice is dealt with in Article 9. Article 9(1) provides that each Party **16.66** shall ensure that any person who considers that his or her request under Article 4 has not been properly dealt with has access to a review procedure before a court of law or another independent and impartial body established by law. Where the review provided is by a court of law, the Party shall ensure that the applicant has access to an expeditious procedure established by law that is free of charge or inexpensive for reconsideration by a public authority or review by an independent and impartial body other than a court of law. Final decisions shall be binding on the public authority holding the information. Reasons shall be stated in writing, at least where information is refused under this paragraph.

Article 9(2) provides that each Party shall ensure that members of the public, hav- **16.67** ing a sufficient interest, have access to a review procedure before a court of law and/or another independent and impartial body established by law to challenge the substantive and procedural legality of any decision, act or omission, with the objective of giving the public concerned wide access to justice within the scope of the Convention. Any non-governmental organization promoting environmental protection and meeting any requirements under national law shall be deemed to have a sufficient interest to bring proceedings.

Article 9(3) provides that in addition to the review procedures referred to in **16.68** paragraphs 1 and 2 of Article 9 each Party shall ensure that where they meet the criteria laid down by national law, members of the public have access to administrative or judicial procedures to challenge acts and omissions by private persons and public authorities which contravene provisions of its national law relating to the environment.

Article 9(4) requires effective remedies, including injunctive relief and Article **16.69** 9(5) requires that information is provided on access to administrative and judicial review procedures and that the Parties shall consider the establishment of appropriate assistance mechanisms to remove or reduce financial and other barriers to access to justice.

The 2002 draft directive on public environmental information

The draft environmental information Directive is currently proceeding through **16.70** the European legislative process. The proposal reached Common Position (agreement by all the member states of a text) at the Environmental Council in June 2001.

16.71   The European Parliament's vote on the second reading took place on 30 May 2002. The Parliament adopted a report drafted by Anneli Korhola and adopted several amendments to the Council's common position. On 5 September 2002 the Commission gave its opinion on the second reading. Of the 47 amendments passed by the European Parliament at the second reading, it stated nine could be accepted by the Commission in full and three in principle. The amendments accepted included the following:

(a)   charges must be reasonable and advance payment should not be required;

(b)   the evaluation period for the Directive should be four years, such evaluation to be based not just on the member states' reports but also in the light of experience gained;

(c)   public authorities are to be obliged, in the case of a refusal of a request, to state the name of the person preparing the answer and if there is a delay and the estimated time needed for completion. In the case of a refusal on the grounds of confidentiality, the latter must be required by national or Community law;

(d)   the grounds for refusal must be interpreted narrowly.[25]

16.72   It is expected that final agreement between the member states and European Parliament should be achieved under the Danish Presidency of the European Union in December 2002. The areas on which there is a possibility of change as a result of continuing negotiations on the draft Directive are:

• charging;
• time limits for responses.

In the meantime the United Kingdom government is undertaking a consultation process on the new draft Environmental Information Regulations. The draft Regulations reflect not only the obligations which the United Kingdom has signed up to in the Aarhus Convention, but the Articles which the United Kingdom government expects to be in the revised Directive.[26]

The 2002 Draft Regulations

16.73   The Department for Environment, Food and Rural Affairs ('DEFRA') in its consultation paper[27] says that the main improvements on the existing regime are:

• the definitions of environmental information and the bodies affected are clarified;

---

[25]   The legislative observatory, procedure file at http://www.db.eurparl.eu.int/oeil/oeil_viewdnl. procedure (26 September 2002).

[26]   The proposals to amend the Directive are discussed at paras 16.73–16.88 below together with the proposed draft Regulations.

[27]   This section is largely based on DEFRA's consultation paper which is at http://www. defra.gov.uk/corporate/consult/default.asp (16 September 2002).

- the time limit for response to a request is reduced to one month in most cases;
- a public interest test is to be introduced which is the same test as applies under the Freedom of Information Act 2000;
- the Information Commissioner and Information Tribunal will provide a strengthened means of review for applicants.

Definitions

The draft Directive adopts a broad definition of 'environmental information' **16.74** which is similar to the definition in the Convention though it is worded differently. The definition in draft regulation 2, which is aimed at clarifying what is and what is not environmental information, is in the following terms:

'environmental information' means information on any of the following—

(a) the state of the elements of the environment, such as
   (i) air and atmosphere,
   (ii) water,
   (iii) soil,
   (iv) land,
   (v) landscape and natural sites, including wetlands, coastal and marine areas, and
   (vi) biological diversity and its components, including genetically modified organisms;
(b) the interaction between the elements listed in sub-paragraph (a);
(c) factors, such as substances, energy, noise, radiation, or waste affecting, or likely to affect, anything mentioned in sub-paragraphs (a) and (b);
(d) emissions, discharges and other releases into the environment;
(e) measures, such as policies, legislation, plans, programmes and environmental agreements, and activities affecting or likely to affect, or intended to protect, anything mentioned in sub-paragraphs (a) and (b);
(f) cost-benefit and other economic analyses and assumptions used in environmental decision-making;
(g) the state of human health and safety, conditions of human life, cultural sites and built structures in as much as they are or may be affected by or through anything mentioned in sub-paragraphs (a) and (b).

The definition of 'public authorities' in the Convention is broad and includes **16.75** bodies such as privatized water authorities and power companies. The 2000 Act defines 'public authorities' as those listed in Schedule 1. The draft Regulations use the Convention definition together with a statement that this includes a public authority within the meaning of section 3 of the Act on the grounds that it both ensures conformity with the Act and allows the Regulations regime to apply more widely as intended by the Convention.

Obligation to make information available on request

The Convention obliges public authorities, upon receiving a request, to make **16.76** environmental information available in the form requested and without an interest having to be stated, unless it is reasonable for the authority to make it available in another form or the information is already publicly available in another form. The draft Directive adds 'or format' after form, and adds the requirement of 'easily accessible' to publicly available material. The draft Regulations also make these additions.[28]

Time limits

16.77   Under the Convention environmental information has to be made available by a public authority as soon as possible after the request has been submitted, and at the latest within one month of the request, with the possibility of a further month's extension in complicated cases. The applicant must be informed of and given reasons to justify the extension. The one month normal deadline is tighter than the existing Regulations, which allow two months. The Act specifies that public authorities must comply promptly and in any event not later than 20 working days after the request.[29] This would usually be very slightly less than a month. The draft Regulations use the 20 working days time limit, which could be extended for voluminous and complicated requests to two months. This has the advantage of ensuring conformity with the Act.

16.78   Under the Convention and the draft Directive the time limits for refusal to supply information are similar to those for the supply of information. In the draft Regulations the 20 working days formula is used for both and all refusals have to be in writing.

Charging

16.79   The Convention states that public authorities may make a charge for supplying information, but if this is done, the charge must not exceed a reasonable amount. In addition, public authorities intending to apply charges must make available to applicants a schedule of charges. While the schedule is new, the underlying principle of 'reasonable amount' is the same as in the existing Regulations. The Freedom of Information Act 2000 makes provision for a charging scheme. Section 9 specifies the steps to be taken in relation to requests for fees, and the implications this has on the time limits for response. The Convention and the draft Directive allow the supply of information to be made conditional on payment. However, unlike the Act they do not allow the clock to stop ticking in relation to time limits for responses. Forthcoming fees regulations will specify limits to charging under the Act. Another difference between the regimes is that section 12 of the Act exempts public authorities from the obligation to provide non-environmental information where the authority estimates that the cost of complying would exceed the appropriate limit specified in the fees regulations. There is no such exemption in the

---

[28]   Draft Regulations, reg 4(3).
[29]   Freedom of Information Act 2000, s 10(1).

Convention or the draft Directive and to introduce one in the new draft Regulations would result in under-implementation of the United Kingdom's obligations. It is not therefore proposed to introduce such an exemption.

DEFRA however anticipates that the procedures and charges for supplying **16.80** information on request up to the amount of the Act limit should, so far as possible, be aligned in practice. DEFRA proposes to set out in guidance ways in which this can be achieved.

The issue of charging is one on which negotiations on the draft Directive are con- **16.81** tinuing. The European Parliament has proposed the replacement of the principle of 'reasonable charge' with 'actual costs of reproduction'. The United Kingdom is negotiating for the retention of 'reasonable charge', taking the line that, in practice this facilitates greater access to environmental information. The government is optimistic that the principle of 'reasonable charge' will be maintained.

Duty to provide advice and assistance

The draft Directive requires public authorities who receive requests formulated in **16.82** too general a manner to ask the applicant to be more specific and to assist him in this task as soon as possible and at the latest within one month after receipt of the applicant's request. Section 16 of the Act imposes a duty to provide advice and assistance. Draft Regulation 6 adopts the same approach as the Act and includes the specific requirement imposed by the draft Directive.

Exceptions

The consultation paper says that the main difference between the draft **16.83** Regulations and the Act is in the treatment of exceptions or exemptions. The potential to refuse a request under the draft Regulations is narrower than under the Act. The consultation paper comments;

> For this reason, however far we may succeed in streamlining and harmonizing procedures and requirements in relation to the supply of information, public authorities will need to turn to the specific legal requirements of each regime whenever they are considering refusal.

The differences are striking. The substantive exceptions only apply where disclosure would have an adverse effect, and there is a public interest test for all substantive exceptions with, in square brackets, a suggestion that there is to be a presumption in favour of disclosure. If this is the right approach for environmental information, it is difficult to see why it is not the right approach for all information. Perhaps in the future the best solution may be to bring the exemptions in the Act into line with the Convention.

The draft Regulations follow the Convention and the draft Directive which clar- **16.84** ify the extent to which reliance can be placed on substantive exceptions to justify refusal of a request for environmental information. The Convention and the draft Directive reformulate the legal proceedings/course of justice exception, limit the availability of the commercial confidentiality exception, and for most exceptions introduce the condition that adverse effect would result from disclosure before the exception may be relied upon. They also introduce a requirement to take into account the public interest every time possible reliance on an exception is being considered.

16.85 The exceptions are set out in regulation 7 of the draft Regulations in the following terms:

(1) A public authority may refuse a request for environmental information where—

(a) it does not hold the information; or

(b) the request is manifestly unreasonable.

(2) A public authority may refuse a request for environmental information where—

(a) the request is formulated in too general a manner; and

(b) it is appropriate to do so in all the circumstances.

(3) A public authority may refuse a request for environmental information where granting the request would involve—

(a) either—

(i)   the disclosure of internal communication within a public authority; or

(ii) the supply of a document or other record which is still in the course of completion; and

(b) in all the circumstances of the case, the public interest in refusing the request outweighs the public interest in disclosing the information.

(4) A public authority may refuse a request for environmental information where—

(a) the disclosure of the information would adversely affect—

(i)   the confidentiality of the deliberations of any public authority;

(ii)   international relations, national defence or public security;

(iii) the course of justice, the ability of a person to receive a fair trial or the ability of a public authority to conduct an enquiry of a criminal or disciplinary nature;

(iv)   intellectual property rights;

(v)   the confidentiality of personal information contained in records held in relation to an individual who has not given his consent to its disclosure;

(vi)   the interests of the person who provided the information where that person—

(aa) was not under, and could not have been put under, any legal obligation to supply it to the public authority;

(bb) did not supply it in circumstances such that the public authority is entitled apart from these Regulations to disclose it; and

(cc) has not consented to its disclosure;

(vii) the environment to which the information relates; and

(b) in all the circumstances of the case (including whether or not the information requested relates to emissions, discharges and other releases into the environment) the public interest in refusing the request outweighs the public interest in disclosing the information.

(5) A public authority may refuse a request for environmental information (except to the extent to which it is a request for information on emissions, discharges and other releases into the environment which is relevant to the protection of the environment) where—

(a) the disclosure of the information would adversely affect the confidentiality of matters to which any commercial or industrial confidentiality attaches to protect a legitimate economic interest; and

(b) in all the circumstances of the case, the public interest in refusing the request outweighs the public interest in disclosing the information.

(6) [For the purposes of paragraphs (4)(b) and (5)(b) above, there shall be a presumption (capable of being rebutted in the circumstances of a particular case) that the public interest in disclosing information outweighs the public interest in refusing a request.]³⁰

(7) Where any environmental information held by an appropriate record authority is environmental information the disclosure of which would adversely affect any of the factors listed in paragraphs (3) (4) or (5) above, any question as to whether the public interest in refusing the request outweighs the public interest in disclosing the information is to be determined by the responsible authority in consultation with the appropriate record authority.

(8) Nothing in the Regulation shall authorise a refusal to make available any environmental information contained in the same record as, or otherwise held with, other information which is withheld by virtue of this regulation unless it is incapable of being separated from the other information for the purpose of making it available.

The commercial confidentiality exemption is of particular interest. The **16.86** Convention, as has been noted, provides for an exception 'where disclosure would adversely affect the confidentiality of commercial and industrial information in order to protect a legitimate economic interest'. It qualifies this exemption with the sentence 'Within this framework, information on emissions which is relevant for the protection of the environment shall be disclosed'. The draft Directive also makes specific reference to statistical confidentiality and tax secrecy in this context. DEFRA's view is that 'statistical confidentiality and tax secrecy' cannot be considered 'legitimate economic interests' within the meaning of the Convention exception. It follows that it would not be appropriate to make specific reference to them in this exception in the new draft Regulations. DEFRA says there are diverging views on how the 'Within this framework. . .' sentence should be interpreted. DEFRA's view is that it provides an exception to the commercial confidentiality exception for information on emissions which is relevant for the

---

³⁰ DEFRA's public consultation paper does not explain the square brackets.

protection of the environment, and the new draft Regulations are drafted accordingly.

Review and enforcement

16.87 The draft Regulations introduce a proper system of review and enforcement. In effect the appeal and enforcement provisions of the Freedom of Information Act 2000 are applied indirectly to requests for environmental information. This meets one of the main criticisms of the Campaign for Freedom of Information.

16.88 It is proposed that under the new regime, the first appeal by an aggrieved applicant should, as now, be to the authority refusing the release of the information. Formalization of such a reconsideration procedure is sufficient to meet the draft Directive and Convention requirements. However the government is proposing to top up this provision. If the applicant is still unsatisfied after the reconsideration procedure, he will be able to apply for review by the Information Commissioner, who constitutes another body established by law under the terms of the Convention. The review procedure will be free of charge and expeditious. The decision of the Commissioner will be binding on both parties unless it is appealed to the Information Tribunal, with a further appeal on a point of law to the High Court. The schedule to the draft Regulations mirrors the provisions in the Act about review and enforcement, such as powers of entry and inspection. In addition provision is made for the amendment of section 77 of the 2000 Act to extend to the draft Regulations the offence of altering records with intent to prevent disclosure.

16.89 The consultation period on the draft Regulations closed on 4 October 2002. The Regulations are expected to be adopted without significant amendment.

B. Other Statutes

16.90 The Act is not the first statute to address the issue of access to information in the broader sense. There have been legally enforceable rights of access to information in specific areas for many years. Successive enactments have required information to be disclosed and collected and have made the records compiled as a result available to the public, to a greater or lesser extent, and usually upon payment of a fee. However, it is significant that most of the information available as a result of this legislation is information about individuals or organizations which has been provided to government or other public authorities under threat of a sanction imposed by the various statutes requiring disclosure of the information in the first place. Few of the other statutes have made available information that would assist in ensuring that public authorities are held to account.

C. The Land Registration Acts

The Land Registry Act 1862

The Land Registry Act 1862 was the first statute to establish a registry of title to **16.91** landed estates. However, registration was voluntary and the information held by the registry was only available upon application to a limited number of people. The specific purpose of the register was to establish an indefeasible title to property. Registered properties could obtain a land certificate which was purely intended to facilitate and simplify conveyancing rather than to make information about ownership of land available to the general public.

Section 137 of the Land Registry Act allowed inspection of any particular entry **16.92** on the register by the registered proprietor of the land concerned or a person authorized by him or pursuant to an order of the court but by no other person. Moreover, there was no general right of inspection and the Act did little to assist in making information generally available to the public; it must accordingly be viewed as a very limited step forward in the process of securing a right of access to information.

The Land Registration Act 1925

The situation improved a little on 1 January 1926 when the Land Registration Act **16.93** 1925 came into force. The Land Transfer Act 1897 had introduced the concept of compulsory registration. The requirement to register was carried forward by the Land Registration Act. However, section 112 again only gave the right to inspect the register of title to the registered proprietor of the property concerned or an authorized person, save for certain specific exceptions.

Between 1925 and 1988 there were numerous further statutes which refined the **16.94** land registration system, including the Land Registration Act 1936, the Land Registration Act 1966, the Land Registration and Land Charges Act 1971 and the Land Registration Act 1986. However, none of these statutes took the crucial step of making the register of title open to public inspection.

The Law Commission's Second Report on Land Registration[31] recommended **16.95** that the register of title kept by HM Land Registry and the documents referred to in it should be open to public inspection. It considered the arguments advanced that an open register would be an invasion of privacy and a departure from the long-standing principle of secret or private conveyancing of land and reached the conclusion that those arguments were outweighed by the many legitimate private and public interests in establishing ownership of land. These included enabling

---

[31] *Inspection of the Register* (Law Com No 148, 1985) para 21.

tenants to identify their immediate and superior landlords or developers to nego-
tiate the purchase of blocks of derelict land in cities.

The Land Registration Act 1988

16.96   The Land Registration Act 1988 gave the public access for the first time to the
Land Register. However, while this went some way to putting an end to secrecy
over land ownership, it did not entirely resolve the matter. In particular, the register of title often recorded no more than the identity of the legal owner. There remained a great deal of other information pertaining to land that was still not
publicly available. For example, overriding interests were not included, and interests capable of subsisting only as minor interests could be created and dealt with
in the same way as if the land affected by them were unregistered. That meant that
third party rights to land could still be concealed notwithstanding the right of
public access to the Land Register. Where there was more than one legal owner the
most that would be revealed by inspecting the register was that the land was held
on trust and, perhaps, whether or not the trustees were also beneficially entitled.
The register did not directly disclose any further information about third party
interests except, possibly, the fact that they existed.

16.97   Minor interests could be protected on the register by the system of notices, cautions, inhibitions and restrictions.[32] The system was not limited in its operation to
the protection of minor interests as a notice, for example, could be associated with
an authorized disposition and, in that context, would protect a legal interest.
However, to a limited extent the nature of the minor interest could be revealed by
the form of protection as the appropriate form was determined primarily by the
nature of the minor interest.

16.98   All registered land was deemed to be subject to such overriding interests as might
for the time being be subsisting in relation to it[33] and the system of land registration allowed those interests either to be overridden, or made binding upon a pur-
chaser, in the same way as if the land were unregistered. The only information that
might be revealed about overriding interests by inspecting the register was the fact
that the land was exempt from land tax, or tithe rentcharge or payments in lieu of
tithe, or from charges or annuities payable for the redemption of tithe rentcharge.

The Land Registration Act 2002

16.99   This statute plainly effects a major reform of the law. Prominent among the
changes which it makes are:

1. It increases substantially the circumstances which give rise to the requirement for
   compulsory registration.

---

[32]   Land Registration Act 1925, Pt IV, ss 48–62.
[33]   ibid, s 70(1).

2. It bestows upon the proprietor unfettered powers of disposition, subject to any entry on the register to the contrary.
3. It significantly reduces in number and extent the range of overriding interests which can affect either the first registered proprietor or a registered disponee. . .[34]

The effect of the statute will be to strengthen the public access approach adopted by the 1988 Act. Section 66 of the 2002 Act provides: **16.100**

(1) Any person may inspect and make copies of, or of any part of—
   (a) the register of title,
   (b) any document kept by the registrar which is referred to in the register of title,
   (c) any other document kept by the registrar which relates to an application to him, or
   (d) the register of cautions against first registration.

Section 66(1)(b) extends the range of documents which may be inspected. It is true that section 66(2) specifies that the right in section 66(1) is subject to rules which may provide for exceptions to the right and impose conditions on its exercise, though no such rules have so far been made.[35]

None of the provisions of the 2002 Act has yet been brought into force. The expectation is that that will be done in stages, and that the first stage is not likely to be reached before October 2003.[36] **16.101**

In any event, there is still a substantial amount of land throughout England and Wales that is unregistered. Any landowner with unregistered title to land may apply voluntarily at any time to register that title and compulsory registration of unregistered land following certain types of transaction has been systematically introduced over the years. Compulsory registration now extends to the whole of England and Wales.[37] Information about unregistered land to which the public have access is to be found on the registers kept in pursuance of the Land Charges Act 1972[38] and the Local Land Charges Act 1975.[39] **16.102**

Land charges

The registers compiled in accordance with the Land Charges Act 1972 are registers of names and registration is effected in the name of the estate owner or other person whose land or estate or interest is intended to be affected by it. All charges and liabilities registrable under the Land Charges Act are registrable in the Land **16.103**

---

[34] I Clarke, *The Land Registration Act 2002: A Practical Guide* (2002) 3–4.
[35] ibid, at 97.
[36] ibid, at vi.
[37] See the Registration of Title Order 1989, SI 1989/1347 (lapsed).
[38] The Land Charges Act 1972 came into force on 29 January 1973: s 19(2); Land Charges Act 1972 (Commencement) Order 1972, SI 1972/2058.
[39] The Local Land Charges Act 1975 came into force on 1 August 1977: s 20(3); Local Land Charges Act 1975 (Commencement) Order 1977, SI 1977/984.

Charges and Agricultural Credits Department of Her Majesty's Land Registry. Any person may, upon completion of the prescribed form and payment of the prescribed fee, inspect an entry.

16.104 The scope of local land charges has been greatly enlarged by statute since the Land Charges Act 1925, the provisions of which were repealed with effect from 1 August 1977 and replaced by the Local Land Charges Act 1975. Section 1 lists the charges and other matters affecting land which may be registered. Any person may search in any local land charges register upon payment of the prescribed fee.

D. The Registration Acts

16.105 A comprehensive system for the registration of births, deaths and marriages was first introduced by the Births and Deaths Registration Act 1836 ('the 1836 Act'). The system of registration established by that statute is now governed by the Registration Acts. Section 21(1) of the Registration Service Act 1953 ('the 1953 Act') consolidated with minor corrections and improvements a number of earlier statutes, in particular the Marriage Act 1949 and the Births and Deaths Registration Act 1953 which, together with the 1953 Act, are now known collectively as the Registration Acts.

16.106 The requirement that the information provided pursuant to the Registration Acts be recorded in registers has meant that that information is available to the general public.

16.107 The particulars required to be registered in each case are prescribed in the Registration of Births and Deaths Regulations 1987[40] and the Registration of Marriages Regulations 1986.[41] The particulars to be given include:

(a) the date and place of the birth, marriage or death;
(b) the name, surname and residence or usual address of the individuals concerned;
(c) certain details about one or both of their parents;
(d) information about sex, marital status, occupation or rank or profession and, where applicable, cause of death;
(e) in relation to births and deaths certain details about the informant.

16.108 All entries on the registers must be notified to the Registrar General and he must make and keep indexes of all certified copies of entries in the General Register Office. Any person is entitled upon payment of the respective fees to search the indexes maintained by the superintendent registrars for each registration district

---

[40] SI 1987/2088.
[41] SI 1986/1442.

and the registers of live births and deaths and register of marriages maintained by the registrars for each sub-district.

In addition to the certified copies of entries in the registers of births, deaths **16.109** and marriages, other records and registers are kept at the General Register Office, including:

(a) the adopted children register;
(b) the parental order register;
(c) the service departments register;
(d) the marine register;
(e) the air and hovercraft registers; and
(f) the consular and United Kingdom High Commissioners' registers.

In the adopted children register must be entered only such entries as are directed **16.110** to be made in it by adoption orders.[42] Similar provisions apply to the parental order register.[43] The Registrar General must also keep such other registers and books, and make such entries in them, as may be necessary to record and make traceable the connection between any entry in the registers of births which had been marked 'Adopted' or marked 'Reregistered by the Registrar General' and any corresponding entry in the adopted children register or the parental order register but those other registers and books are not open to public inspection. The Adoption Act 1976[44] permits the Registrar General to disclose information contained in them either to an adopted person who has reached the age of 18 or under a court order, as the case may be.

The Service Departments Register is a record of the deaths and births occurring **16.111** outside the United Kingdom among, or among the families of:

(a) members of Her Majesty's naval, military or air forces; or
(b) persons serving Her Majesty in, or otherwise employed in any capacity connected with, Her Majesty's naval, military or air forces, or persons belonging to or employed by any organization concerned with the welfare of members of those forces. [45]

Births and deaths at sea or on civil aircraft or hovercraft and deaths on offshore in- **16.112** stallations are similarly recorded separately in either the Marine Register or the Air and Hovercraft Registers.[46]

---

[42] Forms of Adoption Entry Regulations 1975, SI 1975/1959, reg 3(a), Sch 1.
[43] Parental Orders (Human Fertilization and Embryology) Regulations 1994, SI 1994/2767, reg 2, Sch 1 and Forms of Entry for Parental Orders Regulations 1994, SI 1994/2981, reg 2(a), Sch 1.
[44] Adoption Act 1976, s 50(5) and 51 (as amended).
[45] Registration of Births, Deaths and Marriages (Special Provisions) Act 1957 and the Service Departments Registers Order 1959, SI 1959/406.
[46] Merchant Shipping (Returns of Births and Deaths) Regulations 1979, SI 1979/1577; Offshore Installations (Logbooks and Registration of Death) Regulations 1972, SI 1972/1542;

16.113 As can be seen from the foregoing paragraphs, there is a plethora of information concerning individuals collected under the Registration Acts much of which is generally available to public access. However, in some categories, access to the information is restricted. The nature of the restrictions imposed are such that the exemption provided by section 21 of the Freedom of Information Act 2000 may not apply, for example, the information maintained on the Adopted Children and Parental Order Registers is not 'reasonably accessible' to all applicants within the meaning of section 21(2). However, with regard to information currently maintained by the Registrar General that is of no consequence as the Registrar General is not listed in Schedule 1 to the Act.

16.114 There is, of course, the possibility that the Registrar General may be added to Schedule 1 by amendment pursuant to section 4. If such an amendment is made, the personal information that is at present not exempt information by virtue of section 21 will become exempt information in accordance with the provisions of section 40 of the Act.

E. The Census Act 1920

16.115 The Census Act 1920 provided another means by which the general population could be compelled to provide information to government for statistical purposes. The Act gives the monarch the power to direct that a census be taken by Order in Council. Any such Order may prescribe the date upon which the census is to be taken (section 1(1)(a)) and the persons by whom and with respect to whom the returns for the purpose of the census are to be made (section 1(1)(b)). However, section 1(1)(c) limits the particulars that may be required to be stated to those listed in the Schedule to the Act, namely:

(a) names, sex and age;

(b) occupation, profession and trade or employment;

(c) nationality, birthplace, race and language;

(d) place of abode and character of dwelling;

(e) condition as to marriage, relation to head of family and issue born in marriage; and

(f) any other matters with respect to which it is desirable to obtain statistical information with a view to ascertaining the social or civil condition of the population.

By section 1 of the Census (Amendment) Act 2000 the Schedule is amended to insert a new paragraph 5A. That identifies 'Religion' as a matter in respect of

---

Civil Aviation (Births, Deaths and Missing Persons) Regulations 1948, SI 1948/1411 and Hovercraft (Births, Deaths and Missing Persons) Regulations, 1972 SI 1972/1513.

which particulars may be required, but (by an addition to section 8 of the Act) it is provided that no person is to be liable to a penalty for refusing or neglecting to state any particulars in respect of religion.

If any Order directing a census prescribes any particulars with respect to any of the **16.116** matters mentioned in (f), that part of the Order has no effect unless both Houses of Parliament approve that part of the draft Order or, if any modifications in that part are agreed to by both Houses, it has effect as so modified.[47]

By way of example, the Census Order 1990[48] prescribed the particulars that **16.117** should be stated in the returns to be made in the census in 1990. In June 1997 a test questionnaire was circulated which included questions which would provide statistics relating to poverty and wealth for possible inclusion in the 2001 census.[49]

However, a far greater degree of confidentiality attaches to information obtained **16.118** under the Census Act than to information obtained under most other legislation considered in this chapter. The Registrar General is bound to disclose only information about the actual mechanics of the census. Once the information has been collected and collated, the Registrar General must prepare reports[50] on the census returns. Every such report must be printed and laid before both Houses of Parliament. In addition, the Registrar General has a discretion to make certain information available if requested to do so.

If the Registrar General thinks fit, he may, at the request and cost of any local au- **16.119** thority or person, cause abstracts to be prepared containing statistical information which can be derived from the census returns, but which is not contained in his reports and is, in his opinion, reasonably required by that authority or person.[51] However, the information that might be provided in the exercise of this discretion is limited to general statistical information. No 'personal census information' may be disclosed.

'Personal census information' is defined in the Census Act as any census informa- **16.120** tion which relates to an identifiable person or household and 'census information' means any census information which (i) is acquired by any person mentioned in section 8(2)[52] in the course of any work done by him in connection with the discharge of functions under section 2 (as amended) or section 4; (ii) is acquired by any such person in the course of working, for purposes of section 5, with any

---

[47] See the proviso to Census Act 1920, s 1(2).
[48] SI 1990/243.
[49] *Hansard*, HC (series 6) vol 295, col 154 (3 June 1997).
[50] See the Census Act 1920, s 4(1).
[51] ibid, s 4(2).
[52] As substituted by the Census (Confidentiality) Act 1991, s 1.

information acquired as mentioned in (i); or (iii) is derived from any information so acquired.[53]

16.121 If any personal census information is disclosed, the person disclosing it or any person disclosing it to another person knowing that it was disclosed in contravention of the Census Act will be guilty of an offence.[54] However, disclosure of information in connection with proceedings for an offence under the Population (Statistics) Act 1938 or in connection with a report of such proceedings is not an offence.[55] The sanctions imposed for the wrongful disclosure of information obtained under the Census Act underline the emphasis on the confidentiality of personal census information and recognize the need to balance transparency against the preservation of individual privacy. The same theme is discernible in the 2000 Act. Part I and Part II reflect the same balancing exercise. On the one hand, access to information to ensure that illegal or controversial actions by public authorities will be discovered is given by section 1. On the other hand, the sanctity of information held by public authorities which is confidential personal information is preserved either by providing an absolute exemption or by excluding the 'public authority' in question from the scope of the Act.

16.122 As with information obtained and maintained pursuant to the Registration Acts, information obtained under the Census Act of a more general nature, such as statistical information, is accessible upon payment of a fee whereas confidential personal information is protected by section 40 of the 2000 Act.

[53] Census Act 1920, s 8(7) as added by the Census (Confidentiality) Act 1991, s 1.
[54] Census Act 1920, s 8(2) (as substituted, see n 52 above) and 8(3) (as added, see n 53 above).
[55] Population (Statistics) Act 1938, s 4 (as amended).

Part F

FREEDOM OF INFORMATION AND THE COMMERCIAL WORLD

17

IMPLICATIONS FOR BUSINESS

A. Introduction

In his essay 'Freedom of Information: the Implications for Business',[1] Richard **17.01** Thomas[2] wrote (before the freedom of information legislation had completed its passage through Parliament) of the 'opportunities and threats' facing business. The Freedom of Information Act 2000 when in force will present business with enhanced opportunities of access to information held by public authorities, and increased risks (a term here preferred to 'threats') that confidential information supplied by business to such authorities may be accessed by others including competitors. Both opportunities and risks are considered in this chapter, which draws together points concerning the statute's access and exemption provisions that are fully discussed in other chapters.

The effect on business of the operation of freedom of information laws in other **17.02** countries, especially the United States, is also discussed, on the footing that that experience illustrates some of the likely consequences for business in this country,

---

[1] J Beatson and Y Cripps (eds), *Freedom of Expression and Freedom of Information—Essays in Honour of Sir David Williams* (2000).
[2] Then Director of Public Policy at Clifford Chance, now the Information Commissioner.

once the Act is fully operational. It is interesting to note that the experience of the United States is that the main user of their Freedom of Information Act 1966 and Electronic Freedom of Information Act Amendments 1996 is the business community. Around 50–60 per cent of requests are made by commercial bodies seeking information on business competitors.[3] Access has led to a satellite industry with organizations of 'data brokers' or 'surrogate requesters' accessing information on behalf of clients. A substantial number of requests received by NASA, for example, concern contracts, proposals, modifications to contracts and requests for proposals.[4]

B. Access to Information

17.03 In early 1999, the European Commission produced a *Green Paper on Public Sector Information in the Information Society*,[5] which considered access to public information to be essential within a European context both to achieve mobility within the European Union and to enable businesses to take advantage of the internal market. The authors vigorously asserted the need for business to have improved access to public information:

> The ready availability of public information is an absolute prerequisite for the competitiveness of European industry. In this respect, EU companies are at a serious competitive disadvantage compared to their American counterparts which benefit from a highly developed, efficient public information system at all levels of the administration.

17.04 The Green Paper emphasized the need to ensure that businesses were able to obtain information on such matters as administrative procedures, prices, and the quality and safety of products. It stated that taxation provisions needed to be transparent and that citizens of one country should have access to the information which would enable them to buy goods and services from other member states. One example given of the problems to be avoided was the difficulty that people in the British Isles had in obtaining right-hand drive vehicles from the Continent often because of an inability to obtain information and to comply with administrative requirements. The Green Paper described public sector information as being a 'key resource for a very large part of information services'.

17.05 The Green Paper concentrated on practical methods of providing access to information (albeit for the purpose of achieving a 'Citizens' Europe'). Whilst pointing out that the Treaty of Amsterdam had 'firmly anchored [the right of

---

[3] See ME Tankersley, 'How the Electronic Freedom of Information Act Amendments of 1996 update public access for the information age' (1998) 50 Admin Law Review 421–458, reprinted in RG Vaughn (ed): *Freedom of Information* (2000).

[4] Thomas (n 1 above) 406.

[5] COM (98) 585 final, adopted on 20 January 1999.

European citizens] to access documents of the European Parliament, Council and Commission in the EC Treaty' and that there was a European Ombudsman to deal with complaints, the emphasis was upon methods of achieving access. Examples were: the establishment of EUR-Lex displaying the Official Journal for a period of 45 days following publication, the Treaties, the legislation and the case law;[6] the implementation of the European Business Register project to provide basic information on all companies in Europe;[7] and Internet access to the European Patent Office.[8] This kind of practical approach was seen as essential if the right to freedom of information was to be effective.

17.06 The information to which businesses might require access under the Freedom of Information Act might be political, legal or governmental. It might be scientific, technical or medical or it might be concerned with the procedures, needs and requirements of public services. What is needed is a coherent system of access to such information and electronic technology should be used for this purpose. Investment in information technology will be required in order to provide ready access to information held by public authorities. In so far as this has to be paid for, the criterion is surely that the information should be affordable to all, at a price which justifies its exploitation and subject to fair competition. It is to be noted that the Electronic Freedom of Information Act Amendments 1996 were passed in order to provide for electronic access in the United States, but in this country there is no similar provision requiring such access to be provided within the Freedom of Information Act 2000.

C. The Current Position

Opportunities for business

17.07 When the Act is in force, the opportunities which it will create for business are real, and those with US experience will be quick to take advantage of them to gain the competitive advantage which information can give.

17.08 The first question to ask is what information does government have? This question is raised by the Constitution Unit in their paper *Freedom of Information and Business*.[9] They cite a US House of Representatives report[10] in 1978 which they summarize as follows:

---

[6] See http://europa.eu.int/eur-lex
[7] See http://www.ebr.org
[8] See http://www.european-patent-office.org/
[9] Written by Jim Amos and published by the Constitution Unit, School of Public Policy, University College London, 29/30 Tavistock Square, WC1H 9EZ, June 1999.
[10] 95th Congress 2nd Session 1978: House of Representatives Hearings on the Freedom of Information Act, *Requests for business data and reverse FOIA lawsuits*, 1.

A portrayal of every enterprise of any consequence lies in government files, frequently unassembled like pieces of a picture puzzle. Collection and maintenance of such information is a universal characteristic of government operations that regulate private industry, licence commercial activities, purchase and sell goods and services and deal in numerous ways with the Nation's businesses.

17.09 Whitehall has the same information. The House of Commons Select Committee on Public Administration in its 1998 report[11] used three classifications of this information:

(1) Information gathered as a result of regulatory functions or given for monitoring purposes;
(2) Information relating to contracts;
(3) Information relating to commercial activities of the authority itself.

17.10 As the Constitution Unit point out, government has a great deal more information that is relevant to business than is often appreciated. Much of it is the government's own information about the ways in which it is developing and administering policies. Although there are wide exemptions in the Act in relation to the formulation or development of policy and ministerial communications, and the disclosure of information which would inhibit the free and frank provision of advice or exchange of views within public authorities, more information will be available to business under the Act. This will include statistical information used to provide an informed background to the taking of decisions. Indeed much more information is already available than is generally recognized, through the Code of Practice on Access to Government Information ('the Open Government Code'); under the Local Government Acts; under Environmental Directives and Regulations; and from European Institutions under Council Regulation (EC) 1049/2001.

The Open Government Code[12]

17.11 Paragraph 1 of the Open Government Code, which will remain in force until 2005, states that the approach to release of information should in all cases be based on the assumption that information should be released except where disclosure would not be in the public interest as specified in Part II of the Code. It is usually sensible to refer to the Code when seeking information as its provisions are not as widely known in Whitehall as one would expect.

17.12 Paragraph 3 of the Code contains five commitments:

(1) to supply facts and analysis with major policy decisions;
(2) to open up internal guidelines about departments' dealings with the public;
(3) to supply reasons for administrative decisions

---

[11] House of Commons Select Committee on Administration, third report May 1998, Vol 1, xxxvi.
[12] See also the Open Government Code ch 4.

(4) to provide information under the Citizen's Charter about public services, what they cost, targets, performance and redress;

(5) to respond to requests for information.

Those commitments are wide ranging. The provision of major policy decisions **17.13** with facts and analyses should help businesses to foresee more easily the future applications of the policy and thereby to identify business opportunities. The supply of reasons for administrative decisions should enable businesses to understand the viewpoint of the administration and to predict the most likely outcome of future decisions. It may also make it easier to influence future decisions because business can attack, or develop through consultation, the rationale behind decisions. It may even make it easier to challenge decisions by way of judicial review should this be required.

Information concerning public services (costs, targets or performance) should as- **17.14** sist those businesses which contract with public authorities. It should assist in preparing tenders and in predicting future business opportunities. This information may also assist with lobbying.

Part II of the Open Government Code contains 15 exemptions. The exemptions **17.15** which are most relevant to business are disclosure which would harm the frankness and candour of internal advice; disclosure which could prejudice law enforcement and legal proceedings; disclosure which would prejudice the management of the economy and the collection of tax; disclosure which could harm the proper and efficient conduct of the public service and in particular could prejudice the competitive position of a public body, or negotiations or commercial or contractual activities or the awarding of discretionary grants; disclosure of research analysis or statistics which could be misleading or deprive the holder of commercial value; unwarranted disclosure of personal information or disclosure which would constitute an unwarranted invasion of privacy; the disclosure of third party's commercial confidences; and information given in confidence.

A business which is dissatisfied with an answer to an inquiry and cannot obtain **17.16** satisfaction from the department or body concerned may apply through a Member of Parliament to the Ombudsman. The Ombudsman has had considerable success in enforcing the Code and his decisions give a clear indication of the way the Information Commissioner can be expected to apply the Act when it comes fully into force in 2005. Information released as a result of the Ombudsman's investigations have included:

(a) a list of animal carcass incinerator operators who held contracts with the Ministry for Agriculture, Fisheries and Food for the disposal of BSE infected cattle;[13]

---

[13] A33/96, HC 132, session 1997/1998, Fourth Report.

(b) the A36 Salisbury Bypass reassessment report;[14]

(c) details of fees paid to lawyers in the second inquest into the *Marchioness* disaster;[15]

(d) an expert adviser's report on the financial viability of the project for a proposed museum;[16] and

(e) the reasons why the Sports Council for Wales decided not to award a grant to an athlete.[17]

17.17 In chapter 4 there is a detailed discussion of the *Hinduja* case where the Ombudsman eventually extracted proper replies from the Home Office and the Cabinet Office about papers they held in relation to the Hinduja brothers and rejected the Home Office view that this information was covered by the exemption relating to legal proceedings. The Ombudsman decided that the inquiry conducted by Sir Anthony Hammond did not come within the exemption. This decision gives strength to the view that the Ombudsman and the Information Commissioner will have a considerable influence on Whitehall which will lead to greater openness.

17.18 The business community may take some comfort from the *Illisu Dam* cases, which are also considered in depth in chapter 4, where Friends of the Earth failed to obtain information from the Export Credits Guarantee Department about Balfour Beatty's application for export credit support. The Ombudsman concluded that although exemption 13 (third party confidences) applied to the information sought, the harm test within that exemption operated in favour of disclosure. He was unable, however, to recommend disclosure because of legal advice that the information was protected by the law of confidence. This finding is therefore an example of a case where the non-statutory Code cannot override the law. If the case had been brought under the Act the result would have been the same because it would have come within the wider exemption in section 41.[18]

Local government[19]

17.19 Local government is one significant area of the law (the environment, discussed in the next section of this chapter, is another) where access to information has been greatly improved by legislation enacted well before the Freedom of Information Act. In particular, the Local Government (Access to Information) Act 1985 provided for access to local authority meetings (including meetings of committees

---

[14] Parliamentary Commissioner, *Access to Official Information: investigations completed*, 4th report, session 1999–2000, case no A30/96.

[15] ibid, case no A5/97.

[16] ibid, case no C431/96.

[17] ibid, case no A6/97.

[18] See paras 17.51 and 17.52 below.

[19] See also ch 15 above.

and sub-committees), and to agendas, reports, minutes and background papers. There are exceptions for 'exempt' and 'confidential' information, but the access provisions are far-reaching. Similar access provisions were established by the Local Government Act 2000 and the regulations made under it which apply to the new executive structures for local authorities (mayor and cabinet executive, leader and cabinet executive, mayor and council manager executive). These and related statutory provisions are discussed in detail in chapter 15. For the present, a business which seeks to obtain information from a local authority should expect to find greater assistance from the local government legislation than from the Freedom of Information Act.

The fact there is an existing statutory regime for local authorities means that it **17.20** may be difficult to work out the consequences of the interaction of the Local Government (Access to Information) Act 1985, the Local Government Act 2000, the Data Protection Act 1998, and the Freedom of Information Act itself. The present legal position, which 'is somewhat in a state of flux',[20] is likely to be clarified in the near future. The government is 'reviewing the current access to information rules which apply to local authorities to see how they can best be integrated with the new rules under Freedom of Information'.[21] In the meantime, as indicated above, the existing local government statutory regime is likely to provide the best access route to information.

The environment

The Constitution Unit[22] have pointed out some examples of current use by busi- **17.21** ness of information about the environment which is available to the public. The examples are:

(a) companies seeking licences from the Environment Agency for the discharge of noxious substances use the public register to analyse the terms of licences granted to their competitors so that they can argue that the conditions being demanded from them by the Agency are unfairly restrictive;

(b) use of information from the Health and Safety Executive about the extent of enforcement action which has been taken against companies, to help the enquirer assess the qualities of those companies, either as potential suppliers or as candidates for acquisition; and

(c) use of information from the Environment Agency and the Health and Safety Executive to produce 'ethical' profiles of companies to be provided to fund managers who apply specific ethical criteria to their investments.

---

[20] Law Commission, *Publication of Local Authority Reports* (Law Com No 163, 2002) 124, para 88.
[21] Office of the Deputy Prime Minister: *Access to Information in Local Government* (policy paper, September 2002) 5.
[22] J Amos and G Innes, *A Guide for Business to the Freedom of Information Act 2000* (Constitution Unit and Lovells, February 2001) 8–9.

17.22   Access to information about the environment is not governed by the Freedom of Information Act 2000 but by the Aarhus Convention 1998, the Council Directive (EEC) 90/313 on the freedom of access to information on the environment and the Environmental Information Regulations 1992.[23] The Council Directive is about to be replaced, as are the 1992 Regulations to bring both into line with the Aarhus Convention. The operative provisions about access to environmental information are in Article 4 of the Convention, which is the base from which United Kingdom law stems.

17.23   Article 4(1) requires the parties to the Convention to ensure that public authorities make environmental information available to the public in response to a request, including providing copies of actual documentation containing or comprising such information, without an interest having been stated and in the form requested, unless it is reasonable for the authority to make the information available in some other form, or it is already publicly available. The Article provides that:

> A request for environmental information may be refused if the disclosure would adversely affect:
>
> (a) The confidentiality of the proceedings of public authorities, where such confidentiality is provided for under national law;
> (b) International relations, national defence or public security;
> (c) The course of justice, the ability of a person to receive a fair trial or the ability of a public authority to conduct an enquiry of a criminal or disciplinary nature;
> (d) The confidentiality of commercial and industrial information, where such confidentiality is protected by law in order to protect a legitimate economic interest. Within this framework, information on emissions which is relevant for the protection of the environment shall be disclosed;
> (e) Intellectual property rights;
> (f) The confidentiality of personal data and/or files relating to a natural person where that person has not consented to the disclosure of the information to the public, where such confidentiality is provided for in national law;
> (g) The interests of a third party which has supplied the information requested without that party being under or capable of being put under a legal obligation to do so, and where that party does not consent to the release of the material; or
> (h) The environment to which the information relates, such as breeding sites of rare species.
>
> The aforementioned grounds for refusal shall be interpreted in a restrictive way, taking into account whether the information requested relates to emissions into the environment.

17.24   These provisions are to be carried into effect in the United Kingdom by the Environmental Information Regulations 2002, which are close to their final draft.[24] The differences between the new regulations and the Act are notable. First,

---

[23] SI 1992/3240.
[24] See ch 16 at paras 16.73–16.89 below.

the substantive exceptions in the regulations only apply where disclosure would have an adverse effect, and secondly, there is a public interest test for all substantive exceptions, with a presumption in favour of disclosure. Business may therefore find it easier to obtain environmental information than information under the Act.

In chapter 16 there is detailed account of *R v British Coal Corporation, ex p Ibstock* **17.25** *Building Products Ltd*[25] and *R v Secretary of State for the Environment, Transport and the Regions and Midland Expressway Limited, ex p Alliance Against the Birmingham Northern Relief Road*,[26] decisions in which businesses were involved in litigation on the 1992 Environmental Regulations. In the first case the company which owned Ibstock Brick Works sought successfully to find the identity of the person who had told British Coal that naval munitions had been dumped in a mine shaft under the brick works in 1944. In the *Birmingham Northern Relief Road* case protesters represented by the Alliance had the Secretary of State's decision quashed. The judge held that the Alliance was entitled to see part of Midland Expressway's concession agreement. Both these decisions favoured open government and transparency. Freedom of information had arrived, to some extent.

Freedom of information in Europe[27]

The rules concerning access to documents held by the institutions of the **17.26** European Union are contained in Council Regulation (EC) 1049/2001 which was adopted by the European Parliament and the Council of Ministers on 30 May 2001.

The purpose of the Regulation is stated to be to define the principles, conditions **17.27** and limits on grounds of public policy or private interest governing the right of access to European Parliament, Council and Commission documents in such a way as to ensure the widest possible access to documents; to establish rules ensuring the easiest possible exercise of this right; and to promote good administrative practice on access to documents.

Any company having its registered office in a member state has a right to seek ac- **17.28** cess to all documents held by an institution, that is to say, documents drawn up or received by it and in its possession, in all areas of activity of the European Union.

There are of course exceptions to the right of access but they are succinctly stated. **17.29** Those most relevant to business are:

(a) where disclosure would undermine the protection of the financial, monetary or economic policy of the Community or a member state;

---

[25] [1995] JPL 836.
[26] [1999] JPL 231.
[27] See also ch 24 at paras 24.29–24.51 below.

(b) where disclosure would undermine the privacy and the integrity of the individual, in particular in accordance with Community legislation regarding the protection of personal data;

(c) where disclosure would undermine the protection of commercial interests of a natural or legal person (including intellectual property), court proceedings and legal advice, and the purpose of inspections, investigations and audits, unless there is an overriding public interest in disclosure.

17.30 As regards third party documents, the institution is required to consult the third party with a view to ascertaining whether an exception is applicable if there is any doubt whether the documents should be disclosed. This is an important protection to companies giving information to European institutions.

17.31 The Regulation also provides for public access to a register of documents which each institution is required to maintain. There is also a requirement for all basic documents, including Commission proposals and framework positions, to be published in the Official Journal.

17.32 The rights under the Regulation can be enforced by taking proceedings in the European Court of Justice or by an application to the European Ombudsman. The cases[28] which have been decided under the Code which preceded the Regulation[29] demonstrate that the Court will, where necessary, take a firm line with the other institutions. The European Union now has a good freedom of information regime in place.

D. The Position Under the Act

Introduction

17.33 The Constitution Unit point out that:

> Within the business community there has been an increasing recognition of the value and importance of information. In one sense this is not new. It has always been understood that some company information was important and needed to be kept secret. The newer issue is to appreciate the value of information as an asset, to question whether information assets are as well understood as other strategic assets and the degree to which they are properly exploited and protected.[30]

---

[28] Case T-194/94 *Carvel and Guardian Newspapers Ltd v Council of the European Union* [1995] ECR II-02765; Case T-174/95 *Svenska Journalistforbundet v Council of the European Union* [1998] ECR II-02289; Case C-353/99P *Hautala v Council of the European Union* [2002] 1 WLR 1930, ECR II-02765; and Case T-211/00 *Kuijer v Council of the European Union (No 2)* [2002] 1 WLR 1941. These cases are discussed in detail at paras 24.11–24.28 below.

[29] See ch 24 at paras 24.11–24.51 below.

[30] Amos (text and n 9 above) 6.

This part of this chapter takes up this challenge and considers the opportunities and problems which the Act will present to business when it comes fully into force in January 2005.

A statutory right

The fact that everyone will have a statutory right to information is likely to have a much more dramatic effect on the behaviour of public authorities than the little used Open Government Code. **17.34**

The current position concerning freedom of information will change because many more authorities are subject to the Act than were subject to the Open Government Code. The business community has a particular interest in seeing that regulatory bodies are within the scope of the legislation from the outset, and they are.[31] The Financial Services Authority, Office of Fair Trading, Competition Commission, utility regulators, Environment Agency, Health and Safety Commission and Executive, Independent Television Commission, Medicines Control Agency and local authorities with their enforcement functions are all public authorities bound by the Act. One of the first steps for any business to take is to study the list of public authorities in the first Schedule to the Act and identify the relevant authorities from whom information can in future be obtained. **17.35**

Exemptions

Exemptions provide a means of protection for businesses as well as a restriction on access. Exemptions are relevant not only for the purpose of identifying what information cannot be accessed but also for the purpose of trying to protect information of or concerning businesses held by the public authorities. The right of access to information opens up the potential for competitors to obtain information concerning their rivals, and businesses need to be aware of the extent to which exemptions protect such information. There is a balance to be struck between the aim of achieving openness within the operations of government and the need to ensure that confidentiality is maintained so that businesses are not adversely affected by the encouragement of more open and accountable government. **17.36**

The question whether information falls within a statutory exemption is one which must be considered by a public authority when it receives a request for that information. The authority may reach the view that the duty to confirm or deny whether it holds information of the description specified does not arise.[32] Such an exemption will be an absolute exemption if it is created by one of the sections of the Act specified in section 2(3) of the Act. If not, the exemption will only apply **17.37**

---

[31] See ch 5 at paras 5.22–5.29 above.
[32] Freedom of Information Act 2000, s 2(1).

if in all the circumstances of the case the public interest in maintaining the exclusion outweighs the public interest in disclosing whether the information is held.[33] It is likely to be rare that it will be in the public interest not to comply with the duty to confirm or deny since that does not require communication of the information but merely an acknowledgement that the information is or is not held.

17.38　In addition or alternatively the exemption may provide that there is no duty to communicate the information. In this case too, the exemption will be an absolute exemption if it is created by one of the sections of the Act specified in section 2(3). If not, the exemption will only apply if in all the circumstances of the case the public interest in maintaining the exemption outweighs the public interest in disclosing the information.[34] It is this balancing exercise which is more likely to have an adverse result for the person requesting the information.

The public interest test[35]

17.39　The most important exemptions from a business point of view are the exemption in section 41 for information provided in confidence, and the exemption in section 43 for trade secrets and for information the disclosure of which would or would be likely to prejudice the commercial interests of any person. Section 41 is an absolute exemption. Section 43 is not and is subject to the public interest test. Both these sections are considered in detail at paragraphs 17.51 to 17.59 below. The other exemptions of relevance to business which are also subject to the public interest test are:

(a) *section 27,* the information's disclosure would be likely to prejudice international relations or it is confidential information obtained from an overseas state;

(b) *section 29,* the information would be likely to prejudice the country's economic interests or the financial interests of any administration in the UK;

(c) *section 30,* the information is held for the purpose of certain investigations or proceedings as to improper or illegal conduct, fitness or competence;

(d) *section 31,* the information's disclosure would be likely to prejudice law enforcement activities including those relating to tax collection and immigration controls;

(e) *section 33,* the information relates to the audit of public authorities' accounts;

(f) *section 35,* the information relates to the formulation or development of government policy and ministerial communications (although statistical

---

[33] Freedom of Information Act 2000, s 2(1)(b).
[34] ibid, s 2(2)(b).
[35] See ch 6 at paras 6.111–6.113 below.

information used to provide an informed background to the taking of the decision is not to be regarded as exempt information);

(g) *section 36*, the information's disclosure would inhibit the free and frank provision of advice or exchange of views within public authorities;

(h) *section 38*, the information's disclosure would be likely to endanger an individual's health or safety;

(i) *section 42*, the information is legally privileged.

The introduction of this wide-ranging public interest test is a significant change **17.40** from the Open Government Code, and means that much more information will become available. Where the public interest lies will be judged first by the public authority, then by the Information Commissioner, with an appeal to the Information Tribunal; the courts will only get involved in exceptional cases. Business is in as a good a position as anyone else to judge where the public interest will be found to lie. Some help is to be derived from the experience of other jurisdictions.

Public interest—the experience elsewhere

In New Zealand Sir Brian Elwood, the New Zealand Chief Ombudsman, has **17.41** drawn attention to the difficult, sometimes agonizing task of determining whether the public interest in the release of particular information outweighs the prejudice which has been identified, should information be released. He says:

> It is rare indeed for the holder of information once having established a prejudice under section 9[36] to then proceed to acknowledge that the reason for withholding it is outweighed by the public interest. The task of determining the public interest and the weight to be accorded to it, inevitably falls to the review body, in New Zealand the Ombudsman.

The High Court in New Zealand has given some guidance. In *TV3 Network* **17.42** *Services v BSA*, a privacy case, Eichelbaum CJ says:[37]

> it is necessary to draw attention to the distinction between matters properly within the public interest, in the sense of being legitimate concern to the public, and those which are merely interesting to the public on a human level—between what is interesting to the public and what it is in the public interest to be made known.

The Australian Law Reform Commission refer to this decision in the review they **17.43** made of the Australian Act in 1995[38] and also say that the public interest has been described as something that 'is of serious concern or benefit to the public not merely of individual interest'. They add that the public interest is 'an amorphous

---

[36] The section of the New Zealand Freedom of Information Act 1982 which contains exemptions.

[37] [1995] 2 NZLR 720, 733.

[38] *Open Government: a review of the federal Freedom of Information Act 1982* (Report No 77, 1995).

concept' which is not defined in the Australian Act. They list the following factors which they say might be relevant to the public interest:

- the general public interest in government information being accessible;
- whether the document would disclose the reason for the decision;
- whether disclosure would contribute to debate on a matter of public interest; and
- whether disclosure would enhance scrutiny of government decision making processes and thereby improve accountability and participation.

In the Republic of Ireland the public interest has been considered by the Irish Information Commissioner in two recent groups of cases. First, in *Henry Ford & Sons Ltd, Nissan Ireland and Motor Distributors Ltd and the Office of Public Works*[39] the Commissioner accepted that the disclosure by the Office of Public Works of the tender price for army vehicles could prejudice the competitive position of the tenderers as the price quoted could differ from that quoted to other customers and that knowledge of this by those other customers could disrupt the business relationship. He found, however, that the advantages in terms of openness and accountability of disclosing the tender prices outweighed the possible harm to tenderers and that the public interest was better served by disclosing the information.

17.44 The second group of cases is *Eircom plc and the Department of Agriculture and Food, Mark Henry and the Department of Agriculture and Food, Eircom plc and the Department of Finance, and Eircom plc and the Office of the Revenue Commissioners.*[40] An individual sought access to copies of invoices paid to 18 telecommunications companies by Irish government departments. The Irish Information Commissioner accepted that a competitor of Eircom plc, one of the companies, could learn information from the records which it might find useful and that the loss of a substantial part of Eircom's current business with public bodies would result in a material loss to Eircom. He was also satisfied that the release of the information could prejudice the competitive advantage which Eircom enjoyed in the conduct of its business with public bodies.

17.45 The Commissioner found, however, that there was a significant public interest in ensuring that public bodies obtain value for money in purchasing telecommunications services and that this outweighed any public interest in protecting Eircom's ability to do business with public bodies. He also found that there was a public interest in ensuring maximum openness in relation to the use of public funds and in requesters exercising their rights under the Act. He therefore granted access to the documents.

---

[39] Cases 98049, 98056, and 98057, 31 March 1999.
[40] Cases 98114, 98132, 98164, and 98183, 13 January 2000.

In practice it will be very difficult to provide general guidance on the application **17.46**
of the public interest test. It is a balancing exercise and each case will turn on its
own facts and circumstances.

The role of the Information Commissioner

Under the UK Freedom of Information Act 2000 the Information Commissioner **17.47**
has a central role in promoting the observance of the Act and in disseminating
information about its operation to the public. Under section 50 any person ('the
complainant') may apply to the Commissioner for a decision whether a request
for information made by the complainant to a public authority has been dealt
with in accordance with the Act, and the Commissioner is required to decide the
matter. The Commissioner has wide powers. He can issue an information notice
requiring an authority to furnish the Commissioner with specified information
about an application. The Commissioner can under section 52 of the Act issue an
enforcement notice directing a public authority to carry out his decision and if the
notice is not complied with the court can treat the failure to comply as a contempt
of court.

The great advantage of this system is that people, including businesses, seeking **17.48**
information under the Act can obtain a decision on their application from the
Commissioner without incurring the expense usually associated with litigation.
Further there is a right of appeal by the complainant or the public authority to the
Information Tribunal from a decision of the Commissioner which again is an in-
expensive procedure, as the parties do not have to be represented by lawyers. It is
only when a party wishes to appeal from a decision of the Tribunal to the High
Court on a point of law that a business may become involved in full-scale litiga-
tion. This means that business will be able to make full use of the Freedom of
Information Act at acceptable cost.

E. Access to and Protection of Business Information

Information which competitors and others may discover

Stated generally and subject to the proper application of the statutory exemptions, **17.49**
the risks created by the Act are that 'confidential information may become more
easily available to competitors, customers, suppliers and interest groups'.[41]
Among the specific risks that will or may arise are the following:

---

[41] Amos and Innes (n 22 above) 2.

(a) When a business wins a government contract:

- competitors will learn the price of the contract the business won, possibly in detail, and may be able to estimate its costs and profit, together with at least some knowledge of its methodology;
- they may find out the contractual levels of performance to which it is committed;
- they will find out the reasons why it was evaluated the winner rather than one of them;
- they may find out the results of regular performance reviews, so they will be able to see how well/badly it is doing.[42]

(b) When a business loses a bid for such a contract, its competitors may be able to discover the details of its bid (as of all losing bids): in Sweden, for example, such information is generally available.[43]

(c) Quite apart from contract bids, the government may hold information about a company whose position could be damaged if that information became known to competitors and others. Examples might include the fact that the company had been 'the subject of a report, investigation or enforcement notice, relating to product safety, environmental impact, trading standards, market dominance, employment law, transfer pricing to avoid taxation. . .'.[44]

17.50 In order to avoid or reduce the risks businesses will need to be mindful of the statutory exemptions and to take the steps available to them to protect from disclosure the information which they provide to public authorities.

Confidentiality and trade secrets

17.51 So far as business is concerned the most relevant exemptions as we have seen are probably those provided for in sections 41 and 43 of the Act. Section 41 creates an exemption in respect of information provided in confidence, and section 43 exempts trade secrets and information prejudicial to a person's commercial interests.[45] Section 41 confers an absolute exemption with the result that there is no public interest test to be applied to the exclusion of information provided in confidence. There is no such absolute exemption for section 43 of the Act.

17.52 In order to qualify as confidential information:[46]

(a) the information must have been obtained by the public authority from another person;[47] and

---

[42] Amos (text and n 9 above) 18.
[43] ibid.
[44] ibid.
[45] Those exemptions are considered in detail in ch 6 at paras 6.63–6.81 and 6.229–6.239 above.
[46] Freedom of Information Act 2000, s 4(1).
[47] This includes another public authority.

(b) its disclosure would constitute a breach of confidence actionable by the person from whom it was obtained or by any other person.[48]

If or to the extent that a confirmation or denial under section 1(1)(a) would constitute an actionable breach of confidence, the duty to confirm or deny does not arise.[49]

Section 43 of the Act provides exemption for trade secrets and for information the disclosure of which would, or would be likely to, prejudice the commercial interests of any person.[50] As noted above this exemption is not absolute,[51] and the public interest test is to be applied.[52] The duty to confirm or deny does not arise if or to the extent that compliance with section 1(1)(a) would, or would be likely to, prejudice the commercial interests of any person.[53] Trade secrets will, however, be protected by the absolute exemption of section 41 of the Act unless they were disclosed in circumstances which waived or abandoned their confidentiality.

17.53

The term 'trade secrets' is not defined, but it is a term well recognized and understood by the common law. Trade secrets are distinguished from mere confidential information within the context of employment contracts because an employee is under an implied contractual obligation not to use or disclose trade secrets either during or after his employment. In contrast there is no implied term not to use or disclose confidential information short of a trade secret after the employment has ceased. Trade secrets will consist of secret information concerning, for example, manufacturing processes such as chemical formulae or designs or special construction methods. Some information is clearly confidential, such as sales information or information relating to prices, but not so highly confidential that it can be described as a trade secret.[54]

17.54

The interpretation of the test of whether disclosure would, or would be likely to, prejudice the commercial interests of any person may be more open to issue. It is very likely, however, that the phrase 'commercial interests' will be given its ordinary meaning. An interest arises when a person has a stake or concern in something and will be a commercial interest if the stake or concern involves commerce. Commerce is business in its widest sense. It should include financial, mercantile, scientific and technical interests (it is unlikely that the category will ever be closed).

17.55

---

[48] See ch 20, in particular paras 20.11, 20.16, 20.22–20.35 and 20.94–20.100 below for details of actionable breaches of confidence.

[49] See Freedom of Information Act 2000, s 41(2).

[50] ibid, s 43(2)—this includes the public authority holding the information.

[51] ibid, s 2(3) does not include this section and only the sections referred to within s 2(3) are to be regarded as conferring absolute exemption for the purposes of s 2.

[52] ibid, s 2(2)(a) and ch 6 at paras 6.11–6.13 below.

[53] ibid, s 43(3).

[54] See generally *Faccenda Chicken Limited v Fowler* [1987] 1 Ch 117; *Lansing Linde Ltd v Kerr* [1991] 1 WLR 251.

17.56 Once it is established that any person has a commercial interest which is likely to be affected by disclosure of the information sought, the question arises whether disclosure would cause damage or harm to the commercial interest identified. However, section 43 provides no assistance in identifying what damage or harm means. Is it to be limited to competitive harm or is it to be extended, for example, to include disruption of the supply of information? Probably any form of material harm will suffice.

17.57 As to the threshold for determining whether commercial interests would be prejudiced, it is probably sufficient to show that some prejudice would or would be likely to occur and not necessary to show that it will be significant.

17.58 Furthermore the test has to look to what would or would be likely to occur and there is no indication of what level of possibility must be applied. Reasonable foreseeability is the likely test, although the balance of probabilities might be invoked. The New Zealand Court of Appeal has held in the context of comparable provisions in the Official Information Act 1982 that 'likely' means not that the prejudice is more likely than not to eventuate, but that there is 'a distinct or significant possibility' or 'a serious or real and substantial risk' of it.[55] On the basis that the public authority is satisfied that commercial prejudice would or would be likely to occur, the application of the public interest test needs to be considered. This is clearly a matter of assessment and depends upon an understanding of what the public interest is. The Act offers no guidance.

17.59 The public interest in maintaining the exclusion will be based upon the premise that there should not be damage to commercial interests. It will be necessary to consider and weigh the extent of the damage which would or would be likely to occur. The potential consequences will need to be spelt out to the public authority by the business concerned. The starting point in assessing the public interest in disclosing whether the public authority holds the information is the principle that there should be access to information subject to exceptions. However, there will be a need to go further than that and identify specific reasons why in the particular circumstances it is in the interests of the public to have such disclosure. Those reasons are then to be weighed against the identified potential damage.

Experience of the United States of America

17.60 One of the frequently litigated exemptions to the USA's Freedom of Information Act is Exemption 4, which applies to 'trade secrets and commercial or financial information obtained from a person and privileged or confidential'.[56]

---

[55] *Commissioner of Police v Ombudsman* [1988] 1 NZLR 385. See ch 9 at para 9.28 above.
[56] United States Code, Title 5, s 552(b)(4).

In many cases the court has ordered in favour of disclosure, despite the claim that **17.61** the exemption applied. For example in *Center for Public Integrity v Department of Energy*[57] the requester sought disclosure of records relating to the federal government's sale of naval petroleum reserves. The Department argued that the records were not within the Freedom of Information Act's disclosure requirements, by virtue of Exemption 4 (as well as exemption 3: records specifically exempted from disclosure by [another] statute). The court, granting summary judgment to the requester, held that the records were not within the exemptions relied on. As to Exemption 4, the court said[58] that the general approach was to require agencies:

> to disclose information under Exemption 4's competitive harm prong unless they were able to demonstrate that release of the information would be of substantial assistance to competitors in estimating and undercutting a bidder's future bids . . . Those cases in which the courts have not required disclosure of information relating to government contractors typically involved requests not for prices but for more sensitive data, such as audits of private concessions in national parks, . . . profit margins and inventory balances, . . . and appraised values for customs duties assessment of imported parts. . .

In contrast, in *Judicial Watch Inc v United States Department of Commerce*[59] the **17.62** Department relied upon four exemptions in resisting the request. As to Exemption 4, the Department sought to withhold 'confidential commercial information submitted by corporations who wished to be represented on various Commerce Department trade missions'. Submission of the information was evidently a prerequisite for any corporation aspiring to selection for and participation in trade missions. The withheld information included 'commercial plans, project proposals, bid-related information and project values'. Disclosure of the information would, the Department said, 'cause substantial competitive harm to the positions of companies submitting the information'. The court found that the affidavit evidence provided 'sufficient detail of actual competition and likelihood of competitive injury from disclosure to support an Exemption 4 claim'.[60] It is to be noted, however, that the court deferred ruling on whether summary judgment was appropriate (that is, judgment to dismiss the requester's claim) until the Department submitted 'supplemental indices detailing whether documents that are withheld in their entirety under Exemption 4 contain any reasonably segregable information'.[61] So it can be seen that, even where the court is sympathetic to a claim for exemption, its review is exacting as to the extent of the permitted withholding.

---

[57] 191 F Supp 2d 187 (DDC, 2002).
[58] ibid, 194–5.
[59] 83 F Supp 2d 105 (DDC 1999).
[60] ibid, 110–111.
[61] ibid, 111.

17.63 In *McDonnell Douglas Corporation v National Aeronautics and Space Administration*[62] a government contractor claimed (in a 'reverse Freedom of Information Act suit') that NASA's decision to release pricing information relating to its contract was protected from disclosure under [the Act] by [the] exemption for trade secrets and privileged or confidential financial information.[63] The contractual information which the company wished not to be released included satellite launch service prices, cost figures for specific launch service components, overheads, labour rates, profit figures and percentages.[64] The court noted[65] that 'NASA implicitly recognised that it would be to the competitor's advantage to receive McDonnell Douglas' line item price information. Of course, it follows that [McDonnell Douglas] will be competitively harmed by the disclosure.' Accordingly, the company had in law 'every right to insist that its line item prices be withheld as confidential'.[66]

17.64 In this country, it is likely that the balancing of the interests of the requester on the one hand and the provider of the information to the public authority on the other will, in many respects, follow the American pattern. Procedurally, however, the approaches are very different. Most of the relevant decisions of the US courts are made on applications for summary judgment with affidavit evidence. Where there is a 'material fact issue' (that is, a properly arguable issue of fact), or where the factual record is thought to be incomplete (as in the *Judicial Watch* case discussed at paragraph 17.62 above), that issue will be referred ('remanded') for investigation. Under the UK Act it is likely that the issues of fact will have been determined by the Information Commissioner or the Information Tribunal. The court's involvement, if any, is only on questions of law after all factual investigation has been concluded.

17.65 Other countries' experience of operating exemption provisions (including those affecting business) are discussed in chapters 9 and 25.

Protecting information from disclosure

17.66 Businesses which do not want particular information provided by them to public authorities to be disclosed to any third party should try to ensure not only that the information falls within the exemptions of sections 41 and 43 of the Act but also that the public authority is aware of this. Public authorities will take care to ensure compliance with those exemptions, but it is no doubt inevitable that mistakes will occur. The most effective way of seeking to avoid disclosure in error will be to

---

[62] 180 F 3d 303 (DC Cir, 1999).
[63] See the headnote: ibid, 303.
[64] ibid, 304.
[65] ibid, 306–7.
[66] ibid, 307.

mark the information provided as being information in respect of which the provider claims the above-mentioned exemptions (or either of them).

It is to be observed that there is no procedure in the Act requiring the providers of **17.67** information to be contacted before its disclosure. However, the code of practice issued by the Lord Chancellor pursuant to section 45 of the Act deals with this point. Section 45(2)(c) of the Act expressly provides that the code must include provisions relating to consultation with persons to whom the requested information relates and with persons whose interests are likely to be affected by disclosure of the information. Section 45(2)(d) of the Act requires the code to contain provisions concerning the inclusion of terms relating to disclosure within contracts to be entered into by public authorities.

Although the code is only a guide and therefore is not binding upon public au- **17.68** thorities,[67] it is unlikely that public authorities will be able to justify a decision not to consult with those to whom the information relates or whose interests are likely to be affected. Furthermore it is unlikely that a public authority would wish to take such a stance when the consequence might be a claim for damages for breach of confidence. However, the possibility exists and there is no appeal process or stay available to a business adversely affected by a decision.[68]

The Code[69] deals with 'Freedom of Information and Public Sector Contracts' in **17.69** Part VIII. It advises public authorities that they cannot contract out of the Act and terms which purport to restrict the disclosure of information that would otherwise be disclosable under the Act should be rejected. In any event the terms of a contract cannot override the statutory obligations created by the Act and the real issue for those contracting with public authorities is whether any of the exemptions can be relied upon.

The Code refers to the fact that non-public authority contractors may require **17.70** confidentiality clauses. Examples given concern the terms of the contract, its value and performance. The guidance given in paragraph 42 of the Code to the public authorities is that such clauses should be rejected wherever possible. It is accepted that there may have to be non-disclosure provisions but the Code describes these as being exceptional cases. In such cases the Code advises the inclusion of a schedule which identifies clearly the information which will be subject to such a term.

One of those 'exceptional' cases would concern confidential information. **17.71** However, paragraph 43 of the Code emphasizes that public authorities should only agree to such a provision if the information is truly confidential. There must be good reasons for accepting such a clause and the public authority must be in a

---

[67] See further in ch 5 at para 5.145 above.
[68] See ch 7 at paras 7.120–7.136 above.
[69] See ch 5 at paras 5.147–5.149 above and Appendix D below.

position of being able to justify its agreement to such a clause to the Commissioner.

17.72 Those contracting with public authorities must therefore expect to meet robust responses to requests for the inclusion of non-disclosure or confidentiality clauses. It will be necessary to address the issue why such clauses are required for the particular contract and to present the reasons to the public authority for its consideration. It would be prudent to ensure that the clauses are drafted, so far as possible, with reference to specific information. The usual form of general prohibition or exclusion is unlikely to be acceptable if the Code of Guidance is followed.

17.73 The Code is a little more enthusiastic about non-disclosure clauses where they are for the benefit of the public authority; that is, clauses which provide that information that would be exempt from disclosure under the Act should not be disclosed by the contractor. However, even in those cases the Code's guidance is that such constraints should be drafted narrowly in order to avoid secrecy and that terms of secrecy should not otherwise be imposed upon contractors.

17.74 A major problem for businesses wishing to protect the information they have provided is that there is no right to apply to the Commissioner for a decision that the public authority has wrongly failed to apply the exemption. The right to apply conferred by section 50 of the Act only applies to 'the complainant', who is the person who made the request for information. It is not extended to those affected by disclosure. Businesses cannot apply to the Commissioner for a decision that the exemption has not been properly applied and that the public authority has wrongly decided that there is a right of access to the information.

17.75 A business faced with a decision that there is a right of access must look to the court for a remedy. In principle the decision can be challenged by way of judicial review. Alternatively, there could be a claim for damages for breach of confidence. In either case an application for an interim injunction restraining disclosure or use of the information could be made. Such an application would need to establish a serious question to be tried and that the balance of convenience was in favour of the applicant.[70] An undertaking in damages will normally be required, namely an undertaking that if the court later finds that the order has caused loss to the respondent, and decides that the respondent should be compensated for that loss, the applicant will comply with any order the court may make to pay such damage as may result.

17.76 Relevant to the balance of convenience will be the question of whether it is too late for the injunction to have a practical effect. Any challenge to a decision, whether by way of judicial review or by action, faces the potential problem that the

---

[70] The leading authority is *American Cyanamid Co v Ethicon Ltd* [1975] AC 396, HL and see CPR Part 25.

information may have been disclosed before the business could obtain an injunction to restrain disclosure. The only way to avoid this is to act quickly.

F. Practical Notes for Business[71]

Notes on obtaining information

No two businesses are alike: each business will face a different range of opportunities and risks. Subject to that proviso, here is a checklist of steps it may be prudent to take.

    17.77

(a) The public authorities in Schedule 1 to the Act which are likely to have information which is relevant to your business should be identified. But note that the Lord Chancellor may by order amend the Schedule, and also has power to designate as public authorities for the purposes of the statute persons who cannot be added to the Schedule.[72] Publicly-owned companies[73] are also subject to the Act.

(b) Government is likely to hold information about your competitors. This may be derived from export licences, grant applications, applications for regulatory approval, licences and consents, regular reports required by regulators, contract bids, contracts, performance reviews, planning applications, tax returns and negotiated dispensations. How much of this information should you try to obtain?

(c) The European Commission estimates that public procurement represents about 11 per cent of the GDP of the European Union as a whole:[74] it is a huge market. Suppliers looking for new contracts may wish to obtain information on a public authority's procurement history, market intelligence, the studies on which a project is based, prices, service standards and customer needs.

(d) Information about regulatory bodies, including internal guidance, may be available.

(e) Government holds a mass of reports, surveys, statistics, analyses, opinions and recommendations and a great deal of information can be obtained by e-mail or by a simple written or telephoned request.

(f) A request often needs to be reinforced by reference to the Open Government Code. Departments may well be prepared to release now information which they will have to release in 2005.

---

[71] These notes are based on Amos and Innes (n 22 above). This is a very informative publication.
[72] See ch 5 at para 5.47 above.
[73] As defined in s 6 of the Act: see ch 5 at paras 5.52–5.54 above.
[74] Commission Communication, COM(98) 143, Public Procurement, 11 March 1998, 1.

(g) Environmental information can be obtained now under the Environmental Information Regulations. The exceptions under the regulations are tightly drawn and are all subject to a public interest test.

(h) Information from the main institutions of the European Union can be obtained under Council Regulation (EC) 1049/2001, and each institution is required to maintain a register of documents, so it is not difficult to find out what documents they hold.

(i) The publication scheme provisions of the Act were implemented as from November 2002.[75]

Notes on protecting information

17.78 The following is a suggested checklist of steps which a business may want to take to protect its information.

(a) Establish and record who in your business gives what information to which public authority.

(b) Analyse the information provided in terms of confidentiality and risk, for example:
   (i) high risk, always to be subject to tight control;
   (ii) low risk, but could become high risk on occasion (flexible control needed);
   (iii) low risk, with little chance of change (lightest control).

(c) Design suitable processes for managing the provision of information:
   (i) who is authorized to approve submissions of confidential information?
   (ii) who is responsible for ensuring information is properly marked (degree of confidentiality, if any), and submitted to and accepted by the public authority?
   (iii) who is responsible for managing any negotiations with the public authority about the classification of the information both when submitted, and also in response to a request to release it?
   (iv) who is responsible for tracking the handling of the information by the authority and, when necessary, alerting senior management and the legal department to the need for action?

(d) Establish policies and processes for claiming confidentiality and for ensuring that these claims are effective (in place of the widespread practice of marking large quantities of material 'commercial in confidence', a practice which increases the risks of mistakenly releasing genuinely confidential material).

---

[75] See para 5.194 above for the timetable and paras 4.49–4.102 and 5.118–5.125 above for the content of publication schemes.

18

FREEDOM OF INFORMATION
IN COMMERCIAL DISPUTES

A. Introduction

This chapter discusses the ways in which a party involved in a commercial dispute **18.01** may be able to obtain information which will help it to obtain a more successful outcome to its dispute. It is concerned with civil litigation in England and Wales and considers the rules of court and general principles applicable to the disclosure of information within such litigation.

Clearly, where two parties are involved in a commercial dispute, one party may **18.02** hold documents which would be helpful to the other party in obtaining a successful outcome to the dispute. For example, a dispute may turn on what was said at a particular meeting between the parties. One party may have a contemporaneous note of what was said at the meeting which supports the other party's version of events.

There may also be information that would influence a party's attitude to the dis- **18.03** pute. For example, information on a party's financial standing or assets may enable another party to decide whether it is worthwhile embarking on litigation or whether to accept an offer to settle a dispute.

If a party is involved in a commercial dispute with a public authority within the **18.04** scope of the Freedom of Information Act 2000 ('the Act'), it will have the rights

553

to request information from that public authority discussed elsewhere in this book.

18.05 Even if a party (A) is involved in a commercial dispute with another party (B), which is not a public authority within the scope of the Act, public authorities may hold information about B which A can obtain and which would be helpful to A in pursuing the dispute.

18.06 For example, if one party to a commercial dispute is a limited company, it is standard practice for the other party to obtain a company search which will provide information about the financial standing of the company. That information may be relevant to settlement and may also lead to an application for security for costs. Similarly information from the land registry as to the ownership of land may assist one party or the other, for example, by providing information about a party's assets. The Act will itself provide a potential source of information (subject to its exemptions), which may assist a party engaged in a commercial dispute. It should be noted that the public authority to which a request for information is made is not concerned with the motive for that request.

18.07 Given the possible importance of the documents held by the parties to the outcome of a dispute between them, English law has long provided for each party to be able to gain access to some of the other party's documents relevant to litigation between the parties. English law also provides for some circumstances in which one party is able to request information from another party to litigation or require the attendance of a witness at court to give evidence or produce documents.

18.08 The remainder of this chapter gives a broad overview of the rules governing these matters. Those rules apply whether or not either or both parties to the litigation are public bodies within the scope of the Act. Reference should be made to specialist works dealing with civil procedure or specific aspects of that procedure for a more detailed commentary on the relevant rules.

18.09 It should also be noted that modern civil litigation generally provides for substantial exchanges of information between the parties prior to trial in the sense that the parties are required to set out their cases in statements of case and exchange statements of witnesses of fact and expert evidence before trial. The detailed provisions governing this have not been dealt with in this chapter as the information provided by one party to litigation to the other parties in statements of case, witness statements or expert reports is largely a matter for the party providing the document concerned and is not substantially open to influence by the other parties to the litigation.

18.10 There are also other procedures whereby one party to a dispute may be able to obtain information which will help it obtain a more successful outcome to the dispute. For example, the court can in some circumstances order the inspection of property which is relevant to the dispute, the taking of a sample of relevant property or the carrying out of an experiment on or with relevant property.[1] A further example is the court's power to order a person to give evidence by deposition (in other words, to attend before the trial of a claim to be examined).[2] These procedures are encountered less often than the disclosure of documents, requests for information and requiring a witness to attend court. As a result they are not dealt with further in this chapter and reference should be made to specialist works dealing with civil procedure or specific aspects of that procedure for a detailed account of these procedures.

B. The Disclosure of Documents

Introduction

Prior to the introduction of the Civil Procedure Rules ('CPR') on 26 April 1999 **18.11** the process enabling each party to litigation to gain access to some of the other parties' documents relevant to the litigation was known as discovery. With the introduction of the new rules it became known as disclosure.

Disclosure and the inspection of documents is governed by CPR 31 and its **18.12** accompanying Practice Direction.

CPR 31 applies to all claims to which the CPR apply except for claims allocated **18.13** to the small claims track.[3] (The small claims track is the normal track for any claim which has a financial value of not more than £5,000, subject to special provisions for personal injury claims and tenants' claims in respect of disrepair.[4])

CPR 31 distinguishes between the disclosure of documents and their inspection. **18.14**

The meaning of disclosure is given in CPR 31.2 which provides that a party dis- **18.15** closes a document by stating that the document exists or has existed.

The scope of disclosure

Documents are widely defined as anything in which information of any descrip- **18.16** tion is recorded.[5] Accordingly, a tape recording of information,[6] a computer database which contains information which can be retrieved and converted into a

---

[1] Civil Procedure Rules ('CPR') 25.1(1)(c).
[2] CPR 34.8–34.15.
[3] CPR 31.1(2). The CPR apply to all proceedings in county courts, the High Court and the Civil Division of the Court of Appeal except for certain proceedings listed in CPR 2.1(2).
[4] CPR 26.6(1)-(3).
[5] CPR 31.4.
[6] *Grant v Southwestern and County Properties Ltd* [1975] Ch 185, Ch D.

readable form[7] and a word processing file on a computer[8] are all documents. In relation to a document, a copy is anything onto which information recorded in the document has been copied, by whatever means and whether directly or indirectly.[9]

18.17 Prior to the introduction of the Civil Procedure Rules, parties were required to give discovery of all documents relevant to the dispute between them. This included not only documents which supported or adversely affected one party's case but also documents which might lead to a train of inquiry enabling a party either to advance its own case or to damage the case of the other party.[10]

18.18 In complex commercial litigation this test of relevance would sometimes lead to discovery being given of thousands of documents, placing a considerable burden on the parties, their legal advisers and the court. The Civil Procedure Rules sought to reduce the scope of disclosure.

18.19 Accordingly, CPR 31.5(1) provides that, unless the court directs otherwise, an order to give disclosure is an order to give what is described as 'standard disclosure'. The court may dispense with or limit standard disclosure[11] and the parties may agree in writing to dispense with or limit standard disclosure.[12]

18.20 Standard disclosure requires a party to disclose only (a) the documents on which it relies; (b) the documents which adversely affect its own case, adversely affect another party's case or support another party's case; and (c) the documents which it is required to disclose by a relevant Practice Direction.[13] The reference to relevant Practice Directions envisages that provision may be made for certain documents to be disclosed in particular sorts of proceedings.

18.21 When giving standard disclosure a party is required to make a reasonable search for documents which it is required to disclose.[14] The extent of the necessary search will depend on the circumstances of the case.[15] In deciding whether a search is reasonable the factors to be taken into account include (a) the number of documents involved; (b) the nature and complexity of the proceedings; (c) the ease and expense of retrieval of any particular document; and (d) the significance of any document which is likely to be located during the search.[16] In deciding the extent

---

[7] *Derby & Co Ltd v Weldon (No 9)* [1991] 1 WLR 652, Ch D.
[8] *Alliance & Leicester Building Society v Ghahremani* (1992) 32 RVR 198, Ch D.
[9] CPR 31.4.
[10] *Compagnie Financière et Commerciale du Pacifique v Peruvian Guano Co* (1882) 11 QBD 55, CA.
[11] CPR 31.5(2).
[12] CPR 31.5(3).
[13] CPR 31.6.
[14] CPR 31.7(1).
[15] PD (31) 2.1.
[16] CPR 31.7(2).

of the search to make parties should bear in mind the principle of proportionality, that is that the court should deal with cases in ways which are proportionate to (i) the amount of money involved; (ii) the importance of the case; (iii) the complexity of the issues; and (iv) the financial position of each party.[17] It may be reasonable for a party to decide not to search for documents coming into existence before some particular date, for documents other than in some particular place or places or for documents other than those falling into particular categories.[18]

A party is only required to disclose documents which are or have been in its control,[19] where a party has or has had a document in its control if (a) it is or was in its physical possession; (b) it has or has had a right to possession of it; or (c) it has or has had a right to inspect or take copies of it.[20]   **18.22**

In giving standard disclosure a party need not disclose more than one copy of a document.[21] However, a copy of a document which contains a modification, obliteration or other marking or feature (a) on which a party intends to rely, or (b) which adversely affects the party's own case or another party's case or supports another party's case, should be treated as a separate document.[22]   **18.23**

It should be noted that it is open to the court to order that the parties make more extensive disclosure than standard disclosure. This is a power which might, for example, be exercised in a case where there are allegations of fraud where it might be important for the party alleging fraud to have access to those documents which would have been discoverable before the introduction of the Civil Procedure Rules.   **18.24**

How disclosure is given

Standard disclosure is given by a party making and serving on every other party a list of documents.[23] The list must be in the relevant practice form[24] and should identify the documents in a convenient order and manner and as concisely as possible.[25] This will normally mean that documents should be listed in date order, numbered consecutively and each given a concise description, although, where   **18.25**

---

[17] PD (31) 2.1; CPR 1.1(2)(c).
[18] PD (31) 2.1.
[19] CPR 31.8(1).
[20] CPR 31.8(2). It should be noted that documents of which a party can obtain copies under the Act or the Data Protection Act 1998 would constitute documents under the party's control. However, it is likely that in most cases the reasonable search for documents which the party is required to undertake would not extend to such documents.
[21] CPR 31.9(1).
[22] CPR 31.9(2).
[23] CPR 31.10(1) and (2).
[24] CPR 31.10(2). The relevant Practice Form is form N265.
[25] CPR 31.10(3).

there is a large number of documents all falling into a particular category, those documents can be listed as a category rather than individually.[26]

18.26 The list of documents should also include a disclosure statement.[27] This is a statement made by the party disclosing the documents (a) setting out the extent of the search that has been made to locate documents required to be disclosed; (b) certifying that the party understands the duty to disclose documents; and (c) certifying that to the best of the party's knowledge it has carried out that duty.[28] A party, which has not searched for a category or class of documents on the grounds that to do so would be unreasonable, must state this in its disclosure statement and identify the category or class of document concerned.[29] The disclosure statement should expressly state that the party making disclosure believes the extent of the search made for documents to have been reasonable in all the circumstances and, in setting out the extent of the search, should refer to any particular limitations on the extent of the search which were adopted for proportionality reasons and give reasons why those limitations were adopted.[30]

18.27 Where the party making the disclosure statement is a company, firm, association or other organization, the statement should also identify the person making the statement and explain why he or she is considered an appropriate person to make the statement.[31] A disclosure statement may be made by a person who is not a party where this is permitted by a relevant Practice Direction.[32]

18.28 If the party making disclosure has a legal representative acting for it, the legal representative must endeavour to ensure that the person making the disclosure statement understands the duty of disclosure.[33] Proceedings for contempt of court may be brought against a person who makes or causes to be made a false disclosure statement without an honest belief in its truth.[34]

---

[26] PD (31) 3.2.

[27] CPR 31.10(5).

[28] CPR 31.10(6).

[29] CPR 31.7(3).

[30] PD (31) 4.2.

[31] CPR 31.10(7). In those circumstances the disclosure statement should include the name and address of the person making the disclosure statement and the office or position he holds in the party making disclosure or the basis on which the person makes the statement on behalf of the party: PD (31) 4.3.

[32] CPR 31.10(9). PD (31) 4.7 provides that an insurer or the Motor Insurers' Bureau may sign a disclosure statement on behalf of a party where the insurer or Motor Insurers' Bureau has a financial interest in the result of proceedings brought wholly or partially by or against that party.

[33] PD (31) 4.4. A legal representative should also advise as to the importance of not destroying documents which might have to be disclosed: *Rockwell Machine Tool Co Ltd v E P Barrus (Concessionaires) Ltd* [1968] 2 All ER 98 (Note), Ch D. Legal representatives also owe a duty to the court to ensure that proper disclosure is given: *Myers v Elman* [1940] AC 282, HL; *Woods v Martins Bank Ltd* [1959] 1 QB 55, Leeds Assizes.

[34] CPR 31.23. Such proceedings may be brought only by the Attorney-General or with the permission of the court. The procedure to be followed where a party alleges that a disclosure statement is false is set out in PD (32) 28.

The parties may agree in writing to disclose documents without making a list or to disclose documents without the disclosing party making a disclosure statement.[35] Any such written agreement should be lodged with the court.[36] **18.29**

A party's duty of disclosure continues throughout proceedings.[37] Where documents which should be disclosed come to a party's attention after that party's list of documents has been served, those documents should immediately be disclosed to the other parties.[38] This should be done by serving a supplemental list of documents.[39] **18.30**

A party may be permitted to withhold disclosure of a document, which it would otherwise be required to disclose, on the ground that disclosure would damage the public interest. The circumstances in which this arises and the procedure for obtaining permission to withhold disclosure is discussed at paragraph 18.43 and paragraphs 18.54 to 18.64 below. Of greater significance, there are certain documents in respect of which, although they need to be disclosed, a party can claim a right or has a duty to withhold inspection. The circumstances in which this arises are also discussed at paragraphs 18.45 to 18.65 below. **18.31**

A party's list of documents should indicate: **18.32**

(a) those documents in respect of which the party claims a right or duty to withhold inspection;

(b) (i) those documents which are no longer in the party's control; and
    (ii) what has happened to those documents.[40]

Where a party indicates in its list of documents that it claims a right or duty to withhold inspection of a document (or part of a document) the party should state in writing (1) that it has such a right or duty; and (2) the grounds on which it claims that right or duty.[41] This statement should normally be included in the disclosure statement and should identify the document (or part of a document) to which the claim relates.[42]

Inspection

Where one party (A) discloses a document to another (B) (that is states that the document exists or has existed), the latter party, B, has a right to inspect that document except where: **18.33**

---

[35] CPR 31.10(8).
[36] PD (31) 1.4.
[37] CPR 31.11(1).
[38] CPR 31.11(2).
[39] PD (31) 3.3.
[40] CPR 31.10(4).
[41] PD (31) 4.5.
[42] PD (31) 4.6.

(a) the document is no longer in A's control;

(b) A has a right or a duty to withhold inspection of it; or

(c) A considers that it would be disproportionate to the issues in the case to permit inspection of documents within a category or class of document disclosed by A and has stated in its disclosure statement that inspection of those documents will not be permitted on the grounds that to do so would be disproportionate.[43]

18.34 Where a party (A) has a right to inspect a document, A must give the party who disclosed it (B) written notice of its wish to inspect it.[44] B must permit inspection within seven days of receiving any such notice.[45] A may request a copy of the document and, if A undertakes to pay reasonable copying costs, B is obliged to supply A with a copy within seven days of A's request.[46]

Specific disclosure or inspection

18.35 The court may make an order for specific disclosure or specific inspection.[47] An order for specific disclosure is an order that a party do one or more of (a) disclose specified documents or classes of documents; (b) carry out a search to a specified extent; (c) disclose any documents located as a result of that search.[48] An order for specific disclosure may in an appropriate case direct a party to (a) carry out a search for any documents which it is reasonable to suppose may contain information which may (i) enable the party applying for the order either to advance its own case or to damage that of the party giving disclosure; or (ii) lead to a train of enquiry which has either of those consequences; and (b) disclose any documents found as a result of that search.[49]

18.36 An application for an order for specific disclosure will be the remedy where a party believes that the disclosure of documents given by another party is inadequate.[50] The notice making any such application should specify the order that the applicant intends to ask the court to make and the application should be supported by evidence.[51] The grounds on which the order for specific disclosure is sought should be set out in the application notice or in the evidence filed in support of the application.[52] In deciding whether or not to make an order for specific disclosure the court will take into account all the circumstances of the case and, in particu-

---

[43] CPR 31.3.
[44] CPR 31.15(a).
[45] CPR 31.15(b).
[46] CPR 31.15(c).
[47] CPR 31.12(1).
[48] CPR 31.12(2).
[49] PD (31) 5.5.
[50] PD (31) 5.1.
[51] PD (31) 5.2.
[52] PD (31) 5.3.

lar, the overriding objective of enabling the court to deal with cases justly.[53] However, if the court concludes that the party from whom specific disclosure is sought has failed adequately to comply with the obligations imposed by an order for disclosure (whether by failing to make a sufficient search for documents or otherwise) the court will usually make such order as is necessary to ensure that those obligations are properly complied with.[54]

An order for specific inspection is an order that a party permit inspection of a doc-   **18.37** ument, of which that party has stated in its disclosure statement it will not permit inspection on the grounds that it would be disproportionate to do so.[55]

Miscellaneous provisions regarding disclosure or inspection

The court may order, or the parties may agree in writing, that disclosure or inspec-   **18.38** tion or both shall take place in stages.[56]

A party may inspect a document mentioned in a statement of case, a witness state-   **18.39** ment, a witness summary, an affidavit or (subject to an exception) an expert's report.[57] The exception with regard to an expert's report is that, save in specified circumstances, a party is not entitled to inspect a document relating to instructions given to the expert.[58] There are also further provisions relating to the inspection of documents mentioned in an expert's report.[59]

A party may not rely on a document which it has failed to disclose or of which it   **18.40** has failed to permit inspection except with the permission of the court.[60]

In general, a party to whom a document has been disclosed may use the document   **18.41** only for the purposes of the proceedings in which it has been disclosed.[61] There are exceptions to that general rule where the document has been read to or by the court, or referred to, at a hearing which has been held in public; where the court gives permission; or where the party who disclosed the document and the person to whom the document belongs agree.[62] The court can also restrict or prohibit the use of a document which has been disclosed where it has been read to or by the court, or referred to, at a hearing which has been held in public.[63] Any person to

---

[53] PD (31) 5.4; CPR 1.
[54] PD (31) 5.4.
[55] CPR 31.12(3).
[56] CPR 31.13.
[57] CPR 31.14.
[58] CPR 35.10(4).
[59] PD (31) 7.
[60] CPR 31.21.
[61] CPR 31.22(1).
[62] CPR 31.22(1).
[63] CPR 31.22(2). In considering an application for such order (i) the court should start from the principle that very good reasons are required for departing from the normal rule of publicity; (ii) where the application is made in respect of a particular document, the court should take into

whom the document belongs can apply for such an order as well as the parties.[64] Where there is a risk of a party using information disclosed in proceedings for a collateral purpose, the court has an inherent jurisdiction to restrict inspection so as to prevent an abuse of the process of the court.[65]

Withholding inspection or disclosure

18.42 If a party wishes to claim that it has a right or duty to withhold inspection of a document or part of a document, it should state in writing that it has such a right or duty and the grounds on which the right or duty is claimed.[66] That statement should be made in the party's list of documents or, if there is no such list, to the person who wishes to inspect the document.[67] Where a party has claimed a right or duty to withhold inspection of a document, another party can apply to the court to challenge that claim and gain inspection of the document.[68] Such an application should be supported by evidence[69] and, for the purpose of deciding the application, the court may require that the document concerned be produced to the court and may invite any person, whether or not a party, to make representations.[70]

18.43 The Civil Procedure Rules also recognize that there may be situations where the public interest would be damaged by the disclosure of the existence of a document and cannot be adequately protected by the withholding of inspection. In those circumstances a party may apply for an order permitting it to withhold disclosure of a document on the ground that disclosure would damage the public interest.[71] Such an application should be made without notice to any other party[72] and should be supported by evidence.[73] Again, for the purpose of deciding the application, the court may require that the document concerned be produced to the court and may invite any person, whether or not a party, to make representa-

---

account the role that the document has played or will play in the trial and thus its relevance to the process of public scrutiny of proceedings; (iii) the court must bear in mind any 'chilling' effect of an order upon the interests of third parties; (iv) simple assertions of confidentiality and of the damage that will be done by publication should not prevail and specific reasons should be given; and (v) it is highly desirable to avoid the holding of trials in private, or partially in private (*Lilly Icos Ltd v Pfizer Ltd* [2002] 1 All ER 842, CA).

[64] CPR 31.22(3).
[65] *Warner-Lambert Co v Glaxo Laboratories Ltd* [1975] RPC 354, CA; *Church of Scientology v DHSS* [1979] 1 WLR 723, CA.
[66] CPR 31.19(3).
[67] CPR 31.19(4).
[68] CPR 31.19(5).
[69] CPR 31.19(7).
[70] CPR 31.19(6).
[71] CPR 31.19(1).
[72] CPR 31.19(1).
[73] CPR 31.19(7).

tions.[74] Where the court makes an order permitting a party to withhold disclosure of a document, that order must not be served on any other person and must not be open to inspection by any person unless the court orders otherwise.[75]

The Civil Procedure Rules provide that the provisions enabling a party to apply to withhold disclosure of a document or to claim a right or duty to withhold inspection of a document do not affect existing rules of law permitting or requiring a document to be withheld from disclosure or inspection on the ground that its disclosure or inspection would damage the public interest.[76] **18.44**

The grounds for withholding inspection or disclosure

Legal professional privilege

The most common ground on which parties claim the right to withhold inspection of documents is that they are subject to 'legal professional privilege'. **18.45**

Documents which are subject to legal professional privilege can be divided into two categories. The first category (sometimes referred to as legal advice privilege or simply advice privilege) encompasses communications between a party and its legal advisers (including both solicitors and barristers). Such communications (in the ordinary course of professional communications) are privileged whether or not litigation is contemplated or pending if they are confidential and for the purposes of seeking or giving legal advice.[77] **18.46**

The second category of documents which are subject to legal professional privilege are documents which are privileged only if litigation was contemplated or pending when they were made or came into existence. (This sort of privilege is sometimes referred to as litigation privilege.) This category encompasses communications between a party's lawyer and a third party which come into existence after litigation is contemplated or commenced and are made with a view to such litigation (either for the purpose of obtaining or giving advice in connection with the litigation, or of obtaining or collecting evidence to be used in it, or of obtaining information which may lead to the obtaining of such evidence).[78] Certain communications between a party itself and a third party which come into existence after litigation is contemplated or commenced and are made with a view to **18.47**

---

[74] CPR 31.19(6).
[75] CPR 31.19(2).
[76] CPR 31.19(8).
[77] *Gardner v Irvin* (1878) 4 Ex D 49, CA; *Wheeler v Le Marchant* (1881) 17 Ch D 675, CA; *Kennedy v Lyell* (1883) 23 Ch D 387, CA; *O'Shea v Wood* [1891] P 286, CA; *Minter v Priest* [1930] AC 558, HL; *Balabel v Air India* [1988] Ch 317, CA; *R v Manchester Crown Court, ex p Rogers* [1999] 1 WLR 832, DC.
[78] *Anderson v Bank of British Columbia* (1876) 2 Ch D 644, CA.

such litigation are also privileged.[79] Where a document has come into existence for more than one purpose, it is the dominant purpose for which the document came into existence which governs whether the document is privileged.[80]

18.48 The principle behind legal professional privilege is the importance of a party being able to consult its lawyer in confidence and in the knowledge that whatever a party tells its lawyers will not be revealed without its consent.[81] As such, subject to the exceptions referred to in paragraph 18.49 below, legal professional privilege is absolute and cannot be overridden on the basis that it is in the public interest or the interests of justice for it to be so overridden.

18.49 As stated in paragraph 18.48 above, there are limited grounds on which legal professional privilege does not arise or can be overridden. The two most important of these are:

(a) a document which came into existence in pursuance of fraud or crime will not be privileged;[82] and

(b) if a privileged communication is in itself a material fact in proceedings, it will not be privileged. [83]

18.50 Privilege will also be lost if it is waived by a party.[84] It should be noted that the privilege is that of the party and not that of its legal adviser so that privilege can only be waived by the party itself.[85]

18.51 It should also be noted that documents which are subject to legal professional privilege still need to be disclosed in a party's list of documents but the party can claim to withhold inspection of the documents concerned. A party need not list every document which is subject to legal professional privilege separately and it is

---

[79] The exact scope of litigation privilege in this context is not entirely clear. It is clear that, if the party is effectively acting as its lawyer's agent in communicating with a third party for the purpose of the litigation, the communication between the party and the third party will be privileged. Documents obtained by a party for the purpose of submitting them to its lawyer in connection with the litigation will also be privileged. Other communications between a party and a third party for the purpose of the litigation are less likely to be privileged.

[80] *Waugh v British Railways Board* [1980] AC 521, HL.

[81] *R v Derby Magistrates' Court, ex p B* [1996] AC 487, HL.

[82] *R v Cox and Railton* (1884) 14 QBD 153, Crown Case Reserved; *Banque Keyser Ullman SA v Skandia (UK) Insurance Co Ltd* [1986] 1 Lloyd's Rep 336, CA. The reason no privilege arises is because a fraudulent party who communicates with their solicitors for the purposes of the furtherance of a fraud or crime is not communicating with their solicitors in the ordinary course of professional communications.

[83] See, for example, *Conlon v Conlons Ltd* [1952] 2 All ER 462, CA where a party disputed that their solicitors had had authority to settle a claim. It was held that the party could not rely on legal professional privilege to refuse to answer questions about the instructions they had given to their solicitors with regard to the settlement of the claim because communications between a client and their solicitor which the client instructed the solicitor to repeat to the other party to a dispute were not confidential.

[84] *Calcraft v Guest* [1898] 1 QB 759, CA.

[85] *Procter v Smiles* (1886) 55 LJ QB 527, CA.

usual for a party to use general words in its list of documents to describe all of its documents subject to legal professional privilege.[86]

Without prejudice communications

The other category of documents in respect of which a claim to withhold inspection is often made are communications which are 'without prejudice'. These are any communications which contain negotiations between the parties, which negotiations are genuinely aimed at a settlement. The principle behind this privilege is the public policy in encouraging parties to settle disputes rather than litigate them to a finish.[87] Again, the privilege can be waived but it must be waived by both parties to the negotiations. If the negotiations result (or are alleged to result) in a binding settlement between the parties, then the parties may rely on the documents concerned as evidence of the settlement.[88]

18.52

Of course, in most commercial disputes both parties will be aware of the contents of 'without prejudice' communications. In those circumstances the claim to withhold inspection of the documents concerned is of little importance as both parties are likely already to have copies of the documents concerned. Of more relevance in such circumstances is the rule that the documents are not generally admissible as evidence before the court—if the fact that a party had made a concession during negotiations could later be relied on by the other party if the dispute went to trial, parties are likely to be discouraged from making such concessions and thereby reaching negotiated settlements of their disputes. One situation in which the right to withhold inspection may be important is where a claim is brought by a party (A) against more than one party (say, two parties, B and C). If A has reached a settlement with B, C will not be able to obtain inspection of the without prejudice communications between A and B which culminated in the settlement.[89]

18.53

Public interest immunity

There are also documents which are privileged on the ground that production would be injurious to the public interest. This privilege will arise where withholding disclosure or inspection of the documents concerned is necessary for the proper functioning of the public service. In every case the public interest in withholding disclosure or inspection should be balanced against the public interest in the administration of justice not being frustrated. In such a case the privilege is not one that can be waived by a party and, if necessary, the judge should insist on the documents not being produced.

18.54

---

[86] *Derby & Co Ltd v Weldon (No 7)* [1990] 1 WLR 1156, Ch D.
[87] *Cutts v Head* [1984] Ch 290, CA.
[88] *Tomlin v Standard Telephones & Cables Limited* [1969] 1 WLR 1378, CA.
[89] *Rush & Tompkins Ltd v Greater London Council* [1989] AC 1280, HL.

18.55 In some cases the privilege may require that the existence of the documents should not be disclosed. In other cases the privilege may merely require that the documents be withheld from inspection. In this section the term 'disclosure' will be used to refer to both situations.

18.56 This privilege is commonly referred to as public interest immunity (PII). It is a privilege that has long been recognized at common law although previously (as discussed in chapter 1 above) it was referred to as Crown Privilege. Traditionally two different sorts of PII claims have been made: class claims and contents claims. A class claim is that a document should not be disclosed because of the class of documents to which it belongs. When such a claim is made it is immaterial whether the disclosure of the particular document would be contrary to the public interest. In contrast, a contents claim is advanced on the basis that the disclosure of the contents of the particular document would be harmful to the public interest.

18.57 A class claim relies on it being in the public interest that documents in that class should not be disclosed. The rationale advanced for such a claim is often that, if documents in that class were not protected by PII, people would be deterred from acting in a particular way which was in the public interest. For example, at one time the Police Complaints Authority advanced a class claim in respect of material supplied to the authority by a complainant or a witness in the course of a complaint on the basis that, if such a claim was not advanced, potential complainants and their witnesses might be deterred from co-operating with the authority.[90]

18.58 PII claims most frequently arise in the course of litigation where one of the parties is a public authority. However, even in litigation between private parties one party may have documents which may be subject to PII. In such a case the party will normally inform the relevant public authority that it may be required to disclose those documents. The relevant public authority can then take a view as to whether the documents attract PII and, if necessary, intervene in the litigation to advance the PII claim.

18.59 A claim for PII is usually made by a certificate or witness statement put forward by the political head of the public authority concerned. That certificate or witness statement is not however conclusive: the decision as to whether or not to uphold a PII claim is for the court.[91] In some circumstances the court will itself inspect the documents in respect of which the claim is advanced.

18.60 Class claims have attracted a certain amount of criticism, particularly when used in criminal proceedings. This criticism led to the setting up of the 'Scott inquiry'

---

[90] The authority subsequently changed its position as recorded in *R v Chief Constable of West Midlands Police, ex p Wiley* [1995] 1 AC 274, HL.

[91] *Conway v Rimmer* [1968] AC 910, HL.

and its subsequent report.[92] Following the publication of that report, the government published a report in December 1996 setting out a new approach by the government to PII. In that report the government stated in effect that it would no longer advance class claims.[93]

The government has indicated that, in considering whether to advance a PII claim **18.61** in respect of a document, it will adopt a three-stage approach:

(a) a decision will first be taken as to whether or not there is a duty to disclose the document (in other words, whether the document is relevant or potentially relevant to the proceedings concerned);

(b) if there is a duty to disclose, a decision will be taken as to whether the document prima facie attracts PII (in other words, whether the disclosure of the document would be harmful to the public interest);

(c) if the document prima facie attracts PII, a decision will be taken as to the strength of the public interest in disclosure and, if that public interest outweighs the need to withhold disclosure, the document will be disclosed, whereas, if the public interest in disclosure does not outweigh the need to withhold disclosure (or the decision-maker is uncertain), a PII claim will be advanced by certificate.

The December 1996 report states that, in deciding whether to advance a PII **18.62** claim, the government will adopt a fundamental test of whether disclosure would cause real damage. The government confirmed that this was the same as substantial harm, which was the test suggested by Lord Wilberforce in *R v Chief Constable of West Midlands Police, ex p Wiley*.[94]

In considering whether to uphold a PII claim the court is likely to adopt a similar **18.63** approach to the three-stage approach discussed above.

It is difficult to give general rules as to the circumstances in which a PII claim **18.64** should be advanced or upheld given the variety of situations that may arise. Indeed, the exercise of balancing the public interest in withholding disclosure against the public interest in disclosure which has to be undertaken in each case makes any such general rules suspect. However, it can be said that the circumstances in which PII claims have been upheld bear some similarity to some of the exemptions created by the Act. Thus, for example, PII claims have been upheld on the basis of damage to national security, international relations or the effective conduct of public affairs. In general, the fact that a document is confidential will

---

[92] *The Report of the Inquiry into the Export of Defence Equipment and Dual-Use Goods to Iraq and Related Prosecutions* (HC (1995–96) no 115).

[93] This does not, of course, mean that other public authorities may not continue to advance class claims.

[94] [1995] 1 AC 274, 281, HL.

not justify a PII claim[95] although claims advanced to withhold the identity of informants have generally been upheld.[96]

Privilege against incrimination

18.65 As well as the grounds discussed above a party can claim the right to withhold inspection of a document if to produce the document would tend to expose that party (or their spouse) to proceedings for an offence or for the recovery of a penalty under the law of any part of the United Kingdom.[97]

The inadvertent inspection of privileged documents

18.66 If a party inadvertently allows a privileged document to be inspected, the party who has inspected the document may use it or its contents only with the permission of the court.[98]

Disclosure before proceedings start

18.67 Section 33(2) of the Supreme Court Act 1981 gives the High Court power, on the application in accordance with the rules of the court of a person who appears to the High Court to be likely to be a party to subsequent proceedings in that court and in such circumstances as may be specified in those rules, to order another person who appears to the court to be likely to be a party to the proceedings and to be likely to have or to have had in its possession, custody or power any documents which are relevant to an issue arising or likely to arise out of that claim (a) to disclose whether those documents are in its possession, custody or power; and (b) to produce such of those documents as are in its possession, custody or power to the applicant or (on such conditions as may be specified in the order) to the applicant's legal or other advisers. Section 52(2) of the County Courts Act 1984 gives a county court a similar power.[99]

---

[95] See, for example, *Alfred Crompton Amusement Machines Ltd v Commissioners of Customs and Excise* [1974] AC 405, HL.

[96] See, for example, *D v NSPCC* [1978] AC 171, HL.

[97] Civil Evidence Act 1968, s 14. The privilege extends not just to information which might increase the risk of prosecution, but also in respect of any piece of information or evidence on which a prosecuting authority might wish to rely in establishing guilt or in determining whether to prosecute (*Den Norske Bank ASA v Antonatos* [1999] QB 271, CA). The fact that a party is unlikely to be prosecuted does not mean that the privilege does not arise (*Triplex Safety Glass Co Ltd v Lancegaye Safety Glass (1934) Ltd* [1939] 2 KB 395, CA) although only a remote or slight possibility of prosecution will not suffice (*R v Boyes* (1861) 1 B & S 311). The privilege does not attach if the party's protection is adequately secured by other means, such as an order (made with the consent of the Crown Prosecution Service) prohibiting the use of the material in the prosecution of the party (*A T & T Istel Ltd v Tully* [1993] AC 45, HL).

[98] CPR 31.20.

[99] By CPR 48.1, where an application is made for an order under these sections, the general rule is that the court will award the person against whom the order is sought their costs of the application and of complying with any order made on the application. The court may however make a different order having regard to all the circumstances, including the extent to which it was reasonable

CPR 31.16 governs applications made under the provisions referred to in paragraph 18.67 above.[100] Any application under CPR 31.16 must be supported by evidence.[101] The court may make an order under CPR 31.16 only where: **18.68**

(a) the respondent to the application is likely to be a party to subsequent proceedings;

(b) the applicant is also likely to be a party to those proceedings;

(c) if proceedings had started, the respondent's duty by way of standard disclosure would extend to the documents or classes of documents of which the applicant seeks disclosure; and

(d) disclosure before proceedings have started is desirable in order to:
   (i) dispose fairly of the anticipated proceedings;
   (ii) assist the dispute to be resolved without proceedings; or
   (iii) save costs.[102]

Any order made on such an application must specify the documents or the classes of documents which the respondent must disclose and require it, when making disclosure, to specify any of those documents (a) which are no longer in its control or (b) in respect of which it claims a right or duty to withhold inspection.[103] Such an order may require the respondent to indicate what has happened to any document which is no longer in its control and specify the time and place for disclosure and inspection.[104]

Disclosure against a person not a party

Section 34(2) of the Supreme Court Act 1981 gives the High Court power, on the application in accordance with the rules of the court of a party to any proceedings in the High Court and in such circumstances as may be specified in those rules, to order a person who is not a party to the proceedings and who appears to the court to be likely to have in its possession, custody or power any documents which are relevant to an issue arising out of the claim (a) to disclose whether those documents are in its possession, custody or power; and (b) to produce such of those documents as are in its possession, custody or power to the applicant or (on such conditions as may be specified in the order) to the applicant's legal or other advisers. Section 53(2) of the County Courts Act 1984 gives a county court a similar power.[105] **18.69**

---

for the person against whom the order was sought to oppose the application and whether the parties to the application have complied with any relevant pre-action protocols.

[100] CPR 31.16(1).
[101] CPR 31.16(2).
[102] CPR 31.16(3).
[103] CPR 31.16(4).
[104] CPR 31.16(5).
[105] By CPR 48.1, where an application is made for an order under these sections, the general rule is that the court will award the person against whom the order is sought their costs of the application and of complying with any order made on the application. The court may however make a

18.70 CPR 31.17 governs applications made under the provisions referred to in paragraph 18.69 above.[106] Any application under CPR 31.17 must be supported by evidence.[107] The court may make an order under CPR 31.17 only where the documents of which disclosure is sought are likely to support the case of the applicant or adversely affect the case of one of the other parties to the proceedings and disclosure is necessary in order to dispose fairly of the claim or to save costs.[108] Any order made on such an application must specify the documents or the classes of documents which the respondent must disclose and require it, when making disclosure, to specify any of those documents (a) which are no longer in its control; or (b) in respect of which it claims a right or duty to withhold inspection.[109] Such an order may require the respondent to indicate what has happened to any document which is no longer in its control and specify the time and place for disclosure and inspection.[110] In *Re Howglen Ltd*[111] it was held that, before the court makes an order under CPR 31.17 for the disclosure of a class of documents, it must be satisfied that there are documents falling within that class and that those documents are (not might be) documents disclosure of which would support the case of the applicant or adversely affect the case of another party to the proceedings.

Other powers of the court to order disclosure

18.71 CPR 31.16 and 31.17 do not limit any other power which the court may have to order disclosure before proceedings have started and disclosure against a person who is not a party to proceedings.[112] The effect of this is to preserve the inherent jurisdiction of the court to order disclosure in certain circumstances. The circumstances where this is most frequently encountered are where a party seeks the disclosure of the identity of a wrongdoer from a third party.[113]

---

different order having regard to all the circumstances, including the extent to which it was reasonable for the person against whom the order was sought to oppose the application and whether the parties to the application have complied with any relevant pre-action protocols.

[106] CPR 31.17(1).
[107] CPR 31.17(2).
[108] CPR 31.17(3).
[109] CPR 31.17(4).
[110] CPR 31.17(5).
[111] [2001] 1 All ER 376, Ch D.
[112] CPR 31.18.
[113] See, for example, *Norwich Pharmacal v Customs and Excise Commissioners* [1974] AC 133, HL where it was held that, if a person, through no fault of their own, has got mixed up with the tortious acts of others so as to facilitate their wrongdoing, they may incur no personal liability but will come under a duty to assist the person who has been wronged by giving them full information and disclosing the identity of the wrongdoers.

C. Obtaining Further Information

Prior to the introduction of the Civil Procedure Rules on 26 April 1999 there were **18.72** two principal ways in which a party to litigation (A) could seek further information from another party to the litigation (B). The first was where A sought further details of an allegation contained in one of B's pleadings. This was done by a request for further and better particulars of the pleading concerned. The second way in which A could, in some circumstances, seek further information from B was by the service of interrogatories, that is, a series of questions which B was required to answer.

With the introduction of the new rules these two ways of obtaining further **18.73** information from another party to litigation have been combined. The method of obtaining such information is now by a request for further information. This is governed by CPR 18 and its accompanying Practice Direction.

By CPR 18.1(1) the court may at any time order a party to (a) clarify any matter **18.74** which is in dispute in the proceedings, or (b) give additional information in relation to any such matter, whether or not the matter is contained or referred to in a statement of case. The court's power to order the provision of additional information under CPR 18.1(1) is subject to the overriding objective that cases should be dealt with justly.[114] In the remainder of this Part clarification or additional information falling within the scope of CPR 18.1(1) will be referred to as 'further information'.

The power under CPR 18.1(1) is subject to any rule of law to the contrary.[115] This **18.75** means that the court cannot order a party to disclose information disclosure of which cannot as a matter of law be compelled such as where the information concerned is privileged.[116]

Where the court makes an order that a party provide further information, that **18.76** party must file its response and serve it on the other parties within the time specified by the court.[117]

Before a party to litigation (A) applies to the court for an order that another party **18.77** to litigation (B) provide further information, A should serve on B a request for the further information concerned stating a date by which the response to the request should be served.[118] The date must give B a reasonable time to respond.[119] Such a

---

[114] *Toussaint v Mattis* [2001] CP Rep 61, CA.
[115] CPR 18.1(2).
[116] The grounds on which disclosure can be withheld are discussed at paras 18.45 to 18.65 above.
[117] CPR 18.1(3).
[118] PD (18) 1.1.
[119] PD (18) 1.1.

request should be concise and strictly confined to matters which are reasonably necessary and proportionate to enable A to prepare its own case or to understand the case it has to meet.[120]

18.78 Requests should be made as far as possible in a single comprehensive document and not piecemeal.[121] A request may be made by letter if its text is brief but otherwise should be made in a separate document.[122] If a request is made by letter, the letter should state that it contains a request made under CPR 18 and should not deal with other matters.[123] There are also mandatory and suggested provisions as to the format of a request.[124]

18.79 The response to a request should be in writing, dated and signed by B or its legal representative.[125] Where the request was made by letter B may give its response in a letter or in a formal reply.[126] If the response is given by letter, it should identify itself as a response to the request and should deal with no other matters.[127] There are also mandatory provisions as to the format of a response.[128] When B serves the response on A it should serve a copy of the response on every other party to the litigation and file a copy of the request and response with the court.[129]

18.80 If B objects to complying with the whole or part of the request or is unable to do so either at all or within the time specified in the request, it should inform A promptly and in any event within that time.[130] B may do so in a letter or a separate document but in either case must give reasons and, where relevant, give a date by which it expects to be able to comply.[131] Provided B has done this, there is no need for it to apply to the court.[132] If B considers that a request can only be complied with at disproportionate expense and objects to complying for that reason, it should say so in its reply and explain briefly why it has taken that view.[133]

18.81 A party applying for an order that a party provide further information should explain why no informal request[134] was made (if that is the case)[135] and should describe the response (if any) to any informal request.[136]

---

[120] PD (18) 1.2.
[121] PD (18) 1.3.
[122] PD (18) 1.4.
[123] PD (18) 1.5.
[124] PD (18) 1.6.
[125] PD (18) 2.1.
[126] PD (18) 2.2(1).
[127] PD (18) 2.2(2).
[128] PD (18) 2.3.
[129] PD (18) 2.4.
[130] PD (18) 4.1(1).
[131] PD (18) 4.1(2).
[132] PD (18) 4.2(1).
[133] PD (18) 4.2(2).
[134] That is a request under PD (18) 1.1.
[135] PD (18) 5.3(1).
[136] PD (18) 5.3(2).

Where B has made no response to a request served on it, A need not serve the **18.82** application notice (applying for an order that B provide the further information requested) on B and the court may deal with the application without a hearing provided that 14 days have passed since the request was served and the time stated in it for a response has expired.[137]

A response (whether given voluntarily or following an order that the party provide **18.83** the information) should be verified by a statement of truth, that is a statement signed by the party or its legal representative that the facts stated in the response are true.[138]

The court may direct that information provided by a party to another party **18.84** (whether given voluntarily or following an order that the party provide the information) must not be used for any purpose except for that of the proceedings in which it is given.[139]

D. Requiring a Witness to Attend Court to Give Evidence or to Produce Documents to the Court

The provisions providing for the circumstances in which a person may be required **18.85** to attend court to give evidence or to produce documents are contained in CPR 34. The attendance of the person concerned is secured by a witness summons.

A witness summons is a document issued by the court which requires a witness to **18.86** (a) attend court to give evidence; or (b) produce documents to the court.[140] A witness summons should be in the relevant practice form[141] and there must be a separate witness summons for each witness.[142]

A witness summons may require a witness to produce documents to the court **18.87** either on the date fixed for a hearing or on such date as the court may direct.[143] In the latter case the person can only be required to produce documents which they could be required to produce at the hearing.[144]

A witness summons is issued on the date entered on it by the court.[145] The **18.88** summons should be issued by the court where the case in respect of which the

---

[137] PD (18) 5.5.
[138] PD (18) 3; CPR 22.1.
[139] CPR 18.2.
[140] CPR 34.2(1).
[141] CPR 34.2(2).
[142] CPR 34.2(3).
[143] CPR 34.2(4).
[144] CPR 34.2(5).
[145] CPR 34.3(1).

summons is issued is proceeding or where the hearing in question will be held.[146] A party must obtain the court's permission to (a) have a summons issued less than seven days before the date of the trial; (b) have a summons issued for a witness to attend court to give evidence or produce documents on any date except the date fixed for the trial; or (c) have a summons issued for a witness to attend court to give evidence or to produce documents at any hearing except the trial.[147] Otherwise a party can issue a witness summons without the court's permission. The effect of these provisions is that a party can issue a witness summons without permission to require a witness to attend or produce documents at the trial of a claim provided that the summons is issued at least seven days before the trial.

18.89   The court may set aside or vary a witness summons.[148] This enables a witness who is served with a witness summons to apply to the court to set it aside, for example, on the grounds that they have no relevant evidence to give, that the witness summons is oppressive or that it relates to privileged documents.

18.90   A witness summons is binding if it is served at least seven days before the date on which the witness is required to attend the court.[149] The court may, however, direct that a witness summons is to be binding although it will be served less than seven days before the date on which the witness is required to attend the court.[150] A witness summons which is served in accordance with these provisions and requires the attendance of the witness to give evidence is binding until the conclusion of the hearing at which the attendance of the witness is required.[151]

18.91   A witness summons will generally be served by the court.[152] At the time of the service of the witness summons the witness must be offered or paid a sum reasonably sufficient to cover his or her expenses in travelling to and from the court and such sum by way of compensation for loss of time as may be specified in the relevant Practice Direction.[153] Where the court is to serve a witness summons these sums should be deposited in the court office.[154]

---

[146] CPR 34.3(3).
[147] CPR 34.3(2).
[148] CPR 34.3(4).
[149] CPR 34.5(1).
[150] CPR 34.5(2).
[151] CPR 34.5(3).
[152] CPR 34.6(1).
[153] CPR 34.7. The sum to be paid to compensate the witness for their loss of time is based on the sums payable to witnesses attending the Crown Court to give evidence in criminal proceedings (PD (34) 3.2 and 3.3).
[154] CPR 34.6(2).

19

THE INTERNET

A. Introduction

This chapter considers the Internet and its relationship with national and international law, focusing on information and its disclosure. It discusses the use of the Internet by bodies subject to the Freedom of Information Act 2000 and others and outlines some of the potential pitfalls of such use. **19.01**

B. Building the Superhighway

Definitions: I

The Internet is no more or less than a network of computers and of networks of computers spread across the globe which are able to communicate with one another. **19.02**

Early years

19.03 Parallel but unconnected research at the Massachusetts Institute of Technology and in the American defence community in the early to mid 1960s laid the theoretical foundation for the networking of computers.[1] By 1972 the first operational network had been created and in the same year the first e-mail was sent on that network. Research and development continued in both the civil and military spheres through the 1970s and 1980s when most of the key components of the Internet were developed.[2] By the mid 1980s numerous networks existed, almost entirely designed for and used by computer scientists, many of which networks communicated via the first Internet programs.[3]

19.04 Between 1988 and 1995 the necessary conditions for the privatization and the commercialization of the Internet were established.

Definitions: II

19.05 On 24 October 1995 the US Federal Networking Council passed the following resolution defining the Internet:

> The Federal Networking Council (FNC) agrees that the following language reflects our definition of the term 'Internet'. 'Internet' refers to the global information system that—(i) is logically linked together by a globally unique address space based on the Internet Protocol (IP) or its subsequent extensions/follow-ons; (ii) is able to support communications using the Transmission Control Protocol/Internet Protocol (TCP/IP) suite or its subsequent extensions/follow-ons, and/or other IP-compatible protocols; and (iii) provides, uses or makes accessible, either publicly or privately, high level services layered on the communications and related infrastructure described herein.[4]

The Web

19.06 The World Wide Web[5] was invented by Tim Berners-Lee. Through the World Wide Web Consortium[6] that he and others established in 1996, the protocols and programming standards upon which the Web depends were developed.

---

[1] See BM Leiner and others, *A Brief History of the Internet* (version 3.31) at http://www.isoc. org/internet/history/brief.shtml (21 August 2002).

[2] Computer networking had from the first been seen as valuable by the defence community and an early military emphasis on the need for networks to be robust enough to survive the destruction of large numbers of the component computers had a profound effect on the evolution of the Internet.

[3] NSFNET and JANET.

[4] The authors do not think this means any more than the definition at para 19.02 above.

[5] A computer program given that name by Berners-Lee which allows computers to communicate with the result that information received via the Internet can be viewed graphically, ie as a webpage.

[6] Also known as W3C.

C. Using the Web: a Practical and Legal Analysis

The following paragraphs seek to provide a non-technical description of the oper- **19.07** ation of the Internet, as exemplified by the Web, having regard to legal concepts of information, documents, parties, transactions, and jurisdiction.

Internet use is information exchange

From the point of view of any particular computer connected to the Internet, **19.08** Internet communication involves sending information to another computer or computers physically located elsewhere and receiving information from such other computer or computers in return.

Visiting a webpage

'Visiting a webpage' involves a computer requesting information, which request **19.09** is directed via the Internet to the computer or computers where the request indicates the information comprising the webpage is located, or from which it is accessible, and a response from that computer or those computers, which is then decoded and resolved into an image by the computer from which the request originated.

Safe to surf?

The request for information itself necessarily contains information about the **19.10** applicant computer and about the information that is being requested. The full content of the information contained in a request is not normally visible to the person causing the computer to make the request. Users who lack a relatively sophisticated knowledge of the workings of the Internet are unlikely to be aware of the nature and extent of the information about their computers and themselves that they disclose while surfing the Internet. Quite how much information the request does or should disclose and the purposes for which such information may be used[7] are issues raised by those concerned to protect the privacy and confidentiality of Internet communication.[8]

When I press 'send', where does it go?

The path that information takes while crossing the Internet from its original **19.11** sender to its ultimate recipient will normally involve a number of computers, which may be and often are scattered across the world. The links in the chain of transfer and indeed the physical location of either sender or recipient are not

---

[7] See paras 19.18–19.22 below ('Cookies' and 'Spyware').
[8] eg, http://www.epic.org (27 August 2002).

obvious except to themselves. The physical locations of the computers involved are not usually significant in terms of the speed or quality of the communication and establishing the location of the information concerned at any given moment during the process of transmission is practically impossible.[9]

Dispersed resources

19.12 The reference in paragraph 19.09 above to a request to a 'computer or computers' is an indication not only that a number of computers will normally be involved in the transfer of information from original sender to ultimate recipient, but also of the fact that what may appear to be one website or even one webpage is often composed of a number of linked information resources, which may reside on a number of different computers which in turn may be physically located in different jurisdictions.

Information travels, documents don't

19.13 The description of Internet communication above is also couched in terms of the transfer of information and not of a document, even in electronic form. Each link in the chain of computers involved in the transfer receives one or more 'packets' consisting of part of the information being sent and then copies each packet for onward transmission. The packets received are discarded at each transmission point. The copied packets are typically sent to a number of different locations for simultaneous onward transmission and any of those copies (or rather copies of those copies) may form part of the document received by the ultimate recipient computer. This feature of the Internet, that is, that despite appearances no document is ever transferred from A to B, may produce the need to rethink many legal concepts and reinterpret many statutory provisions, in so far as they are applied to Internet communications.

ISPs

19.14 The transfer of information using the Web described above is likely to be facilitated by one or more Internet Service Providers (ISPs). ISPs have the computing and telecommunications resources required to acquire and maintain a point-of-presence on the Internet. This means that an ISP is (theoretically at least) always part of the Internet and is always connected to all other ISPs. The services most commonly provided by ISPs are (a) a link to the Internet for those, namely practically all domestic users and most business users, who do not have their own point-of-presence, and (b) web hosting.

---

[9] This difficulty is inherent in the development of the Internet from its earliest days as a system for delivering information in packets: information is broken down into the equivalent of jigsaw pieces and sent by different routes, with the same piece often being sent simultaneously via a number of paths. See n 2 above in relation to the practical advantages of this.

Web hosting occurs where information resources belonging to a third party are **19.15**
published by and reside upon computers provided by an ISP to those third
parties: its customers, if the ISP is a commercial organization. Thus a website promoting the products of a Swedish engineering company may in fact be composed
of information residing on computers in Norway used by an ISP based in that
jurisdiction.[10]

From this it can be seen that the geographical locations of a computer upon which **19.16**
information resides and of the party who owns or possesses or uses that information may be different. Furthermore it follows that it is often unrealistic to base
legal conclusions relating to Internet transactions on the ownership or location of
the computers and other hardware upon which information resides or from which
it travels or by which it is received.

Virtual reality

For all these reasons it is often convenient to conceptualize information available **19.17**
via the Internet as existing in its own non-geographical but quasi-geographical[11]
world, hence 'the Web' and 'Cyberspace'. Indeed 'the Internet' is another term
which implies the existence of a virtual space, and therefore from a legal stand-
point a term that arguably does more to obscure than it does to describe the nature
of the processes of information exchange and manipulation that it refers to.

Cookies

As indicated above all Internet access involves two-way communication. It is **19.18**
impossible to request information from a website without disclosing at least two
pieces of information: (a) the Internet address of the recipient of the information,[12] and (b) the content of the request. A website may increase the amount of
information it receives during the making of a request for information by placing
a 'cookie' on the computer making the request.

Cookies are small computer files which, if present on the computer making a **19.19**
request for information, are automatically sent to the website from which they
originate along with any request for information from that website. Cookies identify the computer making the request and (for example) the pages of the website
previously visited by that computer. Most websites seek to place one or more
cookies on all computers which visit them.

Thus once a cookie has been placed the website owner is in a position to extract **19.20**
information from those visiting the site about past behaviour while visiting that

---

[10] Or indeed on computers in Thailand used by an ISP based in Germany or vice versa.
[11] And therefore 'virtual'.
[12] The identity of the party making the request may be deliberately hidden using proxy servers
and other devices.

site or other sites. This information is used to 'profile' internet users both for the benefit of those operating relevant websites, for example to improve the design of the site by discovering how it is being used, and by market research companies who sell the information on. Understandably perhaps, not everyone is happy about this.

19.21 Internet software provided with most consumer computers is set by default to accept such cookies without seeking permission from the user.[13] In the United States the practice of placing cookies and extracting information from them for commercial purposes has been the subject of litigation in which class actions have been brought against one of the largest commercial placers and analysers of cookies, initially without success.[14] A settlement now seems likely.[15]

Spyware

19.22 A further attempt to make the most of two-way communication inherent in the use of the Internet is the deployment of spyware,[16] a program embedded in some other piece of software distributed free, which automatically and secretly seeks to connect via the Internet with its 'home' address and convey to that home information about the recipient's computer or Internet usage. An attempt is being made in the United States to control the use of such programmes.[17]

D. The Internet: Legal Issues

19.23 To some the Internet has utopian if not mystical potential. It is argued that because it is practically impossible for any government to control or even to influence the flow of information transmitted by it, the Internet represents a deep and perhaps fatal erosion of the power of the apparatus of the nation state.

A brave new world

19.24 The Internet has been heralded as an unparalleled device to achieve practical democracy, or anarchy or syndicarchy depending upon the political preferences of those concerned. This in turn has engendered debate as to the merits of claims

---

[13] Although the facility to block cookies is being made more accessible on the latest software and hardware.

[14] *In re DoubleClick Inc Privacy Litigation*, 154 F Supp 2d 497, 69 USLW 1604 (SDNY 2001).

[15] See http://www.epic.org (27 August 2002).

[16] A family of programmes including Aureate/ Radiate, see http://grc.com/optout.htm

[17] The Spyware Control and Privacy Protection Act 2001 was introduced as a Bill into the US Senate in January 2001.

that the Internet is or should be self-governing. A discussion of these arguments is beyond the scope of this book.[18]

Legal challenges to Internet freedom

The concept and future of the Internet as an information freeport, where neither **19.25** private law nor public law nor criminal law controls apply at a national or international level and where no such controls can be enforced is being tested by the legislatures of most developed nations and by litigants in those jurisdictions.

Jurisdictional issues

One of the first questions that arises in connection with legal control of the **19.26** Internet is that of jurisdiction. In the course of this chapter mention has been made of the legal problems associated with the fact that Internet communication is geographically opaque and very often involves a number of jurisdictions. Traditional national and international law rely heavily on the ability to ascertain where acts take place.[19] If the location of a legally significant act which takes place 'on the Internet' is analysed on a traditional basis, the result tends to be that the transaction took place either everywhere or at a location which is entirely fortuitous and has no significant geographical link with either party.[20] Although the issue has yet to be grappled with by the English courts, two distinct legal approaches are apparent in reported decisions from other jurisdictions.

Worldwide jurisdiction

One approach is for a national court to accept jurisdiction, at least in some cases, **19.27** over any party whose information is accessible via the Internet to those resident in that country, that is, over the whole world.

The *Yahoo!* and *Chuckleberry* cases

In France a case was brought against Yahoo![21] regarding an Internet auction site **19.28** operated by Yahoo! in the United States upon which Nazi memorabilia was for sale. Such memorabilia could not be legally advertised for sale in France according to French law. Notwithstanding the fact that the website concerned had no French connection, other than the fact that it was accessible via the Internet to

---

[18] See N Weinstock Natanel, 'Cyberspace Self-Governance A Skeptical View from Liberal Democratic Theory' in E Lederman and R Shapira (eds), *Law, Information and Information Technology* (2001).

[19] See eg Art 5 of the Brussels Convention or Arts 4 and 5 of the Rome Convention.

[20] See C Reed, *Internet Law: Text and Materials* (2000), ch 7.

[21] *UEJF and Licra v Yahoo! Inc. and Yahoo France* (*Tribunal de Grande Instance de Paris*, 22 May 2000).

those resident in France, the court ordered Yahoo! to render its site inaccessible to those resident in France or to pay a daily default fine.

19.29 The French court considered that accessibility of the offending advertisements to Internet users resident in France was sufficient to found jurisdiction. It was influenced by the fact that Yahoo! produced a French language version of its website. Yahoo! claimed that the nature of the Internet made 100 per cent compliance with the court's order impossible. The court considered that it was possible to filter out the vast majority of attempted visits to Yahoo!'s auction site by French residents and granted the relief sought. Yahoo!'s response was to cease carrying advertisements for Nazi memorabilia.

19.30 Similarly in the *Chuckleberry* case[22] the US court found that an Italian pornographic website entitled 'Playmen' was in breach of a 15-year-old US injunction against infringing the Playboy trademark in the United States. The publication of 'Playmen' in the form of a magazine in Italy had been held by the Italian courts not to infringe Playboy's intellectual property rights. The US court held that by allowing access by US residents to its website (which access the defendant had solicited in the United States) the defendant was distributing infringing publications within the United States.

A narrower view of jurisdiction

19.31 Some decisions indicate that the court will try to decide on a case by case basis how jurisdictional issues in Internet cases should be resolved on the basis of a forum conveniens style test.

The *Cybersell* case

19.32 In *Cybersell Inc v Cybersell Inc*[23] the US court applied a three-part test in seeking to establish jurisdiction over a non-resident defendant 'present' by reason of Internet activities:

(a) the non-resident defendant must do some act or conclude some transaction within the forum in which the claimant seeks to bring proceedings or perform some act by which he purposefully avails himself of the privilege of conducting activities in the forum, thereby invoking the benefits and protections afforded by the law of the forum;

(b) the claim must be one which arises out of or results from the defendant's forum-related activities; and

(c) exercise of jurisdiction must be reasonable.

---

[22] *Playboy Enterprises v Chuckleberry Publishing*, 939 F Supp 1032 (SDNY 1996).
[23] 130 F 3d 414 (9th Cir 1997).

Liability to the whole world

It follows from the above that a publication of information on a website operated **19.33** from England may expose the publisher to civil or criminal liability in any country of the world on the basis of the law of those countries, whether or not the act complained of would give rise to any right to redress in English law.

The Convention on Cybercrime

On 8 November 2001 the Convention on Cybercrime and its Explanatory **19.34** Report[24] were adopted by the Committee of Ministers of the Council of Europe. The treaty will enter into force when five states, at least three of which are members of the Council of Europe, have ratified it. The United States, as a participant in the drafting of the treaty, will be invited to ratify as well. The Convention represents an international response to social change produced by and involving the use of the Internet:

> The new technologies challenge existing legal concepts. Information and communications flow more easily around the world. Borders are no longer boundaries to this flow. Criminals are increasingly located in places other than where their acts produce their effects. However, domestic laws are generally confined to a specific territory. Thus solutions to the problems posed must be addressed by international law, necessitating the adoption of adequate international legal instruments.[25]

The Convention requires Convention territories to bring into their national law **19.35** criminal legislation on a common template dealing with: unauthorized access to computers,[26] infringements of copyright, computer-related fraud and child pornography. The Convention also outlines legislation to permit states to search, seize and tap information flowing via the Internet within their national boundaries. The Convention will be supplemented by an additional protocol making any publication of racist and xenophobic propaganda via computer networks a criminal offence.

The Convention focuses upon the perceived need to impose criminal sanctions **19.36** on Internet Service Providers, who are not themselves responsible for the crimes to which the Convention relates. By so doing the authors of the Convention recognize that there are practical difficulties in finding and punishing individuals using the Internet for criminal purposes, unless innocent third parties are subject to criminal sanction as part of the investigative process.

---

[24] ETS no 185; http://conventions.coe.int/treaty/EN/projets/FinalCybercrime.htm (27 August 2002).
[25] Explanatory Report (n 24 above) para 6.
[26] ie hacking crimes include possessing passwords or cracking programs with intent to use them to gain unauthorized access.

Adapting the existing law

19.37 Where issues of jurisdiction or of Internet-specific criminal activity do not arise it is reasonable to assume that the English courts will apply the existing law to Internet cases, with such adaptions as are required. This process has been evident in the rash of domain name cases, where those who have opportunistically registered domain names referring to well-known companies or individuals have been ordered to give up those domain names to those whose traditional intellectual property rights have been held to be infringed by the use or threatened use of such names by unconnected parties.[27]

E. Access to Public Information and the Internet

19.38 In countries such as the United States where there is a developed freedom of information culture, the Internet has been regarded by pro-disclosure pressure groups as the delivery system of choice for information to which the public have a right of access.[28]

Some advantages

19.39 The advantages of using the Internet as a delivery system for information for a body subject to the Act are readily apparent. Where categories of information can be identified as being such that any request for that information under the Act would automatically be granted, it serves the purposes of the Act and the needs of the information provider if that information can be published on the Internet. Individual requests for information can also be efficiently managed where the process is conducted via e-mail, with or without the addition of an interactive website.

19.40 Producing documents in electronic form or translating them into that form and rendering those documents accessible via the Internet or an intranet[29] has obvious attractions for any organization which needs to store, access and process significant quantities of information and transmit that information from one operator to another.

---

[27] See *British Telecommunications plc v One in a Million Ltd* [1999] FSR 1.

[28] And this has been given statutory force by the provisions of the US Electronic Freedom of Information Act Amendments 1996. The status of the Internet as a primary medium for effective access to information is assumed in the Report of the Government of Canada's Access to Information Review Task Force. See further chs 9 (at paras 9.21 and 9.99 above) and 25 (at paras 25.289–25.295 below).

[29] A network of computers intended to be accessible only by its member computers.

Some pitfalls

The use of the Internet to store and render accessible large volumes of information, whether or not this information is intended for publication, carries with it a number of potential problems which the courts will have to resolve applying developed principles of confidentiality, privacy and defamation.[30] **19.41**

Convenience versus control

If databases are readily accessible via the Internet it means that anyone with Internet access can obtain the relevant information without further approval or review by the publisher. Thus once information has been published or rendered accessible via the Internet (whether or not for a fee), the information provider abdicates all control in respect of that information over who has access to it and for what purpose. **19.42**

This may prove disastrous in a number of ways. For example, information may be intentionally published which should not have been released on grounds identified in the Freedom of Information Act 2000, or information may be unintentionally published which the Act indicates should have been withheld due to mistakes made by the information provider or by those providing Internet services on its behalf. **19.43**

Defamation by website

In the recent libel litigation between Times Newspapers and Dr Loutchansky[31] it was found that in allowing Internet access to archived articles previously published in *The Times*, which contained material defaming the claimant, the newspaper had libelled the doctor. **19.44**

The *Loutchansky* litigation highlights the fact that any archive may contain material referring to persons whose private law rights would be infringed by making that material publicly accessible on the Internet. The statutory defence of qualified privilege provided to bodies subject to the 2000 Act by section 79 of the Act will apparently only apply to information supplied pursuant to a request under section 1.[32] Information made available otherwise than in response to a specific request will not be covered. Whether ordinary access to a regulated body's website will be found to constitute the making of a request within section 1 in the context of section 79 remains to be seen. A distinction may come to be drawn between access involving an explicit request for information and access that contains only **19.45**

---

[30] For principles relating to privacy and confidentiality, see ch 20 below. For defamation, which is outside the scope of this book, readers are referred to the specialist texts on the subject.
[31] *Loutchansky v Times Newspapers Ltd* [2001] EWCA Civ 1805.
[32] See ch 5 above.

the request implicit in accessing the relevant webpage (see paragraph 19.09 above).

Jurisdiction and enforcement are two different things

19.46 A further consequence of the Internet is that once restricted information has been wrongly exposed to the on-line community, there is very little chance of closing the virtual stable door after the digital horse has bolted, whether by legal means or otherwise. The willingness of courts to accept jurisdiction in Internet cases does not mean that the judgments of those courts are easy to enforce effectively.

19.47 Traditional legal remedies such as an injunction, called upon to restrict, for example, the dissemination of confidential information, are of limited assistance: if the information is interesting enough or valuable enough to make the exercise worth undertaking in the first place, it is likely to have been transferred in a matter of seconds to any number of locations in any number of jurisdictions and either published in such locations or transferred onwards. Identifying any of the persons concerned may be difficult or impossible and there are unlikely to be any practical steps that can be taken to prevent publication or use of the information on a global scale.[33]

Hackers and crackers

19.48 Thus far the issues associated with the disclosure of restricted information to the on-line community have been considered only in relation to disclosures made deliberately or otherwise in response to innocent inquiries over the Internet. Not all requests for information are so benign.

19.49 With a little technical knowledge and appropriate software hackers will try, often successfully, to access files and programs that the proprietors of the computers in question and of the information resident on them intend to remain confidential. Hackers may simply be mischievous or may on the other hand be motivated by the desire to acquire information for commercial or political ends. Attacks may also take the form of blocking legitimate access to Internet resources[34] or of manipulating or mutilating information displayed on a website or resident on linked computers for the advantage or amusement of the intruder.

Viruses

19.50 Viruses, malicious programs designed to produce damaging or unwelcome results on the computers of others, can be spread via the Internet with or without any

---

[33] Injuncting one or more English newspapers from carrying a story is of limited value when Internet publication has occurred as the government discovered when trying to suppress information disclosed by former MI5 operative, David Shayler in 2001. See further ch 12 above.
[34] A so-called denial of service attack.

direct targeting from hackers. Virus protection is necessary both to protect the systems of information providers and to prevent onward transmission of such viruses to others. Negligent transmission of viruses has yet to be the subject of litigation in England but it can only be a matter of time before such actions are commonplace.

F. Conclusion

The Internet will undoubtedly become the primary medium through which   **19.51** information to which the 2000 Act relates is published and requested. Bodies subject to the Act will increasingly use the Internet for internal as well as external communication.

If those charged with designing the systems by which information is released on-   **19.52** line are aware of the nature of the Internet in practical and legal terms and of the pitfalls that attend the use of the Web, it is to be hoped that the Internet will be found to be a tool that can be used safely.

Part G

PRIVACY, CONFIDENTIALITY AND HUMAN RIGHTS

20

PRIVACY AND CONFIDENTIALITY

A. Introduction

Is there today a right of privacy in English law?

In 1991 Glidewell LJ, giving the leading judgment in *Kaye v Robertson*, said:[1] **20.01**

It is well known that in English law there is no right of privacy, and accordingly there is no right of action for breach of a person's privacy.

In 2001 Sedley LJ in *Douglas v Hello! Ltd*[2] said:

. . . we have reached a point at which it can be said with confidence that the law recognises and will appropriately protect a right of personal privacy.[3]

---

[1] [1991] FSR 62.
[2] [2001] QB 967.
[3] ibid, at 997, para 110.

In 2002 the headline for *The Times* law report of the Court of Appeal's decision in *Wainwright v Home Office*[4] was

> Common law does not recognise right of privacy

In 2002 Lord Woolf delivering the judgment of the Court of Appeal in *A v B plc*[5] said that Articles 8 and 10 of the European Convention for the Protection of Human Rights.

> . . . have provided new parameters within which the court will decide, in an action for breach of confidence, whether a person is entitled to have his privacy protected by the court or whether the restriction of freedom of expression which such protection involves cannot be justified.[6]

20.02 How much has changed in the eleven years since *Kaye v Robertson*? The Court of Appeal in the *Douglas* case gave the clearest indication yet that there is a right of privacy in English law. Sedley LJ's recognition of a right of privacy was given tacit support by the President of the Family Division, Dame Elizabeth Butler-Sloss in *Venables v News Group Newspapers Ltd*.[7] Is Sedley LJ's confidence justified or will the caution of other members of the Court of Appeal prevail? What is the effect of the Human Rights Act 1998? These are questions that are in the process of being answered.

20.03 *Douglas* and *Venables* are cases which lie at opposite ends of the spectrum. In both cases there is much discussion of the principle of confidentiality. It is clear from the *Douglas* case that there is no watertight division between the concepts of privacy and confidentiality. If, as Sedley LJ believes, there is a right of privacy in English law it has grown out of the equitable principle of confidentiality.

Kaye v Robertson

20.04 In the case of *Kaye v Robertson*[8] Gordon Kaye, the actor, sued the *Sunday Sport* whose reporter and photographer had invaded the hospital room where Mr Kaye was recovering from serious head injuries. His counsel put his case not as a breach of privacy which it plainly was, but as a case of libel, malicious falsehood, trespass to the person and passing off. The claimant ended up with only an injunction to stop the paper claiming, by way of malicious falsehood, that Mr Kaye had voluntarily given an interview. But as Sedley LJ has pointed out the Court of Appeal did not affirmatively consider and decide whether there is a right of privacy in English law.[9] The Court adopted—for it plainly shared—counsel's assumption that there was none.

---

4 [2002] 3 WLR 405.
5 [2002] 3 WLR 542.
6 ibid, at para 4.
7 [2001] Fam 430.
8 [1991] FSR 62.
9 [2001] QB 967, 998, para 113.

It is nevertheless significant that all the members of the Court were clearly of the **20.05** view that there should be a right of privacy in English law. Thus Glidewell LJ said:

> The facts of the present case are a graphic illustration of the desirability of Parliament considering whether and in what circumstances statutory provision can be made to protect the privacy of individuals.[10]

Bingham LJ, agreeing, said:

> This case nonetheless highlights, yet again, the failure of both the common law of England and statute to protect in an effective way the personal privacy of individual citizens.[11]

Leggatt LJ referred to the way in which the common law had developed in the United States to meet the need which the court on the present occasion was unable to fulfil satisfactorily. He described how over the last 100 years the right to privacy, or the 'right to be let alone', has gained acceptance in most jurisdictions in the United States.[12]

It is not helpful now to speculate whether the Court of Appeal would have reached **20.06** a different view in Gordon Kaye's case if breach of confidence had been fully argued before them. The law has moved on.

Principles which underlie the law of confidentiality

Instead it is appropriate to turn to Lord Scott of Foscote's view as expressed in his **20.07** essay on confidentiality[13] that two basic principles underlie, or ought to underlie, the law of confidentiality. The first is that private individuals are entitled to protection against disclosure without their consent of confidential information about themselves and their activities unless there is a sufficient public interest reason why the information should be disclosed. The second principle is that government, including local authorities and other emanations of government, such as the National Health Service, the Court Service, the Prison Service etc, are not entitled to protection from disclosure of information about themselves and their activities unless there is a sufficient public interest requiring the protection of information from disclosure.

Lord Scott in his essay on confidentiality says: **20.08**

> I regard each of these two principles as self-evidently necessary in a mature democracy. I regard them also as representing the law, properly understood.

---

[10] [1991] FSR 62 at 66.
[11] ibid, at 70.
[12] ibid, at 71.
[13] Published in *Freedom of Expression and Freedom of Information—Essays in Honour of Sir David Williams* (OUP, 2000).

The principles distinguish between private individuals and government. This is a distinction which most people will recognize; a right to some private space and an expectation that a free press and media will pursue the abuse of power in government. The principles mirror the right to respect for private and family life in Article 8 of the European Convention for the Protection of Human Rights and the guarantee of freedom of expression in Article 10. The principles apply as much to a right of privacy as to a right of confidentiality.

The scope of this chapter

20.09   This chapter considers first, the development of this principle of confidentiality, secondly the way in which the media is regulated, thirdly the development of a right of privacy, including a detailed analysis of the new cases, and fourthly when, at common law, government is entitled to protect information from disclosure.

B. The Development of the Principle of Confidentiality

The old cases

20.10   The equitable jurisdiction in cases of breach of confidence is ancient; confidence is the cousin of trust. The Statute of Uses 1535 is framed in terms of 'use confidence or trust'; and a couplet, attributed to Sir Thomas More, Lord Chancellor avers that:

> Three things are to be helpt in Conscience;
> Fraud, Accident and things of Confidence.[14]

20.11   In more recent times the famous case of Prince Albert's etchings and the battle of the Duchess of Argyll against the Duke to retain some privacy established the following propositions:

(a) If information is accepted on the basis that it will be kept secret, the recipient's conscience is bound by the confidence, and it will be unconscionable for him to break his duty of confidence by publishing the information to others.[15]

(b) The court will restrain a breach of confidence independently of any right at law.[16]

(c) The duty can arise independently of property or contract.[17]

(d) The contract or obligation of confidence can be implied.[18]

---

[14] Quoted by Megarry J in *Coco v AN Clark (Engineers) Limited* [1969] RPC 41, 46.
[15] *Prince Albert v Strange* (1849) 1 H & T 1, 23–25.
[16] ibid, at 25; *Argyll v Argyll* [1967] 302, 322.
[17] *Argyll v Argyll* [1967] 1 Ch 302, 322.
[18] ibid.

(e) Information about sexual conduct can be protected as a breach of confidence.[19]

(f) The disclosure of a photograph can be a breach of confidence.[20]

In *Prince Albert v Strange*[21] Queen Victoria and Prince Albert had made drawings **20.12** and etchings of their children and other subjects of interest to the family. Impressions of them had come into the hands of the defendants who proposed to exhibit and publish copies of them and make and publish a catalogue of them. Prince Albert successfully applied to the court for an injunction to restrain them from doing so. One of several grounds on which Lord Cottenham LC granted the injunction was breach of confidence. He rejected the argument that he should follow those cases which held that a title at law must first be established. Of these he said:[22]

> . . . they have no application to cases in which this court exercises an original jurisdiction, not for the protection of a merely legal right, but to prevent what this court considers and treats as a wrong, whether arising from violation of unquestioned right, or from breach of trust, confidence or contract, as in the present case . . .

and he described the case as one '*where privacy is the right invaded*'.[23]

Lord Cottenham also referred to the opinion of Lord Eldon in *Wyatt v Wilson*[24] **20.13** respecting an engraving of George III, during his illness, in which Lord Eldon said:

> If one of the late king's physicians had kept a diary of what he had heard and seen, this Court would not in the king's lifetime, have permitted him to print or publish it.

This was referred to by Ungoed-Thomas J in *Argyll v Argyll*, who commented:[25] **20.14**

> The diary there was the physician's and the only thing which could be described in any sense as the property of the King was the information it contained and to which the physician was given access. If such information can be regarded as within the protection afforded to property then similar confidential information communicated by a wife to her husband could also be so regarded.

The Duchess of Argyll's claim to restrain the publication in a national newspaper **20.15** of intimate marital secrets raised the important question of law, whether secret confidences between husband and wife during their marriage will be protected by

---

[19] *Argyll v Argyll* [1967] 1 Ch 302; *Stephens v Avery* [1988] Ch 449; *Barrymore v News Group Newspapers* Ltd [1997] FSR 600.
[20] *Pollard v Photographic Company* (1889) 40 Ch D 345; *Hellewell v Chief Constable of Derbyshire* [1955] 1 WLR 804, 807.
[21] (1849) 1 H & T 1.
[22] ibid, at 25–26.
[23] (1849) 1 Mac & G 25 at 47 which is to be preferred to (1849) 1 H & T 26.
[24] Lord Chancellor's court, 1820.
[25] [1967] 1 Ch 302, 320.

the court. The judge granted the injunctions sought. The case provides a clear example of protection given to privacy. The decision has been commented on in a number of subsequent cases, including *Douglas* and *Venables*, but its correctness has not been called into question.

The essentials of the doctrine

20.16   *Coco v AN Clark (Engineers) Ltd,*[26] a case about the disclosure of the design for a moped engine, provided the unlikely setting for Megarry J to review *the pure equitable doctrine of confidence*, albeit in the realms of commerce and where no marital relationship arose. Megarry J asked, what were the essentials of the doctrine? From this case and from *Stephens v Avery*[27] it is possible to add the following propositions to the six set out in paragraph 20.11 above:

(g)   The information itself, in the words of Lord Greene in *Saltman Engineering Co Ltd v Campbell Engineering Co Ltd,*[28] must have 'the necessary quality of confidence about it'.[29] It must not be public property already. If it is drawn from information in the public domain there must be some added product of the human brain which is sufficient to confer a confidential nature on the information.

(h)   The information must have been imparted in circumstances importing an obligation of confidence. There will be no protection if the information is blurted out in public. If the circumstances are such that any reasonable man standing in the shoes of the recipient of the information would have realized that upon reasonable grounds the information was being given to him in confidence, then this should be sufficient to impose upon him the equitable obligation of confidence.

(i)   There must be an unauthorized use of the information to the detriment of the person communicating it. Megarry J accepted, however, that there might be cases in which the claimant might have substantial motives for seeking the aid of equity and yet suffer nothing which could fairly be called detriment to him. Megarry J wished to keep open the possibility that no detriment need be shown in such cases.[30]

(j)   The relationship of the parties is not the determining factor.[31]

Further to these propositions an eleventh is suggested:

---

[26]   [1969] RPC 41, 46.

[27]   [1988] Ch 449.

[28]   (1948) 65 RPC 203.

[29]   And see *Terrapin Ltd v Builders's Supply Co (Hayes) Ltd* [1960] RPC 128 and *Seager v Copydex Ltd* [1967] 1 WLR 923.

[30]   As did Lord Goff in *Attorney-General v Guardian Newspapers Ltd (No 2)* [1990] 1 AC 109, 281.

[31]   *Stephens v Avery* [1988] Ch 449.

(k) It is not a necessary precondition of protection against the disclosure of confidential information that the information should have been specifically disclosed by a provider.[32]

Stephens v Avery

In *Stephens v Avery*[33] Sir Nicolas Browne-Wilkinson VC decided that private **20.17** information relating to sexual conduct of an individual (a lesbian relationship) was capable of being protected by the law of confidence. He refused to strike out a claim for damages. He rejected an argument that in the absence of a legally enforceable contract or a pre-existing relationship—such as that of employer and employee, doctor and patient, or priest and penitent—it is not possible to impose a legal duty of confidence on the recipient of the information merely by saying that the information is given in confidence. The Vice-Chancellor held that the basis of equitable intervention to protect confidentiality is that it is unconscionable for a person who has received information on the basis that it is confidential subsequently to reveal that information. Although the relationship between the parties is often important in cases where it is said there is an implied as opposed to an express obligation of confidence, the relationship between the parties is not the determining factor.

Lord Scott's argument

In *Argyll v Argyll* and in *Stephens v Avery* confidential information had been dis- **20.18** closed, in one way or another, by the claimant to the defendant. But as Lord Scott notes in his essay on confidentiality[34] the injunction granted in the *Argyll* case was not limited to information communicated by the Duchess to the Duke. It covered all private information about the Duchess acquired by the Duke from their marital relationship. Lord Scott suggests:

> This would have included information obtained by the Duke from observation of the Duchess, or simply, from sharing the same bed. *Argyll v Argyll* established, therefore, that it is not a necessary pre-condition of protection against the disclosure of confidential information that the information should have been specifically disclosed by a confider. Suppose the Duke had kept private memoirs. Could the Duchess have obtained an injunction restraining him from continuing to do so? Plainly not. Could she have obtained an injunction restraining him from making public the contents of his memoirs? Plainly, yes. So what would have been the position if the Duke's private memoirs had been stolen, and the newspaper had acquired them from the thief? Would a newspaper which had purchased the information from a thief be in a more favourable position than a newspaper which had purchased the information from the confidant? It is surely inconceivable that that, in law, could

---

[32] This is Lord Scott's view, see further para 20.18 below.
[33] [1988] Ch 449.
[34] See n 13 above.

be so. What system of jurisprudence would regard as tortious the disclosure of the material by the Duke but would permit the disclosure of the material by someone who had stolen it from the Duke?

The same point can be made regarding a case like *Stephens v Avery*. If details of the lesbian affair had been confided to the defendant in a letter from the plaintiff, the publication of that letter might, consistently with the views expressed by the Vice-Chancellor, constitute a tortious breach of confidence. How could a thief, who had stolen the letter from the defendant, be in a better position?

20.19 *Francome v Mirror Group Newspapers*[35] was not about a thief, but about people who, without any authority, had bugged the home telephone of Mr Francome, the champion National Hunt jockey, and taped his conversations. The *Daily Mirror* bought the tapes which were alleged to show that the claimant had broken the Jockey Club's rules. The eavesdroppers found themselves in no better position than the confidants in *Argyll v Argyll* and *Stephens v Avery*. The Court of Appeal upheld the grant of an interim injunction restraining the *Daily Mirror* from publishing any article based on the taped conversations.

20.20 The Court of Appeal rejected the argument that there was no cause of action against the newspaper or the eavesdroppers for breach of an obligation of confidentiality. Sir John Donaldson MR said:

> The authority for this rather surprising proposition is said to be *Malone v Metroplitan Police Commissioner* [1979] Ch 344. Suffice it to say that Sir Robert Megarry VC expressly stated, at 384, that he was deciding nothing on the position when tapping was effected for purposes other than the prevention, detection and discovery of crime and criminals or by persons other than the police.

The Court of Appeal recognized that Mr Francome was entitled, prima facie, to have the privacy of his private telephone conversations protected.

20.21 Lord Scott summed up the position in his essay as follows:

> It is, I suggest, now established that private conversations, whether surreptitiously recorded by a party to the conversations, or misappropriated by the theft of some written record, or obtained by the unauthorised tapping of a telephone, will be protected against unwarranted disclosure. So too, would intimate family or personal details known to members of the family be protected against unwarranted disclosure. The cases to which I have referred seem to me to establish that that is so. And there is, in my opinion, no sensible reason in principle or in practice for distinguishing between the eavesdropper who overhears conversations, the 'Peeping Tom' who spies through the bedroom curtains, or the intrusive photographer with his long range telephoto lens. Each of these is, in one way or another, coming into possession of private information. The misuse of that information can be restrained by injunctions (eg *Argyll v Argyll, Francome v Daily Mirror*) or, if dis-

---

[35] [1984] 1 WLR 892.

closure has already occurred, be remedied by an award of damages (*Stephens v Avery*).[36]

But *Kaye v Robertson* stands in the way.

Lord Scott's essay was written before the Human Rights Act 1998 came into force and before the recent Court of Appeal cases which are discussed below in part E. *Kaye v Robertson* may no longer stand in the way.

Defences

Information in the public domain

The principle of confidentiality only applies to information to the extent that it is **20.22** confidential. It is a defence if the information is in the public domain.

This was the basis of the House of Lords decision in *Attorney-General v The* **20.23** *Guardian Newspaper*[37] (the Spycatcher case). Peter Wright was a former member of the British Security Service MI5. Scott J held that the publication of his memoirs in the United States had destroyed any secrecy as to its contents. The Court of Appeal and the House of Lords upheld this finding. Lord Goff said:[38]

> Once it [the information] has entered what is usually called the public domain (which means no more than that the information in question is so generally accessible that in all the circumstances it cannot be regarded as confidential) then, as a general rule, the principle of confidentiality can have no application to it.

The public domain defence may cause problems for private individuals who find **20.24** themselves a target of the media. In *Earl Spencer v The United Kingdom*[39] Earl and Countess Spencer (the Earl is the brother of the late Diana, Princess of Wales) complained to the European Commission of Human Rights about the publication in the *News of the World* on 2 April 1995 of an article entitled *Di's sister-in-law in booze and bulimia clinic*. Close friends of the applicants were referred to as sources. The Spencers also complained about the publication of another article by the *Daily Mirror* on 3 April 1995. They argued before the Commission that by the time the second article was published the matter was in the public domain.

The roles of the parties in *Earl Spencer v The United Kingdom* were the opposite of **20.25** what one might expect. The claimants, who had not sued the newspapers in England, argued that there is no law of privacy in the United Kingdom and that the principle of confidentiality did not give them adequate protection. The government, as respondent to the claim of breach of human rights, argued that the

---

[36] And see the observations of Lord Goff of Chieveley in *Attorney-General v Guardian Newspapers Ltd (No 2)* [1990] 1 AC 109, 286 where he says that the remedy of damages is now available in breach of confidence cases.

[37] [1990] 1 AC 109.

[38] ibid, at 282.

[39] (1998) 25 EHRR CD 105.

claimants had not exhausted their domestic remedies as they were required to do by Article 35(1) of the Convention. The government therefore found itself contending for the protection of individual privacy. This case[40] is a useful starting place for anyone who has to argue that there is no right of privacy in English law.

20.26 The Commission was unimpressed with the argument that the *Daily Mirror* article on 3 April contained material which was in the public domain. The Commission took the pragmatic view that if an injunction had been granted on 2 April restraining the publication of further information that would have had, at least, a deterrent effect on any newspaper which had notice of the injunction. The problem which the Spencers addressed is only a significant one if damages are not available, a topic to be considered below.[41]

No obligation of confidence

20.27 This defence was also relied on in *Earl Spencer v The United Kingdom*. It was said on behalf of the Spencers, in support of the argument that English law did not provide protection, that it must be shown that the relevant newspaper had been put on notice prior to publication that the disclosure amounted to a breach of a duty of confidence owed by their friends to the Spencers. Accordingly they would have had to prove in their case that the newspapers had the requisite notice both of the friends' duty of confidence and of their breach of that duty. Moreover, they argued, such a duty will not exist in the majority of cases of media intrusion and, if it exists, it is difficult to establish. Further this task is rendered more difficult by the protection afforded to newspapers (by Article 10 of the Convention and by domestic law) as regards revealing their sources[42] and the fact that information will often be provided to the newspapers anonymously. If establishing such a duty is possible, it will often relate to some only of the published material and, in such circumstances, the applicants submitted, if a claimant cannot prove that the information was unavailable to the defendant by any other means, the claimant's claim will fail.

20.28 This is a difficult argument in light of the broad circumstances in which the courts will imply a duty of confidence.[43] It found little favour with the Commission in *Earl Spencer v The United Kingdom* and it is unlikely to succeed in the future in view of the tentative recognition of the existence of a right of privacy in English law in the new cases discussed in part E below.

---

[40] Which is considered further at para 20.47 below.
[41] At para 20.31.
[42] See *Goodwin v The United Kingdom* (1996) 22 EHRR 123.
[43] See para 20.11 above.

Public interest

There are limits to the doctrine of confidentiality. There is no confidence in the **20.29** disclosure of iniquity.[44] Beyond that, although the basis of the law's protection of confidence is that there is a public interest in confidences being preserved and protected by the law, nevertheless as Lord Goff made clear in *Attorney-General v Guardian Newspapers (No 2)*,[45] that public interest may be outweighed by some other countervailing public interest which favours disclosure.[46] This has general application.

Remedies

Injunctions

The right of confidentiality is an equitable right which is usually protected by the **20.30** grant of an injunction.[47] The powers of the courts with equitable jurisdiction to grant injunctions are, subject to any relevant statutory restrictions, unlimited.[48] It is well established that misuse of confidential information can be restrained by injunction.[49]

Damages

Under Lord Cairns' Act 1858 damages may be granted in substitution for an **20.31** injunction; yet, as Megarry VC pointed out in *Malone v Metropolitan Police Commissioner*,[50] if there is no case for the grant of an injunction, as where the disclosure has already been made, the unsatisfactory result seems to be that no damage can be awarded under this head.[51]

> In such a case [Megarry VC said] where there is no breach of contract or other orthodox foundation for damages at common law, it seems doubtful whether there is any right to damages as distinct from an account of the profits. It may be, however, that a new tort is emerging (see Goff and Jones, *The Law of Restitution*, 2nd ed (1978) 518, 519, and Gareth Jones (1970) 86 LQR 463, 491) though this has been

---

[44] This is a dictum of Page-Wood VC in *Gartside v Outram* (1856) 26 LJ Ch 113, 114, and see *Initial Services Ltd v Putterill* [1968] 1 QB 396, 405 and *Fraser v Evans* [1969] 1 QB 349, 362.

[45] [1990] 1 AC 109, 282. See also *Beloff v Pressdram Ltd* [1973] 1 All ER 241, 260; *Lion Laboratories Ltd v Evans* [1985] QB, 526, 550; *Malone v Metropolitan Police Commissioner* [1979] 1 Ch 344, 361–362, 377; and *Hellewell v Chief Constable of Derbyshire* [1995] 1 WLR 804, 807.

[46] In *Venables v News Group Newspapers Ltd* [2001] Fam 430, 448 at para 33, Butler-Sloss P suggests that Lord Goff's limiting principle 'cannot stand' in the light of s 12 of the Human Rights Act 1998 and Art 10(1) of the Convention. 'Cannot stand' would mean 'be replaced by' because s 12 requires a similar balancing act.

[47] *Malone v Metropolitan Police Commissioner* [1979] 1 Ch 344, 360.

[48] I Spry, *The Principles of Equitable Remedies* (5th edn, 1997) 323 and see *Broadmoor Special Hospital Authority v Robinson* [2000] QB 775, 786 and the *Venables* case [2001] Fam 430, 447 at para 29.

[49] *Argyll v Argyll* [1967] Ch 303 and *Francome v Mirror Group Newspapers* [1984] 1 WLR 892.

[50] [1979] 1 Ch 344, 360.

[51] See *Proctor v Bayley* (1889) 42 Ch D 390.

doubted: see Street, *The Law of Torts*, 6th ed (1976) 377. Certainly the subject raises many questions which are unresolved.

20.32   Lord Goff, as a member of the House of Lords rather than the joint author of *The Law of Restitution*, dealt with the matter in robust terms in *Attorney-General v Guardian Newspapers Limited (No 2)*:[52]

> The plaintiff's claim to restitution is usually enforced by an account of the profits made by his wrong at the plaintiff's expense. This remedy of an account is an alternative to the remedy of damages, which in cases of breach of confidence is now available despite the equitable nature of the wrong, through a beneficent interpretation of the Chancery Amendment Act 1858 (Lord Cairns' Act), and which by reason of the difficulties attending the taking of an account is often regarded as a more satisfactory remedy, at least in cases where the confidential information is of a commercial nature, and quantifiable damages may therefore have been suffered.

20.33   In the same year the Court of Appeal in New Zealand said that for breach of confidence 'a full range of remedies should be available, as appropriate, no matter whether they originated in common law, equity or statute.'[53]

20.34   The applicants in *Earl Spencer v The United Kingdom*[54] raised doubts as to the availability of damages for breach of confidence where an injunction could not have been granted, citing *Malone v Metropolitan Police Commissioner*. The Commission however considered that the extract quoted from the speech of Lord Goff in *Attorney-General v Guardian Newspapers Limited (No 2)*,[55] handed down more than ten years after the *Malone* case in the High Court, at the very least, shows the developing state of the law relating to the award of damages.

20.35   Lord Scott in his essay on confidentiality[56] says the misuse of information can be restrained by injunction (for example *Argyll v Argyll*,[57] *Francome v Daily Mirror*[58]) or, if disclosure has already occurred, be remedied by an award of damages (*Stephens v Avery*[59]). This must be correct. If English law has reached the conclusion that there is a right of privacy, remedies should not be a problem. There is still life in the equitable maxim *equity will not suffer a wrong to be without a remedy.*[60]

---

[52] [1990] 1 AC 109, 286.
[53] *Acquaculture Corp v New Zealand Green Mussel Co Ltd* [1990] 3 NZLR 299, 301 *per* Cooke P.
[54] [1998] 25 EHRR CD 105, 114.
[55] In paragraph 20.32 above.
[56] See n 13 above.
[57] [1967] 1 Ch 302.
[58] [1984] 1 WLR 892.
[59] [1988] Ch 449.
[60] See *Snell's Equity* (30th edn) 28 at para 3.02.

C. Regulation

The Press Complaints Commission

In 1991 the Press Complaints Commission was set up by the newspaper industry   **20.36**
for the purpose of self-regulation. It offers a claimant against a newspaper an alternative to the hazards of litigation, but it is a body with few teeth. The Commission
is charged with the enforcement of a Code of Conduct which was drafted by the
newspaper industry's code committee and was approved by the Commission in
June 1993. The Code states that members of the press have a duty to maintain the
highest professional standards and that in doing so they should have regard to the
Code of Practice. The Code includes provisions in relation to privacy, harassment,
and listening devices and it contains exceptions to all these clauses based on public interest.

Clause 3 of the Code of Conduct is headed 'Privacy' and provides: **20.37**

   (i) Every one is entitled to respect for his or her private and family life, home, health
       and correspondence. A publication will be expected to justify intrusions into
       any individual's private life without consent.
  (ii) The use of long lens photography to take pictures of people in private places
       without their consent is unacceptable.

Note: Private places are public or private property where there is a reasonable expectation of privacy.

Clause 4 of the Code is headed 'Harassment' and provides: **20.38**

   (i) Journalists and photographers must neither obtain nor seek to obtain informa-
       tion or pictures through intimidation, harassment or persistent pursuit.
  (ii) They must not photograph individuals in private places (as defined by the note
       to clause 3) without their consent, must not persist in telephoning, questioning,
       pursuing or photographing individuals after having been asked to desist, must
       not remain on their property after having been asked to leave and must not fol-
       low them.

Clause 8 deals with listening devices and states: **20.39**

Journalists must not obtain or publish material obtained by using clandestine listening devices or by intercepting private telephone conversations.

These specific provisions of the Code are all subject to public interest exceptions.   **20.40**
'Public interest' is not exhaustively defined but is said to include:

   (i)   Detecting or exposing crime or a serious misdemeanour;
  (ii)   Protecting public health and safety;
  (iii) Preventing the public from being misled by some statement or action of an
       individual or organisation.

If a newspaper has been found to be in breach of the Code of Practice, the news-   **20.41**
paper is bound to print the adjudication by the Commission in full and with due

prominence. However, the Commission has no legal power to prevent the publication of material, to enforce its rulings or to grant any legal remedy against the newspaper in favour of the victim. Notwithstanding these limitations, as the Code has been agreed by the industry, it is likely to be something that the courts will take into account in developing the law of privacy.

Regulation of broadcasting

20.42 The Broadcasting Act 1996 set up a Broadcasting Standards Commission which has a duty to:

> draw up and from time to time review a code giving guidance as to the principles to be observed and the practices to be followed in connection with the avoidance of
> (a) unjust or unfair treatment in programmes . . .
> (b) unwarranted infringement of privacy in or in connection with the obtaining of material contained in such programmes.[61]

All television and radio services provided by the BBC and other television and radio companies in the United Kingdom come within the remit of the Commission.

20.43 The Act establishes a complaints procedure.[62] The Commission investigates complaints involving allegations of infringement of privacy concerning programmes that have been broadcast. It is under a duty to send a statement of its findings to the complainant.[63] It may also give directions for the publication of its findings.[64] Like the Press Complaints Commission it has no power to award compensation to a person whose privacy has been infringed.

D. Protection of Privacy

The Protection from Harassment Act

20.44 Some additional protection for an individual's privacy is now given by the Protection from Harassment Act 1997. Section 1(1) provides that a person must not pursue a course of conduct:

(a) which amounts to harassment of another, and

(b) which he knows or ought to know amounts to harassment of the other.

---

[61] Broadcasting Act 1996, s 107.
[62] ibid, ss 110–120.
[63] ibid, s 115(8) and see *R v Broadcasting Complaints Commission, ex p Barclay* (1997) 9 Admin LR 25; *R v Broadcasting Complaints Commission ex p BBC* The Times, 24 Feb 1995; and *R v Broadcasting Complaints Commission, ex p Channel Four Television* [1995] EMLR 170.
[64] ibid, s 119.

Section 3 provides that an actual or apprehended breach of section 1 may be the subject of a claim in civil proceedings, including a claim for damages by the person who is or may be the victim of the course of conduct in question. For an example of how this will work in practice see the judgment of Buxton LJ in *Wainwright v Home Office*.[65]

From confidentiality to privacy

The argument today is that the tort of breach of confidence contains all that is **20.45** necessary for the fair protection of personal privacy, and that it is now a relatively small step to articulate it in that way as was done four years after *Kaye v Robertson*[66] by Laws J in *Hellewell v Chief Constable of Derbyshire*.[67] He said:

> I entertain no doubt that disclosure of a photograph may, in some circumstances, be actionable as a breach of confidence. If a photographer is hired to take a photograph to be used only for certain purposes but uses it for an unauthorised purpose of his own, a claim will lie against him: *Pollard v Photographic Co.* (1888) 40 Ch D 345 . . . If someone with a telephoto lens were to take from a distance and with no authority a picture of another engaged in some private act, his subsequent disclosure of the photograph would, in my judgment, as surely amount to a breach of confidence as if he had found or stolen a letter or diary in which the act was recounted and proceeded to publish it. In such a case, the law would protect what might reasonably be called a right of privacy, although the name accorded to the cause of action would be breach of confidence.

The judge found in the *Hellewell* case that the photograph of the claimant, which **20.46** was taken while he was in custody and given by the police to a shopkeepers' organization, had been used reasonably by the police for the prevention and detection of crime and that the police would have a public interest defence to any action for breach of confidence. He therefore struck out the action. Laws J's observations about a right of privacy were of course obiter but they have been influential in the thinking of lawyers and commentators. The examples given by Laws J of invasions of privacy in the absence of some extant confidential relationship are taken from the speech of Lord Goff in *Attorney-General v Guardian Newspapers Ltd (No 2)*.[68] Lord Goff said:

> I realise that, in the vast majority of cases, in particular those concerned with trade secrets, the duty of confidence will arise from a transaction or relationship between the parties—often a contract—in which event the duty may arise by reason of either an express or an implied term of the contract. It is in such cases as these that the expressions 'confider' and 'confidant' are perhaps most aptly employed. But it is well settled that a duty of confidence may arise in equity independently of such cases; and I have expressed the circumstances in which the duty may arise in broad terms, not

---

[65] [2002] 3 WLR 405, 420.
[66] [1991] FSR 62.
[67] [1995] 1 WLR 804.
[68] [1990] 1 AC 109, 281 (part of the 'Spycatcher' litigation).

merely to embrace those cases where a third party receives information from a person who is under a duty of confidence in respect of it, knowing that it has been disclosed by that person to him in breach of his duty of confidence, but also to include certain situations, beloved of law teachers—where an obviously confidential document is wafted by an electric fan out of a window into a crowded street, or where an obviously confidential document such as a private diary, is dropped in a public place, and is then picked up by a passer-by. I also have in mind the situations where secrets of importance to national security come into the possession of members of the public . . .

The decision in *Earl Spencer v The United Kingdom*

20.47 The *Earl Spencer v The United Kingdom* case came before the European Commission of Human Rights on 16 January 1998. Some of the arguments which were advanced by the parties have already been considered.[69] The question before the Commission was whether the applicants had exhausted their domestic remedies. The Commission undertook a detailed review of the English authorities, and its own earlier decision in the *Winer* case[70] in which it had expressed the view that the failure to bring a breach of confidence action did not constitute a failure to exhaust domestic remedies in view of the uncertainty as to the precise scope and extent of that remedy. The Commission found that the law had moved on. It found that the domestic courts had extended and developed the relevant principles of confidentiality since the *Winer* decision. The Commission said:

> the parties' submissions indicate that the remedy of breach of confidence (against the newspapers and their sources) was available to the applicants and the applicants have not demonstrated that it was insufficient or ineffective in the circumstances of the cases. It considers that, in so far as relevant doubts remain concerning the financial awards to be made following a finding of breach of confidence, they are not such as to warrant a conclusion that the breach of confidence action is ineffective or insufficient but rather a conclusion that the matter should be put to the domestic courts for consideration in order to allow those courts, through the common law system in the United Kingdom, the opportunity to develop existing rights by way of interpretation.

20.48 The finding of the European Commission of Human Rights echoed what members of the House of Lords had said in *R v Khan (Sultan)*,[71] a case that was largely decided on the question of the admissibility of evidence, but in which the police had installed a listening device. Lord Nicholls said:[72]

> . . . the appellant contended for a right of privacy in respect of private conversations in private houses. I prefer to express no view, either way, on the existence of such a right. This right if it exists, can only do so as part of a larger and wider right of

---

[69] See paras 20.24–20.28 above.
[70] Application 10871/84, (1986) 48 DR 154, 170.
[71] [1997] AC 558.
[72] ibid, at 592.

privacy. The difficulties attendant on this controversial subject are well known. Equally well known is the continuing, widespread concern at the apparent failure of the law to give individuals a reasonable degree of protection from unwarranted intrusion in many situations. I prefer to leave open for another occasion the important question whether the present piecemeal protection of privacy has now developed to the extent that a more comprehensive principle can be seen to exist.

Lord Slynn expressed similar views, as did Lord Browne-Wilkinson who referred **20.49** to the provisions of the European Convention for the Protection of Human Rights, Article 8 of which provides for a right of privacy but always subject to certain exceptions. He also referred to Article 13 which requires that domestic law must provide an effective remedy for any breach of Article 8. He added that in the circumstances, the question whether English law recognizes a right of privacy, and if so what are the limitations of such right, is likely to come before the House of Lords for decision in the future. Until then he preferred to express no view on the question.

The Human Rights Act 1998

The Human Rights Act 1998 was brought into force on 2 October 2000. It **20.50** requires every public authority, including the courts, to act consistently with the European Convention for the Protection of Human Rights and Fundamental Freedoms.[73] What this means is the subject of sharp division and debate among both practising and academic lawyers: does it simply require the courts' procedures to be Convention-compliant, or does it require the law applied by the courts, save where primary legislation plainly says otherwise, to give effect to the Convention principles?[74] The Human Rights Act is the subject of chapter 21 below. Here it is sufficient to say that the Convention rights include Article 8, the right to respect for private and family life, Article 10, freedom of expression and Article 13, the right to an effective remedy. The interplay of these articles is considered in *Douglas v Hello! Ltd*,[75] *Venables v News Group Newspapers Ltd*[76] and *A v B plc*,[77] as is section 12 of the Human Rights Act 1998 which applies if a court is considering whether to grant any relief which, if granted, might affect the exercise of the Convention right to freedom of expression. Section 12(3) provides that no such relief is to be granted so as to restrain publication before trial unless the court is satisfied that the applicant is likely to establish that publication should not be allowed.

---

[73] Human Rights Act 1998, s 6(1).
[74] Sedley LJ in *Douglas v Hello! Ltd* [2001] 2 QB 967, 1001 at para 128.
[75] [2001] QB 967.
[76] [2001] Fam 430.
[77] [2002] 3 WLR 542.

E. The New Cases

The *Douglas* case: the facts

20.51 The *Douglas* case was in effect a battle between the magazines *OK* and *Hello!*. Michael Douglas and Catherine Zeta-Jones agreed to give *OK* the exclusive right to publish photographs of their wedding at the Plaza hotel in New York on 18–19 November 2000. No one else was allowed to take photographs and the couple retained the right to veto any photograph which *OK* wanted to publish. The day after the wedding *Hello!* threatened to publish nine photographs which had been taken surreptitiously, though it was not known whether they were taken by an employee or guest or by an intruder. If the photographs were taken by an intruder there was no relationship of confidence. On 20 November Mr and Mrs Douglas and *OK* were granted an ex parte injunction which was renewed after an inter partes hearing on 21 November. *Hello!* appealed. Robert Walker LJ and Ward LJ could not agree and the case was reargued before a three-judge court. On 23 November the Court of Appeal allowed the appeal. It held that though Mr and Mrs Douglas might establish at trial that publication should not be allowed on grounds of confidentiality, this was likely to be insufficient to tilt the balance against publication; in view of the organized publicity and the retained element of privacy damages would be an adequate remedy.

The *Venables* case: the facts

20.52 *Venables v News Group Newspapers*[78] was a much more serious case. At the age of 11 the claimants, Jon Venables and Robert Thompson, had been convicted of the murder of the two-year-old Jamie Bulger. The case was widely publicized by the media. Shortly before their release from detention at the age of 18 Dame Elizabeth Butler-Sloss had to consider whether injunctions should be granted restraining the publication of information as to the physical appearance, whereabouts or movements of the two young men. In a judgment which reviewed the authorities the President decided that injunctions should be granted against the world. She said:

> . . . in my judgment the case stands or falls on the application to it of the law of confidence.

An analysis of the judgments in the *Douglas* case

Sedley LJ

20.53 Sedley LJ first set out his conclusions. These included: the two first named claimants have a legal right to respect for their privacy, which has been infringed;

---

[78] [2001] Fam 430.

and the circumstances of the infringements are such that the claimants should be left to their remedy in damages.

Then looking at the history of the law of confidentiality he observed[79] that the **20.54** courts have done what they can, using such legal tools as were to hand, to stop the more outrageous invasions of individuals' privacy; but they have felt unable to articulate their measures as a discrete principle of law.

> Nevertheless, [he said] we have reached a point at which it can be said with confidence that the law recognises and will appropriately protect a right of personal privacy.

Sedley LJ gave two reasons for this clear statement. First, equity and the common **20.55** law are today in a position to respond to an increasingly invasive social environment by affirming that everybody has a right to some private space. Secondly and in any event, the Human Rights Act 1998 requires the courts to give appropriate effect to the right to respect for private and family life set out in Article 8 of the European Convention on the Protection of Human Rights. Sections 2 and 6 of the Human Rights Act require the courts of this country to take into account jurisprudence of both the Commission and the European Court of Human Rights which points to a positive institutional obligation to respect privacy; they must themselves act compatibly with that and other Convention rights. This, Sedley LJ says arguably, gives the final impetus to the recognition of a right of privacy in English law.

A right of privacy was material to the *Douglas* case because on the evidence it was **20.56** possible that the photographer was an intruder. If it was an employee or guest the received law of confidence would probably have been sufficient for the claimants.

Sedley LJ reviewed the authorities, ending with the European Commission's conclusion in *Earl Spencer v The United Kingdom*[80] that the tort of breach of confidence was now well established; that its scope and extent, in particular as to damages were still in issue; but that the remedy was available to the applicants and the applicants had not demonstrated that it was insufficient or ineffective in the circumstances of their cases.

Sedley LJ said: **20.58**

> the fact that this unanimous conclusion could emerge from a detailed consideration, after written and oral argument, of the state of the extant English authorities by a body of distinguished European jurists is of real persuasive force. It would not be a happy thing if the national courts were to go back without cogent reason on the United Kingdom's successful exegesis of its own law.

---

[79] [2001] QB 967 at para 110.
[80] 25 EHRR CD 105.

20.59 Sedley LJ's conclusion, at the lowest, was that there was a powerfully arguable case to advance at trial that the first two claimants had a right of privacy which English law would recognize and, where appropriate, protect.

20.60 Sedley LJ summarized his conclusions on the Human Rights Act 1998 in this way:

> For reasons I have given, Mr Douglas and Ms Zeta-Jones have a powerful prima facie claim to redress for invasion of their privacy as a qualified right recognised and protected by English law. The case being one which affects the Convention right of freedom of expression, section 12 of the Human Rights Act 1998 requires the court to have regard to article 10 (as in its absence, would section 6). This, however, cannot, consistently with section 3 and article 17, give the article 10(1) right of freedom of expression a presumptive priority over other rights. What it does is require the court to consider article 10(2) along with article 10(1), and by doing so to bring into the frame the conflicting right to respect for privacy. This right, contained in article 8 and reflected in English law, is in turn qualified in both contexts by the right of others to free expression. The outcome, which self-evidently has to be the same under both articles, is determined principally by considerations of proportionality.

These steps in this closely reasoned passage are considered in detail in the next chapter.

Keene LJ

20.61 Keene LJ was more circumspect. He found it unlikely, because of developments in the common law relating to confidence and the apparent obligation on English courts now to take account of the right to respect for private and family life under Article 8 when interpreting the common law, that *Kaye v Robertson*[81] which held there was no actionable right of privacy in English law would be decided the same way today.[82] He referred to *Argyll v Argyll*[83] and *Attorney-General v Guardian Newspapers Ltd (No 2)*,[84] which do not appear to have been cited to the court in *Kaye v Robertson,* and noted that in the latter decision the House of Lords had made it clear that a duty of confidence could arise from the circumstances in which the information was obtained, so that the recipient was to be precluded from disclosing it to others. Keene LJ therefore concluded:

> Consequently if the present case concerned a truly private occasion, where the persons involved made it clear that they intended it to remain private and undisclosed to the world, then I might well have concluded that in the current state of English law the claimants were likely to succeed at any eventual trial . . . But if persons choose to lessen the degree of privacy attaching to an otherwise private occasion,[85] then the balance to be struck between their rights and other considerations is likely to be affected.

---

[81] [1991] FSR 62.
[82] [2001] QB 967, 1012 at para 167.
[83] [1967] Ch 602.
[84] [1990] 1 AC 109.
[85] eg by arranging, as Mr and Mrs Douglas did, for their wedding to be featured in *OK* magazine.

Brooke LJ

Brooke LJ contented himself with the luxury of identifying difficult issues,[86] with-　**20.62**
out being obliged to solve them, but his judgment points the same way. He said:[87]

> It is well known that this court in *Kaye v Robertson* [[1991] FSR 62] said in uncom-
> promising terms that there was no tort of privacy known to English law. In contrast
> both academic commentary and extra-judicial commentary by judges over the last
> ten years have suggested from time to time that a development of the present fron-
> tiers of a breach of confidence action could fill the gap in English law which is filled
> by privacy in other developed countries. This commentary was given a boost recently
> by the decision of the European Commission of Human Rights in *Earl Spencer v
> United Kingdom* (1998) 25 EHRR CD 105, and by the coming into force of the
> Human Rights Act 1998.

Brooke LJ based his decision on section 12(4) of the Human Rights Act 1998　**20.63**
which provides:

> The court must have particular regard to the importance of the convention right to
> freedom of expression and, where the proceedings relate to material which the
> respondent claims, or which appears to the court to be journalistic, literary or artis-
> tic material (or to conduct connected to such material), to
>
> (a) the extent to which—
>   (i) the material has, or is about to become available to the public; or
>   (i) it is, or would be, in the public interest for the material to be published;
> (b) any relevant privacy code.

Brooke LJ's conclusion was that this provision, read together with the privacy　**20.64**
rules of the Press Complaints Commission's Code of Practice,[88] meant that a
newspaper which flouts clause 3 of the Code is likely to have its claim to an entitlement to freedom of expression trumped by Article 10(2) considerations of privacy. He said he was satisfied that on the present untested evidence the claimants
were likely to establish that publication should not be allowed on confidentiality
grounds.

Injunctive relief refused

All members of the Court were nevertheless agreed that injunctive relief should　**20.65**
not be granted. Keene LJ put the matter in this way:

> In the present case, it is of considerable relevance that very widespread publicity was
> given in any event to the wedding very soon afterwards by way of photographs in
> 'OK!' magazine . . .
>   It may be that a limited degree of privacy remains in such a situation and it
> could be at trial the claimants would succeed in obtaining a permanent injunction.
> There must still be some doubt about that. But even if the claimants had passed that

---

[86] [2001] QB 967, at para 91.
[87] ibid, at para 61.
[88] See para 20.37 above.

threshold of showing that it is likely that they would obtain an injunction at trial, the court in exercising its discretion at the interlocutory stage must still take account of the widespread publicity arranged by the claimant for this occasion. When that organised publicity is balanced against the impact for the defendants of an injunction restraining publication, I have no doubt that the scales come down in this case against prior restraint. This is a matter where any damage to the claimants can adequately be dealt with in monetary terms.

An analysis of the judgment in the *Venables* case

20.66   In the *Venables* case Dame Elizabeth Butler-Sloss P was asked to break new ground in granting injunctions to protect Jon Venables and Robert Thompson. She recognized that in doing so she was extending the law of confidence. She relied on the Human Rights Act and the European Convention for the Protection of Human Rights and followed the lead given by the Court of Appeal in the *Douglas* case. Although the language she used is the language of confidentiality, the rights to which she gave recognition are in essence rights of privacy.

Submissions on behalf of the Attorney-General

20.67   The issue before the court was, is there jurisdiction to grant an injunction in respect of an adult to protect his identity and whereabouts?[89] A number of significant submissions were made on behalf of the Attorney-General. First, that there was an existing law of confidence and it covered identification information which the claimants sought to have protected. Secondly, there did not need to be a formal relationship between the parties. Thirdly, having regard to the case law and to the values enshrined in Article 8 of the Convention, it seemed clear that information the disclosure of which would substantially impair a person's private life and imperil his safety must be capable of protection. Fourthly, a restriction was necessary notwithstanding the general public interest in knowing the identity of those responsible for serious crime.[90]

Application of the Convention

20.68   Before turning to the question of whether there was jurisdiction to grant injunctions, the President considered the preliminary issue of whether the European Convention applied, and concluded in the light of the judgments in the *Douglas* case that she had to apply Article 10 directly to the case.[91] The President held that the claimants could not rely in private law proceedings upon a freestanding application under the Convention, but that they could rely on the tort of breach of confidence which is a recognized cause of action in English law and the court, in

---

[89]   [2001] Fam 430, 441 at para 10.
[90]   ibid, 444 at para 20.
[91]   ibid, 446 at para 26.

light of the Human Rights Act 1998, would be bound to take into account the impact of the Convention on that right.

Article 10: freedom of expression

In section 12 of the Human Rights Act 1998 special provisions are made in rela- **20.69** tion to applications to restrict freedom of expression. Section 12(4) states 'The court must have particular regard to the importance of the Convention right to freedom of expression . . .'. There is no doubt, therefore, that Parliament placed great emphasis upon the importance of Article 10 of the Convention and the protection of freedom of expression, inter alia, for the press and the media. The President said[92] that the Human Rights Act and the Convention reinforce and give greater weight to the principles already established in English case law, and referred to *R v The Secretary of State for the Home Department, ex p Simms*[93] and *R v Central Independent Television plc* where Lord Hoffmann said:[94]

> Freedom means the right to publish things which government and judges, however well motivated, think should not be published. It means the right to say things which 'right-thinking people' regard as dangerous or irresponsible. This freedom is subject only to clearly defined exceptions laid down by common law or statute.

The President also referred[95] to Sedley LJ's judgment in the *Douglas* case where he **20.70** said that section 12 of the Human Rights Act on its proper construction requires the court to consider Article 10(2) along with Article 10(1) and by doing so brings into the frame the conflicting right to respect for privacy. The President said that the conflict that may arise between Articles 10(1) and 10(2) has to be resolved.

The President stated:[96] **20.71**

> The onus of proving the case that freedom of expression must be restricted is firmly upon the applicant seeking relief. The restrictions sought must, in the circumstances of the present case, be shown to be in accordance with the law, justifiable as necessary to satisfy a strong and pressing social need, convincingly demonstrated, to restrain the press in order to protect the rights of the claimants to confidentiality, and proportionate to the legitimate aim pursued. The right to confidence is however, a recognised exception within article 10(2) and the tort of breach of confidence was the domestic remedy upon which the European Commission, in *Earl Spencer v United Kingdom* (1998) 25 EHRR CD 105, declared inadmissible an application by Lord and Lady Spencer on the basis that they had not exhausted their domestic remedies.

---

[92] ibid, 448 at para 36.
[93] [2000] 2 AC 115, 126 *per* Lord Steyn.
[94] [1994] Fam 192, 202–204.
[95] [2001] Fam 430, 450 at para 40.
[96] ibid, 451 at para 44.

Articles 2, 3 and 8

20.72 The President then set out Article 2 (right to life), Article 3 (prohibition of torture) and Article 8 (right to respect for private and family life), and noted that there is to be no derogation from the rights set out in Articles 1 and 3.

Conclusions

20.73 The President stated her conclusions on jurisdiction in section E of her judgment.[97] She said the starting point is the well-recognized position of the press:

> I am being asked to extend the domestic law of confidence to grant injunctions in this case. I am satisfied that I can only restrict the freedom of the media to publish if the need for those restrictions can be shown to fall within the exceptions set out in article 10(2) . . . all the criteria in article 10(2), narrowly interpreted, must be met.

20.74 The President considered each limb in turn, starting with 'in accordance with the law'. She said:

> I am satisfied that, taking into account the effect of the Convention on our law, the law of confidence can extend to cover the injunctions sought in this case and, therefore, the restrictions imposed are in accordance with law. There is a well-established cause of action in the tort of breach of confidence in respect of which injunctions may be granted. The common law continues to evolve, as it has done for centuries, and it is being given considerable impetus to do so by the implementation of the Convention into our domestic law.

20.75 The President was encouraged[98] by the observations of Brooke LJ and Keene LJ in the *Douglas* case[99] that breach of confidence is a developing area of the law, and then came to what she described as the crucial question:[100]

> The duty of confidence may arise in equity independently of a transaction or relationship between the parties. In this case it would be a duty placed upon the media. A duty of confidence does already arise when confidential information comes to the knowledge of the media, in circumstances in which the media have notice of its confidentiality. An example is the medical reports of a private individual . . . the issue is whether the information leading to disclosure of the claimants' identity and location comes within the confidentiality brackets. In answering that crucial question I can properly rely upon the European case law and the duty on the court, where necessary, to take appropriate steps to safeguard the physical safety of the claimants, including the adoption of measures even in the sphere of relations of individuals and/or private organisations between themselves. Under the umbrella of confidentiality there will be information which may require a special quality of protection. In the present case the reason for advancing that special quality is that, if the information was published, the publication would be likely to lead to grave and possibly fatal consequences.

---

[97] [2001] Fam 430, 460 at para 75.
[98] ibid, 461 at para 80.
[99] The passages are [2001] QB 967, 984 at para 61, and 1011 at para 165.
[100] [2001] Fam 430, 462 at para 81.

The President found that the second criterion of Article 10(2) was met. There was **20.76** a strong and pressing social need that the confidentiality of Jon Venables and Robert Thompson be protected.[101]

The President also found that the restrictions sought were proportionate to the **20.77** legitimate aim pursued. This was because she was satisfied that there was a real and serious risk to the rights of the claimants under Articles 2 and 3, that is there was a threat to their lives and a risk that they might suffer inhuman or degrading treatment. The President left open the question whether it would have been right to grant an injunction if these threats had not existed and if only Article 8 was likely to be breached. She said:

> Serious though the breach of the claimants' right to respect for family life and privacy would be, once the journalists and photographers discovered them, and despite the likely serious adverse effect on efforts to rehabilitate them into society, it might not be sufficient to meet the importance of the preservation of the freedom of expression in article 10(1).

To sum up, the decision in the *Venables* case is founded on the principle of confi- **20.78** dentiality and is an extension of that principle. The protection which the court provided is more aptly described as a protection of the claimant's privacy than protection of any confidential information.

Wainwright v Home Office

The claimants in *Wainwright v Home Office*[102] succeeded at first instance in recov- **20.79** ering damages for breach of the right to privacy, the trial judge basing his conclusion in part on the judgment of Sedley LJ in the *Douglas* case and in part on the Human Rights Act 1998. Importantly it was not a case in which the claimants, Mrs Wainwright and her son, complained or could have complained that any breach of confidence had been infringed.

The Wainwrights were strip searched for drugs on a prison visit. The search was **20.80** not conducted according to prison rules, and the claimants were humiliated and distressed. No drugs were found. The son aged 21, who was mentally impaired and suffered from cerebral palsy, developed post-traumatic stress syndrome. The judge awarded both mother and son aggravated damages for infringement of their right of privacy and the son damages for battery. The Home Office was successful in its appeal on the privacy issue.

The prison visit took place before the Human Rights Act came into force. The **20.81** ratio of the Court of Appeal's decision was that there was no right of privacy at common law before the Human Rights Act was passed, and that the Act could not

---

[101] ibid, para 82.
[102] [2002] 3 WLR 405.

be relied on to change substantive law by introducing a retrospective right to privacy which did not exist at common law.

20.82 Lord Woolf pointed out that in the *Douglas* case where Sedley LJ 'in his most instructive judgment was dealing with the question is there a right of privacy in English law' the acts complained of by Michael Douglas and Catherine Zeta-Jones had occurred after the Human Rights Act came into force on 2 October 2000.[103] Lord Woolf did not say expressly whether he agreed with Sedley LJ's judgment.

20.83 Mummery LJ said there was no tort of invasion of privacy. Instead there were torts protecting a person's interest in the privacy of his body, his home and his personal property. There was also available the equitable doctrine of breach of confidence for the protection of personal information, private communications and correspondence.[104] Mummery LJ said:

> As to the future I foresee serious definitional difficulties and conceptual problems in the judicial development of a 'blockbuster' tort vaguely embracing such a potentially wide range of situations. I am not even sure that anybody—the public, Parliament, the press—really wants the creation of a new tort, which could give rise to as many problems as it is sought to solve. A more promising and well trod path is the incremental evolution, both at common law and by statute (eg section 3 of the Protection from Harassment Act 1977), of traditional nominate torts pragmatically crafted as to conditions of liability, specific defences and appropriate remedies, and tailored to suit significantly different privacy interests and infringement situations.

20.84 Buxton LJ in his closely argued judgment agreed that the Home Office's appeal should succeed, but started his judgment by making it clear that if the deplorable conduct meted out to Mrs Wainwright and her son had taken place after the passing of the Protection from Harassment Act 1997 and the Human Rights Act 1998 they would have had a strong case for relief under both Acts: under section 3 of the Harassment Act, and under section 7 of the Human Rights Act by reason of a public authority's lack of regard for Article 8 of the European Convention. The judgment is interesting for its criticisms of the judgment of Sedley LJ in the *Douglas* case, and for its views on the effect of the Human Rights Act, on policy issues concerning privacy and on questions of remoteness of damage.

20.85 Buxton LJ said[105] that all previous investigations of the privacy area were in one way or another cases where confidence can be said to have been broken. That, Buxton LJ said, was of course the case in the *Douglas* case itself. Sedley LJ took a different view. He pointed out that if the photographs of the Douglas wedding were taken by an intruder, there was no relationship of confidence.[106] Sedley LJ's

---

[103] [2002] 3 WLR 405, 412 at para 20.
[104] ibid 419 at para 59.
[105] [2001] QB 967 at para 87.
[106] ibid, at para 112.

observations are not therefore necessarily (as Buxton LJ thought) to be regarded as obiter.

Buxton LJ said that Sedley LJ's observations indubitably demand the closest **20.86** attention. Sedley LJ had said:

> What a conception of privacy does, however, is accord recognition to the fact that the law has to protect not only those persons whose trust has been abused but those who simply find themselves subjected to an unwanted intrusion into their personal lives. The law no longer needs to construct an artificial relationship of confidentiality between the intruder and the victim: it can recognise privacy itself as a legal principle drawn from the fundamental value of personal autonomy.

Buxton LJ commented that Sedley LJ saw the tort as one existing in English private law, independently of the Convention, even though he referred to the 1998 Act as 'arguably [giving] the final impetus to the recognition of a right of privacy in English law'. Buxton LJ, while acknowledging that this was at first sight an attractive prospect, concluded that authority precluded the Court from taking that course and added that there were serious difficulties of principle in the way of judges creating a tort in the terms now suggested.

Buxton LJ criticized the judge for not facing up to the fact that the Convention by **20.87** its terms creates obligations against the state, and not against other private individuals. Buxton LJ pointed out that some have argued that, with the advent of the Human Rights Act 1998, it is possible to use the recognition of the courts as 'public authorities' by section 6(3)(a) of the Human Rights Act to create private law rights broadly in the same verbal terms as the wording of the articles of the Convention. Buxton LJ said there were many difficulties about that contention and he readily adopted Sedley LJ's observation in the *Douglas* case[107] that this was also not the place, without much fuller argument, in which to resolve such a large question. This remains a question for the future. The extent to which the European Convention gives rights against private individuals is a subject which is considered in detail in chapter 21 below. The Convention is not quite as restrictive as Buxton LJ suggests.

Buxton LJ dealt with the substantive provisions of the Human Rights Act in these **20.88** terms:[108]

> . . . it may be convenient to say that, if the events in question had occurred after 2 October 2000, they would in my view have grounded a right to relief for the Wainwrights under section 7(1)(a) of the 1998 Act, by reason of the prison authorities' breach of article 8 of the Convention. That does not, however, engage a private law right in tort, such as the Wainwrights must establish in relation to events occurring before 2 October 2000, because section 7(1)(a) makes the defendants liable on

---

[107] [2001] QB 967, 1001 at para 126.
[108] [2002] 3 WLR 405, 428 at para 93.

the basis of, and only on the basis of, their status as public authorities. I would consider that the right to privacy in article 8(1) had been infringed, and that that breach could not be offset under article 8(2).

Buxton LJ was here rightly accepting that the effect of the Human Rights Act is to give a right of privacy in the terms of Article 8 against public authorities.

20.89 On policy questions Buxton LJ said that what needs to be worked out is the delicate balance, particularly in the area of the publication of information, between the interests on the one hand of the subject and on the other of someone entering his private space, or of the publisher and the latter's audience. He also said that what had to be borne in mind is that what is necessarily proposed is a general tort, available not only to private citizens who simply want to get on with their own lives, like the Wainwrights, but also to corporate bodies that want to keep their affairs private. That, he said, plainly adds a further dimension to attempts to formulate the proper ambit and balance of the tort. In the context of the *Wainwright* case this may well be so, but in the wider context of a tort supported by the European Convention the argument overlooks the fact that the Convention right is a qualified right and Buxton LJ's concerns can be met within the framework of the Convention and the Human Rights Act. This is also true of the concerns which he expressed about remoteness of damage, including the difficult questions he hypothesized: for instance, if non-confidential and true, but private, information is published about someone, with the result that he loses his job, or his marriage.

A v B plc

20.90 *A v B plc*[109] was a case about confidential information. A was a footballer with a premier division football club. B was a national newspaper. C was one of two women with whom A, who is a married man, had affairs. At first instance an injunction was granted to restrain B from publishing the stories which C and the other woman, D, had sold to B recounting their affairs with A. The Court of Appeal, who found that the degree of confidentiality to which the footballer was entitled was very modest, allowed the appeal and discharged the injunction holding that it was most unlikely that a permanent injunction would be granted at trial.

20.91 The judgment of the Court was delivered by Lord Woolf. He said:[110]

> The applications for interim injunctions have now to be considered in the context of articles 8 and 10 of the European Convention for the Protection of Human Rights and Fundamental Freedoms. These articles have provided new parameters within which the court will decide, in an action for breach of confidence, whether a person

---

[109] [2002] 3 WLR 542.
[110] ibid, 546 at para 4.

is entitled to have his privacy protected by the court or whether the restriction of freedom of expression which such protection involves cannot be justified. The court's approach to the issues which the applications raise has been modified because under section 6 of the 1998 Act, the court, as a public authority, is required not to act 'in a way which is incompatible with a Convention right'. The court is able to achieve this by absorbing the rights which articles 8 and 10 protect into the long-established action for breach of confidence. This involves giving a new strength and breadth to the action so that it accommodates the requirements of those articles.

The Court of Appeal was concerned to discourage the excessive citation of author-   **20.92**
ity on applications for interim injunctions and to this end set out guidelines which were intended to assist people to deal with the majority of these applications in a proportionate manner. In particular the Court said that it was most unlikely that any purpose would be served by a judge seeking to decide whether there exists a new cause of action in tort which protects privacy. In the great majority of situations, if not all situations, where the protection of privacy is justified, relating to events after the Human Rights Act 1998 came into force, an action for breach of confidence now will, where this is appropriate, provide the necessary protection. This means that at first instance it can be readily accepted that it is not necessary to tackle the vexed question of whether there is a separate cause of action based upon a new tort involving the infringement of privacy. It is to be hoped that these general words, no doubt well intentioned, will not deter judges from tackling difficult issues of the extent of the new right of privacy where exceptionally these issues arise for decision. In these cases guidelines are no substitute for the consideration of the relevant authorities.

The Court of Appeal also stated[111] that useful guidance on the difficult question   **20.93**
of finding the right balance between privacy and freedom of expression is to be found in the Council of Europe Resolution 1165 of 1998. Detailed consideration is given to the balance to be struck between Articles 8 and 10 of the European Convention for the Protection of Human Rights in chapter 21 below, where the Council of Europe Resolution is further considered. Here it is enough to note that paragraph 12 of the Resolution points out that the right to privacy afforded by Article 8 of the European Convention should not only protect an individual against interference by public authorities, but also against interference by private persons or institutions, including the mass media.

Conclusions

Private individuals are entitled to protection against disclosure without their con-   **20.94**
sent of confidential information about themselves and their activities unless there is a sufficient public interest reason why the information should be disclosed. This

---

[111] ibid, 552 at para 11.

equitable principle affords individuals considerable protection though it was not enough to protect Gordon Kaye.

20.95 Under Article 8 of the European Convention for the Protection of Human Rights everyone has the right to respect for his private and family life, his home and his correspondence. The right is qualified by the matters set out in Article 8(2).

20.96 Under section 6(1) of the Human Rights Act 1998 it is unlawful for a public authority to act in a way that is incompatible with a Convention right. Everyone therefore enjoys a right of privacy against public authorities.[112]

20.97 Paragraph 12 of the Council of Europe Resolution 1165 of 1998 provides that Article 8 should not only protect an individual against interference by public authorities, but also against interference by private persons or institutions, including the mass media. The jurisprudence of the European Court of Human Rights establishes that Article 8 is not restricted to protecting people against public authorities. This is discussed in chapter 21 below. The courts as public authorities are under a positive duty to protect a person against infringements of Convention rights by another private person.[113]

20.98 In *A v B plc* Lord Woolf accepted that the court's approach has been modified because under section 6 of the Human Rights Act 1998, the court, as a public authority, is required not to act 'in a way which is incompatible with a Convention right'. He said the court is able to achieve this by absorbing the rights which Articles 8 and 10 provide into the long-established action for breach of confidence. This involves giving a new strength and breadth to the action so that it accommodates the requirements of those Articles.

20.99 This is very close to the view of Sedley LJ in the *Douglas* case cited in paragraphs 20.53 to 20.60 above, a case in which Keene LJ said that *Kaye v Robertson* would not be decided the same way today.[114] Whilst the matter remains to be considered by the House of Lords the authors' conclusion is that English law will recognize, and where appropriate, protect a right of personal privacy, grounded in the equitable doctrine of breach of confidence, which accords recognition to the fact that the law has to protect not only those whose trust has been abused but also those who find themselves subject to an unwarranted intrusion into their personal lives. The law no longer needs to construct an artificial relationship of confidentiality between intruder and victim: it can recognize privacy as a legal principle drawn from the fundamental value of personal autonomy.[115]

---

[112] See Buxton LJ in *Wainwright v Home Office* [2002] 405, 428 at para 93.
[113] R Clayton, H Tomlinson and C George, *The Law of Human Rights* (2000) ch 5.
[114] [2001] QB 967, 1012 at para 167.
[115] ibid, 1001 at para 126.

The right of personal privacy in English law is qualified by the right of others to **20.100** free expression. Where these rights come into conflict the courts must balance them. The outcome will be determined principally by considerations of proportionality.[116]

F. When Government is Entitled to Protect Information from Disclosure

Lord Scott's second principle

Lord Scott's second principle, it will be remembered,[117] is that government, in the **20.101** widest sense of that term, is not entitled to protection from disclosure of information about itself and its activities unless there is a sufficient public interest requiring the protection of information from disclosure.

Support for this view is to be found in *Attorney-General v Jonathan Cape Ltd*[118] **20.102** where the Court refused to grant an injunction to restrain the publication of the diaries of Richard Crossman. Lord Widgery LCJ said:[119]

> The Attorney-General must show (a) that such publication would be a breach of confidence; (b) that the public interest requires the publication be restrained, and (c) that there are no other facets of the public interest contradictory of and more compelling than that relied upon. Moreover, the court, when asked to restrain such a publication, must closely examine the extent to which relief is necessary to ensure that restrictions are not imposed beyond the strict requirement of public need.

Although this statement has been criticized in an article in the Law Quarterly **20.103** Review,[120] on the grounds that it is contrary to principle and unduly restricts the right of government to restrain disclosure, it was accepted by Mason J in the High Court of Australia in *Commonwealth of Australia v Fairfax & Son Ltd*[121] as correctly elaborating the principle so as to take account of the special character of government.

The Australian view

One of the clearest statements on the matter was made by Mason J in that case **20.104** where he declined to grant an injunction restraining publication of previously

---

[116] *Douglas v Hello! Ltd* [2001] QB 967, 1005 at para 137.
[117] See para 20.07 above.
[118] [1976] QB 752.
[119] ibid, at 770–771.
[120] MW Bryan, 'The Crossman Diaries—Developments in the Law of Breach of Confidence' (1976) 92 LQR 180.
[121] (1980) 147 CLR 39, 50–7.

unpublished communications between the Australian and Indonesian governments on the ground of confidentiality. He said:

> the plaintiff must show, not only that the information is confidential in quality and that it was imparted so as to import an obligation of confidence, but also that there will be 'an unauthorised use of that information to the detriment of the party communicating it' (*Coco v A N Clark (Engineers) Ltd* [1969] RPC 41, 47). The question then, when the executive government seeks the protection given by equity, is: What detriment does it need to show?
>
> The equitable principle has been fashioned to protect the personal, private and proprietary interests of the citizen, not to protect the very different interests of the executive government. It acts, or is supposed to act, not according to standards of private interest, but in the public interest. This is not to say that equity will not protect information in the hands of the government, but it is to say that when equity protects government information it will look at the matter through different spectacles.
>
> It may be a sufficient detriment to the citizen that disclosure of information relating to his affairs will expose his actions to public discussion and criticism. But it can scarcely be a relevant detriment to the government that publication of material concerning its actions will merely expose it to public discussion and criticism. It is unacceptable in our democratic society that there should be a restraint on the publication of information relating to government when the only vice of that information is that it enables the public to discuss, review and criticise government action.
>
> Accordingly, the court will determine the government's claim to confidentiality by reference to the public interest. Unless disclosure is likely to injure the public interest, it will not be protected.
>
> The court will not prevent the publication of information which merely throws light on the past workings of government, even if it be not public property, so long as it does not prejudice the community in other respects. Then disclosure will itself serve the public interest in keeping the community informed and in promoting discussion on public affairs.

A similar approach to the protection from disclosure of confidential information belonging to government was approved in the *Spycatcher* litigation.[122]

The constitutional principle of accountability

20.105 As Lord Scott[123] has said, this is now established as the legally correct approach and corresponds with constitutional principle. Ministers are accountable for what they do as Ministers and for what is done in the departments of which they are in charge. At the heart of the principle of accountability lies an obligation of Ministers to give information about the activities of their departments and about actions and omissions of their civil servants. Sometimes the public interest will require that information be withheld. Information about the operations and per-

---

[122] [1990] 1 AC 109, at first instance (at 151–152), in the Court of Appeal (at 203 and 218) and in the House of Lords (at 257–258, 270 and 283).

[123] See n 13 above.

sonnel of the security and intelligence agencies is an example. But unless there is an acceptable public interest reason for withholding information, the constitutional principle of accountability requires that if information about government or its activities is sought the information should be disclosed. A public interest reason for withholding the information may justify a refusal to disclose it; the confidential character of the information cannot by itself do so.

It seems to Lord Scott that, in principle, no protection should be given against the **20.106** disclosure of confidential information that the government, if asked to do so, ought to disclose. If there is no sufficient public interest to justify the withholding of the information from the public, how can there be a sufficient public interest to restrain the public disclosure of information? In the authors' view there cannot be.

21

THE HUMAN RIGHTS ACT 1998

A. Introduction

Introduction

The Human Rights Act 1998 was brought into force on 2 October 2000. It **21.01** requires every public authority, including the courts, to act consistently with the European Convention for the Protection of Human Rights and Fundamental Freedoms ('the Convention'). The courts will have to do so in relation to the Freedom of Information Act 2000.

Scope of the chapter

21.02   This chapter considers the history of the Convention and the provisions of the Convention which are relevant to freedom of information, and the way in which the Human Rights Act 1998 has incorporated the Convention into English law. It next considers how far, and the extent to which, the Convention gives individuals rights as against other individuals as well as public authorities. The Convention creates by Article 8 a right to respect for private and family life and by Article 10 a right to freedom of expression including the right to receive and impart information and ideas without interference by a public authority and regardless of frontiers. The chapter considers how far these articles have been used by the European Court and Commission for Human Rights to establish a right to know.

21.03   Any freedom of information regime has to grapple with the conflict between the citizen's right to be informed and the right to privacy. Consideration is given to how the European Court of Human Rights ('the Strasbourg Court') has sought to resolve the conflict between Article 8 and Article 10 by applying the principle of proportionality, and what guidance is given to the UK courts about this question by section 12 of the Human Rights Act 1998. Finally the chapter considers the relationship between judicial review in the *Wednesbury* sense and the approach of proportionality applicable in respect of review where Convention rights are at stake, and notes that the English courts are increasingly seeking to find constitutional principles to underlie judicial review. This is a trend which is likely to have consequences for the development of the law of freedom of information.

B. The European Convention for the Protection of Human Rights and Fundamental Freedoms

History

21.04   There was a significant development of human rights law in the aftermath of the Second World War. The Universal Declaration of Human Rights was adopted by 48 members of the United Nations on 10 December 1948. It led the Council of Europe to draft the Convention which was opened for signature in November 1950.

21.05   The United Kingdom played a major part in this process. The Convention was drafted by Sir Oscar Dowson, a former senior legal adviser in the Home Office, and Sir David Maxwell Fyfe QC (who later became the Lord Chancellor, Lord Kilmuir) was a key figure in bringing the project to a successful conclusion.[1] The

---

[1]   A Lester QC, 'Fundamental Rights: the United Kingdom Isolated?' [1984] PL 47.

United Kingdom was the first state to ratify the Convention on 8 March 1951. The Convention came into force on 3 September 1953. The United Kingdom did not, however, adopt the individual right of petition,[2] which gives the Convention its bite, until 1966. The individual right of petition enables citizens to bring governments before the Strasbourg Court. Lord Lester has pointed out[3] that it appears that the timing of the United Kingdom's decision to adopt the individual right of petition was strongly influenced by the wish to prevent an application under the Convention by Burmah Oil to challenge the lawfulness of the War Damage Act 1965 on the ground that it retrospectively overruled the decision of the House of Lords[4] that Burmah Oil was entitled to compensation for wartime damage in Burma.

The Strasbourg Court has taken on an increasing caseload over four decades. As **21.06** Clayton, Tomlinson, and George point out in *The Law of Human Rights,* in the first 20 years of its existence, 1961 to 1981, the Court determined an average of just over two cases a year.[5] In the next decade, this figure rose to nearly 23 a year. By the end of 1999, the total number of cases decided by the Court had reached 1,000, with 177 admissible cases being disposed of in 1999.

Main provisions

Article 1 of the Convention is in the following terms: **21.07**

Obligation to respect human rights
The High Contracting Parties shall secure to everyone within their jurisdiction the rights and freedoms defined in section 1 of this Convention.

The rights and freedoms defined in section 1 of the Convention are those comprised within Articles 2 to 18. The Strasbourg Court in interpreting this provision has not restricted the ambit of the Convention to rights and freedoms against the state. It has construed Article 1 as imposing on states some obligation to provide rights between individuals as well as rights for the individual against the state.[6] In this connection it is to be noted that Article 1 is not included in the 'Convention rights' which are to have effect for the purposes of the Human Rights Act 1998.[7] Its omission from the Human Rights Act reflects the fact that the Act is a domestic human rights instrument. It may have no more significance than that.[8]

---

[2] Article 34.
[3] Lord Lester, 'UK Acceptance of the Strasbourg Jurisdiction: what really went on in Whitehall in 1965' [1998] PL 237.
[4] *Burmah Oil Co Ltd v Lord Advocate* [1965] AC 75.
[5] R Clayton, H Tomlinson and C George, *The Law of Human Rights* (2000) para In.09.
[6] See part D below.
[7] Human Rights Act 1998, s 1(1), (2).
[8] Though Brooke LJ thought it might be significant: *Douglas v Hello! Ltd* [2001] QB 967, 994 at para 91.

21.08   Article 19 establishes the Strasbourg Court and by Article 46 the High Contracting Parties undertake to abide by the final judgments of the Court.

21.09   The following rights and fundamental freedoms set out in the Convention and its Protocols have been ratified by the United Kingdom:[9]

>   the right to life (Article 2);
>   the prohibition of torture (Article 3);
>   the prohibition of slavery and forced labour (Article 4);
>   the right to liberty and security (Article 5);
>   the right to a fair trial (Article 6);
>   no punishment without law (Article 7);
>   the right to respect for private and family life (Article 8);
>   the right to thought, conscience and religion (Article 9);
>   freedom of expression (Article 10);
>   freedom of assembly and association (Article 11);
>   the right to marry (Article 12);
>   the right to an effective remedy (Article 13);[10]
>   the prohibition of discrimination (Article 14);
>   the protection of property (Article 1 of the First Protocol);
>   the right to education (Article 2 of the First Protocol);[11]
>   the right to free elections (Article 3 of the First Protocol);
>   the abolition of the death penalty (Articles 1 and 2 of the Sixth Protocol).

21.10   There is no discrete right to freedom of information under the Convention. The two Articles which come closest to such a right are Articles 8 and 10.[12] Article 8 is in the following terms:

Right to respect for private and family life
1. Everyone has the right to respect for his private and family life, his home and his correspondence.
2. There shall be no interference by a public authority with the exercise of this right except such as is in accordance with the law and is necessary in a democratic society in the interests of national security, public safety or the economic well-being of the country, for the prevention of disorder or crime, for the protection of health or morals, or for the protection of the rights and freedoms of others.

---

[9]   The United Kingdom has not ratified the Fourth and Seventh Protocols which contain the following additional rights and freedoms: prohibition of imprisonment for debt; freedom of movement; prohibition of expulsion of nationals; prohibition of collective expulsion of aliens; procedural safeguards relating to the expulsion of aliens; right of appeal in criminal matters; compensation for wrongful conviction; right not to be tried or punished twice, and equality between spouses.

[10]   The Human Rights Act 1998 does not incorporate Art 13.

[11]   The United Kingdom has entered a reservation to this Article to reflect the principle that children are to be educated in accordance with the wishes of their parents, a principle which is spelt out in the Education Act 1996, s 9. See further Clayton etc (n 5 above) ch 19 from para 19.68.

[12]   These Articles are considered further in part F below.

Article 10 of the Convention is in the following terms: **21.11**

Freedom of Expression

1. Everyone has the right to freedom of expression. This right shall include freedom
   to hold opinions and to receive and impart information and ideas without interference by public authority and regardless of frontiers. This article shall not prevent States from requiring the licensing of broadcasting, television, or cinema
   enterprises.[13]

2. The exercise of these freedoms, since it carries with it duties and responsibilities,
   may be subject to such formalities, conditions, restrictions or penalties as are prescribed by law and are necessary in a democratic society, in the interests of
   national security, territorial integrity or public safety, for the prevention of disorder or crime, for the protection of health or morals, for the protection of the reputation or rights of others, for preventing the disclosure of information received
   in confidence, or for maintaining the authority and impartiality of the judiciary.

Both respect for private and family life and freedom of expression are qualified   **21.12**
rights. Thus in *R(Morgan Grenfell Ltd) v Special Commissioner of Income Tax*[14] the
Court of Appeal, while accepting that legal professional privilege is protected by
Article 8, found that it had to give way to the code established by section 20 of the
Taxes and Management Act 1970 which embodied an investigatory power of
broad ambit conferred by Parliament to counter abuses of the tax system. This was
because Article 8(2) permitted Article 8 rights to be abrogated where it was necessary to do so in the interests of the economic well-being of the country, which
included the public interest in the prompt, fair and complete collection of the
public revenue, and the Human Rights Act did not require the code to be construed otherwise than in accordance with Parliament's manifest intention. Again
in *R v Shayler*[15] the House of Lords held that in view of the special position of
members of the security and intelligence services, and the highly confidential
nature of the information which came into their possession, the interference with
their right to freedom of expression prescribed by the Official Secrets Act 1989
was not greater than was required to achieve the legitimate object of acting in the
interests of national security; and that accordingly sections 1 and 4 of the 1989
Act came within the qualification in Article 10(2) as a justified interference with
the right of free expression guaranteed by Article 10 and were not incompatible
with that Article. The proper application of the Convention requires the court to
balance conflicting rights and qualifications to rights.

---

[13] Regulation of the media is considered briefly in ch 20, part C, above.
[14] [2002] 2 WLR 255.
[15] [2002] 2 WLR 754.

C. The Human Rights Act 1998

A compromise

21.13 The Human Rights Act 1998 is a typical British compromise. It does not incorporate the Convention into English law, which, given the government's intentions, would have been the straightforward thing to do. Instead it requires our courts, as public authorities, to give effect to the Convention (section 6), where possible to interpret Acts of Parliament to comply with the Convention (section 3), to develop the common law to have regard to Convention rights (section 2), and to give effective remedies where there is a breach of those rights (section 8).

21.14 The Lord Chancellor, Lord Irvine was asked to explain, when the Bill was at the report stage in the House of Lords,[16] the difference between all of that and incorporating the Convention. Lord Irvine explained that if the courts found it impossible to construe primary legislation in a way which is compatible with Convention rights, the primary legislation remains in full force and effect. All the courts can do is make a declaration of incompatibility. This means that although the courts are under the interpretative obligation and it is unlawful for public authorities to act in a way which is incompatible with the Convention rights, the Convention itself does not have the force of a UK statute: it does not, therefore, impliedly repeal other statutes.[17] Political pressures seem to have made it necessary to bring the Convention into force in the United Kingdom in a way which did not lay the government open to a charge of surrendering Parliamentary sovereignty. The result is a situation which is more complicated than it needs to be, and which leaves a number of difficult questions to be resolved by the courts.

Convention jurisprudence applies to the common law

21.15 Section 2(1) of the Human Rights Act 1998 provides:

> **Interpretation of Convention Rights**
> 2. (1) A court or tribunal determining a question which has arisen in connection with a Convention right must take into account any—
>> (a) judgment, decision, declaration or advisory opinion of the European Court of Human Rights,
>> (b) opinion of the Commission given in a report under Article 31 of the Convention,[18]
>> (c) decision of the Commission in connection with Article 26 or 27(2) of the Convention,[19] or

---

[16] *Hansard*, HL (series 5) vol 585, cols 421, 422 (29 January 1998).
[17] Clayton etc (n 5 above) ch 3 para 3.89.
[18] ie, a decision on the merits.
[19] ie, a decision on admissibility.

(d) decision of the Committee of Ministers taken under Article 46 of the
    Convention,

whenever made or given, so far as, in the opinion of the court or tribunal, it is
relevant to the proceedings in which that question has arisen.

'Taking into account' is something less than 'being bound by' and it was to be   **21.16**
expected that the Act would take this line because Convention law has no strict
rule of precedence, and the United Kingdom is strictly only bound by cases which
came from the United Kingdom. The courts of England and Wales are, however,
likely to follow decisions of the Strasbourg Court because that court remains the
ultimate arbiter of Convention law. Applicants can still take their cases to the
Strasbourg Court when they have exhausted their local remedies. It therefore
appears, as Clayton, Tomlinson, and George[20] suggest that the effect of section
2(1) is to:

(a) impose a *duty* on the court to take as a starting point relevant Convention case
    law; and

(b) impose a duty to *consider* the relevant case law for the purposes of making its
    adjudication.

It is clear that the Convention does impose such a duty.

Section 2(1) was drafted before the European Court was reorganized by the adop-   **21.17**
tion of the Eleventh Protocol on 1 November 1998. This Protocol amended the
Convention and changed the numbering of the later Articles. It also abolished the
role of the European Commission on Human Rights which had previously determined whether applications were admissible and prepared a report on the merits
of admissible cases which were referred either to the Strasbourg Court or exceptionally to the Council of Ministers of the Council of Europe.[21] The role of the
Commission has been taken over by the Strasbourg Court which now sits full
time,[22] with jurisdiction in all matters regarding the interpretation and application of the Convention including inter-state as well as individual petitions. The
Council of Ministers merely retains a role in supervising the execution of judgments.[23] The new procedure for making an application to the Strasbourg Court is
discussed in *The Law of Human Rights*.[24] One of the tasks of the Commission was
to ascertain the facts. Its reports on the merits are often useful authorities. In the
future, however, it will be to the decisions of the Court that the United Kingdom
courts will chiefly turn.

---

[20] See n 5 above, ch 3 para 3.50.
[21] Under the former Article 32.
[22] Formerly judicial appointments were part time and the Court was not continuously in session.
[23] Former Article 54 now Article 46.
[24] See n 5 above, at ch 23 from para 23.21.

Legislation to be construed as compatible with Convention rights

21.18   Section 3(1) of the Human Rights Act provides that:

> So far as it is possible to do so, primary legislation and subordinate legislation must
> be read and given effect in a way which is compatible with Convention rights.

This is a new rule of construction. The House of Lords has held in *re S (Minors)
(Care Order: Implementation of Care Plan)*[25] that the Human Rights Act reserved
the amendment of primary legislation to Parliament and any purported use of section 3 producing a result which departed substantially from a fundamental feature
of an Act of Parliament was likely to have crossed the boundary between interpretation and amendment. The rule points in a direction in which the courts in
the United Kingdom were already moving. Professor Jeffrey Jowell[26] has pointed
out that rather late in the era of the development of judicial review the courts in
the United Kingdom have begun to base their reasoning upon an explicit recognition of individual democratic rights against the state. One of the clearest statements is in *R v The Secretary of State for the Home Department, ex p Pierson*[27] where
Lord Browne-Wilkinson said:

> A power conferred by Parliament in general terms is not to be taken to authorise the
> doing of acts by the donee of the power which adversely affect the legal rights of the
> citizen or the basic principles on which the law of the United Kingdom is based
> unless the statute conferring the power makes it clear that such was the intention of
> Parliament.

21.19   This formulation is very close to, and perhaps partially explains, the provision in
section 3(1). It is suggested that the only occasions on which a court will be unable
to construe legislation in a way which is compatible with Convention rights is
where the statute uses clear and specific words which have the effect of restricting
the Convention right in question. In these cases the higher courts in the UK may
make a declaration of incompatibility.[28] Where the court is considering whether
to make such a declaration, the Crown is entitled to be heard.[29] A declaration of
incompatibility, however, does not affect the validity, continuing operation or
enforcement of any incompatible legislation.[30]

21.20   If a court has made a declaration of incompatibility the Minister may, by order,
make such amendments to the legislation as he considers necessary to remove the
incompatibility.[31] The procedure is set out in Schedule 2 to the Act.

---

[25]   [2002] 2 WLR 720.

[26]   In 'Beyond the Rule of Law: Towards Constitutional Judicial Review' [2000] PL 671.

[27]   [1998] AC 539, 575.

[28]   Human Rights Act 1998, s 4. For an example of a declaration see *R v Lambert* [2001] 3 WLR
206.

[29]   Human Rights Act 1998, s 5.

[30]   ibid, s 3(2).

[31]   ibid, s 10.

In new legislation a Minister of the Crown in charge of a Bill in either House of **21.21** Parliament has, before the second reading, to make a statement that in his view the provisions of the Bill are compatible with the Convention, or that he is unable to make such a statement, but the government wishes nevertheless to proceed with the Bill.[32]

Public authorities to comply with Convention rights

Section 6(1) of the Human Rights Act 1998 is in the following terms: **21.22**

> It is unlawful for a public authority to act in a way which is incompatible with a Convention right.

This is the central provision of the Act. A 'public authority' is not defined but it is a very wide term which expressly includes a court or tribunal and 'any person certain of whose functions are functions of a public nature'.[33] The fact that the court is a public authority will have an impact on litigation between private individuals.[34]

Section 6(1) is qualified by section 6(2) which is in the following terms: **21.23**

> Subsection (1) does not apply to an act if—
> (a) as the result of one or more provisions of primary legislation, the authority could not have acted differently; or
> (b) in the case of one or more provisions of, or made under, primary legislation which cannot be read or given effect to in a way which is compatible with the Convention rights, the authority was acting so as to give effect to or enforce those provisions.

A person who claims that a public authority has acted in a way which is unlawful **21.24** under section 6, may only bring proceedings in the appropriate court or rely on the Convention rights in any legal proceedings if he is a victim of the unlawful act.[35] A person is a victim for the purposes of the Act if he would be a victim for the purposes of Article 34 of the Convention. In order to establish the status of 'victim' under the Convention, the complainant must show that he is directly affected by the act or omission in issue.[36]

Proceedings and remedies

Section 7(1) of the Human Rights 1998 is in the following terms: **21.25**

> A person who claims that a public authority has acted (or proposes to act) in a way which is made unlawful by section 6(1) may—

---

[32] ibid, s 19.
[33] ibid, s 6(3).
[34] See part D below.
[35] Human Rights Act 1998, s 7(1).
[36] See *Klass v Germany* (1978) 2 EHRR 214.

(a) bring proceedings against the authority under this Act in the appropriate court or tribunal, or

(b) rely on the Convention right or rights concerned in any legal proceedings,

but only if he is (or would be) a victim of the unlawful act.

21.26 Section 8(1) of the Human Rights Act 1998 is in the following terms:

> In relation to any act (or proposed act) of a public authority which the court finds is (or would be) unlawful, it may grant such relief or remedy, or make such order, within its powers as it considers just and appropriate.

21.27 Damages may be awarded only by a court which has power to award damages, or to order the payment of compensation in civil proceedings, section 8(2); no award of damages is to be made unless taking all the circumstances into account, including any other relief granted, it is necessary to afford just satisfaction to the person in whose favour it is made, section 8(3);[37] and the court must take into account the principles applied by the Strasbourg Court in relation to the award of compensation under Article 41[38] of the Convention, section 8(4). Historically, compensation under Article 41 has been low judged by United Kingdom standards.

Freedom of expression

21.28 Section 12 of the Human Rights Act 1998 is of particular relevance to freedom of information. It was introduced into the Bill by the Home Secretary following concerns expressed by the media as to the impact of the privacy rights contained in Article 8 on freedom of the press. Section 12 is considered later in this chapter in part F when the whole relationship of Articles 8 and 10 is discussed.

D. Enforcing the Convention Against Individuals

How far does the Convention apply to rights between individuals?

21.29 The orthodox view is that the Convention confers rights which are primarily exercisable against the state. This was undoubtedly the focus of the draftsmen of the Convention, working as they were in the aftermath of the Second World War. The right to respect for private and family life for example was inspired by the fear of secret policemen arriving in the middle of the night. But this is not the whole story. Article 1 of the Convention provides that the High Contracting Parties

---

[37] See *Maric v Thames Water Utilities Ltd* [2002] 2 WLR 932 where the claimant's garden had repeatedly been flooded and his house adversely affected by sewage discharged as a result of an overloading of a section of the sewerage system maintained by the defendant. The Court of Appeal held that the claimant's Convention rights had been infringed but that the claimant's right to damages at common law was sufficient to afford him just satisfaction under Article 41.

[38] Article 41 deals with just satisfaction.

shall secure to everyone within their jurisdiction the rights and freedoms set out in the Convention, and the Strasbourg Court has been ready to find a positive obligation on states to secure rights for individuals against other individuals.

In *X and Y v The Netherlands*[39] the Strasbourg Court held that, in a case where a prosecutor took no action on a complaint by a father of a sexual assault on his mentally incapacitated daughter of 16, the state had failed to protect a vulnerable individual from a criminal violation of her physical and moral integrity by another private individual. A violation of Article 8 was found. The court said:[40] **21.30**

> The court recalls that although the object of article 8 is essentially that of protecting the individual against arbitrary interference by the public authorities, it does not merely compel the state to abstain from such interference: in addition to this primarily negative undertaking, there may be positive obligations inherent in an effective respect for private or family life. These obligations may involve the adoption of measures designed to secure respect for private life even in the sphere of the relations of individuals between themselves.

In *Osman v The United Kingdom*[41] the Strasbourg Court held that the provisions of Article 2 enjoined a positive obligation upon contracting states to take measures to secure the right to life. In that case the court was concerned with the failure of the police to act to protect a family from criminal acts including murder. **21.31**

The fact that Article 1 of the Convention is not included in the Convention rights defined in section 1 of the Human Rights Act is unlikely to deter the courts in England and Wales from following these decisions of the Strasbourg Court. The expectation must be that the judges will follow Strasbourg's lead. **21.32**

Writers commenting on the Human Rights Act 1998 have said that the fact that section 6(3) provides that the court is a public authority which may not act in a way which is incompatible with a Convention right means that the Human Rights Act will have an impact on litigation between *private* individuals.[42] There has been a sharp division among both practising and academic lawyers. Sedley LJ has put the matter thus:[43] does section 6 require the courts' procedures to be Convention compliant, or does it require the law applied by the courts, save where the primary legislation clearly says otherwise, to give effect to the Convention principles? The question awaits resolution by the highest courts. **21.33**

In the meantime the debate has been conducted in a language of its own. Thus it is said that the approach taken to section 6(3) will determine whether the Human **21.34**

---

[39] (1985) 8 EHRR 235.
[40] ibid, 239–240 at para 23.
[41] (1998) 29 EHRR 245.
[42] See for example Clayton etc (n 5 above) ch 3 para 3.53 and Buxton LJ's reservation of this question in *Wainwright v Home Office* [2002] 3 WLR 405, 428 at para 92.
[43] *Douglas v Hello! Ltd* [2001] QB 967, 1001 at para 128.

Rights Act has only *vertical* application (applying only to the relationship between the individual and the state) or whether it also has *horizontal* application (extending to the regulation of relations between private individuals or bodies, allowing Convention rights to be invoked by them in private law disputes).

21.35 This is not the place for a detailed examination of the debate which at times has achieved a theological intensity. Those who want this will find an admirable summary in *The Law of Human Rights*.[44]

21.36 Clayton, Tomlinson, and George in *The Law of Human Rights*, adopt a middle position and conclude that the Human Rights Act will not enable private litigants to sue each other for breaches of Convention rights but is likely to have horizontal impact on disputes between private litigants in the following cases:

procedural horizontality, which arises where the court as a public authority exercises discretionary powers to control the procedure in private litigation;

remedial horizontality, which arises where the court as a public authority considers the impact on private parties' Convention rights of the granting or withholding of remedies in the context of private litigation;[45]

direct statutory horizontality, which arises where statutes applying between private individuals are interpreted under section 3 of the Human Rights Act (in conjunction with section 6) to give effect whenever possible to Convention rights;

positive rights horizontality, which arises where the court as a public authority is under a positive duty to protect a person against infringements of Convention rights from another private person, compelling it to intervene;

common law horizontality, which arises where the court as a public authority develops the common law as it applies between private parties in a way which is not incompatible with Convention rights.[46]

However, Clayton, Tomlinson, and George say, the Human Rights Act will not produce full or direct horizontality as now exists in Ireland and South Africa. Private litigants will not be able to sue each other for breaches of Convention rights.

21.37 The Human Rights Act has undoubtedly had some effect on the enforcement of Convention rights against private individuals. In *Venables v News Group Newspapers Ltd*[47] (the facts of which are summarized in paragraph 20.52 above) the President had, first, to decide the preliminary issue whether the Convention applied to the case. She said:[48]

---

[44] See n 5 above, at ch 5.
[45] See for example the *Douglas* case ([2001] QB 967) where an injunction was refused; considered further at para 21.67 below.
[46] See *Douglas v Hello! Ltd* [2001] 2 QB 967, 1001 at para 126 where Sedley LJ was prepared to find a common law right of privacy.
[47] [2001] Fam 430.
[48] ibid, 445 at para 24.

It is clear that, although operating in the public domain and fulfilling a public service, the defendant newspapers cannot sensibly be said to come within the definition of public authority in section 6(1) of the Human Rights Act 1998. Consequently, Convention rights are not directly enforceable against the defendants: see section 7(1) and section 8 of the 1998 Act. That is not, however, the end of the matter, since the court is a public authority (see section 6(3)) and must itself act in a way compatible with the Convention (see section 6(1)) and have regard to European jurisprudence: see section 2. In a family law case, *Glaser v United Kingdom* (2000) 3 FCR 193,[49] the European Court of Human Rights, sitting as a Chamber, declared admissible an application by a father seeking the enforcement of contact orders made in private law proceedings between him and the mother of the children. They considered the potential breach of the father's rights under article 8 and article 6. The [Strasbourg] court said, at pp 208–209, para 63:

'The essential object of article 8 is to protect the individual against arbitrary interference by public authorities. There may, however, be positive obligations inherent in an effective *respect* for family life. Those obligations may involve the adoption of measures designed to secure respect for family life even in the sphere of relations between individuals, including both the provision of a regulatory framework of adjudicatory and enforcement machinery protecting individuals' rights and the implementation, where appropriate, of specific steps (see among other authorities, *X and Y v The Netherlands* (1985) 8 EHRR 235 and mutatis mutandis, *Osman v United Kingdom* (1998) 29 EHRR 245). In both the negative and United Kingdom positive contexts, regard must be had to the fair balance which has been struck between the competing interests of the individual and the community, including other concerned third parties, and the state's margin of appreciation (see, among other authorities, *Keegan v Ireland* (1994) 18 EHRR 342, 362, para 49).'

The court held that, in that case, the authorities, including the courts, struck a fair balance between the competing interests and did not fail in their responsibilities to protect the father's right to respect for family life. This decision underlines the positive obligations of the courts including, where necessary, the provision of a regulatory framework of adjudicatory and enforcement machinery in order to protect the right of the individual. The decisions of the European Court of Human Rights in *Glaser's case* and *X and Y v The Netherlands* (1985) 8 EHRR 235, seem to dispose of any argument that a court is not to have regard to the Convention in private law cases.

21.38 This authority decides therefore that although the Convention does not create freestanding causes of action to be used in private law, the fact that the court is obliged to comply with the Convention as a public authority under section 6 of the Human Rights Act means that it must protect the rights of the individual where necessary. The decisions of the Strasbourg Court referred to above mean that the court must have regard to the Convention in private cases. The court in adjudicating upon existing common law causes of action must act positively in a way compatible with the Convention. This is accepted by Lord Woolf in *A v B plc*[50] where he said the court:

---

[49] Also reported at (2001) 33 EHRR 1.
[50] [2002] 3 WLR 542, 546 at para 4.

. . . is required to act 'in a way which is compatible with a Convention right'. The court is able to achieve this by absorbing the rights which articles 8 and 10 protect into the long-established action for breach of confidence.

E. A Convention Right to Information?

Is there a Convention right to freedom of information?

21.39 Under Article 10 the right to freedom of expression includes freedom 'to receive and impart information and ideas without interference by public authority and regardless of frontiers'. This is halfway to a right to freedom of information. Public authorities cannot interfere with the free flow of information which people are prepared to provide yet the Article does not expressly deal with the situation where people are not prepared to hand over information.

21.40 The Strasbourg Court's approach to this omission in Article 10 has been a cautious one. In *Leander v Sweden*[51] the applicant had been refused permanent employment as a museum technician with the Naval Museum on account of certain secret information which allegedly made him a security risk. The applicant invoked Article 10 and maintained that he was entitled to know the content of the secret information which was held against him. The Strasbourg Court rejected his claim and applied the strict wording of the Article. It said:

> The Court observes that the right to freedom to receive information basically prohibits a Government from restricting a person from receiving information that others wish or may be willing to impart to him. Article 10 does not, in circumstances such as those in the present case, confer on an individual a right of access to a register containing information on his personal position, nor does it embody an obligation on the Government to impart such information to the individual.

21.41 In *Gaskin v The United Kingdom*[52] the Strasbourg Court went further towards finding a right to information but it did so in the context of Article 8 rather than Article 10. The Court reaffirmed the views it had expressed in *Leander v Sweden*. Article 10 did not embody an obligation on the state to require Liverpool City Council to impart information held by it to Mr Gaskin against its will. That, however, was not the end of the story.

21.42 Mr Gaskin had been taken into care by Liverpool City Council in December 1959, and remained in its care until December 1977 when he reached the age of 18. During the major part of this period he was boarded out with foster parents. Under the relevant regulations the local authority was under a duty to keep certain confidential records concerning him and his care. Mr Gaskin contended that he

---

[51] (1987) 9 EHRR 433.
[52] (1989) 12 EHRR 36 at para 52.

was ill-treated in care, and had tried to obtain details of the information on these records. Some information had been supplied to him, where the carers involved with his case did not object, but he remained in the dark as to much of what had happened to him and he was not given free access to his records by Liverpool City Council.

The Strasbourg Court decided that persons in the situation of Mr Gaskin had a **21.43** vital interest, protected by the Convention under Article 8, in receiving the information necessary to know and to understand their childhood and early development. This was an example of a positive obligation imposed on the state under Article 8, an obligation which had to be balanced against the public interest in the confidentiality of public records. The Court recognized that such confidentiality is of importance for receiving objective and reliable information, and can also be necessary for the protection of third parties, but found there was no independent person charged with determining whether access had to be granted where the carers involved refused their consent to the release of the information. The Court found in these circumstances, applying the principle of proportionality, that there had been a breach of Article 8.

Guerra v Italy: a step towards a right to information

In 1998 in *Guerra v Italy*[53] the Strasbourg Court had to think again about the pro- **21.44** vision of information by states as a secondary right or obligation derived from the tabulated rights in the Convention. It had to consider the rights of 40 applicants who lived in the town of Manfredonia, approximately 1 kilometre downwind from a chemical factory which produced fertilizers and other chemicals. The applicants complained that the authorities had failed to provide them with relevant information so that they could assess the risks they and their families would run if they continued to live in the town. The Strasbourg Court when the matter was referred to it, in contrast to the Commission at a preliminary hearing, would not accept that the ignorance in which the local people had been kept infringed Article 10 of the Convention. The reason, a narrow one, was that the EC mechanism for accident readiness and public information was in place in Italy; it was just that it had not worked: the case was therefore not one where government was actively obstructing the flow of information.[54] The Commission earlier by a majority of 21 to 8 had taken a much firmer line and found there was a violation of Article 10.[55]

---

[53] (1998) 26 EHRR 357.
[54] The Court in rejecting the Article 10 argument did accept that in cases concerning the restrictions on freedom of the press it had on a number of occasions recognized that the public has a right to receive information as a corollary of the specific function of journalists, which is to impart information and ideas on matters of public interest; see *Observer and Guardian v United Kingdom* (1992) 14 EHRR 153 at para 59(b) and *Thorgeirson v Iceland* (1992) 14 EHRR 843 at para 63.
[55] (1998) 26 EHRR 357, 368. The Court's view though clear is expressed in somewhat perfunctory terms and the argument emerges best from the opinion of the Commission and from the

21.45 The Commission referred in its opinion to resolution 1087 of the Consultative Parliamentary Assembly of the Council of Europe[56] on the consequences of the Chernobyl disaster. Referring not only to the risks associated with the production and use of nuclear energy in the civil sector but also other matters, it stated:

> . . . public access to clear and full information . . . must be viewed as a basic right.

This followed an earlier resolution of the Assembly in 1970[57] when it resolved that the right to freedom of expression in Article 10 involves a:

> corresponding duty for the public authorities to make available information on matters of public interest within reasonable limits and a duty for mass communication media to give complete and general information on public affairs.

21.46 The Commission's opinion may be summarized in this way:

(a) The current state of European law confirms that public information is now an essential tool for protecting public well-being and health in situations of danger to the environment. The Convention must be interpreted in the light of present-day conditions and it is designed to safeguard the individual in a real and practical way as regards those areas with which it deals (paragraph 43).[58]

(b) The importance of a right to information in this field derives from its *raison d'être*, which is to protect the well-being and health of the persons concerned and so, indirectly, rights which are covered by other provisions of the Convention (paragraph 45).

(c) Accordingly in the interdependent fields of the protection of the environment, of public health and of the well-being of individuals, the words 'this right shall include freedom to . . . receive . . . information' contained in the first paragraph of Article 10 should be interpreted as granting an actual right to receive information, in particular from the competent authorities, to persons from sections of the population which have been or which may be affected by an industrial or other activity dangerous to the environment (paragraph 47).

(d) Therefore, Article 10 of the Convention places the state not only under an obligation to make environmental information accessible to the public but also under positive obligations to collect, process and disseminate information which, by its very nature, is not directly accessible and which cannot be known to the public unless the public authorities act accordingly (paragraph 49).

---

dissenting opinion of GH Thune, MA Nowicki, B Conforti and N Bratza (who is now the British judge on the Court), who took the line later adopted by the Court: (1998) 26 EHRR 357, 375.

[56] Adopted on 26 April 1996.
[57] Which was not referred to by the Commission.
[58] See *Airey v Ireland* (1979) 2 EHRR 305 at para 26.

Those who signed the dissenting opinion were of the view that the majority had **21.47** stretched the meaning of Article 10 too wide. In a passage which is more illuminating than the Court's terse decision they said:

> While it is true that the right guaranteed by the Article is expressed to include the freedom to receive information and while we accept that the Article may impose on Member States certain positive obligations to secure the right to freedom of expression, we are unable to accept that the Article can be interpreted as obliging a State to assemble, collate, and disseminate information, even in a case when such measures may be required as a matter of domestic law. Such an interpretation of the article in our view not only distorts the natural meaning of the words of the article but is inconsistent with the established case law of the Court which is to the effect that 'the right to freedom to receive information basically prohibits a Government from restricting a person from receiving information that others could or may be willing to impart to him'.[59]

Sedley LJ in his article, 'Information as a Human Right'[60] comments that distorting the natural meaning of the Article is a respectable strict constructionist's view of the Convention, which perhaps takes too little account of the Strasbourg Court's own view of the Convention in other cases as *a living instrument* capable of growth in changing circumstances. As to the second reason, whilst true, he observes it is an example of Professor Cornford's axiom that nothing should be done for the first time.[61]

However, the result for the people of Manfredonia was not an adverse one. The **21.48** Court went on to hold that Article 8, requiring respect for private and family life, did carry a right to information where, as here, the information was relevant to the enjoyment of the right. Its reasoning, particularly in view of its decision on Article 10, was pretty laconic, namely that the applicants were denied:

> essential information that would have enabled them to assess the risks they and their families might run if they continued to live at Manfredonia, a town particularly exposed to danger in the event of an accident at the factory.

Guerra was thus a positive but short step towards a right to information. It was fol- **21.49** lowed in *McGinley and Egan v United Kingdom*[62] by a stronger assertion of the right, this time in favour of servicemen who had been exposed to nuclear test explosions on Christmas Island—a class of litigants who have found the law of little help. Their claim failed on its facts, but the Strasbourg Court found a positive obligation on the state in these terms:

---

[59] See *Leander v Sweden* (1987) 9 EHRR 433 at para 74 and *Gaskin v The United Kingdom* (1990) 12 EHRR 36 at para 52.
[60] Published in *Freedom of Expression and Freedom of Information, Essays in Honour of Sir David Williams* (OUP, 2000).
[61] FM Cornford, *Microcosmographia Academica* (1908) ch VII.
[62] (1998) 27 EHRR 1, 45 at para 101.

Where a government engages in hazardous activities such as those in issue in the present case, which might have hidden adverse consequences on the health of those involved in such activities, respect for family life under Article 8 requires that an effective and accessible procedure be established which enables such persons to seek all relevant and appropriate information.

21.50   Sedley LJ in his article[63] says:

> ... there is something odd about discovering a right of information in the entrails of Article 8, which says nothing about information, and refusing to discern it in Article 10 which explicitly integrates 'freedom ... to receive ... information and ideas without any interference by public authority' in the right of free expression.

Applying that logical approach it is possible that in time both the Strasbourg Court and the English courts will prefer the approach of the Commission in the *Guerra* case.

The season for growth

21.51   What is clear is that principles of United Kingdom law will be informed and influenced by the Convention as the courts apply sections 3 and 6 of the Human Rights Act 1998. Sedley LJ, in his article, poses the question, where may we look outside Article 8 of the Convention for a nascent right to information? By way of answer he takes the doctrine of informed consent to medical intervention, which will now have to become Convention compliant. How far in English law does the patient's right to know extend? Sedley LJ traces the cases down to *Pearce v United Bristol Healthcare NHS Trust*[64] where Lord Woolf, drawing the threads together, held:

> ... it seems to me to be the law ... that if there is a significant risk which would affect the judgment of a reasonable patient, then, in the normal course it is the responsibility of a doctor to inform the patient of that significant risk ...

Sedley LJ comments that thus information may be coming to feature not as a parasitic requirement of another tabulated right but as a prior requisite if other rights are to have value and substance. He concludes:

> In the field of information and human rights, at least, the space and season for growth—and for accompanying shedding of dead wood—are palpably there.[65]

21.52   The same thought seems to inform Clayton, Tomlinson, and George's cautious assessment:[66]

> It is therefore uncertain whether Article 10 will affect any rights to freedom of information by for example, creating a right to know[67] and widening the exemptions

---

[63] 'Information as a Human Right' (n 60 above) 244.
[64] [1999] PIQR 53, CA.
[65] See further *R (Wilkinson) v RMO Broadmoor* (CA, 22 October 2001).
[66] See n 5 above at para 15.253.
[67] cf *Reynolds v Times Newspapers* [2001] 2 AC 127, 197.

against disclosure in the Freedom of Information Bill[68] or in the Local Government Act 1972.

What seems certain is that the English courts will be asked to construe the **21.53** Freedom of Information Act 2000 against a right to know based on the developing common law, on Articles 8 and 10, and on the principle stated by Lord Scott in his essay on confidentiality, which is discussed in chapter 20.[69] Those who seek to preserve the secrecy of government are unlikely to have as easy a ride in the future as they have in the past. Two Commonwealth cases, which break new bounds, underline this point. First, *TV3 Network v Eveready New Zealand Ltd*[70] where it was held that the right to impart information provided the court with jurisdiction to order a mandatory interlocutory judgment to require a correction of a defamatory television programme and secondly, *Committee for the Commonwealth of Canada v Canada*[71] where the Supreme Court decided that there is a constitutional right to use public property for freedom of expression.

F. Conflicting Rights

Section 12 of the Human Rights Act 1998

The relationship between Article 8 and Article 10 of the European Convention is **21.54** addressed by section 12 of the Human Rights Act, as Jack Straw explained to the House of Commons:

> So far as we are able, in a manner consistent with the Convention and its jurisprudence, we are saying to the courts that whenever there is a clash between article 8 rights and article 10 rights, they must pay particular attention to the article 10 rights.[72]

Section 12 is in the following terms: **21.55**

(1) This section applies if a court is considering whether to grant any relief which, if granted, might affect the exercise of the Convention right to freedom of expression.

(2) If a person against whom the application for relief is made ('the respondent') is neither present nor represented, no such relief is to be granted unless the court is satisfied—

    (a) that the applicant has taken all practicable steps to notify the respondent; or

    (b) that there are compelling reasons why the respondent should not be notified.

---

[68] Now the Freedom of Information Act 2000.
[69] See, eg para 20.07 et seq above.
[70] [1993] 3 NZLR 435.
[71] [1991] 1 SCR 139.
[72] *Hansard*, HC (series 6) vol 315, col 543 (2 July 1998).

(3) No such relief is to be granted so as to restrain publication before trial unless the court is satisfied that the applicant is likely to establish that publication should not be allowed.

(4) The court must have particular regard to the importance of the Convention right to freedom of expression and, where the proceedings relate to material which the respondent claims, or which appears to the court, to be journalistic, literary or artistic material (or to conduct connected with such material), to—

(a) the extent to which—
  (i) the material has, or is about to, become available to the public; or
  (ii) it is, or would be, in the public interest for the material to be published;
(b) any relevant privacy code.

(5) In this section—
'court' includes a tribunal; and
'relief' includes any remedy or order (other than in criminal proceedings).

Article 10 applies between individuals

21.56 Section 12 applies whenever the court is considering whether to grant relief which might affect the exercise of the right to freedom of expression; for example where an injunction is sought to restrain publication of a newspaper article. The first point to make about section 12 is that section 12(4) puts beyond question the direct applicability of at least one article of the Convention (Article 10) as between one party to the litigation and another—in the jargon 'the horizontal effect'.[73]

Section 12 raises the threshold test for interlocutory injunctions

21.57 Section 12(3) is concerned with applications for interim relief to restrain publication before trial. Before the commencement of the Human Rights Act, the test to be applied to an application for a restraining injunction had been the two hurdle approach laid down by the House of Lords in the *American Cyanamid* case.[74] The applicant had to show first that he had a real prospect of succeeding in his claim for a permanent injunction at the trial, and secondly that the balance of convenience lay in favour of making the order.

21.58 It is clear that section 12(3) raises the threshold test for the restraint of publication before trial on the ground that such publication would affect the exercise of the right to freedom of expression: it requires the claimant to establish that he is likely to succeed at trial.

21.59 In the case of *Douglas v Hello! Ltd*[75] Michael Douglas and Catherine Zeta-Jones were seeking an injunction to restrain the publication of unauthorized photographs which were taken at their wedding. Keene LJ dealt with the threshold test in this way:

---

[73] *Douglas v Hello! Ltd* [2001] QB 967, at 1003 para 133 *per* Sedley LJ.
[74] *American Cyanamid Co v Ethicon Ltd* [1975] AC 396.
[75] [2001] QB 967; see para 20.51 and ch 20 passim, above.

It [the section] requires the court to look at the merits of the case and not merely to apply the *American Cyanamid* test. Thus the court has to look ahead to the ultimate stage and be satisfied that the scales are likely to come down in the applicant's favour. That does not conflict with the Convention, since it is merely requiring the court to apply its mind to how one right is to be balanced, on the merits against another right, without building in additional weight on either side.[76]

As to the word 'likely' in section 12(3) further useful guidance is provided by Sir **21.60** Andrew Morritt V-C in *Imutran Ltd v Uncaged Campaigns Ltd.*[77] He said of section 12:

> Counsel for the defendants submitted that the requirement of likelihood imposed a higher standard than that formulated in *American Cyanamid v Ethicon Ltd* [1975] AC 396. I did not understand this to be disputed by counsel for Imutran. He submitted that whatever the standard was his case satisfied it. Theoretically and as a matter of language likelihood is slightly higher in the scale of probability than a real prospect of success. But the difference between the two is so small that I cannot believe that there will be many (if any) cases which would succeed under the *American Cynamid* test but will fail because of the terms of section 12(3). Accordingly I propose to apply the test of likelihood without any further consideration of how much more probable that now has to be.

Section 12 requires the court to have regard to Article 10 and Article 8

The right to freedom of expression contained within Article 10(1) is extremely **21.61** wide. It includes but is not limited to the right to hold opinions and receive or impart information and ideas without interference by public authority. In the case of *Douglas v Hello! Ltd* the Court of Appeal had no hesitation in deciding that photographs of the wedding contained information.

However, Article 10(2) restricts the ambit of the right. It provides that the exercise **21.62** of the right may be subject to:

> . . . such formalities, conditions, restrictions or penalties as are prescribed by law and are necessary in a democratic society . . . for protection of the reputation or rights of others, for preventing the disclosure of information received in confidence, or for maintaining the authority and impartiality of the judiciary.

Section 12(4) does not distinguish between the parts of Article 10, so the court **21.63** must have particular regard to both. Sedley LJ in *Douglas v Hello Ltd* [78] put it this way: when one turns to the Convention right of freedom of expression, it is qualified in favour of the reputation and rights of others and the protection of information received in confidence. In other words you cannot have particular regard to Article 10 without having equally particular regard at the very least to

---

[76] [2001] QB 967, 1008 at para 150.

[77] [2001] 2 All ER 385, 391 at para 17. This passage was approved by the Court of Appeal in *A v B plc* [2002] 3 WLR 542, 549 at para 11(iii).

[78] [2001] QB 967, 1003 at para 133.

Article 8. What this does is to bring into the frame the conflicting rights of privacy and freedom of expression. If the threatened publication would place someone's life in danger the court will have to consider Article 2.

21.64 In the case of *Douglas v Hello! Ltd* the grant of injunctive relief in a claim to invasion of privacy would affect the freedom of expression conferred by Article 10. That meant that *particular regard* would have to be given to both Article 10(1) and 10(2). The application of Article 10(2) meant that the court also had to have particular and equal regard to Article 8 because the exercise of the right to freedom of expression is subject to the rights of privacy conferred by Article 8. Any other approach would be inconsistent with section 3 of the Human Rights Act and Article 17 of the Convention.

21.65 This means that conflicting rights will need to be considered by the court. The outcome will be determined principally by the application of the principles of proportionality.

Balancing conflicting rights

21.66 Any freedom of information regime has to grapple with the inherent conflict between a citizen's right to know and an individual's right to privacy. Under the Freedom of Information Act 2000 this conflict exists between the right of access to information in section 1, and the exemptions set out in Part II of the Act, whether absolute, or dependent on where the public interest lies. Under the Convention the conflict is between the rights contained in Articles 8(1) and 10(1) and the restrictions to those rights in Articles 8(2) and 10(2). Neither Article is a trump card, and the outcome of balancing the conflict self-evidently has to be the same under both Articles. The courts have to consider in each case the principles of legality and proportionality, which as always, constitute the mechanism by which the Strasbourg Court, and now the United Kingdom courts, reach their conclusions on countervailing or qualified rights.[79] Strasbourg principles are increasingly going to inform the decisions of the English courts. Where Convention rights are involved they are required to do so by the provisions of the Human Rights Act 1998 and even where Convention rights are not directly in issue the United Kingdom courts are, as we have seen, increasingly striving to find a constitutional basis for their decisions.[80]

21.67 In *Douglas v Hello! Ltd* the rights of privacy were contrasted with the right of freedom of expression. The former rights might well have prevailed in the circumstances in which the photographs were obtained if Mr and Mrs Douglas had not sold most of their rights to a third party who had the exclusive right to photograph

---

[79] See Sedley LJ in the *Douglas* case [2001] 2 WLR 992, 1029 para 136.
[80] See para 21.18 above and *R v Secretary of State for the Home Department, ex p Pierson* [1998] AC 539, 575.

and publish photographs of the wedding. In these circumstances Mr and Mrs Douglas could not rely upon Article 8 sufficiently to satisfy the court at an interim stage that they were likely to establish at trial that publication should not be allowed. Damages was the more likely remedy.

Before looking further at the principle of proportionality additional practical help **21.68** in holding the balance particularly between Articles 8 and 10 has been given by the Council of Europe's Resolution 1165 of 1990 which has been commended by the Court of Appeal in *A v B plc*.[81] The material paragraphs of the Resolution are:

6. The Assembly is aware that personal privacy is often invaded, even in countries with specific legislation to protect it, as people's lives have become a lucrative commodity for certain sectors of the media. The victims are essentially public figures, since details of their private lives are a stimulus to sales. At the same time, public figures must recognise that the special position they occupy in society—in many cases by choice—automatically entails increased pressure on their privacy.

7. Public figures are persons holding public office and/or using public resources and, more broadly speaking all those who play a role in public life, whether in politics, the economy, the arts, the social sphere, sport or in any other domain.

8. It is often in the name of a one-sided interpretation of the right to freedom of expression, which is guaranteed in article 10 of the European Convention on Human Rights, that the media invade people's privacy, claiming their readers are entitled to know about public figures.

9. Certain facts relating to the lives of public figures, particularly politicians, may indeed be of interest to citizens, and it may therefore be legitimate for readers, who are also voters, to be informed of those facts.

10. It is therefore necessary to find a way of balancing the exercise of two fundamental rights, both of which are guaranteed by the European Convention on Human Rights: the right to respect for one's private life and the right to freedom of expression.

11. The Assembly reaffirms the importance of every person's right to privacy, and of the right to freedom of expression, as fundamental to a democratic society. These rights are neither absolute nor in any hierarchical order, since they are of equal value.

12. However, the Assembly points out that the privacy afforded by article 8 of the European Convention on Human Rights should not only protect an individual against interference by public authorities, but also against interference by private persons or institutions, including the mass media.

The Court of Appeal added:[82]   **21.69**

In drawing up a balance sheet between the respective interests of the parties courts should not act as censors or arbiters of taste. This is the task of others. If there is not a sufficient case for restraining publication the fact that a more lurid approach will be adopted by the publication than the court would regard as acceptable is not relevant.

---

[81] [2002] 3 WLR 542, 552 at para 11(xii).
[82] ibid, 553 at para 11(xiii).

If the contents of the publication are untrue the law of defamation provides a prohibition.

The principle of proportionality

21.70   The criteria for determining the test of proportionality have been analysed in similar terms in the case law of the Court of Justice and the Strasbourg Court. It is not necessary to reinvent the wheel.[83] In *de Freitas v Permanent Secretary of Ministry of Agriculture, Fisheries, Land and Housing*[84] Lord Clyde adopted a precise and concrete analysis of the criteria. The Privy Council was considering the constitutionality of the Civil Service Act in Antigua and Barbuda. Lord Clyde said that in determining whether a limitation is arbitrary or excessive a court should ask itself:

> . . . whether (i) the legislative objective is sufficiently important to justify limiting a fundamental right; (ii) the measures designed to meet the legislative objective are rationally connected to it; and (iii) the means used to impair the right or freedom are no more than is necessary to accomplish the objective.

A four-stage process

21.71   The Privy Council was using proportionality as the test of constitutionality. Professor Jeffrey Jowell in 'Beyond the Rule of Law: Towards Constitutional Judicial Review',[85] an article which was referred to favourably by Lord Steyn in *R (Daly) v Secretary of State for the Home Department*,[86] says proportionality involves a sophisticated, four-stage process, asking the following questions:

(1)   Did the action pursue a legitimate aim?

(2)   Were the means employed suitable to achieve that aim?

(3)   Could the aim have been achieved by a less restrictive alternative?

(4)   Is the derogation justified overall in the interests of a democratic society?

21.72   Professor Jowell explains this process in this way:

> This fourfold test contains a carefully constructed set of criteria which are designed to ensure that a prima facie violation of a fundamental democratic right is not lightly sanctioned. Yet it involves more than a heightened scrutiny of the decision in question. It starts by asking whether the breach is justifiable in terms of the aims it seeks. Some Convention rights can only be violated for a specific purpose (such as national security) and therefore other aims would not be legitimate, whatever their rationale. It then proceeds to consider whether in reality those aims are capable of being achieved. Spurious or impractical aims will not suffice. It then goes on to consider whether less restrictive means could have been employed. The breach must be the minimum necessary. Finally it asks whether the breach is necessary (not merely

---

[83]   *R v A (No 2)* [2001] 2 WLR 1546, 1560 at para 38 *per* Lord Steyn.

[84]   [1999] 1 AC 69, 80.

[85]   [2000] PL 671.

[86]   [2001] 2 AC 532, 547 at para 27.

desirable or reasonable) in the interests of democracy. Only 'a pressing social need' can justify the breach of a fundamental right.

Professor Jowell illustrates how these tests might work in practice by considering **21.73** how they might be applied to the case of *R v Secretary of State for the Home Department, ex p Brind*,[87] the broadcasting ban case. By censoring the direct spoken words of members of a number of terrorist organizations, the Home Secretary in that case infringed Article 10(1), but was held by the House of Lords applying the *Wednesbury* test not to have acted unreasonably. Professor Jowell concludes that the result in *Brind* would have been the same applying the proportionality test. Professor Jowell comments:

> We note the following: first, the Wednesbury approach should not be followed because the decision-maker is in breach of Article 10(1) free speech has been violated. The burden of justifying that violation is now squarely upon the decision-maker. Secondly, the decision-maker has to demonstrate not that his decision was desirable, or possible, or reasonable, or not unreasonable (the criteria of administrative law) but that his decision was necessary to preserve democracy on the grounds of one of the countervailing criteria specified (namely, the interest of national security). It is then for the courts to determine the essentially constitutional question, namely, whether the measure fulfils the constitutive requirements of a modern democracy.

G. Judicial Review and Proportionality

The relationship between proportionality and judicial review

The relationship between proportionality and judicial review has been clarified in **21.74** a number of recent decisions both in the Strasbourg Court and in the English courts, indeed Lord Cooke has suggested that the days of *Wednesbury* unreasonableness could be numbered.[88]

The first case is the Court of Appeal's decision in *R v Ministry of Defence, ex p* **21.75** *Smith*,[89] a case which was decided before the Human Rights Act was even in prospect. The applicants challenged the Ministry of Defence's policy that homosexuality was incompatible with service in the armed forces and that personnel known to be homosexual or engaging in homosexual activity would be administratively discharged. The court's scepticism about the policy is illustrated by Henry LJ's comment[90] that the court was told that the policy had existed throughout the years of conscription (1939 to 1960). This fact, Henry LJ says:

---

[87] [1991] AC 696.
[88] *R (Daly) v Secretary of State for the Home Department* [2001] 2 AC 532.
[89] [1996] QB 517, 554.
[90] ibid, 561.

... may surprise post-war National Servicemen, who I believe to have been generally unaware that a genuine homosexual orientation would have rendered them exempt from compulsory National Service, but their ignorance is explained before us on the basis that the policy did not need to be publicised ...

21.76 The Court of Appeal accepted that it should adopt the approach to irrationality put forward by David Pannick, counsel for three of the applicants:

> The court may not interfere with the exercise of an administrative decision on substantive grounds save where the court is satisfied that the decision is unreasonable in the sense that it is beyond the range of responses open to a reasonable decision-maker. But in judging whether the decision-maker has exceeded this margin of appreciation the human rights context is important. The more substantial the interference with human rights, the more the court will require justification before it is satisfied that the decision is reasonable in the sense outlined above.

Sir Thomas Bingham, Master of the Rolls, said that this submission was an accurate distillation of the principles laid down by the House of Lords in *R v Secretary of State for the Home Department, ex p Bugdaycay*[91] and *R v Secretary of State for the Home Department, ex p Brind.*[92] The court, however, concluded that the policy of excluding homosexuals could not be stigmatized as irrational and the applicants' appeals were dismissed.

21.77 The Strasbourg Court came to the opposite conclusion when the matter came before it entitled *Smith and Grady v United Kingdom.*[93] The Court, first, considered whether the policy could be justified under Article 8(2). It summed up the general principles which applied in this way:[94]

> An interference will be considered 'necessary in a democratic society' for a legitimate aim if it answers a pressing social need and, in particular, is proportionate to the legitimate aim pursued.
>
> Given the matters at issue in the present case, the Court would underline the link between the notion of 'necessity' and that of a 'democratic society', the hallmarks of the latter including pluralism, tolerance and broadmindedness.
>
> The Court recognises that it is for the national authorities to make the initial assessment of necessity, though the final evaluation as to whether the reasons cited for the interference are relevant and sufficient is one for this Court.

21.78 The Strasbourg Court reviewed the facts and concluded neither the investigations conducted into the applicants' sexual orientation, nor their discharge on the grounds of their homosexuality in pursuance of the Ministry of Defence policy, were justified under Article 8(2). The Court then considered whether the applicants had an effective remedy in the United Kingdom. It found:[95]

---

[91] [1987] AC 514.
[92] [1991] 1 AC 696.
[93] (1999) 29 EHRR 493.
[94] ibid, 529 at paras 87, 88.
[95] ibid, 543 at para 138.

... the threshold at which the High Court and the Court of Appeal could find the Ministry of Defence policy irrational was placed so high that it effectively excluded any consideration by the domestic courts of the question of whether the interference with the applicants' rights answered a pressing social need or was proportionate to the national security and public order aims pursued, principles which lie at the heart of the court's analysis of complaints under article 8 of the Convention.

The applicants therefore had no effective remedy and there was a violation of Article 13 as well as Article 8.

R (Daly) v Secretary of State for the Home Department

The House of Lords reviewed the different approaches which were taken by the **21.79** Court of Appeal and the Strasbourg court in the *Smith and Grady* case in *R (Daly) v Secretary of State for the Home Department*.[96] *Daly* is a case about prisoners' rights. The applicant challenged the Home Office policy which was introduced in 1995, which required that prisoners be excluded during cell searches to prevent intimidation and to prevent prisoners acquiring a detailed knowledge of search procedures. The policy provided that officers were to examine but not read any legal correspondence in the cell to check that nothing had been written on it by the prisoner, or stored between its leaves, which was likely to endanger prison security. The House of Lords held the policy provided for a degree of intrusion into the privileged legal correspondence of prisoners which was greater than is justified by the objectives the policy was intended to serve and so violated the common law rights of prisoners.

Lord Bingham said[97] that he reached these conclusions on an orthodox applica- **21.80** tion of common law principles derived from the authorities and an orthodox domestic approach to judicial review. He said that the same result could be achieved by reliance on the Convention, but that the two approaches would not always produce the same result. He referred to the Strasbourg Court's decision in *Smith and Grady v United Kingdom* that the applicants had not been given an effective remedy for breach of their Article 8 rights because the threshold of review had been set too high. He agreed with the speech of Lord Steyn on this part of the case.

Lord Steyn started his speech[98] by referring to argument as to whether certain **21.81** observations of the Master of the Rolls, Lord Phillips in *R (Mahmood) v Secretary of State for the Home Department*[99] were correct. The context was an immigration case involving a decision of the Secretary of State made before the Human Rights Act 1998 came into effect. The Master of the Rolls approached the case as if the

---

[96] [2001] 2 AC 532.
[97] ibid, 545 at paras 21, 23.
[98] ibid, 546 at para 23.
[99] [2001] 1 WLR 840.

Act had been in force and he explained the new approach to be adopted. The Master of the Rolls concluded:[100]

> When anxiously scrutinising an executive decision that interferes with human rights, the court will ask the question, applying an objective test, whether the decision-maker could reasonably have concluded that the interference was necessary to achieve one or more of the legitimate aims recognised by the Convention. When considering the test of necessity in the relevant context, the court must take into account the European jurisprudence in accordance with section 2 of the 1998 Act.

21.82 Lord Steyn said the explanation of the Master of the Rolls in the first sentence of the quoted passage required clarification. It was couched in language reminiscent of the traditional *Wednesbury* grounds of review,[101] and in particular the adaptation of that test in terms of heightened scrutiny in cases involving fundamental rights as formulated in *R v Ministry of Defence, ex p Smith*.[102] Lord Steyn continued:

> There is a material difference between *Wednesbury* and *Smith* grounds of review and the approach of proportionality applicable in respect of review where Convention rights are at stake.

Lord Steyn explained the difference between the two approaches by reference[103] to Lord Clyde's test of proportionality in the *de Freitas* case,[104] to academic public lawyers including Professor Jowell, and to the Strasbourg Court's decision in *Smith and Grady v United Kingdom*.[105] He said that Lord Clyde's criteria were more precise and more sophisticated than the traditional grounds of review. He mentioned three concrete differences. First, the doctrine of proportionality may require the reviewing court to assess the balance which the decision-maker has struck, not merely whether it is within the range of rational or reasonable decisions. Secondly, the proportionality test may go further than the traditional grounds of review inasmuch as it may require attention to be directed to the relative weight to be accorded to interests and considerations. Thirdly, even the heightened scrutiny test developed in *R v Ministry of Defence, ex p Smith*[106] is not necessarily appropriate to the protection of human rights. Lord Steyn concluded that the intensity of the review was guaranteed by the twin requirements that the limitation of the right was necessary in a democratic society, in the sense of meeting a pressing social need, and the question whether the interference was really proportionate to the legitimate aim being pursued. It is therefore important that cases involving Convention rights must be analysed in the correct way, though this does not mean there has been a shift to merits review.

---

[100] [2001] 1 WLR 840, 857 at para 40.
[101] *Associated Picture Houses Ltd v Wednesbury Corp* [1948] 1 KB 223.
[102] [1996] QB 517, 554.
[103] [2001] 2 AC 532 at para 27.
[104] [1999] 1 AC 69.
[105] (1999) 29 EHRR 493.
[106] [1996] QB 517, 554.

This passage from Lord Steyn's speech was endorsed by Lord Bingham in *R v* **21.83**
Shayler.[107] The rigorous and intrusive nature of the review where Convention
rights are at stake was one of the factors which weighed with the House of Lords
in holding that the interference with Mr Shayler's right of freedom of expression
by the Official Secrets Act 1989 was not greater than was required to achieve the
legitimate object of acting in the interests of national security.

Finally Lord Cooke in *Daly* offered brief observations on two matters, less to sup- **21.84**
plement what had been said than to underline its importance. The first is that the
common law by itself is recognized as a sufficient source of the fundamental right
to confidential communication with a legal adviser for the purpose of obtaining
legal advice; thus the decision may prove to be in point in common law jurisdictions not affected by the Convention. Rights similar to those in the Convention
are of course to be found in constitutional documents and other formal affirma-
tions of rights elsewhere.

Lord Cooke said: **21.85**

> The truth is, I think, that some rights are inherent and fundamental to democratic
> civilised society. Conventions, constitutions, bills of rights, and the like respond by
> recognising rather than creating them.

The common law of human rights

Lord Cooke's second observation concerned degrees of judicial review. It is felici- **21.86**
tous and important and must be quoted in full:

> Lord Steyn illuminated the distinctions between 'traditional' (that is to say in terms
> of English law, *Wednesbury*) standards of judicial review and higher standards under
> the European Convention or the common law of human rights. As he indicates often
> the results are the same. But the view that the standards are the same appears to have
> received its quietus in *Smith and Grady v United Kingdom*[108] and *Lustig-Prean and
> Beckett v United Kingdom.*[109] And I think the day will come when it will be more
> widely recognised that *Associated Provincial Picture Houses Ltd v Wednesbury Corp*[110]
> was an unfortunately retrogressive decision in English administrative law, in so far as
> it suggested that there are degrees of unreasonableness and that only a very extreme
> degree can bring an administrative decision within the legitimate scope of judicial
> invalidation. The depth of judicial review and the deference due to administrative
> discretion vary with the subject matter. It may well be, however, that the law can
> never be satisfied in any administrative field merely by a finding that the decision
> under review is not capricious or absurd.

The Court of Appeal gave further consideration to the proper application of **21.87**
the principle of proportionality in *Samaroo v Secretary of State for the Home*

---

[107] [2002] 2 WLR 754, 774 at para 33.
[108] (1999) 29 EHRR 493.
[109] (1999) 29 EHRR 548.
[110] [1948] 1 KB 223.

Department.[111] In that case the applicant, who had been convicted of being knowingly concerned with the importation of a class A drug, challenged the order which the Secretary of State had made for his deportation from the United Kingdom. It was accepted that a deportation order made in respect of a serious criminal offence is a measure taken in pursuance of a legitimate aim, namely the prevention of crime and disorder and (in the case of serious drug trafficking offences) the protection of the health, rights and freedoms of others. The issue that arose was: given that this is a legitimate aim, how should the decision-maker decide whether deportation in a particular case is justified, knowing that it will involve an interference with an Article 8(1) right? It was common ground that it would require a proportionate response. What does proportionality entail in such a context?

21.88 Lord Justice Dyson said that this question usually had to be answered in two distinct stages. At the first stage the question was: could the prevention of crime and disorder and the protection of health and freedom of others be achieved by a means which would interfere less with individual rights? The essential purpose of that stage of the inquiry was to see whether the legitimate aim could be achieved by means that did not interfere, or interfere so much, with a person's rights under the Convention. *Daly* was an example of such a case. At the second stage, it was assumed that the means employed to achieve the legitimate aim was necessary. The question at that stage was: did the measure have an excessive or disproportionate effect on the interests of affected persons? The task for the decision-maker was to strike a fair balance between the legitimate aim on the one hand, and the affected person's Convention rights on the other.

21.89 The onus was on the Secretary of State to show that he had struck a fair balance between the individual's right to respect for family life and prevention of crime and disorder. How much weight he gave to each factor would be the subject of careful scrutiny by the court. The Secretary of State enjoyed a discretion, or margin of appreciation to use Strasbourg language, but the court would interfere with the weight accorded by him where it concluded that the weight accorded was unfair and unreasonable. In that respect the level of scrutiny was undoubtedly more intense than it was when a decision was subject to review on traditional *Wednesbury* lines.

21.90 In *Samaroo* it was common ground that the deportation of Mr Samaroo would have a very adverse affect on his family. It was also accepted on all sides that the rights under Article 8(1) should be given a high degree of constitutional protection. The Court of Appeal, however, had no doubt that the Secretary of State was right to prefer the wider interest of the community to Mr Samaroo's Convention rights.

---

[111] [2001] EWCA Civ 1139.

It remains to be seen whether the two-stage process adopted by Dyson LJ will **21.91** commend itself to the courts in future cases, or whether Professor Jowell's four-stage process will prove more helpful. In *Samaroo* the answer to Professor Jowell's questions would have been:

(1) Did the action pursue a legitimate aim? Yes.
(2) Were the means employed suitable to achieve the aim? Yes.
(3) Could the aim have been achieved by a less restrictive alternative? No.
(4) Is the derogation justified overall in the interests of a democratic society? Yes.

Judicial review and the Freedom of Information Act

How far will the higher standards of judicial review under the Convention and the **21.92** common law of human rights recognized by the House of Lords in *R (Daly) v Secretary of State for the Home Department*[112] apply to decisions made under the Freedom of Information Act 2000?

Section 36 of the Freedom of Information Act 2000 provides that information is **21.93** exempt if in the *reasonable* opinion of a qualified person it might prejudice the effective conduct of public affairs. The courts' instincts will be to construe 'reasonable' in the *Wednesbury* sense, so that the Commissioner will only be able to challenge the decision of the qualified person if it is irrational.

The Freedom of Information Act refers specifically in section 60 to the 'principles **21.94** applied by the courts on an application for judicial review'. Again a court is likely to construe this as a reference to the principles of judicial review in the *Wednesbury* sense, particularly as section 60 is concerned with the conclusive nature of certificates issued by Ministers certifying that exemptions from the right to freedom of information are required for the purpose of safeguarding national security.

These may be special examples. The Freedom of Information Act has its own **21.95** enforcement procedures administered by the Information Commissioner and the Information Tribunal, with an appeal on a point of law to the High Court. It seems probable that, where the courts are concerned whether on appeal or on an application for judicial review, to consider not just rights under the Freedom of Information Act, but also rights to information under Article 8, and possibly under Article 10, the courts will apply the higher test laid down in *R (Daly) v Secretary of State for the Home Department*.

---

[112] [2001] 2 WLR 1622.

Part H

DEVOLUTION

22

SCOTLAND

A. Introduction

The principal purpose of this chapter is to describe the right to obtain access to **22.01** documents held by Scottish public authorities which is conferred by the Freedom of Information (Scotland) Act 2002. It is assumed that that Act will be brought into force in the form in which it was passed and the description of its effect which is given here is based on that assumption.

Some knowledge of the devolution of government from Westminster assists in **22.02** understanding the Scottish Act, as the Freedom of Information (Scotland) Act 2002 is styled in this chapter, and its relationship with the Freedom of Information Act 2000, or the UK Act as it is here called.[1] A brief sketch of the principal bodies of government, legislative and administrative, is therefore essayed at the outset,[2] after which the relationship of the Scottish and UK Acts,

---

[1] In the footnotes the Scottish Act appears as FOI(S)A 2002 and the UK Act as FOIA 2000. But distaste for acronyms has excluded these abbreviations from the text. Occasionally the Scottish Act is referred to in the text by its full title to avoid possible confusion.

[2] For more detailed accounts, see N Burrows, *Devolution* (2000) (including discussion of the arrangements for Wales and Northern Ireland); C Ashton and V Finch, *Constitutional Law in Scotland* (2000) and CMG Himsworth and CR Munro, *The Scotland Act 1998* (2nd edn, 2000)

the operation of the UK Act in Scotland and, at greatest length, the provisions of the Scottish Act are discussed.

22.03 The final parts of the chapter, perhaps perversely to those who esteem chronological order, outline various currently available ways of obtaining access to documents held by public authorities. These comprise the Code of Practice on Access to Scottish Executive Information which forms a type of penumbral precursor to, or dress rehearsal for, the Scottish Act, and some other methods of obtaining access to official information.

B. Government in Scotland

The UK and Scottish Parliaments

22.04 By the Scotland Act 1998, section 1(1) it was enacted that there should be a Scottish Parliament. The Scottish Parliament is a legislative body, whose members are elected, having the power to make laws, known as Acts of the Scottish Parliament.[3] But the legislative competence of the Scottish Parliament is limited. Amongst other limits on that competence, the Scotland Act 1998 specifies a range of topics which are excluded from it; these topics are called reserved matters.[4] An Act of the Scottish Parliament or any provision of it which is outside the legislative competence of the Scottish Parliament is not law.[5] Further, the power of the Scottish Parliament to make laws does not affect the power of the Parliament of the United Kingdom to make laws for Scotland.[6] The Scottish Parliament was, therefore, created by the UK Parliament and derives its legislative power from, and holds it subordinately to, the legislative power of the UK Parliament.

22.05 In this way, power to legislate for Scotland in respect of certain matters is devolved to the Scottish Parliament, but the UK Parliament, in which, of course, MPs returned by Scottish constituencies continue to sit,[7] retains overall competence to legislate for Scotland even in respect of devolved matters. And in respect of reserved matters the UK Parliament holds the sole legislative competence. But,

---

(for that Act with detailed notes). And for an historical analysis, see V Bogdanor, *Devolution in the United Kingdom* (1999).

[3] Scotland Act 1998, s 28(1).

[4] ibid, s 29. For reserved matters, see Sch 5 to the Act (which has effect by virtue of s 30(1)). See s 29(2) for other limits on the Parliament's legislative competence. For an example of a challenge to an Act of the Parliament, see *Anderson, Reid and Doherty v Scottish Ministers* [2001] UKPC D5, 2002 SC (PC) 63, [2002] 3 WLR 1460 (Privy Council), 2001 SC 1 (Inner House).

[5] ibid, s 29(1).

[6] ibid, s 28(7).

[7] Although the Scotland Act 1998, s 86 prepares the way for reduction of the number of Scottish MPs at Westminster by amending the Parliamentary Constituencies Act 1986 so as to remove the rule that Scotland should have not fewer than 71 constituencies.

although the UK Parliament retains competence to legislate for Scotland in respect of devolved matters, the expectation was that it would not normally do so and, in the House of Lords, Lord Sewel, then Parliamentary Under-Secretary of State in the Scottish Office, stated:

> However, as happened in Northern Ireland earlier in the century, we would expect a convention to be established that Westminster would not normally legislate with regard to devolved matters in Scotland without the consent of the Scottish parliament.[8]

The expected convention is also referred to in the Memorandum of Under- **22.06** standing between the United Kingdom government, the Scottish Ministers, the Cabinet of the National Assembly for Wales and the Northern Ireland Executive Committee[9] where it is stated:[10]

> The United Kingdom Parliament retains authority to legislate on any issue, whether devolved or not. It is ultimately for Parliament to decide what use to make of that power. However, the UK Government will proceed in accordance with the convention that the UK Parliament would not normally legislate with regard to devolved matters except with the agreement of the devolved legislature.

The procedure whereby the Scottish Parliament gives its consent to the UK **22.07** Parliament legislating on devolved matters is by passing a motion, known as a 'Sewel motion', permitting the UK Parliament to do so. Guidance on the circumstances in which the consent of the Scottish Parliament should be sought has been given by both the UK government[11] and the Scottish Executive.[12]

The number of occasions on which the UK Parliament has passed legislation con- **22.08** cerning matters which have been devolved has been surprisingly high. A study of the subject[13] reveals that from July 1999 to June 2001 23 Sewel motions concerning 24 separate Bills were agreed by the Scottish Parliament; while during the same period the Scottish Parliament enacted 19 Bills. The balance has tipped in the other direction since the General Election in June 2001. But, as is described in paragraph 22.20 below, in the case of freedom of information, the UK Parliament has observed the boundary of the competence devolved upon the Scottish Parliament.

Like the UK Parliament, the Scottish Parliament is not simply a legislative body. **22.09** The Scottish Ministers, apart from the Law Officers, must be drawn from the members of the Scottish Parliament. Their activities are subject to scrutiny in the

---

[8] *Hansard*, HL (series 5) vol 592, col 791 (21 July 1998).
[9] Cm 5240 (December 2001).
[10] At para 13.
[11] Devolution Guidance Note 10, *Post Devolution Primary Legislation affecting Scotland.*
[12] *'The Sewel Convention': Westminster Legislation in Devolved Areas* (February, 2001).
[13] A Page and A Batey, 'Scotland's Other Parliament: Westminster Legislation about Devolved Matters in Scotland since Devolution' [2002] PL 501.

Parliament. And the Scottish Parliament provides a forum for debate and the airing of grievances. It is entitled to debate non-devolved matters, but the Memorandum of Understanding between the UK government and the devolved administrations requires the devolved executive to encourage the Parliament, when debating non-devolved matters, 'to bear in mind the responsibility of the UK Parliament in these matters'.[14]

The Scottish Parliamentary Corporate Body

22.10 By the Scotland Act 1998, section 21 is established the Scottish Parliamentary Corporate Body, a body corporate whose members are the Presiding Officer[15] and four members of the Parliament appointed in accordance with standing orders. This body is charged with ensuring that the Parliament is provided with the property, staff and services which are required for the Parliament's purposes. Mention is made of this body here because it is a Scottish public authority within the meaning of the Freedom of Information (Scotland) Act 2002.[16]

The Administration in Scotland

22.11 As well as establishing a legislative branch of devolved government in Scotland, the Scotland Act 1998 established a Scottish Executive, whose members are the First Minister, such Ministers as he may appoint,[17] the Lord Advocate and the Solicitor General for Scotland. The members of the Scottish Executive are referred to collectively as the Scottish Ministers.[18]

22.12 The Scottish Administration comprises a wider body of persons.[19] The First Minister may, with the approval of Her Majesty, appoint members of the Parliament to be junior Scottish Ministers.[20] Junior Scottish Ministers do not form part of the Scottish Executive, although they must resign if the Parliament resolves that the Scottish Executive no longer enjoys the confidence of the

---

[14] Cm 5240, para 15.

[15] The Scottish Parliament must, at its first meeting after a general election, elect a Presiding Officer and two deputies, all of whom must be members of the Scottish Parliament; Scotland Act 1998, s 19(1). In outline, the Presiding Officer's functions are to ensure the efficient conduct and administration of Scottish Parliamentary business and to chair sessions of the Scottish Parliament; see *Scotland's Parliament* (Cm 3658, 1997) para 9.5. He is also charged with specific duties under the Scotland Act 1998.

[16] FOI(S)A 2002, s 3(1)(a)(i) and Sch 1, para 3.

[17] Scotland Act 1998, s 44. Power is conferred on the First Minister (who must himself be a member of the Scottish Parliament; see s 45(1)) to appoint Ministers from among the members of the Scottish Parliament by s 47.

[18] Scotland Act 1998, s 44(2).

[19] ibid, s 126(6) to (8).

[20] ibid, s 49.

Parliament.[21] Certain other offices are non-ministerial offices in the Scottish Administration. These include the Registrar General of Births, Deaths and Marriages, the Keeper of the Registers of Scotland and the Keeper of the Records of Scotland. Other offices may be added by order in council.[22] The Scottish Ministers may also appoint persons to be members of the staff of the Scottish Administration.[23] Persons so appointed comprise the civil service for the devolved government of Scotland; service as the holder of any office in the Scottish Administration, other than Ministerial office or as a member of its staff counts as service in the Home Civil Service.

The Scottish Executive may only exercise any function if it does so within its competence. The initial limits of the devolved administrative competence of the Scottish Executive are shaped so as to correspond with the legislative competence of the Scottish Parliament. Thus, to exercise any function is outside devolved competence if a provision of an Act of the Scottish Parliament conferring the function would be outside the legislative competence of the Scottish Parliament.[24] And certain functions previously exercisable by a Minister of the Crown, to the extent that they are exercisable within the devolved competence, are transferred to the Scottish Ministers.[25] But provision is made for the transfer by order in council of other functions presently exercised by a Minister of the Crown in or as regards Scotland to be exercisable by the Scottish Ministers instead of or concurrently with the Minister of the Crown, or for the functions to become exercisable by the Minister of the Crown only with the agreement of, or after consultation with, the Scottish Ministers.[26]

22.13

At Westminster there remains the Secretary of State for Scotland and, as a department of the UK government, the Scotland Office, as the Scottish Office has been renamed. The Scotland Office consists of the offices of the Secretary of State for Scotland and of the Advocate General. The responsibilities of the Secretary of State include:

22.14

> the devolution settlement for Scotland, as set out in the Scotland Act 1998; representing Scottish interests within the UK Government in matters that are reserved to the UK Parliament; managing payments of grant and loans by the UK Government to, and receipts from, the Scottish Consolidated Fund; a number of residual functions in reserved areas such as the conduct and funding of elections in Scotland, the Parliamentary Boundary Commission for Scotland and private legislation procedure on reserved matters.[27]

---

[21] ibid, s 49(4)(c).
[22] ibid, s 126(8).
[23] ibid, s 51.
[24] ibid, s 54(3).
[25] ibid, s 53(1).
[26] ibid, s 63.
[27] *The Scotland Office Charter.* This document is published by the Scotland Office and contains a summary of its functions.

22.15   The Advocate General for Scotland is a post created by the Scotland Act 1998.[28] The Advocate General for Scotland is a Minister of the Crown who acts as the Law Officer to the UK government on matters of Scots law. The need for such an office-holder was caused by the Lord Advocate and Solicitor General for Scotland becoming members of the Scottish Executive. In addition to taking over the functions formerly fulfilled in the UK government by those officers, the Advocate General has specific powers as regards devolution issues. A devolution issue is one which concerns whether a devolved institution has acted within its competence, including whether the Scottish Parliament has acted within its competence in passing an Act.[29] The Advocate General has power to raise proceedings for the determination of a devolution issue, to participate in proceedings in which a devolution issue has arisen and to refer, or caused to be referred, devolution issues to the Judicial Committee of the Privy Council.[30]

Local government

22.16   Since 1 April 1996, when the reorganization enacted by the Local Government etc (Scotland) Act 1994 took effect, there have been 32 council areas in Scotland, for each of which there is one council whose members are elected by the local government electors for the appropriate area.[31] Thus, throughout Scotland there is one tier of elected local authorities.

22.17   But the Scottish Executive has power, in defined circumstances, to create joint boards to carry out certain functions with which local authorities have been charged.[32] A joint board, so created, is a body corporate, constituted for the purposes of a combination of local authorities, which consists of and may only consist of persons appointed by those local authorities.[33]

22.18   The functions formerly exercised by the Secretary of State for Scotland as regards local government are now exercised by the Scottish Executive. How devolved government and local government should demarcate their spheres of activity and responsibility is a developing topic. In 1999 the Commission on Local Government and the Scottish Parliament produced its final report entitled *Moving Forward: Local Government and the Scottish Parliament.* In January 2002 the Executive published a consultation paper on a proposed Local Government Bill.

---

[28] Scotland Act 1998, s 87.

[29] ibid, s 98 and Sch 6, Part I, para 1.

[30] ibid, Sch 6, Part II, paras 4(1), 5, 6 and Part V, paras 33 and 34.

[31] Local Government etc (Scotland) Act 1994, ss 1, 2, 3 and 5.

[32] Local Government (Scotland) Act 1973, ss 62A, 62B and 62C, inserted by the Local Government etc (Scotland) Act 1994, s 20. The power was previously exercisable by the Secretary of State for Scotland.

[33] Local Government (Scotland) Act 1973, s 235(1).

European Union

No account of government in any part of the United Kingdom, however sketchy, **22.19** should omit reference to the European Union as a source of law and as an administrative power. But, for the most part, the main actor on the European stage remains the UK government rather than the devolved administrations.[34] Relations with the European Communities and their institutions is a reserved matter[35] and Ministers of the Crown retain their power to implement EU law in Scotland,[36] albeit that this power is shared with the Scottish Ministers.[37] Coordination between the UK government and the devolved administrations on EU matters is the subject of a Concordat published with the Memorandum of Understanding between those administrations.[38] The Concordat records the wish of the UK government 'to involve the Scottish Executive as directly and fully as possible in decision making on EU matters which touch on devolved areas'. But, relevant to the present topic of freedom of information:

> Participation will be subject to mutual respect for the confidentiality of discussions and adherence by the Scottish executive to the resulting UK line without which it would be impossible to maintain such close working relationships.

C. The United Kingdom Act and the Scottish Act

Demarcation between the UK and Scottish Acts

The Freedom of Information Act 2000, an Act of the United Kingdom **22.20** Parliament, and the Freedom of Information (Scotland) Act 2002, an Act of the Scottish Parliament, dealing with the same subject matter but applying to different public bodies, illustrate the limits on competence imposed by or observed under the system of devolved government created by the Scotland Act 1998. For the Scottish public authorities to which the Scottish Act applies carry out functions which are within the range of the Scottish Parliament's competence. And the UK Act, which extends in its effect to Scotland, only does so in relation to public authorities which operate outside the devolved competence. This achievement of mutual respect results from the fact that the UK Act and the Scottish Act, although distinct in legislative genesis, share, amongst other features, a common method of defining their application by specifically identifying the public bodies

---

[34] For a discussion of whether and how the Scottish Administration might directly intervene in European affairs, see G Clark, 'Scottish Devolution and the European Union' [1999] PL 504.

[35] Scotland Act 1998, s 30 and Sch 5, Part I, para 7(1).

[36] ibid, s 57(1).

[37] Because the power has also been transferred to the Scottish Ministers by s 53. A shared power in this context is not one which must be jointly exercised by both a Minister of the Crown and the Scottish Ministers, but is a power which may be separately exercised by either of them.

[38] Cm 5240 (December 2001).

within their scope and thereby giving that scope clear and definite boundaries. In both cases, the method employed is to define the relevant public authorities as being those:

(a) which are listed in a Schedule to the relevant Act; or

(b) which are designated as a public authority under the UK Act by the Secretary of State or under the Scottish Act by the Scottish Ministers; or

(c) which are publicly-owned companies as defined in similar terms in the two Acts.[39]

22.21 Thus, as it is entitled to do by the UK Act, the UK Parliament has created legislation which has effect in Scotland. But, in doing so, it has observed limits which follow the legislative competence of the Scottish Parliament.

(a) The organs of central or devolved government listed in Schedule 1, Part I, to the UK Act as public authorities for the purpose of the UK Act do not include any institutions created by the Scotland Act 1998 (though by contrast they include the Northern Ireland Assembly and the National Assembly for Wales); nor, by virtue of section 80 of the UK Act, may any of those Scottish institutions be added to Schedule 1 or designated as a public body for the purpose of the UK Act. But some government departments, to which the UK Act applies, carry out activities in Scotland as well as elsewhere in the United Kingdom.

(b) The organs of local government listed in Schedule 1, Part II, to the UK Act as public authorities for the purpose of the UK Act only include authorities and bodies in England and Wales and Northern Ireland.

(c) Similarly Parts III and IV of Schedule 1 to the UK Act, relating to the National Health Service and various educational establishments, list only bodies or persons in England and Wales and Northern Ireland.

(d) Part V of Schedule 1 to the UK Act, being concerned with the police, observes similar limits but also includes the British Transport Police whose remit extends to Scotland and the Ministry of Defence Police whose powers likewise extend to Scotland. The activities of these two bodies relate to reserved matters as defined in the Scotland Act 1998: rail transport security is reserved by Schedule 5, Part II, paragraph E2 and various matters relating to defence and national security by Schedule 5, Part I, paragraph 9 and Part II, paragraph B8.

(e) Part VI of Schedule 1 to the UK Act sets out an uncategorized list of bodies and persons who are public authorities for the purpose of the UK Act. Many of these authorities perform activities in and relating to Scotland. Some of them carry on activities which concern reserved matters, for example, the

---

[39] FOIA 2000, s 3 and FOI(S)A 2002, s 3.

Gaming Board for Great Britain, betting, gaming and lotteries;[40] the Post Office, posts and regulation of postal services;[41] and the Scottish Advisory Committee on Telecommunications, telecommunications and wireless telegraphy.[42] Others have mixed functions, that is they carry on some functions which are reserved but others which are not,[43] such an authority is included within the scope of the UK Act if it is a cross-border public authority, that is one which has been specified as such by an order made pursuant to the Scotland Act 1998, section 88.[44]

Conversely, the Scottish Act observes the limit set by the reservation and the **22.22** exception to it in Schedule 5 to the Scotland Act 1998 concerning public access to information held by public bodies or holders of public offices (including government departments and persons acting on behalf of the Crown).[45] That exception extends to information held by the Scottish Parliament, any part of the Scottish Administration, the Scottish Parliamentary Corporate Body and any Scottish public authority with mixed functions or no reserved functions and accordingly it is to such information that the Scottish Act applies. The exception is itself subject to a proviso contained within it, which is that the information held by one of the identified Scottish bodies should not have been supplied by a Minister of the Crown or government department and be held in confidence. The Scottish Act duly provides that information is not held by a Scottish public authority for the purpose of the Scottish Act if it is held by the authority in confidence, having been supplied by a Minister of the Crown or a department of the government of the United Kingdom.[46]

Principal points of difference between the UK and Scottish Acts

The UK Act and the Scottish Act share a similar structure. In summary, the cen- **22.23** tral features of the two statutory schemes are:

(a) the specific identification of the public bodies to which the statute applies;
(b) the conferring of a general right of access to official information in recorded form;
(c) the exemption from that general right of a series of categories of information, in many but not all cases subject to a public interest test;

---

[40] Scotland Act 1998, Sch 5, Part II, para B9.
[41] ibid, Sch 5, Part II, para C11.
[42] ibid, Sch 5, Part I, para C10.
[43] For the meaning of Scottish public authorities with mixed functions, see the Scotland Act 1998, Sch 5, Part III, para 1(4).
[44] Various authorities have been so specified by the Scotland Act 1998 (Cross-Border Public Authorities) (Specification) Order 1999, SI 1999/1319, many of which appear in Part VI of the Schedule.
[45] Scotland Act 1998, Sch 5, Part I, para B13.
[46] FOI(S)A 2002, s 3(2)(a)(ii).

(d) the imposition of the primary decision whether to claim exemption on the public body from whom the information has been requested;

(e) internal review by that public body of its own decision as a necessary preliminary step to any external appeal;[47]

(f) a scheme of statutory appeal to specialist bodies[48] concerning the treatment of a request for information, with subsequent appeal to the courts of law restricted to points of law;

(g) the promotion and supervision of the scheme by an individual Commissioner;

(h) a duty on public authorities to adopt a publication scheme; and

(i) the amplification of the statute by codes of practice.

22.24 But there are divergences, with varying significance, between the two Acts.

(a) Under the Scottish Act a simple right to be given information requested from a public authority is conferred,[49] whereas under the UK Act a bipartite right to be informed whether the authority holds the requested information and, if it does, to have it communicated is granted.[50] The significance of this is limited. The main purpose of dividing the right in the UK Act is for the purpose of enabling authorities in certain cases not to disclose whether they hold information or not. The Scottish Act provides for the same result but by a different method.[51]

(b) Both Acts confer exemption from disclosure on certain categories of exempt information subject to a public interest test. The tests are expressed slightly differently in the two Acts but the verbal variation does not appear to affect the content of the test.[52]

(c) Some categories of exempt information are defined by reference to the harm which might be caused to a specified interest by disclosure. Under the UK Act information is exempt if its disclosure would or might prejudice the specified interest; under the Scottish Act information is exempt if its disclosure would or might substantially prejudice the specified interest.[53]

(d) Under both Acts decision notices or enforcement notices given by the relevant Commissioner to certain, mainly central government, departments or

---

[47] Under the UK Act any complaints procedure must be exhausted before an appeal may be made to the UK Commissioner, but where the public authority in question had no complaints procedure, this stage would be omitted; see FOIA 2000, s 50(2)(a). Under the Scottish Act, the review is statutorily required; see FOI(S)A 2002, s 20.

[48] Under both Acts, the first appeal is made to the relevant Commissioner; under the UK Act a further layer of appeal exists from the Information Commissioner to the Information Tribunal; see FOIA 2000, s 57.

[49] FOI(S)A 2002, s 1(1).

[50] FOIA 2000, s 1(1).

[51] See paras 22.101–22.103 and 22.173–22.174 below.

[52] Compare FOIA 2000, s 2(1)(b) with FOI(S)A 2002, s 2(1)(b) and see para 22.56 below.

[53] See para 22.58 below.

authorities may be vetoed by a certificate signed by a Minister. The Commissioner may only issue such a notice on the ground that, in the Commissioner's view, the authority to whom the notice was given had failed to comply with the Act. Under the UK Act the Minister must certify that he has on reasonable grounds formed the opinion that there was no relevant failure;[54] under the Scottish Act, the First Minister must, in addition, certify that the information requested is of exceptional sensitivity.[55]

(e) The Scottish Act does not include provision whereby a Minister may certify that information is exempt because it was supplied by a body dealing with security matters. Under the UK Act information which is the subject of such a certificate is absolutely exempt.[56] Information to which that procedure might be applied is likely to be exempt under another head of exemption and, under the Scottish Act, the exemption would have to be claimed under that head. The exemption would then be subject to the public interest test.

(f) A pivotal figure in the schemes created by each of the Acts is the Commissioner who is charged with implementing the pertinent Act and promoting the fulfilment of its aims. But under the UK Act the existing office of Data Protection Commissioner is co-opted for the purpose and the name of that office changed to the Information Commissioner.[57] The Information Commissioner retains his duties under the Data Protection Act 1998.[58] Under the Scottish Act the Scottish Information Commissioner is created as a new officer.[59] His remit does not extend to data protection which, being a reserved matter under the Scotland Act 1998,[60] is outside the legislative competence of the Scottish Parliament.

(g) A Scottish public authority when adopting or reviewing a publication scheme for the purpose of the Scottish Act must have regard to the public interest in allowing public access to information which relates to its provision of services, their costs and standards or consists of facts or analyses on the basis of which decisions of importance to the public have been made by the authority.[61] Public authorities under the UK Act are not enjoined, by the corresponding provision,[62] to have specific regard to these matters. But, in the Scottish Act, these matters are specified as instances of the more general

---

[54] FOIA 2000, s 53(2).
[55] FOI(S)A 2002, s 52(2).
[56] FOIA 2000, ss 23 and 2(3)(b).
[57] ibid, s 18(1).
[58] Some tension might be perceived between the function of protecting data from misuse and promoting freedom of information, in particular in Scotland where data protection is under the remit of the UK Information Commissioner whereas freedom of information is supervised by the Scottish Information Commissioner.
[59] FOI(S)A 2002, s 42(1).
[60] Scotland Act 1998, Sch 5, Part II, para B2.
[61] FOI(S)A 2002, s 23(3)(a)(i) and (ii).
[62] FOIA 2000, s 19(2)(a).

public interest in allowing public access to information held by the authority. Public authorities under the UK Act must have regard to that general interest.

D. Application of the UK Act in Scotland

22.25 The application of the UK Act extends to Scotland, although it may not be made to apply to the Scottish Parliament, any part of the Scottish Administration, the Scottish Parliamentary Corporate Body or any Scottish public authority with mixed functions or no reserved functions within the meaning of the Scotland Act 1998.[63] And by the definition of 'government department' in section 84 of the UK Act the bodies just mentioned do not fall within the meaning of that term for the purpose of the UK Act. But despite these exclusions there are public authorities operating in Scotland to which the UK Act will apply. Such authorities will include any government departments, as defined in the UK Act, which carry out functions in Scotland. In such cases a person seeking information about activities in Scotland will have to make his request under the UK Act. In some, but not all, of these cases, the process of appeal may, as described in paragraph 22.27 below, lead to the Court of Session rather than the English High Court. This will occur where the public authority whose original response to a request for information is under question has its address in Scotland.

22.26 In outline, the process of appeal under the UK Act is as follows. A dissatisfied applicant for information from a public authority may (after exhausting any complaints procedure provided by that public authority) apply to the Information Commissioner for a decision whether his request for information has been dealt with in accordance with the relevant provisions of the Act.[64] The Information Commissioner may, amongst other steps, issue a decision notice, containing his decision for or against the applicant.[65] The Commissioner also has power to issue:

(a) an information notice, for the purpose of seeking further information from the authority either in the context of an individual application or otherwise;[66] or

(b) an enforcement notice, requiring the authority to take specified steps in order to comply with its obligations.[67]

---

[63] FOIA 2000, s 80.
[64] ibid, s 50(1); see s 50(2)(a) for the need to exhaust internal complaints procedures and see generally ch 7 above.
[65] ibid, s 50(3)(b).
[66] ibid, s 51(1).
[67] ibid, s 52(1).

A right of appeal to the Information Tribunal is afforded to whichever party is adversely affected by the decision contained in a decision notice and to any authority to which an information notice or enforcement notice is given.[68]

A further right of appeal, though restricted to points of law, is then afforded from the Information Tribunal to the ordinary courts of law.[69] If the address of the public authority to which the appeal relates is in Scotland, the appeal lies to the Court of Session, but if the address is in England or Wales, the appeal lies to the High Court of Justice in England.[70] **22.27**

E. The Scottish Act

The structure of the statutory scheme created by the Scottish Act is not dissimilar to that created by the UK Act. For the purpose of the following exposition, it is assumed that the Scottish Act will be brought into force in the form in which it was enacted. **22.28**

As with the UK Act, a certain amount of time will pass before the Scottish Act will take full effect. Unless repealed, the UK Act must come into full force on or before 1 December 2005.[71] The UK Act contains no provision for any delay beyond that date. Again subject to repeal, the Scottish Act is to come into full force on a day to be appointed by the Scottish Ministers not later than 31 December 2005, but the Scottish Information Commissioner is empowered to recommend that a later date be appointed and, if he so recommends, to specify the date.[72] **22.29**

The Scottish Act is carefully drafted so as to avoid gender specific language, except with respect to the Queen. The skill of the person who drafted it is most apparent in Parts 3 and 4 of the Act which concern the Scottish Information Commissioner and Enforcement respectively. The authors of the present text have not maintained this approach, but their failure is purely semantic and should not be read as implying any assumption that the Commissioner, or any other individual apart from the Queen, belongs to any particular sex. **22.30**

---

[68] ibid, s 57(1) and (2).
[69] ibid, s 59.
[70] ibid, s 59.
[71] ibid, s 87(3).
[72] FOI(S)A 2002, s 75(1). Different dates may be appointed or specified for different provisions, for different persons or categories of person and for different purposes.

(1) The right of access to information held by Scottish public authorities

The general entitlement

22.31   A person who requests information from a Scottish public authority which holds it is entitled to be given it by the authority.[73] A person making such a request is referred to in the Scottish Act[74] and in this chapter as 'the applicant'. Provision is made for the exercise of the rights conferred by the Act by persons under sixteen.[75]

22.32   Thus, the general entitlement conferred by the Scottish Act is simply to be given the relevant information. The Scottish Act does not reproduce the bipartite right contained in the UK Act whereby the applicant is entitled first to be informed by the authority whether it holds the information and if so to have the information communicated to him.[76] But, the substance of the duty differs little. First, a Scottish public authority may answer a request by giving the applicant notice that it does not hold it[77] while an authority to which the UK Act applies may comply with its bipartite duty simply by communicating the information.[78] Secondly, under the UK Act there are categories of information which, in certain circumstances, carry not only exemption from disclosure but also an exemption from the duty which the authority holding the information would otherwise be under to confirm or deny that it holds the information in question.[79] In respect of such information, an applicant draws a blank from the authority to which he made his request; he neither obtains the information nor learns whether the authority holds it nor even whether the information exists. Under the UK Act the method whereby this is achieved is to provide, in relation to certain categories of information, that the duty to confirm or deny whether the information is held by the authority does not arise. Under the Scottish Act the same result is achieved by providing that, in relation to certain categories of exempt information, the Scottish public authority from whom the information is requested may give a refusal notice which does not disclose whether it holds the information requested.[80]

Scottish public authorities

22.33   For the purpose of the Scottish Act, 'Scottish public authority' means:

(a) any body which, any other person who, or the holder of any office which—
   (i)   is listed in schedule 1; or
   (ii) is designated by order under s 5(1); or

---

[73] FOI(S)A 2002, s 1(1).
[74] ibid, s 1(2).
[75] ibid, s 69.
[76] FOIA 2000, s 1(1).
[77] FOI(S)A 2002, s 16.
[78] FOIA 2000, s 1(5).
[79] ibid, s 2(1).
[80] FOI(S)A 2002, s 18.

(b) a publicly-owned company, as defined by s 6.[81]

Schedule 1 is divided into seven parts.   **22.34**

- Part 1 contains the Scottish Ministers, the Scottish Parliament and the Scottish Parliamentary Corporate Body.
- Part 2 contains various non-ministerial office-holders in the Scottish Administration.
- Part 3 concerns local government and includes, amongst others, councils constituted by the Local Government etc (Scotland) Act 1994 and joint boards as defined by the Local Government (Scotland) Act 1973, section 235(1).
- Part 4 concerns the National Health Service.
- Part 5 comprises various types of educational institutions.
- Part 6 concerns the police.
- Part 7 contains a general list of public bodies, most of them individually identified.

Schedule 1 may be amended by order by the Scottish Ministers so as to add   **22.35** authorities to, or remove them from, it. But they may only add a public authority which is not already listed (thereby avoiding unnecessary duplication[82]) and which is either part of the Scottish Administration or a Scottish public authority with mixed functions or no reserved functions. For the meaning of these terms reference is made to the Scotland Act 1998, Schedule 5, Part III, paragraphs 1(4) and 2.[83] A Scottish public authority some of whose functions relate to reserved matters and some of which do not has mixed functions; such a public authority is not reserved, that is, it is not put outside the legislative competence of the Scottish Parliament, unless it is a cross-border public authority.[84]

The Scottish Ministers are empowered to designate by order any person who is   **22.36** not listed in Schedule 1, cannot be added to it by order under section 4(1) and is neither a public body nor the holder of any public office. To qualify for such designation the person must appear to the Scottish Ministers either to exercise functions of a public nature or to be providing, under a contract made with a Scottish public authority, any service whose provision is a function of that authority. The power, therefore, caters, amongst other things, for the situation where a public authority has contracted one of its otherwise public functions out to a private body. There is an obligation to consult the person to whom the order will relate or persons appearing to represent that person before making the order.

---

[81] FOI(S)A 2002, s 3(1).
[82] The draftsman of FOIA 2000 regarded the Secretary of State as prone to engage in the same excess; see FOIA 2000, s 4(1).
[83] FOI(S)A 2002, s 4(2).
[84] For what is meant by a cross-border public authority, see the Scotland Act 1998, s 88.

22.37 The Scottish Information Commissioner may from time to time make proposals to the Scottish Ministers for the exercise by them of their power under section 4 to amend Schedule 1 to the Act and of their power under section 5 to designate persons as Scottish public authorities.[85]

22.38 A company is a 'publicly-owned company' for the purpose of the Scottish Act if it is wholly owned by the Scottish Ministers or by any other public authority listed in Schedule 1, other than an authority so listed only in relation to information of a specified description. An attempt was made to revise the Bill which preceded the Act so as to extend the definition to include companies which were controlled by public authorities. The amendment would have removed the temptation to which, it was suggested, public authorities might otherwise succumb to evade the legislation by selling a single share in the company[86] but it did not find favour with the Scottish Parliament.

Information

22.39 In this context, 'information' means information which is recorded in any form.[87] Thus the Act provides a right of access to documents and other records as opposed to a right to ask questions and receive information in answer to them.

22.40 The information to which an applicant is entitled is the information held by the authority at the time when his request is received by it.[88] But the authority may amend or delete information contained in its records, even though it has received a request for that information, so long as the amendments or deletions would have been made, regardless of the request, between the time when it received the request and the time when it gives the information.[89] But the authority's power to make such amendments or deletions does not entitle it to destroy the information before it can be given unless the circumstances are such that it is not reasonably practicable to prevent such destruction from occurring.[90] Any tendency to abuse these powers should be tempered by the possibility of prosecution for the offence of altering or destroying a record with the intention of preventing its disclosure.[91]

---

[85] FOI(S)A 2002, s 43(4).
[86] The Campaign for Freedom of Information in Scotland, *Freedom of Information (Scotland) Bill, Stage 3, Briefing on Amendments* (23 April 2002).
[87] FOI(S)A 2002, s 73.
[88] ibid, s 1(4).
[89] ibid, s 1(4).
[90] ibid, s 1(5).
[91] ibid, s 65 (1). See para 22.234 below.

Information to which the entitlement applies

Subject to the exceptions mentioned in the following paragraph, an applicant is **22.41** entitled to obtain disclosure of any information which is held by the Scottish public authority to which he addresses his request. Except where the public authority is the Keeper of the Records of Scotland,[92] information is held by an authority if it is held by the authority otherwise than on behalf of another person or in confidence having been supplied by a Minister of the Crown or by a department of the government of the United Kingdom;[93] or if it is held by a person other than the authority on behalf of the authority.

In the following cases, a public authority is not obliged to comply with a request **22.42** for information:

(a) where the information is exempt from disclosure;[94]
(b) where the authority gives a fees notice to the applicant and the applicant fails to pay the fee;[95]
(c) where the authority estimates that the cost of complying with the request[96] would exceed a prescribed amount;[97]
(d) where the request is vexatious;[98]
(e) where the authority has previously complied with a request for information and a subsequent request is made by the same person which is identical or substantially similar before a reasonable period of time has passed between the request complied with and the subsequent request.[99]

Exempt information is discussed in the following paragraphs. The other cases in which a public authority need not comply with a request are discussed below in the section headed 'Procedure and enforcement'.

Exempt information

The considerations which determine whether particular information is **22.43** exempt vary according to the content of the information. Certain categories of

---

[92] The position relating to the Keeper of the Records of Scotland is discussed further at paras 22.55 and 22.237–22.239 below.
[93] FOI(S)A 2002, s 3(2)(a). Cf the proviso to the exception to para B13 of Sch 5, Part II to the Scotland Act 1998.
[94] By virtue of any provision of Part 2 of FOI(S)A 2002.
[95] FOI(S)A 2002, s 9(3).
[96] In certain circumstances the authority may take two or more requests into account at the same time in estimating the cost of compliance: ibid, s 12(2).
[97] ibid, s 12(1).
[98] ibid, s 14(1).
[99] ibid, s 14(2).

information have absolute exemption from disclosure.[100] In these cases, the question is simply whether the information falls into the relevant category. In all other cases, at least two questions arise: first, does the information fall into the relevant category of exempt information; and secondly, if so, is the public interest in disclosing the information outweighed by the public interest in maintaining the exemption of the information?[101]

Absolute exemptions

22.44 The categories on which absolute exemption from disclosure is conferred are as follows. With one exception, these categories may be divided into two loosely defined groups. The first group concerns information which is or will reasonably soon be made available to the public in some form; the second, information disclosure of which is precluded because of some over-riding rule of law. The rules of law which are recognized as having this effect include rules of law aimed at protecting individual privacy.

The first group of absolute exemptions: information otherwise available

22.45 In two cases information is made absolutely exempt where the information either is or will within a reasonable time be made publicly available. In these cases, there is nothing or little to be gained from putting an authority to the expense of complying with a request for the information. The two cases are:

(a) Information which the applicant can reasonably obtain other than by requesting it under the Act.[102] This category corresponds with that defined in section 21 of the UK Act.

(b) Information which is held, at the time of the applicant's request, with a view to its being published on a date within twelve weeks of the request and which it is reasonable to withhold until the intended date of publication.[103] This category corresponds with that defined in section 22 of the UK Act.

22.46 Personal data to which access may be obtained under the Data Protection Act 1998 will form one of the most important categories of exempt information under the first of the heads mentioned in the preceding paragraph. Under section 7 of that Act an individual who makes a written request and pays the appropriate fee is entitled, amongst other things, to be informed by any data controller whether personal data of which the individual is the data subject are being processed by that data controller and to have the information which constitutes that data communicated to him.[104] The rights are subject to a series of exemptions

---

[100] FOI(S)A 2002, s 2(2).
[101] ibid, s 2(1).
[102] ibid, s 25.
[103] ibid, s 27(1).
[104] Data Protection Act 1998, s 7(1)(a), (c)(i) and s 7(2).

contained in Part IV of the Data Protection Act 1998. A court may order the data controller to comply with the request if he fails to do so.[105]

A case similar to the two heads of exemption mentioned above is that of informa- **22.47**
tion obtained in the course of, or derived from, a programme of research where the programme is continuing with a view to a report of the research being published.[106] The similarity is perhaps limited in that what will be published may not include all the information on which the report is based. But the exemption, which is absolute, is restricted to information obtained in the course of or deriving from the continuing programme of research which, if disclosed, would, or would be likely to, prejudice substantially the programme, the interests of any individual participating in the programme, the interests of the authority which holds the information or the interests of the Scottish public authority which intends to publish the report, if different from the authority which holds the information. Thus the category depends upon the existence or likelihood of harm. This category does not correspond with any identified in the UK Act.

The second group of absolute exemptions: where a rule of law is recognized as over-riding the duty of disclosure

Where the disclosure of information by a Scottish public authority is prohibited **22.48**
by or under an enactment, is incompatible with a Community obligation or would constitute or be punishable as a contempt of court, the information in question is absolutely exempt from disclosure.[107] This category corresponds with that defined in section 44 of the UK Act.

Information is absolutely exempt from disclosure in two cases for the purpose of **22.49**
preserving its legally recognized confidentiality. These cases are:

(a) information in respect of which a claim to confidentiality of communications could be maintained in legal proceedings;[108]
(b) information which was obtained by a Scottish public authority from another person and its disclosure by that authority to the public would constitute a breach of confidence actionable by that person or any other person.[109]

The extent to which there is a legally enforceable rule of law protecting privacy, **22.50**
and, if there is, what its source is, is much debated, but certainly public bodies are required by the Convention right contained in Article 8 of the European Convention on Human Rights to respect individual privacy. That requirement

---

[105] ibid, s 7(9). This jurisdiction is exercisable by the Court of Session or the sheriff; s 15(1).
[106] FOI(S)A 2002, s 27(2).
[107] ibid, s 26.
[108] ibid, s 36(1). This category corresponds with that defined in FOIA 2000, s 42.
[109] FOI(S)A 2002, s 36(2). This category corresponds with that defined in FOIA 2000, s 41.
Such information may be obtainable under the Data Protection Act 1998.

may be categorized for present purposes as a rule of law over-riding the duty to make disclosure and in the following cases, where individual privacy is at stake, information is made absolutely exempt:

(a) information constituting personal data of which the applicant is the data subject;[110]

(b) information constituting personal census information;[111]

(c) information constituting a deceased person's health record;[112]

(d) information which constitutes personal data and which falls within any of paragraphs (a) to (d) of the definition of 'data' in section 1(1) of the Data Protection Act 1998 where disclosure of the information would contravene any of the data protection principles; and information which constitutes personal data not falling within any of paragraphs (a) to (d) of the definition of 'data' in section 1(1) of the Data Protection Act 1998 where disclosure of the information would contravene any of the data protection principles if the exemptions in section 33A(1) of that Act were disregarded.[113] These categories correspond with those defined in section 40(2) of the UK Act.

Court records and other documents created for the purpose of proceedings, inquiries and arbitrations

22.51 The final category of information on which absolute exemption is conferred concerns information contained in documents relating to proceedings before a court, tribunal or other body exercising the judicial power of the state or an inquiry (other than an inquiry instituted under the Fatal Accidents and Sudden Deaths Inquiry (Scotland) Act 1976) or an arbitration where that information is held by a Scottish public authority solely because it is contained in such a document.[114] This category corresponds with that defined in section 32 of the UK Act.

22.52 Perhaps, at least in so far as the exemption relates to particular civil proceedings, it may be justified by considering the basis on which the court or other body holds the documents as being ancillary, or secondary; that is the court or other body holds the information not for its own sake, but for the purpose of resolving the disputes of other persons or facilitating their resolution. If those other persons are or include public authorities, then the information may (if not otherwise exempt) be sought from them rather than the court.

22.53 In one respect the justification just mentioned does not apply. That is the exemption conferred on documents served on or by a Scottish public authority for the

---

[110] FOI(S)A 2002, s 38(1)(a). This category corresponds with that defined in FOIA 2000, s 40(1).

[111] FOI(S)A 2002, s 38(1)(c).

[112] ibid, s 38(1)(d).

[113] ibid, s 38(1)(b).

[114] ibid, s 37.

purposes of proceedings in a cause or matter.[115] In these cases the public authority cannot be said to hold the document on an ancillary basis; it is directly involved in the proceedings at hand. But, perhaps, a duty to disclose such documents would unduly interfere with the authority's ability properly to deal with the proceedings or upset their proper course through the courts.

Information received in confidence from the UK government

Although not an exemption as that word is used in the Act, information which is **22.54** held by a Scottish public authority in confidence, having been supplied by a Minister of the Crown or by a department of the government of the United Kingdom is effectively granted an absolute exemption from the provisions of the Scottish Act. This is conferred by means of the definition of what information is held by an authority. Information of this category in the possession of a Scottish public authority is not held by it for the purpose of the Act.[116] Hence the general entitlement granted to citizens by the Act to obtain information from a Scottish public authority which holds it simply does not apply to such information. However, subject to the exemptions contained in the UK Act, it may be possible to request and obtain the information under that Act directly from the Minister who, or department which, supplied it.

Certain information held by the Keeper of the Records of Scotland

A similar quasi-exemption concerns certain records which have been transferred **22.55** to the Keeper of the Records of Scotland. Records transferred to the Keeper may be designated as open documents. If so, the public may gain access to them without making a request under the Scottish Act. But if the records have not been designated as open documents, then where the records in question were transferred by a Scottish public authority to which the Scottish Act applies, the Keeper must forward the request for access to the public authority which transferred the record to him and that public authority must determine whether an exemption should be claimed in respect of the record.[117] A similar procedure also applies to records transferred before 1 July 1999 by the Secretary of State for Scotland.[118] But other public bodies, not governed by the Scottish Act but governed instead by the UK Act, may also transfer public documents relating to Scotland to the Keeper. If those documents have not been designated as open documents, they are exempted from the application of the Scottish Act because it is provided that the Keeper does not hold such documents within the meaning of the Scottish Act.[119] It is not clear how access to such records may be pursued. For, given that they have been

---

[115] ibid, s 37(1)(a)(iii).
[116] ibid, s 3(2)(a)(ii).
[117] ibid, s 22.
[118] ibid, s 22(6).
[119] ibid, s 3(4).

transmitted to the Keeper, they will no longer be held by the transmitting author-ity[120] and therefore it will not be under any obligation under the UK Act in respect of them.

Other categories of exempt information

22.56 All other categories of exempt information are exempt 'only to the extent that, in all the circumstances of the case, the public interest in disclosing the information is not outweighed by that in maintaining the exemption'.[121] The question to be addressed in any such case is: (in all the circumstances of the case) is the public interest in disclosing the information requested outweighed by the public interest in maintaining the exemption of that information from disclosure? Perhaps this form of question implies that the starting point is recognition of the public inter-est in disclosure, followed by a process of identifying whether there is a contrary public interest detracting from it. Under the UK Act, the issue is couched in the active voice: does the public interest in maintaining the exemption outweigh the public interest in disclosing the information?[122] Doubt is cast on the significance of this verbal reversal by the fact that, where an authority refuses under the Scottish Act to disclose information on the ground that it is exempt (otherwise than under an absolute exemption) the refusal notice 'must state the authority's reason for claiming that, in all the circumstances, the public interest in maintain-ing the exemption outweighs that in disclosure of the information'.[123]

22.57 Categories of exempt information fall into two types:

(a) categories of information which are defined by reference to the subject mat-ter or class of information in question; and

(b) categories of information which are defined by reference to some activity or interest which would or might be harmed if the information in question were disclosed.[124]

22.58 In the latter case, the Scottish Act differs from the UK Act in that it consistently requires that the information is to be exempt from disclosure if its disclosure would, or would be likely to, prejudice *substantially* the activity or interest to be protected. The UK Act only requires that disclosure would, or would be likely to, prejudice such activity or interest.

22.59 The remaining categories of exempt information may also be categorized accord-ing to the topics with which they are concerned and it is by that means that they

---

[120] FOIA 2000, s 1(4).
[121] FOI(S)A 2002, s 2(1)(b).
[122] FOIA 2000, s 2(2)(b) and cf s 2(1)(b).
[123] FOI(S)A 2002, s 16(2).
[124] This classification also applies to the categories of absolute exemptions, only one of which, that relating to research programmes under ibid, s 27(2) is defined by reference to harm.

are now listed under the following headings: (1) national security; (2) defence; (3) international relations; (4) relations between administrations within the United Kingdom; (5) the economy; (6) government policy and public affairs in Scotland; (7) audit functions; (8) investigations and gathering of evidence; (9) law enforcement; (10) commerce; (11) protection of individual health and safety; (12) the environment; and (13) communications with Her Majesty etc and honours. The order in which these categories are listed here does not follow exactly the order of the provisions in the Scottish Act.[125] Although the order is not intended to reflect any moral hierarchy, perhaps it helps indicate the extent to which the exemptions protect governmental concerns, especially those of central government both in Edinburgh and Westminster.

National security

Information is exempt (subject to the public interest test[126]) which is required to be exempt from the general entitlement under section 1(1) for the purpose of safeguarding national security.[127] The requirement for the exemption of particular information is to be proved by a certificate signed by a member of the Scottish Executive certifying that the exemption is, or at any material time was, required for the purpose of safeguarding national security.[128] The certificate forms conclusive proof of the fact that the exemption is so required. A certificate may identify the information to which it applies by means of a general description and may be expressed to have prospective effect.[129] This provision corresponds with section 24 of the UK Act. **22.60**

Laws protecting the secrecy of information relating to national security represent a necessary feature of any responsibly governed state. But the extent of their application may legitimately be debated. In the case of the exemption at hand, external understanding of how the exemption is applied is obstructed by the fact that the Minister's certificate forms conclusive proof that the information needs to be exempt for the purpose of safeguarding national security. If such a certificate is given it would seem unlikely that in many instances the public interest in disclosure will be greater than the public interest in maintaining the exception. Further, even if the Commissioner or the court considered that disclosure should have been made by the Scottish Administration despite the existence of the Minister's certificate and gave or upheld a decision notice requiring disclosure, the First Minister may, pursuant to section 52, over-ride the effect of that notice by giving a further certificate stating that he has on reasonable grounds, after consulting the **22.61**

---

[125] Broadly it follows the order in which the exemptions are set out in FOIA 2000. In both Acts, exemptions relating to governmental interests precede those relating to private concerns.

[126] Under FOI(S)A 2002, s 2(1)(b).

[127] FOI(S)A 2002, s 31(1).

[128] ibid, s 31(2).

[129] ibid, s 31(3).

other members of the Executive, formed the opinion that not disclosing the information did not constitute a failure to comply with the Act and that the information is of exceptional sensitivity. It may be difficult, therefore, even for those who accept the need for special measures to protect national security adequately to judge, if it is appropriate for them to do so, whether the application of this exemption is justified.

Defence

22.62 Information is exempt (subject to the public interest test[130]) the disclosure of which would, or would be likely to, prejudice substantially the defence of the British Islands or of any colony or the capability, effectiveness or security of the armed forces of the Crown, any forces co-operating with those forces or any part of the armed forces of the Crown or of any co-operating forces.[131] This provision corresponds with section 26 of the UK Act. The information to which it relates, although more broadly described, also corresponds with the information to which the prohibition under section 2 of the Official Secrets Act 1989 applies.

International relations

22.63 Information is exempt (subject to the public interest test[132]) the disclosure of which would, or would be likely to, prejudice substantially:

• relations between the United Kingdom and any other state;
• relations between the United Kingdom and any international organization or international court;
• the interests of the United Kingdom abroad; or
• the promotion or protection by the United Kingdom of its interests abroad.[133]

22.64 Information is exempt (subject to the public interest test[134]) which is confidential information obtained from a state other than the United Kingdom or an international organization or international court.[135] Information obtained from a state, organization or court is confidential at any time while the terms on which that information was obtained require it to be held in confidence or the circumstances in which it was obtained make it reasonable for the state, organization or court to expect that it will be held in confidence. The First Minister may veto disclosure by the Scottish Administration of information in this category pursuant to section 52.

22.65 Secrecy remains the norm in the United Kingdom with respect to information relating to international affairs. The Official Secrets Act 1989 creates a number of offences concerned with the unauthorized disclosure of information relating to

---

[130] Under FOI(S)A 2002, s 2(1)(b).
[131] ibid, s 31(4) and (5).
[132] Under FOI(S)A 2002, s 2(1)(b).
[133] ibid, s 32(1)(a).
[134] Under ibid, s 2(1)(b).
[135] ibid, s 32(1)(b).

international affairs. The categories of information relating to this subject which are rendered exempt by the Scottish Act correspond with categories of information referred to in the Official Secrets Act 1989.[136]

The Memorandum of Understanding between the UK government and the **22.66** devolved administrations,[137] after reminding those to whom it is addressed that international affairs and relations with the European Union remain the responsibility of the UK government and the UK Parliament, acknowledges that the devolved administrations have an interest in international and European policy making in relation to devolved matters and states an intention to involve the devolved administrations as fully as possible in discussions about the formulation of the UK's policy position on all EU and international issues which touch on devolved matters.[138] But:

> This must, obviously, be subject to mutual respect for the confidentiality of those discussions and adherence to the resultant UK line, without which it would be impossible to maintain such close working relationships.[139]

The same point is made in the Concordat specifically concerned with co-ordination of EU Policy Issues.[140]

Relations between administrations within the United Kingdom

Information is exempt (subject to the public interest test[141]) the disclosure of **22.67** which would, or would be likely to, prejudice substantially relations between any administration in the United Kingdom and any other such administration.[142] The administrations concerned are the government of the United Kingdom, the Scottish Administration, the Executive Committee of the Northern Ireland Assembly and the National Assembly for Wales.[143] This provision corresponds with section 28 of the UK Act.

In the Memorandum of Understanding the desire is recorded of each administra- **22.68** tion to ensure that the information it supplies to others is subject to appropriate safeguards in order to avoid prejudicing its own interests.[144] Acceptance by the administrations that a duty of confidentiality may arise is recorded and acknowledgement made that the administrations will respect legal requirements of confidentiality because:

---

[136] See the Official Secrets Act 1989, s 3(1) and (5).
[137] Cm 5240.
[138] ibid, paras 17 and 19.
[139] ibid, para 19.
[140] *Devolution: Memorandum of Understanding and Supplementary Agreements* (Cm 5245, December 2001) Part II B 1 para B1.4. Cf para 22.19 above.
[141] Under FOI(S)A 2002, s 2(1)(b).
[142] ibid, s 28(1).
[143] ibid, s 28(2).
[144] Cm 5240, para 11.

Each administration can only expect to receive information if it treats such information with appropriate discretion.[145]

22.69 The Memorandum notes that disclosure of information will be subject to the codes of practice currently in operation concerning access to information held by the UK government and the devolved administrations and to the requirements of future freedom of information regimes. But those receiving information are still enjoined to treat it in accordance with whatever restrictions have been imposed by its supplier. In part the exemption concerning relations between administrations will maintain the required protection against inappropriate disclosure. But further protection is provided by the exclusion from the scope of the Scottish Act of information supplied in confidence by the UK government.[146]

The economy

22.70 Information is exempt (subject to the public interest test[147]) the disclosure of which would, or would be likely to, prejudice substantially:

- the economic interests of the whole or part of the United Kingdom; or
- the financial interest of an administration in the United Kingdom.[148]

This exemption corresponds with that under section 28 of the UK Act.

22.71 In the Franks Report it was suggested that information concerning the currency and reserves should form a category of official secrets, protected against unlawful disclosure by criminal sanction.[149] But when the Official Secrets Act 1989 was passed, it did not include economic information amongst the categories of protected information. In the White Paper preceding the 1989 Act, the government recorded its view that it was not 'considered necessary to protect economic information as a class. Protection will be provided by disciplinary measures and, where necessary, by specific legislation on particular subjects'.[150] But sensitivity in this area remains high. For example, the question whether a Minister, knowing of plans to devalue the currency, must be fully frank to Parliament remains vexed. Some exemption as regards information in this area is, therefore, justified. It remains as true today as in 1972 that:

Certain knowledge of a Government decision to alter the exchange rate would enable speculators to raid the reserves with far greater confidence and on a far greater scale than they could do on the basis of speculation.[151]

---

[145] Cm 5240, para 11.
[146] FOI(S)A 2002, s 3(2)(a)(ii).
[147] Under ibid, s 2(1)(b).
[148] ibid, s 33(2).
[149] *Report of the Departmental Committee on Section 2 of the Official Secrets Act 1911* (Cmnd 5104, September 1972), often called '*The Franks Report*' after its chairman, Lord Franks, paras 135–139.
[150] See the White Paper, *Reform of Section 2 of the Official Secrets Act 1911* (Cm 408, June 1988) para 33.
[151] *The Franks Report* (n 149 above) para 138.

But how far does the exemption extend? Section 64 of the Scotland Act 1998 **22.72** creates a Scottish Consolidated Fund into which the Secretary of State is to make payments of amounts in the discretion of the Secretary of State out of money provided by Parliament. The amount of funds provided to the Secretary of State depends, in certain areas of expenditure, on the application of a formula, known as the Barnett formula, based on changes in expenditure in those areas in England. The funds thereby calculated make up, together with other funds otherwise allocated, the Block grant made available to each of the different territories comprising the United Kingdom. Part of the purpose of the Barnett formula, the use of which was introduced in 1978 by Joel Barnett, then Chief Secretary to the Treasury, was to cause convergence of expenditure per head across the United Kingdom. But spending per head remains higher in Scotland than in England. A study on how devolution might be financed noted that:

> One significant failing of the formula has been the lack of transparency regarding comparable expenditure between the territories. Definitions of English equivalent expenditure have never been published for the two Blocks (Scotland and Wales) nor British comparable expenditure as relates to the Northen Ireland Block. Either the Treasury does not consider territorial expenditure an important issue or the territorial departments want to avoid provoking disputes with the English spending departments.[152]

The financial interest of the Scottish Administration might equally be served by not stirring up similar disputes, the consequence of which might be prejudicial, even seriously so, to the Scottish Administration's interests. Arguably, therefore, the exemption might embrace information, not otherwise available to the public, which would assist in making comparisons between expenditure in England and in Scotland. But, given the nature of the topic, it might be hoped that this would be an instance in which the public interest in disclosure, and the facilitation of informed public debate on an issue of central public interest, would outweigh the public interest in maintaining the exemption. The application of that test in this context might open questions about who the public is whose interest is to be considered. For example, could it be argued that the public interest in maintaining the exemption of such information derived weight from the Scottish public interest in maintaining a higher rate of expenditure per head and thereby outweighed the United Kingdom interest in wider debate? That argument would require decision about who the public is whose interest must be taken into account. The widest constituency of the public would seem to be the better answer.

---

[152] D Bell, S Dow, D King and N Massie, *Financing Devolution* (Hume Papers on Public Policy, vol 4, no 2, Spring 1996).

Government policy and public affairs in Scotland

22.73 Information is exempt (subject to the public interest test[153]) which is held by the Scottish Administration and which relates to the formulation or development of government policy.[154] Government policy means the policy of the Scottish Administration and, in relation to information created before 1 July 1999, the policy of the UK government.[155] This provision corresponds with section 35(1)(a) of the UK Act. Once a decision as to policy has been taken, any statistical information used to provide an informed background to the taking of the decision is no longer to be regarded as relating to the formulation or development of government policy and therefore is no longer within the exemption.[156] And, in determining whether the public interest in disclosure is outweighed by the public interest in maintaining the exemption, the Scottish Administration must have regard to the public interest in the disclosure of factual information which has been used, or is intended to be used, to provide an informed background to the taking of a decision.[157]

22.74 Information is exempt (subject to the public interest test[158]) which is held by the Scottish Administration and which relates to Ministerial communications.[159] Such communications comprise any communications between Ministers and include communications relating to proceedings of the Scottish Cabinet or any of its committees. The Scotland Act 1998 does not include any express reference to a Scottish Cabinet. But in practice one has emerged and is given statutory recognition in the Freedom of Information (Scotland) Act 2002. 'Minister' means a member of the Scottish Executive or a junior Scottish Minister.[160] Statistical information of the nature mentioned in the preceding paragraph is no longer exempt once the policy decision to which it relates has been taken.[161] This provision corresponds with section 35(1)(b) of the UK Act.

22.75 Information is exempt (subject to the public interest test[162]) which is held by the Scottish Administration and which relates to the operation of any Ministerial private office. 'Ministerial private office' means any part of the Scottish Administration which provides personal administrative support to a Minister.[163] Again 'Minister' includes junior Scottish Ministers as well as members of the

---

[153] Under FOI(S)A 2002, s 2(1)(b).
[154] ibid, s 29(1)(a).
[155] ibid, s 29(4).
[156] ibid, s 29(2).
[157] ibid, s 29(3).
[158] Under ibid, s 2(1)(b).
[159] ibid, s 29(1)(b).
[160] ibid, s 29(4).
[161] ibid, s 29(2).
[162] Under ibid, s 2(1)(b).
[163] ibid, s 29(4).

Scottish Executive. This provision corresponds with section 35(1)(d) of the UK Act.

Information is exempt (subject to the public interest test[164]) the disclosure of   **22.76**
which:

- would, or would be likely to, prejudice substantially the maintenance of the convention of the collective responsibility of the Scottish Ministers;
- would, or would be likely to, prejudice substantially the free and frank provision of advice or the free and frank exchange of views for the purposes of deliberation; or
- would otherwise prejudice substantially, or be likely to prejudice substantially, the effective conduct of public affairs.[165]

The group of exemptions set out above are all intended to contribute to good and   **22.77**
effective government. A question faced universally by freedom of information regimes is to what extent the governors and their officials may deliberate in seclusion from public oversight. Deflection from a sensible course, or being locked into a foolish one, might result from premature publication of preliminary views. Opposition, or support, attended by expense and creative of momentum, might mobilize in response to a proposal not yet even half-baked. And, if the governors are denied any officially recognized private territory, they will be driven into the corridors, or canteens, to conduct their crucial exchanges. The exemption concerning the formulation of policy and the curtain to assist the free and frank exchange of views may be justified in terms such as these. The question for the democrat in this area may be not so much 'how much information can I gather?' as 'how much can I participate in the formulation of policy?' Freedom of information is only part of the picture.

More specifically, the exemptions in view aim to protect the collective responsi-   **22.78**
bility of the Scottish Ministers who, though more numerous but generally less swashbuckling than the Three Musketeers, are subject, even in a coalition administration, to a similar ethic of one for all and all for one. Collective responsibility requires collective discretion, as both the Scottish Ministerial Code and the Scottish Executive Guide to Collective Decision Making emphasize:

> The doctrine of collective responsibility bites after a decision has been reached; it does not mean that there must be unanimity (or even a consensus) beforehand. Ministers can express their views frankly in internal discussion of an issue, but their membership of the Executive requires them to maintain a united front once decisions have been reached; to ensure that the privacy of opinions expressed in internal

---

[164] Under ibid, s 2(1)(b).
[165] This provision corresponds with FOIA 2000, s 36(2).

discussions is maintained; and to ensure that the internal processes through which a decision has been made are not disclosed.[166]

22.79 The Guide to Collective Decision Making stipulates that all Cabinet papers, including minutes and agendas, should be protectively marked. They should not be made public but 'should be distributed strictly in accordance with the "need to know" principle'. Departments should not place them in departmental files but handle them separately. Cabinet papers which are no longer required should be disposed of as 'confidential waste'.[167] The Guide refers to the exemption in the Code on Access to Scottish Executive Information concerning internal discussion and advice and to the fact that the Scottish Act will contain a similar exemption, though 'subject to the public interest test'.[168] Scottish Ministers are forbidden from writing books about their Ministerial experience while in office[169] and former Ministers are instructed to submit their manuscripts to the Permanent Secretary and to conform with the principles set out in *The Radcliffe Report* of 1976.[170]

22.80 Nevertheless Ministers are directed to subscribe to the Seven Principles of Public Life,[171] set out in Annexe A to the Scottish Ministerial Code, one of which, entitled 'Openness', enjoins holders of public office to be as open as possible about all the decisions and actions that they take, to give reasons for their decisions and to restrict information only when the wider public interest clearly demands.

22.81 Information is exempt (subject to the public interest test[172]) which is held by the Scottish Administration and which relates to the provision of advice by any of the Law Officers or any request for the provision of such advice.[173] The Law Officers are the Lord Advocate, the Solicitor-General for Scotland, the Advocate-General for Scotland, the Attorney-General, the Solicitor-General and the Attorney-General for Northern Ireland.[174] This provision corresponds with section 35(1)(c) of the UK Act.

22.82 In private life, the confidentiality of legal advice is specially privileged against disclosure. Legal advice, perhaps more than other categories of advice, must be frank and based on frank instructions. This attitude carries over into public life. The Westland Affair of 1986 which engulfed Mrs Thatcher's government in crisis was

---

[166] Guide to Collective Decision Making (June 2002) para 2.2; cf the Scottish Ministerial Code (Feb 2002) para 2.2.

[167] Guide to Collective Decision Making (June 2002) para 4.37.

[168] ibid, para 4.40.

[169] Scottish Ministerial Code, para 8.15.

[170] ibid, para 2.21. *The Radcliffe Report* is the *Report on Ministerial Memoirs* (Cmnd 6386, 1976).

[171] These principles are taken, not from some esoteric branch of speculative philosophy, but from the first report of the Nolan Committee on Standards in Public Life (May 1995).

[172] Under FOI(S)A 2002, s 2(1)(b).

[173] ibid, s 29(1)(c).

[174] ibid, s 29(4).

in large measure exacerbated by allegations that the secrecy of advice given by the Attorney-General had been compromised. But as that instance illustrates, the aim in public life is more to protect the position of the Law Officers than that of the Ministers whom they may have been advising. This aspect is emphasized by the Scottish Ministerial Code:

> The fact and content of opinions or advice given by the Law Officers either individually or collectively must not be disclosed publicly without their authority.[175]

Law Officers, though politically appointed and serving as members of an administration, are required in their role as legal advisers to set partisanship aside and to give counsel according to law. Their ability so to act might be undermined if subjected to immediate public scrutiny and debate. The Scottish Ministerial Code suggests that the written opinions and advice of the Law Officers may be made available to succeeding administrations,[176] but presumably, subject perhaps to lapse of time, the succeeding administration would hold such opinions and advice subject to similar restrictions.

Audit functions

Information is exempt (subject to the public interest test[177]) the disclosure of **22.83** which would, or would be likely to, prejudice substantially the exercise of a Scottish public authority's functions in relation to the audit of the accounts of other Scottish public authorities or the examination of the economy, efficiency and effectiveness with which such authorities use their resources in discharging their functions.[178]

Audits aim to check the accuracy of the accounts under scrutiny. Sometimes they **22.84** reveal dishonesty as well as inaccuracy. The exemption protects the effectiveness of the auditors which might be undermined if those under audit could obtain from the public authority carrying out the audit information about its audit procedures.

Investigations and gathering of evidence

Information is exempt (subject to the public interest test[179]) which has at any time **22.85** been held by a Scottish public authority for the purposes of:

(a) an investigation which the authority has a duty to conduct to ascertain whether a person should be prosecuted for an offence, or whether a person prosecuted for an offence is guilty of it;

---

[175] Scottish Ministerial Code, para 2.23.
[176] ibid, para 2.22.
[177] Under FOI(S)A 2002, s 2(1)(b).
[178] ibid, s 40. This corresponds with FOIA 2000, s 33.
[179] Under FOI(S)A 2002, s 2(1)(b).

    (b) an investigation, conducted by the authority, which in the circumstances may lead to a decision by the authority to make a report to the procurator fiscal to enable it to be determined whether criminal proceedings should be instituted; or

    (c) criminal proceedings instituted in consequence of a report made by the authority to the procurator fiscal.[180]

22.86 Information is exempt (subject to the public interest test[181]) which:

    (a) is held by a Scottish public authority for the purposes of an inquiry instituted under the Fatal Accidents and Sudden Deaths Inquiry (Scotland) Act 1976 but not for the time being concluded; or

    (b) is held at any time by a Scottish public authority for the purposes of any other investigation being carried out by virtue of a duty to ascertain, or for the purpose of making a report to the procurator fiscal as respects, the cause of death of a person.[182]

22.87 The exemptions mentioned in the preceding two paragraphs aim to protect information from disclosure which has been gathered for the purpose of enabling an authority to decide whether criminal proceedings should be brought or as evidence for the purpose of such or other proceedings or inquiry. Premature disclosure would pre-empt the outcome, or might undermine the fairness, of the future proceedings to which the information relates. The information may be used in such subsequent proceedings or it may not. Where it is, disclosure will generally result in the course or at the end of the relevant proceedings or inquiry. Where it is not, the interest of the person under investigation will, generally, favour the non-disclosure of the information.

22.88 Information is exempt (subject to the public interest test[183]) which is held by a Scottish public authority, which relates to the obtaining of information from confidential sources and which was obtained or recorded by the authority for the purposes of investigations, apart from those mentioned in paragraph 22.85 above, conducted for any of the purposes listed in section 35(2).[184]

22.89 This exemption enables public authorities to protect the confidentiality with which informants may be treated.

22.90 Information is exempt (subject to the public interest test[185]) which is obtained or recorded by a Scottish public authority for the purposes of civil proceedings,

---

[180] FOI(S)A 2002, s 34(1).
[181] Under ibid, s 2(1)(b).
[182] ibid, s 34(2).
[183] Under ibid, s 2(1)(b).
[184] ibid, s 34(3).
[185] Under ibid, s 2(1)(b).

brought by or on behalf of the authority which arise out of any investigation mentioned in paragraphs 22.85 or 22.88 above.[186]

22.91 This exemption has a similar rationale to that mentioned in paragraph 22.87 above.

Law enforcement

22.92 Information is exempt (subject to the public interest test[187]) the disclosure of which would, or would be likely to, prejudice substantially:

- the prevention or detection of crime;
- the apprehension or prosecution of offenders;
- the administration of justice;
- the assessment or collection of any tax or duty or of any imposition of a similar nature;
- the operation of the immigration controls;
- the maintenance of security and good order in prisons or other institutions where persons are lawfully detained;
- the exercise by any public authority as defined in the UK Act or Scottish public authority as defined in the Scottish Act of its functions for various specified regulatory purposes;[188]
- any civil proceedings brought and arising out of any investigation conducted for such purpose by or on behalf of any such authority by virtue either of Her Majesty's prerogative or of powers conferred by or under any enactment.[189]

22.93 These exemptions embrace information in a wide range of situations where the authority of the state may be brought to bear against persons natural or legal, citizens or aliens. The exemptions are capable of including generic information about authorities' general policies and procedures, and of applying to specific cases where an authority is taking steps against a particular person. In the latter case, that person will have to look to the procedures applicable to the type of case at hand in order to extract information from the authority. Given the breadth of these exemptions, conscientious application of the public interest test will be required if open government is to be advanced in the departments concerned with the subjects to which the exemptions apply.

---

[186] ibid, s 34(4).
[187] Under ibid, s 2(1)(b).
[188] These purposes are listed in ibid, s 35(2).
[189] FOI(S)A 2002, s 35(1).

Commerce

22.94 Trade secrets are a category of property which would be destroyed by disclosure. Hence, information is exempt (subject to the public interest test[190]) which constitutes a trade secret.[191]

22.95 Information is exempt (subject to the public interest test[192]) the disclosure of which would, or would be likely to, prejudice substantially the commercial interests of any person, including a Scottish public authority.[193] A person's commercial interests may be envisaged as a type of property or private right which should not be detracted from or encroached upon by disclosure of information pertaining to those interests. But, the division between the public domain and the private or commercial is, with contracting out and other forms of providing or financing public services, increasingly blurred. The application of the exemption is likely to create some tension in that context; the interests of those wishing to scrutinize the activities of their governors will conflict with the interest of contractors, and perhaps authorities, to maintain commercial confidentiality.

Protection of individual health and safety

22.96 Information is exempt (subject to the public interest test[194]) if its disclosure would, or would be likely to, endanger the physical or mental health or the safety of an individual.[195]

22.97 This would appear to be a sensible and humane provision. But, under the statute, the individual at risk plays no part in his own protection. He may not even be aware that the request has been made. If an authority decides to disclose to another person information for which it ought to claim this exemption, the individual has no right to seek a review by the authority of its own decision.[196] The question of notifying relevant individuals and taking their views into account should be addressed in the code of practice to be issued under section 60. Maybe, an individual who becomes aware of the request might petition for judicial review of the authority's decision and seek an interdict preventing disclosure in the meantime. Curiously, if the authority refuses to make disclosure in answer to the original request but decides to do so on review, an application by the individual to the Commissioner under section 47 for a decision whether the request was handled in accordance with Part I of the Act would appear to be competent.[197]

---

[190] Under FOI(S)A 2002, s 2(1)(b).
[191] ibid, s 33(1)(a) corresponding with FOIA 2000, s 43(1).
[192] Under FOI(S)A 2002, s 2(1)(b).
[193] ibid, s 33(1)(b) corresponding with FOIA 2000, s 43(2).
[194] Under FOI(S)A 2002, s 2(1)(b).
[195] ibid, s 39(1).
[196] ibid, s 20(1).
[197] ibid, s 47(1); see para 22.201 below.

The environment

Under section 62 of the Scottish Act, the Scottish Ministers are empowered to **22.98** make regulations to incorporate into Scots law certain provisions in the Aarhus Convention concerning access to information about environmental matters which is held by public authorities. When those regulations are made, they will confer a separate right of access to the information to which they relate. To avoid overlap, information which is available under those regulations or which would be if those regulations did not exempt it, is exempt under the Scottish Act.[198] This exemption is subject to the public interest test,[199] but it is also made without prejudice to the absolute exemption conferred by section 25(1)[200] on information which can reasonably be obtained otherwise than by a request under section 1(1).

Information relating to the environment is currently available under the **22.99** Environmental Information Regulations 1992.[201]

Communications with Her Majesty etc and honours

Information is exempt (subject to the public interest test[202]) which relates to com- **22.100** munications with Her Majesty, other members of the Royal Family or the Royal Household, or the exercise by Her Majesty of her prerogative of honour.[203]

Dispensation from revealing whether information is held

In certain cases an authority holding information is released both from the duty **22.101** to give the information to the applicant requesting it and from even disclosing that the authority holds the information. In such cases the applicant seeking the information effectively draws a blank from the public authority from whom he requested it. Under the Scottish Act a blank response may be given where:

- the information is exempt information by virtue of any of sections 28 to 35, 39(1) or 41[204] and
- revealing whether the information exists or is held by the authority would be contrary to the public interest.[205]

Only if both requirements are satisfied may the authority refuse to disclose whether it holds the information. The provision entitling the authority so to refuse to disclose whether it holds the information is permissive. This seems odd:

---

[198] ibid, s 39(2).
[199] Under ibid, s 2(1)(b).
[200] See ibid, s 2(2)(a).
[201] SI 1992/3240 as amended by the Environmental Information (Amendment) Regulations 1998, SI 1998/1447.
[202] Under FOI(S)A 2002, s 2(1)(b).
[203] ibid, s 41.
[204] None of these sections confer absolute exemption; see ibid, s 2(2).
[205] ibid, s 18(1).

if revealing the information would be contrary to the public interest, should the authority not be obliged to maintain its secrecy?

22.102 Under the analogous provision of the UK Act[206] the questions which arise under section 2(1) of that Act are:

- Is the information requested information in respect of which the UK Act provides that the duty to confirm or deny does not arise?
- If yes, does the public interest in maintaining the exclusion of that duty outweigh the public interest in disclosing whether the authority holds the information?

Both questions must be affirmatively answered before the authority may refuse to confirm or deny whether it holds the information.

22.103 What difference does the variation between how the second questions are formulated make? Is there significance in the fact that the second question is, under the Scottish Act, a question for the consideration of the authority to whom the request is made? These questions will remain open until the Acts come into force and their interpretation comes into focus under the scrutiny of the UK and Scottish Commissioners and the courts.

Historical records and the falling away of exemptions with time

22.104 The Scottish Act provides for certain exempt information to cease to be exempt after the lapse of some period of years.

22.105 For the purpose of the Act, a record becomes an 'historical record' at the end of the period of 30 years which began on 1 January of the calendar year following the year in which the record was created.[207] Where records created at different dates are kept together in one file or other assemblage, all the records in that file or assemblage are to be treated as created when the latest of the records contained in the file or assemblage was created.[208] The records must be kept together in the file or assemblage 'for administrative purposes'; so it would be unlawful to create files containing more recent documents or to add more recent documents to a file in order to extend the period before it became a historical record. But determining that such unlawfulness had occurred might prove tricky.

22.106 Once a record has become an historical record information contained in it cannot be exempt by virtue of any of sections 28 to 30, 33(1), 36, 37, 40 and 41(a).[209]

---

[206] FOIA 2000, s 2(1).
[207] FOI(S)A 2002, s 57(1).
[208] ibid, s 57(2).
[209] ibid, s 58(1).

But other exemptions remain effective for longer periods. In the delicate case of **22.107** Her Majesty's exercise of her prerogative of honour, the period is 60 years.[210] And in the case of the exemptions created by sections 34(2)(b), 35 and 38(1)(c) and (d), the period is 100 years.[211] The remaining exemptions appear to remain effective without cease. In some of them, the information may have become otherwise available in the meantime. But this would not necessarily be true of, for example, sections 31, 32, and 33(2), all of which are likely to embrace information of interest, and perhaps value, to historians. They concern, respectively, national security and defence, international relations and the economy.

The Scottish Ministers have power to substitute shorter periods of time.[212] **22.108**

Protection from actions for defamation

Where, in compliance with a request for information, information supplied to a **22.109** Scottish public authority by a third party is communicated by the authority, under section 1, to the applicant, the publication to the applicant of any defamatory matter contained in the information so supplied is privileged unless that publication is shown to have been made with malice.[213]

(2) Environmental information

The Convention on Access to Information, Public Participation in Decision- **22.110** making and Access to Justice in Environmental Matters signed at Aarhus on 25 June 1998, referred to as the 'Aarhus Convention', contains provisions which, once rendered exercisable within a municipal legal system, will create legally enforceable obligations on authorities to disclose relevant information about environmental matters. The Aarhus Convention is discussed in chapter 16 above. Section 62 of the Scottish Act provides for the incorporation of Article 4 of the Convention, together with Articles 3 and 9 as far as they relate to Article 4, into Scots law by regulations issued by the Scottish Ministers. The regulations will relate to information held by or requested from any Scottish public authority. They will provide a right of access to administrative information and documents distinct and separate from the general entitlement conferred by section 1(1) of the Act and will be subject to whatever procedure is laid down in the regulations.

Information which a Scottish public authority is obliged to make publicly avail- **22.111** able under regulations issued pursuant to section 62, or which it would be so obliged to make available but for some exemption contained in those regulations, is exempt from the general entitlement conferred by section 1(1).[214]

---

[210] ibid, s 58(2)(a).
[211] ibid, s 58(2)(b).
[212] ibid, s 59.
[213] ibid, s 67.
[214] ibid, s 39(2).

22.112 Information relating to the environment is currently available under the Environmental Information Regulations 1992.[215]

(3) *General measures promoting freedom of information*

Introduction

22.113 Granting citizens the power to seek and, subject to exemptions, obtain information and documents held by authorities may be a necessary key to opening the closed doors behind which government and its many emanations work. But supporters of open government believe that the doors should not only be opened to those who actively knock and seek entry. Government, on this view, should be continuously open. Under the Scottish Act, as under the UK Act, this aspect of the liberation of governmental information is promoted by a number of measures which are described in this section.

Publication schemes

22.114 Every Scottish public authority must:

- adopt and maintain a publication scheme which relates to the publication of information by the authority and is approved by the Commissioner;
- publish information in accordance with its publication scheme; and
- from time to time review its publication scheme.[216]

22.115 The purposes at which publication schemes are directed are reflected in the matters to which an authority must have regard when adopting or reviewing its publication scheme. In taking those steps the authority must have regard to the public interest in allowing public access to information held by it and in particular to information which relates to the provision of services by it, the cost to it of providing those services or the standards attained by them, or which consists of facts or analyses on the basis of which decisions of importance to the public have been made by it, and to the public interest in the publication of reasons for decisions made by the authority.[217] These purposes are wider than those to which public authorities governed by the UK Act must have regard.[218]An authority must publish its publication scheme, although it may do so in such manner as it thinks fit.[219]

22.116 The publication scheme is a set of rules which must specify:

- classes of information which the authority publishes or intends to publish;

---

[215] SI 1992/3240 as amended by the Environmental Information (Amendment) Regulations 1998, SI 1998/1447.
[216] FOI(S)A 2002, s 23(1).
[217] ibid, s 23(3).
[218] FOIA 2000, s 19(3).
[219] FOI(S)A 2002, s 23(4).

- the manner in which information of each class is, or is intended to be, published; and
- whether the published information is, or is intended to be, available to the public free of charge or on payment.[220]

A publication scheme must be approved by the Commissioner but he may approve a scheme for a limited period.[221] If he has approved a scheme, he may revoke the approval on giving six months' notice.[222] If he refuses to approve a proposed publication scheme or revokes the approval of a publication scheme, he must state his reason for doing so.[223] **22.117**

Every authority need not draft its own scheme from scratch because one of the functions of the Commissioner is to prepare and approve model publication schemes or to approve model schemes prepared by others.[224] Model schemes may be prepared in relation to authorities falling within particular classes. If an authority within the class to which an approved model scheme relates adopts the scheme without modification, no further approval of the Commissioner is required so long as the model scheme remains approved.[225] But the Commissioner's approval is required in relation to any modification of a model scheme. The Commissioner has powers to approve model schemes for specified periods and to revoke approval of model schemes on six months' notice.[226] If he refuses to approve a model scheme prepared by another person or to approve a modification to an approved model scheme or if he revokes approval of a model scheme, he must state his reason for doing so.[227] **22.118**

Provision for publication schemes is made under the UK Act.[228] **22.119**

Codes of practice

A second over-arching element tending towards the promotion of administrative transparency is the obligation, imposed on the Scottish Ministers, to issue codes of practice for the guidance of other Scottish public authorities. Two codes of practice must be issued and may be revised from time to time. The codes, when issued or revised, must be laid before the Scottish Parliament. **22.120**

The first code must provide guidance to Scottish public authorities as to the practice which, in the opinion of the Ministers, it would be desirable for the **22.121**

---

[220] ibid, s 23(2).
[221] ibid, s 23(1) and (5)(a).
[222] ibid, s 23(5)(b).
[223] ibid, s 23(6).
[224] ibid, s 24(1).
[225] ibid, s 24(2).
[226] ibid, s 24(3).
[227] ibid, s 24(4).
[228] FOIA 2000, ss19–20.

authorities to follow in connection with the discharge of the authorities' functions under the Scottish Act.[229] The code must include provision relating to:

(a) the provision of advice and assistance by the authorities to persons who propose to make, or have made requests for information;

(b) the transfer of requests by one of the authorities to another by which the information requested is or may be held;

(c) consultation with persons to whom information requested relates or with persons whose interests are likely to be affected by the disclosure of such information;

(d) the inclusion in contracts entered into by the authorities of terms relating to the disclosure of information;

(e) the provision by the authorities of procedures for dealing with complaints about the handling by the authorities of requests for information; and

(f) the collection and recording by the authorities of statistics as respects the discharge by them of their functions under the Act.[230]

The code may make different provision for different Scottish authorities.[231] Before issuing or revising the code, the Scottish Ministers must consult the Commissioner.[232]

22.122 A code of practice covering the same topics is to be issued under the UK Act by the Secretary of State.[233] Neither the Scottish code nor the UK code are required to include guidance about transferring an applicant's request from a Scottish public authority (governed by the Scottish Act) to a UK public authority (governed by the UK Act) or vice versa.[234] But although not necessary, it might be helpful if some guidance on this were to be included.

22.123 The second code must provide guidance to Scottish public authorities as to the practice which, in the opinion of the Ministers, it would be desirable for the authorities to follow in connection with the keeping, management and destruction of the authorities' records.[235] This code may also include guidance as to the practice to be adopted in relation to the transfer of records to the Keeper of the Records of Scotland; of reviewing records before they are transferred to the Keeper; and to be adopted where one Scottish public authority holds records on behalf of another Scottish public authority.[236] Before issuing or revising this

---

[229] FOI(S)A 2002, s 60(1).
[230] ibid, s 60(2).
[231] ibid, s 60(3).
[232] ibid, s 60(4).
[233] FOIA 2000, s 45(1).
[234] See the FOI(S)A 2002, s 60(2)(b) and FOIA 2000, s 45(2)(b).
[235] FOI(S)A 2002, s 61(1).
[236] ibid, s 61(2).

code the Scottish Ministers must consult both the Commissioner and the Keeper.[237]

This code corresponds with one to be issued by the Lord Chancellor under the UK Act.[238] **22.124**

Authorities' general duty to provide advice and assistance

A third general measure aimed to increase freedom of information is the duty imposed on Scottish public authorities to provide, so far as it is reasonable to expect an authority to do so, advice and assistance to a person who proposes to make, or has made, a request for information to that authority.[239] **22.125**

If an authority complies in providing advice and assistance with the guidance contained in the code of practice issued by the Scottish Ministers, it will be taken to have complied with this duty.[240] A failure by an authority to comply with the duty does not confer a right of action in civil proceedings.[241] **22.126**

A similar duty is imposed by the UK Act.[242] **22.127**

The Commissioner's supervisory role

One of the Scottish Information Commissioner's general functions is to promote the following of good practice by Scottish public authorities with a view to promoting their observance of the Act and of the codes of practice.[243] From time to time he must consult the Keeper of the Records of Scotland about promoting the observance by Scottish public authorities of the provisions of the code of practice issued under section 61 concerning the keeping, management and destruction of records.[244] **22.128**

The Commissioner has power to assess whether a particular authority is following good practice.[245] Good practice means such practice by a Scottish public authority in the discharge of its functions under the Act as appears to the Commissioner to be desirable.[246] It includes but is not limited to compliance with the requirements of the Act and with the provisions of the codes of practice issued under sections 60 or 61. The Commissioner may, if it appears to him that the practice of an authority does not conform with those codes of practice, give a recommendation **22.129**

---

[237] ibid, s 61(5).
[238] FOIA 2000, s 46.
[239] FOI(S)A 2002, s 15(1).
[240] ibid, s 15(2).
[241] ibid, s 55(1).
[242] FOIA 2000, s 16(1).
[243] FOI(S)A 2002, s 43(1).
[244] ibid, s 43(7).
[245] ibid, s 43(3).
[246] ibid, s 43(8).

to the authority concerned. Such a recommendation is called a 'practice recommendation'.[247] It must be in writing and specify the code and the provisions of it with which, in the Commissioner's opinion, the authority's practice does not conform and specify the steps which he thinks the authority ought to take in order to conform.[248] Where the code with which, in the Commissioner's opinion, the authority has failed to conform is that relating to the keeping, management and destruction of records issued under section 61, the Commissioner must consult the Keeper of the Records of Scotland before giving a recommendation notice.[249]

22.130　It appears to be intended that practice recommendations should simply be admonitory. For the Act does not give the Commissioner any means of enforcing his recommendation. Neither does it provide an authority which is aggrieved by the Commissioner's giving it a practice recommendation with any specific means of challenging the Commissioner's act in doing so.

(4)　The Scottish Information Commissioner

Appointment and independence of the Commissioner

22.131　Pivotal to the operation of the Scottish Act is the Scottish Information Commissioner. The Commissioner must be an individual and is appointed by the Queen on the nomination of the Scottish Parliament. The provisions governing the appointment of the Commissioner are contained in section 42.

22.132　To fulfil his functions the Commissioner must maintain his independence and will to challenge, where appropriate, the approach of public authorities to the disclosure of administrative information. Amongst other things, a proper foundation for these qualities in a Commissioner includes security of office and freedom from interference with the exercise of his powers.

22.133　The elements of security of office include the length of the period for which the Commissioner is appointed to office and the methods whereby his appointment may be terminated before that period has expired. By virtue of section 42(3), the term of appointment is for a period of up to five years. The length of the term must be determined by the Scottish Parliamentary Corporate Body at the time of the Commissioner's appointment. Although, therefore, the Act permits the period to be so short as to inhibit or prevent a Commissioner from establishing his authority, it is to be hoped that the approach will be to make appointments for the full five-year term.

22.134　During the Commissioner's appointed period, his office may only be determined in the following instances:

---

[247]　FOI(S)A 2002, s 44(1).
[248]　ibid, s 44(2).
[249]　ibid, s 44(3).

- if he requests that he should be relieved of office;
- if he attains the age of 65;
- if a resolution of the Parliament is passed requiring his removal from office and the number of MSPs who voted for that resolution is equivalent to not less than two-thirds of the total number of seats for members of the Parliament.

Hence, other than by the inevitable passing of years, the Commissioner cannot be removed from office unless there is substantial political momentum behind the desire to remove him.

The Commissioner may be reappointed for a second and, even, third term. But he **22.135** may only be reappointed for a third term if, by reason of special circumstances, his reappointment is desirable in the public interest.

Save with regard to the preparation of accounts, the terms and conditions on **22.136** which members of his staff are appointed and the arrangements made concerning pensions and similar payments to former members of his staff, the Commissioner is not subject to the direction or control of the Scottish Parliamentary Corporate Body, of any member of the Scottish Executive or of the Parliament in the exercise of his functions. Thus, except with regard to the financial matters mentioned, the Act recognizes and protects the formal independence of the Commissioner. But the Commissioner is not exempt from scrutiny. Although the Parliament cannot direct how he should discharge his functions, there is no obstacle to debate in the Parliament about the Commissioner's activity. Nor, obviously, is the Commissioner's power to exercise his functions entirely at large. His decisions may be subject to appeal to the Court of Session under section 56. And it is likely to be the case that, if, in instances where such appeal is not available, he exceeds his powers or otherwise acts unlawfully, a person with the required title and interest may petition the Court of Session for judicial review.

The Act makes provision for the appointment of an acting Commissioner where **22.137** the office of Commissioner is vacant. The appointment of an acting Commissioner is a temporary measure to cover the period until a new Commissioner is appointed. Although an acting Commissioner is to be treated for almost all purposes as the Commissioner, he may be removed from office by the Scottish Parliamentary Corporate Body by notice in writing.

The Commissioner's functions

The Commissioner is charged with a variety of functions under the Act. Some of **22.138** these comprise broad functions exercisable at the Commissioner's initiative for the purpose of promoting the objectives of the Act and supervising its implementation. Others are more specific and arise on an application being made to the Commissioner or his views being sought by consultation.

22.139 At the most general level, the Commissioner should promote the following of good practice by Scottish public authorities.[250] Good practice means such practice in the discharge of an authority's functions under the Act as the Commissioner thinks desirable and includes, but is not limited to, compliance with the provisions of the Act and the codes of practice to be issued under sections 60 and 61.[251] The Commissioner must also publicize the operation of the Act, good practice and other matters within the scope of his functions.[252] And he may give advice about these topics.[253]

22.140 The Commissioner is to assess under section 43(3) whether authorities are following good practice. If he thinks not, he may issue a practice recommendation under section 44. He may give an information notice under section 50 to obtain information to see whether an authority is complying with the Act or the codes of practice. He may also take the more serious step of giving an enforcement notice under section 51.

22.141 He is required to advise the Scottish Ministers on being consulted by them as regards proposed regulations which they are to make pursuant to sections 9(6), 12(5) and 13(3) and when consulted by them about the codes of practice to be issued under sections 60 and 61.[254]

22.142 He may make proposals to the Scottish Ministers for the amendment under section 4 of the list of bodies included in Schedule 1 to the Act and for the designation under section 5 of persons as Scottish public authorities.[255]

22.143 He must approve and supervise publication schemes and model publication schemes under sections 23 and 24.

22.144 He must deal with applications made under section 47 by persons dissatisfied with the treatment of their requests by authorities.

22.145 Once a year he must lay a general report before the Parliament.[256]

22.146 Unlike the Information Commissioner appointed under the UK Act, the Scottish Information Commissioner does not have responsibilities for data protection under the Data Protection Act 1998.

---

[250] FOI(S)A 2002, s 43(1).
[251] ibid, s 43(8).
[252] ibid, s 43(2)(a).
[253] ibid, s 43(2)(b).
[254] ibid, ss 60(4) and 61(5) respectively.
[255] ibid, s 43(4).
[256] ibid, s 46.

(5) Procedure and enforcement

Outline

Where an applicant seeks information held by a Scottish public authority, he must **22.147** make his request to the authority. On receipt of the request, the authority is obliged to deal with it according to the Act.[257] The authority may, if appropriate, require further information from the applicant about his request or may issue a fees notice to him. Substantive responses to the request may involve compliance by supplying the information or giving a refusal notice. In some cases the authority may not need to give a substantive response because the applicant has not supplied further information when required to do so, or has not paid fees duly sought, or has made a vexatious or repeated request, or because the cost of complying with the request would exceed a prescribed amount.

If the applicant is dissatisfied with how the authority handles his request, he must **22.148** require the authority to which the request was made to review the decision.[258] If he is dissatisfied with the result of the review or the authority fails to hold or complete a review, the applicant may apply to the Commissioner for a decision whether his application has been dealt with correctly.[259] The applicant or the authority may appeal, on a point of law, to the Court of Session against the Commissioner's decision.[260] Thus, the system is one under which questions will be adjudicated on by the court only as a last resort and only on points of law; the person with primary responsibility for the satisfactory operation of the system is the Commissioner.

The Commissioner has powers to require Scottish public authorities to provide **22.149** him with information[261] or to take such steps as he may specify so as to comply with the Act. He may require an authority to comply with the Act in consequence of an application by a person dissatisfied with the treatment of his request,[262] but he may also do so where there has been no such individual application.[263] Failure by the authority to comply with the Commissioner's duly made requirement may be treated as if it were a contempt of court.[264] A right of appeal to the Court of Session against a decision by the Commissioner to exercise these powers is afforded to the authority affected.[265]

---

[257] ibid, s 1(1).
[258] ibid, s 20(1).
[259] ibid, s 47(1).
[260] ibid, s 56.
[261] By giving an information notice under ibid, s 50(1).
[262] By specifying steps which the authority must take in his decision notice given pursuant to ibid, section 49(5).
[263] By giving an enforcement notice under ibid, s 51(1).
[264] ibid, s 53.
[265] ibid, s 56(b)(ii) and (c).

22.150   The Commissioner may, in certain instances of non-compliance or where there is suspicion that the offence of altering records has been or is being committed, apply to a sheriff for a warrant authorizing the Commissioner or a member of his staff to enter and search premises, to inspect and seize documents or other material in the premises and to inspect, examine, operate and test any equipment in the premises in which information held by the authority may be recorded.[266]

22.151   Where a request for information has been made to an authority and the applicant is entitled to be given some or all of the information requested, it is an offence for the authority to alter the records held by the authority with the intention of preventing disclosure by the authority of the information to which the applicant is entitled.[267] The offence may also be committed by employees of the authority or persons who are subject to the direction of the authority.

Requests for information

22.152   An applicant must make his request to a single specified Scottish authority.[268] But an applicant may simultaneously make separate requests to different authorities. Such simultaneous requests may be for the same information. For example, it may be unclear which authority holds the information or more than one authority may hold records containing the information sought.

22.153   The request must be made in writing or in some other permanent form which may be later referred to.[269] The example of alternative forms given in the Act is a recording on audio or video tape. If the request is made in text which is transmitted by electronic means, received in legible form and capable of being used for subsequent reference, it is to be treated as made in writing.[270] Thus a request may be made by e-mail.

22.154   The request must state the name of the applicant and an address for correspondence.[271] It must describe the information requested.[272] Although, in this context 'information' is defined as meaning information recorded in some form,[273] it seems clear that the request need not identify the document or other record in which the information is contained but must give a sufficient description to enable the authority to identify what is sought. The request may also state the applicant's preference to receive the information by one or more of the following means of providing it:

---

[266]   FOI(S)A 2002, s 54 and Sch 3.
[267]   ibid, s 65.
[268]   ibid, s 1(1).
[269]   ibid, s 8(1)(a).
[270]   ibid, s 8(2).
[271]   ibid, s 8(1)(b).
[272]   ibid, s 8(1)(c).
[273]   ibid, s 73.

- a copy of the information in permanent form or in another form acceptable to the applicant;
- a digest or summary of the information; or
- a reasonable opportunity to inspect the record containing the information.[274]

Time for compliance

Subject to two exceptions, the Act requires authorities to deal with requests **22.155** promptly.[275] The more specific basic rule, subject to those exceptions, is that an authority must comply with a request not later than the twentieth working day after the request was received.[276] A 'working day' means any day other than a Saturday, a Sunday, Christmas Day or a day which, under the Banking and Financial Dealings Act 1971, is a bank holiday in Scotland.[277] But this rule is displaced where the authority informs the applicant that it requires further information in order to identify and locate the requested information. Provided that the requirement is reasonable, the obligation to comply with the request does not apply until the further information is provided.[278] Only when the authority receives the information does the period for compliance commence and the time for compliance is not later than the twentieth working day after the authority receives the further information.[279] Hence any time which passes between the date when the authority receives the original request and its receiving the further information it requires does not count for the purpose of calculating the time for compliance.

The Scottish Ministers have power to make regulations varying the time for com- **22.156** pliance.[280]

The first exception relates to the Keeper of the Records of Scotland.[281] It is dis- **22.157** cussed further below. But, although in the cases where the exception applies, he is given a dispensation from the general obligation to comply promptly, the more specific effect is only to extend the time for compliance from not later than the twentieth working day after the request or receipt of further information if reasonably required to not later than the thirtieth working day. The Scottish Ministers do not have power to vary the period within which the Keeper is to comply.

---

[274] ibid, s 11(1), (2).
[275] ibid, s 10(1).
[276] ibid, s 10(1)(a).
[277] ibid, s 73.
[278] ibid, s 1(3).
[279] ibid, s 10(1)(b).
[280] ibid, s 10(4), (5).
[281] ibid, s 10(2).

22.158   The second exception is where the authority gives a fees notice to the applicant.[282] Fees notices and their effect are discussed at paragraphs 22.164 to 22.166 below.

Responses to requests

Overview

22.159   There are various responses which an authority may make to an applicant's request for information. The types of responses are described in this section. At the end of the section is a short table setting out the suggested order in which an authority which receives a request for information should consider which substantive response to make.

Requirement by the authority for further information from the applicant

22.160   An applicant's request may not be sufficiently specific to enable the authority to comply with its duty in respect of the request. Where an authority requires further information in order to identify and locate the requested information, it may inform the applicant of this and, in doing so, must specify what the requirement is for further information.[283]

22.161   In other cases where an authority takes a step other than providing the information, it must give particulars of its complaints procedure and the applicant's rights of seeking a review by the authority and of applying to the Commissioner.[284] An authority's notice seeking further information need not contain these particulars.

22.162   If an applicant considered that the requirement of further information was unjustified, because not reasonable, it seems that he could straightaway seek a review, under section 20, by the authority of its action in asking for further information. But also, if in fact the requirement of further information was not reasonable, the period within which the authority must comply with its duty to deal appropriately with the applicant's request is not suspended.[285] Hence, when the time for compliance which applies if the requirement for further information is disregarded expires, the applicant can then seek a review[286] by the authority on the footing that it has failed to deal with his request. There does not seem to be much purpose served in waiting for the later date in order to seek the review.

22.163   Provided that the requirement for further information is reasonable, the authority is not obliged to give the requested information until it has the further information. As described further below, the effect of a requirement for further information is to delay the commencement of the period within which the

---

[282] FOI(S)A 2002, s 10(3).
[283] ibid, s 1(3).
[284] ibid, s 19.
[285] See the proviso in ibid, s 1(3).
[286] Under ibid, s 20.

authority must comply with the applicant's request until the authority receives the further information.[287] Thus, where an authority makes a reasonable requirement for further information, its obligation to deal with the applicant's request is suspended until that information is received. It seems that, if the applicant does not provide the further information which has been required or provides information which does not fulfil that requirement, the authority would not be obliged to take any further step. Where the applicant provided further information but the authority considered that that information was insufficient, it would seem good practice for the authority to inform the applicant of its view. The applicant could then either seek to make good the deficiency or ask the authority to review its decision.

Fees notices

Under section 9 an authority may, within the time allowed for complying with a **22.164** request, give the applicant a notice in writing, called a 'fees notice', stating that a fee of an amount specified in the notice is to be charged by the authority for complying with the request. A fees notice must include particulars of the authority's complaints procedure and about the applicant's rights of application first to the authority for a review and then to the Commissioner if dissatisfied with the result of that review.

It is for the authority to determine the amount of the fee but it must do so in accor- **22.165** dance with regulations made by the Scottish Ministers after they have consulted the Commissioner.

If the authority has given a fees notice to an applicant, it is not obliged to give the **22.166** requested information until the fee is paid. Time for compliance is suspended until the fee is duly paid. The working days[288] in the period beginning with the day on which the fees notice is given and ending with the day on which the fee is received by the authority are to be disregarded in calculating the twentieth working day after receipt of the request. Thus, if the fee is duly paid, the period before the authority gives the fees notice is to be taken into account in calculating when the time for compliance expires. The fee is duly paid if paid within the period of three months beginning with the day on which the fees notice is given. If the fee is not paid by the end of that period, the request will have no further effect and the authority will be released from any obligation to comply with it.

Compliance by providing the information sought

From the applicant's point of view, the most satisfactory outcome of a request is **22.167** that he should be provided with the information which he requested. The information which should be provided is the recorded information, whatever the

---

[287] FOI(S)A 2002, s 10(1)(b).
[288] Defined in ibid, s 73; see para 22.155 above.

form of the record, held by the authority at the date when the request was received.[289] Thus unrecorded information need not be provided. But, the authority may provide the information subject to any amendments or deletions which would have been made, regardless of the request, between the time when it received the request and the time when it gives the information.[290]

22.168 Information may be given by any means which are reasonable in the circumstances but in providing the information the authority must, so far as is reasonably practicable, give effect to the preferred means of providing it stated by the applicant in his request.[291] The possible means which the applicant may ask for are:

- that he be provided with a copy of the information in permanent form or in another form acceptable to the applicant;
- that he be provided with a digest or summary of the information; or
- that he be provided with a reasonable opportunity to inspect the record containing the information.[292]

22.169 In determining what is reasonably practicable the authority may have regard to all the circumstances, including cost. But the authority may not, in applying any test of reasonable practicability detract from any duty which it, as a provider of services, has under or by virtue of section 21 of the Disability Discrimination Act 1995.[293] Where it determines that it is not reasonably practicable to give effect to the preference it must notify the applicant of its reasons.[294] If the applicant is dissatisfied with the authority's failure to give effect to his expressed preference, he may ask the authority to review its decision under section 20 and, if dissatisfied with the outcome of the review, make an application to the Commissioner under section 47. But the authority's notice informing him of its original decision not to give effect to his preference need not include particulars of its complaints procedure and the applicant's rights of seeking a review by the authority and of applying to the Commissioner.[295]

Refusal notices where exempt information is requested

22.170 Where a Scottish public authority holds information which it claims is exempt information, it complies with its duty to the applicant by giving him a refusal notice. Subject to the special case discussed below, a refusal notice is a notice in writing which:

---

[289] FOI(S)A 2002, ss 1(4) and 73.
[290] ibid, s 1(4).
[291] ibid, s 11(1) and (4).
[292] ibid, s 11(2).
[293] ibid, s 11(5).
[294] ibid, s 11(3).
[295] ibid, s 19.

- discloses that the authority holds the information which the applicant requested;
- states that the authority claims that the information is exempt information;
- specifies the exemption in question;
- states, if not otherwise apparent, why the exemption applies;[296] and
- where the provision rendering the information exempt does not confer absolute exemption, states the authority's reason for claiming that, in all the circumstances of the case, the public interest in maintaining the exemption outweighs the public interest in disclosing the information.[297]

The authority need not include a statement explaining why the exemption applies in so far as the statement would disclose information which would itself be exempt information.[298]

A refusal notice must include particulars of its complaints procedure and the applicant's rights of seeking a review by the authority and of applying to the Commissioner.[299]   **22.171**

In some cases an authority may consider that even to reveal that information exists, albeit as exempt information, would be to reveal too much. The Scottish Act provides for such cases by permitting authorities, in certain instances, to give refusal notices which do not disclose whether the authority holds the information requested. Such a notice might be called a blank refusal notice. Whether or not the information exists or is held by the authority, an authority may give a blank refusal notice where, if information existed and was held by the authority: **22.172**

- the authority could give a refusal notice on the basis that the information would be exempt information by virtue of any of sections 28 to 35, 39(1) or 41; and
- the authority considers that to reveal whether the information exists or is held by it would be contrary to the public interest.[300]

A blank refusal notice must be in writing and: **22.173**

- state that the authority claims that the information, if it existed or were held by the authority, would be exempt information;
- specify the exemption in question; and
- state (if not otherwise apparent) why the exemption applies.[301]

---

[296] ibid, s 16(1).
[297] ibid, s 16(2).
[298] ibid, s 16(3).
[299] ibid, s 19.
[300] ibid, s 18(1).
[301] ibid, s 18(2) modifying s 16(1).

A blank refusal notice must also include particulars of its complaints procedure and the applicant's rights of seeking a review by the authority and of applying to the Commissioner.[302]

Notice that the information is not held

22.174   A Scottish public authority must give the applicant a notice stating that it does not hold the information where:

- it receives a request which would require it either to give the information to the applicant or to consider whether the information is exempt under a provision conferring an absolute exemption or if otherwise exempt, whether the public interest in maintaining the exemption outweighs the public interest in disclosing the information; and
- it does not hold the information.[303]

The obligation to give a notice that the requested information is not held does not apply if the authority gives a blank refusal notice under section 18.[304]

22.175   A notice that the requested information is not held must be given within the time for compliance with the request[305] and must include particulars of the authority's complaints procedure and the applicant's rights of seeking a review by the authority and of applying to the Commissioner.[306]

22.176   Provision is to be included in the code of practice to be issued under section 60 for the transfer of requests from one authority to another by which the information is or may be held.[307] Where an authority gives a notice that the requested information is not held by it, it should consider, in accordance with that provision once it is made, whether to transfer the request to another authority.

Other circumstances in which an authority may refuse to give the requested information

22.177   In the following cases, an authority need not comply with a request:

- where the authority gives a fees notice to the applicant and the applicant fails to pay the fee;[308]
- where the authority estimates that the cost of complying with the request would exceed a prescribed amount;[309]

---

[302] FOI(S)A 2002, s 19.
[303] ibid, s 17(1).
[304] ibid, s 17(3).
[305] ibid, s 17(1).
[306] ibid, s 17(2) and s 19.
[307] ibid, s 60(2)(b).
[308] ibid, s 9(3).
[309] ibid, s 12(1).

- where the request is vexatious;[310]
- where the authority has previously complied with a request for information and a subsequent request is made by the same person which is identical or substantially similar before a reasonable period of time has passed between the request previously complied with and the subsequent request.[311]

These cases are discussed in turn below except for the first case, non-payment of **22.178** fees sought by a fees notice, which has been discussed above.[312]

Refusal to give information where the cost would be excessive

The second case arises where an authority estimates that the cost of complying **22.179** with the request would exceed such amount as may be prescribed in regulations made by the Scottish Ministers.[313] In such case, the authority is not obliged to comply with the request but must, within the time for complying with the applicant's request, give him a notice which states that section 12(1) of the Act applies.[314] The notice must give particulars of its complaints procedure and the applicant's rights of seeking a review by the authority and of applying to the Commissioner.[315]

How this dispensation from complying with requests will operate will depend on **22.180** the content of the regulations. Before making the regulations the Scottish Ministers must consult the Commissioner. The regulations may enable an authority to consider two or more requests together for the purpose of estimating the relevant total cost of compliance. The circumstances in which the regulations may enable an authority to consider two or more requests together are capable of impinging adversely on organized campaigns. For one of the circumstances in which the costs of complying with a number of requests may be aggregated is where the requests are made 'by different persons who appear to [the authority] to be acting in concert or whose requests appear to have been instigated wholly or mainly for a purpose other than the obtaining of the information itself'.[316] The purpose for which a regulation might be made to cover this case is no doubt to enable an authority to avoid a barrage of co-ordinated requests which are collectively vexatious but where none of the requests, being from different persons, could individually be classified as vexatious under section 14(1). But the language used is capable of applying to a wider class of cases. Campaigners, and others, will often have a collateral purpose in seeking information. They must be alert, first, to maintain a disciplined use of the entitlement to seek information and, secondly,

---

[310] ibid, s 14(1).
[311] ibid, s 14(2).
[312] See para 22.166 above.
[313] FOI(S)A 2002, s 12(1).
[314] ibid, s 16(4).
[315] ibid, s 19.
[316] ibid, s 12(2)(b).

to monitor the lawfulness of an authority's exercise of such power as it may be granted under the regulations to aggregate requests in order to declare that the cost of complying with them is excessive.

22.181　The other cases where the regulations may enable an authority to consider in the aggregate the cost of complying with two or more requests are where the requests have been made by one person and where they have been made 'by different persons in circumstances where the authority considers it would be reasonable to make the information available to the public at large and elects to do so'.[317] The regulations may, as regards the latter case, provide as to the means by which and the time within which the information is to be made available to the public at large.

22.182　The authority may not take into account any costs which arise in facilitating the provision of information to a disabled person who has requested it.[318]

22.183　The authority may charge for the communication of any information which it is not obliged to give because it estimates that the cost of doing so would be excessive and which it is not otherwise required by law to communicate. The amount of the fee which may be charged is to be determined by the authority in accordance with regulations to be issued by the Scottish Ministers after consulting the Commissioner.[319]

Refusal to comply with vexatious or repeated requests

22.184　Subject to the exception mentioned below, a Scottish public authority which claims that it need not comply with a request because it is vexatious must give the applicant a notice stating that it so claims.[320]

22.185　Where a Scottish public authority has complied with a request from a person for information, it is not obliged to comply with a subsequent request from the same person which is identical or substantially similar unless there has been a reasonable period of time between the making of the request complied with and the making of the subsequent request.[321] Again, subject to the exception mentioned below, where a Scottish public authority claims that it is not obliged to comply with a repeated request in this sense, it must give a notice stating that it so claims.[322]

22.186　In both cases notice must be given within the time for compliance with the applicant's request.[323] Although the Act does not expressly require writing, it is implicit

---

[317]　FOI(S)A 2002, s 12(2)(a) and (c).
[318]　ibid, s 12(6).
[319]　ibid, s 13.
[320]　ibid, s 16(5).
[321]　ibid, s 14(2).
[322]　ibid, s 16(5).
[323]　ibid.

that a notice must be in writing. The notice must give particulars of its complaints procedure and the applicant's rights of seeking a review by the authority and of applying to the Commissioner.[324]

The exception referred to arises where the authority has, in relation to a previous   **22.187** identical or substantially similar request, given the applicant a notice under section 16(5) and it would in all the circumstances be unreasonable to expect it to serve a further such notice in relation to the current request. Where this exception applies, the authority need not give another notice under section 16(5).

Table setting out the order in which an authority might consider the available substantive responses

The suggested order in which an authority might consider the various substantive   **22.188** responses is set out below in eight stages. For the purpose of this table, it is assumed that there is no need to require the applicant to give further information to enable his request to be dealt with; that there are no unpaid fees which have been duly requested by a fees notice; that the cost of complying with the request is not excessive; and that the request is not vexatious or repeated.

Stage one
- Is the requested information exempt information by virtue of one of sections 28 to 35, 39(1) or 41?
- If yes, go to *stage two*.
- If no, go to *stage three*.

Stage two
- Would revealing whether the information exists or is held by the authority be contrary to the public interest?
- If yes, give a blank refusal notice under section 18(1).
- If no, go to *stage three*.

Stage three
- Does the authority hold the requested information?
- If yes, go to *stage four*.
- If no, give a notice under section 17(1) that the requested information is not held by the authority.

Stage four
- Is the requested information exempt information under a provision which confers absolute exemption?[325]

---

[324] FOI(S)A 2002, ss 16(6) and 19.
[325] See FOI(S)A 2002, s 2(2) for the list of provisions conferring absolute exemption.

- If yes, give a refusal notice under section 16(1).
- If no, go to *stage five.*

Stage five

- Is the requested information exempt under a provision which does not confer absolute exemption?[326]
- If yes, go to *stage six.*
- If no, go to *stage seven.*

Stage six

- Does the public interest in maintaining the exemption outweigh the public interest in disclosing the information?
- If yes, give a refusal notice under section 16(1) stating pursuant to section 16(2) the reason why the exemption should be maintained.
- If no, go to *stage seven.*

Stage seven

- Has the applicant expressed a preference for receiving the information by one or more of the means mentioned in section 11(2)?
- If yes, go to *stage eight.*
- If no, provide the information by some reasonable means.

Stage eight

- Is the applicant's preferred means of receiving the information reasonably practicable?
- If yes, provide the information by the applicant's preferred means of receiving it.
- If no, provide the information by some other reasonable means.

Challenging an authority's handling of a request for information

22.189 The structure established by the Act governing challenges to authorities' handling of requests is:

- the applicant must first require the authority to review its own actions or decisions;
- if still dissatisfied, the applicant may apply to the Commissioner for a decision whether his request for information has been dealt with in accordance with the relevant provisions of the Act;
- either the applicant or the authority may appeal to the Court of Session on a point of law against the Commissioner's decision.

---

[326] These provisions will include those already addressed at *stage one.*

These stages are now discussed in that order, together with other aspects of the enforcement of the Act.

The statutory methods of challenging an authority's actions or decisions form a **22.190** code setting out the available methods of mounting such a challenge. For, except for court hearings prompted by a certificate issued by the Commissioner under s 53(1), the Act does not confer any right of action in civil proceedings in respect of failure by a Scottish public authority to comply with a duty imposed by, under or by virtue of the Act.[327]

But the code established by the Act does not exclude proceeding by way of peti- **22.191** tion for judicial review if and where appropriate. In particular, recourse to such proceedings may be necessary where the Commissioner wrongfully exercises his powers, or fails to do so, in circumstances where an appeal under section 56 is not available.[328]

Reviews by authorities of their decisions

Where an applicant who is dissatisfied with the way in which a Scottish public **22.192** authority has dealt with his request wishes to challenge the authority's handling of his request, the first step which he must take is to require a review by the author- ity of its own actions or decisions in relation to that request.[329] Requiring the authority to hold such a review is a necessary pre-condition to taking any com- plaint further because only a person who is dissatisfied with the outcome of the review may make an application to the Scottish Information Commissioner.[330] It would seem that the range of matters in respect of which an applicant may seek a review is unrestricted in that the requirement for review may relate to any of the actions or decisions of the authority, and the references to 'actions' and 'decisions' include inaction and failure to reach a decision.[331]

A requirement for review must **22.193**

- be in writing or in another form which, by reason of its having some perma- nency, is capable of being used for subsequent reference;[332]
- state the name of the applicant and an address for correspondence;

---

[327] FOI(S)A 2002, s 55.
[328] The Commissioner is a Scottish public authority; see item 90 in Sch 1 to the Act. But the power to require the Commissioner to review his own decisions under s 20(1) may only be exercised by an applicant and is only available in respect of the Commissioner's actions or decisions relating to a request made to him for information which he holds.
[329] FOI(S)A 2002, s 20(1).
[330] ibid, s 47(1).
[331] ibid, s 20(9).
[332] Electronic transmission suffices; see ibid, ss 20(4) and 8(2) and cf the requirements relating to the applicant's request discussed at para 22.153 above.

- specify the request for information to which the requirement for review relates; and
- specify the matter which gives rise to the applicant's dissatisfaction.[333]

22.194 The requirement for review must be made by not later than the fortieth working day[334] after:

- the expiry of the time for compliance with the applicant's original request; or
- in a case where the authority purports under the Act to comply with a request for information or to give the applicant a fees notice, a refusal notice or a notice that information is not held but does so after the time for compliance has expired, the receipt by the applicant of the information provided or, as the case may be, the notice.[335]

But a Scottish public authority may comply with a requirement for review made out of time if it considers it appropriate to do so.[336] The Scottish Ministers may make regulations changing the period within which a requirement for review may be made.[337]

22.195 Subject to an exception relating to the Keeper of the Records of Scotland, a Scottish public authority which receives a requirement for review must comply with it promptly.[338] But, in three cases the requirement need not be complied with:

- where the requirement for review is withdrawn by the applicant who made it by notice in writing;[339]
- where the requirement for review is vexatious;
- where the applicant's original request for information to which the requirement for review relates was a request with which the authority was not obliged to comply by virtue of section 14 because that request was itself either vexatious or repetitive.[340]

Where the authority considers that it need not comply with the requirement for review because it is vexatious or relates to a request to which section 14 applied, the authority must give the applicant notice in writing within the time for complying with the requirement for review, that the authority so claims.[341] The notice

---

[333] FOI(S)A 2002, s 20(3).
[334] Defined in ibid, s 73; see para 22.155 above.
[335] FOI(S)A 2002, s 20(5).
[336] ibid, s 20(6).
[337] ibid, s 20(7) and (8).
[338] ibid, s 21(1).
[339] ibid, s 21(3).
[340] ibid, s 21(8).
[341] ibid, s 21(9).

must contain particulars about the rights of application to the Commissioner and of appeal to the Court of Session conferred by sections 47(1) and 56.[342]

Save in the exception mentioned, the authority must comply with the require- **22.196** ment for review by not later that the twentieth working day[343] after receipt by it of the requirement.[344] The Scottish Ministers have power to issue regulations vary- ing the time for compliance.[345]

On the review, the authority may, as respects the request for information to which **22.197** the requirement for review relates:

- confirm the decision complained of, with or without any modifications which the authority considers appropriate;
- substitute a different decision for the decision complained of; or
- reach a decision, where the complaint is that no decision has been reached.[346]

The authority must give the applicant notice in writing of which of these steps it has taken and a statement of its reasons for doing so.[347] The notice must contain particulars about the rights of application to the Commissioner and of appeal to the Court of Session conferred by sections 47(1) and 56.[348]

Applications to the Commissioner for decision

Overview

Subject to three excluded cases, a person who is dissatisfied with a notice given by **22.198** the authority setting out what it has done in response to a requirement for review and its reasons for doing so or with a notice setting out the authority's reasons for not complying with the requirement for review or who is dissatisfied with the authority's failure to give any such notice, may make application to the Commissioner for a decision whether the request for information to which the requirement relates has been dealt with in accordance with Part 1 of the Act.[349] Save in the three excluded cases,[350] the Commissioner must take the following course:

- he must decide whether the application is one which does not require a deci- sion;[351]

---

342 ibid, s 21(10).
343 Defined in ibid, s 73; see para 22.155 above.
344 FOI(S)A 2002, s 21(1).
345 ibid, s 21(6), (7).
346 ibid, s 21(4).
347 ibid, s 21(5).
348 ibid, s 21(10).
349 ibid, s 47(1).
350 ibid, s 48.
351 Pursuant to ibid, s 49(1).

- if he decides that it is, he must inform the applicant and the relevant authority of his decision in writing;[352]
- if he decides that it is not, he must obtain the authority's comments on the application,[353] reach a decision on the application[354] and inform the applicant and the authority of his decision by a notice in writing referred to as a 'decision notice'.[355]

22.199 Further the Commissioner may take steps to encourage the applicant and the authority to settle the dispute which has given rise to the application.[356] And he may issue a notice requiring further information from the authority relating to the application.[357]

Excluded applications

22.200 The three excluded cases mentioned above are where the requirement for review was made to:

- the Commissioner;
- a procurator fiscal; or
- the Lord Advocate, to the extent that the information requested is held by the Lord Advocate as head of the systems of criminal prosecution and investigation of deaths in Scotland.[358]

In these three cases, no application may be made to the Commissioner for a decision under section 47(1). Since the Commissioner may not consider any application in these excluded cases, a dissatisfied applicant has no means of challenging the decisions made on the review under the Act. Whether, and the extent to which, any redress is available by way of petition for judicial review is an open question.

Applications

22.201 The provision creating the right to apply to the Commissioner appears to confer the right to make the application on any person who feels the relevant dissatisfaction; unlike the right to seek a review,[359] it is not only the applicant who made the

---

[352] Pursuant to FOI(S)A 2002, s 49(2).
[353] Pursuant to ibid, s 49(3)(a).
[354] Pursuant to ibid, s 49(3)(b).
[355] Pursuant to ibid, s 49(5).
[356] Pursuant to ibid, s 49(4).
[357] Pursuant to ibid, s 50(1)(a).
[358] FOI(S)A 2002, s 48.
[359] See ibid, s 20(1) and compare the phrase used at ibid, s 56(a) 'the person who applied for that decision' with the definition of 'applicant' in ibid, s 1(2). That definition of 'applicant' only applies to Parts 1, 2 and 7 of the Act; it does not extend to Part 4 which contains the provisions relating to enforcement currently under discussion. Hence the view expressed in the text as to the class of person who may apply to the Commissioner is not affected by use of the word 'applicant' eg in ss 47(2)(b), 49(2) and 49(5).

original request for information who may apply to the Commissioner. No doubt, the Commissioner will require a person other than the applicant who applies for a decision to have some good reason for doing so.

An application to the Commissioner for a decision must: **22.202**

- be in writing or in another form which, by reason of its having some permanency, is capable of being used for subsequent reference;[360]
- state the name of the applicant and an address for correspondence;
- specify the request for information to which the requirement for review relates;
- specify the matter which was specified in the requirement for review as giving rise to the applicant's dissatisfaction; and
- specify the matter which gives rise to the dissatisfaction with the authority's notice given in response to the requirement for review or with its failure to give any such notice.[361]

Where the application concerns a decision notice given by an authority under section 21(5) or a notice given by it under section 21(9) to the effect that it is not obliged to comply with the requirement for review, the application to the Commissioner must be made before the expiry of six months after the date of receipt by the applicant of the notice of which complaint is made.[362] Where the application concerns the failure by an authority to give any notice in response to a requirement for review, the application to the Commissioner must be made before the expiry of six months after the period allowed for complying with the requirement for review has elapsed.[363] But the Commissioner may consider an application made out of time if it is appropriate to do so.[364] The Scottish Ministers may make regulations changing the period within which a requirement for review may be made.[365]

Applications on which no decision is required

There are two cases in which, even though an effective application is made to the **22.203** Commissioner, he need not make a substantive decision in relation to it. These two cases are:

- where, in the opinion of the Commissioner, the application is frivolous or vexatious; or
- where, in the opinion of the Commissioner, the application appears to have been withdrawn or abandoned.[366]

---

[360] Electronic transmission suffices; see ibid, ss 47(3) and 8(2) and cf the requirements relating to the applicant's request discussed at para 22.153 above.
[361] FOI(S)A 2002, s 47(2).
[362] ibid, s 47(4)(a).
[363] ibid, s 47(4)(b).
[364] ibid, s 47(5).
[365] ibid, s 47(6) and (7).
[366] ibid, s 49(1).

The introduction of frivolity as an alternative ground for the Commissioner's not making a decision on an application seems odd, since authorities who receive frivolous but not vexatious requests for information or requirements for review are obliged to deal with them.[367]

22.204 Thus on receiving an application, the Commissioner first must scrutinize it to check whether the application is excluded by section 48 and secondly may consider whether no substantive decision is needed because the application falls into one, or both, of the two cases just mentioned. Where the Commissioner concludes that the application is excluded by section 48, it appears that he need take no further step in relation to it. But it may be good practice for him to inform the applicant of the fact that the application is excluded and therefore incompetent.

22.205 Where the Commissioner forms the opinion that he need not make a substantive decision on an application because it falls into one, or both, of the other two cases mentioned, he must give the applicant and the authority in question notice in writing specifying that no decision falls to be made in relation to the application and the reasons why that is the case.[368] He must give such notice within one month of receiving the application, or within such other period as is reasonable in the circumstances.[369] The notice must contain particulars of the applicant's right to appeal to the Court of Session under section 56.[370]

Applications requiring decisions and decision notices

22.206 In all other cases the Commissioner must deal substantively with the application which has been made to him. In such cases he must give the authority to which the application relates notice in writing of the application and invite its comments.[371] The Act does not specify any period of time within which the authority must respond with its comments. But, since the Commissioner's primary obligation is to give his decision within four months of receiving the application,[372] the authority will have to respond in sufficient time to enable the Commissioner to take its comments into account and comply with the time limit imposed on him. As a matter of practice perhaps the Commissioner will specify a date by which the comments are to be received, but, since no power to impose a time limit is conferred on him, there may be difficulties in excluding from consideration any comments received after such a time limit has expired. The view taken by the authority ought, in any event, to be apparent from the reasons which it gave in the notice,

---

[367] cf FOI(S)A 2002, ss 14(1) and 21(8)(a).
[368] FOI(S)A 2002, s 49(2).
[369] ibid, s 49(2).
[370] ibid, s 49(8).
[371] ibid, s 49(3)(a).
[372] The period is four months from receipt of the application 'or before the expiry of such other period as is reasonable in the circumstances'; see ibid, s 49(3)(b).

given pursuant to section 21(5), of its decision on the review. An authority may decide that those reasons sufficiently set out its position, although it will often be prudent for an authority to reconsider its position in the light of the matters stated in the application to the Commissioner.

Save that it enables the Commissioner to require further information from an authority (but not an applicant) by giving an information notice under section 50(1),[373] the Act does not refer to any other steps to be taken by the Commissioner before he reaches his decision on the application.[374] Hence it would seem that both the applicant and the authority have only one opportunity to set out their contentions: the applicant in the application and the authority in its comments on the application. Whether a more flexible procedure will develop remains to be seen; for example the Commissioner might permit the applicant to respond to the authority's comments or might seek further information on a less formal basis than by an information notice from either party and allow the other to comment on whatever information is then given. But if any such procedure does develop, it is likely to be restrained by the desire to deal with applications simply and without undue procedural elaboration. It appears that all argument is to be conducted in writing. For the Act does not envisage any oral hearing or attendance before the Commissioner and it would seem unlikely that there would be any general development in this regard. Thus, subject to the development of a more flexible procedure, the Commissioner's obligation appears to be to reach a decision on the materials contained or mentioned in the application and the authority's comments on it. **22.207**

Having obtained the material germane to his decision, the Commissioner must, within four months of receiving the application or before the expiry of such other period as is reasonable in the circumstances,[375] reach his decision and give notice of it in writing to the applicant and the authority.[376] The notice is called a decision notice. The Act does not expressly require the decision notice to contain reasons for the conclusion comprised in the decision, but it would seem likely that the Commissioner will give reasons for his decisions. Where the Commissioner decides that the authority has not dealt with a request for information in accordance with Part 1 of the Act, the decision notice must specify: **22.208**

- the provision of Part 1 of the Act with which the authority has failed to comply and the respect in which it has so failed;

---

[373] Information notices may also be given by the Commissioner on his own initiative otherwise than in the course of a particular application; see ibid, s 50(1)(b). Information notices are discussed at para 22.212 below.

[374] See ibid, s 49(3).

[375] FOI(S)A 2002, s 49(3)(b).

[376] ibid, s 49(3)(b) and (5).

- the steps which, in the opinion of the Commissioner, the authority must take to comply with the provision; and
- the time within which those steps must be taken.[377]

A decision notice must contain particulars of the right of appeal conferred by section 56.[378] Where the decision notice specifies steps which the authority must take, the time which is specified as the time within which the authority must take those steps must not expire before the end of the period within which an appeal may be brought under section 56 against the Commissioner's decision and, if such an appeal is brought, no step which is affected by the appeal need be taken before the cause is finally determined.[379]

22.209   The enforcement of a decision notice which requires the authority to which it is addressed to take specified steps is discussed below.[380]

Publication of the Commissioner's decisions?

22.210   The Scottish Act contains no specific provision for the publication of individual decisions made by the Commissioner on applications. Indeed such publication may be precluded by the duty of confidentiality, reinforced by criminal sanction, imposed on the Commissioner and his staff or agents by section 45.[381] But the Commissioner has a general obligation to determine what information it is expedient to give the public concerning the operation of the Act, good practice and other matters within the scope of the Commissioner's functions and must secure the dissemination of that information in an appropriate form and manner.[382] It is to be hoped that, pursuant to that obligation though conformant with the duty of confidentiality, the Commissioner will publish individual decisions so that a body of information about the interpretation of the Act accumulates. Presumably the Commissioner will also provide such information in his annual report.[383]

The Commissioner's power to encourage settlement

22.211   As mentioned in paragraph 22.199 above, the Commissioner may endeavour to effect a settlement between the applicant and the authority to which the application relates during the period allowed for him to reach his decision on the application.[384]

---

[377] FOI(S)A 2002, s 49(6).
[378] ibid, s 49(8).
[379] ibid, s 49(7).
[380] See para 22.225 below.
[381] See ibid, s 45(3) and (4) for the relevant criminal offence and sanctions.
[382] FOI(S)A 2002, s 43(2)(a); see ibid, s 43(8) for the meaning of 'good practice' in relation to a Scottish public authority.
[383] To be laid before the Parliament pursuant to ibid, s 46(1).
[384] FOI(S)A 2002, s 49(4).

Information notices

An information notice is a notice in writing given by the Commissioner to an **22.212** authority requiring it to give the Commissioner, within the time specified in the notice, such information as may be specified in the notice.[385] In this context, 'information' includes unrecorded information.[386] The Commissioner may give an information notice to an authority where he has received an application under section 47(1) for a decision or where he reasonably requires information for the purpose of determining whether the authority has complied or is complying with the provisions of the Act or where he reasonably requires information for the purpose of determining whether the practice of the authority conforms with the code of practice issued under sections 60 or 61.[387] It is not open to the Commissioner to seek information from one authority for the purpose of policing the activities of another authority.

Where the information notice is given because of a pending application under **22.213** section 47(1), the information sought must relate to the application and must contain a statement that the Commissioner has received such an application.[388] Curiously, no statement is required specifying the time within which the information is to be given but presumably the Commissioner will include such a statement in order to enable him to comply with the time limit which he must observe as regards his own decision.[389]

Where the information notice is given pursuant to the general power to police the **22.214** Act or codes of practice, the information must relate to the authority's compliance with the Act or its conformity with the pertinent code of practice and must contain a statement of the purpose for which the Commissioner regards the specified information as relevant; his reasons for so regarding the information; and the time within which the information is to be given.[390] The time so specified must not expire before the end of the period within which an appeal may be brought under section 56 against the information notice; and, if such an appeal is brought, the information need not be given pending the determination or withdrawal of the appeal.[391]

In any case the information notice must contain particulars of the right of appeal **22.215** conferred by section 56.[392]

---

[385] ibid, s 50(1).
[386] ibid, s 50(9).
[387] ibid, s 50(1).
[388] ibid, s 50(1) and (2)(a).
[389] See FOI(S)A 2002, s 49(3)(b) and para 22.208 above.
[390] FOI(S)A 2002, s 50(1) and (2)(b).
[391] ibid, s 50(4).
[392] ibid, s 50(3).

22.216 The Commissioner may cancel an information notice by notice in writing to the authority.[393]

22.217 An authority receiving an information notice is not obliged to give the Commissioner information in respect of:

(a) a communication between professional legal adviser and client in connection with the giving of legal advice to the client with respect to that client's obligations under the Act; or

(b) a communication between professional legal adviser and client, or between such adviser and client and another person, made in connection with or in contemplation of proceedings under or arising out of the Act and for the purpose of such proceedings.[394]

References to a client include references to a person representing that client.[395]

22.218 Although, therefore, legal professional privilege is maintained in respect of advice and proceedings concerning the Act and obligations arising under it, such privilege is otherwise over-ridden. An information notice also over-rides any obligation to maintain secrecy or any other restriction on disclosure however arising or imposed.[396] By virtue of section 45(1) the Commissioner and his staff may not disclose without lawful authority any information obtained by them under the Act. But one instance in which disclosure is lawful is where the disclosure is made for the purpose of proceedings, whether criminal or civil and whether arising under, or by virtue of the Act or otherwise.[397] The power inherent in an information notice might, therefore, seem to intrude deeply into the privacy of the person to whom it is addressed. But this consideration is counter-balanced by the fact that the person to whom it is addressed will be a public authority. Still, difficult questions may arise where the information is sought to be used in the prosecution of an individual who has been an employee or agent of a public authority.

22.219 If an authority fails to comply with an information notice, the Commissioner may certify in writing to the court that the authority has failed to comply with the notice and the Court of Session[398] may then inquire into the matter and, after hearing any witness who may be produced against or on behalf of the authority, and after hearing any statement that may be offered in defence, may deal with the authority as if it had committed a contempt of court.[399] An authority which, in purported compliance with an information notice, makes a statement which it

---

[393] FOI(S)A 2002, s 50(8).
[394] ibid, s 50(5).
[395] ibid, s 50(6).
[396] ibid, s 50(7).
[397] ibid, s 45(2)(d).
[398] ibid, s 53(4).
[399] ibid, s 53(1) and (3).

knows to be false in a material respect or recklessly makes a statement which is false in a material respect is to be taken to have failed to comply with the notice.[400]

Enforcement notices

Where the Commissioner is satisfied that a Scottish public authority has failed to comply with a provision of Part 1 of the Act, he may give the authority an enforcement notice, that is a notice in writing requiring the authority to take, within the time specified in the notice, such steps as are specified for so complying.[401] The time so specified must not expire before the end of the period within which an appeal may be brought under section 56 against the information notice; and, if such an appeal is brought, the notice need not be complied with before the cause is finally determined.[402] **22.220**

An enforcement notice must contain: **22.221**

(a) a statement of the provision with which the Commissioner is satisfied that the authority has failed to comply and the respect in which it has not done so; and
(b) particulars of the right of appeal conferred by section 56.[403]

The Commissioner may cancel an information notice by notice in writing to the authority.[404] **22.222**

Compliance by authorities with decision notices and enforcement notices

Subject to the provision discussed at paragraph 22.225 below, an authority to which a decision notice requiring it to take specified steps or an enforcement notice is given must, subject to the outcome of any appeal which the authority brings, comply with the relevant notice. **22.223**

If an authority fails to comply with any part of a decision notice requiring it to take specified steps or with an enforcement notice, the Commissioner may certify in writing to the court that the authority has failed to comply with the notice and the Court of Session[405] may then inquire into the matter and, after hearing any witness who may be produced against or on behalf of the authority, and after hearing any statement that may be offered in defence, may deal with the authority as if it had committed a contempt of court.[406] **22.224**

The exception mentioned concerns decision notices or enforcement notices which are given to the Scottish Administration and relate to a perceived failure, in **22.225**

---

[400] ibid, s 53(2).
[401] ibid, s 51(1).
[402] ibid, s 51(3).
[403] ibid, s 51(2).
[404] ibid, s 51(4).
[405] ibid, s 53(4).
[406] ibid, s 53(1) and (3).

respect of one or more requests for information, to comply with section 1(1) in respect of information which, by virtue of sections 29, 31(1), 32(1)(b), 34, 36(1) or 41(b) is exempt information. In respect of this collection of cases provision is made for the First Minister of the Scottish Executive to sign and give to the Commissioner a certificate stating that the First Minister has on reasonable grounds formed, after consulting other members of the Executive, the opinion that there was no such failure by the Scottish Administration and that the information requested is of exceptional sensitivity. Where the First Minister signs and gives such a certificate, the decision notice or enforcement notice ceases to have effect. Thus, the First Minister's certificate represents a trump card which, when played, over-rides the Commissioner and even the courts. A similar certification process or trump card is granted to the executive branch under the UK Act.[407]

22.226 The certificate must be signed and given to the Commissioner not later than the thirtieth working day[408] after the day on which the notice was given to the Scottish Administration or, where an appeal against the notice was brought, after the cause was finally determined.[409] The First Minister must lay a copy of his certificate before the Parliament not later than ten days after it was given.[410] Hence if the First Minister plays the trump card comprised in a certificate given under section 52, his doing so may become subject to scrutiny and questions in the Parliament. Where the certificate relates to a decision notice, he must also inform the person to whose application the notice relates of the reasons for the opinion formed, but he is not obliged to do this where he would have to disclose exempt information.[411]

22.227 The First Minister may sign and give such a certificate even after the Scottish Administration has brought an appeal against the relevant notice and, ex hypothesi, failed to succeed in its appeal. The procedure, therefore, transfers effective responsibility to the First Minister and, in a consultative capacity, his ministerial colleagues, subject to subsequent scrutiny in the Parliament.

22.228 The collection of cases to which certification procedure applies comprises information rendered exempt by sections 29, 31(1), 32(1)(b), 34, 36(1) and 41(b). Section 31(1), information exempt for the purpose of safeguarding national security, may seem uncontroversial. A similar view might be taken of section 32(1)(b), confidential information obtained from a state other than the United Kingdom or from an international organization or international court

---

[407] FOIA 2000, s 53.
[408] Defined in FOI(S)A 2002, s 73 and see para 22.155 above.
[409] FOI(S)A 2002, s 52(2).
[410] ibid, s 52(3)(a).
[411] ibid, s 52(3)(b).

and section 34, investigations by Scottish public authorities and proceedings arising out of them. But section 29 concerns, amongst other things, the formulation
or development of government policy, Ministerial communications and the operation of any Ministerial private office. Not only, therefore, is the secrecy of
information relating to the inner processes of Ministerial activity maintained by
the exemption of such information but, in the last resort, the First Minister may
over-ride a direction of the Commissioner, or even the court, that such material
should be disclosed. Section 36(1) concerns information in respect of which a
claim to confidentiality could be maintained in legal proceedings; thus such
information, when held by the Scottish Administration, may be treated with
more deference to its confidentiality than when it would be if held by other
authorities.[412] The last case in respect of which the certification procedure might
be exercised concerns section 41(b), that is information relating to the exercise by
Her Majesty of her prerogative of honour. Although such information may
intrude into the privacy of Her Majesty's subjects and perhaps occasion invidious
comparisons between their individual merits, its selection for the special treatment which it is given does not seem entirely justified when, for example, other
personal data relating to individuals is not similarly treated.

Appeals to the Court of Session

Persons affected by the decisions of the Commissioner may appeal against those   **22.229**
decisions to the Court of Session. But such appeals may only be brought on a
point of law and the appeals which may be brought and the persons who may
bring them are defined as follows:

(a) a person who applied to the Commissioner under section 47(1) for a decision
whether the request for information was dealt with in accordance with Part 1
of the Act may appeal against a decision by the Commissioner under section
49(2) that no decision falls to be made in relation to the application;

(b) a person who applied to the Commissioner under section 47(1) for a decision
whether the request for information was dealt with in accordance with Part 1
of the Act may appeal against a decision by the Commissioner under section
49(3)(b) in respect of the application;

(c) the authority in respect of which a decision by the Commissioner under section 49(3)(b) was made may appeal against the decision;

(d) an authority may appeal against a decision of the Commissioner which
resulted in his giving that authority an information notice or an enforcement
notice.

---

[412] Note that the Commissioner would be able to obtain this information, despite its confidentiality, by giving an information notice; see ibid, s 50(7). The process of certification by the First
Minister does not apply to information notices; see ibid, s 52(1). But the Commissioner might not
be able to make much use of the information.

22.230 The Act does not address the time limits and procedure applicable to such appeals.

The Commissioner's powers of entry and inspection

22.231 The Act enables the Commissioner to seek a warrant authorizing him or a member of his staff to enter and search premises, to inspect and seize any documents or other material found there and to inspect, examine, operate and test any equipment there.[413] The Commissioner may obtain such a warrant from a sheriff who must first be satisfied by evidence on oath supplied by the Commissioner that there are reasonable grounds for suspecting either:

(a) that a Scottish public authority has failed to comply with any of the requirements of Part 1 of the Act, so much of a decision notice given to it by the Commissioner under section 49(5) as requires steps to be taken, an information notice or an enforcement notice; or

(b) that an offence under section 65 of taking steps to alter or destroy records with the intention of preventing its due disclosure has been or is being committed;

and that evidence of such failure to comply or of the commission of such offence is to be found on any premises specified in the evidence adduced before the sheriff.[414]

22.232 Save in cases of urgency the Commissioner must first have given seven days' notice in writing to the occupier of the premises and have been refused access. Other procedural requirements relating to the execution of the warrant are set out in Schedule 3 to the Act.

22.233 The powers of inspection and seizure conferred by a warrant are not exercisable in respect of information which is exempt information by virtue of section 31(1), that is information in respect of which the exemption is required for the purpose of safeguarding national security.[415]

Offence of altering records with the intention of preventing disclosure

22.234 Where a request for information is made to a Scottish public authority and the applicant is entitled under section 1 of the Act to be given the information or any part of it, the authority commits an offence if, with the intention of preventing the disclosure of the information, or part of it, to which the entitlement relates, it

---

[413] FOI(S)A 2002, s 54 and Sch 3.
[414] ibid, Sch 3, para 1(2).
[415] ibid, para 7.

alters, defaces, blocks, erases, destroys or conceals a record held by the authority.[416] The offence may also be committed by any person who is employed by the authority, is an officer of it or is subject to the authority's direction.[417] Such persons include a member of the staff of, or a person acting on behalf of, the Parliament or the Scottish Parliamentary Corporate Body and a member of the staff of the Scottish Administration. But neither the Parliament, the Scottish Parliamentary Corporate Body nor the Scottish Administration is liable to prosecution.[418]

(6) The Keeper of the Records of Scotland

Public records, that is records held for the benefit of the public, have long been maintained in Scotland both locally and centrally in Edinburgh.[419] Since 1948, when the single office of the Keeper of the Registers and Records of Scotland was divided by the Public Registers and Records (Scotland) Act 1948 into two offices relating respectively to registers and records, the office-holder in charge of the central records has been the Keeper of the Records of Scotland. The Keeper is a non-ministerial officer in the Scottish Administration.[420] What used to be known as the Scottish Record Office is now called the National Archives of Scotland. **22.235**

The law pertaining to public records in Scotland is not the subject of systematic legislation and, to some large extent, involves following practices established over time or by the administrative application of rules contained in the Public Records Act 1958 even though they do not, as a matter of law, extend to Scotland.[421] For example, there is no duty imposed on government departments to transmit public records to the Keeper. But under section 5 of the Public Records (Scotland) Act 1937 provision was made rendering it lawful for any government department, board of trustees or other body or person having the custody of any records belonging to His Majesty and relating exclusively or mainly to Scotland to transmit such records to the Keeper. This provision is purely permissive, as is the provision contained in section 3(8) of the Public Records Act 1958 enabling a person holding any public record to transmit it to the Keeper. Nonetheless these provisions 'bring large transmissions each year from Scottish and United Kingdom departments'.[422] Nor is there a statutory definition of 'public records' since the definition laid down in the Public Records Act 1958 and expanded by subsequent orders in council does not apply in Scotland. But, the definition applied by the **22.236**

---

[416] FOI(S)A 2002, s 65(1), (2).
[417] ibid, s 65(2).
[418] ibid, s 68.
[419] See the *Stair Memorial Encyclopedia*, vol 19 under the title 'Public Registers and Records'.
[420] Scotland Act 1998, s 26(8)(a).
[421] See ch 8 above.
[422] *Stair Memorial Encyclopaedia*, vol 19, para 861.

courts, namely records held for the benefit of the public,[423] appears to operate satisfactorily.

22.237 But, whatever may be said of the state of the law, the Keeper is responsible for holding and managing a large body of documents transmitted to him by public authorities. Since he is a Scottish public authority to whom the Freedom of Information (Scotland) Act 2002 applies, anyone may now require the Keeper to give access to any document which he holds. But, because documents held by the Keeper may have been transmitted to him by some other public authority, special provision is made so as to impose on the transmitting authority the duty of determining whether the requested information is exempt. This provision applies to information which is contained in a record transferred to the Keeper by a Scottish public authority and which has not been designated by the authority as open information for the purpose of section 22 of the Scottish Act.[424] When the Keeper receives a request for such information, he must forward it to the authority which transferred the information to him and that authority must determine whether the information is exempt.[425] The time for complying with the request is extended so as to allow this process to be completed before a response is given to the request.[426] Similarly, if the applicant requires a review, the body which must carry out the review is the authority which transmitted the record to the Keeper and the time for the review to be carried out is similarly extended.[427]

22.238 Where information contained in a record was transferred to the Keeper before 1 July 1999 by the Secretary of State for Scotland and is not designated by the Scottish Ministers as open information, the Keeper must forward requests and any subsequent requirements for review to the Scottish Ministers.[428]

22.239 Records may be transferred to the Keeper not only by Scottish public authorities but also by public authorities access to whose records is governed by the UK Act. The right of access to such documents is precluded under the Scottish Act unless the transferring authority has designated that the information is open information or the transferring authority was the Secretary of State for Scotland and the transfer was made before 1 July 1999. This exemption is conferred by providing

---

[423] Further since such documents are *extra commercium* the body to whom they belong may not have its right to recover them cut off by lapse of time; see *Edinburgh Presbytery v University of Edinburgh* (1890) 28 SLR 567 concerning the recovery in 1890 by the Presbytery of its records created prior to 1603 from the University in whose possession they had lain since 1697. The right to recover property *extra commercium* remains imprescriptible; see the Prescription and Limitation (Scotland) Act 1973, ss 7(2) and 8(2) and Sch 3, para (d).

[424] FOI(S)A 2002, s 22(1).

[425] ibid, s 22(2) to (5).

[426] ibid, s 10(2).

[427] ibid, ss 22(4),(5) and 21(2).

[428] ibid, s 22(6).

that the Keeper does not hold information within these categories for the purpose of the Scottish Act.[429]

F. The Code of Practice on Access to Scottish Executive Information

Although, as mentioned in paragraph 22.29 above, it will be some time before the Scottish Act comes into force, much information which will be made available under the Scottish Act is already available to the public. In July 1999 the Scottish Executive published the Code of Practice on Access to Scottish Executive Information. The Code is modelled closely on the Code of Practice on Access to Government Information,[430] and was promulgated in support of the Scottish Ministers' policy of extending access to official information and of responding to reasonable requests for information.[431] The access to information which the Scottish Code affords foreshadows the regime which the Act will create.

22.240

The aims of the Code are:

22.241

- to facilitate policy-making and the democratic process by providing access to the facts and analyses which form the basis for the consideration of proposed policy; and
- to protect the interests of individuals and companies by ensuring that reasons are given for administrative decisions, except where there is statutory authority or established convention to the contrary.

The aims are balanced by the need:

- to maintain high standards of care in ensuring the privacy of personal and commercially confidential information; and
- to preserve confidentiality where disclosure would not be in the public interest or would breach personal privacy or the confidences of a third party, in accordance with statutory requirements and Part II of the Code.

The scope of the Code

The Code of Practice states that it applies to those Scottish public bodies which are within the jurisdiction of the Scottish Parliamentary Commissioner for Administration, referred to here as the Scottish Parliamentary Commissioner,[432]

22.242

---

[429] ibid, s 3(4). See also para 22.55 above.
[430] Discussed in ch 4 above.
[431] Code of Practice on Access to Scottish Executive Information, para 1.
[432] The Scottish Parliamentary Commissioner for Administration is appointed under art 4 of the Scotland Act 1998 (Transitory and Transitional Provisions)(Complaints of Maladministration) Order 1999, SI 1999/1351. He is called 'the Scottish Commissioner' in that Order, but is referred to here as 'the Scottish Parliamentary Commissioner' to prevent confusion with the Scottish Information Commissioner.

and it states that these bodies are listed in Schedule 1 to the Code.[433] Schedule 1 to the Code contains a list in two sections: the first is headed 'Scottish Executive' and lists various of its departments, agencies and other organs; the second section lists a series of Scottish public bodies under the heading 'Other Scottish Authorities'. Under article 8 of the Scotland Act 1998 (Transitory and Transitional Provisions) (Complaints of Maladministration) Order 1999[434] it is provided that the persons, bodies and authorities subject to investigation by the Scottish Parliamentary Commissioner are:

- any member of the Scottish Executive;
- any other office-holder in the Scottish Administration;
- the Parliamentary Corporation[435]
- any Scottish public authority with mixed functions or no reserved functions.[436]

The bodies falling in the last of these categories are listed in Schedule 1 to the Order. This list corresponds with the second section of the Schedule to the Code.

22.243 The Code only applies to government information held by the Scottish public bodies listed in Schedule 1 to the Code. It does not apply to or affect information held by courts or contained in court documents. 'Court' includes tribunals and inquiries.

22.244 If there is any discrepancy between the bodies subject to the Scottish Parliamentary Commissioner's jurisdiction and the list contained in the Schedule to the Code, it would seem, on a strict interpretation, that the list in the Schedule to the Code would be determinative. For example, therefore, it would seem that the Scottish Parliamentary Corporate Body is not subjected to the Code. But, perhaps, given that the Code is a code and not a statute, it will be interpreted more broadly.

The commitment imposed by the Code

22.245 The Code is set out in two parts. Part I contains the operative provisions of the Code. Part II lists a series of exemptions to the Code which identify information which will not be disclosed.

22.246 Paragraph 3 of the Code sets out the general duty imposed by the Code on those bodies to which it applies. It provides that:

subject to the exemptions in Part II, the Code commits those Scottish public bodies falling under the jurisdiction of the Scottish Commissioner:

---

[433] Code of Practice, para 6.
[434] SI 1999/1351.
[435] ie, the Scottish Parliamentary Corporate Body.
[436] Also subject to investigation by the Scottish Parliamentary Commissioner is any cross-border authority which is listed in Sch 2 to the Order; these bodies are not Scottish public bodies and are not subject to the Code.

- to publish the facts and analysis of the facts which Scottish Ministers consider relevant and important in framing major policy decisions; such information will normally be made available when policies are announced;
- to publish, or otherwise make available, explanatory material on the Scottish Executive's and other public bodies' dealings with the public (including such rules, procedures, internal guidance to officials, and similar administrative manuals as will assist better understanding of these bodies' actions in dealing with the public) except where publication could prejudice any matter which should properly be kept confidential under Part II of the Code;
- to give reasons for administrative decisions to those affected;
- to publish full information about how public services are run, how much they cost, who is in charge, and what complaints and redress procedures are available; and full and, where possible, comparable information about what services are being provided, what targets are set, what standards of service are expected and the results achieved;
- to release, in response to specific requests, information relating to their policies, actions and decisions and other matters related to their areas of responsibility.

But the Code does not require the Scottish Executive or other public bodies to acquire information which they do not possess, to provide information which is already published, or to provide information which is provided as part of an existing charged service other than through that service.[437]   **22.247**

Nor does the Code over-ride provisions contained in statutory rights of access to information or records or statutory prohibitions on disclosure. Where information can be sought under an existing statutory right, the terms of the right of access take precedence over the Code.   **22.248**

The Public Records Act 1958 does not apply to the records of any government body which is wholly or mainly concerned with Scottish affairs, or which carries on its activities wholly or mainly in Scotland. But the current practice is to apply the same rules as are imposed by that Act, as they are modified by the White Paper on *Open Government*.[438] The Code does not change this practice.   **22.249**

It is stated that the Code is operated in line with the obligations placed by the European Court of Human Rights on the Scottish Executive.   **22.250**

The exemptions

Part II of the Code consists of a list of categories of information which are exempt from the commitment to provide information imposed by the Code. Some categories identify information by reference to a class of documents. An example is information received in confidence from foreign governments, foreign courts or international organizations. In such cases information falling into the class is   **22.251**

---

[437] Code of Practice, para 4.
[438] Cm 2290.

exempt irrespective of the particular nature of the information or of the particular effect which would or might follow from disclosing the information. But other categories identify exempt information by reference to the harm or prejudice to a specified interest which would or might follow from disclosing the information in question. The reference to harm or prejudice includes both actual harm or prejudice and risk or reasonable expectation of harm or prejudice. An example of such a category is information whose disclosure would harm national security or defence. In such cases the position is that the information should be disclosed 'unless the harm likely to arise from disclosure would outweigh the public interest in making the information available'.

22.252   The Code states that the exemptions will not be interpreted in a way which causes injustice to individuals. This reflects a canon of interpretation which is included in the Code of Practice on Access to Government Information.

22.253   The exemptions are as follows.

22.254   *Defence, security and international relations*

- Information whose disclosure would harm national security or defence.
- Information whose disclosure would harm the conduct of international relations or affairs.
- Information received in confidence from foreign governments, foreign courts or international organisations. (Part II, para 1.)

22.255   These exemptions correspond with those contained in sections 31 and 32 of the Scottish Act.

22.256   *Internal discussion and advice*

Information whose disclosure would harm the frankness and candour of internal discussion, including:
- proceedings of Scottish Cabinet and Scottish Ministerial committees;
- internal opinion, advice, recommendation, consultation and deliberation;
- projections and assumptions relating to internal policy analysis; analysis of alternative policy options and information relating to rejected policy options;
- confidential communications between departments, public bodies and regulatory bodies. (Part II, para 2.)

22.257   This exemption corresponds broadly with certain provisions contained in sections 29 and 30 of the Scottish Act, but the fourth sub-heading overlaps with the quasi-exemption under section 3(2)(a)(ii) of information supplied in confidence by a Minister of the Crown or a department of the UK government and with section 36.

22.258   *Communications with the Royal Household*

Information relating to confidential communications between Ministers and Her Majesty the Queen or other Members of the Royal Household, or relating to confidential proceedings of the Privy Council. (Part II, para 3.)

This provision corresponds with section 41(a) of the Scottish Act but extends further than that section in also protecting certain proceedings of the Privy Council. Since the Privy Council is not a public authority under the UK Act or a Scottish public authority under the Scottish Act, no request for information relating to its proceedings may be made under either statute. **22.259**

Law enforcement and legal proceedings **22.260**

- Information whose disclosure could prejudice the administration of justice (including fair trial), legal proceedings or the proceedings of any tribunal, public inquiry or other formal investigations (whether actual or likely) or whose disclosure is, has been, or is likely to be addressed in the context of such proceedings.
- Information whose disclosure could prejudice the enforcement or proper administration of the law, including the prevention, investigation or detection of crime, or the apprehension or prosecution of offenders.
- Information relating to legal proceedings or the proceedings of any tribunal, public inquiry or other formal investigation which have been completed or terminated, or relating to investigations which have or might have resulted in proceedings.
- Information covered by legal professional privilege.
- Information whose disclosure would harm public safety or public order, or would prejudice the security of any building or penal institution.
- Information whose disclosure could endanger the life or physical safety of any person, or identify the source of information or assistance given in confidence for law enforcement or security purposes.
- Information whose disclosure would increase the likelihood of damage to the environment, or rare or endangered species and their habitats. (Part II, para 4.)

This head covers a wide range of subjects. Largely it corresponds with sections 34 and 35 of the Scottish Act. But under the Act information covered by legal professional privilege is not specifically protected: if it comprised advice from the Law Officers, it would be exempt under section 29(1)(c); otherwise the authority might be entitled to rely on the confidentiality of such information and claim exemption under section 36. Under the Act the exemption relating to individual health and safety is contained in section 39(1). It is no longer linked to the protection of informants which is provided for in section 34(3). The Act does not specifically permit information about the environment to be withheld on the ground of possible damage. But, information concerning environmental matters is to be dealt with under regulations incorporating certain provisions of the Aarhus Convention into Scots law. **22.261**

Immigration and nationality **22.262**

Information relating to immigration, nationality, consular and entry clearance cases. However, information will be provided, though not through access to personal records, where there is no risk that disclosure would prejudice the effective administration of immigration controls or other statutory provisions. (Part II, para 5.)

This corresponds with section 35(1)(e) of the Act. **22.263**

22.264 *Effective management of the economy and collection of tax*

- Information whose disclosure could harm the management of the economy, prejudice the conduct of official market operations, or could lead to improper gain or advantage.
- Information whose disclosure would prejudice the assessment or collection of tax, duties or National Insurance contributions, or assist tax avoidance or evasion. (Part II, para 6.)

22.265 This exemption embraces the exemptions made in the Act in sections 33(2) and 35(1)(d).

22.266 *Effective management and operations of the public service*

- Information whose disclosure could lead to improper gain or advantage or would prejudice: the competitive position of a department or other public body or authority; negotiations or the effective conduct of personnel management, or commercial or contractual activities; or the award of any discretionary grant.
- Information whose disclosure would harm the proper and efficient conduct of the operations of a department or other public body or authority, including NHS organisations, or of any regulatory body. (Part II, para 7.)

22.267 The exemptions under this head appear, in so far as they do appear in the Act, in different forms. Information the disclosure of which would or might substantially prejudice the commercial interests of a Scottish public authority is exempt under section 33(1)(b). The second sub-heading does not correspond with any provision in the Act, but information relating to regulatory activity may be exempt under section 35(1)(g).

22.268 *Public employment, public appointments and honours*

- Personnel records (relating to public appointments as well as employees of public authorities) including those relating to recruitment, promotion and security vetting.
- Information, opinions and assessments given in confidence in relation to public employment and public appointments made by Scottish Ministers, by the Crown on the advice of Ministers, by Ministers in the UK Government or by statutory office holders.
- Information, opinions and assessments given in relation to recommendations for honours. (Part II, para 8.)

22.269 Some of the information covered by these exemptions will be covered by section 38 of the Act which relates to personal data; some may be covered by section 36 relating to confidentiality. Information about the exercise of the prerogative of honour is exempt by virtue of section 41(b).

22.270 *Voluminous or vexatious requests*

Requests for information which are vexatious or manifestly unreasonable or are formulated in too general a manner, or which (because of the amount of information to be processed or the need to retrieve information from files not in current use) would require unreasonable diversion of resources. (Part II, para 9.)

This heading correlates with sections 14 and 12 of the Act.   22.271

Publication and prematurity in relation to publication   22.272

Information which is or will soon be published, or whose disclosure, where the material relates to a planned or potential announcement or publication, could cause harm (for example, of a physical or financial nature). (Part II, para 10.)

This exemption mainly corresponds with sections 25 and 27, but the possibility 22.273 of disclosure causing harm, in so far as it would be suffered by an individual, is covered by section 39(1) and, in so far as it comprised substantial prejudice to commercial interests, by section 33(1)(b).

Research, statistics and analysis   22.274

* Information relating to incomplete analysis, research or statistics, where disclosure could be misleading or deprive the holder of priority of publication or commercial value.
* Information held only for preparing statistics or carrying out research, or for surveillance for health and safety purposes (including food safety), and which relates to individuals, companies or products which will not be identified in reports of that research or surveillance, or in published statistics. (Part II, para 11.)

This corresponds broadly with section 27(2) of the Act, but perhaps also overlaps, 22.275 as regards the first sub-heading, with section 33(1)(b).

Privacy of an individual   22.276

Unwarranted disclosure to a third party of personal information about any person (including a deceased person) or any other disclosure which would constitute or could facilitate an unwarranted invasion of privacy. (Part II, para 12.)

Privacy is not specifically protected under the Act, but the sections relating to per- 22.277 sonal data and confidentiality, respectively sections 38 and 36, cover much of the same area.

Third party's commercial confidences   22.278

Information including commercial confidences, trade secrets or intellectual property whose unwarranted disclosure would harm the competitive position of a third party. (Part II, para 13.)

Trade secrets are exempt under section 33(1)(a) of the Act; information substan- 22.279 tially prejudicing commercial interests is exempt under section 33(1)(b).

Information given in confidence   22.280

* Information held in consequence of having been supplied in confidence by a person who gave the information under a statutory guarantee that its confidentiality would be protected; or who was not under any legal obligation, whether actual or implied, to supply it, and has not consented to its disclosure.
* Information whose disclosure without the consent of the supplier would prejudice the future supply of such information.

- Medical information provided in confidence if disclosure to the subject would harm their physical or mental health, or should only be made by a medical practitioner. (Part II, para 14.)

22.281 These heads do not correspond with any exemptions under the Act although they overlap to varying degrees, under the first sub-heading, with the exemption relating to confidentiality and, under the third, with the exemption relating to the protection of individual health and safety.

22.282 *Statutory and other restrictions*

- Information whose disclosure is prohibited by or under any enactment, regulation, European Community law or international agreement.
- Information whose release would constitute a breach of Parliamentary privilege. (Part II, para 15.)

22.283 The first head corresponds with section 26. No provision relating to information breaching Parliamentary privilege is made in the Scottish Act, although it is in the UK Act.[439] This would not appear to be necessary because, although the House of Lords and the House of Commons are both public authorities within the scope of the UK Act, they are not Scottish public authorities.

Procedure

22.284 The aim under the Code is to provide information as soon as possible. Where the request is simple, twenty working days[440] is set as the target for responding. But where significant search or collation of material is required, the target may be extended. The same period of twenty working days is given to an authority under the Scottish Act. Hence observing the Code will assist authorities in their preparation for the implementation of the Act.

22.285 If information cannot be given, an explanation is normally to be provided.

22.286 Charges may be made in respect of complex requests. The charges are intended to reflect the reasonable costs of making searches or processing or collating information.

22.287 Complaints that information which should have been provided has not been provided, or that unreasonable charges have been demanded, are to be made first to the body from whom the information was requested. If the applicant remains dissatisfied after an internal review, complaints may be made through an MSP to the Scottish Parliamentary Commissioner. The Scottish Parliamentary Commissioner will investigate such complaints in accordance with the procedures provided in the Scotland Act 1998 (Transitory and Transitional Provisions) (Complaints of Maladministration) Order 1999.[441]

---

[439] FOIA 2000, s 34.
[440] cf the definition of 'working day' in FOI(S)A 2002, s 73; see para 22.155 above.
[441] SI 1999/1351.

Operation of the Code

The Scottish Executive publishes an annual report on the operation of the Code. **22.288**
The report on the calendar year 2000 was published on 14 March 2001 and that
for the calendar year 2001 on 17 May 2002. Both reports reveal that the number
of formal requests for information pursuant to the Code is low: 44 in 2000 and 17
in 2001. As the report for 2001 notes, the number of requests is too small to justify any statistical conclusions. No complaints have been investigated by the
Scottish Parliamentary Commissioner.

The reports list other achievements towards open government. For example, in **22.289**
2000, the Scottish Executive published the Scottish Ministerial Code; in the
report for 2001 it is mentioned that the Scottish Arts Council holds its Council
meetings in public.

G. Some Other Methods of Obtaining Access to Official Information in Scotland

The following paragraphs make reference to a number of methods of obtaining **22.290**
official information under existing law.

Local authorities

The Local Government (Scotland) Act 1973[442] confers on the public, subject to **22.291**
exceptions for the protection of confidential information, rights of access to meetings of local authorities and rights of access to documents, including agendas for
meetings of local authorities, reports for meetings and minutes of meetings.

Under sections 53 and 54 of the Local Government (Scotland) Act 1994, a local **22.292**
authority is required to make proper arrangements for the preservation and management of its records, but it has power, subject to consulting the Keeper of the
Records of Scotland, to dispose of any records not considered to be worthy of
preservation. Amongst other things, a local authority may make provision for
enabling persons, with or without charge and subject to such conditions as the
authority may determine, to inspect the records and to make or obtain copies of
them.

---

[442] See ss 50A–50K and Sch 7A as added by s 2 of the Local Government (Access to Information)
Act 1985 and further added to and amended by the Local Government (Access to Information)
(Scotland) Order 1996, SI 1996/2278.

Environmental information held by public bodies

22.293 The Environmental Information Regulations 1992[443] extend to Scotland. The regulations implement Council Directive (EEC) 90/313. They impose an obligation on certain public bodies to make available to anyone who requests it information which they hold in an accessible form and not for the purposes of any judicial or legislative functions and which is not otherwise available.[444] The persons to whom the duty applies are all such Ministers of the Crown, government departments, local authorities and other persons as carry out functions of public administration at a national, regional or local level with responsibilities for the environment.[445] Confidential information is excepted. Information is confidential if and only if it is information the disclosure of which would affect international relations, national defence or public security, would affect matters which are the subject of continuing legal proceedings or an enquiry or of investigations preliminary to proceedings or an inquiry, would affect the confidentiality of the deliberations of a person to whom the duty applies, would involve the supply of a document still in the course of completion or an internal communication of a person to whom the duty applies or would affect the confidentiality of matters to which any commercial or industrial confidentiality attaches, including intellectual property.[446]

Personal data

22.294 Under the Data Protection Act 1998, an individual who is the subject of any personal data is entitled, amongst other things, to have the information constituting that data communicated to him.[447] Such data includes information which is being processed by means of equipment operating automatically in response to instructions given for that purpose, information which is recorded with the intention that it should be processed by such equipment, information which is recorded as part of a filing system structured so as to render the information readily accessible, or which comprises a health record, an educational record or an accessible public record.[448]

22.295 As mentioned above,[449] data protection is a reserved matter and the person primarily charged with the implementation and supervision of the Data Protection

---

[443] SI 1992/3240, amended by the Environmental Information (Amendment) Regulations 1998 SI 1998/1447.

[444] Environmental Information Regulations 1992 (n 443 above) regs 3(1) and 2(1).

[445] ibid, reg 2(3).

[446] ibid, reg 4(2) as substituted by SI 1998/1447, reg 2(1).

[447] Data Protection Act 1998, s 7(1)(c)(i).

[448] ibid, ss 1(1) and 68(1). Fuller discussion of the Data Protection Act 1998 and the terms used in it is provided in ch 10 above.

[449] See para 22.24 above at n 61.

Act 1998 in Scotland as well as England and Wales and Northern Ireland is the Information Commissioner as, by virtue of section 18(1) of the Freedom of Information Act 2000, the Data Protection Commissioner has become.

Information sought for the purpose of civil proceedings

Parties to civil proceedings may obtain documents from public bodies for the **22.296** purpose of pursuing those proceedings. For example, in *P v Tayside Regional Council*[450] the petitioner sought an order under the Administration of Justice (Scotland) Act 1972 for recovery of hospital records pertaining to a child whom the petitioner had fostered and the child's natural mother. The petitioner had contracted hepatitis B, allegedly from the child whose natural mother was an intravenous drug user. The issue to which the documents related was the council's social department's knowledge of the mother's drug use. The council resisted the petition on the basis that the documents were confidential. Lord Sutherland in the Outer House stated:

> It has always been accepted in Scotland that there is no such thing as absolute privilege and in any case the court may over-rule an attempt to prevent the disclosure of information even though there are strong grounds put forward in the public interest for preventing that information being disclosed.

He ruled that 'the public interest in seeing that justice is done in the present case far outweighs the public interest in confidentiality' and made an order for production of the documents to a commissioner in order that he might make relevant excerpts.

---

[450] 1989 SC 38.

23

WALES AND NORTHERN IRELAND

A. Introduction

This chapter is concerned with how the Freedom of Information Act 2000 applies **23.01** to Wales and Northern Ireland. Special consideration had to be given to this issue when the Act was drafted, on account of the devolution of power from Westminster to their respective legislative Assemblies. Although a detailed consideration of devolution is beyond the scope of this book, a brief outline of the basic principles is included to assist in understanding some of the terminology used in the Act and further, to help to explain to some extent why the provisions of the Act dealing with Wales and Northern Ireland are not perfectly symmetrical.

As there are significant similarities between the ways in which Wales and **23.02** Northern Ireland are affected by the Act, the section that discusses Northern Ireland will focus on those provisions which differ from their counterparts in Wales so as to avoid repetition.

B. Wales

(1) The scheme of devolution for Wales

The National Assembly for Wales

The National Assembly for Wales was created by the Government of Wales Act **23.03** 1998. However, the extent to which power has been devolved to this body is subject to limitations; whereas the Scottish Parliament and the Northern Ireland Assembly have power to enact primary legislation, the National Assembly for

Wales has no such right, but only the right to be consulted on Welsh primary legislation as an advisory body. Its own legislative role is confined to specific delegation from the central government in Westminster. Thus, the effect of the Government of Wales Act 1998 is to provide for administrative devolution rather than legislative devolution and accordingly the Assembly is not generally considered to be a Parliament in the true sense of the term.

23.04   The task of the Assembly has effectively been to take over the role of the Secretary of State for Wales and other Ministers in the Welsh Office. This role encompasses forming regulations which are ultimately to be approved by the Assembly after input has been received from the subordinate legislation scrutiny committee.

23.05   The Assembly is made up of 60 members, one of whom is elected by the rest to become Assembly First Secretary. The First Secretary then appoints some of the other members to become Assembly Secretaries. The Assembly acts as the executive and delegates its powers to these Assembly Secretaries. The Assembly Secretaries themselves make up the executive committee which is in essence the Welsh Cabinet. The Assembly First Secretary and Assembly Secretaries have in practice adopted the respective titles First Minister for Wales and Assembly Ministers.

The Welsh Administration Ombudsman

23.06   Section 111 of the Government of Wales Act 1998 provides for an office of Welsh Administration Ombudsman. The Ombudsman's function as set out in Schedule 9 of the 1998 Act is to investigate action taken by the Assembly and a variety of other administrative bodies where a complaint is made to him by a person who claims to have sustained injustice as a result of maladministration.[1]

(2) Freedom of Information in Wales

Public authorities in Wales to which the Act applies

23.07   As noted in earlier chapters of this book, the general right of access to information held by public authorities is set out in section 1(1) of the Freedom of Information Act 2000.[2] The term 'public authority' is defined in section 3(1) as a body or holder of an office which is listed in Schedule 1, or designated by order under section 5, or a publicly-owned company as defined by section 6. Each of these three categories may include Welsh bodies.

---

[1] Government of Wales Act 1998, Sch 9, paras 14 and 17.
[2] See chs 3 and 5 above.

Schedule 1

The National Assembly for Wales is included in Part I of Schedule 1. Accordingly **23.08** the Act applies to the Assembly as it does to the Houses of Parliament and government departments.

Schedule 1 is divided into seven parts,[3] and each of Parts II to V is sub-divided into **23.09** 'England and Wales' and 'Northern Ireland'. Part VI contains all other listed bodies to which the Act applies apart from those in Northern Ireland which are found in Part VII. Below is a list of some of the more important Welsh bodies to which the Act applies:

Part II (Local Government)
- (a) Welsh county councils
- (b) Welsh borough councils
- (c) Welsh community councils

Part V (Police)
- (d) A chief officer of police of a police force in Wales

Part VI (Other Public Bodies)
- (e) The Arts Council of Wales
- (f) The Auditor General for Wales
- (g) The Commission for Local Administration in Wales
- (h) The Countryside Council for Wales
- (i) The Health Service Commissioner for Wales
- (j) Her Majesty's Chief Inspector of Schools in Wales
- (k) The National Museums and Galleries of Wales
- (l) The Sports Council for Wales
- (m) The Welsh Administration Ombudsman
- (n) The Welsh Development Agency.

Section 4(1): amendments to Schedule 1

Pursuant to section 4(1) of the Act, the Lord Chancellor may order any body or **23.10** the holder of any office to be added to Schedule 1 provided that two criteria are satisfied.

The first criterion can be satisfied in one of a number of ways: the body or office **23.11** must be established by virtue of the royal prerogative, by an enactment, or by subordinate legislation, or established in any other way by a Minister of the Crown, by a government department or by the National Assembly for Wales.[4] Thus, a body or office created by the Assembly can be added to Schedule 1 by the Lord Chancellor, although it cannot be added by the Assembly itself.

---

[3] See ch 5 above.
[4] Freedom of Information Act 2000, s 4(2).

23.12   In the case of a body, the second criterion is satisfied where the body is wholly or partly constituted by appointment made by the Crown, by a Minister of the Crown, by a government department or by the National Assembly for Wales. In the case of an office, the appointments to the office must be made by the Crown, by a Minister of the Crown, by a government department or by the National Assembly for Wales.[5]

23.13   Section 4(4) provides that any body or office which is listed in Parts VI or VII shall cease to be a public authority if either of the two criteria ceases to be satisfied.

23.14   Section 4(4) does not require a body or office which loses its public authority status to be formally removed from Schedule 1. However, section 4(5) of the Act confers a discretionary power on the Lord Chancellor to elect to remove a body or office that ceases to meet the two criteria or ceases to exist. This power applies to Parts VI and VII only. It is interesting to note that a body or office, Welsh or otherwise, could be added to Parts I to V of Schedule 1 pursuant to section 4(1) but if at a later date it failed to meet one of the criteria or ceased to exist, there is no provision for its removal from Schedule 1.

23.15   Section 4(7)(a) requires that before making an order pursuant to section 4(1) to add a body or office to Parts II, III, IV or VI of Schedule 1, the Lord Chancellor must consult the National Assembly for Wales if the functions of the body or office-holder are exercisable only or mainly in or as regards Wales. What has yet to be determined, however, is what is meant by 'consult', the Act giving no guidance on this point.

23.16   It can be seen that the mechanism for adding a body or office to Schedule 1 is the same for Wales as for England, save that the National Assembly for Wales will in most cases have to be consulted beforehand. Such a consultation will only be unnecessary if the body or office is being added to Parts I or V of Schedule 1. It seems from the current contents of Part I that only the most important constitutional bodies should be listed here, such as the House of Commons or the Assembly itself. There is however nothing on the face of section 4 to prevent the Lord Chancellor adding a body that satisfies the two criteria in sections 4(2) and (3) into Part I of Schedule 1, thereby avoiding the need for consultation with the National Assembly for Wales. It also seems that the Assembly need not be consulted where the Lord Chancellor is adding a body or office associated with the policing of Wales.[6]

---

[5] Freedom of Information Act 2000, s 4(3).

[6] ibid, Sch 1, Part V would be the most suitable location for such a body or office. Again it appears that there is no obligation on the Lord Chancellor to place such a body or office in Part V.

Section 5 designations as public authorities

There is further potential for a public authority associated with Wales to be cov- **23.17**
ered by the Act in section 5, which gives the Lord Chancellor power to designate
as a public authority a person who is not included in Schedule 1 nor capable of
being added to it under section 4(1). This power can be exercised only where the
person performs a function of a public nature or is providing under a contract
made with a public authority any service whose provision is a function of that
authority.[7] In contrast to most additions under section 4(1),[8] there is no requirement that the National Assembly for Wales must be consulted. Although section
5(3) requires that the Lord Chancellor consult every person[9] to whom the order
relates, it does not follow that the order necessarily relates to the Assembly merely
by virtue of the fact that the public function in question relates to Wales. Given
the express consultation requirements of section 4(7) and 7(4),[10] it seems very
likely that Parliament would have included an express consultation requirement
in section 5 as well had such a condition been intended. However, the scope for
avoiding consultation is limited by the fact that section 5 cannot be used as a substitute for a section 4(1) amendment, that being expressly excluded by the terms
of section 5(1).

Section 7 limitations

Section 7 allows for the confinement of the application of the right of access given **23.18**
by section 1(1) of the Act to just a part of the information held by an authority. By
section 7(3), the Lord Chancellor may by order amend Schedule 1 to limit the
entry relating to a public authority to information of a specific description.
However, if the order relates to the National Assembly for Wales or a Welsh public authority then the Lord Chancellor is under a duty to consult the National
Assembly for Wales first.[11] This section introduces the new term 'Welsh public
authority', the meaning of which is considered in paragraph 23.20 et seq below.

Where section 7 is used to limit the application of the Act when making a section **23.19**
5 designation there is no requirement to consult the National Assembly for
Wales.[12] This is consistent with the absence of such a requirement in section 5
itself.

---

[7] Freedom of Information Act 2000, s 5(1)(a) and (b).
[8] ie, additions to ibid, Sch 1, Parts II, III, IV, and VI: see para 23.15 above.
[9] 'or persons appearing to him to represent such persons'; ibid, s 5(3).
[10] See paras 23.15 above and 23.18 below.
[11] Freedom of Information Act 2000, s 7(4)(a).
[12] ibid, s 7(5) and (6).

Welsh public authorities

23.20   The term 'Welsh public authority' is used in a number of sections of the Act.[13] It is defined in section 83 as meaning any public authority which is listed in Parts II, III, IV or VI of Schedule 1 whose functions are exercisable only or mainly in or as regards Wales (other than an 'excluded authority') or, alternatively, as any public authority which is an Assembly subsidiary as defined by section 99(4) of the Government of Wales Act 1998.

23.21   Section 99(4) of the Government of Wales Act 1998 defines 'Assembly subsidiary' to mean any body corporate or other undertaking[14] of which the Assembly is a parent undertaking,[15] or any trust of which the Assembly is a settlor, or any charitable institution of which the Assembly is a founder but which is neither a body corporate nor a trust.

23.22   An 'excluded authority' is an authority so designated by the Lord Chancellor by an order under section 83(2) of the Freedom of Information Act 2000, although he must consult the National Assembly for Wales before such an order can be made.

23.23   It is interesting to note that whereas the term 'Welsh public authority' is invoked for the purposes of defining the scope of the consultation duty in section 7, it is not used in defining the scope of the consultation duty for the purposes of section 4 amendments in respect of bodies or offices associated with Wales.[16]

23.24   The fact that the Lord Chancellor is not restricted as to which Part of Schedule 1 new bodies or offices may be added to under section 4(1) has the effect that the Lord Chancellor might be able to avoid the need to consult the Assembly for the purposes of section 7(4) simply by adding the body or office in question to Parts I or V so that it does not qualify as a 'Welsh public authority'. It may be that such a decision would be capable of challenge on the basis that it was contrary to the intention of Parliament.

Exempt information

23.25   As discussed in chapter 6 above, certain categories of information are exempt by virtue of Part II of the Act. Wales is specifically referred to in three sections within Part II and is mentioned by implication in one other.

23.26   Section 28(1) provides that information is exempt if its disclosure would be likely to prejudice the relationship between any administration in the United Kingdom

---

[13]   ie, Freedom of Information Act 2000, ss 7(4), 36(5)(h), 53(3)(c), 53(5)(a), and 53(8)(b).
[14]   As defined in the Companies Act 1985, s 259(1).
[15]   Within the meaning of ibid, s 258.
[16]   As found in the Freedom of Information Act 2000, s 4(7)(a): see para 23.15 above.

and any other such administration. Section 28(2) defines 'administration in the United Kingdom' as including the National Assembly for Wales.

Section 29(1)(a) provides that information is exempt if its disclosure would be   **23.27**
likely to prejudice the economic interests of the United Kingdom or any part thereof. Accordingly the Welsh economy enjoys the protection provided by section 29. Protection is also given[17] to the financial interests of any administration in the United Kingdom[18] and as was observed above, this includes the National Assembly for Wales.

Section 35 protects information that relates to the formulation or development of   **23.28**
government policy, Ministerial communications, the provision of advice by any of the Law Officers, and the operation of any Ministerial private office. These classes of exempt information are of direct application since section 35 is expressed to apply where such information is held by the National Assembly for Wales.[19] 'Government policy' includes the policy of the Assembly, 'Ministerial communications' include the proceedings of the executive committee of the Assembly and communications between Assembly Secretaries, and 'Ministerial private office' includes any part of the administration of the Assembly providing personal administrative support to the Assembly First Secretary or an Assembly Secretary.[20] By section 84, 'executive committee' in relation to the National Assembly for Wales is given the same meaning as it has in section 56 of the Government of Wales Act 1998.

Section 36 of the Freedom of Information Act 2000 covers information that is not   **23.29**
covered by section 35, disclosure of which would be prejudicial to the effective conduct of Welsh public affairs. Where information is held by the National Assembly for Wales or any other Welsh public authority, and a qualified person reasonably considers that its disclosure would be likely to prejudice the work of the executive committee of the National Assembly for Wales, or the free and frank exchange of views and provision of advice, or otherwise prejudice the effective conduct of public affairs, then that information is exempt. The expression 'qualified person', defined in section 36(5), refers to the Assembly First Secretary in relation to information held by the National Assembly for Wales, to the public authority itself or any officer or employee of the authority authorized by the Assembly First Secretary, and to the Auditor General for Wales in relation to information held by him.

---

[17]   By ibid, s 29(1)(b).
[18]   As defined in ibid, s 28(2).
[19]   ibid, s 35(1).
[20]   These terms are defined in ibid, s 35(5).

Enforcement

23.30 Enforcement is dealt with in Part IV of the Act.[21] Pursuant to section 50, the Information Commissioner may serve a decision notice on a public authority specifying steps that must be taken by that authority to comply with the Act.[22] If the Information Commissioner requires further information for the purposes of coming to a decision then he may serve the authority with an information notice requiring the authority to furnish such information as is specified.[23] The Information Commissioner may then serve the authority with an enforcement notice if of the view that the authority has failed to comply with any of the requirements of Part I of the Act.[24]

23.31 Section 53 creates an exception to the duty to comply with a decision notice or enforcement notice where it is served on one of the bodies listed in section 53(1)(a). These include the National Assembly for Wales. In fact section 53 can be applied to any public authority by an order made by the Lord Chancellor. Pursuant to section 53(5), the Lord Chancellor is under a duty to consult the National Assembly for Wales where such an order relates to a Welsh public authority.

23.32 The decision notice or enforcement notice can be rendered ineffective if the accountable person in relation to the authority provides the Information Commissioner with a certificate stating that he has on reasonable grounds formed the opinion that there was no failure to comply with section 1(1) of the Act. Thus the Assembly First Secretary[25] is effectively given a power to overrule the Information Commissioner. Section 53(3) requires that where the certificate relates to a decision notice or enforcement notice which has been served on the National Assembly for Wales or any Welsh public authority, a copy of the certificate must be laid before the Assembly.

Appeals

23.33 Part V of the Act sets out an appeals procedure, first to the Information Tribunal[26] and then to the appropriate court.[27] The appropriate court is determined by the address of the public authority so that appeals are to the High Court of Justice in England if the address of the public authority is in England or Wales.

---

[21] See ch 7 above for full details.
[22] Freedom of Information Act 2000, s 50(3) and (4).
[23] ibid, s 51.
[24] ibid, s 52.
[25] The 'accountable person' in relation to the National Assembly for Wales or any Welsh public authority: ibid, s 53(8).
[26] ibid, s 57(1).
[27] ibid, s 59.

Miscellaneous provisions

Section 76 permits the Information Commissioner to disclose information **23.34** obtained under the Act to the Welsh Administration Ombudsman if it appears to the Information Commissioner that the information relates to a matter that could be the subject of an investigation by that Ombudsman under Schedule 9 to the Government of Wales Act 1998.

Section 77 of the Freedom of Information Act 2000 makes it an offence for a pub- **23.35** lic authority or any person who is an officer of, is employed by or is subject to the direction of that authority to alter, deface, block, erase, destroy or conceal any records with the intention of preventing disclosure to any party entitled to information in them. Proceedings for such an offence can only be instituted in Wales by the Information Commissioner or by or with the consent of the Director of Public Prosecutions.

(3) The Code of Practice on Public Access to Information

The Code of Practice on Access to Government Information which applies in **23.36** England is considered in chapter 4 above. However there is a Welsh equivalent that should be considered here—the Code of Practice on Public Access to Information, prepared and adopted in accordance with the Assembly's Standing Order (Number 17). This Code 'sets out the principles which underpin the National Assembly for Wales' approach to the promotion of open government'. The First Minister for Wales announced in March 2000 proposals for the greater openness of the National Assembly and one such proposal was a review of the existing Code.

The second edition of the Code was initially approved by the First Minister and **23.37** his Cabinet, and then formally adopted on 8 May 2001 by the Assembly itself. It is this second edition of the Code that is considered here, although there may well be further revisions in the future. According to paragraph 1.8 of the Code, it will be kept under review to ensure that the National Assembly meets the requirements of the Act and Codes of Practice issued under the provisions of the Act.

It is important to note at the outset that the Code is primarily a statement of **23.38** intent. It does not create rights or override any statutory provisions that pertain to the disclosure of information. However, paragraph 1.5 of the Code expressly states that the Code 'takes account of the key features of the Freedom of Information Act 2000 in advance of its implementation—including the categories of exempt information specified in that Act'. Until the Act is brought into force in January 2005, access to information held by the Assembly should be provided in accordance with the Code, the main provisions of which are similar to, and (as explained at paragraphs 23.44, 23.45 and 23.47 below) in some respects more generous than, those of the Act.

23.39 The most important part of the Code for present purposes is Part 3 which sets out eight principles that the National Assembly should adhere to, and these are considered below.

23.40 *Principle 1: The National Assembly will be as open as possible* This principle is explained as meaning that the National Assembly will make information available unless there are legal or public interest reasons for not so doing. Although the text contains no express reference to the Act, the principle is clearly modelled on the Act's provisions, stating that information can only be withheld if it falls within one of the categories listed in Annexes A and B—which respectively set out the absolute exemptions and non-absolute exemptions found in Part II of the Act.[28] The explanatory text adds that the National Assembly staff will receive the necessary internal guidance and training on 'maximising openness'.

23.41 *Principle 2: Clear language* This principle addresses the issue of information and/or requests for information being in Welsh. The Code states that the National Assembly will produce its documents bilingually in accordance with its Welsh Language Scheme. It also promises that the Assembly will use plain, gender neutral language in dealing with the public and aim to produce brief, easy to read documents without small print.

23.42 *Principle 3: Information on the Internet* This section of the Code (in conjunction with Annexe C) provides useful details of categories of documents which will be published on the National Assembly's website and indicates that an Internet publishing protocol will be developed as part of the publication scheme that the National Assembly will be required to produce pursuant to the Act.[29]

23.43 *Principle 4: The information register* Pursuant to this principle, the National Assembly will maintain an information register which will provide a means by which the public can identify key information produced by the National Assembly in the course of its business.[30] It is not explained how the determination is made as to what information is considered to be 'key'; presumably this is a decision of the Assembly itself. The Code notes, however, that this register is expected to provide the starting point for the publication scheme which the National Assembly is required to produce pursuant to the Act.[31]

23.44 *Principle 5: The laws governing the release of information* The explanatory text states that before responding to a request for information relating to persons

---

[28] In Freedom of Information Act 2000, ss 21, 23, 32, 34, 40, 41, and 44 (Annexe A) and in sections 22, 24, 26, 27, 28, 29, 30, 31, 33, 35, 36, 37, 38, 39, 40, 42, and 43 (Annexe B): see ch 6 above for details.

[29] Under ibid, s 19: see chs 4 and 5 above.

[30] The register can be found at http://www.inforegister.wales.gov.uk (2 December 2002).

[31] This publication scheme can be found at http://www.wales.gov.uk/keypubscheme/index.htm (2 December 2002).

whose interests are likely to be affected by disclosure, the Assembly will consult those persons as appropriate. (The Act of course imposes no such requirement.) Reference is made to a number of pieces of legislation, including the Official Secrets Act 1989, the Data Protection Act 1998, the Human Rights Act 1998, and Part II of the Freedom of Information Act 2000 itself, as examples of laws protecting privacy and confidentiality and otherwise governing the release of information which the National Assembly will 'respect'.

Principle 6: Prompt and comprehensive responses to requests for information **23.45** Whereas the Act imposes a general deadline of 20 working days[32] for responding to a request for information, this principle states that the National Assembly's target for responding will be 15 working days, thus going above and beyond the statutory requirement. However there are a number of limitations to the principle. For example, if the request involves a significant amount of research then the applicant will be informed of the delay and given a date for a full response. What constitutes a 'significant amount of research' is not identified, and neither is the person or body who determines whether the research to be undertaken for a particular request for information is 'significant'. The Code also states that whereas the National Assembly will always be as open and helpful as possible, it will with immediate effect proceed in accordance with the provisions of the Act so far as vexatious and repeat requests for information are concerned.

Principle 7: A right of complaint The Code includes reference to a formal com- **23.46** plaints procedure which is set out in the National Assembly's Code of Practice on Complaints.[33] Where a complainant is unhappy with the outcome of a complaint made about a refusal to provide information, the Code indicates that the complainant may refer the matter to the Welsh Administration Ombudsman until such time as the Information Commissioner assumes the responsibility in accordance with the Act.

Principle 8: Charges for providing information The National Assembly is given **23.47** discretion by the Act to charge for the provision of information,[34] but the Code states the Assembly's current policy is to make no charge (other than the cost of reproducing documents) unless the cost of gathering information exceeds £500, in which case the applicant will be notified and asked if he or she wishes to proceed.

---

[32] Freedom of Information Act 2000, s 10(1).
[33] The e-mail address to send such complaints to is complaints@wales.gsi.gov.uk
[34] Freedom of Information Act 2000, s 9.

C. Northern Ireland

(1) Devolution in Northern Ireland

23.48 Devolution in Northern Ireland has more in common with the scheme used for devolution in Scotland than that adopted in Wales. The Northern Ireland Assembly has a general power to enact primary legislation, subject to a number of specific exceptions, as a result of the Northern Ireland Act 1998.[35]

23.49 The executive is multi-party and is led by a First Minister and Deputy First Minister. Together they can determine the number of Ministerial offices to be held by Northern Ireland Ministers, up to a maximum of 10, and their respective functions.[36] The executive powers of the Northern Ireland Assembly are then delegated to the Ministers.

(2) Freedom of information in Northern Ireland

23.50 Section 88(2) of the Freedom of Information Act 2000 simply states that the Act extends to Northern Ireland. However, there are various specific references to Northern Ireland throughout the Act, which require consideration.

Public authorities in Northern Ireland to which the Act applies

23.51 The list of bodies and offices in Schedule 1 includes numerous references to public authorities in Northern Ireland, the most important of which is in Part I where express reference is made to the Northern Ireland Assembly. In each of Parts II, III, IV and V there is a section set aside for Northern Ireland authorities. Part VII contains all other public bodies and offices related to Northern Ireland. Some of the most important of these authorities are listed below:

Part II (Local Government)
   (a) A district council within the meaning of the Local Government Act (Northern Ireland) 1972

Part III (National Health Service)
   (b) A Health and Social Services Board established under Article 16 of the Health and Personal Social Services (Northern Ireland) Order 1972

---

[35] At the time of writing, the Northern Ireland Assembly was suspended pursuant to the exercise of the Secretary of State's powers under the Northern Ireland Act 2000. During the period of suspension, no one can hold office as a Minister in the devolved administration. This chapter describes what the position would be if at the time the Freedom of Information Act 2000 comes fully into force the devolved institutions had been restored.

[36] The Secretary of State may make an order allowing for the maximum to be greater than 10; Northern Ireland Act 1998, s 17(4).

Part IV (Education)
   (c) The managers of a school within the meaning of Article 2(2) of the Education and Libraries (NI) Order 1986

Part V (Police)
   (d) The Chief Constable of the Police Service of Northern Ireland[37]

Part VII (Other public bodies: Northern Ireland)
   (e) The Assembly Ombudsman for Northern Ireland
   (f) The Law Reform Advisory Committee for Northern Ireland
   (g) The Police Ombudsman for Northern Ireland.

Section 4(1): amendments to Schedule 1

There is no express reference to Northern Ireland in section 4(1) to (6) of the **23.52** Act.[38] This is on account of the fact that 'Minister of the Crown' is defined in section 4(9) to include a Northern Ireland Minister for the purposes of section 4. 'Northern Ireland Minister' is defined to include the First Minister and the deputy First Minister of the Northern Ireland Assembly.[39] The reference to 'subordinate legislation' in section 4(2)(a) means the same as it does in section 21(1) of the Interpretation Act 1978 with the word 'Act' including Northern Ireland legislation.[40] Section 21(1) defines 'subordinate legislation' as meaning Orders in Council, orders, rules, regulations, schemes, warrants, byelaws and other instruments made or to be made under any Act.

Pursuant to section 4(7)(b) of the Freedom of Information Act 2000, before **23.53** adding to Schedule 1 a body or office which would be a Northern Ireland public authority, the Lord Chancellor must consult the First Minister and the deputy First Minister in Northern Ireland.

Northern Ireland public authorities

The term 'Northern Ireland public authority' is defined in section 84 of the Act **23.54** and means any public authority, other than the Northern Ireland Assembly or a Northern Ireland department, whose functions are exercisable only or mainly in or as regards Northern Ireland and relate only or mainly to transferred matters. A 'transferred matter' is defined to have the same meaning as it is given in section 4(1) of the Northern Ireland Act 1998.[41]

---

[37] As the reference in the Freedom of Information Act 2000 to the Royal Ulster Constabulary is required to be construed: Police (Northern Ireland) Act 2000, s 78(2).
[38] See paras 23.10–23.14 above.
[39] Freedom of Information Act 2000, s 84.
[40] ibid.
[41] The definition in the Northern Ireland Act 1998, s 4(1) involves reference to two full schedules to that Act and accordingly is too long to reproduce here.

Publicly-owned companies

23.55 The definition of 'public authorities' to which the Freedom of Information Act 2000 applies includes publicly-owned companies as defined in section 6.[42] The definition of a 'publicly-owned company' is considered elsewhere in the book[43] but where there is a reference to Ministers of the Crown, by virtue of section 6(3) that is deemed to include a Northern Ireland Minister.

Section 7 limitations

23.56 Where the Lord Chancellor makes an order pursuant to section 7(3)[44] which relates to the Northern Ireland Assembly, he must first consult the Presiding Officer of that Assembly.[45] 'Presiding Officer' is defined in section 39 of the Northern Ireland Act 1998. Where the order relates to a Northern Ireland department or a Northern Ireland public authority then the Lord Chancellor must first consult the First Minister and the deputy First Minister in Northern Ireland.[46]

Public Record Office of Northern Ireland

23.57 Throughout the Freedom of Information Act 2000 there are a number of references to the Public Record Office and the Public Records Act 1958, namely in section 15 (special provisions relating to public records transferred to the Public Record Office),[47] section 46 (issue of a code of practice on record management by the Lord Chancellor),[48] section 47 (general functions of the Information Commissioner),[49] section 48 (recommendations as to good practice),[50] section 64 (the removal of exemptions for historical records in public record offices),[51] section 65 (decisions as to refusal of discretionary disclosure of historical records)[52] and section 66 (decisions relating to certain transferred public records).[53] In each case the provisions of these sections are extended to cover Northern Ireland by the inclusion of parallel references to the Public Record Office of Northern Ireland and the Public Records Act (Northern Ireland) 1923. By section 67 of the Freedom of Information Act 2000, Schedule 5 will take effect to make corresponding amendments to both the Public Records Act 1958 and the Public

---

[42] Freedom of Information Act 2000, s 3(1)(b).
[43] In ch 5 above.
[44] See para 23.18 above.
[45] Freedom of Information Act 2000, s 7(4)(b).
[46] ibid, s 7(4)(c).
[47] See ch 8 (at paras 8.32–8.34 above).
[48] See ch 5 above.
[49] See chs 5 and 7 above.
[50] ibid.
[51] See ch 8 (at para 8.27 above).
[52] ibid (at para 8.37 above).
[53] ibid (at paras 8.30–8.36 above).

Records Act (Northern Ireland) 1923 in respect of access to public records in the respective Public Record Offices.[54]

In sections 15, 65 and 66 of the Freedom of Information Act 2000, the references   **23.58**
to the 'appropriate Northern Ireland Minister' (who is given functions reflecting those conferred on the Lord Chancellor by their provisions) mean the Northern Ireland Minister in charge of the Department of Culture, Arts and Leisure in Northern Ireland.[55] He is also required to be consulted by the Lord Chancellor before the section 46 code of practice is issued or revised.[56]

Exempt information

The general provisions on exempt information are discussed in chapter 6 above.   **23.59**
However, there are a number of specific references to Northern Ireland that should be considered.

It will be recalled that section 28 deals with relations within the United Kingdom,   **23.60**
and that information is exempt if its disclosure under the Act would be likely to prejudice relations between administrations in the United Kingdom. The Executive Committee of the Northern Ireland Assembly is deemed to be such an administration.[57]

In section 35(1) (exemption for information relating to formulation of govern-   **23.61**
ment policy, etc) it is to be noted that, whereas there is a specific reference to Wales,[58] there is silence in respect of Northern Ireland. The reason for this is that the section applies to information held by any 'government department' and the term 'government department' is defined in section 84 to include a Northern Ireland department, the Northern Ireland Court Service and any other body or authority exercising statutory functions on behalf of the Crown.[59] For the purposes of that exemption, 'government policy' includes the policy of the Executive Committee of the Northern Ireland Assembly; 'Ministerial communications' includes proceedings of that Committee and also communications between Northern Ireland Ministers; 'Ministerial private office' includes any part of a government department which provides personal administrative support to a Northern Ireland Minister; and 'Law Officers' include the Attorney-General for Northern Ireland.[60]

---

[54] ibid (at para 8.16 above).
[55] As defined in the Freedom of Information Act 2000, s 84.
[56] ibid, s 46(5)(c).
[57] ibid, s 28(2)(c).
[58] See ch 6 at para 6.188 above and para 23.28 above.
[59] Subject to three exceptions: (i) the bodies specified in Freedom of Information Act 2000, s 80(2) ie the Scottish Parliament and other Scottish administrative bodies; (ii) the Security Service, the Secret Intelligence Service and the Government Communications Headquarters; (iii) the National Assembly for Wales.
[60] ibid, s 35(5).

23.62 Section 36[61] applies to Northern Ireland on account of the broad definition of 'government department'. Information is exempt under this section if a qualified person reasonably considers that its disclosure would or would be likely to prejudice (among other things) the work of the Executive Committee of the Northern Ireland Assembly. A 'qualified person' means the Northern Ireland Minister in charge of the department in respect of information held by a Northern Ireland department,[62] the Presiding Officer in respect of information held by the Northern Ireland Assembly,[63] the Comptroller and Auditor General for Northern Ireland in respect of information held by the Northern Ireland Audit Office,[64] and the public authority or any officer or employee thereof authorized by the First Minister and the deputy First Minister in Northern Ireland acting jointly in respect of information held by any Northern Ireland public authority other than the Northern Ireland Audit Office.[65]

Enforcement

23.63 The scheme of decision notices, enforcement notices and certificates for the purposes of section 53 of the Act has already been discussed elsewhere.[66] It should be noted however that this section applies to Northern Ireland as much as it applies to any other part of the United Kingdom.

23.64 Section 53 applies to decision and enforcement notices served on any 'government department'. By section 53(3)(b), in any case where a certificate[67] relating to a decision notice or enforcement notice which has been served on a Northern Ireland department or Northern Ireland public authority is given by the accountable person to the Information Commissioner, a copy must be laid before the Northern Ireland Assembly. In relation to a Northern Ireland department or any Northern Ireland public authority, the accountable person is defined in section 53(8)(a) as being the First Minister and deputy First Minister in Northern Ireland acting jointly. In relation to any other public authority in Northern Ireland the accountable person is the Attorney-General for Northern Ireland.[68]

Appeals

23.65 Section 59 permits a party to appeal a decision of the Information Tribunal on a point of law to the 'appropriate court', which is deemed to be the High Court of

---

[61] See ch 6 at paras 6.196–6.208 above and para 23.29 above.
[62] Freedom of Information Act 2000, s 36(5)(b).
[63] ibid, s 36(5)(f).
[64] ibid, s 36(5)(j).
[65] ibid, s 36(5)(l).
[66] See ch 7 at paras 7.103–7.108 and 23.30–23.32 above.
[67] See Freedom of Information Act 2000, s 53(2).
[68] ibid, s 53(8)(c)(ii).

Justice in Northern Ireland if the address of the public authority in question is in Northern Ireland.[69] However it does not necessarily follow that a public authority exercising an administrative function in relation to Northern Ireland has its address there. For example, if the Act were to be extended to cover the British Board of Film Classification,[70] then an appeal relating to the release of information concerning the censorship and classification of a video recording in Northern Ireland would nevertheless be heard in the High Court of Justice in England.

Miscellaneous provisions

Pursuant to section 75, the Lord Chancellor may order the repeal or amendment **23.66** of any enactment which appears to be capable of preventing the disclosure of information under section 1 of the Act, and for the purposes of section 75 an 'enactment' includes any enactment contained in Northern Ireland legislation or subordinate legislation passed or made before the passing of the Act.[71] It should be noted that where the term 'enactment' appears in other sections of the Act, it is defined to include an enactment contained in Northern Ireland legislation.[72]

Section 76 permits the Information Commissioner to disclose information **23.67** obtained under the Act to the Northern Ireland Commissioner for Complaints if it appears to the Information Commissioner that the information relates to a matter that could be the subject of an investigation by that Commissioner under the Commissioner for Complaints (Northern Ireland) Order 1996.[73] Likewise the Information Commissioner may disclose information to the Assembly Ombudsman for Northern Ireland if it appears to relate to a matter that could be the subject of an investigation under the Ombudsman (Northern Ireland) Order 1996.[74]

Where proceedings are to be commenced in Northern Ireland in respect of a **23.68** section 77 offence,[75] they can only be commenced by the Information Commissioner or by or with the consent of the Director of Public Prosecutions for Northern Ireland.

By section 81(1), each government department is to be treated as a person separate **23.69** from any other government department. This is qualified by section 81(2), which

---

[69] ibid, s 59(c).

[70] As suggested by Lord Falconer of Thoroton on the second reading of the Bill in the House of Lords, (*Hansard*, HL (series 5) vol 612, col 825 (20 April 2000)), although he referred to it as the 'British Board of Film Censorship' as it was then known. The British Board of Film Classification must have regard to the Video Recordings Act 1984 which applies to Northern Ireland by virtue of section 23(3).

[71] Freedom of Information Act 2000, s 75(2)(b).

[72] ibid, s 84.

[73] SI 1996/1297 (NI 7).

[74] SI 1996/1298 (NI 8).

[75] See para 23.35 above.

does not allow reliance on that principle for the purposes of the section 41 exemption[76] (for disclosures that would constitute actionable breaches of confidence). However, section 81(2) differentiates Northern Ireland departments from other government departments. A Northern Ireland department is not permitted to claim that the disclosure of information by it would constitute a breach of confidence actionable by any other Northern Ireland department, and a government department other than a Northern Ireland department cannot claim that the disclosure of information by it would constitute a breach of confidence actionable by any other government department which is not a Northern Ireland department. What section 81(2) does *not* say, however, is that a Northern Ireland department may not claim for the purposes of section 41 that the disclosure of information by it would constitute a breach of confidence actionable by another government department not being a Northern Ireland department, and vice versa. Accordingly, it would appear that section 41 can be relied on in the context of information passing between Northern Ireland departments and other government departments.

---

[76] See ch 6 at paras 6.63–6.81 above.

Part I

THE EUROPEAN UNION
AND OTHER PARTS OF THE WORLD

24

THE EUROPEAN UNION

A. Introduction

The Charter

In December 2000 the European Parliament, the European Council and the **24.01** European Commission jointly signed and proclaimed the Charter of Fundamental Rights of the European Union. Article 42 provides:

> Right of access to documents.

> Any citizen of the Union, and any natural or legal person residing or having its registered office in a Member State, has a right of access to European Parliament, Council and Commission Documents

The Charter is an important statement of intention, but at present it has no legal force. Romano Prodi, the President of the European Commission at the proclamation of the Charter, said it would now 'be possible to envisage calmly how to incorporate the Charter in the founding treaties of the Union'. This remains the intention.

The European Union regulation on access to documents

24.02 For now, however, the law relating to public access to European Union documents has been consolidated and is to be found in Council Regulation (EC) 1049/2001. The Regulation was adopted by the European Parliament and the Council of Ministers on 30 May 2001. It came into force on 3 December 2001 and is directly applicable in all member states.[1]

B. The History

The Maastricht Treaty

24.03 The European Union first seriously addressed the question of access to information in the Treaty on European Union (the Maastricht Treaty), which was signed on 7 February 1992 and came into force on 1 November 1993. The rules about access have developed significantly since then. At Maastricht a declaration on the right of access to information was annexed (as declaration 17) to the final Act of the Treaty. The declaration said:

> The Conference[2] considers that transparency of the decision-making process strengthens the democratic nature of institutions and the public's confidence in the administration. The Conference accordingly recommends that the Commission submits to the Council no later than 1993 a report on measures designed to improve public access to the information available to the institutions.

24.04 The declaration stresses the importance of transparency. Jacob Soderman, the European Union Ombudsman, in his report to the FIDE Conference in Stockholm in 1998 defined 'transparency' as meaning that:

> the processes through which public authorities make decisions should be understandable and open;

> the decisions themselves should be reasoned; and

> as far as possible, the information on which the decisions are based should be made available.

The Code of Conduct

24.05 The Maastricht call for transparency was followed up in 1993 when the European Commission and the Council adopted a joint Code of Conduct about access to

---

[1] On the related matter of the duty of member states to provide environmental information to the European Commission, see: Council Directive (EEC) 91/689 on hazardous waste and Case C–33/01 *EC Commission v Hellenic Republic* [2002] OJ C180/10. Environmental issues are dealt with in ch 16 above.

[2] The Conference was the conference of Member States which led to the Maastricht Treaty.

their documents. The Code was implemented through separate Decisions made by the two institutions, that of the Council being Decision (EC) 93/731.[3] Such decisions have legislative force. The Code of Conduct set out the principle that:

> The public will have the widest possible access to documents held by the Commission and the Council.

'Document' was defined as 'any written text whatever its medium, which contained existing data and was held by the Council or the Commission'. The circumstances which may be relied on by an institution as grounds for rejecting a request for access to documents were listed in the Code of Conduct in the following terms:

1. The institutions will refuse access to any document whose disclosure could undermine: the protection of the public interest (public safety, international relations, monetary stability, court proceedings, inspections and investigations);

   The protection of the individual and of privacy;

   The protection of commercial and industrial secrecy;

   The protection of the Community's financial interests;

   The protection of confidentiality as requested by the natural or legal person who supplied any of the information contained in the document or as required by the legislation of the Member State which supplied that information.

2. Institutions may also refuse access in order to protect the institution's interest in the confidentiality of its proceedings.

24.06 The Ombudsman in his report[4] to the 1998 FIDE Congress drew attention to some shortcomings of the Code. First, he said it gave no right of access to documents which had not originated in the institution to which the request was addressed. So for example, a Commission document contained in a file in the Council could not be disclosed by the latter institution; the request for access had to be addressed to the Commission. Secondly, the Community rules did not expressly provide for the possibility of giving partial access in situations where an exception clause applies only to part of the document requested. This was a defect which was subsequently addressed by the European Court of Justice in *Hautala v Council of the European Union*[5] and *Kuijer v Council of the European Union (No. 2)*[6] (see paragraphs 24.22 and 24.25 below). Thirdly, the rules did not expressly require that registers of documents should be established. The

---

[3] Code of Conduct [1993] OJ L340/41; Council Decision (EC) 93/731 of 20 December 1993 on public access to Council documents [1993] OJ L 340/43; Commission Decision of 8 February 1994 on public access to Commission documents [1994] OJ L 46/58.

[4] *The Citizen, The Administration and Community Law*, general report prepared by the European Ombudsman for the 1998 FIDE Congress, Stockholm, Sweden, 3–6 June 1998.

[5] Case C–353/99 [2002] 1 WLR 1930.

[6] Case T–211/00 [2002] 1 WLR 1941.

Ombudsman said that registers appeared to be an appropriate instrument to attain the objectives underlying a system of rules of public access, since they both facilitate citizens' use of their right of access and promote good administration by preventing the loss of documents.

24.07 The Code remained in force until Council Regulation (EC) 1049/2001 became effective on 3 December 2001. The validity of the Code was upheld by the European Court of Justice in *Netherlands v Council of the European Union.*[7] In that case the European Court of Justice noted that the domestic legislation of most member states now enshrines in a general manner the public's right of access to documents held by public authorities as a constitutional or legislative principle.[8] The Court also referred to a trend at Community level towards a progressive affirmation of individuals' rights of access to documents held by public authorities.[9]

The Treaty of Amsterdam

24.08 This trend is reflected in the Treaty of Amsterdam which was signed on 2 October 1997 and came into force on 1 May 1999. The European Union's commitment to transparency was one of the matters reaffirmed in the Treaty. The Treaty of the European Union was specifically amended at Amsterdam to provide:

> This Treaty marks a new stage in the process of creating an ever closer union among the peoples of Europe, in which decisions are taken as openly as possible and as closely as possible to the citizen.[10]

24.09 The Amsterdam Treaty also paved the way for Council Regulation (EC) 1049/2001 by adding a new Article 191a[11] to the EC Treaty (Treaty of Rome, as amended) concerning citizens' access to documents of the European Parliament, the Council and the Commission. Article 191a provides:

> 1. Any citizen of the Union, and any natural or legal person residing or having its registered office in a member state, shall have a right of access to European Parliament, Council and Commission documents, subject to the principles and the conditions to be defined in accordance with paragraphs 2 and 3.
>
> 2. General principles and limits on grounds of public or private interest governing this right of access to documents shall be determined by the Council, acting in

---

[7] Case C–58/94 [1996] ECR I–2169.

[8] In the United Kingdom the right now probably has the status of both a constitutional and a legislative principle.

[9] Case C–58/94 [1996] ECR I–2169 paras 34–36.

[10] Article 1.

[11] A consolidated version of the EC Treaty (incorporating the amendments made by the Treaty of Amsterdam) has been published by the European Union and Article 191a is renumbered Article 255 in the consolidated EC Treaty.

accordance with the procedure referred to in article 189b[12] [the co-decision procedure[13]] within two years of the entry into force of the Treaty of Amsterdam.

3. Each institution referred to above shall elaborate in its own Rules of Procedure specific provisions regarding access to its documents.

Council Regulation (EC) 1049/2001 is the determination which has been made **24.10** under these provisions. It takes the place of the Code. Before considering its provisions in detail, it is desirable to look at some of the cases which the European Court of Justice has decided under the Code,[14] because although the detailed application of the Code provisions may no longer be relevant, the European Court of Justice's approach to freedom of information questions is likely to have a significant effect on the way the law develops.

C. The Cases

Carvel and Guardian Newspapers Ltd v Council of the European Union

Carvel and Guardian Newspapers Ltd v Council of the European Union[15] was con- **24.11** cerned with Article 4 of Council Decision (EC) 93/731 (the Council Decision which implemented the Code). Article 4 specified exceptions to the principle that the public is to have access to Council documents, distinguishing between the cases referred to in Article 4(1) which were mandatory, in which access might not be granted where its disclosure would undermine interests like public security, international relations, and monetary stability and those referred to in Article 4(2) which were discretionary, in which access might be refused to protect the confidentiality of the Council's proceedings.

In February 1994 John Carvel, the European affairs editor of the *Guardian*, wrote **24.12** to the Secretary-General of the Council and asked for preparatory reports, minutes, the attendance and voting records, and the decisions of three meetings of the Council for Social Affairs, Justice and Agriculture in October and November 1993.[16] He was given the social affairs documents (this was by mistake); he was told that the agriculture documents were not yet available, and he was refused the justice documents on the ground that the documents in question 'directly refer to

---

[12] Article 251 of the consolidated EC Treaty.

[13] The co-decision procedure which was introduced by the Maastricht Treaty provides for the adoption of decisions by the European Parliament jointly with the Council.

[14] That is under the Code and under the Decisions of the Council and the Commission which implemented the Code, see n 3 above.

[15] Case T–194/94 [1995] ECR II–02765.

[16] The composition of the Council of Ministers depends on the subject matter to be discussed, eg at a meeting of the Council to discuss agriculture each member state will be represented by its Minister of Agriculture.

the deliberations of the Council and cannot, under its Rules of Procedure, be disclosed'.

24.13 Mr Carvel renewed his application, making what is called a confirmatory application in respect of the justice documents, that is, he asked the Council to reconsider its decision. His application in respect of all three meetings was refused. The Council explained that if it did allow access it would fail to protect the confidentiality of its proceedings because the documents in question contained confidential information relating to the position taken by the members of the Council during its deliberations.

24.14 The Court found that the Council, under Article 4(2), enjoyed a discretion as to whether or not to refuse a request for access to documents relating to its proceedings. The Court said that the Council must, when exercising its discretion, genuinely balance the interest of citizens in gaining access to its documents against any interest of its own in maintaining the confidentiality of its deliberations. The Council also had a margin of discretion under its Rules of Procedure which it should, in a proper case, use to give effect to its decision under Article 4(2). It could not, by simply not exercising its discretion under its Rules of Procedure, defeat the citizens' rights under Article 4(2).[17]

24.15 The Court went on to consider whether in the case before it the Council had exercised its discretion in compliance with Article 4(2). The Court found it had not done so, and its incorrect interpretation was illustrated by letters to Mr Carvel in which the General Secretariat of the Council wrote, 'I am unable to send you these documents, since they . . . cannot . . . be disclosed' and '. . . access to these documents cannot be allowed . . .', which indicated that the Council considered that it did not have the option of disclosing the documents requested. The Court held that the decision of the Council must be annulled and that the Council should pay the applicant's costs.[18]

Svenska Journalistforbundet v Council of the European Union

24.16 The Campaign for Freedom of Information has pointed out that Sweden's decision to join the European Union was good news for the cause of open government.[19] Its two-hundred-year-old tradition of freedom of information legislation seemed likely to encourage others in the direction of openness. Many Swedes, however, feared the opposite, that Sweden might be pressed to conform with Europe's more secretive culture. Sweden attached a declaration to its accession agreement, stating that access to official documents and the protection of jour-

---

[17] Case T–194/94 [1995] ECR II–02765 paras 64–68.
[18] ibid, paras 73 and 80–81.
[19] The Campaign for Freedom of Information, *Open and Shut Case: Access to Information in Sweden and the EU*, http://www.cfoi.org.uk/sweden1 (22 March 2002).

nalists' sources remain fundamental principles of Sweden's constitutional, political and cultural heritage. In reply the existing member states noted that they took it for granted that Sweden would fully comply with Community law in this respect. This difference of view was one of the issues the Court had to face in *Svenska Journalistforbundet v Council of the European Union*[20] ('the *Journalisten* case').

Following Sweden's accession to the European Union on 1 January 1995 the **24.17** Swedish Union of Journalists' newspaper, *Journalisten*, decided to test the way in which the Swedish authorities applied Swedish citizens' rights of access to information in respect of documents relating to European Union activities. The newspaper applied under Swedish legislation to the Swedish Ministry of Justice and the Police Authority (among others) for a set of twenty documents relating to the setting up of the European Police Office ('Europol'). The applications were successful in 18 out of 20 cases. The Ministry of Justice refused two documents on the ground that they concerned the negotiating positions of the Netherlands and German governments. *Journalisten* then applied to the European Council for the same documents, but only four of them were produced. The Council explained that access to the remaining documents could not be granted because under Article 4(2) of Council Decision (EC) 93/731 their release could be harmful to the public interest (public security) and because they related to the Council's proceedings, including positions taken by members of the Council, and were therefore covered by the duty of confidentiality.

The Council argued that the release of the documents in question by the Swedish **24.18** authorities to the applicant constituted a breach of Community law, since no decision had been taken to authorize disclosure. It would be contrary, it was said, to the system of legal remedies provided by Community law to take advantage of a breach and then to ask the Court to annul a decision whose effects had been circumvented as a consequence of such a breach. Ironically, the Council also argued that the fact that the documents in question were brought into the public domain following an act contrary to Community law should therefore preclude the applicant from bringing an action in the case.[21]

The public domain argument did not appear to find favour with the Court, **24.19** though the Court did not deal specifically with it. The Court, however, held that the objective of Council Decision (EC) 93/731 was to give effect to the principle of the greatest possible access for citizens to information with a view to strengthening the democratic character of the institutions and the trust of the public in the administration. Council Decision (EC) 93/731 did not require members of the public to put forward reasons for seeking access to requested documents. It

---

[20] Case T–174/95 [1998] ECR II–02289.
[21] ibid, paras 56.

followed that a person who was refused access to a document had, by virtue of that very fact, established an interest in the annulment of that decision. The fact that the requested documents were already in the public domain was irrelevant.[22] This decision shows that the Campaign for Freedom of Information's fears that disclosure of information in Sweden might be muzzled by the European institutions may have been exaggerated.[23]

24.20 Turning to the merits of the application before it, the Court annulled the decision of the Council to refuse access to the documents. The Court held that the Council was under a duty to state the reasons for its decision. The Council invoked both the mandatory exception based on the protection of the public interest (public security) and also the discretionary exception based upon the protection of confidentiality, but did not specify whether it was invoking both exceptions in respect of all documents refused or whether it considered that some documents were covered by the first exception while others were covered by the second. The Court held that this was not good enough. The Court held further that most of the documents to which access was refused were concerned only with negotiations on the adoption of the Europol Convention and it was not apparent why the disclosure of the documents would in fact be liable to prejudice a particular aspect of public security. It was thus not possible for the applicant newspaper to know the reasons for the adoption of the measures and therefore to defend its interests. Further, in so far as the decision was based on the discretionary ground of the protection of confidentiality, the contested decision mentioned only the fact that the requested documents related to proceedings of the Council, including the views expressed by members of the Council, without saying whether the Council had made any comparative analysis which sought to balance the interests of citizens seeking information against the criteria for confidentiality of the proceedings of the Council. This was the reasoning which had proved decisive in the *Carvel and Guardian Newspaper* case. The Court therefore annulled the decision.[24]

24.21 The final twist to the *Journalisten* case was that the newspaper had, without consulting its lawyers, published the Council's formal defence on the Internet. It had also published the telephone and fax numbers of the Council's agents and invited the public to send their comments to the agents. The Court found that the newspaper had done this to bring pressure to bear on the Council and to provoke public criticism of the agents. The Court held that this was an abuse of procedure and took the newspaper's conduct into account in considering its costs order. As a result the newspaper did not recover one third of its costs.

---

[22] Case T–174/95 [1998] ECR II–02289, paras 66–69.
[23] As to the position under Council Regulation (EC) 1049/2001 see para 24.41 below.
[24] Case T–174/95 [1998] ECR II–02289 paras 109–127.

Hautala v European Union Council

Ms Hautala, a member of the European Parliament, put written questions to the **24.22**
Parliament in November 1996 asking in particular:

> What will the Council do to put an end to violations of human rights which are
> assisted by arms exports from EU Member States? What are the reasons for the
> secrecy surrounding the guidelines which the Council's working group on conven-
> tional arms exports has proposed to the political committee with a view to clarifying
> the criteria?

In reply the Council referred to a report on criteria for conventional arms exports, **24.23**
drawn up by a working group of the Council's political committee. Ms Hautala
asked for a copy of the report. Ultimately the Council refused to produce the
report on the ground that refusal was necessary for the protection of the public
interest (international relations), the reason stated being that disclosure could be
harmful for the European Union's relations with third countries. In an action by
the applicant, the Court of First Instance of the European Court of Justice
annulled the Council's decision holding that the Council had been under an obligation, but had failed, to consider whether partial access to the report should be
granted so that the parts of the report which would harm international relations
would be concealed but the remainder would be disclosed. The Council appealed.

The European Court of Justice in rejecting the appeal set out the following prin- **24.24**
ciples:[25]

(a) that the Code established by Council Decision (EC) 93/731 concerned not
    only access to documents but also access to the information contained in the
    documents;
(b) an exception to the right of access must be interpreted and applied strictly;
(c) the public have a right of access to items of information contained in a docu-
    ment which items are not covered by one of the exceptions;
(d) the principle of proportionality required the Council to consider partial
    access to a document where disclosure of the whole document would fall
    within one of the exceptions.

The Court held that the Court of First Instance was right to annul the decision.
These principles will also apply to the exemptions in the new Council Regulation
(EC) 1049/2001.

Kuijer v Council of the European Union

Kuijer v Council of the European Union (No. 2)[26] and the *Hautala* case raise similar **24.25**
issues. Aldo Kuijer, a university lecturer and researcher in asylum and immigration

---

[25] Case C–353/99P [2002] 1 WLR 1930 at 1939–1940, paras 23–27 and 31–32.
[26] Case T–211/00 [2002] 1 WLR 1941.

matters, made a request to the European Council for access to, inter alia, certain reports drawn up by or with the Centre for Information, Discussion and Exchange on Asylum and for a list, drawn up by or with the Centre, of the contact persons in the member states involved with asylum cases. He was told that since the reports contained information on political and human rights situations of a number of countries which could be construed as critical of those countries, their disclosure might damage the European Union's relations with those countries. He was also told that disclosure of the list might put the security and private lives of individuals at risk by giving rise to harassment and personal threats. His request was therefore refused on the ground that disclosure of the reports could undermine the protection of the public interest, namely international relations, and the disclosure of the list could undermine the public interest in the functioning of the exchange of information and co-ordination between member states in the field of asylum and immigration.

24.26   The European Court of Justice began its findings with a statement of principle which made clear the Court's general approach to access to information:

> It is first necessary to point out that the principle of transparency is intended to secure a more significant role for citizens in the decision-making process and to ensure that the administration acts with greater propriety, efficiency and responsibility vis-à-vis the citizens in a democratic system. It helps to strengthen the principle of democracy and respect for fundamental rights.

24.27   The Court then set out the conditions in which the public might be denied access to a document. First, it reiterated that the exceptions to the Code must be construed and applied restrictively so as not to defeat the general principle enshrined in the Code. Secondly, the Court said the Council was obliged to consider in respect of each document requested whether, in the light of the information available to it, disclosure was in fact likely to undermine one of the public interests protected by the exceptions provided for in Article 4(1) of Council Decision (EC) 93/731. If those exceptions were to apply, the risk of the public interest being undermined must be reasonably foreseeable and not purely hypothetical. Thirdly, Article 4(1) of Council Decision (EC) 93/731 must be interpreted in the light of the principle of the right to information and the principle of proportionality. Consequently, the Council must consider whether it is appropriate to grant partial access, confined to material which is not covered by exceptions. In exceptional cases a derogation from the obligation to grant partial access might be permissible where the administrative burden of blanking out the parts that may not be disclosed proved to be particularly heavy, thereby exceeding the limits of what might reasonably be required.

24.28   The Court concluded that refusal of access to the reports in question must be founded on an analysis of factors specific to the contents or the context of each report, from which it could be concluded that, because of certain specific circumstances, disclosure of such a document would pose a danger to a particular interest. The Court had in this instance ordered production of the reports at issue and had been able to ascertain that disclosure of a large part of their contents clearly could not be regarded as likely to give rise to tension with the third countries concerned. As to the lists of contact persons, access to these was permitted in certain states. Refusing access to that information was in breach of the principle of proportionality. The Court therefore annulled the decision of the Council.

D. The Council Regulation (EC) 1049/2001

The text

The text of Council Regulation (EC) 1049/2001 is set out in Appendix H.   **24.29**

The recitals

The Recitals to the Regulation deal with many of the criticisms of the Code which   **24.30**
had been made by the Ombudsman and others. These are the salient points the
Recitals make:

(a) Wider access should be granted to documents in cases where the institutions
    are acting in their legislative capacity, including under delegated powers,
    while at the same time preserving the effectiveness of the institutions'
    decision-making process. Such documents should be made directly accessible
    to the greatest possible extent (*Recital 6*).

(b) The right of access also applies to common foreign and security policy and to
    police and judicial co-operation in criminal matters (*Recital 7*).

(c) All agencies established by the institutions should apply the principles laid
    down in this Regulation (*Recital 8*).

(d) In order to bring about greater openness in the work of the institutions, access
    to documents should be granted by the European Parliament, the Council
    and the Commission not only to documents drawn up by the institutions,
    but also to documents received by them. In this context it is recalled that
    Declaration No 35 attached to the Amsterdam Treaty provides that a member state may request the Council or the Commission not to communicate to
    third parties a document originating from that state without its prior agreement (*Recital 10*).

(e) In order to ensure that the right of access is fully respected, a two-stage administrative procedure should apply, with the additional possibility of court proceedings or complaints to the Ombudsman (*Recital 13*).

(f) Each institution should provide access to a register of documents (*Recital 14*).

(g) Even though it is neither the object nor the effect of this Regulation to amend
    national legislation on access to documents, it is nevertheless clear that, by

virtue of the principle of loyal co-operation which governs relations between the institutions and the member states, member states should take care not to hamper the proper application of this Regulation and should respect the security rules of the institutions (*Recital 15*).[27]

Background to the Regulation

24.31 The Regulation was the result of negotiations under the co-decision procedure between the European Parliament, the Council and the Commission. The final version is based on the report by the rapporteur, Michael Cashman, which was approved by the European Parliament on 3 May 2001 by 400 votes to 85 with the Socialist, Liberal and Conservative groups voting in favour. Patrick Birkinshaw comments that the general feeling was that the European Parliament had done well to see through its major proposals although some parties were still disappointed by some of the concessions on sensitive documents.[28] The result is an attractively short document which achieves a clarity of language, which is not a conspicuous feature of the Freedom of Information Act 2000.

The purpose clause

24.32 Article 1 sets out the purpose of the Regulation.[29] It is to define the principles, conditions and limits on grounds of public or private interest governing the right of access to European Parliament, Council, and Commission documents in such a way as to ensure the widest possible access to documents; to establish rules ensuring the easiest possible exercise of this right; and to promote good administrative practice on access to documents. (The European Parliament, Council and Commission are referred to in the Regulation as 'the institutions'.)

Beneficiaries and scope

24.33 Article 2.1 provides that any citizen of the Union, and any natural or legal person residing or having its registered office in a member state, has a right of access to documents of the institutions, subject to the principles, conditions and limits defined in the Regulation. The institutions may also grant access to non-residents.

24.34 Article 2.3 says that the Regulation shall apply to all documents held by an institution, that is to say, documents drawn up or received by it and in its possession, in all areas of activity of the European Union. This is a great improvement on the Code and ensures that the Regulation is comprehensive.

---

[27] The effect of Recital 15 is considered at para 24.41 below.

[28] P Birkinshaw, *Freedom of Information, The Law, the Practice and the Ideal* (3rd edn) 484.

[29] For discussion of purpose clauses in other jurisdictions see ch 9 (at para 9.04) above and ch 25 below.

Definitions

Article 3(a) defines 'document' to mean any content whatever its medium (writ- **24.35** ten on paper or stored in electronic form or as a sound, visual or audiovisual recording) concerning a matter relating to the policies, activities and decisions falling within the institution's sphere of responsibility.

Exceptions

The exceptions in the Regulation mark the sharpest contrast with the Freedom of **24.36** Information Act 2000 and yet they seem to say everything which needs to be said. Perhaps there is a lesson for citizens of the United Kingdom here. Article 4.1 is in the following terms:

> The institutions shall refuse access to a document where disclosure would undermine the protection of:
> (a) the public interest as regards:
> —public security;
> —defence and military matters;
> —international relations;
> —the financial, monetary or economic policy of the Community or a Member State;
> (b) privacy and the integrity of the individual, in particular in accordance with Community legislation regarding the protection of personal data.

Article 4.1, in contradistinction to the following exceptions, is mandatory and is not subject to a public interest test.

Article 4(2) provides: **24.37**

> The institutions shall refuse access to a document where disclosure would undermine the protection of:
> —commercial interests of a natural or legal person, including intellectual property;
> —court proceedings and legal advice;
> —the purpose of inspections investigations and audits,
> —unless there is an overriding public interest in disclosure.

This is a very succinct list of exceptions compared with the Freedom of Information Act 2000, sections 21 to 44, but the subject matter is much the same save that the UK Act surprisingly includes health and safety (section 38).

Article 4(3) provides: **24.38**

> Access to a document drawn up for internal use or received by an institution, which relates to a matter where the decision has not been taken by the institution, shall be refused if disclosure of the document would seriously undermine the institution's decision-making process, unless there is an overriding public interest in disclosure.
> Access to a document containing opinions for internal use as part of deliberations and preliminary consultations with the institution shall be refused even after the

decision has been taken if disclosure of the document would seriously undermine the institution's decision-making process, unless there is an overriding public interest in disclosure.

It is clear from the cases already considered in this chapter that the Court will insist on a genuine balancing of the interest of the citizen and the institution in respect of each document; that the risk of the public interest being undermined by disclosure must be reasonably foreseeable and not merely hypothetical; and that the Court will be prepared to inspect the documents to make sure that genuine consideration has taken place.[30]

24.39 Article 4(4) to (7) is in the following terms:

(4) As regards third-party documents, the institution shall consult the third party with a view to ascertaining whether an exception in paragraph (1) or (2) is applicable, unless it is clear that the document shall or shall not be disclosed.

(5) A Member State may request the institution not to disclose a document originating from that Member State without its prior agreement.

(6) If only parts of the requested documents are covered by any exceptions, the remaining parts of the document shall be released.

(7) The exceptions as laid down in paragraphs (1) to (3) shall only apply for the period during which the protection is justified on the basis of the content of the document. The exceptions may apply for a maximum period of 30 years. In the case of documents covered by the exceptions relating to privacy or commercial interests and in the case of sensitive documents, the exceptions may, if necessary, continue to apply after this period.

24.40 Article 5 is concerned with documents in the member states, a subject which is foreshadowed in Recital 15. It provides that where a member state receives a request for a document in its possession, originating in an institution, unless it is clear that the document shall or shall not be disclosed, the member state shall consult with the institution concerned in order to take a decision that does not jeopardize the attainment of the objectives of the Regulation. The member state may instead refer the request to the institution.

24.41 Recital 15 makes it clear that the object and effect of the Regulation is not to amend national legislation on access to documents. Article 5 does not do so. This must mean for example that it would still be possible, as in the *Journalisten* case, for journalists to obtain European documents under the Swedish legislation though the Swedish authorities should be sensitive to the restrictions in the Regulation. There is no certainty as to where the line will finally be drawn. Perhaps the reality is that the European authorities will be more liberal in the documents which they release, and the national authorities will not be quick to disclose documents which could not properly be disclosed under the Regulation.

---

[30] See paras 24.14, 24.27–24.28 above.

Applications

Article 6 provides that applications can be made in any written form, including   **24.42**
electronic form in one of the languages referred to in Article 314 of the EC Treaty.
The institutions have 15 working days under Article 7 in which to grant access or
state the reasons why access is being refused. If the application relates to a very
long document or to a very large number of documents the institution may confer with the applicant informally, with a view to finding a fair solution. If access is
refused the applicant has 15 working days within which he can make a confirmatory application asking the institution to reconsider its position. If the application
is again refused the institution is required by Article 8 to inform the applicant of
the remedies open to him or her, namely starting court proceedings or making an
application to the European Ombudsman.[31]

Sensitive documents

Article 9 deals with the treatment of sensitive documents. Sensitive documents are   **24.43**
defined as documents, classified as *top secret, secret or confidential* in accordance
with the rules of the institution concerned, which protect essential interests of the
European Union or of one or more of its member states in the areas covered by
Article 4(1)(a), notably public security, defence and military matters. Such applications are only to be handled by persons who have a right to acquaint themselves
with such documents. Article 9(3) provides that sensitive documents shall be
recorded in the register or released only with the consent of the originator, and
Article 9(4) provides that an institution which decides to refuse to release a sensitive document shall give the reasons for its decision in a manner which does not
harm the interests protected in Article 4.

Access

Article 10 provides that an applicant shall have access to documents either by con-   **24.44**
sulting them on the spot or by receiving a copy, including, where available, an
electronic copy, according to the applicant's preference. The cost of producing
and sending copies may be charged to the applicant. The Article provides that this
cost shall not exceed the real cost of producing and sending the copies.
Consultation on the spot, copies of fewer than 20 A4 pages and direct access in
electronic form or through the register are free of charge.

---

[31] The European Ombudsman's website explains how to make a complaint: http://www.euro-
ombudsman.eu.int (31 July 2002).

Registers

24.45 Article 11 provides:

(1) To make citizens' rights under this Regulation effective, each institution shall provide public access to a register of documents. Access to the register should be provided in electronic form. References to documents shall be recorded in the register without delay.

(2) For each document the register shall contain a reference number (including, where applicable, the institutional reference), the subject matter and/or a short description of the content of the document and the date on which it was received or drawn up and recorded in the register. References shall be made in a manner which does not undermine protection of the interests in Article 4.

(3) The institutions shall immediately take the measures necessary to establish a register which shall be operated by June 2002.

24.46 The Freedom of Information Act 2000 does not contain a similar provision. This is understandable because it covers a very wide spread of public authorities. There is much to be said, however, for a similar provision perhaps restricted to government departments and principal local authorities.

24.47 Article 12 provides that legislative documents, that is documents drawn up or received in the course of procedures for the adoption of Acts which are legally binding in or for the member state, should be made directly available in electronic form or through a register. Article 12(3) provides that where possible other documents, notably documents relating to the development of policy or strategy, should be made directly accessible in the same way. Article 12(4) provides that where direct access is not given through the register, the register should as far as possible indicate where the document is located.

Publication in the Official Journal

24.48 Article 13(1) provides for the following documents to be published in the Official Journal:

(a) Commission proposals;

(b) common positions adopted by the Council in accordance with the legislative procedures referred to in Articles 251 and 252 of the EC Treaty and the reasons underlying those common positions, as well as the European Parliament's positions in those procedures;

(c) framework decisions (for the purpose of approximation of the laws and regulations of the member states) and decisions (in pursuit of the other objectives of the Union) referred to in Article 34(2) of the Treaty on European Union;

(d) conventions established by the Council (which it shall recommend to the member states) in accordance with Article 34(2) of the Treaty on European Union;

(e) conventions established by the Council on the basis of Article 293 of the EC Treaty, (which is designed to promote negotiations between member states with a view to the abolition of double taxation, the mutual recognition of companies and firms and the simplification of formalities governing the reciprocal recognition and enforcements of judgments);

(f) international agreements concluded by the Community or in accordance with Article 24 of the Treaty on European Union (which provides that the Council acting unanimously may authorize the President to enter into negotiations in implementation of the Common Foreign and Security Policy).

Article 13(2) provides that as far as possible the following documents shall be pub- **24.49** lished in the Official Journal:

(a) initiatives presented to the Council by a member state pursuant to Article 67(1) of the EC Treaty (these are initiatives under Title IV: *visas, asylum, immigration and other policies relating to the free movement of persons*) or pursuant to Article 34(2) of the Treaty on European Union;

(b) common positions referred to in Article 34(2) of the Treaty on European Union;

(c) Directives, other than those referred to in Article 254(1) and (2) of the EC Treaty, Decisions, other than those referred to in Article 254(1) of the EC Treaty, Recommendations and Opinions. Article 254(1) already provides that legislation shall be published in the Official Journal.

Information and administrative practice

Article 14 requires each institution to take the requisite measures to inform the **24.50** public of the rights they enjoy under the Regulation. Article 15 provides that the institutions shall develop good administrative practices in order to facilitate the exercise of the right of access guaranteed by the Regulation.

Reports

Article 17 provides that each institution shall publish annually a report for the **24.51** preceding year including the number of cases in which the institution refused to grant access to documents, the reasons for such refusals and the number of sensitive documents not recorded in the register.

Conclusion

Michael Cashman, answering questions on his report on the draft Regulation (see **24.52** paragraph 24.31 above), said 'any abuses of the system will be picked up by the yearly review, in which each decision to refuse access to a document has to be justified.'[32] This is likely to be so, and the general conclusion must be that the European Union now has a good freedom of information regime in place.

---

[32] See a report from *EU Observer* (an Internet publication) dated 4 May 2001: http://www.euobserver.com (31 July 2002).

25

THE RIGHT TO KNOW IN AUSTRALIA, CANADA, FRANCE, IRELAND, THE NETHERLANDS, NEW ZEALAND, SWEDEN AND THE UNITED STATES

781

A. Australia

The objects of the Freedom of Information Act

25.01 The Commonwealth of Australia Freedom of Information Act 1982[1] ('the Act') was passed, according to its long title, to give members of the public rights of access to official documents of the government of the Commonwealth and its agencies. The Act is to be interpreted[2] so as to further its expressed object, namely to 'extend as far as possible the right of the Australian community to access to information in the possession of the Government of the Commonwealth' by:

(a) making available information about the operations of departments and public authorities (and, in particular, rules and practices affecting their dealings with members of the public);

(b) 'creating a general right of access to information in documentary form in the possession of Ministers, departments and public authorities, limited only by exceptions and exemptions necessary for the protection of essential public interests and the private and business affairs of persons in respect of whom information is collected and held by departments and public authorities'; and

(c) creating a right to bring about the amendment of records containing incomplete, incorrect, out of date or misleading personal information.[3]

---

[1] The following Acts have been passed at state level to provide for similar rights: Victoria Freedom of Information Act 1982; Australian Capital Territory Freedom of Information Act 1989; New South Wales Freedom of Information Act 1989; South Australia Freedom of Information Act 1991; Tasmanian Freedom of Information Act 1991; Queensland Freedom of Information Act 1992; Western Australia Freedom of Information Act 1992.

[2] Commonwealth of Australia Freedom of Information Act 1982, s 3(2).

[3] ibid, s 3(1).

Section 3(2) of the Act adds that it is Parliament's intention that any discretions **25.02** conferred by the Act 'shall be exercised as far as possible so as to facilitate and promote, promptly and at the lowest reasonable cost, the disclosure of information'.

Development of the Act

The past

Together with the Administrative Decisions (Judicial Review) Act 1977, the **25.03** Administrative Appeals Tribunal Act 1975, and the Ombudsman Act 1976, the Act formed what has been referred to as the 'new administrative law', developed to achieve more open and accountable government at federal level. The 1977 Act had introduced a simplified judicial review procedure and (in section 13) a right for a person entitled to apply for judicial review of a decision to require the decision-maker to furnish a statement setting out its findings on material questions of fact (referring to the material on which they were based) and giving its reasons for the decision. Similar provision was made by section 28 of the 1975 Act in respect of decisions reviewable by the Administrative Appeals Tribunal ('the Tribunal'). Under section 43 of the 1975 Act, the Tribunal may exercise all the powers and discretions which the maker of the decision under review had; it may affirm or vary the original decision, or set it aside and substitute its own. The role of the Tribunal is to examine the merits and reach the correct decision on the material before it.

Freedom of information legislation had been under consideration since the **25.04** 1960s, including by a Royal Commission and two Interdepartmental Committees. A Bill was introduced into the Senate in 1978 which was referred to the Senate Standing Committee on Constitutional and Legal Affairs. Some of its recommendations[4] were reflected in the revised Bill introduced in April 1981, which following minor amendments was enacted on 9 March 1982. The Act commenced operation on 1 December 1982. Since then it has been the subject of a series of substantive amendments as well as lesser procedural ones.[5] The 1983 amendments provided greater rights of access to documents created before the Act's commencement, gave the Tribunal some powers in respect of Ministers' conclusive exemption certificates, narrowed the scope of certain exemptions including that for Cabinet documents, and reduced the time allowed for compliance with requests for access from 60 to 30 days. New fees and charges were introduced in 1986, including a charge for time spent in making a decision on a request as well as search and retrieval activities. The amendments made by the Privacy Act

---

[4] *Freedom of Information. Report by the Senate Standing Committee on Constitutional and Legal Affairs on the Freedom of Information Bill 1978 and aspects of the Archives Bill 1978* (1979).
[5] See, in particular, Freedom of Information Amendment Act 1983; Freedom of Information Laws Amendment Act 1986; Schedule 1 to the Privacy Act 1988; Freedom of Information Amendment Act 1991.

1988 conferred on third parties affected by requests for personal information rights to be consulted and to seek a review of a decision to release the documents sought. The 1991 amendments, made to implement the recommendations of the Senate Standing Committee on Legal and Constitutional Affairs,[6] were aimed at simplifying and clarifying the procedures for making, processing and reviewing access requests.

The future

25.05 In 1994 the Australian Law Reform Commission and Administrative Review Council were asked to conduct a joint review of the Act and report on whether it had achieved its purposes or should be amended to achieve them better. The resulting report[7] ('*the Australian Law Reform Commission report*') concluded that 'more must be done to dismantle the culture of secrecy that still pervades some aspects of Australian public sector administration' and made various recommendations for reform. Draft legislation embodying some of its proposals was subsequently prepared in the form of the Freedom of Information Amendment (Open Government) Bill 2000 ('the Bill'). This was introduced into the Senate as a private member's Bill in September 2000 and referred to the Senate Legal and Constitutional Legislation Committee for inquiry. In their report[8] they endorsed many of the amendments to the Act contained in the Bill, but by no means all, recommending that it proceed subject to significant changes. The Committee was not, however, unanimous, Labor Senators being in favour of amendments (such as alterations to the exemption regime) which the majority did not support and the promoter indicated he would withdraw. The prorogation of Parliament intervened in the progress of the Bill, but it may be reintroduced. Some of the more important reforms proposed by *the Australian Law Reform Commission report* or contained in the Bill are mentioned in chapter 9 above or noted at paragraphs 25.06, 25.07, and 25.27 below. The government is also considering amendments to take account of the impact of outsourcing government functions to private sector bodies.

25.06 One of the key proposals in *the Australian Law Reform Commission report* concerned the wording of the object clause, which the authors criticized for being equivocal and not going far enough to ensure a presumption in favour of disclosure. These criticisms were made against the background of judicial refusals to interpret the existing section 3[9] as requiring a 'leaning' in favour of disclosure,

---

[6] *Freedom of Information Act 1982: Report on the operation and administration of the Freedom of Information legislation* (Senate Standing Committee on Legal and Constitutional Affairs 1987 Report).

[7] *Open Government: A Review of the Federal Freedom of Information Act 1982* ALRC 77 (1995).

[8] *Inquiry into the Freedom of Information Amendment (Open Government) Bill 2000* (April 2001) ('*the Senate Inquiry report*').

[9] See para 25.01 above.

such as characterized the body of US authority to the effect that access provisions are to be given a wide interpretation while exemptions are to be narrowly construed.[10] In the words of Bowen CJ and Fisher J in *News Corp Ltd v National Companies and Securities Commission:*[11]

> In construing our Act we do not favour the adoption of a leaning position. The rights of access and the exemptions are designed to give a correct balance of the competing public interests involved. Each is to be interpreted according to the words used, bearing in mind the stated object of the Act.

According to the judgment of the Court in *Searle Australia Pty Ltd v Public Interest Advocacy Centre,*[12] this meant that while section 3 could assist in interpreting any ambiguities in the legislation (favouring in such cases a construction which would further rather than hinder free access to information), its wording could not prevail over words plainly expressed.[13] Suggestions that a public interest criterion could be implied by reference to section 3 into exemption sections that do not expressly include one have been firmly quashed by the Federal Court.[14]

The Australian Law Reform Commission report recommended[15] various amend- **25.07**
ments to the section, including:

(a) the insertion of an explanation that the underlying rationale of the Act is to underpin Australia's representative democracy by enabling people to participate in the policy and decision-making processes of government, opening the government's activities to scrutiny, and increasing the accountability of the executive;
(b) the insertion of an acknowledgement that information collected and created by public officials is a national resource;
(c) the removal of all reference to exceptions and exemptions, which according to the report leaves the way open for departments and public authorities to regard the statute as being as much about withholding information as providing access to it.

Amendments much to that effect were included in the Bill and received the support of the Senate Committee,[16] having regard to the general agreement among inquiry participants that they would 'send a clear message to agencies that the Act

---

[10] See para 25.286 below.
[11] (1984) 52 ALR 277, 279.
[12] (1992) 36 FCR 111, 115.
[13] In contrast, a 'leaning' position has been inclined towards at state level in the context of similarly worded provisions: see for example the judgments of the Supreme Court of Victoria (Appeal Division) in *Accident Compensation Commission v Croom* [1991] 2 VR 322 and *Sobh v Police Force of Victoria* [1994] 1 VR 41.
[14] See, for example, *Waterford v Dept of Treasury* (1985) 5 FCR 76; *Dept of Industrial Relations v Burchill* (1992) 105 ALR 327; *Commonwealth v Hittich* (1994) 53 FCR 152.
[15] At paras 4.4–4.11.
[16] *The Senate Inquiry report* (n 8 above) paras 3.8–3.11.

is to be interpreted with the concept of pro-disclosure at the fore', and the concerns raised by the Commonwealth Ombudsman who in his *Needs to Know report* had described the problems he identified as 'illustrative of a growing culture of passive resistance to the disclosure of information'.[17]

The right of access

25.08   Subject to the provisions of the Act, every person has a legally enforceable right under section 11 to obtain access to documents of agencies and official documents of Ministers which are not exempt documents. 'Agency' is defined in the interpretation section of the Act, section 4, as meaning a department,[18] a prescribed authority or an eligible case manager.[19] 'Prescribed authorities' include not only those bodies and holders of offices designated as such by regulations, but also bodies and holders of offices established for public purposes by an enactment or Order in Council. Certain agencies (including the Australian Secret Intelligence Service and the Australian Security Intelligence Organization) are altogether exempted from the operation of the Act by section 7 and Schedule 2; others are exempt in relation to particular activities or documents. 'Official document of a Minister' is defined as a document in the possession of a Minister in his Ministerial capacity which relates to the affairs of an agency or department of state.

25.09   The right of access is expressed to be to documents, rather than records or information. However, the definition of 'document' includes 'any article on which information has been stored or recorded, either mechanically or electronically', and 'any other record of information'. It specifically excludes library material maintained for reference purposes and Cabinet notebooks (that is, any records containing notes taken during the course of discussions or deliberations of Cabinet or a Cabinet committee by or under the authority of the Secretary to the Cabinet).

25.10   Section 12(1) of the Act provides that it is not to apply to certain classes of document which are otherwise available to the public: documents which are within the open access period under the Archives Act 1983,[20] or open to public access subject

---

[17]   *Needs to Know: Own motion investigation into the administration of the Freedom of Information Act 1982 in Commonwealth agencies* (Report under s 35A of the Ombudsman Act 1976, June 1999) at para 5.10.

[18]   Defined as a department of the Australian Public Service corresponding to a department of state of the Commonwealth.

[19]   An entity which is, or has been, engaged by the Employment Services Regulatory Authority to assist job seekers to find employment under the scheme established by the Employment Services Act 1994.

[20]   The Archives Act 1983 confers a right of access (free of charge) to Commonwealth records over 30 years old, subject to exemptions which are less restrictive than those in the Commonwealth of Australia FOI Act 1982.

to payment of a charge under some other enactment, or made available for public purchase by an agency.

The extent to which documents which became documents of agencies or official 25.11 documents of Ministers before the commencement of the Act can be made the subject of access requests is dealt with in section 12(2).[21] There are three categories of such documents (and power to add others by regulations):

(a) documents which so became no more than five years before commencement;
(b) documents containing personal information about the applicant, or information relating to his financial, commercial or business affairs;
(c) documents access to which is reasonably necessary to enable proper understanding of documents to which the applicant has lawfully had access.

Making and processing requests

Making the request

A request for access is to be in writing and provide such information as is reason- 25.12 ably necessary to enable identification of the document in question: section 15(2). It must also be accompanied by the application fee payable under the regulations. Agencies are obliged by section 15(3) and (4) to provide reasonable assistance in respect of the making of requests and the redirection as appropriate of requests mistakenly made to them and cannot refuse access on the basis of non-compliance with section 15(2) without having first given the applicant a chance to put matters right: section 24(6). An applicant who has made a request satisfying the requirements of section 15(2) will be entitled to access (subject to payment of all charges payable under the regulations as a condition of access) unless it is for an exempt document: section 18. His reasons for seeking access are immaterial: section 11(2).

Section 18 is, however, subject to sections 24 and 24A, which allow refusal of an 25.13 access request where the agency or Minister is satisfied either that the work involved in processing the request would substantially and unreasonably divert the agency's resources from its other operations, or interfere with the performance of the Minister's functions (section 24), or that (all reasonable steps having been taken to find it without success) the document cannot be found or does not exist (section 24A).

Requests can be transferred from one agency (or Minister) to another if the 25.14 requested document is known to be in that other's possession, or its subject matter is more closely connected with the other's functions: section 16. In certain

---

[21] Extension of the right to all documents under 30 years old was recommended in *the Australian Law Reform Commission report* (n 7 above) para 5.7, to close the 'access gap' between the documents caught by the 1982 Act and the Archives Act respectively, and covered by a clause in the Bill.

circumstances, transfer is mandatory: broadly speaking, where the document sought originated from another entity which enjoys exemption from the Act under section 7 and Schedule 2 and is more closely connected with the functions of that other entity.

Time limits

25.15 The maximum time periods allowed for acknowledging receipt of a request, and notifying the applicant of the substantive response to it, are laid down in section 15(5) as 14 days and 30 days respectively (counting from the date of receipt).[22] However, that is subject to section 15(6), which permits a 30-day extension of time in cases where the Act imposes a duty on the recipient to consult others. There are three such situations. The first occurs where the Commonwealth-state relations exemption[23] might apply and the state in question has made arrangements with the Commonwealth to adopt the consultation provisions of section 26A. Secondly, section 27 prohibits the granting of access to documents concerning individuals' business or professional affairs, or the business, commercial or financial affairs of organizations, unless they have been given a reasonable opportunity to make submissions as to the applicability of the section 43 exemption[24] and regard has been had to any submissions made by them. Thirdly, section 27A makes similar provision in respect of requests for documents containing personal information.[25] Compliance with sections 27 and 27A is excused where it is not reasonably practicable having regard to all the circumstances including the time limits in section 15(5) and (6).

25.16 Sections 26A, 27 and 27A require that notification of a decision to grant access be given to the state in question, or to any affected person who has made submissions against disclosure, so they may exercise their right to apply to the Tribunal for a review of the decision under section 58F, section 59, or section 59A (as the case may be).[26] The same provisions as govern an application for review of a decision to refuse access apply.[27] The decision cannot be implemented until after the expiry of the time allowed for the making of such an application[28] or (if one is made) it has been withdrawn or determined adversely to the applicant.

25.17 Section 21 of the Act permits deferment of access to a document in certain circumstances, namely:

---

[22] Reductions were proposed in *the Australian Law Reform Commission report* and the Bill.
[23] Under s 33A: see para 25.26 below.
[24] See para 25.24 below.
[25] Defined in s 4 as meaning information or an opinion (whether true or not) about an individual whose identity is apparent, or can reasonably be ascertained, from the information or opinion.
[26] An application for internal review may also be an option if the decision was taken other than by the responsible Minister or principal officer of the agency: see s 54(1C)-(1E) and para 25.30 below.
[27] See paras 25.31–25.36 below for details of these.
[28] 30 days after notice of the decision is given.

(a) where its publication is required by law, until the expiry of the period the law allows for publication;

(b) where it has been prepared for presentation to Parliament or making available to a particular person or body, until the expiry of a reasonable period for it to be so presented or made available;

(c) where its premature release would be contrary to the public interest, until such time as its release would not be so contrary;

(d) where a Minister considers that it is of such general public interest that Parliament should be informed of its contents first, until after five sitting days of either House.

Edited copies

Where a decision is taken to withhold access to a document on the ground it is **25.18** exempt, the agency or Minister may nonetheless be under a duty to make an edited copy of it available to the applicant by virtue of section 22. The precondi-tions are that it is both possible to make a copy with such deletions as not to be exempt, and reasonably practicable to do so having regard to the work that would involve and the resources available to do it. The section also imposes an obligation to edit a document containing information which an agency or Minister decides 'would reasonably be regarded as irrelevant to the request' by deleting that information, where possible and reasonably practicable to do so. Section 22 does not bite if the applicant makes it clear that he would not want access to an edited copy. An applicant may not be given an edited copy without being told that it has been edited, and why.

Methods of refusing access

Section 26 requires that particulars of any decision to refuse or defer access be **25.19** given to the applicant in written form. The notice is to state the findings on any material questions of fact (referring to the material on which they were based), and the reasons for the decision; identify the person who took the decision (if on behalf of an agency); and inform the applicant of his rights in respect of the deci-sion.[29] However, that is qualified by section 26(2), which permits the omission of any matter the inclusion of which in a document would attract one of the Act's exemptions. Where information as to the very existence or non-existence of a doc-ument would (if included in a document) attract one of the exemptions in sec-tions 33, 33A and 37(1),[30] the agency or Minister is allowed to give a notice stating that its existence is neither confirmed nor denied, but assuming its existence it would be exempt under such section: section 25.

---

[29] See para 25.29 below.
[30] See paras 25.24–25.26 below.

Methods of providing access

25.20   The various forms in which access can be provided are listed in section 20. If it appears from the request that the applicant desires information which is not available in written form but could be made so available by printing out material stored on computer or transcribing a sound recording, there may be an obligation to do that under section 17. Section 28 requires the designation of government offices throughout Australia as Information Access Offices, and enables a person entitled to access to a document to call for it to be provided at such Information Access Office with suitable facilities as is closest to his place of residence.

Fees and charges

25.21   The primary charging provisions are contained not in the Act itself, but in regulations[31] made by the Governor-General under section 94. That section confers general power to make regulations prescribing all matters that are required or permitted by the Act to be prescribed, or are necessary or convenient to be prescribed for carrying out or giving effect to the Act, but specifies as one particular such matter the making of charges in respect of requests for access and the provision of access to documents under the Act. Section 94(3) provides that if access is given as a result of a request albeit that the applicant would not be entitled to it under the Act, the charges regulations shall apply as if it had been given under the Act.

25.22   Where an agency or Minister decides that a charge is payable under the regulations (other than an application fee), that is for time spent on processing the request and services such as photocopying, a notice is to be served on the applicant giving the particulars prescribed by section 29. These include the amount of any deposit required, a preliminary assessment of the amount of the charge and the basis of the assessment. The applicant is to be informed that he may dispute the assessment, or contend for a reduction or waiver of the charge, and that under section 29(5) the Minister or agency when considering whether to reduce or not impose the charge must take into account financial hardship to the applicant and the public interest in the giving of access. He is allowed 30 days (which can be extended by agreement) to respond in one of three ways; by agreeing to pay the charge, by disputing the assessment or contending for a reduction or waiver (or both), or by withdrawing his request. If he fails to do any of those things he will be taken to have withdrawn his request. If he takes the second course and is unsuccessful, he may apply for an internal or external review of that adverse decision, or complain to the Ombudsman.[32] Section 31 provides for suspension of the period allowed by section 15 for dealing with the request while the issue of what (if any) charge is to be paid is resolved.

---

[31]   The Freedom of Information (Fees and Charges) Regulations 1982 No 197 (as amended).
[32]   Under ss 54, 55 and 57: see paras 25.29–25.36 below.

Section 30A enables an agency or Minister to remit an application fee payable in **25.23** respect of an access request or an application for internal review, either on their own initiative or at the request of the applicant. A rejection of such a request is also subject to the provisions for internal and external review and complaints to the Ombudsman. There is no restriction on the reasons for which a fee can be remitted, but financial hardship to the applicant and public interest in the giving of access are given as specific examples of reasons for which it can be done.

Exemptions

Categories of exemption involving no express public interest test

The provisions relating to exemptions are grouped in Part IV of the Act. **25.24** Considerations of public interest have an express part to play in some, but not the majority of cases. To begin with those exemptions which involve no express public interest test of any kind, a document is exempt if it satisfies any of the criteria summarized below:

(a) if its disclosure:
  (i) would, or could reasonably be expected to,[33] damage the security, defence or international relations of the Commonwealth, or
  (ii) would divulge any information communicated in confidence by or on behalf of a foreign government or international organization: section 33;
(b) if it is:
  (i) a document which has been (or is proposed to be) submitted to the Cabinet[34] or Executive Council for consideration, or
  (ii) an official record of the Cabinet or Executive Council, or
  (iii) a document disclosure of which would involve disclosing any deliberation of the Cabinet or Executive Council, or any decision of the Cabinet or advice of the Executive Council (other than an official publication of such): sections 34, 35;[35]
(c) if its disclosure would, or could reasonably be expected to:
  (i) prejudice the investigation of a breach of the law, or the enforcement or proper administration of the law in a particular case,
  (ii) reveal the existence (or non-existence) or identity of a confidential source of information relating to law enforcement or administration, or

---

[33] The words 'could reasonably be expected to' in the context of Part IV have been interpreted as requiring less than proof on a balance of probabilities that the harm will occur (*A-G's Dept v Cockcroft* (1986) 10 FCR 180), but more than a reasonable possibility of it (*Bartlett v Secretary, Dept of Social Security* (1997) 49 ALD 380).

[34] 'Cabinet' includes a Cabinet committee: s 34(6).

[35] To the extent that they contain purely factual material, documents in category (i) are outside the exemption, unless their disclosure would involve disclosing any deliberation, decision or advice the fact of which has not been officially published: ss 34(1A), 35(1A).

    (iii) endanger the life or physical safety of any person: section 37(1);

(d) if its disclosure would or could reasonably be expected to:

    (i)   prejudice a fair trial or adjudication,

    (ii) disclose lawful methods of preventing and detecting breaches of the law (where that would be reasonably likely to prejudice their effectiveness), or

    (iii) prejudice the maintenance or enforcement of lawful methods of protecting public safety: section 37(2);

(e) if its disclosure to the applicant is prohibited under a provision of another enactment which is listed in Schedule 3 to the Act, or which expressly declares that this exemption applies to documents within its scope: section 38;[36]

(f) if its disclosure would involve the unreasonable disclosure of personal information about any person (alive or dead) other than the applicant: section 41;

(g) if it would be privileged from production in legal proceedings on the ground of legal professional privilege: section 42;

(h) if its disclosure would disclose:

    (i)   trade secrets,

    (ii) information with a commercial value that would, or could reasonably be expected to, be destroyed or diminished by disclosure, or

    (iii) other information concerning an individual's business or professional affairs or the business, commercial or financial affairs of an organization disclosure of which:

        (1) would or could reasonably be expected to unreasonably affect that individual or organization adversely in respect of such affairs, or

        (2) could reasonably be expected to prejudice the future supply of information to the Commonwealth or an agency for administrative purposes: section 43;[37]

(i) if it contains information relating to uncompleted research by an officer of an agency listed in Schedule 4 to the Act, disclosure of which before completion would be likely unreasonably to expose him or the agency to disadvantage: section 43A;

(j) if its disclosure would found an action for breach of confidence by a person other than the Commonwealth: section 45;

(k) if its disclosure would be a contempt of court or infringe Parliamentary privilege: section 46;

(l) if it is a document of certain kinds arising out of companies and securities legislation: section 47;

(m) if it is an electoral roll or related document: section 47A.

---

[36] This section does not apply to the extent that the document contains personal information about the applicant.

[37] The section does not apply if the information concerns only the applicant's own affairs.

Categories of exemption involving an express public interest test

The application of two exemptions depends on disclosure being contrary to the **25.25** public interest. Section 44 exempts a document if its disclosure would be contrary to the public interest *by reason that* it (a) would, or could reasonably be expected to, have a substantial adverse effect on the government's ability to manage the economy, or (b) could reasonably be expected to have undue economic effects by prematurely revealing proposed or possible governmental or Parliamentary action or inaction. Section 36 exempts a document the disclosure of which would disclose opinion, advice or recommendation obtained, prepared or recorded, or consultation or deliberation that has taken place, in the course of, or for the purposes of, the deliberative processes involved in the functions of an agency or a Minister or the government (other than purely factual material) *and* would be contrary to the public interest.

Other documents are exempt if specified criteria are satisfied, but are nonetheless **25.26** to be disclosed if that would, on balance, be in the public interest. There are three classes of such documents:

(a) those disclosure of which:
  (i) would, or could reasonably be expected to, damage Commonwealth-state relations, or
  (ii) would divulge information communicated in confidence by a state government or authority: section 33A;
(b) those disclosure of which would have a substantial adverse effect on the financial or property interests of the Commonwealth or an agency: section 39;
(c) those disclosure of which would, or could reasonably be expected to, prejudice or adversely affect certain activities of agencies, such as audits and the conduct of industrial relations: section 40.

Proposals for reform

The Australian Law Reform Commission report contained recommendations for **25.27** abolition of the exemptions in sections 35, 38, 43A, 44, 47, and 47A and some other modifications, which were reflected in the Bill. However, the Senate Committee conducting the inquiry into the Bill took the view that these changes would be premature and alternative exemption systems (that is, ones not based on individual categories) should be examined before any legislative action is taken in this regard.[38]

Ministerial certificates

Sections 33, 33A and 36 contain provision for Ministers to certify, if so satisfied, **25.28** that the exemption applies. The certificate must specify which of the reasons for

---

[38] *Senate Inquiry report* (n 8 above) paras 3.36, 3.64, 3.137.

refusing disclosure referred to in section 33 or section 33A applies, or (in the case of section 36) the public interest ground relied on. Sections 33 and 33A also empower the Minister to certify that information as to the existence or non-existence of a document would (if contained in a document) cause it to be exempt under that section. The power of certification in respect of the documents of an agency can be delegated to its principal officer.[39] The application of section 34 or section 35 can be certified by the Secretary to the Department of the Prime Minister and Cabinet, or the Secretary to the Executive Council, as appropriate. Such certificates are conclusive for as long as they remain in force (which may be, but has not yet been, limited by regulations made under section 36A), unless revoked in the meantime. The limited powers which the Tribunal has in respect of such certificates are discussed at paragraph 25.33 below.

Reviews and appeals

Options

25.29   An applicant for access who is dissatisfied with a decision of the Minister or agency in respect of his request has up to three avenues to pursue under the Act: internal review, external review by the Tribunal, and investigation by the Commonwealth Ombudsman. Where the first is open to him, he must pursue that before he can have recourse to the second: section 55(2).[40] If he chooses to make a complaint to the Ombudsman, he is precluded from applying to the Tribunal until after he has been informed of the result of the complaint: section 57(3). The existence of the right to apply to the Tribunal does not preclude the Ombudsman from exercising any of his powers under the Ombudsman Act 1976: section 57(2), although if an application has actually been made he will generally decline to proceed with an investigation (see section 6(2) of the Ombudsman Act). However, a complaint can only be made to the Ombudsman where the decision-maker was an agency which is a prescribed authority within the meaning of the Ombudsman Act: section 57(1) and (8) of the Commonwealth of Australia Freedom of Information Act 1982; and his powers are in any event limited to making reports and recommendations to the agency, and including reference to the matter in his annual report or a special report to Parliament.

---

[39]   Defined in s 4 as meaning the Secretary of a department; in the case of a prescribed authority, the officer designated by regulations or (if none) the person entitled to preside at meetings of the authority; in relation to an eligible case manager, he himself (if an individual) or the individual with primary responsibility for its management.

[40]   Abolition of this restriction was recommended in *the Australian Law Reform Commission report* (n 7 above) para 13.6 and included in the Bill, but did not find favour in *the Senate Inquiry report* (n 8 above) para 3.76.

Internal review

The option of internal review is available under section 54 of the Act where the **25.30**
request was made to an agency, and the disputed decision was made otherwise
than by the responsible Minister or principal officer of the agency, pursuant to a
delegation of decision-making power to another officer of the agency in accordance with section 23. A written request for a review of the decision must be made
within 30 days of its notification to the applicant (or such longer period as the
agency agrees). The agency must as soon as practicable arrange for a person other
than the person who made the decision to review it and make a fresh decision. The
provisions of section 26[41] apply to the fresh decision.

Review by the Administrative Appeals Tribunal

An application under section 55 for external review by the Tribunal can be made **25.31**
in respect of an original decision by a Minister or the principal officer of an
agency; a fresh decision made on an internal review; and an original decision in
respect of which an application for internal review has been made but the applicant has not been informed of the result within 30 days. There is another category
of decision in respect of which an application can be made directly to the
Tribunal, and that is a deemed decision to refuse access under section 56(1),
which applies where no actual decision on an access request has been notified to
the applicant within the period allowed by section 15. In such a case the Tribunal
may grant the Minister or agency extra time to deal with the request: section
56(6). The period allowed for an application to the Tribunal is 60 days, running
from notification of an actual decision, or from a deemed decision under section
56, or (where a complaint has been made to the Ombudsman) from notification
of the result of the complaint.

The Administrative Appeals Tribunal Act 1975 governs the Tribunal's powers and **25.32**
procedures, subject to modification by the Act in particular respects. Section 58 of
the Act expressly confers on it specific powers in relation to applications under the
Act in addition to its general powers.[42] It may review any decision made by the
agency or Minister in respect of the request and decide any matter in relation to
the request that could have been or could be decided by the agency or Minister
(except that it has no discretion to order disclosure of an exempt document), and
its decisions have the same effect as those of agencies or Ministers: section 58(1).
It can under section 55(5) require further searches to be carried out where the
ground for refusing access is that the document does not exist or cannot be found
(section 24A).

---

[41] See para 25.19 above.
[42] See para 25.03 above.

25.33 The procedure in respect of challenges to certificates issued under any of sections 33 to 36[43] is laid down in sections 58(3) to (5A) and 58A. The Tribunal lacks power to review the decision to give the certificate, but may determine the question whether there are reasonable grounds for the claim that the document is exempt, or information as to its existence or non-existence would (if contained in a document) attract exemption, or disclosure would be contrary to the public interest (as the case may be). For that purpose it is entitled to require the document to be produced for its inspection: section 58E. If the Tribunal determines that there are no such reasonable grounds, the appropriate Minister[44] has 28 days to decide whether or not to revoke the certificate. In the event of revocation, the claim made in the certificate is taken to have been withdrawn. A decision not to revoke must be notified to the applicant, with a copy of the notice being laid before each House of Parliament within five sitting days, and the Minister has to read the notice to the House in which he sits. The notice is required to state the Minister's findings on any material question of fact, the material on which his findings were based, and the reasons for the decision (but need not contain anything which would, if included in a document of an agency, attract exemption under one of sections 33 to 36). A decision to issue a certificate (and other decisions under the Act) may be amenable to judicial review under the Administrative Decisions (Judicial Review) Act 1977: *Shergold v Tanner*.[45]

25.34 In Tribunal proceedings under Part VI of the Act it is not for the person requesting access to establish that it should be given. Section 61 expressly places the burden of showing that it should not on those who so assert. That is the affected state or other third party on an application under sections 58F, 59 or 59A.[46] In other cases, the agency or Minister has the onus of establishing that a decision given in respect of the request was justified or that the Tribunal should give a decision adverse to the applicant.

25.35 Sections 62 to 64 contain procedural provisions peculiar to the Tribunal's jurisdiction under the Act. Under section 62(2), the Tribunal may declare the particulars given in a notice under section 26[47] to be inadequate, in which case an additional notice containing further and better particulars must be furnished within 28 days. Power to require production of a document for which exemption is claimed so that the Tribunal may inspect it for the purpose of deciding whether it is exempt (or the practicability of producing an edited copy) is conferred by section 64. Sections 64 and 63 place obligations on the Tribunal to take measures to

---

[43] See para 25.28 above.

[44] The Minister who (or whose delegate) gave a certificate under s 33, s 33A or s 36; the Prime Minister, in the case of a certificate under s 34 or s 35.

[45] (2001) 179 ALR 150, FCA, (2002) 188 ALR 302, HC of A.

[46] See para 25.16 above.

[47] See para 25.19 above.

prevent disclosure to the applicant for access or any other person of exempt material. Where necessary for that purpose, the Tribunal may receive evidence and argument in the absence of the applicant or his representative. Additional restrictions are imposed in respect of proceedings relating to documents as to which a certificate is in force under sections 33 to 36: section 58C. In such cases the Tribunal must exclude the applicant, along with his witnesses and legal representatives, from any part of the hearing at which evidence is given or submissions made which involve disclosure of the documents or their contents, and from access to the relevant part of the transcript.[48]

An appeal against a decision of the Tribunal on a question of law may be made to the Federal Court of Australia under section 44 of the Administrative Appeals Tribunal Act 1975. **25.36**

Ancillary provisions

Prescribed publications

The first of the methods of achieving the Act's object specified in section 3(1)[49] forms the subject matter of Part II (sections 8 to 10). Section 8 imposed duties on the Minister responsible for each agency to ensure that statements of various matters relating to the agency were published within 12 months of commencement and brought up to date in every subsequent year. Those matters include particulars of the agency's organization, functions, and decision-making powers; any arrangements for participation by others in its formulation of policy or administration of any enactment or scheme; the categories of documents in its possession which are accessible or available to the public; the facilities it provides for public access to its documents; and its procedures for handling access requests under Part III of the Act. **25.37**

Section 9 requires agencies to make available for inspection and purchase by members of the public copies of manuals and other documents used by them or their officers in making decisions or recommendations under or for the purposes of enactments and schemes administered by them involving the conferment of rights, privileges and benefits or the imposition of obligations, penalties and other detriments. The intention is that members of the public should have the opportunity to apprise themselves of an agency's interpretations, rules, guidelines, practices and procedures. Section 10 provides that a member of the public is not to be subjected to any prejudice by reason of the application to an act or omission of his of a rule, guideline or practice of which he was unaware if the document containing that rule, guideline or practice was not available in accordance with section 9 **25.38**

---

[48] *Dept of Industrial Relations v Forrest* (1990) 91 ALR 417.
[49] See para 25.01 above.

at the date of the act or omission, and, had he been aware of it, he could lawfully have avoided such prejudice.

Correcting personal information

25.39   Part V of the Act is concerned with the right to bring about the amendment of records containing incomplete, incorrect, out of date or misleading personal information referred to in section 3(1)(c).[50] The basic right is conferred by section 48. That section applies where a person has been lawfully provided (whether under the Act or otherwise) with access to a document of an agency or official document of a Minister and claims that it contains personal information about him which satisfies one of the above descriptions and has been or is being used, or is available for use, by the agency or Minister for an administrative purpose. His right is to apply to the agency or Minister for amendment or annotation of the record of that information. The code for making and processing such applications is contained in sections 49 to 51E. Amendment involves the Minister or agency being satisfied that the information is defective and making appropriate alterations or additions. Annotation involves the addition of a statement provided by the applicant specifying the respects in which he claims the information is defective and the corrections he claims are appropriate, without any concession on the part of the Minister or agency to that effect. An application for annotation can only be refused on the ground that the Minister or agency considers the statement to be irrelevant, defamatory or unnecessarily voluminous and where an application for amendment is refused, an annotation must be allowed instead. Decisions to refuse amendment or annotation are subject to the provisions of section 26[51] and reviewable under Part VI of the Act in the same way as refusals to grant access requests under Part III.

Annual reports on the Act

25.40   The Minister administering the Act (who is the Attorney-General) is obliged by section 93 to report annually to Parliament on its operation. All agencies and Ministers are under a duty to furnish him with such information as he requires for the purpose of preparing those reports.

Immunity from proceedings

25.41   Sections 91 and 92 of the Act provide protection against civil and criminal proceedings in respect of the authorizing or giving of access to documents which the Act required to be given, or which was authorized to be given in the bona fide belief that the Act so required.

---

[50] See para 25.01above.
[51] See para 25.19 above.

B. Canada

Purpose and principles

The Canadian Access to Information Act ('the Act') received Royal Assent in July **25.42**
1982 and came into force a year later on 1 July 1983.

The statute defines its purpose in section 2(1) as follows: **25.43**

> The purpose of this Act is to extend the present laws of Canada to provide a right of
> access to information in records under the control of a government institution in
> accordance with the principles that government information should be available to
> the public, that necessary exceptions to the right of access should be limited and spe-
> cific and that decisions on the disclosure of government information should be
> reviewed independently of government.

The right of access

Subject to the various exceptions and exemptions set out in subsequent provisions **25.44**
of the Act, it confers a right to be given access on request to 'any record under the
control of a government institution': section 4(1).

The term 'record' is defined very widely in section 3, to include: **25.45**

> any correspondence, memorandum, book, plan, map, drawing, diagram, pictorial
> or graphic work, photograph, film, microform, sound recording, videotape,
> machine readable record, and any other documentary material, regardless of physi-
> cal form or characteristics, and any copy thereof.

Section 4(3) provides that any record requested under the Act that does not exist **25.46**
but can be produced from a machine readable record under the control of a government institution using computer hardware/software and technical expertise
normally used by the institution shall be deemed to be a record under its control.

The concept of 'access' is explained in section 12(1): a person who is given access **25.47**
to a record under the Act shall (subject to regulations) be given an opportunity to
examine it or be given a copy of it. Section 12(3) (added by amendment in 1992)
provides for a person with a sensory disability (that is, a disability of sight or hearing) to request access in a suitable alternative format (that is, one that allows him
to read or listen to the relevant record), but it may be refused if the institution does
not have it in such a format and the head of the institution does not consider (a)
the giving of access in an alternative format to be necessary to enable him to exercise his access right and (b) the conversion of the record into such a format to be
reasonable.

Originally, the right was confined to Canadian citizens and permanent residents **25.48**
within the meaning of the Immigration Act: section 4(1) of the Access to
Information Act 1982. However, section 4(2) empowers the Governor in Council

to extend the right to others by order, and that power was exercised in 1989 to bring within its scope all individuals and corporations present in Canada.[52]

Government institutions

25.49 'Government institution' is defined in section 3 as meaning any department or ministry of state of the government of Canada or other body or office listed in Schedule I to the Act. Additions to the list may be made by order: section 77(2). Only federal government institutions are affected by the Act. The provinces have their own local access statutes.

25.50 Section 5 requires the publication (at least once a year) and updating (at least twice a year) of a publication describing (a) the organization and responsibilities of each government institution, (b) all classes of records under the control of each institution 'in sufficient detail to facilitate the exercise of the right of access', (c) all manuals used by each institution, (d) the title and address of the officer of each institution to whom requests for access should be sent. The publication and updates are to be made available throughout Canada.

25.51 The head of every government institution[53] is to prepare an annual report for Parliament on the administration of the Act within the institution in the previous financial year: section 72(1). The form of these reports, and the information to be included in them, is to be prescribed by such member of the Privy Council as the Governor in Council designates for the purpose of section 70, who has also to prepare directives and guidelines on the operation of the Act for distribution to government institutions and keep under review the manner in which institutions keep and manage records.[54]

How requests are to be made and dealt with

25.52 A request for access under the Act is to be made in writing, to the government institution with control of the record, in 'sufficient detail to enable an experienced employee of the institution with a reasonable effort to identify the record': section 6.

25.53 The head of the institution receiving a request has 30 days under section 7:

(a) to give written notice whether access will be given; and
(b) if so, to give it;

---

[52] The Access to Information Act Extension Order, No 1 [SOR/89–207].

[53] The head of an institution is (a) in the case of a department or Ministry of state, the member of the Queen's Privy Council for Canada presiding over it or (b) in any other case, the person designated by order in council as such for the purposes of the Act: s 3.

[54] Currently the President of the Treasury Board.

or 15 days to transfer the request to another institution which he considers to have 'a greater interest' in the record, for example because it produced it (section 8). Time can be extended if fees are charged and required to be paid before access is given, as permitted by section 11, or if the institution needs more time to search or consult, or serves notice of the request on an affected third party pursuant to section 27:[55] section 9(1). An extension under section 9 is permitted for 'a reasonable period of time, having regard to the circumstances'. The section is invoked by the head of the institution giving the maker of the request written notice of the extension before the expiry of the initial 30-day period, together with notification of his right to complain about the extension to the Information Commissioner.[56] If the extension exceeds 30 days, it should be notified directly to the Commissioner by the institution concerned: section 9(2).

If the request is refused, the head of the institution may in his section 7 notice **25.54** either (a) state that the record does not exist or (b) say that it does but specify a particular provision of the Act on which the refusal is based or (c) decline to say if it exists or not but specify the provision on which a refusal 'could reasonably be expected to be based' if it does: section 10. The notice must inform the maker of the request that he is entitled to complain to the Information Commissioner about the refusal. Failure to give access within the statutory time limits is deemed to be a refusal of access for the purposes of the Act.

Charging provisions

The charging regime is laid down in section 11 of the Act, as supplemented by reg- **25.55** ulations. A person requesting access to a record under the Act may be required to pay such application fee as is prescribed by regulations (not exceeding $25) at the time of making the request.[57] Before any copies are made, he may be required to pay such fee as is prescribed to reflect the cost of reproduction. Fees are also chargeable at a prescribed rate for producing records in accordance with section 4(3) and conversion into alternative formats under section 12(3).[58] A charge may also be levied for every hour in excess of five hours that is reasonably required to search for a record or prepare it for disclosure.[59] Access may be withheld until after payment and the institution may require a deposit before it even begins to search. However, all of these fees are discretionary and may be waived or refunded by the institution concerned.

---

[55] See para 25.64 below.
[56] See para 25.71 below.
[57] The application fee is currently $5.
[58] See paras 25.46–25.47 above.
[59] The current hourly rate is $10.

Exemptions

25.56 There are a large number of these. Most are in form discretionary, opening with the words 'The head of a government institution may refuse to disclose any record requested under this Act that contains information which . . .', but some are mandatory, replacing the word 'may' with 'shall'. In the former cases, there is no express requirement to balance the public interest in disclosure against the public or private interest in withholding the record.

Interpretation

25.57 The Canadian courts have taken a restrictive approach to the interpretation of the exemption sections on the basis of the policy and objects of the Act and the wording of its purpose clause.[60] This is exemplified in cases such as *Rubin v Canada Mortgage and Housing Cpn*[61] and *Dagg v Canada (Minister of Finance)*:[62]

> The overarching purpose of access to information legislation is to facilitate democracy . . . rights to state held information are designed to improve the workings of government; to make it more effective, responsive and accountable. Consequently, while the Act recognises a broad right of access to any record under the control of a government institution, it is important to have regard to the overarching purposes of the Act in determining whether an exemption to that general right should be granted.[63]

25.58 In *Information Commissioner of Canada and TeleZone Inc v Canada (Minister of Industry)*,[64] the Federal Court of Appeal reiterated the principles that the right of access should be construed broadly in light of the statutory purpose set out in section 2 and, correspondingly, the exceptions should be given as narrow a meaning as is consistent with their purpose and the statutory language in which they are expressed. The right is to be given a 'liberal and purposive construction'. However, a court cannot redraft the exemption provisions to make them narrower where their meaning is plain, but 'must work within the language it has been given'.

The mandatory exemptions

25.59 These apply to records containing any of the following categories of information:

section 13:   information obtained in confidence from (a) a foreign government, (b) an international organization of states, (c) a provincial government, (d) a municipal or regional government, or (e) an aboriginal government; or an institution of any of the above

---

[60] Section 2(1): see para 25.43 above.
[61] [1989] 1 FC 265, 274, FCA, *per* Heald J.
[62] (1997) 148 DLR (4th) 385, SC.
[63] ibid, 403, *per* La Forest J.
[64] Federal Court of Appeal, 29 August 2001.

section 16(3):   information obtained or prepared by the Royal Canadian Mounted Police while performing policing services for a province or municipality which has asked the government not to disclose it

section 19:   personal information as defined in section 3 of the Privacy Act 1982,[65] unless the information is disclosed in accordance with section 8 of that Act[66] or with the consent of the affected individual, or is publicly available

section 20:   third party trade secrets; other confidential information supplied by a third party of a financial/commercial/scientific/technical nature; information the disclosure of which could reasonably be expected to prejudice a third party's competitive position, or interfere with a third party's contractual 'or other' negotiations, or result in material financial loss or gain to a third party:[67] *unless* (i) the third party consents *or* (ii) the record contains the results of product/environmental testing carried out by a government institution *or* (iii) its disclosure would be in the public interest as relating to public health/safety or environmental protection and the public interest in disclosure 'clearly outweighs in importance' the prejudice to the third party: proviso (iii) does not apply to trade secrets

section 24:   information the disclosure of which is prohibited by any enactment listed in Schedule II to the Act.[68]

---

[65] The Privacy Act confers a right of access to government-held personal records comparable to that enjoyed under the UK Data Protection Act. The general definition of 'personal information' in s 3 (illustrated by a series of specific examples) is 'information about an identifiable individual that is recorded in any form'. There are four exceptions for the particular purposes of the Access to Information Act: information about an officer or employee of a government institution that relates to his position or functions; information about an individual providing services under contract to a government institution that relates to the services performed; information relating to any discretionary benefit of a financial nature (including a licence or permit) conferred on an individual; information about an individual who has been dead for more than 20 years.

[66] This section prohibits disclosure of personal information under the control of a government institution without the subject's consent, save for one of the particular purposes enumerated in s 8(2)(a)–(l) inclusive or under s 8(2)(m), the catch-all clause which permits disclosure for any purpose where, in the opinion of the head of the institution, '(i) the public interest in disclosure clearly outweighs any invasion of privacy that could result from the disclosure, or (ii) disclosure would clearly benefit the individual to whom the information relates'.

[67] There is a line of authority, starting with *Canada Packers Inc v Canada (Minister of Agriculture)* [1989] 1 FC 47, (1988) 53 DLR (4th) 246, to the effect that the exceptions in this form are to be interpreted as requiring proof of a reasonable expectation of *probable* (not possible) harm to the specified interest. Consistently with that approach and the principle that exemptions are to be narrowly construed, it has been held that for s 20(1)(d) to apply there must be a reasonable expectation of interference with actual, particular, contractual negotiations, not just hypothetical problems: *Information Commissioner of Canada v Canada (Minister of External Affairs)* [1990] 3 FC 665, 683.

[68] As originally enacted, Sch II listed some 40 such statutory provisions. This was subject to s 24(2) which provided for a Parliamentary committee to review them and report to Parliament on

Non-mandatory exemptions

25.60 These can be divided into two groups, the first consisting of records containing information the disclosure of which could reasonably be expected to do any of the following:

section 14:   be injurious to the conduct of federal-provincial affairs

section 15:   be injurious to (a) the conduct of international affairs, (b) the defence of Canada (or any allied/associated state), or (c) the detection, prevention or suppression of subversive or hostile activities[69]

section 16(1)(c), (d):   be injurious to law enforcement or the conduct of lawful investigations or the security of penal institutions[70]

section 16(2):   facilitate the commission of an offence

section 17:   threaten the safety of individuals

section 18(b):   prejudice the competitive position of a government institution

section 18(c):   deprive an officer/employee of a government institution of priority of publication of the results of scientific/technical research by him

section 18(d):   be materially injurious to the financial interests of the government or its ability to manage the economy, or 'result in undue benefit to any person'.[71]

---

whether they were necessary by 1 July 1986. The review, carried out by the Standing Committee on Justice and the Solicitor General, concluded that the interests protected by these individual prohibitions would be adequately protected by the other general exemptions in the Act and that those prohibitions should be repealed, along with s 24 of and Sch II to the Act, subject to the insertion of new provisions specifically guaranteeing absolute confidentiality in the spheres of income tax records and information supplied by individuals, corporations and trade unions for statistical purposes. These recommendations (to be found in the report *Open and Shut—Enhancing the Right to Know and the Right to Privacy*) have not been followed, and although some of the provisions originally listed in Sch II have been abolished and removed, others have been newly enacted and added by amendment. The total number listed in Sch II has now grown to 66.

[69] The section contains a lengthy list of specific examples of such information (expressed to be without prejudice to the generality of the opening words), and an exhaustive definition of the term 'subversive or hostile activities'.

[70] Applying the principle that exemptions are to be strictly construed, it has been held that it is the conduct of a particular, current or impending, investigation a reasonable expectation of injury to which must be shown; it is not enough that unspecified future investigations or investigative procedures in general may be affected: *Information Commissioner of Canada v Immigration and Refugee Board (Canada)* (1997) 140 FTR 140. Disclosure in a particular case cannot be refused on the basis that it would have a 'chilling effect' on people's willingness to participate in future investigations.

[71] Specific examples are given, some of which obviously would, or could, have an impact on the general economy/government receipts (information relating to currency, government borrowing, contemplated changes in bank interest rates/tariff rates/taxes or other revenue sources); others would seem more to affect individuals or classes of individuals (contemplated changes in the conditions of operation of financial institutions, contemplated sales/purchases of securities, contemplated sales/acquisitions of land/property).

The second group consists of records containing information in any of the fol- **25.61**
lowing categories:

section 16(1)(a):   information obtained or prepared by a government institution
in the course of lawful investigations relating to crime, law
enforcement or suspected threats to national security, if the
record came into existence less than 20 years before the request

section 16(1)(b):   information relating to investigative techniques or plans for
specific investigations

section 18(a):   trade secrets or financial/commercial/scientific/technical
information belonging to the government or a government
institution and having (or being reasonably likely to have)
substantial value

section 21:   materials relating to government deliberations, negotiations,
or advice, if the record came into existence less than 20 years
before the request

section 22:   information relating to testing or auditing procedures/tech-
niques or details of specific tests/audits (if disclosure would
prejudice the use or results of particular tests/audits)

section 23:   information subject to solicitor-client privilege

section 26:   material which the head of the institution believes on reasonable grounds will be published by a government institution,
minister or agent within 90 days of the request.

Severance

Where a request is for a record containing information disclosure of which can be **25.62**
withheld, disclosure is nonetheless to be made of any other part of the record
which is disclosable and can reasonably be severed: section 25.

Third party intervention

The Access to Information Act is very protective of the interests of third parties **25.63**
(defined in section 3 as any person, group of persons or organization other than
the person asking for the record or a government institution). It goes so far as to
give third parties affected by requests rights to intervene in the processing of the
requests from an early stage.

Section 27 requires written notice of intended disclosure of any record which does **25.64**
(or the head of the institution has reason to believe might) fall within any of the
section 20 exemptions to be given to the affected third party within 30 days of
receipt of the request. The third party then has 20 days to make representations to
the head of the institution, who is to decide within 30 days of the giving of the
notice whether to go ahead and disclose: section 28.

25.65 If the decision is to disclose, the third party must be notified and under section 44 he has a right to apply within 20 days to the Federal Court for a review of the matter (to which the person requesting access to the record may appear as a party). The Court can order that the record not be disclosed: section 51.

25.66 The same applies if the original decision was not to disclose, but was changed on the recommendation of the Information Commissioner under section 37.[72] Where access is refused but a complaint is made to the Information Commissioner, the institution is to tell the Commissioner of any third party who was notified under section 27 (or would have been had disclosure been intended); and in any case where a section 20 exemption may apply, if the Commissioner intends to recommend disclosure he must give the affected third party a reasonable opportunity to make representations: sections 33, 35(2)(c).

25.67 Where access is refused, but the person who requested it or the Information Commissioner applies to the Court for a review of the refusal, notice is to be given to any third party who was notified under section 27 (or would have been if there had been an intention to disclose), who may appear as a party to the review: section 43.

The Information Commissioner

25.68 The Commissioner is appointed by the Governor in Council (after approval by both Houses of Parliament) for a seven-year term 'during good behaviour', after which he is eligible for reappointment for a further term of up to seven years.[73] He can be removed at any time by the Governor on address of both Houses.

25.69 He is to rank as and have all the powers of a deputy head of department.[74] He may recommend the appointment of one or more Assistant Information Commissioners (for five-year terms), to carry out such of his functions and duties as he may delegate to them, and is to have such staff as are necessary to enable him to perform his duties and functions.[75] Section 66 confers immunity from any criminal or civil proceedings for anything said or done in good faith in the exercise of his functions under the Act.

25.70 Under sections 38 to 40 he is required to report annually to Parliament on the activities of his office, and may make a special report on matters of urgency or importance at any time in between.

---

[72] See para 25.73 below.
[73] Access to Information Act 1982, s 54.
[74] ibid, s 55.
[75] ibid, ss 56–59.

Functions of the Information Commissioner

His principal duties are to receive and investigate complaints, primarily from dis- **25.71**
gruntled applicants for access whose requests have been refused or who consider
that they have been required to pay too much or wait too long, but also more generally in respect of the section 5 publication[76] and 'any other matter relating to
requesting or obtaining access to records under this Act': section 30(1). Section
30(3) empowers the Commissioner to initiate a complaint himself if 'satisfied
there are reasonable grounds to investigate a matter relating to requesting or
obtaining access to records under this Act'.

If the complaint relates to a request for access, it must be made within one year **25.72**
from the date of receipt of the request.[77] Investigations are to be conducted in private.[78] The Commissioner may determine procedure[79] but has to give a reasonable
opportunity to make representations to the complainant, the head of the institution concerned, and third parties where appropriate (see paragraph 25.66 above),
none of whom are entitled to be present at, have access to, or comment on, each
other's representations.[80] The Commissioner has powers to summon witnesses; to
order production of documents; to administer oaths; and to enter any government institution premises, converse in private with anyone there, and examine or
copy any books or records there.[81] No record to which the Act applies which is
under the control of a government institution can be withheld from his inspection
on any grounds.[82]

If he finds the complaint well-founded, he is to provide the head of the institution **25.73**
with a report containing his findings and 'any recommendations [he] considers
appropriate', and (where appropriate) a request that he be given notice of what the
institution is going to do to implement his recommendations (or an explanation
of why it is not going to do anything). Whether or not he finds it well-founded,
he is to report to the complainant (and any involved third party) on the results of
the investigation, including (where appropriate) the institution's response to his
recommendations.[83] His powers do not extend beyond the making of recommendations; he cannot take action to enforce them. If his recommendations are
ignored, the matter has to go to Court where it is at large.

---

[76] See para 25.50 above.
[77] Access to Information Act 1982, s 31.
[78] ibid, s 35(1).
[79] ibid, s 34.
[80] ibid, s 35.
[81] ibid, s 36(1).
[82] ibid, s 36(2).
[83] ibid, s 37.

The role of the Court

25.74 If the Commissioner does not recommend access be given, or if he does but access is still not given, the person refused access can apply to the Federal Court—Trial Division under section 41 for 'a review of the matter'. Alternatively the Commissioner may apply himself, with the consent of the person refused access: section 42. The time limit for either such application is 45 days from the date of the Commissioner's report to the complainant under section 37 of the Act (subject to extension in the Court's discretion).

25.75 The burden of proof is on the institution to establish that refusal of access is authorized: section 48.[84] The Court may examine any record to which the Act applies,[85] but is to take every reasonable precaution (including receiving ex parte representations and conducting hearings in camera) to avoid disclosure of any material on the basis of which the institution would be entitled to refuse access, or any information as to whether a record exists where the institution has declined to say if it does.[86] There are certain cases in which the application has to be heard in camera and the head of the institution has to be given the opportunity to make ex parte representations: that is, where the ground for refusing access is that the record contains information obtained in confidence from a foreign government or international organization of states, or injury to international relations or defence is anticipated from disclosure (sections 13, 15).[87]

25.76 If the Court determines that the refusal to disclose is not authorized by the Act (or, if the refusal was based on any of sections 14, 15, 16(1)(c) or (d), or 18(d), that the head of the institution did not have reasonable grounds to refuse disclosure), it shall order disclosure 'or make such other order as it deems appropriate': sections 49 and 50.

---

[84] Refusal of access should be justified by affidavit evidence clearly explaining the rationale for exempting each record: *Information Commissioner of Canada v Prime Minister (Canada)* [1993] 1 FC 427, 57 FTR 180. It will not suffice to describe in a general way consequences that could ensue from disclosure. Nor is it any use just affirming a belief (or speculating) that harm will be suffered: *Canadian Broadcasting Corporation v National Capital Commission* (1998) 147 FTR 264.

[85] Access to Information Act 1982, s 46.

[86] ibid, s 47.

[87] ibid, s 52. It has been held that this section absolutely precludes counsel for the person seeking access from seeing the requested records in cases to which it applies, whereas s 47 gives the Court power to allow counsel access for the purposes of preparing his argument: see eg *Hunter v Canada (Minister of Consumer & Corporate Affairs)* [1991] 3 FC 186, FCA; *Maislin Industries Ltd v Minister for Industry Trade & Commerce* [1984] 1 FC 939; *Steinhoff v Canada (Minister of Communications)* (1996) 114 FTR 108. However, the discretion is not necessarily to be exercised by allowing sight of the actual documents; communication of a summary or general description of their contents may be thought to suffice. Conditions can be imposed on such access as is allowed; typically an undertaking not to disclose what counsel has seen to anyone (including his client) will be required, and where appropriate security clearance will be made a precondition.

It is not for the Court to substitute its own opinion for that of the head of the gov-   **25.77**
ernment institution so far as concerns the exercise of the statutory discretion
whether to grant or refuse access where one of the non-mandatory exemptions
applies. However, the Court will intervene if it concludes that the decision is
'clearly wrong', or was made in bad faith, or in breach of natural justice, or on the
basis of irrelevant considerations. Section 48 does not require the head of the institution to prove that the discretion was lawfully exercised, only that the conditions
for its exercise are satisfied.

> When the minister has discharged the burden of establishing that a document falls
> within an exemption, the proceeding must be dismissed unless the applicant satisfies
> the court that the minister has failed lawfully to exercise the discretion to disclose an
> exempted document.[88]

Offences

Section 67 of the Act makes it an offence (punishable on summary conviction by   **25.78**
a fine of up to $1,000) to obstruct the Commissioner or any person acting on his
behalf or under his direction in the performance of his duties and functions under
the Act.

A 1999 amendment added section 67.1, which makes it a criminal offence, pun-   **25.79**
ishable by imprisonment (of up to two years, on indictment) or a fine (maximum
$10,000) or both, to do any of the following with intent to deny a right of access
under the Act: (a) mutilate, destroy, or alter a record; (b) make a false record or fal-
sify a record; (c) conceal a record; or (d) direct, propose, counsel or cause anyone
else to do any of those things.

Exclusions

The application of the Act is altogether excluded by section 68 in relation to pub-   **25.80**
lished materials, materials available for public purchase, and materials in public
archives, libraries, and museums; and by section 69 in respect of confidences of
the Queen's Privy Council for Canada (defined as including Cabinet and Cabinet
committees) that have been in existence for less than 20 years. Following the
September 11 attacks on New York and Washington, the Canadian Parliament
passed the Anti-terrorism Act 2001, section 87 of which derogates from the right
of access conferred by the Act. It adds a new section, 69.1, excluding from the
scope of the Act information disclosure of which has been prohibited by the issue
of a certificate under section 38.13 of the Canada Evidence Act (as amended
by section 43 of the Anti-terrorism Act). Such a certificate may be issued by
the Attorney-General for the purpose of protecting information obtained in

---

[88] *Information Commissioner of Canada and Telezone Inc v Canada (Minister of Industry)* (Federal
Court of Appeal, 29 August 2001).

confidence from, or in relation to, a foreign entity,[89] or protecting national defence or security. It has the effect of automatically discontinuing any existing proceedings under the Act, precluding further investigation by the Commissioner or review by the courts. A party to the proceeding may apply to the Federal Court of Appeal for an order varying or cancelling the certificate, but the jurisdiction is limited to reviewing whether the information subject to the certificate relates to information obtained in confidence from, or in relation to a foreign entity, or to national defence or security, and if and to the extent that the Court determines it does so relate, it is obliged to confirm the certificate.

Reform

25.81 The Act has changed very little since coming into force. Section 75(2) provided that a comprehensive review of the Act's provisions and operation should be undertaken by Parliamentary committee not later than 1 July 1986, to be followed by a report to Parliament with any recommendations for change. Such a review was undertaken by the House of Commons Standing Committee on Justice and the Solicitor General, who produced a unanimous report[90] recommending a number of changes which have not been implemented. Since then various reforms have been proposed by successive Information Commissioners, and there have been a dozen or more private members' Bills proposing amendments which have failed for lack of government support. In August 2000 the government set up a Task Force to review the workings of the Act, which released its report in June 2002.[91]

25.82 The conclusions reached by the Task Force were that the Act is 'still basically sound in concept, structure and balance', but in need of some modernization and amendment; that some administrative practices and attitudes within government institutions need to change; and that the principles of access to information must be embedded in the culture of the public service. To those ends it has made 139 detailed recommendations, many of which are concerned with the practical implementation of the Act rather than its content. No radical alterations in the legislative framework are suggested. References to some of the more significant proposals are to be found in chapter 9 above.

---

[89] Defined as (a) a foreign power, (b) a group or association of foreign powers, or of one or more foreign powers and one or more terrorist groups, or (c) a person acting at the direction of, for the benefit of, or in association with a foreign power or such a group or association.

[90] *Open and Shut—Enhancing the Right to Know and the Right to Privacy*, and see n 68 above.

[91] *Access to Information: Making it work for Canadians.*

C. France

Sources

The primary statute concerning freedom of information in France is the Law no **25.83**
78–753 of 17 July 1978. This statute, as amended by the Law no 2000–321 of
12 April 2000, sets out the principal law concerning access to administrative
documents in France.

Other statutes concerning specific areas of administrative or public activity pro- **25.84**
vide the citizen with means of extracting documents or information from specific
administrative bodies. One of the amendments made in 2000 was to integrate
questions arising under those disparate provisions into the scheme of the Law of
17 July 1978.[92]

A commission called the *Commission d'accès aux documents administratifs* was **25.85**
established under the Law of 17 July 1978. Since the Law came into operation the
commission has published ten reports of its activity,[93] usually on a biennial basis,
the most recent covering 1999 and 2000. The commission's reports contain a
wealth of information and are the source of much of the material in this section.
The commission uses the acronym CADA, although (except in the footnotes) it
is referred to here as the commission.

Illustrations of the operation of the Law are provided by the opinions (*avis*) of the **25.86**
commission given in respect of complaints made to it, advices (*conseils*) provided
by it in response to the questions of administrators or others uncertain how to
comply with the law, and the decisions of the *Conseil d'Etat*.

The right of access to administrative documents

There is no ringing principle contained in the Law of 17 July 1978 that everyone **25.87**
has the right of access to information held by the administration. In its original
version article 1 provided that 'The right of every person to information is secured
by the present title in matters concerning the freedom of access to administrative
documents which do not specifically relate to a named person.' As amended in
2000, article 1 provides that 'The right of every person to information is secured
by the present title in matters concerning the freedom of access to administrative
documents.' (Individual privacy is now protected by article 6-II.) There then follows a list of what counts as an administrative document. Article 2, in its original
form, provided in terms that, subject to the reservations contained in article 6,

---

[92] Article 5–1 of Law no 78–753, as amended. (All following references to articles are references
to articles of this Law unless otherwise identified.)
[93] Pursuant to art 5.

administrative documents originating from administrative bodies of the state,[94] the territorial corporations,[95] public corporations or bodies, even if established under private law, which are charged with carrying out a public service, are disclosable as of right to persons who request their production. As modified in 2000, article 2 provides that, subject to the reservations in article 6, the administrative bodies mentioned in article 1 (where there are now listed the categories previously listed in article 2) are obliged to disclose the administrative documents which are in their possession to any persons who request their production in the circumstances provided for by the statute.

25.88 French law provides a means of access to administrative documents, not to information as such. Applications to administrative bodies may be refused if they do not specify the document sought with sufficient precision or if they are purely requests for information.[96] The commission surmises that the reason why many requests are for *dossiers* (files) is that that is the widest description of document: obtaining the whole file makes it less likely that a document of importance will escape the applicant's attention.[97]

25.89 However, by virtue of the provisions relating to information held on computer, an applicant can, by seeking particular information which is held on a database containing that and other information, require an administrative body to create a new document for the purpose of disclosing the information sought.[98]

Documents in the possession of an administrative body

25.90 Subject to the exclusions and exemptions discussed below, the obligation to disclose documents which have been requested applies to all administrative documents which are in the possession of the body to which the request is made.[99] The body need not be the author of the document. Where, for example, administrative documents created by a local authority are in the possession of the prefecture for the purpose of the prefect's supervising the local authority's activities, the prefecture is obliged to disclose the documents, if requested to do so.[100]

Administrative documents

25.91 To count as an 'administrative document', a document must originate from the state, the territorial corporations, public corporations or bodies established under

---

[94] ie, central government.
[95] ie, local government: the *communes*, the *départements* and the *régions*.
[96] See Table 11 in CADA's report for 1999–2000.
[97] CADA report for 1999–2000, p 65. Nonetheless requests for *dossiers* made up only about one-tenth of requests in each of the years from 1995 to 2000.
[98] See para 25.111 below.
[99] Article 2.
[100] CADA report for 1999–2000, p 19.

public or private law which are charged with the conduct of a public service.[101] In what follows these bodies are referred to compendiously as administrative bodies.

Article 1 contains a list of types of document which for the purpose of the Law of **25.92** 17 July 1978 are considered as administrative documents, namely: all files, reports, research papers, records, minutes, statistics, orders, instructions, circulars, ministerial memoranda and replies which contain an interpretation of substantive rights and liabilities[102] or a description of administrative procedures, opinions, forecasts and decisions. Amongst the information tabulated by the commission in its report of activities is a breakdown by type of the documents of which disclosure has been sought.[103] The table contains 28 different types of documents and a residual category of 'diverse others'. In 2000 the most sought after categories were files (*dossiers*) (8% of all requests), reports (7.8%) and decisions (7.3%). Personal non-medical files and medical files were categorized separately (5.2% and 4% respectively in 2000).

Administrative documents may take the form of writing, aural or visual recording, **25.93** or documents existing in a database or capable of being generated by some currently used computer process.[104]

The following categories of documents do not count as administrative documents **25.94** for the purpose of the Law of 17 July 1978: proceedings of the parliamentary assemblies, opinions of the *Conseil d'Etat* and the administrative courts, documents of the *Cour des comptes*[105] referred to in article L 140–9 of the code governing the courts concerned with public finances and documents of the *chambres régionales des comptes* referred to in article L 241–6 of the same code, documents containing reports about complaints made to the *Médiateur de la République*,[106] and documents prepared for the purpose of granting accreditation to organizations providing health care with regard to article L 710–5 of the code of public health.[107]

The parliamentary assemblies are the National Assembly and the Senate. On the **25.95** basis that the Law of 17 July 1978 is concerned with administrative documents, some documents relating to their proceedings may justifiably be excluded as falling within the legislative branch of government, but other of their activities are concerned with supervision of administrative activity. The exclusion of such documents from the scope of the law might seem less justifiable in principle.

---

[101] Article 1.
[102] The French is *interpretation de droit positif.*
[103] CADA report for 1999–2000, Table 8, p 64.
[104] Article 1.
[105] In France, control over expenditure by public authorities is exercised by a court, rather than a body like the UK National Audit Office.
[106] An office akin to the Ombudsman.
[107] Article 1.

Moreover, under the practice developed by the commission such documents would have been within the scope of the law before the changes made to it in 2000.[108]

25.96   The exclusion of opinions of the *Conseil d'Etat* and the administrative courts may be justified on the footing that these are not administrative documents but documents arising in the course of legal proceedings. In so far as those proceedings concern the activities of administrative bodies which have given rise to the creation of administrative documents, such documents should in any event be disclosable by the body which created them. The central and regional courts of account may equally be regarded as juridical bodies outside the administrative branch at least in respect of their core activities.

25.97   The commission considers that it is not justifiable to exclude the investigation of complaints by the *Médiateur de la République* from the scope of the Law of 17 July 1978. The role of the *Médiateur* is to consider and seek to resolve complaints about administrative activities. Hence the documents in his possession are necessarily administrative documents. They, and the submissions made to him in the course of his drawing up *dossiers* on the complaints of which he is seised, ought to be disclosable. The commission discounts the consideration that such an obligation would interfere with the efficient despatch of business by the *Médiateur* on the ground that, until he was rendered exempt from the Law of 17 July 1978 by the changes made in 2000, he was able to satisfy requests for disclosure under it without undue interference with his principal function.[109]

25.98   The exemption afforded to the process of accrediting health care providers was created to overturn the effect of an opinion expressed by the commission.[110] The commission considers the exemption unjustifiable and causative of suspicion and mistrust.[111]

Exemptions from the obligation to disclose administrative documents

25.99   The right to require disclosure only applies to documents which are in their final form.[112] Drafts of documents need never be disclosed.

25.100   The right does not apply to documents preparatory to an administrative decision which is in the course of being made.[113] A distinction is drawn in this context between drafts of documents and *travaux préparatoires*. Documents prepared for the purpose of reaching an administrative decision may themselves be in final

---

[108]   CADA report for 1999–2000, p 17 and p 39.
[109]   CADA report for 1999–2000, p 40.
[110]   *Conseil* no 19993565 of 18 November 1999.
[111]   CADA report for 1999–2000, p 40.
[112]   Article 2.
[113]   ibid.

form, for example as a report or a collection of statistics, yet they remain, until the decision is taken, documents which are preparatory or instrumental to it. Once the decision has been taken the documents are disclosable. If the body fails over a long time to take any decision relative to which such documents have been prepared, it appears that they may become disclosable.

The commission is not critical of this provision, which, contrary to the aim of **25.101** open government, would seem to have the effect of preventing citizens from seeing documents which would assist them knowledgeably to participate in the making of decisions, but considers, with apparent satisfaction, that it enables administrators to reach their decisions serenely and without external pressure.[114]

Disclosure cannot be required of documents created in the context of a contract **25.102** for the provision of services made on behalf of one or more named persons.[115] The commission considers that this exemption must be read strictly.[116] Its purpose is to cover cases where an administrative body carries out, under contract with a private person or body, some service for that person or body. For example a public body such as the meteorological office might contract to provide particular reports to a private customer in return for payment, just as a private body would. The commercial basis of such contracts would be undermined if third parties could obtain copies of relevant documents by invoking the Law of 17 July 1978. However, the exemption is not applicable where an administrative body contracts with some other person for that other person to provide a service in furtherance of a public function with the conduct of which the administrative body is charged.

Administrative documents are exempt from disclosure if their inspection or dis- **25.103** closure would affect the secrecy of discussions within the government and competent authorities exercising executive power; secrets relating to national defence; the conduct of foreign policy; the security of the state, public safety or the safety of particular persons; the currency and public credit; the conduct of proceedings pending before courts or steps preliminary to such proceedings, unless authorized by the competent authority; the investigation by the competent bodies of offences relating to tax or customs; or generally, secrets protected by statute.[117]

Once an administrative document has been published, the right to require its dis- **25.104** closure may not be exercised.

Restrictions on the disclosure of administrative documents which would or might **25.105** adversely affect specific persons are referred to below in the context of privacy.

---

[114] CADA report for 1999–2000, p 20.
[115] Article 2.
[116] CADA report for 1999–2000, p 23.
[117] Article 6-I.

Protection of privacy

25.106 The French law of privacy is more developed than its English equivalent. Article 9 of the Civil Code provides that everyone has the right to respect for his private life. The range of remedies is broad: judges may, without prejudice to compensation for the damage suffered, grant any form of relief (including sequestration and seizure) which is appropriate to prevent or bring to an end an infringement of privacy; such relief may be granted, in cases of urgency, at an interim stage of proceedings.[118] It would run against the grain if access to administrative documents permitted access to information which would infringe individual privacy. Nor does the Law of 17 July 1978 permit such intrusion.

25.107 Administrative documents containing information which is personal, that is within the categories described below, may only be disclosed to the person to whom the information pertains. The restricted categories are: documents disclosure of which would intrude into the confidentiality of a person's private life and of his personal files, into matters of medical confidentiality and into commercial or industrial matters which are confidential; documents containing an assessment or a value judgment on an individual who is specified by name or easily identifiable; and documents which describe the behaviour of a person in a case where the publication of that behaviour could cause him harm. Where the document contains information of a medical nature disclosure of the document may not be made directly to the person concerned but must be to a doctor whom he has appointed for the purpose.[119]

25.108 Tricky questions arise in the context of seeking to protect privacy. For example, a child who has been taken into care is entitled to obtain disclosure of the files relating to him in order to research his origins; this may involve disclosure of information about his biological mother. Such information will be given, unless the biological mother has expressly requested that it should not. Where the person to whom documents relate is dead, the documents relating to him may be disclosed to direct relatives who can show sufficient interest. Whether disclosure should be made may involve considering the reasons for which it is sought. In general the question why a document is sought is not relevant, and the need for such assessment derogates from the principle that the right of access is an objective right.[120]

---

[118] Article 9 of the Civil Code provides: *Chacun a droit au respect de sa vie privée. Les juges peuvent, sans préjudice de la réparation du dommage subi, prescrire toutes mesures, telles que séquestre, saisie et autres, propres à empêcher ou faire cesser une atteinte à l'intimité de la vie privée: ces mesures peuvent, s'il y a urgence, être ordonnées en référé.*

[119] Article 6-II.

[120] CADA report for 1999–2000, p 30.

Information held on computer databases

Under the Law of 17 July 1978, as originally enacted, it was provided that admin- **25.109** istrative documents might take the form of written documents, audio or visual recordings or data held on computer which did not identify specific persons.[121] Hence, the law could not be invoked in order to obtain information held as data on a computer which identified specific persons. Instead, such data was protected by, and disclosure of it could be sought pursuant to, the statute relating to data protection, that is the Law of 6 January 1978. This might seem reasonable, but it meant that there was a difference in the way in which an application for an administrative document would be treated where the document gave information about a named person: if it was a paper document, a third party could obtain disclosure under the Law of 17 July 1978 (access to administrative documents); if the document formed part of a database, a person wishing to see the document would have to invoke the Law of 6 January 1978 (data protection), under which the document would not be available to third parties. This involved a double offence against reason: in the first case, the privacy of the named person might be infringed; in the second, third parties might be denied information which could be disclosed to them in a form which did not breach legitimate privacy.

The changes made in 2000 to the Law of 17 July 1978 sought to resolve the diffi- **25.110** culty by moving the boundary between the law relating to data protection and that relating to freedom of access to administrative documents. First, the provision which excluded databases which identified specific persons from counting as administrative documents was removed. Administrative documents now include any documents which are recorded in a computer or which are capable of being produced by a data-processing programme in current use.[122] Secondly, the provision in the Law of 6 January 1978 (article 29) preventing data held on a database which identified specific persons from being disclosed to third parties, was modified so as not to apply to a third party who is entitled to see the data by virtue of a right arising under the Law of 17 July 1978. These revisions do not have the effect of opening personal information to any third party who wishes to see it because, by article 6-II of the Law of 17 July 1978, disclosure of administrative documents containing personal information of various categories may only be made to the person interested (or a doctor appointed by him) as described above. Where a document contains information which may be disclosed to a third party as well as information disclosable only to the person interested, the document may be disclosed with the private information redacted.

---

[121] The original for the last category is *traitements automatisés d'informations non nominatives.*
[122] In the original: *de document existant sur support informatique ou pouvant être obtenus par un traitement automatisé d'usage courant.*

25.111 A further consequence of the introduction of the words 'documents . . . capable of being produced by a data-processing programme in current use' is that they have been taken by the commission to mean that an administrative body may be required to create a new document by drawing particular information out of a database containing a wider range of information. Hence not only documents, but, in this context, specifically identified information, are made accessible by the Law of 17 July 1978.

General publication of administrative documents

25.112 All orders, instructions, circulars, Ministerial memoranda and replies which contain an interpretation of substantive rights and liabilities or a description of administrative procedures and the references of administrative documents are to be published regularly. Detailed provision for the publication of these items is made by Decree no 79–834 of 22 September 1979 of the *Conseil d'Etat*.

25.113 Publication of the orders, instructions, circulars, Ministerial memoranda and replies mentioned must be made in certain official publications depending on what governmental body it was which produced the document in question.[123] Such publication in itself satisfies the obligation to publish the reference of the document so published. In relation to other documents, with the exception of files containing documents preparatory to an administrative decision which is not complete, what is required is the publication of their title, their purpose, their date, their origin and the place where they may be consulted or disclosed.[124]

Preventing wrongful use of administrative documents

25.114 Administrative documents are disclosed subject to copyright. The exercise of the right of access does not convey to those taking advantage of it, or third parties, the power to reproduce, disseminate or exploit for commercial purposes the documents which are disclosed.[125]

La Commission d'accès aux documents administratifs

25.115 As mentioned in paragraph 25.85 above, by article 5 of the Law of 17 July 1978 a commission was established called *La Commission d'accès aux documents administratifs* and charged with supervising the freedom of access to administrative documents. The statute provided that the composition of the commission was to be determined by the *Conseil d'Etat*. By decree no 78–1136 of 6 December 1978 the *Conseil d'Etat* ordered that the commission should comprise one member of the *Conseil d'Etat* of at least the rank of *conseiller d'Etat* nominated by the vice-

---

[123] Decree 79–834, arts 1 to 4.
[124] ibid, art 5.
[125] Article 10.

president of the *Conseil d'Etat*, one judge of the *Cour de cassation* nominated by the first president of the *Cour de cassation*, one judge of the *Cour des comptes* nominated by the first president of the *Cour des comptes*, a deputy nominated by the president of the *Assemblée Nationale*, a senator nominated by the president of the Senate, a representative of the Prime Minister, a member of a *conseil general* or of a *conseil municipal* nominated jointly by the president of the Senate and the president of the *Assemblée Nationale*, a professor of higher education nominated by decree, and, ex officio, the director of the *Archives de France* and the director of the *Documentation française*.[126] Thus, the commission, through its members, has ample experience of the workings of administrative bodies from whom disclosure of administrative documents may be sought, but does not include any direct representation of consumer interests. The president of the commission is the member who belongs to the *Conseil d'Etat*. Each member has an alternate, nominated in the same way, save for the two ex officio members. All members and alternates hold office for renewable terms of three years.[127] The president of the commission has power to appoint as rapporteurs judges or civil servants of certain rank.[128] A rapporteur general and a number of rapporteurs have been appointed.

The functions of the commission, as enlarged by the amendments made in 2000, are to supervise the freedom of access to administrative documents under the Law of 17 July 1978, to supervise the freedom of access to the public archives under title II of the Law no 79–18 of 3 January 1979, and to consider questions relating to access to the administrative documents referred to in certain other provisions.[129] The power to consider questions relating to the public archives and the various other statutes represents an extension of the commission's remit and, though this process is incomplete, an attempt to assimilate the right of access to administrative documents under the Law of 17 July 1978 and the various other specific provisions whereby access to administrative documents may be obtained. **25.116**

The principal activities of the commission are to issue opinions (*avis*) on complaints raised by persons seeking access to administrative documents and to give advice (*conseils*) to administrative bodies. In 1999 the total number of cases dealt with by the commission was 4,315 of which 3,770 were complaints seeking opinions and 545, requests for advice; in 2000 the parallel figures were 4,879, 4,244, **25.117**

---

[126] *La Documentation française* is the equivalent of The Stationery Office.
[127] Decree of the *Conseil d'Etat* no 78–1136, art 1.
[128] ibid, art 2.
[129] Article L 2121–26 of the general code of the territorial corporations; art L 28 of the electoral code; art 104, para (b) of the book of fiscal procedures; art L 5 of the law of 1 July 1901 concerning contracts of association; art 2 of the decree of 16 August 1901; art 79 of the civil code governing Alsace-Moselle; and arts L 213–13 and L 332–29 of the city planning code.

and 635. The trend in the number of such cases since the first year of operation (1979–1980), when there was a total of 470, has been constantly upward.[130]

25.118 The largest number of requests for advice come from organs of local government. In 2000 about three-quarters of such requests were made by *communes, départements* and local public bodies (including hospitals).[131] The commission ascribes this proportion to the large number of such bodies and the modesty of their means, presumably in terms of their in-house legal expertise. But the commission encourages administrative bodies to seek its advice. On its website,[132] the commission offers to give rapid and precise advice to any administrative body seeking it: all that is required is that the request for advice is made to the commission in writing.

25.119 About a quarter of the requests for advice come from the state, meaning the departments of central government.[133] The departments giving rise to the largest number of requests in 2000 were (with the number of requests and the percentage which that represents of the total number of requests for advice made by central government departments): Interior (69; 46.6%), Employment (31; 21%), Agriculture (15; 10.1%) and Education (14; 9.5%).[134] The figures were almost identical in 1999.

25.120 The commission may also suggest, either at the request of an administrative body or on its own initiative, any modification of the access laws and any measures which might facilitate the exercise of the rights of access to administrative documents and the public archives and which might promote administrative openness.[135]

Procedure governing applications for access to administrative documents

25.121 Where a person wishes to see an administrative document, he should first apply to the administrative body in whose possession it is. The administrative body is bound to disclose it unless there is good reason not to make disclosure of the document either generally or to the particular applicant. If the administrative body decides not to allow access, it is obliged to inform the applicant of its decision in writing, giving reasons.[136] When a request is made to an administrative body, it ought to respond within one month; if it fails to do so, it is deemed to have refused access.

---

[130] CADA report for 1999–2000, Table 1, p 54. As the commission itself observed in its report for 1995–1998, p 73 (when referring to the number of requests made by telephone) written complaints to it represent '*la partie émergée de l'iceberg*'.

[131] ibid, Table 2, p 55.

[132] http://www.cada.fr

[133] CADA report for 1999–2000, Table 2, p 55.

[134] ibid, Table 3, p 56.

[135] Article 5.

[136] Article 7.

Administrative bodies are not obliged to give effect to requests which are vexa- **25.122**
tious, for example by virtue of their quantity, or their repetitive or extensive
nature.[137]

An administrative body which holds a document may allow access to it either by **25.123**
inspection without charge at the place where it is held, unless the preservation of
the document does not so permit; or, so long as the reproduction does not harm
the safe-keeping of the document, by delivering an accessible copy on a computer
programme identical to that used by the administrative body or a copy on paper,
at the choice of the applicant and on payment of the administrative body's charge,
provided that the charge may not exceed the cost of making the reproduction.[138]
There has in the past been some discrepancy between the charges made by administrative bodies, but a tariff of charges has now been established by order.[139]

Complaints to the commission

If an administrative body refuses to grant access to a document (or is deemed to **25.124**
have done so), the applicant's next step is to complain to the commission. The
complaint must be made within two months from the notification of the refusal
or the expiry of the period for the administrative body's response to the initial
request. Making a complaint to the commission is an obligatory step which must
be taken before commencing any judicial proceedings.[140]

In 2000, 68.3% of those seeking opinions from the commission were individuals, **25.125**
31% were private legal entities and 0.7% were public entities.[141] The same pattern
has obtained since at least 1995. Enthusiasm for seeking opinions varies over
France. Of applications made in 2000, 27.3% came from Île de France, which
includes Paris, 10.3% from Provence-Alpes-Côte-d'Azur, 8% from Rhône-Alpes,
8.8% from Languedoc-Roussillon and 7.3% from Midi-Pyrénées.[142] These
regions represent 43% of the population but generate 60% of the complaints. In
2000 52% of complaints concerned departments of central government or public corporations and 44.4% related to local authorities or local public corporations.[143] The topics causing most complaint were the civil service (*La Fonction
Publique*) (15% of complaints), town planning (13.9%), social matters (13.2%),
the environment (9.5%), public order (7.6%) and the economy and finances
(7%).[144] Similar patterns can be seen in previous years. Requests for documents

---

[137] Article 2.
[138] Article 4.
[139] *Arrêté* of 10 October 2001.
[140] Decree no 88–465 of 28 April 1988 concerning the procedure for obtaining access to administrative documents, art 2.
[141] CADA report for 1999–2000, Table 4, p 57.
[142] ibid, Table 5, p 59.
[143] ibid, Table 6, p 60.
[144] ibid, Table 7, p 62.

relating to *La Fonction Publique* were generally made by *fonctionnaires* concerned about their own careers.

25.126 On receiving a complaint, the commission is obliged to state its opinion on the matter complained of. The period within which the opinion must be given is one month. But, to the commission's regret, it is not able to meet this requirement in many cases. In 2000 the average length of time taken by the commission to give its opinion was 42.2 days. In 1998, the worst year, it was 49.1 days and in 1991, the best, 34.3 days.[145]

25.127 When it gives its opinion, the commission must send it to the administrative body to which it relates. That body is obliged to inform the commission, within one month of receiving the opinion, what it intends to do in relation to the request for access concerned.[146] This reflects the fact that the commission's opinion does not have coercive effect and cannot, as such, be enforced. If the administrative body fails to respond for more than two months from the date when the commission was seised of the applicant's complaint, it is deemed to have refused access.[147]

Recourse to the courts

25.128 An applicant who remains dissatisfied, either because the commission's opinion is unfavourable to him or because, although the opinion is favourable, access is still not permitted by the administrative body concerned, must take his case to the administrative courts by way of a *recours pour excès de pouvoir*. The purpose of such proceedings is to establish that the administrative body of which complaint is made has acted illegally. The remedy is the quashing (*annulation*) of its decision.

25.129 There are three tiers of administrative courts: the *tribunaux administratifs*, the *Cours administratives d'appel* and the *Conseil d'Etat*. Most often, the court of first instance will be an administrative tribunal, from which an appeal may be made to a *Cour administrative d'appel*. The court of appeal's decision may be quashed by the *Conseil d'Etat* for error of law on further application to it by way of *cassation* and the matter remitted to the court of appeal for further hearing in the light of the *Conseil d'Etat*'s guidance on the question of law in respect of which error was made. But where the refusal to give access to an administrative document is made by an administrative body having *competence nationale*, the application should be made directly to the *Conseil d'Etat*.

How well does the French law operate?

25.130 As discussed above, the French law is not primarily a law of freedom of information, but a law providing a right of access to administrative documents. Such a law

---

[145] CADA report for 1999–2000, Table 16: this table only runs from 1989.
[146] Decree no 88–465, art 2.
[147] ibid.

favours those with knowledge of the administrative system over those searching inexpertly for particular information. That the law is much invoked by civil servants concerned about their own affairs has been mentioned. Citizens are doubtless assisted by the cataloguing of administrative documents, but profitable extraction of information from catalogues is not always easily and speedily achieved by the unversed.

These criticisms, essentially of form, should not count for much where adminis- **25.131** trative bodies adopt a positive and helpful attitude. But the commission's view in its report for 1999–2000 is that some administrative bodies show a reticence and lack of enthusiasm in giving access to the documents which they hold.[148] This is evidenced both by the increase in complaints made to the commission and, more tellingly, by the fact that complaint is made to the commission in cases where, in the commission's view, it is obvious that access should be given to the document in question. Complaints should only arise where the question of access raises some point of difficulty. The commission identifies two reasons for the failure of administrative bodies to implement the law: lack of knowledge of the law amongst some bodies, particularly those of local government; and sluggishness in responding to requests for documents and in responding to the commission once complaint has been made to it. The commission made similar points in its previous report for 1995–1998.[149]

The commission considers that some documents are excluded from the law with- **25.132** out good reason, as mentioned above.[150] It would also like to see the provisions of the various laws giving specific rights of access to particular documents or information in particular contexts harmonized more rationally with the general scheme for obtaining access to administrative documents. The architecture of the regime for gaining access to administrative documents remains, in its view, need-lessly complex.[151]

D. Ireland

Introduction

The Freedom of Information Act 1997 ('the Act') was enacted by the Irish **25.133** Parliament (*Oireachtas*) on 21 April 1997.

---

[148] CADA report for 1999–2000, p 45.
[149] CADA report for 1995–1998, p 79.
[150] See paras 25.97–25.98 above.
[151] CADA report for 1999–2000, p 41.

25.134 Save with regard to local authorities and health boards, the Act came into operation on 21 April 1998.[152] With regard to local authorities and health boards, the Act came into operation on 21 October 1998.[153]

25.135 The Act confers powers on 'the Minister' to determine certain matters, to make regulations prescribing other specific matters and 'generally for the purposes of, and for the purpose of giving full effect to' the Act,[154] and to issue guidelines. The Minister concerned is the Minister for Finance. The Minister is sometimes required to act with the consent of other relevant Ministers. So, for example, the date for the Act to come into operation with regard to health boards was a day to be appointed by the Minister with the consent of the Minister for Health.

Rights conferred by the Act

The right of access to records

25.136 The central provision is section 6(1) which provides that, subject to the provisions of the Act, every person has a right to, and shall, on request therefor, be offered access to any record held by a public body. The right conferred by section 6(1) is referred to in the Act as the right of access. It should be noted that the right of access relates to records and not to information. The definition of records is, however, widely drawn, embracing 'any . . . form or thing in which information is held or stored manually, mechanically or electronically'.[155]

Public bodies

25.137 Public bodies for the purposes of the Act are defined (in some cases by list, in others by description) in the First Schedule. The public bodies concerned fall, broadly speaking, into five categories: (1) government departments; (2) certain other national bodies; (3) local authorities; (4) health boards; (5) such additional bodies, organizations and groups of specified kinds as the Minister may prescribe. The Minister's powers extend to any body, organization or group on which functions in relation to the general public or a class of the general public stand conferred by any enactment[156] or which is financed wholly or partly by the government.[157] It is interesting to note that the *Garda Síochána*[158] is not a public body for the purposes of the Act but can be prescribed as such by the Minister. The powers have been exercised in relation to a considerable number of public bodies

---

[152] Freedom of Information Act 1997, s 1(2).
[153] ibid, s 1(3) and the Freedom of Information Act 1997 (Local Authority and Health Board) Commencement Order 1998, SI 1998/397.
[154] Freedom of Information Act 1997, s 3(1)(b).
[155] Section 2(1).
[156] Paragraph 1(5)(f) of the First Schedule.
[157] Paragraph 1(5)(c) of the First Schedule.
[158] The Police Force.

since coming into operation, for example, public voluntary hospitals from Autumn 1999 and universities and regional assemblies from Autumn 2001.

The Act imposes obligations on the 'head' of a public body, whose identity is to be **25.138** ascertained in accordance with the definition in section 2(1). However, the head can delegate his functions under the Act to other members of staff (other than the function of delegation itself or the issuing of certificates under section 25[159] declaring that certain records relating to law enforcement and public safety and security, defence and international relations are exempt records).[160] As the first Irish Information Commissioner, Kevin Murphy, confirmed when giving evidence to the House of Lords Select Committee on the draft Freedom of Information Bill,[161] delegation is the norm and only in 'very, very few cases' would a Minister personally take the decision.

Public bodies are under a duty to give reasonable assistance to a person who is **25.139** seeking a record under the Act in relation to the making of a request for access to the record and, if the person has a disability, so as to facilitate the exercise of his rights under the Act.[162]

Scope of the right of access

The Act applies to records created after the commencement of the Act and such **25.140** earlier records as are prescribed by the Minister.[163] Where, however, access to records created before commencement is necessary or expedient in order to understand records created after commencement, or records created before commencement relate to personal information about the person seeking access to them, there is a right of access in respect of those records.[164] This does not, however, extend to personnel records created more than three years before commencement, which are not being or proposed to be used in a manner or for a purpose that has, or will or may have, an adverse effect on the interests of the employee concerned.[165]

The right of access also extends to records in the possession of a person who is or **25.141** was providing a service for a public body under a contract for services in so far as they relate to the service. Such contracts are deemed to include provisions requiring the contractor to give such records to the public body for retention.[166]

---

[159] See para 25.161 below.
[160] Section 4.
[161] HL Paper (1998–99) no 97, at p 71.
[162] Section 6(2).
[163] Section 6(4).
[164] Section 6(5).
[165] Section 6(6).
[166] Section 6(9).

Other rights

25.142   The Act confers two other rights on members of the public. First, where a record held by a public body contains incomplete, incorrect or misleading personal information, the individual concerned may require the amendment of the record.[167] Secondly, any person affected by an act of a public body who has a material interest in a matter affected by the act, or to which it relates, may apply to the public body for a statement of the reasons for the act and any findings on any material issues of fact made for the purposes of the act.[168] This section confers a general right to reasons on persons affected by the decisions of public bodies, subject however to the Act's exemptions.

Exercise of the right of access

Making requests

25.143   The right of access is exercised by making a request, in writing or in such other form as may be determined by the Minister, addressed to the head of the public body concerned.[169] It must contain sufficient particulars to enable the record to be identified by the taking of reasonable steps. An acknowledgement of receipt must be sent as soon as may be, but not later than two weeks after receipt,[170] together with a summary of the provisions of the Act relating to deemed refusals.[171] Where a request is made to a public body which does not hold the requested records but whose head knows or ought to know that they are held by one or more other public bodies, he is to give a copy of the request to the most appropriate of those other bodies.[172]

25.144   Requests were made at an annual rate of around 8,000 in 1998 (this is an estimated figure as the Act was not in operation for the whole year). 11,531 requests were made under the Act in 1999, increasing to 13,705 in 2000 and 15,428 in 2001. Of these just over half were wholly successful and between 20–25% were partially successful.[173]

Responding to requests

25.145   As soon as may be but not later than four weeks after receiving a request, the head of a public body must (a) decide whether to grant or refuse the request or to grant it in part; (b) if the decision is favourable, determine the form and manner in

---

[167] Section 17.
[168] Section 18.
[169] Section 7(1).
[170] Section 7(2).
[171] Section 41: see para 25.170 below.
[172] Section 7(3) to (6).
[173] The statistics in this section are derived from the Commissioner's annual reports and his report under s 36(2) of the Act on the first three years of its operation.

which the right of access will be exercised; and (c) cause notice of the decision and determination to be given to the requester.[174] The notice must contain certain specified matters.[175] If the request is granted, these include details of the form in which, and the period for which, access will be given, and any fee payable. In the event of a refusal, the notice is to state the reasons for the refusal, and (except in cases where the Act prohibits disclosure by the head of the public body concerned of whether or not the record exists)[176] the provision(s) of the Act pursuant to which the request is refused, the findings on any material issues relevant to the decision and particulars of any matter relating to the public interest taken into consideration for the purposes of the decision. However, the notice is not required to contain any material the inclusion of which in a record would cause it to be exempt from disclosure under the Act.[177]

25.146 Where a request is granted and any necessary fee has already been paid, access to the record concerned shall be offered to the requester forthwith. Where a request is granted but some necessary fee still needs to be paid, access shall be offered to the requester not more than a week after the fee is received. The record is to be made available for a period of four weeks.[178]

25.147 The fee chargeable in respect of the grant of a request for access to a record[179] is equal to the estimated costs as determined by the head of (a) the search for and retrieval of the record and (b) any copy of the record made for the requester.[180] Hourly rates for the costs of search and retrieval and maximum rates for the costs of copying may be prescribed.[181] In certain circumstances the fee may be reduced or waived.[182] Where the cost of search and retrieval is likely to exceed €50.80 a deposit shall be charged and the process of search and retrieval shall not be commenced until the deposit has been paid.[183] Decisions as to fees and deposits are open to review by the public body concerned.[184] Decisions as to fees and deposits exceeding €12.70 are open to review by the Commissioner.[185]

25.148 In deciding whether to grant or refuse a request any reason that the requester gives for the request, and any belief or opinion of the head as to his reasons for making it, are specifically required to be disregarded.[186]

---

[174] Section 8(1).
[175] Section 8(2).
[176] See para 25.159 below.
[177] Section 8(5).
[178] Section 8(3).
[179] Section 47(1).
[180] Section 47(2).
[181] Section 47(3).
[182] Section 47(5) and (6).
[183] Section 47(7).
[184] Section 14(1)(g): see para 25.154 below.
[185] Section 34(1)(c): see paras 25.165–25.167 below.
[186] Section 8(4).

25.149 The head may extend time for the consideration of a request by up to four weeks in certain circumstances. Those circumstances are if in the head's opinion either (a) the request relates to such a number of records, or (b) there are so many other earlier requests relating to the same records or corresponding information outstanding, that it is not reasonably possible to deal with the request in the normal four-week period.[187] It should be noted that the fact that the public body concerned has a large backlog of outstanding requests is not, in itself, a reason for extending the time.

25.150 A request may be refused on certain administrative grounds.[188] They are, broadly, that:

(a) the record concerned does not exist or cannot be found;

(b) the request does not contain sufficient particulars in relation to the information concerned to enable the record to be identified;

(c) granting the request would in the head's opinion require the retrieval and examination of such number of records or an examination of such kinds of records as to cause a substantial and unreasonable interference with or disruption of the other work of the public body;

(d) publication of the record is required by law and is intended to be effected within 12 weeks of the receipt of the request;

(e) the request is in the head's opinion frivolous or vexatious; or

(f) any necessary fee or deposit has not been paid.

25.151 The offering of access can be deferred in certain circumstances,[189] for example if the record is shortly to be laid before or brought to the attention of either House of the *Oireachtas*.

25.152 Access to a record can be given in a number of different ways including by providing a copy of the record, a reasonable opportunity to inspect the record, or a transcript of or computer disk containing the information concerned.[190] If a request is made for access in a particular form or manner, access should be provided in that form or manner except in certain circumstances,[191] namely where the head is satisfied that to do so would damage the record, conflict with a legal obligation of the public body, or prejudice any interest protected by the exemptions from access, or that giving it in another form or manner would be significantly more efficient.

---

[187] Section 9(1).
[188] Section 10(1).
[189] Section 11.
[190] Section 12(1).
[191] Section 12(2).

Where the requested record is an exempt record by reason of the inclusion in it of   **25.153**
some particular matter, the head of the public body should, if practicable, prepare
a copy of the remainder of the record to make available to the requester.[192]

Internal reviews

Where a decision has been made by a person to whom the decision-making func-   **25.154**
tion was delegated, the head of the public body concerned may review it on the
application of the requester.[193] The function of carrying out such reviews can itself
be (and typically is) delegated but the review must be carried out by someone of a
higher rank than the person who made the original decision.[194] The period
allowed for carrying out an internal review is three weeks.[195] Around 14% of
requests in 1998 were subject to such reviews, falling to 11% in 1999 and 7% in
2000 but rising again to 9% in 2001.

Facilitating exercise of the right

Section 15 requires public bodies to publish a reference book containing, among   **25.155**
other things, details of the organization, the sort of records held by it and the
arrangements it makes to enable a person to obtain access to such records. Each
public body is to provide the Minister with a summary of its reference book and
the Minister is to publish a reference book consisting of a collation of those summaries. These reference books are to be updated and republished at intervals not
exceeding three years.

It is the Minister's duty to ensure that public bodies take appropriate measures in   **25.156**
their organization and staff training to facilitate compliance with the Act, and he
is specifically empowered to make regulations concerning the management and
maintenance of their records.[196]

Section 16 requires public bodies to publish the rules, procedures, practices,   **25.157**
guidelines and interpretations used by them and an index of any precedents kept
by them for the purposes of decisions under any enactments or schemes administered by them affecting the rights of members of the public.

Exempt records

Categories of exemption

Part III of the Act, consisting of sections 19 to 32, deals with exempt records.   **25.158**
Exempt records can be broadly categorized as those relating to, or being:

---

[192] Section 13.
[193] Section 14(1) and (2).
[194] Section 14(3).
[195] Section 14(4).
[196] Section 15(5).

- meetings of the government (including advice to, and other documents submitted for the consideration of, Ministers)[197]
- deliberations of public bodies[198]
- the functions and negotiations of public bodies[199]
- records which would be exempt from production in court proceedings on the ground of legal professional privilege[200]
- records disclosure of which would constitute contempt of court[201]
- the private papers of Euro-MPs or members of local authorities or health boards or opinions, advice, recommendations or the results of consultations considered by the *Oireachtas* or its committees[202]
- records relating to law enforcement and public safety[203]
- records relating to security, defence and international relations[204]
- information obtained in confidence[205]
- commercially sensitive information[206]
- personal information[207]
- research and natural resources[208]
- the financial and economic interests of the state and public bodies[209]
- records the non-disclosure of which is authorized or required by any enactment.[210]

25.159 The provisions as to exempt records are detailed and complex and a variety of different tests are applied according to the subject matter. Some provide for an absolute exemption, requiring the head of the public body concerned to refuse access to the exempt record: see, for example, sections 22(1), 26(1)(b), and 32. Other records may be withheld if in the opinion of the head of the public body concerned, prejudice or an adverse effect or a significant adverse effect could reasonably be expected to result from disclosure: for example, prejudice to the effectiveness of audits or investigations conducted by the body,[211] prejudice or impairment to the prevention, detection or investigation of offences,[212] an adverse

---

[197] Section 19.
[198] Section 20.
[199] Section 21.
[200] Section 22(1)(a).
[201] Section 22(1)(b).
[202] Section 22(1)(c).
[203] Section 23.
[204] Section 24.
[205] Section 26.
[206] Section 27.
[207] Section 28.
[208] Section 30.
[209] Section 31.
[210] Section 32.
[211] Section 21(1)(a).
[212] Section 23(1)(a).

effect on the security, defence or international relations of the state or matters relating to Northern Ireland,[213] or a serious adverse effect on the financial interests of the state or the ability of the government to manage the national economy.[214] A number of provisions require the head of the public body concerned not to disclose whether or not a record exists where he is satisfied that the disclosure of the existence or non-existence of the record would be contrary to the public interest[215] or itself have a prejudicial or adverse effect.[216] Other sections contain a proviso disapplying the relevant exemption in a case where, in the opinion of the head of the public body concerned, the public interest would, on balance, be better served by granting than by refusing to grant the request.[217] In one case,[218] it is a precondition of the application of the exemption that the head of the public body should form the opinion that the granting of the request would actually be contrary to the public interest.

The Third Schedule to the Act contains a list of enactments prohibiting the disclosure of information which are excluded from the scope of section 32. These include certain sections of the Irish Official Secrets Act 1963. Section 48 of the Act provides that a person who is, or reasonably believes that he is authorized by the Act to disclose official information is deemed to be duly authorized to communicate that information for the purposes of the 1963 Act and it shall be a defence in a prosecution under those sections to prove that the act to which the charge relates is authorized, or is reasonably believed by the person charged to be authorized, by the Act.   **25.160**

Ministerial certificates

Ministers can issue certificates declaring that a record is an exempt record by virtue of the provisions relating to law enforcement and public safety or security, defence and international relations.[219] Before doing so, they are to be satisfied not just that the record is so exempt, but also that it is of sufficient sensitivity or seriousness to justify taking that step. Such a certificate has the effects that the record concerned is deemed conclusively to be an exempt record and that an application for a review of the decision to refuse the request for access to it shall not lie.[220] Notwithstanding the width of these provisions, there are various safeguards such as the powers of the *Taoiseach* and Ministerial colleagues to review and order the   **25.161**

---

213 Section 24(1).
214 Section 31(1)(a).
215 See ss 19(5) and 22(2).
216 See ss 23(2) and 24(3).
217 See ss 21(2), 23(3), 26(3), 27(3), 28(5), 30(2) and 31(3).
218 Section 20 (records containing matter relating to the deliberative processes of the public body concerned, including policy advice).
219 Section 25.
220 Section 25(3).

revocation of certificates,[221] the requirement that Ministers report annually to the Commissioner on the number of certificates issued by them,[222] and the fact that certificates only remain in force for two years (although they can be renewed).[223] There is also a right of appeal against a certificate to the High Court on a point of law.[224] Only two such certificates were issued in 2000 and one in 2001 and it appears that none had been issued prior to that.

Third parties

25.162 Where the head of a public body proposes to disclose information obtained in confidence, commercially sensitive information or personal information, there are provisions requiring an affected third party to be notified and given an opportunity to make submissions.[225]

Excluded records

25.163 Certain records are excluded from the scope of the Act.[226] These include:

- records held by the courts and certain kinds of tribunal
- records held or created by the Attorney-General or Director of Public Prosecutions or their offices
- records relating to reviews or investigations carried out by the Commissioner, the Ombudsman, or the Comptroller and Auditor-General
- records relating to the President
- records relating to the private papers of members of either House of the *Oireachtas*
- confidential official documents of either House
- records relating to information the disclosure of which could reasonably be expected to reveal the identity of persons who have given information about breaches of the criminal law.

25.164 Nor does the Act apply to records which are available for inspection by members of the public, or of which members of the public can obtain copies otherwise than under the Act.

The Information Commissioner and the courts

The Commissioner

25.165 The Act establishes the office of Information Commissioner.[227] The Commissioner is appointed by the President on the advice of the government following a

---

[221] Section 25(7) and (8).
[222] Section 25(11).
[223] Section 25(13).
[224] Section 42(2).
[225] Section 29.
[226] Section 46.
[227] Section 33(1).

resolution passed by both Houses of the *Oireachtas*.[228] The Act appears to envisage that the Ombudsman might also be Information Commissioner[229] and the first Commissioner has combined both roles.

The Commissioner can review decisions to refuse a request for access to a record **25.166** on the application of the requester.[230] Other classes of decision are also amenable to review by the Commissioner, including decisions to defer access (under section 11), extend time for considering a request (under section 9), give access in a form other than that requested (under section 12), or give access to part only of a record (under section 13). Where section 29 applies, the affected third party may apply to the Commissioner for a review of a decision to disclose. The review provisions also apply to unsuccessful applications under sections 17 and 18.[231] Any right to a review by the public body itself (under section 14) must have been exercised before application is made to the Commissioner. The Commissioner was asked to review the decisions on around 5% of requests at first, falling to around 3% by 2001.

The Commissioner has power to affirm, vary, or annul a decision; in the event of **25.167** annulment, he can substitute such decision as he considers proper.[232] A decision to refuse access under section 7 is presumed not to be justified unless the head of the public body concerned shows to the satisfaction of the Commissioner that it was, while a decision to grant a request to which section 29 applies is presumed to be justified unless the affected third party shows to the Commissioner's satisfaction that it was not.[233] However, the first Commissioner has interpreted his role as 'investigatory' in the sense that he is not confined simply to considering the arguments advanced to him by the parties, on the basis that in exercising the jurisdiction to substitute his own decision he must have regard to the provisions of the Act with a view to ensuring (among other things) that information which is properly exempt should not be disclosed.[234] In similar vein, he told the House of Lords Select Committee on the draft Freedom of Information Bill that he had had cases where the body resisting disclosure had made such a poor case to him that he had applied the Act more rigorously than they: 'I do not think I could get into a position where, because some department was more incompetent than another, information was being released which legitimately should not be released . . . there should be consistency'.[235]

---

228 Section 33(3).
229 Section 33(4) and (5).
230 Section 34.
231 See para 25.142 above.
232 Section 34(2)(b).
233 Section 34(12).
234 In his 1999 annual report.
235 HL Paper (1998–99) no 97, at p 73.

26.168 The Commissioner is also required to keep the operation of the Act under review and can carry out investigations into the practices and procedures adopted by public bodies generally or any particular public body or bodies for the purposes of complying with the Act[236] and enabling persons to exercise the rights conferred by it.[237] A mandatory general investigation had to be carried out within three years of the commencement of the Act.[238] The resulting report was published in July 2001. The Commissioner is required to report to Parliament on an annual basis.[239]

25.169 Section 37 confers on the Commissioner powers to require the production of records and information and to enter premises occupied by public bodies. Non-co-operation is a criminal offence. The procedure for conducting reviews and investigations is largely left to his discretion, but is to be 'as informal as is consistent with the due performance of his functions'.[240]

25.170 Where a public body does not give notice of a decision on a request for access to a record within the statutory time periods, an adverse decision is deemed made.[241] This enables a requester to apply for a review to the public body concerned, or to the Commissioner in the event of a further delay on its part.

Appeals to the High Court

25.171 An appeal lies to the High Court on a point of law from the decision made by the Commissioner on a review[242] or against the issue of a certificate under section 25 or a decision to refuse access to a record which is subject to such a certificate.[243] There are wider provisions for appeals from decisions made by the Commissioner in his capacity as the head of the Office of the Information Commissioner (which is, of course, a public body within the scope of the Act) in relation to records held by that office.[244] The Commissioner may also refer questions of law arising in a review being carried out by him to the High Court for determination.[245] The High Court's decision is final and conclusive.[246]

25.172 Both the Commissioner and the High Court are required to take all reasonable precautions to prevent the disclosure of information contained in an exempt record or, in a case where the Act requires the head of the public body concerned

---

[236] Section 36(1).
[237] Section 36(3).
[238] Section 36(2).
[239] Section 40(1).
[240] Section 36(6).
[241] Section 41.
[242] Section 42(1).
[243] Section 42(2).
[244] Section 42(3).
[245] Section 42(5).
[246] Section 42(8).

not to disclose whether or not a record exists, information as to whether or not a record exists.[247]

Decisions by a public body to disclose records affecting third parties are stayed **25.173** until the time for applying to the Commissioner for a review has expired or any such application has been determined. Similarly, decisions by the Commissioner on a review are stayed until the time for appealing to the High Court has expired or any appeal has been determined.[248]

Immunity from proceedings

Broadly speaking, the Act grants immunity from legal proceedings in respect of **25.174** disclosures of records or information or the furnishing of statements of reasons and findings pursuant to the Act (or which the head of the relevant public body reasonably believed to be required or authorized by the Act).[249]

E. The Netherlands

Introduction

Article 110 of the Dutch Constitution provides that in the exercise of their duties, **25.175** government bodies shall observe the right of public access to information in accordance with rules to be established by Act of Parliament.[250] The relevant Act at present is the Government Information (Public Access) Act of 1991, *Wet Openbaarheid van bestuur*. This Act replaced the Government Information (Public Access) Act of 1978. The 1991 Act made no material changes to the freedom of information regime, but implemented a recommendation that provisions made by regulations under the 1978 Act should appear in the statute itself.

The Government Information (Public Access) Act 1991 (hereafter 'the Act', **25.176** although commonly referred to in the Netherlands as 'the Wob') is divided into eight parts or chapters. Chapter I deals with definitions and identifies the administrative authorities to which the Act applies. Chapter II sets out the general right of public access to government information. Chapter III deals with procedural matters, including the manner in which applications for information and responses thereto should be made. Chapter IV sets out the information which bodies subject to the Act must provide voluntarily, and Chapter V contains exceptions to the general right of access. Chapter VI deals with miscellaneous matters

---

[247] Section 43.
[248] Section 44.
[249] Section 45.
[250] One of the recommendations of the Franken Committee on Fundamental Rights in the Digital Age is an amendment to the constitution to emphasize the importance of public access to information. To date no Bill has been introduced to implement this recommendation.

and the final two chapters are concerned with amendments, repeals and commencement.

25.177   The preamble to the Act states that it was passed 'in the interests of effective, democratic governance'. Administrative authorities subject to the Act have a duty to provide certain information on application (Chapter III, sections 3 to 7) and other information voluntarily (Chapter IV, sections 8 and 9).

25.178   The procedure for reviewing and appealing decisions is to be found not in the Act, but in the General Act on Administrative Law which came into force in 1994, *Algemene wet bestuursrecht Stb 1992, 315* (referred to in the Netherlands as 'the Awb', hereafter 'the Administrative Law Act').

Information to be supplied without request

25.179   The information which must be provided voluntarily by administrative authorities is specified in section 8 of the Act as information on the authority's policy and its preparation and implementation 'whenever the provision of such information is in the interests of effective, democratic governance'. The information should be supplied in a comprehensible form and in such a way as to reach as many interested members of the public as possible sufficiently early to enable them to make their views known to the authority in good time.

25.180   When an administrative body receives policy recommendations from independent advisory committees the recommendations, together with the requests for advice and proposals made to the committees, must be made public no more than four weeks after they have been received by the administrative body. Notice of publication should appear in the *Netherlands Government Gazette* or some other periodical made generally available by the government.[251]

The right of access

25.181   An application may be made for *information* contained in 'documents concerning an administrative matter'.[252] An 'administrative matter' is defined[253] as 'a matter of relevance to the policies of an administrative authority, including the preparation and implementation of such policies'. 'Document' means 'a written document or other material containing data which is deposited with an administrative authority'. This definition is wide enough to include electronic media. The right is unrestricted: anyone may apply.

---

[251]   Government Information (Public Access) Act 1991, s 9.
[252]   ibid, s 3.1.
[253]   Definitions appear in ibid, s 1.

Who must provide information?

The Act applies to Ministers and to government bodies including autonomous   **25.182**
government bodies known as ZBOs, the administrative authorities of provinces,
municipalities and regulatory industrial organizations,[254] and also to agencies or
companies carrying out work for which they are accountable to an administrative
authority.[255] It does not apply to Parliament or judicial bodies.

Applications and decisions

An applicant for information must identify the administrative matter or the   **25.183**
document relevant to the matter about which the information is sought.[256]
Applications need not be in writing. Where an application for information is
made in writing, but submitted to the wrong administrative authority, the recipient is obliged to forward the application to the appropriate authority. If in such a
case the application is made other than in writing, the applicant should be referred
to the appropriate authority.[257]

The decision reached in answer to an application may be given orally or in writ-   **25.184**
ing. If the application was made in writing, a refusal to disclose all or part of the
information sought must be communicated in writing. If the request was made
orally, the applicant may request written notification of a refusal to disclose all or
part of the information sought, and this option must be drawn to the applicant's
attention.[258]

The authority to which application is made is required to reach its decision on the   **25.185**
application at the earliest possible opportunity, and in any event not more than
two weeks after the date of receipt of the application. However, the authority may
take a further two-week period provided that the applicant is notified in writing
of the deferment before the initial two-week period has elapsed. Reasons for the
deferment must be given.[259]

Exceptions and restrictions

These appear in Chapter V, sections 10 and 11.   **25.186**

Absolute exemptions

There is an absolute exemption from disclosure of information where such dis-   **25.187**
closure might endanger the unity of the Crown or damage the security of the state,

---

[254] ibid, s 1a.
[255] ibid, s 3.1.
[256] ibid, s 3.2.
[257] ibid, s 4.
[258] ibid, s 5.
[259] ibid, s 6.

or where it would reveal data relating to companies and manufacturing processes which were furnished to the government in confidence by natural or legal persons.[260]

25.188 The Act also exempts from disclosure personal opinions on policy contained in documents drawn up for the purpose of internal consultation, unless they can be disclosed in a form which cannot be traced back to any individual and disclosure is in the interests of effective democratic governance, although with the agreement of those expressing the opinions such information may be provided in a form which can be traced back to individuals. In the case of a personal opinion on policy contained in the recommendations of a civil service or mixed advisory committee, the information concerning the opinion may be disclosed if the authority concerned informed the committee before its activities commenced that this would be done.[261]

Qualified exemptions

25.189 The Act sets out a broad range of matters which may outweigh the general interest in making the information public.[262] These include:

- relations between the Netherlands and other states or international organizations;
- the economic and financial interests of the state, other bodies constituted under public law or certain administrative bodies;
- the investigation of criminal offences and the prosecution of offenders;
- inspection, control and supervision by administrative authorities;
- respect for personal privacy;
- the prevention of disproportionate advantage or disadvantage to the natural or legal persons concerned or to third parties.

If the importance of the disclosure does not outweigh one of these matters, disclosure need not be made.

How the information is to be provided

25.190 Where information is to be provided in response to an application it may be provided in one of five ways,[263] namely by:

- providing a copy of the documents which contain the information required; or
- conveying the exact substance of the documents which contain the information required in some other form; or
- permitting the applicant to take a note of the contents of the documents; or

---

[260] Government Information (Public Access) Act 1991, s 10.1.
[261] ibid, s 11.
[262] ibid, s 10.2.
[263] ibid, s 7.

- supplying an extract from the documents or a summary of their contents; or
- supplying information contained in the documents.

In choosing between these methods, the authority is to take into account the applicant's preference and the importance of smooth, rapid procedure.

Charges

Public bodies may charge a fee which at state level is limited to the cost price of producing the medium of disclosure, *not* the cost of gathering the information or assessing the request. Up to 6 paper copies are free of charge, between 6 and 13 copies cost €4.50, and more than 14 copies are charged at €0.35 per copy. The fee for electronic files is the cost price of a disk or telephone charge.   **25.191**

Review and appeals

The Administrative Law Act sets out the procedure for objecting to or appealing against decisions reached under the Act. Before a court considers an appeal it is necessary first to lodge an objection to the decision with the administrative body responsible for the decision. This provides that body with an opportunity (and an obligation, provided certain criteria are met) to review its decision. Objection must be made within six weeks of the decision being announced in the prescribed manner. There is no fee for lodging an objection. Unless the objection is manifestly inadmissible or unfounded, the objector is entitled to a hearing. Where a hearing takes place the party raising the objection may file further information no later than ten days beforehand. There is no requirement for the hearing to be in public. Where practicable the review hearing should be undertaken by a party not involved in the original decision. A report is prepared on the hearing and a clear explanation is to be given of the reasons for the decision reached as a result of the hearing.[264]   **25.192**

Where an objector is not satisfied with the outcome of the review procedure, he may appeal to a judge in the district court. The time for appealing is six weeks from the decision on the notice of objection. It is the decision on the notice of objection which is reviewed by the judge, not the original decision. There is a fee for lodging the appeal: €109 for a natural person and €218 for a legal person. The fee may be refunded if the appeal is well founded. The next level of appeal is the Administrative Law Division of the Council of State, where the fee for lodging an appeal is €165 for a natural person and €327 for a legal person.   **25.193**

The future

The right of access to information under the Act is a right of access to information in documents concerning an *administrative matter*. The Dutch government has   **25.194**

---

[264] Administrative Law Act, chs 6 and 7.

indicated its intention to add a new article to the constitution to provide a right of access to '*government information*', thus extending the right beyond administrative matters (subject to appropriate exemptions).[265] To date no Bill has been introduced in this regard.

F. New Zealand

Legislation

25.195 The principal Act is the Official Information Act 1982 (as amended by Official Information Amendment Acts 1983, 1987 and 1993) which makes provision for access to information held by central government and other bodies established to carry out public functions. It applies to Ministers in their official capacity, government departments, and 'organizations', which are defined[266] as the bodies listed in the First Schedule to the 1982 Act and in Part II of the First Schedule to the Ombudsmen Act 1975. State-owned enterprises and Crown health enterprises[267] are subject to its provisions, as are the New Zealand police and the security intelligence service. The Local Government Official Information and Meetings Act 1987 makes particular provision (in very similar terms to the Official Information Act 1982) for access to information held by local authorities. In this chapter, only the Official Information Act 1982 ('the Act') is summarized.

25.196 The Privacy Act 1993 (as amended by Privacy Amendment Acts 1993, 1994, 1996, and 2000) deals (among other things) with requests by natural persons for information about themselves (which were previously dealt with as applications under the Act). The Protected Disclosures Act 2000 has specific provisions relating to whistle-blowing.

Background

25.197 The Official Secrets Act 1951 provided a presumption that official information would be secret unless specifically authorized for disclosure, and made it a criminal offence to communicate, fail to safeguard, or abuse official information. This secrecy of official information was subject to heavy criticism.

25.198 The impetus towards open government came from both local activism[268] and discussions in other jurisdictions (notably Britain, Australia and Canada). In 1977,

---

[265] Press Release of 18 May 2001 http:/www.minbzk.nl (21 August 2002).

[266] In the Official Information Act 1982, s 2.

[267] These were established in a process of reform beginning in the mid–1980s whereby certain functions previously carried out by the government were commercialized or, in some cases, privatized. Privatized bodies are not subject to the Act.

[268] In particular, the opposition of environmental activists to large scale development of natural resources highlighted the difficulty of obtaining official information.

a Freedom of Information Bill was tabled but lapsed after first reading. In 1978, the government established the Danks Committee to consider freedom of information issues.

The Danks Committee produced their report *Towards Open Government* in 1980, **25.199** followed in 1981 by a supplementary report. They firmly recommended a move towards more open government, which, they noted, encouraged public participation in the democratic process and promoted greater accountability for public servants. The Danks Committee produced a draft Bill, which became the Act.

The New Zealand legislation and its implementation seem to be generally **25.200** regarded as something of a success story. The New Zealand Law Commission produced an extensive report in 1997, declaring itself satisfied that, in general, the Act works relatively effectively to further its stated purposes.[269]

Structure of the Official Information Act 1982

The Act was divided into seven Parts entitled (I) Purposes and Criteria; (II) **25.201** Requests for Access to Official Information; (III) Publication of, and Access to, Certain Documents and Information; (IV) Right of Access to Personal Information; (V) Review of Decisions; (VI) Information Authority;[270] (VII) Miscellaneous Provisions.[271]

The notable features of the New Zealand legislation include (1) the principle of **25.202** availability, which is explicitly linked with an express purpose clause; (2) a consequential, flexible approach to exemptions; and (3) a right of application for review to the Ombudsmen.

Purpose

The Act has both a long title and a section expressing the purposes of the statute. **25.203** The long title reads:

> An Act to make official information more freely available, to provide for proper access by each person to official information relating to that person, to protect official information to the extent consistent with the public interest and the preservation of personal privacy, to establish procedures for the achievement of those purposes, and to repeal the Official Secrets Act 1951.

---

[269] New Zealand Law Commission, *Review of the Official Information Act 1982* (Law Com Report 40, 1997).

[270] The Information Authority (which had been set up to review the working of the Act and to consider whether the protections accorded by other statutes to official information were reasonable and compatible with the purposes of the Act) was dissolved and Part VI expired on 30 June 1988 pursuant to s 53.

[271] Part I is ss 4–11; Part II is ss 12–19; Part III is ss 20–23; Part IV is ss 24–27; Part V is ss 28–36; Part VI was ss 37–45; Part VII is ss 46–53.

The purposes of the Act are set out in section 4:

> Purposes—The purposes of this Act are, consistently with the principle of the
> Executive Government's responsibility to Parliament,—
>> (a) To increase progressively the availability of official information to the people
>> of New Zealand in order—
>>> (i) To enable their more effective participation in the making and adminis-
>>> tration of laws and policies; and
>>> (ii) To promote the accountability of Ministers of the Crown and offi-
>>> cials,—
> and thereby to enhance respect for the law and to promote the good government of
> New Zealand.
>> (b) To provide for proper access by each person to official information relating to
>> that person.
>> (c) To protect official information to the extent consistent with the public inter-
>> est and the preservation of personal privacy.

25.204 The section is striking in the emphasis that it places on the rationale for access to information, namely that it is both part of and advantageous to the democratic process. Further, although protection of official information is expressed to be a distinct purpose, that is an aim which is always limited by considerations of public policy and personal privacy.

Principle of availability

25.205 Section 5 sets out the principle of availability, namely, that the question of whether any official information is to be made available *shall be determined*, except where otherwise provided, *in accordance with the purposes of the Act* and the principle that the *information shall be made available unless there is good reason* for withholding it. This provision reverses the former presumption under the Official Secrets Act 1951 (which was repealed by the Act). It should also be noted that the point of reference for the Act is 'official information'[272] rather than 'documents' or 'records'.

Exemptions

25.206 A good reason for withholding information is established by showing either a conclusive reason within section 6 (or section 7) or another reason within section 9. A conclusive reason within section 6 (or section 7) is akin to an absolute exemp-

---

[272] 'Official information' is defined in s 2 by reference to various categories of information; 'information' is not defined. See *Commissioner of Police v Ombudsman* [1985] 1 NZLR 578, 586, *per* Jeffries J, 'Perhaps the most outstanding feature of the definition is that the word "information" is used which dramatically broadens the scope of the whole Act. The stuff of what is held by Departments, Ministers, or organizations is not confined to the written word but embraces any knowledge, however gained or held, by the named bodies in their official capacities. The omission, undoubtedly deliberate, to define the word "information" serves to emphasise the intention of the legislature to place few limits on relevant knowledge.'

tion whereas another reason within section 9 is akin to a qualified exemption, in that it is subject to a public interest test.

Section 6 provides that a good reason exists if the making available of the informa- **25.207** tion *would be likely to*:

(a) prejudice national security or defence or international relations;
(b) prejudice entrusting of confidential information to New Zealand by other countries or international organizations;
(c) prejudice the maintenance of law;
(d) endanger the safety of any person; or
(e) damage seriously the economy of New Zealand by prematurely disclosing decisions to change or continue government economic or financial policies.

Section 7 deals specifically with information relating to the Cook Islands, Tokelau, or Niue, or the Ross Dependency. In *Commissioner of Police v Ombudsman*[273] it was held that 'likely to' did not mean 'more likely than not' but was to be construed as meaning no more than a distinct or significant possibility.

Section 9 provides that good reason exists where the withholding of information **25.208** *is necessary to* achieve one of a number of listed aims *unless* the withholding of information is outweighed by *other considerations* which render it *desirable*, in the *public interest, to make that information available.* In *Television New Zealand Ltd v Ombudsman*[274] Heron J stated that (although not expressing any concluded view) he thought that, in the context, 'necessary' meant 'reasonably necessary' rather than 'strictly necessary'.

The listed aims are: **25.209**

(a) to protect the privacy of natural persons (including deceased natural persons);
(b) to protect information where the making available of the information would
    (i) disclose a trade secret; or
    (ii) be likely unreasonably to prejudice the commercial position of the person who supplied or who is the subject of the information;
(ba) to protect information which is subject to an obligation of confidence or which any person has been or could be compelled to provide under the authority of any enactment where the making available of the information would be likely—
    (i) to prejudice the supply of similar information, or information from the same source and it is in the public interest that such information should continue to be supplied; or

---

[273] [1988] 1 NZLR 385, CA.
[274] [1992] 1 NZLR 106, 118.

    (ii) otherwise to damage the public interest;

(c) to avoid prejudice to measures protecting the health or safety of members of the public;

(d) to avoid prejudice to the substantial economic interests of New Zealand;

(e) to avoid prejudice to measures that prevent or mitigate material loss to members of the public;

(f) to maintain the constitutional conventions for the time being which protect—

    (i) the confidentiality of communications by or with the Sovereign or her representative;

    (ii) collective and individual Ministerial responsibility;

    (iii) the political neutrality of officials;

    (iv) the confidentiality of advice tendered by Ministers and officials;

(g) to maintain the effective conduct of public affairs through—

    (i) the free and frank expression of opinions by or between or to Ministers or members of an organization or officers and employees of any department or organization in the course of their duty; or

    (ii) the protection of such Ministers, members of organizations, officers and employees from improper pressure or harassment;

(h) to maintain legal professional privilege;

(i) to enable a Minister or any department or organization holding the information to carry out, without prejudice or disadvantage, commercial activities;

(j) to enable a Minister or any department or organization holding the information to carry on, without prejudice or disadvantage, negotiations (including commercial and industrial negotiations);

(k) to prevent the disclosure or use of official information for improper gain or improper advantage.

25.210 The listed aims are noticeably widely drafted. The exemption provisions have been characterized as consequential rather than categorical. Their effect is that a holder of official information (or the Ombudsman[275]) must consider the full matrix of circumstances in deciding whether or not to withhold information. They reflect a conscious decision to retain flexibility:

> Judgments cannot, in our view, be properly and satisfactorily made all at one time by legislation. We were faced early in our work, with the choice of trying to design a once and for all static mechanism, with a complex set of exceptions, or a more flexible mechanism, operating by reference to principles and competing criteria that reflect a continuing shift away from a presumption of secrecy. We opted for a flexible process.[276]

---

[275] See para 25.223 below.
[276] Danks Committee 1980 report (see para 25.199 above).

The Committee recognized the possible pitfalls of this approach in potentially '[creating] a bureaucratic monster fed by the unreasonable antics of those seeking information and those seeking to deny it'.

By section 10, a department, Minister or organization to whom a request is made **25.211** may refuse to confirm or deny the existence of the information, if satisfied that (a) an exemption within section 6 (or section 7) or the exemption in section 9(2)(b) (trade secrets or confidential information) applies (or would apply if the information existed) and (b) the interest protected by the relevant exemption would be *likely to be prejudiced* by the disclosure of the existence or non-existence of the information.

Requests for access to official information

Part II deals with requests for information. A request can be made not only by a **25.212** New Zealand citizen or body corporate, but also by a permanent resident of New Zealand, or any person who is in New Zealand, or by a foreign body corporate which has a place of business in New Zealand: section 12. The information sought is to be specified with due particularity. By section 12(1A), any request by a natural person for information about himself is deemed to be a request under the Privacy Act 1993 (which extends to requests for information held in the private, in addition to the public, sector) and is to be dealt with exclusively under that Act.

The department, Minister or organization to whom the request is made must **25.213** decide whether to grant it, and notify the person who made the request of that decision, as soon as reasonably practicable and in any case within 20 working days.[277] A failure to respond within the time allowed, or undue delay in making the information available thereafter, is deemed to be a refusal to make it available for the purposes of section 28, triggering the Ombudsmen's powers of investigation and review.

A request can only be refused in one of a number of specified circumstances,[278] **25.214** most importantly (a) if there is a good reason for withholding disclosure within sections 6, 7 or 9. The other reasons for refusal are:
(b) that, by virtue of section 10, the department, Minister or organization does not confirm or deny the existence or non-existence of the information requested;
(c) that the making available of the information requested would—
  (i) be contrary to the provisions of a specified enactment; or

---

[277] Official Information Act 1982, s 15. Section 15A provides for an extension of the time limits in certain circumstances, broadly speaking where the request is for a large quantity of information or necessitates searches or consultations which cannot reasonably be carried out within them.
[278] Section 18.

    (ii) constitute contempt of court or of the House of Representatives;

(d) that the information requested is or will soon be publicly available;

(e) that the document alleged to contain the information requested does not exist or cannot be found;

(f) that the information requested cannot be made available without substantial collation or research;

(g) that the information requested is not held by that department, Minister or organization and the person dealing with the request has no grounds for believing that the information is either

    (i) held by another department, Minister or organization or a local authority, or

    (ii) connected more closely with the functions of another department, Minister or organization or of a local authority;[279]

(h) that the request is frivolous or vexatious or that the information requested is trivial.

25.215 Section 18(f) and 18(h) recognizes that there are situations where the administrative burdens of providing information outweigh the aims of access to information.[280]

> The granting of access to official information, even information which of its nature clearly need not be withheld, cannot be an absolute priority to which all other functions of administration must yield. Especially in times of financial and staff restraints on government activities, some limitation of the resources available for providing information to members of the public is inevitable.

25.216 Reason(s) for refusal must be given (unless the existence of the information is being neither confirmed nor denied under section 10).[281] If a request is refused for a good reason within sections 6, 7 or 9, the person dealing with the request must, if requested to do so by the applicant, notify him of the grounds in support of the reason(s) and in the case of section 9 the grounds on which it is said that there is no countervailing public interest.[282]

25.217 Section 15(1A) and (3) empowers Ministers, departments and organizations to charge for the supply of official information under the Act, and to require payment in advance. Such charges must be 'reasonable'.[283] Decisions about charging are subject to review by the Ombudsmen.

---

[279] The existence of such a belief would trigger a duty to transfer the request to such other Minister, department, organization or local authority: s14.

[280] Danks Committee supplementary report 1981 (see para 25.199 above).

[281] Section 19.

[282] Section 19(a)(ii). The person dealing with the request can refuse to give the grounds, if the giving of the grounds would, of itself, prejudice the protected interest.

[283] Section 15(2).

Publication of, and access to, certain documents and information

Section 20 provides for the compulsory publication by the State Services **25.218**
Commission in respect of every department and organization of a description of
its structure and functions; a description of the categories of documents held by
it; a description of all manuals and the like which contain policies, rules and
guidelines in accordance with which its decisions are made; and a statement showing how members of the public can request official information from it. By
section 21, a person is entitled to be given access to this information, without
qualification.

Section 22 provides for a right of access to any document which contains policies, **25.219**
principles, rules or guidelines in accordance with which decisions or recommendations are made in respect of any person or body of persons in his or its personal
capacity. This information can only be withheld for a good reason under the provisions of sections 6, 7 and some parts of section 9.[284] Subject to section 10,
reasons must be given for refusal, and if requested, grounds in support of those
reasons.

Section 23 provides a right of access for a person affected by a decision or recom- **25.220**
mendation of a department, Minister or organization to the reasons for it. This
information can only be withheld for a good reason under the provisions of sections 6, 7 or 9(2)(b).[285]

Right of access to personal information

Part IV of the Act used to provide both natural persons and bodies corporate with **25.221**
a right of access to personal information[286] about themselves which was held by a
department, Minister or organization.[287] Since the enactment of the Privacy Act
1993, however, all requests by natural persons for information about themselves
are dealt with under that Act; a body corporate may still take advantage of the provisions of Part IV of the Official Information Act 1982. A Part IV request can be
refused only in specified circumstances, most importantly if (a) the disclosure
would be likely to prejudice any of the interests protected by section 6(a) to (d), section 7 or section 9(2)(b)[288] (and, in the case of an interest under section 9(2)(b)
there is no countervailing public interest in favour of disclosure). The other
grounds for refusal are:[289]

---

[284] Where the withholding of information is necessary to (a) protect the privacy of any person;
(b) protect a trade secret or confidential information; (i) enable a Minister, department or organization to carry out, without prejudice or disadvantage, commercial activities; or (j) enable a Minister,
department or organization to carry on, without prejudice or disadvantage, negotiations.

[285] Trade secrets or confidential information.

[286] Meaning information from which an individual is identifiable: s 2.

[287] Section 24 created the right.

[288] Trade secrets or confidential information.

[289] Section 27: grounds (d)–(f) have been repealed.

(b) the disclosure of the information would involve the unwarranted disclosure of the affairs of another person or of a deceased person; or

(c) the disclosure of the information or of information identifying the person who supplied it, being evaluative material, would breach an express or implied promise—

(i) which was made to the person who supplied the information; and

(ii) which was to the effect that the information or the identity of the person who supplied it or both would be held in confidence; or

(g) the disclosure of the information would breach legal professional privilege; or

(h) the request is frivolous or vexatious, or the information requested is trivial.

25.222   Part IV also provides a body corporate given access under section 24 to personal information held by a department, Minister or organization which it believes is inaccurate, or incomplete and misleading, a right to request that it be corrected (section 26).

Complaint to Ombudsmen

25.223   Part V provides for a right of complaint to the Ombudsmen in relation to a decision under Part II or a notice under section 10 of the Act. The Ombudsmen are appointed by the New Zealand Parliament. Their primary purpose is to inquire into complaints raised against New Zealand central, regional and local government organizations or agencies. They are independent review authorities and are accountable to Parliament, not the government of the day.[290] The Ombudsmen have various investigatory powers under the Ombudsmen Act and the Official Information Act 1982, including the right under section 29A of the Act to require a department, Minister or organization to produce information or documents relating to an inquiry into a complaint. On completion of an investigation, the Ombudsman may make a recommendation as to whether the information should be disclosed.[291]

25.224   A department, Minister or organization is under a 'public duty' to comply with the recommendation of the Ombudsman[292] (in the rare case of non-compliance with that public duty, it is usual for the Solicitor-General to institute proceedings). However, the Cabinet, collectively, may override the Ombudsman's recommendation by Order in Council;[293] if it does so the Order in Council must be published in the *Gazette* and laid before Parliament as soon as practicable, with

---

[290] Ombudsmen Act 1975. There are now three Ombudsmen, currently Sir Brian Elwood, CBE, Judge Anand Satyanand and Mel Smith.

[291] Official Information Act 1982, s 30.

[292] Section 32.

[293] The collective veto was introduced in place of the previous system of veto by individual Ministers by the Official Information Amendment Act 1987.

reasons and grounds in support of those reasons.[294] These must be reasons which were relied on before the Ombudsman; new ones cannot be introduced at this stage. If an Order in Council is made, it can be subject to a judicial review (and appeal, thereafter, to the Court of Appeal) at the instance of the person making the request.[295]

A person may seek judicial review of a decision as to the disclosure or non-disclosure of information, but only after the Ombudsman has made a recommendation.[296] It has been judicially recognized that it is only in the rarest of cases that the court should intervene. **25.225**

> Parliament delegated to the Chief Ombudsman tasks, which at times are complex and even agonising, with no expectation that the Courts would sit on his shoulder about those judgments which are essentially balancing exercises involving competing interests. The Courts will only intervene when the Chief Ombudsman is plainly and demonstrably wrong, and not because he preferred one side against another.[297]

The Ombudsmen may also investigate decisions under Parts III and IV and make recommendations to the appropriate department or Minister or organization. If no adequate action is taken, the Ombudsmen may further report to the Prime Minister.[298] **25.226**

G. Sweden

The origins of the right of free access to information

The Kingdom of Sweden may justifiably claim to have led the world in the field of freedom of information. Swedish citizens have enjoyed access to official documents and information on administrative matters since 1766.[299] **25.227**

The right of free access to information lies at the heart of the Swedish Constitution. Chapter 2 of the Instrument of Government lays down the fundamental rights of every Swedish citizen. Article 1 of that Chapter provides that: **25.228**

> Every citizen shall be guaranteed the following rights and freedoms in his relations with the public institutions . . .
>
> 2. freedom of information: that is, the freedom to procure and receive information and otherwise acquaint oneself with the utterances of others.

---

[294] Section 32A.
[295] Sections 32B and 32C.
[296] Section 34.
[297] *Wyatt Co (NZ) Ltd v Queenstown-Lakes District Council* [1991] 2 NZLR 180, 191, *per* Jeffries J.
[298] Section 35.
[299] With the exception of the years 1772–1774 and 1792–1810.

25.229 The fundamental constitutional principle of freedom of information is reinforced and developed in Chapter 2 of the Freedom of the Press Act 1949 ('the 1949 Act') which is entitled 'On the public nature of official documents'. The 1949 Act forms one of Sweden's four fundamental laws. These are:

- the Instrument of Government
- the Act of Succession
- the Freedom of the Press Act
- the Fundamental Law on Freedom of Expression.

These laws serve as a basis for how Sweden is ruled.

25.230 The 1949 Act runs to a total of 14 Chapters and is concerned, primarily, with guaranteeing freedom of speech. That Act has been variously amended, the last occasion being 1998. It has to be read in conjunction with the Secrecy Act 1980[300] ('the Secrecy Act'), a separate 'special act of law' which establishes the exceptions to the principle of free access to information. When taken together the two Acts establish the three basic principles which may be identified as common to freedom of information legislation in most jurisdictions. These are:

- the right of the citizen to disclosure of official information
- material which it is deemed necessary, in the public interest, should remain secret is exempt from disclosure
- there is machinery for appealing against the refusal of officials to supply information.

The Freedom of the Press Act 1949

The overriding principle

25.231 Article 1 of Chapter 2 of the 1949 Act establishes the essential right of Swedish citizens to access to official documents. The Article, which consists of a single sentence, provides:

> To encourage the free exchange of opinion and availability of comprehensive information, every Swedish citizen shall be entitled to have free access to official documents.

The remainder of Chapter 2 is concerned with defining the extent and limits of the right.

Who may have access?

25.232 The terms of Article 1 appear to restrict the right of access to official documents to those who are Swedish citizens. However, Article 5 of Chapter 14 of the Act (which is entitled 'General Provisions') provides that 'Except as otherwise pro-

---

[300] Swedish Code of Statutes 1980:100.

vided in this Act or elsewhere in law, foreign nationals shall be equated with Swedish Citizens'. Thus, despite the words of Article 1, the right of free access to official documents is open to everyone. In any event, there is no obligation on an individual who seeks access to official documents in Sweden to identify him or herself (unless the document falls within a class governed by the Secrecy Act, in which case the authority is entitled to seek sufficient information to determine whether the document should be released[301]) and therefore there exists no power for officials to determine the nationality of an applicant before deciding whether the material in question should be released.

What is an 'official document'?

The definition of 'document' is to be found in Article 3 of Chapter 2 of the 1949 **25.233** Act: 'any written or pictorial matter or recording which may be read, listened to, or otherwise comprehended only using technical aids'. This definition of what constitutes a document may be compared favourably with the broad definition of 'information' to be found in section 84 of the United Kingdom Freedom of Information Act 2000. The width of the definition appears to bring the potentially restrictive right of 'free access to official *documents*' found in Article 1 into line with the constitutional principle of 'freedom of *information*: that is, the freedom to procure and receive *information*'.

Guidance on the operation of the 1949 Act and its sister legislation, the Secrecy **25.234** Act, published by the Swedish Ministry of Justice gives the word 'document' a generous interpretation as follows:

> a presentation in writing or images but also a recording that one can read listen to or comprehend in another way only by means of technical aids. The word 'document' consequently refers not only to paper and writing or images but also, for example, to a tape recording or an EDP [electronic data processing] recording. One can say that a document is an object which contains information of some kind.[302]

A 'document' is 'official' if it is held by a public authority or is deemed, by Articles **25.235** 6 and 7 of the Chapter, to have been received or drawn up by that authority. What constitutes a 'public authority' for these purposes is not defined in the Act. However, Article 5 of the Chapter states that the *Riksdag* (the Swedish Parliament) and any local government assembly having decision-making powers is to be 'equated' with a public authority for the purposes of the freedom of information legislation.

Where a document falls within the category of a 'recording' for the purposes of **25.236** Article 3 it is deemed to be held by the public authority in question if it is available

---

[301] See the Swedish Ministry of Justice publication, *The Right of Access to Official Documents in Sweden*.

[302] The Swedish Ministry of Justice, *Public Access to Information and Secrecy with Swedish Authorities* (2000), ch 2.1.

to the authority using technical aids (which the authority itself uses) for communication in such form that it may be read, listened to or otherwise comprehended. Thus a 'document' created in electronic form is an 'official document' if the authority in question has and uses the software for displaying that document, but not otherwise. This is so whether or not the public authority holds that information on its own computer systems or has access to it through some form of computer connection.

25.237 There is excluded from this definition any 'recording' which forms part of a register of persons if, because of any law, statutory instrument or 'special decision taken by virtue of law', the authority is not entitled to make that communication public. In this context a 'register of persons' is to be understood as meaning any 'register, list or other record containing information concerning a private person which can be related back to any person'.

25.238 This safeguard has proved necessary in light of the Swedish experience. While the doctrine of openness in the Swedish Constitution may be praised, it has been suggested that organs of the state have tended to collect significant amounts of data on individual citizens, an endeavour assisted by the fact that each Swedish citizen has an official 10-digit 'person number' enabling information on individuals to be obtained and recorded with ease.[303] It has been reported anecdotally that the openness of the system and the ease with which information relating to an individual might be traced has led to abuse, with information on the health and tax positions of individuals being obtained by others. In one instance the government agreed to waive the usual restrictions on access to health and criminal records to enable a social research project, entitled Project Metropolitan, to be carried out by sociologists in Stockholm. As a result the researchers were able to compile a detailed record of information relating to 15,000 citizens each of whom could be identified by their 'person number'. The researchers were subsequently instructed by the Data Inspection Board to depersonalize their findings.[304]

25.239 By virtue of Article 4 there is included in the definition of an 'official document' any letter or communication addressed to the holder of an office in an authority provided that the communication relates to matters falling within the remit of the authority. However, the document will not be an 'official document' if it is sent to the office-holder only in his capacity as the holder of some other position. An example of this distinction is given by the Ministry of Justice in its guidance: a document received by a public official (such as an elected councillor or trade union representative serving on a municipal board) which relates to the activities of the authority in question will not be an official document where it is received

---

[303] *Disclosure of Official Information—A report on overseas practice* (HMSO, London, 1979).
[304] *International Herald Tribune*, 13 March 1986.

by the individual in question exclusively in his or her capacity as a politician or trade unionist.[305]

Articles 6 and 7 of Chapter 2 of the 1949 Act contain deeming provisions in **25.240** respect of the receipt and drawing up of official documents for the purpose of determining when they become subject to the right of inspection.

Under Article 6 a document is deemed to have been received by the public author- **25.241** ity when it is received by them or when it reaches the hands of a competent offi- cial. Where the document is a 'recording' as defined by Article 3 the document is received when it has been made available to the authority 'in such form that it may be read, listened to or otherwise comprehended'. However, to avoid obvious problems of commercial confidentiality tender documents delivered under a sealed cover are not deemed received until the time appointed for their opening.

Article 7 is designed to protect policy guidance, draft documents and work in **25.242** progress. By virtue of that article a document is only deemed to have been drawn up (and thus to be an 'official document' within the meaning of Article 1) in the following circumstances:

- when it has been despatched by the authority
- when the matter or case to which it relates has been finally settled by the author- ity
- if the document does not relate to a particular matter or case, when the docu- ment has been finally checked and approved by the authority or has otherwise received final form.

A document is also deemed to have been drawn up in the following circum- **25.243** stances:

- in the case of day-books, ledgers and registers or lists kept on an ongoing basis, when the document is ready for entry or registration in the ledger, list or register
- in the case of court or other decisions which require to be despatched or pronounced as a matter of law (together with related documents), when the decision is pronounced or despatched
- in the case of other records or memoranda held by a public authority, when the document has been finally checked and approved or has otherwise received final form.

In an attempt to ensure that advice given to politicians and public officials **25.244** remains confidential, there is specifically excluded from this last category of doc- uments deemed to have been drawn up the records of *Riksdag* (Parliamentary) committees, Parliamentary and local authority auditors, state commissions and

---

[305] Swedish Ministry of Justice (n 302 above) ch 2.1.

local authorities where these relate solely to the preparation of a matter for decision.

25.245 As part of the protection for advice and work in progress, Article 9 exempts from the definition of 'official documents' all memoranda which have been prepared at a public authority but not yet despatched notwithstanding that, by virtue of Article 7, they would otherwise be deemed to have been 'drawn up', unless the memorandum in question has been accepted for filing and registration. 'Memorandum' in this context means any 'aide memoire or note or recording produced solely for the preparation or oral presentation of a matter', but excluding any factual information within it. Similarly, preliminary outlines or drafts of decisions or official communications of a public authority (together with other like documents) do not fall within the category of documents which have been 'drawn up'.

25.246 In the case of associated or connected public bodies, Article 8 excludes from the definition of 'official documents' documents passed between them unless they act as separate entities from one another.

What documents are exempt from disclosure?

25.247 Like freedom of information legislation in other jurisdictions, Sweden's Freedom of the Press Act exempts from disclosure certain categories of document. Article 2 of Chapter 2 of the Act defines the seven categories of document the right of access to which:

> may be restricted only if restriction is necessary having regard to:
> - the security of the Realm or its relations with another state or international organization;
> - the central fiscal, monetary or currency policy of the Realm;
> - the inspection, control or other supervisory activities of a public authority;
> - the interest of preventing or prosecuting crime;
> - the economic interest of public institutions;
> - the protection of the personal or economic circumstances of private subjects;
> - the preservation of animal or plant species.

25.248 However, these provisions state only the broad categories of documents which may be made subject to an exemption from disclosure. In order for a document to be exempt from the obligations imposed by the 1949 Act further provision has to be made.

> Any restriction of the right of access to official documents shall be scrupulously specified in the provisions of a special act of law, or, if this is deemed more appropriate in a particular case, in another act of law to which the special act of law refers. With authority in such provisions, the Government may however issue more precise provisions for its application in a statutory instrument.[306]

---

[306] 1949 Act, Ch 2, Art 2.

The special act of law referred to is the Secrecy Act.

Article 11 of Chapter 2 of the 1949 Act also defines certain categories of docu- **25.249**
ments which are exempt from disclosure by reason of their being deemed not to
be 'official documents'. These are:

(1) letters, telegrams, and other such documents delivered to or drawn up by a public authority solely for the purpose of forwarding a communication;

(2) notices or other documents delivered to or drawn up by a public authority solely
for the purpose of publication in a periodical published under the auspices of the
authority;

(3) printed matter, recordings of sound or pictures, or other documents forming
part of a library or deposited by a private person in a public archive solely for the
purpose of care and safe keeping, or for research and study purposes, and private
letters, written matter or recordings otherwise surrendered to a public authority
solely for the purposes referred to above;

(4) recordings of the contents of documents under point 3, if such recordings are
held by a public authority, where the original document would not be deemed
to be an official document.

The operation of the Secrecy Act

The Secrecy Act runs to 16 Chapters and governs all secrecy in public activities. It **25.250**
is a consolidating measure which replaces the previous Secrecy Act of 1937 and
regulations governing the duties of confidentiality owed by those working within
state or municipal bodies. However, the Act does not legislate in respect of secrecy
in court proceedings. The question of when a court can sit in camera is governed
by the Code of Judicial Procedure.[307]

The Secrecy Act imposes upon all public authorities a duty to observe secrecy in **25.251**
accordance with its terms. As in the Freedom of the Press legislation no definition
of 'public authority' is given. However, state and municipal decision-making
bodies such as the *Riksdag* and county councils and municipal assemblies are again
equated with public authorities for this purpose.[308] Private individuals and companies are also to be treated as public authorities where they carry out public functions. So, for example, notaries public are treated as public authorities for the
purposes of the Act, as is the Swedish Motor Vehicle Inspection Company.[309]

Individuals in public service or who are undertaking public service duties (such as **25.252**
those undergoing compulsory military service) are also subject to the duties of
secrecy imposed by the Secrecy Act. As might be expected the duty of secrecy is a
continuing obligation after employment in the public service has ceased.

---

[307] The Swedish Code of Judicial Procedure: Ds 1998:65: Part 1, Chapter 5.
[308] As they are for the purposes of the 1949 Act by virtue of Article 5 of Chapter 2 of that Act.
[309] Swedish Ministry of Justice (n 302 above) ch 3.2.2.

25.253   The obligation of secrecy imposed by the Secrecy Act involves a prohibition on the disclosure of information, whether orally, in writing or in any other way. The effect of the Act is two-fold: it both restricts the right of the public to have access to certain official information and forbids public officials from making that information public. Where an obligation of secrecy is imposed in respect of a document or category of documents, the Secrecy Act prohibits that information being made available to individuals except where the Act permits it. The Act also operates to prevent the sharing of such information between or within public authorities except in those cases where the Act permits it.

25.254   It is a criminal offence to breach the provisions of the Secrecy Act. Article 3 of Chapter 20 of the Swedish Penal Code[310] creates an offence of 'breach of professional confidentiality' and provides:

> A person who discloses information which he is duty-bound by Law or other statutory instrument or by order or provision issued under a Law or statutory instrument to keep secret, or if he unlawfully makes use of such secret, he shall, if the act is not otherwise specially subject to punishment, be sentenced for breach of professional confidentiality to a fine or imprisonment for at most one year. A person who through carelessness commits an act described in the first paragraph shall be sentenced to a fine. In petty cases, however, punishment shall not be imposed. (Law 1980:102).

25.255   Where an obligation of secrecy applies to a category of documents by virtue of the Secrecy Act, it may be either an absolute obligation or a conditional obligation. The imposition of a conditional obligation of secrecy depends upon there being some stated risk of damage or harm arising if the information is disclosed. In turn the requirement of damage may be stated as 'straight' or 'reverse'.

25.256   In cases falling within the 'straight requirement of damage' category of conditional secrecy, the documents in question will not be subject to secrecy unless it can be assumed that their release will cause damage to the individual or organization in question. Conversely, where a class of documents is subject to a 'reverse requirement of damage', their release is presumed to be harmful unless the contrary can be shown. So, for example, in cases of occupational injury or partial pensions insurance:

> Secrecy shall apply to matters concerning occupational injury insurance or partial pension insurance for information concerning an individual's business or operational circumstances, if it can be assumed that disclosure of the information would cause damage to the individual.

Whereas, in cases involving social services:

> Secrecy applies within the social services to information concerning an individual's personal circumstances, unless it is manifestly evident that the information may be disclosed without the individual or a person closely related to him being harmed.

---

[310] The Swedish Penal Code: Ds 1999:36.

The period of secrecy imposed in respect of a document or class of documents **25.257**
may be between 2 and 70 years, depending on the nature of the interest which
requires to be protected. By way of example the Swedish Ministry of Justice, in its
guidance on this area of the law, suggests that the secrecy period will usually be one
of 50 to 70 years where the personal affairs of an individual are in issue, and 20
years where a public or private individual's financial circumstances are involved.[311]

Gaining access to official documents

The procedural provisions relating to access to official documents are to be found **25.258**
in Articles 12 to 14 of Chapter 2 of the 1949 Act. To assist the public to gain access
to information, public authorities are required to maintain a register of official
documents.[312] However, the fact that a document does not yet appear in the
register will not prevent it being an 'official document' for the purposes of the
legislation.

Article 12 provides for an official document to which the public has access to be **25.259**
made available, on request, 'forthwith' or 'as soon as possible' at the place where it
is held. Access to the document is to be provided free of charge to any person wishing to examine it 'in such form that it can be read, listened to, or otherwise comprehended'. A document may be copied, reproduced, or used for sound
transmission. Where the original document cannot be made available without
disclosing those parts of it which constitute classified material, the authority is
entitled to give disclosure by means of a transcript or copy of the unclassified
parts.

The public authority is relieved of the obligation to make the document available **25.260**
at the place where it is held where to do so would present 'serious difficulty'. This
imprecise exception is nowhere defined in the Act.

Article 13 provides that a person who wishes to examine an official document may **25.261**
obtain a transcript or copy of that document on payment of a fixed fee.[313]
However, the authority is not bound to release a recording for automatic data processing except in the form of a printout. An authority is obliged to deal with a
request for a transcript or copy of an official document 'promptly'.

A request to inspect an official document is to be made to the authority which **25.262**
holds the document and the request is to be considered by that authority: see
Article 14. Ordinarily the request for inspection will be made, in the first instance,
to the Registrar responsible for maintaining the public register of official

---

[311] Swedish Ministry of Justice (n 302 above) ch 3.3.3.
[312] Secrecy Act, Ch 15.
[313] Where the document does not exceed nine pages in length, the authority is bound to provide
a copy free of charge: *The Right of Access to Official Documents in Sweden* (n 301 above).

documents within the public authority in question. Where the Registrar refuses to disclose the document the application may be referred to the authority in question for a decision whether it should be released.

25.263   However, by virtue of the enabling provisions of paragraph 2 of Article 2 in respect of the categories of documents potentially excluded from disclosure, provision may be made by statutory instrument for another authority to consider and approve any request to examine an official document which falls within one of the exemptions. In the case of documents relating to national security, Article 14 permits provision to be made by statutory instrument for a particular authority to have exclusive jurisdiction in determining whether those documents may be released.

25.264   The remainder of Article 14 prohibits an authority from inquiring into the identity of a person seeking disclosure of an official document. Nor may the authority inquire into the purpose of the request unless the document falls within one of the categories of exemption from disclosure set out in Article 2 of Chapter 2 of the 1949 Act. In such case the authority may enquire into the identity of the applicant and the purpose for which he requires the document only to such extent as is necessary to establish whether there is any obstacle to its release.

25.265   An authority to which an application is made for disclosure of a document falling within an exemption may nevertheless agree to release that document subject to conditions or 'reservations'. Those reservations may restrict the use to which the applicant may put the information. The imposition of a reservation is as much subject to a right of appeal as an outright refusal to supply the document.

The right of appeal against a refusal to disclose

25.266   In common with other jurisdictions, the Swedish legislation on freedom of information provides for a right of appeal against the refusal of a public authority to give access to an official document. Article 15 of Chapter 2 of the 1949 Act provides:

> Should anyone other than the *Riksdag* or the Government reject a request to examine an official document, or release such a document with a proviso restricting the applicant's right to disclose its contents or otherwise dispose of it, the applicant may appeal against the decision.

25.267   Where the decision to refuse access to a document is made by a government minister, any appeal is lodged with the government and may ultimately be determined by the Cabinet. Where the refusal to disclose is that of another authority, an appeal is lodged with 'a court of law'. Under the Swedish legal system the appeal falls to be determined within the distinct administrative court system. An appeal will be lodged with the first instance county administrative courts (the *Länsrätter*). The *Länsrätter* generally consists of a legally qualified judge assisted by three lay assessors. An appeal against the decision of that court may be made to one of four administrative courts of appeal (the *Kammarrätter*). Ordinarily a 'special permission of appeal' is required to appeal to the *Kammarrätter*. The court of final appeal for administrative matters is the *Regeringsrätten*, or Supreme Administrative Court.

A continuing commitment to free access to information

The commitment of the Swedish government to ensuring free access to official information has not, it seems, been dimmed by the passage of time since the enactment of the original Freedom of the Press Act 1766. The rights enshrined in the Swedish Constitution by the 1949 Act continue to be regarded by the government of Sweden as being of fundamental importance to Swedish society. As recently as November 2000 the Swedish Ministry of Justice published a factsheet setting out a summary of its submissions to the European Commission on free access to information held by EU institutions[314] in which it was said: **25.268**

> For more than two centuries Swedish Citizens have enjoyed the right of access to official documents. Sweden believes that this right is vital in a modern democracy. Democracy requires public participation in informed discussions on matters of common public interest. It also demands that citizens have the means to exercise control over the administration in order to promote its efficiency and deter corruption. A democracy must therefore ensure openness within the public administration and guarantee the right of public access to official information.

The publication of the Ministry of Justice paper in which the Swedish government set out its concerns about the proposed EU Regulation governing access to EU documents coincided with the introduction of the Swedish government's 'Open Sweden' campaign, a government initiative designed to ensure 'better transparency in Swedish public administration and a vitalised communication between the public institutions and the citizens'.[315] **25.269**

The 'Open Sweden' initiative stemmed from a perception held by journalists, trade unions, professional organizations and the Swedish public at large that, despite the longevity of Swedish freedom of information legislation, there was a general lack of knowledge of both the principle of public access to official information and its practical application. The campaign was intended to heighten awareness on the part of the public and the civil service of the right of the Swedish citizen to access to public documents, a right which the government described as being 'one of the cornerstones of a democratic society'. **25.270**

---

[314] The Swedish Ministry of Justice, *The Swedish Approach to Public Access to Documents*, Article no Ju 00.14e (November 2000).
[315] Quoted from the Swedish contribution to the OECD report *Strengthening Government–Citizen Connections* (June 2001).

25.271 The objectives of the 'Open Sweden' campaign were:

- to achieve a better application of the public access to information principle
- to increase openness within the public sector
- to cultivate public knowledge and awareness
- to encourage involvement and debate.

The campaign was targeted at civil servants throughout the public sector to encourage greater openness from bureaucrats as well as informing the general public about their rights.

25.272 In the paper which was submitted by the Swedish government to the OECD and forms part of the OECD report *Strengthening Government–Citizen Connections* published in June 2001, the Swedish government suggested three criteria which demonstrate the proper application of the principle of open access to public documents. These are:

- that managers and civil servants are accessible, generous in providing information and have a good knowledge of the regulations;
- that information is easy to find and written in a clear and easy-to-read language;
- that work-place organization and routines support easy access to information.

25.273 The autonomy of Swedish public institutions prevented the initiative from being imposed by central government on its own agencies and on local government. Participation in the campaign by public sector organizations was necessarily voluntary. Nevertheless the Swedish government was able to report to the OECD in June 2001 that within one year of the start of the campaign 230 out of a possible 400 government bodies had joined in the initiative.

25.274 The 'Open Sweden' campaign drew to a close on 30 June 2002, by when it was hoped to have established 'genuine development processes within the public institutions that will continue for a long time, raising the general level of "openness" '.

H. The United States

Introduction

25.275 Though the primary statute is the Freedom of Information Act 1966,[316] the American concern with keeping a watchful eye on the agencies of government is long established. 'The generation that made the nation thought secrecy in government one of the instruments of Old World tyranny and committed itself to the principle that a democracy cannot function unless the people are permitted to

---

[316] US Code, Title 5, s 552.

know what their government is up to'.[317] Prior to the 1966 Act the operative statute was the Administrative Procedure Act 1946, which, though it represented a major advance towards open government, established rights and remedies in a narrowly circumscribed form. In particular it provided (by section 3) that 'matters of official record shall . . . be made available to persons properly or directly concerned . . .', and (by section 10) that any 'person suffering legal wrong because of any agency action, or adversely affected or aggrieved by such action within the meaning of any relevant statute, shall be entitled to judicial review thereof'.

The Freedom of Information Act 1966 ('the Act') has been amended several times.[318] The greatest changes were made by the Electronic Freedom of Information Act Amendments 1996, which are considered in paragraphs 25.289 to 25.295 below. The Privacy Act 1974 and other related statutes are briefly discussed in paragraphs 25.303 to 25.313 below. **25.276**

The Act provides that 'any person' (not limited to US citizens or to the 'properly or directly concerned' persons specified by the Administrative Procedure Act 1946) has the right to request access to records or information held by federal agencies. An agency, on receiving a written request, must disclose the relevant records unless it can show that they are within one of the nine exemptions set out in the Act. **25.277**

The Act is a federal statute which applies only to agencies within the executive branch of the federal government.[319] It does not provide access to records held by the judicial or legislative branches, or by private businesses or individuals. All the states have their own statutes concerning access to state and local records. There is no central federal office for receiving and processing requests under the Act: each agency responds to requests for its own records.[320] **25.278**

Exemptions

The federal agencies are authorized by the Act to withhold information within the following nine categories:[321] **25.279**

(1) classified national defence and foreign policy information;

---

[317] *EPA v Mink*, 410 US 73, 80, *per* Douglas J (1973), quoting the historian Henry Steele Commager. Though Douglas J was dissenting in *Mink*, this passage was referred to approvingly in the opinion of the Supreme Court in *Dept of Justice v Reporters Comm*, 489 US 749, 772; 103 L Ed 2d 774 (1989).
[318] In 1974, 1976, 1986 and 1996.
[319] 'Agency' is defined in 5 USC §551(1) and 5 USC §552(f)(1) as including 'any executive department, military department, Government corporation, Government controlled corporation or other establishment in the executive branch of the Government (including the Executive Office of the President), or any independent regulatory agency'.
[320] US Department of Justice, *Freedom of Information Act Reference Guide* (August 2000) 1.
[321] 5 USC §552(b)(1) to (9).

(2) internal agency rules and practices;

(3) information the disclosure of which is prohibited by another federal statute;

(4) trade secrets and privileged or confidential commercial or financial information;

(5) inter-agency or intra-agency communications that are protected by legal
privilege;

(6) information (personnel, medical and similar files) involving matters of personal privacy;

(7) certain records or information compiled for law enforcement purposes if disclosure would result in specified kinds of harm;

(8) information relating to the regulation or supervision of financial institutions;

(9) certain geological and geophysical information and data.

It is to be noted that even if the information sought is within one of the statutory
exemptions, the relevant agency may, as a matter of administrative discretion,
disclose it.[322]

Response to a request

25.280 Agencies are required to respond to a request under the Act within 20 business
days.[323] Time begins to run when the agency's Freedom of Information Act office
receives the request. The agency is not obliged to respond by providing the
requested document within the 20 days; it can send a letter informing the
requester of its favourable decision and provide the document within a reasonable
time thereafter.

25.281 The Act[324] enables the agency, or a 'component' of an agency[325] to extend the
response time by a further 10 days in any of the following circumstances:

(1) the agency needs to collect relevant records from field officers; or

(2) the request involves a 'voluminous' quantity of records which must be
located, compiled or reviewed, or

(3) the agency must consult another agency which has a substantial interest in the
material needed to answer the requests.

25.282 In any of the foregoing circumstances the requester must be notified in writing
and offered the opportunity of (a) modifying or limiting the request, or (b) agreeing a different timetable. If the process just described has not led to agreement, the
requester may decide to challenge the outcome in court (as to which see paragraph
25.285 below). Such a challenge carries the risk of the court finding that the

---

[322] 'The Justice Department strives to achieve maximum possible information disclosure
through this discretionary disclosure policy': *Reference Guide* (n 320 above) 8.

[323] Excluding Saturdays, Sundays and public holidays: 5 USC §552(6)(A).

[324] 5 USC §552(6)(B).

[325] Such as the FBI, a component of the Department of Justice.

agency's failure to comply within the statutory period is justified. Furthermore the court may accept the agency's delay or adjourn consideration of the lawsuit where the agency can show that it has an accumulation of requests received before the one in issue, and is making reasonable progress in dealing with the requests in the order in which they were received.

Expedited access

The Act provides that requests are to be processed on an expedited basis in cases **25.283** in which the requester demonstrates a compelling need (and in other cases determined by the agency). 'Compelling need' means either that a failure to obtain requested records on an expedited basis could reasonably be expected to pose a threat to an individual's life or physical safety, or that the request is made by a person (not necessarily a representative of the news media) primarily engaged in disseminating information to the public and the information is urgently needed to inform the public about some actual or alleged government activity.[326]

Appeals

A disappointed requester is able to appeal an agency's withholding of information **25.284** or its failure to locate additional records or to grant expedited access. The initial step is an administrative appeal, which is an internal determination carried out within the agency in question.

Judicial review

Any further challenge to the agency's decision must be pursued in the federal **25.285** court. The court conducts a complete rehearing of the case, and the agency carries the burden of justifying its refusal to supply the information sought.[327]

The approach of the court is to construe the disclosure requirements of the Act **25.286** widely, and the exemptions strictly: 'The Legislative plan creates a liberal disclosure requirement limited only by specific exemptions, which are to be narrowly construed'.[328]

Success for the plaintiff requester may result in the court ordering the agency to **25.287** supply the information sought. A lesser but still significant degree of success may lead to the agency being required to provide a *Vaughn* index, that is, an itemized index in which the agency sets out its detailed justification of its claims, correlating each document (or part thereof) sought to be withheld with a specific exemption under the Act.[329] 'Practically speaking, the mere prospect of a

---

[326] 5 USC §552(a)(6)(E).
[327] ibid, §552(a)(4)(B).
[328] *Getman v NLRB*, 450 F 2d 670, 672 (1971); *Bristol-Myers v FTC*, 424 F 2d 935, 938 (1970).
[329] First ordered by the court in *Vaughn v Rosen* 484 F 2d 820 (1973).

court-mandated *Vaughn* procedure may provide the agencies with far more incentive to disclose than does [the Act's] presumption of disclosure. If the index is not sufficiently detailed, the court may . . . require a more detailed index'.[330] The process of identifying the desired documents and considering the exemptions which may apply is often pursued informally, in 'oral *Vaughn*' discussions between the parties.[331]

Third party suits

25.288 Where a third party wishes to prevent an agency from handing over information concerning him to a requester, he can apply for judicial review of the agency's decision. This form of litigation, known as a reverse Freedom of Information Act suit, originated with the Administrative Procedure Act 1946.[332]

The 1996 Amendments

25.289 The Electronic Freedom of Information Act Amendments 1996[333] effected a substantial change of emphasis. The classic means of obtaining information for the previous thirty years had entailed (a) making a request, and (b) waiting for an answer. The 1996 Amendments now required the agencies to anticipate requests and make broad categories of records immediately available to the public, both at agency record depositories and, using telecommunications technology, via the requesters' home computers.[334]

25.290 The change reflected not only the need to improve access to information and the availability of new technology to satisfy that need, but also a change in legislative purpose. The core purpose of the 1966 Act was identified by the Supreme Court as that of 'contribut[ing] significantly to public understanding of the operations or activities of the government' by permitting the people 'to know what their government is up to'.[335] The 1996 Amendments contained (in section 2) their own statement of legislative purpose: '. . . to require agencies . . . to make certain agency information available . . . for any public or private purpose'.[336]

---

[330] AC Aman and WT Mayton, *Administrative Law* (2nd edn, 2001) 656.

[331] P Birkinshaw, *Freedom of Information* (3rd edn, 2001) 66.

[332] See the 1946 Act, s 10 and the discussion in *Campaign for Family Farms v Glickman*, 200 F 3d 1180, 1184–1185 (8th Cir 2000).

[333] Codified in 5 USC §552 (originally Supp II 1996).

[334] ME Tankersley, 'How the Electronic Freedom of Information Act Amendments of 1996 update public access for the information age' (1998) 50 Admin L Rev 421, 423, reprinted in RG Vaughn (ed), *Freedom of Information* (2000).

[335] *US Dept of Justice v Reporters Committee for Freedom of the Press* 489 US 749, 103 L Ed 2d 774 (1989).

[336] See the discussion in JT O'Reilly: 'Expanding the Purpose of Federal Records Access' (1998) 50 Admin L Rev 371, 376, 379, also reprinted in Vaughn (n 334 above). O'Reilly says that the effect of the 1996 legislative purpose statement 'is to turn the FOIA from a window for oversight of the actions of government into a library of resources about others'.

The 1996 Amendments also filled what had been a surprising gap in the 1966 Act, namely the absence of any definition of 'record'. The Act, as amended, however, defines records so as to include 'any information that would be an agency record subject to the requirement of this section when maintained by an agency in any format, including an electronic format'.[337]   **25.291**

The 1996 Amendments required agencies to expand the types of records which must be either published or offered for sale, or deposited in agency reading rooms, where requesters could examine an index of the records and inspect and copy the records that interested them. The Amendments specified that such records should include those identified in response to a previous request 'which, because of the nature of their subject matter, the agency determines have become or are likely to become the subject of subsequent requests for substantially the same records'.[338]   **25.292**

Besides having to expand their conventional reading rooms, agencies were required by the Amendments to establish, by 1 November 1997, electronic reading rooms in order to make recent records in agency reading rooms available in electronic format. If an agency did not have the means to make the relevant materials available online, then they had to be made available in some other electronic form, such as CD-ROM or disk.[339]   **25.293**

By March 2001, the General Accounting Office found that most agencies had established electronic reading rooms, and that in general the 1996 regime was operating satisfactorily.[340]   **25.294**

In one particular respect the Amendments may fall short of expectations: the intention had been to strengthen the requester's hand when confronted by agency delay in dealing with his request. In reality, the requester must either pursue a negotiation in which he is at a disadvantage (the agency knows, and he does not, how much time is essential for processing his request) or take the risks as to costs, time and outcome in going to court. In the blunt summary of one commentator: 'The critical problem for FOIA requesters is that the [1966] statute provides no meaningful sanctions to deter unreasonable delay in processing requests. The 1996 Amendments continue to provide none.'[341]   **25.295**

Use of the Freedom of Information Act

It might have been expected that the press and other media would have been the main users of the Act. In fact they account for only 5 to 8% of requests. The business community is by far the main user: 50–60% of requests are made by   **25.296**

---

[337] 5 USC §552(f)(2)
[338] 5 USC §552(a)(2)(D), and see Tankersley (n 334 above) 426–427.
[339] Tankersley (n 334 above) 427–428.
[340] Birkinshaw (n 331 above) 71.
[341] Tankersley (n 334 above) 94.

commercial bodies seeking information on business competitors.[342] Antonin Scalia[343] commented in 1982 that the Act and its amendments 'were promoted as a boon to the press, the public interest group, the little guy; they have been used most frequently by corporate lawyers'.[344] The Defence and Health Departments and their agencies have received the greatest number of requests. Taking a single agency by way of example, NASA receives about 3,000 requests a year. 'About 80% of these are commercial and are concerned with contracts, proposals, and modifications to contracts and requests for proposals.'[345] After business, the next largest user is the public, making some 20–25% of requests. About 80% of all requests are granted in full.[346]

25.297   By no means all requests are made directly by the person or organization seeking the information. A satellite industry has grown up, with organizations of 'data brokers' or 'surrogate requesters' who acquire information under the Act and sell it on to persons interested.[347]

25.298   Though the Act is often said to have generated a huge and expensive industry in making and answering requests, Birkinshaw suggests that the annual costs are (or were in the 1980s) comparable with the costs of maintaining golf courses on military bases. The government's annual expenditure on publicity and public relations was some thirty times greater.

Criticism of the Freedom of Information Act

25.299   In its 1966 form the Act was widely regarded as weak: Antonin Scalia[348] described it as 'a relatively toothless beast, sometimes kicked about shamelessly by the agencies', which was unable to deal effectively with delays, arbitrary denials and overclassification of documents. It is true that the courts were able to effect some strengthening of the statutory regime, in particular when they required agencies to produce a *Vaughn* index.[349] However, Congressional support for strengthening the Act (which might have prevailed in any event) was reinforced by the Watergate investigations, and the 1974 Amendments to the Act were in conference committee when President Nixon resigned.[350]

---

[342]   Birkinshaw (n 331 above) 69.
[343]   Then a professor of law; from 1986 a Justice of the Supreme Court of the United States.
[344]   'The Freedom of Information Act has no clothes', in *Regulation: AEI Journal on Government and Society* (March/April 1982) 16, reprinted in Vaughn (n 334 above).
[345]   R Thomas, 'Freedom of Information: Implications for Business' in J Beatson and Y Cripps (eds), *Freedom of Expression and Freedom of Information* (2000) 406–7.
[346]   Birkinshaw (n 331 above) 69.
[347]   ibid, 70.
[348]   See nn 343 and 344 above.
[349]   See n 329 above.
[350]   Aman and Mayton (n 330 above) 637.

The 1974 Amendments 'gave practicable and enforceable life to the 1966 FOIA **25.300** mandate, making it much more difficult for the agencies to avoid their legal duty to search and disclose'.[351]

The changes effected by the Electronic Freedom of Information Act Amendments **25.301** 1996, and the continuing criticism of agency delays, have already been discussed.[352]

In a balanced assessment, which records the Drug Enforcement Administration's **25.302** claim that 60 per cent of the information requests it received were from imprisoned or known drug traffickers, Aman and Mayton reach a favourable view of the workings of the Act as amended, concluding that:

> by requiring de novo judicial review and placing the burden of proving exemption status on the agency, citizen access to information has been greatly facilitated.[353]

Related statutes

Federal Advisory Committee Act 1972

By this statute[354] Congress extended the requirement of openness to the advisory **25.303** committees which are often a source of advice to agencies. The members of the committees are private citizens, many of them having scientific, technical or professional expertise. The Act provides that advisory committees must give notice of their meetings, which must be held in public.[355]

Government in the Sunshine Act 1976

The Sunshine Act[356] directs its attention to meetings of the agencies themselves **25.304** (plainly of greater consequence than the advisory committee meetings addressed by the 1972 Act). The Act provides that 'every portion of every meeting of an agency shall be open to public observation', unless the subject matter of the meeting is within one of the exempted categories. The exemptions substantially overlap those of the Freedom of Information Act.[357]

---

[351] ibid, 637–638. See ibid, 638–643 for discussion of later amendments to the Act.

[352] See paras 25.289–25.295 above.

[353] Aman and Mayton (n 330 above) 691–693.

[354] 5 USCA App 1.

[355] For Supreme Court consideration of the Act's provisions, see *Public Citizen v US Dept of Justice*, 491 US 440, 105 L Ed 2d 377 (1989).

[356] 5 USCA 552b. The derivation of the statute's full title is attributed to some phrases of Louis Brandeis (before he became Brandeis J), who wrote a piece for *Harper's Weekly* in 1913 in which he observed: 'Publicity is justly commended as a remedy for social and industrial diseases. Sunlight is said to be the best of disinfectants; electric light the most efficient policeman': see Aman and Mayton (n 330 above) 728.

[357] See para 25.279 above. Exemption 5 under the 1966 Act, ie inter- or intra-agency memoranda, is not included in the Sunshine Act, since they are among the materials intended to be exposed to the light.

25.305 Most of the Act is concerned with setting out the procedures for announcing meetings in advance, closing meetings which are exempt, and providing for public access to non-exempt portions of otherwise closed meetings.

25.306 The agencies have closed about 40 per cent of their meetings, relying on one or more of the exempt categories.[358]

25.307 Where violation of open meeting requirements is alleged, the complainant can seek judicial review.[359] In fact the statute has not been frequently litigated in its first quarter-century of life.

The Privacy Act 1974

25.308 This statute[360] gives individuals the right to see and copy records about themselves maintained by federal agencies, and to ask for correction of inaccurate, incomplete or irrelevant information contained in those records.[361] An agency must keep a list noting each disclosure outside the agency within the previous five years, and must make that list available to the subject of the record when so requested.[362]

25.309 Further constraints on the agencies are that they can collect only such information as is relevant and necessary to accomplish an agency function, and that they must collect the information to the 'greatest extent practicable' from the subject himself.[363]

25.310 Records may be disclosed to third parties (that is, to someone other than the subject of the record) only if specifically permitted by the Act or authorized in writing by the subject of the record.[364]

25.311 A complainant alleging failure by an agency to release information to him or to correct information about him or otherwise comply with the Act can seek de novo judicial review by the district court.[365]

25.312 The Act enables agencies to make rules under which entire categories of records can be exempted from disclosure: such exemptions cover CIA, secret service, security and law enforcement records.[366]

25.313 Until the Privacy Act was amended in 1984, it was treated by some agencies as an exempting statute under the Freedom of Information Act.[367] So where the

---

[358] Aman and Mayton (n 330 above) 733–734.
[359] 5 USCA §552b(d)–(m).
[360] ibid, §552a.
[361] ibid, §552a(d)(2)–(4).
[362] ibid, §552a(c).
[363] ibid, §552a(e)(2).
[364] ibid, §552a(b).
[365] ibid, §552a(g).
[366] Aman and Mayton (n 330 above) 702–703.
[367] See para 25.279 above.

requester sought information which was within a Privacy Act exemption, the Freedom of Information Acts provided no separate help. Congress, however, amended the Privacy Act to provide that no agency should rely on any exemption in the Privacy Act 'to withhold from an individual any record which is otherwise accessible to [him]' under the Freedom of Information Act. The amended Privacy Act 'now provides an individual requester with the maximum information accessible under either or both Acts—no matter how the request is characterized'.[368]

---

[368] Aman and Mayton (n 330 above) 708. See ibid, 708–709 for a helpful discussion of the courts' approach to the interrelationship between the Privacy Act and the Freedom of Information Act.

PART J

THE FUTURE

26

THE FUTURE

A. Introduction

A constitutional right

The views expressed in this chapter are the personal views of the author.[1] The **26.01** Freedom of Information Act was one of a range of constitutional reforms introduced by the Labour government which was elected in 1997. It followed devolution to Scotland and Wales, a new form of government for London, the introduction of a form of proportional representation for the European elections, the Human Rights Act and, as the first stage of the reform of the second chamber, the curtailing of the right of hereditary peers to attend and vote.

The Human Rights Act 1998 has provided a framework of basic rights for United **26.02** Kingdom citizens. It requires every public authority, including the courts, to act consistently with the European Convention. The most material articles of the Convention for freedom of information are Article 8, which includes a right to privacy, and Article 10, which gives a right to freedom of expression. The weakness of Article 10 as a touchstone is that it has not yet been interpreted by the European Court of Human Rights as giving a general right of access to public information. This weakness is put right by the Freedom of Information Act, and the task for the courts is to balance the right to freedom of expression and the right

---

[1] John Macdonald QC.

to know against the right to privacy. They are all constitutional rights and the courts should therefore apply the principle of proportionality in reviewing the action of public authorities under the Freedom of Information Act rather than the traditional *Wednesbury* irrationality test.[2] If necessary the Act should be amended to make this clear. This is not a major step, it is in line with Lord Cooke's view expressed in *R(Daly) v Secretary of State for the Home Department*[3] that the days of the *Wednesbury* test may be numbered.

B. The Civil Service

The role of the civil service

26.03 The success of freedom of information legislation will ultimately depend in great part on the attitude of civil servants. It is therefore encouraging that those in the public service have been given such a clear lead by the Lord Chancellor, his department and the Information Commissioner who between them are responsible for the implementation of the Act. The roadshows which the department has held have demonstrated how seriously the Act is being taken by a wide range of public authorities. The department has emphasized that the principle underlying the Act is the principle of accountability. The better informed the electorate is, the better placed they are to make a judgment on those they have elected to represent them. Open government is likely to be better government.

Record keeping

26.04 Good record keeping too lies at the heart of freedom of information. If a public authority is to pass information on it is essential that it should know what information it has, what it receives, what it creates and what it keeps. The great Departments of State have long kept meticulous records. Anyone for example who is interested in the affairs of Ocean Island[4] or Barbuda will find in the Public Record Office (subject to the thirty years rule) every dispatch which passed between the administrators on those islands and London, together with the Colonial Office memoranda and minutes which determined the policy to be applied to them. Public authorities of course extend way beyond the Departments of State. It has been estimated by the Lord Chancellor's Department that there are more than 100,000 of them and they do not all have good record systems. The Act does not say much about how records are to be kept. There is nothing comparable to Article 11 of the European Regulation[5] which requires each institution of the

---

[2] This is discussed further at paras 21.74–21.95 above.
[3] [2001] 2 AC 532, 549 para 32.
[4] Which are discussed in *Tito v Waddell* [1977] Ch 106.
[5] Council Regulation (EC) 1049/2001.

European Union to provide public access to a register of documents, and for the register to contain a reference number, the subject matter and a short description of the document, and the date on which it was received or drawn up and recorded in the register. A formal regime of this kind has some attractions, but on balance the greater flexibility of the United Kingdom system, which depends on the guidance given in the Code of Practice on the Management of Records under section 46 of the Act, is perhaps to be preferred because it allows smaller authorities to find the system that is best for them. There is a real danger that a system which is appropriate for Europe would prove too bureaucratic and expensive if it were applied to all public authorities.

Publication schemes

Section 19 of the Act requires public authorities to adopt and maintain a publication scheme which has to be approved by the Information Commissioner. This is an important new development because the best way to ensure that a freedom of information regime works smoothly is for public authorities to take the initiative in publishing information before they are asked. As a result fewer questions will need to be asked, and time and costs will be saved. The government has stressed the importance it attaches to the publication schemes and authorities have been able to concentrate on them in the period before the Act comes into force. The schemes tend to be published first on the Internet and some of the pilot schemes, understandably perhaps, are designed to show the department concerned in a good light. Public authorities, however, must resist the temptation to use their schemes as public relations exercises. What is needed is information, not spin, with a clear demarcation line between fact and comment. Public authorities must be scrupulous about this. **26.05**

C. A Simple Act with a Clear Structure

A purpose clause

So far so good. The attitude of the civil service, good records and a willingness by government to disclose information before it is sought will all be crucial to the quality of freedom of information. But there are improvements which can be made. The most important changes which need to be made are to simplify the structure and language of the Act. To start with the Act would be better if it contained a purpose clause. **26.06**

The purpose clause should perhaps be based on the clause in the New Zealand Act[6] and should state the principle contained in section 5 of that Act that information **26.07**

---

[6] Freedom of Information Act 1982, s 4, set out at para 9.04 above.

held by public authorities should be made available unless there is good reason for withholding it. This sums up what the Act is all about. The principle has of course to be balanced against the consideration that private individuals are entitled to protection against the disclosure without their consent of confidential information about themselves and their activities unless there is a sufficient public interest reason why the information should be disclosed.[7]

Structure

26.08 The structure of the Act is unnecessarily complicated. This is something which the authors of this book have come to know only too well. It comes about chiefly because the right to receive information is in two parts, and the draftsman has chosen to deal with both parts in every exemption. The applicant is entitled under section 1, first, to be informed whether the public authority holds the information he seeks and secondly, if it does hold the information, to have the information communicated to him. The structure of the Act is that rights have effect not directly but subject to section 2 which is entitled 'Effect of the exemptions in Part II'.

26.09 Section 2(1) says that where any provision in Part II states that the duty to confirm or deny does not arise, and the effect of the provision is that it confers an absolute exemption, or the public interest is against disclosure, the right to be told whether the information exists does not apply. Section 2(2) provides that in respect of any information which is exempt information by virtue of any provision in Part II, and the information is exempt information or the public interest is against disclosure, the right to receive the information does not apply. This involved formulation means, as has been seen, that each section which contains an exemption deals with both the right to be told whether the information exists, and the right to receive the information. This makes the Act much more complicated and much harder to understand than it needs to be. The EC Regulation which secures access to information held by the institutions of the European Union (see paragraph 26.04 above) and the UK Regulations which deal with environmental information are much simpler and much clearer.

26.10 The Act should state the rights in simple terms: there is a general right to access of information 'held' by public authorities. This includes both a right to be told whether information exists as well as a right to receive information. The Act should then state the exemptions and list the exceptional circumstances in which authorities do not even have to disclose whether they hold information. Scotland and New Zealand seem to have managed things better.

---

[7] See Richard Scott, 'Confidentiality' in J Beatson and Y Cripps (eds), *Freedom of Expression and Freedom of Information: Essays in Honour of Sir David Williams* (OUP, 2000) 267.

The exemptions

The Act provides for a number of absolute exemptions where public authorities **26.11**
are not required to release information, though they may still do so. These exemptions are not subject to the public interest test. There seems no good reason for this.

One of the features of both the Aarhus Convention and the draft Environmental **26.12**
Information Regulations 2002 is that all the exemptions are subject to a public interest test. If the government was prepared to accept this position for environmental information it is strange that it adopted a more restrictive scheme in the Act. It would be better if the same rule applied to all information. If all the exemptions are subject to a public interest test this means that the disclosure of information has to be as a thinking, rather than an automatic, process. That is as it should be. Whether or not information is disclosed should depend on the consequences of disclosure rather than on whether the information falls within a particular category. This is the approach in New Zealand.

Under the New Zealand Official Information Act 1982 all the substantive exemp- **26.13**
tions are framed by reference to the consequences of disclosure, rather than categories of information, and their application has accordingly to be judged on a case by case basis depending on the particular circumstances. This reflects a conscious decision to retain flexibility by the Danks Committee which prepared the legislation:

> Judgments cannot, in our view, be properly and satisfactorily made all at one time by legislation. We were faced early in our work, with the choice of trying to design a once and for all static mechanism, with a complex set of exceptions, or a more flexible mechanism, operating by reference to principles and competing criteria that reflect a continuing shift away from a presumption of secrecy. We opted for a flexible process.[8]

A flexible approach is to be preferred.[9]

If this approach is adopted environmental information could be brought within **26.14**
the framework of the Act. This would make life simpler for everyone. Two of the exemptions, section 21 (information accessible to applicants by other means) and section 22 (information intended for future publication), are not true exemptions because in both cases the public is entitled to the information, but by another route and at another time. It would be better if these matters were separated out. It is important that the structure of the Act should be as simple and easy to follow as possible. There is another point about section 22: it only applies if it is

---

[8] *Towards Open Government*—The Committee on Official Information's report (1980).
[9] This is the view of commentators in Canada who are critical of the way comparable provisions in the Canadian Act have worked: see para 9.34 above.

reasonable in all the circumstances that the information should be withheld from disclosure until the intended date of publication. There is no express time limit. Canada and Ireland have similar provisions but they both have time limits: the time limit is 90 days in Canada[10] and 12 weeks in Ireland.[11] A time limit could prove a salutary discipline for public authorities.

26.15 The list of exemptions in the Act could be pruned with advantage. Section 28 (relations within the United Kingdom) and section 37 (communications with the Queen) should be dispensed with. Where such relations and communications need to be protected, reliance can quite safely be placed on other exemptions.

Policy advice and the conduct of public affairs

26.16 Perhaps the two most controversial exemptions are those contained in section 35 (formulation of policy) and section 36 (prejudice to effective conduct of public affairs). Everyone agrees that good government can only be achieved if there can be a full and frank exchange of views between Ministers and their advisers. Neither does anyone disagree that whenever possible factual information used to provide an informed background to decision-taking should be made available. But there is a grey area in the middle, where there is little agreement. The Act solves this by drawing the exemption in wide terms and making it subject to the public interest test. And applying that test in this context, the Act requires that regard should specifically be paid to the particular public interest in disclosure of factual information which has been used or is intended to be used to provide an informed background to decision-taking.

26.17 While it would be good to see factual information excluded altogether from the exemption it is probably sensible to see how the Information Commissioner and the public authorities apply the test, and where they draw the line, before suggesting any changes. It is important to appreciate that the section as it stands does not impose a blanket ban on the disclosure of information and that under the public interest test each question has to be looked at in the light of its own circumstances.

26.18 As to section 36 the government puts forward two arguments. First, once it is accepted that there should be some protection to enable open and frank conversations to take place between officials and Ministers in central government, it seems right that the same protection should be given to public authorities which are not part of central government. Secondly, the government said, there may be more than 50,000 public authorities covered by the Act.[12] They will all be under an obligation

---

[10] Access to Information Act 1982, s 26.

[11] Freedom of Information Act 1997, s 10(1)(d).

[12] This estimate, given by Lord Falconer in the debates on the Bill, *Hansard* HL (series 5) vol 619, col 240 (14 November 2000), may need to be revised to over 100,000.

to give people the right to know, and some sort of exemption should be given to prevent them having to make disclosure in situations which may arise, but cannot be foreseen, which would in fact prejudice the effective conduct of public affairs.

The argument for the policy advice exemption to apply to all public authorities is **26.19** well made, but a general exemption to prevent disclosure which would be prejudicial to the effective conduct of public affairs, even if it is subject to the public interest test, is much too wide. It should go.

It would be helpful if the remaining exemptions were drafted with as much **26.20** clarity and economy as those in Article 4 of Council Regulation (EC) 1049/2001 for documents held by the institutions of the European Union.

Appeals and the role of the Information Commissioner

The central role given to the Information Commissioner is one of the good features of the Act. It is the Commissioner who will decide whether a request for **26.21** information has been dealt with in accordance with the Act. The scheme, under which the first decision as to whether or not information should be disclosed is taken by the public authority and the decision can be reviewed by the authority before it goes to the Commissioner, seems to get the balance right. It should ensure that decisions are made and reviewed with the minimum of red tape and expense. The Commissioner has been given adequate powers to make sure that he can police the Act effectively. It is less clear whether the Information Tribunal, which will hear appeals from the Commissioner, has a useful role to play. There is a danger that having an elaborate appeals structure will lead to procrastination by public authorities. The fear is that authorities will appeal to the Tribunal in order to put off having to disclose information which may prove embarrassing. Time will tell. One way of countering this threat is for appeals to the Tribunal to be permitted only with the consent of the Commissioner or the Tribunal. It is very important to keep the appeal procedure simple and informal so that people who use the Act do not have to waste time and money on what can quickly become full-scale litigation.

It is important that the Information Commissioner is appointed in a way which **26.22** best secures his or her independence. In a constitution where reliance is placed on checks and balances it is not satisfactory to have the Commissioner appointed by the executive, which is likely to be involved in many of the disputes that come before the Commissioner. It would be better if the Commissioner is appointed by a joint committee of both Houses of Parliament. He or she should be appointed for a fixed term and should only be capable of being removed from office during this term by an affirmative vote of each House of Parliament.

The Act provides for an appeal from the Tribunal to the High Court on a point of **26.23** law. This is only likely to happen in exceptional cases where a point of principle is at issue. In these test cases, which will affect many other people, it is important that legal aid should be available for those who are impecunious, so that the parties are on an equal footing.

Third parties

26.24   The Act proceeds on the basis that whether information should be disclosed is a matter to be resolved between the person requesting the information and the authority to whom the request is made. No provision is made in the Act for third parties to whom requested information may relate to intervene before the information is disclosed. This is a defect in the Act. It is surprising that the matter was not dealt with specifically because it has proved a contentious issue in the United States, where what is called a 'reverse freedom of information application' has become an established part of the regime. The Code of Practice to be issued by the Lord Chancellor under section 45 requires that before disclosing the information which affects third parties, an authority should consult those parties. Although this fills the gap to some extent, it is not enough. A third party should have the rights recognized in the Act to be informed of any request for information which affects his interests before disclosure of that information is made, to intervene to protect his interests and, in the event of differences remaining between him and the applicant who made the request or the authority to whom it was made, to apply to the Information Commissioner for a decision resolving such differences. And the third party should be recognized as a person entitled to make further appeals to the Tribunal and, on points of law, to the courts.

The executive override

26.25   There was much discussion in Parliament about the executive override which is in section 53 of the Act. The Constitution Unit[13] describes the executive override in these terms:

> In exceptional circumstances an 'accountable person', may issue a certificate stating that they have formed, on reasonable grounds, the view that the authority did not fail to comply with the requirements of the Act. In this case, the authority need not comply with a decision or enforcement notice (relating to the public interest test) issued by the Commissioner. Such a certificate, which applies just to Central Government, can only be issued by a Cabinet Minister or by the Attorney General and as soon as practicable a copy of the certificate must be laid before each House of Parliament. The authority must also inform the applicant of the reasons for its decision.

If the suggestion that has been made earlier in this chapter that the public interest test should be extended to all exemptions is adopted, governments will argue that an executive override is even more important. This may not be the strongest of

---

[13]   Jim Amos, Dick Baxter, Jeremy Croft and Robert Hazell, *A Practical Guide to the Freedom of Information Act 2000* (The Constitution Unit, March 2001).

arguments, but the political reality is that any government will want an override to safeguard it against some unforeseen situation where it wishes to play safe and disclose nothing. Even so the override should be closely prescribed. The fact that a certificate under the Act can only be issued by a member of the Cabinet or the Attorney-General and the fact that it has to be reported to Parliament ensures publicity and the protection which publicity brings, but the override should not be absolute. It should be subject to a reference to the High Court which should review the decision, applying the principle of proportionality, rather than the *Wednesbury* test. The Court's review should be final.

D. Conclusions

To sum up, the following changes in the Act are proposed in this chapter: **26.26**

(a) The addition of a purpose clause to the Act stating the principle that information held by public authorities should be made available unless there is good reason for withholding it.

(b) The structure of the Act should be simplified. The rights should be set out in plain terms followed by the exemptions. The Act should list separately the exceptional circumstances in which authorities do not have to disclose that they hold information.

(c) There should be no absolute exemptions. All exemptions should be subject to a public interest test.

(d) Environmental information should be dealt with in the same way as other information.

(e) There should be a time limit on the exemption for information which is to be published in the future.

(f) The exemptions should be pruned. Relations within the United Kingdom and communications with the Royal family should not be separate exemptions. Such information should only be withheld if it falls within one of the other exemptions.

(g) Policy advice for local government and other public authorities outside Whitehall should be protected, but the exemption in section 36 which prevents disclosure which would prejudice the efficient conduct of public affairs is too wide, and should go.

(h) The Information Commissioner should be appointed by a joint committee of both Houses of Parliament for a fixed term and should only be capable of being removed from office during that term by an affirmative vote of each House of Parliament.

(i) Appeals to the Information Tribunal should only take place with the permission of the Information Commissioner or the Tribunal (to prevent authorities from bringing appeals as a delaying tactic).

(j) The rights of third parties who may be affected by disclosure of information should be recognized and measures created enabling them to intervene before such disclosure is made.

(k) Executive override certificates should be referred to the High Court which should review such certificates, applying the principle of proportionality. The decision of the court should be final.

As Aristotle said:

> Even when laws have been written down, they ought not always to remain unaltered.

APPENDICES

I: Practical Guides

II: Materials

I: PRACTICAL GUIDES

APPENDIX A

Good Practice Guide for Public Authorities

A. Introduction

Purpose

This guide is designed primarily for officials in central and local government who **A.01** find themselves involved in dealing with requests for information but who are not specialists on the Freedom of Information Act 2000.

Basic Questions

It is sensible to start with some basic questions. Asking and answering these ques- **A.02** tions will start you on the right course.

(a) What information do you have?
(b) Where is it?
(c) How is it organized?
(d) What information are people likely to want from you?
(e) How should you provide it?
(f) Do you publish now, or wait to be asked?
(g) Have you identified information which should not be disclosed?
(h) What are the reasons for this?
(i) Are the reasons readily available for anyone dealing with the information?

> Have you read the Code on Record Management issued by the Lord Chancellor under section 46? (see Appendix E)

> Help and advice about record management is available from the Public Record Office. Consult the Public Record Office website at www.pro.gov.uk.

Publication Schemes

Use your publication scheme to publish on a regular basis as much as possible of **A.03** the information which the public is likely to want. There will always be a demand to see the facts and statistics on which policy decisions are taken. Make sure that reports and memoranda are written so that facts and statistics are separated from the advice and conclusions, and can therefore be published without compromising the confidentiality inherent in the advice process.

> Let the facts speak for themselves. It is good public relations to give people straight information, not an account of what information is held.

The Act does not stand alone

A.04 The Act does not provide a complete code for supplying information. Public Authorities are also required to supply information under the Data Protection Act 1998, Environmental Regulations 2002,[1] and Local Government legislation.[2] You will have to decide which regime applies.

Data protection

A.05 Many requests for information will concern personal data. Personal data is generally exempt under section 40 of the Act. Requests for 'my personal file' should be treated as requests under the Data Protection Act. The Freedom of Information Act *does* apply to requests for personal information about third parties but data protection principles also apply. Some requests will need to be handled under both Acts.

> The eight Data Protection Principles are set out and discussed in paras 10.16–10.34 above.

Environmental Information Regulations

A.06 The main difference between the Regulations and the Freedom of Information Act is in the treatment of exceptions or exemptions. The potential to refuse a request under the Regulations is narrower than under the Act. There are no absolute exemptions to the right to environmental information. There is a public interest test for *all* substantive exceptions. Substantive exceptions only apply where disclosure would have an adverse effect.

> The definition of environmental information in the draft Regulations is set out at para 16.74 above.

---

[1] These regulations are in draft at the time of writing. They will replace the Environmental Regulations 1992 (amended 1998).
[2] Local Government (Access to Information) Act 1985 and the Local Government Act 2000.

> The exceptions to the right to environmental information in Regulation 7 are set out and discussed in paras 16.85–16.86 above.

The definition of environmental information is very broad and local authorities **A.07** should consider in particular whether requests for information about development and planning matters should be dealt with under the Environmental Regulations.

Local Authorities

The government is undertaking a comprehensive review of the inter-relationship **A.08** of the Local Government statutes with the Freedom of Information Act with the aim of providing a clear and comprehensive code.[3] You should, of course, consult this code when it is published.[4]

Local Authorities have been under a statutory duty to disclose information since **A.09** 1985. The public has rights of access to meetings, reports and documents, subject to specified confidentiality provisions. These rights are now backed up by the 2000 Act.

> The special rules relating to local authorities are set out and discussed in part B of chapter 15 paras 15.03–15.53.

B. Handling Requests

Procedures

Public authorities should publish their procedures for dealing with requests for **A.10** information. The right to disclosure contained in section 1 of the Act operates in two stages. First the entitlement that a public authority 'confirm or deny' whether it holds the information specified in the request under section 1(1)(a); and secondly, the distinct entitlement 'to have that information communicated', under section (1)(1)(b). The procedures must cover both stages. As a practical matter they should also include an address, including an e-mail address where possible, to which applicants may direct requests for information or assistance. A telephone number should also be provided, where possible that of a named individual, who can provide assistance. The procedure for the applicant should be made as clear

---

[3] In September 2002 the Office of the Deputy Prime Minister produced a policy paper *Access to Information in Local Government*, which invited comments from councils and user groups.
[4] The website address of the Office of the Deputy Prime Minister is: htpp://www.odpm.gov.uk

and straightforward as possible. Where possible establish direct contact with the applicant and find out what he really wants. This will save time in the long run and avoid misunderstandings.

The request

A.11 To be valid the request has to be in writing,[5] but any writing will suffice and will start the timetable laid down by the Act running. The request must contain the applicant's name and address and describe the information which the applicant wishes to obtain. The information must be information held by the authority and the request must not be vexatious or repetitious.[6]

Advice and assistance

A.12 Public authorities are under a duty to provide advice and assistance to applicants.[7] People may need help in framing their request so that it is possible to identify the information which is sought.

> The Code issued by the Lord Chancellor under section 45 suggests that appropriate assistance might include:
>
> —providing an outline of the different kinds of information which might meet the terms of the request;
>
> —providing access to detailed catalogues and indexes, where these are available, to help the applicant ascertain the nature and extent of the information held by the authority.

> It may make sense to suggest that the applicant calls in to explain his request in person, or that he seeks help from an agency such as a Citizens Advice Bureau in framing his request.

A.13 If it is still not possible to identify or locate the information, you should disclose what information you can and explain why you cannot take the matter any further.

A.14 Authorities should be aware that the aim of providing assistance is to clarify the nature of the information sought not to determine the aims or motivation of the applicant. The applicant does not have to give reasons for his request or any indication of the use to which the information will be put.

---

[5] S7.
[6] S9.
[7] S16.

Handling an organized campaign

Where applications for information appear to be part of an organized campaign **A.15** you should accept that and consider putting the information on your website and giving each applicant a brief notification of the website address. This will save money. People taking part in an organized campaign have as much right to information as anyone else.

Timing

The time limits are very tight. Normally the deadline for replying to a request is **A.16** 20 days. Applications should be dealt with as soon as possible. Do not wait until day 20. In cases where the information is subject to an exemption and the authority is required to consider the balance of the public interest, then the response does not have to be within 20 days but must be within a reasonable time. You are still required to issue a notice within the 20 day period stating that an exemption applies and including an estimate of the date by which the decision will have been made. Authorities will be expected to keep to their estimates.

Fees

Remember the Act does not require fees to be charged for supplying information. **A.17** An authority may charge a fee calculated in accordance with the Fees Regulations.[8] The maximum fee must not exceed 10% of the prescribed costs and disbursements. *Prescribed costs* means the costs reasonably incurred in locating and retrieving the information. They do not include any costs spent deciding how much information to release, nor the costs of consulting third parties. *Disbursements* are the direct costs of communicating the information. Where the prescribed costs are £550 or more, the authority is not obliged to comply with the request.

Transfer of requests

If an authority to whom the original request was made believes that some or all of **A.18** the information requested is held by another authority the first authority should consider what is the most helpful way of assisting the applicant with his request. It may be to transfer the request to the other authority, or to invite the applicant to apply direct to the other authority. You should always deal with any part of the request which relates to information you hold. You should also consult with the applicant and with the other authority before you act.

---

[8] These are still in draft at the time of writing.

A.19 All transfers of requests should take place as soon as is practicable and the applicant should be informed when this has been done. The second authority will have 20 days from the day it receives the request to comply with it.

Considering the request

A.20 Having determined the request is valid, the first question is whether the authority holds the information. If it does you should then ask the following questions:

(a) Have any certificates been issued under the Act which will help to answer the questions which the authority faces?

Certificates

A minister may issue a certificate under sections 23 and 24 of the Act which is conclusive evidence that information about security matters falls within one or other of these sections.[9] The Speaker and the Clerk of the Parliaments can issue certificates in relation to matters of Parliamentary privilege and information held by Parliament in its conduct of public affairs.[10]

(b) Is the information exempt under any of the grounds set out in Part II of the Act. If it is not the authority is under a duty to release it.

(c) Does the information fall within any of the absolute exemptions specified in section 2(3)?

Absolute exemptions:

s.21 Information accessible to applicants by other means.[11]

s.23 Information supplied by, or relating to, bodies dealing with security matters.[12]

s.32 Court records.[13]

s.34 Parliamentary privilege.[14]

s.36 Prejudice to effective conduct of public affairs (applying to information held by the House of Commons or House of Lords[15]).

(continuous)

---

[9] See paras 6.22–6.27 and 6.139–6.142 above.
[10] See para 3.25 and 6.53–6.54 above.
[11] See paras 6.13–6.18 above.
[12] See paras 6.19–6.27 above.
[13] See paras 6.28–6.40 above.
[14] See paras 6.41–6.54 above.
[15] See paras 6.55–6.56 above.

(continued)

s.40 Personal information (principally where the applicant is the subject of that information[16]).

s.41 Information provided in confidence.[17]

s.44 Prohibitions on disclosure (as a result of any enactment, community obligation or contempt of court).[18]

If information does fall within one of these absolute exemptions it should not be disclosed.[19]

(d) In any event the authority should consider the separate question of whether it is under a duty to confirm or deny that it holds the information. It is necessary to look at the terms of each exemption in order to answer this question.

The exemptions in section 21 and 40 do not deprive the applicant of information: **A.21** it is likely he will be entitled to it, but by a different route, in the case of section 21 from the public source of the information and in the case of section 40 under the Data Protection Act 1988. The other absolute exemption on which authorities are most likely to be able to rely is section 41: information provided in confidence. The exemption only applies if the disclosure would constitute an actionable breach of confidence.[20]

Conditional exemptions

The next question is does the information fall within any of the conditional ex- **A.22** emptions? All the conditional exemptions are subject to a public interest test, and some of them only apply where prejudice is or is likely to be caused by disclosure of the information.

The conditional exemptions are set out in paras 6.114 above.

The conditional exemptions which only apply if prejudice is shown are:

s.26 Defence.[21]

s.27 International relations.[22]

(continuous)

---

[16] See paras 6.57–6.62 above.
[17] See paras 6.63–6.81 above.
[18] See paras 6.82–6.110 above.
[19] The Authority's decision may be overruled by the Information Commissioner or the Tribunal.
[20] See para 6.66 above.
[21] See paras 6.144–6.146 above.
[22] See paras 6.147–6.153 above.

(continued)

s.28 Relations within the United Kingdom.[23]

s.29 The economy.[24]

s.31 Law enforcement.[25]

s.33 Audit functions.[26]

s.36 The conduct of public affairs.[27]

s.38 Health and safety.[28]

s.43 Commercial interests.[29]

A.23 The last five of these together with the exemption in section 30 (investigations and proceedings conducted by public authorities) and the exemption applying under the Regulations to environmental information are the exemptions with which local authorities are most likely to be concerned. If the information falls within any of the exemptions which depend on prejudice, the question arises: would disclosure cause or be likely to cause prejudice? If not, then the exemption will not arise.

A.24 If the information falls within any of the conditional exemptions, it is necessary to apply the public interest test.

The public interest test

A.25 The next questions are therefore whether the balance of public interest is in favour of disclosure:

(a) of the existence of the information?

(b) of the information?

The public interest test is discussed in paras 2.07–2.10, 3.09–3.11, 6.11–6.113 and 17.41–17.46 above (look at para 17.41 first).

---

[23] See paras 6.154–6.156 above.
[24] See paras 6.157–6.161 above.
[25] See paras 6.176–6.182 above.
[26] See paras 6.183–6.187 above.
[27] See 6.196–6.208 above.
[28] See paras 6.212–6.217 above.
[29] See paras 6.229–6.239 above.

> Factors which would favour disclosure
>
> - government does not hold information for itself but on behalf of its citizens
> - the information may reveal reasons for decisions
> - disclosure would contribute to a debate on a matter of public interest
> - disclosure would enhance scrutiny of government decision-making processes and thereby improve accountability and participation
> - potential or actual embarrassment to government is not a valid criterion.

If the balance of public interest favours disclosure the information should be disclosed. If it does not the authority must then consider whether it is in the public interest to confirm or deny that it holds the information.

Consultation with third parties

In some cases the disclosure of information pursuant to a request may affect the **A.26** legal rights of a third party, for example where information is subject to the common law duty of confidence or where it constitutes personal data within the meaning of the Data Protection Act 1998. The Freedom of Information Act says little about third parties but the section 45 Code reminds public authorities that unless an exemption applies in relation to any particular information they will be obliged to disclose the information in response to a request.

The section 45 Code places a duty on public authorities to consult with third par- **A.27** ties who may be affected before releasing information, and this is so whether or not the third party has any legal rights in the information. The decision whether or not to release the information remains that of the authority. Consultation is particularly important where the views of the third party may assist you to determine whether an exemption under the Act applies to the information requested or where the public interest lies.

> The duty under the Code to consult third parties is discussed in paras 5.145–5.146 above.

The authority's discretion

Remember even if an exemption applies nothing in the Act is to be taken to limit **A.28** the powers of a public authority to disclose information held by it.[30] Subject to the law of confidence an authority can release information if it wishes to do so.

---

[30] S78 of the Act.

The release of information

A.29 If no exemption applies, then information should be released, subject to the payment of any charges which are required. So far as is practicable you should release the information using the means preferred by the applicant.

The refusal of a request

A.30 If you decide to refuse the request you must comply with the provisions of section 17. This means giving the applicant a notice which specifies the exemption on which you rely and explains why the exemption applies. The notice must also give details of the authority's complaints procedure and inform the applicant of his right to appeal to the Information Commissioner.

Complaints procedure[31]

A.31 Complaints should not be handled by the person who took the original decision. They should be dealt with by someone who is more senior. The procedure must be seen to be capable of changing or amending the original decisions. Complaints should be handled promptly according to published target times. They should be properly recorded. A complaint should be seen as an opportunity to demonstrate the professionalism of the authority.

C. Regulation and Help

The role of the Information Commissioner

A.32 The Information Commissioner is responsible for the smooth running of the Act. It is important to ensure that you have good lines of communication with the office of the Commissioner.

> The Commissioner's responsibilities:
> - approve and revoke publication schemes
> - promote good practice
> - ensure compliance with the Act
> - disseminate information and give advice about the Act
> - assess, with the consent of an authority, whether it is following good practice
> - report to Parliament once a year.

---

[31] See paras 7.58–7.66 above.

An applicant can apply to the Commissioner for a decision that a request for **A.33** information has not been dealt with in accordance with the requirements of the Act. The Commissioner may issue a decision notice to an authority requiring compliance.

The Commissioner may issue an information notice requiring an authority to **A.34** provide specific information to help the Commissioner determine a complaint.

Where the Commissioner is satisfied that the authority has failed to comply with **A.35** the Act, he may issue an enforcement notice requiring the authority to comply within a specific time-scale. Failure to comply with notices will be treated as a contempt of court.[32]

Appeals

The Information Tribunal can receive appeals either from an applicant or from a **A.36** public authority. There is no right of appeal for third parties. The Tribunal may allow or dismiss an appeal. An appeal from the Tribunal lies to the High Court on a point of law.[33]

Ministerial override

In exceptional circumstances a cabinet minister or the Attorney-General can issue **A.37** a certificate overriding the decision of the Information Commissioner in a particular case. This power only applies to decisions relating to central government.[34]

Help

Help and advice can be obtained from the Information Commissioner's Office **A.38** and from the Lord Chancellor's Department. The Constitution Unit offers a range of training and consultancy services on the administration of Freedom of Information.

> Lord Chancellor's Department
> Freedom of Information and Data Protection Division
> Room 151 Selbourne House
> London SW1E 6QW
> Telephone: 0207 210 8755
> Fax: 0207 210 1415
> E-mail: fidp@lcdhq.gsi.gov.uk
> Website: htpp://www.lcd.gov.uk

---

[32] See paras 7.109–7.116 above.
[33] See paras 7.90–7.102 above.
[34] See paras 7.103–7.108 above.

Information Commissioner
Wycliff House
Water Lane
Wilmslow, Cheshire
SK9 5AF
Telephone: 01625 545 700
Fax: 01625 524 510
E-mail: data@dataprotection.gov.uk
Website: htpp://www.dataprotection.gov.uk

The Constitution Unit
School of Public Policy
University College London
29/30 Tavistock Square
London WC1H 9QU
Telephone: 0207 679 4977
E-mail: constitution@ucl.ac.uk
Website: http:// www.ucl.ac.uk/constitution-unit

A.39 From time to time requests for information will raise difficult legal issues, which will have to be considered by senior management, who may need to seek outside legal advice. Everyone dealing with enquiries must be aware of this.

APPENDIX B

Guide to Applying for Information under the Act

Purpose

This is a practical guide for business people and others seeking to obtain information pursuant to the right conferred by the Act. **B.01**

The right to know

> The right to know is dealt with in paras 5.09–5.13 above.

The right created by section 1 of the Act is a right to be informed in writing by a **B.02** public authority whether it holds information of the description specified in the request and if that is the case to have the information communicated to him.

Who is bound by the Act

> The meaning of 'public authorities' is discussed in chapter 5 part C paras 5.22–5.58 above.

Either ask the public authority or turn to Schedule 1 to the Act to ascertain **B.03** whether the public authority concerned is subject to the right and whether the right of access is limited to specified information only, bearing in mind that:

(a) Schedule 1 can be amended by order of the Lord Chancellor;[1]
(b) The Lord Chancellor can also designate a person as a public authority by order even if they do not qualify to be in Schedule 1;[2]
(c) public authorities include publicly owned companies, which in summary are wholly owned by the Crown or by a public authority listed in Schedule 1 other than a government department or an authority listed only in relation to particular information;[3]

---

[1] S 4 of the Act.
[2] S 5 of the Act.
[3] S 6 of the Act.

(d) in the case of government departments, section 81(1) of the Act provides that each government department is to be treated as being an individual entity distinct from any other government department.

Restrictions on the right to know

> Restrictions are discussed in general terms in paras 6.01–6.02 above.

B.04 There will be a right to have the information communicated only if the information is held by the public authority concerned; such communication is not prevented by an exemption contained in Part II of the Act; any fees required in accordance with section 9 of the Act have been paid; the cost exemptions of section 12 of the Act do not apply; and the request is neither vexatious nor repetitious: if it falls within either category the authority is not obliged to comply with the request—see section 14 of the Act.

Useful documents

B.05 Before making a request an applicant should consider the following documents. This will assist in identifying the information required, preparing the request and dealing with the public authority concerned:

(a) the public authority's publication scheme which is required to be approved by the Information Commissioner and which must specify classes of information which the public authority publishes or intends to publish, the manner of publication and whether the material is intended to be free of charge;[4]

(b) the Code of Practice issued by the Lord Chancellor to provide guidance to public authorities as to the discharge of their functions, which is in Appendix 2;[5]

(c) the Code of Practice issued by the Lord Chancellor as guidance in respect of the keeping, management and destruction of records of a public authority which is in Appendix 2;[6]

(d) the information issued to the public by the Information Commissioner about the operation of the Act and good practice.[7]

Apply in writing

> The form of the request is discussed in paras 5.65–5.67 above.

---

[4] S 19 of the Act.
[5] S 45 of the Act.
[6] S 46 of the Act.
[7] S 47 of the Act.

The request for information must be in writing[8] and **B.06**

(a) state the name of the applicant and the address for correspondence;

(b) ensure that the description of the information required is sufficiently clear and detailed to enable the public authority to provide access;[9]

(c) if required, state a preference for any one or more of the following methods by which the information can be accessed, namely by being provided with a copy in a permanent or other form acceptable to the applicant, or a reasonable opportunity to inspect a record containing the information or a digest or summary of the information in a permanent or other form acceptable to the applicant.[10]

The duty of disclosure only applies to information held by the authority at the date of the request.

The authority's response

Insofar as may be necessary request advice and assistance from the public author-ity in fulfilment of its statutory duty created by section 16 of the Act and in ac-cordance with the guidance provided by the Lord Chancellor's Code of Practice. **B.07**

Wait for the public authority to fulfil its duty to confirm or deny whether it holds the information and, if so, whether the business is entitled to have access to it.[11] **B.08**

In the event of undue delay or a refusal to provide access to the information, ex-haust the internal complaints procedures of the public authority concerned before making an application to the Information Commissioner pursuant to section 50 of the Act for a decision whether the request for information has been dealt with in accordance with the requirements of Part I of the Act. **B.09**

Advice and assistance

> Advice and assistance is discussed in paras 5.72–5.79 above.

Reference has been made to the duty under section 16 of the Act to provide advice and assistance. This duty should not be under-estimated and the Lord Chancellor's Code of Guidance provides considerable guidance. However, it is to be noted that the duty is to provide advice and assistance '*so far as it would be rea-sonable to expect the authority to do so*'. It is to be anticipated that businesses will **B.10**

---

[8] It can be transmitted electronically provided it is received in a legible form and is capable of being used for subsequent reference, see s 8(2) of the Act.

[9] S 1 of the Act.

[10] S 11(1) of the Act—the public authority is only required to comply with the preference in so far as it is reasonably practical to do so.

[11] S 1(1) and 1(6) of the Act.

normally be expected to have a better knowledge of, and ability to comply with, the Act than the ordinary man in the street. It might be that in the case of requests from businesses the public authority will take the view that the applicant can afford to obtain professional advice and that the duty under section 16 will be satisfied by directing the applicant to the appropriate source of such advice. Whether this will occur and whether it would be appropriate will depend upon the circumstances. However, as a general observation it is reasonable to assert that public authorities should not avoid their duty in such a manner. It is the public authority that knows whether it has the relevant information and it is for the authority to provide advice and assistance in enabling the applicant to obtain access to it.

Timing—possible delays

> Time for compliance is discussed in paras 5.89–5.97 above.

B.11 The public authority is required to comply promptly with the duty to confirm or deny and in any event not later than the twentieth working day following receipt of the request.[12] However:

(i) the time period can be suspended if:
  (a) the public authority serves a notice requesting further information in order to identify and locate the information requested until after that further information is provided;
  (b) the public authority decides to charge a fee and gives a written notice (a 'fees notice') stating that a fee of a specified amount will be charged; where that happens the authority is not obliged to comply unless the fee is paid within three months beginning with the day on which the fee notice is given to avoid the duty ending;[13]

(ii) the public authority is exempted from compliance where it estimates that the cost will exceed the appropriate limit to be prescribed by the Lord Chancellor by regulation;[14]

(iii) where a request is refused, the applicants must be given a notice of refusal of the request which must comply with section 17;

(iv) a public authority is not obliged to comply with:
  (a) vexatious requests or

---

[12] S 10 of the Act unless otherwise stated within the following sub-paragraphs.
[13] S 9 of the Act.
[14] Which may vary between different cases.

(b) requests previously made in identical or substantially similar terms by the same person without a reasonable period elapsing between compliance with the previous request and the making of the current request.[15]

Charges

> Fees are discussed in part F of chapter 5 see paras 5.80–5.87 above.

It is to be observed that the Act does not require a public authority to make charges for the information requested. However, there will be Fees Regulations made under sections 9, 12 and 13 of the Act. The public authority will have a discretion to charge applicants a fee in accordance with those Regulations.   **B.12**

New information

> The date of information to be provided is discussed in paras 5.62–5.64 above.

The public authority is only required to provide information held at the time the request is received.[16] Section 1(4) of the Act provides that a public authority in performing its duty may (ie, it has a discretion) take account of any amendment or deletion made between the time of the request and the time the information is to be communicated, being an amendment or deletion which would have occurred regardless of the request. This does not appear to refer to new material; it is only concerned with the amendment or deletion of the material existing at the time of the request. So it is for the applicant to ensure that updated information is requested. If such a further request is necessary, it should not lead to the exemption described in sub-paragraph (iv) (b) above being invoked (requests previously made in identical or substantially similar terms without a reasonable period elapsing) provided the information requested is limited to information in existence between the date of the old request and the date of the new request.   **B.13**

Transfer of requests

> Transferring requests is discussed in paras 5.98–5.100 above.

---

[15] S 14 of the Act.
[16] S 1(4) of the Act.

B.14 The Act does not refer to transfers of requests between public authorities. However the Code issued under section 45 of the Act, gives guidance to public authorities on this issue under Part VI. In essence:

(i) it does not excuse compliance with the Act insofar as a public authority has part of the information requested—the duty to confirm or deny must be complied with in any event and a transfer can only be made in respect of information not held by the authority to whom the request is made; subject to that compliance;

(ii) insofar as information is held by another public authority in most cases it will be appropriate to advise the applicant to re-apply to the authority that holds the information, providing contact details; but

(iii) the request may be transferred without permission if the public authority reasonably concludes that the applicant would not object;

(iv) otherwise the transfer should not take place without consent;

(v) the transferred request is to be treated by the receiving authority in the same way as an original request by the applicant and time for dealing with the request starts with the day of its receipt;

(vi) all transfers should take place as soon as practicable and the applicant should be informed as soon as possible once the transfer has occurred.

Reason for requests are immaterial

B.15 In some cases the public authority may be concerned with the reasons why a request is being made. It is in fact sufficient for businesses and any other applicant to identify the information required. The Act is not concerned with motive and the Lord Chancellor's Code of Practice at paragraph 9 emphasizes strongly that:

> the aim of providing assistance is to clarify the nature of the information sought, *not* to determine the aims or motives of the applicant. Care should be taken not to give the applicant the impression that he or she is obliged to disclose the nature of his or her interest or that he or she will be treated differently if he or she does.

B.16 At the end of the day the question for the applicant must be whether, as a matter of common sense, the public authority is assisting or not. If not, the process of complaints and appeals will need to be considered.

Complaints

Complaints procedure is discussed in paras 7.58–7.66 above.

B.17 Difficulties in obtaining information or assistance should be met with the appropriate complaint, for example that the public authority is failing to fulfil its statutory duty to confirm or deny, or its statutory duty to provide advice and assistance. The latter duty is prescribed by section 16 of the Act. Although it is limited by the proviso 'so far as it would be reasonable to expect the authority to do so', it is an important part of the scheme of the Act and provides substantive assistance for the right of access.

The Code of Practice issued by the Lord Chancellor pursuant to the requirements **B.18** of section 45 of the Act includes provisions relating to procedures to be implemented by public authorities in order to deal with complaints. These procedures must be exhausted before a complaint can be made to the Information Commissioner. Thereafter, on the basis that the request continues to be thwarted or refused, the remedy is to make an application for a decision to the Commissioner.

Enforcement

> Applications for decisions by the Information Commission are discussed at paras 7.67–7.77 above.

The procedure prescribed by Part IV of the Act (enforcement) for the purposes of **B.19** obtaining such a decision can be summarized as follows:

(i) make an application for a decision as to whether the request has been dealt with in accordance with the requirements of Part I of the Act;[17]

(ii) await a decision by the Commissioner subject to him deciding to serve an information notice[18] on the public authority requiring information relating to the application, to compliance with Part I of the Act or to conformity with the code of practice as may be specified in the notice.

The decision sought will be that there has been a failure to communicate informa- **B.20** tion or to provide confirmation or denial or to comply with the requirements for the method of communication specified in section 11 of the Act or with the requirements for the refusal of a request specified in section 17 of the Act.

Decision Notices

> Decision notices are discussed in paras 7.70–7.77 above.

If such a decision is made, the decision notice must specify the steps which must **B.21** be taken by the public authority in order to comply with its statutory duty.[19] A

---

[17] S 50 of the Act.
[18] S 51 of the Act.
[19] S 50(4) of the Act.

period for such compliance will also be specified, although time will not run if an appeal is made which would affect the steps required to be taken. Nor must the time for the period be less than the period for bringing an appeal.[20]

Enforcement Notices

Enforcement notices are discussed in paras 7.39–7.43 above.

B.22 The Commissioner may also serve an enforcement notice requiring such compliance[21] and the same rules concerning time and appeals apply. It will be important that the application is made promptly because one of the grounds which entitle the Commissioner to refuse to make a decision is that there has been undue delay. Other grounds for refusal are (a) a failure to exhaust a complaints procedure provided by the public authority in compliance with the code of practice (b) the application appearing to be frivolous or vexatious or (c) the withdrawal or abandoning of the application.[22]

Appeals

Appeals are considered at paras 7.78–7.102 above.

B.23 Appeals by the complainant or the public authority against a decision notice, and by a public authority against an information notice or an enforcement notice, are made to the Information Tribunal. Appeals are to be determined by deciding whether the notice appealed is in accordance with law or whether any discretion exercised by the Commissioner in respect of the decision notified ought to have been exercised differently. The Tribunal may review any finding of fact. A decision of the Tribunal can be appealed on a point of law to the High Court in England if the address of the public authority is in England or Wales or to the Court of Session if in Scotland or to the High Court of Justice in Northern Ireland if there.[23]

---

[20] S 50(6) of the Act.
[21] S 52 of the Act, noting that exceptions from the duty to comply with the decision or the notice may arise pursuant to s 53 of the Act.
[22] S 50(2) of the Act.
[23] Ss 57 to 59 of the Act.

II: MATERIALS

APPENDIX C

The Act is printed as amended by the Transfer of Functions (Miscellaneous) Order 2001, SI 2001/3500 and the Freedom of Information (Additional Public Authorities) Order 2002, SI 2002/2623. Additions are underlined, and deleted words and phrases are shown struck through.

Freedom of Information Act 2000

2000 CHAPTER 36

ARRANGEMENT OF SECTIONS

PART I

ACCESS TO INFORMATION HELD BY PUBLIC AUTHORITIES

Right to information

PART II
EXEMPT INFORMATION

21. Information accessible to applicant by other means.
22. Information intended for future publication.
23. Information supplied by, or relating to, bodies dealing with security matters.
24. National security.
25. Certificates under ss. 23 and 24: supplementary provisions.
26. Defence.
27. International relations.
28. Relations within the United Kingdom.
29. The economy.
30. Investigations and proceedings conducted by public authorities.
31. Law enforcement.
32. Court records, etc.
33. Audit functions.
34. Parliamentary privilege.
35. Formulation of government policy, etc.
36. Prejudice to effective conduct of public affairs.
37. Communications with Her Majesty, etc. and honours.
38. Health and safety.
39. Environmental information.
40. Personal information.
41. Information provided in confidence.
42. Legal professional privilege.
43. Commercial interests.
44. Prohibitions on disclosure.

PART III
GENERAL FUNCTIONS OF SECRETARY OF STATE, LORD CHANCELLOR AND INFORMATION COMMISSIONER

45. Issue of code of practice by Secretary of State.
46. Issue of code of practice by Lord Chancellor.
47. General functions of Commissioner.
48. Recommendations as to good practice.
49. Reports to be laid before Parliament.

PART IV
ENFORCEMENT

50. Application for decision by Commissioner.
51. Information notices.
52. Enforcement notices.
53. Exception from duty to comply with decision notice or enforcement notice.
54. Failure to comply with notice.
55. Powers of entry and inspection.
56. No action against public authority.

PART V
APPEALS

PART VI
HISTORICAL RECORDS AND RECORDS IN PUBLIC RECORD OFFICE OR THE PUBLIC RECORD OFFICE OF NORTHERN IRELAND

PART VII
AMENDMENTS OF DATA PROTECTION ACT 1998

Amendments relating to personal information held by public authorities

Other amendments

PART VIII
MISCELLANEOUS AND SUPPLEMENTAL

87. Commencement.
88. Short title and extent.

SCHEDULES

An Act to make provision for the disclosure of information held by public authorities or by persons providing services for them and to amend the Data Protection Act 1998 and the Public Records Act 1958; and for connected purposes.

[30th November 2000]

BE IT ENACTED by the Queen's most Excellent Majesty, by and with the advice and consent of the Lords Spiritual and Temporal, and Commons, in this present Parliament assembled, and by the authority of the same, as follows:—

PART I

ACCESS TO INFORMATION HELD BY PUBLIC AUTHORITIES

Right to information

General right of access to information held by public authorities

1. (1) Any person making a request for information to a public authority is entitled—
    (a) to be informed in writing by the public authority whether it holds information of the description specified in the request, and
    (b) if that is the case, to have that information communicated to him.

(2) Subsection (1) has effect subject to the following provisions of this section and to the provisions of sections 2, 9, 12 and 14.

(3) Where a public authority—
    (a) reasonably requires further information in order to identify and locate the information requested, and

    (b) has informed the applicant of that requirement,

the authority is not obliged to comply with subsection (1) unless it is supplied with that further information.

    (4) The information—

      (a) in respect of which the applicant is to be informed under subsection (1)(a), or

      (b) which is to be communicated under subsection (1)(b),

is the information in question held at the time when the request is received, except that account may be taken of any amendment or deletion made between that time and the time when the information is to be communicated under subsection (1)(b), being an amendment or deletion that would have been made regardless of the receipt of the request.

    (5) A public authority is to be taken to have complied with subsection (1)(a) in relation to any information if it has communicated the information to the applicant in accordance with subsection (1)(b).

    (6) In this Act, the duty of a public authority to comply with subsection (1)(a) is referred to as 'the duty to confirm or deny'.

Effect of the exemptions in Part II

2. (1) Where any provision of Part II states that the duty to confirm or deny does not arise in relation to any information, the effect of the provision is that where either—

    (a) the provision confers absolute exemption, or

    (b) in all the circumstances of the case, the public interest in maintaining the exclusion of the duty to confirm or deny outweighs the public interest in disclosing whether the public authority holds the information,

section 1(1)(a) does not apply.

    (2) In respect of any information which is exempt information by virtue of any provision of Part II, section 1(1)(b) does not apply if or to the extent that—

    (a) the information is exempt information by virtue of a provision conferring absolute exemption, or

    (b) in all the circumstances of the case, the public interest in maintaining the exemption outweighs the public interest in disclosing the information.

    (3) For the purposes of this section, the following provisions of Part II (and no others) are to be regarded as conferring absolute exemption—

    (a) section 21,

    (b) section 23,

    (c) section 32,

    (d) section 34,

    (e) section 36 so far as relating to information held by the House of Commons or the House of Lords,

    (f) in section 40—

      (i) subsection (1), and

      (ii) subsection (2) so far as relating to cases where the first condition referred to in that subsection is satisfied by virtue of subsection (3)(a)(i) or (b) of that section,

    (g) section 41, and

    (h) section 44.

Public authorities

3. (1) In this Act 'public authority' means—

    (a) subject to section 4(4), any body which, any other person who, or the holder of any office which—

    (i) is listed in Schedule 1, or

    (ii) is designated by order under section 5, or

  (b) a publicly-owned company as defined by section 6.

(2) For the purposes of this Act, information is held by a public authority if—

  (a) it is held by the authority, otherwise than on behalf of another person, or

  (b) it is held by another person on behalf of the authority.

Amendment of Schedule 1

4. (1) ~~The Secretary of State~~ Lord Chancellor may by order amend Schedule 1 by adding to that Schedule a reference to any body or the holder of any office which (in either case) is not for the time being listed in that Schedule but as respects which both the first and the second conditions below are satisfied.

(2) The first condition is that the body or office—

  (a) is established by virtue of Her Majesty's prerogative or by an enactment or by subordinate legislation, or

  (b) is established in any other way by a Minister of the Crown in his capacity as Minister, by a government department or by the National Assembly for Wales.

(3) The second condition is—

  (a) in the case of a body, that the body is wholly or partly constituted by appointment made by the Crown, by a Minister of the Crown, by a government department or by the National Assembly for Wales, or

  (b) in the case of an office, that appointments to the office are made by the Crown, by a Minister of the Crown, by a government department or by the National Assembly for Wales.

(4) If either the first or the second condition above ceases to be satisfied as respects any body or office which is listed in Part VI or VII of Schedule 1, that body or the holder of that office shall cease to be a public authority by virtue of the entry in question.

(5) The ~~Secretary of State~~ Lord Chancellor may by order amend Schedule 1 by removing from Part VI or VII of that Schedule an entry relating to any body or office—

  (a) which has ceased to exist, or

  (b) as respects which either the first or the second condition above has ceased to be satisfied.

(6) An order under subsection (1) may relate to a specified person or office or to persons or offices falling within a specified description.

(7) Before making an order under subsection (1), the ~~Secretary of State~~ Lord Chancellor shall—

  (a) if the order adds to Part II, III, IV or VI of Schedule 1 a reference to—

    (i) a body whose functions are exercisable only or mainly in or as regards Wales, or

    (ii) the holder of an office whose functions are exercisable only or mainly in or as regards Wales,

consult the National Assembly for Wales, and

  (b) if the order relates to a body which, or the holder of any office who, if the order were made, would be a Northern Ireland public authority, consult the First Minister and deputy First Minister in Northern Ireland.

(8) This section has effect subject to section 80.

(9) In this section 'Minister of the Crown' includes a Northern Ireland Minister.

Further power to designate public authorities

5. (1) The ~~Secretary of State~~ Lord Chancellor may by order designate as a public authority for the purposes of this Act any person who is neither listed in Schedule 1 nor capable of being added to that Schedule by an order under section 4(1), but who—

(a) appears to the ~~Secretary of State~~ Lord Chancellor to exercise functions of a public nature, or

(b) is providing under a contract made with a public authority any service whose provision is a function of that authority.

(2) An order under this section may designate a specified person or office or persons or offices falling within a specified description.

(3) Before making an order under this section, the ~~Secretary of State~~ Lord Chancellor shall consult every person to whom the order relates, or persons appearing to him to represent such persons.

(4) This section has effect subject to section 80.

Publicly-owned companies

6. (1) A company is a 'publicly-owned company' for the purposes of section 3(1)(b) if—

  (a) it is wholly owned by the Crown, or

  (b) it is wholly owned by any public authority listed in Schedule 1 other than—

    (i) a government department, or

    (ii) any authority which is listed only in relation to particular information.

(2) For the purposes of this section—

  (a) a company is wholly owned by the Crown if it has no members except—

    (i) Ministers of the Crown, government departments or companies wholly owned by the Crown, or

    (ii) persons acting on behalf of Ministers of the Crown, government departments or companies wholly owned by the Crown, and

  (b) a company is wholly owned by a public authority other than a government department if it has no members except—

    (i) that public authority or companies wholly owned by that public authority, or

    (ii) persons acting on behalf of that public authority or of companies wholly owned by that public authority.

(3) In this section—

'company' includes any body corporate;

'Minister of the Crown' includes a Northern Ireland Minister.

Public authorities to which Act has limited application

7. (1) Where a public authority is listed in Schedule 1 only in relation to information of a specified description, nothing in Parts I to V of this Act applies to any other information held by the authority.

(2) An order under section 4(1) may, in adding an entry to Schedule 1, list the public authority only in relation to information of a specified description.

(3) The ~~Secretary of State~~ Lord Chancellor may by order amend Schedule 1—

  (a) by limiting to information of a specified description the entry relating to any public authority, or

  (b) by removing or amending any limitation to information of a specified description which is for the time being contained in any entry.

(4) Before making an order under subsection (3), the ~~Secretary of State~~ Lord Chancellor shall—

  (a) if the order relates to the National Assembly for Wales or a Welsh public authority, consult the National Assembly for Wales,

  (b) if the order relates to the Northern Ireland Assembly, consult the Presiding Officer of that Assembly, and

  (c) if the order relates to a Northern Ireland department or a Northern Ireland public authority, consult the First Minister and deputy First Minister in Northern Ireland.

(5) An order under section 5(1)(a) must specify the functions of the public authority designated by the order with respect to which the designation is to have effect; and nothing in Parts I to V of this Act applies to information which is held by the authority but does not relate to the exercise of those functions.

(6) An order under section 5(1)(b) must specify the services provided under contract with respect to which the designation is to have effect; and nothing in Parts I to V of this Act applies to information which is held by the public authority designated by the order but does not relate to the provision of those services.

(7) Nothing in Parts I to V of this Act applies in relation to any information held by a publicly-owned company which is excluded information in relation to that company.

(8) In subsection (7) 'excluded information', in relation to a publicly-owned company, means information which is of a description specified in relation to that company in an order made by the ~~Secretary of State~~ Lord Chancellor for the purposes of this subsection.

(9) In this section 'publicly-owned company' has the meaning given by section 6.

Request for information

8. (1) In this Act any reference to a 'request for information' is a reference to such a request which—
    (a) is in writing,
    (b) states the name of the applicant and an address for correspondence, and
    (c) describes the information requested.

(2) For the purposes of subsection (1)(a), a request is to be treated as made in writing where the text of the request—
    (a) is transmitted by electronic means,
    (b) is received in legible form, and
    (c) is capable of being used for subsequent reference.

Fees

9. (1) A public authority to whom a request for information is made may, within the period for complying with section 1(1), give the applicant a notice in writing (in this Act referred to as a 'fees notice') stating that a fee of an amount specified in the notice is to be charged by the authority for complying with section 1(1).

(2) Where a fees notice has been given to the applicant, the public authority is not obliged to comply with section 1(1) unless the fee is paid within the period of three months beginning with the day on which the fees notice is given to the applicant.

(3) Subject to subsection (5), any fee under this section must be determined by the public authority in accordance with regulations made by the ~~Secretary of State~~ Lord Chancellor.

(4) Regulations under subsection (3) may, in particular, provide—
    (a) that no fee is to be payable in prescribed cases,
    (b) that any fee is not to exceed such maximum as may be specified in, or determined in accordance with, the regulations, and
    (c) that any fee is to be calculated in such manner as may be prescribed by the regulations.

(5) Subsection (3) does not apply where provision is made by or under any enactment as to the fee that may be charged by the public authority for the disclosure of the information.

Time for compliance with request

10. (1) Subject to subsections (2) and (3), a public authority must comply with section 1(1) promptly and in any event not later than the twentieth working day following the date of receipt.

(2) Where the authority has given a fees notice to the applicant and the fee is paid in accordance with section 9(2), the working days in the period beginning with the day on which the fees notice is given to the applicant and ending with the day on which the fee is received by the authority are to be disregarded in calculating for the purposes of subsection (1) the twentieth working day following the date of receipt.

(3) If, and to the extent that—
    (a) section 1(1)(a) would not apply if the condition in section 2(1)(b) were satisfied, or
    (b) section 1(1)(b) would not apply if the condition in section 2(2)(b) were satisfied,

the public authority need not comply with section 1(1)(a) or (b) until such time as is reasonable in the circumstances; but this subsection does not affect the time by which any notice under section 17(1) must be given.

(4) The ~~Secretary of State~~ Lord Chancellor may by regulations provide that subsections (1) and (2) are to have effect as if any reference to the twentieth working day following the date of receipt were a reference to such other day, not later than the sixtieth working day following the date of receipt, as may be specified in, or determined in accordance with, the regulations.

(5) Regulations under subsection (4) may—
    (a) prescribe different days in relation to different cases, and
    (b) confer a discretion on the Commissioner.

(6) In this section—
'the date of receipt' means—
    (a) the day on which the public authority receives the request for information, or
    (b) if later, the day on which it receives the information referred to in section 1(3);

'working day' means any day other than a Saturday, a Sunday, Christmas Day, Good Friday or a day which is a bank holiday under the Banking and Financial Dealings Act 1971 in any part of the United Kingdom.

Means by which communication to be made

11. (1) Where, on making his request for information, the applicant expresses a preference for communication by any one or more of the following means, namely—
    (a) the provision to the applicant of a copy of the information in permanent form or in another form acceptable to the applicant,
    (b) the provision to the applicant of a reasonable opportunity to inspect a record containing the information, and
    (c) the provision to the applicant of a digest or summary of the information in permanent form or in another form acceptable to the applicant,

the public authority shall so far as reasonably practicable give effect to that preference.

(2) In determining for the purposes of this section whether it is reasonably practicable to communicate information by particular means, the public authority may have regard to all the circumstances, including the cost of doing so.

(3) Where the public authority determines that it is not reasonably practicable to comply with any preference expressed by the applicant in making his request, the authority shall notify the applicant of the reasons for its determination.

(4) Subject to subsection (1), a public authority may comply with a request by communicating information by any means which are reasonable in the circumstances.

Exemption where cost of compliance exceeds appropriate limit

12. (1) Section 1(1) does not oblige a public authority to comply with a request for information if the authority estimates that the cost of complying with the request would exceed the appropriate limit.

(2) Subsection (1) does not exempt the public authority from its obligation to comply with paragraph (a) of section 1(1) unless the estimated cost of complying with that paragraph alone would exceed the appropriate limit.

(3) In subsections (1) and (2) 'the appropriate limit' means such amount as may be prescribed, and different amounts may be prescribed in relation to different cases.

(4) The ~~Secretary of State~~ Lord Chancellor may by regulations provide that, in such circumstances as may be prescribed, where two or more requests for information are made to a public authority—

(a) by one person, or

(b) by different persons who appear to the public authority to be acting in concert or in pursuance of a campaign,

the estimated cost of complying with any of the requests is to be taken to be the estimated total cost of complying with all of them.

(5) The ~~Secretary of State~~ Lord Chancellor may by regulations make provision for the purposes of this section as to the costs to be estimated and as to the manner in which they are to be estimated.

Fees for disclosure where cost of compliance exceeds appropriate limit

13. (1) A public authority may charge for the communication of any information whose communication—

(a) is not required by section 1(1) because the cost of complying with the request for information exceeds the amount which is the appropriate limit for the purposes of section 12(1) and (2), and

(b) is not otherwise required by law,

such fee as may be determined by the public authority in accordance with regulations made by the ~~Secretary of State~~ Lord Chancellor.

(2) Regulations under this section may, in particular, provide—

(a) that any fee is not to exceed such maximum as may be specified in, or determined in accordance with, the regulations, and

(b) that any fee is to be calculated in such manner as may be prescribed by the regulations.

(3) Subsection (1) does not apply where provision is made by or under any enactment as to the fee that may be charged by the public authority for the disclosure of the information.

Vexatious or repeated requests

14. (1) Section 1(1) does not oblige a public authority to comply with a request for information if the request is vexatious.

(2) Where a public authority has previously complied with a request for information which was made by any person, it is not obliged to comply with a subsequent identical or substantially similar request from that person unless a reasonable interval has elapsed between compliance with the previous request and the making of the current request.

Special provisions relating to public records transferred to Public Record Office, etc

15. (1) Where—

(a) the appropriate records authority receives a request for information which relates to information which is, or if it existed would be, contained in a transferred public record, and

(b) either of the conditions in subsection (2) is satisfied in relation to any of that information,

that authority shall, within the period for complying with section 1(1), send a copy of the request to the responsible authority.

(2) The conditions referred to in subsection (1)(b) are—

(a) that the duty to confirm or deny is expressed to be excluded only by a provision of Part II not specified in subsection (3) of section 2, and

(b) that the information is exempt information only by virtue of a provision of Part II not specified in that subsection.

(3) On receiving the copy, the responsible authority shall, within such time as is reasonable in all the circumstances, inform the appropriate records authority of the determination required by virtue of subsection (3) or (4) of section 66.

(4) In this Act 'transferred public record' means a public record which has been transferred—

(a) to the Public Record Office,

(b) to another place of deposit appointed by the Lord Chancellor under the Public Records Act 1958, or

(c) to the Public Record Office of Northern Ireland.

(5) In this Act—

'appropriate records authority', in relation to a transferred public record, means—

(a) in a case falling within subsection (4)(a), the Public Record Office,

(b) in a case falling within subsection (4)(b), the Lord Chancellor, and

(c) in a case falling within subsection (4)(c), the Public Record Office of Northern Ireland;

'responsible authority', in relation to a transferred public record, means—

(a) in the case of a record transferred as mentioned in subsection (4)(a) or (b) from a government department in the charge of a Minister of the Crown, the Minister of the Crown who appears to the Lord Chancellor to be primarily concerned,

(b) in the case of a record transferred as mentioned in subsection (4)(a) or (b) from any other person, the person who appears to the Lord Chancellor to be primarily concerned,

(c) in the case of a record transferred to the Public Record Office of Northern Ireland from a government department in the charge of a Minister of the Crown, the Minister of the Crown who appears to the appropriate Northern Ireland Minister to be primarily concerned,

(d) in the case of a record transferred to the Public Record Office of Northern Ireland from a Northern Ireland department, the Northern Ireland Minister who appears to the appropriate Northern Ireland Minister to be primarily concerned, or

(e) in the case of a record transferred to the Public Record Office of Northern Ireland from any other person, the person who appears to the appropriate Northern Ireland Minister to be primarily concerned.

Duty to provide advice and assistance

16. (1) It shall be the duty of a public authority to provide advice and assistance, so far as it would be reasonable to expect the authority to do so, to persons who propose to make, or have made, requests for information to it.

(2) Any public authority which, in relation to the provision of advice or assistance in any case, conforms with the code of practice under section 45 is to be taken to comply with the duty imposed by subsection (1) in relation to that case.

Refusal of request

17. (1) A public authority which, in relation to any request for information, is to any extent relying on a claim that any provision of Part II relating to the duty to confirm or deny is relevant to the request or on a claim that information is exempt information must, within the time for complying with section 1(1), give the applicant a notice which—

(a) states that fact,

(b) specifies the exemption in question, and

(c) states (if that would not otherwise be apparent) why the exemption applies.

(2) Where—

    (a) in relation to any request for information, a public authority is, as respects any information, relying on a claim—

        (i) that any provision of Part II which relates to the duty to confirm or deny and is not specified in section 2(3) is relevant to the request, or

        (ii) that the information is exempt information only by virtue of a provision not specified in section 2(3), and

    (b) at the time when the notice under subsection (1) is given to the applicant, the public authority (or, in a case falling within section 66(3) or (4), the responsible authority) has not yet reached a decision as to the application of subsection (1)(b) or (2)(b) of section 2,

the notice under subsection (1) must indicate that no decision as to the application of that provision has yet been reached and must contain an estimate of the date by which the authority expects that such a decision will have been reached.

(3) A public authority which, in relation to any request for information, is to any extent relying on a claim that subsection (1)(b) or (2)(b) of section 2 applies must, either in the notice under subsection (1) or in a separate notice given within such time as is reasonable in the circumstances, state the reasons for claiming—

    (a) that, in all the circumstances of the case, the public interest in maintaining the exclusion of the duty to confirm or deny outweighs the public interest in disclosing whether the authority holds the information, or

    (b) that, in all the circumstances of the case, the public interest in maintaining the exemption outweighs the public interest in disclosing the information.

(4) A public authority is not obliged to make a statement under subsection (1)(c) or (3) if, or to the extent that, the statement would involve the disclosure of information which would itself be exempt information.

(5) A public authority which, in relation to any request for information, is relying on a claim that section 12 or 14 applies must, within the time for complying with section 1(1), give the applicant a notice stating that fact.

(6) Subsection (5) does not apply where—

    (a) the public authority is relying on a claim that section 14 applies,

    (b) the authority has given the applicant a notice, in relation to a previous request for information, stating that it is relying on such a claim, and

    (c) it would in all the circumstances be unreasonable to expect the authority to serve a further notice under subsection (5) in relation to the current request.

(7) A notice under subsection (1), (3) or (5) must—

    (a) contain particulars of any procedure provided by the public authority for dealing with complaints about the handling of requests for information or state that the authority does not provide such a procedure, and

    (b) contain particulars of the right conferred by section 50.

The Information Commissioner and the Information Tribunal

18. (1) The Data Protection Commissioner shall be known instead as the Information Commissioner.

(2) The Data Protection Tribunal shall be known instead as the Information Tribunal.

(3) In this Act—

    (a) the Information Commissioner is referred to as 'the Commissioner', and

    (b) the Information Tribunal is referred to as 'the Tribunal'.

(4) Schedule 2 (which makes provision consequential on subsections (1) and (2) and amendments of the Data Protection Act 1998 relating to the extension by this Act of the functions of the Commissioner and the Tribunal) has effect.

(5) If the person who held office as Data Protection Commissioner immediately before the day on which this Act is passed remains in office as Information Commissioner at the end of the period of two years beginning with that day, he shall vacate his office at the end of that period.

(6) Subsection (5) does not prevent the re-appointment of a person whose appointment is terminated by that subsection.

(7) In the application of paragraph 2(4)(b) and (5) of Schedule 5 to the Data Protection Act 1998 (Commissioner not to serve for more than fifteen years and not to be appointed, except in special circumstances, for a third or subsequent term) to anything done after the passing of this Act, there shall be left out of account any term of office served by virtue of an appointment made before the passing of this Act.

Publication schemes

19. (1) It shall be the duty of every public authority—
- (a) to adopt and maintain a scheme which relates to the publication of information by the authority and is approved by the Commissioner (in this Act referred to as a 'publication scheme'),
- (b) to publish information in accordance with its publication scheme, and
- (c) from time to time to review its publication scheme.

(2) A publication scheme must—
- (a) specify classes of information which the public authority publishes or intends to publish,
- (b) specify the manner in which information of each class is, or is intended to be, published, and
- (c) specify whether the material is, or is intended to be, available to the public free of charge or on payment.

(3) In adopting or reviewing a publication scheme, a public authority shall have regard to the public interest—
- (a) in allowing public access to information held by the authority, and
- (b) in the publication of reasons for decisions made by the authority.

(4) A public authority shall publish its publication scheme in such manner as it thinks fit.

(5) The Commissioner may, when approving a scheme, provide that his approval is to expire at the end of a specified period.

(6) Where the Commissioner has approved the publication scheme of any public authority, he may at any time give notice to the public authority revoking his approval of the scheme as from the end of the period of six months beginning with the day on which the notice is given.

(7) Where the Commissioner—
- (a) refuses to approve a proposed publication scheme, or
- (b) revokes his approval of a publication scheme,

he must give the public authority a statement of his reasons for doing so.

Model publication schemes

20. (1) The Commissioner may from time to time approve, in relation to public authorities falling within particular classes, model publication schemes prepared by him or by other persons.

(2) Where a public authority falling within the class to which an approved model scheme relates adopts such a scheme without modification, no further approval of the Commissioner is required so long as the model scheme remains approved; and where such an authority adopts such a scheme with modifications, the approval of the Commissioner is required only in relation to the modifications.

(3) The Commissioner may, when approving a model publication scheme, provide that his approval is to expire at the end of a specified period.

(4) Where the Commissioner has approved a model publication scheme, he may at any time publish, in such manner as he thinks fit, a notice revoking his approval of the scheme as from the end of the period of six months beginning with the day on which the notice is published.

(5) Where the Commissioner refuses to approve a proposed model publication scheme on the application of any person, he must give the person who applied for approval of the scheme a statement of the reasons for his refusal.

(6) Where the Commissioner refuses to approve any modifications under subsection (2), he must give the public authority a statement of the reasons for his refusal.

(7) Where the Commissioner revokes his approval of a model publication scheme, he must include in the notice under subsection (4) a statement of his reasons for doing so.

PART II
EXEMPT INFORMATION

Information accessible to applicant by other means

21. (1) Information which is reasonably accessible to the applicant otherwise than under section 1 is exempt information.

(2) For the purposes of subsection (1)—
    (a) information may be reasonably accessible to the applicant even though it is accessible only on payment, and
    (b) information is to be taken to be reasonably accessible to the applicant if it is information which the public authority or any other person is obliged by or under any enactment to communicate (otherwise than by making the information available for inspection) to members of the public on request, whether free of charge or on payment.

(3) For the purposes of subsection (1), information which is held by a public authority and does not fall within subsection (2)(b) is not to be regarded as reasonably accessible to the applicant merely because the information is available from the public authority itself on request, unless the information is made available in accordance with the authority's publication scheme and any payment required is specified in, or determined in accordance with, the scheme.

Information intended for future publication

22. (1) Information is exempt information if—
    (a) the information is held by the public authority with a view to its publication, by the authority or any other person, at some future date (whether determined or not),
    (b) the information was already held with a view to such publication at the time when the request for information was made, and
    (c) it is reasonable in all the circumstances that the information should be withheld from disclosure until the date referred to in paragraph (a).

(2) The duty to confirm or deny does not arise if, or to the extent that, compliance with section 1(1)(a) would involve the disclosure of any information (whether or not already recorded) which falls within subsection (1).

Information supplied by, or relating to, bodies dealing with security matters

23. (1) Information held by a public authority is exempt information if it was directly or indirectly supplied to the public authority by, or relates to, any of the bodies specified in subsection (3).

(2) A certificate signed by a Minister of the Crown certifying that the information to which it applies was directly or indirectly supplied by, or relates to, any of the bodies specified in subsection (3) shall, subject to section 60, be conclusive evidence of that fact.

(3) The bodies referred to in subsections (1) and (2) are—

    (a) the Security Service,

    (b) the Secret Intelligence Service,

    (c) the Government Communications Headquarters,

    (d) the special forces,

    (e) the Tribunal established under section 65 of the Regulation of Investigatory Powers Act 2000,

    (f) the Tribunal established under section 7 of the Interception of Communications Act 1985,

    (g) the Tribunal established under section 5 of the Security Service Act 1989,

    (h) the Tribunal established under section 9 of the Intelligence Services Act 1994,

    (i) the Security Vetting Appeals Panel,

    (j) the Security Commission,

    (k) the National Criminal Intelligence Service, and

    (l) the Service Authority for the National Criminal Intelligence Service.

(4) In subsection (3)(c) 'the Government Communications Headquarters' includes any unit or part of a unit of the armed forces of the Crown which is for the time being required by the Secretary of State to assist the Government Communications Headquarters in carrying out its functions.

(5) The duty to confirm or deny does not arise if, or to the extent that, compliance with section 1(1)(a) would involve the disclosure of any information (whether or not already recorded) which was directly or indirectly supplied to the public authority by, or relates to, any of the bodies specified in subsection (3).

National security

24. (1) Information which does not fall within section 23(1) is exempt information if exemption from section 1(1)(b) is required for the purpose of safeguarding national security.

(2) The duty to confirm or deny does not arise if, or to the extent that, exemption from section 1(1)(a) is required for the purpose of safeguarding national security.

(3) A certificate signed by a Minister of the Crown certifying that exemption from section 1(1)(b), or from section 1(1)(a) and (b), is, or at any time was, required for the purpose of safeguarding national security shall, subject to section 60, be conclusive evidence of that fact.

(4) A certificate under subsection (3) may identify the information to which it applies by means of a general description and may be expressed to have prospective effect.

Certificates under ss. 23 and 24: supplementary provisions

25. (1) A document purporting to be a certificate under section 23(2) or 24(3) shall be received in evidence and deemed to be such a certificate unless the contrary is proved.

(2) A document which purports to be certified by or on behalf of a Minister of the Crown as a true copy of a certificate issued by that Minister under section 23(2) or 24(3) shall in any legal proceedings be evidence (or, in Scotland, sufficient evidence) of that certificate.

(3) The power conferred by section 23(2) or 24(3) on a Minister of the Crown shall not be exercisable except by a Minister who is a member of the Cabinet or by the Attorney General, the Advocate General for Scotland or the Attorney General for Northern Ireland.

Defence

26. (1) Information is exempt information if its disclosure under this Act would, or would be likely to, prejudice—

    (a) the defence of the British Islands or of any colony, or

    (b) the capability, effectiveness or security of any relevant forces.

(2) In subsection (1)(b) 'relevant forces' means—
  (a) the armed forces of the Crown, and
  (b) any forces co-operating with those forces,

or any part of any of those forces.

(3) The duty to confirm or deny does not arise if, or to the extent that, compliance with section 1(1)(a) would, or would be likely to, prejudice any of the matters mentioned in subsection (1).

International relations

27. (1) Information is exempt information if its disclosure under this Act would, or would be likely to, prejudice—
  (a) relations between the United Kingdom and any other State,
  (b) relations between the United Kingdom and any international organisation or international court,
  (c) the interests of the United Kingdom abroad, or
  (d) the promotion or protection by the United Kingdom of its interests abroad.

(2) Information is also exempt information if it is confidential information obtained from a State other than the United Kingdom or from an international organisation or international court.

(3) For the purposes of this section, any information obtained from a State, organisation or court is confidential at any time while the terms on which it was obtained require it to be held in confidence or while the circumstances in which it was obtained make it reasonable for the State, organisation or court to expect that it will be so held.

(4) The duty to confirm or deny does not arise if, or to the extent that, compliance with section 1(1)(a)—
  (a) would, or would be likely to, prejudice any of the matters mentioned in subsection (1), or
  (b) would involve the disclosure of any information (whether or not already recorded) which is confidential information obtained from a State other than the United Kingdom or from an international organisation or international court.

(5) In this section—
'international court' means any international court which is not an international organisation and which is established—
  (a) by a resolution of an international organisation of which the United Kingdom is a member, or
  (b) by an international agreement to which the United Kingdom is a party;

'international organisation' means any international organisation whose members include any two or more States, or any organ of such an organisation;
'State' includes the government of any State and any organ of its government, and references to a State other than the United Kingdom include references to any territory outside the United Kingdom.

Relations within the United Kingdom

28. (1) Information is exempt information if its disclosure under this Act would, or would be likely to, prejudice relations between any administration in the United Kingdom and any other such administration.

(2) In subsection (1) 'administration in the United Kingdom' means—
  (a) the government of the United Kingdom,
  (b) the Scottish Administration,
  (c) the Executive Committee of the Northern Ireland Assembly, or
  (d) the National Assembly for Wales.

(3) The duty to confirm or deny does not arise if, or to the extent that, compliance with section 1(1)(a) would, or would be likely to, prejudice any of the matters mentioned in subsection (1).

The economy

29. (1) Information is exempt information if its disclosure under this Act would, or would be likely to, prejudice—

(a) the economic interests of the United Kingdom or of any part of the United Kingdom, or

(b) the financial interests of any administration in the United Kingdom, as defined by section 28(2).

(2) The duty to confirm or deny does not arise if, or to the extent that, compliance with section 1(1)(a) would, or would be likely to, prejudice any of the matters mentioned in subsection (1).

Investigations and proceedings conducted by public authorities

30. (1) Information held by a public authority is exempt information if it has at any time been held by the authority for the purposes of—

(a) any investigation which the public authority has a duty to conduct with a view to it being ascertained—

(i) whether a person should be charged with an offence, or

(ii) whether a person charged with an offence is guilty of it,

(b) any investigation which is conducted by the authority and in the circumstances may lead to a decision by the authority to institute criminal proceedings which the authority has power to conduct, or

(c) any criminal proceedings which the authority has power to conduct.

(2) Information held by a public authority is exempt information if—

(a) it was obtained or recorded by the authority for the purposes of its functions relating to—

(i) investigations falling within subsection (1)(a) or (b),

(ii) criminal proceedings which the authority has power to conduct,

(iii) investigations (other than investigations falling within subsection (1)(a) or (b)) which are conducted by the authority for any of the purposes specified in section 31(2) and either by virtue of Her Majesty's prerogative or by virtue of powers conferred by or under any enactment, or

(iv) civil proceedings which are brought by or on behalf of the authority and arise out of such investigations, and

(b) it relates to the obtaining of information from confidential sources.

(3) The duty to confirm or deny does not arise in relation to information which is (or if it were held by the public authority would be) exempt information by virtue of subsection (1) or (2).

(4) In relation to the institution or conduct of criminal proceedings or the power to conduct them, references in subsection (1)(b) or (c) and subsection (2)(a) to the public authority include references—

(a) to any officer of the authority,

(b) in the case of a government department other than a Northern Ireland department, to the Minister of the Crown in charge of the department, and

(c) in the case of a Northern Ireland department, to the Northern Ireland Minister in charge of the department.

(5) In this section—

'criminal proceedings' includes—

(a) proceedings before a court-martial constituted under the Army Act 1955, the Air Force Act 1955 or the Naval Discipline Act 1957 or a disciplinary court constituted under section 52G of the Act of 1957,

    (b) proceedings on dealing summarily with a charge under the Army Act 1955 or the Air Force Act 1955 or on summary trial under the Naval Discipline Act 1957,

    (c) proceedings before a court established by section 83ZA of the Army Act 1955, section 83ZA of the Air Force Act 1955 or section 52FF of the Naval Discipline Act 1957 (summary appeal courts),

    (d) proceedings before the Courts-Martial Appeal Court, and

    (e) proceedings before a Standing Civilian Court;

'offence' includes any offence under the Army Act 1955, the Air Force Act 1955 or the Naval Discipline Act 1957.

  (6) In the application of this section to Scotland—

    (a) in subsection (1)(b), for the words from 'a decision' to the end there is substituted 'a decision by the authority to make a report to the procurator fiscal for the purpose of enabling him to determine whether criminal proceedings should be instituted',

    (b) in subsections (1)(c) and (2)(a)(ii) for 'which the authority has power to conduct' there is substituted 'which have been instituted in consequence of a report made by the authority to the procurator fiscal', and

    (c) for any reference to a person being charged with an offence there is substituted a reference to the person being prosecuted for the offence.

Law enforcement

31. (1) Information which is not exempt information by virtue of section 30 is exempt information if its disclosure under this Act would, or would be likely to, prejudice—

    (a) the prevention or detection of crime,

    (b) the apprehension or prosecution of offenders,

    (c) the administration of justice,

    (d) the assessment or collection of any tax or duty or of any imposition of a similar nature,

    (e) the operation of the immigration controls,

    (f) the maintenance of security and good order in prisons or in other institutions where persons are lawfully detained,

    (g) the exercise by any public authority of its functions for any of the purposes specified in subsection (2),

    (h) any civil proceedings which are brought by or on behalf of a public authority and arise out of an investigation conducted, for any of the purposes specified in subsection (2), by or on behalf of the authority by virtue of Her Majesty's prerogative or by virtue of powers conferred by or under an enactment, or

    (i) any inquiry held under the Fatal Accidents and Sudden Deaths Inquiries (Scotland) Act 1976 to the extent that the inquiry arises out of an investigation conducted, for any of the purposes specified in subsection (2), by or on behalf of the authority by virtue of Her Majesty's prerogative or by virtue of powers conferred by or under an enactment.

  (2) The purposes referred to in subsection (1)(g) to (i) are—

    (a) the purpose of ascertaining whether any person has failed to comply with the law,

    (b) the purpose of ascertaining whether any person is responsible for any conduct which is improper,

    (c) the purpose of ascertaining whether circumstances which would justify regulatory action in pursuance of any enactment exist or may arise,

    (d) the purpose of ascertaining a person's fitness or competence in relation to the management of bodies corporate or in relation to any profession or other activity which he is, or seeks to become, authorised to carry on,

    (e) the purpose of ascertaining the cause of an accident,

(f) the purpose of protecting charities against misconduct or mismanagement (whether by trustees or other persons) in their administration,

(g) the purpose of protecting the property of charities from loss or misapplication,

(h) the purpose of recovering the property of charities,

(i) the purpose of securing the health, safety and welfare of persons at work, and

(j) the purpose of protecting persons other than persons at work against risk to health or safety arising out of or in connection with the actions of persons at work.

(3) The duty to confirm or deny does not arise if, or to the extent that, compliance with section 1(1)(a) would, or would be likely to, prejudice any of the matters mentioned in subsection (1).

Court records

32. (1) Information held by a public authority is exempt information if it is held only by virtue of being contained in—

(a) any document filed with, or otherwise placed in the custody of, a court for the purposes of proceedings in a particular cause or matter,

(b) any document served upon, or by, a public authority for the purposes of proceedings in a particular cause or matter, or

(c) any document created by—
  (i) a court, or
  (ii) a member of the administrative staff of a court,

for the purposes of proceedings in a particular cause or matter.

(2) Information held by a public authority is exempt information if it is held only by virtue of being contained in—

(a) any document placed in the custody of a person conducting an inquiry or arbitration, for the purposes of the inquiry or arbitration, or

(b) any document created by a person conducting an inquiry or arbitration, for the purposes of the inquiry or arbitration.

(3) The duty to confirm or deny does not arise in relation to information which is (or if it were held by the public authority would be) exempt information by virtue of this section.

(4) In this section—

(a) 'court' includes any tribunal or body exercising the judicial power of the State,

(b) 'proceedings in a particular cause or matter' includes any inquest or post-mortem examination,

(c) 'inquiry' means any inquiry or hearing held under any provision contained in, or made under, an enactment, and

(d) except in relation to Scotland, 'arbitration' means any arbitration to which Part I of the Arbitration Act 1996 applies.

Audit functions

33. (1) This section applies to any public authority which has functions in relation to—

(a) the audit of the accounts of other public authorities, or

(b) the examination of the economy, efficiency and effectiveness with which other public authorities use their resources in discharging their functions.

(2) Information held by a public authority to which this section applies is exempt information if its disclosure would, or would be likely to, prejudice the exercise of any of the authority's functions in relation to any of the matters referred to in subsection (1).

(3) The duty to confirm or deny does not arise in relation to a public authority to which this section applies if, or to the extent that, compliance with section 1(1)(a) would, or would be likely to,

prejudice the exercise of any of the authority's functions in relation to any of the matters referred to in subsection (1).

Parliamentary privilege

34. (1) Information is exempt information if exemption from section 1(1)(b) is required for the purpose of avoiding an infringement of the privileges of either House of Parliament.

(2) The duty to confirm or deny does not apply if, or to the extent that, exemption from section 1(1)(a) is required for the purpose of avoiding an infringement of the privileges of either House of Parliament.

(3) A certificate signed by the appropriate authority certifying that exemption from section 1(1)(b), or from section 1(1)(a) and (b), is, or at any time was, required for the purpose of avoiding an infringement of the privileges of either House of Parliament shall be conclusive evidence of that fact.

(4) In subsection (3) 'the appropriate authority' means—
    (a) in relation to the House of Commons, the Speaker of that House, and
    (b) in relation to the House of Lords, the Clerk of the Parliaments.

Formulation of government policy, etc

35. (1) Information held by a government department or by the National Assembly for Wales is exempt information if it relates to—
    (a) the formulation or development of government policy,
    (b) Ministerial communications,
    (c) the provision of advice by any of the Law Officers or any request for the provision of such advice, or
    (d) the operation of any Ministerial private office.

(2) Once a decision as to government policy has been taken, any statistical information used to provide an informed background to the taking of the decision is not to be regarded—
    (a) for the purposes of subsection (1)(a), as relating to the formulation or development of government policy, or
    (b) for the purposes of subsection (1)(b), as relating to Ministerial communications.

(3) The duty to confirm or deny does not arise in relation to information which is (or if it were held by the public authority would be) exempt information by virtue of subsection (1).

(4) In making any determination required by section 2(1)(b) or (2)(b) in relation to information which is exempt information by virtue of subsection (1)(a), regard shall be had to the particular public interest in the disclosure of factual information which has been used, or is intended to be used, to provide an informed background to decision-taking.

(5) In this section—
'government policy' includes the policy of the Executive Committee of the Northern Ireland Assembly and the policy of the National Assembly for Wales;
'the Law Officers' means the Attorney General, the Solicitor General, the Advocate General for Scotland, the Lord Advocate, the Solicitor General for Scotland and the Attorney General for Northern Ireland;
'Ministerial communications' means any communications—
    (a) between Ministers of the Crown,
    (b) between Northern Ireland Ministers, including Northern Ireland junior Ministers, or
    (c) between Assembly Secretaries, including the Assembly First Secretary,

and includes, in particular, proceedings of the Cabinet or of any committee of the Cabinet, proceedings of the Executive Committee of the Northern Ireland Assembly, and proceedings of the executive committee of the National Assembly for Wales;

'Ministerial private office' means any part of a government department which provides personal administrative support to a Minister of the Crown, to a Northern Ireland Minister or a Northern Ireland junior Minister or any part of the administration of the National Assembly for Wales providing personal administrative support to the Assembly First Secretary or an Assembly Secretary;

'Northern Ireland junior Minister' means a member of the Northern Ireland Assembly appointed as a junior Minister under section 19 of the Northern Ireland Act 1998.

Prejudice to effective conduct of public affairs

36. (1) This section applies to—

    (a) information which is held by a government department or by the National Assembly for Wales and is not exempt information by virtue of section 35, and

    (b) information which is held by any other public authority.

(2) Information to which this section applies is exempt information if, in the reasonable opinion of a qualified person, disclosure of the information under this Act—

    (a) would, or would be likely to, prejudice—

      (i) the maintenance of the convention of the collective responsibility of Ministers of the Crown, or

      (ii) the work of the Executive Committee of the Northern Ireland Assembly, or

      (iii) the work of the executive committee of the National Assembly for Wales,

    (b) would, or would be likely to, inhibit—

      (i) the free and frank provision of advice, or

      (ii) the free and frank exchange of views for the purposes of deliberation, or

    (c) would otherwise prejudice, or would be likely otherwise to prejudice, the effective conduct of public affairs.

(3) The duty to confirm or deny does not arise in relation to information to which this section applies (or would apply if held by the public authority) if, or to the extent that, in the reasonable opinion of a qualified person, compliance with section 1(1)(a) would, or would be likely to, have any of the effects mentioned in subsection (2).

(4) In relation to statistical information, subsections (2) and (3) shall have effect with the omission of the words 'in the reasonable opinion of a qualified person'.

(5) In subsections (2) and (3) 'qualified person'—

    (a) in relation to information held by a government department in the charge of a Minister of the Crown, means any Minister of the Crown,

    (b) in relation to information held by a Northern Ireland department, means the Northern Ireland Minister in charge of the department,

    (c) in relation to information held by any other government department, means the commissioners or other person in charge of that department,

    (d) in relation to information held by the House of Commons, means the Speaker of that House,

    (e) in relation to information held by the House of Lords, means the Clerk of the Parliaments,

    (f) in relation to information held by the Northern Ireland Assembly, means the Presiding Officer,

    (g) in relation to information held by the National Assembly for Wales, means the Assembly First Secretary,

    (h) in relation to information held by any Welsh public authority other than the Auditor General for Wales, means—

      (i) the public authority, or

      (ii) any officer or employee of the authority authorised by the Assembly First Secretary,

(i) in relation to information held by the National Audit Office, means the Comptroller and Auditor General,

(j) in relation to information held by the Northern Ireland Audit Office, means the Comptroller and Auditor General for Northern Ireland,

(k) in relation to information held by the Auditor General for Wales, means the Auditor General for Wales,

(l) in relation to information held by any Northern Ireland public authority other than the Northern Ireland Audit Office, means—

   (i) the public authority, or

   (ii) any officer or employee of the authority authorised by the First Minister and deputy First Minister in Northern Ireland acting jointly,

(m) in relation to information held by the Greater London Authority, means the Mayor of London,

(n) in relation to information held by a functional body within the meaning of the Greater London Authority Act 1999, means the chairman of that functional body, and

(o) in relation to information held by any public authority not falling within any of paragraphs (a) to (n), means—

   (i) a Minister of the Crown,

   (ii) the public authority, if authorised for the purposes of this section by a Minister of the Crown, or

   (iii) any officer or employee of the public authority who is authorised for the purposes of this section by a Minister of the Crown.

(6) Any authorisation for the purposes of this section—

(a) may relate to a specified person or to persons falling within a specified class,

(b) may be general or limited to particular classes of case, and

(c) may be granted subject to conditions.

(7) A certificate signed by the qualified person referred to in subsection (5)(d) or (e) above certifying that in his reasonable opinion—

(a) disclosure of information held by either House of Parliament, or

(b) compliance with section 1(1)(a) by either House,

would, or would be likely to, have any of the effects mentioned in subsection (2) shall be conclusive evidence of that fact.

Communications with Her Majesty, etc. and honours

37. (1) Information is exempt information if it relates to—

(a) communications with Her Majesty, with other members of the Royal Family or with the Royal Household, or

(b) the conferring by the Crown of any honour or dignity.

(2) The duty to confirm or deny does not arise in relation to information which is (or if it were held by the public authority would be) exempt information by virtue of subsection (1).

Health and safety

38. (1) Information is exempt information if its disclosure under this Act would, or would be likely to—

(a) endanger the physical or mental health of any individual, or

(b) endanger the safety of any individual.

(2) The duty to confirm or deny does not arise if, or to the extent that, compliance with section 1(1)(a) would, or would be likely to, have either of the effects mentioned in subsection (1).

Environmental information

39. (1) Information is exempt information if the public authority holding it—

(a) is obliged by regulations under section 74 to make the information available to the public in accordance with the regulations, or

(b) would be so obliged but for any exemption contained in the regulations.

(2) The duty to confirm or deny does not arise in relation to information which is (or if it were held by the public authority would be) exempt information by virtue of subsection (1).

(3) Subsection (1)(a) does not limit the generality of section 21(1).

Personal information

40. (1) Any information to which a request for information relates is exempt information if it constitutes personal data of which the applicant is the data subject.

(2) Any information to which a request for information relates is also exempt information if—

(a) it constitutes personal data which do not fall within subsection (1), and

(b) either the first or the second condition below is satisfied.

(3) The first condition is—

(a) in a case where the information falls within any of paragraphs (a) to (d) of the definition of 'data' in section 1(1) of the Data Protection Act 1998, that the disclosure of the information to a member of the public otherwise than under this Act would contravene—

　(i) any of the data protection principles, or

　(ii) section 10 of that Act (right to prevent processing likely to cause damage or distress), and

(b) in any other case, that the disclosure of the information to a member of the public otherwise than under this Act would contravene any of the data protection principles if the exemptions in section 33A(1) of the Data Protection Act 1998 (which relate to manual data held by public authorities) were disregarded.

(4) The second condition is that by virtue of any provision of Part IV of the Data Protection Act 1998 the information is exempt from section 7(1)(c) of that Act (data subject's right of access to personal data).

(5) The duty to confirm or deny—

(a) does not arise in relation to information which is (or if it were held by the public authority would be) exempt information by virtue of subsection (1), and

(b) does not arise in relation to other information if or to the extent that either—

　(i) the giving to a member of the public of the confirmation or denial that would have to be given to comply with section 1(1)(a) would (apart from this Act) contravene any of the data protection principles or section 10 of the Data Protection Act 1998 or would do so if the exemptions in section 33A(1) of that Act were disregarded, or

　(ii) by virtue of any provision of Part IV of the Data Protection Act 1998 the information is exempt from section 7(1)(a) of that Act (data subject's right to be informed whether personal data being processed).

(6) In determining for the purposes of this section whether anything done before 24th October 2007 would contravene any of the data protection principles, the exemptions in Part III of Schedule 8 to the Data Protection Act 1998 shall be disregarded.

(7) In this section—

'the data protection principles' means the principles set out in Part I of Schedule 1 to the Data Protection Act 1998, as read subject to Part II of that Schedule and section 27(1) of that Act;

'data subject' has the same meaning as in section 1(1) of that Act;

'personal data' has the same meaning as in section 1(1) of that Act.

Information provided in confidence

41. (1) Information is exempt information if—
    - (a) it was obtained by the public authority from any other person (including another public authority), and
    - (b) the disclosure of the information to the public (otherwise than under this Act) by the public authority holding it would constitute a breach of confidence actionable by that or any other person.

(2) The duty to confirm or deny does not arise if, or to the extent that, the confirmation or denial that would have to be given to comply with section 1(1)(a) would (apart from this Act) constitute an actionable breach of confidence.

Legal professional privilege

42. (1) Information in respect of which a claim to legal professional privilege or, in Scotland, to confidentiality of communications could be maintained in legal proceedings is exempt information.

(2) The duty to confirm or deny does not arise if, or to the extent that, compliance with section 1(1)(a) would involve the disclosure of any information (whether or not already recorded) in respect of which such a claim could be maintained in legal proceedings.

Commercial interests

43. (1) Information is exempt information if it constitutes a trade secret.

(2) Information is exempt information if its disclosure under this Act would, or would be likely to, prejudice the commercial interests of any person (including the public authority holding it).

(3) The duty to confirm or deny does not arise if, or to the extent that, compliance with section 1(1)(a) would, or would be likely to, prejudice the interests mentioned in subsection (2).

Prohibitions on disclosure

44. (1) Information is exempt information if its disclosure (otherwise than under this Act) by the public authority holding it—
    - (a) is prohibited by or under any enactment,
    - (b) is incompatible with any Community obligation, or
    - (c) would constitute or be punishable as a contempt of court.

(2) The duty to confirm or deny does not arise if the confirmation or denial that would have to be given to comply with section 1(1)(a) would (apart from this Act) fall within any of paragraphs (a) to (c) of subsection (1).

PART III

GENERAL FUNCTIONS OF SECRETARY OF STATE, LORD CHANCELLOR AND INFORMATION COMMISSIONER

Issue of code of practice by ~~Secretary of State~~ Lord Chancellor

45. (1) The ~~Secretary of State~~ Lord Chancellor shall issue, and may from time to time revise, a code of practice providing guidance to public authorities as to the practice which it would, in his opinion, be desirable for them to follow in connection with the discharge of the authorities' functions under Part I.

(2) The code of practice must, in particular, include provision relating to—
    - (a) the provision of advice and assistance by public authorities to persons who propose to make, or have made, requests for information to them,

(b) the transfer of requests by one public authority to another public authority by which the information requested is or may be held,

(c) consultation with persons to whom the information requested relates or persons whose interests are likely to be affected by the disclosure of information,

(d) the inclusion in contracts entered into by public authorities of terms relating to the disclosure of information, and

(e) the provision by public authorities of procedures for dealing with complaints about the handling by them of requests for information.

(3) The code may make different provision for different public authorities.

(4) Before issuing or revising any code under this section, the ~~Secretary of State~~ Lord Chancellor shall consult the Commissioner.

(5) The ~~Secretary of State~~ Lord Chancellor shall lay before each House of Parliament any code or revised code made under this section.

Issue of code of practice by Lord Chancellor

46. (1) The Lord Chancellor shall issue, and may from time to time revise, a code of practice providing guidance to relevant authorities as to the practice which it would, in his opinion, be desirable for them to follow in connection with the keeping, management and destruction of their records.

(2) For the purpose of facilitating the performance by the Public Record Office, the Public Record Office of Northern Ireland and other public authorities of their functions under this Act in relation to records which are public records for the purposes of the Public Records Act 1958 or the Public Records Act (Northern Ireland) 1923, the code may also include guidance as to—

(a) the practice to be adopted in relation to the transfer of records under section 3(4) of the Public Records Act 1958 or section 3 of the Public Records Act (Northern Ireland) 1923, and

(b) the practice of reviewing records before they are transferred under those provisions.

(3) In exercising his functions under this section, the Lord Chancellor shall have regard to the public interest in allowing public access to information held by relevant authorities.

(4) The code may make different provision for different relevant authorities.

(5) Before issuing or revising any code under this section the Lord Chancellor shall consult—

(a) the ~~Secretary of State~~,[1]

(b) the Commissioner, and

(c) in relation to Northern Ireland, the appropriate Northern Ireland Minister.

(6) The Lord Chancellor shall lay before each House of Parliament any code or revised code made under this section.

(7) In this section 'relevant authority' means—

(a) any public authority, and

(b) any office or body which is not a public authority but whose administrative and departmental records are public records for the purposes of the Public Records Act 1958 or the Public Records Act (Northern Ireland) 1923.

General functions of Commissioner

47. (1) It shall be the duty of the Commissioner to promote the following of good practice by public authorities and, in particular, so to perform his functions under this Act as to promote the observance by public authorities of—

(a) the requirements of this Act, and

---

[1] Ceases to have effect by virtue of Transfer of functions (Miscellaneous) Order 2001 (2001/3500)

(b) the provisions of the codes of practice under sections 45 and 46.

(2) The Commissioner shall arrange for the dissemination in such form and manner as he considers appropriate of such information as it may appear to him expedient to give to the public—

(a) about the operation of this Act,

(b) about good practice, and

(c) about other matters within the scope of his functions under this Act,

and may give advice to any person as to any of those matters.

(3) The Commissioner may, with the consent of any public authority, assess whether that authority is following good practice.

(4) The Commissioner may charge such sums as he may with the consent of the ~~Secretary of State~~ Lord Chancellor determine for any services provided by the Commissioner under this section.

(5) The Commissioner shall from time to time as he considers appropriate—

(a) consult the Keeper of Public Records about the promotion by the Commissioner of the observance by public authorities of the provisions of the code of practice under section 46 in relation to records which are public records for the purposes of the Public Records Act 1958, and

(b) consult the Deputy Keeper of the Records of Northern Ireland about the promotion by the Commissioner of the observance by public authorities of those provisions in relation to records which are public records for the purposes of the Public Records Act (Northern Ireland) 1923.

(6) In this section 'good practice', in relation to a public authority, means such practice in the discharge of its functions under this Act as appears to the Commissioner to be desirable, and includes (but is not limited to) compliance with the requirements of this Act and the provisions of the codes of practice under sections 45 and 46.

Recommendations as to good practice

48. (1) If it appears to the Commissioner that the practice of a public authority in relation to the exercise of its functions under this Act does not conform with that proposed in the codes of practice under sections 45 and 46, he may give to the authority a recommendation (in this section referred to as a 'practice recommendation') specifying the steps which ought in his opinion to be taken for promoting such conformity.

(2) A practice recommendation must be given in writing and must refer to the particular provisions of the code of practice with which, in the Commissioner's opinion, the public authority's practice does not conform.

(3) Before giving to a public authority other than the Public Record Office a practice recommendation which relates to conformity with the code of practice under section 46 in respect of records which are public records for the purposes of the Public Records Act 1958, the Commissioner shall consult the Keeper of Public Records.

(4) Before giving to a public authority other than the Public Record Office of Northern Ireland a practice recommendation which relates to conformity with the code of practice under section 46 in respect of records which are public records for the purposes of the Public Records Act (Northern Ireland) 1923, the Commissioner shall consult the Deputy Keeper of the Records of Northern Ireland.

Reports to be laid before Parliament

49. (1) The Commissioner shall lay annually before each House of Parliament a general report on the exercise of his functions under this Act.

(2) The Commissioner may from time to time lay before each House of Parliament such other reports with respect to those functions as he thinks fit.

PART IV

ENFORCEMENT

Application for decision by Commissioner

50. (1) Any person (in this section referred to as 'the complainant') may apply to the Commissioner for a decision whether, in any specified respect, a request for information made by the complainant to a public authority has been dealt with in accordance with the requirements of Part I.

(2) On receiving an application under this section, the Commissioner shall make a decision unless it appears to him—

    (a) that the complainant has not exhausted any complaints procedure which is provided by the public authority in conformity with the code of practice under section 45,

    (b) that there has been undue delay in making the application,

    (c) that the application is frivolous or vexatious, or

    (d) that the application has been withdrawn or abandoned.

(3) Where the Commissioner has received an application under this section, he shall either—

    (a) notify the complainant that he has not made any decision under this section as a result of the application and of his grounds for not doing so, or

    (b) serve notice of his decision (in this Act referred to as a 'decision notice') on the complainant and the public authority.

(4) Where the Commissioner decides that a public authority—

    (a) has failed to communicate information, or to provide confirmation or denial, in a case where it is required to do so by section 1(1), or

    (b) has failed to comply with any of the requirements of sections 11 and 17,

the decision notice must specify the steps which must be taken by the authority for complying with that requirement and the period within which they must be taken.

(5) A decision notice must contain particulars of the right of appeal conferred by section 57.

(6) Where a decision notice requires steps to be taken by the public authority within a specified period, the time specified in the notice must not expire before the end of the period within which an appeal can be brought against the notice and, if such an appeal is brought, no step which is affected by the appeal need be taken pending the determination or withdrawal of the appeal.

(7) This section has effect subject to section 53.

Information notices

51. (1) If the Commissioner—

    (a) has received an application under section 50, or

    (b) reasonably requires any information—

        (i) for the purpose of determining whether a public authority has complied or is complying with any of the requirements of Part I, or

        (ii) for the purpose of determining whether the practice of a public authority in relation to the exercise of its functions under this Act conforms with that proposed in the codes of practice under sections 45 and 46,

he may serve the authority with a notice (in this Act referred to as 'an information notice') requiring it, within such time as is specified in the notice, to furnish the Commissioner, in such form as may be so specified, with such information relating to the application, to compliance with Part I or to conformity with the code of practice as is so specified.

(2) An information notice must contain—

    (a) in a case falling within subsection (1)(a), a statement that the Commissioner has received an application under section 50, or

933

(b) in a case falling within subsection (1)(b), a statement—

    (i) that the Commissioner regards the specified information as relevant for either of the purposes referred to in subsection (1)(b), and

    (ii) of his reasons for regarding that information as relevant for that purpose.

(3) An information notice must also contain particulars of the right of appeal conferred by section 57.

(4) The time specified in an information notice must not expire before the end of the period within which an appeal can be brought against the notice and, if such an appeal is brought, the information need not be furnished pending the determination or withdrawal of the appeal.

(5) An authority shall not be required by virtue of this section to furnish the Commissioner with any information in respect of—

    (a) any communication between a professional legal adviser and his client in connection with the giving of legal advice to the client with respect to his obligations, liabilities or rights under this Act, or

    (b) any communication between a professional legal adviser and his client, or between such an adviser or his client and any other person, made in connection with or in contemplation of proceedings under or arising out of this Act (including proceedings before the Tribunal) and for the purposes of such proceedings.

(6) In subsection (5) references to the client of a professional legal adviser include references to any person representing such a client.

(7) The Commissioner may cancel an information notice by written notice to the authority on which it was served.

(8) In this section 'information' includes unrecorded information.

Enforcement notices

52. (1) If the Commissioner is satisfied that a public authority has failed to comply with any of the requirements of Part I, the Commissioner may serve the authority with a notice (in this Act referred to as 'an enforcement notice') requiring the authority to take, within such time as may be specified in the notice, such steps as may be so specified for complying with those requirements.

(2) An enforcement notice must contain—

    (a) a statement of the requirement or requirements of Part I with which the Commissioner is satisfied that the public authority has failed to comply and his reasons for reaching that conclusion, and

    (b) particulars of the right of appeal conferred by section 57.

(3) An enforcement notice must not require any of the provisions of the notice to be complied with before the end of the period within which an appeal can be brought against the notice and, if such an appeal is brought, the notice need not be complied with pending the determination or withdrawal of the appeal.

(4) The Commissioner may cancel an enforcement notice by written notice to the authority on which it was served.

(5) This section has effect subject to section 53.

Exception from duty to comply with decision notice or enforcement notice

53. (1) This section applies to a decision notice or enforcement notice which—

    (a) is served on—

        (i) a government department,

        (ii) the National Assembly for Wales, or

        (iii) any public authority designated for the purposes of this section by an order made by the ~~Secretary of State~~ Lord Chancellor, and

(b) relates to a failure, in respect of one or more requests for information—

    (i) to comply with section 1(1)(a) in respect of information which falls within any provision of Part II stating that the duty to confirm or deny does not arise, or

    (ii) to comply with section 1(1)(b) in respect of exempt information.

(2) A decision notice or enforcement notice to which this section applies shall cease to have effect if, not later than the twentieth working day following the effective date, the accountable person in relation to that authority gives the Commissioner a certificate signed by him stating that he has on reasonable grounds formed the opinion that, in respect of the request or requests concerned, there was no failure falling within subsection (1)(b).

(3) Where the accountable person gives a certificate to the Commissioner under subsection (2) he shall as soon as practicable thereafter lay a copy of the certificate before—

(a) each House of Parliament,

(b) the Northern Ireland Assembly, in any case where the certificate relates to a decision notice or enforcement notice which has been served on a Northern Ireland department or any Northern Ireland public authority, or

(c) the National Assembly for Wales, in any case where the certificate relates to a decision notice or enforcement notice which has been served on the National Assembly for Wales or any Welsh public authority.

(4) In subsection (2) 'the effective date', in relation to a decision notice or enforcement notice, means—

(a) the day on which the notice was given to the public authority, or

(b) where an appeal under section 57 is brought, the day on which that appeal (or any further appeal arising out of it) is determined or withdrawn.

(5) Before making an order under subsection (1)(a)(iii), the ~~Secretary of State~~ Lord Chancellor shall—

(a) if the order relates to a Welsh public authority, consult the National Assembly for Wales,

(b) if the order relates to the Northern Ireland Assembly, consult the Presiding Officer of that Assembly, and

(c) if the order relates to a Northern Ireland public authority, consult the First Minister and deputy First Minister in Northern Ireland.

(6) Where the accountable person gives a certificate to the Commissioner under subsection (2) in relation to a decision notice, the accountable person shall, on doing so or as soon as reasonably practicable after doing so, inform the person who is the complainant for the purposes of section 50 of the reasons for his opinion.

(7) The accountable person is not obliged to provide information under subsection (6) if, or to the extent that, compliance with that subsection would involve the disclosure of exempt information.

(8) In this section 'the accountable person'—

(a) in relation to a Northern Ireland department or any Northern Ireland public authority, means the First Minister and deputy First Minister in Northern Ireland acting jointly,

(b) in relation to the National Assembly for Wales or any Welsh public authority, means the Assembly First Secretary, and

(c) in relation to any other public authority, means—

    (i) a Minister of the Crown who is a member of the Cabinet, or

    (ii) the Attorney General, the Advocate General for Scotland or the Attorney General for Northern Ireland.

(9) In this section 'working day' has the same meaning as in section 10.

Failure to comply with notice

54. (1) If a public authority has failed to comply with—
    (a) so much of a decision notice as requires steps to be taken,
    (b) an information notice, or
    (c) an enforcement notice,

the Commissioner may certify in writing to the court that the public authority has failed to comply with that notice.

(2) For the purposes of this section, a public authority which, in purported compliance with an information notice—
    (a) makes a statement which it knows to be false in a material respect, or
    (b) recklessly makes a statement which is false in a material respect,

is to be taken to have failed to comply with the notice.

(3) Where a failure to comply is certified under subsection (1), the court may inquire into the matter and, after hearing any witness who may be produced against or on behalf of the public authority, and after hearing any statement that may be offered in defence, deal with the authority as if it had committed a contempt of court.

(4) In this section 'the court' means the High Court or, in Scotland, the Court of Session.

Powers of entry and inspection

55. Schedule 3 (powers of entry and inspection) has effect.

No action against public authority

56. (1) This Act does not confer any right of action in civil proceedings in respect of any failure to comply with any duty imposed by or under this Act.

(2) Subsection (1) does not affect the powers of the Commissioner under section 54.

Part V
Appeals

Appeal against notices served under Part IV

57. (1) Where a decision notice has been served, the complainant or the public authority may appeal to the Tribunal against the notice.

(2) A public authority on which an information notice or an enforcement notice has been served by the Commissioner may appeal to the Tribunal against the notice.

(3) In relation to a decision notice or enforcement notice which relates—
    (a) to information to which section 66 applies, and
    (b) to a matter which by virtue of subsection (3) or (4) of that section falls to be determined by the responsible authority instead of the appropriate records authority,

subsections (1) and (2) shall have effect as if the reference to the public authority were a reference to the public authority or the responsible authority.

Determination of appeals

58. (1) If on an appeal under section 57 the Tribunal considers—
    (a) that the notice against which the appeal is brought is not in accordance with the law, or
    (b) to the extent that the notice involved an exercise of discretion by the Commissioner, that he ought to have exercised his discretion differently,

the Tribunal shall allow the appeal or substitute such other notice as could have been served by the Commissioner; and in any other case the Tribunal shall dismiss the appeal.

(2) On such an appeal, the Tribunal may review any finding of fact on which the notice in question was based.

Appeals from decision of Tribunal

59. Any party to an appeal to the Tribunal under section 57 may appeal from the decision of the Tribunal on a point of law to the appropriate court; and that court shall be—
- (a) the High Court of Justice in England if the address of the public authority is in England or Wales,
- (b) the Court of Session if that address is in Scotland, and
- (c) the High Court of Justice in Northern Ireland if that address is in Northern Ireland.

Appeals against national security certificate

60. (1) Where a certificate under section 23(2) or 24(3) has been issued—
- (a) the Commissioner, or
- (b) any applicant whose request for information is affected by the issue of the certificate,

may appeal to the Tribunal against the certificate.

(2) If on an appeal under subsection (1) relating to a certificate under section 23(2), the Tribunal finds that the information referred to in the certificate was not exempt information by virtue of section 23(1), the Tribunal may allow the appeal and quash the certificate.

(3) If on an appeal under subsection (1) relating to a certificate under section 24(3), the Tribunal finds that, applying the principles applied by the court on an application for judicial review, the Minister did not have reasonable grounds for issuing the certificate, the Tribunal may allow the appeal and quash the certificate.

(4) Where in any proceedings under this Act it is claimed by a public authority that a certificate under section 24(3) which identifies the information to which it applies by means of a general description applies to particular information, any other party to the proceedings may appeal to the Tribunal on the ground that the certificate does not apply to the information in question and, subject to any determination under subsection (5), the certificate shall be conclusively presumed so to apply.

(5) On any appeal under subsection (4), the Tribunal may determine that the certificate does not so apply.

Appeal proceedings

61. (1) Schedule 4 (which contains amendments of Schedule 6 to the Data Protection Act 1998 relating to appeal proceedings) has effect.

(2) Accordingly, the provisions of Schedule 6 to the Data Protection Act 1998 have effect (so far as applicable) in relation to appeals under this Part.

PART VI
HISTORICAL RECORDS AND RECORDS IN PUBLIC RECORDS OFFICE OR PUBLIC RECORD OFFICE IN NORTHERN IRELAND

Interpretation of Part VI

62. (1) For the purposes of this Part, a record becomes a 'historical record' at the end of the period of thirty years beginning with the year following that in which it was created.

(2) Where records created at different dates are for administrative purposes kept together in one

file or other assembly, all the records in that file or other assembly are to be treated for the purposes of this Part as having been created when the latest of those records was created.

(3) In this Part 'year' means a calendar year.

Removal of exemptions: historical records generally

63. (1) Information contained in a historical record cannot be exempt information by virtue of section 28, 30(1), 32, 33, 35, 36, 37(1)(a), 42 or 43.

(2) Compliance with section 1(1)(a) in relation to a historical record is not to be taken to be capable of having any of the effects referred to in section 28(3), 33(3), 36(3), 42(2) or 43(3).

(3) Information cannot be exempt information by virtue of section 37(1)(b) after the end of the period of sixty years beginning with the year following that in which the record containing the information was created.

(4) Information cannot be exempt information by virtue of section 31 after the end of the period of one hundred years beginning with the year following that in which the record containing the information was created.

(5) Compliance with section 1(1)(a) in relation to any record is not to be taken, at any time after the end of the period of one hundred years beginning with the year following that in which the record was created, to be capable of prejudicing any of the matters referred to in section 31(1).

Removal of exemptions: historical records in public record offices

64. (1) Information contained in a historical record in the Public Record Office or the Public Record Office of Northern Ireland cannot be exempt information by virtue of section 21 or 22.

(2) In relation to any information falling within section 23(1) which is contained in a historical record in the Public Record Office or the Public Record Office of Northern Ireland, section 2(3) shall have effect with the omission of the reference to section 23.

Decisions as to refusal of discretionary disclosure of historical records

65. (1) Before refusing a request for information relating to information which is contained in a historical record and is exempt information only by virtue of a provision not specified in section 2(3), a public authority shall—

    (a) if the historical record is a public record within the meaning of the Public Records Act 1958, consult the Lord Chancellor, or

    (b) if the historical record is a public record to which the Public Records Act (Northern Ireland) 1923 applies, consult the appropriate Northern Ireland Minister.

(2) This section does not apply to information to which section 66 applies.

Decisions relating to certain transferred public records

66. (1) This section applies to any information which is (or, if it existed, would be) contained in a transferred public record, other than information which the responsible authority has designated as open information for the purposes of this section.

(2) Before determining whether—

    (a) information to which this section applies falls within any provision of Part II relating to the duty to confirm or deny, or

    (b) information to which this section applies is exempt information,

the appropriate records authority shall consult the responsible authority.

(3) Where information to which this section applies falls within a provision of Part II relating to the duty to confirm or deny but does not fall within any of the provisions of that Part relating to that duty which are specified in subsection (3) of section 2, any question as to the application of subsec-

tion (1)(b) of that section is to be determined by the responsible authority instead of the appropriate records authority.

(4) Where any information to which this section applies is exempt information only by virtue of any provision of Part II not specified in subsection (3) of section 2, any question as to the application of subsection (2)(b) of that section is to be determined by the responsible authority instead of the appropriate records authority.

(5) Before making by virtue of subsection (3) or (4) any determination that subsection (1)(b) or (2)(b) of section 2 applies, the responsible authority shall consult—

  (a) where the transferred public record is a public record within the meaning of the Public Records Act 1958, the Lord Chancellor, and

  (b) where the transferred public record is a public record to which the Public Records Act (Northern Ireland) 1923 applies, the appropriate Northern Ireland Minister.

(6) Where the responsible authority in relation to information to which this section applies is not (apart from this subsection) a public authority, it shall be treated as being a public authority for the purposes of Parts III, IV and V of this Act so far as relating to—

  (a) the duty imposed by section 15(3), and

  (b) the imposition of any requirement to furnish information relating to compliance with Part I in connection with the information to which this section applies.

Amendments of public records legislation

67. Schedule 5 (which amends the Public Records Act 1958 and the Public Records Act (Northern Ireland) 1923) has effect.

PART VII

AMENDMENTS OF DATA PROTECTION ACT 1998

Amendments relating to personal information held by public authorities

Extension of meaning of 'data'

68. (1) Section 1 of the Data Protection Act 1998 (basic interpretative provisions) is amended in accordance with subsections (2) and (3).

(2) In subsection (1)—

  (a) in the definition of 'data', the word 'or' at the end of paragraph (c) is omitted and after paragraph (d) there is inserted 'or
    (e) is recorded information held by a public authority and does not fall within any of paragraphs (a) to (d);', and

  (b) after the definition of 'processing' there is inserted—
    ' "public authority" has the same meaning as in the Freedom of Information Act 2000;'.

(3) After subsection (4) there is inserted—

  '(5) In paragraph (e) of the definition of "data" in subsection (1), the reference to information "held" by a public authority shall be construed in accordance with section 3(2) of the Freedom of Information Act 2000.

  (6) Where section 7 of the Freedom of Information Act 2000 prevents Parts I to V of that Act from applying to certain information held by a public authority, that information is not to be treated for the purposes of paragraph (e) of the definition of "data" in subsection (1) as held by a public authority.'

(4) In section 56 of that Act (prohibition of requirement as to production of certain records), after subsection (6) there is inserted—

  '(6A) A record is not a relevant record to the extent that it relates, or is to relate, only to personal data falling within paragraph (e) of the definition of "data" in section 1(1).'

(5) In the Table in section 71 of that Act (index of defined expressions) after the entry relating to processing there is inserted—

'public authority   section 1(1).'

Right of access to unstructured personal data held by public authorities

69. (1) In section 7(1) of the Data Protection Act 1998 (right of access to personal data), for 'sections 8 and 9' there is substituted 'sections 8, 9 and 9A'.

(2) After section 9 of that Act there is inserted—

'Unstructured personal data held by public authorities.

9A. (1) In this section "unstructured personal data" means any personal data falling within paragraph (e) of the definition of "data" in section 1(1), other than information which is recorded as part of, or with the intention that it should form part of, any set of information relating to individuals to the extent that the set is structured by reference to individuals or by reference to criteria relating to individuals.

(2) A public authority is not obliged to comply with subsection (1) of section 7 in relation to any unstructured personal data unless the request under that section contains a description of the data.

(3) Even if the data are described by the data subject in his request, a public authority is not obliged to comply with subsection (1) of section 7 in relation to unstructured personal data if the authority estimates that the cost of complying with the request so far as relating to those data would exceed the appropriate limit.

(4) Subsection (3) does not exempt the public authority from its obligation to comply with paragraph (a) of section 7(1) in relation to the unstructured personal data unless the estimated cost of complying with that paragraph alone in relation to those data would exceed the appropriate limit.

(5) In subsections (3) and (4) "the appropriate limit" means such amount as may be prescribed by the Secretary of State by regulations, and different amounts may be prescribed in relation to different cases.

(6) Any estimate for the purposes of this section must be made in accordance with regulations under section 12(5) of the Freedom of Information Act 2000.'

(3) In section 67(5) of that Act (statutory instruments subject to negative resolution procedure), in paragraph (c), for 'or 9(3)' there is substituted ', 9(3) or 9A(5)'.

Exemptions applicable to certain manual data held by public authorities

70. (1) After section 33 of the Data Protection Act 1998 there is inserted—

'Manual data held by public authorities.

33A. (1) Personal data falling within paragraph (e) of the definition of "data" in section 1(1) are exempt from—

(a) the first, second, third, fifth, seventh and eighth data protection principles,

(b) the sixth data protection principle except so far as it relates to the rights conferred on data subjects by sections 7 and 14,

(c) sections 10 to 12,

(d) section 13, except so far as it relates to damage caused by a contravention of section 7 or of the fourth data protection principle and to any distress which is also suffered by reason of that contravention,

(e) Part III, and

(f) section 55.

(2) Personal data which fall within paragraph (e) of the definition of "data" in section 1(1) and relate to appointments or removals, pay, discipline, superannuation or other personnel matters, in relation to—

(a)   service in any of the armed forces of the Crown,

(b)   service in any office or employment under the Crown or under any public authority, or

(c)   service in any office or employment, or under any contract for services, in respect of which power to take action, or to determine or approve the action taken, in such matters is vested in Her Majesty, any Minister of the Crown, the National Assembly for Wales, any Northern Ireland Minister (within the meaning of the Freedom of Information Act 2000) or any public authority,

are also exempt from the remaining data protection principles and the remaining provisions of Part II.'

(2) In section 55 of that Act (unlawful obtaining etc. of personal data) in subsection (8) after 'section 28' there is inserted 'or 33A'.

(3) In Part III of Schedule 8 to that Act (exemptions available after 23rd October 2001 but before 24th October 2007) after paragraph 14 there is inserted—

'14A. (1) This paragraph applies to personal data which fall within paragraph (e) of the definition of "data" in section 1(1) and do not fall within paragraph 14(1)(a), but does not apply to eligible manual data to which the exemption in paragraph 16 applies.

(2) During the second transitional period, data to which this paragraph applies are exempt from—

(a)   the fourth data protection principle, and

(b)   section 14(1) to (3).'

(4) In Schedule 13 to that Act (modifications of Act having effect before 24th October 2007) in subsection (4)(b) of section 12A to that Act as set out in paragraph 1, after 'paragraph 14' there is inserted 'or 14A'.

Particulars registrable under Part III of Data Protection Act 1998

71. In section 16(1) of the Data Protection Act 1998 (the registrable particulars), before the word 'and' at the end of paragraph (f) there is inserted—

'(ff) where the data controller is a public authority, a statement of that fact,'.

Availability under Act disregarded for purpose of exemption

72. In section 34 of the Data Protection Act 1998 (information available to the public by or under enactment), after the word 'enactment' there is inserted 'other than an enactment contained in the Freedom of Information Act 2000'.

Other amendments

Further amendments of Data Protection Act 1998

73. Schedule 6 (which contains further amendments of the Data Protection Act 1998) has effect.

PART VIII
MISCELLANEOUS AND SUPPLEMENTAL

Power to make provision relating to environmental information

74. (1) In this section 'the Aarhus Convention' means the Convention on Access to Information, Public Participation in Decision-making and Access to Justice in Environmental Matters signed at Aarhus on 25th June 1998.

(2) For the purposes of this section 'the information provisions' of the Aarhus Convention are Article 4, together with Articles 3 and 9 so far as relating to that Article.

(3) The Secretary of State may by regulations make such provision as he considers appropriate—

(a) for the purpose of implementing the information provisions of the Aarhus Convention or any amendment of those provisions made in accordance with Article 14 of the Convention, and

(b) for the purpose of dealing with matters arising out of or related to the implementation of those provisions or of any such amendment.

(4) Regulations under subsection (3) may in particular—

(a) enable charges to be made for making information available in accordance with the regulations,

(b) provide that any obligation imposed by the regulations in relation to the disclosure of information is to have effect notwithstanding any enactment or rule of law,

(c) make provision for the issue by the Secretary of State of a code of practice,

(d) provide for sections 47 and 48 to apply in relation to such a code with such modifications as may be specified,

(e) provide for any of the provisions of Parts IV and V to apply, with such modifications as may be specified in the regulations, in relation to compliance with any requirement of the regulations, and

(f) contain such transitional or consequential provision (including provision modifying any enactment) as the Secretary of State considers appropriate.

(5) This section has effect subject to section 80.

Power to amend or repeal enactments prohibiting disclosure of information

75. (1) If, with respect to any enactment which prohibits the disclosure of information held by a public authority, it appears to the ~~Secretary of State~~ Lord Chancellor that by virtue of section 44(1)(a) the enactment is capable of preventing the disclosure of information under section 1, he may by order repeal or amend the enactment for the purpose of removing or relaxing the prohibition.

(2) In subsection (1)—

'enactment' means—

(a) any enactment contained in an Act passed before or in the same Session as this Act, or

(b) any enactment contained in Northern Ireland legislation or subordinate legislation passed or made before the passing of this Act;

'information' includes unrecorded information.

(3) An order under this section may do all or any of the following—

(a) make such modifications of enactments as, in the opinion of the ~~Secretary of State~~ Lord Chancellor, are consequential upon, or incidental to, the amendment or repeal of the enactment containing the prohibition;

(b) contain such transitional provisions and savings as appear to the ~~Secretary of State~~ Lord Chancellor to be appropriate;

(c) make different provision for different cases.

Disclosure of information between Commissioner and ombudsmen

76. (1) The Commissioner may disclose to a person specified in the first column of the Table below any information obtained by, or furnished to, the Commissioner under or for the purposes of this Act or the Data Protection Act 1998 if it appears to the Commissioner that the information relates to a matter which could be the subject of an investigation by that person under the enactment specified in relation to that person in the second column of that Table.

Ombudsman	*Enactment*
The Parliamentary Commissioner for Administration.	The Parliamentary Commissioner Act 1967 (c. 13).
The Health Service Commissioner for England.	The Health Service Commissioners Act 1993 (c. 46).
The Health Service Commissioner for Wales.	The Health Service Commissioners Act 1993 (c. 46).
The Health Service Commissioner for Scotland.	The Health Service Commissioners Act 1993 (c. 46).
A Local Commissioner as defined by section 23(3) of the Local Government Act 1974.	Part III of the Local Government Act 1974 (c. 7).
The Commissioner for Local Administration in Scotland.	Part II of the Local Government (Scotland) Act 1975 (c. 30).
The Scottish Parliamentary Commissioner for Administration.	The Scotland Act 1998 (Transitory and Transitional Provisions) (Complaints of Maladministration) Order 1999 (S.I. 1999/1351).
The Welsh Administration Ombudsman.	Schedule 9 to the Government of Wales Act 1998 (c. 38).
The Northern Ireland Commissioner for Complaints.	The Commissioner for Complaints (Northern Ireland) Order 1996 (S.I. 1996/1297 (N.I. 7)).
The Assembly Ombudsman for Northern Ireland.	The Ombudsman (Northern Ireland) Order 1996 (S.I. 1996/1298 (N.I. 8)).

(2) Schedule 7 (which contains amendments relating to information disclosed to ombudsmen under subsection (1) and to the disclosure of information by ombudsmen to the Commissioner) has effect.

Offence of altering etc. records with intent to prevent disclosure

77. (1) Where—
   (a) a request for information has been made to a public authority, and
   (b) under section 1 of this Act or section 7 of the Data Protection Act 1998, the applicant would have been entitled (subject to payment of any fee) to communication of any information in accordance with that section,

any person to whom this subsection applies is guilty of an offence if he alters, defaces, blocks, erases, destroys or conceals any record held by the public authority, with the intention of preventing the disclosure by that authority of all, or any part, of the information to the communication of which the applicant would have been entitled.

(2) Subsection (1) applies to the public authority and to any person who is employed by, is an officer of, or is subject to the direction of, the public authority.

(3) A person guilty of an offence under this section is liable on summary conviction to a fine not exceeding level 5 on the standard scale.

(4) No proceedings for an offence under this section shall be instituted—
   (a) in England or Wales, except by the Commissioner or by or with the consent of the Director of Public Prosecutions;
   (b) in Northern Ireland, except by the Commissioner or by or with the consent of the Director of Public Prosecutions for Northern Ireland.

Saving for existing powers

78. Nothing in this Act is to be taken to limit the powers of a public authority to disclose information held by it.

Defamation

79. Where any information communicated by a public authority to a person ('the applicant') under section 1 was supplied to the public authority by a third person, the publication to the applicant of any defamatory matter contained in the information shall be privileged unless the publication is shown to have been made with malice.

Scotland

80. (1) No order may be made under section 4(1) or 5 in relation to any of the bodies specified in subsection (2); and the power conferred by section 74(3) does not include power to make provision in relation to information held by any of those bodies.

    (2) The bodies referred to in subsection (1) are—
      (a) the Scottish Parliament,
      (b) any part of the Scottish Administration,
      (c) the Scottish Parliamentary Corporate Body, or
      (d) any Scottish public authority with mixed functions or no reserved functions (within the meaning of the Scotland Act 1998).

Application to government departments, etc

81. (1) For the purposes of this Act each government department is to be treated as a person separate from any other government department.

    (2) Subsection (1) does not enable—
      (a) a government department which is not a Northern Ireland department to claim for the purposes of section 41(1)(b) that the disclosure of any information by it would constitute a breach of confidence actionable by any other government department (not being a Northern Ireland department), or
      (b) a Northern Ireland department to claim for those purposes that the disclosure of information by it would constitute a breach of confidence actionable by any other Northern Ireland department.

    (3) A government department is not liable to prosecution under this Act, but section 77 and paragraph 12 of Schedule 3 apply to a person in the public service of the Crown as they apply to any other person.

    (4) The provisions specified in subsection (3) also apply to a person acting on behalf of either House of Parliament or on behalf of the Northern Ireland Assembly as they apply to any other person.

Orders and regulations

82. (1) Any power of the <u>Lord Chancellor or the</u> Secretary of State to make an order or regulations under this Act shall be exercisable by statutory instrument.

    (2) A statutory instrument containing (whether alone or with other provisions)—
      (a) an order under section 5, 7(3) or (8), 53(1)(a)(iii) or 75, or
      (b) regulations under section 10(4) or 74(3),
shall not be made unless a draft of the instrument has been laid before, and approved by a resolution of, each House of Parliament.

    (3) A statutory instrument which contains (whether alone or with other provisions)—

(a)   an order under section 4(1), or

(b)   regulations under any provision of this Act not specified in subsection (2)(b),

and which is not subject to the requirement in subsection (2) that a draft of the instrument be laid before and approved by a resolution of each House of Parliament, shall be subject to annulment in pursuance of a resolution of either House of Parliament.

(4)   An order under section 4(5) shall be laid before Parliament after being made.

(5)   If a draft of an order under section 5 or 7(8) would, apart from this subsection, be treated for the purposes of the Standing Orders of either House of Parliament as a hybrid instrument, it shall proceed in that House as if it were not such an instrument.

Meaning of 'Welsh public authority'

83. (1) In this Act 'Welsh public authority' means—

(a)   any public authority which is listed in Part II, III, IV or VI of Schedule 1 and whose functions are exercisable only or mainly in or as regards Wales, other than an excluded authority, or

(b)   any public authority which is an Assembly subsidiary as defined by section 99(4) of the Government of Wales Act 1998.

(2)   In paragraph (a) of subsection (1) 'excluded authority' means a public authority which is designated by the ~~Secretary of State~~ Lord Chancellor by order as an excluded authority for the purposes of that paragraph.

(3)   Before making an order under subsection (2), the Lord Chancellor ~~Secretary of State~~ shall consult the National Assembly for Wales.

Interpretation

84. In this Act, unless the context otherwise requires—

'applicant', in relation to a request for information, means the person who made the request;

'appropriate Northern Ireland Minister' means the Northern Ireland Minister in charge of the Department of Culture, Arts and Leisure in Northern Ireland;

'appropriate records authority', in relation to a transferred public record, has the meaning given by section 15(5);

'body' includes an unincorporated association;

'the Commissioner' means the Information Commissioner;

'decision notice' has the meaning given by section 50;

'the duty to confirm or deny' has the meaning given by section 1(6);

'enactment' includes an enactment contained in Northern Ireland legislation;

'enforcement notice' has the meaning given by section 52;

'executive committee', in relation to the National Assembly for Wales, has the same meaning as in the Government of Wales Act 1998;

'exempt information' means information which is exempt information by virtue of any provision of Part II;

'fees notice' has the meaning given by section 9(1);

'government department' includes a Northern Ireland department, the Northern Ireland Court Service and any other body or authority exercising statutory functions on behalf of the Crown, but does not include—

(a)   any of the bodies specified in section 80(2),

(b)   the Security Service, the Secret Intelligence Service or the Government Communications Headquarters, or

(c)   the National Assembly for Wales;

'information' (subject to sections 51(8) and 75(2)) means information recorded in any form;

'information notice' has the meaning given by section 51;

'Minister of the Crown' has the same meaning as in the Ministers of the Crown Act 1975;

'Northern Ireland Minister' includes the First Minister and deputy First Minister in Northern Ireland;

'Northern Ireland public authority' means any public authority, other than the Northern Ireland Assembly or a Northern Ireland department, whose functions are exercisable only or mainly in or as regards Northern Ireland and relate only or mainly to transferred matters;

'prescribed' means prescribed by regulations made by the ~~Secretary of State~~ Lord Chancellor;

'public authority' has the meaning given by section 3(1);

'public record' means a public record within the meaning of the Public Records Act 1958 or a public record to which the Public Records Act (Northern Ireland) 1923 applies;

'publication scheme' has the meaning given by section 19;

'request for information' has the meaning given by section 8;

'responsible authority', in relation to a transferred public record, has the meaning given by section 15(5);

'the special forces' means those units of the armed forces of the Crown the maintenance of whose capabilities is the responsibility of the Director of Special Forces or which are for the time being subject to the operational command of that Director;

'subordinate legislation' has the meaning given by subsection (1) of section 21 of the Interpretation Act 1978, except that the definition of that term in that subsection shall have effect as if 'Act' included Northern Ireland legislation;

'transferred matter', in relation to Northern Ireland, has the meaning given by section 4(1) of the Northern Ireland Act 1998;

'transferred public record' has the meaning given by section 15(4);

'the Tribunal' means the Information Tribunal;

'Welsh public authority' has the meaning given by section 83.

Expenses

85. There shall be paid out of money provided by Parliament—

   (a) any increase attributable to this Act in the expenses of the ~~Secretary of State~~ Lord Chancellor in respect of the Commissioner, the Tribunal or the members of the Tribunal,

   (b) any administrative expenses of the ~~Secretary of State~~ Lord Chancellor attributable to this Act,

   (c) any other expenses incurred in consequence of this Act by a Minister of the Crown or government department or by either House of Parliament, and

   (d) any increase attributable to this Act in the sums which under any other Act are payable out of money so provided.

Repeals

86. Schedule 8 (repeals) has effect.

Commencement

87. (1) The following provisions of this Act shall come into force on the day on which this Act is passed—

   (a) sections 3 to 8 and Schedule 1,

   (b) section 19 so far as relating to the approval of publication schemes,

   (c) section 20 so far as relating to the approval and preparation by the Commissioner of model publication schemes,

   (d) section 47(2) to (6),

   (e) section 49,

   (f) section 74,

   (g) section 75,

    (h)   sections 78 to 85 and this section,

    (i)   paragraphs 2 and 17 to 22 of Schedule 2 (and section 18(4) so far as relating to those paragraphs),

    (j)   paragraph 4 of Schedule 5 (and section 67 so far as relating to that paragraph),

    (k)   paragraph 8 of Schedule 6 (and section 73 so far as relating to that paragraph),

    (l)   Part I of Schedule 8 (and section 86 so far as relating to that Part), and

    (m) so much of any other provision of this Act as confers power to make any order, regulations or code of practice.

(2) The following provisions of this Act shall come into force at the end of the period of two months beginning with the day on which this Act is passed—

    (a)   section 18(1),

    (b)   section 76 and Schedule 7,

    (c)   paragraphs 1(1), 3(1), 4, 6, 7, 8(2), 9(2), 10(a), 13(1) and (2), 14(a) and 15(1) and (2) of Schedule 2 (and section 18(4) so far as relating to those provisions), and

    (d)   Part II of Schedule 8 (and section 86 so far as relating to that Part).

(3) Except as provided by subsections (1) and (2), this Act shall come into force at the end of the period of five years beginning with the day on which this Act is passed or on such day before the end of that period as the ~~Secretary of State~~ Lord Chancellor may by order appoint; and different days may be appointed for different purposes.

(4) An order under subsection (3) may contain such transitional provisions and savings (including provisions capable of having effect after the end of the period referred to in that subsection) as the Lord Chancellor ~~Secretary of State~~ considers appropriate.

(5) During the twelve months beginning with the day on which this Act is passed, and during each subsequent complete period of twelve months in the period beginning with that day and ending with the first day on which all the provisions of this Act are fully in force, the ~~Secretary of State~~ Lord Chancellor shall—

    (a)   prepare a report on his proposals for bringing fully into force those provisions of this Act which are not yet fully in force, and

    (b)   lay a copy of the report before each House of Parliament.

Short title and extent

88. (1) This Act may be cited as the Freedom of Information Act 2000.

(2) Subject to subsection (3), this Act extends to Northern Ireland.

(3) The amendment or repeal of any enactment by this Act has the same extent as that enactment.

Schedules

SCHEDULE 1
PUBLIC AUTHORITIES

PART I
GENERAL

1. Any government department.

2. The House of Commons.

3. The House of Lords.

4. The Northern Ireland Assembly.

5. The National Assembly for Wales.

6. The armed forces of the Crown, except—
    (a) the special forces, and
    (b) any unit or part of a unit which is for the time being required by the Secretary of State to assist the Government Communications Headquarters in the exercise of its functions.

PART II
LOCAL GOVERNMENT

England and Wales

7. A local authority within the meaning of the Local Government Act 1972, namely—
    (a) in England, a county council, a London borough council, a district council or a parish council,
    (b) in Wales, a county council, a county borough council or a community council.

8. The Greater London Authority.

9. The Common Council of the City of London, in respect of information held in its capacity as a local authority, police authority or port health authority.

10. The Sub-Treasurer of the Inner Temple or the Under-Treasurer of the Middle Temple, in respect of information held in his capacity as a local authority.

11. The Council of the Isles of Scilly.

12. A parish meeting constituted under section 13 of the Local Government Act 1972.

13. Any charter trustees constituted under section 246 of the Local Government Act 1972.

14. A fire authority constituted by a combination scheme under section 5 or 6 of the Fire Services Act 1947.

15. A waste disposal authority established by virtue of an order under section 10(1) of the Local Government Act 1985.

16. A port health authority constituted by an order under section 2 of the Public Health (Control of Disease) Act 1984.

17. A licensing planning committee constituted under section 119 of the Licensing Act 1964.

18. An internal drainage board which is continued in being by virtue of section 1 of the Land Drainage Act 1991.

19. A joint authority established under Part IV of the Local Government Act 1985 (fire services, civil defence and transport).

20. The London Fire and Emergency Planning Authority.

21. A joint fire authority established by virtue of an order under section 42(2) of the Local Government Act 1985 (reorganisation of functions).

22. A body corporate established pursuant to an order under section 67 of the Local Government Act 1985 (transfer of functions to successors of residuary bodies, etc.).

23. A body corporate established pursuant to an order under section 22 of the Local Government Act 1992 (residuary bodies).

24. The Broads Authority established by section 1 of the Norfolk and Suffolk Broads Act 1988.

25. A joint committee constituted in accordance with section 102(1)(b) of the Local Government Act 1972.

26. A joint board which is continued in being by virtue of section 263(1) of the Local Government Act 1972.

27. A joint authority established under section 21 of the Local Government Act 1992.

28. A Passenger Transport Executive for a passenger transport area within the meaning of Part II of the Transport Act 1968.

29. Transport for London.

30. The London Transport Users Committee.

31. A joint board the constituent members of which consist of any of the public authorities described in paragraphs 8, 9, 10, 12, 15, 16, 20 to 31, 57 and 58.

32. A National Park authority established by an order under section 63 of the Environment Act 1995.

33. A joint planning board constituted for an area in Wales outside a National Park by an order under section 2(1B) of the Town and Country Planning Act 1990.

34. A magistrates' court committee established under section 27 of the Justices of the Peace Act 1997.

35. The London Development Agency.

Northern Ireland

36. A district council within the meaning of the Local Government Act (Northern Ireland) 1972.

PART III
THE NATIONAL HEALTH SERVICE

England and Wales

37. A Health Authority established under section 8 of the National Health Service Act 1977.

38. A special health authority established under section 11 of the National Health Service Act 1977.

39. A primary care trust established under section 16A of the National Health Service Act 1977.

40. A National Health Service trust established under section 5 of the National Health Service and Community Care Act 1990.

41. A Community Health Council established under section 20 of the National Health Service Act 1977.

42. The Dental Practice Board constituted under regulations made under section 37 of the National Health Service Act 1977.

43. The Public Health Laboratory Service Board constituted under Schedule 3 to the National Health Service Act 1977.

44. Any person providing general medical services, general dental services, general ophthalmic services or pharmaceutical services under Part II of the National Health Service Act 1977, in respect of information relating to the provision of those services.

45. Any person providing personal medical services or personal dental services under arrangements made under section 28C of the National Health Service Act 1977, in respect of information relating to the provision of those services.

Northern Ireland

46. A Health and Social Services Board established under Article 16 of the Health and Personal Social Services (Northern Ireland) Order 1972.

47. A Health and Social Services Council established under Article 4 of the Health and Personal Social Services (Northern Ireland) Order 1991.

48. A Health and Social Services Trust established under Article 10 of the Health and Personal Social Services (Northern Ireland) Order 1991.

49. A special agency established under Article 3 of the Health and Personal Social Services (Special Agencies) (Northern Ireland) Order 1990.

50. The Northern Ireland Central Services Agency for the Health and Social Services established under Article 26 of the Health and Personal Social Services (Northern Ireland) Order 1972.

51. Any person providing general medical services, general dental services, general ophthalmic services or pharmaceutical services under Part VI of the Health and Personal Social Services (Northern Ireland) Order 1972, in respect of information relating to the provision of those services.

Part IV
Maintained schools and other educational institutions

England and Wales

52. The governing body of a maintained school, within the meaning of the School Standards and Framework Act 1998.

53. (1) The governing body of—
    (a) an institution within the further education sector,
    (b) a university receiving financial support under section 65 of the Further and Higher Education Act 1992,
    (c) an institution conducted by a higher education corporation,
    (d) a designated institution for the purposes of Part II of the Further and Higher Education Act 1992 as defined by section 72(3) of that Act, or
    (e) any college, school, hall or other institution of a university which falls within paragraph (b).

    (2) In sub-paragraph (1)—
    (a) 'governing body' is to be interpreted in accordance with subsection (1) of section 90 of the Further and Higher Education Act 1992 but without regard to subsection (2) of that section,
    (b) in paragraph (a), the reference to an institution within the further education sector is to be construed in accordance with section 91(3) of the Further and Higher Education Act 1992,
    (c) in paragraph (c), 'higher education corporation' has the meaning given by section 90(1) of that Act, and
    (d) in paragraph (e) 'college' includes any institution in the nature of a college.

Northern Ireland

54. (1) The managers of—
    (a) a controlled school, voluntary school or grant-maintained integrated school within the meaning of Article 2(2) of the Education and Libraries (Northern Ireland) Order 1986, or
    (b) a pupil referral unit as defined by Article 87(1) of the Education (Northern Ireland) Order 1998.

    (2) In sub-paragraph (1) 'managers' has the meaning given by Article 2(2) of the Education and Libraries (Northern Ireland) Order 1986.

55. (1) The governing body of—

    (a) a university receiving financial support under Article 30 of the Education and Libraries (Northern Ireland) Order 1993,

    (b) a college of education maintained in pursuance of arrangements under Article 66(1) or in respect of which grants are paid under Article 66(2) or (3) of the Education and Libraries (Northern Ireland) Order 1986, or

    (c) an institution of further education within the meaning of the Further Education (Northern Ireland) Order 1997.

(2) In sub-paragraph (1) 'governing body' has the meaning given by Article 30(3) of the Education and Libraries (Northern Ireland) Order 1993.

56. Any person providing further education to whom grants, loans or other payments are made under Article 5(1)(b) of the Further Education (Northern Ireland) Order 1997.

PART V
POLICE

England and Wales

57. A police authority established under section 3 of the Police Act 1996.

58. The Metropolitan Police Authority established under section 5B of the Police Act 1996.

59. A chief officer of police of a police force in England or Wales.

Northern Ireland

60. The Police Authority for Northern Ireland.

61. The Chief Constable of the Royal Ulster Constabulary.

Miscellaneous

62. The British Transport Police.

63. The Ministry of Defence Police established by section 1 of the Ministry of Defence Police Act 1987.

64. Any person who—

    (a) by virtue of any enactment has the function of nominating individuals who may be appointed as special constables by justices of the peace, and

    (b) is not a public authority by virtue of any other provision of this Act,

in respect of information relating to the exercise by any person appointed on his nomination of the functions of a special constable.

PART VI
OTHER PUBLIC BODIES AND OFFICES: GENERAL

The Adjudication Panel for Wales

The Adjudicator for the Inland Revenue and Customs and Excise.

The Administration of Radioactive Substances Advisory Committee.

The Advisory Board on Family Law.

The Advisory Board on Restricted Patients.

The Advisory Board on the Registration of Homoeopathic Products.

The Advisory Committee for Cleaner Coal Technology.

The Advisory Committee for Disabled People in Employment and Training.

The Advisory Committee for the Public Lending Right.

The Advisory Committee for Wales (in relation to the Environment Agency).

The Advisory Committee on Advertising.

The Advisory Committee on Animal Feedingstuffs.

The Advisory Committee on Borderline Substances.

The Advisory Committee on Business and the Environment.

The Advisory Committee on Business Appointments.

The Advisory Committee on Conscientious Objectors.

The Advisory Committee on Consumer Products and the Environment.

The Advisory Committee on Dangerous Pathogens.

The Advisory Committee on Distinction Awards.

An Advisory Committee on General Commissioners of Income Tax.

The Advisory Committee on the Government Art Collection

The Advisory Committee on Hazardous Substances.

The Advisory Committee on Historic Wreck Sites.

An Advisory Committee on Justices of the Peace in England and Wales.

The Advisory Committee on the Microbiological Safety of Food.

The Advisory Committee on NHS Drugs.

The Advisory Committee on Novel Foods and Processes.

The Advisory Committee on Overseas Economic and Social Research.

The Advisory Committee on Packaging.

The Advisory Committee on Pesticides.

The Advisory Committee on Releases to the Environment.

The Advisory Council on Libraries.

The Advisory Council on the Misuse of Drugs.

The Advisory Council on Public Records.

The Advisory Group on Hepatitis.

The Advisory Panel on Standards for the Planning Inspectorate.

The Aerospace Committee.

An Agricultural Dwelling House Advisory Committee.

An Agricultural Wages Board for England and Wales.

An Agricultural Wages Committee.

The Agriculture and Environment Biotechnology Commission.

The Airborne Particles Expert Group.

The Alcohol Education and Research Council.

The All-Wales Medicines Strategy Group.

The Ancient Monuments Board for Wales.

The Animal Procedures Committee.

The Animal Welfare Advisory Committee.

The Apple and Pear Research Council.

The Armed Forces Pay Review Body.

The Arts Council of England.

The Arts Council of Wales.

The Audit Commission for Local Authorities and the National Health Service in England and Wales.

The Auditor General for Wales.

The Authorised Conveyancing Practitioners Board.

The Bank of England, in respect of information held for purposes other than those of its functions with respect to—
  (a) monetary policy,
  (b) financial operations intended to support financial institutions for the purposes of maintaining stability, and
  (c) the provision of private banking services and related services.

The Better Regulation Task Force.

The Biotechnology and Biological Sciences Research Council.

Any Board of Visitors established under section 6(2) of the Prison Act 1952.

The Britain–Russia Centre and East–West Centre.

The British Association for Central and Eastern Europe.

The British Broadcasting Corporation, in respect of information held for purposes other than those of journalism, art or literature.

The British Coal Corporation.

The British Council.

The British Educational Communications and Technology Agency.

The British Hallmarking Council.

The British Library.

The British Museum.

The British Pharmacopoeia Commission.

The British Potato Council.

The British Railways Board.

British Shipbuilders.

The British Tourist Authority.

The British Waterways Board.

The British Wool Marketing Board.

The Broadcasting Standards Commission.

The Building Regulations Advisory Committee.

The Care Council for Wales.

The Central Advisory Committee on War Pensions.

The Central Council for Education and Training in Social Work (UK).

The Central Rail Users' Consultative Committee.

The Certification Officer.

The Channel Four Television Corporation, in respect of information held for purposes other than those of journalism, art or literature.

The Children and Family Court Advisory and Support Service.

The Children's Commissioner for Wales.

The Civil Aviation Authority.

The Civil Justice Council.

The Civil Procedure Rule Committee.

The Civil Service Appeal Board.

The Civil Service Commissioners.

The Coal Authority.

The Commission for Architecture and the Built Environment.

The Commission for Health Improvement.

The Commission for Local Administration in England.

The Commission for Local Administration in Wales.

The Commission for Racial Equality.

The Commission for the New Towns.

The Commissioner for Integrated Transport.

The Commissioner for Public Appointments.

The Commissioners of Northern Lighthouses.

The Committee for Monitoring Agreements on Tobacco Advertising and Sponsorship.

The Committee of Investigation for Great Britain.

The Committee on Agricultural Valuation.

The Committee on Carcinogenicity of Chemicals in Food, Consumer Products and the Environment.

The Committee on Chemicals and Materials of Construction For Use in Public Water Supply and Swimming Pools.

The Committee on Medical Aspects of Food and Nutrition Policy.

The Committee on Medical Aspects of Radiation in the Environment.

The Committee on Mutagenicity of Chemicals in Food, Consumer Products and the Environment.

The Committee on Standards in Public Life.

The Committee on Toxicity of Chemicals in Food, Consumer Products and the Environment.

The Committee on the Medical Effects of Air Pollutants.

The Committee on the Safety of Medicines.

The Commonwealth Scholarship Commission in the United Kingdom.

The Community Development Foundation.

The Competition Commission, in relation to information held by it otherwise than as a tribunal.

The Construction Industry Training Board.

Consumer Communications for England.

The Consumer Council for Postal Services.

The Consumer Panel.

The consumers' committee for Great Britain appointed under section 19 of the Agricultural Marketing Act 1958.

The Council for Professions Supplementary to Medicine.

The Council for the Central Laboratory of the Research Councils.

The Council for Science and Technology.

The Council on Tribunals.

The Countryside Agency.

The Countryside Council for Wales.

The Covent Garden Market Authority.

The Criminal Cases Review Commission.

The Criminal Injuries Compensation Authority.

The Criminal Injuries Compensation Appeals Panel, in relation to information held by it otherwise than as a tribunal.

The Criminal Justice Consultative Council.

The Crown Court Rule Committee.

The Dartmoor Steering Group and Working Party.

The Darwin Advisory Committee.

The Defence Nuclear Safety Committee.

The Defence Scientific Advisory Council.

The Design Council.

The Development Awareness Working Group.

The Diplomatic Service Appeal Board.

The Disability Living Allowance Advisory Board.

The Disability Rights Commission.

The Disabled Persons Transport Advisory Committee.

The Economic and Social Research Council.

The Education Transfer Council.

The Electoral Commission.

The Energy Advisory Panel.

The Engineering Construction Industry Training Board.

The Engineering and Physical Sciences Research Council.

The English National Board for Nursing, Midwifery and Health Visiting.

English Nature.

The English Sports Council.

The English Tourist Board.

The Environment Agency.

The Equal Opportunities Commission.

The Expert Advisory Group on AIDS.

The Expert Group on Cryptosporidium in Water Supplies.

An Expert Panel on Air Quality Standards.

The Export Guarantees Advisory Council.

The Family Proceedings Rules Committee.

The Farm Animal Welfare Council.

The Fire Services Examination Board.

The Firearms Consultative Committee.

The Food Advisory Committee.

Food from Britain.

The Football Licensing Authority.

The Fuel Cell Advisory Panel.

The Further Education Funding Council for Wales.

The Gaming Board for Great Britain.

The Gas Consumers' Council.

The Gas and Electricity Consumer Council.

The Gene Therapy Advisory Committee.

The General Chiropractic Council.

The General Dental Council.

The General Medical Council.

The General Osteopathic Council.

The General Social Care Council.

The General Teaching Council for Wales.

The Genetic Testing and Insurance Committee.

The Government Hospitality Advisory Committee for the Purchase of Wine.

The Government Chemist.

The Great Britain–China Centre.

The Health and Safety Commission.

The Health and Safety Executive.

The Health Service Commissioner for England.

The Health Service Commissioner for Wales.

Her Majesty's Chief Inspector of Schools in Wales.

The Higher Education Funding Council for England.

The Higher Education Funding Council for Wales.

The Hill Farming Advisory Committee.

The Hill Farming Advisory Sub-committee for Wales.

The Historic Buildings Council for Wales.

The Historic Buildings and Monuments Commission for England.

The Historic Royal Palaces Trust.

The Home-Grown Cereals Authority.

The Honorary Investment Advisory Committee.

The Horserace Betting Levy Board.

The Horserace Totalisator Board.

The Horticultural Development Council.

Horticulture Research International.

The House of Lords Appointments Commission.

Any housing action trust established under Part III of the Housing Act 1988.

The Housing Corporation.

The Human Fertilisation and Embryology Authority.

The Human Genetics Commission.

The Immigration Services Commissioner.

The Imperial War Museum.

The Independent Board of Visitors for Military Corrective Training Centres.

The Independent Case Examiner for the Child Support Agency.

The Independent Living Funds.

The Independent Television Commission.

The Indian Family Pensions Funds Body of Commissioners.

The Industrial Development Advisory Board.

The Industrial Injuries Advisory Council.

The Information Commissioner.

The Inland Waterways Amenity Advisory Council.

The Insolvency Rules Committee.

The Insurance Brokers Registration Council.

Investors in People UK.

The Joint Committee on Vaccination and Immunisation.

The Joint Nature Conservation Committee.

The Joint Prison/Probation Accreditation Panel.

The Judicial Studies Board.

The Know-How Fund Advisory Board.

The Land Registration Rule Committee.

The Law Commission.

The Legal Services Commission.

The Legal Services Consultative Panel.

The Legal Services Ombudsman.

The Library and Information Services Council (Wales).

The Local Government Boundary Commission for Wales.

The Local Government Commission for England.

A local probation board established under section 4 of the Criminal Justice and Court Services Act 2000.

The London Pensions Fund Authority.

The Low Pay Commission.

The Magistrates' Courts Rules Committee.

The Marshall Aid Commemoration Commission.

The Measurement Advisory Committee.

The Meat and Livestock Commission.

The Medical Practices Committee.

The Medical Research Council.

The Medical Workforce Standing Advisory Committee.

The Medicines Commission.

The Milk Development Council.

The Millennium Commission.

The Museum of London.

The National Army Museum.

The National Audit Office.

The National Biological Standards Board (UK).

The National Care Standards Commission.

The National Consumer Council.

The National Council for Education and Training for Wales.

The National Crime Squad.

The National Employers' Liaison Committee.

The National Endowment for Science, Technology and the Arts.

The National Expert Group on Transboundary Air Pollution.

The National Gallery.

The National Heritage Memorial Fund.

The National Library of Wales.

The National Lottery Charities Board.

The National Lottery Commission.

The National Maritime Museum.

The National Museum of Science and Industry.

The National Museums and Galleries of Wales.

The National Museums and Galleries on Merseyside.

The National Portrait Gallery.

The National Radiological Protection Board.

The Natural Environment Research Council.

The Natural History Museum.

The New Deal Task Force.

The New Opportunities Fund.

The Occupational Pensions Regulatory Authority.

The Oil and Pipelines Agency.

The OSO Board.

The Overseas Service Pensions Scheme Advisory Board.

The Panel on Standards for the Planning Inspectorate.

The Parliamentary Boundary Commission for England.

The Parliamentary Boundary Commission for Scotland.

The Parliamentary Boundary Commission for Wales.

The Parliamentary Commissioner for Administration.

The Parole Board.

The Particle Physics and Astronomy Research Council.

The Pensions Compensation Board.

The Pensions Ombudsman.

The Pharmacists' Review Panel.

The Place Names Advisory Committee.

The Poisons Board.

The Police Complaints Authority.

The Police Information Technology Organisation.

The Police Negotiating Board.

The Political Honours Scrutiny Committee.

The Post Office.

The Post Office Users' Councils for Scotland, Wales and Northern Ireland.

The Post Office Users' National Council.

The Property Advisory Group.

The Qualifications, Curriculum and Assessment Authority for Wales.

The Qualifications Curriculum Authority.

The Race Education and Employment Forum.

The Race Relations Forum.

The Radio Authority.

The Radioactive Waste Management Advisory Committee.

Any Rail Passengers' Committee established under section 2(2) of the Railways Act 1993

A Regional Cultural Consortium.

Any regional development agency established under the Regional Development Agencies Act 1998, other than the London Development Agency.

Any regional flood defence committee.

The Registrar of Occupational and Personal Pension Schemes.

The Registrar of Public Lending Right.

Remploy Ltd.

The Renewable Energy Advisory Committee.

Resource: The Council for Museums, Archives and Libraries.

The Review Board for Government Contracts.

The Review Body for Nursing Staff, Midwives, Health Visitors and Professions Allied to Medicine.

The Review Body on Doctors and Dentists Remuneration.

The Reviewing Committee on the Export of Works of Art.

The Royal Air Force Museum.

The Royal Armouries.

The Royal Botanic Gardens, Kew.

The Royal Commission on Ancient and Historical Monuments of Wales.

The Royal Commission on Environmental Pollution.

The Royal Commission on Historical Manuscripts.

The Royal Military College of Science Advisory Council.

The Royal Mint Advisory Committee on the Design of Coins, Medals, Seals and Decorations.

The School Teachers' Review Body.

The Scientific Committee on Tobacco and Health.

The Scottish Advisory Committee on Telecommunications.

The Scottish Committee of the Council on Tribunals.

The Sea Fish Industry Authority.

The Senior Salaries Review Body.

The Sentencing Advisory Panel.

The Service Authority for the National Crime Squad.

Sianel Pedwar Cymru, in respect of information held for purposes other than those of journalism, art or literature.

Sir John Soane's Museum.

The Skills Task Force.

The social fund Commissioner appointed under section 65 of the Social Security Administration Act 1992.

The Social Security Advisory Committee.

The Social Services Inspectorate for Wales Advisory Group.

The Spongiform Encephalopathy Advisory Committee.

The Sports Council for Wales.

The Standards Board for England.

The Standing Advisory Committee on Industrial Property.

The Standing Advisory Committee on Trunk Road Assessment.

The Standing Dental Advisory Committee.

The Standing Nursing and Midwifery Advisory Committee.

The Standing Medical Advisory Committee.

The Standing Pharmaceutical Advisory Committee.

The Steering Committee on Pharmacy Postgraduate Education.

The Strategic Rail Authority.

The subsidence adviser appointed under section 46 of the Coal Industry Act 1994.

The Substance Misuse Advisory Panel.

The Sustainable Development Commission.

The Sustainable Development Education Panel.

The Tate Gallery.

The Teacher Training Agency.

The Theatres Trust.

The Traffic Commissioners, in respect of information held by them otherwise than as a tribunal.

The Treasure Valuation Committee.

The UK Advisory Panel for Health Care Workers Infected with Bloodborne Viruses.

The UK Sports Council.

The United Kingdom Atomic Energy Authority.

The United Kingdom Central Council for Nursing, Midwifery and Health Visiting.

The United Kingdom Register of Organic Food Standards.

The United Kingdom Xenotransplantation Interim Regulatory Authority.

The Unlinked Anonymous Serosurveys Steering Group.

The Unrelated Live Transplant Regulatory Authority.

The Urban Regeneration Agency.

The Veterinary Products Committee.

The Victoria and Albert Museum.

The Wales New Deal Advisory Task Force.

The Wales Tourist Board.

The Wallace Collection.

The War Pensions Committees.

The Water Regulations Advisory Committee.

The Welsh Administration Ombudsman.

The Welsh Advisory Committee on Telecommunications.

The Welsh Committee for Professional Development of Pharmacy.

The Welsh Dental Committee.

The Welsh Development Agency.

The Welsh Industrial Development Advisory Board.

The Welsh Language Board.

The Welsh Medical Committee.

The Welsh National Board for Nursing, Midwifery and Health Visiting.

The Welsh Nursing and Midwifery Committee.

The Welsh Optometric Committee.

The Welsh Pharmaceutical Committee.

The Welsh Scientific Advisory Committee.

The Westminster Foundation for Democracy.

The Wilton Park Academic Council.

The Wine Standards Board of the Vintners' Company.

The Women's National Commission.

The Youth Justice Board for England and Wales.

The Zoos Forum.

PART VII
OTHER PUBLIC BODIES AND OFFICES: NORTHERN IRELAND

An Advisory Committee on General Commissioners of Income Tax (Northern Ireland).

The Advisory Committee on Justices of the Peace in Northern Ireland.

The Advisory Committee on Juvenile Court Lay Panel (Northern Ireland).

The Advisory Committee on Pesticides for Northern Ireland.

The Agricultural Research Institute of Northern Ireland.

The Agricultural Wages Board for Northern Ireland.

The Arts Council of Northern Ireland.

The Assembly Ombudsman for Northern Ireland.

The Belfast Harbour Commissioners.

The Board of Trustees of National Museums and Galleries of Northern Ireland.

Boards of Visitors and Visiting Committees.

The Boundary Commission for Northern Ireland.

The Certification Officer for Northern Ireland.

The Charities Advisory Committee.

The Chief Electoral Officer for Northern Ireland.

The Civil Service Commissioners for Northern Ireland.

The Commissioner for Public Appointments for Northern Ireland.

The Construction Industry Training Board.

The consultative Civic Forum referred to in section 56(4) of the Northern Ireland Act 1998.

The Council for Catholic Maintained Schools.

The Council for Nature Conservation and the Countryside.

The County Court Rules Committee (Northern Ireland).

The Disability Living Allowance Advisory Board for Northern Ireland.

The Distinction and Meritorious Service Awards Committee.

The Drainage Council for Northern Ireland.

An Education and Library Board established under Article 3 of the Education and Libraries (Northern Ireland) Order 1986.

Enterprise Ulster.

The Equality Commission for Northern Ireland.

The Family Proceedings Rules Committee (Northern Ireland).

The Fire Authority for Northern Ireland.

The Fisheries Conservancy Board for Northern Ireland.

The General Consumer Council for Northern Ireland.

The Health and Safety Agency for Northern Ireland.

The Historic Buildings Council.

The Historic Monuments Council.

The Independent Assessor of Military Complaints Procedures in Northern Ireland.

The Independent Reviewer of the Northern Ireland (Emergency Provisions) Act.

The Independent Commissioner for Holding Centres.

The Industrial Development Board for Northern Ireland.

The Industrial Research and Technology Unit.

The Juvenile Justice Board.

The Labour Relations Agency.

The Laganside Corporation.

The Law Reform Advisory Committee for Northern Ireland.

The Lay Observer for Northern Ireland.

The Legal Aid Advisory Committee (Northern Ireland).

The Livestock & Meat Commission for Northern Ireland.

The Local Enterprise Development Unit.

The Local Government Staff Commission.

The Londonderry Port and Harbour Commissioners.

The Magistrates' Courts Rules Committee (Northern Ireland).

The Mental Health Commission for Northern Ireland.

The Northern Ireland Advisory Committee on Telecommunications.

The Northern Ireland Audit Office.

The Northern Ireland Building Regulations Advisory Committee.

The Northern Ireland Civil Service Appeal Board.

The Northern Ireland Commissioner for Complaints.

The Northern Ireland Community Relations Council.

The Northern Ireland Consumer Committee for Electricity.

The Northern Ireland Council for the Curriculum, Examinations and Assessment.

The Northern Ireland Council for Postgraduate Medical and Dental Education.

The Northern Ireland Crown Court Rules Committee.

The Northern Ireland Economic Council.

The Northern Ireland Fishery Harbour Authority.

The Northern Ireland Higher Education Council.

The Northern Ireland Housing Executive.

The Northern Ireland Human Rights Commission.

The Northern Ireland Insolvency Rules Committee.

The Northern Ireland Local Government Officers' Superannuation Committee.

The Northern Ireland Museums Council.

The Northern Ireland Pig Production Development Committee.

The Northern Ireland Supreme Court Rules Committee.

The Northern Ireland Tourist Board.

The Northern Ireland Transport Holding Company.

The Northern Ireland Water Council.

The Parades Commission.

The Police Ombudsman for Northern Ireland.

The Probation Board for Northern Ireland.

The Rural Development Council for Northern Ireland.

The Sentence Review Commissioners appointed under section 1 of the Northern Ireland (Sentences) Act 1998.

The social fund Commissioner appointed under Article 37 of the Social Security (Northern Ireland) Order 1998.

The Sports Council for Northern Ireland.

The Staff Commission for Education and Library Boards.

The Statistics Advisory Committee.

The Statute Law Committee for Northern Ireland.

The Training and Employment Agency.

Ulster Supported Employment Ltd.

The Warrenpoint Harbour Authority.

The Youth Council for Northern Ireland.

SCHEDULE 2

THE COMMISSIONER AND THE TRIBUNAL

PART I

PROVISION CONSEQUENTIAL ON S. 18(1) AND (2)

General

1. (1) Any reference in any enactment, instrument or document to the Data Protection Commissioner or the Data Protection Registrar shall be construed, in relation to any time after the commencement of section 18(1), as a reference to the Information Commissioner.

(2) Any reference in any enactment, instrument or document to the Data Protection Tribunal shall be construed, in relation to any time after the commencement of section 18(2), as a reference to the Information Tribunal.

2. (1) Any reference in this Act or in any instrument under this Act to the Commissioner shall be construed, in relation to any time before the commencement of section 18(1), as a reference to the Data Protection Commissioner.

(2) Any reference in this Act or in any instrument under this Act to the Tribunal shall be construed, in relation to any time before the commencement of section 18(2), as a reference to the Data Protection Tribunal.

Public Records Act 1958 (c. 51)

3. (1) In Part II of the Table in paragraph 3 of Schedule 1 to the Public Records Act 1958 (definition of public records), the entry relating to the Data Protection Commissioner is omitted and there is inserted at the appropriate place—
     'Information Commissioner.'

(2) In paragraph 4(1) of that Schedule, for paragraph (nn) there is substituted—
     '(nn) records of the Information Tribunal;'.

Parliamentary Commissioner Act 1967 (c. 13)

4. In Schedule 2 to the Parliamentary Commissioner Act 1967 (departments etc. subject to investigation), the entry relating to the Data Protection Commissioner is omitted and there is inserted at the appropriate place—
     'Information Commissioner'.

5. In Schedule 4 to that Act (tribunals exercising administrative functions), for the entry relating to the Data Protection Tribunal there is substituted—
     'Information Tribunal constituted under section 6 of the Data Protection Act 1998.'†

Superannuation Act 1972 (c. 11)

6. In Schedule 1 to the Superannuation Act 1972 (employment with superannuation scheme), for 'Data Protection Commissioner' there is substituted 'Information Commissioner'.

Consumer Credit Act 1974 (c. 39)

7. In section 159 of the Consumer Credit Act 1974 (correction of wrong information), in subsections (7) and (8)(b), for 'Data Protection Commissioner', in both places where it occurs, there is substituted 'Information Commissioner'.

House of Commons Disqualification Act 1975 (c. 24)

8. (1) In Part II of Schedule 1 to the House of Commons Disqualification Act 1975 (bodies whose members are disqualified), the entry relating to the Data Protection Tribunal is omitted and there is inserted at the appropriate place—
    'The Information Tribunal'.

(2) In Part III of that Schedule (disqualifying offices), the entry relating to the Data Protection Commissioner is omitted and there is inserted at the appropriate place—
    'The Information Commissioner'.

Northern Ireland Assembly Disqualification Act 1975 (c. 25)

9. (1) In Part II of Schedule 1 to the Northern Ireland Assembly Disqualification Act 1975 (bodies whose members are disqualified), the entry relating to the Data Protection Tribunal is omitted and there is inserted at the appropriate place—
    'The Information Tribunal'.

(2) In Part III of that Schedule (disqualifying offices), the entry relating to the Data Protection Commissioner is omitted and there is inserted at the appropriate place—
    'The Information Commissioner'.

Tribunals and Inquiries Act 1992 (c. 53)

10. In paragraph 14 of Part I of Schedule 1 to the Tribunals and Inquiries Act 1992 (tribunals under direct supervision of Council on Tribunals)—
    (a) in sub-paragraph (a), for 'The Data Protection Commissioner' there is substituted 'The Information Commissioner', and
    (b) for sub-paragraph (b) there is substituted—
    '(b) the Information Tribunal constituted under that section, in respect of its jurisdiction under—
    (i) section 48 of that Act, and
    (ii) section 57 of the Freedom of Information Act 2000.'

Judicial Pensions and Retirement Act 1993 (c. 8)

11. In Schedule 5 to the Judicial Pensions and Retirement Act 1993 (retirement provisions: the relevant offices), in the entry relating to the chairman and deputy chairman of the Data Protection Tribunal, for 'the Data Protection Tribunal' there is substituted 'the Information Tribunal'.

12. In Schedule 7 to that Act (retirement dates: transitional provisions), in paragraph 5(5)(xxvi) for 'the Data Protection Tribunal' there is substituted 'the Information Tribunal'.

Data Protection Act 1998 (c. 29)

13. (1) Section 6 of the Data Protection Act 1998 (the Data Protection Commissioner and the Data Protection Tribunal) is amended as follows.

(2) For subsection (1) there is substituted—
    '(1) For the purposes of this Act and of the Freedom of Information Act 2000 there shall be an officer known as the Information Commissioner (in this Act referred to as "the Commissioner").'

(3) For subsection (3) there is substituted—
    '(3) For the purposes of this Act and of the Freedom of Information Act 2000 there shall be a tribunal known as the Information Tribunal (in this Act referred to as "the Tribunal").'

14. In section 70(1) of that Act (supplementary definitions)—

(a) in the definition of 'the Commissioner', for 'the Data Protection Commissioner' there is substituted 'the Information Commissioner', and

(b) in the definition of 'the Tribunal', for 'the Data Protection Tribunal' there is substituted 'the Information Tribunal'.

15. (1) Schedule 5 to that Act (the Data Protection Commissioner and the Data Protection Tribunal) is amended as follows.

(2) In paragraph 1(1), for 'Data Protection Commissioner' there is substituted 'Information Commissioner'.

(3) Part III shall cease to have effect.

PART II
AMENDMENTS RELATING TO EXTENSION OF FUNCTIONS OF COMMISSIONER AND TRIBUNAL

Interests represented by lay members of Tribunal

16. In section 6(6) of the Data Protection Act 1998 (lay members of Tribunal)—

(a) for the word 'and' at the end of paragraph (a) there is substituted—
'(aa) persons to represent the interests of those who make requests for information under the Freedom of Information Act 2000,', and

(b) after paragraph (b) there is inserted 'and
(bb) persons to represent the interests of public authorities.'

Expenses incurred under this Act excluded in calculating fees

17. In section 26(2) of that Act (fees regulations), in paragraph (a)—

(a) after 'functions' there is inserted 'under this Act', and

(b) after 'Tribunal' there is inserted 'so far as attributable to their functions under this Act'.

Information provided to Commissioner or Tribunal

18. In section 58 of that Act (disclosure of information to Commissioner or Tribunal), after 'this Act' there is inserted 'or the Freedom of Information Act 2000'.

19. (1) Section 59 of that Act (confidentiality of information) is amended as follows.

(2) In subsections (1) and (2), for 'this Act', wherever occurring, there is substituted 'the information Acts'.

(3) After subsection (3) there is inserted—
'(4) In this section 'the information Acts' means this Act and the Freedom of Information Act 2000.'

Deputy commissioners

20. (1) Paragraph 4 of Schedule 5 to that Act (officers and staff) is amended as follows.

(2) In sub-paragraph (1)(a), after 'a deputy commissioner' there is inserted 'or two deputy commissioners'.

(3) After sub-paragraph (1) there is inserted—
'(1A) The Commissioner shall, when appointing any second deputy commissioner, specify which of the Commissioner's functions are to be performed, in the circumstances referred to in paragraph 5(1), by each of the deputy commissioners.'

Exercise of Commissioner's functions by others

21. (1) Paragraph 5 of Schedule 5 to that Act (exercise of functions of Commissioner during vacancy etc.) is amended as follows.

(2) In sub-paragraph (1)—

    (a) after 'deputy commissioner' there is inserted 'or deputy commissioners', and

    (b) after 'this Act' there is inserted 'or the Freedom of Information Act 2000'.

(3) In sub-paragraph (2) after 'this Act' there is inserted 'or the Freedom of Information Act 2000'.

Money

22. In paragraph 9(1) of Schedule 5 to that Act (money) for 'or section 159 of the Consumer Credit Act 1974' there is substituted ', under section 159 of the Consumer Credit Act 1974 or under the Freedom of Information Act 2000'.

SCHEDULE 3
POWERS OF ENTRY AND INSPECTION

Issue of warrants

1. (1) If a circuit judge is satisfied by information on oath supplied by the Commissioner that there are reasonable grounds for suspecting—

    (a) that a public authority has failed or is failing to comply with—

        (i) any of the requirements of Part I of this Act,

        (ii) so much of a decision notice as requires steps to be taken, or

        (iii) an information notice or an enforcement notice, or

    (b) that an offence under section 77 has been or is being committed,

and that evidence of such a failure to comply or of the commission of the offence is to be found on any premises specified in the information, he may, subject to paragraph 2, grant a warrant to the Commissioner.

(2) A warrant issued under sub-paragraph (1) shall authorise the Commissioner or any of his officers or staff at any time within seven days of the date of the warrant—

    (a) to enter and search the premises,

    (b) to inspect and seize any documents or other material found there which may be such evidence as is mentioned in that sub-paragraph, and

    (c) to inspect, examine, operate and test any equipment found there in which information held by the public authority may be recorded.

2. (1) A judge shall not issue a warrant under this Schedule unless he is satisfied—

    (a) that the Commissioner has given seven days' notice in writing to the occupier of the premises in question demanding access to the premises, and

    (b) that either—

        (i) access was demanded at a reasonable hour and was unreasonably refused, or

        (ii) although entry to the premises was granted, the occupier unreasonably refused to comply with a request by the Commissioner or any of the Commissioner's officers or staff to permit the Commissioner or the officer or member of staff to do any of the things referred to in paragraph 1(2), and

    (c) that the occupier, has, after the refusal, been notified by the Commissioner of the application for the warrant and has had an opportunity of being heard by the judge on the question whether or not it should be issued.

(2) Sub-paragraph (1) shall not apply if the judge is satisfied that the case is one of urgency or that compliance with those provisions would defeat the object of the entry.

3. A judge who issues a warrant under this Schedule shall also issue two copies of it and certify them clearly as copies.

Execution of warrants

4. A person executing a warrant issued under this Schedule may use such reasonable force as may be necessary.

5. A warrant issued under this Schedule shall be executed at a reasonable hour unless it appears to the person executing it that there are grounds for suspecting that the evidence in question would not be found if it were so executed.

6. (1) If the premises in respect of which a warrant is issued under this Schedule are occupied by a public authority and any officer or employee of the authority is present when the warrant is executed, he shall be shown the warrant and supplied with a copy of it; and if no such officer or employee is present a copy of the warrant shall be left in a prominent place on the premises.

(2) If the premises in respect of which a warrant is issued under this Schedule are occupied by a person other than a public authority and he is present when the warrant is executed, he shall be shown the warrant and supplied with a copy of it; and if that person is not present a copy of the warrant shall be left in a prominent place on the premises.

7. (1) A person seizing anything in pursuance of a warrant under this Schedule shall give a receipt for it if asked to do so.

(2) Anything so seized may be retained for so long as is necessary in all the circumstances but the person in occupation of the premises in question shall be given a copy of anything that is seized if he so requests and the person executing the warrant considers that it can be done without undue delay.

Matters exempt from inspection and seizure

8. The powers of inspection and seizure conferred by a warrant issued under this Schedule shall not be exercisable in respect of information which is exempt information by virtue of section 23(1) or 24(1).

9. (1) Subject to the provisions of this paragraph, the powers of inspection and seizure conferred by a warrant issued under this Schedule shall not be exercisable in respect of—
   (a) any communication between a professional legal adviser and his client in connection with the giving of legal advice to the client with respect to his obligations, liabilities or rights under this Act, or
   (b) any communication between a professional legal adviser and his client, or between such an adviser or his client and any other person, made in connection with or in contemplation of proceedings under or arising out of this Act (including proceedings before the Tribunal) and for the purposes of such proceedings.

(2) Sub-paragraph (1) applies also to—
   (a) any copy or other record of any such communication as is there mentioned, and
   (b) any document or article enclosed with or referred to in any such communication if made in connection with the giving of any advice or, as the case may be, in connection with or in contemplation of and for the purposes of such proceedings as are there mentioned.

(3) This paragraph does not apply to anything in the possession of any person other than the professional legal adviser or his client or to anything held with the intention of furthering a criminal purpose.

(4) In this paragraph references to the client of a professional legal adviser include references to any person representing such a client.

10. If the person in occupation of any premises in respect of which a warrant is issued under this Schedule objects to the inspection or seizure under the warrant of any material on the grounds that it consists partly of matters in respect of which those powers are not exercisable, he shall, if the person executing the warrant so requests, furnish that person with a copy of so much of the material in relation to which the powers are exercisable.

Return of warrants

11. A warrant issued under this Schedule shall be returned to the court from which it was issued—
    (a) after being executed, or
    (b) if not executed within the time authorised for its execution;

and the person by whom any such warrant is executed shall make an endorsement on it stating what powers have been exercised by him under the warrant.

Offences

12. Any person who—
    (a) intentionally obstructs a person in the execution of a warrant issued under this Schedule, or
    (b) fails without reasonable excuse to give any person executing such a warrant such assistance as he may reasonably require for the execution of the warrant,

is guilty of an offence.

Vessels, vehicles etc.

13. In this Schedule 'premises' includes any vessel, vehicle, aircraft or hovercraft, and references to the occupier of any premises include references to the person in charge of any vessel, vehicle, aircraft or hovercraft.

Scotland and Northern Ireland

14. In the application of this Schedule to Scotland—
    (a) for any reference to a circuit judge there is substituted a reference to the sheriff, and
    (b) for any reference to information on oath there is substituted a reference to evidence on oath.

15. In the application of this Schedule to Northern Ireland—
    (a) for any reference to a circuit judge there is substituted a reference to a county court judge, and
    (b) for any reference to information on oath there is substituted a reference to a complaint on oath.

SCHEDULE 4
APPEAL PROCEEDINGS: AMENDMENTS OF SCHEDULE 6 TO DATA PROTECTION ACT 1998

Constitution of Tribunal in national security cases

1. In paragraph 2(1) of Schedule 6 to the Data Protection Act 1998 (constitution of Tribunal in national security cases), at the end there is inserted 'or under section 60(1) or (4) of the Freedom of Information Act 2000'.

2. For paragraph 3 of that Schedule there is substituted—
    '3. The Tribunal shall be duly constituted—
    (a) for an appeal under section 28(4) or (6) in any case where the application of paragraph 6(1) is excluded by rules under paragraph 7, or
    (b) for an appeal under section 60(1) or (4) of the Freedom of Information Act 2000,

if it consists of three of the persons designated under paragraph 2(1), of whom one shall be designated by the Lord Chancellor to preside.'

Constitution of Tribunal in other cases

3. (1) Paragraph 4 of that Schedule (constitution of Tribunal in other cases) is amended as follows.

(2) After sub-paragraph (1) there is inserted—

'(1A) Subject to any rules made under paragraph 7, the Tribunal shall be duly constituted for an appeal under section 57(1) or (2) of the Freedom of Information Act 2000 if it consists of—

(a) the chairman or a deputy chairman (who shall preside), and

(b) an equal number of the members appointed respectively in accordance with paragraphs (aa) and (bb) of section 6(6).'

(3) In sub-paragraph (2), after '(1)' there is inserted 'or (1A)'.

Rules of procedure

4. (1) Paragraph 7 of that Schedule (rules of procedure) is amended as follows.

(2) In sub-paragraph (1), for the words from 'regulating' onwards there is substituted 'regulating—

(a) the exercise of the rights of appeal conferred—

(i) by sections 28(4) and (6) and 48, and

(ii) by sections 57(1) and (2) and section 60(1) and (4) of the Freedom of Information Act 2000, and

(b) the practice and procedure of the Tribunal.'

(3) In sub-paragraph (2), after paragraph (a) there is inserted—

'(aa) for the joinder of any other person as a party to any proceedings on an appeal under the Freedom of Information Act 2000,

(ab) for the hearing of an appeal under this Act with an appeal under the Freedom of Information Act 2000,'.

SCHEDULE 5
AMENDMENTS OF PUBLIC RECORDS LEGISLATION

PART I
AMENDMENTS OF PUBLIC RECORDS ACT 1958

Functions of Advisory Council on Public Records

1. In section 1 of the Public Records Act 1958 (general responsibility of the Lord Chancellor for public records), after subsection (2) there is inserted—

'(2A) The matters on which the Advisory Council on Public Records may advise the Lord Chancellor include matters relating to the application of the Freedom of Information Act 2000 to information contained in public records which are historical records within the meaning of Part VI of that Act.'

Access to public records

2. (1) Section 5 of that Act (access to public records) is amended in accordance with this paragraph.

(2) Subsections (1) and (2) are omitted.

(3) For subsection (3) there is substituted—

'(3) It shall be the duty of the Keeper of Public Records to arrange that reasonable facilities are available to the public for inspecting and obtaining copies of those public records in the Public Record Office which fall to be disclosed in accordance with the Freedom of Information Act 2000.'

(4) Subsection (4) and, in subsection (5), the words from 'and subject to' to the end are omitted.

3. Schedule 2 of that Act (enactments prohibiting disclosure of information obtained from the public) is omitted.

Power to extend meaning of 'public records'

4. In Schedule 1 to that Act (definition of public records) after the Table at the end of paragraph 3 there is inserted—

'3A.—(1) Her Majesty may by Order in Council amend the Table at the end of paragraph 3 of this Schedule by adding to either Part of the Table an entry relating to any body or establishment—

    (a) which, at the time when the Order is made, is specified in Schedule 2 to the Parliamentary Commissioner Act 1967 (departments, etc. subject to investigation), or

    (b) in respect of which an entry could, at that time, be added to Schedule 2 to that Act by an Order in Council under section 4 of that Act (which confers power to amend that Schedule).

(2) An Order in Council under this paragraph may relate to a specified body or establishment or to bodies or establishments falling within a specified description.

(3) An Order in Council under this paragraph shall be subject to annulment in pursuance of a resolution of either House of Parliament.'

PART II
AMENDMENT OF PUBLIC RECORDS ACT (NORTHERN IRELAND) 1923

5. After section 5 of the Public Records Act (Northern Ireland) 1923 (deposit of documents in Record Office by trustees or other persons) there is inserted—

'Access to public records

5A. It shall be the duty of the Deputy Keeper of the Records of Northern Ireland to arrange that reasonable facilities are available to the public for inspecting and obtaining copies of those public records in the Public Record Office of Northern Ireland which fall to be disclosed in accordance with the Freedom of Information Act 2000.'

SCHEDULE 6
FURTHER AMENDMENTS OF DATA PROTECTION ACT 1998

Request by data controller for further information

1. In section 7 of the Data Protection Act 1998 (right of access to personal data), for subsection (3) there is substituted—

'(3) Where a data controller—

    (a) reasonably requires further information in order to satisfy himself as to the identity of the person making a request under this section and to locate the information which that person seeks, and

    (b) has informed him of that requirement,

the data controller is not obliged to comply with the request unless he is supplied with that further information.'

Parliament

2. After section 35 of that Act there is inserted—

'Parliamentary privilege

35A. Personal data are exempt from—

(a) the first data protection principle, except to the extent to which it requires compliance with the conditions in Schedules 2 and 3,

(b) the second, third, fourth and fifth data protection principles,

(c) section 7, and

(d) sections 10 and 14(1) to (3),

if the exemption is required for the purpose of avoiding an infringement of the privileges of either House of Parliament.'

3. After section 63 of that Act there is inserted—

'Application to Parliament.

63A. (1) Subject to the following provisions of this section and to section 35A, this Act applies to the processing of personal data by or on behalf of either House of Parliament as it applies to the processing of personal data by other persons.

(2) Where the purposes for which and the manner in which any personal data are, or are to be, processed are determined by or on behalf of the House of Commons, the data controller in respect of those data for the purposes of this Act shall be the Corporate Officer of that House.

(3) Where the purposes for which and the manner in which any personal data are, or are to be, processed are determined by or on behalf of the House of Lords, the data controller in respect of those data for the purposes of this Act shall be the Corporate Officer of that House.

(4) Nothing in subsection (2) or (3) is to be taken to render the Corporate Officer of the House of Commons or the Corporate Officer of the House of Lords liable to prosecution under this Act, but section 55 and paragraph 12 of Schedule 9 shall apply to a person acting on behalf of either House as they apply to any other person.'

4. In Schedule 2 to that Act (conditions relevant for the purposes of the first data protection principle: processing of any personal data) in paragraph 5 after paragraph (a) there is inserted—

'(aa) for the exercise of any functions of either House of Parliament,'

5. In Schedule 3 to that Act (conditions relevant for the purposes of the first data protection principle: processing of sensitive personal data) in paragraph 7 after paragraph (a) there is inserted—

'(aa) for the exercise of any functions of either House of Parliament,'.

Honours

6. In Schedule 7 to that Act (miscellaneous exemptions) in paragraph 3(b) (honours) after honour' there is inserted 'or dignity'.

Legal professional privilege

7. In paragraph 10 of that Schedule (legal professional privilege), for the words 'or, in Scotland, to confidentiality as between client and professional legal adviser,' there is substituted 'or, in Scotland, to confidentiality of communications'.

Extension of transitional exemption

8. In Schedule 14 to that Act (transitional provisions), in paragraph 2(1) (which confers transitional exemption from the prohibition on processing without registration on those registered under the Data Protection Act 1984) the words 'or, if earlier, 24th October 2001' are omitted.

SCHEDULE 7
DISCLOSURE OF INFORMATION BY OMBUDSMEN

The Parliamentary Commissioner for Administration

1. At the end of section 11 of the Parliamentary Commissioner Act 1967 (provision for secrecy of information) there is inserted—

'(5) Information obtained from the Information Commissioner by virtue of section 76(1) of the Freedom of Information Act 2000 shall be treated for the purposes of subsection (2) of this section as obtained for the purposes of an investigation under this Act and, in relation to such information, the reference in paragraph (a) of that subsection to the investigation shall have effect as a reference to any investigation.'

2. After section 11A of that Act there is inserted—

'Disclosure of information by Parliamentary Commissioner to Information Commissioner.

11AA.(1) The Commissioner may disclose to the Information Commissioner any information obtained by, or furnished to, the Commissioner under or for the purposes of this Act if the information appears to the Commissioner to relate to—

    (a) a matter in respect of which the Information Commissioner could exercise any power conferred by—

        (i) Part V of the Data Protection Act 1998 (enforcement),

        (ii) section 48 of the Freedom of Information Act 2000 (practice recommendations), or

        (iii) Part IV of that Act (enforcement), or

    (b) the commission of an offence under—

        (i) any provision of the Data Protection Act 1998 other than paragraph 12 of Schedule 9 (obstruction of execution of warrant), or

        (ii) section 77 of the Freedom of Information Act 2000 (offence of altering etc. records with intent to prevent disclosure).

    (2) Nothing in section 11(2) of this Act shall apply in relation to the disclosure of information in accordance with this section.'

The Commissions for Local Administration in England and Wales

3. In section 32 of the Local Government Act 1974 (law of defamation, and disclosure of information) after subsection (6) there is inserted—

'(7) Information obtained from the Information Commissioner by virtue of section 76 of the Freedom of Information Act 2000 shall be treated for the purposes of subsection (2) above as obtained for the purposes of an investigation under this Part of this Act and, in relation to such information, the reference in paragraph (a) of that subsection to the investigation shall have effect as a reference to any investigation.'

4. After section 33 of that Act there is inserted—

'Disclosure of information by Local Commissioner to Information Commissioner.

33A.—(1) A Local Commissioner may disclose to the Information Commissioner any information obtained by, or furnished to, the Local Commissioner under or for the purposes of this Part of this Act if the information appears to the Local Commissioner to relate to—

    (a) a matter in respect of which the Information Commissioner could exercise any power conferred by—

        (i) Part V of the Data Protection Act 1998 (enforcement),

        (ii) section 48 of the Freedom of Information Act 2000 (practice recommendations), or

        (iii) Part IV of that Act (enforcement), or

    (b) the commission of an offence under—

        (i) any provision of the Data Protection Act 1998 other than paragraph 12 of Schedule 9 (obstruction of execution of warrant), or

        (ii) section 77 of the Freedom of Information Act 2000 (offence of altering etc. records with intent to prevent disclosure).

    (2) Nothing in section 32(2) of this Act shall apply in relation to the disclosure of information in accordance with this section.'

The Health Service Commissioners

5. At the end of section 15 of the Health Service Commissioners Act 1993 (confidentiality of information) there is inserted—

'(4) Information obtained from the Information Commissioner by virtue of section 76 of the Freedom of Information Act 2000 shall be treated for the purposes of subsection (1) as obtained for the purposes of an investigation and, in relation to such information, the reference in paragraph (a) of that subsection to the investigation shall have effect as a reference to any investigation.'

6. After section 18 of that Act there is inserted—

'Disclosure of information to Information Commissioner.

18A.—(1) The Health Service Commissioner for England or the Health Service Commissioner for Wales may disclose to the Information Commissioner any information obtained by, or furnished to, the Health Service Commissioner under or for the purposes of this Act if the information appears to the Health Service Commissioner to relate to—

    (a) a matter in respect of which the Information Commissioner could exercise any power conferred by—

        (i) Part V of the Data Protection Act 1998 (enforcement),

        (ii) section 48 of the Freedom of Information Act 2000 (practice recommendations), or

        (iii) Part IV of that Act (enforcement), or

    (b) the commission of an offence under—

        (i) any provision of the Data Protection Act 1998 other than paragraph 12 of Schedule 9 (obstruction of execution of warrant), or

        (ii) section 77 of the Freedom of Information Act 2000 (offence of altering etc. records with intent to prevent disclosure).

    (3) Nothing in section 15 (confidentiality of information) applies in relation to the disclosure of information in accordance with this section.'

The Welsh Administration Ombudsman

7. In Schedule 9 to the Government of Wales Act 1998 (the Welsh Administration Ombudsman), at the end of paragraph 25 (confidentiality of information) there is inserted—

'(5) Information obtained from the Information Commissioner by virtue of section 76 of the Freedom of Information Act 2000 shall be treated for the purposes of sub-paragraph (1) as obtained for the purposes of an investigation and, in relation to such information, the reference in paragraph (a) of that subsection to the investigation shall have effect as a reference to any investigation.'

8. After paragraph 27 of that Schedule there is inserted—

'Disclosure of information to Information Commissioner

28. (1) The Welsh Administration Ombudsman may disclose to the Information Commissioner any information obtained by, or furnished to, the Welsh Administration Ombudsman under or for the purposes of this Schedule if the information appears to the Welsh Administration Ombudsman to relate to—

    (a) a matter in respect of which the Information Commissioner could exercise any power conferred by—

        (i) Part V of the Data Protection Act 1998 (enforcement),

        (ii) section 48 of the Freedom of Information Act 2000 (practice recommendations), or

        (iii) Part IV of that Act (enforcement), or

    (b) the commission of an offence under—

        (i) any provision of the Data Protection Act 1998 other than paragraph 12 of Schedule 9 (obstruction of execution of warrant), or

(ii) section 77 of the Freedom of Information Act 2000 (offence of altering etc. records with intent to prevent disclosure).

(2) Nothing in paragraph 25(1) applies in relation to the disclosure of information in accordance with this paragraph.'

The Northern Ireland Commissioner for Complaints

9. At the end of Article 21 of the Commissioner for Complaints (Northern Ireland) Order 1996 (disclosure of information by Commissioner) there is inserted—

'(5) Information obtained from the Information Commissioner by virtue of section 76 of the Freedom of Information Act 2000 shall be treated for the purposes of paragraph (1) as obtained for the purposes of an investigation under this Order and, in relation to such information, the reference in paragraph (1)(a) to the investigation shall have effect as a reference to any investigation.'

10. After that Article there is inserted—

'Disclosure of information to Information Commissioner

21A.—(1) The Commissioner may disclose to the Information Commissioner any information obtained by, or furnished to, the Commissioner under or for the purposes of this Order if the information appears to the Commissioner to relate to—

(a) a matter in respect of which the Information Commissioner could exercise any power conferred by—
  (i) Part V of the Data Protection Act 1998 (enforcement),
  (ii) section 48 of the Freedom of Information Act 2000 (practice recommendations), or
  (iii) Part IV of that Act (enforcement), or
(b) the commission of an offence under—
  (i) any provision of the Data Protection Act 1998 other than paragraph 12 of Schedule 9 (obstruction of execution of warrant), or
  (ii) section 77 of the Freedom of Information Act 2000 (offence of altering etc. records with intent to prevent disclosure).

(2) Nothing in Article 21(1) applies in relation to the disclosure of information in accordance with this Article.'

The Assembly Ombudsman for Northern Ireland

11. At the end of Article 19 of the Ombudsman (Northern Ireland) Order 1996 there is inserted—

'(5) Information obtained from the Information Commissioner by virtue of section 76 of the Freedom of Information Act 2000 shall be treated for the purposes of paragraph (1) as obtained for the purposes of an investigation under this Order and, in relation to such information, the reference in paragraph (1)(a) to the investigation shall have effect as a reference to any investigation.'

12. After that Article there is inserted—

'Disclosure of information to Information Commissioner

19A.—(1) The Ombudsman may disclose to the Information Commissioner any information obtained by, or furnished to, the Omubudsman under or for the purposes of this Order if the information appears to the Ombudsman to relate to—

(a) a matter in respect of which the Information Commissioner could exercise any power conferred by—
  (i) Part V of the Data Protection Act 1998 (enforcement),
  (ii) section 48 of the Freedom of Information Act 2000 (practice recommendations), or
  (iii) Part IV of that Act (enforcement), or
(b) the commission of an offence under—
  (i) any provision of the Data Protection Act 1998 other than paragraph 12 of Schedule 9 (obstruction of execution of warrant), or

(ii) section 77 of the Freedom of Information Act 2000 (offence of altering etc. records
with intent to prevent disclosure).

(2) Nothing in Article 19(1) applies in relation to the disclosure of information in accordance
with this Article.'

The Commissioner for Local Administration in Scotland

13. In section 30 of the Local Government (Scotland) Act 1975 (limitation on disclosure of
information), after subsection (5) there is inserted—

'(5A) Information obtained from the Information Commissioner by virtue of section 76 of the
Freedom of Information Act 2000 shall be treated for the purposes of subsection (2) as obtained for the purposes of an investigation under this Part of this Act and, in relation to such
information, the reference in subsection (2)(a) to the investigation shall have effect as a reference to any investigation.'

SCHEDULE 8
REPEALS

PART I
REPEAL COMING INTO FORCE ON PASSING OF ACT

Chapter	Short title	Extent of repeal
1998 c. 29	The Data Protection Act 1998.	In Schedule 14, in paragraph 2(1), the words 'or, if earlier, 24th October 2001'.

PART II
REPEALS COMING INTO FORCE IN ACCORDANCE WITH SECTION 87(2)

Chapter	Short title	Extent of repeal
1958 c. 51.	The Public Records Act 1958.	In Schedule 1, in Part II of the Table in paragraph 3, the entry relating to the Data Protection Commissioner.
1967 c. 13.	The Parliamentary Commissioner Act 1967.	In Schedule 2, the entry relating to the Data Protection Commissioner.
1975 c. 24.	The House of Commons Disqualification Act 1975.	In Schedule 1, in Part III, the entry relating to the Data Protection Commissioner.
1975 c. 25.	The Northern Ireland Assembly Disqualification Act 1975.	In Schedule 1, in Part III, the entry relating to the Data Protection Commissioner.
1998 c. 29.	The Data Protection Act 1998.	In Schedule 5, Part III. In Schedule 15, paragraphs 1(1), 2, 4, 5(2) and 6(2).

PART III
REPEALS COMING INTO FORCE IN ACCORDANCE WITH SECTION 87(3)

Chapter	Short title	Extent of repeal
1958 c. 51	The Public Records Act 1958.	In section 5, subsections (1), (2) and (4) and, in subsection (5), the words from 'and subject to' to the end. Schedule 2.
1975 c. 24.	The House of Commons Disqualification Act 1975.	In Schedule 1, in Part II, the entry relating to the Data Protection Tribunal.
1975 c. 25.	The Northern Ireland Assembly Disqualification Act 1975.	In Schedule 1, in Part II, the entry relating to the Data Protection Tribunal.
1998 c. 29.	The Data Protection Act 1998.	In section 1(1), in the definition of 'data', the word 'or' at the end of paragraph (c). In Schedule 15, paragraphs 1(2) and (3), 3, 5(1) and 6(1).

APPENDIX D

Lord Chancellor's Code of Practice on the Discharge of Public Authorities' Functions under Part I of the Freedom of Information Act 2000, Issued under Section 45 of the Act

NOVEMBER 2002

PRESENTED TO PARLIAMENT BY THE
LORD CHANCELLOR
PURSUANT TO SECTION 45(5) OF THE
FREEDOM OF INFORMATION ACT 2000

CONTENTS

FOREWORD

INTRODUCTION

1. The Code of Practice, to which this is a foreword, fulfils the duty on the Lord Chancellor set out in section 45 of the Freedom of Information Act 2000, to provide guidance to public authorities as to the practice which it would, in his opinion, be desirable for them to follow in connection with the discharge of their functions under Part I of the Act. It is envisaged that Regulations to be made with respect to environmental information will make provision for the issue by the Secretary of State of a Code of Practice applying to the discharge of authorities' functions under those Regulations.

2. This foreword does not form part of the Code itself.

3. The Government is committed to greater openness in the public sector. The Freedom of Information Act will further this aim by helping to transform the culture of the public sector to one of greater openness, enabling members of the public to question the decisions of public authorities more closely and ensuring that services provided by the public sector are more efficiently and properly delivered. Conformity with the Code will assist this.

4. The Code is a supplement to the provisions in the Act. It is not a substitute for legislation. Public authorities should seek legal advice as considered necessary on general issues relating to the implementation of the Act, or its application to individual cases.

Practice Recommendations

5. Under the provisions of section 47 of the Act, the Information Commissioner has a duty to promote the observance of this Code by public authorities. If it appears to the Commissioner that the practice of a public authority in the exercise of its functions under Part I of the Act does not conform with that proposed in the Code of Practice, he may give to the authority a recommendation, under section 48 (known as a 'practice recommendation'), specifying the steps which should, in his opinion, be taken to promote such conformity.

6. A practice recommendation must be given in writing and must refer to the particular provisions of the Code of Practice with which, in the Commissioner's opinion, the public authority's practice does not conform. A practice recommendation is simply a recommendation and cannot be directly enforced by the Information Commissioner. However, a failure to comply with a practice recommendation may lead to a failure to comply with the Act. Further, a failure to take account of a practice recommendation may lead to an adverse comment in a report to Parliament by the Commissioner.

7. It should be noted that because the provisions of the Act relating to the general right of access will not be brought into force until 1 January 2005, the Commissioner's powers to issue practice recommendations in relation to the handling of individual requests for information under the general right of access will not take effect before that date.

Information Notices

8. The Information Commissioner determines whether the practice of a public authority conforms to the Code. Under section 51 of the Act, he may serve an information notice on the authority, requiring it to provide information relating to its conformity with the Code.

9. Under the provisions of section 54 of the Act, if a public authority fails to comply with an information notice, the Commissioner may certify in writing to the court that the public authority has failed to comply with that notice. The court may then inquire into the matter and, after hearing any witnesses who may be produced against or on behalf of, the public authority, and after hearing any statement that may be offered in defence, deal with the authority as if it had committed a contempt of court.

Duty to provide advice and assistance

10. Section 16 of the Act places a duty on public authorities to provide advice and assistance to applicants. A public authority is deemed to have complied with this duty in any particular case if it has conformed with the Code in relation to the provision of advice and assistance in that case. The duty to assist and advise is enforceable by the Information Commissioner. If a public authority fails in its statutory duty, the Commissioner may issue a decision notice under section 50, or an enforcement notice under section 52.

11. Public authorities should not forget that other Acts of Parliament may be relevant to the way in which authorities provide advice and assistance to applicants or potential applicants, e.g. the Disability Discrimination Act 1995 and the Race Relations Act 1976 (as amended by the Race Relations (Amendment) Act 2000).

MAIN FEATURES OF THE ACT

12. The main features of the Freedom of Information Act 2000 are:
   i. a general right of access to recorded information held by public authorities, subject to certain conditions and exemptions;
   ii. in cases where information is exempted from disclosure, except where an absolute exemption applies, a duty on public authorities to:

   a. inform the applicant whether they hold the information requested, and
   b. communicate the information to him or her,

   unless the public interest in maintaining the exemption in question outweighs the public interest in disclosure;

   iii. a duty on every public authority to adopt and maintain a scheme, approved by the Commissioner, which relates to the publication of information by the authority, and to publish information in accordance with the scheme. An authority may adopt a model scheme approved by the Commissioner, which may have been prepared by the Commissioner or by other persons;
   iv. a new office of Information Commissioner with wide powers to enforce the rights created by the Act and to promote good practice, and a new Information Tribunal;
   v. a duty on the Lord Chancellor to promulgate Codes of Practice for guidance on specific issues.

COPYRIGHT

13. Public authorities should be aware that information which is disclosed under the Act may be subject to copyright protection. If an applicant wishes to use any such information in a way that would infringe copyright, for example by making multiple copies, or issuing copies to the public, he or she would require a licence from the copyright holder. HMSO have issued guidance on this subject in relation to Crown Copyright, which is available on HMSO's website at (http://www.hmso.gov.uk/g-note19.htm) or by contacting HMSO at:

HMSO Licensing Division
St Clements House
2–16 Colegate
Norwich
NR3 1BQ

Tel: 01613 621000
Fax: 01603 723000
e-mail: hmsolicensing@cabinet-office.x.gsi.gov.uk

TRAINING

14. All communications in writing to a public authority, including those transmitted by electronic means, potentially amount to a request for information within the meaning of the Act, and if they do, they must be dealt with in accordance with the provisions of the Act. It is therefore essential that everyone working in a public authority who deals with correspondence, or who otherwise may be required to provide information, is familiar with the requirements of the Act and the Codes of Practice issued under its provisions and takes account of any relevant guidance on good practice issued by the Commissioner. Authorities should ensure that proper training is provided in this regard.

15. In planning and delivering training authorities should be aware of other provisions affecting the disclosure of information such as Environmental Information Regulations and the Data Protection Act 1998.

Code of Practice
On the Discharge of the Functions of Public Authorities under Part I of the Freedom of Information Act 2000

The Lord Chancellor, after consulting the Information Commissioner, issues the following Code of Practice pursuant to section 45 of the Act.

Laid before Parliament on 20 November 2002 pursuant to section 45(5) of the Freedom of Information Act 2000.

I INTRODUCTION

1. This code of practice outlines to public authorities the practice which it would, in the opinion of the Lord Chancellor, be desirable for them to follow in connection with the discharge of their functions under Part I (Access to information held by public authorities) of the Freedom of Information Act 2000 ('the Act').

2. The aims of the Code are to:
    —facilitate the disclosure of information under the Act by setting out good administrative practice that it is desirable for public authorities to follow when handling requests for information, including, where appropriate, the transfer of a request to a different authority;
    —protect the interests of applicants by setting out standards for the provision of advice which it would be good practice to make available to them and to encourage the development of effective means of complaining about decisions taken under the Act;
    —ensure that the interests of third parties who may be affected by any decision to disclose information are considered by the authority by setting standards for consultation; and
    —ensure that authorities consider the implications for Freedom of Information before agreeing to confidentiality provisions in contracts and accepting information in confidence from a third party more generally.

3. Although there is a statutory duty on the Lord Chancellor to issue the Code, the provisions of the Code themselves do not have statutory force. However, authorities are expected to abide by the Code unless there are good reasons, capable of being justified to the Information Commissioner, why it would be inappropriate to do so. The statutory requirements for dealing with requests for information are contained in the Act and regulations made under it and public authorities must comply with

these statutory provisions at all times. However, section 47 of the Act places a duty on the Information Commissioner to promote the following of good practice by public authorities ('good practice' includes compliance with the provisions of the Code), and section 48 of the Act enables the Information Commissioner to issue a 'practice recommendation' to a public authority if it appears to him that the practice of the authority does not conform with that proposed in the Code. Further, section 16 of the Act places a duty on public authorities to provide advice and assistance to applicants and potential applicants. Authorities will have complied with this duty in any particular case if they have conformed with the Code in relation to the provision of advice or assistance in that case.

4. Words and expressions used in this Code have the same meaning as the same words and expressions used in the Act.

II The provision of advice and assistance to persons making requests for information

5. Every public authority should be ready to provide advice and assistance, including but not necessarily limited to the steps set out below, to those who propose to make, or have made requests to it, in order to facilitate their use of the Act. The duty on the public authority is to provide advice and assistance 'so far as it would be reasonable to expect the authority to do so'. Any public authority which conforms with this Code in relation to the provision of advice and assistance in any case will be taken to comply with this duty in relation to that case.

6. Public authorities should publish their procedures for dealing with requests for information. These procedures may include what the public authority's usual procedure will be where it does not hold the information requested. (See also VI—'Transferring requests for information') It may also alert potential applicants to the fact that the public authority may need to consult other public authorities and/or third parties in order to reach a decision on whether the requested information can be released, and therefore alert potential applicants that they may wish to be notified before any transfer of request or consultation is made and if so, they should say so in their applications. (See also VII—'Consultation with third parties'.) The procedures should include an address or addresses (including an e-mail address where possible) to which applicants may direct requests for information or for assistance. A telephone number should also be provided, where possible that of a named individual who can provide assistance. These procedures should be referred to in the authority's publication scheme.

7. Staff working in public authorities in contact with the public should bear in mind that not everyone will be aware of the Act, or Regulations made under it, and they will need to draw these to the attention of potential applicants who appear unaware of them.

8. A request for information under the Act's general right of access must be made in writing (which includes a request transmitted by electronic means which is received in legible form and is capable of being used for subsequent reference). Where a person is unable to frame their request in writing, the public authority should ensure that appropriate assistance is given to enable that person to make a request for information. Depending on the circumstances, appropriate assistance might include:

   —advising the person that another person or agency (such as a Citizens Advice Bureau) may be able to assist them with the application, or make the application on their behalf;

   —in exceptional circumstances, offering to take a note of the application over the telephone and then send the note to the applicant for confirmation (in which case the written note of the telephone request, once verified by the applicant and returned, would constitute a written request for information and the statutory time limit for reply would begin when the written confirmation was received).

This list is not exhaustive, and public authorities should be flexible in offering advice and assistance most appropriate to the circumstances of the applicant.

9. Where the applicant does not describe the information sought in a way which would enable the public authority to identify or locate it, or the request is ambiguous, the authority should, as far as practicable, provide assistance to the applicant to enable him or her to describe more clearly the information requested. Authorities should be aware that the aim of providing assistance is to clarify the nature of the information sought, *not* to determine the aims or motivation of the applicant. Care should be taken not to give the applicant the impression that he or she is obliged to disclose the nature of his or her interest or that he or she will be treated differently if he or she does. It is important that the applicant is contacted as soon as possible, preferably by telephone, fax or e-mail, where more information is needed to clarify what is sought.

10. Appropriate assistance in this instance might include:

—providing an outline of the different kinds of information which might meet the terms of the request;

—providing access to detailed catalogues and indexes, where these are available, to help the applicant ascertain the nature and extent of the information held by the authority;

—providing a general response to the request setting out options for further information which could be provided on request.

This list is not exhaustive, and public authorities should be flexible in offering advice and assistance most appropriate to the circumstances of the applicant.

11. In seeking to clarify what is sought public authorities should bear in mind that applicants cannot reasonably be expected to possess identifiers such as a file reference number, or a description of a particular record, unless this information is made available by the authority for the use of applicants.

12. If, following the provision of such assistance, the applicant still fails to describe the information requested in a way which would enable the authority to identify and locate it, the authority is not expected to seek further clarification. The authority should disclose any information relating to the application which has been successfully identified and found for which it does not wish to claim an exemption. It should also explain to the applicant why it cannot take the request any further and provide details of the authority's complaints procedure and the applicant's rights under section 50 of the Act (see 'Complaints Procedure' in section XII below).

13. Where the applicant indicates that he or she is not prepared to pay the fee notified in any fees notice given to the applicant, the authority should consider whether there is any information that may be of interest to the applicant that is available free of charge.

14. Where an authority is not obliged to comply with a request for information because, under section 12(1) and regulations made under section 12(4), the cost of complying would exceed the 'appropriate limit' (i.e. cost threshold), and where the public authority is not prepared to comply on a discretionary basis because of the cost of doing so, the authority should consider providing an indication of what information could be provided within the cost ceiling.

15. An authority is not expected to provide assistance to applicants whose requests are vexatious within the meaning of section 14 of the Act.

III HANDLING REQUESTS FOR INFORMATION WHICH APPEAR TO BE PART OF AN ORGANISED CAMPAIGN

16. Where an authority is not required to comply with a number of related requests because, under section 12(1) and regulations made under section 12(4), the cumulative cost of complying with the requests would exceed the 'appropriate limit' (i.e. cost threshold) prescribed in Fees Regulations, the authority should consider whether the information could be disclosed in another, more cost-effective, manner. For example, the authority should consider if the information is such that publication on the authority's website, and a brief notification of the website reference to each applicant, would bring the cost within the appropriate limit.

IV Timeliness in dealing with requests for information

17. Public authorities are required to comply with all requests for information promptly and they should not delay responding until the end of the 20 working day period under section 10(1) if the information could reasonably have been provided earlier.

18. Public authorities should aim to make *all* decisions within 20 working days, including in cases where a public authority needs to consider where the public interest lies in respect of an application for exempt information. However, it is recognised there will be some instances where it will not be possible to deal with such an application within 20 working days. Although there is no statutory time limit on the length of time the authority may take to reach a decision where the public interest must be considered, it must, under section 17(2), give an estimate of the date by which it expects to reach such a decision. In these instances, authorities are expected to give estimates which are realistic and reasonable in the circumstances of the particular case, taking account, for example, of the need to consult third parties where this is necessary. Public authorities are expected to comply with their estimates unless there are good reasons not to. If the public authority exceeds its estimate, it should apologise to the applicant and explain the reason(s) for the delay. If a public authority finds, while considering the public interest, that the estimate given is proving unrealistic, it should keep the applicant informed. Public authorities should keep a record of instances where estimates are exceeded, and where this happens more than occasionally, take steps to identify the problem and rectify it.

V Charging fees

19. The Act does not require charges to be made, but public authorities have discretion to charge applicants a fee in accordance with Fees Regulations made under sections 9, 12 and 13 of the Act in respect of requests made under the general right of access.

20. The Fees Regulations do not apply:

> —to material made available under a publication scheme under section 19;
> —to information which is reasonably accessible to the applicant by other means within the meaning of the exemption provided for at section 21; or
> —where provision is made by or under any enactment as to the fee that may be charged by the public authority for disclosure of the information as provided in sections 9(5) and 13(3) of the Act.

Public authorities should ensure that any charges they make in cases falling outside those covered by the Fees Regulations are in accordance with any relevant legislation and are within the terms of any relevant guidance which has been issued or approved by HM Treasury and which is applicable to the public authority, or any relevant guidance issued or approved by the Northern Ireland Department of Finance and Personnel applicable to devolved public bodies in Northern Ireland.

VI Transferring requests for information

21. A request can only be transferred where a public authority receives a request for information which it does not hold, within the meaning of section 3(2) of the Act, but which is held by another public authority. If a public authority in receipt of a request holds some of the information requested, a transfer can only be made in respect of the information it does not hold (but is held by another public authority).

22. Public authorities should bear in mind that 'holding' information includes holding a copy of a record produced or supplied by another person or body (but does not extend to holding a record on behalf of another person or body as provided for in section 3(2)(a) of the Act).

23. The authority receiving the initial request must always process it in accordance with the Act in respect of such information relating to the request as it holds. The authority should also advise the applicant that it does not hold part of the requested information, or all of it, whichever applies. But before doing this, the authority must be certain as to the extent of the information relating to the request which it holds itself.

24. If the authority to whom the original request was made believes that some or all of the information requested is held by another public authority, the authority should consider what would be the most helpful way of assisting the applicant with his or her request. In most cases this is likely to involve:

—contacting the applicant and informing him or her that the information requested may be held by another public authority;

—suggesting that the applicant re-applies to the authority which the original authority believes to hold the information;

—providing him or her with contact details for that authority.

25. However, in some cases the authority to whom the original request is made may consider it to be more appropriate to transfer the request to another authority in respect of the information which it does not hold. In such cases, the authority should consult the other authority with a view to ascertaining whether it does hold the information and, if so, consider whether it should transfer the request to it. A request (or part of a request) should not be transferred without confirmation by the second authority that it holds the information.

26. Before transferring a request for information to another authority, the authority should consider:

—whether a transfer is appropriate; and if so

—whether the applicant is likely to have any grounds to object to the transfer.

If the authority reasonably concludes that the applicant is not likely to object, it may transfer the request without going back to the applicant, but should tell him or her it has done so.

27. Where there are reasonable grounds to believe an applicant is likely to object, the authority should only transfer the request to another authority with his or her consent. If the authority is in any doubt, it may prefer contact the applicant with a view to suggesting that he or she makes a new request to the other authority, as in paragraph 23 above.

28. Where a request or part of a request is transferred from one public authority to another, the receiving authority must comply with its obligations under Part I of the Act in the same way as it would for a request that is received direct from an applicant. The time for complying with such a request will be measured from the day that the receiving authority receives the request.

29. All transfers of requests should take place as soon as is practicable, and the applicant should be informed as soon as possible once this has been done.

30. Where a public authority is unable either to advise the applicant which public authority holds, or may hold, the requested information or to facilitate the transfer of the request to another authority (or considers it inappropriate to do so) it should consider what advice, if any, it can provide to the applicant to enable him or her to pursue his or her request.

VII CONSULTATION WITH THIRD PARTIES

31. In some cases the disclosure of information pursuant to a request may affect the legal rights of a third party, for example where information is subject to the common law duty of confidence or where it constitutes 'personal data' within the meaning of the Data Protection Act 1998 ('the DPA'). Public authorities must always remember that unless an exemption provided for in the Act applies in relation to any particular information, they will be obliged to disclose that information in response to a request.

32. Where a disclosure of information cannot be made without the consent of a third party (for example, where information has been obtained from a third party and in the circumstances the disclosure of the information without their consent would constitute an actionable breach of confidence such that the exemption at section 41 of the Act would apply), the authority should consult that third party with a view to seeking their consent to the disclosure, unless such a consultation is not practicable, for example because the third party cannot be located or because the costs of consulting them would be disproportionate.

33. Where information constitutes 'personal data' within the meaning of the DPA, public authorities should have regard to section 40 of the Act which makes detailed provision for cases in which a request relates to such information and the interplay between the Act and the DPA in such cases.

34. Where the interests of the third party which may be affected by a disclosure do not give rise to legal rights, consultation may still be appropriate.

35. Consultation should take place where:

—the views of the third party may assist the authority to determine whether an exemption under the Act applies to the information requested; or
—the views of the third party may assist the authority to determine where the public interest lies under section 2 of the Act.

36. A public authority may consider that consultation is not appropriate where the cost of consulting with third parties would be disproportionate. In such cases, the authority should consider what is the most reasonable course of action for it to take in light of the requirements of the Act and the individual circumstances of the request.

37. Consultation will be unnecessary where:

—the public authority does not intend to disclose the information relying on some other legitimate ground under the terms of the Act;
—the views of the third party can have no effect on the decision of the authority, for example, where there is other legislation preventing or requiring the disclosure of this information;
—no exemption applies and so under the Act's provisions, the information must be provided.

38. Where the interests of a number of third parties may be affected by a disclosure and those parties have a representative organisation which can express views on behalf of those parties, the authority may, if it considers consultation appropriate, consider that it would be sufficient to consult that representative organisation. If there is no representative organisation, the authority may consider that it would be sufficient to consult a representative sample of the third parties in question.

39. The fact that the third party has not responded to consultation does not relieve the authority of its duty to disclose information under the Act, or its duty to reply within the time specified in the Act.

40. In all cases, it is for the public authority, not the third party (or representative of the third party) to determine whether or not information should be disclosed under the Act. A refusal to consent to disclosure by a third party does not, in itself, mean information should be withheld.

VIII Freedom of information and public sector contracts

41. When entering into contracts public authorities should refuse to include contractual terms which purport to restrict the disclosure of information held by the authority and relating to the contract beyond the restrictions permitted by the Act. Public authorities cannot 'contract out' of their obligations under the Act. Unless an exemption provided for under the Act is applicable in relation to any particular information, a public authority will be obliged to disclose that information in response to a request, regardless of the terms of any contract.

42. When entering into contracts with non-public authority contractors, public authorities may be under pressure to accept confidentiality clauses so that information relating to the terms of the contract, its value and performance will be exempt from disclosure. Public authorities should reject such clauses wherever possible. Where, exceptionally, it is necessary to include non-disclosure provisions in a contract, an option could be to agree with the contractor a schedule of the contract which clearly identifies information which should not be disclosed. But authorities will need to take care when drawing up any such schedule, and be aware that any restrictions on disclosure provided for could potentially be overridden by their obligations under the Act, as described in the paragraph above.

43. In any event, public authorities should not agree to hold information 'in confidence' which is not in fact confidential in nature. Authorities should be aware that the exemption provided for in section 41 only applies if information has been obtained by a public authority from another person, and the disclosure of the information to the public, otherwise than under the Act would constitute a breach of confidence actionable by that, or any other person.

44. Any acceptance of such confidentiality provisions must be for good reasons and capable of being justified to the Commissioner.

45. It is for the public authority to disclose information pursuant to the Act, and not the non-public authority contractor. However, the public authority may wish to protect from disclosure by the contractor, by appropriate contractual terms, information which the authority has provided to the contractor which would clearly be exempt from disclosure under the Act, by appropriate contractual terms. In order to avoid unnecessary secrecy, any such constraints should be drawn as narrowly as possible, and according to the individual circumstances of the case. Apart from such cases, public authorities should not impose terms of secrecy on contractors.

46. Section 5(1)(b) of the Act empowers the Lord Chancellor to designate as public authorities for the purposes of the Act, persons (or bodies) who provide under a contract made with a public authority, any service whose provision is a function of that authority. Thus, some non-public authority contractors will be regarded as public authorities within the meaning of the Act, although only in respect of the services provided under the contract. As such, and to that extent, the contractor will be required to comply with the Act like any other public authority.

IX ACCEPTING INFORMATION IN CONFIDENCE FROM THIRD PARTIES

47. A public authority should only accept information from third parties in confidence if it is necessary to obtain that information in connection with the exercise of any of the authority's functions and it would not otherwise be provided. In addition, public authorities should not agree to hold information received from third parties 'in confidence' which is not confidential in nature. Again, acceptance of any confidentiality provisions must be for good reasons, capable of being justified to the Commissioner.

X CONSULTATION WITH DEVOLVED ADMINISTRATIONS

48. Public authorities should consult with the relevant devolved administration before disclosing information provided by or directly concerning that administration, except where:

—the views of the devolved administration can have no effect on the decision of the authority (for example where there is other legislation requiring the disclosure of the information), or there is no applicable exemption so the information must be disclosed under the Act; or
—in the circumstances, consultation would be disproportionate.

49. Similarly, the devolved administrations should consult with the relevant non-devolved public authority before disclosing information provided by or directly concerning that authority, except

where the views of the public authority can have no effect on the decision whether to disclose, or where consultation would be disproportionate in the circumstances.

XI Refusal of request

50. Where a request for information is refused in reliance on an exemption, the Act requires that the authority notifies the applicant which exemption has been claimed, and if it would otherwise not be apparent, why that exemption applies. Public authorities should not (subject to the proviso in section 17(4) i.e. if the statement would involve the disclosure of information which would itself be exempt information) merely paraphrase the wording of the exemption. The Act also requires authorities, when withholding information (other than under an 'absolute' exemption), to state the reasons for claiming that the public interest in maintaining the exemption outweighs the public interest in disclosure. Public authorities should specify the public interest factors (for and against disclosure) which they have taken into account before reaching the decision (again, subject to the proviso in section 17(4)).

51. For monitoring purposes public authorities should keep a record of all applications where either all or part of the requested information is withheld. In addition to a record of the numbers of applications involved where information is withheld, senior managers in each public authority need information on each case to determine whether cases are being properly considered, and whether the reasons for refusals are sound. This could be done by requiring all staff who refuse a request for information to forward the details to a central point in the organisation for collation. Details of information on complaints about applications which have been refused (see XII—'Complaints procedure' below) could be collected at the same central point.

XII Complaints procedure

52. Each public authority should have a complaints procedure in place by the date that its duties in respect of the publication scheme provisions of the Act come into effect. The complaints procedure may then be used by any person who perceives that the authority is not complying with its publication scheme. If the matter cannot be dealt with satisfactorily on an informal basis, the public authority should inform such persons if approached by them of the details of its internal complaints procedure, and how to contact the Information Commissioner, if the complainant wishes to write to him about the matter. The authority should also explain that although the complainant cannot apply to the Commissioner for a decision under section 50 of the Act, the Commissioner may investigate the matter at his discretion.

53. When the provisions of the Act relating to the general right of access come into force, the complaints procedure will also be required for dealing with complaints from people who consider that their request has not been properly handled, or who are otherwise dissatisfied with the outcome of the consideration of their request, and where the issue is such that it cannot be resolved informally in discussion with the official dealing with the request. If a public authority has failed to introduce a complaints procedure, an applicant is entitled, under the Act, to complain directly to the Commissioner.

54. When communicating any decision made in relation to a request under the Act's general right of access, public authorities are obliged, under section 17(7) of the Act, to notify the applicant of their rights of complaint. They should provide details of their own complaints procedure, including how to make a complaint and inform the applicant of the right to complain to the Commissioner under section 50 if he or she is still dissatisfied following the authority's review.

55. Any written reply from the applicant (including one transmitted by electronic means) expressing dissatisfaction with an authority's response to a valid request for information should be treated as a complaint, as should any written communication from a person who perceives the authority is not complying with its publication scheme. These communications should be handled in accordance with the authority's complaints procedure, even if, in the case of a request for information under the general right of access, the applicant does not state his or her desire for the authority to review their decision or their handling of the application.

56. The complaints procedure should be a fair and impartial means of dealing with handling problems and reviewing decisions taken pursuant to the Act, including decisions taken about where the public interest lies in respect of exempt information. It should be possible to reverse or otherwise amend decisions previously taken. Complaints procedures should be clear and not unnecessarily bureaucratic. They should be capable of producing a prompt determination of the complaint.

57. Where the complaint concerns a request for information under the general right of access, the review should be handled by a person who was not a party to the original decision, where this is practicable. If this is not possible (for example in a very small public authority), the circumstances should be explained to the applicant. Where the decision on the application was taken by someone in a position where a review cannot realistically be undertaken (e.g. a Minister), the public authority may consider whether to waive the internal review procedure (and inform the applicant if this is what is decided), so that the applicant is free to approach the Commissioner.

58. In all cases, complaints should be acknowledged and the complainant should be informed of the authority's target date for determining the complaint. Where it is apparent that determination of the complaint will take longer than the target time (for example because of the complexity of the particular case), the authority should inform the applicant and explain the reason for the delay. The complainant should always be informed of the outcome of his or her complaint.

59. Authorities may set their own target times for dealing with complaints but these should be reasonable, defensible, and subject to regular review. Each public authority should publish its target times for determining complaints and information as to how successful it is with meeting those targets.

60. Records should be kept of all complaints and of their outcome. Authorities should have procedures in place for monitoring complaints and for reviewing, and, if necessary, amending, procedures for dealing with requests for information where such action is indicated by more than occasional reversals of initial decisions.

61. Where the outcome of a complaint is that information should be disclosed which was previously withheld, the information in question should be disclosed as soon as practicable and the applicant should be informed how soon this will be.

62. Where the outcome of a complaint is that the procedures within an authority have not been properly followed by the authority's staff, the authority should apologise to the applicant. The authority should also take appropriate steps to prevent similar errors occurring in future.

63. Where the outcome of a complaint is that an initial decision to withhold information is upheld, or is otherwise in the authority's favour, the applicant should be informed of his or her right to apply to the Commissioner, and be given details of how to make an application, for a decision on whether the request for information has been dealt with in accordance with the requirements of Part I of the Act.

APPENDIX E

Lord Chancellor's Code of Practice on the Management of Records under Section 46 of the Freedom of Information Act 2000

NOVEMBER 2002

PRESENTED TO PARLIAMENT BY THE LORD CHANCELLOR PURSUANT TO SECTION 46(6) OF THE FREEDOM OF INFORMATION ACT 2000

CONTENTS

FOREWORD

General

(i) This Code of Practice (hereafter referred to as 'the Code') provides guidance to all public authorities as to the practice which it would, in the opinion of the Lord Chancellor, be desirable for them to follow in connection with the discharge of their functions under the Freedom of Information Act 2000 (FOIA). The Code applies also to other bodies that are subject to the Public Records Act 1958 and the Public Records Act (NI) 1923.

(ii) The Code fulfils the duty of the Lord Chancellor under section 46 of the FOIA.

(iii) Any freedom of information legislation is only as good as the quality of the records to which it provides access. Such rights are of little use if reliable records are not created in the first place, if they cannot be found when needed or if the arrangements for their eventual archiving or destruction are inadequate. Consequently, all public authorities are strongly encouraged to pay heed to the guidance in the Code.

(iv) The Code is a supplement to the provisions in the FOIA. But its adoption will help authorities to comply with their duties under that Act. It is not a substitute for legislation. Public authorities should seek legal advice as appropriate on general issues relating to the implementation of the FOIA, or its application to individual cases. The Code is complemented by the Code of Practice under section 45 of the FOIA and by Memoranda of Understanding setting out how the consultation requirements of section 66 of the FOIA will be put into effect.

(v) The Information Commissioner will promote the observance of the Code by public authorities, acting as required by the FOIA. If it appears to the Commissioner that the practice of an authority in relation to the exercise of its functions under the FOIA does not conform with that set out in the Code, he may issue a practice recommendation under section 48 of the Act. A practice recommendation must be in writing and must specify the provisions of the Code which have not been met and the steps which should, in his opinion, be taken to promote conformity with Code.

(vi) If the Commissioner reasonably requires any information for the purpose of determining whether the practice of a public authority in relation to the exercise of its functions under the FOIA conforms with that proposed in this Code, he may serve on the authority a notice (known as an 'information notice') under the provisions of section 51 of the Act. This requires it, within such time as is specified in the notice, to furnish the Commissioner, in such form as may be so specified, with such information relating to conformity with the Code of Practice as is so specified.

(vii) An information notice must contain a statement that the Commissioner regards the specified information as relevant for the purpose of deciding whether the practice of the authority conforms with that proposed in the Code of Practice and of his reasons for regarding that information as relevant for that purpose. It must also contain particulars of the rights of appeal conferred by section 57 of the FOIA.

(viii) Authorities should note that if they are failing to comply with the Code, they may also be failing to comply with the Public Records Acts 1958 and 1967, the Local Government (Records) Act 1962, the Local Government Act 1972, the Local Government (Access to Information) Act 1985 or other record-keeping or archives legislation, and they may consequently be in breach of their statutory obligations.

(ix) The Public Records Act (NI) 1923 sets out the duties of public record bodies in Northern Ireland in respect of the records they create and requires that records should be transferred to, and preserved by, the Public Record Office of Northern Ireland.

Main features of the FOIA

(x) The main features of the FOIA are:

1. a general right of access to recorded information held by a wide range of bodies across the public sector, subject to certain conditions and exemptions. The right includes provisions in respect of historical records which are more than 30 years old.

2. in relation to most exempt information, the information must nonetheless be disclosed unless the public interest in maintaining the exemption in question outweighs the public interest in disclosure.

3. a duty on every public authority to adopt and maintain a scheme which relates to the publication of information by the authority and is approved by the Information Commissioner. Authorities must publish information in accordance with their publication schemes. This scheme must specify:

   a. classes of information which the public authority publishes or intends to publish;

   b. the manner in which information of each class is, or is intended to be, published; and

   c. whether the material is, or is intended to be, available to the public free of charge, or on payment.

4. a new office of Information Commissioner and a new Information Tribunal, with wide powers to enforce the rights created and to promote good practice;

5. a duty on the Lord Chancellor to promulgate Codes of Practice for guidance on specific issues;

6. the amendment of the public records system to integrate it with the new right of access under the FOIA.

Training

(xi) All communications in writing (including by electronic means) to a public authority fall within the scope of the FOIA, if they seek information, and must be dealt with in accordance with the provisions of the Act. It is therefore essential that everyone working in a public authority is familiar with the provisions of the FOIA, the Codes of Practice issued under its provisions, any relevant Memoranda of Understanding, and any relevant guidance on good practice issued by the Commissioner. Authorities should ensure that proper training is provided.

(xii) In planning and delivering training, authorities should be aware of other provisions affecting the disclosure of information, such as the Environmental Information Regulations 1992 and their successors which, for example, do not require requests to be in writing.

Authorities subject to the Public Records Acts

(xiii) The guidance on records management and on the transfer of public records in the Code should be read in the context of existing legislation on record-keeping. In particular, the Public Records Act 1958 (as amended) gives duties to public record bodies in respect of the records they create. It also requires the Keeper of Public Records to supervise the discharge of those duties. Authorities that are subject to the Public Records Acts 1958 and 1967 should note that if they are failing to comply with the Code, they may also be failing to comply with those Acts.

(xiv) The Public Records Act (NI) 1923 sets out the duties of public record bodies in Northern Ireland in respect of the records they create and requires that records should be transferred to, and preserved by, the Public Record Office of Northern Ireland.

(xv) The Information Commissioner will promote the observance of the Code in consultation with the Keeper of Public Records when dealing with bodies which are subject to the Public Records Acts 1958 and 1967 and with the Deputy Keeper of the Records of Northern Ireland for bodies subject to the Public Records Act (NI) 1923.

(xvi) If it appears to the Commissioner that the practice of an authority in relation to the exercise of its functions under the FOIA does not conform with that set out in the Code, he may issue a practice recommendation under Section 48 of the Act. Before issuing such a recommendation to a body subject to the Public Records Acts 1958 and 1967 or the Public Records Act (NI) 1923, the Commissioner shall consult the Keeper of Public Records or the Deputy Keeper of the Records of Northern Ireland.

(xvii) The content of this Code has been agreed by the Deputy Keeper of Records of Northern Ireland. Part Two, in particular, describes the roles which public record bodies should perform to ensure the timely and effective review and transfer of public records to the Public Record Office or to places of deposit (as defined in Section 4 of the Public Records Act 1958) or to the Public Record Office of Northern Ireland (under the Public Records Act 1958 or the Public Records Act (NI) 1923). For the avoidance of doubt the term 'public records' includes Welsh public records as defined by Sections 116–118 of the Government of Wales Act 1998.

Role of the Lord Chancellor's Advisory Council on Public Records and of the Public Record Office

(xviii) To advise authorities on the review of public records, the Lord Chancellor, having received the advice of his Advisory Council on Public Records, (hereafter 'the Advisory Council') may prepare and issue guidance. This may include advice on the periods of time for which the Advisory Council considers it appropriate to withhold categories of sensitive records beyond the 30 year period. In Northern Ireland similar guidance shall be issued by the Deputy Keeper of the Records of Northern Ireland following consultation with the Departments responsible for the records affected by the guidance.

(xix) The Public Record Office will provide support as appropriate to the Advisory Council in its consideration of applications from authorities in respect of public records and in its preparation of guidance to authorities. In Northern Ireland the Public Record Office of Northern Ireland will provide similar support to the Sensitivity Review Group.

Code of Practice
On (1) The Management of Records by Public Authorities and (2) the Transfer and Review of Public Records under the Freedom of Information Act 2000

The Lord Chancellor, after consulting the Information Commissioner and the appropriate Northern Ireland Minister, issues the following Code of Practice pursuant to section 46 of the Freedom of Information Act.

Laid before Parliament on 20 November 2002 pursuant to section 46(6) of the Freedom of Information Act 2000.

Introduction

1 The aims of the Code are:

(1) to set out practices which public authorities, and bodies subject to the Public Records Act 1958 and the Public Records Act (NI) 1923, should follow in relation to the creation, keeping, management and destruction of their records (Part One of the Code), and

(2) to describe the arrangements which public record bodies should follow in reviewing public records and transferring them to the Public Record Office or to places of deposit or to the Public Record Office of Northern Ireland (Part Two of the Code).

2 This Code refers to records in all technical or physical formats.

3 Part One of the Code provides a framework for the management of records of public authorities and of bodies subject to the Public Records Act 1958 and the Public Records Act (NI) 1923, and Part Two deals with the review and transfer of public records. More detailed guidance on both themes may be obtained from published standards. Those which support the objectives of this Code most directly are listed at Annex A.

4 Words and expressions used in this Code have the same meaning as the same words and expressions used in the FOIA.

Part one: records management

5 Functional Responsibility

5.1 The records management function should be recognised as a specific corporate programme within an authority and should receive the necessary levels of organisational support to ensure effectiveness. It should bring together responsibilities for records in all formats, including electronic records, throughout their life cycle, from planning and creation through to ultimate disposal. It should have clearly defined responsibilities and objectives, and the resources to achieve them. It is desirable that the person, or persons, responsible for the records management function should also have either direct responsibility or an organisational connection with the person or persons responsible for freedom of information, data protection and other information management issues.

6 Policy

6.1 An authority should have in place an overall policy statement, endorsed by top management and made readily available to staff at all levels of the organisation, on how it manages its records, including electronic records.

6.2 This policy statement should provide a mandate for the performance of all records and information management functions. In particular, it should set out an authority's commitment to create, keep and manage records which document its principal activities. The policy should also outline the role of records management and its relationship to the authority's overall strategy; define roles and responsibilities including the responsibility of individuals to document their actions and decisions in the authority's records, and to dispose of records; provide a framework for supporting standards, procedures and guidelines; and indicate the way in which compliance with the policy and its supporting standards, procedures and guidelines will be monitored.

6.3 The policy statement should be reviewed at regular intervals (at least once every three years) and, if appropriate, amended to maintain its relevance.

7 Human Resources

7.1 A designated member of staff of appropriate seniority should have lead responsibility for records management within the authority. This lead role should be formally acknowledged and made known throughout the authority.

7.2 Staff responsible for records management should have the appropriate skills and knowledge needed to achieve the aims of the records management programme. Responsibility for all aspects of record keeping should be specifically defined and incorporated in the role descriptions or similar documents.

7.3 Human resource policies and practices in organisations should address the need to recruit and retain good quality staff and should accordingly support the records management function in the following areas:

- the provision of appropriate resources to enable the records management function to be maintained across all of its activities;

- the establishment and maintenance of a scheme, such as a competency framework, to identify the knowledge, skills and corporate competencies required in records and information management;
- the regular review of selection criteria for posts with records management duties to ensure currency and compliance with best practice;
- the regular analysis of training needs;
- the establishment of a professional development programme for staff with records management duties;
- the inclusion in induction training programmes for all new staff of an awareness of records issues and practices.

8. Active Records Management

Record Creation

8.1 Each operational/business unit of an authority should have in place an adequate system for documenting its activities. This system should take into account the legislative and regulatory environments in which the authority works.

8.2 Records of a business activity should be complete and accurate enough to allow employees and their successors to undertake appropriate actions in the context of their responsibilities, to

- facilitate an audit or examination of the business by anyone so authorised,
- protect the legal and other rights of the authority, its clients and any other person affected by its actions, and
- provide authenticity of the records so that the evidence derived from them is shown to be credible and authoritative.

8.3 Records created by the authority should be arranged in a record keeping system that will enable the authority to obtain the maximum benefit from the quick and easy retrieval of information.

Record Keeping

8.4 Installing and maintaining an effective records management programme depends on knowledge of what records are held, in what form they are made accessible, and their relationship to organisational functions. An information survey or record audit will meet this requirement, help to promote control over the records, and provide valuable data for developing records appraisal and disposal procedures.

8.5 Paper and electronic record keeping systems should contain metadata (descriptive and technical documentation) to enable the system and the records to be understood and to be operated efficiently, and to provide an administrative context for effective management of the records.

8.6 The record-keeping system, whether paper or electronic, should include a set of rules for referencing, titling, indexing and, if appropriate, security marking of records. These should be easily understood and should enable the efficient retrieval of information.

Record Maintenance

8.7 The movement and location of records should be controlled to ensure that a record can be easily retrieved at any time, that any outstanding issues can be dealt with, and that there is an auditable trail of record transactions.

8.8 Storage accommodation for current records should be clean and tidy, and it should prevent damage to the records. Equipment used for current records should provide storage which is safe from unauthorised access and which meets fire regulations, but which allows maximum accessibility to the information commensurate with its frequency of use. When records are no longer required for the conduct of current business, their placement in a designated records centre rather than in offices may be a more economical and efficient way to store them. Procedures for handling records should take full account of the need to preserve important information.

8.9 A contingency or business recovery plan should be in place to provide protection for records which are vital to the continued functioning of the authority.

9 Disposal Arrangements

9.1 It is particularly important under FOI that the disposal of records—which is here defined as the point in their lifecycle when they are either transferred to an archives or destroyed—is undertaken in accordance with clearly established policies which have been formally adopted by authorities and which are enforced by properly authorised staff.

Record Closure

9.2 Records should be closed as soon as they have ceased to be of active use other than for reference purposes. As a general rule, files should be closed after five years and, if action continues, a further file should be opened. An indication that a file of paper records or folder of electronic records has been closed should be shown on the record itself as well as noted in the index or database of the files/folders. Wherever possible, information on the intended disposal of electronic records should be included in the metadata when the record is created.

9.3 The storage of closed records awaiting disposal should follow accepted standards relating to environment, security and physical organisation.

Appraisal Planning and Documentation

9.4 In order to make their disposal policies work effectively and for those to which the FOIA applies to provide the information required under FOI legislation, authorities need to have in place systems for managing appraisal and for recording the disposal decisions made. An assessment of the volume and nature of records due for disposal, the time taken to appraise records, and the risks associated with destruction or delay in appraisal will provide information to support an authority's resource planning and workflow arrangements.

9.5 An appraisal documentation system will ensure consistency in records appraisal and disposal. It should show what records are designated for destruction, the authority under which they are to be destroyed and when they are to be destroyed. It should also provide background information on the records, such as legislative provisions, functional context and physical arrangement. This information will provide valuable data for placing records selected for preservation into context and will enable future records managers to provide evidence of the operation of their selection policies.

Record Selection

9.6 Each authority should maintain a selection policy which states in broad terms the functions from which records are likely to be selected for permanent preservation and the periods for which other records should be retained. The policy should be supported by or linked to disposal schedules which should cover all records created, including electronic records. Schedules should be arranged on the basis of series or collection and should indicate the appropriate disposal action for all records (e.g. review after x years; destroy after y years).

9.7 Records selected for permanent preservation and no longer in regular use by the authority should be transferred as soon as possible to an archival institution that has adequate storage and public access facilities (see Part Two of this Code for arrangements for bodies subject to the Public Records Acts).

9.8 Records not selected for permanent preservation and which have reached the end of their administrative life should be destroyed in as secure a manner as is necessary for the level of confidentiality or security markings they bear. A record of the destruction of records, showing their reference, description and date of destruction should be maintained and preserved by the records manager. Disposal schedules would constitute the basis of such a record.

9.9 If a record due for destruction is known to be the subject of a request for information, destruction should be delayed until disclosure has taken place or, if the authority has decided not to disclose the information, until the complaint and appeal provisions of the FOIA have been exhausted.

10 Management of Electronic Records

10.1 The principal issues for the management of electronic records are the same as those for the management of any record. They include, for example the creation of authentic records, the tracking of records and disposal arrangements. However, the means by which these issues are addressed in the electronic environment will be different.

10.2 Effective electronic record keeping requires:

- a clear understanding of the nature of electronic records;
- the creation of records and metadata necessary to document business processes: this should be part of the systems which hold the records;
- the maintenance of a structure of folders to reflect logical groupings of records;
- the secure maintenance of the integrity of electronic records;
- the accessibility and use of electronic records for as long as required (which may include their migration across systems);
- the application of appropriate disposal procedures, including procedures for archiving; and
- the ability to cross reference electronic records to their paper counterparts in a mixed environment.

10.3 Generic requirements for electronic record management systems are set out in the 1999 Public Record Office statement *Functional Requirements and Testing of Electronic Records Management Systems.* (*see*: http://www.pro.gov.uk/recordsmanagement/eros/invest/default.htm). Authorities are encouraged to use these, and any subsequent versions, as a model when developing their specifications for such systems.

10.4 Audit trails should be provided for all electronic information and documents. They should be kept securely and should be available for inspection by authorised personnel. The BSI document *Principles of Good Practice for Information Management (PD0010)* recommends audits at predetermined intervals for particular aspects of electronic records management.

10.5 Authorities should seek to conform to the provisions of BSI DISC PD0008—*A Code of Practice for Legal Admissibility and Evidential Weight of Information Stored Electronically (2nd edn)*—especially for those records likely to be required as evidence.

Part two: review and transfer of public records

11.1 This part of the Code relates to the arrangements which authorities should follow to ensure the timely and effective review and transfer of public records. Accordingly, it is relevant only to authorities which are subject to the Public Records Acts 1958 and 1967 or to the Public Records Act (NI) 1923. The general purpose of this part of the Code is to facilitate the performance by the Public Record Office, the Public Record Office of Northern Ireland and other public authorities of their functions under the Freedom of Information Act.

11.2 Under the Public Records Acts, records selected for preservation may be transferred either to the Public Record Office or to places of deposit appointed by the Lord Chancellor. This Code applies to all such transfers. For guidance on which records may be transferred to which institution, and on the disposition of UK public records relating to Northern Ireland, see the Public Record Office *Acquisition Policy* (1998) and the Public Record Office *Disposition Policy* (2000).

11.3 In reviewing records for public release, authorities should ensure that public records become available to the public at the earliest possible time in accordance with the FOIA.

11.4 Authorities which have created or are otherwise responsible for public records should ensure that they operate effective arrangements to determine

a) which records should be selected for permanent preservation; and

b) which records should be released to the public.

These arrangements should be established and operated under the supervision of the Public Record Office or, in Northern Ireland, in conjunction with the Public Record Office of Northern Ireland. The objectives and arrangements for the review of records for release are described in greater detail below.

11.5 In carrying out their review of records for release to the public, authorities should observe the following points:

11.5.1 transfer to the Public Record Office must take place by the time the records are 30 years old, unless the Lord Chancellor gives authorisation for them to be retained for a longer period of time (see section 3 (4) of the Public Records Act 1958). By agreement with the Public Record Office, transfer and release may take place before 30 years;

11.5.2 review—for selection and release—should therefore take place before the records in question are 30 years old.

11.5.3 in Northern Ireland transfer under the Public Records Act (NI) 1923 to the Public Record Office of Northern Ireland is normally at 20 years.

11.6 In the case of records to be transferred to the Public Record Office or to a place of deposit appointed under section 4 of the Public Records Act 1958, or to the Public Record Office of Northern Ireland, the purpose of the review of records for release to the public is to:

- consider which information must be available to the public on transfer because no exemptions under the FOIA apply
- consider which information must be available to the public at 30 years because relevant exemptions in the FOIA have ceased to apply;
- consider whether the information must be released in the public interest, notwithstanding the application of an exemption under the FOIA; and
- consider which information merits continued protection in accordance with the provisions of the FOIA.

11.7 If the review results in the identification of specified information which the authorities consider ought not to be released under the terms of the FOIA, the authorities should prepare a schedule identifying this information precisely, citing the relevant exemption(s), explaining why the information may not be released and identifying a date at which either release would be appropriate or a date at which the case for release should be reconsidered. Where the information is environmental information to which the exemption at Section 39 of the FOIA applies, the schedule should cite the appropriate exception in the Environmental Information Regulations. This schedule must be submitted to the Public Record Office or, in Northern Ireland, to the Public Record Office of Northern Ireland prior to transfer which must be before the records containing the information are 30 years old (in the case of the Public Record Office) or 20 years old (in the case of the Public Record Office of Northern Ireland). Authorities should consider whether parts of records might be released if the sensitive information were blanked out.

11.8 In the first instance, the schedule described in 11.7 is to be submitted to the Public Record Office for review and advice. The case in favour of withholding the records for a period longer than 30 years is then considered by the Advisory Council. The Advisory Council may respond as follows:

a) by accepting that the information may be withheld for longer than 30 years and earmarking the records for release or rereview at the date identified by the authority;

b) by accepting that the information may be withheld for longer than 30 years but asking the authority to reconsider the later date designated for release or re-review;

c) by questioning the basis on which it is deemed that the information may be withheld for longer than 30 years and asking the authority to reconsider the case;

d) by advising the Lord Chancellor if it is not satisfied with the responses it receives from authorities on particular cases;

e) by taking such other action as it deems appropriate within its role as defined in the Public Records Act.

In Northern Ireland there are separate administrative arrangements requiring that schedules are submitted to a Sensitivity Review Group consisting of representatives of different departments. The Sensitivity Review Group has the role of advising public authorities as to the appropriateness or otherwise of releasing records.

11.9 For the avoidance of doubt, none of the actions described in this Code affects the statutory rights of access established under the FOIA. Requests for information in public records transferred to the Public Record Office or to a place of deposit appointed under section 4 of the Public Records Act 1958 or to the Public Record Office of Northern Ireland will be dealt with on a case by case basis in accordance with the provisions of the FOIA.

11.10 Where records are transferred to the Public Record Office or a place of deposit before they are 30 years old, they should be designated by the transferring department or agency for immediate release unless an exemption applies: there will be no formal review of these designations.

11.11 When an exemption has ceased to apply under section 63 of the FOIA the records will become automatically available to members of the public on the day specified in the finalised schedule (i.e. the schedule after it has been reviewed by the Advisory Council). In other cases, if the authority concerned wishes further to extend the period during which the information is to be withheld in accordance with the FOIA, it should submit a further schedule explaining the sensitivity of the information. This is to be done before the expiry of the period stated in the earlier schedule. The Public Record Office and Advisory Council will then review the schedule in accordance with the process described in paragraph 11.8 above. In Northern Ireland, Ministerial approval is required for any further extension of the stated period.

11.12 In reviewing records an authority may identify those which are appropriate for retention within the department, after they are 30 years old, under section 3(4) of the Public Records Act 1958. Applications must be submitted to the Public Record Office for review and advice. The case in favour of retention beyond the 30 year period will then be considered by the Advisory Council. The Advisory Council will consider the case for retaining individual records unless there is already in place a standing authorisation by the Lord Chancellor for the retention of a whole category of records. It will consider such applications on the basis of the guidance in chapter 9 of the White Paper *Open Government* (Cm 2290, 1993) or subsequent revisions of government policy on retention.

Annex A

Standards accepted in records management

British Standards (BSI)

BS 4783	Storage, transportation and maintenance of media for use in data processing and information storage
BS 7799	Code of practice for information security management
BS ISO 15489–1	Information and Documentation—Records Management—Part 1: General
BSI DISC PD 0008	Code of practice for legal admissibility and evidential weight of information stored on electronic document management systems
BSI DISC PD0010	Principles of good practice for information management
BSI DISC PD0012	Guide to the practical implications of the Data Protection Act 1998

Public Record Office standards for the management of public records

The Public Record Office publishes standards, guidance and toolkits on the management of public records, in whatever format, covering their entire life cycle. They are available on the Public Record Office website (http://www.pro.gov.uk/recordsmanagement).

APPENDIX F

THE LORD CHANCELLOR'S DEPARTMENT
Freedom of Information

Open Government

CODE OF PRACTICE ON ACCESS TO GOVERNMENT INFORMATION

SECOND EDITION 1997

Applies to those bodies who come within the jurisdiction of the Parliamentary Commissioner for Administration, as it is he who enforces the Code. The full text of the revised Code of Practice follows, and an **explanatory leaflet** is also available.

Free copies of the Code of Practice Guidance on Interpretation can be obtained from the Freedom of Information Unit.

© Crown Copyright 1999, 2000, 2001

THE LORD CHANCELLOR'S DEPARTMENT
Freedom of Information

Code of Practice on Access to Government Information

PART 1

Purpose

1. This Code of Practice supports the Government's policy under the **Citizen's Charter** of extending access to official information, and responding to reasonable requests for information. The

1001

approach to release of information should in all cases be based on the assumption that information should be released except where disclosure would not be in the public interest, as specified in **Part II** of this Code.

2. The aims of the Code are:

- to improve policy-making and the democratic process by extending access to the facts and analyses which provide the basis for the consideration of proposed policy;
- to protect the interests of individuals and companies by ensuring that reasons are given for administrative decisions, except where there is statutory authority or established convention to the contrary; and
- to support and extend the principles of public service established under the **Citizen's Charter**.

These aims are balanced by the need:

- to maintain high standards of care in ensuring the privacy of personal and commercially confidential information; and
- to preserve confidentiality where disclosure would not be in the public interest or would breach personal privacy or the confidences of a third party, in accordance with statutory requirements and **Part II** of the Code.

Information the Government will release

3. Subject to the exemptions in **Part II**, the Code commits departments and public bodies under the jurisdiction of the **Parliamentary Commissioner for Administration** (the Ombudsman):[1]

   i. to publish the facts and analysis of the facts which the Government considers relevant and important in framing major policy proposals and decisions; such information will normally be made available when policies and decisions are announced;

  ii. to publish or otherwise make available, as soon as practicable after the Code becomes operational, explanatory material on departments' dealings with the public (including such rules, procedures, internal guidance to officials, and similar administrative manuals as will assist better understanding of departmental action in dealing with the public) except where publication could prejudice any matter which should properly be kept confidential under **Part II** of the Code;

  iii. to give reasons for administrative decisions to those affected;[2]

  iv. to publish in accordance with the **Citizen's Charter**:

- full information about how public services are run, how much they cost, who is in charge, and what complaints and redress procedures are available;
- full and, where possible, comparable information about what services are being provided, what targets are set, what standards of service are expected and the results achieved.

  v. to release, in response to specific requests, information relating to their policies, actions and decisions and other matters related to their areas of responsibility.

4. There is no commitment that pre-existing documents, as distinct from information, will be made available in response to requests. The Code does not require departments to acquire information they do not possess, to provide information which is already published, or to provide information which is provided as part of an existing charged service other than through that service.

---

[1] In Northern Ireland, the **Parliamentary Commissioner for Administration and the Commissioner for Complaints**.

[2] There will be a few areas where well-established convention or legal authority limits the commitment to give reasons, for example decisions on citizenship applications (see s44(2) of the British Nationality Act 1981) or certain decisions on merger and monopoly cases or on whether to take enforcement action.

Responses to requests for information

5. Information will be provided as soon as practicable. The target for response to simple requests for information is 20 working days from the date of receipt. This target may need to be extended when significant search or collation of material is required. Where information cannot be provided under the terms of the Code, an explanation will normally be given.

Scope

6. The Code applies to those Government departments and other bodies within the **jurisdiction of the Ombudsman** (as listed in Schedule 2 to the Parliamentary Commissioner Act 1967)[3]. The Code applies to agencies within departments and to functions carried out on behalf of a department or public body by contractors. The Security and Intelligence Services are not within the scope of the Code, nor is information obtained from or relating to them.

Charges

7. Departments, agencies and public bodies will make their own arrangements for charging. Details of charges are available from departments on request. Schemes may include a standard charge for processing simple requests for information. Where a request is complex and would require extensive searches of records or processing or collation of information, an additional charge, reflecting reasonable costs may be notified.

Relationship to statutory access rights

8. This Code is non-statutory and cannot override provisions contained in statutory rights of access to information or records (nor can it override statutory prohibitions on disclosure) Where the information could be sought under an existing statutory right, the terms of the right of access takes precedence over the Code. There are already certain access rights to health, medical and educational records, to personal files held by local authority housing and social services departments, and to personal data held on computer. There is also a right of access to environmental information. It is not envisaged that the **Ombudsman** will become involved in supervising these statutory rights.

The White Paper on Open Government (Cm 2290) proposed two new statutory rights to information:

> an access right to personal records, proposed in Chapter 5;
> an access right to health and safety information, proposed in Chapter 6.

Where a statutory right is proposed but has yet to be implemented, access to relevant information may be sought under the Code, but the Code should not be regarded as a means of access to original documents or personal files.

Public records

9. The Code is not intended to override statutory provisions on access to public records, whether over or under thirty years old. Under s12(3) of the Parliamentary Commissioner Act 1967, the Ombudsman is not required to question the merits of a decision if it is taken without maladministration by a Government department or other body in the exercise of a discretion vested in it. Decisions on public records made in England and Wales by the Lord Chancellor, or in Scotland and Northern Ireland by the Secretary of State, are such discretionary decisions.

---

[3] In Northern Ireland the Code applies to public bodies under the jurisdiction of the Northern Ireland **Parliamentary Commissioner for Administration and the Commissioner for Complaints**, with the exception of local government and health and personal social services bodies, for which separate arrangements are being developed as in Great Britain. Some Northern Ireland departments and bodies are expressly subject to the jurisdiction of the Parliamentary Commissioner under the 1967 Act.

Jurisdiction of courts, tribunals or inquiries

10. The Code only applies to Government-held information. It does not apply to or affect information held by courts or contained in court documents. ('Court' includes tribunals, inquiries and the Northern Ireland Enforcement of Judgements Office). The present practice covering disclosure of information before courts, tribunals and inquiries will continue to apply.

Investigation of complaints

11. Complaints that information which should have been provided under the Code has not been provided, or that unreasonable charges have been demanded, should be made first to the department or body concerned. If the applicant remains dissatisfied, complaints may be made through a Member of Parliament to the **Ombudsman**. Complaints will be investigated at the Ombudsman's discretion in accordance with the procedures provided in the 1967 Act.[4]

THE LORD CHANCELLOR'S DEPARTMENT
Freedom of Information

Code of Practice on Access to Government Information

PART 2

Reasons for confidentiality

The following categories of information are exempt from the commitments to provide information in this Code. In those categories which refer to harm or prejudice, the presumption remains that information should be disclosed unless the harm likely to arise from disclosure would outweigh the public interest in making the information available.

References to harm or prejudice include both actual harm or prejudice and risk or reasonable expectation of harm or prejudice. In such cases it should be considered whether any harm or prejudice arising from disclosure is outweighed by the public interest in making information available.

The exemptions will not be interpreted in a way which causes injustice to individuals.

1. Defence, security and international relations

- Information whose disclosure would harm national security or defence.
- Information whose disclosure would harm the conduct of international relations or affairs.
- Information received in confidence from foreign governments, foreign courts or international organisations.

2. Internal discussion and advice

Information whose disclosure would harm the frankness and candour of internal discussion, including:

- proceedings of Cabinet and Cabinet committees;
- internal opinion, advice, recommendation, consultation and deliberation;

---

[4] Separate arrangements will apply in Northern Ireland.

- projections and assumptions relating to internal policy analysis; analysis of alternative policy options and information relating to rejected policy options;
- confidential communications between departments, public bodies and regulatory bodies.

3. Communications with the Royal Household

Information relating to confidential communications between Ministers and Her Majesty the Queen or other Members of the Royal Household, or relating to confidential proceedings of the Privy Council

4. Law enforcement and legal proceedings

Information whose disclosure could prejudice the administration of justice (including fair trial), legal proceedings or the proceedings of any tribunal, public inquiry or other formal investigations (whether actual or likely) or whose disclosure is, has been, or is likely to be addressed in the context of such proceedings.

Information whose disclosure could prejudice the enforcement or proper administration of the law, including the prevention, investigation or detection of crime, or the apprehension or prosecution of offenders.

Information relating to legal proceedings or the proceedings of any tribunal, public inquiry or other formal investigation which have been completed or terminated, or relating to investigations which have or might have resulted in proceedings.

Information covered by legal professional privilege.

Information whose disclosure would harm public safety or public order, or would prejudice the security of any building or penal institution.

Information whose disclosure could endanger the life or physical safety of any person, or identify the source of information or assistance given in confidence for law enforcement or security purposes.

Information whose disclosure would increase the likelihood of damage to the environment, or rare or endangered species and their habitats.

5. Immigration and nationality

Information relating to immigration, nationality, consular and entry clearance cases. However, information will be provided, though not through access to personal records, where there is no risk that disclosure would prejudice the effective administration of immigration controls or other statutory provisions.

6. Effective management of the economy and collection of tax

Information whose disclosure would harm the ability of the Government to manage the economy, prejudice the conduct of official market operations, or could lead to improper gain or advantage.

Information whose disclosure would prejudice the assessment or collection of tax, duties or National Insurance contributions, or assist tax avoidance or evasion.

7. Effective management and operations of the public service

Information whose disclosure could lead to improper gain or advantage or would prejudice:

- the competitive position of a department or other public body or authority;
- negotiations or the effective conduct of personnel management, or commercial or contractual activities;
- the awarding of discretionary grants.

Information whose disclosure would harm the proper and efficient conduct of the operations of a department or other public body or authority, including NHS organisations, or of any regulatory body.

8. Public employment, public appointments and honours

Personnel records (relating to public appointments as well as employees of public authorities) including those relating to recruitment, promotion and security vetting.

Information, opinions and assessments given in confidence in relation to public employment and public appointments made by Ministers of the Crown, by the Crown on the advice of Ministers or by statutory office holders.

Information, opinions and assessments given in relation to recommendations for honours.

9. Voluminous or vexatious requests

Requests for information which are vexatious or manifestly unreasonable or are formulated in too general a manner, or which (because of the amount of information to be processed or the need to retrieve information from files not in current use) would require unreasonable diversion of resources.

10. Publication and prematurity in relation to publication

Information which is or will soon be published, or whose disclosure, where the material relates to a planned or potential announcement or publication, could cause harm (for example, of a physical or financial nature).

11. Research, statistics and analysis

Information relating to incomplete analysis, research or statistics, where disclosure could be misleading or deprive the holder of priority of publication or commercial value.

Information held only for preparing statistics or carrying out research, or for surveillance for health and safety purposes (including food safety), and which relates to individuals, companies or products which will not be identified in reports of that research or surveillance, or in published statistics.

12. Privacy of an individual

Unwarranted disclosure to a third party of personal information about any person (including a deceased person) or any other disclosure which would constitute or could facilitate an unwarranted invasion of privacy.

13. Third party's commercial confidences

Information including commercial confidences, trade secrets or intellectual property whose unwarranted disclosure would harm the competitive position of a third party.

14. Information given in confidence

Information held in consequence of having been supplied in confidence by a person who:

- gave the information under a statutory guarantee that its confidentiality would be protected; or
- was not under any legal obligation, whether actual or implied, to supply it, and has not consented to its disclosure.

Information whose disclosure without the consent of the supplier would prejudice the future supply of such information.

Medical information provided in confidence if disclosure to the subject would harm their physical or mental health, or should only be made by a medical practitioner.

15. Statutory and other restrictions

Information whose disclosure is prohibited by or under any enactment, regulation, European Community law or international agreement.

Information whose release would constitute a breach of Parliamentary Privilege.

APPENDIX G

Convention on Access to Information, Public Participation in Decision-Making and Access to Justice in Environmental Matters

The Parties to this Convention,

Recalling principle 1 of the Stockholm Declaration on the Human Environment,

Recalling also principle 10 of the Rio Declaration on Environment and Development,

Recalling further General Assembly resolutions 37/7 of 28 October 1982 on the World Charter for Nature and 45/94 of 14 December 1990 on the need to ensure a healthy environment for the well-being of individuals,

Recalling the European Charter on Environment and Health adopted at the First European Conference on Environment and Health of the World Health Organization in Frankfurt-am-Main, Germany, on 8 December 1989,

Affirming the need to protect, preserve and improve the state of the environment and to ensure sustainable and environmentally sound development,

Recognizing that adequate protection of the environment is essential to human well-being and the enjoyment of basic human rights, including the right to life itself,

Recognizing also that every person has the right to live in an environment adequate to his or her health and well-being, and the duty, both individually and in association with others, to protect and improve the environment for the benefit of present and future generations,

Considering that, to be able to assert this right and observe this duty, citizens must have access to information, be entitled to participate in decision-making and have access to justice in environmental matters, and acknowledging in this regard that citizens may need assistance in order to exercise their rights,

Recognizing that, in the field of the environment, improved access to information and public participation in decision-making enhance the quality and the implementation of decisions, contribute to public awareness of environmental issues, give the public the opportunity to express its concerns and enable public authorities to take due account of such concerns,

Aiming thereby to further the accountability of and transparency in decision-making and to strengthen public support for decisions on the environment,

Recognizing the desirability of transparency in all branches of government and inviting legislative bodies to implement the principles of this Convention in their proceedings,

Recognizing also that the public needs to be aware of the procedures for participation in environmental decision-making, have free access to them and know how to use them,

Recognizing further the importance of the respective roles that individual citizens, non-governmental organizations and the private sector can play in environmental protection,

Desiring to promote environmental education to further the understanding of the environment and sustainable development and to encourage widespread public awareness of, and participation in, decisions affecting the environment and sustainable development,

Noting, in this context, the importance of making use of the media and of electronic or other, future forms of communication,

Recognizing the importance of fully integrating environmental considerations in governmental decision-making and the consequent need for public authorities to be in possession of accurate, comprehensive and up-to-date environmental information,

Acknowledging that public authorities hold environmental information in the public interest,

Concerned that effective judicial mechanisms should be accessible to the public, including organizations, so that its legitimate interests are protected and the law is enforced,

Noting the importance of adequate product information being provided to consumers to enable them to make informed environmental choices,

Recognizing the concern of the public about the deliberate release of genetically modified organisms into the environment and the need for increased transparency and greater public participation in decision-making in this field,

Convinced that the implementation of this Convention will contribute to strengthening democracy in the region of the United Nations Economic Commission for Europe (ECE),

Conscious of the role played in this respect by ECE and recalling, inter alia, the ECE Guidelines on Access to Environmental Information and Public Participation in Environmental Decision-making endorsed in the Ministerial Declaration adopted at the Third Ministerial Conference 'Environment for Europe' in Sofia, Bulgaria, on 25 October 1995,

Bearing in mind the relevant provisions in the Convention on Environmental Impact Assessment in a Transboundary Context, done at Espoo, Finland, on 25 February 1991, and the Convention on the Transboundary Effects of Industrial Accidents and the Convention on the Protection and Use of Transboundary Watercourses and International Lakes, both done at Helsinki on 17 March 1992, and other regional conventions,

Conscious that the adoption of this Convention will have contributed to the further strengthening of the 'Environment for Europe' process and to the results of the Fourth Ministerial Conference in Aarhus, Denmark, in June 1998,

Have agreed as follows:

[*Article 1*]

Objective

In order to contribute to the protection of the right of every person of present and future generations to live in an environment adequate to his or her health and well-being, each Party shall guarantee the rights of access to information, public participation in decision-making, and access to justice in environmental matters in accordance with the provisions of this Convention.

[*Article 2*]

Definitions

For the purposes of this Convention,

1. 'Party' means, unless the text otherwise indicates, a Contracting Party to this Convention;

2. 'Public authority' means,

   (a) Government at national, regional and other level;
   (b) Natural or legal persons performing public administrative functions under national law, including specific duties, activities orservices in relation to the environment;
   (c) Any other natural or legal persons having public responsibilities or functions, or providing public services, in relation to the environment, under the control of a body or person falling within subparagraphs (a) or (b)above;
   (d) The institutions of any regional economic integration organization referred to in article 17 which is a Party to this Convention.

This definition does not include bodies or institutions acting in a judicial or legislative capacity.

3. 'Environmental information' means any information in written, visual, aural, electronic or any other material form on:

(a) The state of elements of the environment, such as air and atmosphere, water, soil, land, landscape and natural sites, biologicaldiversity and its components, including genetically modified organisms, and the interaction among these elements;

(b) Factors, such as substances, energy, noise and radiation, and activities or measures, including administrative measures, environmental agreements, policies, legislation, plans and programmes, affecting or likely to affect the elements of the environment within the scope of subparagraph (a) above, and cost-benefit and other economic analyses and assumptions used in environmental decision-making;

(c) The state of human health and safety, conditions of human life,cultural sites and built structures, inasmuch as they are or may be affected by the state of the elements of the environment or, through these elements, by the factors, activities or measures referred to in subparagraph (b) above.

4. 'The public' means one or more natural or legal persons, and, in accordance with national legislation or practice, their associations,organizations or groups.

5. 'The public concerned' means the public affected or likely to be affected by, or having an interest in, the environmental decision-making; for the purposes of this definition, non-governmental organizations promoting environmental protection and meeting any requirements under national law shall be deemed to have an interest.

[*Article 3*]

General provisions

1. Each Party shall take the necessary legislative, regulatory and other measures, including measures to achieve compatibility between the provisions implementing the information, public participation and access-to-justice provisions in this Convention, as well as proper enforcement measures, to establish and maintain a clear, transparent and consistent framework to implement the provisions of this Convention.

2. Each Party shall endeavour to ensure that officials and authorities assist and provide guidance to the public in seeking access to information, in facilitating participation in decision-making and in seeking access to justice in environmental matters.

3. Each Party shall promote environmental education and environmental awareness among the public, especially on how to obtain access to information, to participate in decision-making and to obtain access to justice in environmental matters.

4. Each Party shall provide for appropriate recognition of and support to associations, organizations or groups promoting environmental protection and ensure that its national legal system is consistent with this obligation.

5. The provisions of this Convention shall not affect the right of a Party to maintain or introduce measures providing for broader access to information, more extensive public participation in decision-making and wider access to justice in environmental matters than required by this Convention.

6. This Convention shall not require any derogation from existing rights of access to information, public participation in decision-making and access to justice in environmental matters.

7. Each Party shall promote the application of the principles of this Convention in international environmental decision-making processes and within the framework of international organizations in matters relating to the environment.

8. Each Party shall ensure that persons exercising their rights in conformity with the provisions of this Convention shall not be penalized, persecuted or harassed in any way for their involvement. This provision shall not affect the powers of national courts to award reasonable costs in judicial proceedings.

9. Within the scope of the relevant provisions of this Convention, the public shall have access to information, have the possibility to participate in decision-making and have access to justice in environmental matters without discrimination as to citizenship, nationality or domicile and, in the case of a legal person, without discrimination as to where it has its registered seat or an effective centre of its activities.

[Article 4]

Access to environmental information

1. Each Party shall ensure that, subject to the following paragraphs of this article, public authorities, in response to a request for environmental information, make such information available to the public, within the framework of national legislation, including, where requested and subject to subparagraph (b) below, copies of the actual documentation containing or comprising such information:

   (a) Without an interest having to be stated;
   (b) In the form requested unless:

      (i) It is reasonable for the public authority to make it available in another form, in which case reasons shall be given for making it available in that form; or
      (ii) The information is already publicly available in another form.

2. The environmental information referred to in paragraph 1 above shall be made available as soon as possible and at the latest within one month after the request has been submitted, unless the volume and the complexity of the information justify an extension of this period up to two months after the request. The applicant shall be informed of any extension and of the reasons justifying it.

3. A request for environmental information may be refused if:

   (a) The public authority to which the request is addressed does not hold the environmental information requested;
   (b) The request is manifestly unreasonable or formulated in too general a manner; or
   (c) The request concerns material in the course of completion or concerns internal communications of public authorities where such an exemption is provided for in national law or customary practice, taking into account the public interest served by disclosure.

4. A request for environmental information may be refused if the disclosure would adversely affect:

   (a) The confidentiality of the proceedings of public authorities, where such confidentiality is provided for under national law;
   (b) International relations, national defence or public security;
   (c) The course of justice, the ability of a person to receive a fair trial or the ability of a public authority to conduct an enquiry of a criminal or disciplinary nature;
   (d) The confidentiality of commercial and industrial information, where such confidentiality is protected by law in order to protect a legitimate economic interest. Within this framework, information on emissions which is relevant for the protection of the environment shall be disclosed;
   (e) Intellectual property rights;
   (f) The confidentiality of personal data and/or files relating to a natural person where that person has not consented to the disclosure of the information to the public, where such confidentiality is provided for in national law;
   (g) The interests of a third party which has supplied the information requested without that party being under or capable of being put under a legal obligation to do so, and where that party does not consent to the release of the material; or
   (h) The environment to which the information relates, such as the breeding sites of rare species.

The aforementioned grounds for refusal shall be interpreted in a restrictive way, taking into account the public interest served by disclosure and taking into account whether the information requested relates to emissions into the environment.

5. Where a public authority does not hold the environmental information requested, this public authority shall, as promptly as possible, inform the applicant of the public authority to which it believes it is possible to apply for the information requested or transfer the request to that authority and inform the applicant accordingly.

6. Each Party shall ensure that, if information exempted from disclosure under paragraphs 3 (c) and 4 above can be separated out without prejudice to the confidentiality of the information exempted, public authorities make available the remainder of the environmental information that has been requested.

7. A refusal of a request shall be in writing if the request was in writing or the applicant so requests. A refusal shall state the reasons for the refusal and give information on access to the review procedure provided for in accordance with article 9. The refusal shall be made as soon as possible and at the latest within one month, unless the complexity of the information justifies an extension of this period up to two months after the request. The applicant shall be informed of any extension and of the reasons justifying it.

8. Each Party may allow its public authorities to make a charge for supplying information, but such charge shall not exceed a reasonable amount. Public authorities intending to make such a charge for supplying information shall make available to applicants a schedule of charges which may be levied, indicating the circumstances in which they may be levied or waived and when the supply of information is conditional on the advance payment of such a charge.

[Article 5]

Collection and dissemination of environmental information

1. Each Party shall ensure that:

   (a) Public authorities possess and update environmental information which is relevant to their functions;

   (b) Mandatory systems are established so that there is an adequate flow of information to public authorities about proposed and existing activities which may significantly affect the environment;

   (c) In the event of any imminent threat to human health or the environment, whether caused by human activities or due to natural causes, all information which could enable the public to take measures to prevent or mitigate harm arising from the threat and is held by a public authority is disseminated immediately and without delay to members of the public who may be affected.

2. Each Party shall ensure that, within the framework of national legislation, the way in which public authorities make environmental information available to the public is transparent and that environmental information is effectively accessible, inter alia, by:

   (a) Providing sufficient information to the public about the type and scope of environmental information held by the relevant public authorities, the basic terms and conditions under which such information is made available and accessible, and the process by which it can be obtained;

   (b) Establishing and maintaining practical arrangements, such as:

   (i) Publicly accessible lists, registers or files;

   (ii) Requiring officials to support the public in seeking access to information under this Convention; and

   (iii) The identification of points of contact; and

   (c) Providing access to the environmental information contained in lists, registers or files as referred to in subparagraph (b) (i) above free of charge.

3. Each Party shall ensure that environmental information progressively becomes available in electronic databases which are easily accessible to the public through public telecommunications networks. Information accessible in this form should include:

(a) Reports on the state of the environment, as referred to in paragraph 4 below;

(b) Texts of legislation on or relating to the environment;

(c) As appropriate, policies, plans and programmes on or relating to the environment, and environmental agreements; and

(d) Other information, to the extent that the availability of such information in this form would facilitate the application of national law implementing this Convention, provided that such information is already available in electronic form.

4. Each Party shall, at regular intervals not exceeding three or four years, publish and disseminate a national report on the state of the environment, including information on the quality of the environment and information on pressures on the environment.

5. Each Party shall take measures within the framework of its legislation for the purpose of disseminating, inter alia:

(a) Legislation and policy documents such as documents on strategies, policies, programmes and action plans relating to the environment, and progress reports on their implementation, prepared at various levels of government;

(b) International treaties, conventions and agreements on environmental issues; and

(c) Other significant international documents on environmental issues, as appropriate.

6. Each Party shall encourage operators whose activities have a significant impact on the environment to inform the public regularly of the environmental impact of their activities and products, where appropriate within the framework of voluntary eco-labelling or eco-auditing schemes or by other means.

7. Each Party shall:

(a) Publish the facts and analyses of facts which it considers relevant and important in framing major environmental policy proposals;

(b) Publish, or otherwise make accessible, available explanatory material on its dealings with the public in matters falling within the scope of this Convention; and

(c) Provide in an appropriate form information on the performance of public functions or the provision of public services relating to the environment by government at all levels.

8. Each Party shall develop mechanisms with a view to ensuring that sufficient product information is made available to the public in a manner which enables consumers to make informed environmental choices.

9. Each Party shall take steps to establish progressively, taking into account international processes where appropriate, a coherent, nationwide system of pollution inventories or registers on a structured, computerized and publicly accessible database compiled through standardized reporting. Such a system may include inputs, releases and transfers of a specified range of substances and products, including water, energy and resource use, from a specified range of activities to environmental media and to on-site and offsite treatment and disposal sites.

10. Nothing in this article may prejudice the right of Parties to refuse to disclose certain environmental information in accordance with article 4, paragraphs 3 and 4.

[*Article 9*]

Access to justice

1. Each Party shall, within the framework of its national legislation, ensure that any person who considers that his or her request for information under article 4 has been ignored, wrongfully refused, whether in part or in full, inadequately answered, or otherwise not dealt with in accordance with the provisions of that article, has access to a review procedure before a court of law or another independent and impartial body established by law.

In the circumstances where a Party provides for such a review by a court of law, it shall ensure that such a person also has access to an expeditious procedure established by law that is free of charge or inexpensive for reconsideration by a public authority or review by an independent and impartial body other than a court of law.

Final decisions under this paragraph 1 shall be binding on the public authority holding the information. Reasons shall be stated in writing, at least where access to information is refused under this paragraph.

2. Each Party shall, within the framework of its national legislation, ensure that members of the public concerned

(a) Having a sufficient interest or, alternatively,

(b) Maintaining impairment of a right, where the administrative procedural law of a Party requires this as a precondition,

have access to a review procedure before a court of law and/or another independent and impartial body established by law, to challenge the substantive and procedural legality of any decision, act or omission subject to the provisions of article 6 and, where so provided for under national law and without prejudice to paragraph 3 below, of other relevant provisions of this Convention.

What constitutes a sufficient interest and impairment of a right shall be determined in accordance with the requirements of national law and consistently with the objective of giving the public concerned wide access to justice within the scope of this Convention. To this end, the interest of any non-governmental organization meeting the requirements referred to in article 2, paragraph 5, shall be deemed sufficient for the purpose of subparagraph (a) above. Such organizations shall also be deemed to have rights capable of being impaired for the purpose of subparagraph (b) above.

The provisions of this paragraph 2 shall not exclude the possibility of a preliminary review procedure before an administrative authority and shall not affect the requirement of exhaustion of administrative review procedures prior to recourse to judicial review procedures, where such a requirement exists under national law.

3. In addition and without prejudice to the review procedures referred to in paragraphs 1 and 2 above, each Party shall ensure that, where they meet the criteria, if any, laid down in its national law, members of the public have access to administrative or judicial procedures to challenge acts and omissions by private persons and public authorities which contravene provisions of its national law relating to the environment.

4. In addition and without prejudice to paragraph 1 above, the procedures referred to in paragraphs 1, 2 and 3 above shall provide adequate and effective remedies, including injunctive relief as appropriate, and be fair, equitable, timely and not prohibitively expensive. Decisions under this article shall be given or recorded in writing. Decisions of courts, and whenever possible of other bodies, shall be publicly accessible.

5. In order to further the effectiveness of the provisions of this article, each Party shall ensure that information is provided to the public on access to administrative and judicial review procedures and shall consider the establishment of appropriate assistance mechanisms to remove or reduce financial and other barriers to access to justice.

APPENDIX H

REGULATION (EC) NO 1049/2001 OF THE EUROPEAN PARLIAMENT AND OF THE COUNCIL OF 30 MAY 2001

regarding public access to European Parliament, Council and Commission documents

THE EUROPEAN PARLIAMENT AND THE COUNCIL OF THE EUROPEAN UNION,

Having regard to the Treaty establishing the European Community, and in particular Article 255(2) thereof,

Having regard to the proposal from the Commission[1],

Acting in accordance with the procedure referred to in Article 251 of the Treaty[2],

Whereas:

(1) The second subparagraph of Article 1 of the Treaty on European Union enshrines the concept of openness, stating that the Treaty marks a new stage in the process of creating an ever closer union among the peoples of Europe, in which decisions are taken as openly as possible and as closely as possible to the citizen.

(2) Openness enables citizens to participate more closely in the decision-making process and guarantees that the administration enjoys greater legitimacy and is more effective and more accountable to the citizen in a democratic system. Openness contributes to strengthening the principles of democracy and respect for fundamental rights as laid down in Article 6 of the EU Treaty and in the Charter of Fundamental Rights of the European Union.

(3) The conclusions of the European Council meetings held at Birmingham, Edinburgh and Copenhagen stressed the need to introduce greater transparency into the work of the Union institutions. This Regulation consolidates the initiatives that the institutions have already taken with a view to improving the transparency of the decisionmaking process.

(4) The purpose of this Regulation is to give the fullest possible effect to the right of public access to documents and to lay down the general principles and limits on such access in accordance with Article 255(2) of the EC Treaty.

(5) Since the question of access to documents is not covered by provisions of the Treaty establishing the European Coal and Steel Community and the Treaty establishing the European Atomic Energy Community, the European Parliament, the Council and the Commission should, in accordance with Declaration No 41 attached to the Final Act of the Treaty of Amsterdam, draw guidance from this Regulation as regards documents concerning the activities covered by those two Treaties.

(6) Wider access should be granted to documents in cases where the institutions are acting in their legislative capacity, including under delegated powers, while at the same time preserving the effectiveness of the institutions' decision-making process. Such documents should be made directly accessible to the greatest possible extent.

(7) In accordance with Articles 28(1) and 41(1) of the EU Treaty, the right of access also applies to documents relating to the common foreign and security policy and to police and judicial cooperation in criminal matters. Each institution should respect its security rules.

---

[1] OJ C 177 E, 27.6.2000, p. 70.
[2] Opinion of the European Parliament of 3 May 2001 (not yet published in the Official Journal) and Council Decision of 28 May 2001.

(8) In order to ensure the full application of this Regulation to all activities of the Union, all agencies established by the institutions should apply the principles laid down in this Regulation.

(9) On account of their highly sensitive content, certain documents should be given special treatment. Arrangements for informing the European Parliament of the content of such documents should be made through interinstitutional agreement.

(10) In order to bring about greater openness in the work of the institutions, access to documents should be granted by the European Parliament, the Council and the Commission not only to documents drawn up by the institutions, but also to documents received by them. In this context, it is recalled that Declaration No 35 attached to the Final Act of the Treaty of Amsterdam provides that a Member State may request the Commission or the Council not to communicate to third parties a document originating from that State without its prior agreement.

(11) In principle, all documents of the institutions should be accessible to the public. However, certain public and private interests should be protected by way of exceptions. The institutions should be entitled to protect their internal consultations and deliberations where necessary to safeguard their ability to carry out their tasks. In assessing the exceptions, the institutions should take account of the principles in Community legislation concerning the protection of personal data, in all areas of Union activities.

(12) All rules concerning access to documents of the institutions should be in conformity with this Regulation.

(13) In order to ensure that the right of access is fully respected, a two-stage administrative procedure should apply, with the additional possibility of court proceedings or complaints to the Ombudsman.

(14) Each institution should take the measures necessary to inform the public of the new provisions in force and to train its staff to assist citizens exercising their rights under this Regulation. In order to make it easier for citizens to exercise their rights, each institution should provide access to a register of documents.

(15) Even though it is neither the object nor the effect of this Regulation to amend national legislation on access to documents, it is nevertheless clear that, by virtue of the principle of loyal cooperation which governs relations between the institutions and the Member States, Member States should take care not to hamper the proper application of this Regulation and should respect the security rules of the institutions.

(16) This Regulation is without prejudice to existing rights of access to documents for Member States, judicial authorities or investigative bodies.

(17) In accordance with Article 255[3] of the EC Treaty, each institution lays down specific provisions regarding access to its documents in its rules of procedure. Council Decision 93/731/EC of 20 December 1993 on public access to Council documents[3], Commission Decision 94/90/ECSC, EC, Euratom of 8 February 1994 on public access to Commission documents[4], European Parliament Decision 97/632/EC, ECSC, Euratom of 10 July 1997 on public access to European Parliament documents[5], and the rules on confidentiality of Schengen documents should therefore, if necessary, be modified or be repealed,

HAVE ADOPTED THIS REGULATION:

---

[3] OJ L 340, 31.12.1993, p. 43. Decision as last amended by Decision 2000/527/EC (OJ L 212, 23.8.2000, p. 9).

[4] OJ L 46, 18.2.1994, p. 58. Decision as amended by Decision 96/ 567/EC, ECSC, Euratom (OJ L 247, 28.9.1996, p. 45).

[5] OJ L 263, 25.9.1997, p. 27.

[*Article 1*]

Purpose

The purpose of this Regulation is:

(a) to define the principles, conditions and limits on grounds of public or private interest governing the right of access to European Parliament, Council and Commission (hereinafter referred to as 'the institutions') documents provided for in Article 255 of the EC Treaty in such a way as to ensure the widest possible access to documents,

(b) to establish rules ensuring the easiest possible exercise of this right, and

(c) to promote good administrative practice on access to documents.

[*Article 2*]

Beneficiaries and scope

1. Any citizen of the Union, and any natural or legal person residing or having its registered office in a Member State, has a right of access to documents of the institutions, subject to the principles, conditions and limits defined in this Regulation.

2. The institutions may, subject to the same principles, conditions and limits, grant access to documents to any natural or legal person not residing or not having its registered office in a Member State.

3. This Regulation shall apply to all documents held by an institution, that is to say, documents drawn up or received by it and in its possession, in all areas of activity of the European Union.

4. Without prejudice to Articles 4 and 9, documents shall be made accessible to the public either following a written application or directly in electronic form or through a register. In particular, documents drawn up or received in the course of a legislative procedure shall be made directly accessible in accordance with Article 12.

5. Sensitive documents as defined in Article 9(1) shall be subject to special treatment in accordance with that Article.

6. This Regulation shall be without prejudice to rights of public access to documents held by the institutions which might follow from instruments of international law or acts of the institutions implementing them.

[*Article 3*]

Definitions

For the purpose of this Regulation:

(a) 'document' shall mean any content whatever its medium (written on paper or stored in electronic form or as a sound, visual or audiovisual recording) concerning a matter relating to the policies, activities and decisions falling within the institution's sphere of responsibility;

(b) 'third party' shall mean any natural or legal person, or any entity outside the institution concerned, including the Member States, other Community or non-Community institutions and bodies and third countries.

[*Article 4*]

Exceptions

1. The institutions shall refuse access to a document where disclosure would undermine the protection of:

(a) the public interest as regards:
— public security,
— defence and military matters,

— international relations,

— the financial, monetary or economic policy of the Community or a Member State;

(b) privacy and the integrity of the individual, in particular in accordance with Community legislation regarding the protection of personal data.

2. The institutions shall refuse access to a document where disclosure would undermine the protection of:

— commercial interests of a natural or legal person, including intellectual property,

— court proceedings and legal advice,

— the purpose of inspections, investigations and audits,

unless there is an overriding public interest in disclosure.

3. Access to a document, drawn up by an institution for internal use or received by an institution, which relates to a matter where the decision has not been taken by the institution, shall be refused if disclosure of the document would seriously undermine the institution's decision-making process, unless there is an overriding public interest in disclosure.

Access to a document containing opinions for internal use as part of deliberations and preliminary consultations within the institution concerned shall be refused even after the decision has been taken if disclosure of the document would seriously undermine the institution's decision-making process, unless there is an overriding public interest in disclosure.

4. As regards third-party documents, the institution shall consult the third party with a view to assessing whether an exception in paragraph 1 or 2 is applicable, unless it is clear that the document shall or shall not be disclosed.

5. A Member State may request the institution not to disclose a document originating from that Member State without its prior agreement.

6. If only parts of the requested document are covered by any of the exceptions, the remaining parts of the document shall be released.

7. The exceptions as laid down in paragraphs 1 to 3 shall only apply for the period during which protection is justified on the basis of the content of the document. The exceptions may apply for a maximum period of 30 years. In the case of documents covered by the exceptions relating to privacy or commercial interests and in the case of sensitive documents, the exceptions may, if necessary, continue to apply after this period.

[*Article 5*]

Documents in the Member States

Where a Member State receives a request for a document in its possession, originating from an institution, unless it is clear that the document shall or shall not be disclosed, the Member State shall consult with the institution concerned in order to take a decision that does not jeopardise the attainment of the objectives of this Regulation.

The Member State may instead refer the request to the institution.

[*Article 6*]

Applications

1. Applications for access to a document shall be made in any written form, including electronic form, in one of the languages referred to in Article 314 of the EC Treaty and in a sufficiently precise manner to enable the institution to identify the document. The applicant is not obliged to state reasons for the application.

2. If an application is not sufficiently precise, the institution shall ask the applicant to clarify the application and shall assist the applicant in doing so, for example, by providing information on the use of the public registers of documents.

3. In the event of an application relating to a very long document or to a very large number of documents, the institution concerned may confer with the applicant informally, with a view to finding a fair solution.

4. The institutions shall provide information and assistance to citizens on how and where applications for access to documents can be made.

[Article 7]

Processing of initial applications

1. An application for access to a document shall be handled promptly. An acknowledgement of receipt shall be sent to the applicant. Within 15 working days from registration of the application, the institution shall either grant access to the document requested and provide access in accordance with Article 10 within that period or, in a written reply, state the reasons for the total or partial refusal and inform the applicant of his or her right to make a confirmatory application in accordance with paragraph 2 of this Article.

2. In the event of a total or partial refusal, the applicant may, within 15 working days of receiving the institution's reply, make a confirmatory application asking the institution to reconsider its position.

3. In exceptional cases, for example in the event of an application relating to a very long document or to a very large number of documents, the time-limit provided for in paragraph 1 may be extended by 15 working days, provided that the applicant is notified in advance and that detailed reasons are given.

4. Failure by the institution to reply within the prescribed time-limit shall entitle the applicant to make a confirmatory application.

[Article 8]

Processing of confirmatory applications

1. A confirmatory application shall be handled promptly. Within 15 working days from registration of such an application, the institution shall either grant access to the document requested and provide access in accordance with Article 10 within that period or, in a written reply, state the reasons for the total or partial refusal. In the event of a total or partial refusal, the institution shall inform the applicant of the remedies open to him or her, namely instituting court proceedings against the institution and/or making a complaint to the Ombudsman, under the conditions laid down in Articles 230 and 195 of the EC Treaty, respectively.

2. In exceptional cases, for example in the event of an application relating to a very long document or to a very large number of documents, the time limit provided for in paragraph 1 may be extended by 15 working days, provided that the applicant is notified in advance and that detailed reasons are given.

3. Failure by the institution to reply within the prescribed time limit shall be considered as a negative reply and entitle the applicant to institute court proceedings against the institution and/or make a complaint to the Ombudsman, under the relevant provisions of the EC Treaty.

[Article 9]

Treatment of sensitive documents

1. Sensitive documents are documents originating from the institutions or the agencies established by them, from Member States, third countries or International Organisations, classified as 'TRÈS SECRET/TOP SECRET', 'SECRET' or 'CONFIDENTIEL' in accordance with the rules of the institution concerned, which protect essential interests of the European Union or of one or more of its Member States in the areas covered by Article 4(1)(a), notably public security, defence and military matters.

2. Applications for access to sensitive documents under the procedures laid down in Articles 7 and 8 shall be handled only by those persons who have a right to acquaint themselves with those documents. These persons shall also, without prejudice to Article 11(2), assess which references to sensitive documents could be made in the public register.

3. Sensitive documents shall be recorded in the register or released only with the consent of the originator.

4. An institution which decides to refuse access to a sensitive document shall give the reasons for its decision in a manner which does not harm the interests protected in Article 4.

5. Member States shall take appropriate measures to ensure that when handling applications for sensitive documents the principles in this Article and Article 4 are respected.

6. The rules of the institutions concerning sensitive documents shall be made public.

7. The Commission and the Council shall inform the European Parliament regarding sensitive documents in accordance with arrangements agreed between the institutions.

[*Article 10*]

Access following an application

1. The applicant shall have access to documents either by consulting them on the spot or by receiving a copy, including, where available, an electronic copy, according to the applicant's preference. The cost of producing and sending copies may be charged to the applicant. This charge shall not exceed the real cost of producing and sending the copies. Consultation on the spot, copies of less than 20 A4 pages and direct access in electronic form or through the register shall be free of charge.

2. If a document has already been released by the institution concerned and is easily accessible to the applicant, the institution may fulfil its obligation of granting access to documents by informing the applicant how to obtain the requested document.

3. Documents shall be supplied in an existing version and format (including electronically or in an alternative format such as Braille, large print or tape) with full regard to the applicant's preference.

[*Article 11*]

Registers

1. To make citizens' rights under this Regulation effective, each institution shall provide public access to a register of documents. Access to the register should be provided in electronic form. References to documents shall be recorded in the register without delay.

2. For each document the register shall contain a reference number (including, where applicable, the interinstitutional reference), the subject matter and/or a short description of the content of the document and the date on which it was received or drawn up and recorded in the register. References shall be made in a manner which does not undermine protection of the interests in Article 4.

3. The institutions shall immediately take the measures necessary to establish a register which shall be operational by 3 June 2002.

[*Article 12*]

Direct access in electronic form or through a register

1. The institutions shall as far as possible make documents directly accessible to the public in electronic form or through a register in accordance with the rules of the institution concerned.

2. In particular, legislative documents, that is to say, documents drawn up or received in the course of procedures for the adoption of acts which are legally binding in or for the Member States, should, subject to Articles 4 and 9, be made directly accessible.

3. Where possible, other documents, notably documents relating to the development of policy or strategy, should be made directly accessible.

4. Where direct access is not given through the register, the register shall as far as possible indicate where the document is located.

[Article 13]

Publication in the Official Journal

1. In addition to the acts referred to in Article 254(1) and (2) of the EC Treaty and the first paragraph of Article 163 of the Euratom Treaty, the following documents shall, subject to Articles 4 and 9 of this Regulation, be published in the Official Journal:

 (a) Commission proposals;
 (b) common positions adopted by the Council in accordance with the procedures referred to in Articles 251 and 252 of the EC Treaty and the reasons underlying those common positions, as well as the European Parliament's positions in these procedures;
 (c) framework decisions and decisions referred to in Article 34(2) of the EUTreaty;
 (d) conventions established by the Council in accordance with Article 34(2) of the EUTreaty;
 (e) conventions signed between Member States on the basis of Article 293 of the EC Treaty;
 (f) international agreements concluded by the Community or in accordance with Article 24 of the EUTreaty.

2. As far as possible, the following documents shall be published in the Official Journal:

 (a) initiatives presented to the Council by a Member State pursuant to Article 67(1) of the EC Treaty or pursuant to Article 34(2) of the EUTreaty;
 (b) common positions referred to in Article 34(2) of the EU Treaty;
 (c) directives other than those referred to in Article 254(1) and (2) of the EC Treaty, decisions other than those referred to in Article 254(1) of the EC Treaty, recommendations and opinions.

3. Each institution may in its rules of procedure establish which further documents shall be published in the Official Journal.

[Article 14]

Information

1. Each institution shall take the requisite measures to inform the public of the rights they enjoy under this Regulation.

2. The Member States shall cooperate with the institutions in providing information to the citizens.

[Article 15]

Administrative practice in the institutions

1. The institutions shall develop good administrative practices in order to facilitate the exercise of the right of access guaranteed by this Regulation.

2. The institutions shall establish an interinstitutional committee to examine best practice, address possible conflicts and discuss future developments on public access to documents.

[Article 16]

Reproduction of documents

This Regulation shall be without prejudice to any existing rules on copyright which may limit a third party's right to reproduce or exploit released documents.

1020

[*Article 17*]

Reports

1. Each institution shall publish annually a report for the preceding year including the number of cases in which the institution refused to grant access to documents, the reasons for such refusals and the number of sensitive documents not recorded in the register.

2. At the latest by 31 January 2004, the Commission shall publish a report on the implementation of the principles of this Regulation and shall make recommendations, including, if appropriate, proposals for the revision of this Regulation and an action programme of measures to be taken by the institutions.

[*Article 18*]

Application measures

1. Each institution shall adapt its rules of procedure to the provisions of this Regulation. The adaptations shall take effect from 3 December 2001.

2. Within six months of the entry into force of this Regulation, the Commission shall examine the conformity of Council Regulation (EEC, Euratom) No 354/83 of 1 February 1983 concerning the opening to the public of the historical archives of the European Economic Community and the European Atomic Energy Community[6] with this Regulation in order to ensure the preservation and archiving of documents to the fullest extent possible.

3. Within six months of the entry into force of this Regulation, the Commission shall examine the conformity of the existing rules on access to documents with this Regulation.

[*Article 19*]

Entry into force

This Regulation shall enter into force on the third day following that of its publication in the *Official Journal of the European Communities*.

It shall be applicable from 3 December 2001.

This Regulation shall be binding in its entirety and directly applicable in all Member States.

Done at Brussels, 30 May 2001.

For the European Parliament
The President
N. Fontaine

For the Council
The President
B. Lejon

---

[6] OJ L 43, 15.2.1983, p. 1.

APPENDIX I

United States Code

TITLE 5—GOVERNMENT ORGANIZATION AND EMPLOYEES
PART I—THE AGENCIES GENERALLY

CHAPTER 5—ADMINISTRATIVE PROCEDURE
SUBCHAPTER II—ADMINISTRATIVE PROCEDURE

Sec. 552. Public information; agency rules, opinions, orders, records, and proceedings

(a) Each agency shall make available to the public information as follows:

(1) Each agency shall separately state and currently publish in the Federal Register for the guidance of the public—

(A) descriptions of its central and field organization and the established places at which, the employees (and in the case of a uniformed service, the members) from whom, and the methods whereby, the public may obtain information, make submittals or requests, or obtain decisions;

(B) statements of the general course and method by which its functions are channeled and determined, including the nature and requirements of all formal and informal procedures available;

(C) rules of procedure, descriptions of forms available or the places at which forms may be obtained, and instructions as to the scope and contents of all papers, reports, or examinations;

(D) substantive rules of general applicability adopted as authorized by law, and statements of general policy or interpretations of general applicability formulated and adopted by the agency; and

(E) each amendment, revision, or repeal of the foregoing. Except to the extent that a person has actual and timely notice of the terms thereof, a person may not in any manner be required to resort to, or be adversely affected by, a matter required to be published in the Federal Register and not so published. For the purpose of this paragraph, matter reasonably available to the class of persons affected thereby is deemed published in the Federal Register when incorporated by reference therein with the approval of the Director of the Federal Register.

(2) Each agency, in accordance with published rules, shall make available for public inspection and copying—

(A) final opinions, including concurring and dissenting opinions, as well as orders, made in the adjudication of cases;

(B) those statements of policy and interpretations which have been adopted by the agency and are not published in the Federal Register;

(C) administrative staff manuals and instructions to staff that affect a member of the public;

(D) copies of all records, regardless of form or format, which have been released to any person under paragraph (3) and which, because of the nature of their subject matter, the agency determines have become or are likely to become the subject of subsequent requests for substantially the same records; and

(E) a general index of the records referred to under subparagraph (D); unless the materials are promptly published and copies offered for sale. For records created on or after November 1, 1996, within one year after such date, each agency shall make such records available, including by computer telecommunications or, if computer telecommunications means have not been established by the agency, by other electronic means. To the extent required to prevent a clearly unwarranted invasion of personal privacy, an agency may delete identifying details when it makes available or publishes an opinion, statement of policy, interpretation, staff manual, instruction, or copies of records referred to in subparagraph (D). However, in each case the justification for the deletion shall be explained fully in writing, and the extent of such deletion shall be indicated on the portion of the record which is made available or published, unless including that indication would harm an interest protected by the exemption in subsection (b) under which the deletion is made. If technically feasible, the extent of the deletion shall be indicated at the place in the record where the deletion was made. Each agency shall also maintain and make available for public inspection and copying current indexes providing identifying information for the public as to any matter issued, adopted, or promulgated after July 4, 1967, and required by this paragraph to be made available or published. Each agency shall promptly publish, quarterly or more frequently, and distribute (by sale or otherwise) copies of each index or supplements thereto unless it determines by order published in the Federal Register that the publication would be unnecessary and impracticable, in which case the agency shall nonetheless provide copies of such index on request at a cost not to exceed the direct cost of duplication. Each agency shall make the index referred to in subparagraph (E) available by computer telecommunications by December 31, 1999. A final order, opinion, statement of policy, interpretation, or staff manual or instruction that affects a member of the public may be relied on, used, or cited as precedent by an agency against a party other than an agency only if—

(i) it has been indexed and either made available or published as provided by this paragraph; or

(ii) the party has actual and timely notice of the terms thereof.

(3)

(A) Except with respect to the records made available under paragraphs (1) and (2) of this subsection, each agency, upon any request for records which (i) reasonably describes such records and (ii) is made in accordance with published rules stating the time, place, fees (if any), and procedures to be followed, shall make the records promptly available to any person.

(B) In making any record available to a person under this paragraph, an agency shall provide the record in any form or format requested by the person if the record is readily reproducible by the agency in that form or format. Each agency shall make reasonable efforts to maintain its records in forms or formats that are reproducible for purposes of this section.

(C) In responding under this paragraph to a request for records, an agency shall make reasonable efforts to search for the records in electronic form or format, except when such efforts would significantly interfere with the operation of the agency's automated information system.

(D) For purposes of this paragraph, the term 'search' means to review, manually or by automated means, agency records for the purpose of locating those records which are responsive to a request.

(4)

(A)

(i) In order to carry out the provisions of this section, each agency shall promulgate regulations, pursuant to notice and receipt of public comment, specifying the schedule of fees applicable to the processing of requests under this section and establishing procedures and guidelines for determining when such fees should be waived or reduced. Such schedule shall conform to the guidelines which shall be promulgated, pursuant to notice and receipt of public comment, by the Director of the Office of Management and Budget and which shall provide for a uniform schedule of fees for all agencies.

(ii) Such agency regulations shall provide that—

(I) fees shall be limited to reasonable standard charges for document search, duplication, and review, when records are requested for commercial use;

(II) fees shall be limited to reasonable standard charges for document duplication when records are not sought for commercial use and the request is made by an educational or noncommercial scientific institution, whose purpose is scholarly or scientific research; or a representative of the news media; and

(III) for any request not described in (I) or (II), fees shall be limited to reasonable standard charges for document search and duplication.

(iii) Documents shall be furnished without any charge or at a charge reduced below the fees established under clause (ii) if disclosure of the information is in the public interest because it is likely to contribute significantly to public understanding of the operations or activities of the government and is not primarily in the commercial interest of the requester.

(iv) Fee schedules shall provide for the recovery of only the direct costs of search, duplication, or review. Review costs shall include only the direct costs incurred during the initial examination of a document for the purposes of determining whether the documents must be disclosed under this section and for the purposes of withholding any portions exempt from disclosure under this section. Review costs may not include any costs incurred in resolving issues of law or policy that may be raised in the course of processing a request under this section. No fee may be charged by any agency under this section—

(I) if the costs of routine collection and processing of the fee are likely to equal or exceed the amount of the fee; or

(II) for any request described in clause (ii) (II) or (III) of this subparagraph for the first two hours of search time or for the first one hundred pages of duplication.

(v) No agency may require advance payment of any fee unless the requester has previously failed to pay fees in a timely fashion, or the agency has determined that the fee will exceed $250.

(vi) Nothing in this subparagraph shall supersede fees chargeable under a statute specifically providing for setting the level of fees for particular types of records.

(vii) In any action by a requester regarding the waiver of fees under this section, the court shall determine the matter de novo: Provided, That the court's review of the matter shall be limited to the record before the agency.

(B) On complaint, the district court of the United States in the district in which the complainant resides, or has his principal place of business, or in which the agency records are situated, or in the District of Columbia, has jurisdiction to enjoin the agency from withholding agency records and to order the production of any agency records improperly withheld from the complainant. In such a case the court shall determine the matter de novo, and may examine the contents of such agency records in camera to determine whether such records or any part thereof shall be withheld under any of the exemptions set forth in subsection (b) of this section, and the burden is on the agency to sustain its action. In addition to any other matters to which a court accords substantial weight, a court shall accord substantial weight to an affidavit of an agency concerning the agency's determination as to technical feasibility under paragraph (2)(C) and subsection (b) and reproducibility under paragraph (3)(B).

(C) Notwithstanding any other provision of law, the defendant shall serve an answer or otherwise plead to any complaint made under this subsection within thirty days after service upon the defendant of the pleading in which such complaint is made, unless the court otherwise directs for good cause shown.

(D) Repealed. Pub. L. 98-620, title IV, Sec. 402(2), Nov. 8, 1984, 98 Stat. 3357.)

(E) The court may assess against the United States reasonable attorney fees and other litigation costs reasonably incurred in any case under this section in which the complainant has substantially prevailed.

(F) Whenever the court orders the production of any agency records improperly withheld from the complainant and assesses against the United States reasonable attorney fees and other litigation costs, and the court additionally issues a written finding that the circumstances surrounding the withholding raise questions whether agency personnel acted arbitrarily or capriciously with respect to the withholding, the Special Counsel shall promptly initiate a proceeding to determine whether disciplinary action is warranted against the officer or employee who was primarily responsible for the withholding. The Special Counsel, after investigation and consideration of the evidence submitted, shall submit his findings and recommendations to the administrative authority of the agency concerned and shall send copies of the findings and recommendations to the officer or employee or his representative. The administrative authority shall take the corrective action that the Special Counsel recommends.

(G) In the event of noncompliance with the order of the court, the district court may punish for contempt the responsible employee, and in the case of a uniformed service, the responsible member.

(5) Each agency having more than one member shall maintain and make available for public inspection a record of the final votes of each member in every agency proceeding.

(6)

(A) Each agency, upon any request for records made under paragraph (1), (2), or (3) of this subsection, shall—

(i) determine within 20 days (excepting Saturdays, Sundays, and legal public holidays) after the receipt of any such request whether to comply with such request and shall immediately notify the person making such request of such determination and the reasons therefor, and of the right of such person to appeal to the head of the agency any adverse determination; and

(ii) make a determination with respect to any appeal within twenty days (excepting Saturdays, Sundays, and legal public holidays) after the receipt of such appeal. If on appeal the denial of the request for records is in whole or in part upheld, the agency shall notify the person making such request of the provisions for judicial review of that determination under paragraph (4) of this subsection.

(B)

(i) In unusual circumstances as specified in this subparagraph, the time limits prescribed in either clause (i) or clause (ii) of subparagraph (A) may be extended by written notice to the person making such request setting forth the unusual circumstances for such extension and the date on which a determination is expected to be dispatched. No such notice shall specify a date that would result in an extension for more than ten working days, except as provided in clause (ii) of this subparagraph.

(ii) With respect to a request for which a written notice under clause (i) extends the time limits prescribed under clause (i) of subparagraph (A), the agency shall notify the person making the request if the request cannot be processed within the time limit specified in that clause and shall provide the person an opportunity to limit the scope of the request so that it may be processed within that time limit or an opportunity to arrange with the agency an alternative time frame for processing the request or a modified request. Refusal by the person to reasonably modify the request or arrange such an alternative time frame shall be considered as a factor in determining whether exceptional circumstances exist for purposes of subparagraph (C).

(iii) As used in this subparagraph, 'unusual circumstances' means, but only to the extent reasonably necessary to the proper processing of the particular requests—

(I) the need to search for and collect the requested records from field facilities or other establishments that are separate from the office processing the request;

(II) the need to search for, collect, and appropriately examine a voluminous amount of separate and distinct records which are demanded in a single request; or

(III) the need for consultation, which shall be conducted with all practicable speed, with another agency having a substantial interest in the determination of the request or among two or more components of the agency having substantial subject-matter interest therein.

(iv) Each agency may promulgate regulations, pursuant to notice and receipt of public comment, providing for the aggregation of certain requests by the same requestor, or by a group of requestors acting in concert, if the agency reasonably believes that such requests actually constitute a single request, which would otherwise satisfy the unusual circumstances specified in this subparagraph, and the requests involve clearly related matters. Multiple requests involving unrelated matters shall not be aggregated.

(C)

(i) Any person making a request to any agency for records under paragraph (1), (2), or (3) of this subsection shall be deemed to have exhausted his administrative remedies with respect to such request if the agency fails to comply with the applicable time limit provisions of this paragraph. If the Government can show exceptional circumstances exist and that the agency is exercising due diligence in responding to the request, the court may retain jurisdiction and allow the agency additional time to complete its review of the records. Upon any determination by an agency to comply with a request for records, the records shall be made promptly available to such person making such request. Any notification of denial of any request for records under this subsection shall set forth the names and titles or positions of each person responsible for the denial of such request.

(ii) For purposes of this subparagraph, the term 'exceptional circumstances' does not include a delay that results from a predictable agency workload of requests under this section, unless the agency demonstrates reasonable progress in reducing its backlog of pending requests.

(iii) Refusal by a person to reasonably modify the scope of a request or arrange an alternative time frame for processing a request (or a modified request) under clause (ii) after being given an opportunity to do so by the agency to whom the person made the request shall be considered as a factor in determining whether exceptional circumstances exist for purposes of this subparagraph.

(D)

(i) Each agency may promulgate regulations, pursuant to notice and receipt of public comment, providing for multitrack processing of requests for records based on the amount of work or time (or both) involved in processing requests.

(ii) Regulations under this subparagraph may provide a person making a request that does not qualify for the fastest multitrack processing an opportunity to limit the scope of the request in order to qualify for faster processing.

(iii) This subparagraph shall not be considered to affect the requirement under subparagraph (C) to exercise due diligence.

(E)

(i) Each agency shall promulgate regulations, pursuant to notice and receipt of public comment, providing for expedited processing of requests for records—

(I) in cases in which the person requesting the records demonstrates a compelling need; and

(II) in other cases determined by the agency.

(ii) Notwithstanding clause (i), regulations under this subparagraph must ensure—

(I) that a determination of whether to provide expedited processing shall be made, and notice of the determination shall be provided to the person making the request, within 10 days after the date of the request; and

(II) expeditious consideration of administrative appeals of such determinations of whether to provide expedited processing.

(iii) An agency shall process as soon as practicable any request for records to which the agency has granted expedited processing under this subparagraph. Agency action to deny or affirm denial of a request for expedited processing pursuant to this subparagraph, and failure by an agency to respond in a timely manner to such a request shall be subject to judicial review under paragraph (4), except that the judicial review shall be based on the record before the agency at the time of the determination.

(iv) A district court of the United States shall not have jurisdiction to review an agency denial of expedited processing of a request for records after the agency has provided a complete response to the request.

(v) For purposes of this subparagraph, the term 'compelling need' means—

(I) that a failure to obtain requested records on an expedited basis under this paragraph could reasonably be expected to pose an imminent threat to the life or physical safety of an individual; or

(II) with respect to a request made by a person primarily engaged in disseminating information, urgency to inform the public concerning actual or alleged Federal Government activity.

(vi) A demonstration of a compelling need by a person making a request for expedited processing shall be made by a statement certified by such person to be true and correct to the best of such person's knowledge and belief.

(F) In denying a request for records, in whole or in part, an agency shall make a reasonable effort to estimate the volume of any requested matter the provision of which is denied, and shall provide any such estimate to the person making the request, unless providing such estimate would harm an interest protected by the exemption in subsection (b) pursuant to which the denial is made.

(b) This section does not apply to matters that are—

(1)

(A) specifically authorized under criteria established by an Executive order to be kept secret in the interest of national defense or foreign policy and (B) are in fact properly classified pursuant to such Executive order;

(2) related solely to the internal personnel rules and practices of an agency;

(3) specifically exempted from disclosure by statute (other than section 552b of this title), provided that such statute (A) requires that the matters be withheld from the public in such a manner as to leave no discretion on the issue, or (B) establishes particular criteria for withholding or refers to particular types of matters to be withheld;

(4) trade secrets and commercial or financial information obtained from a person and privileged or confidential;

(5) inter-agency or intra-agency memorandums or letters which would not be available by law to a party other than an agency in litigation with the agency;

(6) personnel and medical files and similar files the disclosure of which would constitute a clearly unwarranted invasion of personal privacy;

(7) records or information compiled for law enforcement purposes, but only to the extent that the production of such law enforcement records or information (A) could reasonably be expected to interfere with enforcement proceedings, (B) would deprive a person of a right to a fair trial or an impartial adjudication, (C) could reasonably be expected to constitute an unwarranted invasion of personal privacy, (D) could reasonably be expected to disclose the identity of a confidential source, including a State, local, or foreign agency or authority or any private institution which furnished information on a confidential basis, and, in the case of a record or information compiled by criminal law enforcement authority in the course of a criminal investigation or by an agency conducting a lawful national security intelligence investigation, information furnished by a confidential source, (E) would disclose techniques and procedures for law enforcement investigations or prosecutions, or would disclose guidelines for law enforcement investigations or prosecutions if such disclosure could reasonably be expected to risk circumvention of the law, or (F) could reasonably be expected to endanger the life or physical safety of any individual;

(8) contained in or related to examination, operating, or condition reports prepared by, on behalf of, or for the use of an agency responsible for the regulation or supervision of financial institutions; or

(9) geological and geophysical information and data, including maps, concerning wells. Any reasonably segregable portion of a record shall be provided to any person requesting such record after

deletion of the portions which are exempt under this subsection. The amount of information deleted shall be indicated on the released portion of the record, unless including that indication would harm an interest protected by the exemption in this subsection under which the deletion is made. If technically feasible, the amount of the information deleted shall be indicated at the place in the record where such deletion is made.

(c)

(1) Whenever a request is made which involves access to records described in subsection (b)(7)(A) and—

(A) the investigation or proceeding involves a possible violation of criminal law; and

(B) there is reason to believe that (i) the subject of the investigation or proceeding is not aware of its pendency, and (ii) disclosure of the existence of the records could reasonably be expected to interfere with enforcement proceedings, the agency may, during only such time as that circumstance continues, treat the records as not subject to the requirements of this section.

(2) Whenever informant records maintained by a criminal law enforcement agency under an informant's name or personal identifier are requested by a third party according to the informant's name or personal identifier, the agency may treat the records as not subject to the requirements of this section unless the informant's status as an informant has been officially confirmed.

(3) Whenever a request is made which involves access to records maintained by the Federal Bureau of Investigation pertaining to foreign intelligence or counterintelligence, or international terrorism, and the existence of the records is classified information as provided in subsection (b)(1), the Bureau may, as long as the existence of the records remains classified information, treat the records as not subject to the requirements of this section.

(d) This section does not authorize withholding of information or limit the availability of records to the public, except as specifically stated in this section. This section is not authority to withhold information from Congress.

(e)

(1) On or before February 1 of each year, each agency shall submit to the Attorney General of the United States a report which shall cover the preceding fiscal year and which shall include—

(A) the number of determinations made by the agency not to comply with requests for records made to such agency under subsection (a) and the reasons for each such determination;

(B)

(i) the number of appeals made by persons under subsection (a)(6), the result of such appeals, and the reason for the action upon each appeal that results in a denial of information; and

(ii) a complete list of all statutes that the agency relies upon to authorize the agency to withhold information under subsection (b)(3), a description of whether a court has upheld the decision of the agency to withhold information under each such statute, and a concise description of the scope of any information withheld;

(C) the number of requests for records pending before the agency as of September 30 of the preceding year, and the median number of days that such requests had been pending before the agency as of that date;

(D) the number of requests for records received by the agency and the number of requests which the agency processed;

(E) the median number of days taken by the agency to process different types of requests;

(F) the total amount of fees collected by the agency for processing requests; and

(G) the number of full-time staff of the agency devoted to processing requests for records under this section, and the total amount expended by the agency for processing such requests.

(2) Each agency shall make each such report available to the public including by computer telecommunications, or if computer telecommunications means have not been established by the agency, by other electronic means.

(3) The Attorney General of the United States shall make each report which has been made available by electronic means available at a single electronic access point. The Attorney General of the United States shall notify the Chairman and ranking minority member of the Committee on Government Reform and Oversight of the House of Representatives and the Chairman and ranking minority member of the Committees on Governmental Affairs and the Judiciary of the Senate, no later than April 1 of the year in which each such report is issued, that such reports are available by electronic means.

(4) The Attorney General of the United States, in consultation with the Director of the Office of Management and Budget, shall develop reporting and performance guidelines in connection with reports required by this subsection by October 1, 1997, and may establish additional requirements for such reports as the Attorney General determines may be useful.

(5) The Attorney General of the United States shall submit an annual report on or before April 1 of each calendar year which shall include for the prior calendar year a listing of the number of cases arising under this section, the exemption involved in each case, the disposition of such case, and the cost, fees, and penalties assessed under subparagraphs (E), (F), and (G) of subsection (a)(4). Such report shall also include a description of the efforts undertaken by the Department of Justice to encourage agency compliance with this section.

(f) For purposes of this section, the term—

(1) 'agency' as defined in section 551(1) of this title includes any executive department, military department, Government corporation, Government controlled corporation, or other establishment in the executive branch of the Government (including the Executive Office of the President), or any independent regulatory agency; and

(2) 'record' and any other term used in this section in reference to information includes any information that would be an agency record subject to the requirements of this section when maintained by an agency in any format, including an electronic format.

(g) The head of each agency shall prepare and make publicly available upon request, reference material or a guide for requesting records or information from the agency, subject to the exemptions in subsection (b), including—

(1) an index of all major information systems of the agency;

(2) a description of major information and record locator systems maintained by the agency; and

(3) a handbook for obtaining various types and categories of public information from the agency pursuant to chapter 35 of title 44, and under this section.

APPENDIX J

[year] No.

Freedom of Information

THE FREEDOM OF INFORMATION (FEES AND APPROPRIATE LIMIT)
REGULATIONS [YEAR]

Made	*[date]*
Laid before Parliament	*[date]*
Coming into force	*[date]*

The Lord Chancellor[1], in exercise of the powers conferred on him by sections 9(3) and (4), 12(3), (4) and (5) and 13(1) and (2) of the Freedom of Information Act 2000[2], hereby makes the following Regulations:

Citation and commencement

1. These Regulations may be cited as the Freedom of Information (Fees and Appropriate Limit) Regulations 2000 and shall come into force on [*date*].

Interpretation

2. —(1) In these Regulations—

'the Act' means the Freedom of Information Act 2000;

'disbursements', in relation to any request for information, means any costs directly and reasonably incurred by a public authority in informing the applicant whether it holds information of the description specified in the request and in communicating any such information to him; and any reference to disbursements includes a reference to such disbursements as the public authority reasonably estimates would be incurred in relation to the request;

'prescribed costs', in relation to any request for information, means any costs reasonably incurred by a public authority in determining whether it holds information of the description specified in the request, in locating and retrieving any such information and in giving effect to any preference expressed by the applicant as to the means of communication of such information, including the cost of associated staff time, but does not include the cost of staff time incurred in determining whether the public authority is obliged to comply with the request for information; and any reference to prescribed costs includes a reference to such costs as the public authority reasonably estimates would be incurred in relation to the request.

---

[1] The powers conferred on the Secretary of State under the Freedom of Information Act 2000 (c. 36) were transferred to the Lord Chancellor by the Transfer of Functions (Miscellaneous) Order 2001 (S.I. 2001/) which came into force on [*date*].

[2] (b) 2000 c. 36.

(2) References in these Regulations to sections are references to sections of the Act.

Calculation of fee

3. The costs to be taken into account by a public authority when determining any fee to be charged under section 9(1) or 13(1) are—

(a) the prescribed costs; and
(b) the disbursements;

that would be incurred by the public authority in complying with the request for information to which the fee relates.

Maximum fee

4. The fee which may be charged by a public authority under section 9(1) shall not exceed the sum of—

(a) 10% of the prescribed costs; and
(b) the disbursements;

referred to in regulation 3 above.

5. The fee which may be charged by a public authority under section 13(1) shall not exceed the sum of—

(a) 10% of the prescribed costs, for the first £550 of such costs; and
(b) the prescribed costs, for such costs over £550; and
(c) the disbursements;

referred to in regulation 3 above.

Appropriate limit

6.—(1) The appropriate limit for the purposes of section 12(1) and (2) shall be £550.

(2) The costs to be taken into account by a public authority when estimating the cost of complying with a request for information for the purposes of section 12(1) or (2) are the prescribed costs that it would incur in complying with the request.

Aggregation of costs

7. The circumstances prescribed for the purposes of section 12(4) are that—

(a) the two or more requests referred to in that section are for information which is on the same subject matter or is otherwise related;

(b) the last of the requests is received by the public authority before the twentieth working day following the date of receipt of the first of the requests; and

(c) it appears to the public authority that the requests have been made in an attempt to ensure that the prescribed costs of complying separately with each request would not exceed the appropriate limit.

Signed by the authority of the Lord Chancellor

Parliamentary Secretary
Lord Chancellor's Department

[*date*]

Explanatory Note

(This note is not part of the Regulations)

These Regulations prescribe a number of matters in relation to the fees which may be charged by public authorities before complying with a request for information under the Freedom of Information Act 2000 ('the Act').

Regulation 4 prescribes the maximum fee which may be charged for complying with a request for information under section 1(1) of the Act. Regulation 5 prescribes the maximum fee which may be charged for the communication of information where such communication is not required by virtue of section 12(1) of the Act because the estimated cost of complying with the request would exceed the appropriate limit.

Regulation 6 sets the appropriate limit for the purposes of section 12 of the Act at £550. Regulation 7 prescribes the circumstances in which, under section 12(4) of the Act, the estimated cost of complying with separate requests for information can be aggregated for the purpose of determining whether the estimated cost of complying with any of the requests would exceed the appropriate limit.

APPENDIX K

DRAFT REGULATIONS AS AT 1 JULY 2002: SUBJECT TO PUBLIC CONSULTATION

Draft Regulations laid before Parliament under paragraph 2(2) of Schedule 2 to the European Communities Act 1972 and section 82(2) of the Freedom of Information Act 2000, for approval by resolution of each House of Parliament.

DRAFT STATUTORY INSTRUMENTS

2002 No.
Freedom of Information

THE ENVIRONMENTAL INFORMATION REGULATIONS 2002

Made	*[ ] 2002*
Coming into force	*[ ] 2002*

Whereas a draft of these Regulations has been approved by resolution of each House of Parliament in pursuance of paragraph 2(2) of Schedule 2 to the European Communities Act 1972[1] and section 82(2) of the Freedom of Information Act 2000[2];

Now, therefore, the Secretary of State, being a Minister designated[3] for the purposes of subsection (2) of section 2 of the European Communities Act in relation to freedom of access to, and the dissemination of, information on the environment held by public authorities or bodies with public responsibilities for the environment and which are under the control of a public authority, in exercise of the powers conferred on her by that subsection and by section 74(3) of the Freedom of Information Act 2000, makes the following Regulations:

Citation and commencement

1. These Regulations may be cited as the Environmental Information Regulations 2002 and shall come into force on [ ].

Interpretation

2. In these Regulations—
'the 2000 Act' means the Freedom of Information Act 2000;
'applicant' means any natural or legal person requesting environmental information;
['appropriate record authority' has the same meaning as under section 15(5) of the 2000 Act;]
'the code of practice' means the code of practice issued from time to time by the Secretary of State in accordance with regulation 11 below;
'the Commissioner' means the Information Commissioner, whose office was reconstituted by section 18(1) of the 2000 Act;

---

[1] 1972 c.68.
[2] 2000 c. 36.
[3] S.I.1992/1711.

'environmental information' means information on any of the following.

(a) the state of the elements of the environment, such as—

    (i) air and atmosphere,

    (ii) water,

    (iii) soil,

    (iv) land,

    (v) landscape and natural sites, including wetlands, coastal and marine areas, and

    (vi) biological diversity and its components, including genetically modified organisms;

(b) the interaction between the elements listed in sub-paragraph (a);

(c) factors, such as substances, energy, noise, radiation or waste affecting, or likely to affect, anything mentioned in sub-paragraphs (a) and (b);

(d) emissions, discharges and other releases into the environment;

(e) measures, such as policies, legislation, plans, programmes and environmental agreements, and activities affecting or likely to affect, or intended to protect, anything mentioned in sub-paragraphs (a) and (b);

(f) cost-benefit and other economic analyses and assumptions used in environmental decision-making;

(g) the state of human health and safety, conditions of human life, cultural sites and built structures in as much as they are or may be affected by or through anything mentioned in sub-paragraphs (a) and (b);

'information' (subject to paragraph 2(8) of the Schedule to these Regulations) includes anything contained in any records in whatever form;

'information held for a public authority' means environmental information which is physically held by a natural or legal person on behalf of a public authority;

'measures' includes administrative measures;

'public authority' means—

(a) any Minister of the Crown, government department or local authority;

(b) any other person that is, from time to time, a 'public authority' within the meaning of section 3(1) of the 2000 Act;

(c) any other person carrying out functions of public administration in relation to the environment pursuant to any enactment; and

(d) any person with public responsibilities or functions of public administration in relation to the environment which does not fall within sub-paragraphs (a) and (b) above but is under the control of a person falling within those sub-paragraphs;

['records' includes—

(a) any record created, received or maintained.

    (i) as evidence;

    (ii) in pursuance of a legal obligation;

    (iii) in the furtherance of the functions of a public authority; or

    (iv) in the transaction of business by or with a public authority; and

(b) registers, reports and returns and any other written records whatsoever;

(c) computer records and records in any other electronic form whatsoever; and

(d) records kept otherwise than in a document.]

['responsible authority' has the same meaning as under section 15(5) of the 2000 Act;]

'statutory provision' means any provision made by or under any enactment other than the 2000 Act; ['transferred public record' has the same meaning as under section 15(4) of the 2000 Act;] and 'the Tribunal' means the Information Tribunal, as reconstituted by section 18(2) of the 2000 Act.

Application

3. These Regulations shall not apply—

   (a) to any of the following bodies—

      (i) the Scottish Parliament,
      (ii) any part of the Scottish Administration,
      (iii) the Scottish Parliamentary Corporate Body, or
      (iv) any Scottish public authority with mixed functions or no reserved functions (within the meaning of the Scotland Act 1998[4]); or

   (b) to any public authority acting in a judicial or legislative capacity.

Obligation to make environmental information available on request

4.—(1) Subject to the following provisions of these Regulations, a public authority that holds any environmental information shall make that information available to every person who requests it.

(2) It shall be the duty of every public authority that holds environmental information to make such arrangements for giving effect to paragraph (1) above are necessary to ensure that the requirements of paragraphs (3) to (15) below are met.

(3) Information shall be made available in the form or format requested unless—

   (a) it is reasonable for the public authority to make the information available in another form or format; or

   (b) the information is already publicly available and easily accessible in another form or format.

(4) A request shall be complied with or refused.

   (a) as soon as possible; and

   (b) subject to paragraphs (6) and (7) below, in any event not later than the twentieth working day after the date on which the request is received, unless.

      (i) the complexity of the information requested makes it impracticable for a response to be given within that period, in which case the request may be complied with or refused within the period of the two months beginning with the day on which the request is received; or

      (ii) the volume of the information requested makes it impracticable for the request to be complied with within that period, in which case the request may be complied with within the period of the two months beginning with the day on which the request is received.

(5) Where the period within which a request is to be complied with or refused is extended in accordance with paragraph (4)(b)(i) or (4)(b)(ii) above, the applicant shall be informed of the delay and the justification for it.

(6) Where a request is transferred from one public authority to another in accordance with paragraph (11) below, the period within which the request is to be complied with by the authority to which the request is transferred shall begin with the day on which the request is received by the authority to which the request is transferred.

---

[4] 1998 c.46.

(7) Where a public authority asks an applicant to specify a request in accordance with regulation 6(2) below, the period within which the request is to be complied with by the authority shall be treated as beginning with the day on which the specified request is received by the authority.

(8) Where the response to a request contains a refusal to make information available, the refusal shall—

    (a) be in writing; and

    (b) specify the reasons for the refusal, including.

        (i) the exception relied upon;

        (ii) if it would not otherwise be apparent, the basis on which the exception applies; and

        (iii) if the exception relied upon is one of those listed in regulation 7(3), 7(4) or 7(5) below, the reasons for claiming that, in all the circumstances, the public interest in maintaining the exception outweighs the public interest in disclosing the information.

(9) Where the response to a request contains a refusal to make information available in the form or format requested, the refusal shall—

    (a) be in writing; and

    (b) specify the reasons for the refusal.

(10) Where the response to a request contains a refusal to make information available or to make information available in the form or format requested, the applicant shall be given—

    (a) particulars of the procedure provided by the public authority pursuant to regulation 8 below;

    (b) where the request was made on or after [*to be determined*], particulars of the rights conferred by regulation 9 below and by the Schedule to these Regulations; and

    (c) information on the possibility of making a legal challenge to the refusal;

(11) Subject to paragraph (12) below, where a public authority refuses a request under regulation 7(1)(a) below and, at the time when the refusal is made, that authority believes that the environmental information requested may be held by or for another public authority, it shall as soon as possible—

        (i) inform the applicant which authority may hold that information; or

        (ii) transfer the request to that other authority and inform the applicant accordingly.

(12) Paragraph (11) above shall not apply where the applicant has indicated in his request that it is not to be transferred to another public authority.

(13) The obligation of a public authority to make environmental information available in pursuance of paragraph (1) above—

    (a) is only to make that information available at such times and places as may be reasonable; and

    (b) is, in particular, a duty owed to the applicant.

(14) Public authorities shall make all reasonable efforts to maintain environmental information held by or for them in forms or formats that are readily reproducible and accessible by computer telecommunications or by other electronic means.

(15) Subject to the remaining provisions of these Regulations, where any statutory provision or rule of law imposes any restriction or prohibition on the disclosure of information by any person, that restriction or prohibition shall not apply to any disclosure of information in pursuance of these Regulations.

Charging

5. The arrangements made by a public authority for giving effect to regulation 4(1) above may.

    (a) include provision for the imposition of a charge on any person in respect of the costs reasonably attributable to the supply of information to that person in pursuance of that paragraph; and

(b) make the supply of any information in pursuance of that paragraph conditional on the payment of such a charge,

provided that the public authority makes available to all persons requesting environmental information a schedule of the charges that may be levied which indicates when charges may be levied and when the supply of information will be conditional on the payment of a charge.

Duty to provide advice and assistance

6.—(1) Subject to paragraphs (2) and (3) below, it shall be the duty of a public authority to provide advice and assistance, so far as it would be reasonable to expect the authority to do so, to persons who propose to make or have made requests for information to it.

(2) Without prejudice to regulation 7(2) below, if a request is formulated in too general a manner, the public authority shall, as soon as possible and in any event not later than 20 working days after the request is made, ask the applicant to specify the request and shall assist the applicant in doing so.

(3) To the extent that a public authority conforms to the code of practice in relation to the provision of advice or assistance in a particular case, it shall be taken to have complied with the duty imposed by paragraphs (1) and (2) above.

Exceptions to right to environmental information

7.—(1) A public authority may refuse a request for environmental information where.
    (a) it does not hold the information; or
    (b) the request is manifestly unreasonable.

(2) A public authority may refuse a request for environmental information where.

    (a) the request is formulated in too general a manner; and
    (b) it is appropriate to do so in all of the circumstances.

(3) A public authority may refuse a request for environmental information where granting the request would involve—

    (a) either—
        (i) the disclosure of internal communication within a public authority; or
        (ii) the supply of a document or other record which is still in the course of completion; and
    (b) in all the circumstances of the case, the public interest in refusing the request outweighs the public interest in disclosing the information.

(4) A public authority may refuse a request for environmental information where.

    (a) the disclosure of the information would adversely affect.

        (i) the confidentiality of the deliberations of any public authority;
        (ii) international relations, national defence or public security;
        (iii) the course of justice, the ability of a person to receive a fair trial or the ability of a public authority to conduct an enquiry of a criminal or disciplinary nature;
        (iv) intellectual property rights;
        (v) the confidentiality of personal information contained in records held in relation to an individual who has not given his consent to its disclosure;
        (vi) the interests of the person who provided the information where that person.
            (aa) was not under, and could not have been put under, any legal obligation to supply it to the public authority;
            (bb) did not supply it in circumstances such that the public authority is entitled apart from these Regulations to disclose it; and
            (cc) has not consented to its disclosure; or
        (vii) the environment to which the information relates; and

(b) in all the circumstances of the case (including whether or not the information requested relates to emissions, discharges and other releases into the environment), the public interest in refusing the request outweighs the public interest in disclosing the information.

(5) A public authority may refuse a request for environmental information (except to the extent to which it is a request for information on emissions, discharges and other releases into the environment which is relevant for the protection of the environment) where—

(a) the disclosure of the information would adversely affect the confidentiality of matters to which any commercial or industrial confidentiality attaches to protect a legitimate economic interest; and

(b) in all the circumstances of the case, the public interest in refusing the request outweighs the public interest in disclosing the information.

(6) [For the purposes of paragraphs (4)(b) and (5)(b) above, there shall be a presumption (capable of being rebutted in the circumstances of a particular case) that the public interest in disclosing information outweighs the public interest in refusing a request.]

(7) Where any environmental information held by an appropriate record authority is environmental information the disclosure of which would adversely affect any of the factors listed in paragraph (3), (4) or (5) above, any question as to whether the public interest in refusing the request outweighs the public interest in disclosing the information is to be determined by the responsible authority in consultation with the appropriate record authority.

(8) Nothing in this regulation shall authorise a refusal to make available any environmental information contained in the same record as, or otherwise held with, other information which is withheld by virtue of this regulation unless it is incapable of being separated from the other information for the purpose of making it available.

Reconsideration by public authorities

8.—(1) Where it appears to a person who has requested a public authority for information that the authority has not complied with the requirements of these Regulations, that person may make representations to that effect to the authority, provided that he does so within two months beginning with the date on which the alleged failure to comply with the requirements of these Regulations occurred.

(2) It shall be the duty of the public authority to whom the representations are made in accordance with paragraph (1) above—

(a) to consider them and any supporting evidence which the person making them provides;
(b) to take a decision as to whether it accepts it has not complied with the requirements of these Regulations; and
(c) to serve on the person notice of that decision within a period of two months beginning with the day on which the representations are received by the authority.

(3) Where representations are made in accordance with paragraph (1) above and the public authority concerned accepts it has not complied with the requirements of these Regulations, it shall remedy the breach immediately.

Enforcement provisions

9. The provisions of the Schedule to these Regulations shall apply where.

(a) a person has requested a public authority for information and has made representations in accordance with regulation 8 above in relation to that request;
(b) the request for information was made on or after [*to be determined*];
(c) it appears to the person who requested the information that the public authority concerned either—

(i) did not accept, within the period specified in regulation 8(3)(c) above, that it has not complied with the requirements of these Regulations, or

(ii) failed to remedy the breach within a reasonable period.

Proactive dissemination

10.—(1) Subject to paragraph (2) below, public authorities shall make all reasonable efforts to organise the environmental information which is relevant to their functions and which is held by or for them, with a view to its active and systematic dissemination to the public, in particular by means of computer telecommunication or electronic technology (or by both means).

(2) Paragraph (1) above shall not apply to information collected before the date on which these Regulations come into force unless the information is already available in electronic form.

(3) The information to be made available and disseminated shall be updated as appropriate and shall include—

(a) texts of international treaties, conventions or agreements, and of Community, national, regional or local legislation, on the environment or relating to it;

(b) policies, plans and programmes relating to the environment;

(c) progress reports on the implementation of the items referred to in (a) and (b) when prepared by public authorities;

(d) reports on the state of the environment;

(e) data or summaries of data derived from the monitoring of activities affecting, or likely to affect, the environment.

Issue of a code of practice by the Secretary of State

11.—(1) The Secretary of State shall issue, and may from time to time revise, a code of practice providing guidance to public authorities as to the practice which it would, in his opinion, be desirable for them to follow in connection with the discharge of the authorities. functions under these Regulations.

(2) The code may make different provision for different public authorities.

(3) Before issuing or revising any code under this section, the Secretary of State shall consult the Commissioner.

(4) The Secretary of State shall lay before each House of Parliament any code or revised code issued under this regulation.

Functions of the Commissioner: promotion of good practice

12.—(1) It shall be the duty of the Commissioner to promote the following of good practice by public authorities and, in particular, so to perform his functions under these Regulations as to promote the observance by public authorities of—

(a) the requirements of these Regulations, and

(b) the provisions of the code of practice.

(2) The Commissioner shall arrange for the dissemination in such form and manner as he considers appropriate of such information as it may appear to him expedient to give to the public—

(a) about the operation of these Regulations,

(b) about good practice, and

(c) about other matters within the scope of his functions under Regulations,

(d) and may give advice to any person as to any of those matters.

(3) The Commissioner may, with the consent of any public authority, assess whether that authority is following good practice.

(4) The Commissioner may charge such sums as he may with the consent of the Lord Chancellor determine for any services provided by the Commissioner under this regulation.

(5) For the purposes of this regulation, .good practice., in relation to a public authority, means such practice in the discharge of its functions under these Regulations as appears to the Commissioner to be desirable and includes (but is not limited to) compliance with the requirements of these Regulations and the provisions of the code of practice.

Functions of the Commissioner: enforcement

13.—(1) If it appears to the Commissioner that the practice of a public authority in relation to the exercise of its functions under these Regulations does not conform with that proposed in the code of practice, he may give to the authority a recommendation (referred to in this regulation as a 'practice recommendation') specifying the steps which ought in his opinion to be taken for promoting such conformity.

(2) A practice recommendation must be given in writing and must refer to the particular provisions of the code of practice with which, in the Commissioner's opinion, the public authority's practice does not conform.

(3) The provisions of the Schedule to these Regulations shall apply in relation to the Commissioner's enforcement functions under these Regulations.

Functions of the Commissioner: reports to Parliament

14.—(1) The Commissioner shall lay annually before each House of Parliament a general report on the exercise of his functions under these Regulations.

(2) The Commissioner may from time to time lay before each House of Parliament such other reports with respect to those functions as he thinks fit.

Offences

15.—(1) A person is guilty of an offence if he —

  (a) intentionally obstructs a person in the execution of a warrant issued under Part III of the Schedule to these Regulations, or
  (b) fails without reasonable excuse to give any person executing such a warrant such assistance as he may reasonably require for the execution of the warrant.

(2) A person guilty of an offence under paragraph (1) above is liable on summary conviction to a fine not exceeding level 5 on the standard scale.

(3) No proceedings for an offence under paragraph (1) above shall be instituted—

  (a) in England or Wales, except by the Commissioner or by or with the consent of the Director of Public Prosecutions;
  (b) in Northern Ireland, except by the Commissioner or by or with the consent of the Director of Public Prosecutions for Northern Ireland.

Amendments to the Freedom of Information Act 2000

16.—(1) The 2000 Act shall be amended in accordance with the following paragraph.

(2) In section 77(2) of the 2000 Act (offence of altering etc records with intent to prevent disclosure)—

  (a) immediately after the words 'section 1 of this Act', there shall be inserted a comma and the words 'the Environmental Information Regulations 2002', and
  (b) immediately after the word 'fee', there shall be inserted the words 'or charge'.

Revocation of Regulations

17. The Environmental Information Regulations 1992[5], the Environmental Information (Amendment) Regulations 1998[6], the Environmental Information Regulations (Northern Ireland) 1993[7] and the Environmental Information (Amendment) Regulations (Northern Ireland)[8] are revoked.

One of Her Majesty's Principal Secretaries of State
Department for Environment, Food and Rural Affairs

[*Date*]

SCHEDULE
ENFORCEMENT PROVISIONS

PART I
POWERS OF THE COMMISSIONER

Application for decision by Commissioner

1.—(1) Any person (referred to in this Schedule as 'the complainant') may apply to the Commissioner for a decision whether, in any specified respect, a request for information made by the complainant to a public authority has been dealt with in accordance with the requirements of these Regulations.

(2) On receiving an application under this section, the Commissioner shall make a decision unless it appears to him—

    (a) that the complainant has not exhausted any complaints procedure which is provided by the public authority in conformity with the code of practice,

    (b) that there has been undue delay in making the application,

    (c) that the application is frivolous or vexatious, or

    (d) that the application has been withdrawn or abandoned.

(3) Where the Commissioner has received an application under this paragraph, he shall either.

    (a) notify the complainant that he has not made any decision under this paragraph as a result of the application and of his grounds for not doing so, or

    (b) serve notice of his decision (referred to in this Schedule as a 'decision notice') on the complainant and the public authority.

(4) Where the Commissioner decides that a public authority—

    (a) has failed to provide information in a case where it is required to do so by these Regulations, or

    (b) has failed to comply with any of the requirements of these Regulations,

    the decision notice must specify the steps which must be taken by the authority for complying with that requirement and the period within which they must be taken.

(5) A decision notice must contain particulars of the right of appeal conferred by Part II of this Schedule.

(6) Where a decision notice requires steps to be taken by the public authority within a specified period, the time specified in the notice must not expire before the end of the period within which an

---

[5] S.I. 1992/3240.
[6] S.I. 1998/1447.
[7] S.R. 1993 No. 45.
[8] S.R. 1998 No. 238.

appeal can be brought against the notice and, if such an appeal is brought, no step which is affected by the appeal need be taken pending the determination or withdrawal of the appeal.

Information notices

2.—(1) If the Commissioner—

    (a) has received an application under paragraph 1 above, or

    (b) reasonably requires any information—

        (i) for the purpose of determining whether a public authority has complied or is complying with any of the requirements of these Regulations, or

        (ii) for the purpose of determining whether the practice of a public authority in relation to the exercise of its functions under these Regulations conforms with that proposed in the code of practice, he may serve the authority with a notice (referred to in this Schedule as 'an information notice') requiring it, within such time as is specified in the notice, to furnish the Commissioner, in such form as may be so specified, with such information relating to the application, to compliance with these Regulations or to conformity with the code of practice as is so specified.

    (2) An information notice must contain.

    (a) in a case falling within sub-paragraph (1)(a) above, a statement that the Commissioner has received an application under paragraph 1 above, or

    (b) in a case falling within sub-paragraph (1)(b) above, a statement.

        (i) that the Commissioner regards the specified information as relevant for either of the purposes referred to in sub-paragraph (1)(b) above, and

        (ii) of his reasons for regarding that information as relevant for that purpose.

    (3) An information notice must also contain particulars of the right of appeal conferred by Part II of this Schedule.

    (4) The time specified in an information notice must not expire before the end of the period within which an appeal can be brought against the notice and, if such an appeal is brought, the information need not be furnished pending the determination or withdrawal of the appeal.

    (5) An authority shall not be required by virtue of this section to furnish the Commissioner with any information in respect of—

    (a) any communication between a professional legal adviser and his client in connection with the giving of legal advice to the client with respect to his obligations, liabilities or rights under these Regulations, or

    (b) any communication between a professional legal adviser and his client, or between such an adviser or his client and any other person, made in connection with or in contemplation of proceedings under or arising out of these Regulations (including proceedings before the Tribunal) and for the purposes of such proceedings.

    (6) In sub-paragraph (5) above, references to the client of a professional legal adviser include references to any person representing such a client.

    (7) The Commissioner may cancel an information notice by written notice to the authority on which it was served.

    (8) In this paragraph, 'information' includes unrecorded information.

Enforcement notices

3.—(1) If the Commissioner is satisfied that a public authority has failed to comply with any of the requirements of these Regulations, the Commissioner may serve the authority with a notice (referred to in these Regulations as 'an enforcement notice') requiring the authority to take, within such time as may be specified in the notice, such steps as may be so specified for complying with those requirements.

(2) An enforcement notice must contain—

   (a) a statement of the requirement or requirements of these Regulations with which the Commissioner is satisfied that the public authority has failed to comply and his reasons for reaching that conclusion, and

   (b) particulars of the right of appeal conferred by Part II of this Schedule.

(3) An enforcement notice must not require any of the provisions of the notice to be complied with before the end of the period within which an appeal can be brought against the notice and, if such an appeal is brought, the notice need not be complied with pending the determination or withdrawal of the appeal.

(4) The Commissioner may cancel an enforcement notice by written notice to the authority on which it was served.

Failure to comply with notice

4.—(1) If a public authority has failed to comply with—

   (a) so much of a decision notice as requires steps to be taken,

   (b) an information notice, or

   (c) an enforcement notice,

the Commissioner may certify in writing to the court that the public authority has failed to comply with that notice.

(2) For the purposes of this section, a public authority which, in purported compliance with an information notice.

   (a) makes a statement which it knows to be false in a material respect, or

   (b) recklessly makes a statement which is false in a material respect, is to be taken to have failed to comply with the notice.

(3) Where a failure to comply is certified under sub-paragraph (1) above, the court may inquire into the matter and, after hearing any witness who may be produced against or on behalf of the public authority, and after hearing any statement that may be offered in defence, deal with the authority as if it had committed a contempt of court.

(4) In this paragraph, 'the court' means the High Court or, in Scotland, the Court of Session.

No action against public authority

5. Subject to paragraph 4 above, these Regulations do not confer any right of action in civil proceedings in respect of any failure to comply with any duty imposed by or under these Regulations.

PART II
APPEALS TO THE TRIBUNAL

Appeal against notices served under Part I

6.—(1) Where a decision notice has been served, the complainant or the public authority may appeal to the Tribunal against the notice.

(2) A public authority on which an information notice or an enforcement notice has been served by the Commissioner may appeal to the Tribunal against the notice.

Determination of appeals

7.—(1) If on an appeal under this Part, the Tribunal considers—

(a) that the notice against which the appeal is brought is not in accordance with the law, or

(b) to the extent that the notice involved an exercise of discretion by the Commissioner, that he ought to have exercised his discretion differently,

the Tribunal shall allow the appeal or substitute such other notice as could have been served by the Commissioner; and in any other case the Tribunal shall dismiss the appeal.

(2) On such an appeal, the Tribunal may review any finding of fact on which the notice in question was based.

Appeals from decision of Tribunal

8.—(1) Any party to an appeal to the Tribunal under this Part may appeal from the decision of the Tribunal on a point of law to the appropriate court; and that court shall be—

(a) the High Court of Justice in England if the address of the public authority is in England or Wales,

(b) the Court of Session if that address is in Scotland, and

(c) the High Court of Justice in Northern Ireland if that address is in Northern Ireland.

Appeal proceedings

9. The provisions of Schedule 6 to the Data Protection Act 1998 shall have effect (so far as applicable) in relation to appeals under this Part.

PART III

POWERS OF ENTRY AND INSPECTION

Issue of warrants

10.—(1) If a circuit judge is satisfied by information on oath supplied by the Commissioner that there are reasonable grounds for suspecting that—

(a) a public authority has failed or is failing to comply with.

(i) any of the requirements of these Regulations,

(ii) so much of a decision notice as requires steps to be taken, or

(iii) an information notice or an enforcement notice; and

(b) that evidence of such a failure to comply is to be found on any premises specified in the information,

he may, subject to sub-paragraph (2) below, grant a warrant to the Commissioner.

(2) A warrant issued under sub-paragraph (1) above shall authorise the Commissioner or any of his officers or staff at any time within seven days of the date of the warrant.

(a) to enter and search the premises,

(b) to inspect and seize any documents or other material found there which may be such evidence as is mentioned in that sub-paragraph, and

(c) to inspect, examine, operate and test any equipment found there in which information held by the public authority may be recorded.

11.—(1) A judge shall not issue a warrant under this Part unless he is satisfied—

(a) that the Commissioner has given seven days. notice in writing to the occupier of the premises in question demanding access to the premises, and

(b) that either—

(i) access was demanded at a reasonable hour and was unreasonably refused, or

(ii) although entry to the premises was granted, the occupier unreasonably refused to comply with a request by the Commissioner or any of the Commissioner's officers or staff to permit the Commissioner or the officer or member of staff to do any of the things referred to in paragraph 10(2) above, and

(c) that the occupier, has, after the refusal, been notified by the Commissioner of the application for the warrant and has had an opportunity of being heard by the judge on the question whether or not it should be issued.

(2) Sub-paragraph (1) shall not apply if the judge is satisfied that the case is one of urgency or that compliance with those provisions would defeat the object of the entry.

12. A judge who issues a warrant under this Part shall also issue two copies of it and certify them clearly as copies.

Execution of warrants

13. A person executing a warrant issued under this Part may use such reasonable force as may be necessary.

14. A warrant issued under this Part shall be executed at a reasonable hour unless it appears to the person executing it that there are grounds for suspecting that the evidence in question would not be found if it were so executed.

15.—(1) If the premises in respect of which a warrant is issued under this Part are occupied by a public authority and any officer or employee of the authority is present when the warrant is executed, he shall be shown the warrant and supplied with a copy of it; and if no such officer or employee is present a copy of the warrant shall be left in a prominent place on the premises.

(2) If the premises in respect of which a warrant is issued under this Part are occupied by a person other than a public authority and he is present when the warrant is executed, he shall be shown the warrant and supplied with a copy of it; and if that person is not present a copy of the warrant shall be left in a prominent place on the premises.

16.—(1) A person seizing anything in pursuance of a warrant under this Part shall give a receipt for it if asked to do so.

(2) Anything so seized may be retained for so long as is necessary in all the circumstances but the person in occupation of the premises in question shall be given a copy of anything that is seized if he so requests and the person executing the warrant considers that it can be done without undue delay.

Matters exempt from inspection and seizure

17.—(1) Subject to the provisions of this paragraph, the powers of inspection and seizure conferred by a warrant issued under this Part shall not be exercisable in respect of—

(a) any communication between a professional legal adviser and his client in connection with the giving of legal advice to the client with respect to his obligations, liabilities or rights under these Regulations, or

(b) any communication between a professional legal adviser and his client, or between such an adviser or his client and any other person, made in connection with or in contemplation of proceedings under or arising out of these Regulations (including proceedings before the Tribunal) and for the purposes of such proceedings.

(2) Sub-paragraph (1) applies also to—

(a) any copy or other record of any such communication as is there mentioned, and

(b) any document or article enclosed with or referred to in any such communication if made in connection with the giving of any advice or, as the case may be, in connection with or in contemplation of and for the purposes of such proceedings as are there mentioned.

(3) This paragraph does not apply to anything in the possession of any person other than the professional legal adviser or his client or to anything held with the intention of furthering a criminal purpose.

(4) In this paragraph references to the client of a professional legal adviser include references to any person representing such a client.

18. If the person in occupation of any premises in respect of which a warrant is issued under this Part objects to the inspection or seizure under the warrant of any material on the grounds that it consists partly of matters in respect of which those powers are not exercisable, he shall, if the person executing the warrant so requests, furnish that person with a copy of so much of the material in relation to which the powers are exercisable.

Return of warrants

19. A warrant issued under this Part shall be returned to the court from which it was issued—

(a) after being executed, or
(b) if not executed within the time authorised for its execution;

and the person by whom any such warrant is executed shall make an endorsement on it stating what powers have been exercised by him under the warrant.

Vessels, vehicles etc

20. In this Part, 'premises' includes any vessel, vehicle, aircraft or hovercraft, and references to the occupier of any premises include references to the person in charge of any vessel, vehicle, aircraft or hovercraft.

Scotland and Northern Ireland

21. In the application of this Part to Scotland—

(a) for any reference to a circuit judge there is substituted a reference to the sheriff, and
(b) for any reference to information on oath there is substituted a reference to evidence on oath.

22. In the application of this Part to Northern Ireland—

(a) for any reference to a circuit judge there is substituted a reference to a county court judge, and
(b) for any reference to information on oath there is substituted a reference to an application.

INDEX

Information Commissioner (*cont.*):
national security certificates, power to appeal
against 3.23, 7.95
ombudsmen, exchange of information with
3.65, 23.34, 23.67
parliamentary privilege 6.54
practice assessments 7.26
practice recommendations 7.27–7.29
prosecutions 5.174, 7.119, 10.88, 23.35,
23.68
public authorities
good practice guide A.32-A.35
public authority, as a 7.25
public interest, determining balance of 2.06,
2.07, 3.109, 9.27
publication schemes 4.91, 4.93, 4.96,
4.102–4.103, 5.119–5.125, 7.23
review of public authorities' decisions
consequences of 7.74
nature of 7.73
role under Freedom of Information Act 2000
3.32–3.50, 7.02–7.03, 7.17–7.19,
9.103–9.107, 17.47–17.48,
26.21–26.23
search warrants 7.45–7.51, 10.89
criminal offence of obstructing execution
7.51
Section 45 and Section 46 Codes of Practice
duty to promote observance of 3.36–3.37,
5.131, 5.163, 7.08, 7.20–7.21
enforcement notices, unavailability of 7.08,
7.29, 7.41
entitlement to be consulted about 5.127,
7.12, 7.14, 7.21
information notices 7.08, 7.31, 7.33
Keeper of Public Records, duty to consult
3.23, 5.163, 7.27
practice recommendations 3.38,
5.131–5.132, 7.08, 7.27–7.29
seizure 5.183, 7.50
statutory obligations 7.20–7.25
statutory powers 7.26–7.51
third parties 7.67, 7.120–7.136, 17.74, 26.24
White Paper *'Your Right to Know'* 1.50,
7.16–7.17
information notices *see also* Information
Commissioner
appeals to Information Tribunal against
3.51–3.52, 7.35–7.36, 7.80–7.82
contempt of court, non-compliance treated as
3.50, 7.38, 7.109–7.112, 7.114–7.116
contents of 3.43, 7.31–7.33, 7.35–7.37,
7.111
data protection 10.91–10.96
special 10.92, 10.94–10.96
grounds for serving 3.43, 7.08, 7.31

Information Commissioner, service by 3.43,
7.31–7.38, 7.71
legal professional privilege 7.37, 10.93
Scottish Information Commissioner 22.207,
22.212–22.219
unrecorded information 3.44, 7.34,
9.15–9.17
information technology *see also* Internet
business 17.06
Canada 9.99
technological revolution 1.48
United States 1.48, 9.21, 17.02, 17.06,
25.276, 25.289–25.295, 25.301
Information Tribunal 3.32–3.33, 9.105, 17.48
appeals from Information Commissioner
3.51–3.52, 7.35, 7.43, 7.75–7.89
grounds for 3.52
nature of 7.81–7.82
notices, substitution of 7.82
appeals to High Court from 3.53, 7.90–7.93,
26.23
composition of 7.84, 10.90
costs 7.87
data protection 4.106, 10.90, 10.98
national security certificates, appeals against
3.23–3.24, 3.83, 6.24, 6.27, 6.139,
7.95–7.102, 9.41, 10.70
Northern Ireland 23.65
role of 26.21
rules of procedure 7.85–7.88
third parties 7.132–7.133
time limits 7.88
injunctions
confidential information 20.12, 20.15,
20.19, 20.26, 20.30–20.35,
20.90–20.93
freedom of expression 20.51–20.52,
20.65–20.78, 20.90–20.93
threshold test for interim 21.57–21.60
government, protection from disclosure by
20.102–20.104
Human Rights Act 1998 21.57–21.60
newspapers 20.52, 20.67–20.78,
20.90–20.93, 21.56
photographs 20.51, 20.65, 21.59
privacy 20.51–20.52, 20.65–20.78,
20.90–20.93
publication before trial, restraining 20.51,
21.55–21.60, 21.65
Spycatcher case 1.10, 20.104
third parties seeking to prevent disclosure
6.07–6.08, 6.80–6.81, 6.237, 7.135,
17.74–17.76
interim injunction, applications for
17.75–17.76
inquiries 6.173, 22.51–22.53, 22.86–22.87